POET'S MARKET
KEY TO SYMBOLS

N this market is recently established and appearing for the first time in *Poet's Market*

★ this market did not appear in the previous edition of *Poet's Market*

this market is located in Canada

🌐 this market is located outside the U.S. and Canada

▣ this market publishes primarily online

$ this market pays a monetary amount

○ this market welcomes submissions from beginning poets

◐ this market prefers submissions from skilled, experienced poets; will consider work from beginning poets

◉ this market prefers submissions from poets with a high degree of skill and experience

◎ this market has a specialized focus

⊘ this market does not consider unsolicited submissions

∅ this market is currently closed to *all* submissions

● indicates market information of special note

(For words and expressions relating specifically to writing and publishing, see the Glossary in the back of this book.)

— TEAR ALONG PERFORATION

2009 POET'S MARKET
KEY TO SYMBOLS

TEAR ALONG PERFORATION

Thank you for purchasing *Poet's Market*. Visit PoetsMarket.com for updates and access to other useful features.

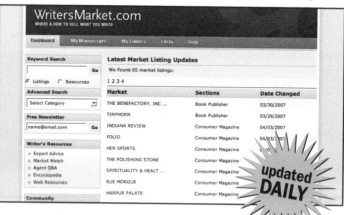

2009

POET'S MARKET ®

From the Editors of Writer's Digest Books

WRITER'S DIGEST BOOKS
CINCINNATI, OH

Editorial Director, Writer's Digest Books: Jane Friedman
Managing Editor, Writer's Digest Market Books: Alice Pope

Poet's Market Web page: wwww.poetsmarket.com
Writer's Market Web site: www.writersmarket.com
Writer's Digest Web site: www.writersdigest.com
F+W Publications Bookstore: http://fwbookstore.com

Distributed in Canada by Fraser Direct
100 Armstrong Ave.
Georgetown, ON, Canada L7G 5S4
Tel: (905) 877-4411

Distributed in the U.K. and Europe by David & Charles
Brunel House, Newton Abbot, Devon, TQ12 4PU, England
Tel: (+44) 1626 323200, Fax: (+44) 1626 323319
E-mail: postmaster@davidandcharles.co.uk

Distributed in Australia by Capricorn Link
P.O. Box 704, Windsor, NSW 2756, Australia
Tel: (02) 4577-3555

Distributed in New Zealand by David Bateman Ltd.
P.O. Box 100-242, N.S.M.C., Auckland 1330, New Zealand
Tel: (09) 415-7664, Fax: (09) 415-8892

Distributed in South Africa by Real Books
P.O. Box 1040, Auckland Park 2006, Johannesburg, South Africa
Tel: (011) 837-0643, Fax: (011) 837-0645
E-mail: realbook@global.co.za

ISSN: 0883-5470
ISBN-13: 978-1-58297-544-3
ISBN-10: 1-58297-544-2

Cover design by Claudean Wheeler
Interior design by Clare Finney
Production coordinated by Greg Nock
Photographs on selected pages © Frédéric Cirou/PhotoAlto

Attention Booksellers: This is an annual directory of F+W Publications.
Return deadline for this edition is December 31, 2009.

F+W PUBLICATIONS, INC.

Contents

RESOURCES

INDEXES

From the Editor

Besides my experience as a young reader spending time with *A Child's Garden of Verses* and *Where the Sidewalk Ends*, I didn't give poetry much thought until high school when I was confronted with poetry written by my peers.

My friend David (who often wrote under the name "Apollyon," which he said was some sort of Jim Morrison reference) and my best friend Lisa's boyfriend Chris both penned plenty of poetry as teens. David read his poems to Lisa and me; we discussed them. Lisa showed me Chris' poetry which he generally mailed to her; we squealed at the adolescent sort-of-love-poems.

The thing was—I never really understood those poems. I just didn't get them. They were moody and deep, full of big words, and oh-so-intelligent, thought I. Poetry just wasn't my thing. I did enjoy some of the poems I later studied in college (particularly the romantics—Keats, Byron, Shelley), but I felt like the majority of the poets I read were over my head.

But years ago as I began looking over material for *Poet's Market*, seeing snippets of poems, reading interviews with their creators, I began to see something. Poetry doesn't have to be a high-falutin' art reserved for intellectuals. It can be accessible. It can be dark. It can be lovely. It can be deeply sad. It can be fun. It can be comforting. It can be whatever a poet needs it to be.

Open Books co-owner Christine Deavel put it so well in her interview on page 17: "In the entryway of our store we have a quotation by Emily Dickinson: 'If I read a book and it makes my whole body so cold no fire can ever warm me, I know that is poetry.' That sentiment has bothered several folks, who believe that poetry should always be warm and embracing. But engagement with art is always a risk. And out of that risk can come astounding reward. However, I'm also all in favor of the ditty, the witty, the silly bit of sonic nonsense. It's all poetry. It all offers something that matters to human existence."

The 2009 edition of *Poet's Market* aims to make the editors and publishers of poetry accessible to you, the poets. Our articles, interviews (with the likes of Mary Karr, page 60; Keith Flynn, page 148; Diane Glancy, page 194; and others) along with hundreds of updated listings are all here to help you help your poems find a home in print and, ultimately, in the hearts of readers.

As for those high school poems by David and Chris, decades later I brought them up with Lisa. She admitted that she didn't get them either—which made me feel so much better. And even happier about the Mary Oliver and e.e. cummings volumes on my night stand.

Alice Pope
Managing Editor
Writer's Digest Market Books
poetsmarket@fwpubs.com

Getting Started

(and Using This Book)

Delving into the pages of *Poet's Market* indicates a commitment—you've decided to take that big step and begin submitting your poems for publication. How do you *really* begin, though? Here are eight quick tips to help make sense of the marketing/submission process:

1. Be an avid reader. The best way to hone your writing skills (besides writing) is to immerse yourself in poetry of all kinds. It's essential to study the masters; however, from a marketing standpoint, it's equally vital to read what your contemporaries are writing and publishing. Read journals and magazines, chapbooks and collections, anthologies for a variety of voices; scope out the many poetry sites on the Internet. Develop an eye for quality, and then use that eye to assess your own work. Don't rush to publish until you know you're writing the best poetry you're capable of producing.

2. Know what you like to write—and what you write best. Ideally, you should be experimenting with all kinds of poetic forms, from free verse to villanelles. However, there's sure to be a certain style with which you feel most comfortable, that conveys your true "voice." Whether you favor more formal, traditional verse or avant-garde poetry that breaks all the rules, you should identify which markets publish work similar to yours. Those are the magazines and presses you should target to give your submissions the best chance of being read favorably—and accepted. (See the Subject Index beginning on page 530 to observe how some magazines and presses specify their needs.)

3. Learn the "business" of poetry publishing. Poetry may not be a high-paying writing market, but there's still a right way to go about the "business" of submitting and publishing poems. Learn all you can by reading writing-related books and magazines. Read the articles and interviews in this book for plenty of helpful advice. Surf the Internet for a wealth of sites filled with writing advice, market news and informative links. (See Additional Resources on page 466 for some leads.)

4. Research the markets. Study the listings in *Poet's Market* thoroughly; these present submission guidelines, editorial preferences and editors' comments as well as contact information (names, postal and e-mail addresses, Web site URLs). The Magazines/Journals section begins on page 41, the Book/Chapbook Publishers section on page 321, with the Contests & Awards section following on page 353. In addition, the indexes in the back of this book provide insights into what an editor or publisher may be looking for.

However, studying market listings alone won't cut it. The best way to gauge the kinds of poetry a market publishes is to read several issues of a magazine/journal or several of a press's books to get a feel for the style and content of each. If the market has a Web site, log on and take a look. Web sites may include poetry samples, reviews, archives of past issues, exclusive content, and especially submission guidelines. (If the market is an online publication, the current issue will be available in its entirety.) If the market has no online presence, send for guidelines and sample copies (include a SASE—self-addressed stamped envelope—for guidelines; include appropriate cost for sample copy).

Submission guidelines are pure gold for the specific information they provide. However you acquire them—by SASE or e-mail, online, or in a magazine itself—make them an integral part of your market research.

5. Start slowly. It may be tempting to send your work directly to *The New Yorker* or *Poetry*, but try to adopt a more modest approach if you're just starting out. Most listings in this book display symbols that reflect the level of writing a magazine or publisher prefers to receive. The (◯) symbol indicates a market that welcomes submissions from beginning or unpublished poets. As you gain confidence and experience (and increased skill in your writing), you can move on to markets coded with the (◑) symbol. Later, when you've built a publication history, submit to the more prestigious magazines and presses (the ◉ markets). Although it may tax your patience, slow and steady progress is a proven route to success.

6. Be professional. Professionalism is not something you should "work up to." Make it show in your first submission, from the way you prepare your manuscript to the attitude you project in your communications with editors.

Follow those guidelines. Submit a polished manuscript. (See "Frequently Asked Questions" on page 7 for details on manuscript formatting and preparation.) Choose poems carefully with the editor's needs in mind. *Always* include a SASE with any submission or inquiry. Such practices show respect for the editor, the publication and the process; and they reflect *your* self-respect and the fact that you take your work seriously. Editors love that; and even if your work is rejected, you've made a good first impression that could help your chances with your next submission.

7. Keep track of your submissions. First, do *not* send out the only copies of your work. There are no guarantees your submission won't get lost in the mail, misplaced in a busy editorial office, or vanish into a black hole if the publication or press closes down. Create a special file folder for poems you're submitting. Even if you use a word processing pro-

2009 POET'S MARKET KEY TO SYMBOLS

Ⓝ this market is recently established and appearing for the first time in *Poet's Market*

✕ this market did not appear in the previous edition of *Poet's Market*

♦ this market is located in Canada

⊕ this market is located outside the U.S. and Canada

▣ this market publishes primarily online

$ this market pays a monetary amount

◯ this market welcomes submissions from beginning poets

◑ this market prefers submissions from skilled, experienced poets; will consider work from beginning poets

◉ this market prefers submissions from poets with a high degree of skill and experience

◎ this market has a specialized focus

⊘ this market does not consider unsolicited submissions

⊘ this market is currently closed to *all* submissions

• indicates market information of special note

ms, mss manuscript(s)

b&w black & white (art/photo)

SASE self-addressed, stamped envelope

IRC International Reply Coupon (replaces return postage when mailing to countries other than your own)

(For words and expressions relating specifically to poetry and submissions, see the Glossaries in the back of this book.)

Find a handy pull-out bookmark, a quick reference to the icons used in this book, right inside the front cover.

Articles & Information

Submission Tracker

Poem Title	Publication/ Contest	Editor/Contact	Date Sent	Date Returned	Date Accepted	Date Published	Pay Received	Comments

gram and store your manuscripts on disk, keep a hard copy file as well (and be sure to back up your electronic files).

Second, establish a tracking system so you always know which poems are where. This can be extremely simple: index cards, a chart created with word processing or database software, or even a simple notebook used as a log. (You can enlarge and photocopy the Submission Tracker on page 4 or use it as a model to design your own version.) Note the titles of the poems submitted (or the title of the collection if you're submitting a book/chapbook manuscript); the name of the publication, press, or contest; date sent; estimated response time; and date returned *or* date accepted. Additional information you may want to log: the name of the editor/contact, date the accepted piece is published and/or issue number of the magazine, type/amount of pay received, rights acquired by the publication or press, and any pertinent comments.

Without a tracking system, you risk forgetting where and when manuscripts were submitted. This is even more problematic if you simultaneously send the same manuscripts to different magazines, presses or contests. And if you learn of an acceptance by one magazine or publisher, you *must* notify the others that the poem or collection you sent them is no longer available. You run a bigger chance of overlooking someone without an organized approach. This causes hard feelings among editors you may have inconvenienced, hurting your chances with these markets in the future.

8. Don't fear rejection. Learn from it. No one enjoys rejection, but every writer faces it. The best way to turn a negative into a positive is to learn as much as you can from your rejections. Don't let them get you down. A rejection slip isn't a permission slip to doubt yourself, condemn your poetry or give up.

Look over the rejection. Did the editor provide any comments about your work or reasons why your poems were rejected? Probably he or she didn't. Editors are extremely busy and don't necessarily have time to comment on rejections. If that's the case, move on to the next magazine or publisher you've targeted and send your work out again.

If, however, the editor *has* commented on your work, pay attention. It counts for something that the editor took the time and trouble to say anything, however brief, good or bad. And consider any remark or suggestion with an open mind. You don't have to agree, but you shouldn't automatically disregard the feedback, either. Tell your ego to sit down and be quiet, then use the editor's comments to review your work from a new perspective. You might be surprised by how much you'll learn from a single scribbled word in the margin; or how encouraged you'll feel from a simple "Try again!" written on the rejection slip.

Keep these eight tips in mind as you prepare your poetry submissions, and keep *Poet's Market* at hand to help you along. Believe in yourself and don't give up! As the number of listings in this book shows, there are many opportunities for beginning poets to become published poets.

GUIDE TO LISTING FEATURES

On page 6 is an example of a Magazines/Journal listing (Book/Chapbook Publishers listings follow a similar format). Note the callouts that identify various format features of the listing. A key to the symbols displayed at the beginning of each listing is located on page 3, on the inside covers of this book and on a pull-out bookmark just inside the front cover.

Articles & Information

EASY-TO-USE
REFERENCE
ICONS

TYPES OF
POETRY
CONSIDERED

DETAILED
SUBMISSION
GUIDELINES

WEB SITES

SPECIFIC
CONTACT
NAMES

EDITOR'S
COMMENTS

☑ SLANT: A JOURNAL OF POETRY

Box 5063, University of Central Arkansas, 201 Donaghey Ave., Conway AR 72035-5000. (501)450-5107. Web site: www. uca.edu/english/Slant/. Established 1987. **Contact:** James Fowler, editor.

Magazine Needs *Slant: A Journal of Poetry*, published annually in May, aims "to publish a journal of fine poetry from all regions of the United States and beyond." Wants "traditional and 'modern' poetry, even experimental; moderate length, any subject on approval of Board of Readers." Doesn't want "haiku, translations." Has published poetry by Susan H. Case, Philip Dacey, Elizabeth Howrd, Timothy Martin, Gilbert Wesley Purdy, and Nancy Scott. *Slant* is 120 pages, professionally printed on quality stock, flat-spined, with matte card cover. Receives about 1,400 poems/year, accepts 70-80. Press run is 175 (70-100 subscribers). Sample: $10.

How to Submit Submit up to 5 poems at a time. Lines/poem: poems should be of moderate length. No previously published poems or simultaneous submissions. Submissions should be typed; include SASE. "Put name, address (including e-mail if available), and phone number at the top of each page." Reads submissions September 1-November 15. Comments on rejected poems "on occasion." Guidelines available in magazine, for SASE, or on Web site. Responds in 3-4 months from November 15 deadline. Pays one contributor's copy. Poet retains rights.

Advice "We tend to publish those poems whose execution, line by line, does full justice to their conception. Often the decision to accept comes down to the matter of craft, language."

Frequently Asked Questions

The following FAQ (Frequently Asked Questions) section provides the expert knowledge you need to submit your poetry in a professional manner. Answers to most basic questions, such as "How many poems should I send?", "How long should I wait for a reply?" and "Are simultaneous submissions okay?" can be found by simply reading the listings in the Magazines/Journals and Book/Chapbook Publishers sections. See the introduction to each section for an explanation of the information contained in the listings. Also, see the Glossary of Listing terms on page 476.

Is it okay to submit handwritten poems?

Usually, no. Now and then a publisher or editor makes an exception and accepts handwritten manuscripts. However, check the preferences stated in each listing. If no mention is made of handwritten submissions, assume your poetry should be typed or computer-generated.

How should I format my poems for submission to magazines and journals?

If you're submitting poems by regular mail (also referred to as *land mail*, *postal mail* or *snail mail*), follow this format (also see sample on page 8):

Poems should be typed or computer-printed on white 8½×11 paper of at least 20 lb. weight. Left, right and bottom margins should be at least one inch. Starting ½ inch from the top of the page, type your name, address, telephone number, e-mail address (if you have one) and number of lines in the poem in the *upper right* corner, in individual lines, single-spaced. Space down about six lines and type the poem title, either centered or flush left. The title may appear in all caps or in upper and lower case. Space down another two lines (at least) and begin to type your poem. Poems are usually single-spaced, although some magazines may request double-spaced submissions. (Be alert to each market's preferences.) Double-space between stanzas. Type one poem to a page. For poems longer than one page, type your name in the *upper left* corner; on the next line type a key word from the title of your poem, the page number, and indicate whether the stanza begins or is continued on the new page (i.e., MOTHMAN, Page 2, continue stanza *or* begin new stanza).

If you're submitting poems by e-mail (also see sample on page 9):

First, make sure the publication accepts e-mail submissions. This information, when available, is included in all *Poet's Market* listings. In most cases, editors will request that poems be pasted within the body of your e-mail, *not* sent as attachments. Many editors prefer this format because of the danger of viruses, the possibility of software incompatibility, and other concerns associated with e-mail attachments. Editors who consider e-mail attachments taboo may even delete the message without opening the attachment.

Articles & Information

Mailed Submission Format

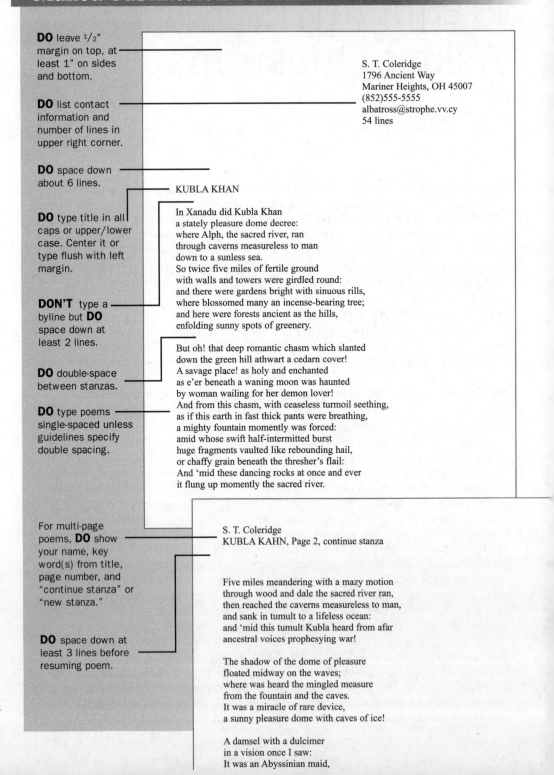

DO leave ¹/₂" margin on top, at least 1" on sides and bottom.

DO list contact information and number of lines in upper right corner.

DO space down about 6 lines.

DO type title in all caps or upper/lower case. Center it or type flush with left margin.

DON'T type a byline but **DO** space down at least 2 lines.

DO double-space between stanzas.

DO type poems single-spaced unless guidelines specify double spacing.

For multi-page poems, **DO** show your name, key word(s) from title, page number, and "continue stanza" or "new stanza."

DO space down at least 3 lines before resuming poem.

S. T. Coleridge
1796 Ancient Way
Mariner Heights, OH 45007
(852)555-5555
albatross@strophe.vv.cy
54 lines

KUBLA KHAN

In Xanadu did Kubla Khan
a stately pleasure dome decree:
where Alph, the sacred river, ran
through caverns measureless to man
down to a sunless sea.
So twice five miles of fertile ground
with walls and towers were girdled round:
and there were gardens bright with sinuous rills,
where blossomed many an incense-bearing tree;
and here were forests ancient as the hills,
enfolding sunny spots of greenery.

But oh! that deep romantic chasm which slanted
down the green hill athwart a cedarn cover!
A savage place! as holy and enchanted
as e'er beneath a waning moon was haunted
by woman wailing for her demon lover!
And from this chasm, with ceaseless turmoil seething,
as if this earth in fast thick pants were breathing,
a mighty fountain momently was forced:
amid whose swift half-intermitted burst
huge fragments vaulted like rebounding hail,
or chaffy grain beneath the thresher's flail:
And 'mid these dancing rocks at once and ever
it flung up momently the sacred river.

S. T. Coleridge
KUBLA KAHN, Page 2, continue stanza

Five miles meandering with a mazy motion
through wood and dale the sacred river ran,
then reached the caverns measureless to man,
and sank in tumult to a lifeless ocean:
and 'mid this tumult Kubla heard from afar
ancestral voices prophesying war!

The shadow of the dome of pleasure
floated midway on the waves;
where was heard the mingled measure
from the fountain and the caves.
It was a miracle of rare device,
a sunny pleasure dome with caves of ice!

A damsel with a dulcimer
in a vision once I saw:
It was an Abyssinian maid,

E-mail Submission Format

DO use a basic typeface and point size.

DO use the appropriate e-mail address.

DO consult guidelines for special instructions about formatting the subject line.

DO follow basic guidelines for a good cover letter.

DO provide contact information, including regular mail address.

DO be aware that formatting can become lost in an electronic submission. Keep it simple.

DO paste all poems within one message, one after the other, unless guidelines specify otherwise.

DON'T send submissions by e-mail unless editor says it's okay (in market listing or guidelines).

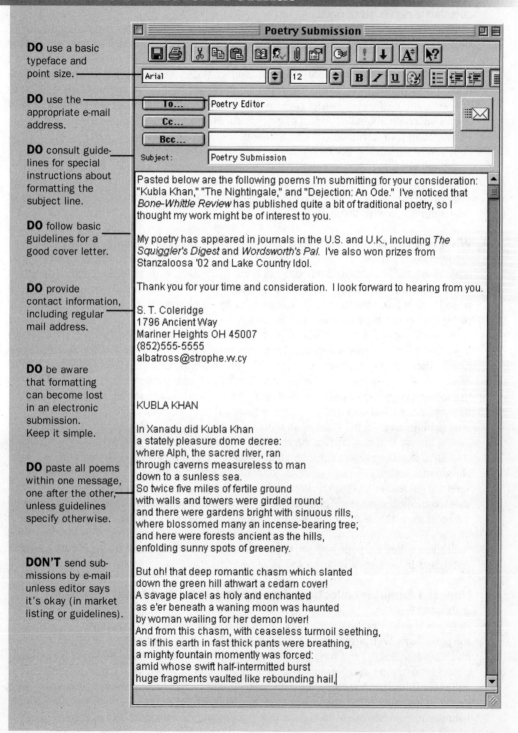

Poetry Submission

Arial   12   **B** *I* <u>U</u>

To... Poetry Editor
Cc...
Bcc...
Subject: Poetry Submission

Pasted below are the following poems I'm submitting for your consideration: "Kubla Khan," "The Nightingale," and "Dejection: An Ode." I've noticed that *Bone-Whittle Review* has published quite a bit of traditional poetry, so I thought my work might be of interest to you.

My poetry has appeared in journals in the U.S. and U.K., including *The Squiggler's Digest* and *Wordsworth's Pal.* I've also won prizes from Stanzaloosa '02 and Lake Country Idol.

Thank you for your time and consideration. I look forward to hearing from you.

S. T. Coleridge
1796 Ancient Way
Mariner Heights OH 45007
(852)555-5555
albatross@strophe.w.cy

KUBLA KHAN

In Xanadu did Kubla Khan
a stately pleasure dome decree:
where Alph, the sacred river, ran
through caverns measureless to man
down to a sunless sea.
So twice five miles of fertile ground
with walls and towers were girdled round:
and there were gardens bright with sinuous rills,
where blossomed many an incense-bearing tree;
and here were forests ancient as the hills,
enfolding sunny spots of greenery.

But oh! that deep romantic chasm which slanted
down the green hill athwart a cedarn cover!
A savage place! as holy and enchanted
as e'er beneath a waning moon was haunted
by woman wailing for her demon lover!
And from this chasm, with ceaseless turmoil seething,
as if this earth in fast thick pants were breathing,
a mighty fountain momently was forced:
amid whose swift half-intermitted burst
huge fragments vaulted like rebounding hail,

Of course, other editors do accept, and even prefer e-mail submissions as attachments. This information should be clearly stated in the market listing. If it's not, you're probably safer submitting your poems in the body of the e-mail. (All the more reason to pay close attention to details given in the listings.)

Note, too, the number of poems the editor recommends including in the e-mail submission. If no quantity is given specifically for e-mails, go with the number of poems an editor recommends submitting in general. Identify your submission with a notation in the subject line. While some editors simply want the words "Poetry Submission," others want poem titles. Check the market listing for preferences. **Note:** Because of spam, filters and other concerns, some editors are strict about what must be printed in the subject line and how. If you're uncertain about any aspect of e-mail submission formats, double-check the Web site (if available) for information or contact the publication for directions.

If you're submitting poems on disk:

Submit poems on disk *only* when the publication indicates this is acceptable. Even then, if no formatting preferences are given, contact the publisher for specifics before sending the disk. Make sure your disk is virus-free. Always include a hard copy (i.e., printed copy) of your submission with the disk.

What is a chapbook? How is it different from a regular poetry book?

A chapbook is a booklet, averaging 24-50 pages in length (some are shorter), usually digest-sized ($5^1/_2 \times 8^1/_2$, although chapbooks can come in all sizes, even published within the pages of a magazine). Typically, a chapbook is saddle-stapled with a soft cover (card or special paper); chapbooks can also be produced with a plain paper cover the same weight as the pages, especially if the booklet is photocopied.

A chapbook is a much smaller collection of poetry than a full-length book (which runs anywhere from 50 pages to well over 100 pages, longer for "best of" collections and retrospectives). There are probably more poetry chapbooks being published than full-length books, and that's an important point to consider. Don't think of the chapbook as a poor relation to the full-length collection. While it's true a chapbook won't attract big reviews, qualify for major prizes or find national distribution through chain bookstores, it's a terrific way for a poet to build an audience (and reputation) in increments, while developing the kind of publishing history that may attract the attention of a book publisher one day.

Although some presses consider chapbooks through a regular submission process, many choose manuscripts through competitions. Check each publisher's listing for requirements, send for guidelines or visit the Web site (absolutely vital if a competition is involved), and check out some sample chapbooks the press has already produced (usually available from the press itself). Most chapbook publishers are as choosy as book publishers about the quality of work they accept. Submit your best poems in a professional manner. (See the Chapbook Publishers Index on page 482 for markets that consider chapbook manuscripts; the Book Publishers Index begins on page 486.)

How do I format a collection of poems to submit to a book/chapbook publisher?

Before you send a manuscript to a book/chapbook publisher, request guidelines (or consult the publisher's Web site, if available). Requirements vary regarding formatting, query letters and samples, length, and other considerations. Usually you will use $8^1/_2 \times 11$, 20 lb. white paper; set left, right and bottom margins of at least one inch; put your name and title of your collection in the top left corner of every page; limit poems to one per page (although poems certainly may run longer than one page); and number pages consecutively. Individual publisher requirements might include a title page, table of contents, credits page (indicating where previously published poems originally appeared) and biographical note.

If you're submitting your poetry book or chapbook manuscript to a competition, you *must* read and follow the guidelines. Failure to do so could disqualify your manuscript. Guidelines for a competition might call for an official entry form to accompany the submission, a special title page, a minimum and maximum number of pages, and specific formatting instructions (such as paginating the manuscript and not putting the poet's name on any of the manuscript pages).

What is a cover letter? Do I have to send one? What should it say?

A cover letter is your introduction to the editor, telling him a little about yourself and your work. Most editors indicate their cover letter preferences in their listings. If an editor states a cover letter is "required," absolutely send one! It's also better to send one if a cover letter is "preferred." Experts disagree on the necessity and appropriateness of cover letters, so use your own judgment when preferences aren't clear in the listing.

A cover letter should be professional but also allow you to present your work in a personal manner. (See the fictional cover letter on page 12 as an example.) Keep your letter brief, no more than one page. Address your letter to the correct contact person. (Use "Poetry Editor" if no contact name appears in the listing.) Include your name, address, phone number and e-mail address (if available). If a biographical note is requested, include 2-3 lines about your background, interests, why you write poetry, etc. Avoid praising yourself or your poems in your letter (your submission should speak for itself). Include titles (or first lines) of the poems you're submitting. You may list a few of your most recent publishing credits, but no more than five; and keep in mind that some editors find publishing credits tiresome—they're more interested in the quality of the work you're submitting to *them*.

Show your familiarity with the magazine to which you're submitting: comment on a poem the magazine published, tell the editor why you chose to submit to her magazine, mention poets the magazine has published. Use a business-style format for a professional appearance, and proofread carefully; typos, misspellings and other errors make a poor first impression. Remember that editors are people, too. Respect, professionalism and kindness go a long way in poet/editor relationships.

What is a SASE? An IRC (with SAE)?

A SASE is a self-addressed, stamped envelope—and you should never send a submission by regular mail without one. Also include a SASE if you send an inquiry to an editor. If your submission is too large for an envelope (for instance, a bulky book-length collection of poems), use a box and include a self-addressed mailing label with adequate return postage paper-clipped to it.

An IRC is an International Reply Coupon, enclosed with a self-addressed envelope for manuscripts submitted to foreign markets. Each coupon is equivalent in value to the minimum postage rate for an unregistered airmail letter. IRCs may be exchanged for postage stamps at post offices in all foreign countries that are members of the Universal Postal Union (UPU). When you provide the adequate number of IRCs and a self-addressed envelope (SAE), you give a foreign editor financial means to return your submission (U.S. postage stamps cannot be used to send mail *to* the United States from outside the country). Purchase price is $2 per coupon. Call your local post office to check for availability (sometimes only larger post offices sell them).

Important note about IRCs: Foreign editors sometimes find the IRCs have been stamped incorrectly by the U.S. post office when purchased. This voids the IRCs and makes it impossible for the foreign editor to exchange the coupons for return postage for your manuscript. When buying IRCs, make sure yours have been stamped correctly before you leave the

Important

Preparing Your Cover Letter

DO type on one side of 8 1/2 x 11 20 lb. paper.

DO proofread carefully.

DO use a standard 12-point typeface (like Times New Roman).

DO list the poems you're submitting for consideration.

DO mention something about the magazine and about yourself.

DO be brief!

Perry Lineskanner
1954 Eastern Blvd.
Pentameter, OH 45007
(852) 555-5555
soneteer@trochee.vv.cy

April 24, 2009

Spack Saddlestaple, Editor
The Squiggler's Digest
Double-Toe Press
P.O. Box 54X
Submission Junction, AZ 85009

Dear Mr. Saddlestaple:

Enclosed are three poems for your consideration for *The Squiggler's Digest*: "The Diamond Queen," "The Boy Who Was Gromit," and "The Maker of Everything."

Although this is my first submission to your journal, I'm a long-time reader of *The Squiggler's Digest* and enjoy the scope of narrative poetry you feature. I especially enjoyed Sydney Dogwood's poetry cycle in Issue 4.

My own poetry has appeared recently in *The Bone-Whittle Review*, *Bumper-Car Reverie*, and *Stock Still*.

Thank you for considering my manuscript. I look forward to hearing from you.

Sincerely,

Perry Lineskanner

Note: The names used in this letter are intended to be fictional; any resemblance to real people, publications or presses is purely coincidental.

counter. (The Postal Service clerk must place a postmark in the block with the heading *control stamp of the country of origin*.) More information about International Reply Coupons is available on the USPS Web site (www.usps.com).

To save time and money, poets sometimes send disposable manuscripts to foreign markets and inform the editor to discard the manuscript after it's been read. Some enclose an IRC and SAE for reply only; others establish a deadline after which they will withdraw the manuscript from consideration and market it elsewhere.

How much postage does my submission need?

As much as it takes—you do *not* want your manuscript to arrive postage due. Purchase a postage scale or take your manuscript to the post office for weighing. Remember, you'll need postage on two envelopes: the one containing your submission and SASE, and the return envelope itself. Submissions without SASEs usually will not be returned (and possibly may not even be read).

Note: New postage rates went into effect on May 12, 2008. There is now a new fee structure for First-Class Postage. For letters and cards (including business-size envelopes), the First-Class rate is 42 cents for the first ounce, and 17 cents per additional ounce up to and including 3.5 ounces. **Letter-sized mail that weighs more than 3.5 ounces is charged the "flats" rate** ("flats" include any envelope large enough to mail an $8\frac{1}{2} \times 11$ manuscript page unfolded) of 83 cents for the first ounce, and 17 cents for each additional ounce up to and including 13 ounces. This means if you send a large envelope that weighs only one ounce, it costs 83 cents at the First-Class flats rate instead of the 42 cents charged for First-Class letters and cards. (See the charts on page 14 for First-Class rates for letters and flats, or go to www.usps.com for complete information on all rates questions.)

The USPS also offers its Click-N-Ship® program, which allows a customer to print domestic and international shipping labels with postage, buy insurance and pay for postage by credit card. See the USPS Web site for a one-time software download, to check system requirements and to register for an account.

The Web site is also your source for ordering supplies (such as postage scale and labels), reviewing postal regulations, calculating postage and more. Canada Post information and services are available at www.canadapost.com.

What does it mean when an editor says "no previously published" poems? Does this include poems that have appeared in anthologies? What if one of my poems appeared online through a group or forum?

If your poem appears *anywhere* in print for a public audience, it's considered "previously" published. That includes magazines, anthologies, Web sites and online journals, and even printed programs (say for a church service, wedding, etc.). See the explanation for rights below, especially *second serial (reprint) rights* and *all rights* for additional concerns about previously published material.

One exception to the above guidelines is if your poem appears online in a *private* poetry forum, critique group, etc. As long as the site is private (i.e., a password is required to view and participate), your poem isn't considered "published." However, if your poem is printed on an online forum or bulletin board that's available for public viewing, even if you must use a password to post the poem or to comment, then your poem is considered "published" as far as rights are concerned.

What rights should I offer for my poems? What do these different rights mean?

Editors usually indicate in their listings what rights they acquire. Most journals and magazines license *first rights* (a.k.a. *first serial rights*), which means the poet offers the right to publish

Postage Information

First-Class Mail Rates: Letters & Cards

1 ounce	$0.42	3 ounces	0.76
2 ounces	$0.59	3.5 ounces	0.93
		Postcard	0.27

First-Class Mail Rates: Flats

Weight not over (ounces)	Rate	Weight not over (ounces)	Rate
1	$0.83	8	2.02
2	1.00	9	2.19
3	1.17	10	2.36
4	1.34	11	2.53
5	1.51	12	2.70
6	1.68	13	2.87
7	1.85		

Source: Web site of the United States Postal Service (www.usps.com)

U.S. and Canadian Postal Codes

AL	Alabama	MN	Minnesota	VA	Virginia
AK	Alaska	MS	Mississippi	WA	Washington
AZ	Arizona	MO	Missouri	WV	West Virginia
AR	Arkansas	MT	Montana	WI	Wisconsin
CA	California	NE	Nebraska	WY	Wyoming
CO	Colorado	NV	Nevada		
CT	Connecticut	NH	New Hampsire	**Canada**	
DE	Delaware	NJ	New Jersey	AB	Alberta
DC	District of	NM	New Mexico	BC	British Columbia
	Columbia	NY	New York	MB	Manitoba
FL	Florida	NC	North Carolina	NB	New Brunswick
GA	Georgia	ND	North Dakota	NL	Newfoundland &
GU	Guam	OH	Ohio		Labrador
HI	Hawaii	OK	Oklahoma	NS	Nova Scotia
ID	Idaho	OR	Oregon	NT	Northwest
IL	Illinois	PA	Pennsylvania		Territories
IN	Indiana	PR	Puerto Rico	NU	Nunavut
IA	Iowa	RI	Rhode Island	ON	Ontario
KS	Kansas	SC	South Carolina	PE	Prince Edward
KY	Kentucky	SD	South Dakota		Island
LA	Louisiana	TN	Tennessee	QC	Quebec
ME	Maine	TX	Texas	SK	Saskatchewan
MD	Maryland	UT	Utah	YT	Yukon
MA	Massachusetts	VT	Vermont		
MI	Michigan	VI	Virgin Islands		

the poem for the first time in any periodical. All other rights to the material remain with the poet. (Note that some editors state that rights to poems "revert to poets upon publication" when first rights are acquired.) When poems are excerpted from a book prior to publication and printed in a magazine/journal, this is also called *first serial rights*. The addition of *North American* indicates the editor is the first to publish a poem in a U.S. or Canadian periodical. The poem may still be submitted to editors outside of North America or to those who acquire reprint rights.

When a magazine/journal licenses *one-time rights* to a poem (also known as *simultaneous rights*), the editor has *nonexclusive* rights to publish the poem once. The poet may submit that same poem to other publications at the same time (usually markets that don't have overlapping audiences).

Editors/publishers open to submission of work already published elsewhere seek *second serial (reprint) rights*. The poet is obliged to inform them where and when the poem previously appeared so they can give proper credit to the original publication. In essence, chapbook or book collections license reprint rights, listing the magazines in which poems previously appeared somewhere in the book (usually on the copyright page or separate credits page).

If a publisher or editor requires you to relinquish *all rights*, be aware that you're giving up ownership of that poem or group of poems. You cannot resubmit the work elsewhere, nor can you include it in a poetry collection without permission or by negotiating for reprint rights to be returned to you. Before you agree to this type of arrangement, ask the editor first if he or she is willing to acquire first rights instead of all rights. If you receive a refusal and you don't want to relinquish all rights, simply write a letter withdrawing your work from consideration. Some editors will reassign rights to a writer after a given amount of time, such as one year.

With the growth in Internet publishing opportunities, *electronic rights* have become very important. These cover a broad range of electronic media, including online magazines, CD recordings of poetry readings and CD-ROM editions of magazines. When submitting to an electronic market of any kind, find out what rights the market acquires upfront (many online magazines also stipulate the right to archive poetry they've published so it's continually available on their Web sites).

What is a copyright? Should I have my poems copyrighted before I submit them for publication?

Copyright is a proprietary right that gives you the power to control your work's reproduction, distribution and public display or performance, as well as its adaptation to other forms. In other words, you have the legal right to the exclusive publication, sale or distribution of your poetry. What's more, your "original works of authorship" are protected as soon as they are "fixed in a tangible form of expression," i.e., written down or recorded. Since March 1989, copyright notices are no longer required to secure protection, so it's not necessary to include them on your poetry manuscript. Also, in many editors' minds, copyright notices signal the work of amateurs who are distrustful and paranoid about having work stolen.

If you still want to indicate copyright, use the © symbol or the word *copyright*, your name and the year. If you wish, you can register your copyright with the Copyright Office for a $45 fee, using Form TX (directions and form available for download from www.copyright.gov). Since paying $45 per poem is costly and impractical, you may prefer to copyright a group of unpublished poems for that single fee. Further information is available from the U.S. Copyright Office, Library of Congress, 101 Independence Ave. S.E., Washington DC 20559-6000; by download from www.copyright.gov; or by calling (202)707-3000 between 8:30 a.m. and 5:00 p.m. (EST) weekdays.

Special note regarding Copyright Office mail delivery: The "effective date of registration'' for copyright applications is usually the day the Copyright Office actually receives all elements of an application (application form, fee and copies of work being registered). Because of security concerns, all USPS and private-carrier mail is screened off-site prior to arrival at the Copyright Office. This can add 3-5 days to delivery time and could, therefore, impact the effective date of registration. See the Web site for details about proper packaging, special handling and other related information.

Open Books

Seattle's Thriving Bookstore for Poets

Photo © Michael Dylan Welch

by Michael Dylan Welch

Seattle is a city where more than half the adult population has a college degree, where the city's new library is a stunning architectural wonder, and where a nationally known librarian, Nancy Pearl, has her own action figure, complete with shushing index finger. Seattle even tops the country in number of bookstores per 10,000 people. In short, Seattle is a city whose population loves books and loves to read. So it's no wonder that Seattle boasts a poetry-only bookstore, one of only two in the country (the other is Grolier's, in Cambridge, Massachusetts). Indeed, Open Books: A Poem Emporium (www.openpoetrybooks.com) is one of the country's greatest poetry treasures—a place that poet Peter Pereira has called a "sacred site."

Open Books is located on a slight hill in a semi-residential area of Seattle's Wallingford neighborhood, just west across the I-5 freeway from the University district. There's a gas station, grocery store, and a famous burger joint named Dick's just down the street, intermingled with single-family homes. The store carries 9,000+ carefully selected titles, all poetry or poetry-related. Visitors could spend days perusing it all, yet the owners know much of their stock and welcome questions. Open Books is also a hangout for the local poetry community, where it's easy to talk with other store visitors because you know you share a common passion. What's more, locally or even nationally known poets are likely to walk into the store while you're browsing. It's a place where you want to listen in on other conversations because of the poetry news or gossip you're likely to hear.

One factor that helps Open Books thrive is the Pacific Northwest's rich poetry tradition. Theodore Roethke casts the longest shadow, having influenced other notable poets with current or past Seattle ties, including James Wright, Carolyn Kizer, David Wagoner, and Richard Hugo (Seattle's renowned literary arts center is named for Hugo). Denise Levertov was prominent here in her last years; and Heather McHugh, Richard Kenney, and Linda Beirds at the University of Washington are well known. Jim Harrison has called Copper Canyon Press in nearby Port Townsend the best publisher of poetry in America. Joshua Beckman of Wave Books is a recent Seattle transplant, and nearby San Juan Islander Sam

MICHAEL DYLAN WELCH has published his haiku, tanka, and longer poetry in hundreds of journals and anthologies in more than a dozen languages. His work appears in two Norton poetry anthologies, in such journals as *Rivet*, *StringTown*, *Pontoon*, *Floating Bridge Review*, and *Modern Haiku*, and has won first place in numerous contests. He is a director of the Haiku North America conference (www.haikunorthamerica.com), which he cofounded. He lives with his wife and two children near Seattle, Washington, and is also a board member of the Washington Poets Association, editor of *Tundra: The Journal of the Short Poem*, and of Press Here haiku and tanka books.

Green was just appointed as the first poet laureate of Washington State. Much of the current poetry populace regularly beats a path to Open Books.

But what makes Open Books tick? It's the dedication and generosity of its husband-and-wife owners, J.W. Marshall and Christine Deavel, who founded the store in 1995. They make visitors feel part of the community; and they themselves attend numerous readings and events at other venues around Seattle, sometimes even presenting their own work. And through it all, despite the seeming folly of running an independent bookstore (let alone one focused on poetry), their small but vibrant enterprise is thriving—and much loved.

This talk with Marshall and Deavel reveals some of their secrets and shows how they're dedicated to running their unique store—and quietly making a mark with their own poetry.

Contrary to national trends and what the National Endowment for the Arts would have us believe about the decline of books and reading, Seattle has been cited as having more readers per capita than any other city in the country. Do you think it's because of the rain?

JWM: Seattle is definitely a literate city. We have the wonders of nature all around us, but the weather really is conducive to staying indoors for several months of the year. I think also the city has a well-educated populace, and some large employers attract educated folk, paying them pretty well. And maybe something in the western migration mindset still lingers, a willingness to seek adventure, to engage curiosity. Reading is a natural outlet for that kind of mind.

Is having such a strong local concentration of highly educated people and dedicated book lovers part of the Open Books success story? What makes the store work in Seattle where it might not in other cities?

JWM: I'm not sure that a poetry-only bookstore couldn't work in most, if not all, major American cities. It seems to me more people are interested in poetry, actually interested enough to buy and read books, than is generally imagined.

I grew up here, arriving in 1959 when I was 7; so while I love Seattle, I may not be able to see what sets it apart. Aren't all cities like this? But what makes Open Books work in Seattle is, I think, a combination of our willingness to listen to and learn from and engage our customers, and our continued love for the art form of poetry. We still get excited by some books and some writers, and our customers appreciate that our interest is not solely in the sales potential of the books. That said, we need to sell books to keep the store open, and we make no secret of it. We are involved in a business, not some communal experience of the bliss of poetry.

CD: Unromantic a fact as it is, the price of real estate also makes a difference. The book business operates on a fairly small margin, making it difficult to hold on if you are in an expensive city. We were able to find a good store location before prices leapt in Seattle. It might be more challenging were we to start out here now. Still, compared to New York City or San Francisco, I imagine a marginal business like ours has an easier go of it here.

Also, Seattle is a tourist destination. We benefit from folks who come to ride the ferries, see the mountains, and stop by the poetry-only bookstore. We could not exist on our Seattle customers alone. We also ship to those folks who visit, and to people who have never set foot in the bookstore but have learned about us through friends, articles, or our Web site.

How does Open Books survive in the face of competition, volume buying, and price cutting from the chain bookstores?

JWM: The two of us know poetry. That sets our store apart from others, particularly the large chains and Internet monsters. I had a guy come in the store once looking for a book by a woman named Gold that had something to do with cells. A computer database, given this information, might have come up with some books for him to look over, but I figured he meant *The Gold Cell* by Sharon Olds and was right. We have been selling books for 20 years, and reading poetry closely for a lot longer than that; so our store of knowledge is pretty good, and our brains are still supple enough to make some sharp connections.

In this age of price being the marketplace god, we don't discount the price of books. We do include used books in our inventory, which usually cost less than new books. As for volume buying, that is meaningful only if you sell a large number of whatever title you buy in large numbers. The beauty of our store is the breadth of choices, another factor that sets us apart from other stores. Generally, some people are willing to pay a touch more for a book than they would from a discounter, knowing they benefit from our degree of expertise. And some people like helping the store stay in business, too.

CD: We try very hard to maintain a vast and varied stock. I like to think that the store is agenda-less, except to stock as much poetry as possible. We can't have everything—there's not enough room—but we want our shelves to have breadth, from tiny chapbooks to best-sellers; books published decades ago and those hot off the press; a variety of languages and aesthetics. Poetry is a big tent, and we want the store to reflect that.

I would also add that we run a pretty spare and, some might say, quirky operation. We have no employees—the person who orders the books is also the one who cleans (occasionally) the toilet. It definitely helps that we're committed to each other as well as the store. Those late nights working on the newsletter are done together in the house we share. We each understand the other's poetry mania. And our customers, the many who've hung with us, understand that for us to stay with it, we need to not burn out, which means that we

Photo © Michael Dylan Welch

Open Books, one of only two poetry-only bookstores in the country, stocks more than 9,000 poetry-related titles, including books by both well-known and emerging poets, used, and even out-of-print books.

cannot offer the extensive hours that a chain bookstore would, and that we close the store occasionally to get away for a few days.

Please describe Open Books. How do you have publications arranged? And would you want a bigger space, perhaps?

JWM: It is a relatively small space, long and narrow, about 450 square feet. The cash register is near the front door, and we greet pretty much everyone who comes in. Across the register is a display of recently received books and a cabinet of rarer books—first editions, some signed. We have a poetry-community bulletin board on one side and a display of sale books on the other; then the store gets a little wider with bookcases along all the walls. We have new and used books arranged together by author moving alphabetically around the room. The last four sets of shelves have anthologies, arranged by focus—meaning the haiku anthologies are together, the women's anthologies are together, that kind of thing. We also have displays of chapbooks and one display with magazines, mostly local.

As for wanting a bigger site, this store is perfect as it is. But a fantasy arrangement would have the store located in a larger building (with parking), which also housed a café with a liquor license, and a theater space for readings.

CD: But that is definitely a fantasy! It is indeed an intimate space, but I like to think that's part of its charm. And it's manageable (more or less) at this size. We are trying not to be foolish about what we can do.

What advice would you have for poets and small press publishers who struggle to sell and distribute their work?

JWM: I try to point out to fledgling poets that all writers start out, and most remain, as local writers. That doesn't necessarily mean writing about locale, but the community you live in will be your basis of support. Those are the people who are likely to come hear you read or who will buy your poetry.

That's the way to think about publishing, too. Begin with local magazines. And read them, don't just submit your poems to them. Attend readings whether or not you take part. Your poetry will improve through studying others. And, of course, read up a storm. Read everything. If you like a poem, figure out why. If you don't like a poem, figure out why. Talk to other people who are enthusiastic about poetry. Thinking about all writing, about what works and what doesn't work, is fine exercise for the creative mind.

I guess what I'm saying is don't let the act of making your work public become your highest priority. Study the craft. Enjoy it. Read and write, stay focused on the art, and associate with others who are into that, too. Somehow making the work public will happen.

What I've said about the poet's role is true for publishers, too. Fledgling small press publishers almost have it harder. It's easy, given some money, to get books printed. Getting them into the public's hands, and getting the public to want them in their hands, is not easy. Publishing poets whose work is known in a community is the best thing you can do. Community is vital, both geographically and aesthetically. Develop relationships with bookstores and reviewers and the poetry-buying public at large. And remember, no one owes you anything. And perhaps they don't share your vision of great work. Oh, well. Find your audience and treat them well. With perseverance you may find yourself enjoying your life as a publisher. I'd suggest not setting out to become New Directions; set out to publish some writers who deserve publishing. Focus on the art form, including the art of book design, and study what those publishers you consider to be successful are doing.

The thing to keep in mind, both for poets and small press publishers, is that there is no winning or losing. Engage in the process of creating, which is truly its own reward.

CD: I would encourage fledgling poets and publishers to learn as much as possible about the book business. If you hope to have a bookstore stock your book, you would be wise to know—in advance of approaching a bookseller—what to expect and what you want to offer. As with writers seeking out other writers to listen to and talk with, small press publishers in particular are well served by talking with others in their community. Community is key in the world of poetry, I think!

I would also encourage a Web presence. It needn't be elaborate. That's how I'm tracking down some interesting small presses I hear about by word of mouth. And certainly there are a number of ways to publish work online. That eliminates the struggle of distribution, but it also eliminates the wonderfulness that is a book.

How would you describe your own approaches to poetry, and how do you balance that with a need to be somewhat "agnostic" in support of varying genres and perspectives—or "agenda-less," as one of you said earlier? Are there some titles or types of poetry that you simply won't stock?

CD: My job as a bookseller is not to have everyone read what I read. It's to help people navigate their reading lives in ways that are satisfying to them. In the process I learn much from others, a true boon. The longer I've been reading and listening to and writing poetry, the more I can find to appreciate in all sorts of writing. The perfect poem is rare; we have to take our pleasures where we can.

I don't think we would rule out any particular type of poetry. We have been known to resist poetry books written by celebrities and published by mega-publishers, but even there we don't have a rule. We have limited space, so we make what we hope are wise judgments, not only about what will eventually interest at least one customer, but also what just feels right to have on the shelf.

In addition to running the store, you also have your own poetry careers. John, in 2007 you won the Field Poetry Prize from Oberlin College, a prestigious honor. In March of 2008, Oberlin University Press published *Meaning a Cloud*, your first full-length poetry collection. What did winning this prize mean to you, and how has it affected your poetic career?

JWM: Winning the Field Poetry Prize meant a great deal to me. It's lovely to think I have a book that potentially has national distribution and review attention. I like many of the poems, love some of them, and now they have their chance on a larger stage.

That book is a lesson in perseverance. *Field* magazine was one of my favorites literally decades ago, starting probably in the early 1980s. I sent them poems since I liked their taste, and was rejected. I tried every so often for years because I continued to read and admire the poems they printed, and the books they published, both in translation and by American poets. Then, nearly 20 years after my first rejection from them, they chose three poems for publication. So I tried their book contest, my first attempt with a manuscript, and was a finalist. I sent the magazine more poems and hit with another, so I gave my manuscript a major tweaking and sent again, two years after being the finalist. This time it hit. I am extra pleased to be published by Oberlin because I have retained such respect for the magazine and the books they've published.

Christine, your work has appeared in numerous journals, including *The American Poetry Review*, *Fence*, *The Iowa Review*, *Ploughshares*, *Talisman*, and *Volt*. In 2005, LitRag Press published your book *Box of Little Spruce*. What's next for you?

CD: I am a slow writer, often quiet for months, and even slower at pursuing publication. I've been grateful to be able to participate in the local poetry community, which has often spurred me to write. I continue to be amazed and buoyed by the generative power of artistic dialogue. While publication either on the page or the stage has been a gratifying part of my writerly life, my deepest satisfaction comes from the writing process itself, which is mysterious and invigorating—and at times frustrating and frightening. It's a journey that starts out in the unknown and ends somewhere that I hope will feel inevitable to me, and maybe a reader. There's no journey like it, at least for me.

How did the two of you meet, and what keeps you together—in addition to poetry? Are you ever poetically competitive with each other?

JWM: Though we each have a degree from the University of Iowa, we met here, in Seattle. We were introduced to each other by a mutual friend at a concert. She thought we would hit it off, and we did.

In addition to poetry, what holds us together, I think, is mutual respect. After 20 years of marriage, we know each other awfully well; and I believe each of us admires the choices the other makes in living a life. That, and we have similar caustic senses of humor. As for competing, we have learned that when we show each other a poem in progress, it is best to ask for what we want to hear. Do we want a critique or an appreciation of the piece? This has helped us talk about each other's work. Otherwise, we certainly do each want the other to get whatever success the other is looking for. And we each like the other's writing, which is very helpful.

CD: If there's a formula, it might be to not take ourselves overly seriously but to take each other quite seriously. How we spend our days is both avocation and vocation. That's a wonderful thing to practice as individuals—and to share.

You've met a tremendous number of prominent poets over the years. Any interesting anecdotes about these experiences? How often do major poets just walk into the store?

JWM: You're right, the list is very long. We have sold books at events ranging aesthetically from Barbara Guest to Billy Collins. (Open Books is the official bookseller for the Seattle Arts & Lectures poetry series, among other events.) It has been, and continues to be, quite a ride. Seamus Heaney and John Ashbery have each been in the store to do book signings. A friend who was driving Gwendolyn Brooks around town brought her in. She was delightfully magical. The late great American surrealist poet Philip Lamantia was brought to the store, and he, too, was quite a magical character. There are countless stories, but one vision that sticks with me is of looking down at Seamus Heaney's name printed on a gold card when he was buying a book. I felt like I was taking part in an American Express commercial.

How can poetry be more relevant to American culture? Do you see it as a problem for a poet to be "popular" (one thinks of Billy Collins)? And how should poets balance accessibility with erudition or challenge? I think of Owen Barfield who refers to "strangeness" in poetry—that it's only when poetry feels "strange" that the reader can grow by leaving his or her comfort level.

CD: Poetry can't be any more relevant to American culture, or to any culture. It is what it is; it has been written for millennia and it will continue to be written, no matter what happens. Poets shouldn't do any balancing; they should write what they need to write. They will find their community of readers, which may be one other person, if they're lucky. In the entryway of our store we have a quotation by Emily Dickinson: "If I read a book and it makes my whole body so cold no fire can ever warm me, I know that is poetry." That sentiment has bothered several folks, who believe that poetry should always be warm and embracing. But engagement with art is always a risk. And out of that risk can come astounding reward.

However, I'm also all in favor of the ditty, the witty, the silly bit of sonic nonsense. It's all poetry. It all offers something that matters to human existence.

JWM: I do love the strange, and have always felt that I get surprised as a reader of a poem when the poet has been surprised during the writing of it. I look for that.

The whole notion that a poet "should" do anything but write is a bit disquieting. The poet Dobby Gibson has a sweet piece in his book *Polar* that begins "It may be true that everything / has already been said, / but it's just as true that not everyone / has had a chance to say it." I find that a lovely sentiment. Before Nike told people to "Just Do It," Elizabeth Bishop told herself to "Write it."

Studying the art, poetry and all other art, is good for the writer, and should be pleasurable too. Worrying overly about the reception of the poem is unlikely to make for good art.

What are some of the best rewards of running a bookstore devoted to poetry?

CD: The books and the people, the people and the books. I am basically a private person. The poetry books here I might have been able to find elsewhere, but the people who have come into my life because of Open Books, the numerous and wonderful ways that they have broadened my life and my ever-evolving understanding of poetry, that would have been impossible without this store. I have the key to a place where poetry is paramount, where people read it, think about it, weep, laugh, and argue over it, and respect it profoundly. That continues to astound and delight me.

JWM: What more is there to say? I am astounded and delighted, too. What a lovely way to live.

The Greenville Poets

A Writer's Group That Does It Right

by Jane K. Kretschmann

I n west-central Ohio there's a small but very well published poetry group that sets the bar high for what such groups can accomplish. Founded over 20 years ago, the Greenville Poets boast 11 books in print (including a Pulitzer nomination), and have good advice to share about how to form and sustain a writers' group. Currently the Greenville Poets include five members—Myrna Stone, Belinda Rismiller, David Lee Garrison, Lianne Spidel, and Cathryn Essinger. They meet once a month to critique each other's poetry, share publishing information and provide the encouragement which, as Spidel says, "is the only way to sustain writing, knowing you have these people on your side."

Collectively, the members of Greenville Poets have won five Ohio Arts Council grants, two Walt McDonald First-Book Awards, and two Darke County Lowell Thomas Literary Awards. Four members have been named Ohio Poet of the Year. Their poems have appeared on *Poetry Daily*, *Verse Daily* and *The Writer's Almanac*, and have been choreographed by the Dayton Contemporary Dance Company in its 2006 piece *In a Word*.

THE CRITIQUE PROCESS

"We're dedicated, we work hard and we are all good friends who support each other's work," says Stone of the group's success. Their critique process is standard. Taking turns, each writer passes around copies of a poem turned face down, reads the poem aloud, gives everyone time to read the work silently, and then listens as the others make comments for the poet to consider in the revision process. "We try to offer each other the best criticism, but we also have to be sensitive," Stone explains. "Raking someone over the coals doesn't help." All agree that it is important to be absolutely honest, though, for the critique to be of benefit.

It's then up to the writer to decide which advice, if any, to follow. David Lee Garrison recalls Deanna Pickard, a member of the group until her death in 2004. "I'm not sure she ever took any of our suggestions," he says with a laugh. "I, on the other hand, am shameless about following advice. When I've taken a poem as far as I can go, I'm ready to have someone else look at it."

"You have to know when to stick to your guns, though," counters fellow member Belinda Rismiller. "If you think what you have is fine no matter what the group says, you have to stay with it."

JANE K. KRETSCHMANN teaches at a community college in Ohio. Her poems have been broadcast on NPR and WKCR in New York and published in journals such as *Ibbetson Street* and *The Ledge Poetry & Fiction Magazine*. Her chapbook is *Imagining a Life* (FootHills Publishing, 2006).

The development of this confident critical sense has taken time. In 1985, Stone decided the writing group she was then in was not providing adequate critique of her poetry. She joined with Rismiller and poet Miriam Vermilya to form the Greenville Poets.

In 1989 they invited Spidel, impressed with work she had submitted to a contest. Spidel is glad she joined for many reasons, one of which is the comfort of knowing that, when she's getting rejection letters, "these people are getting rejected, too, and I know that's just the way it works."

Cathryn Essinger, whose creative writing course had gotten Stone started as a poet, also joined the group in 1989. Later Erika Tweed, a German instructor from Troy, became a member, bringing the group to six.

The unexpected death of founding member Vermilya in January 1999 posed a new challenge: The group's members worked to overcome their grief by shepherding her manuscript into publication. As the Greenville Poets said in the book's afterword, "There was no time in which we didn't consider her presence among us—where she remains, witty, wise, a stickler for correct grammar, young at heart." When Vermilya's *Heartwood* was published in 2000 by Texas Tech University Press, it was nominated for the Pulitzer Prize, a tribute not only to the quality of Vermilya's poems but to the value of working with a small group of committed writers.

Cathryn Essinger thinks the group has worked together so successfully because of both the friendship and commitment of its members. "We have grown to be great friends, certainly; but when we come together, we are all focused on the poetry. And I think it helps that when we leave on Sunday evening, we go separate ways. We don't work together or even see each other much socially. So this is our special time together; we value it and make the most of it." She recommends that any writers considering forming a critique group develop such dedication.

Keeping the size of the group small is important, too. "If you have more than five or six members, you don't have time to be effective," Rismiller stresses. "It takes us the whole afternoon to give each poem its due." And since the poets meet alternately in two members' homes, the number of people who can sit comfortably around the table is a factor.

Meeting regularly is essential as well. "I was in a group before this one," Garrison says, "but it fell apart because it met irregularly, and that eventually became never." He believes that meeting every month "nudges you to produce, so it keeps you writing."

TAKING ON NEW MEMBERS

When the Greenville Poets consider adding a new member, they invite the poet as a guest to see how she—or he, in Garrison's case—interacts with the group and whether that person can take and give criticism effectively. They look for writers who are at least at the members' own level, and they consider what unique talent the potential member could bring to the group. Tweed brought her special knowledge of classical mythology, metrics and word derivations. Stone says that Pickard, with her interest in superstitions and cultural heritage, "quite simply inspired everyone." Garrison, the sole male in the group, is a foreign language professor, editor and translator.

Members emphasize that it's important to invite writers who are producing good work on a regular basis and possess a strength the rest of the group can learn from.

In the last several years, the Greenville Poets have enjoyed steadily growing state and national reputations. In addition to the many poems that have appeared in well-respected journals, members collectively have published three poetry chapbooks, eight books of poems, a volume of translation and an anthology of food poems. Interestingly enough, none of these successful poets have a MFA or an academic degree with an emphasis on poetry. They continue to educate themselves by attending workshops, reading a great deal, doing hands-on critiques, and revising, revising.

Belinda Rismiller's work has appeared in *The Bitter Oleander*. Her honors include Professional Assistance Awards from the Ohio Arts Council and the Darke County Endowment for the Arts, a Scholarship from the Catskill Writers' Conference, and two first-place awards in the Edison Community College poetry contests.

Myrna Stone's poems have appeared in *Poetry*, *Ploughshares* and *TriQuarterly*, among others, and have been anthologized in *Flora Poetica: The Chatto Book of Botanical Verse*. In 2004, two of her poems were named Distinguished Entries in the Campbell Corner Poetry Contest sponsored by Sarah Lawrence College. She is the recipient of a Full Fellowship to Vermont Studio Center and the 2002 Dr. O. Marvin Lewis Poetry Award from *Weber Studies*.

Lianne Spidel is a former Greenville High School teacher. Her poems have appeared in such journals as *Poetry*, *Southern Poetry Review* and *Shenandoah* and have been featured on *Poetry*'s Web site. Her work has also been anthologized in *I Have My Own Song For It: Modern Poems of Ohio*.

Cathryn Essinger's poems have been anthologized in *The Poetry Anthology, 1912-2002: Ninety Years of America's Most Distinguished Verse Magazine* and in *Poetry Daily: 366* Poems. Her work has appeared in such journals as *Poetry*, *The Southern Review* and *Quarterly* West. Essinger has received a scholarship to the Sewanee Writer's Conference. She teaches writing at Edison Community College in Piqua.

Read the Greenville Poets

David Lee Garrison:
- *Blue Oboe* (The Vincent Brothers Company, 1984)
- *Inside the Sound of Rain* (The Vincent Brothers Company, 1997)
- *Certain Chance* (by Pedro Salinas, translated by Garrison, Bucknell University Press, 2000)
- *Taste and See: Food Poems* (Edited by Garrison & Terry Hermsen (Bottom Dog Press, 2003)
- *Sweeping the Cemetery* (Browser Books Publishing, 2007)

Cathryn Essinger:
- *A Desk in the Elephant House* (Texas Tech University Press, 1998)
- *My Dog Does Not Read Plato* (Main Street Rag Publishing Company, 2004)

Myrna Stone:
- *The Art of Loss* (Michigan State University Press, 2001)
- *How Else to Love the World* (Browser Books Publishing, 2007)

Deanna Pickard:
- *In Dreams We Kiss Ourselves Good-bye* (Luquer Street Press, 2003)
- *Lose Them If You Can* (The Vincent Brothers Company, 2003)

Miriam Vermilya:
- *Heartwood* (Texas Tech University Press, 2000)

Lianne Spidel:
- *Chrome* (Finishing Line Press, 2006)

David Lee Garrison, the recipient of three Montgomery County Individual Artist Fellowships, teaches Spanish and Portuguese at Wright State University. He has taught poetry workshops at Sinclair Community College, Antioch University and the University of Dayton. His poems have appeared in publications such as *The Vincent Brothers Review, Colorado Review* and *The Nation*.

While celebrating their individual successes, the Greenville Poets have supported each other in their losses. Erika Tweed passed away less than a year after Deanna Pickard's death in December 2004. Whenever Essinger gives a public reading of her own work, she often reads some of Tweed's and Pickard's poems as well. "This is my way of honoring their work as Greenville Poets, and their friendship," Essinger explains. In addition, she is editing a chapbook of Tweed's poetry and will be submitting it for publication.

The Greenville Poets have begun to market themselves as a group. Garrison, for one, is "pleasantly surprised at how much interest there is in hearing what we have to offer." In 2004 they presented a program at the convention of the National Federation of State Poetry Societies (NFSPS) in Columbus, Ohio. In 2006 they were featured speakers at the West Virginia Writers' Conference. The Greenville Poets do group readings and have been the featured speakers at libraries and local and regional colleges, where they explain how a group inspires, critiques work and encourages poets to write and publish.

As Kathleen Burgess of the NFSPS has said, "The Greenville Poets group is the model of what a critiquing group should do and how to do it well. The members are friends who work with intensity and plenty of laughter over good food and even better poetry."

Editor's note: The Greenville Poets are available to meet with a class, conduct a workshop, provide a manuscript critique, give a poetry reading, or provide a panel discussion about how to form a writers' group or how to publish a book. For more information about fees and schedules, contact them through the group's Web site at www.greenvillepoets.org.

Publishing Poetry

A Reality Check

by Nancy Breen

As editor of *Poet's Market*, I got a lot of questions about the whole process of writing and submitting poetry. Often similar questions were forwarded to me from *Writer's Market*. Regardless of the source, I tried to treat all such queries with respect and genuine concern for passing along what I hoped was valued information.

There were certain questions, though, that I dreaded receiving—because my answers invariably lead to disillusionment and disappointment as I splashed cold reality into the faces of unsuspecting (and uninformed) poets. Read further if you're curious about these questions—I address them below.

Is there any money in poetry?

It really hurts to tell ambitious writers that their efforts will result in little monetary gain. However, that's the brutal truth about poetry: There's no money in it, at least not for the average hard-working (and even widely published) poet.

Most poetry appears in little magazines and literary journals. These markets are unlikely to pay cash for the poetry they print, offering instead a copy or two of the issue in which the poet's work appears (called a *contributor's copy*). Online literary magazines usually don't pay at all, although many poets see the worldwide exposure of Internet publication as a type of compensation. While there are a few larger literary magazines that do pay, they're quite prestigious and receive thousands of submissions per year while choosing a small percentage for publication. That means intense competition and high rates of rejection. The same is true of the few commercial magazines that publish poetry, such as *The New Yorker* and *The Atlantic Monthly*.

In truth, if you had a poem accepted by every paying magazine and journal, you probably still wouldn't make a decent income.

The situation in poetry book publishing is just as financially grim. Few of the "major" publishers put out many volumes of poetry; and those volumes usually are by our best known, established poets, talented up-and-comers, and major prizewinners. (A few celebrity poetry books may be in the mix; but, obviously, you have to become a celebrity *first* for publishers to take interest in your poetry.)

Most poetry publishers are literary presses, often run through universities and colleges;

NANCY BREEN is the former editor of *Poet's Market* (www.poetsmarket.com). Her chapbooks include: *Rites and Observances* (Finishing Line Press) and *How Time Got Away* (Pudding House Publications). She blogs at www.salmag undiexpress.wordpress.com.

or they're independent smaller presses. In either case, they don't have large sums of money to throw around for advances and royalties.

If you're disappointed, and even depressed by the low financial rewards of poetry publishing, ask yourself: When was the last time you bought a literary magazine or book of poetry? Few readers in America spend their dollars on poetry (and too often that includes the poets themselves).

Can you recommend a publisher for my 300-poem book manuscript?

First, reread the preceding section, especially the paragraphs about book publishers.

Next, if you haven't looked at the poetry shelves of your local bookstore lately, do a little market research. How many 300-poem books do you see? If you find one, is it by a single poet or is it an anthology? If the book is the work of one poet, review the biographical note for the poet's age, publishing history, academic background, awards won and hints about his or her standing in the literary community. If you don't have a similar biography as a poet, don't even think about trying to get such a massive collection of poems published.

Also, if you've never published any of your poems in literary magazines, don't start shopping for a book publisher just yet. The established route poets follow is to publish individual poems in magazines and journals (in print and online) before assembling a collection of any length. By publishing in magazines first, you establish some necessary credentials:

- You demonstrate you're familiar with the world of poetry publishing because you've been an active participant—publishers appreciate that.
- You prove that someone else has read and appreciated your work besides you, your friends and your family.
- You establish a track record of having worked successfully with editors.

There are occasional exceptions to the publish-in-magazines-first approach. The aforementioned celebrity poetry books are one example. And every few years there's a publishing phenomenon like Mattie Stepanek, the young boy with muscular dystrophy who sold millions of copies of his poetry books before his death at 14 in 2004. Such situations are unique unto themselves and represent exceptions, rather than the rule.

Keep in mind, too, that most poets progress from publishing in magazines to assembling a chapbook, rather than book manuscript. What is a chapbook? It's a soft cover publication of about 24-32 pages. Although bookstores don't stock chapbooks (even independent stores don't favor chapbooks because there's no spine showing the title—chapbooks are usually folded and saddle-stapled), chapbooks have become a very popular format. Production values range from simple to extravagant (depending on paper and cover stock), they can be produced and sold economically, and they're easy to offer for sale at readings. No, they don't make money for the poet *or* the press; but as I said earlier, money should never be a primary concern if you're serious about poetry.

Can you recommend an agent who can represent my poetry book?

As I said, there's little money in poetry. Agents work on commission, i.e., a percentage of what the poet is paid. Consequently, 15% of nothing doesn't make poetry attractive to agents.

As always, there may be exceptions. A highly successful poet may have an agent, especially if the poet does other writing that *does* benefit from representation. A beginning poet, though—especially a beginning poet with a manuscript of 300 previously unpublished poems—probably is not going to find an agent. In fact, any poet who comes across an agent who does express interest should be wary. Ask questions, do your homework, don't sign anything until you've thoroughly researched the agent. And *never* pay for representation.

How can I get my self-published book of poetry into bookstores?

Whether your book is truly self-published or printed by a vanity publisher or print-on-demand publisher (known as POD, wherein a publisher stores your book digitally and prints out copies as they're purchased), distribution is going to be a challenge. Bookstores usually work with professional distributors to stock their shelves, an avenue that may be closed to poets who self-publish. Similarly, vanity publishers can't get your books into bookstores without a distributor, no matter what they may claim. POD publishers may rely more on their own online bookstores and author Web sites than working with a distributor.

In most bookstores, a limited amount of shelf space is devoted to poetry. Sometimes independent bookstores (i.e., not owned by national chains) are more open to stocking small press and self-published books; this is especially true if the poet is a local author.

Poets shouldn't focus on bookstores as a sole source of sales. Other methods of selling include offering books through a personal Web site; scheduling readings at coffeehouses, bookstores or even your own church or community center (where you can offer your book for sale to the audience); and sending promotional postcards to potential customers with information about how to order by mail. To learn more, and to brainstorm additional ideas for selling and promotion, try your library for books on self-publishing; or enter "selling self-published books" or similar phrases into a search engine for a range of information and perspectives on the Web.

And about those anthologies . . .

No reality check for poets would be complete without a mention of those poetry operations that sponsor contests and Web sites, the ones that publish huge anthologies of "winning" poems. If you choose to participate, that's your decision, but be aware of these points:

- *Everyone* who submits a poem to such contests is "chosen" to appear in an anthology, so there's no quality standard.
- Having a poem published in such an anthology is *not* a legitimate publishing credit (that is, serious publishers don't take such publishing credits seriously).
- If your poem(s) appear in such an anthology, or on an associated public Web site, your work is considered "published" and cannot be submitted to any magazine or contest that does not accept previously published work.

Some poets appreciate the sense of community they find at such Web sites. They simply enjoy seeing their work in print and online, and they don't mind spending huge sums for copies of the anthologies (or for the plaques, coffee mugs and other merchandise that may be available). And that's their prerogative, as long as those poets aren't deceiving themselves about what such publication means. If they use their anthology appearances as selling points to prospective editors and publishers, though, they may find that they and their poetry are not going to be taken seriously.

What are your objectives?

Be realistic about what the world of poetry publishing has to offer and what you hope to achieve. If writing good poetry is more important to you than money, recognition and the other trappings of high stakes publication, then you're on the right path. If, on the other hand, you hope to achieve fame and fortune through your poetry, well—you need a reality check.

Mistakes Poets Make

I n putting together listings for *Poet's Market*, we ask editors for any words of advice they want to share with our readers. Often the editors' responses include comments about what poets should and shouldn't do when submitting work—the same comments, over and over. That means a lot of poets are repeating similar mistakes when they send out their poems for consideration.

The following list includes the most common of those mistakes—the ones poets should work hardest to avoid.

Not reading a publication before submitting work

Researching a publication is essential before submitting your poetry. Try to buy a sample copy of a magazine (by mail, if necessary) or at least see if an issue is available at the library. It may not be economically feasible for poets to purchase a copy of every magazine they target, especially if they send out a lot of poems. However, there are additional ways to familiarize youself with a publication.

Read the market listing thoroughly. If guidelines are available, send for them by e-mail or regular mail, or check for them online. A publication's Web site often presents valuable information, including sample poems, magazine covers—and guidelines.

Submitting inappropriate work

Make good use of your research so you're sure you understand what a magazine publishes. Don't rationalize that a journal favoring free verse might jump at the chance to consider your long epic poem in heroic couplets. Don't convince yourself your experimental style will be a good fit for the traditional journal filled with rhyming poetry. Don't go into denial about whether a certain journal and your poetry are made for each other. It's counterproductive and ultimately wastes postage (not to mention time—yours and the editor's).

Submitting an unreasonable number of poems

If an editor recommends sending three to five poems (a typical range), don't send six. Don't send a dozen poems and tell the editor to pick the five she wants to consider. If the editor doesn't specify a number (or the listing says "no limit"), don't take that as an invitation to mail off 20 poems. The editors and staff of literary magazines are busy enough as it is, and they may decide they don't have time to cope with you. (When submitting book or chapbook manuscripts to publishers, make sure your page count falls within the range they state.)

Don't go to the other extreme and send only *one* poem, unless an editor says it's okay (which is rare). One poem doesn't give an editor much of a perspective on your work, and it doesn't give you very good odds on getting the piece accepted.

Ignoring the editor's preferences regarding formats

If an editor makes a point of describing a preferred manuscript format, follow it, even if that format seems to contradict the standard. (Standard format includes using $8\frac{1}{2} \times 11$ white paper and conventional typeface and point size; avoid special graphics, colors or type flourishes; put your name and address on every page.) Don't devise your own format to make your submission stand out. Keep everything clean, crisp and easy to read (and professional).

Be alert to e-mail submission formats. Follow directions regarding what the editor wants printed in the subject line, how many poems to include in a single e-mail, whether to use attachments or paste work in the body of the message, and other elements. Editors have good reasons for outlining their preferences; ignoring them could mean having your e-mail deleted before your poems are even read.

Omitting a self-addressed stamped envelope (SASE)

Why do editors continuously say "include a SASE with your submission"? Because so many poets don't do it. Here's a simple rule: Unless the editor gives alternate instructions, include a #10 SASE, whether submitting poems or sending an inquiry.

Writing bad cover letters (or omitting them completely)

Cover letters have become an established part of the submission process. There are editors who remain indifferent about the necessity of a cover letter, but many consider it rude to be sent a submission without any other communication from the poet.

Unless the editor says otherwise, send a cover letter. Keep it short and direct, a polite introduction of you and your work. (See "Frequently Asked Questions" on page 7 for more tips on cover letters, and an example.) Here are a few important Don'ts:

- **Don't** list all the magazines where your work has appeared; limit yourself to five magazine titles. The work you're submitting has to stand on its own.
- **Don't** tell the editor what a good poet you are—or how good someone else thinks you are.
- **Don't** tell the editor how to edit, lay out or print your poem. Some of those decisions are up to the editor, assuming she decides to accept your poem in the first place.
- **Don't** point out the poem is copyrighted in your name or include the copyright symbol. All poems are automatically copyrighted in the poet's name as soon as they're "fixed" (i.e., written down), and editors know this.

Not maintaining good editor/poet relations

Most editors are hard-working poetry lovers dedicated to finding and promoting good work. They aspire to turn submissions around as quickly as possible and to treat all poets with respect. They don't want to steal your work. Often they aren't paid for their labor and may even have to dip into their own pockets just to keep their magazines going.

Poets should finesse their communications with editors regarding problems, especially in initial letters and e-mail. Editors (and their magazines and presses) aren't service-oriented businesses, like the phone company. Getting huffy with an editor as if arguing with your cable provider about an overcharge is inappropriate. Attitude isn't going to get you anywhere; in fact, it could create additional obstacles.

That's not to say poets shouldn't feel exasperated when they're inconvenienced or ill treated. None of us likes to see our creations vanish, or to pay good money for something we're never going to receive (like a subscription or sample copy). However, exasperated is one thing; outraged is another. Too often poets go on the offensive with editors and make matters worse. Experts on how to complain effectively recommend you keep your cool and stay professional, no matter what kind of problem you're trying to work out.

For additional advice on editor/poet relations, see "Dealing With Problem Editors" on page 33.

Dealing With Problem Editors

There *are* problem editors out there, and we've all encountered them at one time or another. Some rip people off, prey on poets' desires to be published, or treat poets and their work with flagrant disregard. Fortunately, such editors are very much in the minority.

Now and then you may discover the disorganized editor or the overwhelmed editor; these two cause heartache (and heartburn) by closing up shop without returning manuscripts, or failing to honor paid requests for subscriptions and sample copies. More often than not, their transgressions are rooted in chaos and irresponsibility, not malicious intent. Frustrating as such editors are, they're not out to get you.

There are many instances, too, where larger circumstances are beyond an editor's control. For example, a college-oriented journal may be student-staffed, with editors changing each academic year. Funds for the journal may be cut unexpectedly by administration belt-tightening, or a grant could be cancelled. The editorial office may be moved to another part of the university. An exam schedule could impact a publishing schedule. All of these things cause problems and delays.

Then again, a literary journal may be a one-person, home-based operation. The editor may get sick or have an illness in the family. Her regular job may suddenly demand lots of overtime. There may be divorce or death with which the editor has to cope. A computer could crash. Or the editor may need to scramble for money before the magazine can go to the printer. Emergencies happen, and they take their toll on deadlines. The last thing the editor wants is to inconvenience poets and readers, but sometimes life gets in the way.

Usually, difficulties with these kinds of "problem" editors can be resolved satisfactorily through communication and patience. There are always exceptions, though. Here are a few typical situations with problem editors and how to handle them:

An editor is rude. If it's a matter of bad attitude, take it with a grain of salt. Maybe he's having a rotten day. If there's abusive language and excessive profanity involved, let us know about it. (See the complaint procedure on page 34.)

An editor harshly criticizes your poem. If an editor takes time to comment on your poetry, even if the feedback seems overly critical, consider the suggestions with an open mind and try to find something valid and useful in them. If, after you've given the matter fair consideration, you think the editor was out of line, don't rush to defend your poetry or wave your bruised ego in the editor's face. Allow that the editor has a right to her opinion (which you're not obligated to take as the final word on the quality of your work), forget about it and move on.

An editor is slow to respond to a submission. As explained above, there may be many reasons why an editor's response takes longer than the time stated in the market listing or guidelines. Allow a few more weeks to pass beyond the deadline, then write a polite inquiry to the editor about the status of your manuscript. (Include a SASE if sending by regular mail.) Understand an editor may not be able to read your letter right away if deadlines are pressing or if he's embroiled in a personal crisis. Try to be patient. If you haven't received a reply to your inquiry after a month or so, however, it's time for further action.

An editor won't return your manuscript. Decide whether you want to invest any more time in this journal or publisher. If you conclude you've been patient long enough, write a firm but professional letter to the editor withdrawing your manuscript from consideration. Request that the manuscript be returned; but know, too, a truly indifferent editor probably won't bother to send it back or reply in any way. Keep a copy of your withdrawal letter for your files, make a new copy of your manuscript and look for a better market.

Also, contact *Poet's Market* by letter or e-mail with details of your experience. We always look into problems with editors, although we don't withdraw a listing on the basis of a single complaint unless we discover further evidence of consistent misbehavior. We do, however, keep complaints on file and watch for patterns of unacceptable behavior from any specific market.

An editor takes your money. If you sent a check for a subscription or sample copy and you haven't received anything, review your bank statement to see if the check has been cashed. If it has, send the editor a query. Politely point out the editor has cashed your check, but you haven't yet received the material you were expecting. Give the editor the benefit of the doubt: An upcoming issue of a magazine could be running late, your subscription could have been overlooked by mistake, or your copy could have been lost in transit or sent in error to the wrong address.

If your check has *not* been cashed, query the editor to see if your order was ever received. It may have been lost (in the mail or on the editor's desk), the editor may be holding several checks to cash at one time, or the editor may be waiting to cash checks until a tardy issue is finally published.

Complaint Procedure

Important

If you feel you have not been treated fairly by a market listed in *Poet's Market*, we advise you to take the following steps:

- First, try to contact the market. Sometimes one phone call, letter, or e-mail can quickly clear up the matter. Document all your communications with the market.

- When you contact us with a complaint, provide the details of your submission, the date of your first contact with the market and the nature of your subsequent communication.

- We will file a record of your complaint and further investigate the market.

- The number and severity of complaints will be considered when deciding whether or not to delete a market from the next edition of *Poet's Market*.

If you get an unsatisfactory response from the editor (or no response at all), wait a few weeks and try again. If the matter still isn't resolved, let us know about it. We're especially interested in publishers who take money from poets but don't deliver the goods. Be sure to send us all the details of the transaction, plus copies of any correspondence (yours and the editor's). We can't pursue your situation in any legal way or act as mediator, but we can ban an unscrupulous publisher from *Poet's Market* and keep the information as a resource in case we get later complaints.

Should you continue trying to get your money back from such editors? That's your decision. If your loss is under $10 (say, for a subscription or sample copy), it might cost you less in the long run to let the matter go. And the fee for a "stop payment" order on a check can be hefty—possibly more than the amount you sent the editor in the first place. Yes, it's infuriating to be cheated, but sometimes fighting on principle costs more than it's worth.

If your monetary loss is significant (for instance, you shelled out a couple hundred dollars in a subsidy publishing agreement), consider contacting your state attorney general's office for advice about small claims court, filing a complaint and other actions you can take.

Is It a 'Con'?

Think Before You Trust

What is a "con"? Con is short for "confidence," an adjective defined by Webster's as "of, relating to, or adept at swindling by false promise," as in "confidence man" or "confidence game." While the publishing world is full of legitimate opportunities for poets to gain honor and exposure for their work, there are also plenty of "cons." How can you tell the difference? The following are some of the most common situations that cost poets disappointment, frustration—and cash. Learn to spot them before submitting your work, and don't let your vanity be your guide.

ANTHOLOGIES

Has this happened to you? You see an ad in a perfectly respectable publication announcing a poetry contest with big cash prizes. You enter, and later you receive a glowing letter congratulating you on your exceptional poem, which the contest sponsor wants to include in his deluxe hardbound anthology of the best poetry submitted to the contest. The anthology costs only, say, $65. You don't have to buy it—they'll still publish your poem—but wouldn't you be proud to own one? And wouldn't it be nice to buy additional copies to give to family and friends? And for an extra charge you can include a biographical note. And so on . . .

Of course, when the anthology arrives, the quality of the poetry may not be what you were expecting, with several poems crammed unattractively onto a page. Apparently everyone who entered the contest was invited to be published; you basically paid cash to see your poem appear in a phone book-like volume with no literary merit whatsoever.

Were you conned? Depends on how you look at it. If you bought into the flattery and believed you were being published in an exclusive, high-quality publication, no doubt you feel duped. On the other hand, if all you were after was seeing your poem in print, even knowing you'd have to pay for the privilege, then you got what you wanted. (Unless you've deceived yourself into believing you've truly won an honor and now have a worthy publishing credit; you don't.)

If you don't want to add insult to injury, resist additional spiels, like having your poem printed on coffee mugs and t-shirts (you can do this yourself through print shops or online services like www.cafepress.com) or spending large sums on awards banquets and conferences. And, before you submit a single line of poetry, find out what rights the contest sponsor acquires. You may be relinquishing all rights to your poem simply by mailing it in or submitting it through a Web site. If the poem no longer belongs to you, the publisher can do whatever he wishes with it. Don't let your vanity propel you into a situation you'll always regret.

READING AND CONTEST FEES

Suppose you notice a promising market for your poetry, but the editor requires a set fee just to consider your work. Or you see a contest that interests you, but you have to pay the sponsor a fee just to enter. Are you being conned?

In the case of reading fees, keep these points in mind: Is the market so exceptional that you feel it's worth risking the cost of the reading fee to have your work considered? What makes it so much better than markets that do *not* charge fees? Has the market been around awhile, with an established publishing schedule? What are you paid if your work is accepted? Are reasonably priced samples available so you can judge the production values and quality of the writing?

Reading fees don't necessarily signal a suspicious market. In fact, they're increasingly popular as editors struggle with the costs of publishing books and magazines, including the man-hours required to read loads of (often bad) submissions. However, fees represent an additional financial burden on poets, who often don't receive any monetary reward for their poems to begin with. It's really up to individual poets to decide whether paying a fee is beneficial to their publishing efforts. Think long and hard about fee-charging markets that are new and untried, don't pay poets for their work (at the very least a print publication should offer a contributor's copy), charge high prices for sample copies or set fees that seem unreasonable.

Entry fees for contests often fund prizes, judges' fees, honorariums and expenses of running and promoting the contest (including publishing a "prize" collection or issue of a magazine). Other kinds of contests charge entry fees, from Irish dancing competitions to bake-offs at a county fair. Why not poetry contests?

That's not to say you shouldn't be cautious. Watch out for contests that charge higher-than-average fees, especially if the fees are out of proportion to the amount of prize money being given. (Look through the Contests & Awards section beginning on page 353 to get a sense of what most competitions charge; you'll also find contests in other sections of this book by consulting the Additional Contests & Awards index on page 421.) Find out how long the contest has been around, and verify whether prizes have been awarded each year and to whom. In the case of book and chapbook contests, send for one of the winning publications to confirm that the publisher puts out a quality product. Regard with skepticism any contest that tells you you've won something, then demands payment for an anthology, trophy or other item. (It's okay if a group offers an anthology for a modest price without providing winners with free copies. Most state poetry societies have to do this; but they also present cash awards in each category of the contest, and their entry fees are low.)

SUBSIDY PUBLISHERS, PRINT-ON-DEMAND

Poetry books are a hard sell to the book-buying public. Few of the big publishers handle these books, and those that do feature the "name" poets (i.e., the major prize winners and contemporary masters with breathtaking reputations). Even the small presses publish only so many books per year—far less than the number of poets writing.

No wonder so many poets decide to pay to have their poetry collections published. While some may self-publish (i.e., take full control of their book, working directly with a printer), others turn to subsidy publishers (also called "vanity publishers") and print-on-demand (POD) publishers.

There are many differences between subsidy publishing and POD publishing, as well as similarities (having to pay to get published is a big one). Whether or not you get conned is entirely up to you. *You* have to take responsibility for asking questions, doing research on presses, and reading the fine print on the contract to make sure you know exactly what you're paying for. There are landmines in dealing with subsidy and POD publishers, and you have to investigate thoroughly and intelligently to avoid damage.

Some questions to keep in mind: Are fees inflated compared to the product and services you'll be receiving? Will you still own the rights to your book? Does the publisher put out a quality product that's attractive and cleanly printed? (Get a sample copy and find out.) How many copies of the book will you receive? How much will you have to pay for additional copies? How will your book be sold and distributed? (Don't count on seeing your volume in bookstores.)

Will you receive royalties? How much? Does the publisher offer any kind of promotional assistance or is it all up to you? Will those promotion efforts be realistic and results-oriented? (Sometimes "promotion" means sending out review copies, which is a waste—such volumes are rarely reviewed.) Don't wait until *after* you've signed a contract (and a check) to raise these issues. Do your homework first.

Obviously, poets who don't stay on their toes may find themselves preyed upon. And a questionable publishing opportunity doesn't have to be an out-and-out rip-off for you to feel cheated. In every situation, you have a choice *not* to participate. Exercise that choice, or at least develop a healthy sense of skepticism before you fling yourself and your poetry at the first smooth talker who compliments your work. Poets get burned because they're much too impatient to see their work in print. Calm your ego, slow down and devote that time, energy and money toward reading other poets and improving your own writing. You'll find that getting published will eventually take care of itself.

Helpful Web sites

For More Info

The following Web sites include specific information about questionable poetry publishers and awards. For more Web sites of value to poets, see Additional Resources on page 466.

- An Incomplete Guide to Print On Demand Publishers offers articles on POD publishing, comparisons of POD publishers (contracts, distribution, fees, etc.) and an online forum: *http://booksandtales.com/ pod/index.php*

- Answers to frequently asked questions about poetry awards from the Academy of American Poets: *www.poets.org/page.php/prmID/116*

- Poets will find warnings and other valuable publishing information on the Preditors & Editors Web site: *www.anotherealm.com/prededitors/*

- Writer Beware tracks contests, publishers and literary agents: *www.sfwa.org/beware*

- "Literary Contest Caution" at *http://windpub.com/literary.scams*

Promote Your Work

Attracting Readers Is Up to You

These days, all writers have to promote themselves and their work in order to attract readers. This is especially true for poets. Does the idea of "putting yourself out there" make you uncomfortable? Think of self-promotion as a means of sharing poetry as well as promoting it. Here are a few suggestions to get you started:

Meet the public.

Do poetry readings and book signings. Get in touch with bookstores and coffeehouses: call, send postcards (see below) or press releases, let them know you're available. Find out when and where open mic readings are scheduled. Sign up, read your poems. If you've published a book or chapbook, be creative about handselling your collection. It's hard to break into the big chain bookstores, but independent stores may be happy to stock your publication (especially if you're a local author) and arrange a book signing.

Widen your scope: Would the local historical society be interested in an appearance? Is there a community group who might enjoy having you read and sign books as part of their meeting program? Would a friend be willing to sponsor a "poetry night" house party with you as the featured reader?

Create poetry postcards.

Think specially designed postcards, not the plain ones you buy at the post office. You can create postcards on your computer, or paste up a master design from typewritten copy and clip art. (You could even use rubber stamps to dress up a plain printed card.) If you design the postcards on your computer, you can print them out yourself as well. (Special perforated postcard stock for home printers is available in various sizes at your local office supply store.) Or you can take your master design to a quick print shop and have the postcards printed there. (If you're printing a lot of postcards, this might be the less expensive option.)

Postcards can be informational (i.e., used to announce a reading or new publication), but they can also be used to share your poetry. Simply type one of your poems on one side of the card, using an attractive, readable font. Leave the other side blank; or, if the poem is from a book or chapbook you want to promote, indicate the title of the collection and include ordering information. Keep all text and design elements on the far left side of the postcard back so they don't interfere with the addressee portion of the card.

Postcard mailings get results, but remember that postcards don't have to be mailed to be effective. Don't be shy about giving out postcards at readings, especially your poem postcards. Offer to sign them. Your audience will enjoy having a personalized souvenir of your reading, and they may decide later to order your book or chapbook.

Use poetry postcards for personal communications, too. Turn a simple note into a chance to enhance someone's day with poetry.

Step into the media spotlight.

It doesn't have to be a *big* spotlight. Your community newspaper probably prints "news-maker" tidbits like award and publication announcements, and it may even be interested in doing a feature on a "local poet." (Regional magazines are another possibility.) Newspapers usually have calendar sections where you can list a reading or bookstore appearance. (Be sure to provide all the necessary details.) TV and radio stations may also broadcast arts and entertainments calendars, and locally produced programs may be very happy to schedule a poet for an interview segment or to promote a reading. You never know until you ask. (Be polite, never pushy.)

Create a Web site. Start a blog.

It's helpful to have a URL to list on press releases, business cards and postcards. A Web site or blog is a shortcut for anyone who wants to know more about you, from biographical information to samples of your poetry. Your "place on the Web" can be as complicated or as simple as you wish. There are plenty of books and software programs available to help, even if you're a first-timer with few computer skills. There's also a lot of free information on the Web, including free blog-hosting sites that make it easy to become a "poet-blogger."

Whether you try these approaches or come up with some new, creative techniques of your own, don't hesitate to promote yourself and your work. Every reading, book signing, interview, and Web site is an opportunity to attract new readers to poetry.

Important Market Listing Information

Important

- Listings are based on questionnaires completed by editors, and on subsequent verified copy. Listings are not advertisements, *nor* are markets necessarily endorsed by the editors of this book.

- Information in the listings comes directly from the publishers and is as accurate as possible. However, publications and editors come and go, and poetry needs fluctuate between the publication date of this directory and the date of purchase.

- If you are a poetry publisher and would like to be considered for a listing in the next edition, e-mail us at poetsmarket@fwpubs.com or send a SASE (or SAE and IRC) to *Poet's Market*—QR, 4700 East Galbraith Road, Cincinnati OH 45236.

- *Poet's Market* reserves the right to exclude any listing that does not meet its requirements.

Magazines/ Journals

L iterary magazines and journals usually provide a poet's first publishing success. In fact, you shouldn't be thinking about book/chapbook publication until your poems have appeared in a variety of magazines, journals and zines (both print and online). This is the preferred way to develop an audience, build publishing credits and learn the ins and outs of the publishing process.

In this section you'll find hundreds of magazines and journals that publish poetry. They range from small black-and-white booklets produced on home computers to major periodicals with high production values and important reputations. To help you sort through these markets and direct your submissions most effectively, we've organized information in each listing according to a basic format.

HOW LISTINGS ARE FORMATTED

Content of each market listing was provided or verified by a representative of the publication (editor, poetry editor, managing editor, etc.). Here is how that content is arranged within the listing:

Symbols. Icons at the beginning of each listing offer visual signposts to specific information about the publication: (**N**) this market is recently established and new to *Poet's Market*; (**✪**) this market did not appear in the 2008 edition; (**▣**) this market publishes primarily online (although it may also produce an annual print version or a "best of" anthology); (**✦**) this market is located in Canada or (**⊕**) outside the U.S. and Canada; (**$**) this market pays a monetary amount (as opposed to contributor's copies); (**◯**) this market welcomes submissions from beginning poets; (**◐**) this market prefers submissions from skilled, experienced poets, will consider work from beginning poets; (**◑**) this market prefers submissions from poets with a high degree of skill and experience; (**◎**) this market has a specialized focus (listed in parentheses after magazine/journal title); (**⊘**) this market does not consider unsolicited submissions; and (**⊘**) this market is closed to *all* submissions. (Keys to these symbols are listed on the inside covers of this book and on page 3.)

Contact information. Depending on what was provided by each editor, contact information includes: magazine/journal title (in bold) with areas of specialization noted in parentheses where appropriate; regular mail address; telephone number; fax number; e-mail address; Web site address; year the publication was established; the name of the person to contact (or an editorial title); and membership in small press/publishing organizations. (**Note:** If a magazine/journal publishes only online and/or wants submissions by e-mail exclusively, no street address may be given.)

Magazine Needs. It's important to study this section as you research potential markets.

Here you'll find such helpful information as the editor's overview of the publication, with individual poetry needs and preferences; a list of recently published poets; production information (number of pages, printing/binding details, type of cover); the number of poetry submissions the publication receives vs. the number accepted; and press run, distribution and price information.

How to Submit. This section focuses on the specific details of submitting work: how many poems to send; minimum/maximum number of lines per poem; whether previously published poems or simultaneous submissions are considered; submission format preferences (including whether to submit by e-mail, and how); response times; payment; rights acquired and more.

Additional Information. Editors may use this section to explain other publishing activities, elaborate on some aspect of the magazine/journal, suggest future plans—anything beyond the basic details that readers may find of interest.

Contest/Award Offerings. This section discusses prizes and competitions associated with the publication, with either brief guidelines or a cross-reference to a separate listing in the Contests & Awards section.

Also Offers. Describes additional offerings associated with this publication (i.e., sponsored readings, Web site activities such as blogs and forums, related poetry groups, etc.).

Advice. Provides direct quotes from editors about everything from pet peeves to tips on writing to perspectives on the state of poetry today.

GETTING STARTED, FINDING MARKETS

If you don't have a certain magazine or journal in mind, read randomly through the listings, making notes as you go. (Don't hesitate to write in the margins, underline, use highlighters; it also helps to flag markets that interest you with Post-It Notes). Browsing the listings is an effective way to familiarize yourself with the kind of information presented and the publishing opportunities that are available at various skill levels.

If you have a specific market in mind, however, begin with the General Index. Here all the book's listings are alphabetized along with additional references that may be buried within a listing (such as a press name or competition title). Also, markets from the 2008 edition that don't appear in this book are included in the General Index, accompanied by a two-letter code explaining the market's absence (a key to these codes appears at the beginning of the General Index). Furthermore, publications that have changed names since the 2008 edition are listed in the General Index, cross-referenced to the new titles.

REFINE YOUR SEARCH

To supplement the General Index, we provide the following indexes to help you refine your marketing plan for submitting your poems to publications. Not every listing appears in one of these indexes, so use them only to reinforce your other research efforts:

Openness to Submissions Index categorizes markets according to the icons (☐ ◑ ◔ ◎) that appear at the beginning of each listing—signposts that indicate the level of writing an editor prefers to see. (For an explanation of these symbols, see page 3, the inside covers of this book or the handy tear-out bookmark just inside the front cover.)

Geographical Index sorts magazines and journals by state or by countries outside the U.S. Some markets are more open to poets from their respective regions, so this index is helpful when pinpointing local opportunities.

Subject Index groups markets according to areas of special focus. These include all specialized markets (appearing with the ◎ symbol) as well as broader categories such as online markets, poetry for children, markets that consider translations and others. When you want to submit a poem that features a certain topic or theme, is written in a specific form or style or addresses a unique audience, check this index first.

THE NEXT STEP

Once you know how to interpret the listings in this section and identify markets for your work, the next step is to start submitting your poems. See "Getting Started (and Using This Book)" on page 2 and "Frequently Asked Questions" on page 7 for advice, guidelines for preparing your manuscript and proper submissions procedures.

ADDITIONAL FEATURES

The Magazines/Journals section includes seven Insider Reports that cover a wide range of artists and topics: Lauren Mosko interviews poet **Mary Karr** about how her love of the world supports her poetry (page 60); Brian Daldorph interviews **John Mark Eberhart** about his double life as a journalist and a poet (page 92); Mosko interviews poet and *Asheville Poetry Review* editor **Keith Flynn** about his devotion to the process of writing (page 148); Nancy Breen interviews poet **Diane Glancy** about her involvement in the National Federation of State Poetry Societies (page 194); poet **Sandra Soli** writes about the prose poem (page 238); and Breen interviews poet-dentist **Daniel Thomas Moran** about life juggling a pen and dental surgery (page 280).

Ⓝ ▣ ☻ (A BRILLIANT) RECORD MAGAZINE

1055 Granville, Chicago IL 60660. (312)361-5057. E-mail: northsider2402@hotmail.com. Web site: www.recordblog.blogspot.com. Established 2007. **Contact:** Godfrey Logan.

Magazine Needs *(A Brilliant) Record Magazine*, published 2 times/year online and by e-mail, prints "quality poetry and short stories outside the box. If another magazine says it's not what they're looking for, then it's likely that I want it." *(A Brilliant) Record Magazine* (e-mail version) is about 20 pages. "Will accept 50% of what I receive." Press run is 200; "copies of the magazine are sent via e-mail; but if print copies are requested, they go first to those who have been accepted more than once on blog/site, and after that to those who request copies from what is left of run (4 copies at are sent out in that case)."

How to Submit Submit 5-6 poems at a time. Lines/poem: 5-10. Considers simultaneous submissions; no previously published poems (does not consider poems posted on a public Web site/blog/forum or on a private, password-protected forum to be previously published). Accepts e-mail submissions (pasted into body of message); no disk submissions. Cover letter is preferred. "Just a few words about publishing history or inspiration for work. Will be included in publication." Reads submissions year round. Time between acceptance and publication is 1 week. Never comments on rejected poems. "Please see previous work on blog/site to know what I'm looking for." Sometimes publishes theme issues. Upcoming themes available by e-mail. Guidelines available by e-mail or on Web site. Responds in 1 week. Pays 1-4 contributor's copies. Acquires one-time rights. Rights revert to poets upon publication. "Will not accept books for review but will accept well written reviews no more than 500 words."

Advice "Never give up on your dream of writing! Be patient! I have published at several different online publications, and it doesn't get any easier. Always support your literary magazines!"

Ⓐ ◎ THE AARDVARK ADVENTURER (Specialized: light verse; humor; subscribers given preference)

Pickle Gas Press, 31 Rolling Meadows Way, Penfield NY 14526. (585)388-6968. E-mail: thearmchair aesthete@yahoo.com or bypaul@frontiernet.net. Established 1996. **Contact:** Paul Agosto, editor.

Magazine Needs *The Aardvark Adventurer*, published 3 times/year, is "a family-fun digest-style zine of humor, thought, and verse. Very short stories (less than 500 words) are sometimes included." Wants "light, brief humorous verse; any style; any 'family-acceptable' subject matter." Does not want anything "obscene, overly forboding; no graphic gore or violence." Submission MUST be accompanied by a SASE (#10 envelope). Has published poetry by Chris Brown, Laverne and Carol Frith, Lydia Williams, Andrew Bynom, and Douglas Empringham. *The Aardvark Adventurer* is 12 pages, digest-sized, photocopied, saddle-stapled. Receives about 500 poems/year, accepts about 40%. Press run is 150. Single copy: $5 postpaid and 2 First-Class stamps; subscription: $8/3 issues. Make checks payable to Paul Agosto. **"Subscription not required, but subscribers given preference."**

How to Submit Lines/poem: 16 maximum. Considers previously published poems and simultaneous submissions, if indicated. Accepts e-mail submissions (pasted into body of message). Cover letter is preferred. Time between acceptance and publication is up to 12 months. Seldom comments on rejected poems. Guidelines available for SASE. Responds in 2 months. Pays 1 contributor's copy. Acquires one-time rights.

Advice "*The Aardvark Adventurer*, a digest-style publication with a very playful format, is a perfect opportunity for the aspiring poet."

Ⓐ ABBEY

5360 Fallriver Row Court, Columbia MD 21044. E-mail: greisman@aol.com. Established 1970. **Contact:** David Greisman, editor.

Magazine Needs *Abbey* is "a more-or-less informal zine looking for poetry that does for the mind what the first sip of Molson Ale does for the palate." Does not want "pornography or politics." Has published poetry by Richard Peabody, Ruth Moon Kempher, Carol Hamilton, Harry Calhoun, Wayne Hogan, and Edmund Conti. *Abbey* is usually 20-26 pages, magazine-sized, photocopied, and held together with 1 low-alloy metal staple in the top left corner. Receives about 1,000 poems/ year, accepts about 150. Press run is 200. Subscription: $2. Sample: 50¢.

How to Submit Responds in 1 month "except during baseball season." Pays 1-2 contributor's copies.

Additional Information Abbey Cheapochapbooks come out once or twice every 5 years, averaging 10-15 pages. For chapbook consideration, query with 4-6 sample poems, bio, and list of publications. Responds in 2 months "including baseball season." Pays 25-50 author's copies.

Advice "I'm definitely seeing poetry from 2 schools—the nit'n'grit school and the textured/reflective school. I much prefer the latter."

▣ ☑ ABRAMELIN, THE JOURNAL OF POETRY AND MAGICK

P.O. Box 337, Brookhaven NY 11719. E-mail: nessaralindaran@aol.com. Web site: www.abramelin .net. Established 2006. **Contact:** Vanessa Kittle, editor.

Magazine Needs *Abramelin, the Journal of Poetry and Magick*, published biannually online and a yearly best of edition each December, offers "literary poetry and essays concerning the western esoteric traditions." Wants "poetry that shows rather than tells. Poems that make me jealous of the writer. Poems that are inspired with wonderful language and imagery. In short—literature. Poetry submissions needn't be about magick at all. I feel that real poetry is magick. In fact, poetry that is literally magickal in theme has to be twice as good." Does not want "rhyming poems. Very short fiction. But beware, I learned from the best." Considers poetry by teens. Has published poetry by Simon Perchik, Rich Kostelanetz, and Lyn Lifshin. *Abramelin* receives about 1,000 poems/year, accepts about 5%. Distributed free online. Number of unique visitors: 3,000/issue.

How to Submit Submit 1-5 poems at a time. Lines/poem: no minimum/maximum. Considers previously published poems and simultaneous submissions (with notification). Accepts e-mail (pasted into body of message) and disk submissions. Cover letter is preferred. Reads submissions year round. Submit seasonal poems 2 months in advance. Time between acceptance and publication is 1-3 months. Often comments on rejected poems. Sometimes publishes theme issues. Upcoming themes available in magazine or on Web site. Guidelines available by e-mail or on Web site. Responds in 1 month. Pays 1 contributor's copy. Acquires one-time rights, with option to include in a yearly print anthology. Rights revert to poets upon publication.

Additional Information Publishes an annual print anthology—40 pages, digest-sized, professionally printed, perfect-bound, with glossy full color cover. Single copy: $9.50. Make checks payable to Vanessa Kittle.

Advice "Bring the reader into the moment. Be as specific as possible."

✪ ☑ ◎ ABRAXAS (Specialized: contemporary lyric; experimental)

P.O. Box 260113, Madison WI 53726-0113. (608)238-0175. E-mail: abraxaspress@hotmail.com. Web site: www.geocities.com/abraxaspress/. Established 1968. **Contact:** Ingrid Swanberg, editor/ publisher.

• *ABRAXAS* **does not consider unsolicited material, except as announced as projects arise.**

Magazine Needs *ABRAXAS*, published "irregularly; 9- to 12-month intervals or much longer," is interested in poetry that's "contemporary lyric, experimental, and poetry in translation. When submitting translations, please include poems in the original language as well." Does not want "political posing; academic regurgitations." Has published poetry by Ivan Argüelles, Denise Levertov, César Vallejo, d.a. levy, T.L. Kryss, and Andrea Moorhead. *ABRAXAS* is up to 80 pages (160-page double issues), digest-sized, litho-offset-printed, flat-spined (saddle-stapled for smaller issues), with matte card cover with original art. Press run is 600. Subscription: $16 USD (4 issues); $20 Canada, Mexico, and overseas (surface mail); $29 Canada and Mexico, $36 overseas (air mail). Sample: $4 USD ($8 double issues); add $3 shipping for foreign orders.

How to Submit *ABRAXAS* will announce submission guidelines as projects arise. "Please check Web site for reading periods." Pays 1 contributor's copy, 40% discount on additional copies.

❍ ◎ THE ACORN (Specialized: young authors)

1530 Seventh St., Rock Island IL 61201. (309)788-3980. Established 1988. **Contact:** Betty Mowery, poetry editor.

Magazine Needs *The Acorn*, published quarterly, is a "publication for young authors, as well as teachers or anyone else interested in our young authors." Considers poetry and fiction from children and teens in grades K-12. "Young authors submitting to *The Acorn* should put either age or grade on manuscripts." Accepts well over half of submitted mss. Press run is 100. Subscription: $10. Sample: $3. Make all checks payable to *The Oak*.

How to Submit Submit up to 5 poems at a time. Lines/poem: 35 maximum. Considers previously published poems and simultaneous submissions. Include SASE with all submissions. Responds in 1 week. "*The Acorn* does not pay in dollars or copies, but you need not purchase to be published." Acquires first or second rights. All rights revert to poet upon publication.

Contest/Award Offerings Sponsors numerous poetry contests. Guidelines available for SASE.

⊠ ▦ ☑ ACUMEN MAGAZINE

Ember Press, 6 The Mount, Higher Furzeham, Brixham, South Devon TQ5 8QY England. E-mail: patricia@acumen-poetry.co.uk. Web site: www.acumen-poetry.co.uk. Established 1971 (press), 1984 (*Acumen*). **Contact:** Patricia Oxley, poetry editor.

Magazine Needs *Acumen*, published 3 times/year in January, May, and September, is "a general literary magazine with emphasis on good poetry." Wants "well-crafted, high-quality, imaginative poems showing a sense of form." Does not want "experimental verse of an obscene type." Has published poetry by Ruth Padel, William Oxley, Hugo Williams, Peter Porter, Danielle Hope, and Leah Fritz. *Acumen* is 120 pages, A5, perfect-bound. Receives about 12,000 poems, accepts about 120. Press run is 650. Subscription: $45 surface/$50 air. Sample: $15.

How to Submit Submit 5-6 poems at a time. Considers simultaneous submissions (if not submitted to UK magazines); no previously published poems. "If a reply is required, please send IRCs. One IRC for a decision, 3 IRCs if work is to be returned." Willing to reply by e-mail to save IRCs. Responds in 3 months. Pays "by negotiation" and 1 contributor's copy. Staff reviews books of poetry in up to 300 words (single-book format) or 600 words (multi-book format). Send materials for review consideration to Glyn Pursglove, 25 St. Albans Rd., Brynmill, Swansea, West Glamorgan SA2 0BP Wales.

Advice "Read *Acumen* carefully to see what kind of poetry we publish. Also, read widely in many poetry magazines, and don't forget the poets of the past—they can still teach us a great deal."

▣ ☑ THE ADIRONDACK REVIEW

521 56th St., 2F, Brooklyn NY 11220. E-mail: diane@blacklawrencepress.com (inquiries); tarpoetry @blacklawrencepress.com (submissions). Web site: www.adirondackreview.homestead.com. Established 2000. **Contact:** Diane Goettel, editor.

Magazine Needs *The Adirondack Review*, published quarterly online, is a literary journal dedicated to quality free verse poetry and short fiction as well as book and film reviews, art, photography, and interviews. "We are open to both new and established writers. Our only requirement is excellence. We would like to publish more French and German poetry translations as well as original poems in these languages. We publish an eclectic mix of voices and styles, but all poems should show attention to craft. We are open to beginners who demonstrate talent, as well as established voices. The work should speak for itself." Wants "well-crafted, thoughtful writing full of imagery." Does not want "religious, overly sentimental, horror/gothic, rhyming, greeting card, pet-related, humor, or science fiction poetry." Has published poetry by Bob Hicok, Timothy Liu, Lola Haskins, D.C. Berry, David Rigsbee, and Paul Guest. Accepts about 3-5% of poems submitted.

How to Submit Submit 2-7 poems at a time. Considers simultaneous submissions (with notification); no previously published poems. Accepts e-mail submissions only. "All submissions should be pasted into the body of an e-mail (no attached files, please). We no longer accept postal submissions. All postal submissions will be discarded unread." Cover letter is preferred. Reads submissions year round. Submit seasonal poems 3 months in advance. Time between acceptance and publication is 1-3 months. Seldom comments on rejected poems. Guidelines available on Web site. Responds in 1 week to 4 months. Acquires first or one-time rights. Rights revert to poet upon publication. "We reserve the right to reprint the work in the event of a print-based anthology at a later date." Reviews books of poetry. Send materials for review consideration.

Contest/Award Offerings With Black Lawrence Press, offers The Fiddlehead Poetry Prize (see separate listing in Contests & Awards).
Advice "Get your hands on all the good writing you can, including international, past, contemporary, Web-based, and print. Read much, write well, and send us what you love."

☐ ADVOCATE, PKA'S PUBLICATION

1881 Little West Kill Rd., Prattsville NY 12468. (518)299-3103. Established 1987.
Magazine Needs *Advocate, PKA's Publication*, published bimonthly, is an advertiser-supported tabloid using "original, previously unpublished works, such as feature stories, essays, 'think' pieces, letters to the editor, profiles, humor, fiction, poetry, puzzles, cartoons, or line drawings." Wants "nearly any kind of poetry, any length. Poetry ought to speak to people and not be so oblique as to have meaning only to the poet. If I had to be there to understand the poem, don't send it. Also looking for horse-related poems, stories, drawings, and photos." Does not want "religious or pornographic poetry." Considers poetry by children and teens (when included with release form signed by adult). Accepts about 25% of poems received. Circulation is 10,000; all distributed free. Subscription: $16.50 (6 issues). Sample: $4 (includes guidelines).
How to Submit Submit any number of poems at a time. Lines/poem: open. No previously published poems or simultaneous submissions. "Please, no work that has appeared on the Internet." Submissions may be typed or legibly handwritten. "Send a SASE with your submission; no postcards, please." Time between acceptance and publication is up to 6 months. Occasionally comments on rejected poems. Responds in 2 months. Guidelines available with sample copy ($4). Pays 2 contributor's copies. Acquires first rights only.
Advice "Always looking for horse/equine-oriented works."

$ ☑ AGNI

Boston University, 236 Bay State Rd., Boston MA 02215. (617)353-7135. Fax: (617)353-7134. E-mail: agni@bu.edu. Web site: www.agnimagazine.org. Established 1972. **Contact:** Sven Birkerts, editor.
- Work published in *AGNI* has been included regularly in *The Best American Poetry* and *The Pushcart Prize*.

Magazine Needs *AGNI*, published semiannually, prints poetry, fiction, and essays "by both emerging and established writers. We publish quite a bit of poetry in forms as well as 'language' poetry, but we don't begin to try and place parameters on the 'kind of work' that *AGNI* selects." Wants readable, intelligent poetry—mostly lyric free verse (with some narrative and dramatic)—that somehow communicates tension or risk. Has published poetry by Patricia Goedicke, Stephen Dunn, Kim Addonizio, Kate Northrop, Matt Donovan, and Seamus Heaney. *AGNI* is typeset, offset-printed, perfect-bound. Circulation is 3,000 for subscriptions, mail orders, and bookstore sales. Subscription: $20. Sample: $10 ($12 for *30th Anniversary Poetry Anthology*).
How to Submit Submit no more than 5 poems at a time. Considers simultaneous submissions; no previously published poems. No e-mail submissions. Cover letter is required ("brief, sincere"). "No fancy fonts, gimmicks. Include SASE or e-mail address; no preformatted reply cards." Reads submissions September 1-May 31. Pays $20/page ($150 maximum), a 1 year subscription, and for print publication: 2 contributor's copies and 4 gift copies. Acquires first serial rights.

▣ ☑ AGNIESZKA'S DOWRY (AGD)

A Small Garlic Press (ASGP), 5445 N. Sheridan Rd., #3003, Chicago IL 60640. E-mail: marek@entera ct.com and ketzle@ketzle.net (send submissions to both e-mail addresses simultaneously). Web site: http://asgp.org. Established 1995. **Contact:** Marek Lugowski and Katrina Grace Craig, co-editors.
Magazine Needs *Agnieszka's Dowry (AgD)* is "a magazine published both in print and as a permanent Internet installation of poems and graphics, letters to Agnieszka. The print version consists of professionally crafted chapbooks. The online version comprises fast-loading pages employing an intuitive, if uncanny, navigation in an interesting space, all conducive to fast and comfortable reading. No restrictions on form or type. We use contextual and juxtapositional tie-ins with other

material in making choices, so visiting the online AgD or reading a chapbook of an AgD issue is required of anyone making a submission." Single copy: $3 plus $3 shipping, if ordered from Web site by an individual. Make checks payable to A Small Garlic Press.

How to Submit Submit 5-10 poems at a time. Accepts e-mail submissions only (NOTE: pasted into body of message in plain text, sent to both editors simultaneously; no attachments). "Prisoners may make submissions by regular mail, and we will waive the requirement that they read a print issue." Sometimes comments on rejected poems. Guidelines and annotated catalog available on Web site only. Responds by e-mail or SASE, usually within 2 months. Pays 1 contributor's copy. Acquires one-time rights where applicable.

Additional Information A Small Garlic Press (ASGP) publishes up to 3 chapbooks of poetry/year. Query with a full online ms, ASCII (plain text) only.

☐ THE AGUILAR EXPRESSION

1329 Gilmore Ave., Donora PA 15033. (724)379-8019. E-mail: xyz0@access995.com. (inquiries only). Web site: www.wordrunner.com/xfaguilar. Established 1986. **Contact:** Xavier F. Aguilar, editor/publisher.

Magazine Needs *The Aguilar Expression*, published semiannually in summer and winter, encourages "poetics that deal with now, which our readers can relate to. In publishing poetry, I try to exhibit the unique reality that we too often take for granted and acquaint as mediocre." Has published poetry by Martin Kich and Gail Ghai. *The Aguilar Expression* is 4-20 pages, 5×7, typeset, printed on 20 lb. paper. Receives about 10-15 poems/month, accepts about 10-15/year. Circulation is 200. Sample: $8. Make checks payable to Xavier Aguilar.

How to Submit Submit up to 3 poems at a time. Lines/poem: 30 maximum. No e-mail submissions. Cover letter is required (include writing background). SASE (for contact purposes) is required. Manuscripts should be submitted in clear, camera-ready copy. Submit copies, not originals; mss will not be returned. "We encourage all writers to send a SASE for writer's guidelines before submitting." Responds in 2 months. Pays 2 contributor's copies.

$☑ ◎ AIM MAGAZINE (Specialized: racial harmony & peace)

P.O. Box 390, Milton WA 90354-0390. E-mail: apiladoone@aol.com. Web site: www.aimmagazine. org. Established 1974. **Contact:** Ruth Apilado, poetry editor.

Magazine Needs *Aim Magazine*, published quarterly, is "dedicated to racial harmony and peace." Uses 3-4 poems ("poetry with social significance mainly") in each issue. Considers poetry by high school students. Has published poetry by J. Douglas Studer, Wayne Dowdy, Ned Pendergast, and Maria DeGuzman. *Aim* is magazine-sized with glossy cover. Receives about 30 submissions/year, accepts about half. Press run is 10,000. Single copy: $5; subscription: $20.

How to Submit Considers simultaneous submissions. Lines/poem: 32 average. Publishes theme issues. Upcoming themes available for SASE. Guidelines available on Web site. Responds in 6 weeks. Pays $10/poem and 1 contributor's copy. Does not send an acceptance notice: "We simply send payment and magazine copy."

Advice "Read the work of published poets."

☑ ALASKA QUARTERLY REVIEW

University of Alaska Anchorage, 3211 Providence Dr., Anchorage AK 99508. Phone/fax: (907)786-6916. E-mail: ayaqr@uaa.alaska.edu. Web site: www.uaa.alaska.edu/aqr. Established 1981. **Contact:** Ronald Spatz, executive editor.

  • Poetry published in *Alaska Quarterly Review* has been selected for inclusion in *The Best American Poetry*, *The Pushcart Prize*, and *Beacon's Best* anthologies.

Magazine Needs *Alaska Quarterly Review*, published in 2 double issues/year, is "devoted to contemporary literary art. We publish both traditional and experimental fiction, poetry, literary nonfiction, and short plays." Wants all styles and forms of poetry, "with the most emphasis perhaps on voice and content that displays 'risk,' or intriguing ideas or situations." Has published poetry by Maxine Kumin, Jane Hirshfield, David Lehman, Pattiann Rogers, Albert Goldbarth, and Billy Collins. *Alaska Quarterly Review* is 224-300 pages, digest-sized, professionally printed, perfect-bound, with card cover with color or b&w photo. Receives up to 5,000 submissions/year, accepts 40-90. Press run is 2,800. Subscription: $18. Sample: $6.

How to Submit No fax or e-mail submissions. Reads submissions mid-August to mid-May; manuscripts are *not* read May 15-August 15. Responds in up to 5 months, "sometimes longer during peak periods in late winter." Pay depends on funding. Acquires first North American serial rights.

Additional Information Guest poetry editors have included Stuart Dybek, Jane Hirshfield, Stuart Dischell, Maxine Kumin, Pattiann Rogers, Dorianne Laux, Peggy Shumaker, Olena Kalytiak Davis, Nancy Eimers, Michael Ryan, and Billy Collins.

☑ ◎ ALBATROSS (Specialized: environmental & nature poetry)

The Anabiosis Press, 2 South New St., Bradford MA 01835. (978) 469-7085. E-mail: rsmyth@anabio sispress.org. Web site: www.anabiosispress.org. **Contact:** Richard Smyth, editor.

Magazine Needs *Albatross*, published "as soon as we have accepted enough quality poems to publish an issue—about 1 per year," considers the albatross "to be a metaphor for the environment. The journal's title is drawn from Coleridge's *The Rime of the Ancient Mariner* and is intended to invoke the allegorical implications of that poem. This is not to say that we publish only environmental or nature poetry, but that we are biased toward such subject matter. We publish mostly free verse, and we prefer a narrative style." Wants "poetry written in a strong, mature voice that conveys a deeply felt experience or makes a powerful statement." Does not want "rhyming poetry, prose poetry, or haiku." Has published poetry by Mitchell LesCarbeau, Joan Colby, Simon Perchik, Jackie White, and Fredrick Zydek. *Albatross* is 28 pages, digest-sized, laser-typeset, with linen cover. Subscription: $8 for 2 issues. Sample: $5.

How to Submit Submit 3-5 poems at a time. Lines/poem: 200 maximum. No simultaneous submissions. Accepts e-mail submissions if included in body of message (but is "often quicker at returning mailed submissions"). Name and address must accompany e-mail submissions. Cover letter is not required. "We do, however, need bio notes and SASE for return or response. Poems should be typed single-spaced, with name, address, and phone number in upper left corner." Time between acceptance and publication is up to 6 months to a year. Guidelines available for SASE or on Web site. Responds in 1-2 months. Pays 1 contributor's copy. Acquires all rights. Returns rights provided that "previous publication in *Albatross* is mentioned in all subsequent reprintings."

Contest/Award Offerings The Anabiosis Press Chapbook Contest (see separate listing Contests & Awards).

Advice "We expect a poet to read as much contemporary poetry as possible. We want to be moved. When you read our poetry, we hope that it moves you in the same way that it moves us. We try to publish the kind of poetry that you would want to read again and again."

☑ ◎ ALIMENTUM, THE LITERATURE OF FOOD (Specialized: poems about/referencing food; menupoems; recipe poems)

P.O. Box 776, New York NY 10163. E-mail: submissions@alimentumjournal.com. (inquiries only). Web site: www.alimentumjournal.com. Established 2005. **Contact:** Cortney Davis, poetry editor.

Magazine Needs *Alimentum, The Literature of Food*, published semiannually in winter and summer, is "the only literary journal all about food." Wants "fiction, creative nonfiction, and poetry all around the subject of food." Has published poetry by Dick Allen, Stephen Gibson, Carly Sachs, Jen Karetnik, Virginia Chase Sutton. *Alimentum* is 128 pages, $6 \times 7\frac{1}{2}$, perfect-bound, with matte coated cover with 4-color art, interior b&w illustration includes ads. Receives about 1,000 poems/year, accepts about 30-40. Press run is 2,000. Single copy: $10 ($14 Canada/foreign); subscription: $18 for 1 year ($24 Canada/foreign). Make checks payable to *Alimentum* (payment available online through credit card or PayPal).

How to Submit Submit no more than 5 poems at a time. Lines/poem: no minimum or maximum. Considers simultaneous submissions; no previously published poems. No e-mail submissions; postal submissions only. Include SASE. Reads submissions year round. Check guidelines available on Web site. Responds 1-3 months. Pays contributor's copy. Acquires First North American Serial rights. Rights revert to poets upon publication.

Also Offers Publishes an annual broadside of "menupoems" for restaurants during National Poetry Month in April.

Advice "While food is our subject, we like poems to be about more than just the food. As in the stories we publish, the poems should also carry a personal element, even a story, not just a list of ingredients. Some special poem categories that we look for are menupoems and recipe poems."

⚡ ◻ ALWAYS LOOKING MAGAZINE/YA'SOU

P.O. Box 77463, Columbus OH 43207. Established 2000. **Contact:** David D. Bell, editor.

Magazine Needs "Our purpose is to celebrate life. We like thought-provoking and uplifting material in any style and subject matter. We would like to see poetry essays, short stories, articles, and black-and-white artwork." Does not want "sexually explicit, pornographic, or violent poetry." Considers poetry by children and teens; parental consent required. Receives about 200 poems/year, accepts about 90%.

How to Submit Submit 5 poems at a time. Lines/poem: 30 maximum. Considers previously published poems and simultaneous submissions. Cover letter is preferred. "Your name and complete address should be at the top left corner of every poem. Work should be camera-ready. SASE required." **Reading fee:** $1/poem, "or design your own page ($8\frac{1}{2} \times 11$) with as many poems as you wish for $5." Reads submissions year round. Time between acceptance and publication varies. "All work is read and chosen by the editor." Pays 1 contributor's copy.

Advice "Let your own unique voice be heard. Remember, express your heart, live your soul, and celebrate life."

⚡ ◈ $◻ AMBIT

17 Priory Gardens, Highgate, London N6 5QY England. (44)(208)340-3566. E-mail: info@ambitmag azine.co.uk (inquiries only). Web site: www.ambitmagazine.co.uk **Contact:** Martin Bax, Carol Ann Duffy, and Henry Graham, poetry editors.

Magazine Needs *Ambit*, published quarterly, is a 96-page quarterly of avant-garde, contemporary, and experimental work. *Ambit* is perfect-bound, with 2-color cover with artwork. Accepts about 3% of submissions received. Subscription: £25 UK, £27/€48 rest of Europe, £29/$56 overseas (individuals); £36 UK, £38/€64 rest of Europe, £40/$73 overseas (institutions). Sample: £6.50 UK, £7/€15 rest of Europe, £8/$18 overseas.

How to Submit Submit up to 6 poems at a time. No previously published poems or simultaneous submissions. No e-mail submissions. "SAE vital for reply;" include IRCs when submitting from outside of UK. Poems should be typed, double-spaced. Never comments on rejected poems. Guidelines available in magazine or on Web site. Responds in 3-4 months. Pays small token plus 2 contributor's copies. Staff reviews books of poetry. Send materials for review consideration to review editor.

Advice "Read a copy of the magazine before submitting!"

◻ ◎ THE AMERICAN DISSIDENT (Specialized: engaged writing; poetry in English, French, Spanish)

1837 Main St., Concord MA 01742. E-mail: todslone@yahoo.com. Web site: www.TheAmericanDis sident.org. Established 1998. **Contact:** G. Tod Slone, editor.

Magazine Needs *The American Dissident*, published 2 times/year, provides "a forum for examining the dark side of the established order academic/literary milieu, which not only seems to have been discouraging vigorous debate, cornerstone of democracy, but also outright censoring voices and ideas from the literary agora to the detriment of American Literature." Wants "poetry, reviews, and short (1,000 words) essays in English, French, or Spanish, written on the edge with a dash of personal risk and stemming from personal experience, conflict with power, and/or involvement." Submissions should be "iconoclastic and parrhesiastic in nature." *The American Dissident* is 56-64 pages, digest-sized, offset-printed, perfect-bound, with card cover. Press run is 200. Single copy: $8; subscription: $16.

How to Submit Submit 3 poems at a time. Considers simultaneous submissions; no previously published poems. No e-mail submissions. "Include SASE and cover letter containing not credits, but rather personal dissident information and specific events that may have pushed you to reject indoctrination and 'go upright and vital, and speak the rude truth in all ways' (Emerson)." Time between acceptance and publication is up to 2 months. Almost always comments on rejected poems. Guidelines available for SASE. Responds in 1 month. Pays 1 contributor's copy. Acquires first North American serial rights. Reviews books/chapbooks of poetry and other magazines in 250 words, single-book format. Send materials for review consideration.

Advice "For the sake of democracy, poetry needs to be much more than safe, comfortable, diversionary intellectual entertainment, and poets much more than public court jesters. If only the latter endeavored to be more than just working the poem and filling out applications for grants, fellowships, and contests. If only they questioned and challenged, rather than accepted. If only they heeded Villon ('*Estoit-il lors temps de moy taire*'), Thoreau ('Let your life be a counter friction to stop the machine'), Wole Soyinka ('Criticism, like charity, starts at home'), Sinclair Lewis ('Every Compulsion is put upon writers to become safe, polite, obedient, and sterile'), Yevtushenko ('A Poet is always in danger when he lives too safely'), Hemingway ('Writers are forged in injustice as a sword is forged') and James Baldwin ('The peculiar nature of this [the writer's] responsibility is that he must never cease warring with it [society], for its sake and for his own'). Do not be afraid to name names!"

☑ AMERICAN LITERARY REVIEW

University of North Texas, P.O. Box 311307, Denton TX 76203-1307. (940)565-2755. E-mail: americanliteraryreview@yahoo.com. Web site: www.engl.unt.edu/alr. **Contact:** Bruce Bond and Corey Marks, poetry editors.

Magazine Needs *American Literary Review*, published semiannually, considers all forms and modes of poetry, nonfiction, and fiction. "We are especially interested in originality, substance, imaginative power, and lyric intensity." Has published poetry by Kathleen Pierce, Mark Irwin, Stephen Dunn, William Olsen, Dave St. John, and Cate Marvin. *American Literary Review* is about 120 pages, digest-sized, attractively printed, perfect-bound, with color card cover with photo. Subscription: $10/year, $18 for 2 years. Sample: $6.

How to Submit Submit up to 5 typewritten poems at a time. Considers simultaneous submissions. No fax or e-mail submissions. Cover letter is required. Include author's name, address, phone number, and poem titles. Reads mss September 1-May 1. Guidelines available on Web site. Responds in up to 3 months. Pays 2 contributor's copies.

Contest/Award Offerings Send SASE for details.

☑ THE AMERICAN POETRY JOURNAL

P.O. Box 2080 Aptos CA 95001-2080. E-mail: editor@americanpoetryjournal.com. Web site: www.americanpoetryjournal.com. Established 2004. **Contact:** J.P. Dancing Bear, editor.

Magazine Needs *The American Poetry Journal*, published annually (July), seeks "to publish work using poetic device, favoring image, metaphor, and good sound. We like alliteration, extended metaphors, image, movement, and poems that can pass the 'so what' test. *The American Poetry Journal* has in mind the reader who delights in discovering what a poem can do to the tongue and what the poem paints on the cave of the mind." Wants poems "that exhibit strong, fresh imagery, metaphor, and good sound." Does not want "narratives about family, simplistic verse, annoying word hodge-podges." Has published poetry by C.J. Sage, Natasha Sage, Lola Haskins, Dorianne Laux, and Jennifer Juneau. *The American Poetry Journal* is 50 pages, digest-sized. Accepts about 1% of poems submitted. Single copy: $12; subscription: $12. Make checks payable to J.P. Dancing Bear.

How to Submit Submit 3-5 poems at a time. Considers simultaneous submissions; no previously published poems. E-mail submissions are preferred. Cover letter is preferred. Considers unsolicited submissions September 1-April 30 (poets may submit no more than twice during the reading period). "We consider submissions from subscribers year round." Time between acceptance and publication is 6 months. "Poems are read first for clarity and technique, then read aloud for sound quality." Seldom comments on rejected poems. Guidelines available on Web site. Responds in 2 months. Pays one contributor's copy. Acquires first rights.

Contest/Award Offerings Offers The American Poet Prize and *The American Poetry Journal* Book Prize (see separate listings in Contests & Awards).

Advice "Know your target before submitting. It's not that difficult, but it helps your odds when the editor can tell that you get what the magazine is about. Reading an issue is the easiest way to do this."

⬤ ◎ AMERICAN TANKA (Specialized: English-language tanka)

P.O. Box 120-024, Staten Island NY 10312. E-mail: editorsdesk@americantanka.com. Web site: www.americantanka.com. Established 1996. **Contact:** Laura Maffei, editor. Executive Director: Tim Younce.

Magazine Needs *American Tanka*, published annually, is devoted to single English-language tanka. Wants "concise and vivid language, good crafting, and echo of the original Japanese form, but with unique and contemporary content." Does not want anything that's not tanka. Considers poetry by children and teens. Has published poetry by Sanford Goldstein, Marianne Bluger, Michael Mc-Clintock, Michael Dylan Welch, Jane Reichhold, and George Swede. *American Tanka* is 95-120 pages, digest-sized, perfect-bound, with glossy cover. Single copy: $12; subscription: $20 for 2 issues, $28 for 3 issues. Make checks/money orders payable to *American Tanka* and send to Tim Younce, 4906 W. State Route 55, Troy OH 45373.

How to Submit Submit up to 5 poems at a time (1 submission/reading period). No previously published poems or simultaneous submissions. Accepts submissions by e-mail (pasted into body of message). Guidelines available for SASE, by e-mail, or on Web site. Responds in up to 4 months. Acquires first North American serial rights.

Advice "Become familiar with the tanka form by reading both translations and English-language tanka. In your own tanka, be natural and concrete and vivid. Avoid clichés, overcrowded imagery, or attempting to imitate Japanese poems."

$⬤ ◎ ANCIENT PATHS (Specialized: Christian)

P.O. Box 7505, Fairfax Station VA 22039. E-mail: SSBurris@msn.com. Web site: www.editorskylar.com. Established 1998. **Contact:** Skylar H. Burris, editor.

Magazine Needs *Ancient Paths*, published biennially in odd-numbered years, provides "a forum for quality Christian literature and contains poetry, short stories, and art." Wants "traditional rhymed/metrical forms and free verse; subtle Christian themes. I seek poetry that makes the reader both think and feel." Does not want " 'preachy' poetry, inconsistent meter, or forced rhyme; no stream of conscious or avant-garde work; no esoteric academic poetry." Has published poetry by Giovanni Malito, Ida Fasel, Diane Glancy, Walt McDonald, and Donna Farley. *Ancient Paths* is 80+ pages, digest-sized, photocopied, perfect-bound, with cardstock cover. Receives about 600 poems/year, accepts about 7%. Press run is 175; 90 distributed free to churches, libraries, and authors. Single copy: $12. Make checks payable to Skylar Burris.

How to Submit Submit up to 5 poems at a time. Lines/poem: 60 maximum. Considers previously published poems and simultaneous submissions. Accepts e-mail submissions "only if you reside outside the U.S.; submissions should be pasted directly into the message, single-spaced, 1 poem per message, using a small or normal font size, with name and address at the top of each submission. Use subject heading: ANCIENT PATHS SUBMISSION, followed by your title." For postal submissions, poems should be single-spaced; "always include name, address, and line count on first page of all submissions, and note if the poem is previously published and what rights (if any) were purchased." Check Web site for reading period for Issue 15. Time between acceptance and publication is up to one year. Often comments on rejected poems. Guidelines available for SASE or on Web site. Responds in 3-4 weeks "if rejected, longer if being seriously considered." Pays $2/poem and 1 contributor's copy; offers contributors discount off cover price for pre-ordered copies. Acquires one-time or reprint rights.

Advice "Read the great religious poets: John Donne, George Herbert, T.S. Eliot, Lord Tennyson. Remember not to preach. This is a literary magazine, not a pulpit. This does not mean you do not communicate morals or celebrate God. It means you are not overbearing or simplistic when you do so."

⊘ ◎ ⊘ **ANGEL FACE (Specialized: poems arranged according to Mysteries of the Rosary)**

% MaryAnka Press, P.O. Box 102, Huffman TX 77336. Web site: www.maryanka.com. Established 2004. **Contact:** Mary Agnes Dalrymple, editor.

Magazine Needs *Angel Face*, published annually in the spring, prints poems "arranged according to the pattern of the Rosary (according to the Rosary Mysteries), but submitting poets need not be Catholic or Christian. I am open to many different viewpoints and have published poetry by Jewish and other non-Christian poets, as well as Catholic and Protestant poets. My goal is to bring the Rosary 'into life.' " Wants "poetry written from the life of the poet, but I am also open to poems written from the Biblical and traditional source material of the Rosary Mysteries. Some themes of the Rosary are birth, rebirth, joy, light, sorrow, abandonment, death, epiphany, redemption, resurrection, hope, transformation, forgiveness, the seasons of nature, the cycle of life, and the search for God in everyday life. Additional Rosary information can be found through the links page of my Web site." Does not want "rhyming or didactic poems. Also nothing negative or derogatory." *Angel Face* is 50 pages, digest-sized, desktop-published, hand-bound by the editor with waxed Irish linen thread, with cardstock cover with color artwork. Receives about 300 submissions/year, accepts about 40 poems. Press run is 100. Single copy: $7; subscription: $14 for 2 copies. Make checks payable to Mary Agnes Dalrymple.

How to Submit Submit up to 5 poems at a time. Lines/poem: about 60 maximum. Considers previously published poems and simultaneous submissions. Accepts submissions by postal mail only. "For information on why I do not accept e-mailed submissions, go to guidelines page of Web site and click on the Editor's Notes." Cover letter is preferred. Reads submissions year round. Time between acceptance and publication is 4 months to one year. Sometimes comments on rejected poems. "If I see something I like but think it still needs work, I will comment." Guidelines available for SASE or on Web site. Responds in about 3 months ("longer when I am putting an issue together"). Pays one contributor's copy. Acquires one-time rights. Rights revert to poet upon publication. **Currently not accepting admissions. On Hiatus.**

Advice "Write it, and then rewrite it. Consider each poem to be a child. No responsible person would send a child out half-naked on an empty stomach with no way to get back home. Poetry shouldn't be sent out that way, either. Provide the right size SASE with proper postage. Most of the poems published in *Angel Face* were not written with the Rosary in mind. Send your best poems, even if you are not sure they will fit the Rosary prayer pattern."

⊠ ⊠ ⊘ **THE ANTIGONISH REVIEW**

P.O. Box 5000, Antigonish NS B2G 2W5 Canada. (902)867-3962. Fax: (902)867-5563. E-mail: TAR@ stfx.ca. Web site: www.antigonishreview.com. Established 1970. **Contact:** Jeanette Lynes, co-editor.

Magazine Needs *The Antigonish Review*, published quarterly, tries "to produce the kind of literary and visual mosaic that the modern sensibility requires or would respond to. Subject matter can be anything; the style is traditional, modern, or post-modern limited by typographic resources. Purpose is not an issue." Does not want "erotica, scatalogical verse, excessive propaganda toward a certain subject." Has published poetry by Andy Wainwright, W.J. Keith, Michael Hulse, Jean McNeil, M. Travis Lane, and Douglas Lochhead. *The Antigonish Review* is 144 pages, digest-sized, offset-printed, flat-spined, with glossy card cover with art. Receives 2,500 submissions/year, accepts about 10%. Press run is 1,000. Subscription: $24 CAD, $30 CAD elsewhere. Sample: $7 CAD.

How to Submit Submit 5-10 poems at a time. Lines/poem: "not over 80, i.e., 2 pages." No previously published poems or simultaneous submissions. Accepts fax submissions; no e-mail submissions. Include SASE (SAE and IRCs if outside Canada; "we cannot use U.S. postage"). Time between acceptance and publication is up to 8 months. Sometimes comments on rejected poems. Guidelines available for SASE, by e-mail, or on Web site. Responds in up to 6 months. Pays $30 CAD per page and 2 contributor's copies. Acquires first North American serial rights.

$⊠ **THE ANTIOCH REVIEW**

P.O. Box 148, Yellow Springs OH 45387. (937)769-1365. Web site: www.review.antioch.edu. Established 1941. **Contact:** Judith Hall, poetry editor.

• Work published in *The Antioch Review* has been included frequently in *The Best American Poetry* and *The Pushcart Prize*.

Magazine Needs *The Antioch Review* "is an independent quarterly of critical and creative thought. For well over 50 years, creative authors, poets, and thinkers have found a friendly reception—regardless of formal reputation. We get far more poetry than we can possibly accept, and the competition is keen. Here, where form and content are so inseparable and reaction is so personal, it is difficult to state requirements or limitations. Studying recent issues of *The Antioch Review* should be helpful." Does not want " 'light' or inspirational verse." Has published poetry by Lucille Clifton, Terrance Hayes, W.S. Merwin, Wislawa Szymborska, and Susan Wheeler. Receives about 3,000 submissions/year. Circulation is 5,000; 70% distributed through bookstores and newsstands. Subscription: $40. Sample: $7.

How to Submit Submit 3-6 poems at a time. No previously published poems or simultaneous submissions. Include SASE with all submissions. Reads submissions September 1-May 1 only. Guidelines available on Web site. Responds in 8-10 weeks. Pays $15/published page plus 2 contributor's copies; additional copies available at 40% discount.

▣ $◻ ◎ AOIFE'S KISS (Specialized: fantasy; science fiction)

P.O. Box 782, Cedar Rapids IA 52406-0782. E-mail: aoifeskiss@yahoo.com. Web site: www.samsdotpublishing.com. Established 2002. **Contact:** Tyree Campbell, managing editor. Member: The Speculative Literature Foundation (http://SpeculativeLiterature.org).

Magazine Needs *Aoife's Kiss*, published quarterly in print and online (the 2 versions are different), prints "fantasy, science fiction, sword and sorcery, alternate history, horror short stories, poems, illustrations, and movie and book reviews." Wants "fantasy, science fiction, spooky horror, and speculative poetry with minimal angst." Does not want "horror with excessive blood and gore." Considers poetry by children and teens. Has published poetry by Bruce Boston, Karen A. Romanko, Mike Allen, Corrine De Winter, Julie Shiel, and Marge B. Simon. *Aoife's Kiss* (print version) is 32 pages, magazine-sized, offset-printed, saddle-stapled, with color paper cover, includes ads. Receives about 300 poems/year, accepts about 50 (17%). Press run is 140; 5 distributed free to reviewers. Single copy: $7; subscription: $18/year, $34 for 2 years. Make checks payable to Tyree Campbell/Sam's Dot Publishing.

How to Submit Submit up to 5 poems at a time. Lines/poem: prefers less than 100. Considers previously published poems; no simultaneous submissions. Accepts e-mail submissions (pasted into body of message); no disk submissions. "Submission should include snail mail address and a short (1-2 lines) bio." Reads submissions year round. Submit seasonal poems 6 months in advance. Time between acceptance and publication is 2-5 months. Often comments on rejected poems. Guidelines available on Web site. Responds in 4-6 weeks. Pays $5/poem, $3/reprint, $1 for scifaiku and related forms, and 1 contributor's copy. Acquires first North American serial rights. Reviews books/chapbooks of poetry. Send materials for review consideration to Tyree Campbell.

Advice "It's up to the writer to take the first step and submit work. Some of our best poems have come from poets who weren't sure if they were good enough. Horror poetry is a difficult sell with us."

◻ APALACHEE REVIEW

Apalachee Press, P.O. Box 10469, Tallahassee FL 32302. Web site: www.apalacheereview.org. Established 1971. **Contact:** Michael Trammell, editor; Laura Newton and Dominika Wrozynski, poetry editors. Member: CLMP, AAP.

Magazine Needs *Apalachee Review*, published about twice/year, appears "as soon as we have enough good material." Has published poetry by Rita Mae Reese and Charles Harper Webb. *Apalachee Review* is 120 pages, digest-sized, professionally printed, perfect-bound, with card cover. Press run is 700. Subscription: $15 for 2 issues ($30 foreign). Sample: $5.

How to Submit Submit 3-5 poems at a time. Considers simulaneous submissions. Accepts submissions by postal mail only. "Submit clear copies, with name and address on each." SASE required. Reads submissions year round. Sometimes comments on rejected poems. Guidelines available for SASE or on Web site. Responds in 4 months, "but sometimes we get bogged down." Pays 2 contributor's copies. Poet retains rights. Staff reviews books of poetry. Send materials for review consideration.

▣ ⬆ ◨ APPLE VALLEY REVIEW: A JOURNAL OF CONTEMPORARY LITERATURE

E-mail: editor@leahbrowning.net. Web site: www.applevalleyreview.com. Established 2005. **Contact:** Leah Browning, editor. Member: Council of Literary Magazines and Presses (CLMP).

Magazine Needs *Apple Valley Review: A Journal of Contemporary Literature*, published semiannually online, features "beautifully crafted poetry, short fiction, and essays." Wants "work that has both mainstream and literary appeal. All work must be original, previously unpublished, and in English. Translations are welcome if permission has been granted. Preference is given to short (under 2 pages), non-rhyming poetry." Does not want "erotica, work containing explicit language or violence, or work that is scholarly, critical, inspirational, or intended for children." Considers poetry by children and teens; "all work is considered regardless of the author's age." Has published poetry by Anna Evans, Rob Hardy, Ona Gritz, Rosa Salazar, Karen Schubert, and David Cazden. Receives about 5,000+ poems/year, accepts less than 1%.

How to Submit Submit 2-6 poems at a time. Lines/poem: "no limit, though we prefer short poems (under 2 pages). No previously published poems or simultaneous submissions. Accepts e-mail submissions (pasted into body of message, with "poetry" in subject line); no disk submissions. Cover letter is preferred. "Include name, address, phone number, e-mail address, and a short biography (maximum 150 words)." Reads submissions year round. Submit seasonal poems 6 months in advance, "though our interest in seasonal poems is very limited." Time between acceptance and publication is 1-6 months. Sometimes comments on rejected poems. Guidelines available by e-mail or on Web site. Responds in 1 week to 3 months. Sometimes sends prepublication galleys. "This is not a paying market. However, all work published in the *Apple Valley Review* during a given calendar year will be considered for the annual *Apple Valley Review* Editor's Prize [see below]." Acquires first rights and first serial rights and retains the right to archive the work online for an indefinite period of time. "As appropriate, we may also choose to nominate published work for awards or recognition. Author retains all other rights."

Contest/Award Offerings Offers the annual *Apple Valley Review* Editor's Prize. Award varies. "In 2007, the prize was $100 and a book of poetry." Submit 2-6 poems. **Entry fee:** none. **Deadline:** rolling; all submissions to the *Apple Valley Review*, and all work published during a given calendar year will be considered for the prize.

Advice "Try to read as much as possible, and submit to markets that are publishing work that you enjoy. They are more likely to be a good fit."

⬆ ▦ ◨ ◨ AQUARIUS

Flat 4, Room B, 116 Sutherland Ave., London W9 2QP England. Web site: www.geocities.com/eddielinden **Contact:** Eddie Linden, editor.

Magazine Needs *Aquarius*, published irregularly, prints poetry, fictional prose, essays, interviews, and reviews. Single copy: $10; subscription: $50 (U.S.). Special issue on the poets/writers George Barker and W.S. Graham available for £6 plus £1.25 p&p in United Kingdom.

How to Submit "Please note the magazine will not accept work unless writers have bought the magazine and studied the style/form of the work published." Payment is by arrangement.

⬆ $◨ ARC POETRY MAGAZINE

P.O. Box 81060, Ottawa ON K1P 1B1 Canada. E-mail: arc@arcpoetry.ca. Web site: www.arcpoetry.ca. Established 1978. **Contact:** Pauline Conley, managing editor.

Magazine Needs *Arc Poetry Magazine*, published semiannually, prints poetry, poetry-related articles, interviews, and book reviews. "Tastes are eclectic. International submissions are welcome and encouraged." Has published poetry by Evelyn Lau, Michael Crummey, Erin Mouré, Patricia Young, and Joelene Heathcote. *Arc Poetry Magazine* is 130-160 pages, perfect-bound, printed on matte white stock "with a crisp, engaging design and a striking visual art portfolio in each issue." Receives about 1,000 submissions/year, accepts about 40-50 poems. Press run is 1,500. Single copy: $12.50 CAD, $18 CAD (U.S.), $20 CAD (overseas); subscription: 2 issues/1 year—$17.95 CAD (in Canada); 4 issues/2 years—$34.95 CAD (in Canada), $42.95 USD, $45.95 USD (overseas). Online ordering available for subscriptions and single copies (with occasional promotions).

How to Submit Submit 4-8 poems at a time. No previously published poems or simultaneous submissions. No e-mail submissions. Cover letter is required. Submissions should be single-spaced, with name and address on each page. Publishes theme issues. Upcoming themes available in magazine or on Web site. Guidelines available for SAE and IRC or on Web site. Responds in 4-6 months. Pays $40 CAD/page plus 2 contributor's copies. Acquires first Canadian serial rights.

Contest/Award Offerings The Confederation Poets Prize is an annual award of $200 for the best poem published in *Arc* that year. *Arc* also sponsors an international Poem of the Year Contest: 1st Prize: $1,500 CAD; 2nd Prize: $1,000 CAD; 3rd Prize: $750 CAD. Guidelines available on Web site. **Entry fee:** $23 CAD for 4 poems. **Deadline:** June 30. Other awards include the Lampman-Scott Award for Poetry, Critic's Desk Award, and the Diana Brebner Prize for Poetry.

⚡ ARDENT!

Poetry in the Arts, 1909 Hollow Ridge Dr, Cedar Park, TX 78613. (512)699-8821. E-mail: rimer777@gmail.co. Web site: www.ardent.poetryinarts.org. Established 1985. **Contact**: Dillon McKinsey, editor.

Magazine Needs *Ardent!*, published semiannually, is a journal of poetry and art. All forms and styles are considered. *Ardent!* is perfect-bound.

How to Submit Accepts e-mail submissions, "but must adhere to the guidelines. See the *Ardent!* Web site for details." Submission by postal mail should be sent ℅ *Ardent!* editors to the address listed above. Pays contributor's copies.

Contest/Award Offerings An annual award will be given for the best published submission of both poetry and art.

🖊 ARIES: A JOURNAL OF CREATIVE EXPRESSION

Dept. of Languages and Literature, Texas Wesleyan University, 1201 Wesleyan St., Fort Worth TX 76105-1536. (817)531-4907. Fax: (817)531-6503. E-mail: sneeley@txwes.edu (inquiries only; no submissions). Web site: www.department.txwes.edu/aries. Established 1985. **Contact:** Stacia Dunn Neeley, general editor.

Magazine Needs *Aries: A Journal of Creative Expression*, published annually in August, prints quality poetry, b&w art, fiction, creative non-fiction, essays, and one-act plays. Wants poetry in all forms up to 50 lines. "Special: Original poetry in languages other than English welcome if submitted with English translation as companion." Does not want erotica. Has published poetry by Virgil Suárez, Richard Robbins, Susan Smith Nash, Gerald Zipper, and Lynn Veach Sadler. *Aries* is 60 pages, digest-sized, offset-printed, perfect-bound, with heavy cardstock cover and b&w art (1,500 dpi scans). Receives about 800 poems/year, accepts about 10%. Press run is 300. Single copy: $7; subscription: $7. Make checks payable to Aries @ Texas Wesleyan University.

How to Submit Submit 5 submissions maximum per year. Lines/poem: 3 minimum, 50 maximum. Considers simultaneous submissions; no previously published poems. No fax, e-mail, or disk submissions. Cover letter with titles of submissions and 100-word bio required; no names allowed on submissions themselves. Accepts submissions September 1-January 31 only. Notification April/May; publication July/August. "At least 3 reviewers read every submission via blind review. Personal response to every submission accompanied by a SASE or functioning e-mail address." Always comments on rejected poems. Guidelines available in magazine, for SASE, by e-mail, or on Web site. Responds in up to 6 months (notification of acceptance in April). Offers 50% off 2 contributor's copies. Acquires first rights.

Advice "Write in the voice that speaks from your unique position in the world. Our editors tend to choose works that show 'there's something at stake.'"

🖥 $🖊 ◎ ARKANSAS LITERARY FORUM (Specialized: AR resident writers only)

Henderson State University, Box 7601, Arkadelphia AR 71999-0001. (870)230-5272. E-mail: beggsm @hsu.edu. Web site: www.hsu.edu/alf. Established 1999. **Contact:** Marck L. Beggs, editor.

Magazine Needs *Arkansas Literary Forum*, published annually online in October, brings "the best of Arkansas to the world." Wants "well-written, image-rich poetry that surprises the reader" **from Arkansas residents only**. Does not want "message-oriented or sentimental poetry." Has published poetry by Miller Williams, Michael Heffernan, Andrea Hollander Budy, Jo McDougall, Terry Wright, and Jennifer Horne. Receives about 200 poems/year, accepts about 20-30.

How to Submit Submit 2-4 poems at a time. Lines/poem: no limit. No previously published poems or simultaneous submissions. Accepts e-mail submissions (pasted into body of message or as attachment in Word or WordPerfect); no disk submissions. Cover letter is preferred. "The cover letter should clarify the poet's connection to Arkansas." Reads submissions during January and February only. Time between acceptance and publication is 6-8 months. Poems are circulated to an editorial board. Never comments on rejected poems. Guidelines available in magazine or on Web site. Responds in 1-2 months. Always sends prepublication galleys. Pays $25/poem upon publication. Acquires first rights. Rights revert to poet upon publication.

Advice "Read everything you can get your hands on; however, don't read about how to write poems, read *poems*."

☐ ◎ ARKANSAS REVIEW: A JOURNAL OF DELTA STUDIES (Specialized: work that evokes 7-state Mississippi River Delta region)

P.O. Box 1890, State University AR 72467-1890. (870)972-3043. Fax: (870)972-3045. E-mail: tswillia @astate.edu. Web site: www.clt.astate.edu/arkreview. Established 1968 (as *Kansas Quarterly*). **Contact:** Tom Williams, general editor & creative materials editor.

Magazine Needs *Arkansas Review: A Journal of Delta Studies*, published 3 times/year, is "a regional studies journal devoted to the 7-state Mississippi River Delta. Interdisciplinary in scope, we publish academic articles, relevant creative material, interviews, and reviews. Material must respond to or evoke the experiences and landscapes of the 7-state Mississippi River Delta (St. Louis to New Orleans)." Has published poetry by Greg Fraser, Jo McDougall, and Catherine Savage Brosman. *Arkansas Review* is 92 pages, magazine-sized, photo offset-printed, saddle-stapled, with 4-color cover. Receives about 500 poems/year, accepts about 5%. Press run is 600; 50 distributed free to contributors. Subscription: $20. Sample: $7.50. Make checks payable to ASU Foundation.

How to Submit Submit any number of poems at a time. No previously published poems or simultaneous submissions. Accepts e-mail and disk submissions. Cover letter is preferred. Include SASE. Time between acceptance and publication is about 6 months. "The Creative Materials Editor makes the final decision based, in part, on recommendations from other readers." Often comments on rejected poems. Occasionally publishes theme issues. Guidelines available for SASE or by e-mail. Responds in 4 months. Pays 3 contributor's copies. Acquires first rights. Staff reviews books/chapbooks of poetry "that are relevant to the Delta" in 500 words, single- and multi-book format. Send materials for review consideration to Tom Williams ("inquire in advance").

☑ THE ARMCHAIR AESTHETE

Pickle Gas Press, 31 Rolling Meadows Way, Penfield NY 14526. (585)388-6968. E-mail: thearmchair aesthete@yahoo.com or bypaul@frontiernet.net. Established 1996. **Contact:** Paul Agosto, editor.

Magazine Needs *The Armchair Aesthete*, published 3 times/year, is a zine of "thoughtful, well-crafted, concise fiction and poetry. Interested in both fiction and poetry." *The Armchair Aesthete* is 60-80 pages, digest-sized, desktop-published, photocopied, with card cover and plastic spiral bound. Receives about 300 poems/year, accepts about 25-30%. Submission must be accompanied by a SASE (#10 envelope). Recently published work by Chris Brown, Laverne and Carol Frith, Lydia Williams, Andrew Bynom, and Douglas Empringham. Subscription: $18/3 issues. Sample: $6.95 postpaid and 5 First-Class stamps. Make checks payable to Paul Agosto.

How to Submit Lines/poem: 60 maximum. Fiction: 4,500 words maximum. Considers previously published poems and simultaneous submissions, if indicated. Accepts e-mail submissions (pasted into body of message or attached MS Word file). Cover letter is preferred. Time between acceptance and publication is up to 12 months. Seldom comments on rejected poems. Guidelines available for SASE. Responds in 2 months. Pays 1 contributor's copy. Acquires one-time rights.

☑ ART TIMES: A LITERARY JOURNAL AND RESOURCE FOR ALL THE ARTS

P.O. Box 730, Mt. Marion NY 12456. Phone/fax: (845)246-6944. E-mail: info@arttimesjournal.com. (inquiries only). Web site: www.arttimesjournal.com. Established 1984. **Contact:** Raymond J. Steiner, poetry editor.

Magazine Needs *Art Times*, published monthly (combining Jan/Feb and July/Aug), is a tabloid newspaper devoted to the fine and performing arts. Focuses on cultural and creative articles and essays, but also publishes some poetry and fiction. Wants "poetry that strives to express genuine observation in unique language. All topics, all forms." *Art Times* is 20-26 pages, newsprint, includes ads. Receives 300-500 poems/month, accepts about 40-50/year. Circulation is 27,000; most distribution is free through galleries, performing arts centers, schools, museums, theatres, etc., in the Northeast Corridor of the U.S. Subscription: $15/year. Sample: $1 with 9×12 SAE and 3 First-Class stamps.

How to Submit Submit 4-5 typed poems at a time. Lines/poem: up to 20. No e-mail submissions. Include SASE with all submissions. Has an 18-month backlog. Guidelines available for SASE. Responds in 6 months. Pays 6 contributor's copies plus one-year subscription.

$⊘ ARTS & LETTERS JOURNAL OF CONTEMPORARY CULTURE

Campus Box 89, Georgia College & State University, Milledgeville GA 31061. (478)445-1289. E-mail: al@gcsu.edu. Web site: http://al.gcsu.edu. Established 1999. **Contact:** Laura Newbern, poetry editor. Editor: Martin Lammon.

- Work published in *Arts & Letters Journal* has received the Pushcart Prize.

Magazine Needs *Arts & Letters Journal of Contemporary Culture*, published semiannually, is devoted to contemporary arts and literature, featuring ongoing series such as The World Poetry Translation Series and The Mentors Interview Series. Wants work that is of the highest literary and artistic quality. Does not want genre fiction, light verse. Has published poetry by Margaret Gibson, Marilyn Nelson, Stuart Lishan, R.T. Smith, Laurie Lamon, and Miller Williams. *Arts & Letters Journal of Contemporary Culture* is 180 pages, offset-printed, perfect-bound, with glossy cover with varied artwork, includes ads. Receives about 4,000 poems/year, accepts about .5%. Press run is 1,500. Single copy: $8 plus $1 postage for current issue; subscription: $15 for 2 issues (one year). Sample: $5 plus $1 postage for back issue. Make checks payable to Georgia College & State University.

How to Submit Submit 5 poems at a time. Considers simultaneous submissions "if notified immediately of publication elsewhere"; no previously published poems. No fax, e-mail, or disk submissions. Cover letter is preferred. Include SASE. Reads submissions September 1-March 1. "Poems are screened, discussed by group of readers, then if approved, submitted to poetry editor for final approval." Seldom comments on rejected poems. Guidelines available in magazine, for SASE, by e-mail, or on Web site. Responds in 1-2 months. Always sends prepublication galleys. Pays $10/published page ($50 minimum) plus 2 contributor's copies and one-year subscription. Acquires one-time rights. Reviews books of poetry in 500 words, single-book format. Query first to Martin Lammon.

Contest/Award Offerings Offers the annual Arts & Letters/Rumi Prize for Poets (see separate listing in Contests & Awards).

▣ ⟐ ⊘ ASCENT ASPIRATIONS MAGAZINE

1560 Arbutus Dr., Nanoose Bay BC V9P 9C8 Canada. (250)468-7313. E-mail: ascentaspirations@shaw.ca. Web site: www.ascentaspirations.ca. Established 1997. **Contact:** David Fraser, editor.

Magazine Needs *Ascent Aspirations Magazine*, published quarterly online (February, May, August, November) and semiannually in print (late fall and late spring), specializes in poetry, short fiction, essays, and visual art. "A quality electronic and print publication, *Ascent* is dedicated to encouraging aspiring poets and fiction writers. We accept all forms of poetry on any theme. Poetry needs to be unique and touch the reader emotionally with relevant human, social, and philosophical imagery." Does not want poetry "that focuses on mainstream overtly religious verse." Considers poetry by children and teens. Has published poetry by Janet Buck and Taylor Graham. Work is considered for the print editions of *Ascent* through contests (see below). Receives about 1,500 poems/year, accepts about 15%.

How to Submit Submit 1-5 poems at a time. Considers previously published poems and simultaneous submissions. Prefers e-mail submissions (pasted into body of message or as attachment in Word); no disk submissions. "If you must submit by postal mail because it is your only avenue, provide a SASE with IRCs or Canadian stamps." Reads submissions on a quarterly basis year round. Time between acceptance and publication is 3 months. Editor makes decisions on all poems. Seldom comments on rejected poems. Occasionally publishes theme issues. Upcoming themes available on Web site. Responds in 3 months. Acquires one-time rights.

Contest/Award Offerings To fund the printing of the 2 semiannual anthologies, *Ascent* offers a contest for poetry and fiction. 1st Prize: $100 CAD; 2nd Prize: $75 CAD; 3rd Prize: $50 CAD; 4th Prize: $25 CAD; 5 Honorable Mentions: $10 CAD each. All winners and honorable mentions receive 1-2 copies of anthology; all other entrants published in anthology receive 1 free copy. Guidelines available for SASE, by e-mail, or on Web site. **Entry fee:** $5 CAD/poem or $10 CAD/3 poems. **Deadlines:** "these vary for each contest." **NOTE: "Fee, awards, and the number of copies for winners of contests can change. Refer always to the Web site for the most up-to-date information."**

Advice "Write with passion for your material. In terms of editing, always proofread to the point where what you submit is the best it can possibly be. Never be discouraged if your work is not accepted; it may be just not the right fit for the current publication."

☑ ASHEVILLE POETRY REVIEW

P.O. Box 7086, Asheville NC 28802. (828)649-0217. E-mail: editor@ashevillereview.com. Web site: www.ashevillereview.com. Established 1994. **Contact:** Keith Flynn, founder/managing editor.

Magazine Needs *Asheville Poetry Review*, published annually, prints "the best regional, national, and international poems we can find. We publish translations, interviews, essays, historical perspectives, and book reviews as well." Wants "quality work with well-crafted ideas married to a dynamic style. Any subject matter is fit to be considered so long as the language is vivid with a clear sense of rhythm. We subscribe to the Borges dictum that great poetry is a combination of 'algebra and fire.' " Has published poetry by Sherman Alexie, Eavan Boland, Gary Snyder, Colette Inez, Robert Bly, and Fred Chappell. *Asheville Poetry Review* is 160-200 pages, digest-sized, perfect-bound, laminated, with full-color cover. Receives about 8,000 submissions/year, accepts about 5%. Press run is 2,000. Subscription: $22.50 for 2 years, $43.50 for 4 years. Sample: $13. **"We prefer poets purchase a sample copy prior to submitting."**

How to Submit Submit 3-5 poems at a time. No previously published poems or simultaneous submissions. No e-mail submissions. Cover letter is required. Include comprehensive bio, recent publishing credits, and SASE. Reads submissions January 15-July 15. Time between acceptance and publication is up to one year. Poems are circulated to an editorial board. Seldom comments on rejected poems. Occasionally publishes theme issues. Guidelines available for SASE or on Web site. Responds in up to 7 months. Pays 1 contributor's copy. Rights revert back to author upon publication. Reviews books/chapbooks of poetry. Send materials for review consideration.

■ ☑ ◎ ASININE POETRY (Specialized: humor, satire

Mongrel Publications, P.O. Box 1349, New York NY 10276. E-mail: editor@asininepoetry.com. Web site: www.asininepoetry.com. Established 1998 (print), 2001 (online). **Contact:** R. Narvaez, editor.

Magazine Needs *asinine poetry*, published monthly online, "features 10-12 new poems each month. We specialize in poetry that does not take itself too seriously." Wants "any form of poetry, but for us the poetry must be in a humorous, parodic, or satirical style. Many submissions to our site are slapdash, too broad, or funny on just one snickering level. We prefer well-crafted poems that may contain serious elements or cover serious subjects—but which are also amusing, absurd, or hilarious. We also love topical and occasional poems." Does not want serious, straightforward poems. Has published poetry by Hal Sirowitz, William Trowbridge, Allan Planz, Graham Everett, and Colonel Drunky Bob. Receives about 800 poems/year, accepts about 10%.

How to Submit Submit 3-4 poems at a time. Lines/poem: 50 maximum. Considers previously published poems and simultaneous submissions. Accepts e-mail (pasted into body of message) and disk submissions. Reviews books/chapbooks of poetry. Send materials for review consideration.

Contest/Award Offerings Sponsors 2 contests/year. Guidelines available on Web site.

☑ ATLANTA REVIEW

P.O. Box 8248, Atlanta GA 31106. E-mail: dan@atlantareview.com. (inquiries only). Web site: www.atlantareview.com. Established 1994. **Contact:** Dan Veach, editor/publisher.

• Work published in *Atlanta Review* has been included in *The Best American Poetry* and *The Pushcart Prize*.

Mary Karr

'A poet loves the world'

Photo © Marion Ettlinger

Mary Karr lives in New York City's Garment District, which she calls the last bastion of the working class in Manhattan, a place full of every kind of wonderful smell, sound, and sight. The daughter of a portrait painter, she's especially drawn to faces—affluent and indigent, every shape, color, denomination and attitude. On good days, she says, she steps out onto the street and feels like Walt Whitman.

"The city for me is very rich," she says, recalling Lorca's *Poet in New York* and the work of Hart Crane. "The city puts its little hypodermic needle in my brain stem every time I walk out the door."

Her voice takes on a note of wonder and reverence as she recounts the synesthesia she experienced when passing a man selling rolls of mandarin orange, cherry and lime embroidered Chinese silks out of a cardboard box. "It looked like organ pipes; there was something about all the different noises of those colors."

A moment later, she's laughing about a pick-up line tossed to her by a guy on the street: *Baby, you look like a dentist's wife.* "What a great line. I don't even know what that means."

Her passion, as well as her poetic sensibility (a delicate dance of the sacred and absurd), is obvious in these anecdotes, just as it is in her four collections of poetry—*Abacus* (Wesleyan University Press), *The Devil's Tour* (New Directions), *Viper Rum* (New Directions), and *Sinner's Welcome* (HarperCollins)—and her two acclaimed memoirs, the PEN/Martha Albrand Award-winning *The Liar's Club* (Viking Adult) and *Cherry*. Although most of the world knows Karr for her prose writing, she considers herself foremost a poet and explains why this distinction is important.

"The difference between a poet and a prose writer is that a poet loves the world and a prose writer wants to create an alternate world, because they kind of hate the world," Karr says. "And so I'm, to varying degrees, in love with the world."

"I'm drawn to beauty—wherever you find it. Every now and then you catch a glimpse of something, like the fabric rolled up like organ pipes in a cardboard box, and you have a sense that in one moment you can sort of experience the whole range of human feeling."

All these little glimpses and moments, a noise or a phrase or a mood or a tone, become her "obsessions," recorded in Karr's notebooks to become the seeds of future poems. She's at work on her poetry all the time, whether she's sitting at her desk or stealing time in airplanes or cars. For her, the most important part of the creative process is revision, and it's not unusual for her to rewrite each poem between 40 and 60 times.

"I'm not a very good writer; I'm a little bulldog of a rewriter," she says. "The joke I always make to my students is that every poem I've ever written is essentially 'I'm sad. The end. by Mary Karr.' And the rest of the revision comes in making that more specific.''

Although it's true that an undercurrent of sadness runs through much of Karr's early poetry, which, like her memoirs, reflects upon love and its loss, family trauma and grief, and spiritual desolation, her religious awakening and conversion to Catholicism in 1996 (the subject of her latest book of poetry *Sinners Welcome* and the essay ''Facing Altars'' published in *Poetry* magazine in 2005) has challenged her to ''accommodate joy as part of her literary enterprise.'' Despite the pleasure and comfort she takes in rituals like the Mass and meditation on the Bible and the life of Christ, she admits it's a struggle that probably has as much to do with history and culture as it does her own life.

''The last century was so much about genocide and the holocaust—not that this century won't also be about genocide and a new form of holocaust, it looks like it's already happened—but, you know, I really do believe the vast majority of us, what's truest about us is that lit up place that's in each of us,'' she says. ''It's hard to capture that light unless you throw it against the background of darkness. Satan in *Paradise Lost* is the most interesting character. After book three when he goes out and it's just Adam and Eve . . . it's like ho-hum, whatever. Evil has agency. I still find that difficult, although I write much more about joy than I used to.

''I think poets have been just traditionally a very dark lot. My mother gave me Sartre's *Nausea* when I was 12 years old, and I think a lot of us in my generation come out of that French Existentialist continental philosophy—nihilistic, we're going to die, and if there is a God, he's cruel, etc. etc. A kind of secular misery-ism. I'm sure in some ways, against the clippity-clop of the Victorian prettiness, it had a job to do, but now it's become a cliché. Being a drunk, miserable poet is a cliché. The poetry has to accommodate a broader spectrum of feeling.''

In addition to this cliché of the miserable poet, Karr, the Jesse Truesdell Peck Professor of Literature at Syracuse University, cautions her students against a few other ''evils'' that threaten poetry's growth: a lack of clarity and a lack of unity. If she were to write a follow-up to her 1991 essay ''Against Decoration,'' published originally in *Parnassus* and again in *Viper Rum*, Karr says she'd call it ''Against the Fragment.''

''People publish poems now and if there's one to six lines in a poem they like, they consider it a successful poem,'' she says. ''What about a poem that has an actual shape? I mean, not necessarily rhythmical, formal—a sonnet or a villanelle—but what about having a poem that *advances* instead of just being stream of consciousness or a series of moments completely tied around some theme.

''There are so many people that say, 'I *love* this book!' And I'll say, 'Show me the poem that's great in this book.' And they'll say, 'Well, these six lines.' Six lines? What about having a *whole poem*? What about [Yeats's] 'The Second Coming'? What about 'The Fish,' by Elizabeth Bishop? What about 'Black Stone Lying on a White Stone,' by César Vallejo? What about all these poems in which every single line is great *and* the poem advances in some way so that the end of it is completely different and new and fresh from the beginning? You have the sense of a whole work of art as opposed to a handful of interesting lines.

''There's still an astonishing lack of clarity,'' she adds. ''I don't understand how people can publish poems other people don't understand. I mean, what's the point? I don't get it. It's a wicked mistake.'' Karr attributes some of this fragmentation and obfuscation to poets being afraid of using the autobiographical *I*.

''There's a way where, in order to avoid using the autobiographical *I*, people just bring in references to the stuff they've read. And they assume that, because they're just referring to things they've read instead of events that actually happened to them, they have some kind of intellectual cache that pays the freight. *As though*," she laughs, "what you've read is not part of your autobiographical experience."

Much of the power of Karr's poetry comes from a fearless embracing of autobiographical experience, and no one in academia or the poetry community or the media has scolded her for her honesty and unvarnished language; although she fondly recalls a review for *Viper Rum* in which the critic accused her of trying to "cash in" on the celebrity of *The Liar's Club* with a book of poetry. "It was really funny, the idea that if you were going to cash in on something, it would be with poetry," she says. "Smart marketing move, to write a book of poems and really make a lot of money. You're going to *really sell out* with poetry."

This memorable review aside, she disregards the trappings of the marketplace. Other than when she gives public readings, Karr refuses to read her published work because she finds it "humiliating."

"The marketplace which is so in your face—especially where I live in New York City—it seems so urgently important, but it's highly possible that in 50 years nobody will know who John Ashbery is the way that nobody knows now who Robert Lowell is," she says.

"I remember [in graduate school] just being so desperate to publish a book. There was this girl who was sleeping with a really famous poet, and I remember going to [my teacher] Louise Gluck and saying, 'Well she's sleeping with this poet and she's publishing here and she's publishing there.' And Louise said, 'She'll sink like a stone.' And I said, 'What does that mean?' And she said, 'Well, the people who get into place through connections and through meeting people are interested in something else. It's not really about the poetry so much. And the people who keep writing, all those people publishing, have to be passionately engaged with the work. It doesn't always pay off in the end in the marketplace, but it's the interest in the work that sustains you.' "

To listen to Karr talk about studying the historical context of the poets she loves or discussing poetry with her colleagues at Syracuse or drawing inspiration from works of art, there's no doubt she thrives in her writing. "I always say, if you can give up writing, go for it. If just taking a stupid job is going to make you stop writing, then you didn't want to write that damn bad," she says. "I just had to have it. There was nothing else that kept me happy."

And like a true artist, Karr is always focused on the work. "I don't feel like I've been neglected, I feel rather that I really haven't written that much or as well as I'd like to write, in any genre," she says. "By the time I'd published a book, I really didn't care. I wanted great reviews, I wanted everybody to buy the book, blah blah blah—none of which *happened*. For many, many years. But none of that really mattered. I continued worrying the bone of the work."

For her, the only gift of the marketplace is the ability to be engaged in the dialogue of the literary community. "I can have a conversation with people that I would otherwise maybe not be able to have a conversation with," she says. "Don DeLillo *talks* to me. George Saunders *talks* to me. Brooks Haxton *talks* to me. Brenda Hillman *talks* to me. And I'm glad to have that."

Despite already earning the Whiting Writer's Award, grants from the NEA, a Radcliffe Bunting Fellowship, and a Guggenheim, Karr continues to set the bar high for herself. "This week, I reread *Richard II*—Shakespeare. If I could write one poem half as good as his great speeches in that play, I could die happy," she says. "Or someone like Dickinson, someone who could create in a single instant a heightened state of feeling in me. Literally, after I read a play like that, I walk outside and, I swear to God, the stars are lower to the ground. People's faces are more luminous. It really changes the possibility of the world. That's what I'd like to do. Plus, you know, sell a million books. Win a MacArthur and a Pulitzer. It's not that I'm not venal; I want all those things too. But if I could get to have that level of conversation with the English language, that would be pretty perfect."

Mary Karr's latest memoir, *Lit*, about overcoming her alcoholism and developing a spiritual life, is forthcoming from Viking. She is also at work on a fifth collection of poetry.

—*Lauren Mosko*

Lauren Mosko is an editor at Writer's Digest Books and formerly the editor of *Novel & Short Story Writer's Market*.

Magazine Needs *Atlanta Review*, published semiannually, is devoted primarily to poetry, but occasionally features interviews and b&w artwork. Wants "quality poetry of genuine human appeal." Has published poetry by Seamus Heaney, Billy Collins, Derek Walcott, Maxine Kumin, Alicia Stallings, and Thomas Lux. *Atlanta Review* is 128 pages, digest-sized, professionally printed on acid-free paper, flat-spined, with glossy color cover. Receives about 10,000 poems/year, accepts about 1%. Press run is 2,500. Single copy: $6; subscription: $10. Sample: $5.

How to Submit Submit no more than 5 poems at a time. No previously published poems. No e-mail submissions from within the U.S.; postal submissions only. Include SASE for reply. "Authors living outside the United States and Canada may submit work via e-mail." Cover letter is preferred. Include brief bio. Put name and address on each poem. Reads submissions according to the following deadlines: June 1 for Fall; December 1 for Spring. "While we do read year round, response time may be slower during summer and the winter holidays." Time between acceptance and publication is 6 months. Seldom comments on rejected poems. Guidelines available for SASE, by e-mail, or on Web site. Responds in 1 month. Pays 2 contributor's copies, author's discounts on additional copies. Acquires first North American serial rights.

Contest/Award Offerings *Atlanta Review* sponsors the Poetry 2009 International Poetry Competition (see separate listing in Contests & Awards).

$⬛ THE ATLANTIC MONTHLY

P.O. Box 130149, Boston MA 02113. Web site: www.theatlantic.com. Established 1857. **Contact:** David Barber, poetry editor.

Magazine Needs *The Atlantic Monthly* publishes some of the most distinguished poetry in American literature. "We read with interest and attention every poem submitted to the magazine and, quite simply, we publish those that seem to us to be the best." Wants "the broadest possible range of work: traditional forms and free verse, the meditative lyric and the 'light' or comic poem, the work of the famous and the work of the unknown." Has published poetry by Maxine Kumin, Stanley Plumly, Linda Gregerson, Philip Levine, Ellen Bryant Voigt, and W.S. Merwin. Has a circulation of 500,000. Receives about 60,000 poems/year, accepts about 30-35. Subscription: $24.50 for 10 issues. Sample: $7.50 (back issue).

How to Submit Submit 2-6 poems at a time. No previously published poems or simultaneous submissions. No e-mail or disk submissions; postal submissions only. SASE required. Responds in 2-6 weeks. Always sends prepublication galleys. Pays about $4/line. Acquires first North American serial rights only.

Advice "We have long been committed to the discovery of new poets. Our one limitation is length; we are unable to publish very long poems, and authors should consult back issues of the magazine for precedents."

⬛ ◎ THE AUROREAN (Specialized: seasonal focus)

Encircle Publications LLC, P.O. Box 187, Farmington ME 04938. (207)778-0467. E-mail: Aurorean@ encirclepub.com. (inquiries only). Web site: www.encirclepub.com. Established 1992 (Encircle Publications); 1995 (*The Aurorean*). **Contact:** Cynthia Brackett-Vincent, editor.

Magazine Needs *The Aurorean*, published semiannually (spring/summer, fall/winter), uses "well crafted upbeat poetry. Seasonal/New England theme, but open to other subjects." Wants "short poems (4-6 lines). Publishes haiku section each issue. "Mostly free verse and occasional rhyme. We publish newer poets alongside the biggest names in the small press." Does not want "hateful, overly religious." Has published poetry by Mary Buchinger, Alan Catlin, Joyce Odam, and Thomas R. Smith. *The Aurorean* is digest-sized, professionally printed, perfect-bound. Press run is 500-550. Single copy: $11 U.S., $12 international; subscription: $21 U.S. (2 issues), $25 international. Sample: back issues from previous quarterly format, $3 each; back issues of current semiannual format, $7 each. Make checks payable to Encircle Publications, LLC.

How to Submit Submit 1-5 poems at a time. Lines/poem: 40 maximum. Considers previously published poems. "Discourages simultaneous submissions "as we always reply in 3 months maximum. If you must submit simultaneously, be aware that none can be withdrawn once we have typeset/mailed a proof." Cover letter with brief introduction is preferred. "Fold cover letter separately and fold poems together. Poems folded individually cannot be reviewed." Include SASE with sufficient postage for return/reply. Manuscripts are acknowledged with a postcard or by e-mail upon receipt (e-mail address appreciated). Reads submissions August 16-February 15 for spring/summer; February 15-August 15 for fall/winter. Sends proofs with instructions on how to submit bios for each issue. Pays 2 contributor's copies per poem published (maximum 4 copies/issue). Acquires one-time rights. Appreciates credit if later published elsewhere. Two featured poets each issue (superb execution of poetic craft; in some way seasonally/New England reflective) receive publication of up to 3 poems with 100-word bio; 10 copies of magazine and 1-year subscription.

Contest/Award Offerings Open Submissions cannot be acknowledged or returned; same deadlines as above: 1) Seasonal Poetic Quote: send 4 seasonal lines maximum from not-too-obscure poet; source MUST be cited to verify. Winner receives 2 free issues. 2) Editor's Chapbook Choice: send poetry chapbooks; editor recommends 1/issue ("small blurb and ordering information; not a review; do not send books for review"). Must have been published within the previous year. Specialized/Other: 1) Creative Writing Program Students. Winner receives publication of his/her haiku, 3 copies of magazine, $10, and award certificate. Submissions MUST be sent per guidelines on contest page of Web site. 2) Best Poem of Last Issue: Independent Judge picks "Best Poem" from previous issue; winner receives $30.

Additional Information Editor recommends 1 chapbook/issue ("small blurb and ordering information; we do not publish reviews"). Chapbook must have been published within the last 6 months; cannot be acknowledged or returned. Query via e-mail for more information.

Also Offers *The Unrorean* broadsheet, appears twice/year beginning of January and July for poems too long, experimental, or dark for magazine. "Still, nothing hateful." 2-4 11×17 pages, laser-printed. Sample: $2 postpaid. Include SASE for return/reply. No proofs, bios; open submission dates. Pays 1 contributor's copy/poem, 1 "editor's pick" receives 2. "Poets may submit for the magazine or broadsheet individually (work submitted individually for broadsheet is not acknowledged by postcard or e-mail). Work sent to the magazine will also be considered for the broadsheet, unless otherwise requested in cover letter."

Advice "Be familiar with your markets; don't submit blindly. Keep writing. Support the markets that support poets. *Poet's Market* is your best friend."

▣ ◻ ◎ AUTUMN LEAVES (Specialized: poems from Native Americans)

E-mail: sjball@mindspring.com. Web site: www.sondra.net/al. Established 1996. **Contact:** Sondra Ball, publisher.

Magazine Needs *Autumn Leaves*, published twice/month, is a "magazine of original poetry, mostly by Native American authors, although I accept and publish poems by other people also." Wants "poetry of all styles." Does not want "anti-Indian poetry; seldom publish pro-war poetry." Considers poetry written by children "under 14 for my 'kids' section. I want to be told the age of the child." Has published poetry by Johnny Rustywire, Larry Kibby, Harvest McCampbell, Richard Vallance, Shigeki Matsumura, and John Christina Hopkins. Receives about 7,000 poems/year, accepts about 15%.

How to Submit Submit 1-4 poems at a time. Lines/poem: no limit, "although I probably would not publish a book-length poem." Considers previously published poems and simultaneous submissions. Accepts e-mail submissions (pasted into body of message); no disk submissions. Cover letter is preferred. "If a person is a Native American (or First Nations) person, I would like to be told that, and also told what nation they are affiliated with." Reads submissions year round. Submit seasonal poems 2 months in advance. Time between acceptance and publication "anywhere from 2 months to a year." Sometimes comments on rejected poems. Sometimes publishes theme issues. "I publish theme issues on unexpected current events (such as Katrina) if I receive enough submissions on that issue; but I don't usually plan it beforehand." Guidelines available by e-mail. Responds in 2-3 months. No payment, "but I do send the author the URL of the individual poems." Acquires one-time rights. Rights revert to poet upon publication.

AVOCET, A JOURNAL OF NATURE POEMS (Specialized: nature; spirituality)

P.O. Box 1717, Southold NY 11971. Web site: www.avocetreview.com. Established 1997. **Contact:** Peter C. Leverich, editor; Pat Swenson, founder & editor emeritus.

Magazine Needs *Avocet, A Journal of Nature Poems*, published quarterly, is "devoted to poets seeking to understand the beauty of nature." Wants "poetry that shows man's interconnectedness with nature; discovering the Divine in nature." Does not want "poems that have rhyme or metrical schemes, cliché, abstraction, or sexual overtones." Has published poetry by Barbara Bennett, Gary Every, Judy Snow, Greg Gregory, John Grey, and Lorraine Vail. *Avocet* is 36 pages, $4\frac{1}{4} \times 5\frac{1}{2}$, professionally printed, saddle-stapled, with card cover. Single copy: $6; subscription: $24. Make checks payable to Peter C. Leverich.

How to Submit Submit 3-5 poems at a time. Considers previously published poems, if acknowledged; no simultaneous submissions. Cover letter is required. Include SASE for reply only; mss will not be returned. Time between acceptance and publication is up to 3 months. Responds in up to 2 months. Pays 1 contributor's copy.

THE AWAKENINGS REVIEW (Specialized: people living with mental illness)

Box 177, Wheaton, IL 60187. E-mail: awakeningsreview@aol.com. Web site: www.theawakenings project.org. Established 1999. **Contact:** Robert Lundin, editor.

Magazine Needs *The Awakenings Review*, published annually, prints works by people living with mental illness. Poet "must live with mental illness: consumer, survivor, family member, ex-patient." Wants "meaningful work, good use of the language. Need not be *about* mental illness." Has published poetry by Joan Rizzo, Wanda Washko, Ben Beyerlein, and Trish Evers. *The Awakenings Review* is 150 pages, digest-sized, perfect-bound, with glossy b&w cover. Receives about 800 poems/year, accepts about 10%. Press run is 1,000; 300 distributed free to contributors, friends. Single copy: $12 postpaid; subscription: $35. Make checks payable to *The Awakenings Review*.

How to Submit Submit 5 poems at a time. No previously published poems or simultaneous submissions. No e-mail submissions. Cover letter is preferred. Include SASE and short bio. Submit seasonal poems 6 months in advance. Time between acceptance and publication is 8 months. Poems are read by a board of editors. Often comments on rejected poems. Occasionally publishes theme issues. Guidelines available in magazine, for SASE, by e-mail, or on Web site. Responds in 1 month. Pays 1 contributor's copy, plus discount on additional copies. Acquires first rights. Send materials for review consideration.

Advice "Write a cover letter outlining your relationship to mental illness: consumer, survivor, ex-patient, family member, therapist."

AXE FACTORY REVIEW

Cynic Press, P.O. Box 40691, Philadelphia PA 19107. E-mail: cynicpress@yahoo.com. Established 1986 (*Axe Factory Review*), 1996 (Cynic Press). **Contact:** Joseph Farley, editor/publisher.

Magazine Needs *Axe Factory Review*, published 1-4 times/year, spreads "the disease known as literature. The content is mostly poetry and essays, but we use short stories, too." Wants "eclectic work. Will look at anything but suggest potential contributors purchase a copy of the magazine first to see what we're like." Does not want "greeting card verse." Has published poetry by Taylor Graham, A.D. Winans, Normal, and John Sweet. *Axe Factory Review* is 20-40 pages, magazine-sized, neatly printed, saddle-stapled, with light card cover. Press run is 200. Single copy: $9 (current issue); subscription: $24 for 4 issues. Sample: $8 (back issue). Make checks payable to Cynic Press or Joseph Farley.

How to Submit Submit up to 10 poems at a time. Considers previously published poems ("sometimes, but let me know up front") and simultaneous submissions. Cover letter is preferred, "but not a form letter; tell me about yourself." Often comments on rejected poems. Pays 1-2 contributor's copies; " 'featured poet' receives more." Reserves right to anthologize poems under Cynic Press; all other rights returned. Reviews books of poetry in 10-1,000 words. Send materials for review consideration.

Additional Information Cynic Press occasionally publishes chapbooks. Has published *Childhood* by B.Z. Niditch, *Rule of Thumb* by Kelley Jean White, M.D., *Yellow Flower Girl* by Xu Juan, *Under the Dogwoods* by Joseph Banford, *Ceiling of Mirrors* by Shane Allison, and *13 Ways of Looking at Godzilla* by Michael Hafer. **Reading fee:** $20. Make checks payable to Cynic Press. **No guarantee of publication.** Several anthologies planned; upcoming themes available in magazine, for SASE, or by e-mail.

Contest/Award Offerings Contest information available by e-mail.

Advice "Writing is a form of mental illness, spread by books, teachers, and the desire to communicate."

▣ ◳ ◎ BABEL: THE MULTILINGUAL, MULTICULTURAL ONLINE JOURNAL AND COMMUNITY OF ARTS AND IDEAS (Specialized: bilingual/foreign language)

E-mail: submissions@towerofbabel.com. Web site: www.towerofbabel.com. Established 1995. **Contact:** Jennifer Low, submissions editor.

Magazine Needs "*Babel* is an electronic zine recognized by the UN as one of the most important social and human sciences online periodicals. Publishes regional reports from international stringers all over the planet, as well as features, round table discussions, fiction, columns, poetry, erotica, travelogues, and reviews of all the arts and editorials. We want to see poetry from all over the world, including multicultural or multilingual work, as well as poetry that has been translated from or into another language, as long as it is also in English. We also appreciate gay/lesbian and bisexual poetry. Writers whose work discriminates against the opposite sex, different cultures, or belief systems will not be considered."

How to Submit Submit no more than 10 poems at a time. Considers previously published poems and simultaneous submissions. Accepts e-mail submissions only. Cover letter is required. "Please send submissions with a résumé or bio as a Microsoft Word or RTF document attached to e-mail." Time between acceptance and publication varies; "usually no more than a month or 2 depending on how busy we are." Seldom comments on rejected poems. Guidelines available on Web site. Responds in 2-4 weeks. Reviews books/chapbooks of poetry and other magazines, single- and multi-book format. Open to unsolicited reviews. Send materials for review consideration.

Advice "We would like to see more poetry with first person male characters written by female authors as well as more poetry with first person female characters written by male authors. We would also like to see that dynamic in action when it comes to other languages, cultures, races, classes, sexual orientations, and ages. The best advice we could give to writers wanting to be published in our publication is simply to know what you're writing about and to write passionately about it."

$▢ ◎ BABYBUG MAGAZINE (Specialized: children ages 6 months-2 years)

Carus Publishing, 70 E. Lake St., Suite 300, Chicago IL 60601. Web site: www.cricketmag.com. Established 1994. **Contact:** Submissions Editor.

Magazine Needs *BABYBUG Magazine*, published 10 times/year, is a read-aloud magazine for ages 6 months to 2 years. Wants "rhythmic, rhyming" short poems. *BABYBUG* is 24 pages, $6^{1}/_{4} \times 7$, printed on cardstock with nontoxic glued spine. Receives more than 1,200 submissions/month, accepts 25-30. Circulation is 48,000. Subscription: $35.97/year (10 issues). Sample: $5; sample pages available on Web site.

How to Submit Submit no more than 5 poems at a time. Lines/poem: 8 lines maximum. Considers previously published poems. Include SASE. Guidelines available for SASE or on Web site. Responds in 6 months. Pays $25 minimum on publication. Acquires North American publication rights for previously published poems; rights vary for unpublished poems.

Advice "Before attempting to write for *BABYBUG*, be sure to familiarize yourself with this age child and with the magazine itself."

☐ BABYSUE®

P.O. Box 15749, Chattanooga, TN 37415. Web site: www.babysue.com and www.LMNOP.com. **Contact:** Don W. Seven, editor/publisher.

Magazine Needs *babysue®*, published twice/year, offers obtuse humor for the extremely open-minded. "We are open to all styles, but prefer short poems." No restrictions. Has published poetry by Edward Mycue, Susan Andrews, and Barry Bishop. *babysue®* is 32 pages, offset-printed. "We print prose, poems, and cartoons. We usually accept about 5% of what we receive." Sample: $5. Payment may be made in either cash, check, or money order payable to M. Fieve.

How to Submit Considers previously published poems and simultaneous submissions. Deadlines are March 30 and September 30 of each year. Seldom comments on rejected poems. Responds "immediately, if we are interested." Pays 1 contributor's copy. "We do occasionally review other magazines."

☑ BACKSTREET

P.O. Box 1377, Berthoud CO 80513. E-mail: backstreetqtrly@earthlink.net. Established 2004. **Contact:** Ray Foreman, editor.

Magazine Needs *Backstreet*, published 6 times/year, wants "strong, clear narrative poems relevant to the times and the human condition, and appropriate for a readership of experienced poets. We are a 'poet's magazine for poets' whose purpose is keeping them writing by providing an easy and regular publishing outlet. We are privately subsidized, never run contests, and offer subscriptions at minimal cost to poets who read other poets' work." Does not want "poems that are obscure in any way or poems that have meaning only to the writer." Has published poetry by A.D. Winans, Anselm Brocki, Charles Ries, Laurel Speer, Arthur Gotlieb, and Steven Levi. *Backstreet* "has a special layout that has the equivalent content of a 36-page magazine," laser-printed, stapled, with paper cover. Receives about 600 poems/year, accepts about 200. Press run is 150. Single copy: $2; subscription: $10 for 10 issues. Make checks payable to R. Foreman.

How to Submit Submit 3 poems at a time. Lines/poem: 15 minimum, 50 maximum. "Maximum width is 65 characters per line." Considers previously published poems and simultaneous submissions. No e-mail or disk submissions. "SASE for first submission only. No cover letter, bio, or credits list. No graphic layout. Flush left, preferably in Times Roman or Garamond. No long skinnys. Disposable sharp hard copies. Your work speaks for you." Reads submissions year round. Time between acceptance and publication is 3 months. Sometimes comments on rejected poems. Responds in one week to one month. Acquires one-time rights. Rights revert to poet upon publication.

Advice "To write better poems, read poems in current anthologies to get a feel for what is good. It almost never happens at most poetry readings. Poetry is essentially an abbreviated short story literary art on the page."

☐ BARBARIC YAWP

Boneworld Publishing, 3700 County Rt. 24, Russell NY 13684. (315)347-2609. Established 1996. **Contact:** John and Nancy Berbrich, editors.

Magazine Needs *Barbaric Yawp*, published quarterly, prints "the best fiction, poetry, and essays available." Encourages beginning writers. "We are not preachers of any particular poetic or literary school. We publish any type of quality material appropriate for our intelligent and wide-awake audience; all types considered: blank, free, found, concrete, traditional rhymed and metered forms." Does not want "any pornography, gratuitous violence, or any whining, pissing, or moaning." Considers poetry by teens. Has published poetry by Nancy Henry, Mark Spitzer, and Jeff Grimshaw. *Barbaric Yawp* is a 60-page booklet, stapled, with 67 lb. cover. Receives 2,000 poems/year, accepts about 5%. Press run is 150. Single copy: $4; subscription: $15/year (4 issues). Make checks payable to John Berbrich.

How to Submit Submit up to 5 poems at a time. Lines/poem: 50 maximum. Considers previously published poems and simultaneous submissions. Cover letter is preferred (1 page). Include a short publication history (if available) and a brief bio. Include SASE. Reads submissions year round. Time between acceptance and publication is up to 6 months. Often comments on rejected poems. Guidelines available for SASE. Responds in up to 2 months. Pays 1 contributor's copy. Acquires one-time rights.

Advice "Read a lot—Dead White Males and Living Black Females—and everyone in-between. Write often, summon the Muse, and don't fear rejection!"

▣ ◑ ◎ THE BAREFOOT MUSE (Specialized: formal/metrical verse only)

P.O. Box 115, Hainesport NJ 08036. E-mail: submissions@barefootmuse.com. Web site: www.barefootmuse.com. Established 2005. **Contact:** Anna Evans, editor.

Magazine Needs *The Barefoot Muse*, published semiannually online, prints "only formal/metrical poetry (rhyme is optional). Poems in formal structures are most welcome. These include (but are not limited to) sonnets, villanelles, sestinas, triolets, pantoums, and rondeaus." Does not want "free verse; also, please do not send me rhyming poetry without first finding out what meter is." Has published poetry by Denise Duhamel, Jared Carter, Gail White, X.J. Kennedy, and Annie Finch. Receives about 1600 poems/year, accepts about 3%.

How to Submit Submit up to 5 poems at a time. Lines/poem: less than 40 preferred. Considers previously published poems ("by invitation only") and simultaneous submissions ("with notification"). Accepts e-mail submissions (pasted into body of message). Reads submissions year round. Time between acceptance and publication is up to 6 months. Sometimes comments on rejected poems. Guidelines available on Web site. Responds in 2 months. Always sends prepublications galleys. Acquires one-time rights. Rights revert to poet upon publication.

▣ $◑ BARNWOOD

4604 47th Ave. S., Seattle WA 98118-1824. (206)225-6887. E-mail: barnwoodpress@earthlink.net. Web site: www.barnwoodpress.org. Established 1975. **Contact:** Tom Koontz, editor.

Magazine Needs *Barnwood*, published online, "serves poets and readers by publishing excellent poems." Does not want "expressions of prejudice such as racism, sexism." Has published poetry by Bly, Goedicke, Friman, and Stafford. Receives about 3,000 poems/year, accepts about 1%.

How to Submit Submit 1-3 poems at a time. Considers simultaneous submissions; no previously published poems. "E-mail: paste poems into body of message with bio note and send to barnwoodsubmit@earthlink.net. Postal: Include SASE or no response." Reads submissions September 1-May 31 only. Time between acceptance and publication is one day. Seldom comments on rejected poems. Responds within 1 month. Pays $25/poem. Acquires one-time rights.

Advice "Emphasize imagination, passion, engagement, artistry."

◑ BARROW STREET

P.O. Box 1831, New York NY 10156. E-mail: info@barrowstreet.org. Web site: www.barrowstreet.org. Established 1998. **Contact:** Lorna Blake, Patricia Carlin, Peter Covino, and Melissa Hotchkiss, editors.

● Poetry published in *Barrow Street* is often selected for *The Best American Poetry*.

Magazine Needs *Barrow Street*, published semiannually, "is dedicated to publishing new and established poets." Wants "poetry of the highest quality; open to all styles and forms." Has published poetry by Molly Peacock, Lyn Hejinian, Carl Phillips, Marie Ponsot, Charles Bernstein, and Stephen Burt. *Barrow Street* is 96-120 pages, digest-sized, professionally printed, perfect-bound, with glossy cardstock cover with color or b&w photography. Receives about 3,000 poems/year, accepts about 3%. Press run is 1,000. Subscription: $15/year, $28 for 2 years, $42 for 3 years. Sample: $8.

How to Submit Submit up to 5 poems at a time. Considers simultaneous submissions (when notified); no previously published poems. Cover letter is preferred. Include brief bio. Must have name, address, e-mail, and phone on each page submitted or submission will not be considered. Reads submissions September 1 - May 31. Poems are circulated to an editorial board. Sometimes comments on rejected poems. Occasionally publishes theme issues. Guidelines available for SASE or on Web site. Responds in up to 9 months. Always sends prepublication galleys. Pays 2 contributor's copies. Acquires first rights.

Contest/Award Offerings The Barrow Street Press Book Contest (see separate listing in Contests & Awards).

Advice "Submit your strongest work."

◻ BATHTUB GIN

Pathwise Press, P.O. Box 1164, Champaign IL 61824. E-mail: pathwisepress@hotmail.com. Web site: www.pathwisepress.com. Established 1997. **Contact:** Christopher Harter, editor.

> • **PLEASE NOTE:** "*Bathtub Gin*/Pathwise Press are on hiatus through 2008; interested parties should contact the magazine to check on status."

Magazine Needs *Bathtub Gin*, published semiannually in April and October, has "an eclectic aesthetic—we want to keep you guessing what is on the next page." Wants poetry that "takes a chance with language or paints a vivid picture with its imagery, has the kick of bathtub gin, which can be experimental or a sonnet." Does not want "trite rhymes, Bukowski wannabes (let the man rest), or confessionals." Has published poetry by Kell Robertson, Tom Kryss, Mike James, and Richard Krech. *Bathtub Gin* is about 60 pages, digest-sized, laser-printed, saddle-stapled, with 80 lb. coverstock cover. Receives about 1,200 poems/year, accepts about 5%. Press run is 300-350; 10 distributed free to reviewers, other editors, and libraries. Single copy: $5; subscription: $8. Sample: $3.50 (back issue). Foreign orders add $2. Make checks payable to Christopher Harter.

How to Submit Submit 4-6 poems at a time. Considers previously published poems and simultaneous submissions. Accepts e-mail submissions (pasted into body of message). Cover letter is required. "Three- to five-line bio required if you are accepted for publication; if none provided, we make one up." Include SASE. Reads submissions June 1-September 15 only, but accepts contributions for 2 issues. Time between acceptance and publication is up to 8 months. Sometimes comments on rejected poems. Guidelines available in magazine, for SASE, by e-mail, or on Web site. Responds in up to 2 months. Pays 2 contributor's copies. "We also sell extra copies to contributors at a discount, which they can give away or sell at full price."

Additional Information Pathwise Press's goal is to publish chapbooks, broadsides, and "whatever else tickles us." Has published *The Levelling Wind* by Kell Robertson, *Nothing But Love* by Mike James, *The United Colors of Death* by Mark Terrill, and *Living Room, Earth* by Carmen Germain. Guidelines available for SASE or on Web site.

Also Offers "We feature a 'News' section where people can list their books, presses, events, etc."

✷ ◻ BAYOU

% Genre editor, English Dept., University of New Orleans, 2000 Lakeshore Dr., New Orleans, LA 70148. E-mail: bayou@uno.edu. Established 1975 as *The Panhandler* (University of West Florida); 2002 as *Bayou* (co-published by University of West Florida and University of New Orleans). *Bayou* is now solely published by the University of New Orleans. **Contact:** Joanna Leake, editor (University of New Orleans, Lakefront). Member: CLMP (Council of Literary Magazines and Presses).

Magazine Needs *Bayou Magazine*, published biannually, is "a young publication with an old soul. Each issue contains stunningly beautiful fiction, nonfiction, and poetry. One issue a year contains an award-winning play from the annual Tennessee Williams/New Orleans Literary Festival One-Act Play competition. From quirky shorts to more traditional stories, we are committed to publishing solid work. Regardless of style, at *Bayou* we are always interested first in a well-told tale. Our poetry and prose are filled with memorable characters observing their world, acknowledging both the mundane and the sublime, often at once, and always with an eye toward beauty. Contains a range of material from established, award-winning authors as well as new voices on the rise." Has published poetry by Eric Trethewey, Virgil Suáréz, Marilyn Hacker, Sean Beaudoin, Tom Whalen, and Mark Doty. *Bayou* is 130 pages, digest-sized, professionally printed, perfect-bound, with matte cardstock cover (artwork varies). Receives "hundreds of submissions," accepts "very few." Press run is 500; distributed free to students and faculty of University of West Florida and University of New Orleans. Single copy: $8; subscription: $15. Make checks payable to the UNO Foundation.

How to Submit Submit no more than 5 poems at a time. Lines/poem: "We have no strict length restrictions, though obviously it is harder to fit in very long poems." Considers simultaneous submissions; no previously published poems. No e-mail or disk submissions. "A brief cover letter is necessary, but don't tell us your life story, explain your poems, or tell us how wonderful your poems are. Do give us your contact information." Reads submissions year round, "but we tend to slow down in the summer months." Time between acceptance and publication varies "but we give the author a general idea when the work is accepted." Poems are circulated to an editorial board. Never comments on rejected poems. Guidelines available in magazine, for SASE, or by e-mail. Responds in 4 months. Pays 2 contributor's copies. Acquires first North American serial rights.

◐ ◎ BEAR CREEK HAIKU (Specialized: haiku/senryu; poems under 15 lines)

P.O. Box 3787, Boulder CO 80307. Established 1991. **Contact:** Ayaz Daryl Nielsen, editor.

Magazine Needs *bear creek haiku* prints haiku/senryu and any form/style less than 15 lines. Has published poetry by Quinn Rennerfeldt, Carl Mayfield, Heyoka, and Sean Perkins. *bear creek haiku* is 24 pages, photocopied on legal-sized blue paper cut in thirds lengthwise, stacked 3-high, folded, and stapled. Receives about 6,000 poems/year, accepts about 5%. Press run is about 200/issue. Single copy: free for SASE; subscription: $5. Make checks payable to Daryl Nielsen.

How to Submit Submit 5-20 poems at a time. Considers previously published poems and simultaneous submissions. "Include name, address, and several poems on each page. Keep your postage expenses at two First-Class stamps, one of which is on the SASE." Reads submissions year round. Time between acceptance and publication varies. Response time varies. Pays 2 contributor's copies. Acquires first rights.

Advice "We appreciate receiving your own personal favorites, be they simultaneously submitted or published elsewhere or never seen before. Write, create your poems—the heart, spirit, shadow, ancestors, readers, other poets, an occasional editor, etc., will benefit deeply."

$◎ THE BEAR DELUXE (Specialized: nature/ecology)

P.O. Box 10342, Portland OR 97296-0342. (503)242-1047. E-mail: bear@orlo.org. Web site: www.orlo.org. Established 1993. **Contact:** Casey Bush, poetry editor. Editor: Tom Webb.

- *The Bear Deluxe* is published by Orlo, a nonprofit organization exploring environmental issues through the creative arts.

Magazine Needs *The Bear Deluxe*, published quarterly, provides "a fresh voice amid often strident and polarized environmental discourse. Street-level, non-dogmatic, and solution-oriented, *The Bear Deluxe* presents lively creative discussion to a diverse readership." Wants poetry "with innovative environmental perspectives." Has published poetry by Judith Barrington, Robert Michael Pyle, Mary Winters, Stephen Babcock, Carl Hanni, and Derek Sheffield. *The Bear Deluxe* is 48 pages, 9×12, newsprint, saddle-stapled, with brown Kraft paper cover. Receives about 1,200 poems/year, accepts about 20-30. Press run is 20,000; 18,000 distributed free on the streets of the western U.S. and beyond. Subscription: $16. Sample: $5. Make checks payable to Orlo.

How to Submit Submit 3-5 poems at a time. Lines/poem: 50 maximum. Considers previously published poems and simultaneous submissions "so long as noted." Accepts e-mail submissions (pasted into body of message). "We can't respond to e-mail submissions but do look at them." Poems are reviewed by a committee of 3-5 people. Publishes 1 theme issue/year. Guidelines available for SASE. Responds in 6 months. Pays $20/poem, 1 contributor's copy (more if willing to distribute), and subscription. Acquires first or one-time rights.

⊕ ◐ ◎ THE BEATNIK COWBOY (Specialized: Beat-influenced poetry)

Ruamchoke Condoview 2, 37/447 Moo 2, Khao Pratumnak Rd., Nongprue, Banglamung, Chonburi 20150 Thailand. E-mail: beatnik_cowboy@yahoo.com.au. Established 2004. **Contact:** Mr. Randall Rogers.

Magazine Needs *The Beatnik Cowboy*, published quarterly, wants "Beat-influenced poetry from all poets. We are a young and vibrant magazine, seeking to publish poems from poets all around the world." Has published poetry by Steve Dalchinsky, Herschell Silverman, Randall Rogers, and Joe Speer. *The Beatnik Cowboy* is 32 pages, magazine-sized, computer-generated, side-stapled (will be bound in the future), includes ads. Receives about 200 poems/year. Press run is 30; 15 distributed free. Single copy: $6 USD. Make checks payable to Randall Rogers.

How to Submit Submit 5 poems at a time. Lines/poem: short poems preferred. Considers previously published poems and simultaneous submissions. Accepts e-mail (as attachment) and disk submissions. Cover letter is preferred. SAE with IRCs required for return of poems. Reads submissions year round. Submit seasonal poems 2 months in advance. Time between acceptance and publication is 3 months. Never comments on rejected poems. Guidelines available in magazine, for SASE, or by e-mail. Responds in 2 months. Acquires one-time rights.

▣ ◎ BELL'S LETTERS POET (Specialized: subscribers preferred)

P.O. Box 2187, Gulfport MS 39505-2187. E-mail: jimbelpoet@aol.com. Established 1956. **Contact:** Jim Bell, editor/publisher.

Magazine Needs *Bell's Letters Poet*, published quarterly, **must be purchased by contributors before they can be published.** "Many say they stop everything the day [the magazine] arrives." Wants "clean writing in good taste; no vulgarity, no artsy vulgarity." Has published poetry by Betty Wallace, Paul Pross, Carrie Quick, and Kalman Gayler. *Bell's Letters Poet* is about 60 pages, digest-sized, photocopied on plain bond paper (including cover), saddle-stapled. Single copy: $6; subscription: $24. Sample: $5. "Send a poem (20 lines or under, in good taste) with your sample order, and we will publish it in our next issue."

How to Submit Submit 4 poems at a time. Lines/poem: 4-20. Considers previously published poems "if cleared by author with prior publisher"; no simultaneous submissions. No e-mail submissions; accepts submissions by postal mail only. Submission deadline is 2 months prior to publication. Accepted poems by subscribers are published immediately in the next issue. Guidelines available in magazine or for SASE. No payment for accepted poetry, but "many patrons send cash awards to the poets whose work they especially like." Reviews books of poetry by subscribers.

Contest/Award Offerings "The Ratings" is a competition in each issue. Readers are asked to vote on their favorite poems, and the "Top 40" are announced in the next issue, along with awards sent to the poets by patrons. News releases are then sent to subscriber's hometown newspaper.

Also Offers *Bell's Letters Poet* also features a telephone and e-mail exchange among poets, a birthdate listing, and a profile of its poets.

Advice "Tired of seeing no bylines this year? Subscription guarantees a byline in each issue."

◻ ◎ BELLEVUE LITERARY REVIEW (Specialized: humanity, health, and healing)

New York University School of Medicine, OBV-A612, 550 First Ave., New York NY 10016. (212)263-3973. E-mail: info@BLReview.org. Web site: www.BLReview.org. Established 2001. **Contact:** Stacy Bodziak, managing editor. Member: CLMP.

• Work published in *Bellevue Literary Review* has appeared in *The Pushcart Prize*.

Magazine Needs *Bellevue Literary Review*, published semiannually, prints "works of fiction, nonfiction, and poetry that touch upon relationships to the human body, illness, health, and healing." Has published poetry by Rafael Campo, Sharon Olds, James Tate, Rick Moody, John Stone, and Floyd Skloot. *Bellevue Literary Review* is 160 pages, digest-sized, perfect-bound, includes ads. Receives about 1,100 poems/year, accepts about 3%. Press run is 5,000; distributed free to lit mag conferences, promotions, and other contacts. Single copy: $7; subscription: $12/year, $30 for 3 years (plus $5/year postage to Canada, $8/year postage foreign). Make checks payable to *Bellevue Literary Review*.

How to Submit Submit up to 3 poems at a time. Lines/poem: prefers poems of one page or less. Considers simultaneous submissions. No previously published poems; work published on personal blogs or Web sites will be considered on a case-by-case basis. No e-mail or disk submissions. "We accept poems via regular mail and through our Web site; when submitting via regular mail, please include SASE." Cover letter is preferred. Reads submissions year round. Time between acceptance and publication is about 6-7 months. "Poems are reviewed by two independent readers, then sent to an editor." Sometimes comments on rejected poems. Sometimes publishes theme issues. Upcoming themes available on Web site. Guidelines available for SASE or on Web site. Responds in 3-5 months. Always sends prepublication galleys. Pays 2 contributor's copies and one-year subscription for author, plus one-year gift subscription for friend. Acquires first North American serial rights. Rights revert to poet upon publication.

Contest/Award Offerings The annual Magliocco Prize for Poetry (see separate listing in Contests & Awards).

✴ ☑ BELLOWING ARK

Bellowing Ark Press, P.O. Box 55564, Shoreline WA 98155. (206)440-0791. E-mail: bellowingark@b ellowingark.org. Web site: www.bellowingark.org. Established 1984. **Contact:** Robert R. Ward, editor.

Magazine Needs *Bellowing Ark*, published bimonthly, is a literary tabloid that prints "only poetry which demonstrates in some way the proposition that existence has meaning or, to put it another way, that life is worth living. We have no strictures as to length, form, or style; only that the work we publish is, to our judgment, life-affirming." Does not want "academic poetry, in any of its manifold forms." Has published poetry by Jerry Austin, Robert King, Paula Milligan, Esther Cameron, Mary Jo Balistrieri, Dolores Stewart, and Jacqueline Hill. Beginning in 2008 two cash awards, The Lois and Marine Robert Warden (poetry) and The Michael L. Newell (black and white line art), will be given. *Bellowing Ark* is 32 pages, tabloid-sized, printed on electrobright stock. Press run is 1,000. Subscription: $20/year. Sample: $4.

How to Submit Submit 3-6 poems at a time. "Absolutely no simultaneous submissions." No e-mail submissions; accepts postal submissions only. Guidelines available for SASE or on Web site. Responds in up to 3 months; publishes accepted work within the next 2 issues. Occasionally comments on rejected poems if they "seem to display potential to become the kind of work we want." Sometimes sends prepublication galleys. Pays 2 contributor's copies. Reviews books of poetry. Send materials for review consideration.

Additional Information Bellowing Ark Press publishes collections of poetry by **invitation only**.

☑ BELOIT POETRY JOURNAL

P.O. Box 151, Farmington ME 04938. (207)778-0020. E-mail: sharkey@maine.edu. (inquiries only). Web site: www.bpj.org. Established 1950. **Contact:** John Rosenwald and Lee Sharkey, editors.

- Poetry published in the *Beloit Poetry Journal* has been included in *The Best American Poetry, Best New Poets*,and *The Pushcart Prize*.

Magazine Needs *Beloit Poetry Journal*, published quarterly, prints "the most outstanding poems we receive, without bias as to length, school, subject, or form. For more than 58 years of continuous publication, we have been distinguished for the extraordinary range of our poetry and our discovery of strong new poets." Wants "visions broader than the merely personal; language that makes us laugh and weep, recoil, resist—and pay attention. We're drawn to poetry that grabs hold of the whole body, not just the head." Has published poetry by Mark Doty, Albert Goldbarth, Patricia Goedicke, Karl Elder, John Haines, Sonia Sanchez, and Susan Tichy. *Beloit Poetry Journal* is about 48 pages, digest-sized, saddle-stapled, attractively printed, with "beautiful" 4-color covers. Circulation is 1,250. Subscription: $18/year, $48 for 3 years (individuals); $23/year, $65 for 3 years (institutions). Sample: $5.

How to Submit No previously published poems or simultaneous submissions. No e-mail submissions. "Submit any time, without query, in any legible form; no bio necessary. Unless it's a long poem, send what will go in a business envelope for 1 stamp. Don't send your life's work. We respond to most submissions within 2 weeks. Manuscripts under active consideration we keep for up to 4 months, circulating them among our readers, and continuing to winnow. At the quarterly meetings of the Editorial Board, we read aloud all the surviving poems and put together an issue of the best we have." Complete guidelines available on Web site. Pays 3 contributor's copies. Acquires first serial rights. Editor for Reviews and Exchanges reviews books by and about poets. Send books for review consideration to Marion Stocking, 24 Berry Cove Rd., Lamoine ME 04605.

Additional Information "To diversify our offerings, we occasionally publish chapbooks (most recently, the *Split This Rock* Chapbook of political poetry); these are almost never the work of a single poet."

Contest/Award Offerings Awards the Chad Walsh Poetry Prize ($3,000) to a poem or group of poems published in the calendar year. "Every poem we publish in 2009 will be considered for the 2009 prize."

Advice "We are always watching for fresh music, live forms and language."

■ $◎ BELTWAY POETRY QUARTERLY (Specialized: Washington, D.C.-area poets)

E-mail: beltway.poetry@juno.com. Web site: www.beltwaypoetry.com. Established 2000. **Contact:** Kim Roberts, editor.

Magazine Needs *Beltway Poetry Quarterly*, published online, "features poets who live or work in the greater Washington, D.C., metro region. *Beltway* showcases the richness and diversity of Washington, D.C., authors, with poets from different backgrounds, races, ethnicities, ages, and sexual orientations represented. We have included Pulitzer Prize-winners and those who have never previously published. We publish academic, spoken word, and experimental authors—and those whose work defies categorization." Takes unsolicited submissions only for special themed issues. Themes change annually; check Web site for details. Has published poetry by Cornelius Eady, Anthony Hecht, E. Ethelbert Miller, Jane Shore, Sharan Strange, and Hilary Tham.

How to Submit *"Other than annual themed issue, we consider poems by invitation only.* Theme issues have included poetic responses to Walt Whitman, the war in Iraq, and D.C. Places. 2 issues per year feature 5 poets from the greater-D.C. region, and these issues are open only by invitation. 1 issue per year is guest-edited." Never comments on rejected poems. Guidelines available on Web site.

Also Offers "Monthly Poetry News section has information on new publications, calls for entries, workshops, readings, and performances. Extensive links also include the most complete listing anywhere of artist residency programs in the U.S."

$□ ◎ BEYOND CENTAURI (Specialized: fantasy, science fiction, & mild horror for older children and teens)

P.O. Box 782, Cedar Rapids IA 52406-0782. E-mail: beyondcentauri@yahoo.com. Web site: www.samsdotpublishing.com. Established 2003. **Contact:** Tyree Campbell, managing editor. Member: The Speculative Literature Foundation.

Magazine Needs *Beyond Centauri*, published quarterly, contains "fantasy, science fiction, sword and sorcery, very mild horror short stories, poetry, and illustrations for readers ages 9-18." Wants "fantasy, science fiction, spooky horror, and speculative poetry for younger readers." Does not want "horror with excessive blood and gore." Considers poetry by children and teens. Has published poetry by Bruce Boston, Bobbi Sinha-Morey, Debbie Feo, Dorothy Imm, Cythera, and Terrie Leigh Relf. *Beyond Centauri* is 32 pages, magazine-sized, offset-printed, saddle-stapled, with paper cover with color art, includes ads. Receives about 200 poems/year, accepts about 50 (25%). Press run is 100; 5 distributed free to reviewers. Single copy: $6; subscription: $20/year, $37 for 2 years. Make checks payable to Tyree Campbell/Sam's Dot Publishing.

How to Submit Submit up to 5 poems at a time. Lines/poem: prefers less than 100. Considers previously published poems; no simultaneous submissions. Accepts e-mail submissions (pasted into body of message); no disk submissions. "Submission should include snail mail address and a short (1-2 lines) bio." Reads submissions year round. Submit seasonal poems 6 months in advance. Time between acceptance and publication is 1-2 months. Often comments on rejected poems. Guidelines available on Web site. Responds in 4-6 weeks. Pays $2/original poem, plus 1 contributor's copy. Acquires first North American serial rights. Reviews books/chapbooks of poetry. Send materials for review consideration to Tyree Campbell.

Advice "We like to see submissions from younger writers."

$☑ ◎ BIBLE ADVOCATE (Specialized: Christian)

P.O. Box 33677, Denver CO 80233. E-mail: bibleadvocate@cog7.org. Web site: www.cog7.org/BA. Established 1863. **Contact:** Sherri Langton, associate editor.

Magazine Needs *Bible Advocate*, published 8 times/year, features "Christian content—to be a voice for the Bible and for the church." Wants "free verse, some traditional, with Christian/Bible themes." Does not want "avant-garde poetry." *Bible Advocate* is 32 pages, magazine-sized. Receives about 30-50 poems/year, accepts about 10-20. Press run varies; all distributed free.

How to Submit Submit no more than 5 poems at a time. Lines/poem: 5 minimum, 20 maximum. Considers previously published poems (with notification) and simultaneous submissions. Prefers e-mail submissions. Cover letter is preferred. "No handwritten submissions, please." Time between acceptance and publication is up to 1 year. "I read them first and reject those that won't work for us. I send good ones to editor for approval." Seldom comments on rejected poems. Publishes theme issues. Guidelines available for SASE or on Web site. Responds in 2 months. Pays $20 and 2 contributor's copies. Acquires first, reprint, electronic, and one-time rights.

Advice "Avoid trite or forced rhyming. Be aware of the magazine's doctrinal views (send for doctrinal beliefs booklet)."

☻ ◎ ⊘ BIBLIOPHILOS (Specialized: bilingual/foreign language; nature/ecology; social issues)

200 Security Building, Fairmont WV 26554. Established 1981. **Contact:** Gerald J. Bobango, editor.

Magazine Needs *"Bibliophilos* is an academic journal for the literati, illuminati, *amantes artium*, and those who love animals; scholastically oriented, for the liberal arts. Topics include fiction and nonfiction, literature and criticism, history, art, music, theology, philosophy, natural history, educational theory, contemporary issues and politics, sociology, and economics. Published in English, French, German, and Romanian." Also publishes 1 all-poetry issue per year, containing the winners of an annual poetry contest (see below). Wants "traditional forms, formalism, structure, rhyme; also blank verse. Aim for concrete visual imagery, either in words or on the page." Does not want "inspirational verse, or anything that Ann Landers or Erma Bombeck would publish." Considers poetry by children ages 10 and up. Has published poetry by Anselm Brocki, Esther Cameron, Paul Bray, Jack C. Wolf, Eugene C. Flinn, and Bernie Bernstein. *Bibliophilos* is 72 pages, digest-sized, laser-photography-printed, saddle-stapled, with light card cover, includes ads. Receives about 200 poems/year, accepts about 30%. Press run is 300. Subscription: $18/year, $35 for 2 years. Sample: $5.25. Make checks payable to The Bibliophile. West Virginia residents, please add 6% sales tax.

How to Submit *Closed to unsolicited submissions.* Query first with SASE and $5.25 for sample and guidelines. Then, if invited, submit 3-5 poems at a time, with name and address on each page. Considers previously published poems and simultaneous submissions. Cover letter with brief bio is preferred. Time between acceptance and publication is up to 1 year. Often comments on rejected poems. Guidelines available for SASE. Responds in 2 weeks. Pays 2 contributor's copies. Acquires first North American serial rights. Staff reviews books/chapbooks of poetry in 750-1,000 words, single-book format. Send materials for review consideration.

Contest/Award Offerings Sponsors an annual poetry contest. 1st Prize: $25 plus publication. Guidelines available for SASE.

Advice "Do not send impressionistic, 'Why did he/she leave me, I can't live without him/her' poems about 'relationships,' which have no meaning beyond the author's psyche. Send poetry lamenting the loss of millions of acres of farmland to miserable Wal-Marts, or the lives lost by industrial rape and pollution."

✪ ◪ BIG TOE REVIEW

E-mail: submissions@bigtoereview.com. Web site: www.bigtoereview.com. Established 2004. **Contact:** Joshua Michael Stewart, editor.

Magazine Needs *Big Toe Review*, published online ("a new issue goes up when there are enough strong poems to warrant a new issue"), considers "all types of poems, but we really, really want prose poems. If you write in traditional forms, you better be doing something new with them." Does not want "anything trite." Has published poetry by Ellen Doré Watson, Ryan G. Van Cleave, David Dodd Lee, and Mary Koncel.

How to Submit Submit 3-5 poems at a time. "The shorter the poem, the better your chances." Considers previously published poems and simultaneous submissions. Accepts e-mail submissions only (pasted into body of message; "never, never attach document"); no disk submissions. Cover letter is required. Reads submissions year round. Sometimes comments on rejected poems. Guidelines available by e-mail or on Web site. Responds "as soon as possible." No payment. Acquires first North American serial rights.

Also Offers "There's a page dedicated to giving free advertisement for the books/chapbooks of poets who are contributors to the magazine, with links to where to buy the book in question."

Advice "Buy and read as much poetry as you write."

▣ ◪ ◎ THE BIG UGLY REVIEW (Specialized: theme-driven issues)

490 Second St., Suite 200, San Fransisco CA 94107. E-mail: info@biguglyreview.com (inquiries); poetry@biguglyreview.com (submissions). Web site: www.biguglyreview.com. Established 2004. **Contact:** Miriam Pirone, poetry editor.

Magazine Needs *The Big Ugly Review*, published 2 times/year online, showcases "emerging and established writers, photographers, filmmakers, and musicians. Each issue includes fiction (short stories and flash fiction), creative nonfiction, poetry, photo-essays, short films of 5 minutes or less, and downloadable songs, all related to that issue's theme." Wants "vivid and accurate poetry of any style, form, or length." Has published poetry by Edward Smallfield, Jennifer C. Chapis, Valerie Coulton, Stephen Hemenway, Diana Der-Hovanessian, and James Cihlar. Receives about 750-1,000 poems/year, accepts about 20.

How to Submit Submit no more than 6 poems at a time. Considers previously published poems and simultaneous submissions. Accepts e-mail submissions (pasted into body of message and as attachment); no disk submissions. "Send documents in Word or Word-readable attachments. Also paste the poems into the body of the e-mail text. Include your name, address, phone number, and e-mail on the first page." Cover letter is preferred. Reads submissions year round. Time between acceptance and publication is 1-2 months. Sometimes comments on rejected poems. Regularly publishes theme issues. Guidelines available on Web site. Responds "approximately 1 month after close of the issue's submission deadline." No payment. Author retains all rights.

◪ THE BITTER OLEANDER

4983 Tall Oaks Dr., Fayetteville NY 13066-9776. (315)637-3047. Fax: (315)637-5056. E-mail: info@bitteroleander.com. Web site: www.bitteroleander.com. Established 1974. **Contact:** Paul B. Roth, editor/publisher.

• Poetry published in *The Bitter Oleander* has been included in *The Best American Poetry*; recognized by Public Radio's *Excellence In Print* award for best literary journal of 2005.

Magazine Needs *The Bitter Oleander*, published semiannually in April and October, seeks "highly imaginative poetry whose language is serious. Particularly interested in translations." Has published poetry by Alan Britt, George Kalamaras, Duane Locke, Silvia Scheibli, Shawn Fawson, Anthony Seidman, and Christine Boyka Kluge. *The Bitter Oleander* is 128 pages, digest-sized, offset-printed, perfect-bound, with glossy 4-color cover with art, includes ads. Receives about 12,000 poems/year, accepts less than 1%. Press run is 1,500. Single copy: $8; subscription: $15. Make checks payable to Bitter Oleander Press.

How to Submit Submit up to 8 poems at a time. Lines/poem: 30 maximum. No previously published poems or simultaneous submissions. No e-mail submissions unless outside U.S. Cover letter is preferred. Include name and address on each page of ms. Does not read mss during July. Time between acceptance and publication is 6 months. "All poems are read by the editor only, and all decisions are made by this editor." Often comments on rejected poems. Guidelines available for SASE or on Web site. Responds within 1 month. Pays 1 contributor's copy.

Contest/Award Offerings Sponsors the Frances Locke Memorial Poetry Award (see separate listing in Contests & Awards).

Advice "We simply want poetry that is imaginative and serious in its delivery of language. So much flat-line poetry is written today that anyone reading one magazine after another cannot tell the difference."

$◪ BLACK WARRIOR REVIEW

P.O. Box 862936, Tuscaloosa AL 35486-0027. (205)348-4518. E-mail: bwr@ua.edu. Web site: www.bwr.ua.edu. Established 1974. **Contact:** Dave Welch, poetry editor.

• Poetry published in *Black Warrior Review* has been included in *The Best American Poetry* and *The Pushcart Prize*.

Magazine Needs *Black Warrior Review*, published semiannually in March and October, prints poetry, fiction, and nonfiction by up-and-coming as well as accomplished writers. Has published poetry by Aimee Nezhukumatathil, Bob Hicok, Rachel Zucker, Tony Tost, Joshua Beckman, and Carol Guess. *Black Warrior Review* is 180 pages, digest-sized. Press run is 2,000. Subscription: $16/

year, $28 for 2 years, $40 for 3 years. Sample: $10. Make checks payable to the University of Alabama.

How to Submit Submit up to 7 poems at a time. Considers simultaneous submissions if noted. No e-mail or disk submissions. Responds in up to 5 months. Pays up to $75 and one-year subscription. Acquires first rights. Reviews books of poetry in single- or multi-book format. Send materials for review consideration.

Advice "Subscribe or purchase a sample copy to see what we're after. For 33 years, we've published new voices alongside Pulitzer Prize winners. Freshness and attention to craft, rather than credits, impress us most."

☑ BLACKWIDOWS WEB OF POETRY

87788 Blek Dr., Veneta OR 97487. E-mail: sunris2set@aol.com. Web site: www.geocities.com/blackwidowswebofpoetry1/BlackWidowsMagazine.index.html. Established 2001. **Contact:** J. Margiotta, chief editor.

- Blackwidows Web of Poetry is on temporary hiatus until September 2008.

Magazine Needs *Blackwidows Web of Poetry*, published 3 times/year, is "a growing magazine striving to open the door to beginning poets, dedicated to publishing great poetry. We now also accept short stories (less than 2 pages)." Wants well-crafted poetry, all styles and forms. "We love unique, strong imagery and have a soft spot for nature, humor, narrative, etc. Rhyming less likely. We encourage all subject matters." Does not want overly religious, sexual, political poems; no racist/violent poetry. Has published poetry by Cleo Griffith, Debra J. Harmes-Kurth, Robert Demaree, and Gary Miron. *Blackwidows Web of Poetry* is 40-60 pages, digest-sized, laser-printed, photocopied, saddle-stapled, with color cover on 65 lb. cardstock with smooth finish. Receives about 1,00 poems/year, accepts about 40%. Press run is 200; 25 distributed free to coffeehouses, local areas of interest. Single copy: $7; subscription: $17. Make checks payable to J. Margiotta.

How to Submit Submit 5 poems at a time; haikus 10 to a page. Lines/poem: 3 minimum, 30 maximum ("very long line length not encouraged"). Considers previously published poems; no simultaneous submissions. No e-mail or disk submissions. Cover letter is required. "Include a brief bio, name, address, and phone number. SASE is required. Overseas poets will receive an e-mail response only; no SASE is needed." Reads submissions all year. Submit seasonal poems 3 months in advance. Time between acceptance and publication is 4 months. "Do not send unfinished work for critique. Read the guidelines carefully! We do not accept careless submissions. Poems are in review for opinion, style, content, originality, punctuation, etc." Often comments on rejected poems ("I like personal contact with each poet"). "We recommend you invest in a copy to see what we're all about, but it's not required. We appreciate all your support now and in the future." Guidelines available on Web site only. Responds in 1 month or less. Sometimes sends prepublication galleys. Pays 1 contributor's copy. "No payment is able to be made to overseas contributors due to funds, though copies are available for purchase—and we appreciate those who have." Acquires one-time rights with future credit to *Blackwidow's Web of Poetry*. Reviews other magazines/journals.

Advice "Trust yourself, write what you know, keep your pen alive, and revise, revise!"

☑ ◎ BLUE COLLAR REVIEW (Specialized: social, political, & working class issues)

Partisan Press, P.O. Box 11417, Norfolk VA 23517. E-mail: red-ink@earthlink.net. (inquiries only). Web site: www.partisanpress.org. Established 1997 (*Blue Collar Review*); 1993 (Partisan Press). **Contact:** A. Markowitz, editor. Co-Editor: Mary Franke.

Magazine Needs *Blue Collar Review (Journal of Progressive Working Class Literature)*, published quarterly, contains poetry, short stories, and illustrations "reflecting the working class experience—a broad range from the personal to the societal. Our purpose is to promote and expand working class literature and an awareness of the connections between workers of all occupations and the social context in which we live. Also to inspire the creativity and latent talent in 'common' working people." Wants "writing of high quality that reflects the working class experience from delicate internal awareness to the militant. We accept a broad range of style and focus—but are generally progressive, political/social." Does not want anything "racist, sexist-misogynist, right wing, or overly religious. No 'bubba' poetry, nothing overly introspective or confessional, no academic/

abstract or 'Vogon' poetry. No simple beginners rhyme or verse." Has published poetry by Simon Perchik, Joya Lonsdale, Kathryn Kirkpatrick, Marge Piercy, Alan Catlin, and Rob Whitbeck. *Blue Collar Review* is 60 pages, digest-sized, offset-printed, saddle-stapled, with colored card cover, includes ads. Receives hundreds of poems/year, accepts about 30%. Press run is 500. Subscription: $15/year, $25 for 2 years. Sample: $5. Make checks payable to Partisan Press.

How to Submit Submit up to 4 poems at a time; "no complete manuscripts, please." Considers previously published poems; no simultaneous submissions. No e-mail submissions; postal submissions only. Cover letter is preferred. Include full-size SASE for response. "Poems should be typed as they are to appear upon publication. Author's name and address should appear on every page. Overly long lines reduce chances of acceptance as line may have to be broken to fit the page size and format of the journal." Time between acceptance and publication is 3 months to a year. Poems are reviewed by editor and co-editor. Seldom comments on rejected poems. Guidelines available on Web site. Responds in 3 months. Sends prepublication galleys only upon request. Pays 1-3 contributor's copies. Considers reviews of chapbooks and journals.

Additional Information Partisan Press looks for "poetry of power that reflects a working class consciousness and moves us forward as a society. Must be good writing reflecting social/political issues." Publishes about 3 chapbooks/year; not presently open to unsolicited submissions. "Submissions are requested from among the poets published in the *Blue Collar Review*." Has published *A Possible Explanation* by Peggy Safire and *American Sounds* by Robert Edwards. Chapbooks are usually 20-60 pages, digest-sized, offset-printed, saddle-stapled or flat-spined, with card or glossy covers. Sample chapbooks are $5 and listed on Web site.

Contest/Award Offerings Sponsors the annual Working People's Poetry Competition (see separate listing in Contests & Awards).

Advice "Don't be afraid to try. Read a variety of poetry and find your own voice. Write about reality, your own experience, and what moves you."

✪ ⊘ BLUE UNICORN, A TRI-QUARTERLY OF POETRY

22 Avon Rd., Kensington CA 94707. (510)526-8439. Web site: www.blueunicorn.org. Established 1977. **Contact:** Ruth G. Iodice, John Hart, and Fred Ostrander, editors.

Magazine Needs *Blue Unicorn, A Tri-Quarterly of Poetry*, published in October, February, and June, is "distinguished by its fastidious editing, both with regard to contents and format." Wants "well-crafted poetry of all kinds, in form or free verse, as well as expert translations on any subject matter. We shun the trite or inane, the soft-centered, the contrived poem. Shorter poems have more chance with us because of limited space." Has published poetry by James Applewhite, Kim Cushman, Patrick Worth Gray, Joan LaBombard, James Schevill, and Gail White. *Blue Unicorn* is 56 pages, narrow digest-sized, finely printed, saddle-stapled. Receives more than 3,500 submissions/year, accepts about 200. Single copy: $7 (foreign add $3); subscription: $18 for 3 issues (foreign add $6).

How to Submit Submit 3-5 poems at a time. No previously published poems or simultaneous submissions. Cover letter is "OK, but will not affect our selection." Submit poems typed on $8^{1}/_{2} \times 11$ paper. Sometimes comments on rejected poems. Guidelines available for SASE. Responds in up to 3 months (generally within 6 weeks). Pays one contributor's copy.

Contest/Award Offerings Sponsors an annual (spring) contest with prizes of $150, $75, $50, and sometimes special awards; distinguished poets as judges; publication of top 3 poems and 6 honorable mentions in the magazine. Guidelines available for SASE. **Entry fee:** $6 for first poem, $3 for each additional poem.

Advice "We advise beginning poets to read and study poetry—poets both of the past and of the present; concentrate on technique; and discipline yourself by learning forms before trying to do without them. When your poem is crafted and ready for publication, study your markets and then send whatever of your work seems to be compatible with the magazine you're submitting to."

✪ ◎ BLUELINE (Specialized: poems about the Adirondacks & similar regions)

125 Morey Hall, Dept. of English and Communication, SUNY Potsdam, Potsdam NY 13676. Fax: (315)267-2043. E-mail: blueline@potsdam.edu. Established 1979. **Contact:** Rick Henry, editor-in-chief. Poetry Editor: Stephanie Coyne DeGhett. Member: CLMP.

Magazine Needs *Blueline*, published annually in May, is "dedicated to prose and poetry about the Adirondacks and other regions similar in geography and spirit." Wants "clear, concrete poetry that goes beyond mere description. We prefer a realistic to a romantic view." Does not want "sentimental or extremely experimental poetry." Uses poems on "nature in general, Adirondack Mountains in particular. Form may vary, can be traditional or contemporary." Has published poetry by L.M. Rosenberg, John Unterecker, Lloyd Van Brunt, Laurence Josephs, Maurice Kenny, and Nancy L. Nielsen. *Blueline* is 200 pages, digest-sized. Press run is 600. Sample: $7 (back issue).

How to Submit Submit 3 poems at a time. Lines/poem: 75 maximum; "occasionally we publish longer poems." No simultaneous submissions. Submit September 1-November 30 only. Include short bio. Poems are circulated to an editorial board. Sometimes comments on rejected poems. Guidelines available for SASE or by e-mail. Responds in up to 3 months. "Decisions in early February." Pays 1 contributor's copy. Acquires first North American serial rights. Reviews books of poetry in 500-750 words, single- or multi-book format.

Advice "We are interested in both beginning and established poets whose poems evoke universal themes in nature and show human interaction with the natural world. We look for thoughtful craftsmanship rather than stylistic trickery."

✪ BOGG: A JOURNAL OF CONTEMPORARY WRITING

Bogg Publications, 422 N. Cleveland St., Arlington VA 22201-1424. Established 1968. **Contact:** John Elsberg (USA), Wilga Rose (Australia: 13 Urara Rd., Avalon Beach, NSW 2107 Australia), and Sheila Martindale (Canada: 36114 Talbot Line, Shedden ON N0L 2E0 Canada), contributing editors.

Magazine Needs *Bogg: A Journal of Contemporary Writing*, published twice/year, combines "innovative American work with a range of writing from England and the Commonwealth. It features poetry (including haiku and tanka, prose poems, and experimental/visual poems), very short experimental or satirical/wry fiction, interviews, essays on the small press scene, reviews, review essays, and line art. We also publish occasional free-for-postage pamphlets." Uses a great deal of poetry in each issue (with featured poets). Wants "poetry in all styles, with a healthy leavening of shorts (under 10 lines). *Bogg* seeks original voices." Considers all subject matter. "Some have even found the magazine's sense of play offensive. Overt religious and political poems have to have strong poetical merits—statement alone is not sufficient." *Bogg* started in England and in 1975 began including a supplement of American work; it is now published in the U.S. and mixes U.S., Canadian, Australian, and UK work with reviews of small press publications from all of those areas. Has published poetry by Richard Peabody, Ann Menebroker, LeRoy Gorman, Marcia Arrieta, Kathy Ernst, and Steve Sneyd. *Bogg* is 56 pages, digest-sized, typeset, saddle-stapled, in a format "that leaves enough white space to let each poem stand and breathe alone." Receives more than 10,000 American poems/year, accepts about 100-150. Press run is 850. Single copy: $6; subscription: $15 for 3 issues. Sample: $4.

How to Submit Submit 6 poems at a time. Considers previously published poems "occasionally, but with a credit line to the previous publisher"; no simultaneous submissions. Cover letter is preferred ("it can help us get a 'feel' for the writer's intentions/slant"). SASE required or material will be discarded ("no exceptions"). Prefers hard copy mss, with author's name and address on each sheet. Guidelines available for SASE. Responds in 1 week. Pays 2 contributor's copies. Acquires one-time rights. Reviews books/chapbooks of poetry and other magazines/journals in 250 words. Send materials to relevant editor (by region) for review consideration.

Additional Information Bogg Publications occasionally publishes pamphlets and chapbooks **by invitation only**, with the author receiving 25% of the print run. Recent chapbooks include *Cleft Brow Totem* by Dave Wright, *South Jersey Shore* by David Check and John Elsberg, and *78 RPM* by John Yamrus. Obtain free chapbook samples by sending digest-sized SASE with 2 ounces worth of postage.

Advice "Become familiar with a magazine before submitting to it. Long lists of previous credits irritate us. Short notes about how the writer has heard about *Bogg* or what he or she finds interesting or annoying in the magazine are welcome."

⚡ ☑ ◎ **BORDERLANDS: TEXAS POETRY REVIEW (Specialized: TX & Southwest writers; bilingual)**

P.O. Box 33096, Austin TX 78764. E-mail: borderlands_tpr@hotmail.com. Web site: www.borderlands.org. Established 1992. **Contact:** Editor.

Magazine Needs *Borderlands: Texas Poetry Review*, published semiannually, prints "high-quality, outward-looking poetry by new and established poets, as well as brief reviews of poetry books and critical essays. Cosmopolitan in content, but particularly welcomes Texas and Southwest writers." Wants "outward-looking poems that exhibit social, political, geographical, historical, feminist, or spiritual awareness coupled with concise artistry. We also seek poems in 2 languages (one of which must be English), where the poet has written both versions." Does not want "introspective work about the speaker's psyche, childhood, or intimate relationships." Has published poetry by Walter McDonald, Naomi Shihab Nye, Mario Susko, Wendy Barker, Larry D. Thomas, and Reza Shirazi. *Borderlands* is 100-150 pages, digest-sized, offset-printed, perfect-bound, with 4-color cover. Receives about 2,000 poems/year, accepts about 120. Press run is 1,000. Subscription: $20/year, $34 for 2 years. Sample: $12.

How to Submit Submit 4 typed poems at a time. No previously published poems or simultaneous submissions. No e-mail submissions. Include SASE (or SAE and IRCs) with sufficient return postage. Seldom comments on rejected poems. Guidelines available for SASE or on Web site. Responds in 6 months. Pays 1 contributor's copy. Acquires first rights. Reviews books of poetry in 1 page. Send materials for review consideration to Editors, *Borderlands*.

▣ ☑ **BORN MAGAZINE**

E-mail: editors@bornmagazine.org. Web site: www.bornmagazine.org. Established 1996. **Contact:** Anmarie Trimble, editor. Contributing Editors: David J. Daniels, Tenaya Darlington, Jennifer Grotz, Michael Robins, Bruce Smith.

Magazine Needs *Born Magazine*, published quarterly online, is "an experimental venue that marries literary arts and interactive media. We publish 4 to 8 multimedia 'interpretations' of poetry and prose in each issue, created by interactive artists in collaboration with poets and writers." Wants poems suited to "interpretation into a visual or interactive form. Due to the unusual, collaborative nature of our publication, we represent a variety of styles and forms of poetry." Has published poetry by Edward Hirsch, Marvin Bell, Michele Glazer, Crystal Williams, Major Jackson, and Joyelle McSweeney.

How to Submit Submit 2-5 poems at a time. Considers previously published poems; no simultaneous submissions. Accepts e-mail submissions only (as Word documents or .txt files). Reads submissions year round. Submit seasonal poems 6 months in advance. Time between acceptance and publication is 3-6 months. "Poems must be accepted by the editor and 1 contributing editor. Selected works are forwarded to our art department, which chooses an artist partner to work with the writer. Artist and writer collaborate on a concept, to be realized by the artist. We also accept proposals for collaborating with an artist to create a piece from scratch." Never comments on rejected poems. Guidelines available on Web site. Responds in 3 weeks to e-mail queries. Always sends prepublication galleys. No payment. "We can offer only the experience of participating in a collaborative community, as well as a broad audience (we average 40,000 readers to our site per month)." Acquires one-time rights.

Advice "We accept new and previously published work. *Born*'s mission is to nurture creativity and co-development of new literary art forms on the Web."

⚡ $☑ **BOSTON REVIEW**

35 Medford St., Suite 302, Somerville MA 02143. (617)591-0505. Fax: (617)591-0440. E-mail: review@bostonreview.net. (inquiries only). Web site: www.bostonreview.net. Established 1975. **Contact:** Timothy Donnelly, poetry editor.

• Poetry submitted to *Boston Review* has been included in *The Best American Poetry* Anthology.

Magazine Needs *Boston Review*, published bimonthly, is a tabloid-format magazine of arts, culture, and politics. "We are open to both traditional and experimental forms. What we value most is originality and a strong sense of voice." Has published poetry by Frank Bidart, Lucie Brock-Broido,

Peter Gizzi, Jorie Graham, Allen Grossman, John Koethe, and Karen Volkman. Receives about 5,000 submissions/year, accepts about 30 poems/year. Circulation is 15,000 nationally. Single copy: $5; subscription: $25. Sample: $5.

How to Submit Submit 5-6 poems at a time. No e-mail submissions; postal submissions (and inquiries) only. Cover letter is encouraged. Include brief bio. Time between acceptance and publication is 6 months to one year. Responds in 3 months. Pays $25/poem and 5 contributor's copies. Acquires first serial rights. Reviews books of poetry, solicited reviews only. Send materials for review consideration.

Contest/Award Offerings The *Boston Review* Annual Poetry Contest (see separate listing in Contests & Awards).

$☐ ◎ BRAVE HEARTS (Specialized: inspiring, upbeat, humorous poetry)

Ogden Publications, 1503 SW 42nd St., Topeka KS 66609-1265. (785)274-4300. Fax: (785)274-4305. Web site: www.braveheartsmagazine.com. Established 1879. **Contact:** K.C. Compton, editor-in-chief.

Magazine Needs *Brave Hearts*, published quarterly in February, May, August, and November, is an inspirational magazine featuring themes and humorous or inspiring poems. "Poems should be short." Sample: $4.95.

How to Submit Lines/poem: 16 or less. Upcoming themes available in magazine or for SASE. Guidelines available for SASE or on Web site. Pays $5-12/poem; additional payment of $2 if poem is used on Web site.

Advice "Poems chosen are upbeat, sometimes humorous, always easily understood. Short poems of this type fit our format best."

◨ ◎ THE BRIAR CLIFF REVIEW

Briar Cliff College, 3303 Rebecca St., Sioux City IA 51104-2340. E-mail: jeanne.emmons@briarcliff.edu. (inquiries only). Web site: www.briarcliff.edu/bcreview. Established 1989. **Contact:** Jeanne Emmons, poetry editor. Managing Editor: Tricia Currans-Sheehan. Member: CLMP; American Humanities Index; EBSCO/Humanities International Complete.

Magazine Needs *The Briar Cliff Review*, published annually in April, is "an attractive, eclectic literary and cultural magazine." Wants "quality poetry with strong imagery; especially interested in regional, Midwestern content with tight, direct, well-wrought language." Has published poetry by James Doyle, Lois Harrod, and Barry Ballard. *The Briar Cliff Review* is 100 pages, magazine-sized, professionally printed on 100 lb. Altima Satin text paper, perfect-bound, with 4-color cover on dull stock. Receives about 1,000 poems/year, accepts about 30. Press run is 1,000. Sample: $12.

How to Submit Considers simultaneous submissions, but expects prompt notification of acceptance elsewhere; no previously published poems. No e-mail submissions; postal submissions only. Cover letter is required. "Include short bio. Submissions should be typewritten or letter quality, with author's name and address on each page. No manuscripts returned without SASE." Reads submissions August 1-November 1 only. Time between acceptance and publication is up to 6 months. Seldom comments on rejected poems. Guidelines available on Web site. Responds in 6-8 months. Pays 2 contributor's copies. Acquires first serial rights.

Contest/Award Offerings The *Briar Cliff Review* Annual Fiction, Poetry and Creative Nonfiction Contest (see separate listing in Contests & Awards).

◸ ▣ ◨ BRICK & MORTAR REVIEW

E-mail: submit@bmreview.com. Web site: www.bmreview.com. Established 2003. **Contact:** Jack Stull, senior editor.

Magazine Needs *Brick & Mortar Review*, published quarterly online, seeks poetry "that is grounded in concrete language, i.e., that uses images. Avoid the use of empty, fluffy language such as 'beautiful,' 'freedom,' 'amazed,' 'spectacular,' 'love,' etc. Of course, these words can be used in the right context, but sparingly. We don't mind an occasional rhyme, but we don't want poetry that is forced into rhyme schemes."

How to Submit Submit 3 or more (up to 10) poems at a time. Considers simultaneous submissions if notified when poetry is accepted elsewhere; no previously published poems. Accepts e-mail submissions only (pasted into body of message); no disk submissions. "We accept and respond only via e-mail." Please include a brief bio (a few sentences about yourself). Reads submissions year round. Time between acceptance and publication can be months. "The editors independently review the submissions and then meet to discuss and vote." Seldom comments on rejected poems. Guidelines available on Web site. Responds in 2 months. No payment. Acquires one-time rights.

Contest/Award Offerings Offers annual award of 1st Prize: $1,000; 2nd Prize: $250; 3rd Prize: $100; plus possible Honorable Mentions. All winning poetry is published on the Web site. Considers simultaneous submissions (with notification of acceptance elsewhere). Submit 3 or more poems of any length. "If submitting by e-mail, make sure it's clear where each poem begins and ends; also write 'contest' in the subject box (see Web site for more details on submitting)." Guidelines available on Web site. **Entry fee:** $5/poem. **Deadline:** "We accept entries year round. Awards are given at the beginning of Fall." Judges: the editors.

BRILLIANT CORNERS: A JOURNAL OF JAZZ & LITERATURE (Specialized: jazz-related literature)

Lycoming College, Williamsport PA 17701. (570)321-4279. Fax: (570)321-4090. E-mail: feinstein@lycoming.edu. Web site: www.lycoming.edu/BrilliantCorners. Established 1996. **Contact:** Sascha Feinstein, editor.

Magazine Needs *Brilliant Corners*, published semiannually, features jazz-related poetry, fiction, and nonfiction. "We are open as to length and form." Wants "work that is both passionate and well crafted—work worthy of our recent contributors." Does not want "sloppy hipster jargon or improvisatory nonsense." Has published poetry by Amiri Baraka, Jayne Cortez, Yusef Komunyakaa, Philip Levine, Sonia Sanchez, and Al Young. *Brilliant Corners* is 100 pages, digest-sized, commercially printed, perfect-bound, with color card cover with original artwork, includes ads. Accepts about 5% of work received. Press run is 800. Subscription: $12. Sample: $7.

How to Submit Submit 3-5 poems at a time. No previously published poems or simultaneous submissions. No e-mail or fax submissions. Cover letter is preferred. Reads submissions September 1-May 15 only. Seldom comments on rejected poems. Responds in 2 months. Pays 2 contributor's copies. Acquires first North American serial rights. Staff reviews books of poetry. Send materials for review consideration.

BRYANT LITERARY REVIEW

Faculty Suite F, Bryant University, Smithfield RI 02917. Web site: http://web.bryant.edu/~blr. Established 2000. **Contact:** Tom Chandler, editor. Member: CLMP.

Magazine Needs Bryant Literary Review, published annually in May, features poetry, fiction, photography, and art. "Our only standard is quality." Has published poetry by Michael S. Harper, Mary Crow, Denise Duhamel, and Baron Wormser. Bryant Literary Review is 125 pages, digest-sized, offset-printed, perfect-bound, with 4-color cover with art or photo. Receives about 3,000 poems/year, accepts about 1%. Press run is 2,500. Single copy: $8; subscription: $8.

How to Submit Submit 3-5 poems at a time. Cover letter is required. "Include SASE; please submit only once each reading period." Reads submissions September 1-December 31. Time between acceptance and publication is 5 months. Seldom comments on rejected poems. Guidelines available in magazine or on Web site. Responds in 3 months. Pays 2 contributor's copies. Acquires one-time rights.

Advice "No abstract expressionist poems, please. We prefer accessible work of depth and quality."

BUFFALO CARP

1715 Second Ave., Rock Island IL 61201. (309)793-1213. Fax: (309)793-1265. E-mail: rcollins@quadcityarts.com. Web site: www.quadcityarts.com. Established 1998. **Contact:** Ryan Collins, managing editor.

Magazine Needs *Buffalo Carp* is "a national literary journal featuring the best unpublished writing in the genres of poetry, fiction, and narrative nonfiction." Wants "any style of poetry as long as it is well crafted, vivid, and accessible." Has published poetry by John E. Smelcer, Jack R. Ridl,

Carolyn Brook Morrell, Terry Savoie, and Matt Schumacher. *Buffalo Carp* is 50-90 pages, digest-sized, offset-printed, perfect-bound, with coated, full-color cover with jury-selected, original art-work. Press run is 500; distributed free to selected libraries and schools. Single copy: $10. Sample: $5. Make checks payable to Quad City Arts.

How to Submit Submit up to 5 poems or 5 pages at a time between April 1 and October 31. Lines/poem: any. Considers simultaneous submissions "if notified immediately of other acceptance"; no previously published poems. Accepts e-mail submissions; no fax or disk submissions. Cover letter is preferred. Include SASE for acknowledgment only; "we do not return work." Reads submissions September-March. "We respond in July/August with acceptance or rejection." Time between acceptance and publication is about 6 months. Poems are circulated to an editorial board. Sometimes comments on rejected poems. "Although we can't comment on all submissions, we do offer advice to writers whose work shows promise." Guidelines available in magazine and on Web site. Pays 2 contributor's copies. Acquires first North American serial rights.

Advice "Send us your best, most interesting work. Worry less about how you would classify the work and more about it being high-quality and stand-out. We are looking to go in new directions with upcoming issues, so send us what you think best represents you and not who your influences are. *Buffalo Carp* is not interested in blending in, and has no interest in homogenized work. Blow us away!"

◙ BURNSIDE REVIEW

P.O. Box 1782, Portland OR 97207. E-mail: sid@burnsidereview.org. Web site: www.burnsidereview.org. Established 2004. **Contact:** Sid Miller, editor.

Magazine Needs *Burnside Review*, published every 9 months, prints "the best poetry we can get our hands on." Each issue includes 1 featured poet with an interview and new poems. "We tend to publish poetry that finds beauty in truly unexpected places; that combines urban and natural imagery; that breaks the heart." Open to all forms. Translations are encouraged. "Would like to see more lyric poetry." Has published poetry by Linda Bierds, Dorianne Laux, Christopher Howell, Kim Addonizio, Paul Guest, and Larissa Szporluk. *Burnside Review* is 80 pages, 6×6, professionally printed, perfect-bound. Receives about 2,500 poems/year, accepts about 50. Press run is 500. Single copy: $8; subscription: $13. Make checks payable to *Burnside Review* or order online.

How to Submit Submit 3-5 poems at a time. Considers simultaneous submissions; no previously published poems. Accepts e-mail only. "E-mailed submissions should include all poems and cover letter in 1 Word or RTF file sent as an attachment. The subject line should read 'Poetry Submission.' Send to submissions@burnsidereview.org. Check Web site for complete details. Please put name and address on each poem." Reads submissions year round. Submit seasonal poems 3-6 months in advance. Time between acceptance and publication is up to 9 months. "Editors read all poems." Seldom comments on rejected poems. Guidelines available on Web site. Responds in 2-4 months. Pays 1 contributor's copy. Acquires first rights.

Contest/Award Offerings The *Burnside Review* Chapbook Competition (see separate listing in Contests & Awards).

$◙ BUTTON MAGAZINE

P.O. Box 77, Westminster MA 01473. E-mail: sally@moonsigns.net. Web site: http://moonsigns.net. Established 1993. **Contact:** Maude Piper, poetry editor.

Magazine Needs *Button*, published annually, is "New England's tiniest magazine of fiction, poetry, and gracious living." Wants "poetry that incises a perfect figure eight on the ice, but also cuts beneath that mirrored surface. Minimal use of vertical pronoun." Does not want "sentiment; no 'musing' on who or what done ya wrong." Has published poetry by Amanda Powell, Brendan Galvin, Jean Monahan, Mary Campbell, Kevin McGrath, and Ed Conti. *Button* is 30 pages, 4¼×5½, saddle-stapled, with cardstock offset cover with illustrations that incorporate 1 or more buttons. Press run is 1,200. Subscription: $5 for 4 issues, $25 lifetime. Sample: $2 and 1 First-Class stamp.

How to Submit Submit no more than 2 poems at a time. "Do not submit more than twice in one year." No previously published poems. Cover letter is required. Time between acceptance and publication is up to 6 months. Poems are circulated to an editorial board. Often comments on rejected poems. Guidelines available by e-mail. Responds in 4 months. Pays honorarium, subscription, and at least 5 contributor's copies. Acquires first North American serial rights.

Advice "Writing as therapy is fine. Publishing as therapy is not. Take the vertical pronoun (I) and write your poem without it. Still got something to say? Also, *Button* tries to reflect a world one would want to live in—this does not mean we make the space for various uncatalogued human vices (self-pity, navel gazing). If you can be really amusing about those, that's another story. Finally, writers who need to say they've published 1,200 poems in various magazines and then name all of the magazines—well, we don't really need to know. Aim high, write often, but refine, refine, refine."

$ ☑ ◎ BYLINE MAGAZINE (Specialized: writers & writing)

P.O. Box 111, Albion NY 14411. (585)355-3290. E-mail: dmarbach@rochester.rr.com. Web site: www.bylinemag.com. Established 1981. **Contact:** Donna M. Marbach, poetry editor.

Magazine Needs *ByLine*, published monthly, is a magazine for the encouragement of writers and poets. Uses 6-10 poems/issue. Wants "any subject, any style; must be well-crafted." Has published poetry by Patricia Fargnoli, Kathryn Howd Machan, Dee Shapiro, Allen Britt, C.E. Chaffin, and Thomas Holmes. *ByLine* is magazine-sized, professionally printed, includes ads. Receives about 2,500 poetry submissions/year, accepts about 100. Subscription: $29. Sample: $6.

How to Submit Submit up to 3 poems at a time. Lines/poem: less than 30 preferred. No previously published poems. Accepts e-mail submissions (preferred). Guidelines available for SASE or on web site. Pays $10/poem. Acquires first North American serial rights. Reviews books about the writing or marketing of poetry in 250-500 words. Pays $25/review.

Additional Information Also seeking poetry-related how-to articles. Pays $35/article (500-700 words) and $50/article (1,500-1,800 words).

Contest/Award Offerings Sponsors up to 20 poetry contests and a biennial chapbook contest. Guidelines available for #10 SASE or on Web site.

Advice "Because our primary goal is to assist writers in improving and growing their craft, we are looking for poetry that is top-quality and shows skillful knowledge of poetic devices, techniques, and forms. Articles and book reviews should focus on poetic craft and the submission process. While we encourge new writers and are happy to work with them, we are seeking poetry that is concise, original, and a positive model for other poets."

☑ CALIFORNIA QUARTERLY

P.O. Box 7126, Orange CA 92863-7126. (949)854-8024. E-mail: jipalley@aol.com. (inquiries only). Web site: www.californiaquarterly.blogspot.com. Established 1972. **Contact:** The Editors.

Magazine Needs *California Quarterly*, the official publication of the California State Poetry Society (an affiliate of the National Federation of State Poetry Societies), is designed "to encourage the writing and dissemination of poetry." Wants poetry on any subject. "No geographical limitations. Quality is all that matters." Has published poetry by Michael L. Johnson, Lyn Lifshin, and Joanna C. Scott. *California Quarterly* is 64 pages, digest-sized, offset-printed, perfect-bound, with heavy paper cover with art. Receives 3,000-4,000 poems/year, accepts about 5%. Press run is 500. Membership in CSPS is $30/year and includes a subscription to *California Quarterly*. Sample: $6 (includes guidelines).

How to Submit Submit up to 6 poems at a time. Lines/poem: 60 maximum. No previously published poems. Accepts submissions by postal mail only; no e-mail submissions. Put name and address on each sheet, include SASE. Seldom comments on rejected poems. Guidelines available for SASE. Responds in up to 8 months. Pays 1 contributor's copy. Acquires first rights. Rights revert to poet after publication.

Advice "Since our editor changes with each issue, we encourage poets to resubmit."

☑ ◎ CALLALOO: A JOURNAL OF AFRICAN DIASPORA ARTS & LETTERS (Specialized: poetry dealing with African Diaspora)

Dept. of English, Texas A&M University, 4212 TAMU, College Station TX 77843-4227. (979)458-3108. Fax: (979)458-3275. E-mail: callaloo@tamu.edu. Web site: http://callaloo.tamu.edu. Established 1976. **Contact:** Charles H. Rowell, editor.

• Poetry published in *Callaloo* has been included frequently in volumes of *The Best American Poetry*.

Magazine Needs *Callaloo: A Journal of African Diaspora Arts & Letters*, published quarterly, is devoted to poetry dealing with the African Diaspora, including North America, Europe, Africa, Latin and Central America, South America, and the Caribbean. Has published poetry by Aimé Césaire, Lucille Clifton, Rita Dove,Yusef Komunyakaa, Natasha Tretheway, and Carl Phillips. Features about 15-20 poems (all forms and styles) in each issue along with short fiction, interviews, literary criticism, and concise critical book reviews. Circulation is 1,600 subscribers of which half are libraries. Subscription: $39, $107 for institutions.

How to Submit Submit complete ms in triplicate. No fax or e-mail submissions. Include cover letter with name, mailing address, e-mail address if available, and SASE. Responds in 6 months. Pays copies.

☐ ◎ CALYX, A JOURNAL OF ART AND LITERATURE BY WOMEN (Specialized: poetry by & about women; multicultural)

Calyx Books, P.O. Box B, Corvallis OR 97339-0539. (541)753-9384. Fax: (541)753-0515. E-mail: calyx@proaxis.com. Web site: www.calyxpress.org. Established 1976. **Contact:** Beverly McFarland, senior editor.

Magazine Needs *CALYX, A Journal of Art and Literature by Women*, published 3 times every 18 months, contains poetry, prose, art, book reviews, essays, and interviews by and about women. Wants "excellently crafted poetry that also has excellent content." Has published poetry by Maurya Simon, Diane Averill, Carole Boston Weatherford, and Eleanor Wilner. *CALYX* is 6×8, handsomely printed on heavy paper, flat-spined, with glossy color cover. Single copy: $9.50 plus shipping; subscription: $21/volume (3 issues), $39 for 2 volumes (6 issues). Sample: $12.50. See Web site for foreign and institutional rates.

How to Submit Send up to 6 poems at a time. Considers previously published poems "occasionally" and simultaneous submissions "if kept up-to-date on publication." No fax or e-mail submissions. Include SASE and short bio. "We accept copies in good condition and clearly readable. *CALYX* is edited by a collective editorial board." Reads submissions postmarked October 1-December 31 only. **Manuscripts received outside of reading period will be returned unread.** Guidelines available for SASE, by e-mail, or on Web site. Responds in 9 months. Pays one contributor's copy/poem, plus subscription. Send materials for review consideration.

Additional Information CALYX Books publishes one book of poetry/year. All work published is by women. Has published *Storytelling in Cambodia* by Willa Schneberg and *Black Candle: Poems about Women from India, Pakistan, and Bangladesh* by Chitra Banerjee Divakaruni. **Closed to submissions until further notice.**

Contest/Award Offerings The annual Lois Cranston Memorial Poetry Prize (see separate listing in Contests & Awards).

Advice "Read the publication and be familiar with what we have published."

◘ $◪ ◎ CANADIAN WRITER'S JOURNAL (Specialized: poetry writing)

White Mountain Publications, Box 1178, New Liskeard ON P0J 1P0 Canada. (705)647-5424. Fax: (705)647-8366. E-mail: cwj@cwj.ca. Web site: www.cwj.ca. **Contact:** Deborah Ranchuk, editor.

Magazine Needs *Canadian Writer's Journal*, published bimonthly, uses a few "short poems or portions thereof as part of 'how-to' articles relating to the writing of poetry, and occasional short poems with tie-in to the writing theme. We try for 90% Canadian content but prefer good material over country of origin or how well you're known." *Canadian Writer's Journal* is digest-sized. Subscription: $35/year, $67.50 for 2 years (add 7% GST in Canada). Sample: $9.

How to Submit Submit up to 5 poems at a time. No previously published poems. Accepts e-mail submissions (pasted into body of message, with 'Submission' in the subject line). Include SASE with postal submissions. "U.S. postage accepted; do not affix to envelope. Poems should be titled. Hard copy and SASE required if accepted." Responds in 3-6 months. Pays $2-5/poem and 1 contributor's copy.

⊠ $⊘ THE CAPILANO REVIEW (Specialized: avant-garde, experimental)
2055 Purcell Way, North Vancouver BC V7J 3H5 Canada. (604)984-1712. E-mail: tcr@capcollege.bc
.ca. Web site: www.thecapilanoreview.ca. Established 1972. **Contact:** Submissions.
Magazine Needs *The Capilano Review*, published 3 times/year, is a literary and visual arts review.
Wants "avant-garde, experimental, previously unpublished poetry of sustained intelligence and
imagination. We are interested in poetry that is new in concept and in execution." Has published
poetry by bill bissett, Phyllis Webb, and Michael Ondaatje. *The Capilano Review* is 90-100 pages,
digest-sized, finely printed, perfect-bound, with glossy full-color card cover. Circulation is 800.
Sample: $10 CAD prepaid.
How to Submit Submit 5-6 poems minimum. No simultaneous submissions. No e-mail or disk
submissions. Cover letter is required. Include SAE with IRCs; "submissions with U.S. postage will
not be considered." Responds in up to 3 months. Pays $50-200 CAD, subscription, and 2 contributor's copies. Acquires first North American serial rights.
Advice "Read the magazine and web site before you submit. *The Capilano Review* receives dozens
of manuscripts each week; unfortunately, the majority of them are simply inappropriate for the
magazine."

$◯ ◎ CAPPER'S (Specialized: everyday situations; upbeat, humorous)
Ogden Publications, 1503 SW 42nd St., Topeka KS 66609-1265. (785)274-4300. Fax: (785)274-4305.
Web site: www.cappers.com. Established 1879. **Contact:** K.C. Compton, editor-in-chief.
Magazine Needs *Capper's*, published monthly, is a tabloid (newsprint) going to 240,000 mail subscribers, mostly small-town and rural families. Wants short poems (4-16 lines preferred, lines of
one-column width) "relating to everyday situations, nature, inspirational, humorous. Most poems
used in *Capper's* are upbeat in tone and offer the reader a bit of humor, joy, enthusiasm, or encouragement." Considers poetry by children ages 12 and under. Has published poetry by Elizabeth
Searle Lamb, Robert Brimm, Margaret Wiedyke, Helena K. Stefanski, Sheryl L. Nelms, and Claire
Puneky. Sample: $1.95. Not available on newsstand.
How to Submit Submit 5-6 poems at a time. Lines/poem: 14-16. No simultaneous submissions. No
e-mail or fax submissions. Returns mss with SASE. Publishes seasonal theme issues. Guidelines
available for SASE or on Web site. Responds in 3 months. Pays $10-15/poem; additional payment
of $5 if poem is used on Web site. Acquires one-time rights.
Advice "Poems chosen are upbeat, sometimes humorous, always easily understood. Short poems
of this type fit our format best."

◯ ◎ THE CARIBBEAN WRITER (Specialized: Caribbean focus)
University of the Virgin Islands, RR 1, P.O. Box 10,000, Kingshill, St. Croix USVI 00850. (340)692-
4152. Fax: (340)692-4026. E-mail: info@thecaribbeanwriter.org. Web site: www.thecaribbeanwrite
r.org. Established 1987. **Contact:** Ms. Quilin Mars.
   • Poetry published in *The Caribbean Writer* has appeared in The Pushcart Prize.
Magazine Needs *The Caribbean Writer*, published annually, is a literary anthology with a Caribbean
focus (Caribbean must be central to the literary work, or the work must reflect a Caribbean heritage,
experience, or perspective). Has published poetry by Jacqueline Johnson Bishop, McDonald Dixon,
Susan Broili and Thomas Reiter. *The Caribbean Writer* is 300+ pages, digest-sized, handsomely
printed on heavy stock, perfect-bound, with glossy card cover. Press run is 1,200. Single copy: $15
plus $4 postage; subscription: $25. Sample: $7 plus $4 postage. (Note: postage to and from the
Virgin Islands is the same as within the US.)
How to Submit Submit up to 5 poems at a time. Considers simultaneous submissions; no previously
published poems. Accepts e-mail as attachment; no fax submissions. Blind submissions only: name,
address, phone number, e-mail address, and title of ms should appear in cover letter along with brief
bio. Title only on ms. Reads submissions by November 31 annual deadline. Guidelines available in
magazine, for SASE, by e-mail, or on Web site. Pays 2 contributor's copies. Acquires first North
American serial rights. Reviews books of poetry and fiction in 1,000 words. Send materials for
review consideration.
Contest/Award Offerings All submissions are eligible for the Daily News Prize ($300) for the best

poem or poems, The Marguerite Cobb McKay Prize to a Virgin Island author ($200), the David Hough Literary Prize to a Caribbean author ($500), the Canute A. Brodhurst Prize for Fiction ($400), and the Charlotte and Isidor Paiewonsky Prize ($200) for first-time publication.

Ⓝ $▢ ◎ CAT TALES: FANTASTIC FELINE FICTION (Specialized: fantasy, crime, and horror involving cats)

9710 Traville Gateway Dr. #234, Rockville MD 20850. E-mail: g-scithers@sff.net. Web site: www.weirdtalesmagazine.com. Established 2008. **Contact:** George H. Scithers, editor.

Magazine Needs *Cat Tales: Fantastic Feline Fiction*, published twice per year, is a trade paperback anthology which prints "fantasy, crime, and horror fiction involving cats, with some poetry on those subjects." Wants "poetry touching on fantasy, crime, or horror, involving cats. Both serious and humor accepted, inlucing limericks and double dactyls." Accepts poetry by children and teens. *Cat Tales: Fantastic Feline Fiction* is 176 pages, trade paperback sized, offset-printed, perfect-bound with a process color cover. Accepts about 3 poems per issue. Press run is 5,000.

How to Submit Submit up to 5 poems at a time. No previously published poems or simultaneous submissions. E-mail preferred. Include author address on every poem. Time between acceptance and publication varies. Poems are circulated to an editorial board. Seldom comments on rejected poems. Never publishes theme issues. Guidelines available for SASE or by e-mail. Responds in 1 month. Pays $1 or less/line and 2 contributor's copies. Acquires first North American serial rights.

Advice "Follow standard manuscript format."

⬜ CAVEAT LECTOR

400 Hyde St., Apt. 606, San Francisco CA 94109-7445. Phone/fax: (415)928-7431. E-mail: editors@caveat-lector.org. Web site: www.caveat-lector.org. Established 1989. **Contact:** Christopher Bernard and Anna Sears, principals.

Magazine Needs *Caveat Lector*, published 2 times/year, "is devoted to the arts and cultural and philosophical commentary. We publish visual art and music as well as literary and theoretical texts. Our Web site includes an art gallery and a multimedia section offering video and audio." Wants poems "on any subject, in any style, as long as the work is authentic in feeling and appropriately crafted. We are looking for accomplished poems, something that resonates in the mind long after the reader has laid the poem aside. We want work that has authenticity of emotion and high craft; poems that, whether raw or polished, ring true—and if humorous, are actually funny, or at least witty. Classical to experimental. Note: We sometimes request authors for audio of work we publish to post on our Web site." Has published poetry by Joanne Lowery, Simon Perchik, Les Murray, Alfred Robinson, and Ernest Hilbert. *Caveat Lector* is 24-32 pages, $11 \times 4^{1}/_{4}$, photocopied, saddle-stapled, with b&w cover. Receives 200-600 poems/year, accepts about 2%. Press run is 250. Single copy: $3.50; subscription: $15 for 4 issues. Sample: $3.

How to Submit Submit up to 6 short poems, 3 medium-length poems, or 1 long poem at a time. Lines/poem:short, up to 50 each; medium, 51-100; long, up to 500. Considers simultaneous submissions, "but please inform us." Cover letter is required. "Place name, address, and (optional) telephone number on each page. Include SASE and brief bio (100 words or less)." Reads submissions January-June. Time between acceptance and publication is 1 year. Sometimes comments on rejected poems. Guidelines available for SASE. Responds in 1 month. Pays 2 contributor's copies. Acquires first publication rights.

Advice "The 2 rules of writing are: 1) Revise it again. 2) Revise it again. The writing level of most of our submissions is pleasingly high. A rejection by us is not always a criticism of the work, and we try to provide comments to our more promising submitters."

⬜ CC&D/CHILDREN, CHURCHES AND DADDIES

(formerly *Children, Churches and Daddies*), Scars Publications, 829 Brian Court, Gurnee IL 60031. E-mail: ccandd96@scars.tv. Web site: http://scars.tv. Established 1993. **Contact:** Janet Kuypers, editor/publisher.

Magazine Needs *CC&D/Children, Churches and Daddies (The Unreligious, Non-Family-Oriented Literary Magazine)*, published monthly, contains poetry, prose, art, and essays. "Also run electronic issues and collection books. We accept poetry of almost any genre, but no rhyme or religious poems (look at our current issue for a better idea of what we're like). We are okay with gay/lesbian/bisexual, nature/rural/ecology, political/social issues, women/feminism." Does not want "racist, sexist (therefore we're not into pornography, either), or homophobic stuff." Has published poetry by Mel Waldman, Pat Dixon, Angeline Hawkes-Craig, Cheryl Townsend, Kenneth DiMaggio. *CC&D/Children, Churches and Daddies* (print) has ranged from 30 to 100 pages, been both digest-sized and standard-sized, photocopied, saddle-stapled; currently 40 pages, saddle-stitched and laser-printed. Receives hundreds of poems/year, accepts about 40%. Sample: $6 (print); free electronic sample online. Make checks payable to Janet Kuypers.

How to Submit Lines/poem: accepts longer works, "within 2 pages for an individual poem is appreciated." Considers previously published poems and simultaneous submissions. Accepts e-mail submissions (preferred, pasted into body of message or as attachment in Microsoft Word .doc file) or disk submissions. "When submitting via e-mail in body of message, explain in preceding paragraph that it is a submission; for disk submissions, mail floppy disk with ASCII text, or Macintosh disk." Comments on rejected poems "if asked." Guidelines available for SASE, by e-mail, or on Web site. Responds in 2 weeks.

Contest/Award Offerings Scars Publications sometimes sponsors a contest "where writing appears in an annual book." Write or e-mail (editor@scars.tv) for information.

Also Offers Also able to publish electronic chapbooks. Additional information available by e-mail or on Web site.

Advice "The Web site is a more comprehensive view of what *CC&D/Children, Churches and Daddies* does. All the information is there."

☐ CEREMONY, A JOURNAL OF POETRY AND OTHER ARTS

Dance of My Hands Publishing, 120 Vista Dr., Warminster PA 18974. E-mail: danceofmyhands@aol .com. Web site: www.danceofmyhands.com. **Contact:** Melanie M. Eyth, editor.

Magazine Needs *Ceremony, a Journal of Poetry and Other Arts*, published semiannually, encourages "all expression and articism. We do not judge or criticize submissions, but publish most work offered. Beginning poets are especially encouraged." Wants poetry, short pieces of prose, photography, drawings, and other printable arts. Considers poetry by children and teens. *Ceremony* is digest-sized, home computer-printed on 20 lb. standard white paper, stapled. Receives about 100 submissions/year, accepts "nearly as many." Single copy: $2.50.

How to Submit Submit up to 6 poems at a time. Considers previously published poems and simultaneous submissions. Accepts e-mail submissions only. Reads submissions year round. Time between acceptance and publication is 1-2 years. Sometimes comments on rejected poems. Sometimes publishes theme issues. Guidelines available in magazine and on Web site. Pays 1 contributor's copy. Rights revert to poet upon publication.

◪ THE CHAFFIN JOURNAL

Dept. of English, Case Annex 467, Eastern Kentucky University, Richmond KY 40475-3102. (859)622-3080. Web site: www.english.eku.edu/chaffin_journal. Established 1998. **Contact:** Robert W. Witt, editor.

Magazine Needs *The Chaffin Journal*, published annually in December, prints quality short fiction and poetry by new and established writers/poets. Wants any form, subject matter, or style. Does not want "poor quality." Has published poetry by Taylor Graham, Diane Glancy, Judith Montgomery, Simon Perchik, Philip St. Clair, and Virgil Suárez. *The Chaffin Journal* is 120 pages, digest-sized, offset-printed, perfect-bound, with plain cover with title only. Receives about 500 poems/year, accepts about 10%. Press run is 300; 40-50 distributed free to contributors. Single copy: $6; subscription: $6/year. Sample (back issue): $5. Make checks payable to *The Chaffin Journal*.

How to Submit Submit 5 poems at a time. Considers simultaneous submissions (although not preferred); no previously published poems. No e-mail or disk submissions. Cover letter is preferred. "Submit typed pages with only one poem per page. Enclose SASE." Reads submissions June 1-October 1. Time between acceptance and publication is 6 months. Poems are reviewed by the general editor and 2 poetry editors. Never comments on rejected poems. Guidelines available in magazine

or on Web site. Responds in 3 months. Pays 1 contributor's copy. Acquires one-time rights.
Advice "Submit quality work during our reading period; include cover letter and SASE."

▧ ▢ ◎ CHALLENGER INTERNATIONAL (Specialized: poetry for/by teens)
(250)991-5567. E-mail: danlukiv@sd28.bc.ca. Web site: http://challengerinternational.20m.com/
index.html. Established 1978. **Contact:** Dan Lukiv, editor.

Magazine Needs *Challenger international*, published annually, contains "poetry and (on occasion) short fiction." Wants "any type of work, especially by teenagers (our mandate: to encourage young writers, and to publish their work alongside established writers), providing it is not pornographic, profane, or overly abstract." Has published poetry from Canada, the continental U.S., Hawaii, Switzerland, Russia, Malta, Italy, Slovenia, Ireland, England, Korea, Pakistan, Australia, Zimbabwe, Argentina, and Columbia. *Challenger international* is generally 20-50 pages, magazine-sized, laser-printed, side-stapled. Press run is 50. *Challenger international* is distributed free to McNaughton Centre Secondary Alternate School sudents.

How to Submit Considers previously published poems and simultaneous submissions. Cover letter is required. Include list of credits, if any. Accepts e-mail submissions only; no postal submissions. "Sometimes we edit to save the poet rejection." Responds in 6 months. Payment is 1 e-copy (sent as an e-mail attachment) of the issue in which the author's work appears. Poet retains rights.

Additional Information Island Scholastic Press publishes chapbooks by authors featured in *Challenger international*. Pays 3 author's copies. Copyright remains with author. Distribution of free copies through McNaughton Centre.

Advice "We like imagistic poetry that makes sense."

$▢ ◎ CHAMPAGNE SHIVERS (Specialized: horror poetry only)
E-mail: ChampagneShivers@hotmail.com (accepts submissions by e-mail only). Web site: http://samsdotpublishing.com/vineyard/Champagne%20Shivers.htm. Established 2002. **Contact:** Cathy Buburuz, editor.

Magazine Needs *Champagne Shivers* is "a classy horror magazine. This is not the place to submit offensive language. We prefer poetic, well-written horror." Wants "horror poetry only. We prefer poems that do not rhyme, but all verse will be considered. Long poems stand the best chance for acceptance, especially if they're scary and entertaining." Does not want "anything that isn't horror related, and always proof and edit before you send your submission. If your work does not have high entertainment or high impact, do not send it here." Has published poetry by Lee Clark Zumpe, Nancy Bennett, Steve Vernon, Kurt Newton, W.B. Vogel III, and Keith W. Sikora. *Champagne Shivers* is 40-60 pages, magazine-sized, professionally printed, saddle-stapled, with b&w cover with scary art. Receives about 1,000 poems/year, accepts 7 poems/issue. Press run and subscriber base vary; the only free copies go to reviewers and contributors. Single copy: $12 U.S. and Canada. Sample: $10 U.S. and Canada. ("Foreign countries, please inquire about costs." Make checks payable to Tyree Campbell, Sam's Dot Publishing, P.O. Box 782, Cedar Rapids IA 52406-0782 (for subscriptions and sample copies only; DO NOT SEND SUBMISSIONS TO THIS ADDRESS).

How to Submit Submit 1 poem at a time. Lines/poem: 20-30. Considers previously published poems; no simultaneous submissions. Accepts e-mail submissions only (pasted into body of message; DO NOT SEND ATTACHMENTS) to ChampagneShivers@hotmail.com. Does not accept snail mail submissions. Cover letter is preferred. "Submit 1 poem with a bio written in the third person, your mailing address, and your e-mail address." Reads submissions year round. Submit seasonal poems 4 months in advance. Time between acceptance and publication is less than 6 months. Always comments on rejected poems. Guidelines available by e-mail or on Web site. Pays 10¢/line for unpublished poems; 5¢/line for previously published poems (let the editor know where and when the poem appeared), plus 1 contributor's copy. Acquires first North American serial rights to unpublished poems, one-time rights to previously published poems. All rights revert back to the writer upon publication.

Contest/Award Offerings Sam's Dot Publishing offers The James Award (Trophy) annually. "Submit one poem per e-mail, but submit as often as you like." **Entry fee:** "None—it's free." **Deadline:** December 31. Guidelines available on Web site. "Never send snail mail submissions; always submit in the body of an e-mail after reading the information under How to Submit above.''

Also Offers *Expressions (A Newsletter for Creative People Worldwide)*, edited by Cathy Buburuz (visit the Web site at www.samsdotpublishing.com/expressions.htm).

Advice "Submit horror poems only. I love psychological horror poetry, horror poetry about the Old West, horror poems about asylums, or anything that's just plain scary. I do not want poems about werewolves, vampires, ghosts, or traditional monsters. I want to read poetry that's fresh and exciting. Most of all, send me something that's high in entertainment, that's never been done before. Send poems that will give me and my audience the shivers.''

▣ ◯ CHANTARELLE'S NOTEBOOK

E-mail: chantarellesnotebook@yahoo.com. Web site: www.chantarellesnotebook.com. Established 2005. **Contact:** Kendall A. Bell and Christinia Bell, editors.

Magazine Needs *Chantarelle's Notebook*, published quarterly online, seeks "quality work from undiscovered poets. We enjoy poems that speak to us—poems with great sonics and visuals.'' Wants "all styles of poetry, as long as it's quality work.'' Does not want "infantile rants, juvenile confessionals, greeting card-styled verse, political posturing, or religious outpourings.'' Considers poetry by children and teens. "There are no age restrictions, but submissions from younger people will be held to the same guidelines and standards as those from adults.'' Has published poetry by Patrick Carrington, Kristina Marie Darling, Jeanpaul Ferro, Taylor Graham, Corey Mesler, and Simon Perchik. Receives about 500 poems/year, accepts about 20%. Sample: see Web site for latest issue.

How to Submit Submit 3-5 poems at a time. Lines/poem: "shorter poems have a better chance, but long poems are fine.'' Considers previously published poems; no simultaneous submissions. Accepts e-mail submissions (pasted into body of message; "we will not open any attachments—they will be deleted''). Cover letter is required. "Please include a short bio of no more than 75 words, should we decide to accept your work.'' Reads submissions year round. Submit seasonal poems 2-3 months in advance. "The editors will review all submissions and make a decision within a week's time.'' Never comments on rejected poems. Guidelines available on Web site. "Please follow the guidelines—all the information is there!'' Responds in 1 week. Acquires one-time rights. Rights revert to poets upon publication. *"Chantarelle's Notebook* is also accepting photo submissions. Please visit the Web site for guidelines on how to submit your photos to us.''

Also Offers *"Chantarelle's Notebook* will publish a 'best of' print journal that will cull poems from each of the previous 4 quarterly issues in the past year. The authors of the poems chosen will receive 1 contributor's copy and can buy additional copies at half price.''

Advice "Read as much poetry as you can. Immerse yourself in work other than your own. Turn off your television. Write from the pit of your stomach. Revise. Edit. Rewrite. Do not let rejections keep you off your path. The only way to become a great poet is to learn from all experiences, good and bad.''

▦ ◪ ◎ CHAPMAN (Specialized: Scottish culture)

Chapman Publishing, 4 Broughton Place, Edinburgh EH1 3RX Scotland. (44)(131)557-2207. E-mail: chapman-pub@blueyonder.co.uk. Web site: www.chapman-pub.co.uk. Established 1970. **Contact:** Dr. Joy Hendry, editor.

Magazine Needs *Chapman*, published 3 times/year, "is controversial, influential, outspoken, and intelligent. Established in 1970, it has become a dynamic force in Scottish culture covering theatre, politics, language, and the arts. Our highly respected forum for poetry, fiction, criticism, review, and debate makes it essential reading for anyone interested in contemporary Scotland. *Chapman* publishes the best in Scottish writing—new work by well-known Scottish writers in the context of lucid critical discussion. It also, increasingly, publishes international writing. With our strong commitment to the future, we energetically promote new writers, new ideas, and new approaches.'' Also interested in receiving poetry dealing with women's issues and feminism. Has published poetry by Liz Lochhead, Sorley MacLean, Edwin Morgan, Willa Muir, Tom Scott, and Una Flett. *Chapman* is 144 pages, digest-sized, professionally printed in small type on matte stock, perfect-bound, with glossy card cover. Press run is 2,000. Receives "thousands'' of poetry submissions/year, accepts about 200. Single copy: £6.50 including post; subscription: £24 ($60). Sample: £7.50, $15 (overseas). Payment also via PayPal.

How to Submit Submit 4-10 poems at a time. No simultaneous submissions. Cover letter is required. "Submissions must be accompanied by a SASE/IRC or provide e-mail address for reply. Please send sufficient postage to cover the return of your manuscript. Do not send foreign stamps. Limit 1 poem/page. We do not usually publish single poems." Responds "as soon as possible." Always sends prepublication galleys. Pays a small fee and/or contributor's copies at discount. Staff reviews books of poetry. Send materials for review consideration.

Additional Information *Chapman Publishing is currently not accepting submissions of books or chapbooks.*

Advice "Poets should not try to court approval by writing poems especially to suit what they perceive as the nature of the magazine. They usually get it wrong and write badly."

$◨ THE CHARITON REVIEW (Specialized: subscribers preferred)

821 Camino de Jemez, Santa Fe NM 87501. Established 1975. **Contact:** Jim Barnes, editor.

Magazine Needs *The Chariton Review*, published semiannually, prints "open and closed forms—traditional, experimental, mainstream. We do not consider verse, only poetry in its highest sense, whatever that may be." Does not want "the sentimental and the inspirational. Also, no more 'relativism' (short stories and poetry centered around relatives)." Has published poetry by Michael Spence, Kim Bridgford, Sam Maio, Kenneth Lincoln, Wayne Dodd, and Lynne McMahon. *The Chariton Review* is 100+ pages, digest-sized, professionally printed, flat-spined, with glossy cover with photographs. Receives 8,000-10,000 submissions/year, accepts about 35-50. Press run is about 600. Subscription: $10/year, $18 for 2 years.

How to Submit Submit 3-5 poems at a time. No simultaneous submissions. Poems should be typed single-spaced. Do not write for guidelines. Responds "quickly"; accepted poems often appear within a few issues of notification. Always sends prepublication galleys. Pays $5/printed page when funds are available. Acquires first North American serial rights. **Contributors are expected to subscribe or pay $5 reading fee for each submission.**

⬧ $◨ THE CHATTAHOOCHEE REVIEW

Georgia Perimeter College, 2101 Womack Rd., Dunwoody GA 30338. (770)274-5145. E-mail: gpccr @gpc.edu. Web site: www.chattahoochee-review.org. Established 1980. **Contact:** Marc Fitten, editor-in-chief.

Magazine Needs *The Chattahoochee Review*, published quarterly, prints poetry, short fiction, essays, reviews, and interviews. "We publish a number of Southern writers, but *The Chattahoochee Review* is not by design a regional magazine. All themes, forms, and styles are considered as long as they impact the whole person: heart, mind, intuition, and imagination." Has recently published work by George Garrett, Jim Daniels, Jack Pendarvis, Ignacio Padilla, and Kevin Canty. *The Chattahoochee Review* is 160 pages, digest-sized, professionally printed, flat-spined, with four-color silk-matte card cover. Press run is 1,250; 300 are complimentary copies sent to editors and "miscellaneous VIPs." Subscription: $20/year. Sample: $6.

How to Submit Submit 3-5 poems at a time. No previously published poems or simultaneous submissions. No e-mail or disk submissions. Cover letter is "encouraged, but not required." Include bio material when sending cover letter. Poems should be typed on one side of page with poet's name clearly visible. No reply without SASE. Time between acceptance and publication is up to 4 months. Publishes theme issues. Guidelines available for SASE or on Web site. Responds in 1 week to 6 months. Pays $50/poem and 2 contributor's copies. Acquires first rights. Staff reviews books of poetry and short fiction in 1,500 words, single- or multi-book format. Send materials for review consideration.

◨ CHAUTAUQUA LITERARY JOURNAL

P.O. Box 613, Chautauqua NY 14722. E-mail: CLJEditor@aol.com. Web site: http://writers.ciweb.org. Established 2003. **Contact:** Richard Foerster, editor.

- Poetry published in *Chautauqua Literary Journal* has been included in *The Pushcart Prize* anthology.

Magazine Needs *Chautauqua Literary Journal*, published annually in June, prints poetry, short fiction, creative nonfiction, and book reviews. "We welcome poems that exhibit the writer's craft and attention to language, employ striking images and metaphors, engage the mind as well as the emotions, and reveal insights into the larger world of human concerns. The editor invites traditional as well as experimental work." Does not want "hackneyed inspirational versifying; poems typed in all capitals or on pastel paper." Has published poetry by Patricia Smith, Karl Shapiro, Douglas Goetsch, William Heyen, Robert Cording, and Randall Watson. *Chautauqua Literary Journal* is 178 pages, digest-sized, offset-printed, with notch adhesive binding and glossy cover with original artwork, includes ads. Receives about 4,000 poems/year, accepts about 40. Press run is 2,000; 300 distributed free to contributors and others. Single copy: $10; subscription: $18. Make checks payable to *Chautauqua Literary Journal*.

How to Submit Submit 4 poems maximum at a time. Considers simultaneous submissions (if notified); no previously published poems. No e-mail or disk submissions. Cover letter is preferred. "We prefer single-spaced manuscripts in 12 pt. font. Cover letters should be brief and mention recent publications (if any). SASE is mandatory." Reads submissions year round. Time between acceptance and publication is up to 1 year. "The editor is the sole arbiter, but we do have advisory editors who periodically make recommendations." Sometimes comments on rejected poems. Guidelines available on Web site. Responds in 3 months or less. Always sends prepublication galleys. Pays 2 contributor's copies. Acquires first rights "plus one-time non-exclusive rights to reprint accepted work in an anniversary issue." Reviews books/chapbooks of poetry in 750-1,000 words, single- and multi-book format. Send materials for review consideration to *Chautauqua Literary Journal*/Reviews, P.O. Box 2039, York Beach ME 03910.

Advice "Poets who are not avid readers of contemporary poetry will most likely not be writing anything of interest to us."

N ☑ THE CHERRY BLOSSOM REVIEW

E-mail: thecherryblossomreview@yahoo.com. Web site: http://www.geocities.com/thecherryblossomreview/. Established 2007. **Contact:** Jennifer LeBlanc, editor

Magazine Needs *The Cherry Blossom Review*, published quarterly in print and online, is dedicated to publishing quality poetry. Poems that contain metaphors, imagery, and lyrical quality are appreciated. Wants mostly free verse. "Interested in metaphors, imagery, and lyrical quality." Does not want "not interested in sexual content or inappropriate language. No rhyming poems, please." Considers poetry by teens. *The Cherry Blossom Review* is approximately 28-32 pages, digest-sized and online, photocopied, saddle-stapled, with stock cover. Receives about 600 poems/year, accepts about 20%. Press run is 25; 15 distributed free to contributors and friends. Single copy: $4.50; subscription: $18. Make checks payable to Jennifer LeBlanc. Send e-mail asking for postal address.

How to Submit Submit 1-3 poems at a time. Considers simultaneous submissions. Does not consider previously published work (Considers poetry posted on a public Web site/blog/forum and poetry posted on a private, password-protected forum as published). Accepts e-mail submissions (as attachment); no fax or disk submissions. Cover letter is required. "Send poetry submissions to thecherryblossomreview@yahoo.com. Do *not* send submissions to postal address. They will not be read. Please include a short, third person biography to be published with accepted poems." Reads submissions mid-May-midsummer. Check Web site for dates. Time between acceptance and publication is up to 10 months. Seldom comments on rejected poems. Never publishes theme issues. Guidelines available on Web site. Responds in 2 weeks. Pays 1 contributor's copy. Acquires one-time publishing rights, "which includes publication on the Web site and in the corresponding print issue. Poetry will remain on the Web site for up to 1 year. Rights revert to poets upon publication."

Advice "Read contemporary poetry, write often, and proofread your work!"

N ☑ ◎ CHEST (Specialized: Medical themes)

3300 Dundee Rd, Northbrook IL 60062.800-343-2222. E-mail: poetrychest@aol.com. Web site: www.chestjournal.org. Established 1937. **Contact**: Michael Zack, M.D., poetry editor.

John Mark Eberhart

Journalism by day, poetry by night

According to Robert Jones, editor of Mid-America Press, John Mark Eberhart has established himself as "a careful and readable poet." Poet Philip Miller says that in Eberhart's poetry the reader "discovers the unexpected and essential in the familiar." For Robert Stewart, poet and editor of *New Letters*, Eberhart's passionate poems "do not leave us where they found us. We are moved." Eberhart's poetry has appeared in many journals, including *Coal City Review*, *New Letters*, *Mid-America Poetry Review*, *New Millennium Writings*, and *I-70 Review*. He is the author of two poetry collections, *Night Watch* (Mid-America Press), and the forthcoming *Broken Time*.

While he has enjoyed success publishing his poetry and has had praise bestowed upon his work as a poet, Eberhart's bread and butter lies in journalism. Born in 1960 in St. Joseph, Missouri, Eberhart earned a bachelor's degree in journalism from the University of Missouri, Columbia, in 1983, and an MA in English from the University of Missouri-Kansas City in 1998. He has worked for the *Kansas City Star* since 1987 and has been book review editor since 2000.

Eberhart has had a long-time love affair with literature, one he attributes to his family's blue-collar background. Books, he says, "were magical things written by people who weren't like me. I started reading for pleasure as soon as I could, so much that a teacher would write on my report card, regarding extracurricular activities at school, 'reads almost all his spare time.' "

Writing started out as something Eberhart did simply to earn a good grade. But around the time he was finishing high school and starting college he figured out that writing was what he did best. "I loved literature but felt journalism was a good way to make a living, and working for a paper, making deadlines, talking to people, sounded exciting."

His interest in poetry came along later as he got into his 20s and had more time to read on his own. Eberhart started writing poems when he was about 30, "or at least there are poems that survive from that period," he says. "I destroyed some earlier work, things written in my early 20s that thoroughly embarrassed me after a couple of years."

Here Eberhart talks about balancing the journalism and the creative, poetry's place in contemporary cultures, his advice to young poets, and more. Visit his Web site, www.johnm arkeberhart.com.

How do you balance your career as a journalist and your work on poetry?

Well, I'm afraid it's a lot more journalism than poetry, simply because there's a level at which I have to contribute at the paper. I'm half writer and half editor at *The Star*. In my first two or three years as Books Editor, I was producing more than 200 bylines a year. That quickly led to burnout. The other half of my job is producing the weekly books pages, and that involves editing, budgeting, choosing photos, etc. So I have to write at a reasonable level to make time for the editing side, but I'm still trying to produce at least 12 bylines a month, or about 150 a year.

I only *wish* I could write 150 poems a year. My output in 2007 was more like 50 or 60, I think. But a poem takes a great deal of time to produce. It's the thinking that takes the time. A poem must have great depth, the language must be spot-on, and so on. Not that journalism shouldn't be well crafted, but its main function is to transmit information. A poem's main function is to transport the reader or listener away from the real world to the imagined world.

Do you feel that your writing as a journalist and your "creative writing" are separate and come from "different sides" of your brain?

Separate? No. Different? Yes. Journalism, if it's good writing, does require creativity. In fact, these days I try much harder, when I'm writing a profile or an interview piece or a book review, to invest it with fresh language, rhythmic syntax, and strong ideas and imagery. Even a metaphor or simile now and then, if I can sneak one in! But poetry, because it must be imagined, does draw deeper from the creative well.

How do you find time to pursue two related but separate "careers"?

The short answer: Journalism by day, poetry by night—and weekends. The long answer: I have to pursue the verse on my own time, but I certainly don't regard that as a burden.

Which poets have been inspirational for you?

Emily Dickinson, Coleridge, Yeats, Stevie Smith, Philip Larkin. Living: Ted Kooser, Dorianne Laux, Al Young, Margaret Atwood, Richard Newman, Philip Miller, Philip Stephens. And I am very grateful to H.L. Hix for his friendship and the ongoing dialogue I've had with him about verse. We communicate pretty sporadically—he lives in Wyoming now—but he makes me think about things, especially the power of investing description with emotion, at which he is very good.

Please note that the people I've cited are the ones who've had some sort of influence on me; there are many others I love but whose work is so different from what I do. Ginsberg, Eliot, Blake—great poets, but I can't say they've inspired my own poems, simply because they live in realms so strange.

What directions do you think you will explore in poetry in the near future?

I'm trying to get more and more "outside" my own experience and draw more on research, observation, even eavesdropping, when it comes to dialogue, for example. I continue to write quite often in the first person, but these voices are not "me." Even with *Night Watch*, my first book, the speakers are not me; they are variations, created. But I do want to keep moving away from direct experience.

Please select one poem which you think best characterizes your work, and tell us how you came to write it.

In the poem "Killing Rabbits," a middle-aged man reflects on his life—he has been a hunter but no longer kills. In the poem, his dogs one morning find some baby rabbits and kill them before he can intervene. We then find out his father served in WWII, in Germany, and for awhile was forced to live off the game or face starvation. The poem concludes with the speaker recalling his father saying, "I know how it feels to be the rabbit."

In the first drafts I wrote, the speaker said this man who knew how it felt to be the rabbit was his uncle. That didn't work. It had to be a stronger connection, a father/son poem, so I changed it.

Killing Rabbits

I don't do that anymore, but I did
in my youth, when a shotgun blast
sounded like manhood to me.

As always, this morning, I brewed coffee.
The dogs mined the field behind the farmhouse.
The smaller dog found the hole in the ground,
worried his nose into it, pulled them into the light:
Four baby rabbits. He played with them
till they died, barked and stood over them.

My father hated rabbits—hated hunting them,
couldn't abide the smell. In Germany,
in World War II, he'd lived part of a bitter
December on rabbits, raw, their bones
poking through the skin after he'd
stripped off their fur with his bayonet.

I don't think of him much anymore.
But I remember something he used to say:
"I know how it feels to be the rabbit."

(from *Night Watch* [Mid-America Press, ©2005; reprinted with permission])

What place do you think poetry has in contemporary American culture?
Unfortunately, I think it is growing smaller. Whether this can be reversed, I don't know. As the NEA has demonstrated, reading itself is now at risk in this country, or at least reading for pleasure is. And poetry, I think, now seems very foreign to a solid majority of the American public. Even dedicated readers tell me, on occasion, that they don't read poetry.

Who do you see as the audience for poetry?
Other poets. I'm kidding, but not smiling much when I write that. A lot of people who read it also seem to have an interest in writing it. Basically, the true answer: Anyone who, somehow, has a deep interest in literature, to the point of some kind of participation, is more likely to read poetry.

How would you characterize the publishing opportunities for poets?
I think they're pretty good. But by that, I mean getting published in periodicals—journals, basically. Getting a book published by a legitimate press is much, much harder. And getting that first book out there is no guarantee of continued success. I know of poets who have seen eight, nine years pass since their first books and can't find a home for their second. They're good poets, too. The market does not support that many poetry books in a given year.

What advice would you give to a "young" poet?

Don't be in a hurry. That's good advice for all writers. As Ted Kooser says, no one is champing at the bit to get your verse in print, so take your time with it and make it good. Don't force poetry either—though it is good to write down your good ideas. Keep a "commonplace book." If you have four lines and know there are ten more out there somewhere, wait for those ten.

—Brian Daldorph

Brian Daldorph teaches at the University of Kansas, Lawrence. His three full-length poetry collections are *The Holocaust and Hiroshima: Poems* (Mid-America Press), *Outcasts* (Mid-America Press) and *Senegal Blues* (219 Press). Daldroph also has taught in Japan, England, Senegal, Zambia and at the Douglas County Jail (Kansas). He edits *Coal City Review*. Contact him at briandal@ku.edu.

Magazine Needs *Chest*, published monthly, "is the official medical journal of the American College of Chest Physicians, the world's largest medical journal for pulmonologists, sleep, and critical care specialists, with over 22,000 subscribers." Wants "poetry with themes of medical relevance." *Chest* is approximately 300 pages, magazine-sized, perfect-bound, with a glossy cover, and includes ads. Press run is 22,000. Number of unique visitors: 900,000 to Web site. Subscription: $192. Make checks payable to American College Chest Physicians.

How to Submit Submit up to 3 poems at a time, between 10 and 80 lines. Only accepts e-mail submissions (as attachment or in body of e-mail); no fax or disk submissions. Brief cover letter preferred. Reads submissions year round. Poems are circulated to an editorial board. Sometimes comments on rejected poems. Never publishes theme issues. Guidelines available in magazine and on Web site. Responds in 2 months; always sends prepublication galleys. Retains all rights.

$◎ CHILDREN'S DIGEST (Specialized: children ages 10-12)

Children's Better Health Institute, 1100 Waterway Blvd., Indianapolis IN 46202. Web site: www.cbh i.org. or www.childrensdigestmag.org.

Magazine Needs *Children's Digest*, published bimonthly for The Children's Better Health Network, is a magazine for ages 10-12. "Prepares kids for the teen years." Wants light-hearted poetry appropriate for the age group. Reviews submissions for possible use in all Children's Better Health Institute publications.

How to Submit Manuscripts must be typewritten with poet's contact information in upper right-hand corner of each poem's page. SASE required. Submit seasonal material at least 8 months in advance. Guidelines available for SASE or on Web site. Responds in about 3 months. Pays $25 minimum for poetry. Acquires all rights.

Advice "We receive too many poetry submissions that are about kids, not for kids. Or, the subject matter is one that adults think children would or should like. Reading our guidelines is not enough. Careful study of current issues will acquaint writers with each title's 'personality.'"

$◎ CHILDREN'S PLAYMATE (Specialized: children ages 6-8)

Children's Better Health Institute, 1100 Waterway Blvd., Indianapolis IN 46202. Web site: www.cbh i.org. or www.childrensplaymatemag.org.

Magazine Needs *Children's Playmate*, published bimonthly by The Children's Better Health Institute, is a magazine for ages 6-8. "Strives to make learning fun." Wants light-hearted poetry appropriate for the age group. Reviews submissions for possible use in all Children's Better Health Institute publications.

How to Submit Manuscripts must be typewritten with poet's contact information in upper right-hand corner of each poem's page. SASE required. Submit seasonal material at least 8 months in advance. Guidelines available for SASE or on Web site. Responds in about 3 months. Pays $25 minimum for poetry. Acquires all rights.

Advice "We receive too many poetry submissions that are about kids, not for kids. Or, the subject matter is one that adults think children would or should like. Reading our guidelines is not enough. Careful study of current issues will acquaint writers with each title's 'personality.' "

⬛ ◪ CHIRON REVIEW

522 E. South Ave., St. John KS 67576-2212. (620)786-4955. E-mail: ChironSubmissions@hotmail.c om. Web site: www.geocities.com/SoHo/Nook/1748/. Established 1982 as *The Kindred Spirit*. **Contact:** Geraled and Zachary Locklin, poetry editors.

Magazine Needs *Chiron Review*, published quarterly, is a tabloid using photographs of featured writers. No taboos. Has published poetry by Quentin Crisp, Felice Picano, Edward Field, Wanda Coleman, and Marge Piercy. Press run is about 1,000. Subscription: $16/year (4 issues).

How to Submit Submit up to 6 poems at a time. No longer accepts e-mail submissions. Guidelines available for SASE or on Web site. Responds in 2 months. Pays 1 contributor's copy, discount on additional copies. Acquires first-time rights. Reviews books of poetry in 500-700 words.

Additional Information Will also publish occasional chapbooks; see Web site for details.

⬛ $◪ ◉ THE CHRISTIAN CENTURY (Specialized: Christian; social issues)

104 S. Michigan Ave., Suite 700, Chicago IL 60603. (312)263-7510. Fax: (312)263-7540. Web site: www.ChristianCentury.org. Established 1884; named *The Christian Century* 1900, established again 1908, joined by *New Christian* 1970. **Contact:** Jill Peláez Baumgaertner, poetry editor.

Magazine Needs *The Christian Century*, an "ecumenical biweekly," is a liberal, sophisticated journal of news, articles of opinion, and reviews. Uses approximately 1 poem/issue, not necessarily on religious themes but in keeping with the literate tone of the magazine. Wants "poems that are not statements but experiences, that do not talk about the world but show it. We want to publish poems that are grounded in images and that reveal an awareness of the sounds of language and the forms of poetry even when the poems are written in free verse." Does not want "pietistic or sentimental doggerel." Has published poetry by Jeanne Murray Walker, Ida Fasel, Kathleen Norris, Luci Shaw, J. Barrie Shepherd, and Wendell Berry. The *Christian Century* is about 48 pages, magazine-sized, printed on quality newsprint, saddle-stapled, includes ads. Sample: $3.50.

How to Submit Lines/poem: 20 maximum. "Prefer shorter poems." No simultaneous submissions. Submissions without SASE (or SAE and IRCs) will not be returned. Submit poems typed, double-spaced, one poem/page. Include name, address, and phone number on each page. Pays usually $20/poem plus 1 contributor's copy and discount on additional copies. Acquires all rights. Inquire about reprint permission. Reviews books of poetry in 300-400 words, single-book format; 400-500 words, multi-book format.

◪ ◉ THE CHRISTIAN GUIDE (Specialized: Christian)

P.O. Box 14622, Knoxville TN 37914. Established 1989. **Contact:** J. Brian Long, poetry editor.

Magazine Needs *The Christian Guide*, published quarterly, features articles, announcements, advertisements, photographs, and poetry. Wants "positive, accessible poetry that concerns itself with the interaction between God and the nature of (and surrounding) mankind in micro- or macrocosm. All poems themed to the gentler tenets of the devotion reciprocated between Heaven and Earth are welcomed, but only the most well-crafted will be accepted." Does not want forced, trite rhyme. Has published poetry by Jill Alexander Essbaum, C.E. Chaffin, Teresa White, and Charles Semones. *The Christian Guide* is magazine-sized, with full-color cover with photographs and/or artwork, includes ads. Press run is 25,000.

How to Submit Submit 1-5 poems at a time. Lines/poem: 200 maximum. Considers previously published poems and simultaneous submissions. No e-mail or disk submissions. Cover letter is required. "Include brief bio, list of publishing credits, and a SASE." Reads submissions year round. Submit seasonal poems 6 months in advance. Seldom comments on rejected poems. Responds in 3 months. Pays 2 contributor's copies. Acquires one-time rights.

Advice "Subtlety. Subtlety. Subtlety. We are seeking poems that inspire awe, but do so by speaking to (and through) the reader with that 'small, still voice.' "

$☑ THE CHRISTIAN SCIENCE MONITOR

The Home Forum Page, One Norway St., Boston MA 02115. E-mail: homeforum@csmonitor.com. Web site: www.csmonitor.com. Established 1908. **Contact:** Judy Lowe, Home Forum editor.

Magazine Needs *The Christian Science Monitor*, an international daily newspaper, regularly features poetry in The Home Forum section. Wants "finely crafted poems that explore and celebrate daily life; that provide a respite from daily news and from the bleakness that appears in so much contemporary verse." Does not want "work that presents people in helpless or hopeless states; poetry about death, aging, or illness; or dark, violent, sensual poems. No poems that are overtly religious or falsely sweet." Considers free verse and fixed forms. Has published poetry by Diana Der-Hovanessian, Marilyn Krysl, and Michael Glaser. Publishes 1-4 poems/week.

How to Submit Submit up to 5 poems at a time. Lines/poem: "For us, 20 lines is a long poem." No previously published poems or simultaneous submissions. Accepts e-mail submissions only (by attachment in MS Word, 1 poem/e-mail). Pays $20/haiku; $40/poem.

☑ ◎ CHRISTIANITY AND LITERATURE (Specialized: Christian; spirituality/inspirational)

Humanities Division, Pepperdine University, 24255 Pacific Coast Highway, Malibu CA 90263. Web site: www.pepperdine.edu/sponsored/ccl/journal. **Contact:** Julia S. Kasdorf, poetry editor (Pennsylvania State University, English Dept., 114 Burrows Bldg, University Park, PA 16802).

Magazine Needs *Christianity and Literature*, a quarterly scholarly journal, publishes about 4-6 poems/issue. Press run is 1,100. Single copy: $10; subscription: $25/year, $45 for 2 years. Make checks payable to CCL.

How to Submit Submit 1-6 poems at a time. No previously published poems or simultaneous submissions. Accepts submissions by surface mail only. Cover letter is required. Submissions must be accompanied by SASE. Time between acceptance and publication is 6-12 months. "Poems are chosen by our poetry editor." Guidelines available on Web site. Responds within 4 months. Pays 2 contributor's copies "and a dozen offprints to poets whose work we publish." Rights revert to poets upon written request. Reviews collections of literary, Christian poetry occasionally in some issues (no chapbooks).

Advice "We look for poems that are clear and surprising. They should have a compelling sense of voice, formal sophistication (though not necessarily rhyme and meter), and the ability to reveal the spiritual through concrete images. We cannot return submissions that are not accompanied by SASE."

$☑ ◎ CHRYSALIS READER (Specialized: spirituality; themes)

1745 Gravel Hill Rd., Dillwyn VA 23936. Fax: (434)983-1074. E-mail: chrysalis@hovac.com. Web site: www.swedenborg.com/chrysalis. Established 1985. **Contact:** Robert F. Lawson, poetry editor. Editor: Carol S. Lawson.

Magazine Needs *Chrysalis Reader*, published annually in September by the Swedenborg Foundation, is a "contribution to the search for spiritual wisdom, a book series that challenges inquiring minds through the use of literate and scholarly fiction, essays, and poetry." Wants "poetry that surprises, that pushes the language, gets our attention." Does not want anything "overly religious or sophomoric." Has published work by Robert Bly, Linda Pastan, Wesley McNair, Wyn Cooper, William Kloefkorn, and Virgil Suárez. *Chrysalis Reader* is 208 pages, 7×10, professionally printed on archival paper, perfect-bound, with coated coverstock. Receives about 1,000 submissions/year, accepts about 16 poems. Press run is 3,500. Sample: $10. (Sample poems available on Web site.)

How to Submit Submit no more than 5-6 poems at a time. Considers simultaneous submissions "if notified immediately when work is accepted elsewhere"; no previously published poems. Include SASE. Reads submissions year round. Time between acceptance and publication is typically 18 months. Regularly publishes theme issues (the 2009 issue theme is "Lenses"). Themes and guidelines available with SASE or on Web site. Responds in 3 months. Always sends prepublication galleys. Pays $25 and 3 contributor's copies. Acquires first-time rights. "We expect to be credited for reprints after permission is given."

Contest/Award Offerings The Bailey Prize (see separate listing in Contests & Awards).

Advice ''Purchase a back issue or request your bookstore to order a reading copy so that you can better gauge what to submit.''

$☐ ◎ CICADA MAGAZINE (Specialized: teens, ages 14 and up)

Carus Publishing, 70 E. Lake St., Suite 300, Chicago IL 60601. Web site: www.cricketmag.com. Established 1998. **Contact:** Submissions Editor.

Magazine Needs *CICADA Magazine*, published semimonthly, is ''the groundbreaking teen literary magazine that raises the issues that today's young adults find most important; a high-quality literary magazine for ages 14 and up.'' Wants ''serious or humorous poetry; rhymed or free verse.'' Considers poetry by teens. *CICADA* is 128 pages, digest-sized, perfect-bound, with full-color cover. Receives more than 1,200 submissions/month, accept 25-30. Circulation is 17,000. Subscription: $35.97/year (6 issues). Sample: $8.50; sample pages available online.

How to Submit Submit no more than 5 poems at a time. Lines/poem: up to 25. Considers previously published poems. Show line count on each poem submitted. Include SASE. Guidelines available for SASE or on Web site. Responds in 6 months. Pays up to $3/line on publication. Acquires North American publication rights for previously published poems; rights vary for unpublished poems.

Also Offers ''The Slam,'' an online writing forum ''for young writers who want the world to see what they can do with words.''

Advice ''Our standards are very high, and we will accept only top-quality material. Please familiarize yourself with *CICADA* before submitting.''

◢ CIDER PRESS REVIEW

777 Braddock Lane, Halifax PA 17032. E-mail: editor@ciderpressreview.com. (inquiries only). Web site: http://ciderpressreview.com. Established 1999. **Contact:** Caron Andregg and Robert Wynne, co-editors.

Magazine Needs *Cider Press Review*, published annually, features ''the best new work from contemporary poets.'' Wants ''thoughtful, well-crafted poems with vivid language and strong images. We prefer poems that have something to say. We would like to see more well-written humor. We also encourage translations.'' Does not want ''didactic, inspirational, greeting card verse, empty word play, therapy, or religious doggerel.'' Has published poetry by Robert Arroyo, Jr., Virgil Suárez, Linda Pastan, Kathleen Flenniken, Tim Seibles, Joanne Lowery, Thomas Lux, and Mark Cox. *Cider Press Review* is 128 pages, digest-sized, offset-printed, perfect-bound, with 4-color coated card cover. Receives about 2,500 poems/year, accepts about 3%. Press run is 750. Single copy: $12; subscription: $20 for 2 issues (1 journal, 1 book from the *Cider Press Review* Book Award). Sample: $10 (journal).

How to Submit Submit up to 5 poems at a time. No previously published poems or simultaneous submissions. Submit by postal mail or through online submission form at Web site. ''International authors or special needs, please query via e-mail. Do not send unsolicited disk or e-mail submissions.'' Cover letter is preferred. Include short bio (50 words maximum). SASE required for reply. Reads submissions April 1-August 31 only. Time between acceptance and publication is 6-9 months. Poems are circulated to an editorial board. Guidelines available for SASE or on Web site. Responds in 1-4 months. Always sends prepublication galleys. Pays 1 contributor's copy. Acquires first North American serial rights.

Contest/Award Offerings The *Cider Press Review* Book Award (see separate listing in Contests & Awards).

$◢ THE CINCINNATI REVIEW

P.O. Box 210069, Cincinnati OH 45221-0069. (513)556-3954. E-mail: editors@cincinnatireview.com. Web site: www.cincinnatireview.com. Established 2003. **Contact:** Don Bogen, poetry editor.

Magazine Needs *The Cincinnati Review*, published semiannually, is devoted ''to publishing the best new poetry and literary fiction, as well as book reviews, essays, and interviews. Open to any schools, styles, forms—as long as the poem is well made and sophisticated in its language use and subject matter.'' *The Cincinnati Review* is 180-200 pages, digest-sized, perfect-bound, with matte paperback cover with full-color art, includes ads. Press run is 1,000. Single copy: $9 (current issue); subscription: $15. Sample: $7 (back issue).

How to Submit Submit up to 10 pages of poetry at a time. Considers simultaneous submissions with notification; no previously published poems. No e-mail or disk submissions. Cover letter is preferred. SASE required. Reads submissions September 1-May 31. Time between acceptance and publication is 6 months. "First-round reading by small, trained staff. Final decisions made by genre editors." Seldom comments on rejected poems. Guidelines available for SASE or on Web site. Responds in 6 weeks. Always sends prepublication galleys. Pays $30/page and 2 contributor's copies. Acquires first North American serial rights. Reviews books of poetry in 1,500 words, single-book format.

◖ ◎ CLARK STREET REVIEW (Specialized: narrative and prose poetry)

P.O. Box 1377, Berthoud CO 80513. E-mail: clarkreview@earthlink.net. Established 1998. **Contact:** Ray Foreman, editor.

Magazine Needs *Clark Street Review*, published 8 times/year, uses narrative poetry and short shorts. Tries "to give writers and poets cause to keep writing by publishing their best work." Wants "narrative poetry under 100 lines that reaches readers who are mostly published poets and writers. Subjects are open." Does not want "obscure or formalist work." Has published poetry by Charles Ries, Anselm Brocki, Ed Galling, Ellaraine Lockie, and J. Glenn Evans. *Clark Street Review* is 20 pages, digest-sized, photocopied, saddle-stapled, with paper cover. Receives about 1,000 poems/year, accepts about 10%. Press run is 200. Single copy: $2; subscription: $10 for 10 issues postpaid for writers only. Make checks payable to R. Foreman.

How to Submit Submit 1-5 poems at a time. Lines/poem: 20 minimum, 75 maximum. Considers previously published poems and simultaneous submissions. Send "disposable sharp copies. Maximum width—65 characters. Include SASE for reply. No cover letter." Time between acceptance and publication is 4 months. "Editor reads everything with a critical eye of 30 years of experience in writing and publishing small press work." Often comments on rejected poems. Guidelines available for SASE or by e-mail. Responds in 3 weeks. Acquires one-time rights.

Advice *"Clark Street Review* is geared to the more experienced poet and writer deeply involved in the writer's life. There are tips and quotes throughout each issue that writers appreciate. As always, the work we print speaks for the writer and the magazine. We encourage communication between our poets by listing their e-mail addresses. Publishing excellence and giving writers a reason to write is our only aim. Well-crafted, interesting, and accessible human narrative poems will see ink in *CSR.*"

◖ COAL CITY REVIEW

English Dept., University of Kansas, Lawrence KS 66045. E-mail: briandal@ku.edu. Established 1989. **Contact:** Brian Daldorph, editor.

Magazine Needs *Coal City Review*, published annually in the fall, prints poetry, short stories, reviews, and interviews—"the best material I can find. As Pound said, 'Make it new.' " Does not want "experimental poetry, doggerel, five-finger exercises, or beginner's verse." Has published poetry by Gary Lechliter, Phil Miller, Cheela Chilala, Maggie Sawkins, and Denise Low. *Coal City Review* is 100 pages, digest-sized, professionally printed on recycled paper, perfect-bound, with colored card cover. Accepts about 5% of material received. Press run is 200. Subscription: $10. Sample: $6.

How to Submit Submit 6 poems at a time. Considers previously published poems "occasionally"; no simultaneous submissions. No e-mail submissions. "Please do not send list of prior publications." Include name and address on each page. Seldom comments on rejected poems. Guidelines available for SASE. Responds in up to 3 months. Pays 1 contributor's copy. Reviews books of poetry in 300-1,000 words, mostly single-book format. Send materials for review consideration.

Additional Information *Coal City Review* also publishes occasional books and chapbooks as issues of the magazine, but **does not accept unsolicited book/chapbook submissions**. Most recent book is *Bird's Horn* by Kevin Rabas.

Advice "Care more (much more) about writing than publication. If you're good enough, you'll publish."

$⊚ COBBLESTONE MAGAZINE (Specialized: American history; children/teens ages 9-14)

Editorial Dept., Cobblestone Publishing, 30 Grove St., Suite C, Peterborough NH 03458. Web site: www.cricketmag.com. **Contact:** Meg Chorlian.

Magazine Needs *COBBLESTONE Magazine*, published 9 times/year, is a magazine of American history for children ages 9-14. "All material must relate to the theme of a specific upcoming issue in order to be considered." Wants "clear, objective imagery. Serious and light verse considered. Must relate to theme." Subscription: $29.95/year (9 issues). Sample: $5.95 plus $2.00 s&h (include 10×13 SASE); sample pages available on Web site.

How to Submit Query first. Lines/poem: up to 100. No e-mail submissions or queries. Include SASE. Reads submissions according to deadlines for queries (see Web site for schedule and details). Always publishes theme issue. Guidelines available on Web site. Pays varied rates. Acquires all rights.

Advice "Writers are encouraged to study recent back issues for content and style."

$⊘ COLORADO REVIEW

Center for Literary Publishing, Dept. of English, Colorado State University, Fort Collins CO 80523. (970)491-5449. E-mail: creview@colostate.edu. Web site: http://coloradoreview.colostate.edu. Established 1956 (as *Colorado Review*), 1966 (resurrected as *Colorado State Review*), 1985 (renamed *Colorado Review*). **Contact:** Donald Revell, Sasha Steensen, and Matthew Cooperman, poetry editors. General Editor; Stephanie G'Schwind.

• Poetry published in *Colorado Review* has been included in *The Best American Poetry* and *Pushcart Prize Anthology*.

Magazine Needs *Colorado Review*, published 3 times/year, prints short fiction, poetry, and personal essays. Has published poetry by Robert Creeley, Kazim Ali, Rusty Morrison, Lucie Brock-Broido, Cynthia Cruz, and Fanny Howe. *Colorado Review* is about 224 pages, digest-sized, professionally printed, notch-bound, with glossy card cover. Press run is 1,300. Receives about 10,000 submissions/year, accepts about 2%. Subscription: $24/year. Sample: $10.

How to Submit Submit no more than 5 poems at a time. Considers simultaneous submissions, "but you must notify *Colorado Review* immediately if accepted elsewhere"; no previously published poems. No e-mail submissions. SASE required for response. Reads submissions September 1-May 1 only. Responds in 2 months, "often sooner." Pays $5/printed page. Acquires first North American serial rights. Reviews books of poetry, fiction, and nonfiction. "Most book reviews are solicited, but feel free to query." Send materials for review consideration.

Contest/Award Offerings Colorado Prize for Poetry (see separate listing in Contests & Awards).

⊘ COLUMBIA: A JOURNAL OF LITERATURE AND ART

(212)854-4216. Fax: (212)854-7704. E-mail: info@columbiajournal.org. Web site: www.columbiajo urnal.org. Established 1977. **Contact:** Dawn Marie Knopf, editor.

Magazine Needs *Columbia: A Journal of Literature and Art*, published annually, will consider "any poem that is eclectic and spans from traditional to experimental genres." Has published poetry by Louise Gluck, James Tate, Eamon Grennan, Mary Jo Salter, and Yuse Komunyakaa. *Columbia* is 176 pages, digest-sized, offset-printed, notch-bound, with glossy cover, includes ads. Receives about 2,000 poems/year, accepts about 2%. Press run is 2,000. Subscription: $10/year, $15 for 2 years. Sample: $8; back issue: $5.

How to Submit Submit up to 5 poems at a time. Considers simultaneous submissions when noted; no previously published poems. Accepts submissions through Web site only. Cover letter is preferred. Reads submissions year round. Poems are circulated to an editorial board. Seldom comments on rejected poems. Guidelines available in magazine or on Web site. Responds in 3-4 months. Pays 2 contributor's copies. Acquires first North American serial rights.

Contest/Award Offerings Sponsors annual contest with an award of $500. Submit no more than 5 poems/entry. **Entry fee:** $10. **Deadline:** see Web site or recent journal issue. All entrants receive a copy of the issue publishing the winners.

☑ COMMON GROUND REVIEW

40 Prospect St. Unit C1, Westfield, MA 01085. Web site: www.cgreview.org. Established 1999. **Contact:** Larry O'Brien, editor.

• *Common Ground Review* is affiliated with Western New England College.

Magazine Needs *Common Ground Review*, published semiannually, prints poetry and original artwork by the art editor Alice Ahrens Williams. Wants poetry with strong imagery; well-written free or traditional forms. Does not want greeting card verse, overly sentimental or political poetry. Has published poetry by James Doyle, Martin Galvin, Lyn Lifshin, Virgil Suárez, and Rennie McQuilken. *Common Ground Review* is 60 pages, digest-sized, perfect-bound, with 4-color cover. Receives about 1,000 poems/year, accepts less than 10%. Press run is 125-150. Single copy: $12.50 (includes S&H). Orders: Make checks payable to *Common Ground Review* and send to 43 Winton Rd., East Windsor CT 06088.

How to Submit Submit 1-5 poems at a time. Lines/poem: 60 maximum. No previously published poems or simultaneous submissions. No disk or e-mail submissions. Cover letter is required, as is biography. "Poems should be single-spaced; include name, address, phone number, e-mail address, brief biography, and SASE (submissions without SASE will not be notified)." Reads submissions year round, but deadline for non-contest submissions is August 31. Submit seasonal poems 6 months in advance. Time between acceptance and publication is 4-6 months. "Editor reads and culls submissions. Final decisions made by editorial board." Seldom comments on rejected poems. Guidelines available in magazine or on Web site. Responds in 2 months. Pays 1 contributor's copy. Acquires one-time rights.

Contest/Award Offerings Sponsors an annual poetry contest. Offers 1st Prize: $150; 2nd Prize: $75; 3rd Prize: $50; Honorable Mentions. **Entry fee:** $10 for 1-3 unpublished poems. **Deadline:** February 28 for contest submissions only. All contest submissions are considered for publication in *Common Ground Review*.

Advice "Read journal before submitting. Beginning poets need to read what's out there, get into workshops, and work on revising. Attend writers' conferences. Listen and learn."

☐ ◎ COMMON THREADS (Specialized: submissions by members only)

3520 State Route 56, Mechanicsburg OH 43044. (937)834-2666. Web site: www.ohiopoetryassn.com. Established 1928. **Contact:** Amy Jo Zook, editor.

Magazine Needs *Common Threads*, published semiannually in April and October, is the Ohio Poetry Association's member poetry magazine. **Only members of OPA may submit poems.** "We use beginners' poetry, but would like it to be good, tight, revised. In short, not first drafts. We'd like poems to make us think as well as feel something. I really treasure short poems for spacing's sake." Does not want to see poetry that is highly sentimental, overly morbid, religiously coercive, or pornograpic. Considers poetry by teens "if members or high school contest winners." Has published poetry by Bill Reyer, Michael Bugeja, Timothy Russell, Yvonne Hardenbrook, and Dalene Stull. *Common Threads* is 52 pages, digest-sized, computer-typeset, with matte card cover. "*Common Threads* is a forum for our members, and we do use reprints so new members can get a look at what is going well in more general magazines." Subscription: annual OPA dues, including 2 issues of *Common Threads* are $18; $15 for seniors (over age 65). Single copy: $2; $8 for students (through college).

How to Submit Lines/poem: "nothing over 40 (unless exceptional)." Considers previously published poems, if "author is upfront about them." Accepts submissions by postal mail only. Reads submissions year round. Frequently publishes seasonal poems. Guidelines available for SASE. All rights revert to poet after publication.

Advice "Read a lot to see what is being done by good poets nationally. Write what you know and love. Revise!!"

☑ THE COMSTOCK REVIEW

4956 St. John Dr., Syracuse NY 13215. (315)488-8077. E-mail: poetry@comstockreview.org. (inquiries only). Web site: www.comstockreview.org. Established 1987 (as *Poetpourri*). **Contact:** John M. Bellinger, managing editor.

Magazine Needs *The Comstock Review*, published semiannually (Volume I in summer, Volume II in winter) by the Comstock Writers' Group, Inc., seeks "well-written free and traditional verse." Wants "metaphor and fresh, vivid imagery." Does not want "obscene, obscure, patently religious, or greeting card verse. Few haiku." Has published poetry by Melanie Almeder, Robert Cooperman, Barbara Crooker, Elton Glaser, Richard Jones, and Enid Shomer. *The Comstock Review* is about 100 pages, digest-sized, professionally printed, perfect-bound. Press run is 600. Single copy: $9; subscription: $16/year, $28/2 years. Sample: through year 2004, $6 each.

How to Submit Submit 3-6 poems at a time. Lines/poem:up to 40. No previously published poems or simultaneous submissions. No e-mail submissions; postal submissions only. Cover letter is preferred. Include short bio. Put name, address, and phone number or e-mail address on each page. Reads submissions January 1-March 15 only (at present; check Web site). Acceptances mailed out 6-8 weeks after close of reading period. "Rejections may receive editorial commentary and may take slightly longer." Guidelines available in magazine, for SASE, or on Web site. Pays 1 contributor's copy. Acquires first North American serial rights.

Contest/Award Offerings The annual Muriel Craft Bailey Memorial Award and the Jesse Bryce Niles Memorial Chapbook Award (see separate listings in Contests & Awards).

☑ CONCHO RIVER REVIEW

P.O. Box 10894, Angelo State University, San Angelo TX 76909. (915)942-2273. Fax: (915)942-2155. E-mail: jerry.bradley@lamar.edu. Web site: www.angelo.edu/dept/english/publications/concho_river_review.htm. Established 1984. **Contact:** Jerry Bradley, poetry editor. Editor: Mary Ellen Hartje.

Magazine Needs *Concho River Review*, published twice/year, is a literary journal "particularly looking for poems with distinctive imagery and imaginative forms and rhythms. The first test of a poem will be its imagery. We prefer shorter poems; few long poems accepted." Has published poetry by Walt McDonald, Robert Cooperman, Mary Winters, William Wenthe, and William Jolliff. *Concho River Review* is 120-138 pages, digest-sized, professionally printed, flat-spined, with matte card cover. Receives 1,000 poems/year, accepts 60. Press run is 300 (200 subscribers, 10 libraries). Subscription: $14. Sample: $5.

How to Submit Submit 3-5 poems at a time. No simultaneous submissions. Accepts e-mail submissions (as attachment in Word). "No reply without SASE or e-mail address. No handwritten manuscripts accepted." Responds in 2-3 months. Pays 1 contributor's copy. Acquires first rights.

Advice "We're always looking for good, strong work—from well-known poets and those who have never been published before."

$☑ CONFRONTATION MAGAZINE

English Dept., C.W. Post Campus, Long Island University, 720 Northern Blvd., Brookville NY 11548-1300. (516)299-2720. Fax: (516)299-2735. E-mail: martin.tucker@liu.edu. (inquiries only). Web site: www.liu.edu/confrontation. Established 1968. **Contact:** Isaac Cates, poetry editor. Editor-in-Chief: Martin Tucker.

Magazine Needs *Confrontation Magazine*, published semiannually, is interested "in all forms. Our only criterion is high literary merit. We think of our audience as an educated, lay group of intelligent readers. We prefer lyric poems." Does not want "sentimental verse." Considers poetry by children and teens. Has published poetry by David Ray, T. Alan Broughton, David Ignatow, Philip Appleman, Jane Mayhall, and Joseph Brodsky. *Confrontation* is about 300 pages, digest-sized, professionally printed, flat-spined. Receives about l,200 submissions/year, accepts about 150. Circulation is 2,000. Subscription: $10/year. Sample: $3.

How to Submit Submit no more than 10 pages of poetry at a time. Lines/poem: "length generally should be kept to 2 pages." No previously published poems. "Prefer single submissions. Clear copy." No e-mail submissions; postal submissions only. Reads submissions September-May. "Do not submit mss June through August." Publishes theme issues. Upcoming themes available for SASE. Guidelines available on Web site. Responds in 2 months. Sometimes sends prepublication galleys. Pays $5-50 and 1 contributor's copy with discount available on additional copies. Staff reviews books of poetry. Send materials for review consideration.

Additional Information Occasionally publishes "book" issues or "anthologies." Most recent "occasional" book is *Life as a novice* by Jeffrey Kane, a poetic sequence on the transcendence of guilt.
Advice "We want serious poetry, which may be humorous and light-hearted on the surface."

$🖉 THE CONNECTICUT POETRY REVIEW

P.O. Box 392, Stonington CT 06378. Established 1981. **Contact:** J. Claire White and Harley More, poetry editors.
Magazine Needs *The Connecticut Poetry Review*, published annually, looks for "poetry of quality that is both genuine and original in content. No specifications except length: 10-40 lines." Has published poetry by John Updike, Robert Peters, Diane Wakoski, and Marge Piercy. *The Connecticut Poetry Review* is 45-60 pages, digest-sized, flat-spined, "printed letterpress by hand on a Hacker Hand Press from Monotype Bembo." Receives more than 2,500 submissions/year, accepts about 20. Press run is 400. Sample: $5.
How to Submit Lines/poem: 10 minimum, 40 maximum. Reads submissions April-June and September-December only. Responds in 3 months. Pays $5/poem plus 1 contributor's copy.
Advice "Study traditional and modern styles. Study poets of the past. Attend poetry readings and write. Practice on your own."

🖉 CONNECTICUT REVIEW

Southern Connecticut State University, 501 Crescent St., New Haven CT 06515. (203)392-6737. Fax: (203)392-5748. E-mail: ctreview@southernct.edu. (inquiries only). Established 1968. **Contact:** Vivian Shipley, editor.
   • Poetry published in *Connecticut Review* has been included in *The Best American Poetry* and *The Pushcart Prize* anthologies; has received special recognition for Literary Excellence from Public Radio's series *The Poet and the Poem*; and has won the Phoenix Award for Significant Editorial Achievement from the Council of Editors of Learned Journals (CELJ).
Magazine Needs *Connecticut Review*, published semiannually, contains essays, poetry, articles, fiction, b&w photographs, and color artwork. Has published poetry by Jack Bedell, Colette Inez, Maxine Kumin, Tony Fusco, Dana Gioia, and Marilyn Nelson. *Connecticut Review* is 208 pages, digest-sized, offset-printed, perfect-bound, with glossy 4-color cover. Receives about 2,500 poems/year, accepts about 5%. Press run is 3,000; 1,000 distributed free to Connecticut State libraries and high schools. Sample: $8. Make checks payable to Connecticut State University.
How to Submit Submit 3-5 typed poems at a time. Accepts submissions by postal mail only. Name, address, and phone number in the upper left corner of each page. Include SASE for reply only. Guidelines available for SASE. Pays 2 contributor's copies. Acquires first or one-time rights.

🖉 CONNECTICUT RIVER REVIEW

53 Pearl Street, New Haven, CT 06511. Web site: http://ct-poetry-society.org/publications.htm. Established 1978. **Contact:** Tony Fusco, editor.
Magazine Needs *Connecticut River Review*, published annually in July or August by the Connecticut Poetry Society, prints "original, honest, diverse, vital, well-crafted poetry." Wants "any form, any subject. Translations and long poems welcome." Has published poetry by Marilyn Nelson, Jack Bedell, Maria Mazziotti Gillan, and Vivian Shipley. *Connecticut River Review* is digest-sized, attractively printed, perfect-bound. Receives about 2,000 submissions/year, accepts about 100. Press run is about 300. Membership: $25 per year; includes *Connecticut River Review* and *Long River Run*, a members-only magazine.
How to Submit Submit no more than 3-5 poems at a time. Considers simultaneous submissions if notified of acceptance elsewhere; no previously published poems. Cover letter is preferred. Include bio. "Complete contact information typed in upper right corner; SASE required." Reads submissions October 1-April 15. Guidelines available for SASE or on Web site. Responds in up to 8 weeks. Pays 1 contributor's copy. "Poet retains copyright."
Advice "Read as much good poetry as you can before you write."

N ▣ ◿ CONTE, AN ONLINE JOURNAL OF NARRATIVE WRITING

E-mail: poetry@conteonline.net. Web site: http://www.conteonline.net. Established 2005. **Contact:** Adam Tavel, poetry editor.

Magazine Needs *Conte, an Online Journal of Narrative Writing*, published semiannually online, prints "narrative writing of the highest quality. Writing that displays some degree of familiarity with our journal is likely to attract our attention, so make sure your work has a narrative bent." Has published poetry by Laura McCullough, R.T. Castleberry, Ann Iverson, Paul Hostovsky, Robin Greene, and Lyn Lifshin. Receives about 1,500 poems/year, accepts about 24. Number of unique visitors: approximately 1,000/month.

How to Submit Submit up to 3 poems at a time. "Query before sending poems over 100 lines in length." Considers simultaneous submissions ("please state clearly in your cover letter that your work is under consideration elsewhere and notify us immediately if it is accepted by another publication"); does not accept previously published poems (considers poetry posted on a public Web site/blog/forum and poetry posted on a private, password-protected forum as published). Accepts e-mail submissions (pasted into body of message); no fax or disk submissions. Cover letter is preferred. "Here at *Conte*, it is obvious when a writer is unfamiliar with our narrative mission, because he/she will rave about our 'avant-garde style' or 'embrace of the experimental.' Be aware of your own aesthetic leanings and send work to publications that are a snug fit. Cover letters are optional for some magazines, but we like to know a little about our submitters. The type of things you should probably include are: 1) how you learned about our journal; 2) a few places you have been published previously, if at all; and 3) whether or not you are sending a simultaneous submission." Reads submissions year round. Time between acceptance and publication is typically 2-4 months. "Since *Conte* is a small journal, it is truly a labor of love for our 2 editors. While we occasionally share work with one another during the screening process, primarily we rely on our respective expertise in poetry and prose when making editorial selections. Ultimately, a good poem is fresh and engaging from its very first line, so the chief responsibility for any poetry editor is to sift through cliché and mediocrity to share the best submitted work with the world." Sometimes comments on rejected poems. Sometimes publishes theme issues. Upcoming themes and guidelines available on Web site. Responds in 3 months. Sometimes sends prepublication galleys. Acquires one-time rights. Rights revert to poets upon publication.

$ ☑ ◎ CONTEMPORARY HAIBUN (Specialized: haibun, haiga)

P.O. Box 2461, Winchester VA 22604-1661. (540)722-2156. E-mail: jim.kacian@redmoonpress.com (inquires only). Web site: www.redmoonpress.com. Established 1999 (as *American Haibun & Haiga*). **Contact:** Jim Kacian, editor/publisher.

Magazine Needs *contemporary haibun*, published annually in April, is the first Western journal dedicated to haibun and haiga. Considers poetry by children and teens. Has published poetry by Steven Addiss, Kuniharu Shimizu, Marjorie Buettner, and Ray Rasmussen. *contemporary haibun* is 128 pages, digest-sized, offset-printed on quality paper, with 4-color heavy-stock cover. Receives several hundred submissions/year, accepts about 5%. Print run is 1,000. Subscription: $16.95 plus $4 p&h. Sample available for SASE or by e-mail.

How to Submit Submit up to 3 haibun or haiga at a time. Considers previously published poems. Accepts submissions online at www.poetrylives.com/cho/ as well as disk and postal submissions. Include SASE for postal submissions. Time between acceptance and publication varies according to time of submission. Poems are circulated to an editorial board. "Only haibun and haiga will be considered. If you are unfamiliar with the form, consult *Journey to the Interior*, edited by Bruce Ross, *contemporary haibun online* (at www.redmoonpress.com), or previous issues of *contemporary haibun*, for samples and some discussion." Guidelines available in magazine, for SASE, by e-mail, or on Web site. Pays $1/page. Acquires first North American serial rights.

Also Offers Publishes *The Red Moon Anthology*, "an annual volume of the finest English-language haiku and related work published anywhere in the world." (See separate listing in this section.)

Advice "It is best if you familiarize yourself with what is happening in the genre (and its close relatives) today before submitting. We strive to give all the work we publish plenty of space in which to resonate, and to provide a forum where the best of today's practitioners can be published with dignity and prestige."

◖ COTTONWOOD (Specialized: Midwest emphasis)

Cottonwood Magazine and Press, 1301 Jayhawk Blvd., Room 400, Kansas Union, University of Kansas, Lawrence KS 66045. (7850)864-3777. E-mail: pwedge@ku.edu. Established 1965. **Contact:** Philip Wedge, poetry editor.

Magazine Needs *Cottonwood*, published semiannually, emphasizes the Midwest "but publishes the best poetry received regardless of region." Wants poems "on daily experience, perception; strong narrative or sensory impact, non-derivative." Does not want " 'literary,' not 'academic.' " Has published poetry by Rita Dove, Virgil Suárez, Walt McDonald, and Luci Tapahonso. *Cottonwood* is 112 pages, digest-sized, printed from computer offset, flat-spined. Receives about 3,000 submissions/year, accepts about 20. Press run is 500-600. Single copy: $8.00. Sample: $5.

How to Submit Submit up to 5 pages of poetry at a time with SASE. Lines/poem: 60 maximum. No simultaneous or e-mailed submissions. Sometimes comments on rejected poems. Responds in up to 5 months. Pays 1 contributor's copy.

Additional Information Cottonwood Press "is auxiliary to *Cottonwood Magazine* and publishes material by authors in the region. **Material is usually solicited.**" Has published *Violence and Grace* by Michael L. Johnson and *Midwestern Buildings* by Victor Contoski.

Advice "Read the little magazines and send to ones you like."

✗ ◖ CRAB CREEK REVIEW

7315 34th Ave NW, Seattle WA 98117. E-mail: editors@crabcreekreview.org. Web site: www.crabc reekreview.org. Established 1983. **Contact:** Editors.

Magazine Needs *Crab Creek Review*, published biannually. "Send us poetry and fiction that takes us somewhere unexpected, keeps us engaged, and stays with us beyond the initial reading. We appreciate lyrical and narrative forms of poetry, with a slight bias toward free verse. Translations are welcome—please submit with a copy of the poem in its original language, if possible." Has published poetry by Oliver de la Paz, Dorianne Laux, Greg Nicholl, and translations by Ilya Kaminsky and Matthew Zapruder. Fiction by Karen Heuler and Daniel Homan. *Crab Creek Review* is an 80- to 120-page, perfect-bound paperback. Subscription: $15/year. Sample: $6.

How to Submit "Please refer to our Web site as our contest/open submission periods have changed significantly." No e-mail submissions. Cover letter is preferred. Include SASE; "without one we will not consider your work." Responds in up to 6 months. Pays 2 contributor's copies.

$◖ CRAB ORCHARD REVIEW

Dept. of English, Mail Code 4503, Faner Hall 2380, Southern Illinois University Carbondale, 1000 Faner Dr., Carbondale IL 62901. Web site: www.siu.edu/~crborchd. Established 1995. **Contact:** Allison Joseph, editor and poetry editor.

- *Crab Orchard Review* received a 2007 Literary Award and a 2007 Operating Grant from the Illinois Arts Council; poetry published in *Crab Orchard Review* has appeared in *The Best American Poetry* and *Beacon's Best of 1999* and *2000*.

Magazine Needs *Crab Orchard Review*, published semiannually in February and August, prints poetry, fiction, creative nonfiction, interviews, book reviews, and novel excerpts. Wants all styles and forms from traditional to experimental. Does not want greeting card verse; literary poetry only. Has published poetry by Luisa A. Igloria, Erinn Batykefer, Jim Daniels, Bryan Tso Jones. *Crab Orchard Review* is 280-300 pages, digest-sized, professionally printed, perfect-bound, with (usually) glossy card cover with color photos. Receives about 12,000 poems/year, accepts about 1%. Press run is 2,500; 100 exchanged with other journals; remainder in shelf sales. Subscription: $20. Sample: $12.

How to Submit Submit up to 5 poems at a time. Considers simultaneous submissions with notification; no previously published poems. Postal submissions only. Cover letter is preferred. "Indicate stanza breaks on poems of more than 1 page." Reads submissions April-November for Summer/Fall special theme issue, February-April for regular, non-thematic Winter/Spring issue. Time between acceptance and publication is 6 months to a year. "Poems that are under serious consideration are discussed and decided on by the managing editor and poetry editor." Seldom comments on rejected poems. Publishes theme issues. Upcoming themes available in magazine, for SASE, or on Web site.

Magazines/Journals

Guidelines available for SASE or on Web site. Responds in up to 9 months. Pays $20/page ($50 minimum), 2 contributor's copies, and 1 year's subscription. Acquires first North American serial rights. Staff reviews books of poetry in 500-700 words, single-book format. Send materials for review consideration to Jon C. Tribble, Managing Editor.

Contest/Award Offerings The Crab Orchard Series in Poetry Open Competition Awards, The Crab Orchard Series in Poetry First Book Award, and The Richard Peterson Poetry Prize (see separate listings in Contests & Awards).

Advice "Do not send any submissions via e-mail! Include SASE (#10 or larger) with all submissions and all queries—no postcards or small envelopes. Before you send work, check the Web site to see what issue we are currently reading submissions for. Being familiar with our reading schedule will help you submit appropriate work at the right time."

$⊘ CRAZYHORSE

Dept. of English, College of Charleston, 66 George St., Charleston SC 29424. (843)953-7740. E-mail: crazyhorse@cofc.edu. Web site: http://crazyhorse.cofc.edu. Established 1960. **Contact:** Garrett Doherty and Carol Ann Davis, poetry editors.

● Poetry published in *Crazyhorse* has appeared in *The Best American Poetry* and *The Pushcart Prize*.

Magazine Needs *Crazyhorse*, published semiannually, prints fine fiction, poetry, and essays. "Send your best words our way. We like to print a mix of writing regardless of its form, genre, school, or politics. We're especially on the lookout for writing that doesn't fit the categories. Before sending, ask 'What's reckoned with that's important for other people to read?'" Has published poetry by David Wojahn, Mary Ruefle, Nance Van Winkle, Dean Young, Marvin Bell, and A.V. Christie. *Crazyhorse* is 160 pages, $8^{3}/_{4} \times 8^{1}/_{2}$, perfect-bound, with 4-color glossy cover. Receives about 15,000 poems/year. Circulation is 2,000. Single copy: $9; subscription: $16/year, $27 for 2 years, $36 for 3 years. Sample: $6. Make checks payable to *Crazyhorse*.

How to Submit Submit 3-5 poems at a time. Considers simultaneous submissions; no previously published poems. No fax, e-mail, or disk submissions. Cover letter is preferred. Reads submissions year round. "We read slower in summer." Time between acceptance and publication is 6 months. Seldom comments on rejected poems. Guidelines available in magazine, for SASE, by e-mail, or on Web site. Responds in 3 months. Sometimes sends prepublication galleys. Pays $20/page, 2 contributor's copies, and one-year subscription (2 issues). Acquires first North American serial rights.

Contest/Award Offerings The annual Lynda Hull Memorial Poetry Prize (see separate listing in Contests & Awards).

Advice "Feel strongly; then write."

⊘ THE CREAM CITY REVIEW

Dept. of English, University of Wisconsin—Milwaukee, P.O. Box 413, Milwaukee WI 53201. (414)229-4708. E-mail: info@creamcityreview.org(inquiries only). Web site: www.creamcityreview.org. **Contact:** Ellen Elder and Dawn Tefft, poetry editors.

● Poetry published in *The Cream City Review* has been included in *The Best American Poetry*.

Magazine Needs *The Cream City Review*, published twice/year, seeks "all forms of writing, from traditional to experimental. We strive to produce issues that are challenging, diverse, and of lasting quality." Does not want "sexist, homophobic, racist, or formulaic writings." Has published poetry by Elizabeth Bradfield, Annie Finch, Timothy Liu, Thylias Moss, Lee Ann Roripaugh, and Larissa Szporluk. *The Cream City Review* is about 200 pages, digest-sized, perfect-bound, with full-color cover on 70 lb. paper. Press run is 1,000. Single copy: $12; subscription: $22/year, $41 for 2 years ($35/year for institutions). Sample: $7.

How to Submit Submit no more than 5 poems at a time. Considers simultaneous submissions when notified. No e-mail submissions; postal submissions only. Include SASE. Cover letter is preferred. "Please include a few lines about your publication history and other information you think of interest." Reads submissions August 1-April 1 only. Sometimes comments on rejected poems. Publishes theme issues; "inquire regularly." Guidelines available for SASE or on Web site. Responds in 6-8 months. Payment includes one-year subscription. Acquires first rights. Reviews books of poetry in 1-2 pages. Send materials for review consideration to the book review editor.

Contest/Award Offerings Sponsors an annual poetry contest, The Beau Boudreaux Prize. Awards $1000 plus publication. **Entry fee:** $15 for 3-5 poems. All entries are considered for publication. Guidelines available on Web site.

CREATIVE CONNECTIONS (Specialized: psychology, sociology, philosophy, spirituality)

(formerly *Mr. Marquis' Museletter*), Kwil Kids Publishing, Box 98037, 135 Davie St., Vancouver BC V6Z 2Y0 Canada. E-mail: Creative-Connections@hotmail.com. Web site: http://creative-connections.spaces.live.com Established 1996. **Contact:** Kalen Marquis, editor.

Magazine Needs *Creative Connections*, published quarterly, is a newsletter that prints "essays, articles, short stories, poems, book reviews, dialogues, letters, sidebar lists, and black and white ink sketches." Wants "woven words of wisdom, wonder, and wellness. We promote 'creativity' and 'connection' as well as human growth and development through joy, compassion, and cheerleading—not criticism." Interested in psychology, sociology, philosophy, and spirituality "in the broadest sense" as well as "long-standing universal human themes." *Creative Connections* is 10 pages. Receives about 400 submissions/year, accepts about 80%. Press run is 200. Subscription: $20 CAD (4 issues). Make checks payable to Kalen Marquis.

How to Submit Submit 5 poems at a time. Accepts e-mail submissions (pasted into body of message; no attachments). Cover letter is preferred. Include SASE (or SAE with IRC for those submitting outside of Canada). Reads submissions year round. Time between acceptance and publication is up to 3 months. Always comments on rejected poems. "Kwil always provides encouragement and personalized response with SASE (or SAE and IRC)." Guidelines available for SASE (Canadian-stamped envelope, or IRC, or $1 USD for Canadian postage) or by e-mail. Responds in April, August, and December. Pays 1 contributor's copy. Acquires one-time rights.

Advice "Submit best and submit often; provide Canadian-stamped envelope; sign permission card; have fun writing."

CREOSOTE

Dept. of English, Eastern Arizona College, Thatcher AZ 85552.Established 2000. **Contact:** Ken Raines, editor.

Magazine Needs *Creosote*, published annually, prints poetry, fiction, and literary nonfiction. Wants "more traditional forms, but interested in any and all quality poems. Biased against confessional and beat-influenced poetry, but will consider anything." Considers poetry by children and teens. "No age restrictions." Has published poetry by William Wilborn, Ruth Moose, Barry Ballard, Ryan G. Van Cleave, Michael Trammell, and others. *Creosote* is 48 pages, digest-sized, offset printed, saddle-stapled, with card cover stock including color photography and artwork. Receives about 500 poems; accepts 25-30. Press run is 500; 400 distributed free. Single copy: $5; subscription: $5. Make checks payable to Eastern Arizona College.

How to Submit Submit up to 5 poems at a time. Considers simultaneous submissions. Cover letter is preferred. Reads submissions year round. Time between acceptance and publication is 2-3 months. Poems are circulated to an editorial board. Sometimes comments on rejected poems. Guidelines available in magazine, for SASE, or by e-mail. Responds in 3-6 months. Sometimes sends prepublication galleys. Pays 3-6 contributor's copies. Acquires one-time rights.

$ CRICKET MAGAZINE (Specialized: for young reades ages 9-14)

Carus Publishing, 70 E. Lake St., Suite 300, Chicago IL 60601. Web site: www.cricketmag.com. Established 1973. **Contact:** Submissions Editor.

Magazine Needs *CRICKET Magazine*, published monthly, is a literary magazine for young readers ages 9-14. Wants "serious and humorous poetry, nonsense rhymes." Does not want "forced or trite rhyming or imagery that doesn't hang together to create a unified whole." *CRICKET* is 64 pages, 8×10, saddle-stapled, with color cover. Circulation is 73,000. Subscription: $35.97/year (12 issues). Sample: $5; sample pages available on Web site.

How to Submit Submit no more than 5 poems at a time. Lines/poem: 50 (2 pages) maximum. Considers previously published poems. Put line count on each poem submitted. Include SASE. Guidelines available for SASE or on Web site. Responds in 6 months. Payment is up to $3/line on publication. Acquires North American publication rights for previously published poems; rights vary for unpublished poems.

Contest/Award Offerings Sponsors poetry contests for readers.

Advice "Our standards are very high, and we will accept only top-quality material. Before attempting to write for *CRICKET*, be sure to familiarize yourself with this age child and with the magazine itself."

☑ CRUCIBLE

Barton College, College Station, Wilson NC 27893. (252)399-6344. E-mail: tgrimes@barton.edu. Established 1964. **Contact:** Terrence L. Grimes, editor.

Magazine Needs *Crucible*, published annually in November, uses "poetry that demonstrates originality and integrity of craftsmanship as well as thought. Traditional metrical and rhyming poems are difficult to bring off in modern poetry. The best poetry is written out of deeply felt experience which has been crafted into pleasing form." Wants "free verse with attention paid particularly to image, line, stanza, and voice." Does not want "very long narratives, poetry that is forced." Has published poetry by Robert Grey, R.T. Smith, and Anthony S. Abbott. *Crucible* is 100 pages, digest-sized, professionally printed on high-quality paper, with matte card cover. Press run is 500. Sample: $7.

How to Submit Submit 5 poems at a time. No previously published poems or simultaneous submissions. "We require 3 unsigned copies of the manuscript and a short biography including a list of publications, in case we decide to publish the work." Reads submissions between Christmas and mid-April only. Responds in up to 4 months. Pays in contributor's copies.

Contest/Award Offerings The Sam Ragan Prize ($150), in honor of the former Poet Laureate of North Carolina, and other contests (prizes of $150 and $100). Guidelines available for SASE.

⊕ ☑ CURRENT ACCOUNTS

16-18 Mill Lane, Horwich, Bolton BL6 6AT England. Phone/fax: (44)(120 4)669858. E-mail: bswscribe@aol.com. Web site: http://hometown.aol.co.uk/bswscribe/myhomepage/newsletter.html. Established 1994. **Contact:** Rod Riesco, editor.

Magazine Needs *Current Accounts*, published semiannually, prints poetry, fiction, and nonfiction by members of Bank Street Writers, and other contributors. Open to all types of poetry. "No requirements, although some space is reserved for members." Considers poetry by children and teens. Has published poetry by Pat Winslow, M.R. Peacocke, and Gerald England. *Current Accounts* is 52 pages, A5, photocopied, saddle-stapled, with card cover with b&w or color photo or artwork. Receives about 300 poems/year, accepts about 5%. Press run is 80; 8 distributed free to competition winners. Subscription: £6. Sample: £3. Make checks payable to Bank Street Writers (sterling checks only).

How to Submit Submit up to 6 poems at a time. Lines/poem: 100 maximum. No previously published poems (unpublished poems preferred) or simultaneous submissions. Prefers e-mail submissions (pasted into body of message). Cover letter is required. SAE or IRC essential for postal submissions. Time between acceptance and publication is 6 months. Seldom comments on rejected poems. Guidelines available for SASE, by fax, e-mail, or on Web site. Responds in 3 months. Pays 1 contributor's copy. Acquires first rights.

Also Offers Bank Street Writers meets once/month and offers workshops, guest speakers, and other activities. Write for details.

Advice "We like originality of ideas, images, and use of language. No inspirational or religious verse unless it's also good in poetic terms."

✖ ☐ CURRICULUM VITAE

Simpson Publications, P.O. Box 1082, Franklin PA 16323. E-mail: simpub@hotmail.com. Established 1995. **Contact:** Amy Dittman, managing editor.

Magazine Needs *Curriculum Vitae*, published semiannually in January and July, is "a zine where quality work is always welcome. We'd like to see more metrical work, especially more translations, and well-crafted narrative free verse is always welcome. We do not want to see rambling Bukowski-esque free verse or poetry that overly relies on sentimentality." *Curriculum Vitae* is 40 pages, digest-sized, photocopied, saddle-stapled, with 2-color cardstock cover. Receives about 500 poems/year, accepts about 75. Press run is 1,000. Subscription: $6 for 4 issues. Sample: $4.

How to Submit Submit 3 poems at a time. Considers previously published poems and simultaneous submissions. Cover letter is preferred ("to give us an idea of who you are"). "Submissions without a SASE cannot be acknowledged due to postage costs." Time between acceptance and publication is 8 months. Poetry is circulated among 3 board members. Often comments on rejected poems. Publishes theme issues. Guidelines available for SASE or by e-mail. Responds within 1 month. Pays 2 contributor's copies plus one-year subscription.

Additional Information "We're also interested in expanding our list of innovative side projects, books, graphic novels, chapbooks like *The Iowa Monster*, and the CV Poetry Postcard Project." Simpson Publications publishes about 5 chapbooks/year. Query with full manuscripts or well-thought-out plans with clips. Include SASE.

Also Offers "We are currently looking for poets who would like to be part of our Poetry Postcard series."

☑ CUTBANK

English Dept., University of Montana, Missoula MT 59812. (406)243-6156. E-mail: cutbank@umont ana.edu. Web site: www.cutbankonline.org. Established 1973. **Contact:** Poetry Editor.

Magazine Needs *CutBank*, published semiannually, prints regional, national, and international poetry, prose, interviews, and artwork. Has published poetry by Richard Hugo, Carl Phillips, Sandra Alcosser, and Virgil Suarez. Press run is 1000. Single copy: $10; subscription: $12/2 issues. Sample: $4.

How to Submit Submit up to 5 poems at a time. Considers simultaneous submissions ("discouraged, but accepted with notification"). Poems should be single-spaced; include SASE. Reads submissions October 1-February 28 only. Accepts submissions December 1-February 28 for Patricia Goedicke Prize in Poetry, guest-judged Contest, $500 award plus publication. Guidelines available for SASE or on Web site. Responds in up to 4 months. Pays 2 contributor's copies. All rights return to author upon publication.

❀ ☑ DALHOUSIE REVIEW

Dalhousie University, Halifax NS B3H 4R2 Canada. (902)494-2541. Fax: (902)494-3561. E-mail: dalhousie.review@dal.ca. Web site: http://dalhousiereview.dal.ca. Established 1921. **Contact:** Anthony Stewart, editor.

Magazine Needs *Dalhousie Review*, published 3 times/year, is a journal of criticism publishing poetry and fiction. Considers poetry from both new and established writers. *Dalhousie Review* is 144 pages, digest-sized. Accepts about 5% of poems received. Press run is 500. Single copy: $15 CAD; subscription: $22.50 CAD, $28 USD. Make checks payable to *Dalhousie Review*.

How to Submit Lines/poem: 40. No previously published poems. No e-mail submissions except from outside North America (all other initial submissions are by means of hard copy only). "Submissions should be typed on plain white paper, double-spaced throughout. Spelling preferences are those of *The Canadian Oxford Dictionary*: catalogue, colour, program, travelling, theatre, and so on. Beyond this, writers of fiction and poetry are encouraged to follow whatever canons of usage might govern the particular story or poem in question, and to be inventive with language, ideas, and form. Please enclose a SASE (or SAE and IRC) for response." Reads submissions year round. Seldom comments on rejected poems. Occasionally publishes theme issues. Guidelines available for SAE and IRC or on Web site. Pays 2 contributor's copies and 10 off-prints.

⊞ ☑ ◎ DANDELION ARTS MAGAZINE (Specialized: member-subscribers only)

Fern Publications, 24 Frosty Hollow, East Hunsbury, Northants NN4 0SY England. Fax: (44)(160)470-1730. Established 1978. **Contact:** Jacqueline Gonzalez-Marina, M.A, editor/publisher.

Magazines/Journals

Magazine Needs *Dandelion Arts Magazine*, published semiannually in May and December, is "a platform for new and established poets and prose writers to be read throughout the world." **Poets must become member-subscribers of *Dandelion Arts Magazine* and poetry club in order to be published.** Wants poetry that is "modern but not wild." Does not want "bad language poetry, religious or political, nor offensive to any group of people in the world." Has published poetry by Andrew Duncan, Paul Wilkins, Andrew Pye, John Brander, etc. *Dandelion Arts* is about 40 pages, A4, thermal-bound, with original cover design. Receives about 200-300 poems/year, accepts about 40%. Press run is up to 1,000; some distributed free to chosen organizations. Subscription: £17 UK, £30 Europe, $90 U.S. Sample: half price of subscription. Make checks payable to Fern Publications.
How to Submit Submit 4-6 poems at a time. Lines/poem: 40-60 maximum. Considers simultaneous submissions; no previously published poems. No fax submissions. Cover letter is required. "Submissions must be typed out clearly and ready for publication, if possible, accompanied by a SAE or IRC to cover the cost of postage for the reply." Reads submissions year round. Time between acceptance and publication is 2-6 months. "The material sent to Fern Publications is read by the editor when it arrives, and a decision is made straight away." Sometimes offers "constructive" comments on rejected poems. Guidelines available for SASE (or SAE and IRC) or by fax. Responds within 3 weeks. Reviews books of poetry. Send materials for review consideration.
Additional Information Fern Publications is a press for artistic, poetic, and fiction books. Books are usually 50-80 pages, A5 or A4, thermal-bound or hand-finished. Query first with 6-10 poems. **Requires authors to subscribe to *Dandelion Arts Magazine*.** Responds to queries and mss in 3 weeks. Subsidizes costs for books, paying no royalties. **"All books are published at a cost agreed on beforehand and paid in advance."**
Also Offers *Dandelion Arts* includes information on poetry competitions and art events.
Advice "Consider you are submitting material for an international magazine where subjects such as war or religious issues or bad language are not accepted."

◎ DARKLING MAGAZINE (Specialized: poetry of a dark nature)

Darkling Publications, RR 3, Box 67, Colome SD 57528. (605)842-1402. E-mail: darkling@mitchellte lecom.net. Established 2005. **Contact:** James C. Van Oort, editor-in-chief.
Magazine Needs *Darkling Magazine*, published annually in June, is "primarily interested in poetry. All submissions should be dark in nature. Horror poetry is acceptable but not a requisite. All poetry submissions should help expose the darker side of man. Poetry of any form, style, etc., that is either dark or depressing will be strongly considered." Does not want "poetry aimed at making one feel good or experience the warm fuzzies. Such submissions will be trash-canned and will merit no response. 'Dark nature' does not mean whiny or overly murderous, and certainly being depressed does not make an artist's work dark. Pornography will not be considered and will merit no response. Profanity that is meritless or does not support the subject of any piece is unacceptable." Has published poems by Robert Cooperman, Kenneth DiMaggio, Cathy Porter and Simon Perchik, among others. Subscription: $15 with s&h. Make checks payable to Darkling Publications.
How to Submit Submit up to 8 poems at a time. Lines/poem: any length is acceptable, but "epic poems must be of exceptional quality." Considers previously published poems and simultaneous submissions. Will accept e-mail submissions; no disk submissions. Cover letter is required. Reads submissions October to April. Time between acceptance and publication is 2-3 months. Poems are circulated to an editorial board. Sometimes comments on rejected poems. Sometimes publishes theme issues. Guidelines available in magazine. Announces rejections and acceptance in April or May. Pays 1 contributor's copy. All rights revert to author upon publication.
Advice "We are always looking for new poets who have a voice we feel needs to be heard. Do not be afraid to ask questions. Our editorial staff will be very happy to communicate with you."

◢ THE DERONDA REVIEW

P.O. Box 55164, Madison WI 53705. E-mail: drndrev@execpc.com. Web site: www.pointandcircum ference.com. Established 1995. **Contact:** Esther Cameron, editor. Co-Editor for Israel: Mindy Aber Barad, P.O.B. 7731, Jerusalem 91077.
Magazine Needs *The Deronda Review*, published semiannually, seeks to "promote poetry of intro-

spection, dialogue, and social concern." Wants "poetry of beauty and integrity with emotional and intellectual depth, commitment to subject matter as well as language, and the courage to ignore fashion. Welcome: well-crafted formal verse, social comment (including satire), love poems, philosophical/religious poems. *The Deronda Review* has a standing interest in work that sees Judaism as a source of values and/or reflects on the current situation of Israel and of Western civilization. Open, in principle, to writers of all ages." Has published poetry by Yakov Azriel, Ruth Blumert, Ida Fasel, Constance Rowell Mastores, Richard Moore, and Marc Widershien. *The Deronda Review* is 28-32 pages, magazine-sized, photocopied, saddle-stapled, with cardstock cover. Press run is 275. Single copy: $6; subscription: $10.

How to Submit Submit 3-5 poems at a time. Considers simultaneous submissions and previously published poems "on rare occasions." Cover letter is unnecessary. "Do include SASE with sufficient postage to return all manuscripts or with 'Reply Only" clearly indicated. First-time contributors in the U.S. are requested to submit by surface mail. Poets whose work is accepted will be asked for titles of books available, to be published in the magazine." Time between acceptance and publication is up to 1 year. Often comments on rejected poems. Does not offer guidelines because "the tradition is the only 'guideline.' We do encourage contributors to write for a sample." Responds in up to 4 months. Pays 2 contributor's copies. Acquires first rights.

Additional Information *The Deronda Review* publishes the addresses of poets who would welcome correspondence. "Poets can also submit longer selections of work for publication on the 'Point and Circumference' Web site."

Advice "The poem should speak to the ear and to the understanding, and it should be understood that understanding has social consequences. Like all our social functioning, poetry today suffers from a loss of community, which translates into a lack of real intimacy with the reader. Poets can work against this trend by remaining in touch with the poetry of past generations, by forming relationships in which poetry can be employed as the language of friendship, and by at least contemplating the concept of covenant. Publication should be an afterthought."

◙ DESCANT: FORT WORTH'S JOURNAL OF POETRY AND FICTION

English Dept., Texas Christian University, Box 297270, Fort Worth TX 76129. Fax: (817)257-6239. E-mail: descant@tcu.edu. Web site: www.descant.tcu.edu. Established 1956. **Contact:** Dave Kuhne, editor.

Magazine Needs *descant: Fort Worth's Journal of Poetry and Fiction*, published annually during the summer, seeks "well-crafted poems of interest. No restrictions as to subject matter or form." *descant* is 100+ pages, digest-sized, professionally printed and bound, with matte card cover. Receives about 3,000 poems/year. Press run is 500. Single copy: $12 ($18 outside U.S.). Sample: $10.

How to Submit Lines/poem: 60 or fewer, "but sometimes longer." No simultaneous submissions. No fax or e-mail submissions. Reads submissions September-March only. Responds in 6 weeks. Pays 2 contributor's copies.

Contest/Award Offerings Sponsors the annual Betsy Colquitt Award for Poetry, offering $500 to the best poem or series of poems by a single author in a volume. *descant* also offers a $250 award for an outstanding poem in an issue. No application process or reading fee; all published submissions are eligible for consideration.

✖ ◘ ◎ DESERT VOICES (Specialized: interested in the Desert Southwest)

Palo Verde College, One College Dr., Blythe CA 92225. (760)921-5449. Fax: (760)922-0230. E-mail: aminyard@paloverde.edu. **Contact:** Applewhite Minyard and Joe Jondrea, co-editors.

Magazine Needs *Desert Voices*, published annually, is a "non-profit literary magazine featuring short fiction, essays, and poetry." *Desert Voices* is 60 pages, digest-sized, offset-printed, stapled. Receives about 100 poems/year, accepts about 20. Press run is 1,000; some distributed free to students. Single copy: $3. Make checks payable to Palo Verde College.

How to Submit Submit 3-5 poems at a time. Lines/poem: 1 page or less/poem. Considers simultaneous submissions; no previously published poems. Accepts mail and e-mail (attachment in MS Word) submissions; no fax submissions. Cover letter is preferred. Include SASE for return or reply.

Reads submissions September-June. "Include brief biography, contact information (post, phone, e-mail), and SASE for return or reply. Guidelines available via e-mail or post with SASE. Accepts submissions year-round. Acceptance and rejection notices sent in December. Never comments on rejected submissions. Occasionally publishes theme issues. Guidelines available for SASE or by e-mail. Responds in 2 months. Pays 2 contributor's copies. Acquires one-time rights.

Advice "*Desert Voices* readers demand high-quality, original, distinct poetic voices that have a thematic revelation. Desert Voices does not accept poetry that is cliché, romantic, sentimental, epic, obscene, or profane. Our audience desires intelligence and craft with vivid description, emotion, insights, and language that capture and maintain their attention."

✪ ◪ DI-VÊRSÉ-CITY

P.O. Box 41224, Austin TX 78704. E-mail: aipfinfo@aipf.org. Web site: www.aipf.org. Established 1993. **Contact:** Susan Stockton.

Magazine Needs *di-vêrsé-city*, published annually in April, seeks "eclectic, well-crafted poems that touch not only the heart, but also the mind. Surprise us!" *di-vêrsé-city* is about 100 pages, digest-sized, professionally printed, perfect-bound, with glossy cardstock cover with original art. Receives about 600 poems/year, accepts about 15%. Make checks payable to Austin International Poetry Festival.

How to Submit Submit 3 poems at a time. Lines/poem: 48 maximum. No previously published poems or simultaneous submissions. Poets use the online submission form. "Follow Web site instructions carefully." Reads submissions December-February. Submit seasonal poems by February 1. Poems are circulated to an editorial board. Never comments on rejected poems. To submit, poets must register online at www.aipf.org and pay festival registration fee (see Web site). "You do not have to attend the festival to have a poem in *di-vêrsé-city*, but you must pay the fee." Guidelines available on Web site. Acquires first rights. Rights revert to poet upon publication.

Contest/Award Offerings Sponsors the annual Christina Sergeyevna Award. Offers cash prizes. **Entry fee:** all poems accepted for *di-vêrsé-city* are eligible. **Deadline:** February 1. Uses outside judge.

▣ ◪ DIAGRAM

648 Crescent NE, Grand Rapids MI 49503. E-mail: editor@thediagram.com. Web site: www.thediagram.com. Established 2000. **Contact:** Ander Monson, editor. Member: CLMP.

- Work appearing in *DIAGRAM* has been reprinted on the Poetry Daily and Verse Daily Web sites.

Magazine Needs *DIAGRAM*, published semimonthly online, prints "poetry, prose, and schematic (found or created), plus nonfiction, art, and sound. We're especially interested in unusual forms and structures, and work that blurs genre boundaries." Does not want light verse. Has published poetry by Arielle Greenberg, Anne Boyer, Jason Bredle, GC Waldrep, Simone Muench, and Medbh McGuckian. Receives about 1,000 poems/year, accepts about 10%. Number of unique visitors:1,500/day.

How to Submit Submit 3-6 poems at a time. Lines/poem: no limit. Considers simultaneous submissions; no previously published poems. Electronic submissions accepted through submissions manager; no e-mail, disk, or fax submissions. Electronic submissions MUCH preferred; print submissions must include SASE." Cover letter is preferred. Reads submissions year round. Time between acceptance and publication is 1-10 months. Poems are circulated to an editorial board. Sometimes comments on rejected poems. Sometimes publishes theme issues. Guidelines available on Web site. Responds in 1-3 months. Always sends prepublication galleys. Acquires first rights and first North American serial rights. Rights revert to poet upon publication. Reviews books/chapbooks of poetry in 500-1,500 words, single- or multi-book format. Send materials for review consideration to Aaron Welborn, reviews editor.

Additional Information *DIAGRAM* also publishes periodic perfect-bound print anthologies.

Contest/Award Offerings Sponsors the annual *DIAGRAM*/Michigan Press Chapbook Contest (see separate listing in Contests & Awards).

■ ○ ◎ **DIAMOND DUST E-ZINE (Specialized: poetry for/by teens; Christian; inspirational)**

E-mail: DiamondEditor@yahoo.com. Web site: www.freewebs.com/diamonddustmagazine. Established 2005. **Contact:** Laura and Stephanie Rutlind, co-editors.

Magazine Needs *Diamond Dust E-zine*, published bi-monthly online, is "a magazine and e-newsletter for teens and adults. Our goal is to inspire our readers in their Christian walk." Wants "poetry, short fiction, articles, book and music reviews, and fillers. Poetry of all types and all topics is considered. Submissions are not required to be religious, but we ask that they include good morals and clean content. 'Inspirational' is key." Does not want "to see anything that does not have clean content or high morals, or anything that is not inspirational." Considers poetry by teens. "Teens are encouraged to submit their work, but they must include their age and name or pen name." Accepts 24 poems/year. Available for free online.

How to Submit Submit 3 poems at a time. Lines/poem: less than 30. Considers previously published poems. Requires e-mail submissions (pasted into body of e-mail). Cover letter is required. "Tell us who you are and what you write. Include bio. If you're a teen, please include your age." Reads submissions year round. Submit seasonal poems 4 months in advance. Time between acceptance and publication is approximately 1-3 months ("unless held for a future seasonal or theme issue"). Sometimes publishes theme issues. Guidelines and themes available by e-mail or on Web site. Responds within 3 weeks. No payment, but will include an author bio and contact links on Web site. "We acquire one-time electronic rights. All rights are given back to the author after publication. All pieces remain on our Web site for 2 months and then they are deleted."

Advice "We love to work with beginning writers, so take a look at our current issue online. If you follow our guidelines and themes list, your submission has a good chance of achieving publication."

◙ ◎ **JAMES DICKEY NEWSLETTER (Specialized: life & works of James Dickey)**

Dept. of English, University of South Carolina, Columbia SC 29208. (803)777-4203. Fax: (803)777-9064. E-mail: thorne@sc.edu. Web site: www.jamesdickey.org. Established 1984 (newsletter), 1990 (society). **Contact:** Thorne Compton, editor.

Magazine Needs *James Dickey Newsletter*, published semiannually in the spring and fall by the James Dickey Society, is "devoted to critical articles/studies of James Dickey's works/biography and bibliography." Publishes "a few poems of high quality. No poems lacking form, meter, or grammatical correctness." Has published poetry by Henry Taylor, Fred Chappell, George Garrett, and Dave Smith. *James Dickey Newsletter* is 50 pages, $8^{1}/_{2} \times 5^{1}/_{2}$, neatly offset (back and front), saddle-stitched, with card back-cover. Single copy: $8; subscription: $12/year for individuals (includes membership in the James Dickey Society), $14 for U.S. institutions, $15.50 for foreign institutions.

How to Submit Accepts fax and e-mail (pasted into body of message/as attachment) submissions. "However, if poet wants written comments/suggestions line by line, send manuscript by postal mail with SASE." Cover letter is required. "Contributors should follow MLA style and standard manuscript format, sending one copy, double-spaced." Guidelines available in magazine or on Web site. Pays 2 contributor's copies. Acquires first rights. Reviews "only works on Dickey or that include Dickey."

Also Offers The James Dickey Society is devoted to discussions, dissemination, and interpretive scholarship and research concerning the works of James Dickey. Additional information available on Web site.

Advice "Consult issues [of newsletter] and guidelines [before submitting]."

$ ◎ **DIG MAGAZINE (Specialized: archeology & exploration; theme-specific; children/teens ages 9-14)**

d Editorial Dept., Cobblestone Publishing, 30 Grove St., Suite C, Peterborough NH 03458. Web site: www.cricketmag.com. **Contact:** Rosalie Baker.

Magazine Needs *DIG Magazine*, published 9 times/year in partnership with *Archeology* magazine, features archeology and exploration for children ages 9-14. "All material must relate to the theme of a specific upcoming issue in order to be considered." Wants "clear, objective imagery. Serious and light verse considered. Must relate to theme.'' Subscription: $32.97/year (9 issues). Sample: $5.95 plus $2.00 s&h (include 10×13 SASE); sample pages available on Web site.

How to Submit Query first. Lines/poem: up to 100. No e-mail submissions or queries. Include SASE. Reads submissions according to deadlines for queries (see Web site for schedule and details). Always publishes theme issue. Themes and guidelines available on Web site. Pays varied rates. Acquires all rights.

Advice ''Writers are encouraged to study recent back issues for content and style.''

N P ✍ THE DIRTY NAPKIN

E-mail: Jeremy@dirtynapkin.com. Web site: www.dirtynapkin.com. Established 2007. **Contact:** Jeremy C. Ellis, managing director.

Magazine Needs ''Have you ever felt the urgency to write while you were out, at a restaurant, say, and scribbled a thought down on a napkin or the closest thing you could find? Have you ever told your friends to 'hang on a sec' until you finished that thought? As writers, we do not know when the muse will slap us silly. Luckily, there are many napkins filling the world waiting for us to dirty them. The *Dirty Napkin*, published quarterly online, seeks to publish the best poetry, fiction, and letters in four issues a year. What are the best poems, stories, and letters, you ask? You tell us. The *Dirty Napkin* acknowledges that writing cannot be separate from the voice, breath, and the personality of the author; that should a piece of writing be separated from this literal voice, much power will be lost. Therefore, the *Dirty Napkin* seeks to include voice by having each author read their work online.'' Wants ''any length and style, though the shorter amount of time it takes to cripple us with your brilliance, the better.'' Does not want ''unfinished or undeveloped note taking.'' Has published poetry by Alicia Ostriker, Jane Mead, F.D. Reeve, Gerry LaFemina, Paula McLain, John Hoppenthaler. Single copy: $20 for print on demand, subscription $20 (includes access to all author recordings, discounts on special events, one free submission to Gerald Stern Poetry Prize, and much more).

How to Submit Submit 3 poems at a time. Accepts e-mail submissions (through online form); no fax or disk submissions. Cover letter is preferred. Reads submissions year round. Time between acceptance and publication is 2 months. Poems are circulated to an editorial board. Sometimes comments on rejected poems. Sometimes publishes theme issues. Upcoming themes and guidelines available on Web site. Responds in 1 month. Acquires first North American serial and electronic rights. Rights revert to poets upon publication.

Contest/Award Offerings The Gerald Stern Poetry Prize, offered annually, offers a 1st prize of $250 and a book chosen by Gerald Stern. Submit 4-8 poems. Wants ''poems that show in Gerald's own words, 'courage, audacity, originality, humility, intelligence, and honesty.' '' Guidelines available in magazine and on Web site. **Entry fee**: $5 and **Deadline**: March 1.

Also Offers ''Each issue will feature one writer on its cover. The piece we like the best out of the pool of accepted writers wins the coveted cover. There are no entry fees or application materials other than the regular submission of your manuscript. If you win the *Cover Prize*, we will ask that you handwrite your piece on a napkin of your choosing. Your work will also appear typed inside.''

P ✍ DMQ REVIEW

E-mail: editors@dmqreview.com. Web site: www.dmqreview.com. **Contact:** Sally Ashton, editor-in-chief.

Magazine Needs *DMQ Review*, published quarterly online, is ''a quality magazine of poetry presented with visual art.'' Wants ''finely crafted poetry that represents the diversity of contemporary poetry.'' Has published poetry by David Lehman, Ellen Bass, Amy Gerstler, Bob Hicok, Ilya Kaminsky, and Jane Hirshfield. Receives about 3,000-5,000 poems/year, accepts about 1%.

How to Submit Submit up to 3 poems at a time (''no more than once per quarter''). Considers simultaneous submissions (with notifications only); no previously published poems. Accepts e-mail submissions (pasted into body of message; no attachments will be read) only. ''Please read and follow complete submission guidelines on our Web site.'' Reads submissions year round. Time between acceptance and publication is 1-3 months. Poems are circulated to an editorial board. Never comments on rejected poems. Responds within 3 months. Acquires first rights.

Additional Information Nominates for the Pushcart Prize. ''We also consider submissions of visual art, which we publish with the poems in the magazine, with links to the artists' Web sites.''

Advice ''Read recent issues of *DMQ Review* before submitting, follow our guidelines, and send your best work.''

▣ $◎ DOVETAIL: A JOURNAL BY AND FOR JEWISH/CHRISTIAN FAMILIES (Specialized: Jewish/Christian interfaith marriage)

775 Simon Greenwell Lane, Boston KY 40107. (800)530-1596. E-mail: DI-IFR@bardstown.com. Web site: www.dovetailinstitute.org. Established 1991. **Contact:** Julie Aziz, editor.

Magazine Needs *Dovetail: A Journal by and for Jewish/Christian Families*, published quarterly online, provides ''strategies and resources for interfaith couples, their families, and friends.'' Wants poetry related to Jewish/Christian marriage issues; uses some material related to other sorts of interfaith marriage, especially Muslim/Christian and Muslim/Jewish. Does not want poetry on general religious themes. Has published work by Janet Landman, Donald R. Stoltz, and Eric Wolk Fried. Receives about 10 poems/year, accepts about 1%. Press run is 1,000. Single copy: $5.50; subscription: $39.95. Sample: available to download free online. Make checks payable to DI-IFR.

How to Submit Submit 1 poem at a time. Considers previously published poems and simultaneous submissions. Accepts e-mail (pasted into body of message) submissions. Time between acceptance and publication is up to 1 year. Poems are circulated to an editorial board. ''Clergy and other interfaith professionals review draft issues.'' Seldom comments on rejected poems. Publishes theme issues. Guidelines available for SASE or by e-mail or fax. Responds in 1 month. Pays $10-20. Acquires first North American serial rights. Reviews other magazines in 500 words, single- and multi-book format.

Advice ''We get 20 inappropriately denomination-oriented poems for every 1 that actually relates to interfaith marriage. Don't waste your time or ours with general Christian or 'inspirational' themes.''

▣ ◯ DOWN IN THE DIRT

Scars Publications, 829 Brian Court, Gurnee IL 60031. E-mail: alexrand@scars.tv. Web site: http://scars.tv. Established 2000. **Contact:** Alexandria Rand, editor.

Magazine Needs *Down in the Dirt*, published monthly online, prints ''good work that makes you think, that makes you feel like you've lived through a scene instead of merely read it.'' Also can consider poems. Does not want smut, rhyming poetry, or religious writing. Has published work by I.B. Rad, Jennifer Rowan, Cheryl A. Townsend, Tom Racine, David-Matthew Barnes, and Michael Estabrook. *Down in the Dirt* is published ''electronically as well as in print, either on the Web or in e-book form (PDF file).'' Sample: available on Web site.

How to Submit Lines/poem: any length is appreciated. Considers previously published poems and simultaneous submissions. Accepts e-mail submissions (vastly preferred to snail mail; pasted into body of message or as Microsoft Word .doc file attachment) and disk submissions (formatted for Macintosh). Guidelines available for SASE, by e-mail, or on Web site. No payment. ''Currently, accepted writings get their own web page in the ''writings'' section at http://scars.tv, and samples of accepted writings are placed into an annual collection book Scars Publications produces.''

Contest/Award Offerings Scars Publications sponsors a contest ''where accepted writing appears in a collection book. Write or e-mail (editor@scars.tv) for information.''

Additional Information Also able to publish electronic chapbooks. Write for more information.

Advice ''The Web site is a more comprehensive view of what *Down in the Dirt* does. All the information is there.''

Ⓝ ▣ ◖ DROWN IN MY OWN FEARS

E-mail: karinabowman@gmail.com. Web site: http://drowninmyownfears.angelfire.com. Established 2007. **Contact:** Karina Bowman, editor.

Magazine Needs *Drown In My Own Fears*, published quarterly online, ''is a poetry journal about the human condition, therefore, we want poems reflecting that. Poems submitted should be about love, hate, pain, sorrow, etc. We don't want maudlin sentimentality, we want the depths of your very being. We want well-written, deeply conceived pieces of work. Anything that isn't about the human condition really isn't for us.'' Wants ''all styles of poetry, as long as it's your best work.''

Does not want "syrupy sweet, gooey nonsense, religious rants, political grandstandings." Considers poetry by teens. Has published poetry by Kendall A. Bell, MK Chavez, Taylor Graham, Natalie Lorenzo, Michael Keshigian, and Corey Mesler. Receives about 300 poems/year, accepts about 10%.

How to Submit Submit 3-5 poems at a time. "We prefer short poems, but long ones are ok." Considers previously published poems; no simultaneous submissions. Accepts e-mail submissions (pasted into body of e-mail message); no fax or disk submissions. Cover letter is rquired. Include a brief bio with your submission. Reads submissions year round. Submit seasonal poems 3 months in advance. Time between acceptance and publication is 1-2 months. Never comments on rejected poems. Sometimes publishes theme issues. Upcoming themes and guidelines available on Web site. Responds in 2-4 weeks. Acquires first rights. Rights revert to poets upon publication.

Advice "Try different writing styles and don't limit your poetic view to one way of thinking. Read lots of different poets. Write on little pieces of paper when an idea or a line comes. If you can't finish a poem in one sitting, come back to it later. You might find more inspiration in a day or two. Always rewrite and find avenues to workshop your poems. Several sets of eyes can certainly give you invaluable advice. True poets write because they must."

N E O EARTHSHINE

PO Box 245, Hummelstown PA 17036.E-mail: poetry@ruminations.us. Web site: www.ruminations .us. Established 2007. **Contact:** Sally Zaino and Julie Moffitt, poetry editors.

Magazine Needs *Earthshine*, published irregularly in print, and online, features poetry and 1-2 pieces of cover art per volume. "When the online journal is full, a printed volume is produced and offered for sale. Subscriptions will be available as the publication becomes regular. The voice of *Earthshine* is one of illumination, compassion, humanity, and reason. Please see submission guidelines Web page for updated information. Poems are the ultimate rumination, and if the world is to be saved, the poets will be needed, they who see the connections between all things, and the patterns shared. We seek poetry of high literary quality which will generate its own light for our readers." Has published poetry by Rachel Barroso, Fredrik Zydek, Steven Klepetar, Mario Susko.

How to Submit Submit no more than 6 poems at a time. Considers previously published poems; no simultaneous submissions. (Considers poetry posted on a public Web site/blog/forum and poetry posted on a private, password-protected forum as published.) "We prefer poems that have not been published elsewhere, but occasionally make exceptions. If a work has been published elsewhere, including on a personal Web site, please include the publication history." Accepts e-mail submissions (pasted into body of message); no fax or disk submissions. Cover letter is preferred. "Please let us know where you heard about *Earthshine*. If submitting by mail, please include a SASE for reply only. Please do not send the only copy of your work." Reads submissions year round. Submit seasonal poems 1 month in advance. Time between acceptance and publication is" online publication is almost immediate, printed publication TBD." Sometimes comments on rejected poems. Never publishes theme issues. Guidelines available in magazine, for SASE, and on Web site. Responds in 1-2 months. Pays 1 contributor copy. Acquires first rights, one-time rights, electronic rights (publication rights include online publication and publication in 1 printed volume. Request first rights if poem is previously unpublished; one-time rights if poem has appeared elsewhere. Archive rights negotiated separately." Rights revert to poets upon publication.

Also Offers "The parent of *Earthshine* is also at Ruminations.us, and offers full editing and review services for a fee."

C O THE ECLECTIC MUSE (Specialized: rhyme; neo-classicist revival)

Suite 307, 6311 Gilbert Rd., Richmond BC V7C 3V7 Canada. (604)277-3864. E-mail: jrmbooks@hot mail.com. Web site: www.thehypertexts.com. Established 1985. **Contact:** Joe M. Ruggier, publisher.

Magazine Needs *The Eclectic Muse*, published annually at Christmas, is devoted "to publishing all kinds of poetry (eclectic in style and taste) but specializing in rhyme- and neo-classicist revival." Does not want "bad work (stylistically bad or thematically offensive)." Has published poetry by Mary Keelan Meisel, John Laycock, Philip Higson, Roy Harrison, Michael Burch, and Ralph O.

Cunningham. *The Eclectic Muse* is magazine-sized, digitally copied, saddle-stapled, with paper cover. The number of pages varies from year to year (32 minimum to 56 maximum). Receives about 300 poems/year, accepts about 15%. Press run is 200; distributed free to all contributing authors plus selected gift subscription recipients. Single copy: $8; subscription: $25. Make checks payable to Joe M. Ruggier.

How to Submit Submit no more than 5 poems at a time. Lines/poem: 60 maximum; "please consult if longer." Considers previously published poems and simultaneous submissions. Accepts e-mail submissions (preferred, as a single .doc or .rtf attachment containing all 5 poems) and disk submissions. "Send your submission by regular mail only if you have no access to a computer or you are computer illiterate. Typeset everything in Times New Roman 12 point. If your poetry features indents and special line spacing, please make sure you reproduce these features yourself in your data entry since it will not be possible for the editor to determine your intentions." Cover letter is preferred. "Include brief bio (100 words maximum) with your name, credentials (degrees, etc.), occupation and marital status, your most major publication credits only, and any hobbies or interests." Provide SASE plus clear e-mail and postal addresses for communication and for sending contributor's copy. Reads submissions year round. Time between acceptance and publication is 1 year. Poems are circulated to an editorial board. Sometimes comments on rejected poems. **"If authors wish to have a manuscript carefully assessed and edited, the fee is $250 USD; will respond within 8 weeks."** Guidelines available in magazine or on Web site. Responds in 2 months. Pays 2 contributor's copies. Reviews books/chapbooks of poetry and other magazines/journals in 900 words. Send materials for review consideration to Joe M. Ruggier, managing editor.

Also Offers "Look us up on www.thehypertexts.com, where myself and my services are listed (featured) permanently. The host of this splendid poetry Web site is my U.S. associate, Mr. Michael Burch. He features, on this site, most of the leading names in contemporary North America."

Advice "An author's style is really the only thing which belongs to him as an artist to manipulate for his own purposes as he pleases. Truths and feelings do not belong to him exclusively and may not be bent or manipulated for his own purposes as he pleases. We do not want bad work where the poet feels that the message matters but the style is bad (not good workmanship), nor do we wish to publish work which seems to us to distort and bend truths and human feelings far too much."

EDGZ

Edge Publications, P.O. Box 799, Ocean Park WA 98640. Established 2000. **Contact:** Blaine R. Hammond, editor/publisher; Debra Brimacombe, associate editor.

Magazine Needs *Edgz*, published semiannually in (or around) May and November, prints "poetry of all sorts of styles and schools. Our purpose is to present poetry with transpersonal intentions or applications, and to put poets on a page next to other poets they are not used to appearing next to." Wants "a broad variety of styles with a transpersonal intent. *Edgz* has two main reasons for existence: Our weariness with the attitude that whatever kind of poetry someone likes is the only legitimate poetry; and our desire to present poetry addressing large issues of life. Must be engaged; intensity helps." Does not want "anything with a solely personal purpose; dense language poetry; poetry that does not take care with the basics of language, or displays an ignorance of modern poetry. No clichés, gushing, sentimentalism, or lists of emotions. Nothing vague or abstract. No light verse or doggerel, but humor is fine." Has published poetry by Barry Ballard, Joseph Barker, Leonard Cirino, Joan Payne Kincaid, and R. Yurman. *Edgz* is digest-sized, laser-printed on recycled paper, saddle-stapled, with 80 lb. cardstock cover with art/graphics. Single copy: $8; subscription: $15 for 2 issues. Sample: $4. Make checks payable to Edge Publications.

How to Submit Submit 3-5 poems at a time ("a longer poem may be submitted by itself"). Lines/poem: no length restrictions. Considers simultaneous submissions; no previously published poems. Cover letter is "not required, but if we find something interesting in yours, it may appear in the magazine. We don't mind more than one poem to a page or well-traveled submissions; these are ecologically sound practices. We like recycled paper. Submissions without SASE will be gratefully used as note paper. No postcards in place of SASE. Please do not fold poems separately. Handwritten poems OK if poet is poor or incarcerated." Reads submissions by February 1 and August 1 deadlines.

Time between acceptance and publication is 1-6 months. Comments on rejected poems "as we feel like it. We don't provide criticism services." Guidelines available for SASE. Responds in up to 6 months. Pays 1 contributor's copy/published poem, with discounts on additional copies. Acquires first rights plus anthology rights ("just in case").

Advice "It's one thing to require subscriptions in order to be published. It's something else to charge reading fees. In a world that considers poetry valueless, reading fees say it is less than valueless—that editors should be compensated for being exposed to it. I beg such editors to cease the practice. I advise everyone else not to submit to them, or the practice will spread. My most common rejection note is 'too personal for my thematic focus.' "

EKPHRASIS (Specialized: ekphrastic verse)

Frith Press, P.O. Box 161236, Sacramento CA 95816-1236. E-mail: frithpress@aol.com. (inquiries only). Web site: www.hometown.aol.com/ekphrasis1. Established 1995 (Frith Press) and 1997 (*Ekphrasis*). **Contact:** Laverne Frith and Carol Frith, editors.

• Poems from *Ekphrasis* have been featured on *Poetry Daily*.

Magazine Needs *Ekphrasis*, published semiannually in March and September, is an "outlet for the growing body of poetry focusing on individual works from any artistic genre." Wants "poetry whose main content is based on individual works from any artistic genre. Poetry should transcend mere description. Open to all forms." Does not want "poetry without ekphrastic focus. No poorly crafted work. No archaic language." Has published poetry by Jeffrey Levine, Peter Meinke, David Hamilton, Barbara Lefcowitz, Molly McQuade, and Annie Boutelle. *Ekphrasis* is 40-50 pages, digest-sized, photocopied, saddle-stapled. Subscription: $12/year. Sample: $6. Make checks payable, in U.S. funds, to Laverne Frith.

How to Submit Submit 3-7 poems at a time. Considers previously published poems "infrequently, must be credited"; no simultaneous submissions. Accepts submissions by postal mail only. Cover letter is required, including short bio with representative credits and phone number. Include SASE. Time between acceptance and publication is up to 1 year. Seldom comments on rejected poems. Guidelines available for SASE or on Web site. Responds in 4 months. Pays 1 contributor's copy. Nominates for Pushcart Prize. Acquires first North American serial or one-time rights.

Additional Information Until further notice, Frith Press will publish **occasional chapbooks by invitation only**.

Contest/Award Offerings The Ekphrasis Prize, which awards $500 and publication for a single poem, is sponsored and judged by the editors of *Ekphrasis*. Guidelines available for SASE or on Web site. 2007 winner was Jeffrey Levine ("Half Matter in a Material World").

Advice "With the focus on ekphrastic verse, we are bringing attention to the interconnections between various artistic genres and dramatizing the importance and universality of language. Study in the humanities is essential background preparation for the understanding of these interrelations."

EMRYS JOURNAL

P.O. Box 8813, Greenville SC 29604. E-mail: lydia.dishman@gmail.com. Web site: www.emrys.org. Established 1982. **Contact:** Poetry Editor. Editor: L.B. Dishman.

• **Will begin reading submissions again August 1, 2008**.

Magazine Needs *Emrys Journal*, published annually in May, prints "literary or narrative poetry of less than 36 lines. Rhyming needs to be oustanding to be considered." Has published poetry by Kristin Berkey-Abbott, Adriano Scopino, John Popielaski, J. Morris, and Terri McCord. *Emrys Journal* is up to 120 pages, digest-sized, handsomely printed, flat-spined. Press run is 400 (250 subscribers, 10 libraries). Sample: $12 and 7×10 SASE with 4 First-Class stamps.

How to Submit *No mss will be read until August 1, 2008*. Submit up to 5 poems at a time (per author). No previously published poems or simultaneous submissions. Accepts e-mail submissions (as attachment). Include SASE. Reads submissions August 1-November 1 only; no mss will be read outside the reading period. Time between acceptance and publication is up to 8 months. Guidelines available for SASE or on Web site. Responds "by the end of the reading period." Pays 5 contributor's copies.

Contest/Award Offerings Sponsors the annual Nancy Dew Taylor Award for excellence in the art of poetry. Offers $250 prize to the author of the best poem published in *Emrys Journal* that year.

✍ ENGLISH JOURNAL

Interdisciplinary Studies in Curriculum & Instruction, National-Louis University, Tampa, FL 33609. (941)629-0541. Fax: (941)629-0541. E-mail: EJPoetry@nl.edu (submissions); asullivan@nl.edu (inquiries). **Contact:** Anne McCrary Sullivan, poetry editor.

Magazine Needs *English Journal,* established 1912, published 6 times annually by The National Council of Teachers of English, is a professional education journal, circulation over 20,000. "Issues are themed, and poetry submissions that respond to these themes, either implicitly or explicitly, are encouraged. Themes are announced in every issue and at the NCTE Web site: http://www.engli shjournal.colostate.edu/issuetopics.htm. Poems may be in any form or style, serious or humorous." English Journal accepts fewer than 10% of submissions.

How to Submit Submissions are accepted electronically only. "Send by email attachment, for blind review, up to 5 poems with only phone number and initials on the page. In your e-mail message, include brief biographical information." No previously published poems or simultaneous submissions. Seldom comments on rejected poems. Responds in 2-4 months. Pays 2 contributor's copies.

✍ EPICENTER: A LITERARY MAGAZINE

P.O. Box 367, Riverside CA 92502. E-mail: poetry@epicentermagazine.org. Web site: www.epicent ermagazine.org. Established 1994. **Contact:** Rowena Silver.

Magazine Needs *Epicenter: A Literary Magazine,* published semiannually, is open to all styles. "*Epicenter* is looking for poetry, essays, short stories, creative nonfiction, and artwork. We publish new and established writers." Considers translations. Does not want "angst-ridden, sentimental, or earthquake poetry. We are not adverse to graphic images as long as the work contains literary merit." Has published poetry by Virgil Suarez, Alba Cruz-Hacher, B.Z. Niditch, Egon Lass, and Zdravka Evtimova. *Epicenter* is 100 pages, perfect-bound. Receives about 2,000 submissions/year, accepts about 5%. Press run is 800. Single copy: $7. Make checks payable to *Epicenter: A Literary Magazine.*

How to Submit Submit up to 5 poems at a time. Considers previously published poems and simultaneous submissions. Accepts e-mail submissions. Include SASE with sufficient postage for return of materials. Seldom comments on rejected poems. Guidelines available in magazine, for SASE, by e-mail, or on Web site. Pays 1 contributor's copy. Acquires one-time and electronic rights.

✍ ◎ EPITOME (Specialized: northeastern OH women writers only)

Implosion Press, 4975 Comanche Trail, Stow OH 44224-1217. (330)836-7808. E-mail: epitomepoetry @aol.com. Web site: http://epitomemag.com. Established 1984. **Contact:** Cheryl Townsend, poetry editor.

Magazine Needs *epitome* is a regional publication for and by northeastern OH women. Wants "poetry that addresses the power of women to overcome social obstacles and injustices; poetry that is not subserviant to anyone. Poetry that celebrates being a woman. Material should be straight from the gut, uncensored and real. Any length as long as it works. All subjects OK, providing there are no 'isms.' We publish **ONLY** northeastern Ohio women in our Poetry and Featured Artist sections." Does not want rhymed verse. Sample: $5. Make checks payable to Implosion Press.

How to Submit Submit 3-8 poems at a time. Lines/poem: prefers "shorter, to-the-point work." Considers previously published poems if noted as such (include when and where each poem was originally published). Accepts e-mail submissions (pasted into body of message). Appreciates "a cover letter that tells how the poet found out about our magazine." Include name and address on each page; SASE for reply/return. Time between acceptance and publication is generally 5 months. Guidelines available for SASE, by e-mail, or on Web site. Responds within 4 months. Acquires one-time rights. Reviews books of poetry. Send materials for review consideration.

Additional Information In addition to *epitome,* Implosion Press publishes chapbooks by northeastern OH women writers.

Advice "Know your market. Request guidelines and/or a sample copy."

$✍ EPOCH

251 Goldwin Smith Hall, Cornell University, Ithaca NY 14853. (607)255-3385. Web site: www.arts.c ornell.edu/english/epoch.html. Established 1947. **Contact:** Nancy Vieira Couto, poetry editor.

Magazine Needs *Epoch*, published 3 times/year, has a distinguished and long record of publishing exceptionally fine poetry and fiction. Has published poetry by Kevin Prufer, Peter Dale Scott, Martin Walls, Maxine Kumin, Heather McHugh, and D. James Smith. *Epoch* is 128 pages, digest-sized, professionally printed, perfect-bound, with glossy color cover. Accepts less than 1% of the many submissions received each year. Has 1,000 subscribers. Subscription: $11/year domestic, $15/year foreign. Sample: $5.

How to Submit No simultaneous submissions. Manuscripts not accompanied by SASE will be discarded unread. Reads submissions September 15-April 15. Responds in up to 10 weeks. Occasionally provides criticism on mss. Pays 3 contributor's copies and at least $10/page. "We pay more when we have more!" Acquires first serial rights.

Advice "Read the magazine."

★ ⊕ ☑ ◎ EUROPEAN JUDAISM (Specialized: emphasis on European Jewish theology/philosophy/literature/history)

Leo Baeck College, The Sternberg Centre, 80 East End Rd., London N3 2SY England. Web site: www.berghahnbooks.com/journals/ej. Established 1966. **Contact**: Ruth Fainlight, poetry editor.

Magazine Needs *European Judaism*, published twice/year, is a "glossy, elegant magazine with emphasis on European Jewish theology/philosophy/literature/history, with some poetry in every issue. Poems should (preferably) be short and have some relevance to matters of Jewish interest." Has published poetry by Linda Pastan, Elaine Feinstein, Daniel Weissbort, and Dannie Abse. *European Judaism* is 110 pages, digest-sized, flat-spined. Press run is 950 (about 500 subscribers, over 100 libraries). Subscription: $45 individual, $20 student, $162 institution.

How to Submit Submit 3-4 poems at a time. Lines/poem: short poems preferred. "I prefer unpublished poems, but poems from published books are acceptable." Cover letter is required. "No material is read or returned if not accompanied by SASE (or SAE with IRCs). We cannot use American stamps." Pays 1 contributor's copy.

$☑ ◎ EVANGEL (Specialized: Christian)

Light and Life Communications, P.O. Box 535002, Indianapolis IN 46253-5002. Established 1897. **Contact**: J. Innes, editor.

Magazine Needs *Evangel*, published weekly, is an adult Sunday school paper. "Devotional in nature, it lifts up Christ as the source of salvation and hope. The mission of *Evangel* is to increase the reader's understanding of the nature and character of God and the nature of a life lived for Christ. Material that fits this mission and isn't longer than one page will be considered." Does not want rhyming work. *Evangel* is 8 pages, digest-sized (two $8^{1}/_{2} \times 11$ sheets folded), printed in 4-color, unbound. Accepts about 5% of poetry received. Press run is about 10,000. Subscription: $2.49/quarter (13 weeks). Sample: free for #10 SASE.

How to Submit Submit no more than 5 poems at a time. Considers simultaneous submissions. Cover letter is preferred. "Poetry must be typed on $8^{1}/_{2} \times 11$ white paper. In the upper left-hand corner of each page, include your name, address, phone number, and social security number. In the upper right-hand corner of cover page, specify what rights you are offering. One-eighth of the way down the page, give the title. All subsequent material must be double-spaced, with one-inch margins." Submit seasonal poems 1 year in advance. Seldom comments on rejected poems. Guidelines available for #10 SASE. "Write 'guidelines request' on your envelope so we can sort it from the submissions." Responds in up to 2 months. Pays $10 plus 2 contributor's copies. Acquires one-time rights.

Advice "Poetry is used primarily as filler. Send for sample and guidelines to better understand what and who the audience is."

☑ THE EVANSVILLE REVIEW

1800 Lincoln Ave., Evansville IN 47722. Phone/fax: (812)488-1042. E-mail: evansvillereview@evansville.edu. Web site: http://english.evansville.edu/EvansvilleReview.htm. Established 1989. **Contact**: Kirby Snell, poetry editor.

• Poetry published in *The Evansville Review* has been included in *The Best American Poetry* and *The Pushcart Prize*.

Magazine Needs *The Evansville Review*, published annually in April, prints "prose, poems, and drama of literary merit." Wants "anything of quality." No excessively experimental work; no erotica. Has published poetry by Joseph Brodsky, J.L. Borges, John Updike, Willis Barnstone, Rita Dove, and Vivian Shipley. *The Evansville Review* is 140-200 pages, digest-sized, perfect-bound, with art on cover. Receives about 2,000 poems/year, accepts about 2%. Press run is 1,500. Sample: $5.

How to Submit Submit 3-5 poems at a time. Considers previously published poems and simultaneous submissions. No fax or e-mail submissions; postal submissions only. Cover letter is required. Include brief bio. Manuscripts not returned without SASE. Reads submissions September 1-December 1 only. Time between acceptance and publication is 3 months. Poems are circulated to an editorial board. Seldom comments on rejected poems. Guidelines available for SASE or on Web site. Responds within 3 months of the deadline. Pays 2 contributor's copies. Rights remain with poet.

Contest/Award Offerings The Willis Barnstone Translation Prize (see separate listing in Contests & Awards).

⊚ EXIT 13 (Specialized: geography/travel)

P.O. Box 423, Fanwood NJ 07023-1162. (908)889-5298. E-mail: exit13magazine@yahoo.com. Established 1987. **Contact:** Tom Plante, editor.

Magazine Needs *Exit 13*, published annually, uses poetry that is "short, to the point, with a sense of geography." Has published poetry by A.D. Winans, Adele Kenny, Edwin Romond, Penny Harter, Brent Fisk, and Charles Rammelkamp. *Exit 13* is about 76 pages. Press run is 300. Sample: $7.

How to Submit Considers simultaneous submissions and previously published poems. Accepts e-mail submissions (no attachments). Guidelines available in magazine or for SASE. Responds in 4 months. Pays 1 contributor's copy. Acquires one-time and possible anthology rights.

Advice "*Exit 13* looks for adventure, a living record of places we've experienced. Every state, region, country, and ecosystem is welcome. Write about what you know and have seen. Send a snapshot of an 'Exit 13' road sign and receive a free copy of the issue in which it appears."

▣ ◲ FAILBETTER.COM

2022 Grove Ave., Richmond VA 23220. E-mail: submissions@failbetter.com. Web site: www.failbetter.com. Established 2000. **Contact:** Mary Donnelly and Ben Gantcher, poetry editors. Publisher: Thom Didato. Member: CLMP.

• Works published in *failbetter* have received recognition in various award anthologies including *Best American Poetry*, *The Pushcart Prize* and *Best of the Net*.

Magazine Needs *failbetter.com*, published online, seeks "that which is at once original and personal. When choosing work to submit, be certain that what you have created could only have come from you." Publishes translations and interviews with such poets as Paul Muldoon, Marie Ponsot, Mary Jo Salter, and Billy Collins. Has published poetry by J. Allyn Rosser, Terrance Hayes, Mary Donnely, and Thaddeus Rutkowski. Receives about 2,000 poetry submissions/year, accepts about 9-12. Publishes 3-4 poets/issue.

How to Submit Submit 4-6 poems at a time. Lines/poem: "we're not concerned with length—one good sentence may find a home here, as the bulk of mediocrity will not." Considers simultaneous submissions; no previously published poems. Encourages e-mail submissions (pasted into body of message). "Send to submissions@failbetter.com only! Please read and follow submission guidelines posted on Web site. All e-mail submissions should include title in header. All poetry submissions must be included in the body of your e-mail. Please do not send attached files." Also accepts postal submissions; "please note, however, any materials accepted for publication must ultimately be submitted in electronic format in order to appear on our site." Cover letter is preferred. Reads submissions year round. Time between acceptance and publication is 4 months minimum and upward. Poems are circulated to an editorial board. Often comments on rejected poems. "It's not unusual to ask poets to re-submit, and their subsequent submissions have been accepted." Guidelines available on Web site. Responds in up to 4 months to e-mail submissions; up to 6 months by regular mail. "We will not respond to any e-mail inquiry regarding receipt confirmation or status of any work under consideration." No payment. Acquires exclusive first-time Internet rights; works will also be archived online. All other rights, including opportunity to publish in traditional print form, revert to the poet.

Advice "With a readership of more than 60,000 per issue, *failbetter* is one of the Web's widely read literary magazines, offering exposure of poets' works to a much broader, worldwide audience than the typical print journal. For both established and emerging poets our advice remains the same: We strongly recommend that you not only read the previous issue, but also sign up on our e-mail list (subscribe@failbetter.com) to be notified of future publications."

▣ ◪ THE FAIRFIELD REVIEW

544 Silver Spring Rd., Fairfield CT 06824-1947. (203)256-1960. E-mail: fairfieldreview@hpmd.com. Web site: www.fairfieldreview.org. Established 1997. **Contact:** Janet and Edward Granger-Happ and Pamela Pollak, editors.

Magazine Needs *The Fairfield Review*, published twice/year online, features poetry, short stories, and essays from new and established authors. "Wants "free style poems, approachable on first reading, but with the promise of a rich vein of meaning coursing along under the consonants and vowels." Does not want "something better suited for a Hallmark card." Considers poetry written by children and teens; requires parents' permission/release for children under 18. Has published poetry by Taylor Graham, Lyn Lifshin, and John Jeffrey. Receives about 630 poems/year, accepts about 6%.

How to Submit Submit 3 poems at a time. Lines/poem: 75 maximum. Considers previously published poems with permission; no simultaneous submissions. Accepts e-mail submissions (**strongly preferred**; as attachment). "Notifications are sent exclusively via e-mail. An e-mail address is required with all submissions." Cover letter is preferred. Reads submissions continually. Time between acceptance and publication is "usually less than 2 months." Poems are circulated to an editorial board. Sometimes comments on rejected poems, if requested and submitted via e-mail. Guidelines available on Web site. Responds in up to 1 year. Always sends prepublication galleys (online only). Acquires first rights, right to retain publication in online archive issues, and the right to use in "Best of *The Fairfield Review*" anthologies. Occasionally reviews books of poetry. "We consider reviews of books from authors we have published or who are referred to us."

Contest/Award Offerings "We select poems from each issue for 'Editor's Choice' awards, plus 'Reader's Choice' awards based on readership frequency."

Advice "Read our article 'Writing Qualities to Keep in Mind.' "

◪ FAULTLINE

Dept. of English & Comparative Literature, University of California, Irvine, Irvine CA 92697-2650. (949)824-1573. E-mail: faultline@uci.edu. Web site: www.humanities.uci.edu/faultline. Established 1991. **Contact:** Collier Nogues, poetry editor.

• Poetry published by *Faultline* has been included in *The Pushcart Prize*.

Magazine Needs *Faultline*, published annually each spring, features new poetry, fiction, and translation. Has published poetry by C.K. Williams, Larissa Szporluk, Yusef Komunyakaa, Amy Gerstler, and Killarney Clary. *Faultline* is about 200 pages, digest-sized, professionally printed on 60 lb. paper, perfect-bound, with 80 lb. coverstock. Receives about 5,000 poems/year, accepts less than 1%. Press run is 1,000. Single copy: $10. Sample: $5.

How to Submit Submit up to 5 poems at a time. Considers simultaneous submissions, "but please note in cover letter that the manuscript is being considered elsewhere." No fax or e-mail submissions. Cover letter is required. Include name, postal and e-mail addresses, and titles of work submitted; do not put name and address on ms pages themselves. SASE required. Reads submissions September 15-February 15 only. Poems are selected by a board of up to 6 readers. Seldom comments on rejected poems. Guidelines available for SASE or on Web site. Responds in 3 months. Pays 2 contributor's copies. Acquires first or one-time serial rights.

▣ FEELINGS OF THE HEART

3317 SE Emerson St., Topeka KS 66605. (785)969-0321. E-mail: apoetesswitch28@aol.com or allypo etesswitch@yahoo.com. Web site: www.freewebs.com/feelingsoftheheartliteraryjournal. Established 1999. **Contact:** Alice M. Harnisch, editor/publisher/founder/poetess.

Magazine Needs *Feelings of the Heart*, published 2 times/year, seeks "poetry from the heart." Considers poetry by children and teens. Has published poetry by Mark Hurley, Jerry S. Reynolds, and Sharon Kroenlein. *Feelings of the Heart* is 50 pages, newsletter format, magazine-sized, computer-printed, stapled, includes ads. Receives about 100 poems/year, accepts about 95%. Press run is 100+. Single copy: $6; subscription: $18/year, $36 for 2 years (2-year subscribers receive free gift with order). Make checks payable to Alice M. Harnisch.

How to Submit Submit 5 poems at a time. Lines/poem: 20-40. Considers previously published poems and simultaneous submissions. Accepts e-mail (pasted into body of message or as attachment in Word) and disk submissions. Cover letter is "important." Include name and address on every poem submitted. "Please enclose SASE or IRC with all postal correspondence. No SASE or IRC, no reply!" Submit seasonal poems 2 months in advance. Time between acceptance and publication is less than 2 weeks with SASE or e-mail. Poems "are read by me, the editor, and decided by the poetic intent of poetry submitted." Often comments on rejected poems. "If asked why rejected, you will receive an answer." Guidelines available for SASE, by e-mail, or on Web site. Sometimes sends prepublication galleys. Acquires first rights. Reviews books/chapbooks of poetry and other magazines/journals in 200 words or less, single-book format. Send materials for review consideration.

Contest/Award Offerings Holds annual contests for cash prizes. Guidelines available on Web site.

Also Offers Prints poetry chapbooks for those interested **in being self-published**. Write for details.

Advice "Write poetry for yourself; publish for everyone else!"

▣ ◎ FEMINIST STUDIES (Specialized: feminism)

0103 Taliaferro Hall, University of Maryland, College Park MD 207427726. (301)405-7415. Fax: (301)405-8395. E-mail: creative@feministstudies.org. Web site: www.feministstudies.org. Established 1969. **Contact:** Minnie Bruce Pratt, creative writing editor.

Magazine Needs *Feminist Studies*, published 3 times/year, welcomes "all forms of written creative expression, which may include but is not limited to poetry and short fiction." Has published poetry by Dawn McDuffie, Liz Robbins, Maria Mazziotti Gillan, Mary Ann Wehler, Barbara Wiedemann, and Paola Corso. *Feminist Studies* is 250 pages, elegantly printed, flat-spined, paperback. Press run is 8,000. Sample: $17.

How to Submit No previously published poems ("we only consider original work that is not under review elsewhere") or simultaneous submissions. No fax submissions. Send 1 hard copy of submission as well as an electronic version (disk, CD, or e-mail). "We will not process creative submissions until we receive both a hard copy and electronic version." Retain a copy; work will not be returned. Reads submissions twice/year according to May 1 and December 1 deadlines. Responds by July 15 and February 15 with notice of board's decision. Regularly publishes theme issues. Guidelines available on Web site. Always sends prepublication galleys. Pays 2 contributor's copies.

▣ ▣ ◎ FICKLE MUSES (Specialized: myth and legend)

E-mail: editor@ficklemuses.com. Web site: www.ficklemuses.com. Established 2006. **Contact:** Sari Krosinsky, editor.

Magazine Needs *Fickle Muses*, published weekly online, is a journal of myth and legend printing poetry, fiction, reviews, essays, and art. Open to all styles and forms. Has published poetry by Jeannine Hall Gailey, Robert Arthur Reeves, Carol L. MacKay, and Margarita Engle. Accepts about 10% of poems received. Number of unique visitors: 125/week.

How to Submit Submit up to 5 poems at a time. Lines/poem: no limits on length. Considers previously published poems and simultaneous submissions. Accepts e-mail submissions (pasted into body of message preferred, unless special formatting requires an attachment); no disk submissions. Cover letter is preferred. Reads submissions year round. Time between acceptance and publication is 3 months. Never comments on rejected poems. Guidelines available by e-mail or on Web site.

Responds in up to 3 months. Acquires one-time rights. Rights revert to poets upon publication. Reviews books/chapbooks of poetry and other magazines/journals in 500 words, single-book format. For review consideration, query by e-mail.

$☑ FIELD: CONTEMPORARY POETRY AND POETICS

Oberlin College, 50 N. Professor St., Oberlin OH 44074. (440)775-8408. E-mail: oc.press@oberlin.edu. (inquiries only). Web site: www.oberlin.edu/ocpress. Established 1969. **Contact:** David Young.

• Work published in *FIELD* has been included frequently in *The Best American Poetry*.

Magazine Needs *FIELD: Contemporary Poetry and Poetics*, published semiannually in April and October, is a literary journal with "emphasis on poetry, translations, and essays by poets." Wants the "best possible" poetry. Has published poetry by Marianne Boruch, Miroslav Holub, Charles Wright, Franz Wright, Charles Simic, and Jean Valentine. *FIELD* is 100 pages, digest-sized, printed on rag stock, flat-spined, with glossy color card cover. Subscription: $14/year, $24 for 2 years. Sample: $7 postpaid.

How to Submit Submit up to 5 poems at a time. No previously published poems or simultaneous submissions. No e-mail submissions. Include cover letter and SASE. Reads submissions year round. Seldom comments on rejected poems. Guidelines available for SASE, by e-mail, or on Web site. Responds in 4-6 weeks. Always sends prepublication galleys. Pays $15/page and 2 contributor's copies. Staff reviews books of poetry. Send materials for review consideration.

Additional Information Oberlin College Press publishes books of translations in the FIELD Translation Series. Books are usually flat-spined paperbacks averaging 150 pages. Query regarding translations. Also publishes books of poetry in the FIELD Poetry Series, **by invitation only**. Has published *Meaning a Cloud* by J.W. Marshall, *Lie Awake Lake* by Beckian Fritz Goldberg, *Chez Nous* by Angie Estes, *Stubborn* by Jean Gallagher, and *Red Studio* by Mary Cornish. Write for catalog or visit Web site to buy sample books.

Contest/Award Offerings Sponsors the annual FIELD Poetry Prize for a book-length collection of poems (see separate listing in Contests & Awards).

Advice "A sampling of 3-5 poems is desirable. Be sure to include enough postage on SASE if you want poems returned. We try to read promptly; please wait to submit poems elsewhere."

▣ $☐ ◎ THE FIFTH DI... (Specialized: fantasy; science fiction)

E-mail: fifth@samsdotpublishing.com. Web site: www.samsdotpublishing.com. Established 1994. **Contact:** J. Alan Erwine, editor.

• Honored by Preditors & Editors as Best Fiction Zine.

Magazine Needs *The Fifth Di...*, published quarterly online, features fiction and poetry from the science fiction and fantasy genres. Open to most forms, but all poems must be science fiction or fantasy. Does not want horror, or anything that is not science fiction or fantasy. Considers poetry by children and teens. Has published poetry by Bruce Boston, Cathy Buburuz, Marge Simon, Aurelio Rico Lopez III, Terrie Relf, and John Bushore. Receives about 200 poems/year, accepts about 20.

How to Submit Submit 1 poem at a time. Lines/poem: no limit. No previously published poems or simultaneous submissions. Accepts e-mail submissions only (as attachment); no disk submissions. Cover letter is preferred. Reads submissions year round. Time between acceptance and publication is 1 month. Sometimes comments on rejected poems. Guidelines available on Web site. Responds in 1-3 months. Pays $5. Acquires first rights.

☑ FIGHT THESE BASTARDS

Platonic 3 Way Press, P.O. Box 844, Warsaw IN 46581. (317)457-3505. E-mail: evilgenius@platonic3waypress.com. Web site: www.Platonic3WayPress.com. Established 2005. **Contact:** Oren Wagner, Steve Henn, and Don Winter, co-editors.

Magazine Needs *Fight These Bastards*, published semiannually, seeks "poetry of revolt, against the Academy, against the poetic mainstream." Wants "poetry accessible beyond the ivory towers of academia and outside the bounds of religious or politically correct restrictions. We enjoy poetry that celebrates honesty and humor. We enjoy poetry with some bite to it. We enjoy poetry that claims to represent the interests, views, or tastes of the common person, particularly as distinct

from those of the rich and powerful." Does not want "cute bunny poems; no overtly political poems, no knee-jerk, poorly executed anti-(fill-in-the-blank) poems." Has published poetry by Linda McCarriston, Lyn Lifshin, Fred Voss, Gerald Locklin, Mike Kriesel, Gary Goude and others. *Fight These Bastards* is about 20-30 pages, magazine-sized, photocopied in high resolution, side-stapled, with cover with artwork, includes ads. Accepts about 2% of poems submitted. Press run is 250. Single copy: $4; subscription: $10 (3 issues). Make checks payable to Platonic 3Way Press.
How to Submit Submit 3-5 poems at a time. Considers previously published poems ("if given the name of the journal where poem was published") and simultaneous submissions ("if so noted"). No e-mail or disk submissions. Cover letter is required. Reads submissions year round. Time between acceptance and publication is up to 1 year. Poems are circulated to an editorial board. Sometimes comments on rejected poems. Guidelines available in magazine or on Web site. Responds in 2 weeks to 6 months. Sometimes sends prepublication galleys. Pays 1 contributor's copy. Acquires one-time rights. Rights revert to poet upon publication. Reviews books/chapbooks of poetry and other magazines/journals in 250 words or less, single- and/or multi-book format.
Contest/Award Offerings Sponsors the annual Evil Genius Chapbook Contest (see separate listing in Contests & Awards).
Advice "Make it new; trust your gut. We like poetry that is wedded to the street, not the classroom. We like poetry without foreign phrases, myriad obscure allusions, and cross-references."

◯ ◎ FIGHTING CHANCE MAGAZINE (Specialized: horror; science fiction/fantasy)
Suzerain Enterprises, P.O. Box 60336, Worcester MA 01606. Established 1994. **Contact:** Milton Kerr, editor/publisher.
Magazine Needs *Fighting Chance Magazine*, published 3 times/year, gives "unpublished writers a chance to be published." Wants dark fiction, horror, and science fiction. Does not want "porn, ageism, sexism, racism, children in sexual situations." Has published poetry by A.H. Ferguson, Wayne Adams, Gary McGhee, Robert Donald Spector, Cecil Boyce, and Ellaraine Lockie. *Fighting Chance Magazine* is 15-30 pages, magazine-sized, photocopied, side-stapled, with computer-designed paper cover. Receives about 500 poems/year, accepts about 10%. Press run is 100. Subscription: $12/year. Sample: $4. Make checks payable to Suzerain Enterprises.
How to Submit Submit 3 poems at a time. Lines/poem: 20 maximum. Considers previously published poems and simultaneous submissions. Cover letter is preferred. "Proofread for spelling errors, neatness; must be typewritten in standard manuscript form. No handwritten manuscripts." Time between acceptance and publication is 3 months. Often comments on rejected poems. Guidelines available for SASE. Responds in 6 weeks. Acquires first or one-time rights.
Advice "Proofread your work. Edit carefully. Always include business-sized SASE with correct postage. Don't let rejection slips get you down. Keep submitting and don't give up. Don't be afraid to write something different."

▨ ▨ ◪ FILLING STATION
P.O. Box 22135, Bankers Hall, Calgary AB T2P 4J5 Canada. (403)234-0336. E-mail: editor@fillingstation.ca or general@fillingstation.ca. Web site: www.fillingstation.ca. Established 1993. **Contact:** Natalie Walschots, managing editor. Laurie Fuhr, general editor.
Magazine Needs *filling Station*, published 3 times/year, prints contemporary poetry, fiction, visual art, film stills, interviews, reviews, and articles. "We are looking for all forms of contemporary writing, but especially that which is original and/or experimental." Has published poetry by Fred Wah, Larissa Lai, Margaret Christakos, Robert Kroetsch, Ron Silliman, Susan Holbrook, and many more. *filling Station* is 80 pages, magazine-sized, perfect-bound, with card cover, includes photos and artwork. Receives about 100 submissions for each issue, accepts approximately 10%. Press run is 600. Subscription: $22/year, $38 for 2 years. Sample: $8.
How to Submit E-mailed submissions for text is strongly encouraged. Submissions should include author's name, address, e-mail, and a short biography. Only successful submissions will receive a reply; no rejections sent and unaccepted submissions will not be returned. Considers simultaneous submissions, provided this is noted on submissions and they are withdrawn elsewhere if accepted by *filling Station*. No previously published material. Accepts submissions year round; deadlines

vary. E-mail editor for next deadline. Guidelines available in magazine, for SASE, by e-mail, or on Web site. Responds in 6 months. Pays one-year subscription. Acquires first North American serial rights and non-exclusive rights to reprint and/or electronically publish material published in *filling Station*. All copyrights remain with that author or artist. "*filling Station* does not accept submissions that are racist, misogynist, and/or homophobic."

Advice "You stop between these 'fixed' points on the map to get an injection of something new, something fresh that's going to get you from point to point...We want to be a kind of connection between polarities: a link."

☑ FIRST CLASS

Four-Sep Publications, P.O. Box 86, Friendship IN 47021. E-mail: christopherm@four-sep.com. Web site: www.four-sep.com. Established 1994. **Contact:** Christopher M., editor.

Magazine Needs *First Class*, published in February and August, prints "excellent/odd writing for intelligent/creative readers." Wants "short postmodern poems." Does not want "traditional work." Has published poetry by Bennett, Locklin, Roden, Splake, Catlin, and Huffstickler. *First Class* is 48-56 pages, $4\frac{1}{4} \times 11$, printed, saddle-stapled, with colored cover. Receives about 1,500 poems/year, accepts about 30. Press run is 300-400. Sample: $6 (includes guidelines), or mini version $1. Make checks payable to Christopher M.

How to Submit Submit 5 poems at a time. Considers previously published poems and simultaneous submissions. No fax or e-mail submissions. Cover letter is preferred. "Manuscripts will not be returned." Time between acceptance and publication is 2-4 months. Often comments on rejected poems. Guidelines available in magazine, for SASE, or on Web site. Responds in 3 weeks. Pays 1 contributor's copy. Acquires one-time rights. Reviews books of poetry and fiction. Send materials for review consideration.

Additional Information Chapbook production available.

Advice "Belt out a good, short, thought-provoking, graphic, uncommon piece."

✖ ⊕ FIRST OFFENSE

Syringa, Stodmarsh, Canterbury, Kent CT3 4BA England. E-mail: Tim@firstoffense.co.uk. Web site: www.firstoffense.co.uk. Established 1985. **Contact:** Tim Fletcher, editor.

Magazine Needs *First Offense*, published 1-2 times/year, is "for contemporary poetry and is not traditional, but is received by most ground-breaking poets." Wants "contemporary, language, and experimental poetry and articles." *First Offense* is photocopied, "so we need well typed or word-processed manuscripts." Press run is 300. Subscription: £6.50 plus 75p for postage, or $9.50 plus $5 airmail, or equivalent in Euros. Make checks payable to Tim Fletcher.

How to Submit No previously published poems. "No reply without SAE."

Advice "Always buy a copy for research before submitting so as not to waste everyone's time."

☑ 5 AM

P.O. Box 205, Spring Church PA 15686. Web site: www.5ampoetry.com. Established 1987. **Contact:** Ed Ochester and Judith Vollmer, editors.

Magazine Needs *5 AM*, published twice/year, is a poetry publication open in regard to form, length, subject matter, and style. Does not want religious poetry or "naive rhymers." Has published poetry by Virgil Suárez, Nin Andrews, Alicia Ostriker, Edward Field, Billy Collins, and Denise Duhamel. *5 AM* is 24-pages, tabloid size, offset-printed. Receives about 5,000 poems/year, accepts about 2%. Press run is 1,200. Subscription: $15 for 4 issues. Sample: $5.

How to Submit No previously published poems or simultaneous submissions. Seldom comments on rejected poems. Responds within 6 weeks. Pays 2 contributor's copies. Acquires first rights.

Advice "Read the magazine before submitting."

✖ $☑ FIVE POINTS

Georgia State University, P.O. Box 3999, Atlanta GA 30302-3999. (404)413-5833. Fax: (404)413-5877. Web site: www.webdelsol.com/Five_Points. Established 1996. **Contact:** Megan Sexton, editor.

Magazine Needs *Five Points*, published 3 times/year, prints "quality poetry, fiction, nonfiction, interviews, and art by established and emerging writers." Wants "poetry of high quality that shows evidence of an original voice and imagination." Has published poetry by Charles Wright, Kim Addonizio, and Philip Levine. *Five Points* is about 200 pages, digest-sized, professionally printed, perfect-bound, with 4-color card cover, includes ads. Receives about 2,000 poems/year, accepts about 5%. Press run is 2,000. Single copy: $7 plus $1.50 shipping.

How to Submit Submit no more than 3 poems at a time (accepts 2 submissions/reading period). Lines/poem: 50 maximum. No previously published poems or simultaneous submissions. Cover letter is preferred. Reads submissions September 1-April 30 only. Time between acceptance and publication is 3 months. Poems are circulated to an editorial board. "First reader culls poems, then sends them to the final reader." Seldom comments on rejected poems. Guidelines available for SASE or on Web site. Responds in 3 months. Always sends prepublication galleys. Pays $50/poem, 2 contributor's copies, and one-year subscription. Acquires first North American serial rights.

Contest/Award Offerings The James Dickey Prize for Poetry (see separate listing).

☑ FLINT HILLS REVIEW

Dept. of English, Box 4019, Emporia State University, 1200 Commercial St., Emporia KS 66801. Fax: (620)341-5547. E-mail: krabas@emporia.edu. Web site: www.emporia.edu/fhr/index.htm. Established 1995. **Contact:** The Editors.

Magazine Needs *Flint Hills Review*, published annually in late summer, is "a regionally focused journal presenting writers of national distinction alongside new authors." Wants all forms of poetry except rhyming. Does not want sentimental or gratuitous verse. Has published poetry by E. Ethelbert Miller, Elizabeth Dodd, Walt McDonald, and Gwendolyn Brooks. *Flint Hills Review* is about 100 pages, digest-sized, offset-printed, perfect-bound, with glossy card cover with b&w photo. Receives about 2,000 poems/year, accepts about 5%. Single copy: $7.

How to Submit Submit 3-5 poems at a time. Considers simultaneous submissions; no previously published poems. Accepts submissions by fax or e-mail (pasted into body of message). Cover letter is required. Include SASE. Reads submissions January-March only. Time between acceptance and publication is about one year. Seldom comments on rejected poems. Occasionally publishes theme issues. Guidelines available for SASE or on Web site. Pays 1 contributor's copy. Acquires first rights.

Contest/Award Offerings FHR hosts an annual nonfiction contest. **Entry Fee**: $10. **Deadline:** March 15.

Advice "Send writing with evidence of a strong sense of place."

☑ FLYWAY, A JOURNAL OF WRITING AND ENVIRONMENT

206 Ross Hall, Iowa State University, Ames IA 50011-1201. Fax: (515)294-6814. E-mail: flyway@iast ate.edu. Web site: www.flyway.org. Established 1961. **Contact:** Stephen Pett, editor-in-chief.

Magazine Needs *Flyway, A Journal of Writing and Environment*, published 3 times/year, "is one of the best literary magazines for the money. It's packed with some of the most readable poems being published today—all styles, forms, lengths, and subjects." Does not want "elite-sounding free verse with obscure meanings, and pretty-sounding formal verse with obvious meanings." *Flyway* is 112 pages, digest-sized, professionally printed, perfect-bound, with matte card cover with color. Press run is 600. Subscription: $18. Sample: $7.

How to Submit Submit 4-6 poems at a time. Cover letter is preferred. "We do not read manuscripts between the first of May and the end of August." Responds in 6 weeks (often sooner). Pays 2 contributor's copies. Acquires first rights.

Contest/Award Offerings Sponsors an annual award for poetry, fiction, and nonfiction. Details available for SASE or on Web site.

ⓝ ▣ ☑ THE FOLIATE OAK ONLINE

University of Arkansas, Arts and Humanities, Monticello AK 71656.870-460-1247. E-mail: foliateoak @uamont.edu. Web site: www.foliateoak.uamont.edu. Established 1970. **Contact:** Diane Payne

Magazine Needs *The Foliate Oak Online*, published monthly online, prints prose, poetry, and artwork reviewed by college students, edited and added to the Web site. Wants "all genres and forms of poetry are accepted." Does not want: "we're not interested in homophobic, religious rants, or pornographic, violent stories. Please avoid using offensive language." Considers poetry by teens. Has published poetry by Joe Mills, Gary Beck, Janet Butler, Francis Raven, Nadine Nettmann, David LaBounty. Receives about 300 poems/year, accepts about 100. Number of unique visitors: 500 monthly.

How to Submit Submit no more than 5 poems at a time, maximum 30 lines. Considers previously published poems, no simultaneous submissions.(Considers poetry posted on a public Web site/blog/forum and poetry posted on a private, password-protected forum as published.) Accepts e-mail submissions as attachment); no fax or disk submissions. Cover letter is unnecessary. See Web site for guidelines; Word documents are preferred, submit a third person bio. Reads submissions year round. Submit seasonal poems 1 months in advance. Time between acceptance and publication is 2-3 weeks. Poems are circulated to an editorial board. Always comments on rejected poems. Never publishes theme issues. Guidelines available on Web site. Responds in 1 week. Acquires one-time rights. Reviews other magazines/journals.

Additional Information "We are accepting submissions at this time! If accepted, the work will be posted in our monthly magazine for a minimum of 4 weeks. Send us what you have via e-mail."

Advice "Be original, have fun with it; if you are rejected, just keep sending us your work - we enjoy reading them!"

▣ ☑ FORPOETRY.COM

E-mail: poems@forpoetry.com. Web site: www.forpoetry.com. Established 1999. **Contact:** Jackie Marcus, editor.

Magazine Needs *ForPoetry.Com*, published online with daily updates, seeks "to promote new and emerging poets, with or without MFAs. We will be publishing established poets, but our primary interest is in publishing excellent poetry, prose, and reviews." Wants "lyric poetry, vivid imagery, open form, natural landscape, philosophical themes—but not at the expense of honesty and passion." Does not want "city punk, corny sentimental fluff, or academic workshop imitations." Has published poetry by Sherod Santos, John Koethe, Robert Hass, Kim Addonizio, and Brenda Hillman.

How to Submit Submit no more than 2 poems at a time. Considers simultaneous submissions; no previously published poems. Accepts e-mail submissions only (pasted into body of message; no attachments). Cover letter is preferred. Reads submissions September-May only. Time between acceptance and publication is 2-3 weeks. "We'll read all submissions and then decide together on the poems we'll publish." Comments on rejected poems "as often as possible. We receive lots of submissions and are very selective about acceptances, but we will always try to send a note back on rejections." Guidelines available on Web site. Responds in 2 weeks. Reviews books/chapbooks of poetry and other magazines in 800 words.

Advice "As my friend Kevin Hull said, 'Get used to solitude and rejection.' Sit on your poems for several months or more. Time is your best critic."

◎ ⊘ 4*9*1 ELITE IMAGINATIVE POETRY & ART (Specialized: neo-naive poetry)

E-mail: wilokilts@aol.com. Web site: www.491.20m.com. Established 1997. **Contact:** Donald Ryburn and Juan Beauregaard-Montez, co-editors.

Magazine Needs *4*9*1 Imaginative Poetry & Art*, published online, features poetry, art, photography, essays, and interviews. Wants "work of neo-naive genre." Does not want "academic poetry; limited and fallacious language. No sentimental post-modernism." **Considers submmissions by invitation only.** Has published poetry by Duane Locke and Jesus Morales-Montez.

How to Submit Submit 3-6 poems at a time. Considers previously published poems and simultaneous submissions. Accepts e-mail by invitation only. Instructions included in invitation. Time between acceptance and publication varies. Response time varies. Payment varies. Acquires first or one-time rights. Reviews books and chapbooks of poetry and other magazines. Send materials for review consideration.

Also Offers Sponsors a series of creative projects. Write or visit the Web site for details.

THE FOURTH RIVER

Chatham University, Woodland Rd., Pittsburgh PA 15232. E-mail: 4thriver@gmail.com. Web site: http://fourthriver.chatham.edu. Established 2005. **Contact:** Christy Diulus, editor.

Magazine Needs *The Fourth River*, an annual publication of the MFA program at Chatham University, features "literature that engages and explores the relationship between humans and their environments." Wants "writings that are richly situated at the confluence of place, space, and identity, or that reflect upon or make use of landscape and place in new ways." *The Fourth River* is digest-sized, perfect-bound, with full-color cover by various artists. Accepts about 30-40 poems/year. Press run is 500. Single copy: $10; subscription: $18 for 2 years. Make checks payable to Chatham University.

How to Submit Submit 7 poems at a time. Lines/poem: submit 25 pages maximum. No previously published poems. No e-mail or disk submissions. Cover letter is preferred. "SASE is required for response." Reads submissions August 1-February 15. Time between acceptance and publication is 5-8 months. Poems are circulated to an editorial board. Sometimes comments on rejected poems. Sometimes publishes theme issues. Guidelines available on Web site. Responds in 3-5 months. Acquires first North American serial rights.

FREE LUNCH

P.O. Box 717, Glenview IL 60025-0717. Web site: www.poetsfreelunch.org. Established 1988. **Contact:** Ron Offen, editor.

Magazine Needs *Free Lunch*, published 2 times/year, is "interested in publishing the whole spectrum of what is currently being produced by American poets. Features a 'Mentor Series,' in which an established poet introduces a new, unestablished poet. Mentor poets are selected by the editor and have included Maxine Kumin, Denise Duhamel, Billy Collins, Lucille Clifton, Donald Hall, Carolyn Forché, Wanda Coleman, Lyn Lifshin, Stephen Dunn, and Edward Hirsch. *Free Lunch* is especially interested in experimental work and work by unestablished poets." Wants "metaphors, similes, arresting images, and a sensitive and original use of language. We are interested in all genres—experimental poetry, protest poetry, formal poetry, etc. No restriction on form (except no haikus, please), length, style, purpose. No aversion to form, rhyme." Has published poetry by Jared Carter, Donald Hall, James Reiss, Stephen Dunn, Lisel Mueller, and Cathy Song. *Free Lunch* is 32-40 pages, digest-sized, attractively printed and designed, saddle-stapled. Press run is 1,200. Subscription: $12 ($15 foreign). Sample: $5 ($6 foreign). "*Free Lunch* seeks to provide all serious poets living in the U.S. with a free subscription. For details on free subscription, send SASE."

How to Submit Submit no more than 3 poems at a time. Considers simultaneous submissions; no previously published poems. Cover letter is preferred. "Although a cover letter is not mandatory, I like them. I especially want to know if a poet is previously unpublished, as I like to work with new poets." Reads submissions September 1-May 31. "Submissions sent at other times will be returned unread." Always comments on rejected poems. Responds in 2-3 months. Guidelines available for SASE or on Web site. Pays 1 contributor's copy plus subscription.

Contest/Award Offerings The Rosine Offen Memorial Award, a prize of $200, is awarded to 1 poem in each issue of *Free Lunch*. Winners are selected solely by the Board of Directors of Free Lunch Arts Alliance, and are announced in the following issue.

Advice "Archibald MacLeish said, 'A poem should not mean/But be.' I have become increasingly leery of the ego-centered lyric that revels in some past wrong, good-old-boy nostalgia, or unfocused ecstatic experience. Not receptive to art- or literature-referenced poems or poems about writing poems, other poems, poetry reading, etc. Poetry is concerned primarily with language, rhythm, and sound; fashions and trends are transitory and to be eschewed. Perfecting one's work is often more important than publishing it."

$ FREEFALL MAGAZINE

Alexandra Writers' Centre Society, 922 Ninth Ave. SE, Calgary AB T2G 0S4 Canada. (403)264-4730. E-mail: FreeFallmagazine@yahoo.ca. Web site: www.freefallmagazine.ca. Established 1990. **Contact:** Micheline Maylor, editor. Managing Editor: Lynn Fraser. Member: AMPA and Magazines Canada.

Magazine Needs *FreeFall Magazine*, published in April and October, contains fiction, nonfiction, poetry, and interviews related to writers/writing, and artwork and photographs suitable for b&w reproduction. *"FreeFall's* mandate is to encourage the voices of new, emerging, and experienced writers and provide an outlet for their work." Wants "poems in a variety of forms with a strong voice, effective language, and fresh images." Has published poetry by Christopher Wiseman, Sharon Drummond, Edna Alford, Joan Clarke, and Barry Butson. *FreeFall* is 100-120 pages, digest-sized, perfect-bound, glossy, with 60 lb. paper cover. Receives about 100 poems/year, accepts about 15%. Press run is 500; 30 distributed free to contributors, promotion. Single copy: $12.50 USD, $10 CAD; subscription: $25 USD, $20 CAD. Sample: $10 USD, $10 CAD.

How to Submit Submit up to 5 poems at a time. No previously published poems or simultaneous submissions. Accepts postal and disk submissions (ASCII, text format, must include hard copy); no e-mail submissions. Cover letter is required. Include 2-line bio and SASE. Reads submissions in January and July only. Time between acceptance and publication is 3 months. "All submissions are read by 8 editors." Seldom comments on rejected poems. Occasionally publishes theme issues. Guidelines available by mail request, for SAE and IRC, by e-mail, or on Web site. Responds in 3 months. Pays 1 contributor's copy and a nominal amount per page. Acquires first North American serial rights.

Additional Information See Web site for information about the Alexandra Writers' Centre Society activities and services, and for additional information about *FreeFall Magazine*.

Contest/Award Offerings Hosts an annual fiction and poetry contest. **Deadline:** December 31. Guidelines available by e-mail or on Web site.

✦ ▣ ◪ FREEXPRESSION

P.O. Box 4, West Hoxton, NSW 2171 Australia. (61)(2)9607-5559. E-mail: frexprsn@tpg.com.au. Web site: www.freexpression.net. Established 1993. **Contact:** Peter F. Pike, managing editor.

Magazine Needs *FreeXpresSion*, published monthly, contains "creative writing, how-to articles, short stories, and poetry including cinquain, haiku, etc., and bush verse." Open to all forms. "Christian themes OK. Humorous material welcome. No gratuitous sex; bad language OK. We don't want to see anything degrading." Has published poetry by Ron Stevens, Ellis Campbell, John Ryan, and Ken Dean. *FreeXpresSion* is 28 pages, magazine-sized, offset-printed, saddle-stapled, with paper cover. Receives about 2,500 poems/year, accepts about 30%. Press run is 500. Single copy: $3.50 AUS; subscription: $42 AUS ($66 AUS overseas airmail). Sample: A4 SAE with $1 stamp (Australia) or 2 IRCs (overseas).

How to Submit Submit 3-4 poems at a time. Lines/poem: "very long poems are not desired but would be considered." Considers previously published poems and simultaneous submissions. Accepts e-mail (pasted into body of message) and disk submissions. Cover letter is preferred. Time between acceptance and publication is 2 months. Seldom comments on rejected poems. Publishes theme issues. Upcoming themes available in magazine, by e-mail, or on Web site. Guidelines available in magazine, for SAE and IRC, or by fax or e-mail. Responds in 2 months. Sometimes sends prepublication galleys. Pays 1 contributor's copy; additional copies available at half price. Acquires first Australian rights only. Reviews books of poetry in 500 words. Send materials for review consideration.

Additional Information *FreeXpresSion* also publishes books up to 200 pages **through subsidy arrangements with authors**. "Some poems published throughout the year are used in *Yearbooks* (annual anthologies)."

Contest/Award Offerings Sponsors an annual contest with 3 categories for poetry: blank verse (up to 60 lines); traditional verse (up to 80 lines), and haiku. 1st Prize in blank verse: $200 AUS; 2nd Prize: $100 AUS; 1st Prize in traditional rhyming poetry: $250 AUS; 2nd Prize: $150 AUS; 3rd Prize: $100 AUS. Haiku, one prize $100 AUS. Guidelines and entry form available by e-mail.

Advice "Keep it short and simple."

▣ ◖ THE FROGMORE PAPERS

21 Mildmay Road, Lewes, East Sussex BN71PJ, England. Web site: www.frogmorepress.co.uk. Established 1983. **Contact:** Jeremy Page, poetry editor.

Magazines/Journals

Magazine Needs *The Frogmore Papers*, published semiannually, is a literary magazine with emphasis on new poetry and short stories. "Quality is generally the only criterion, although pressure of space means very long work (over 100 lines) is unlikely to be published." Has published poetry by Marita Over, Brian Aldiss, Carole Satyamurti, John Mole, Linda France, and Tobias Hill. *The Frogmore Papers* is 46 pages, photocopied in photo-reduced typescript, saddle-stapled, with matte card cover. Accepts 2% of poetry received. Press run is 500. Subscription: £10 ($20). Sample: £2.50 ($5). U.S. payments should be made in cash, not check.

How to Submit Submit 5-6 poems at a time. Lines/poem: rarely accepts poems over 100 lines. Considers simultaneous submissions. Rarely comments on rejected poems. Responds in 6 months. Pays 1 contributor's copy. Staff reviews books of poetry in 2-3 sentences, single-book format.

Contest/Award Offerings Sponsors the annual Frogmore Poetry Prize. Write for information.

Advice "My advice to people starting to write poetry is: Read as many recognized modern poets as you can, and don't be afraid to experiment."

FROGPOND: JOURNAL OF THE HAIKU SOCIETY OF AMERICA (SPECIALIZED: HAIKU AND RELATED FORMS; TRANSLATIONS)

Haiku Society of America, P.O. Box 122, Nassau NY 12123. E-mail: gswede@ryerson.ca. Web site: www.hsa-haiku.org. Established 1978. **Contact:** George Swede, editor.

Magazine Needs *Frogpond*, published triannually (February, June, October), is the international journal of the Haiku Society of America. Wants "contemporary English-language haiku, ranging from 1-4 lines or in a visual arrangement, focusing on a moment keenly perceived and crisply conveyed, using clear images and non-poetic language." Also considers "related forms: senryu, sequences, linked poems, and haibun. We welcome translations of any of these forms." Considers poetry by children and teens. Has published poetry by all of the foremost haiku poets. *Frogpond* is 96 pages, digest-sized, perfect-bound. Receives about 20,000 submissions/year, accepts about 500. *Frogpond* goes to 800 subscribers as well as to over a dozen foreign countries. Sample: $7 U.S. (back issue), $9 ROW. Make checks payable to Haiku Society of America.

How to Submit Submissions by e-mail preferred. No simultaneous submissions. Include SASE with postal submissions. Guidelines available for SASE or on Web site. Detailed instructions on Web site. Responds within 1 month. Reviews books of poetry, usually in 1,000 words or less.

Contest/Award Offerings The "best of issue" prize is awarded to a poem from each issue of *Frogpond* through a gift from the Museum of Haiku Literature, located in Tokyo. The Haiku Society of America also sponsors The Harold G. Henderson Haiku Award Contest, the Gerald Brady Senryu Award Contest, the Bernard Lionel Einbond Memorial Renku Contest, the Nicholas A. Virgilio Memorial Haiku Competition for High School Students, the Mildred Kanterman Merit Book Awards for outstanding books in the haiku field. Guidelines available on Web site.

Advice "Submissions to *Frogpond* are accepted from both members and nonmembers, although familiarity with the journal will aid writers in discovering what it publishes."

$ FUGUE

200 Brink Hall, University of Idaho, P.O. Box 441102, Moscow ID 83844. E-mail: fugue@uidaho.edu. Web site: www.uidaho.edu/fugue. Established 1990. **Contact:** Laura Powers, poetry editor.

Magazine Needs *Fugue*, published semiannually in summer and winter, is a literary magazine of the University of Idaho. "There are no limits on type of poetry; however, we are not interested in trite or quaint verse." Has published poetry by Sonia Sanchez, Simon Perchik, Denise Duhamel, Dean Young, and W.S. Merwin. *Fugue* is up to 200 pages, perfect-bound. Receives about 400 poems/semester, accepts only 15-20 poems/issue. Press run is 250. There is also an online version. Sample: $8.

How to Submit Submit 3-5 poems at a time (10 pages maximum). No previously published poems. Considers simultaneous submissions "with the explicit provision that the writer inform us immediately if the work is accepted for publication elsewhere." No e-mail submissions. Cover letter is required. "Include name, address, e-mail, phone number, poem titles, and a brief bio citing any awards/publications. Submissions without a #10 SASE will not be considered." Reads submissions September 1-May 1 only. Time between acceptance and publication is up to 1 year. "Submissions are reviewed by staff members and chosen with consensus by the editorial board. No major changes are made to a manuscript without authorial approval." Publishes theme issues. Guidelines available for SASE or on Web site. Responds in up to 5 months. Pays at least 1 contributor's copy plus an honorarium (up to $25 as funds allow). Acquires first North American serial rights.

Contest/Award Offerings "For information regarding our spring poetry contest, please visit our Web site."

Advice "We are looking for poetry that takes risks while demonstrating powerful voice and careful attention to language and craft. Proper manuscript format and submission etiquette are expected; submissions without proper SASE will not be read or held on file."

FULCRUM: AN ANNUAL OF POETRY AND AESTHETICS

421 Huron Ave., Cambridge MA 02138. (617)864-7874. E-mail: editor@fulcrumpoetry.com. Web site: www.fulcrumpoetry.com. Established 2002. **Contact:** Philip Nikolayev, Katia Kapovich, editors. Member: CLMP.

Magazine Needs *Fulcrum: an annual of poetry and aesthetics* is "a one-of-a-kind international serial anthology of poetry and criticism, with a philosophical bent." Wants "poetry that exhibits a strong aesthetic compulsion and comes from a deep place. All forms and styles; no 'schools.' " Does not want "gibberish, 'metapoetry' (pensive poems about poems) or 'based-on' poetry." Has published poetry by Ben Mazer, Stephen Sturgeon, Jeet Thayil, Joe Green, and Vivek Narayanan. *Fulcrum* is 500 pages, digest-sized, professionally printed, flat-spined, with glossy cover with b&w art. Accepts about .5% of poems submitted. Press run is 2,000. Single copy: (postpaid domestic) $17 for individuals, $42 for libraries. Make checks payable to *Fulcrum* or subscribe through Web site.

How to Submit No e-mail or disk submissions. Cover letter is preferred. Include SASE (SAE with IRCs for international submissions) for reply only (manuscripts cannot be returned). Reads submissions June-August only. Time between acceptance and publication is 6-8 months. "All poems and essays are accepted or rejected by the editors. Read *Fulcrum* before submitting!" Seldom comments on rejected poems. Guidelines available on Web site. Responds in 1-6 months. Always sends pre-publication galleys. Pays 1 contributor's copy. Acquires first world rights.

Advice "There are no 'schools'—life is a vacation!"

FULLOSIA PRESS

The Rockaway Park Philosophical Society, P.O. Box 280, Ronkonkoma NY 11779. E-mail: deanofRP PS@aol.com. Web site: http://rpps_fullosia_press.tripod.com. Established 1971. **Contact:** jd collins.

Magazine Needs *Fullosia Press*, published monthly online, presents news, information, satire, and right/conservative perspective. Wants any style of poetry. "If you have something to say, say it. We consider many different points of view." Does not want "anti-American, anti-Christian." Considers poetry by children with parental consent. Has published poetry by Awesome David Lawrence, Peter Vetrano, Michael Levy, Dr. Kelley White, and Taylor Graham. Receives about 50 poems/ year, accepts about 40%. Single copy: $15 and SASE (free online); subscription: $25/year (free online). Make checks payable to RPPS-Fullosia Press.

How to Submit Accepts e-mail (pasted into body of message) and disk submissions. "E-mail preferred. Final submission by disk or e-mail only." Cover letter is required. Reads submissions when received. Submit seasonal poems 1 month in advance. Time between acceptance and publication varies. "I review all poems: 1) Do they say something?; 2) Is there some thought behind it?; 3) Is it more than words strung together?" Always comments on rejected poems. Publishes theme issues. Guidelines available for SASE, by e-mail, or on Web site. Responds in 1 month. Acquires one-time rights. Reviews books/chapbooks of poetry and other magazines/journals. Send materials for review consideration to RPPS-Fullosia Press.

Advice "Say what you have in mind without tripping over your own symbolism. We like poems that are clear, concise, to the point; American traditional heroes; Arthurian legend; American states. Everybody sings about Texas; has anyone written a poem to New Jersey?"

▣ ◖ THE FURNACE REVIEW

E-mail: submissions@thefurnacereview.com. Web site: www.thefurnacereview.com. Established 2004. **Contact:** Ciara LaVelle, editor.

Magazine Needs *The Furnace Review*, published quarterly online, is "dedicated to new writers and unique or groundbreaking work." Wants "all forms, from haiku to sonnets to free verse to totally experimental. Just make it interesting." Has published poetry by Sarah Lynn Knowles, David Gruber, Curtis Evans, and Richard Matthes. Receives about 500 pieces/year, accepts about 30.

How to Submit Submit up to 5 poems at a time. Lines/poem: 75 maximum. Considers simultaneous submissions; no previously published poems. Accepts e-mail submissions; no disk submissions. Cover letter is preferred. "Include a short biography with all submissions." Reads submissions year round. Time between acceptance and publication is 3 months. Poems are circulated to an editorial board. Sometimes comments on rejected poems. Guidelines available on Web site. Responds in 4 months. Acquires first North American serial rights.

◖ GARGOYLE MAGAZINE

Paycock Press, 3819 N. 13th St., Arlington VA 22201. (202)234-3287. E-mail: gargoyle@gargoylemagazine.com. Web site: www.gargoylemagazine.com. Established 1976. **Contact:** Richard Peabody and Lucinda Ebersole, co-editors.

Magazine Needs *Gargoyle Magazine*, published annually, has always been a scallywag magazine, a maverick magazine, a bit too academic for the underground and way too underground for the academics. We generally run short, one-page poems. We like wit, imagery, killer lines." Has published poetry by Naomi Ayala, Nicole Blackman, Kate Braverman, Laura Chester, Thaisa Frank, Thylias Moss, Elizabeth Swados, and Paul West. *Gargoyle* is about 500 pages, digest-sized, offset-printed, perfect-bound, with color cover, includes ads. Accepts about 10% of the poems received each year. Press run is 2,000. Subscription: $30 for 2 issues (individuals); $40 (institutions). Sample: $10.

How to Submit Submit 5 poems at a time. Considers simultaneous submissions. Accepts e-mail submissions (preferred; pasted into body of message). Reads submissions "all summer—June, July, and August." Time between acceptance and publication is 12 months. "The 2 editors make some concessions but generally concur." Often comments on rejected poems. Responds in 3 months. Always sends prepublication galleys. Pays 1 contributor's copy and offers 50% discount on additional copies. Acquires first rights.

Additional Information Paycock Press has published 22 additional titles since 1976 and is **not currently seeking mss.**

◖ GECKO

E-mail: geckogalpoet@hotmail.com. Established 1998. **Contact:** Rebecca Lu Kiernan, editor.

• "Due to the overwhelming response of *Poet's Market* readers and personal projects of the editor, we are currently closed to unsolicited manuscripts. We hope to change this in the future when an assistant will assume some of the editor's duties."

◖ ◉ GENIE (Specialized: humorous poetry)

1753 Fisher Ridge, Horse Cave KY 42749. Established 2005. **Contact:** David Rogers, editor.

Magazine Needs *Genie*, published annually in August, features humorous poetry, "although good poems that are not funny are considered as well." Wants "poems that are humorous, satirical, or erotic. Short (200-300 words) political/social commentary. The editor has a bias toward liberal causes but will seriously consider any well-written satirical piece as long as it is genuinely funny. Feel free to blur the distinction between poetry and prose." Does not want "pornography (but erotica is good—know the difference) or anything that encourages violence or hate." Considers poetry by children and teens. "Don't care much about the age of the writer, as long as it's good." Has published poetry by Merlin Freehand, George Held, Alan Catlin, and Dave Church. *Genie* is 15 or more pages ("depending on the number of good submissions that come in"), 4¼×5½, laser-printed, saddle-stapled or perfect-bound, with cardstock cover with color printing. Receives about 150 poems/year, accepts about 10%. Press run is 100; 50 distributed free to contributors or "anyone who's interested.'' Single copy: $2; subscription: $6. Make checks payable to David Rogers.

How to Submit Submit up to 5 poems at a time. Lines/poem: 100. Considers previously published poems and simultaneous submissions (''but PLEASE do not withdraw submitted poems''). No disk submissions. Cover letter is required. Reads submissions year round. Time between acceptance and publication is up to 1 year. Never comments on rejected poems. Guidelines available in magazine. Responds in up to 6 months. Pays 1 or more contributor's copies. Acquires one-time rights. Reviews books/chapbooks of poetry in 100 words. Send materials for review consideration to David Rogers.

Advice ''Be funny. Watch Comedy Central and read Hal Sirowitz and Billy Collins (see his 'Another Reason Why I Don't Keep a Gun in the House')—not to imitate, but for inspiration. A good humorous poem often resembles a bit from a stand-up comedy act in surprising ways.''

☑ GEORGETOWN REVIEW

Box 227, 400 E. College St., Georgetown KY 40324. (502)863-8308. Fax: (502)868-8888. E-mail: gtownreview@georgetowncollege.edu. Web site: http://georgetownreview.georgetowncollege.edu. Established 1993. **Contact:** Steven Carter, editor. Member: CLMP.

Magazine Needs *Georgetown Review*, published annually in May, is a literary journal of poetry, fiction, and creative nonfiction. ''We have no specific guidelines concerning form or content of poetry, but are always eager to see poetry that is insightful, rooted in reality, and human.'' Does not want ''work that is merely sentimental, political, or inspirational.'' Considers poetry by children and teens. Has published poetry by Denise Duhamel, X.J. Kennedy, William Greenway, Fred Chappell, John Tagliabue, and Frederick Smock. *Georgetown Review* is 192 pages, digest-sized, offset-printed, perfect-bound, with 60 lb. glossy 4-color cover with art/graphics, includes ads. Receives about 1,000 poems/year, accepts about 50-60. Press run is 1,000. Single copy: $5; subscription: $5. Make checks payable to *Georgetown Review*.

How to Submit Submit 1-10 poems at a time. Lines/poem: open. Considers simultaneous submissions; no previously published poems. No fax, e-mail, or disk submissions. Cover letter is preferred. ''In cover letter, please include short bio and a list of publications. Also, must include SASE for reply.'' Reads submissions September 1-March 15. Submit seasonal poems 1 year in advance. Time between acceptance and publication is 1-2 months. Poems are circulated to an editorial board. ''The first reader passes the poem along to the poetry editor, and then a final decision is made by the poetry editor and the head editor.'' Seldom comments on rejected poems. Guidelines available for SASE, by e-mail, or on Web site. Responds in 1-3 months. Pays 2 contributor's copies. Acquires first North American serial rights. Reviews books/chapbooks of poetry in 1,000 words, multi-book format.

Contest/Award Offerings Sponsors annual contest, offering $1,000 prize and publication; runners-up also receive publication. Guidelines available for SASE, by e-mail, or on Web site. **Entry fee:** $10/poem, $5 for each additional poem.

$☑ THE GEORGIA REVIEW

The University of Georgia, 012 Gilbert Hall, Athens GA 30602-9009. (706)542-3481. E-mail: garev@uga.edu. Web site: www.uga.edu/garev. Established 1947. **Contact:** The Editors.

Magazine Needs *The Georgia Review*, published quarterly, seeks ''the very best work we can find, whether by Nobel laureates and Pulitzer Prize-winners or by little-known (or even previously unpublished) writers. All manuscripts receive serious, careful attention. We have featured first-ever publications by many new voices over the years, but encourage all potential contributors to become familiar with past offerings before submitting.'' Has published poetry by Rita Dove, Stephen Dunn, Margaret Gibson, Albert Goldbarth, and Lola Haskins. *The Georgia Review* is 200-232 pages, 7×10, professionally printed, flat-spined, with glossy card cover. Publishes 60-70 poems/year, less than .5% of those received. Press run is 4,500. Subscription: $30/year. Sample: $8.

How to Submit Submit 3-5 poems at a time. No simultaneous submissions. Reads year-round, but submissions postmarked May 15-August 15 will be returned unread. Guidelines available for SASE or on Web site. Responds in 2-3 months. Always sends prepublication galleys. Pays $3/line, one-year subscription, and 1 contributor's copy. Acquires first North American serial rights. Reviews books of poetry. ''Our poetry reviews range from 500-word 'Book Briefs' on single volumes to 5,000-word essay reviews on multiple volumes.''

Advice "Needless to say, competition is extremely tough. All styles and forms are welcome, but response times can be slower during peak periods in the fall and late spring."

◌ GERONIMO REVIEW

E-mail: geronimoreview@att.net. Web site: www.sanjeronimofnd.org. Established 1998. Contact: S. Bass, editor. Secretary: g. bassetti.

Magazine Needs *geronimo review*, published online, will "publish on its Web site virtually everything submitted. Submit whatever strikes your fancy. Literally. Anything. Overt pornography, hate speech, etc., taken under editorial advisement." Has 2 submission categories: Open (these submissions are graded "mercilessly" by both editors and readers) and Amateur ("graded on an appropriate scale"). Wants "politics and political satire. Anything of unusual excellence, especially the short lyric." Has published poetry by Mark C. Peery, dada rambass, zeninubasho, geronimo bassetti, Élan B. Yergmoul, "and innumerable others."

How to Submit Submit 3 poems at a time. Lines/poem: 100 maximum (or the length demanded by the poem). Considers simultaneous submissions; no previously published poems. Accepts submissions by e-mail only (as Word attachment or pasted into body of message). Submissions in html will appear with poet's formatting. Reads submissions all year. Time between acceptance and publication is 2 weeks. Guidelines available on Web site. Responds in 3 weeks ("maybe"). Acquires all rights; returns to poet "on request." Send materials for review consideration.

Additional Information MaoMao Press will publish essays on and reviews of poetry in the future. **"Not presently accepting book submissions—watch our Web site.** *GR* will soon allow poets to post their work directly online, and will allow readers to comment on and vote, allowing superior material to float to the top." Artists will also be encouraged to post their art. Poets who have published a book may, on request, get their own page on the site.

Also Offers Plans anthology of *geronimo review* material.

Advice "Don't be Susan Wheeler. Be in the tradition of Yeats, Frost, Carroll, Stevens, and be really original and inspire strong reactions."

◧ ◎ GERTRUDE (Specialized: gay, lesbian, bisexual, transgendered, queer-identified & allied)

P.O. Box 83948, Portland OR 97283. E-mail: poetry@gertrudepress.org. Web site: www.gertrudepress.org. Established 1998. **Contact:** Steve Rydman, poetry editor. Founding Editor: Eric Delehoy.

Magazine Needs *Gertrude*, published semiannually, is the literary publication of Gertrude Press (see separate listing in Books/Chapbooks), "a nonprofit 501(c)(3) organization showcasing and developing the creative talents of lesbian, gay, bisexual, trans, queer-identified, and allied individuals." Has published poetry by Judith Barrington, Deanna Kern Ludwin, Casey Charles, Michael Montlack, Megan Kruse, and Noah Tysick. *Gertrude* is 64-112 pages, digest-sized, offset-printed, perfect-bound, with glossy 4-color cardstock cover with art. Receives about 500 poems/year, accepts about 6-8%. Press run is 300; 50 distributed free. Single copy: $8.25; subscription: $15/year, $27 for 2 years. Sample: $6.25. Make checks payable to Gertrude Press.

How to Submit Submit 6 poems at a time. Lines/poem: open. Considers simultaneous submissions; no previously published poems. Accepts e-mail submissions via the Web site only; no disk submissions. Cover letter is preferred. Include short bio and SASE. Reads submissions year round. Time between acceptance and publication is 3-6 months. Poems are circulated to an editorial board. Sometimes comments on rejected poems. Guidelines available in magazine, by e-mail, or on Web site. Responds in 3 months. Sometimes sends prepublication galleys. Pays 1 contributor's copy plus discount on additional copies/subscriptions. Acquires one-time rights. Rights revert to poets upon publication.

Contest/Award Offerings The Gertrude Press Poetry Chapbook Contest (see separate listing in Contests & Awards).

Advice "*Gertrude* publishes the best poetry that is received. While we are a queer publication, poetry need not be lesbigay-specific, and publication is open to all poets regardless of background."

Magazines/Journals

$ ☑ THE GETTYSBURG REVIEW

Gettysburg College, Gettysburg PA 17325. (717)337-6770. Fax: (717)337-6775. E-mail: mdrew@gett ysburg.edu. Web site: www.gettysburgreview.com. Established 1988. **Contact:** Peter Stitt, editor.

• Work appearing in *The Gettysburg Review* has been included frequently in *The Best American Poetry* and *The Pushcart Prize*. Editor Peter Stitt won the first PEN/Nora Magid Award for Editorial Excellence.

Magazine Needs *The Gettysburg Review*, published quarterly, considers "well-written poems of all kinds." Has published poetry by Rita Dove, Beckian Fritz Goldberg, Charles Wright, Michelle Boisseau, Mark Doty, and Charles Simic. Accepts 1-2% of submissions received. Press run is 4,500. Subscription: $24/year. Sample: $7.

How to Submit Submit 3-5 poems at a time. Considers simultaneous submissions; no previously published poems. Cover letter is preferred. Include SASE. Reads submissions September-May only. Occasionally publishes theme issues. "Response time can be slow during heavy submission periods, especially in the late fall." Pays $2.50/line, one-year subscription, and 1 contributor's copy. Essay-reviews are featured in most issues. Send materials for review consideration.

▣ ☑ GHOTI MAGAZINE

E-mail: editors@ghotimag.com. Web site: www.ghotimag.com. Established 2005. **Contact:** CL Bledsoe, Donna Epler, and Jillian Meyer, editors.

Magazine Needs *Ghoti Magazine*, published quarterly online, prints "fiction, nonfiction, poetry, book reviews, and interviews with up-and-coming writers or those who have been ignored by the mainstream. *Ghoti Magazine* also publishes recipes by writers." Wants "fiction, poetry, nonfiction, and reviews of recent books. We are open to experimental and traditional styles, but our main criterion is quality. Is this piece of writing going to stay with a reader? In five years, will it be worth reading again? If so, *Ghoti Magazine* wants it." Does not want "self-absorbed work. If it's boring to you, it's boring to us." Has published poetry by Simon Perchik, Lyn Lifshin, Arlene Ang, Jo McDougall, Ace Boggess, and Barry Ballard. Receives about 1,000 poems/year, accepts about 40-50.

How to Submit Submit 3-5 poems at a time. Lines/poem: "there is no line limit, but longer poems must be able to sustain their length." Considers simultaneous submissions; no previously published poems. Accepts e-mail submissions only (pasted into body of message; "if the poems have complicated formatting, please paste them into the body of the e-mail and attach them to the e-mail as well"). Cover letter is preferred. Reads submissions year round. Submit seasonal poems 3 months in advance. Time between acceptance and publication is 3-6 months. "We have 3 editors. Generally at least 2 editors read each submission." Often comments on rejected poems. Guidelines available on Web site. Responds in 2 months. Acquires electronic rights. Rights revert to poet upon publication. Reviews books/chapbooks of poetry in 250-500 words, single-book format. "For review materials, contact the editors."

Advice "We are open to the prosaic, performance-oriented poetry that seems to mainly be written today, but we would much prefer to see poetry that experiments with language and sound, instead of just stating a case. Prosody is not a bad thing. We rarely publish political rants or anything that seems to be beating us over the heads with meaning. We judge each submission based on quality of the work, regardless of how many credits the author has."

▣ ☑ GOOD FOOT MAGAZINE

P.O. Box 681, Murray Hill Station, New York NY 10156. E-mail: info@goodfootmagazine.com. Web site: www.goodfootmagazine.com. Established 2000. **Contact:** Amanda Lea Johnson and Carmine Simmons, editors.

Magazine Needs *Good Foot Magazine* "seeks vibrant contemporary poetry that is compelling and utterly readable. We invite a wide cross-section of work without restriction in form, style, or subject." Has published poetry by Doug Ramspeck, Matthea Harvey, David Trinidad, Susanna Childress, Tony Tost, and Simon Perchik. *Good Foot* is about 120 pages, 7×8½, professionally offset-printed, perfect-bound, with color matte card cover. Receives about 1,200 poems/year. Single copy: $8; subscription: $14. Make checks payable to *Good Foot Magazine* or order at Web site via PayPal.

How to Submit Submit no more than 3 poems at a time. Considers simultaneous submissions ("please contact us by e-mail if work is accepted elsewhere"); absolutely no previously published poems. No e-mail submissions. "Name and contact information should appear on every sheet of paper you submit. Include brief bio in cover letter. Please help us by following these guidelines." All responses via e-mail; manuscripts will not be returned. Reads submissions February 1-October 31. Submissions received during November, December, and January will be returned unread. Time between acceptance and publication "averages" 6 months. "All submissions are read by the editors." Seldom comments on rejected poems. Responds in up to 6 months. Pays 1 contributor's copy. Acquires first North American serial rights. Check Web site for more information and announcement of 2008 contest.

✪ ⇄ $⃠ GRAIN

P.O. Box 67, Saskatoon SK S7K 3K1 Canada. (306)244-2828. Fax: (306)244-0255. E-mail: grainmag @sasktel.net. (inquiries only). Web site: www.grainmagazine.ca. Established 1973. **Contact:** Gerry Hill, poetry editor.
Magazine Needs *Grain*, published quarterly, "strives for artistic excellence." Wants "poetry that is well-crafted, imaginatively stimulating, distinctly original." Has published poetry by Lorna Crozier, Don Domanski, Cornelia Haeussler, Patrick Lane, Karen Solie, and Monty Reid. *Grain* is 128-144 pages, digest-sized, professionally printed. Press run is 1,400. Receives about 2,400 submissions/year. Subscription: $29.95 CAD/year, $46 CAD for 2 years. Sample: $13 CAD. (See Web site for U.S. and foreign postage fees.)
How to Submit Submit up to 8 poems at a time. No previously published poems or simultaneous submissions. No fax or e-mail submissions; postal submissions only. Cover letter is required. "Poems should be typed, single-spaced, on $8^1/2 \times 11$ paper, 1 side only. Indicate the number of poems submitted, and include your address (with postal or ZIP code), phone number, e-mail address, and SASE (or SAE and IRC) for response (if you do not want your submission returned, provide an e-mail address for electronic response; we will recycle your manuscript)." Reads submissions September-May only. "Manuscripts postmarked between June 1 and September 1 will be returned unread." Guidelines available in magazine, for SASE (or SAE and IRC), by fax, e-mail, or on Web site. Responds in 2-4 months. Pays $50-225 CAD (depending on number of pages) and 2 contributor's copies. Acquires first Canadian serial rights only. Copyright remains with the author.
Advice "Only work of the highest literary quality is accepted. Read several back issues."

⃠ THE GREAT AMERICAN POETRY SHOW

The Muse Media, P.O. Box 69506, West Hollywood CA 90069. (323)969-4905. E-mail: info@tgaps.n et. Web site: www.tgaps.net. Established 2002. **Contact:** Larry Ziman, editor/publisher.
Magazine Needs *The Great American Poetry Show*, published about every 3 years, is an $8^1/2 \times 11$ hardcover serial poetry anthology. Wants poems on any subject, in any style, of any length. Has published poetry by Sara Berkeley, Alan Britt, Hector E. Estrada, Heidi Nye, Tom Smith, and Sarah Brown Weitzman. *The Great American Poetry Show* is 150 pages, sheet-fed offset-printed, perfect-bound, with cloth cover with art/graphics. "For our first volume, we read about 8,000 poems from about 1,400 poets and accepted only 113 poems from 83 poets." Press run is 1,000. Single copy: $35 (print), $7.50 (e-book, download only).
How to Submit Submit any number of poems at a time. Considers previously published poems and simultaneous submissions. Accepts e-mail submissions (as attachment). Cover letter is optional. Include SASE. "If we reject a submission of your work, please send us another group to go through. We have 3 editors who can handle a lot of submissions." Responds in 1-3 months ("depends on how busy we are"). Pays 1 contributor's copy.
Also Offers "Please visit our message boards where anyone can have us post poetry news, reviews, essays, articles, and recommended books."
Advice "We are very hard to please. But we are very easy to submit to. Do not get discouraged by rejections from us. Just keep sending us more poems to consider. Hopefully, we will find something we want to publish in your submissions. If we reject everything you send us, still do not get discouraged. Send your poems to other publishers until you find one who wants to publish your poetry."

▣ ☑ GREEN HILLS LITERARY LANTERN

McClain Hall, Truman State University, Kirksville MO 63501. (660)785-4513. E-mail: jbeneven@tru
man.edu. Web site: http://ll.truman.edu/ghllweb/. **Contact:** Joe Benevento, poetry editor.

Magazine Needs *Green Hills Literary Lantern*, published annually online in June, is "an open-access journal of short fiction and poetry of exceptional quality." Wants "the best poetry, in any style, preferably understandable. There are no restrictions on subject matter. Both free and formal verse forms are fine, though we publish more free verse overall." Does not want "haiku, limericks, or anything over 2 pages. Pornography and gratuitous violence will not be accepted. Obscurity for its own sake is also frowned upon." Has published poetry by Jim Thomas, Phillip Dacey, Susan Terris, Louis Philips, Francine Tolf, and Julie Lechevsky. Sample: $7 (back issue).

How to Submit Submit 3-7 poems at a time. Considers simultaneous submissions, "but not preferred"; no previously published poems. No e-mail submissions. Cover letter is preferred. Include list of publication credits. Type poems one/page. Often comments on rejected poems. Guidelines available for SASE, by e-mail, or on Web site. Responds within 4 months. Always sends prepublication galleys. Pays 2 contributor's copies. Acquires one-time rights.

Advice "Read the best poetry and be willing to learn from what you encounter. A genuine attempt is made to publish the best poems available, no matter who the writer. First-time poets, well-established poets, and those in between, all can and have found a place in the *Green Hills Literary Lantern*. We try to supply feedback, particularly to those we seek to encourage."

☑ GREEN MOUNTAINS REVIEW

Johnson State College, Johnson VT 05656. (802)635-1350. Fax: (802)635-1210. E-mail: gmr@jsc.e
du. Web site: http://greenmountainsreview.jsc.vsc.edu. Established 1975. **Contact:** Neil Shepard, poetry editor.

● Poetry published in *Green Mountains Review* has been included in *The Best American Poetry* and *The Pushcart Prize* anthologies.

Magazine Needs *Green Mountains Review*, published twice/year, includes poetry (and other writing) by well-known authors and promising newcomers. Has published poetry by Carol Frost, Sharon Olds, Carl Phillips, David St. John, and David Wojahn. *Green Mountains Review* is 150-200 pages, digest-sized, flat-spined. Receives about 5,000 submissions/year, publishes 30 authors. Press run is 1,800. Single copy: $9.50; subscription: $15/year. Sample: $7 (back issue).

How to Submit Submit no more than 5 poems at a time. Considers simultaneous submissions. No e-mail submissions. Reads submissions September 1-March 1 only. Sometimes comments rejected poems. Publishes theme issues. Guidelines available for SASE. Responds in up to 6 months. Pays 2 contributor's copies plus one-year subscription. Acquires first North American serial rights. Send materials for review consideration.

☑ THE GREENSBORO REVIEW

MFA Writing Program, 3302 Hall for Humanities and Research Administration, University of North Carolina at Greensboro, P.O. Box 26170, Greensboro NC 27402. (336)334-5459. E-mail: anseay@un
cg.edu. Web site: www.greensbororeview.org. Established 1966. **Contact:** Jim Clark, editor.

● Work published in *The Greensboro Review* has been consistently anthologized or cited in *Best American Short Stories*, *New Stories from the South*, *The Pushcart Prize*, and *Prize Stories: The O. Henry Awards*.

Magazine Needs *The Greensboro Review*, published twice/year, showcases well-made verse in all styles and forms, though shorter poems (under 50 lines) are preferred. Has published poetry by Stephen Dobyns, Natasha Trethewey, Claudia Emerson, Thomas Lux, Stanley Plumly, and Alan Shapiro. *The Greensboro Review* is 144 pages, digest-sized, professionally printed, flat-spined, with colored matte cover. Subscription: $10/year, $25 for 3 years. Sample: $5.

How to Submit Submit no more than 5 poems at a time. Lines/poem: under 50 lines preferred. No previously published poems or simultaneous submissions. No fax or e-mail submissions. Cover letter is preferred. Include number of poems submitted. Provide SASE for reply; sufficient postage for return. Reads submissions according to the following deadlines: mss must arrive by September 15 to be considered for the Spring issue (acceptances in December), or February 15 to be considered for the Fall issue (acceptances in May). "Manuscripts arriving after those dates will be held for consideration for the next issue." Guidelines available in magazine, for SASE, or on Web site. Responds in 4 months. Always sends prepublication galleys. Pays 3 contributor's copies. Acquires first North American serial rights.

Advice "We want to see the best being written regardless of theme, subject, or style."

N $⊠ THE GROVE REVIEW

1631 NE Broadway, PMB #137, Portland OR 97232.Web site: www.thegrovereview.org. Established 2004. **Contact:** Jess Dolan, poetry editor.

Magazine Needs *The Grove Review*, published semiannually, features the work of poets, fiction writers, and visual artists. Wants all styles and forms except haiku. Has published poetry by Ursula K. Le Guin, David Biespiel, Michael Collier, Tess Gallagher. *The Grove Review* is 136 pages in a 6×9format, one-color interior printing on high quality stock, perfect-bound, with full color cover with matte finish, includes ads. Receives about 600 poems/year, accepts about 10%. Press run is 1500. Single copy: $11; subscription: $20. Make checks payable to *The Grove Review*.

How to Submit Submit no more than 5 poems at a time. Considers simultaneous submissions No fax, e-mail, or disk submissions. Cover letter is preferred. Include SASE. Reads submissions year round. Submit seasonal poems 6 months in advance. Time between acceptance and publication is 6 months. Poems are circulated to an editorial board. Sometimes comments on rejected poems. Sometimes publishes theme issues. Upcoming themes and guidelines available on Web site. Responds in 2-4 months, sometimes sooner. Pays $50 and 2 contributor's copies. Acquires first North American serial rights, electronic rights for use on Web site, and other rights for use in marketing and PR materials. Rights revert to poets upon publication.

$⊠ GULF COAST: A JOURNAL OF LITERATURE AND FINE ARTS

Dept. of English, University of Houston, Houston TX 77204-3013. (713)743-3223. Web site: www.gulfcoastmag.org. Established 1986. **Contact:** Darin Ciccotelli, managing editor; Nicole Zaza, associate editor; Paul Otremba, Brian Russell, Kent Shaw, poetry editors.

Magazine Needs *Gulf Coast: A Journal of Literature and Fine Arts*, published twice/year in April and October, includes poetry, fiction, essays, interviews, and color reproductions of work by artists from across the nation. While the journal features work by a number of established poets, editors are also interested in "providing a forum for new and emerging writers who are producing well-crafted work that takes risks." Has published poetry by Anne Carson, Terrance Hayes, Srikanth Reddy, Karen Volkman, Susan Wheeler, and Dean Young. *Gulf Coast* is 230 pages, 7×9, offset-printed, perfect-bound. Single copy: $8; subscription: $14/year, $26 for 2 years. Sample: $7.

How to Submit Submit up to 5 poems at a time. Considers simultaneous submissions with notification; no previously published poems. Cover letter is required. List previous publications "if any" and include a brief bio. Reads submissions September-April. Guidelines available for SASE or on Web site. Responds within 6 months. Pays $50/poem and 2 contributor's copies. Returns all rights (except electronic) upon publication.

Contest/Award Offerings Sponsors an annual poetry contest, awarding $1,000 and publication. **Entry fee:** $20 (includes one-year subscription). Make checks payable to *Gulf Coast*. Guidelines available on Web site.

⊠ HAIGHT ASHBURY LITERARY JOURNAL (Specialized: thematic issues)

558 Joost Ave., San Francisco CA 94127. (415)584-8264. E-mail: poetship@comcast.net. (inquiries only). Established 1979-1980. **Contact:** Indigo Hotchkiss, Alice Rogoff, Gail Mitchell, and Cesar Love, editors.

Magazine Needs *Haight Ashbury Literary Journal*, published 1-2 times/year, is a newsprint tabloid that uses "all forms [of poetry]. Subject matter sometimes political, but open to all subjects. Poems of background—prison, minority experience—often published, as well as poems of protest. Few rhymes." Has published poetry by Dan O'Connell, Diane Frank, Dancing Bear, Lee Herrick, Al Young, and Laura Beausoleil. *Haight Ashbury* is 16 pages, includes ads. Press run is 2,500. Subscription: $16 for 4 issues; $40 for a lifetime subscription (all future and 9 back issues). Sample: $3.

How to Submit Submit up to 6 poems at a time. No e-mail submissions; postal submissions only. "Please type 1 poem to a page, put name and address on every page, and include SASE. No bio." Always publishes theme issues (each issue changes its theme and emphasis). Guidelines available for SASE. Responds in 4 months. Pays 3 contributor's copies, plus small monetary amount to featured writers. Rights revert to author.

Additional Information An anthology of past issues, *This Far Together*, is available for $15.

Advice "Do not send work that is longer than our magazine!"

HANDSHAKE (Specialized: science fiction; fantasy; horror)

5 Cross Farm, Station Rd. N., Fearnhead, Warrington, Cheshire WA2 0QG England. Established 1992. **Contact:** J.F. Haines.

Magazine Needs *Handshake*, published irregularly, "is a newsletter for science fiction poets." Wants "science fiction/fantasy poetry of all styles. Prefer short poems." Does not want "epics or foul language." Has published poetry by Cardinal Cox, Neil K. Henderson, Andrew Dallington, Peter Day, Steve Sneyd, John Light, and Joanne Tolson. *Handshake* is 1 sheet of A4 paper, photocopied, includes ads. "It has evolved into being 1 side of news and information and 1 side of poetry." Receives about 50 poems/year, accepts up to 50%. Print run 100, 5 sent to official archives). Subscription: SAE with IRC. Sample: SAE with IRC.

How to Submit Submit 2-3 poems. No previously published poems or simultaneous submissions. Cover letter is preferred. Poems must be typed and camera-ready. Time between acceptance and publication varies. Editor selects "whatever takes my fancy and is of suitable length." Seldom comments on rejected poems. Occasionally publishes theme issues. Responds ASAP. Pays 1 contributor's copy. Acquires first rights. Reviews books/chapbooks of poetry or other magazines/journals of very short length. Send material for review consideration. Time-sensitive material may not be accepted unless received well in advance.

Also Offers *Handshake* is also the newsletter for The Eight Hand Gang, an organization for British science fiction poets established in 1991. Currently has 100 members. Information about the organization available in *Handshake*.

$ HANGING LOOSE

Hanging Loose Press, 231 Wyckoff St., Brooklyn NY 11217. Web site: www.hangingloosepress.com. Established 1966. **Contact:** Robert Hershon, Dick Lourie, and Mark Pawlak, poetry editors.

Magazine Needs *Hanging Loose*, published in April and October, "concentrates on the work of new writers." Wants "excellent, energetic" poems. Considers poetry by teens ("one section contains poems by high-school-age poets"). Has published poetry by Sherman Alexie, Paul Violi, Donna Brook, Kimiko Hahn, Harvey Shapiro, and Ha Jin. *Hanging Loose* is 120 pages, offset-printed on heavy stock, flat-spined, with 4-color glossy card cover. Sample: $11.

How to Submit Submit 4-6 poems at a time. No simultaneous submissions. "Would-be contributors should read the magazine first." Responds in 3 months. Pays small fee and 2 contributor's copies.

Additional Information Hanging Loose Press does not consider unsolicited book mss or artwork.

HARP-STRINGS POETRY JOURNAL (Specialized: traditional forms of poetry)

Verdure Publications, P.O. Box 640387, Beverly Hills FL 34464-0387. E-mail: verdure@tampabay.rr. com. Established 1989. **Contact:** Madelyn Eastlund, editor.

Magazine Needs *Harp-Strings Poetry Journal*, published quarterly, features traditional forms of poetry. Wants "narratives, lyrics, prose poems, haibun, ballads, sestinas, and other traditional forms." Does not want "anything 'dashed off' or trite; no broken prose masquerading as poetry." Has published poetry by Ruth Harrison, Daniel Blackston, Howard F. Stein, Robert Cooperman, and Barry Ballard. *Harp-Strings* is 24-28 pages, digest-sized, professionally printed on quality colored matte stock, saddle-stapled, with matte card cover. Accepts about 1% of poems received. Press run is 200. Subscription: $14. Sample: $4.00.

How to Submit Submit 3-5 poems at a time. Lines/poem: 14 minimum, 80 maximum. "Best chance with poems to 40 lines; over 40 really need to make each word in each line count - no padding!" Considers previously published poems **by invitation only**; no simultaneous submissions. Accepts e-mail submissions (pasted into body of message or as Word attachment); no disk submissions. Cover letter is "not necessary, but if enclosed should contain information on poet or poems. *Harp-Strings* does use brief contributor notes. Always include a SASE—lately poets seem to forget." Reads submissions in February, May, August, and November only. Responds at the end of each reading period. Accepted poems will appear in the next issue being planned following each reading period. Seldom comments on rejected poems. "A poem might not be right for us, but right for another publication. Rejection does not necessarily imply poem needs revisions." Pays 1 contributor's copy. Acquires one-time rights.

Contest/Award Offerings Sponsors the annual Edna St. Vincent Millay "Ballad of the Harp Weaver" Award (see separate listing in Contests & Awards). "We may also sponsor a special contest during each quarter." Contest guidelines available for SASE.

Advice "Some things I've noticed in the past year or 1 are the number of submissions with no SASE, submissions stuffed into very small envelopes, lack of return postage on return envelope, failure to put the poet's name on each page submitted...and, evidently, attention not paid to what the magazine lists as 'needs,' because we get haiku, tanka, and other short verse. We also get 8-12 poems submitted with a note that 'this is from my book,' or worse—we get entire manuscripts, especially by e-mail, which we must return because we are not a press. It looks like many poets 'gun shot' their submissions."

◎ ❷ **HARTWORKS (SPECIALIZED: POETRY FOR TEENS; AFRICAN AMERICAN ISSUES)**
D.C. Creative Writing Workshop, 601 Mississippi Ave. SE, Washington DC 20032. (202)445-4280. E-mail: info@dccww.org. Web site: www.dccww.org. Established 2000. **Contact:** Nancy Schwalb, artistic director.

- **Although this journal doesn't accept submissions from the general public, it's included here as an outstanding example of what a literary journal can be (for anyone of any age).**

Magazine Needs *hArtworks* appears 3 times/year. "We publish the poetry of Hart Middle School students (as far as we know, Hart may be the only public middle school in the U.S. with its own poetry magazine) and the writing of guest writers such as Nikki Giovanni, Alan Cheuse, Arnost Lustig, Henry Taylor, Mark Craver, and Cornelius Eady, along with interviews between the kids and the grown-up pros. We also publish work by our writers-in-residence, who teach workshops at Hart, and provide trips to readings, slams, museums, and plays." Wants "vivid, precise, imaginative language that communicates from the heart as well as the head." Does not want "poetry that only 'sounds' good; it also needs to say something meaningful." Has published poetry by Luqman Abdullah, Reginald Conway, Nichell Kee, James Saunders, Monae Smith, and Renita Williams. *hArtworks* is 60 pages, magazine-sized, professionally printed, saddle-stapled, with card cover. Receives about 1,000 poems/year, accepts about 20%. Press run is 500; 100 distributed free to writers, teachers. Single copy: $10; subscription: $25. Make checks payable to D.C. Creative Writing Workshop.

How to Submit "Writers-in-residence solicit most submissions from their classes, and then a committee of student editors makes the final selections. Each year, our second issue is devoted to responses to the Holocaust."

Advice "Read a lot; know something about how other writers approach their craft. Write a lot; build an understanding of yourself as a writer. Don't be so stubborn you settle into the same old poem you perfected in the past. Writing is not some static machine, but a kind of experience, a kind of growing."

❷ **HAWAI'I PACIFIC REVIEW**
1060 Bishop St., Honolulu HI 96813. (808)544-1108. Fax: (808)544-0862. E-mail: pwilson@hpu.edu. Web site: www.hpu.edu. Established 1987. **Contact:** Patrice M. Wilson, editor.

Magazine Needs *Hawai'i Pacific Review*, published annually in August or September by Hawai'i Pacific University, prints "quality poetry, short fiction, and personal essays from writers worldwide. Our journal seeks to promote a world view that celebrates a variety of cultural themes, beliefs, values, and viewpoints. We wish to further the growth of artistic vision and talent by encouraging sophisticated and innovative poetic and narrative techniques." Has published poetry by Wendy

Bishop, Rick Bursky, Virgil Suárez, Bob Hikok, Daniel Gutstein, and Linda Bierds. *Hawai'i Pacific Review* is 80-120 pages, digest-sized, professionally printed on quality paper, perfect-bound, with coated card cover. Receives 800-1,000 poems/year, accepts up to 30-40. Press run is about 500 (100 shelf sales). Single copy: $8.95. Sample: $5.

How to Submit Submit up to 5 poems at a time. Lines/poem: 100 maximum. No previously published poems or simultaneous submissions. No fax or e-mail submissions. Cover letter is required. Include 5-line professional bio including prior publications. SASE required. "One submission per issue. No handwritten manuscripts. Include name on all pages." Reads submissions September 1-December 31 annually. Seldom comments on rejected poems. Guidelines available for SASE, by e-mail, or on Web site. Responds within 3 months. Pays 2 contributor's copies. Acquires first North American serial rights. Rights revert to poet upon publication. "Must acknowledge *Hawai'i Pacific Review* as first publisher."

Advice "We'd like to receive more experimental verse. Good poetry is eye-opening; it investigates the unfamiliar or reveals the spectacular in the ordinary. Good poetry does more than simply express the poet's feelings; it provides both insight and unexpected beauty. Send us your best work!"

ℕ ◌ ◎ HEART: A JOURNAL OF SPIRITUAL WRITING (Specialized: spiritual themes)

% Mary H. Ber, Oro Valley AZ 85737.(520) 544-2832. E-mail: Maryhber@aol.com. Established 2008. **Contact:** Mary H. Ber, editor.

Magazine Needs *Heart: A Journal of Spiritual Writing*, published biannually, "is a non-denominational literary magazine dedicated to the affirmation of the meaning of life and to the qualities of the heart as a means of living life fully. People from many spiritual paths are now pointing at the human heart as the center of personal and global transformation." Wants poems "that promote these affirmations. We are hoping to get writing that mirrors many spiritual traditions and also writing from seekers involved in no specific traditions." Does not want "proselytizing pieces or the conventional kind of 'inspirational writing.' We will not accept writing that exhibits sentimentality or the simplification of complex issues." Considers poetry by children and teens. *Heart* is 36-48 pages, digest-sized, saddle-stitched, with glossy cover containing artwork or photography. Single copy: $6; subscription: $12. Make checks payable to Mary H. Ber.

How to Submit Submit 3 poems at a time. Considers previously published poems and simultaneous submissions. Accepts e-mail submissions (pasted into body of message); no fax or disk submissions. Cover letter is preferred. Reads submissions year round. Submit seasonal poems 6 months in advance. Time between acceptance and publication is 1 year. Poems are circulated to an editorial board. Always comments on rejected poems. Sometimes publishes theme issues. Guidelines available in magazine, for SASE, and by fax. Responds in 1 week. Pays 1 contributor's copy. Acquires one-time rights.

✴ ◉ ⌀ HEELTAP

Pariah Press, 604 Hawthorne Ave. E., St. Paul MN 55101. Established 1985 (Pariah Press), 1997 (*Heeltap*). **Contact:** Richard Houff, editor.

Magazine Needs *Heeltap*, published 2 times/year, features "social issues: people connecting with people, surviving chaos and government brain washing, re-establishing a literate society and avoiding the corporate machine." Wants all kinds of poetry. "We don't believe in censorship." Does not want "early- to mid-19th-century rhyme about mother's lilacs, etc." Has published poetry by Tom Clark, Gerald Locklin, Albert Huffstickler, Theodore Enslin, Charles Plymell, and Marge Piercy. *Heeltap* is 48-64 pages ("varies depending on finances"), digest-sized, laser/high-speed-printed, saddle-stapled, with cardstock cover designed by Mama Rue Day, includes ads. Receives about 10,000 poems/year, accepts about 2-5%. Press run is 500. Single copy: $5; subscription: $18 for 4 issues. Sample: $5 postage paid. Make checks payable to Richard Houff.

How to Submit "We encourage poets to buy samples before submitting. The amount of inappropriate material we receive is stagnating."

Additional Information *Pariah Press publishes only solicited material.*Has published *Cosmology of Madness* by Albert Huffstickler, *Art & Life* and *Henry's Gift & Other Poems* by Gerald Locklin,

The Clam Diggers & Other Poems by John Garmon, and *Scorched Hands Anthology*. Published 12 titles in 2000 (number of books published per year "varies depending on cash flow"). Chapbooks are 24 pages, laser/high-speed-printed, saddle-stapled, with covers that vary from 150-lb. glossy to card stock. No unsolicited mss. "We solicit established poets and writers to send a complete manuscript." Responds to queries in 2 months. Pays 50 author's copies (out of a press run of 500). Order sample chapbooks by sending $5 (postage paid) to Richard Houff.

Advice "The beginning poet should study the classics, from the early Greek tradition to the present. On the current scene, try to be yourself. Draw inspiration from others and you'll eventually find your voice. Let Bukowski rest—there are thousands of clones. Buk wouldn't approve."

☑ HIDDEN OAK

402 S. 25th St., Philadelphia PA 19146. E-mail: hiddenoak@verizon.net. Established 1999. **Contact:** Louise Larkins, editor.

Magazine Needs *Hidden Oak*, published 2 or 3 times/year, seeks "well-crafted poems that make imaginative use of imagery to reach levels deeper than the immediate and personal. Both traditional forms and free verse are accepted. Especially welcome are poems which include time-honored poetic devices and reveal an ear for the music of language." *Hidden Oak* is 68-72 pages, digest-sized, photocopied, stapled, with original art/photograph on cover. Receives about 600 poems/year, accepts up to 40%. Press run is 100+. Single copy: $5; subscription: $12. Sample: $4. Make checks payable to Louise Larkins.

How to Submit Submit 3-6 poems at a time. Lines/poem: 30 maximum. Considers previously published poems (occasionally); no simultaneous submissions. Accepts e-mail submissions; no disk submissions. Cover letter is preferred. Include SASE. Submit seasonal poems 2-3 months in advance. Time between acceptance and publication is up to 3 months. Seldom comments on rejected poems. Might publish theme issues in the future. Guidelines available for SASE or by e-mail. Responds in 3 weeks. Pays 1 contributor's copy. Does not review books or chapbooks.

☑ HIRAM POETRY REVIEW

P.O. Box 162, Hiram OH 44234. (330)569-7512. Fax: (330)569-5166. E-mail: greenwoodwp@hiram.edu. Established 1966. **Contact:** Willard Greenwood, poetry editor.

Magazine Needs *Hiram Poetry Review*, published annually in spring, features "distinctive, beautiful, and heroic poetry." Wants "works of high and low art. We tend to favor poems that are pockets of resistance in the undeclared war against 'plain speech,' but we're interested in any work of high quality." Press run is 400 (300 subscribers, 150 libraries). Subscription: $9/year; $23/3 years.

How to Submit Send 3-5 poems at a time. Lines/poem: under 50 (3 single-spaced pages or less). Considers simultaneous submissions. No e-mail submissions. Cover letter is required. Include brief bio. Reads submissions year round. Responds in up to 6 months. Pays 2 contributor's copies. Acquires first North American serial rights. Rights return to poets upon publication. Reviews books of poetry in single- or multi-book format, no set length. Send materials for review consideration.

$☑ THE HOLLINS CRITIC

P.O. Box 9538, Hollins University, Roanoke VA 24020-1538. (540)362-6275. Web site: www.hollins.edu/grad/eng_writing/critic/critic.htm. Established 1964. **Contact:** Cathryn Hankla, poetry editor.

Magazine Needs *The Hollins Critic*, published 5 times/year, prints critical essays, poetry, and book reviews. Uses a few short poems in each issue, interesting in form, content, or both. Has published poetry by William Miller, R.T. Smith, David Huddle, Margaret Gibson, and Julia Johnson. *The Hollins Critic* is 24 pages, magazine-sized. Press run is 500. Subscription: $9/year ($11 outside U.S.). Sample: $2.

How to Submit Submit up to 5 poems at a time. "Must be typewritten, with SASE." Reads submissions September 1-December 15. Submissions received at other times will be returned unread. Responds in 6 weeks. Pays $25/poem plus 5 contributor's copies.

☑ HOME PLANET NEWS

P.O. Box 455, High Falls NY 12440. Web site: www.homeplanetnews.org. Established 1979. **Contact:** Donald Lev, editor.

Magazine Needs *Home Planet News*, published 3 times/year, aims "to publish lively and eclectic poetry, from a wide range of sensibilities, and to provide news of the small press and poetry scenes, thereby fostering a sense of community among contributors and readers." Wants "honest, well-crafted poems, open or closed form, on any subject." Does not want "any work which seems to us to be racist, sexist, ageist, anti-Semitic, or imposes limitations on the human spirit." Considers poetry by children and teens. Has published poetry by Enid Dame, Antler, Lyn Lifshin, Gerald Locklin, Hal Sirowitz, and Janine Pommy Vega. *Home Planet News* is 24 pages, tabloid, Web offset-printed, includes ads. Receives about 1,000 poems/year, accepts up to 3%. Press run is 1,000 (300 subscribers). Single copy: $4; subscription: $10/3 issues, $18/6 issues.

How to Submit Submit 3-6 poems at a time. Lines/poem: no limit on length, "but shorter poems (under 30 lines) stand a better chance." No previously published poems or simultaneous submissions. Cover letter is preferred. "SASE is a must." Time between acceptance and publication is 1 year. Seldom comments on rejected poems. Occasionally publishes theme issues. Upcoming themes available in magazine. Guidelines available for SASE or on Web site; "however, it is usually best to simply send work." Responds in 4 months. Pays one-year gift subscription plus 3 contributor's copies. Acquires first rights. Rights revert to poet upon publication. Reviews books/chapbooks of poetry and other magazines in 1,200 words, single- and multi-book format. Send materials for review consideration to Donald Lev. "Note: we do have guidelines for book reviewers; please write for them or check Web site. Magazines are reviewed by a staff member."

Advice "Read many publications, attend readings, feel yourself part of a writing community, learn from others."

⬙ HOMESTEAD REVIEW

Box A-5, 156 Homestead Ave., Hartnell College, Salinas CA 93901. (831)755-6943. Fax: (831)755-6751. E-mail: homesteadreview@gmail.com. Web site: www.hartnell.cc.ca.us/homestead_review. Established 1985. **Contact:** Maria Garcia Teutsch, editor.

Magazine Needs *Homestead Review*, published semiannually in December and May, seeks "avant-garde poetry as well as fixed form styles of remarkable quality and originality." Does not want "Hallmark-style writing or first drafts." Considers poetry written by children and teens. Has published poetry by Ray Gonzalez, Kathryn Kirkpatrick, Dana Garrett, Virgil Suárez, Daphne Gottlieb, and Hal Sirowitz. Receives about 1,000 poems/year, accepts about 15%. Press run is 500 (300 subscribers/libraries); 200 are distributed free to poets, writers, bookstores. Single copy: $10; subscription: $20/year. Make checks payable to *Homestead Review*.

How to Submit Submit 3 poems at a time. No previously published poems or simultaneous submissions. No fax, e-mail, or disk submissions. Cover letter is required. "A brief bio should be included in the cover letter." Reads submissions year round. Submit seasonal poems 3 months in advance. Time between acceptance and publication is up to 5 months. "Manuscripts are read by the staff and discussed. Poems/fiction accepted by majority consensus." Often comments on rejected poems. Guidelines available for SASE. Responds in 5 months. Pays 1 contributor's copy. Acquires one-time rights.

Contest/Award Offerings Contest with categories for poetry and fiction. Offers 1st Prize: $150 plus publication in *Homestead Review*; 2nd Prize: $100; 3rd Prize: $50. All entries will be considered for publication in *Homestead Review*. Guidelines available on Web site. **Entry fee:** $15 for 3 poems. **Deadline:** see Web site for current dates.

Advice "Poetry is language distilled; do not send unpolished work. Join a workshop group if at all possible."

▦ ▣ ◻ ◎ HOSPITAL DRIVE (Specialized: Medical/Healthcare)

Charlottesville VA 22908. (434)924-5856. Fax: (434)924-5986. E-mail: mhi-mag@virginia.edu. Web site: http://hospitaldrive.med.virginia.edu. Established 2006. **Contact:** Dr. Daniel Becker, editor.

Magazine Needs *Hospital Drive*, published twice/year online, "encourages original creative work that examines themes of health, illness, and healing. Summer 2007 marked the release of the inaugural issue. Submissions will be accepted from anyone involved with providing, teaching, studying, or researching patient care. Poems, short fiction, personal essays, reviews, photography, and visual art (painting, drawing, sculpture, mixed media) will be considered.'' Wants any poetry, so long as ''contributors are involved with health care in some fashion.''

How to Submit Submit up to 5 poems at a time. Considers simultaneous submissions. Accepts e-mail submissions as attachment); no fax or disk submissions. Cover letter is unnecessary. ''All works must be submitted by e-mail, accompanied by basic contact information, including the contributor's health care affiliation and the titles of each piece. Attach each poem as a separate document to 1 e-mail. Put ''poetry submission'' in the e-mail subject line.'' Reads submissions year round. Time between acceptance and publication is 3-6 months. All submissions will be reviewed anonymously by the editorial board, ''and only the highest quality work will be published.'' Never comments on rejected poems. Sometimes publishes theme issues. Guidelines available on Web site. Responds in 2-3 months.

⊕ ◐ HQ POETRY MAGAZINE (THE HAIKU QUARTERLY)

The Day Dream Press, 39 Exmouth St., Kingshill, Swindon, Wiltshire SN1 3PU England. (44)(179)352-3927. Web site: www.noggs.dsl.pipex.com/hq/. Established 1990. **Contact:** Kevin Bailey, editor.

Magazine Needs *HQ Poetry Magazine*, published quarterly, is ''a platform from which new and established poets can speak and have the opportunity to experiment with new forms and ideas.'' Wants ''any poetry of good quality.'' Considers poetry by children and teens. Has published poetry by Al Alvarez, D.M. Thomas, James Kirkup, Cid Corman, Brian Patten, and Penelope Shuttle. *HQ Poetry Magazine* is 48-64 pages, A5, perfect-bound, includes ads. Accepts about 5% of poetry received. Press run is 500-600. Subscription: (4 issues) £10 UK, £13 foreign. Sample: £3.00.

How to Submit No previously published poems or simultaneous submissions. Cover letter is required. Must include SASE (or SAE and IRCs). Time between acceptance and publication is 3-6 months. Often comments on rejected poems. Responds ''as time allows.'' Pays 1 contributor's copy. Reviews books of poetry in about 1,000 words, single-book format. Send materials for review consideration.

Also Offers Sponsors ''Piccadilly Poets'' in London, and ''Live Poet's Society'' based in Bath, Somerset, England. Also acts as ''advisor to Poetry on the Lake Annual Poetry Festival in Orta, Italy.''

◑ HUBBUB

5344 SE 38th Ave., Portland OR 97202. Established 1983. **Contact:** L. Steinman and J. Shugrue, editors.

Magazine Needs *Hubbub*, published once/year in the spring, is designed ''to feature a multitude of voices from interesting contemporary American poets.'' Wants ''poems that are well-crafted, with something to say. We have no single style, subject, or length requirement and, in particular, will consider long poems.'' Does not want light verse. Has published poetry by Madeline DeFrees, Cecil Giscombe, Carolyn Kizer, Primus St. John, Shara McCallum, and Alice Fulton. *Hubbub* is 50-70 pages, digest-sized, offset-printed, perfect-bound, with cover art. Receives about 1,200 submissions/year, accepts up to 2%. Press run is 350. Subscription: $7/year. Sample: $3.35 (back issues), $7 (current issue).

How to Submit Submit 3-6 typed poems at a time. No previously published poems or simultaneous submissions. Include SASE. Guidelines available for SASE. Responds in 4 months. Pays 2 contributor's copies. Acquires first North American serial rights. ''We review 2-4 poetry books/year in short (3-page) reviews; all reviews are solicited. We do, however, list books received/recommended.'' Send materials for review consideration.

Contest/Award Offerings Outside judges choose poems from each volume for 3 awards: Vi Gale Award ($100), Stout Award ($50), and Kenneth O. Hanson Award ($75). There are no special submission procedures or entry fees involved.

$◑ THE HUDSON REVIEW

684 Park Ave., New York NY 10065. Web site: www.hudsonreview.com. **Contact:** Julia Powers, assistant editor.

- Work published in *The Hudson Review* has been included in *The Best American Poetry*.

Magazine Needs *The Hudson Review*, published quarterly, is considered one of the most prestigious and influential journals in the nation. Editors welcome all styles and forms; however, competition is extraordinarily keen. Has published poetry by Marilyn Nelson, Hayden Carruth, Louis Simpson, and Dana Gioia. *The Hudson Review* is 176 pages, flat-spined. Subscription: $36/year ($44 foreign), institutions $38/year ($42 foreign). Sample: $10.

How to Submit Submit no more than 10 poems at a time. No previously published poems or simultaneous submissions. **Nonsubscribers may submit poems April 1-June 30 only.** "Manuscripts submitted by subscribers who so identify themselves will be read throughout the year." Guidelines available in magazine, for SASE, or on Web site. Responds in 3 months. Always sends prepublication galleys. Pays 50¢/line and 2 contributor's copies.

Advice "Read the magazine to ascertain our style/sensibility."

$ ◎ HUMPTY DUMPTY'S MAGAZINE (Specialized: children ages 4-6)

Children's Better Health Institute, 1100 Waterway Blvd., Indianapolis IN 46202. Web site: www.cbhi.org. or www.humptydumptymag.org.

Magazine Needs *Humpty Dumpty's Magazine*, published bimonthly by The Better Health Institute, is for ages 4-6. "Designed to keep young minds growing and active bodies healthy and fit." Wants light-hearted poetry appropriate for the age group. Reviews submissions for possible use in all Children's Better Health Institute publications.

How to Submit Manuscripts must be typewritten with poet's contact information in upper right-hand corner of each poem's page. SASE required. Submit seasonal material at least 8 months in advance. Guidelines available for SASE or on Web site. Responds in about 3 months. Pays $25 minimum for poetry. Acquires all rights.

Advice "We receive too many poetry submissions that are about kids, not for kids. Or, the subject matter is one that adults think children would or should like. Reading our guidelines is not enough. Careful study of current issues will acquaint writers with each title's 'personality.' "

$ ▢ ◎ HUNGUR MAGAZINE (Specialized: vampires)

P.O. Box 782, Cedar Rapids IA 52406-0782. E-mail: hungurmagazine@yahoo.com. Web site: www.samsdotpublishing.com. Established 2004. **Contact:** Terrie Leigh Relf. Member: The Speculative Literature Foundation (http://SpeculativeLiterature.org).

Magazine Needs *Hungur Magazine*, published biannually, features "stories and poems about vampires, and especially about vampires on other worlds." Prefers a "decadent literary style." Does not want "horror with excessive blood and gore." *Hungur Magazine* is 32 pages, magazine-sized, offset-printed, saddle-stapled, with paper cover with color art, includes ads. Receives about 200 poems/year, accepts about 20 (10%). Press run is 100/issue. Single copy: $8; subscription: $14/year. Make checks payable to Tyree Campbell/Sam's Dot Publishing.

How to Submit Submit up to 5 poems at a time. Lines/poem: prefers less than 200. No previously published poems or simultaneous submissions. Accepts e-mail submissions (pasted into body of message); no disk submissions. "Submission should include snail mail address and a short (1-2 lines) bio." Reads submissions year round. Submit seasonal poems 6 months in advance. Time between acceptance and publication is 3-4 months. Editor: Terrie Leigh Relf. Often comments on rejected poems. Guidelines available on Web site. Responds in 4-6 weeks. Pays $4/poem and 1 contributor's copy. Acquires first North American serial rights. Reviews books and chapbooks of poetry. Send materials for review consideration to Tyree Campbell.

Advice "It's up to the writer to take the first step and submit work. Some of our best poems have come from poets who weren't sure if they were good enough."

◪ THE HURRICANE REVIEW: A NATIONAL JOURNAL OF POETRY AND SHORT FICTION

English/Communications Dept., Pensacola Junior College, 1000 College Blvd., Pensacola FL 32504. (850)484-1424. Fax: (850)484-1149. E-mail: mwernicke@pjc.edu. Web site: www.pjc.edu/academics/departments/english/hurricane.html. Established 1986. **Contact:** Marian Wernicke, faculty editor.

Magazine Needs *The Hurricane Review, A National Journal of Poetry and Short Fiction,* published annually in the fall, features poetry and short fiction. Wants poetry of "any style, any length. No biases other than quality." Does not want "inspirational or greeting card verse." Has published poetry by R.T. Smith, Sue Walker, Larry Rubin, and Simon Perchik. *The Hurricane Review* is 100 pages, digest-sized, professionally printed, perfect-bound, with matte card cover. Receives about 1,000 poems/year, accepts about 50-60. Press run is 500. Subscription: $4. Sample: $4.

How to Submit Submit 3-5 poems at a time. No previously published poems or simultaneous submissions. Cover letter is preferred. Include bio and/or publication history. SASE required. Reads submissions August 1-May 15 only. Responds in 3 months, faster when possible. Pays 3 contributor's copies. Acquires first rights.

Advice "As David Kirby says, a poem should be well punctuated and give evidence of careful proofreading. It should be understandable to a reader who is not the poet."

☑ IBBETSON ST. PRESS

25 School St., Somerville MA 02143-1721. (617)628-2313. E-mail: dougholder@post.harvard.edu. Web site: http://homepage.mac.com/rconte. Established 1999. **Contact:** Doug Holder, editor. Submissions Editor: Robert K. Johnson.

Magazine Needs *Ibbetson St. Press,* published semiannually in June and November, prints " 'down to earth' poetry that is well-written; has clean, crisp images; with a sense of irony and humor." Wants "mostly free verse, but are open to rhyme." Does not want "maudlin, trite, overly political, vulgar for vulgar's sake work." Has published poetry by Afaa Michael Weaver, Sarah Hannah, Gloria Mindock, Harris Gardner, and Abbot Ikeler, Robert K. Johnson, and others. *Ibbetson St. Press* is 50 pages, magazine-sized, desktop-published, with glossy white cover, includes ads. Receives about 1,000 poems/year, accepts up to 30%. Press run is 200. Also archived at Harvard, Brown, University of Wisconsin, Poets House-NYC, and Buffalo University Libraries. Single copy: $7; subscription: $13. Make checks payable to *Ibbetson St. Press.*

How to Submit Submit 3-5 poems at a time. Considers previously published poems; no simultaneous submissions. No e-mail submissions; postal submissions only. Cover letter is required. Time between acceptance and publication is up to 5 months. "3 editors comment on submissions." Guidelines available for SASE. Responds in 2 months or more. Pays 1 contributor's copy. Acquires one-time rights. Reviews books/chapbooks of poetry and other magazines in 250-500 words. Send materials for review consideration.

Additional Information *Does not accept unsolicited chapbook mss.* Has published *Louisa Solano: The Grolier Poetry Book Shop* by Doug Holder/Steve Glines, *From Mist to Shadow* by Robert K. Johnson, and *Blood Soaked Dresses* by Gloria Mindock. Responds to queries in 1 month.

Advice "Please buy a copy of the magazine you submit to—support the small press. In your work, be honest."

$☑ THE ICONOCLAST

1675 Amazon Rd., Mohegan Lake NY 10547-1804. Established 1992. **Contact:** Phil Wagner, editor/publisher.

Magazine Needs *The Iconoclast,* published 6 times/year, is a general interest literary journal. Wants "poems that have something to say—the more levels the better. Try for originality; if not in thought, then expression. Look for the unusual in the usual, parallels in opposites, the capturing of what is unique or often unnoticed in an ordinary, or extraordinary, moment; what makes us human—and the resultant glories and agonies. Our poetry is accessible to a thoughtful reading public." Does not want "greeting card verse or noble religious sentiments. Nothing sentimental, obscure, or self-absorbed." *The Iconoclast* is 64-96 pages, magazine-sized, photo offset-printed on 50 lb. white paper, includes ads. Receives about 2,000 poems/year, accepts up to 3%. Press run is 1,000-3,000. Subscription: $18 for 8 issues. Sample: $5.

How to Submit Submit 3-4 poems at a time. Time between acceptance and publication is 4 months to one year. Sometimes comments on rejected poems. Guidelines available for SASE. Responds in 1 month. Pays $2-5/poem for first North American rights (on publication), 1 contributor's copy per published page or poem, offers 40% discount on extras. Reviews books of poetry in 250 words, single-book format.

Keith Flynn

Devotion to the process

In "Apostrophes," a poem from his collection *The Book of Monsters*, Keith Flynn writes:

> *We have to stay connected*
> *to a will, a person, a focus, a feeling*
> *When all about us disengages*
> *When the streetlights fail and blink out*
> *steaming in protest*
> *we have to stay*
> *and stay connected*

This devotion to and reverence for connection threads through Flynn's entire career as a musician, editor and poet.

As lyricist and front man for the acclaimed rock band The Crystal Zoo, he held the group together and propelled them to tour extensively. Flynn produced the albums *Swimming Through Lake Eerie*, *Pouch* and the spoken-word and music compilation, *Nervous Splendor*.

As editor of the *Asheville Poetry Review*, Flynn unites distinct groups of artists in a burgeoning North Carolina literary scene and continues to provide a rare outlet for poetry, one without agenda or pretense, seeking only work that shares Flynn's passion for image and rhythm.

And as an award-winning author of four collections of poetry—*The Talking Drum* (Metropolis Communications), *The Book of Monsters* (Urthona Press), *The Lost Sea* (Iris Press), and *The Golden Ratio* (Iris Press), as well as a collection of essays entitled *The Rhythm Method, Razzmatazz and Memory: How to Make Your Poetry Swing* (Writer's Digest Books, 2007; in the interest of full disclosure, I should note that I edited this book)—he seamlessly blends the aesthetic offerings of roots music, surrealist art and language into work that enters the bodies of its readers and listeners, becoming as close to them as the cadence of their own heartbeat and breath. To watch Flynn perform—the event itself a dynamic coupling of verse and *a cappella* song—is to witness poetry that cannot thrive without such connection.

In addition to these accomplishments, Flynn has been awarded the Sandburg Prize for poetry (at the ripe old age of 23), the ASCAP Emerging Songwriter Prize, and the Paumanok Poetry Award, and was twice named the Gilbert-Chappell Distinguished Poet for North Carolina. He slowed down for a minute to talk to us about his writing and his experiences as a working poet and editor.

You told Matt Mullins at Unstable Euphony (http://unstableeuphony.blogspot .com) that you can teach anybody to be a better writer, but you can't make them burn with it. What is it about poetry that first consumed—and continues to consume—you?

My first dramatic inclination to write poems came after I had absorbed the mighty aphorisms of William Blake's *Marriage of Heaven and Hell*. Those sentences stared me down. They challenged all my assumptions and tore them asunder. And this power was musical, rhythmic, honorable and obscene at once.

Every poet can remember the moment that words began to come out of them, when the gush released their deepest emotions, the collapse of held secrets, the blown-open vault of their creative imagination. Poetry is the language of hidden things in commerce with one another, I believe. Cocteau said, "All poets are mediums and workhands of this mysterious force that inhabits them."

In the beginning, I was at the mercy of words and the endless variations of sounds. My poetic voice rose out of my singing voice; and since I had grown up in the church, learning to find my voice in the choir, I saw no difference between a poem and a hymn. Because poetry is language with a shape, and requires constant improvisation, its challenges are infinite. Perhaps I'm in love with flux, the beauty and mystery of constantly becoming, because the search is the thing, not the arrival. It is the hunt for the poem that should challenge us, shaping time into orderly forms, though it sometimes feels like herding fleas into a water glass.

Where does the process begin for you? From what seeds does a Keith Flynn poem root?

I usually become entranced by a phrase or idea and then build around that kernel.

I have never been able to start a poem by believing I knew exactly what I wanted to write about and then logically erecting the poem's architecture on the foundation of that thought. I never know what sentences I've written will become the scaffolding of a poem. But I am always trying to make the tightest, smallest sentences and to condense the amount of dross. This is the infernal chase, to make poems where the artifice of labor disappears and the seams dissolve. All art is the elimination of the unnecessary.

My method is to take copious notes, sometimes dozens of pages or drafts, and compose the poem from the top down. An 18-line poem may have begun as a couple of hundred lines or more, but they are slowly whittled away as the poem reveals its identity. Sometimes several fragments, years apart, may begin to move toward one another and can be judged as family. This way, I track the poem through hundreds of ideas—word by word. The poem leads me, not the other way around.

Since poems have to live in the air, reading them aloud will uncover whether they will creak or fly. In my office, in the middle of my desk, is an ancient cassette recorder. As I compose a poem, I recite it aloud, over and over, and listen to the recording for fault lines in the sonic structure of the piece. I walk round and round that old table, circling the poem like a vulture, ready to pounce on and eradicate any dead parts that do not lift. You should have a devotion to the process, the idea of creating the poem as a ceremony, where nothing you conceive is ultimately sacred.

Are there any themes or images you find yourself returning to in your poetry?

Well, I do have a lot of mirrors, rivers and flying things in my poems—particularly bees, because the hive is attractive to me in its symmetries and systems. But my poems are usually so dense with imagery that it's hard to say any symbol will stand for the same thing twice. I do have a fascination for the macabre or monstrous, and music is a moral law for me that stands in for other laws.

It's been written that I do have an unnerving sympathy for the underdog, unnerving perhaps to the friendly fascists who surround us every day, trying to squash the individualism out of our culture. And like most Southern poets, I have my ongoing conversations with the Divine; but poetry does not seek to change the world, but to embrace it in all its forms and richness. All art is action, usually born of a painful awareness, and is naturally averse to the swell of conformity from every age.

So I see that my poetry is a quarrel with the world as it exists; and it becomes political at times, no matter how hard I try to listen without prejudice. That's why poetry is appreciated by an immense minority, because in our present culture, somewhat addled by fear and addicted to convenience, finding the right words in the right order, and trying to lend a little light, is not convenient at all.

One of the most remarkable works in your latest collection, *The Golden Ratio*, is "Chang and Eng"—a historical feat of poetic acrobatics in nine parts, starring the Bunker twins of Wilkesboro, North Carolina. What attracted you to the story of these Siamese twins? Several of the poems are written from Eng's perspective—why did you choose this brother?

I first saw a picture of these amazing brothers when I was eight or nine years old, in a Grolier encyclopedia, perhaps. I never forgot their look of quiet dignity, almost to the point of glacial indifference to the camera. And the stillness of that famous photograph, coupled with the finery of their dress, was memorable to a naïve country boy.

The poem itself was written slowly over a 14-year period, through dozens and dozens of drafts, and seemed to lack a central focus. Allowing one brother to speak in first person humanized them and solved my perspective problem. It was a strategy I had employed in previous books with some success, particularly the Picasso voice in "The Painter as Mantis Sings the Blues" [from *The Lost Sea*], and I have learned a lot about the idea of voice from the poetry of Ai and Russell Edson, whose *I* is never certain, but remains unforgettable.

As [*The Golden Ratio*] became more and more about the imbalances in our world—both natural and synthetic, as well as financial, sexual and spiritual—giving Eng his own struggle in opposition to his brother's excesses made his plight feel universal. And of course, the idea of never being alone is a haunting concept for a poet, whose finest moments occur when he is most alone. That's why the end is so jarring; Eng's only solitary moment comes as he is face to face with death, when he is borne aloft by a flood of memories as his brother succumbs.

You were barely 20 years old when you began your public career as a poet. How has the poetry biz changed since you first entered the game? What's remained constant?

When I first started getting published and giving readings in the early 1980s, there was not the proliferation of workshops, MFA pit stops, literary salon blogs, support groups, *Poetry for Dummies*, open mike nights and ubiquitous art zines and poetry rags like you see today. There was really no one who thought of being a poet as a career decision; it sort of happened to you, like the Ebola virus, and then you had to figure out how to make a real living at something else while you whittled away at the poetry in your down time.

But now, maybe for the first time ever, you can actually be a professional poet and support yourself. With the advent of rap and hip-hop, poetry is constantly on the radio. The revitalization of many urban centers and the focus on the downtown areas have created coffee shops and art galleries where poets can perform. The Slam Poetry movement has organized those performers.

But you have to travel, do readings, publish books, teach workshops, etc.; and there is only a handful of poets who sell enough books to sustain themselves from their royalties. Of course, talking about what "a living" is will differ from region to region, and some folks need to be more comfortable than others. In 2003, about 1,400 poets made money from their work. I told an editor friend of mine that statistic, and he was incredulous: "That many?" In a nation of nearly 350 million people, that's a damn shame. I do about 50 to 70 workshops and readings a year, as many as 150 or more in the years that I have books or albums out; but even with that murderous schedule, I am forced to diversify with other work on occasion to become remotely comfortable.

What has not changed is the nepotism of the Biz and the preconceived notions of the academic sector. Most poets still teach to support themselves. There is still no one who rushes home to tell his parents that he is a poet and then is subsequently swamped with congratulations and financial support.

How has your own poetry evolved? How do you continue to challenge yourself?
The challenge comes from a willingness to try anything, to allow the poem to be a vessel for experimentation and growth, to squeeze every sonic possibility out of the sentences. I've become much more patient as I've grown older, with less sense of an urgency than before. When I was younger, I was constantly afraid of losing the gift, or that I would die before I could realize any of my potential; but learning to surrender is the first step toward deliverance. It's become less important to me what others think of my work, and so I can wait for the poem to emerge organically, without the need to write toward a subject or a deadline. When you stop having to prove yourself, the proof of your poetry reflects and constitutes its own reward.

I'm also less interested in using my own biography as the subject matter for the poetry, and I believe I have become more accepting of my Appalachian heritage as I've aged. Geography is history, and we are made from the circumstances of our surroundings. Southern-ness is otherness, and the crazy colloquialisms and unnerving stories are part of my genetic makeup. I'm no longer embarrassed by having grown up on a dead-end dirt road in a trailer. It's part of the path that led me to this place, in this time. Though I've traveled all over this continent, and a couple of others, performing and teaching, my community became more valuable in my absence from it, just as Eden was more precious to Adam after the Fall. And when I returned to Madison County after 20 years of living on the road and being ensconced in Nashville and New York, I realized that I was carrying this Eden inside me as I traveled, sharing and defining it by my interactions with anyone who might aspire to this state of grace or empathize with the struggles of our people.

What inspired you to start the *Asheville Poetry Review*?
When I moved back to Western North Carolina in 1993, I landed right in the middle of this incredible literary and artistic renaissance that was taking place in Asheville. There was an explosion of activity in the downtown area, which had been unsafe a few years before. Coffee shops, art galleries and record stores were springing up on every street corner. Three distinct groups were already meeting and talking actively about their writing. The performance poets had regular slam teams practicing at the Green Door, a multilevel gallery and performance space. There was a vibrant women's group centered around Malaprop's Bookstore, and the creative writing programs at UNC-Asheville, Western Carolina University and Warren Wilson College were gaining national prominence.

I had already published one book and was about to release a second, *The Book of*

Monsters. I realized that no one was documenting or publishing all the amazing work that was being produced. Since I had relationships with all the artists and belonged to no one group in particular, I was the obvious choice to bring these slightly disparate elements into a single forum. I asked each of the various leaders to meet with me and discuss the possibilities of a literary journal. There was an enormous groundswell of support. I did fundraisers with my band and organized readings and begged and borrowed and put up my own money for the first issue. We released that issue in June 1994 at the Asheville Poetry Festival and sold every copy we had.

I wanted the *Review* to have no political agenda; the only criteria for inclusion would be quality. My idea was to include translations in every issue to broaden the cultural exposure for poets outside the country, and to include a rich sampling of work from the region itself. We always wanted to have different graphic artists competing for the cover space, and that would hopefully keep the artistic community interested in our efforts and help to give the journal a distinctive visual appearance. I have gradually tried to include more essays, interviews and book reviews to give the *Review* more of a critical voice and create dialogue and historical perspective. We have no university affiliation or nonprofit status. We receive no federal funds or grant monies. We subsist entirely on retail sales and subscriptions.

From those humble and unexpected origins, the *Asheville Poetry Review* has grown into an international journal that has published more than 1,500 writers from 25 different countries and is distributed in both North America and Europe. It has been quite a ride.

When you're reading through the 8,000 submissions you receive per year, what makes a poem stand out for you?

I'm always looking for poems with the right Borgesian combination of "algebra and fire." And my only criterion for admission is interesting subject matter married to a clear sense of rhythm. What the editor wants is transformation—to be surprised, knocked off center, silenced. The best poems stop us in our tracks, shut us up, make us read the poem again and again, because it has suddenly opened a new room in our brain that was hidden to us before.

All editing is subjective. I have been submitting my poems to other editors since I was 18 years old and have known firsthand the pain of that rejection letter. So I treat prospective contributors to my journal the same way I would want to be treated myself, and I hope that my approach bears the quality of tenderness. Genius makes its own rules, however, and memorable poems are gateways that engage all the senses. Their agility and music propel them into the reader's body, but their transformative power rides upon the willful use of subversive metaphoric and symbolic details, and is filled with moments of startling associations. What the reader wants are unexpected astonishments, non-logical leaps forward that are proven durable by working backward toward known principles. Only the rebellious can do it. And there is a rebel lurking in every successful poet.

Does reading all those submissions affect your own work? How do you maintain room in your head for your own words?

We are what we read. I welcome the opportunity to read poetry, even bad poetry, because it always makes me linger on the possibilities that could make the poem better.

It keeps my axe sharp. But to maintain the integrity and originality of your own poems, you have to have a place where no one else is allowed to putter around, where you go to create alone. Then you have to set aside the time to work every day. I made a vow when I was 19 that I would write something down every day of my life (believing I had forged a blood bond with my Muses), and I have stuck to that, more or less, for the last 25 years. I usually begin around midnight and work for as long as I am able, or until I shimmy down another rabbit hole.

Once after a particularly well-placed shot upon the green, Jack Nicklaus heard a fan yell, "Lucky!" He turned to the gallery and said, "The more I practice, the luckier I get." You have to become intimately acquainted with the discipline that will allow you to try anything, to approach the blank page without fear, what Hemingway called "the white bull." Just like the dance of the toreador with that two-ton animal, the mind has a muscle memory. Like a singer whose voice gets more nimble and durable the more the throat is used, the imagination will arrive at its appointed hour if a routine has been established. My whole body begins to change and focus as my allotted time with the work draws near.

I also maintain several projects at once, several poems or essays or books that I'm working toward, so that on any given evening I will hopefully have something useful to work on and a variance in my attention.

Being an editor, is it difficult to allow yourself to be edited by those that publish your collections? What advice would you give poets about understanding the necessity of the editorial process and revision?
I've always welcomed criticism of my work and have several readers whose opinions are honored and occasionally obeyed. The most valuable ally any poet can have is a reader who will tell him the truth, regardless of their relationship. Getting any objectivity about your own work is very difficult, because as hard as I try I will never be able to read a poem as if I hadn't written it; but I trust my instincts implicitly.

Every poem should have its own structure, intuitively created or artificially crammed into a preexisting structure of sonnet or villanelle or pantoum, what have you. I think a poem should be a long piece of hungry momentum pushing headlong down the page, admitting no impediment to its flow, and using the active verbs as little turbines propelling the larger engines of the sentences. "Form is never more than an extension of content," decreed Robert Creeley, and I pretty much adhere to that maxim, preferring to create my own music, rather than relying on a premeditated traditional structure. All of the writers I admire accomplished their work in the same way, by the force of their will upon the words, unwilling to settle for the first thought or effort, continually sharpening their tools and allowing the idea of gratification to come from a devotion to the process.

Compose in a flood, I say, edit in a trickle. It's hard to be wise and in love at the same time. Every poem has thousands of decisions that must be made, and a poet should be ready, willing and able to defend each of those choices. Being an editor is subjective and thankless, but it is never personal. Every editor wants that next envelope to contain the best poem he has ever seen and is poised for that outcome. That's a damn lot of disappointment to sift through, but editors are the most jaded, and yet optimistic, creatures you will ever talk to.

While we were working on *The Rhythm Method* together, I was continually amazed by the breadth and depth of knowledge you possess about the intertwining histories of poetry, art and music. When did you start studying these things? What do you think other poets gain from such interdisciplinary education?
Yeats said that poets should know all philosophy and then keep it out of their work. That's a classic example, in his case, of do what I say and not what I do. I've always believed that a poem could contain everything and be about anything, that no subject matter was unfit to be considered in a poem. I also believe that we do not create out of a fear of death, but to find out who we are and what we know.

Poetry is a translation of feelings or perceptions that are, in some ways, previously unsayable. We have been conditioned to believe that our external reality is true, and does not match our internal reality. But our brains are lit by what we see and what we think we see, making the process of the past just as real as the lived moment viewed by the eyes. The brain processes 400 billion bits of information per second, but we are only aware of about 2,000 of those. We spend the majority of our time eliminating waste, disposing of random sensory projections, accepting the symbols and imagery that occur the most or serve our body best. The integration of reality is always slower than its actuality. It takes silence to create poetry and the space to dream, and dreaming in America is nursed in darkness and viewed with suspicion.

It is important to have several arrows for one's bow, since Truth has a protean face; and the poet is unable to stand transfixed before the velocity of Truth for any protracted length of time. So we fix our sights as best we can, accept our inability to trap our quarry and move forward, changing with it, so that the poem's structures and equations are invisible and seamless, soaking down into the darkness of its reader, unimpeded by analysis.

I also take John Coltrane for a model here, who as a sax player used dense, rapidly changing chords with complex extensions built on each note of the chord, and played with remarkable speed and dexterity. I want my poems to operate much the same way, clusters of associations that hint at the connectedness of all things, but stated musically, matter-of-factly in several voicings and textures, gaining momentum as the narrative passes, the way songs do. Surrealism is one strategy to achieve these multilayers, but not the only one; among the holies of consilience it is widely known that there is more than one ghost.

You do numerous public performances each year. What are the best and worst things about reading poetry in front of an audience? Why is it a necessary part of a poet's art?

Poetry matters, even if its confused public face is sometimes defined as childish diary entries mundanely rendered by the entangled minds of arrogant geeks. Whether we are mistaking poetry "performance" for the reading of true poetry, as some would suggest, is irrelevant. The fact that audiences are interested in the spoken word helps maintain a sense of literary community in an atmosphere where fewer large publishers are taking the time to publish books of poetry, and where book reviews of these collections have mostly disappeared from the mainstream media.

If the dire prognostications of the NEA are to be believed, fewer people are reading books of any kind than ever before, even though more books are being published than at any time in history. Almost the only way to attract an audience for a poet (or to sell books of poems) is by giving readings of your work, in much the same way that rock bands used to tour incessantly before releasing an album. "The power of music that poetry lacks is the ability to persuade without argument," said William Matthews. But the best poems, when read aloud, hide their argument, as well as their form. The successful performance of a poem elicits the mysterious bond between the audience and the poem's mechanics, slipping in and out of the listener, inviting him or her back to read it again and again, coaxing the imagination out like energy in a spring, or the underground flow of lava coursing under the earth's skin.

Boris Pasternak believed that "poetry searches for music amidst the tumult of the dictionary." The best readers of their poems do the same, stringing the sounds along the tension of the lines like birds on a wire, making a melody that is immediate and universal, resonating in the body of the bewitched audience long after the poet has ceased to sing.

For more information on Keith Flynn and Asheville Poetry Review, *visit keithflynn.net and asheville review.com.*

—Lauren Mosko

Lauren Mosko is an editor at Writer's Digest Books and the former editor of *Novel & Short Story Writer's Market*.

Advice "Poets merely collecting another credit need not apply. Show us you care about something other than self-mythologizing. And if we've already published you, it helps if you can indicate you actually read the work of anyone else in that issue."

▦ ◻ ◎ IDIOM 23 (Specialized: Central Queensland region of Australia)

Regional Centre of the Arts, Central Queensland University, Rockhampton 4702 Australia. E-mail: l.hawryluk@cqu.edu.au. Established 1988. **Contact:** Dr. Lynda Hawryluk, editorial board.

Magazine Needs *Idiom 23*, published annually, is "named for the Tropic of Capricorn and is dedicated to developing the literary arts throughout the Central Queensland region. Submissions of original short stories, poems, articles, and black-and-white drawings and photographs are welcomed by the editorial collective. *Idiom 23* is not limited to a particular viewpoint but, on the contrary, hopes to encourage and publish a broad spectrum of writing. The collective seeks out creative work from community groups with as varied backgrounds as possible. The magazine hopes to reflect and contest idiomatic fictional representations of marginalized or non-privileged positions and values." Considers poetry written by children and teens (10 years of age and older). *Idiom 23* is about 140 pages, 7¾×10, professionally printed, perfect-bound, with 4-color cover, includes ads. Single copy: $15.

How to Submit Considers previously published poems. Cover letter is required. Poems are circulated to an editorial board. Reviews books of poetry in single-book format. Send materials for review consideration to Dr. Lynda Hawryluk.

Contest/Award Offerings Sponsors the Bauhinia Literary Awards for short stories and poetry in 3 categories: Open, Regional, and Student. Submit up to 3 poems, 50 lines maximum each. "Where possible, please e-mail entries or send on a CD." Send SAE and IRC for complete details. **Entry fee:** $6. **Deadline:** June 27 (postmark). Winning entries will be announced at the CQ Multicultural Fair and CQU Open Day in August. Outstanding entries will be published in *Idiom 23*.

▦ ◻ ILLOGICAL MUSE

P.O. Box 63, Buchanan MI 49107. E-mail: illogicalmuse@yahoo.com. Web site: www.geocities.com/illogicalmuse. Established 2004. **Contact:** Amber Rothrock, editor.

Magazine Needs *Illogical Muse*, published quarterly, welcomes "submissions of poetry, fiction, essays and artwork. Looks for well-crafted, intelligent verse in any form and on any subject." Does not want "anything overly graphic or explicit in content." Considers poetry written by children and teens. Has published poetry by Michael Lee Johnson, Sandra Hedin, B.Z. Niditch, Sara Crawford, and Marianne Lavalle-Vincent. Home Computer printed and stapled. Accepts 90% of the material received. Single copy: $5 U.S., $10 Foreign. Subscription: $20 U.S., $40 Foreign.

How to Submit Submit up to 6 poems at a time. Lines/poem: no more than 100. Considers previously published poems and simultaneous submissions. Absolutely no multiple submissions. Accepts e-mail submissions (pasted into body of message); no disk submissions. Cover letter is preferred. Include SASE, IRC's or valid e-mail for response. Work will be returned if proper postage is provided. Reads submissions year round. Submit seasonal poems 6 months in advance. Time between acceptance and publication is up to 1 year. Sometimes comments on rejected poems. "Current theme is Nature but there are special requirements for this issue so check guidelines before submitting. Guidelines available for SASE or on Web site. Responds in 6 months. Pays 1 contributor's copy. Reviews books/chapbooks of poetry and fiction and other magazine/journals. Send materials for review consideration. Acquires one-time rights and electronic/archival rights for Web site.

Also Offers Creative writing exercises each quarter. These are available on the blog. Link from the Web site.

Advice "Sometime in the near future *Illogical Muse* will be going on hiatus as I go back to school for my BFA. The exact date is not known at this time, but will be posted on the Web site as soon as it becomes available."

$◻ ◎ ILLUMEN (Specialized: speculative poetry)

P.O. Box 782, Cedar Rapids IA 52406-0782. E-mail: illumensdp@yahoo.com. Web site: www.samsdotpublishing.com. Established 2004. **Contact:** Karen L. Newman, editor. Member: The Speculative Literature Foundation.

Magazine Needs *Illumen*, published biannually, contains speculative poetry and articles about speculative poetry. "Speculative poetry includes, but is not limited to, fantasy, science fiction, sword and sorcery, alternate history, and horror." Wants "fantasy, science fiction, spooky horror, and speculative poetry with minimal angst." Does not want "horror with excessive blood and gore." Considers poetry by children and teens. Has published poetry by Ian Watson, Bruce Boston, Sonya Taaffe, Mike Allen, Marge B. Simon, and David C. Kopaska-Merkel. *Illumen* is 50 pages, digest-sized, offset-printed, perfect-bound, with color cover with color art, includes ads. Receives about 200 poems/year, accepts about 50 (25%). Press run is 100/issue (20 subscribers, 50 shelf sales); 5 distributed free to reviewers. Single copy: $9; subscription: $15/year. Make checks payable to Tyree Campbell/Sam's Dot Publishing.

How to Submit Submit up to 5 poems at a time. Lines/poem: prefers less than 200. Considers previously published poems; no simultaneous submissions. Accepts e-mail submissions (pasted into body of message); no disk submissions. "Submission should include snail mail address and a short (1-2 lines) bio." Reads submissions year round. Submit seasonal poems 6 months in advance. Time between acceptance and publication is 1-2 months. Often comments on rejected poems. Guidelines available on Web site. Responds in 4-6 weeks. Pays 2 cents/word (minimum: $3) for original poems and 1 contributor's copy. Acquires first North American serial rights. Reviews books/chapbooks of poetry. Send materials for review consideration to Tyree Campbell.

Advice "It's up to the writer to take the first step and submit work. Some of our best poems have come from poets who weren't sure if they were good enough. Horror poetry is a difficult sell with us."

★ ☑ ILLUMINATIONS: An International Magazine of Contemporary Writing

Dept. of English, College of Charleston, 66 George St., Charleston SC 29424-0001. (843)953-1920. Fax: (843)953-3180. E-mail: lewiss@cofc.edu. Web site: www.cofc.edu/Illuminations. Established 1982. **Contact:** Simon Lewis, editor.

Magazine Needs *Illuminations: An International Magazine of Contemporary Writing*, published annually, provides "a forum for new writers alongside already established ones." Open as to form and style, and to translations. Does not want to see anything "bland or formally clunky." Has published poetry by Peter Porter, Michael Hamburger, Geri Doran, and Anne Born. *Illuminations* is 64-88 pages, digest-sized, offset-printed, perfect-bound, with 2-color card cover. Receives about 1,500 poems/year, accepts up to 5%. Press run is 500. Subscription: $15/2 issues. Sample: $10.

How to Submit Submit up to 6 poems at a time. No previously published poems or simultaneous submissions. Accepts fax, e-mail (pasted into body of message, no attachments), and disk submissions. Cover letter is preferred (brief). Time between acceptance and publication "depends on when received. Can be up to a year." Occasionally publishes theme issues. Guidelines available by e-mail or on Web site. Responds within 2 months. Pays 2 contributor's copies plus 1 subsequent issue. Acquires all rights. Returns rights on request.

$☺ ◎ IMAGE: ART, FAITH, MYSTERY (Specialized: religious faith; Judeo-Christian)

3307 3rd Ave. W., Seattle WA 98119. E-mail: image@imagejournal.org. Web site: www.imagejournal.org. Established 1989. **Contact:** Gregory Wolfe, publisher.

Magazine Needs *Image: Art, Faith, Mystery*, published quarterly, "explores and illustrates the relationship between faith and art through world-class fiction, poetry, essays, visual art, and other arts." Wants "poems that grapple with religious faith, usually Judeo-Christian." Has published poetry by Philip Levine, Scott Cairns, Annie Dillard, Mary Oliver, Mark Jarman, and Kathleen Norris. *Image* is 136 pages, 10×7, printed on acid-free paper, perfect-bound, with glossy 4-color cover, includes ads. Receives about 800 poems/year, accepts up to 2%. Has 4,200 subscribers (100 are libraries). Subscription: $39.95. Sample: $16 postpaid.

How to Submit Submit up to 4 poems at a time. No previously published poems. No e-mail submissions. Cover letter is preferred. Time between acceptance and publication is 1 year. Guidelines available on Web site. Responds in 3 months. Always sends prepublication galleys. Pays 4 contributor's copies plus $2/line ($150 maximum). Acquires first North American serial rights. Reviews books of poetry in 2,000 words, single- or multi-book format. Send materials for review consideration.

▣ ☑ IN OUR OWN WORDS

d Burning Bush Publications, P.O. Box 4658, Santa Rosa CA 95402. Web site: www.bbbooks.com. **Contact:** Abby Bogomolny, editor.

Magazine Needs *In Our Own Words*, published two times/year online, seeks poetry and prose poems for its literary e-zine. Wants "thought-provoking, creative, alternative writing. We choose work that inspires compassion, peace, and respect for diversity in original and unexpected ways." Does not want "manuscripts of full-length books." Sample: past issues available on Web site.

How to Submit Cover letter is required. "Send submissions to us by U.S. mail only. Include SASE. If you want us to reply via e-mail, include your e-mail address! We will ask you for a digital file via e-mail, if we want to publish your submission." Reads submissions according to the following deadlines: May 30 for Fall edition, December 22 for Spring edition. Guidelines available on Web site. Rights revert to poet upon publication.

Contest/Award Offerings The Burning Bush Poetry Prize (see separate listing in Contests & Awards).

Advice "Our readers are interested in love, social and economic justice, liberation movements, and improving the quality of life in all communities."

⊠ ☑ ◎ IN THE GROVE (Specialized: poetry by CA writers)

P.O. Box 16195, Fresno CA 93755. (559)442-4600, ext. 8105. Fax: (559)265-5756. E-mail: leeherrick @hotmail.com. Web site: www.inthegrove.net. Established 1996. **Contact:** Lee Herrick.

Magazine Needs *In the Grove*, published annually, publishes "short fiction, essays, and poetry by new and established writers currently living in the Central Valley and throughout California." Wants "poetry of all forms and subject matter. We seek the originality, distinct voice, and craft of a poem." Does not want "greeting card verse or forced rhyme. Be fresh. Take a risk." Has published poetry by Andres Montoya, Corrinne Clegg Hales, Daniel Chacon, Lawson Fusao Inada, Amy Uyematsu, and Charles Harper Webb. *In the Grove* is 80-100 pages, digest-sized, photocopied, perfect-bound, with heavy cardstock cover. Receives about 500 poems/year, accepts up to 10%. Press run is 200 (50 subscribers, 100 shelf sales); 50 distributed free to contributors, colleagues. Subscription: $12. Sample: $6.

How to Submit Submit 3-5 poems at a time. Considers previously published poems ("on occasion") and simultaneous submissions ("with notice"). Cover letter is preferred. Time between acceptance and publication is up to 6 months. "Poetry editor reads all submissions and makes recommendations to editor, who makes final decisions." Seldom comments on rejected poems. Guidelines available for SASE or on Web site. Responds in 3-6 months. Pays 1 contributor's copy. Acquires first or one-time rights as well as right to publish on Web site. Rights return to poets upon publication.

☑ ◎ INDEFINITE SPACE (Specialized: experimental, visual, minimalistic)

P.O. Box 40101, Pasadena CA 91114. Established 1992. Web site: www.indefinitespace.net. **Contact:** Marcia Arrieta, editor/publisher.

Magazine Needs *Indefinite Space*, published annually, prints experimental, visual, and minimalistic poetry. Does not want rhyming poetry. Has published poetry by Marthe Reed, Anne Blonstein, Kevin Magee, Petra Backonja, Peter Layton, and Jill Magi. *Indefinite Space* is 48 pages, digest-sized. Single copy: $7; subscription: $12 for 2 issues. Make checks payable to Marcia Arrieta.

How to Submit Considers simultaneous submissions; no previously published poems. Seldom comments on rejected poems. Guidelines available on Web site. Responds in up to 3 months. Poet retains copyright.

⊠ $☑ INDIANA REVIEW

Ballantine Hall 465, 1020 E. Kirkwood Ave., Bloomington IN 47405-7103. (812)855-3439. E-mail: inreview@indiana.edu. Web site: www.indiana.edu/ ~ inreview. Established 1976. **Contact:** Jenny Burdge, editor.

• Poetry published in *Indiana Review* has been included in *The Best American Poetry* and *The Pushcart Prize*.

Magazine Needs *Indiana Review*, published semiannually, includes prose, poetry, creative nonfiction, book reviews, and visual art. "We look for an intelligent sense of form and language, and admire poems of risk, ambition, and scope." Wants "all types of poems—free verse, traditional, experimental. Reading a sample issue is the best way to determine if *Indiana Review* is a potential home for your work. Any subject matter is acceptable if it is written well. Translations are welcome." Has published poetry by Denise Duhamel, Sherman Alexie, Marilyn Chin, Julianna Baggott, and Alberto Rios. *Indiana Review* is 160 pages, digest-sized, professionally printed, flat-spined, with color matte cover. Receives more than 9,000 submissions/year, accepts up to 60. Has 2,000 subscribers. Subscription: $17/year, $28 for 2 years. Sample: $9.

How to Submit Submit 4-6 poems at a time. Lines/poem: "do not send more than 10 pages of poetry per submission." Considers simultaneous submissions with notification; no previously published poems. Cover letter with brief bio is desired. SASE is mandatory for response. Guidelines available on Web site. "We try to respond to manuscripts in 3-4 months. Reading time is often slower during summer and holiday months." Pays $5/page ($10 minimum), 2 contributor's copies, and remainder of year's subscription. Acquires first North American serial rights only. Reviews books of poetry. Send materials for review consideration.

Contest/Award Offerings Holds yearly poetry and prose-poem contests. Guidelines available for SASE or on Web site.

✪ $□ INKWELL

Manhattanville College, 2900 Purchase St., Purchase NY 10577. (914)323-7239. Fax: (914)323-3122. E-mail: inkwell@mville.edu. Web site: www.inkwelljournal.org. Established 1995. **Contact:** Poetry Editor. Member: CLMP.

- *Inkwell* is produced in affiliation with the Master of Arts in Writing program at Manhattanville College, and is staffed by faculty and graduate students of the program.

Magazine Needs *Inkwell*, published semiannually, features "emerging writers, high quality poems and short stories, creative nonfiction, artwork, literary essays, memoir and interviews on writing by established figures, and yearly compeitions in poetry and fiction." Wants "serious work—very well made verse, any form, any genre." Does not want "doggerel, light or humorous verse." Has published poetry by Thomas Lux, Penelope Scambly Schott, Katherine Mosby, Jim Daniels, John Hoppenthaler, and Jennifer Perrine. *Inkwell* is 150 pages, digest-sized, press-printed, perfect-bound, with cover with illustration/photography. Receives about 2,500 poems/year, accepts about 40. Press run is 1,000. Single copy: $8; subscription: $16/year. Sample: $6 (back issue). Make checks payable to Manhattanville College—*Inkwell*.

How to Submit Submit up to 5 poems at a time. Lines/poem: 70 maximum. Considers simultaneous submissions; no previously published poems. ("Previously published" work includes poetry posted on a public Web site/blog/forum, but not on a private, password-protected forum.) No fax, e-mail, or disk submissions. Cover letter is required. "Omit name of author from text." Include SASE. Reads submissions August 1-November 30. Time between acceptance and publication is 5 months. Poems are circulated to an editorial board. Sometimes comments on rejected poems. Guidelines available for SASE or on Web site. Responds in 3 months. Pays $10/page and 2 contributor's copies. Acquires first North American serial rights. Rights revert to poets upon publication.

Contest/Award Offerings The Inkwell Annual Poetry Competition (see separate listing in Contests & Awards).

▦ ◗ INTERPRETER'S HOUSE

19 The Paddox, Oxford OX2 7PN England. Web site: www.interpretershouse.org.uk. Established 1996. **Contact:** Merryn Williams.

- Business correspondence (including subscriptions) should go to Matt Bright, Upper Flat, 251 Abingdon Rd., Oxford OX1 4TH England.

Magazine Needs *Interpreter's House*, published 3 times/year in February, June, and October, prints short stories and poetry. Wants "good poetry, not too long." Does not want "Christmas-card verse or incomprehensible poetry." Has published poetry by Dannie Abse, Tony Curtis, Pauline Stainer, Alan Brownjohn, Peter Redgrove, and R.S. Thomas. *Interpreter's House* is 74 pages, A5, with attractive cover design. Receives about 1,000 poems/year, accepts up to 5%. Press run is 300 (200

subscribers). Single copy: £3 plus 55p. postage; subscription: £12 for 3 issues. Sample: £3.50.
How to Submit Submit 5 poems at a time. No previously published poems or simultaneous submissions. Cover letter is preferred. Time between acceptance and publication is 2 weeks to 3 months. Often comments on rejected poems. Guidelines available for SASE (or SAE and IRC). Responds "fast." Pays 1 contributor's copy.
Contest/Award Offerings Sponsors the Bedford Open Poetry Competition. Send SAE and IRC for details.

⚡ ◎ INTRO (Specialized: students in college writing programs)
AWP, MS 1E3, George Mason University, Fairfax VA 22030. Web site: http://awpwriter.org. Established 1970. **Contact:** Supriya Bhatnagar, director of publications.
Magazine Needs Students in college writing programs belonging to The Association of Writers & Writing Programs (AWP) may submit to this consortium of magazines publishing student poetry, fiction, and creative nonfiction. Open as to the type of poetry submitted, except they do not want "non-literary, haiku, etc. In our history, we've introduced Dara Wier, Carolyn Forché, Greg Pope, Norman Dubie, and others."
How to Submit All work must be submitted through the program director of your college. Programs nominate *Intro* works in the fall. Ask your program director for more information or go to www.awp writer.org. for guidelines.

◐ ◎ INVERTED-A HORN (Specialized: traditional poetry with meter and rhyme)
Inverted-A, Inc., P.O. Box 267, Licking MO 65542. E-mail: amnfn@well.com. Established 1977. **Contact:** Nets Katz and Aya Katz, editors.
Magazine Needs *Inverted-A Horn*, published irregularly, welcomes political topics, social issues, and science fiction. Wants traditional poetry with meter and rhyme. Does not want to see anything "modern, formless, existentialist." *Inverted-A Horn* is usually 9 pages, magazine-sized, offset-printed. Press run is 300. Sample: SASE with postage for 2 ounces (subject to availability).
How to Submit Considers simultaneous submissions. Accepts e-mail submissions (as attachment, ASCII). Responds in 4 months. Pays 1 contributor's copy; offers 40% discount on additional copies.
Additional Information Inverted-A, Inc. is a very small press that evolved from publishing technical manuals for other products. "Our interests center on freedom, justice, and honor." Publishes 1 chapbook/year.
Advice "I strongly recommend that would-be contributors avail themselves of this opportunity to explore what we are looking for. Most of the submissions we receive do not come close."

◐ IODINE POETRY JOURNAL
P.O. Box 18548, Charlotte NC 28218-0548. (704)595-9526. E-mail: iodineopencut@aol.com. Web site: www.iodinepoetryjournal.com. Established 2000. **Contact:** Jonathan K. Rice, editor/publisher.
• Poetry published in *Iodine Poetry Journal* has been selected for inclusion in *The Best American Poetry*.
Magazine Needs *Iodine Poetry Journal*, published semiannually, provides "a venue for both emerging and established poets." Wants "good poetry of almost any style, including form (e.g., pantoum and sestina) and experimental." Does not want rhyme, religion, or pornography. Has published poetry by Fred Chappell, David Chorlton, Robert Cooperman, Colette Inez, and R.T. Smith. *Iodine Poetry Journal* is 64 pages, digest-sized, perfect-bound, with full-color laminated cover, includes ads. Receives about 2,000 poems/year, accepts about 60 poems/issue. Press run is 350. Single copy: $7; subscription: $12/year (2 issues) $22 for 2 years (4 issues). Sample: "Back issues vary in price." Make checks payable to *Iodine Poetry Journal*.
How to Submit Submit 3-5 poems at a time. Lines/poem: 40 or less preferred, "but not totally averse to longer poems." No previously published poems or simultaneous submissions. Accepts e-mail submissions from international poets only; no disk submissions. Cover letter is preferred. "Always include SASE, and specify if SASE is for return of manuscript or reply only. I like a brief introduction of yourself in the cover letter." Reads submissions year round. Submit seasonal poems 6 months in advance. Time between acceptance and publication is 6 months to 1 year. Poems are

circulated to an editorial board. "I occasionally have other readers assist in the selection process, but editor makes the final decision." Sometimes comments on rejected poems. Guidelines available in magazine, for SASE, or on Web site. Responds in 1-2 months. Sometimes sends prepublication galleys. Pays 1 contributor's copy and discounts extra copies of the issue in which work appears. Acquires first North American serial rights.

Also Offers "Shorter work is published in *Open Cut*, the summer broadside. Payment is 3 copies of the broadside. The broadside is 11×17 folded to pamphlet size, which will fit into a #10 envelope. It's a free publication that appears between the Spring and Fall issues of *Iodine* and is distributed to subscribers and at poetry readings hosted by the editor. Sample copies can be obtained by sending a #10 SASE. *Open Cut* is archived in the Special Collections of some university libraries."

✪ ⊕ ⊘ IOTA

Ragged Raven Press, 1 Lodge Farm, Snitterfield, Warwicks CV37 0LR England. (44)(1789)730320. E-mail: iotapoetry@aol.com. Web site: www.iotapoetry.co.uk. Established 1988. **Contact:** Janet Murch and Bob Mee, editors.

Magazine Needs *iota*, published quarterly, considers "any style and subject; no specific limitations as to length." Has published poetry by Jane Kinninmont, John Robinson, Tony Petch, Chris Kinsey, Christopher James, and Michael Kriesel. *iota* is 56 pages, professionally printed, perfect-bound, with b&w photograph litho cover. Receives 6,000 poems/year, accepts about 300. Press run is 300. Single copy: £3 UK, £4 rest of Europe, £4.50 ROW; subscription: £12 UK, £16 rest of Europe, £18 ROW ("UK sterling only; payment can also be made by credit card via our Web site").

How to Submit Submit 4-6 poems at a time. No previously published poems or simultaneous submissions. Accepts e-mail submissions (pasted into body of message). Cover letter is required. Prefers name and address on each poem, typed. "No SAE, no reply." Responds in 2 months (unless production of the next issue takes precedence). Pays 1 contributor's copy. Reviews books of poetry. Send materials for review consideration.

Additional Information The editors also run Ragged Raven Press (www.raggedraven.co.uk), which publishes poetry collections, nonfiction, and an annual anthology of poetry linked to an international competition.

Contest/Award Offerings Sponsors an annual poetry competition, offering 1st Prize: £200; 2nd and 3rd Prize: £25; publication in *iota* and on Web site. Guidelines available on Web site. **Entry fee**: free for up to 2 poems for subscribers, £2 for each subsequent poem; £2/poem for non-subscribers. **Deadline:** April 15.

Advice "Read poetry, particularly contemporary poetry. Edit your own poems to tighten and polish."

$⊘ THE IOWA REVIEW

308 EPB, University of Iowa, Iowa City IA 52242. (319)335-0462. E-mail: iowa-review@uiowa.edu. Web site: www.iowareview.org. Established 1970. **Contact:** David Hamilton, editor.

• Poetry published in *The Iowa Review* has appeared often in *The Best American Poetry* and *The Pushcart Prize*.

Magazine Needs *The Iowa Review*, published 3 times/year, prints fiction, poetry, essays, reviews, and, occasionally, interviews. "We simply look for poems that, at the time we read and choose, we find we admire. No specifications as to form, length, style, subject matter, or purpose. Though we print work from established writers, we're always delighted when we discover new talent." *The Iowa Review* is 192 pages, professionally printed, flat-spined. Receives about 5,000 submissions/year, accepts up to 100. Press run is 2,900; 1,500 distributed to stores. Subscription: $25. Sample: $9.

How to Submit Submit 3-6 poems at a time. No e-mail submissions. Cover letter (with title of work and genre) is encouraged. SASE required. Reads submissions "only during the Fall semester, September through November, and then contest entries in the spring." Time between acceptance and publication is "around a year." Occasionally comments on rejected poems or offers suggestions on accepted poems. Responds in up to 4 months. Pays $25 for the first page and $15 for each subsequent page, 2 contributor's copies, and a one-year subscription. Acquires first North American serial rights, non-exclusive anthology rights, and non-exclusive electronic rights.

Contest/Award Offerings *The Iowa Review* Award in Poetry, Fiction, and Essay (see separate listing in Contests & Awards).

$⬛ ◎ ISOTOPE: A JOURNAL OF LITERARY NATURE AND SCIENCE WRITING

Dept. of English, Utah State University, 3200 Old Main Hill, Logan UT 84322-3200. (435)797-3697. Fax: (435)797-3797. E-mail: lbrown@cc.usu.edu. Web site: http://isotope.usu.edu. Established 2003. **Contact:** Leslie Brown, managing editor. Member: CLMP.

Magazine Needs *Isotope*, published semianually, features literary nature and science writing. Has published poetry by Pattiann Rogers, Susan Maurer, Joanne Lowery, John Gilgun, Jim Fisher, and Thomas Joswick. *Isotope* is 52 pages, magazine-sized, offset-printed, saddle-stapled, with coverstock cover with color artwork. Receives about 1,200 poems/year, accepts about 20. Press run is 1,400 (1,000 subscribers, 15 libraries, 200 shelf sales); 300 distributed free to contributors, funders, and reviewers. Single copy: $5; subscription: $10. Make checks payable to *Isotope*.

How to Submit Submit 5 poems at a time. Considers simultaneous submissions; no previously published poems. No fax, e-mail, or disk submissions. Cover letter is preferred. "Include SASE, brief bio in cover letter." Reads submissions September 1-November 30. Time between acceptance and publication is 6-18 months. "Decisions are made by Poetry Editor and Magazine Editor." Rarely comments on rejected poems. Sometimes publishes theme issues. Guidelines available for SASE or on Web site. Responds in 6-9 months. Sends prepublication galleys. Pays $50/poem, 4 contributor's copies, and one-year subscription. Acquires first North American serial rights. Rights revert to poet upon publication.

Contest/Award Offerings *Isotope* sponsors an Editors' Prize in poetry. Offers annual award of $300 and publication. Submit up to 5 poems totaling no more than 10 pages. All entries are considered for publication. Guidelines available for SASE or on Web site. **Entry fee:** $15 (includes 2 year magazine subscription). **Deadline:** submit September 1-November 30 (postmark).

◎ ITALIAN AMERICANA (Specialized: Italian culture)

URI/CCE, 80 Washington St., Providence RI 02903-1803. (401)277-5306. Fax: (401)277-5100. E-mail: bonomoal@ital.uri.edu. Web site: www.italianamericana.com. Established 1974. **Contact:** Michael Palma, poetry editor.

Magazine Needs *Italian Americana*, published twice/year, uses 16-20 poems of "no more than 3 pages." Does not want "trite nostalgia about grandparents." Has published poetry by Mary Jo Salter and Jay Parini. *Italian Americana* is 150-200 pages, digest-sized, professionally printed, flat-spined, with glossy card cover. Press run is 1,000. Singly copy: $10; subscription: $20/year, $35 for 2 years. Sample: $7.

How to Submit Submit no more than 3 poems at a time. No previously published poems or simultaneous submissions. Cover letter is not required "but helpful." Name on first page of ms only. Occasionally comments on rejected poems. Responds in 6 weeks. Acquires first rights. Reviews books of poetry in 600 words, multi-book format. Send materials for review consideration to Prof. John Paul Russo, English Dept., University of Miami, Coral Gables, FL 33124.

Contest/Award Offerings Along with the National Italian American Foundation, *Italian Americana* co-sponsors the annual $1,000 John Ciardi Award for Lifetime Contribution to Poetry. *Italian Americana* also presents $250 fiction or memoir award annually; and $1,500 in history prizes.

Advice "Single copies of poems for submissions are sufficient."

$◎ JACK AND JILL (Specialized: children ages 7-10)

Children's Better Health Institute, 1100 Waterway Blvd., Indianapolis IN 46202. Web site: www.cbhi.org. or www.jackandjillmag.org. Established 1938.

Magazine Needs *Jack and Jill*, published bimonthly by The Children's Better Health Network, is a magazine for ages 7-10. Wants light-hearted poetry appropriate for the age group. Reviews submissions for possible use in all Children's Better Health Institute publications.

How to Submit Manuscripts must be typewritten with poet's contact information in upper right-hand corner of each poem's page. SASE required. Submit seasonal material at least 8 months in advance. Guidelines available for SASE or on Web site. Responds in about 3 months. Pays $25 minimum for poetry.

Advice "We receive too many poetry submissions that are about kids, not for kids. Or, the subject matter is one that adults think children would or should like. Reading our guidelines is not enough. Careful study of current issues will acquaint writers with each title's 'personality.' "

■ ◙ ◎ JERRY JAZZ MUSICIAN (Specialized: mid-20th century America)

2207 NE Broadway, Portland OR 97232. (503)287-5570. Fax: (801)749-9896. E-mail: jm@jerryjazz.c om. Web site: www.jerryjazz.com.

Magazine Needs *Jerry Jazz Musician*, published monthly online, "celebrates mid-20th century America, with an emphasis on jazz, film, literature, art, civil rights history, and politics of the era. Open to all topics and poetic forms." Considers poetry by children and teens. Has published poetry by Pablo Neruda, Jim Harrison, Kenneth Rexroth, Golda Soloman, and Bunny M. Receives about 300 poems/year, accepts about 50. Has 4,000 subscribers; distributed free to 150,000 unique Inter net visitors/month.

How to Submit Submit 1-2 poems at a time. Lines/poem: 6-100. Considers previously published poems and simultaneous submissions. Accepts e-mail submissions. "Would prefer e-mail submissi ons pasted into message; however, if font and style are essential to the poem's success, will accept a Microsoft Word attachment." Cover letter is preferred. Reads submissions year round. Submit seasonal poems 4 months in advance. Time between acceptance and publication is 1 month. "Editor consults with a variety of readers, or may make choice on his own." Often comments on rejected poems. Guidelines available on Web site. Responds in 1 month. Poet retains all rights.

✦ ◙ ◎ JEWISH CURRENTS (Specialized: translations of Yiddish & Hebrew; Jewish subj ects)

45 E. 33rd St., 4th Floor, New York NY 10016. (212)889-2523. E-mail: jewishcurrents@circle.org. Web site: www.jewishcurrents.org. Established 1946. **Contact:** Lawrence Bush, editor.

Magazine Needs *Jewish Currents*, published 6 times/year, prints articles, reviews, fiction, and poetry "pertaining to Jewish subjects or presenting a Jewish point of view on an issue of interest, including translations from Yiddish and Hebrew (original texts should be submitted with transla-tions)." Considers poetry by children and teens. *Jewish Currents* is 48 pages, magazine-sized, offset-printed, saddle-stapled. Press run is 12,500. Subscription: $30/year. Sample: $5.

How to Submit Submit 1 poem at a time. No previously published poems or simultaneous submis-sions. Cover letter is required. "Include brief bio with author's publishing history." Poems should be typed, double-spaced; include SASE. Time between acceptance and publication is up to 2 years. Often comments on rejected poems. Responds within 3 months. Always sends prepublication gal-leys. Pays 6 contributor's copies. Reviews books of poetry.

Advice "Be intelligent, original, unexpected, comprehensible."

$◙ ◎ JEWISH WOMEN'S LITERARY ANNUAL (Specialized: poetry by Jewish women only)

820 Second Ave., New York NY 10017. (212)751-9223. Established 1994. **Contact:** Dr. Henny Wenk-art, editor.

Magazine Needs *Jewish Women's Literary Annual*, published in April, prints poetry and fiction by Jewish women. Wants "poems by Jewish women on any topic, but of the highest literary quality." Has published poetry by Linda Zisquit, Merle Feld, Helen Papell, Enid Dame, Marge Piercy, and Lesléa Newman. *Jewish Women's Literary Annual* is 230 pages, digest-sized, perfect-bound, with laminated card cover. Receives about 1,500 poems/year, accepts about 10%. Press run is 1,500. Subscription: $18 for 3 issues. Sample: $7.50.

How to Submit No previously published poems. Poems are circulated to an editorial board. Often comments on rejected poems. Guidelines available for SASE. Responds in up to 5 months. Pays 1 contributor's copy plus a small honorarium. Rights remain with the poet.

Advice "Send only your very best. We are looking for humor, as well as other things, but nothing cutesy or smart-aleck. We do no politics; prefer topics other than 'Holocaust'."

⬇ ☑ JONES AV.

OEL Press, 88 Dagmar Ave., Toronto ON M4M 1W1 Canada. (416)461-8739. E-mail: oel@interlog.c om. Web site: www.interlog.com/~oel. Established 1994. **Contact:** Paul Schwartz, editor/publisher.

Magazine Needs *Jones Av.*, published quarterly, contains "poems from the lyric to the ash can; starting poets and award winners." Wants poems "concise in thought and image. Prose poems sometimes. Rhymed poetry is very difficult to do well these days; it better be good." Has published poetry by Bert Almon, Michael Estabrook, John Grey, Bernice Lever, B.Z. Niditch, and Elana Wolff. *Jones Av.* is 24 pages, digest-sized, photocopied, saddle-stapled, with card cover. Receives about 300 poems/year, accepts 30-40%. Press run is 100. Subscription: $12. Sample: $3. Make checks payable to Paul Schwartz.

How to Submit Submit 3-5 poems at a time. Lines/poem: up to 30. No previously published poems or simultaneous submissions. Accepts e-mail submissions (pasted into body of message). Cover letter is required. Include bio and SASE (or SAE with IRCs). "Remember, U.S. stamps cannot be used in Canada." Time between acceptance and publication is up to 1 year. Often comments on rejected poems. Occasionally publishes theme issues. Upcoming themes available in magazine. Guidelines available for SASE or on Web site. Responds in 3 months. Pays 1 contributor's copy. Acquires first rights. Staff reviews books/chapbooks of poetry and other magazines/journals in 50-75 words, multi-book format. Send materials for review consideration.

Advice "Request and study a sample issue of the publication if you are not familiar with the editor's taste."

⬛ ☑ ◎ THE DAVID JONES JOURNAL (Specizlied: David Jones; the Great War; mythology; visual arts)

The David Jones Society, 22 Gower Rd., Sketty, Swansea, W. Glam SA2 9BY Wales. (44)(179)220-6144. Fax: (44)(179)247-5037. E-mail: anne.price-owen@sihe.ac.uk. Established 1997. **Contact:** Anne Price-Owen, editor.

Magazine Needs *The David Jones Journal*, published annually, features "material related to painter-poet David Jones, War, mythology, religion, poetry, and the visual arts." Wants "anything in the spirit of David Jones." Has published poetry by Seamus Heaney, John Mole, John Montague, R.S. Thomas, Rowan Williams. *The David Jones Journal* is about 200 pages, digest-sized, camera ready-printed, perfect-bound, with full-color card cover. Receives about 30 poems/year, accepts about 12%. Press run is 400 (300 subscribers). Single copy: £10/$25; subscription: £20/$35. Make checks payable to The David Jones Society.

How to Submit Submit 1 poem at a time. Considers simultaneous submissions; no previously published poems. Accepts e-mail and disk submissions. Cover letter is preferred. Time between acceptance and publication is 6 months. "Two editors agree on publication." Occasionally publishes theme issues. Guidelines available by e-mail. Responds in 6 weeks. Sometimes sends prepublication galleys. Pays 2 contributor's copies. Acquires first rights. Reviews books/chapbooks of poetry and other magazines in 750 words, single-book format. Open to unsolicited reviews. Send materials for review consideration.

☑ ◎ JOURNAL OF NEW JERSEY POETS (Specialized: of, by, for NJ poets)

English Dept., County College of Morris, 214 Center Grove Rd., Randolph NJ 07869-2086. (973)328-5471. Fax: (973)328-5425. E-mail: szulauf@ccm.edu. Established 1976. **Contact:** Sander Zulauf, editor. Associate Editors: North Peterson, Debra DeMattio, and Gina Serafin.

Magazine Needs *Journal of New Jersey Poets*, published annually in April, is "not necessarily about New Jersey—but of, by, and for poets from New Jersey." Wants "serious work that conveys the essential, real, whole emotional moment of the poem to the reader without sentimentality." Has published poetry by Joe Weil, X.J. Kennedy, Marvin Silbersher, Tina Kelley, Gerald Stern, Kenneth Burke, and Catherine Doty. *Journal of New Jersey Poets* is about 90 pages, perfect-bound, offset-printed on recycled stock. Press run is 600. Single copy: $10; subscription: $16 for 2 issues ($16/issue for institutions). Sample: $5.

How to Submit Submit up to 3 poems at a time. Accepts fax and e-mail submissions, "but they will not be acknowledged nor returned. Include SASE with sufficient postage for return of manuscript, or provide instructions to recycle.'' Annual deadline for submissions: September 1. Time between acceptance and publication is within 1 year. Guidelines available for SASE or by e-mail. Responds in up to 1 year. Pays 2 contributor's copies and a one-year subscription. Acquires first North American serial rights. All reviews are solicited. Send 2 copies of books for review consideration.

Advice ''Read the *Journal* before submitting. Realize we vote on everything submitted, and rejection is mostly an indication of the quantity of submissions received and the enormous number of New Jersey poets submitting quality work.''

🗀 ◎ JOURNAL OF REGIONAL CRITICISM (Specialized: surrealism; science fiction/ fantasy; spirituality; symbols)

Arjuna Library Press, 1025 Garner St., D, Space 18, Colorado Springs CO 80905-1774. E-mail: pfupho ff@earthlink.net. Web site: http://home.earthlink.net/~pfuphoff/. Established 1963 (library), 1979 (press). **Contact:** Ct. Pf. Joseph A. Uphoff, Jr., executive director.

Magazine Needs *Journal of Regional Criticism*, published frequently in varied format, features ''surrealist prose poetry, visual poetry, dreamlike, short and long works; no obscene, profane (will criticize but not publish), unpolished work.'' Has published work by Aliya Mehdi, Carlos Ponce-Melendez, James Livingston, Jane Stuart, Randall Brock, Janette Patterson-Schafer, and Ronald Orszag. *Journal of Regional Criticism* is published in JPG files (on CD-ROM) of collage, writing, mathematical, fine art theory, and criticism.

How to Submit Send 1 or 2 short poems at a time. ''Upon request will treat material as submitted for reprint, one-time rights.'' Accepts submissions by postal mail only, including CD-ROM: PDF or JPG, ASF. Cover letter is required. Include SASE. Guidelines (on sample CD) available for SASE. Reviews books of poetry ''occasionally.'' Send materials for review consideration.

Additional Information ''The Arjuna Library Press is avant-garde, designed to endure the transient quarters and marginal funding of the literary phenomenon (as a tradition) while presenting a context for the development of current mathematical ideas in regard to theories of art, literature, and performance; publication is now by CD-ROM, JPG, and ASF files. Each disk is unique. The poet is sent a color Xerox hard copy, poems illustrated by photographic and artistic experiments in an irregular format. Photocopy printing allows for very limited editions and irregular format. Quality is maintained as an artistic materialist practice.'' Publishes 6-12 disks/year, averaging 600 MB (50 pages) each. Sample: $10.

Also Offers ''The Arjuna Library Digital Visual Dream Laboratory and Acoustic Studio is extending publication beyond photocopy printing while maintaining respect for artistic relics such as manuscript copies and original photographs or papers. The format will remain varied and irregular (poetic, stream of consciousness production). Poetry is published in writing and with video of poets reading their works. Austerity is due to limited resources and expense of equipment and supplies. Works are now illustrated in color. Development work is continuing of the publication of poetry by the writers listed (Mehdi, Ponce-Melendez, et. al.).''

Advice ''Web site exhibition of visual poetics and literature has proceeded through the Mail Art phenomenon. This is an excellent means of contacting the public in an impersonal way; it remains true that there are other venues to develop the commercial profile. As a general rule, we should use principles of scientific observation (minimum interference) such that the proferred dimensions are not strained or reconfigured. If the membership grows too large, rather than excluding contributors by pyramidal elitism, more organization can be founded. In this way, an accurate assessment can be maintained as to how many individuals are requesting service. Instead of redesigned organization, the pyramidal elitism can be established by supplemental organization. It follows that acceptance then rises to the level of competency of the artist or writer within a system that provides continuing adequate support for newcomers and advancing practitioners. Thus, we do not need a surrender by vulgar insults: irony can be separated from the other reputable constructs. The audience can gravitate to protected interests. Some of the *Journal of Regional Criticism* will be published and exhibited by the internet including sites such as Artmajeur, eSnips, and Flickr.''

⏻ ◎ JOURNAL OF THE AMERICAN MEDICAL ASSOCIATION (JAMA) (Specialized: poetry related to a medical experience)

515 N. State St., Chicago IL 60610. (312)464-444. Fax: (312)464-5824. E-mail: jamams@jama-archives.org. Web site: www.jama.com. Established 1883. **Contact:** Charlene Breedlove, associate editor.

Magazine Needs *Journal of the American Medical Association (JAMA)*,published weekly, includes a poetry and medicine column and publishes poetry "in some way related to a medical experience, whether from the point of view of a health care worker or patient, or simply an observer. No unskilled poetry." Has published poetry by Jack Coulehan, Floyd Skloot, and Walt McDonald. *JAMA* is magazine-sized, flat-spined, with glossy paper cover. Receives about 750 poems/year, accepts about 7%. Has 360,000 subscribers (369 libraries). Subscription: $66. Sample: free, "no SASE needed."

How to Submit No previously published poems or simultaneous submissions. Accepts submissions by fax or through *JAMA*'s Web-based submissions and review system at http://manuscripts.jama.com. (or click the "Information for Authors/Reviewers" button on the www.jama.com. home page). "I always appreciate inclusion of a brief cover letter. Mention of other publications and special biographical notes are always of interest." Publishes theme issues (i.e., in 2007: access to care; malaria; chronic diseases of children; violence/human rights; medical education; poverty and human development). "However, we would rather that poems relate obliquely to the theme." Guidelines available on Web site. Pays 1 contributor's copy, more by request. "We ask for a signed copyright release, but publication elsewhere is always granted."

⚡ $⏻ THE JOURNAL

Dept. of English, The Ohio State University, 164 W. 17th Ave., Columbus OH 43210. (614)292-4076. Fax: (614)292-7816. E-mail: thejournal@osu.edu. Web site: http://english.osu.edu/research/journals/thejournal/. Established 1972. **Contact:** Kathy Fagan and Michelle Herman, co-editors.

Magazine Needs *The Journal*, published twice/year, includes reviews, quality fiction and nonfiction, and poetry. "We're open to all forms; we tend to favor work that gives evidence of a mature and sophisticated sense of the language." Has published poetry by Beckian Fritz Goldberg, Terrance Hayes, Bob Hicok, and Linda Bierds. *The Journal* is 128-144 pages, digest-sized, professionally printed on heavy stock. Receives about 4,000 submissions/year, accepts about 200. Press run is 1,900. Subscription: $12. Sample: $7.

How to Submit Considers simultaneous submissions, "but please notify us of this at time of submission." No fax or e-mail submissions. Occasionally comments on rejected poems. Occasionally publishes theme issues. Guidelines available on Web site. Responds in up to 3 months. Pays 2 contributor's copies "and an honorarium of $20-50 when funds are available." Acquires first North American rights and electronic rights. Returns rights on publication. Reviews books of poetry.

Contest/Award Offerings Chooses the winning ms in the Ohio State University Press/*The Journal Award* (see separate listing in Contests & Awards).

Advice "However else poets train or educate themselves, they must do what they can to know our language. Too much of the writing we see indicates poets do not, in many cases, develop a feel for the possibilities of language, and do not pay attention to craft. Poets should not be in a rush to publish—until they are ready."

🌐 ⏻ THE JOURNAL

Original Plus Press, 17 High St., Maryport, Cumbria CA15 6BQ England. E-mail: smithsssj@aol.com. Web site: http://members.aol.com/smithsssj/index.html. Established 1994. **Contact:** Sam Smith.

Magazine Needs *The Journal*, published annually, features English poetry/translations, reviews, and articles. Wants "new poetry howsoever it comes; translations and original English-language poems." Does not want "staid, generalized, all form/no content." Has published poetry by David H. Grubb, Gary Allen, and Ozdemir Asaf. *The Journal* is 40 pages, A4, offset-printed, stapled. Receives about 1,000 poems/year, accepts about 5%. Press run is 100-150. Single copy: £3; subscription: £8 for 3 issues. Outside UK, single copy: £4; subscription: £11 for 3 issues. Make checks payable to Sam Smith or through PayPal. Back issues £2.

How to Submit Submit up to 6 poems at a time. Considers previously published poems and simultaneous submissions. Accepts e-mail submissions. Cover letter is preferred. "Please send 2 IRCs with hard-copy submissions." Time between acceptance and publication is up to 1 year. Often comments on rejected poems. Guidelines available for SASE (or SAE and IRC). Responds in 1 month. Always sends prepublication galleys. Pays 1 contributor's copy.

Additional Information In 1997, Original Plus Press began publishing collections of poetry. Has published books by Richard Wonnacott, James Turner, Don Ammons, Idris Caffrey, and RG Bishop. Send SASE (or SAE and IRC) or e-mail for details.

Advice "I prefer poetry that has been written with thought—both to what it is saying and how it is being said."

◖ ◎ KAIMANA: LITERARY ARTS HAWAI'I (Specialized: HI, Pacific references)

Hawai'i Literary Arts Council, P.O. Box 11213, Honolulu HI 96828. Web site: www.hawaii.edu/hlac. Established 1974. **Contact:** Tony Quagliano, editor.

- Poets published in *Kaimana* have received the Pushcart Prize, the Hawaii Award for Literature, the Stefan Baciu Award, the Cades Award, and the John Unterecker Award.

Magazine Needs *Kaimana: Literary Arts Hawai'i*, published annually, is the magazine of the Hawai'i Literary Arts Council. Wants poems with "some Pacific reference—Asia, Polynesia, Hawai'i—but not exclusively." Has published poetry by Kathryn Takara, Howard Nemerov, Anne Waldman, Reuel Denney, Haunani-Kay Trask, and Simon Perchik. *Kaimana* is 64-76 pages, $7^{1}/_{2} \times 10$, saddle-stapled, with high-quality printing. Press run is 1,000. Subscription: $15, includes membership in HLAC. Sample: $10.

How to Submit Cover letter is preferred. Sometimes comments on rejected poems. Guidelines available in magazine or on Web site. Responds with "reasonable dispatch." Pays 2 contributor's copies.

Advice "Hawai'i gets a lot of 'travelling regionalists,' visiting writers with inevitably superficial observations. We also get superb visiting observers who are careful craftsmen anywhere. *Kaimana* is interested in the latter, to complement our own best Hawai'i writers."

$◎ KALEIDOSCOPE: EXPLORING THE EXPERIENCE OF DISABILITY THROUGH LITERATURE AND THE FINE ARTS (SPECIALIZED: DISABILITY THEMES)

701 S. Main St., Akron OH 44311-1019. (330)762-9755. Fax: (330)762-0912. E-mail: mshiplett@udsakron.org. Web site: www.udsakron.org/kaleidoscope.htm. Established 1979. **Contact:** Gail Willmott, editor-in-chief.

Magazine Needs *Kaleidoscope: Exploring the Experience of Disability through Literature and the Fine Arts*, published twice/year in January and July, is based at United Disability Services, a not-for-profit agency. Poetry should deal with the experience of disability, but is not limited to that experience when the writer has a disability. Wants high-quality poetry with vivid, believable images and evocative language. Does not want "stereotyping, patronizing, or offending language about disability." Has published poetry by Gerald Wheeler, Jeff Worley, Barbara Crooker, and Sheryl L. Nelms. *Kaleidoscope* is 64 pages, magazine-sized, professionally printed, saddle-stapled, with 4-color semigloss card cover. Press run is 1,500 (for libraries, social service agencies, health care professionals, universities, and individual subscribers). Single copy: $6; subscription: $10 individual, $15 agency.

How to Submit Submit up to 6 poems at a time. Considers previously published poems and simultaneous submissions "as long as we are notified in both instances." Accepts fax and e-mail submissions. Cover letter is required. Send photocopies with SASE for return of work. "All submissions must be accompanied by an autobiographical sketch and should be double-spaced, with pages numbered and author's name on each page." Reads submissions by March 1 and August 1 deadlines. Publishes theme issues. Upcoming themes available in magazine, for SASE, by fax, e-mail, or on Web site. Guidelines available for SASE, by fax, e-mail, and on Web site. Responds within 3 weeks; acceptance or rejection may take 6 months. Pays $10-25 plus 2 contributor's copies. Rights revert to author upon publication. Staff reviews books of poetry. Send materials for review consideration.

◙ KARAMU

Dept. of English, Eastern Illinois University, Charleston IL 61920. Web site: www.eiu.edu/~kara mu. Established 1966. **Contact:** Olga Abella, editor.

- *Karamu* has received grants from the Illinois Arts Council, and has won recognition and money awards in the IAC Literary Awards competition.

Magazine Needs *Karamu*, published annually in May or June, aims to "provide a forum for the best contemporary poetry and fiction that comes our way. We especially like to print the works of new writers. We like to see poetry that shows a good sense of what's being done with poetry currently." Wants "poetry that builds around real experiences, real images, and real characters, and that avoids abstraction, overt philosophizing, and fuzzy pontifications. We prefer well-structured free verse, poetry with an inner, sub-surface structure as opposed to, let's say, the surface structure of rhymed quatrains. We have definite preferences in terms of style and form, but no such preferences in terms of length or subject matter." Does not want "the openly didactic poem. We don't want poems that preach against or for some political or religious viewpoint. The poem should first be a poem." Has published poetry by Becky Kennedy, Bill Brown, Peggy Miller, Michael Salcman, Paula Weld-Cary, and Peter Desy. *Karamu* is 150 pages, digest-sized, handsomely printed (narrow margins), with matte cover. Receives submissions from about 300 poets each year, accepts 40-50 poems. Press run is 500 (300 subscribers, 15 libraries). Single copy: $8. Sample: $6 for 2 back issues.

How to Submit Submit no more than 5 poems at a time. No previously published poems or simultaneous submissions. "Always include a SASE for reply and return of material. Sufficient postage is necessary for return of work." Reads submissions September 1-February 15 only; "for fastest decision, submit January through February 15." Critiques "a few of the better poems. We want the poet to consider our comments and then submit new work." Time between acceptance and publication is up to 1 year. Occasionally publishes theme issues. Guidelines available for SASE. Pays 1 contributor's copy. Acquires first serial rights.

Advice "Follow the standard advice: Know your market. Read contemporary poetry and the magazines you want to be published in. Be patient."

☐ ◎ KELSEY REVIEW (Specialized: Mercer County, NJ writers only)

Liberal Arts Division, Mercer County Community College, P.O. Box B, Trenton NJ 08690. E-mail: kelsey.review@mccc.edu. Web site: www.mccc.edu/community_kelsey-review.shtml. Established 1988. **Contact:** Ed Carmien or Holly-Katharine Johnson, editors.

Magazine Needs *Kelsey Review*, published annually in September by Mercer County Community College, serves as "an outlet for literary talent of people living and working in Mercer County, New Jersey only." Has no specifications as to form, length, subject matter, or style. Fiction: 4,000 word limit. Poetry: Not more than 6 pages. Non-Fiction: 2,500 word limit. Black and White art. Does not want to see poetry "about kittens and puppies." Has published poetry by Vida Chu, Carolyn Foote Edelmann, and Mary Mallery. *Kelsey Review* is about 90 glossy pages, 7×11, with paper cover. Receives 100+ submissions/year, accepts 10. Press run is 2,000; all distributed free to contributors, area libraries, bookstores, and schools.

How to Submit Submit up to 6 poems at a time. No previously published poems or simultaneous submissions. No fax or e-mail submissions. Manuscripts must be typed. Submit poems by May 1 deadline. Guidelines available by e-mail. Responds in August of each year. Pays 5 contributor's copies. All rights revert to authors.

$◙ THE KENYON REVIEW

Walton House, Kenyon College, Gambier OH 43022. (740)427-5208. Fax: (740)427-5417. E-mail: kenyonreview@kenyon.edu. Web site: www.KenyonReview.org. Established 1939. **Contact:** David Lynn, editor.

Magazine Needs *The Kenyon Review*, published quarterly, contains poetry, fiction, essays, criticism, reviews, and memoirs. Features all styles, forms, lengths, and subject matters. Considers translations. Has published poetry by Billy Collins, Diane Ackerman, John Kinsella, Carol Muske-Dukes, Diane di Prima, and Seamus Heaney. *The Kenyon Review* is 180 pages, digest-sized, flat-spined.

Magazines/Journals

Receives about 4,000 submissions/year. Press run is 6,000. Sample: $12 (includes postage).

How to Submit Submit up to 6 poems at a time. No previously published poems or simultaneous submissions. Accepts submissions **through online registration only** at www.kenyon-review.org/submissions (group poems in a single document; do not submit poems individually). Reads submissions September 1-January 31 (for unsolicited work). Guidelines available on Web site. Responds in up to 4 months. Payment for accepted work is made upon publication. Author retains rights and will receive a contract upon acceptance. Does not consider unsolicited reviews.

Advice "Read recent issues of the *Review* to become familiar with the type and quality of writing being published before submitting your work."

▣ ☑ KING LOG

E-mail: davidcase@earthlink.net. Web site: www.angelfire.com/il/kinglog. Established 1997. **Contact:** David Case, David Starkey, and Carolie Parker-Lopez, editors.

Magazine Needs *King Log*, published quarterly online, seeks "accomplished poetry by American and Anglophone writers, whether experimental, confessional, or formalist." Seeks "poetry that captures the confusion of work/writing, romantic attachments, popular and high culture, history, and political and philosophical idealism and disillusion—comedy, irony, and passion." Does not want "gushy, sentimental, macho, or precious" work. Has published poetry by Jim Daniels, Barry Spacks, Katherine Swiggart, Walt McDonald, Evelyn Perry, and Paul Willis. Receives about 400 poems/year, accepts about 60.

How to Submit Submit 3-5 poems at a time. No previously published poems or simultaneous submissions. Accepts e-mail submissions only (pasted into body of message). Cover letter is required. Reads submissions year round. Time between acceptance and publication is 3 months. Poems are read by "3 editors who broadly share a consensus." Seldom comments on rejected poems. Guidelines available on Web site. Responds in 3 weeks. No payment. Acquires one-time rights.

$▢ THE KIT-CAT REVIEW

244 Halstead Ave., Harrison NY 10528-3611. (914)835-4833. E-mail: kitcatreview@gmail.com. Established 1998. **Contact:** Claudia Fletcher, editor.

Magazine Needs *The Kit-Cat Review*, published quarterly, is named "after the 18th-century Kit-Cat Club whose members included Addison, Steele, Congreve, Vanbrugh, and Garth. Its purpose is to promote/discover excellence and originality." Wants quality work—traditional, modern, experimental. Has published poetry by Coral Hull, Virgil Suárez, Margret J. Hoehn, Louis Phillips, Chayym Zeldis, and Marin Sorescu. *The Kit-Cat Review* is 75 pages, digest-sized, laser-printed/photocopied, saddle-stapled, with colored card cover. Receives about 1,000 poems/year. Press run is 500. "*The Kit-Cat Review* is part of the collections of the University of Wisconsin (Madison) and the State University of New York (Buffalo)." Subscription: $25. Sample: $7. Make checks payable to Claudia Fletcher.

How to Submit Submit any number of poems at a time. Considers previously published poems and simultaneous submissions. "Cover letter should contain any relevant bio." Time between acceptance and publication is 2 months. Responds within 2 months. Pays up to $100/poem plus 2 contributor's copies. Acquires first or one-time rights.

▣ ▢ ◎ KOTAPRESS LOSS JOURNAL (Specialized: grief & healing in relation to death of a child)

(206)251-6706. E-mail: editor@kotapress.com. Web site: www.kotapress.com. Established 1999. **Contact:** Kara L.C. Jones, editor.

Magazine Needs *KotaPress Loss Journal*, published monthly online, provides support "of the grief and healing process after the death of a child. We publish *only* non-fictional poetry that somehow relates to grief and healing in relation to the death of a child. Please do not make up poems about this kind of loss and send them just to get in the magazine; it is insulting to many of our readers who are living this reality. As always, our interest is more in the content and story rather than one's ability to write in form; more in the ideas of poetry therapy rather than the academic, critique, competitive ideas normally fostered in universities.'' Has published poetry by John Fox, Poppy Hullings, Patricia Wellingham-Jones, Carol Jo Horn, and Sarah Bain.

How to Submit ''Please read current and some archived issues of the *Loss Journal* before sending anything. Then send a letter explaining your interest in contributing. We are interested in knowing how your personal experiences with death, dying, grief, and healing are playing out in the specific poems you are submitting. Include a bio if you wish to see one published with your poems after acceptance. Send your letter, poems, and bio as text all in one e-mail. Multiple e-mails will be ignored. File attachments will be deleted without ever being opened or acknowledged. Make sure the subject line of your e-mail says 'Loss Journal Submission'—we get over 600 e-mails a day, most of them spam, so we sort and read based on the subject line.'' Reads submissions year round on a rolling basis. Time between acceptance and publication is up to 2 months. Guidelines available on Web site. Responds in 2 months. Acquires one-time electronic rights and archive rights. ''We do not remove works from our archives. Please see our Web site to find out more about us and about what we offer. We look forward to hearing from you and reading your poetry.''

Advice ''If you are interested in contributing to our *Loss Journal*, it is really important that you read the journal first. This will tell you a lot about the voice of the work we publish and how your poems might 'fit the bill' for us. Please understand that while we acknowledge that all losses are difficult, we do not equate pet loss with child loss—and we do not equate fictional ideas about loss with the reality of death and dying. Read the journal first. Then submit your poems if you feel they fit the mission of our journal.''

⊕ ◐ KRAX

63 Dixon Lane, Leeds, Yorkshire LS12 4RR England. Established 1971. **Contact:** Andy Robson, editor.

Magazine Needs *Krax*, published annually in the summer, prints contemporary poetry from England and America. Wants ''poetry that is light-hearted and witty; original ideas.'' All forms and styles considered. Does not want ''haiku, religious, or topical politics.'' Has published poetry by Dean Blehert, Gail Holmes, and Salena Godden. *Krax* is 72 pages, digest-sized, offset-printed, saddle-stapled. Receives up to 700 submissions/year, accepts about 10%. Single copy: £3.50 ($7); subscription: £10 ($20). Sample: $1 (75p).

How to Submit Submit 6 poems maximum at a time. Lines/poem: 2,000 words maximum. No previously published poems or simultaneous submissions. No disk submissions. Cover letter is preferred. ''Writer's name on same sheet as poem. SASE or SAE with IRC encouraged but not vital.'' Responds in 2 months. Pays 1 contributor's copy. Reviews books of poetry (''brief, individual comments; no outside reviews''). Send materials for review consideration.

Advice ''Rewrite only to improve structure or format—unnecessary rewriting usually destroys the original spontaneity and rhythm.''

ℕ ◻ ◎ LACHRYMA: MODERN SONGS OF LAMENT (Specialized: Lament)

P.O. Box 9675, Canton OH 44714. E-mail: submissions@lachryma.com. Web site: www.lachryma.com. Established 2007. **Contact:** Lizzie Joy Lukens, editor.

Magazine Needs *Lachryma: Modern Songs of Lament*, published semiannually in April and October, prints poetry ''on the topic of suffering, grief, sadness, disappointment with God, etc, either fictional or based on real life experiences.'' Wants ''poetry of any form. Formal verse, rhyme, or free verse are all okay. Also accepting short stories or prose up to 2,500 words, and b&w artwork.'' Does not want ''anything that is merely an attempt to fix the problem by providing pat answers.'' *Lachryma* is magazine-sized, staple-bound, with b&w artwork; includes ads. Receives about 100 poems/year, accepts about 30%. Press run is 300. Single copy: $6.50; subscription: $11.95. Sample: $5 (back issue). Make checks payable to Lachryma Publishing.

How to Submit Submit up to 3 poems at a time. Considers previously published poems and simultaneous submissions. Accepts e-mail submissions (pasted into body of message); no fax or disk submissions. Cover letter is unnecessary. Include mailing address and 2-3 sentence bio. Include SASE with mailed submissions. Reads submissions April - September. Time between acceptance and publication is up to 1 year. Poems are circulated to an editorial board. Never comments on rejected poems. Guidelines available in magazine and on Web site. Responds in 8 weeks. Pays 1 contributor's copy. Acquires one-time rights. Rights revert to poets upon publication.

Advice "There are a lot of ways one could go with this topic—feel free to think outside the box. Poetry for publication should be well-edited and crafted, not something simply spewed off after a bad day."

$☐ ◎ LADYBUG MAGAZINE (Specialized: children ages 2-6)

Carus Publishing, 70 E. Lake St., Suite 300, Chicago IL 60601. Web site: www.cricketmag.com. Established 1990. **Contact:** Submissions Editor.

Magazine Needs *LADYBUG Magazine*, published monthly, is a reading and listening magazine for young children (ages 2-6). Wants poetry that is "rhythmic, rhyming; serious, humorous, active." *LADYBUG* is 40 pages, 8×10, staple-bound, with full color cover. Receives more than 1,200 submissions/month, accepts 25-30. Circulation is 120,000. Subscription: $35.97/year (12 issues). Sample: $5; sample pages available on Web site.

How to Submit Submit no more than 5 poems at a time. Lines/poem: up to 20. Considers previously published poems. Include SASE. Responds in 6 months. Guidelines available for SASE or on Web site. Pays $3/line ($25 minimum) on publication. Acquires North American publication rights for previously published poems; rights vary for unpublished poems.

Advice "In evaluating manuscripts, we look for beauty of language and a sense of joy or wonder. Before attempting to write for *LADYBUG*, be sure to familiarize yourself with this age child and with the magazine itself."

◢☐ LAKE EFFECT: A JOURNAL OF THE LITERARY ARTS

School of Humanities & Social Sciences, Penn State Erie, 5091 Station Rd., Erie PA 16563-1501. (814)898-6281. Fax: (814)898-6032. E-mail: gol1@psu.edu. Web site: www.pserie.psu.edu/lakeeffect. Established 1978 (as *Tempus*; renamed *Lake Effect* in 2001). **Contact:** George Looney, editor-in-chief. Member: CLMP.

Magazine Needs *Lake Effect*, published annually in March/April, provides "an aesthetic venue for writing that uses language precisely to forge a genuine and rewarding experience for our readers. *Lake Effect* wishes to publish writing that rewards more than 1 reading, and to present side-by-side the voices of established and emerging writers." Wants "poetry aware of, and wise about, issues of craft in forming language that is capable of generating a rich and rewarding reading experience." Does not want "sentimental verse reliant on clichés." Has published poetry by Norman Dubie, Richard Jackson, David Kirby, Susan Ludvigson, Harry Humes, and Chase Twichell. *Lake Effect* is 180 pages, digest-sized, offset-printed, perfect-bound, with gloss-by-flat film lamination cover. Receives about 3,000 poems/year, accepts about 1%. Press run is 800 (300 shelf sales); 300 distributed free to contributors and writing programs. Single copy: $6; subscription: $6. Make checks payable to The Pennsylvania State University.

How to Submit Submit 3-5 poems at a time. Considers simultaneous submissions; no previously published poems. No fax, e-mail, or disk submissions. Cover letter is required. Reads submissions year round. Time between acceptance and publication is up to 4 months. "The poetry staff reads the poems, meets and discusses them to come to a consensus. Poetry editor, along with editor-in-chief, makes final decisions." Occasionally comments on rejected poems. Guidelines available in magazine or on Web site. Responds in up to 4 months. Pays 2 contributor's copies. Acquires first North American serial rights.

Advice "*Lake Effect* strives to provide an attractive venue for the good work of both established and emerging writers. We care about the integrity of poetry, and care for the poems we accept."

⊞ ◎ LANDFALL: NEW ZEALAND ARTS AND LETTERS (Specialized: work by & about New Zealand writers)

Otago University Press, P.O. Box 56, Dunedin New Zealand. (64)(3)479-8807. Fax: (64)(3)479-8385. E-mail: landfall@otago.ac.nz. Web site: www.otago.ac.nz/press/landfall. Established 1947; originally published by Caxton Press, then by Oxford University Press, now published by Otago University Press. **Contact:** Richard Reeve, *Landfall* coordinator.

Magazine Needs *Landfall: New Zealand Arts and Letters*, published twice/year in May and November, focuses "primarily on New Zealand literature and arts. It publishes new fiction, poetry, commentary, and interviews with New Zealand artists and writers, and reviews of New Zealand books." Single issue: $29.95 NZD; subscription: $45 NZD (2 issues) for New Zealand subscribers, $30 AUD for Australian subscribers, $30 USD for other overseas subscribers.

How to Submit No fax or e-mail submissions. "Once accepted, contributions should, if possible, also be submitted on disk." Submissions must be typed and include SASE. Publishes theme issues. Guidelines available for SASE. New Zealand poets should write for further information.

◼ ◿ LANGUAGEANDCULTURE.NET

E-mail: review@languageandculture.net. Web site: www.languageandculture.net. Established 2001. **Contact:** Liz Fortini, editor.

Magazine Needs *Languageandculture.net*, published twice/year online, prints contemporary poetry in English. Also accepts translations of Spanish, French, German, Italian, and Russian; "other languages under review." No restrictions on form. Considers poetry by teens. Publishes 20-40 poems/issue.

How to Submit Submit up to 5 poems at a time. Lines/poem: 70 maximum. Considers previously published poems and simultaneous submissions. Accepts e-mail submissions; no disk submissions. "Return e-mail address must be included." Cover letter is preferred. Include brief bio. Reads submissions "yearly." Time between acceptance and publication "varies; no longer than 5 months." Poems are circulated to an editorial board. Comments on rejected poems. No payment. Acquires one-time electronic rights.

Advice "Enrich your lives with different perspectives and poetry styles."

◻ ◎ LAURELS (Specialized: work by members only)

West Virginia Poetry Society, % Debra J. Harmes-Kurth, 1050A McGhee St, Milton WV, 25541. E-mail: djharmeskurth@hotmail.com. Web site: http://laurels.wvpoetrysociety.org. Contact: Debra J. Harmes-Kurth, editor or Lola Warren, co-editor.

Magazine Needs *Laurels*, published quarterly, is the journal of the West Virginia Poetry Society, with poetry and line drawings. **Considers work from WVPS members only.** " *Laurels* was established by Jim Bush and the Ripley Chapter, which starts out each meeting with the words of their founder: 'We gather together,/ for better or worse, / but mainly to better / our amateur verse.' *Laurels* was established in that spirit, to showcase the work of the members who are constantly striving to better their craft." Wants "any form, any style, most subjects." Does not want "anything hostile, prejudiced, or erotic." Considers poetry by children and teens, if members. Editor will need parental consent for anyone under the age of 18. Has published poetry by Kirk Judd, Salvatore Buttaci, Ann Gasser, "Granny Sue" Susanna Holstein, Jim Bush, and Tovli Simiryan. *Laurels* is usually 50 pages, digest-sized, stapled, with a cardstock cover with pen and ink drawings. Accepts about 70% of submissions. Press run is 300. Single copy: $7 "when available, e-mail first to be sure." Subscription: $20, includes full membership to WVPS. Make checks payable to WVPS-Treasurer.

How to Submit Submit up to 4 poems at a time, no more than 40 lines. Considers previously published poems and simultaneous submissions. Accepts e-mail submissions (pasted into body of email message); no fax or disk. Cover letter is preferred. Include brief bio. **Writers should request and read guidelines before submitting.** "Telephone numbers or e-mail addresses included with submissions would be helpful if there is a question." Reads submissions year round. Submit seasonal poems 6 months in advance. Time between acceptance and publication is 4 months or more. "*Laurels* is open to members only, but we'd love for people to join WVPS even if it's only to contribute to *Laurels* and submit to annual contests." Sometimes comments on rejected poems. Guidelines available for SASE, in magazine, and on Web site. Responds in up to 6 months. Pays 1 contributor's copy. Acquires one-time rights. Rights revert to poets upon publication.

Contest/Award Offerings West Virginia Poetry Society (WVPS) sponsors an annual contest for members. See Web site for more information. **Entry fee:** no fee for current WVPS members.

Advice "Poets/writers of all skill levels will be accepted. As a poetry society and a community, we have a unique opportunity to learn from one another."

⊠ ▣ ○ ◎ LAURELS ONLINE (Specialized: West Virginia or Appalacian Themed Poems)

℅ Holly Cross, Nitro WV 25143. E-mail: wvpoetrysociety.org. Web site: http://laurelsonline.wvpoet rysociety.org. Established 2008 **Contact:** Holly Cross, online editor.

Magazine Needs *Laurels Online*, published quarterly online, prints West Virginia or Appalachian themed poems, preferably by poets from Appalachia, American South, or West Virginia. "Unlike the WVPS print publication, *Laurels*, which is open only to member submissions, *Laurels Online* accepts submissions from non-members. We seek to create an Appalachian-themed e-zine that supports Appalachian poets and explores Appalachian themes." Wants all forms, all styles. "Appalachian themes; partial to West Virginia specific poems." Does not want "anything derogatory about the south or Appalachia. *Laurels Online* is a celebration of Appalachia." Considers poetry by children and teens "with parental consent for anyone under the age of 18."

How to Submit Submit up to 3 poems at a time, preferably less than 40 lines but will consider longer. Considers previously published poems and simultaneous submissions. (Considers poetry posted on a public Web site/blog/forum and poetry posted on a private, password-protected forum as published.) Accepts e-mail submissions (pasted into body of message); no fax or disk submissions. Cover letter is preferred. "In your cover letter, please tell us a little about your background/ heritage. If you don't live in Appalachia now, tell us when you did, when you visited, where and why. Tell us about your motivation to write about Appalachian themes. If you submit via snail mail, please enclose an SASE." Reads submissions year round. Submit seasonal poems 4 months in advance. Time between acceptance and publication is up to 6 months. Often comments on rejected poems. Sometimes publishes theme issues; upcoming themes available in magazine and on Web site. Guidelines available in magazine, by e-mail, and on Web site. Responds in 2 - 3 months. Acquires one-time rights. Rights revert to poets upon publication. Reviews books and chapbooks of poetry. Send materials for review consideration "the same as you would a poem. We only review chapbooks and books or publish reviews by Appalachian writers. We will accept reviews written by members and other poets. Reviews must be very well-written, thoughtful, and insightful."

Contest/Award Offerings The WVPS sponsors annual contests, prize varies. See Web site for guidelines. **Entry fee**: no fee for WVPS members; $1 per poem for everyone else. **Deadline**: July of each year.

Also Offers *Laurel*, a print version of the publication for the WVPS. See separate listing in Magazines/Journals.

Advice "If you do not read poetry, you cannot write poetry. E-zines give everyone the opportunity to read the most contemporary and current poetry available, usually without spending a dime. Read new poetry every day and you will begin to see where your voice fits into the culture of modern poetry. Ignoring what is out there is (I find) the most common mistake young poets make. Read, read, read!"

✪ $○ ◎ LEADING EDGE (Specialized: science fiction/fantasy only)

CRWH, Provo UT 84602. E-mail: fiction@leadingedgemagazine.com. Web site: www.leadingedge magazine.com. **Contact:** Matt Gibbons, poetry director.

Magazine Needs *Leading Edge*, published biannually in April and October, is a journal of science fiction and fantasy. Wants "high-quality poetry reflecting both literary value and popular appeal. We accept traditional science fiction and fantasy poetry, but we like innovative stuff." Does not want "graphic sex, violence, or profanity." Considers poetry by children and teens. Has published poetry by Michael Collings, Tracy Ray, Susan Spilecki, and Bob Cook. *Leading Edge* is 170 pages, digest-sized. Receives about 60 poems/year, accepts about 4. Press run is 500 (100 subscribers, 10 libraries, 400 shelf sales). Single copy: $5.95; subscription: $10 (2 issues), $20 (4 issues), $27.50 (6 issues).

How to Submit Submit 1 or more poems at a time. No simultaneous submissions or previously published poems. No e-mail submissions. Cover letter is preferred. "Include name, address, phone number, length of poem, title, and type of poem at the top of each page. Please include SASE with every submission." Guidelines available in magazine, for SASE, or on Web site. Responds in 2-4 months. Always sends prepublication galleys. Pays $10 for the first 4 typeset pages, $1.50 for each additional page, plus 2 contributor's copies. Acquires first North American serial rights.

Advice "Poetry is given equal standing with fiction; it is not treated as filler, but as art."

ⓃⒹ LEAGUE OF LABORING POETS, THE

19850 Arrow Hwy, #C10, Covina CA 91724.626-966-2329. E-mail: laboringpoets@yahoo.com. Established 2007 **Contact**: Tom Conroy, publisher/editor.

Magazine Needs *The League of Laboring Poets*, published quarterly, "includes chapbook reviews, interviews with poets, some photography." Wants "all types of poetry, favors free verse, haiku, and tanka." Does not want "religious, sentimental, defamatory or bigoted poems." *The League of Laboring Poets* is 28 pages, digest-sized, offset, stiched binding, with color photograph cover. Receives about 600 poems/year, accepts about 10%. Press run is 250; distributed free to 22. Single copy: $3.50; subscription: $10/year. Make checks payable to Tom Conroy.

How to Submit Submit 3-5 poems at a time, maximum 80 lines, though will go over for a great poem. Considers previously published poems and simultaneous submissions. Considers poetry posted on a public Web site/blog/forum and poetry posted on a private, password-protected forum as published. Accepts e-mail submissions; no fax or disk submissions. Cover letter is preferred. Reads submissions year round. Time between acceptance and publication is up to 8 weeks. Poems are circulated to an editorial board. Never comments on rejected poems. Guidelines available in magazine or for SASE. Responds in 2 weeks. Pays 2 contributor copies, 1 poem in the Best Of issue awarded $25. Acquires one-time rights. Rights revert to poets upon publication. Reviews books and chapbooks of poetry in 600-800 words.

Additional Information Also seeking submissions for a trifold insert included with each issue featuring haiku and tanka.

Contest/Award Offerings Best of Issue offered quarterly offers a $25 prize for best poem in each issue. All poems submitted are considered. No entry fee. Deadline: January 1, April 1, August 1, and October 1.

Advice "Strong imagery and well crafted words/sounds are appreciated. No gimmicky poetry accepted."

Ⓓ THE LEDGE

40 Maple Ave., Bellport NY 11713. E-mail: tkmonaghan@aol.com. Web site: www.theledgemagazine.com. Established 1988. **Contact:** Timothy Monaghan, editor-in-chief/publisher.

Magazine Needs *The Ledge* seeks "poems that utilize language and imagery in a fresh, original fashion. We favor poems that speak to the human experience." Wants "inspired, imaginative, well-crafted verse, and we're open to all styles and schools of writing. Each issue of *The Ledge* features a wide and eclectic range of work by poets of all backgrounds and persuasions. Excellence is the ultimate criterion." Has published poetry by Elton Glaser, Robert Fanning, Jennifer Perrine, Tony Gloeggler, Melody Lacina, and Lynne Knight. *The Ledge* is 240 pages, 6×9, typeset, perfect-bound, with glossy cover. Accepts 3% of poetry received. Press run is 1,500. Single copy: $10; subscription: $18 for 2 issues, $32 for 4 issues, $42 for 6 issues.

How to Submit Submit 3-5 poems at a time. Considers simultaneous submissions; no previously published poems. Include SASE. Reads submissions September-May. Responds in 3-6 months. Pays 1 contributor's copy. Acquires one-time rights.

Contest/Award Offerings *The Ledge* Poetry Awards Competition and *The Ledge* Poetry Chapbook Contest (see separate listings in Contests & Awards).

Ⓓ LEFT BEHIND, A JOURNAL OF SHOCK LITERATURE

832 Shasta Dr., Colton CA 92324. E-mail: Jeffery@epicentermagazine.org. Established 2007. **Contact:** Jeff Green, editor.

Magazine Needs *Left Behind, A Journal of Shock Literature*, published semiannually, prints poetry, short stories, short plays, screenplays, and essays. Wants "the work you thought was too racy to ever admit you wrote. The blasphemous, erotic, misanthropic, political incorrectable, homoerotic, homophobic, homo-habilis, scatological—you know, the good stuff. Formal, free verse, experimental, visual/concrete are all welcome. Surprise us. The serious and dark are encouraged, but the humorous is prized. Make us blush and say, 'Jeez, did we print that?' Imagine Bukowski, but without the soft touch." *Left Behind* is 80 pages, digest-sized, full-color laser-printed, perfect-bound, with color cover, includes ads. Press run is 1000. Single copy: $8. Make checks payable to Jeff Green.

How to Submit Submit 6 poems at a time. Lines/poem: "no range limit; but we are only 80 pages, so if it's long, it's got to be good." Considers previously published poems and simultaneous submissions. Accepts e-mail submissions (as attachment; "Left Behind" should be in subject line) and disk submissions; no fax. Cover letter is preferred. Reads submissions year round. Time between acceptance and publication is 8 months. Poems are circulated to an editorial board. Sometimes comments on rejected poems. Guidelines available in magazine or for SASE. Responds in 2 months. Pays 2 contributor's copies. Acquires one-time rights. Rights revert to poets upon publication. Reviews books/chapbooks of poetry and other magazines/journals in single-book format. Send materials for review consideration to Jeff Green.

Advice "For humorous work, read it to your friends and see if they laugh before submitting it to *Left Behind*. For poetry, attend an open mic and see how the audience responds. If there are no open mics in your area, start one."

✪ ☑ ◎ LEFT CURVE (Specialized: political; social issues)

P.O. Box 472, Oakland CA 94604-0472. (510)763-7193. E-mail: editor@leftcurve.org. Web site: www.leftcurve.org. Established 1974. **Contact:** Csaba Polony, editor.

Magazine Needs *Left Curve*, published "irregularly, about every 10 months," addresses the "problem(s) of cultural forms, emerging from the crisis of modernity, that strives to be independent from the control of dominant institutions, and free from the shackles of instrumental rationality." Wants poetry that is "critical culture, social, political, 'post-modern.' We will look at any form of poetry, from experimental to traditional." Does not want "purely formal, too self-centered, poetry that doesn't address in sufficient depth today's problems." Has published poetry by Jon Hillson, Devorah Major, W.K. Buckley, and Jack Hirschman. *Left Curve* is 144 pages, magazine-sized, offset-printed, perfect-bound, with Durosheen cover, includes ads. Press run is 2,000 (250 subscribers, 100 libraries, 1,600 shelf sales). Subscription: $30/3 issues (individuals) , $45/3 issues (institutions). Sample: $10.

How to Submit Submit up to 5 poems at a time. Lines/poem: "most of our published poetry is 1 page in length, though we have published longer poems of up to 8 pages." Accepts e-mail or disk submissions. Cover letter is required. "Explain why you are submitting." Publishes theme issues. Guidelines available for SASE, by e-mail, or on Web site. Responds in up to 6 months. Pays 3 contributor's copies. Send materials for review consideration.

☑ ◎ LIGHT (Specialized: light verse)

P.O. Box 7500, Chicago IL 60680. Web site: www.lightquarterly.com. Established 1992. **Contact:** John Mella, editor.

Magazine Needs *Light*, published quarterly, prints "light and occasional verse, satire, wordplay, puzzles, cartoons, and line art." Does not want "greeting card verse, cloying or sentimental verse." *Light* is 64 pages, perfect-bound. Single copy: $6; subscription: $22/year, $34 for 2 years, $38/year international ($28/year, $46 for 2 years for institutions). Sample (back issue): $5 plus $2 for first-class postage.

How to Submit No previously published poems or simultaneous submissions. Submit 1 poem/page. Include name, address, poem title, and page number on each page. Seldom comments on rejected poems. Guidelines available for #10 SASE. Responds in 6 months or less. Always sends prepublication galleys. Pays 2 contributor's copies to domestic contributors, 1 to foreign contributors. Send materials for review consideration.

✪ ◎ LILITH MAGAZINE: INDEPENDENT, JEWISH & FRANKLY FEMINIST (SPECIALIZED: WOMEN; JEWISH)

250 W. 57th St., Suite 2432, New York NY 10107-0172. (212)757-0818. Fax: (212)757-5705. E-mail: info@lilith.org. Web site: www.lilith.org. Established 1976. **Contact:** Poetry Editor.

Magazines/Journals

Magazine Needs *Lilith Magazine: Independent, Jewish & Frankly Feminist*, published quarterly, is "an independent magazine with a Jewish feminist perspective" that uses poetry by Jewish women "about the Jewish woman's experience." Does not want poetry on other subjects. "Generally we use short rather than long poems." Has published poetry by Irena Klepfisz, Lyn Lifshin, Marcia Falk, Adrienne Rich, and Muriel Rukeyser. *Lilith Magazine* is 48 pages, magazine-sized, with glossy color cover. Publishes about 4 poems/year. Press run is about 10,000 (about 6,000 subscribers). Subscription: $21/year. Sample: $6.

How to Submit Send up to 3 poems at a time. Considers simultaneous submissions "if advised." No e-mail submissions. "Please put name and contact info on each sheet submitted. Copy should be neatly typed and proofread for typos and spelling errors. Short cover letters only." Sometimes comments on rejected poems. Guidelines available for SASE or on Web site. Responds in up to 6 months.

Advice "Read a copy of the publication before you submit your work. Please be patient."

LILLIPUT REVIEW (Specialized: poems of 10 lines or less; short Eastern forms)

282 Main St., Pittsburgh PA 15201-2807. E-mail: lilliputreview@gmail.com. Web site: http://donw7 14.tripod.com/lillieindex.html. Established 1989. **Contact:** Don Wentworth, editor.

Magazine Needs *Lilliput Review*, published 8-10 times/year, is "shipped 2 issues at a time, every fourth issue being a broadside that features the work of a single poet." Wants poems in any style or form, no longer than 10 lines. Has published poetry by Pamela Miller Ness, Albert Huffstickler, Charlie Mehrhoff, and John Martone. *Lilliput Review* is 12-16 pages, $4\frac{1}{4} \times 3\frac{1}{2}$, laser-printed on colored paper, stapled. Press run is 400. Subscription: $5 for 6 issues, $10 for 15 issues; $12 for institutions (12 issues). Sample: $1 or SASE. Make checks payable to Don Wentworth.

How to Submit Submit up to 3 poems at a time. Lines/poem: 10 maximum. Considers previously published poems if noted as such. SASE required. Editor comments on submissions "occasionally; I always try to establish human contact." Guidelines available for SASE or on Web site. Responds within 90 months. Pays 2 contributor's copies/poem. Acquires first rights.

Additional Information The Modest Proposal Chapbook Series began in 1994, publishing 1 chapbook/year, 18-24 pages in length. Has published *Now Now* by Cid Corman. **Chapbook submissions are by invitation only.** Query with standard SASE. Sample chapbook: $3.

Advice "A note above my desk reads 'Clarity & resonance, not necessarily in that order.' The perfect poem for *Lilliput Review* is simple in style and language, and elusive/allusive in meaning and philosophy. *Lilliput* is open to all short poems in approach and theme, including any of the short Eastern forms, traditional or otherwise."

LIPS

7002 Blvd. East, #2-26G, Guttenberg NJ 07093. (201)662-1303. E-mail: LBoss79270@aol.com. Established 1981. **Contact:** Laura Boss, poetry editor.

Magazine Needs *Lips*, published twice/year, takes pleasure "in publishing previously unpublished poets as well as the most established voices in contemporary poetry. We look for quality work: the strongest work of a poet; work that moves the reader; poems that take risks that work. We prefer clarity in the work rather than the abstract. Poems longer than 6 pages present a space problem." Has published poetry by Robert Bly, Allen Ginsberg, Michael Benedikt, Maria Gillan, Stanley Barkan, Lyn Lifshin, and Ishmael Reed. *Lips* is about 150 pages, digest-sized, flat-spined. Receives about 16,000 submissions/year, accepts about 1%. Press run is 1,000 (200 subscribers, 100 libraries). Sample: $10 plus $2 for postage.

How to Submit Submit 6 pages maximum at a time. Poems should be typed. Reads submissions September-March only. Guidelines available for SASE. Responds in 1 month (but has gotten backlogged at times). Sometimes sends prepublication galleys. Pays 1 contributor's copy. Acquires first rights.

Advice "Remember the 2 T's: Talent and Tenacity."

THE LISTENING EYE

Kent State Geauga Campus, 14111 Claridon-Troy Rd., Burton OH 44021. (440)286-3840. E-mail: grace_butcher@msn.com. Web site: www.geocities.com/Athens/3716. Established 1970 (for student work), 1990 (as national publication). **Contact:** Grace Butcher, editor.

Magazine Needs *The Listening Eye*, published annually in early fall, prints poetry, short fiction, creative nonfiction, and art. Wants "high literary-quality poetry. Any subject, any style." Does not want "trite images or predictable rhyme." Considers poetry by children and teens if high literary quality. Has published poetry by Alberta Turner, Virgil Suárez, Walter McDonald, and Simon Perchik. *The Listening Eye* is 52-60 pages, digest-sized, professionally printed, saddle-stapled, with card stock cover with b&w or color art. Receives about 200 poems/year, accepts about 5%. Press run is 200. Single copy: $4. Make checks payable to Grace Butcher.

How to Submit Submit up to 4 poems at a time. Lines/poem: "prefer shorter poems (less than 2 pages), but will consider longer if space allows." Accepts previously published poems "occasionally"; no simultaneous submissions. No e-mail submissions "unless from overseas." Cover letter is required. Poems should be typed, single-spaced, 1 poem/page—name, address, phone number, and e-mail address in upper left-hand corner of each page—with SASE for return of work. Reads submissions January 1-April 15 only. Time between acceptance and publication is up to 6 months. Poems are circulated to the editor and 2 assistant editors who read and evaluate work separately, then meet for final decisions. Occasionally comments on rejected poems. Guidelines available in magazine or for SASE. Responds in 1 month. Pays 2 contributor's copies. Acquires first or one-time rights.

Contest/Award Offerings Awards $30 to the best sports poem in each issue.

Advice "I look for tight lines that don't sound like prose; unexpected images or juxtapositions; the unusual use of language; noticeable relationships of sounds; a twist in viewpoint; an ordinary idea in extraordinary language; an amazing and complex idea simply stated; play on words and with words; an obvious love of language. Poets need to read the 'Big 3'—Cummings, Thomas, Hopkins—to see the limits to which language can be taken. Then read the 'Big 2'—Dickinson to see how simultaneously tight, terse, and universal a poem can be, and Whitman to see how sprawling, cosmic, and personal. Then read everything you can find that's being published in literary magazines today, and see how your work compares to all of the above."

🖥 🖉 LITERAL LATTÉ

200 E. 10th St., Suite 240, New York NY 10003. (212)260-5532. E-mail: litlatte@aol.com. Web site: www.literal-latte.com. Established 1994. **Contact:** Dorie Davidson, assistant editor.

Magazine Needs *Literal Latté*, published continually online, is a literary journal of "pure prose, poetry, and art. Open to all styles of poetry—quality is the determining factor." Has published poetry by Allen Ginsberg, Carol Muske, Amy Holman, and John Updike. Receives about 3,000 poems/year, accepts 1%.

How to Submit Considers simultaneous submissions; no previously published poems. No e-mail submissions; postal submissions only. Cover letter is required. Include bio and SASE (or e-mail for response only). Time between acceptance and publication is within 1 year. Often comments on rejected poems. Guidelines available by e-mail or on Web site. Responds in 5 months.

Additional Information "We will publish an anthology in book form at the end of each year, featuring the best of our Web magazine."

Contest/Award Offerings *Literal Latté* Poetry Awards and *Literal Latté* Food Verse Awards (see separate listings in Contests & Awards).

🖥 🖉 ◎ LITERARY MAMA (Specialized: writing by mothers about mothering)

E-mail: poetry@literarymama.com (submissions) or info@literarymama.com (inquiries). Web site: www.literarymama.com. Established 2003. **Contact:** Sharon Kraus, poetry editor.

Magazine Needs *Literary Mama*, published monthly online, prints fiction, poetry, and creative nonfiction by writers of all ages who are "self-identified" mothers. "We also publish literary criticism, book reviews, and profiles about mother writers. *Literary Mama* is doing something for mama-centric literature that no one else is doing. The poetry, fiction, and creative nonfiction that may be too long, too complex, too ambiguous, too deep, too raw, too irreverent, too ironic, too body-conscious, and too full of long words for the general reader will find a home with us. While there are plenty of online literary magazines that publish writing like this, none devote themselves exclusively to writing about motherhood." Wants poems of any form that are "extraordinary for their vision, craftsmanship, integrity, and originality; centered around parenting; written by writers who are also self-identified mothers: biological, non-biological, step, transgender, adoptive.'' Receives about 70 poems/month, accepts about 10-15%.

How to Submit Submit 4 poems maximum at a time. Considers previously published poems (if they are not otherwise available on the Web) and simultaneous submissions. Accepts e-mail submissions (pasted into body of message; no attachments); no disk submissions. Include full name plus the word "submission" in your subject line. Cover letter is required. "Please include name, brief bio, and contact information." Reads submissions year round except for December and June. Time between acceptance and publication is 2-8 weeks. "The final decision about all poetry submissions is made by the poetry editor." Sometimes comments on rejected poems. Guidelines available on Web site. Responds in 8-12 weeks. No payment. Acquires first rights for previously unpublished work, non-exclusive one-time rights for reprints. Reviews books/chapbooks of poetry. Query via e-mail prior to sending materials for review consideration.

☑ THE LITERARY REVIEW: AN INTERNATIONAL JOURNAL OF CONTEMPORARY WRITING

Fairleigh Dickinson University, 285 Madison Ave., Madison NJ 07940. (973)443-8564. Fax: (973)443-8364. E-mail: tlr@fdu.edu. Web site: www.theliteraryreview.org. Established 1957. **Contact:** Walter Cummins, editor-in-chief.

Magazine Needs *The Literary Review*, published quarterly, seeks "work by new and established poets that reflects a sensitivity to literary standards and the poetic form." No specifications as to form, length, style, subject matter, or purpose. Has published poetry by David Citino, Rick Mulkey, Virgil Suárez, Gary Fincke, and Dale M. Kushner. *The Literary Review* is about 180 pages, digest-sized, professionally printed, flat-spined, with glossy color cover. Receives about 1,200 submissions/year, accepts 100-150. Press run is 2,000 (800 subscribers, one-third are overseas). Sample: $7 domestic, $8 outside U.S.; request a "general issue."

How to Submit Submit up to 5 typed poems at a time. Accepts only online submissions at www.theliteraryreview.org/submit.html. Considers simultaneous submissions. No fax or e-mail submissions. **Read-time September 1 through January 31**. Sometimes comments on rejected poems. Publishes theme issues. Responds in 4-6 months. Always sends prepublication galleys. Pays 2 contributor's copies. Acquires first rights. Reviews books of poetry in 500 words, single-book format. Send materials for review consideration.

Also Offers *TLR Online*, available on the Web site, features original work not published in the print edition. Has published poetry by Renée Ashley and Catherine Kasper.

Advice "Read a general issue of the magazine carefully before submitting."

▣ ⊕ ◯ LIVING POETS MAGAZINE

Dragonheart Press, 11 Menin Rd., Allestree, Derby DE22 2NL England. E-mail: submissions@dragonheartpress.com. Web site: www.dragonheartpress.com. Established 1995. **Contact:** Sean Woodward, executive editor.

Magazine Needs *Living Poets Magazine*, published irregularly online, provides a showcase for poetry. Wants "crafted poetry with strong imagery." Does not want "constrained rhyming structures." Receives about 400 poems/year, accepts about 20%. Digital sample: $10 (printable from PDF). Make checks payable to S. Woodward or via PayPal.

How to Submit Submit 3 poems at a time. Considers previously published poems and simultaneous submissions. Accepts e-mail submissions. Cover letter is preferred. Include bio and publication credits. Time between acceptance and publication is 1-2 months. Often comments on rejected poems. Publishes theme issues. Guidelines available for SASE, by e-mail, or on Web site. Responds in 3 months. Pays 1 contributor's copy. Reviews books/chapbooks of poetry or other magazines in single-book format. Send materials for review consideration to Review Editor, Dragonheart Press.

Contest/Award Offerings Sponsors Dragonheart Press Annual Poetry Competition. **Deadline:** December 31. Guidelines available for SASE (or SAE and IRC) or by e-mail (competition@dragonheartpress.com).

☑ LONE STARS MAGAZINE

4219 Flint Hill St., San Antonio TX 78230-1619. E-mail: lonestarsmagazine@yahoo.com. Web site: www.lonestarsmagazine.net. Established 1992. **Contact:** Milo Rosebud, editor/publisher.

Magazine Needs *Lone Stars*, published 3 times/year, features "contemporary poetry." Wants poetry "that holds a continuous line of thought." Does not want "profanity." Considers poetry by children and teens. Has published poetry by Bernie Bernstein, Crayton Moody, Eve J. Blohm, and Cecil Boyce. *Lone Stars* is 25 pages, magazine-sized, photocopied, saddle-stapled, bound with tape. Press run is 200. Single copy: $6; subscription: $20 for 4 issues. Sample: $5.50.

How to Submit Submit 3-5 poems at a time. Considers previously published poems and simultaneous submissions. Cover letter is preferred. Submit poems on any subject, formatted and "typed the way you want them in print." **Charges reading fee of $1 per poem.** Time between acceptance and publication is 6 months. Guidelines available for SASE. Responds within 3 months. Acquires one-time rights.

Contest/Award Offerings Sponsors annual "Songbook" Lyric Poetry Contest. Details available for SASE.

Advice "Submit poetry that expresses a reasonable train of thought."

▣ ◉ LONG ISLAND QUARTERLY (Specialized: Long Island, NY poets)

P.O. Box 114, Northport NY 11768. E-mail: Liquarterly@aol.com. Web site: www.poetrybay.com. Established 1990. **Contact:** George Wallace, editor/publisher.

Magazine Needs *Long Island Quarterly*, published online, is a journal of poetry (mostly lyric free verse) by people on or from Long Island. "Surprise us with fresh language. No conventional imagery, self-indulgent confessionalism, compulsive article-droppers." Has published poetry by Edmund Pennant and David Ignatow.

How to Submit Submit 3 poems at a time. Accepts e-mail submissions (preferred; pasted into body of message; "no attachments will be opened"). Include name and address on each page for postal entries; submissions without SASE are not returned. Cover letter with brief bio stating connection to Long Island region is required. Responds in 3 months.

Advice "1) Go beyond yourself; 2) Don't be afraid to fictionalize; 3) Don't write your autobiography—if you're worth it, maybe someone else will."

✪ ☑ LONG STORY SHORT, AN E-ZINE FOR WRITERS

P.O. Box 475, Lewistown MT 59457. E-mail: camel1ss@comcast.net. Web site: www.longstoryshort.us. Established 2003. **Contact:** Linda Barnett-Johnson, poetry editor.

Magazine Needs *Long Story Short, An E-zine for Writers*, published monthly online, is "eclectic—open to all forms and styles" of poetry. Does not want "profanity; overly explicit sex." Considers poetry by children (ages 10 and up) and teens. Has published poetry by Carolyn Howard-Johnson, Patricia Wellingham-Jones, Floriana Hall, Russell Bittner, and Marie Delgado Travis.

How to Submit Submit 2 poems at a time. Lines/poem: 32 maximum. Considers previously published poems and simultaneous submissions. Accepts e-mail submissions only ("paste poems in the body of your e-mail; no attachments will be opened"). Include a brief biography and permission to use e-mail address for reader contact. Reads submissions year round. Submit seasonal poems 4 months in advance. Time between acceptance and publication is one month. "Poems are reviewed and chosen by the poetry editor." Often comments on rejected poems. Guidelines available on Web site. ("Read them! It's obvious when you haven't." All rights reserved by author.

Also Offers Free newsletter with poetry of the month chosen by poetry editor; includes author's bio and Web page listed in the e-zine. Also provides resource page on Web site. Offers light critique of submissions upon request, and a free writing forum.

Advice "*Long Story Short* is an e-zine dedicated to the advancement of women writers, although we gladly welcome submissions from men as well."

☑ LOS

150 N. Catalina St., No. 2, Los Angeles CA 90004. E-mail: lospoesy@earthlink.net. Web site: http://home.earthlink.net/~lospoesy. Established 1991. **Contact:** The Editors.

Magazine Needs *Los*, published 4 times/year, features poetry. Has published poetry by John P. Campbell, Jean Esteve, Mary Kasimor, Bill Knott, Kevin Roddy, and Charles Wuest. *Los* is digest-sized and saddle-stapled. Press run is 100.

How to Submit Accepts e-mail submissions (pasted into body of message or as attachment). Time between acceptance and publication is up to 1 month. Guidelines available on Web site. Responds in 3 months. Pays 1 contributor's copy.

✪ ◎ THE LOUISIANA REVIEW (Specialized: LA poets, LA-related poetry)

Division of Liberal Arts, Louisiana State University at Eunice, P.O. Box 1129, Eunice LA 70535. (337)550-1315. E-mail: bfonteno@lsue.edu. Web site: www.lsue.edu/LA-Review/. Established 1999. **Contact:** Dr. Billy Fontenot, editor.

Magazine Needs *The Louisiana Review*, published annually during the fall or spring semester, offers "Louisiana poets, writers, and artists a place to showcase their most beautiful pieces. Others may submit Louisiana- or Southern-related poetry, stories, and b&w art, as well as interviews with Louisiana writers. We want to publish the highest-quality poetry, fiction, art, and drama." Wants "strong imagery, metaphor, and evidence of craft." Does not want "sing-song rhymes, abstract, religious, or overly sentimental work." Has published poetry by Gary Snyder, Antler, David Cope, and Catfish McDaris. *The Louisiana Review* is 100-200 pages, digest-sized, professionally printed, perfect-bound. Receives up to 2,000 poems/year, accepts 40-50. Press run is 300-600. Single copy: $5.

How to Submit Submit up to 5 poems at a time. No previously published poems. No fax or e-mail submissions. "Include cover letter indicating your association with Louisiana. Name and address should appear on each page." Reads submissions year round. Time between acceptance and publication is up to 2 years. Pays one contributor's copy. Poets retain all rights.

Advice "Be true to your own voice and style."

✪ ◎ THE LOUISVILLE REVIEW

Spalding University, 851 S. Fourth St., Louisville KY 40203. (502)585-9911, ext. 2777. E-mail: louisvillereview@spalding.edu. Web site: www.louisvillereview.org. Established 1976. **Contact:** Poetry Editor. Associate Editor: Kathleen Driskell.

Magazine Needs *The Louisville Review*, published twice/year, prints all kinds of poetry. Has a section devoted to children's poetry (grades K-12) called The Children's Corner. Considers poetry by children and teens. Has published poetry by Wendy Bishop, Gary Fincke, Michael Burkard, and Sandra Kohler. *The Louisville Review* is 100 pages, digest-sized, flat-spined. Receives about 700 submissions/year, accepts about 10%. Single copy: $8; subscription: $14/year, $27/2 years, $40/3 years (foreign subscribers add $6/year for s&h). Sample: $5.

How to Submit Considers simultaneous submissions; no previously published poems. No e-mail submissions. Include SASE for reply only. "Poetry by children must include permission of parent to publish if accepted. Address those submissions to The Children's Corner." Reads submissions year round. Time between acceptance and publication is up to 3 months. Submissions are read by 3 readers. Guidelines available on Web site. Responds in 3-5 months. Pays 2 contributor's copies.

Advice "We look for the striking metaphor, unusual imagery, and fresh language."

◻ ◎ LOVE'S CHANCE MAGAZINE (Specialized: love/romance)

Suzerain Enterprises, P.O. Box 60336, Worcester MA 01606. Established 1994. **Contact:** Milton Kerr, editor/publisher.

Magazine Needs *Love's Chance Magazine*, published 3 times/year, gives "unpublished writers a chance to be published." Wants romance. Does not want "porn, ageism, sexism, racism, children in sexual situations." Has published poetry by A.H. Ferguson, Wayne Adams, Robert Donald Spector, Cecil Boyce, and Ellaraine Lockie. *Love's Chance Magazine* is 15-30 pages, magazine-sized, photocopied, side-stapled, with computer-designed paper cover. Receives about 500 poems/year, accepts about 10%. Press run is 100. Subscription: $12/year. Sample: $4. Make checks payable to Suzerain Enterprises.

How to Submit Submit 3 poems at a time. Lines/poem: 20 maximum. Considers previously published poems and simultaneous submissions. Cover letter is preferred. "Proofread for spelling errors, neatness; must be typewritten in standard manuscript form. No handwritten manuscripts." Time between acceptance and publication is 3 months. Often comments on rejected poems. Guidelines available for SASE. Responds in 6 weeks. Acquires first or one-time rights.

Advice "Proofread your work. Edit carefully. Always include business-sized SASE with correct postage. Don't let rejection slips get you down. Keep submitting and don't give up. Don't be afraid to write something different."

$☐ LUCIDITY POETRY JOURNAL (Specialized: submission fee required)

Bear House Press, 14781 Memorial Dr., #10, Houston TX 77079-5210. (281)920-1795. E-mail: tedbadger1@yahoo.com. Established 1985. **Contact:** Ted O. Badger, editor.

Magazine Needs *Lucidity Poetry Journal*, published semiannually, **requires a submission fee—$1/poem for "juried" selection** by a panel of judges, or **$2/poem to compete for cash awards** of $15, $10, and $5. All winners paid in both cash and copies. Also publishes 6 pages of Succint Verse—poems of 12 lines or less—in most issues. "We expect them to be pithy and significant, and there is no reading/entry fee if sent along with Cash Award or Juried poems. Just think of all poetic forms that are 12 lines or less: cinquain, limerick, etheree, haiku, senryu, lune, etc., not to mention quatrain, triolet, and couplets." In addition, a few guest contributors are invited to submit to each issue. Contributors are encouraged to subscribe or buy a copy of the magazine. No restrictions on form; space limit due to format. "We look for poetry that is life-related and has clarity and substance. We dedicate our journal to publishing those poets who express their thoughts, feelings, and impressions about the human scene with clarity and substance." Does not want "religious, butterfly, or vulgar poems." *Lucidity* is 72 pages, digest-sized, photocopied from typescript, saddle-stapled, with matte card cover. Press run is 280 (225 subscribers); some distributed free to selected winners. Subscription: $7. Sample: $2 (including guidelines).

How to Submit Submit 3-5 poems in each category at a time. Lines/poem: 36 maximum (including spaces). Considers simultaneous submissions. No e-mail submissions. Time between acceptance and publication is 6 months to a year. Guidelines available for SASE or by e-mail. Responds in 12-18 months. Pays cash and 1 contributor's copy. Acquires one-time rights.

Additional Information Bear House Press is "**a self-publishing arrangement** by which poets can pay to have booklets published in the same format as *Lucidity* (but with perfect binding), with prices beginning at 100 copies of 32 pages for $336." Publishes about 6 chapbooks/year.

Also Offers Sponsors the *Lucidity* Poets' Ozark Retreat, a 3-day retreat held during the month of April in Eureka Springs, AR.

Advice "Small press journals offer the best opportunity to most poets for publication and recognition."

☑ LULLWATER REVIEW

Emory University, P.O. Box 22036, Atlanta GA 30322. (404)727-6184. E-mail: LullwaterReview@yahoo.com. Established 1990. **Contact:** Amy Cheng and Erin Crews, editor-in-chief.

Magazine Needs *Lullwater Review*, published in May and December, prints poetry, short fiction, and artwork. Wants poetry of any genre with strong imagery, original voice, on any subject. Does not want profanity or pornographic material. Has published poetry by Amy Greenfield, Peter Serchuk, Katherine McCord, Virgil Suárez, and Ha Jin. *Lullwater Review* is 60-80 pages, magazine-sized, with full-color cover, includes b&w and color pictures. Press run is 1,200. Subscription: $8 for individuals, $10 for institutions. Sample: $5.

How to Submit Submit 6 or fewer poems at a time. Considers simultaneous submissions; no previously published poems. Cover letter is preferred. Prefers poems single-spaced with name and contact info on each page. "Poems longer than 1 page should include page numbers. We must have a SASE with which to reply." Reads submissions September 1-May 15 only. Time between acceptance and publication is up to 6 months. Poems are circulated to an editorial board. Seldom comments on rejected poems. Guidelines available for SASE. Responds in 5 months maximum. Pays 3 contributor's copies. Acquires first North American serial rights.

Advice "Keep writing, find your voice, don't get frustrated. Please be patient with us regarding response time. We are an academic institution."

◨ LUNGFULL!MAGAZINE (SPECIALIZED: ROUGH DRAFT TO FINISHED POEM)

316 23rd St., Brooklyn NY 11215. E-mail: lungfull@rcn.com. Web site: http://lungfull.org. Established 1994. **Contact:** Brendan Lorber, editor/publisher.

• *LUNGFULL!* was the recipient of a grant from the New York State Council for the Arts.

Magazine Needs *LUNGFULL!magazine*, published annually, prints "the rough draft of each poem, in addition to the final, so that the reader can see the creative process from start to finish. We recommend you get a copy before submitting." Wants "any style as long as it's urgent, immediate, playful, probing, showing great thought while remaining vivid and grounded. Poems should be as interesting as conversation." Does not want "empty poetic abstractions." Has published poetry by Alice Notley, Lorenzo Thomas, Tracie Morris, Hal Sirowitz, Eileen Myles, and John Ashbery. *LUNGFULL!* is 200 pages, 8½×7, offset-printed, desktop-published, perfect-bound, with glossy waterproof 2-color cover, includes ads. Receives about 1,000 poems/year, accepts 3%. Press run is 3,000 (600 subscribers, 2300 shelf sales); 100 distributed free to contributors. Single copy: $9.95; subscription: $39.80 for 4 issues, $19.90 for 2 issues. Sample: $12.95. Make checks payable to Brendan Lorber, or order online.

How to Submit Submit up to 6 poems at a time. Considers previously published poems and simultaneous submissions (with notification; "however, other material will be considered first and stands a much greater chance of publication"). Accepts e-mail submissions. "We prefer hard copy by USPS—but e-submissions can be made in the body of the e-mail itself; submissions with attachments will be deleted unread." Cover letter is preferred. Time between acceptance and publication is up to 8 months. "The editor looks at each piece for its own merit and for how well it will fit into the specific issue being planned based on other accepted work." Guidelines available by e-mail. Responds in 1 year. Pays 2 contributor's copies.

Also Offers "Each copy of *LUNGFULL!magazine* contains a Cultural Attache Sticker—they can be removed from the magazine and placed on any flat surface to make it a little less flat. Previous stickers contain statements like 'Together we can keep the poor poor' and 'You only live once—just not as long as in countries with free healthcare.' "

Advice "Failure demands a certain dedication. Practice makes imperfection, and imperfection makes room for the amazing. Only outside the bounds of acceptable conclusions can the astounding transpire, can writing contain anything beyond twittering snack food logic and the utilitarian pistons of mundane engineering."

✪ ◨ ◎ THE LUTHERAN DIGEST (Specialized: Christian; inspirational; short poems)

P.O. Box 4250, Hopkins MN 55343. (952)933-2820. Fax: (952)933-5708. E-mail: tldi@lutherandigest.com. Web site: www.lutherandigest.com. Established 1953. **Contact:** David Tank, editor.

Magazine Needs *The Lutheran Digest,* published quarterly, aims to "entertain and encourage believers and to subtly persuade non-believers to embrace the Christian faith. We publish short poems that will fit in a single column of the magazine. Most are inspirational, but that doesn't necessarily mean religious." Does not want "avant-garde poetry." Considers poetry by children and teens. Has published poetry by Kathleen A. Cain, William Beyer, Margaret Peterson, Florence Berg, and Erma Boetkher. *The Lutheran Digest* is 64 pages, digest-sized, offset-printed, saddle-stapled, with 4-color paper cover, includes local ads. Receives about 200 poems/year, accepts 20%. Press run is 100,000; some distributed free to Lutheran churches. Subscription: $14/year, $22/2 years. Sample: $3.50.

How to Submit Submit 3 poems at a time. Lines/poem: 25 maximum. Considers previously published poems and simultaneous submissions. Accepts fax and e-mail (as attachment) submissions. Cover letter is preferred. "Include SASE if return is desired." Time between acceptance and publication is up to 9 months. "Poems are selected by editor and reviewed by publication panel." Guidelines available for SASE or on Web site. Responds in 3 months. Pays credit and 1 contributor's copy. Acquires one-time rights.

Advice "Poems should be short and appeal to senior citizens. We also look for poems that can be sung to traditional Lutheran hymns."

⊠ ▣ ✏ LYRIC POETRY REVIEW

P.O. Box 2494, Bloomington IN 47402. E-mail: lyric@lyricreview.org. Web site: www.lyricreview.o rg. Established 2001. **Contact:** Nathaniel Perry, editor. Member: CLMP.

• Poems published in *Lyric Poetry Review* have appeared in *The Best American Poetry* and *The Pushcart Prize* as well as on the Poetry Daily and Verse Daily Web sites.

Magazine Needs *Lyric Poetry Review*, published semiannually, presents "poetry by Americans and translations of both little-known and celebrated poets from around the world." Also publishes interviews and literary essays on poetry or poetics. Wants "poetry that has strong musicality and lyricism. We are open to all styles, including longer poems and lyrical narratives. We tend to publish more than 1 poem by any given author and try to find a group of poems that demonstrates both range and consistency of voice." Has published poetry by Marilyn Hacker, Maurice Manning, Czeslaw Milosz, Jean Valentine, Alicia Ostriker, and Gerald Stern. *Lyric Poetry Review* is 96 pages, digest-sized, perfect-bound, with full-color cover with original artwork. Receives about 2,500 poems/year, accepts about 5%. Press run is 1,000. Single copy: $9; subscription: $15/year (subscribers outside U.S. add $5 postage). Make checks payable to *Lyric Poetry Review*.

How to Submit Submit 3-6 poems at a time. Considers simultaneous submissions if notified; no previously published poems. No e-mail or disk submissions. Cover letter is required. Reads submissions year round. Response time may be considerably slower in the summer months. Time between acceptance and publication is up to 1 year. "We strongly advise that those submitting work read a recent issue first." Seldom comments on rejected poems. Occasionally publishes theme issues. Upcoming themes available by e-mail. Guidelines available in magazine, for SASE, or on Web site. Responds in up to 4 months. Always sends prepublication galleys. Pays 2 contributor's copies. Acquires first rights. Solicits reviews.

✏ ◎ THE LYRIC (Specialized: rhymed poetry, traditional)

P.O. Box 110, Jericho Corners VT 05465. Phone/fax: (802)899-3993. E-mail: Lyric@sover.net. Established 1921. **Contact:** Jean Mellichamp-Milliken, editor.

Magazine Needs *The Lyric*, published quarterly, is "the oldest magazine in North America in continuous publication devoted to traditional poetry." Prints about 55 poems/issue. Wants "rhymed verse in traditional forms, for the most part, with an occasional piece of blank or free verse. Our themes are varied, ranging from religious ecstasy to humor to raw grief, but we feel no compulsion to shock, embitter, or confound our readers. We also avoid poems about contemporary political or social problems—'grief but not grievances,' as Frost put it. Frost is helpful in other ways: If yours is more than a lover's quarrel with life, we are not your best market. And most of our poems are accessible on first or second reading. Frost again: 'Don't hide too far away.' " Has published poetry by Rhina P. Espaillat, Gail White, Joseph Awad, Alfred Dorn, Ruth Harrison, and Glenna Holloway. *The Lyric* is 32 pages, digest-sized, professionally printed with varied typography, with matte card cover. Press run is 750 (600 subscribers, 40 libraries). Receives about 3,000 submissions/year, accepts 5%. Subscription: $15/year, $28/2 years, $38/3 years (U.S.), $17/year for Canada and other countries (in U.S. funds only). Sample: $4.

How to Submit Submit up to 6 poems at a time. Lines/poem: 40 maximum. Considers simultaneous submissions (although "not preferred"); no previously published poems. Cover letter is "often helpful, but not required. Subscription will not affect publication of submitted poetry." Guidelines available for SASE or by e-mail. Responds in 3 months ("average; inquire after 6 months"). Pays 1 contributor's copy.

Contest/Award Offerings All contributors are eligible for quarterly and annual prizes totaling $750. Also offers the Lyric College Contest, open to undergraduate students. Awards prize of $400. **Deadline:** December 15. Send entries to Tanya Cimonetti, 1393 Spear St., S., Burlington VT 05403.

Advice "Our *raison d'étre* has been the encouragement of form, music, rhyme, and accessibility in poetry. As we witness the growing tide of appreciation for traditional/lyric poetry, we are proud to have stayed the course for 88 years, helping keep the roots of poetry alive."

✏ THE MACGUFFIN

Schoolcraft College, 18600 Haggerty Rd., Livonia MI 48152-2696. (734)462-4400, ext. 5327. Fax: (734)462-4679. E-mail: macguffin@schoolcraft.edu. Web site: www.schoolcraft.edu/macguffin. Established 1984. **Contact:** Carol Was, poetry editor.

Magazine Needs *The MacGuffin*, published 3 times/year, prints "the best poetry, fiction, nonfiction, and artwork we find. We have no thematic or stylistic biases. We look for well-crafted poetry." Does not want "pornography, triteness, and sloppy poetry. We do not publish haiku, concrete, or light verse." Has published poetry by Susan Terris, Gabriel Welsch, Linda Nemec Foster, Conrad Hilberry, and Laurence Lieberman. *The MacGuffin* is 160 pages, 6×9, perfect-bound, with color cover. Press run is 500; the rest are local sales, contributor copies, and distribution to college offices. Subscription: $22. Sample: $6.

How to Submit Submit no more than 5 poems at a time. Lines/poem: 400 maximum. Considers simultaneous submissions if informed; no previously published poems. Accepts fax, e-mail (as Word attachment only; do not paste into body of message), and disk/CD submissions. Cover letter is required. "List titles and brief bio in cover letter. Do not staple work." Poems should be typed, single-spaced, 1 per page. Poet's name, address, and e-mail should appear on each page. Include SASE. Guidelines available for SASE, by fax, e-mail, or on Web site. Responds in 4-6 months. Pays 2 contributor's copies plus discount on additional copies. Rights revert to poets upon publication.

Contest/Award Offerings The National Poet Hunt Contest (see separate listing in Contests & Awards).

◩ MAD POETS REVIEW

Mad Poets Society, P.O. Box 1248, Media PA 19063-8248. E-mail: Madpoets@comcast.net. (inquiries only). Web site: www.madpoetssociety.com. Established 1987. **Contact:** Eileen M. D'Angelo, editor.

Magazine Needs *Mad Poets Review*, published annually in October/November, aims "to promote thought-provoking, moving poetry, and encourage beginning poets. We don't care if you have a 'name' or a publishing history if your poetry is well-crafted. We are anxious for work with *joie de vivre* that startles and inspires." No restrictions on subject, form, or style. "Just because our name is *Mad Poets Review* doesn't mean we want mad ramblings masquerading under the guise of poetry." Does not want obscenities simply for shock value. Has published poetry by Daniel Hoffman, Gerald Stern, Naomi Shihab Nye, Greg Djanikian, Harry Humes, and Nathalie Anderson. *Mad Poets Review* is about 200 pages, digest-sized, attractively printed, perfect-bound, with glossy, full-color laminated cover. Receives about 2,000 poems/year, accepts 150. Press run is 500. Single copy: $12. Sample: $14 (includes p&h). Make checks payable to Mad Poets Society.

How to Submit Submit up to 8 poems at a time. Considers previously published poems and simultaneous submissions. "If published previously, please include prior publication information on the same page as the poem." No e-mail submissions; postal submissions only. "Must include a short 3-4 sentence bio about yourself suitable for our Bio Notes section; no full resumes please. Mark envelope 'contest' or 'magazine.' Poems without a SASE with adequate postage will not be returned or acknowledged." Reads submissions January 1-June 1 only. Time between acceptance and publication is 8 months. Often comments on rejected poems. Responds in 3 months. Pays 1 contributor's copy. Acquires one-time rights.

Contest/Award Offerings Sponsors the annual *Mad Poets Review* Poetry Competition. Awards cash prizes determined by the number of entries received. Grand Prize winner and finalists will be published in an upcoming issue of *Mad Poets Review*. Submissions must be unpublished. See guidelines for complete entry requirements. **Entry fee:** $10 for up to 6 poems. "There is no fee to submit to the magazine, only for the contest." Make checks payable to Mad Poets Society. **Deadline:** June 30. Guidelines available on Web site.

Also Offers "The Mad Poets Society is an active organization in Pennsylvania. We run approximately 80 events per year, including many feature readings, workshops, open mikes, and critique circles which are free and open to the public. Mad poets also coordinate a children's contest through Delaware County School system; run an annual poetry festival the first Sunday in October; sponsor Mad Poets Bonfires for local poets and musicians. Membership in Mad Poets Society is $20/yr and includes 10-12 page newsletters that offer the most comprehensive listing of arts and poetry events available anywhere in the tri-state area, as well as quarterly meetings for members for critique and club business."

Advice "It is advised that if someone is going to submit, they see what kind of poetry we publish."

✦ ◨ THE MADISON REVIEW

University of Wisconsin-Madison, Dept. of English, 6193 Helen C. White Hall, 600 N. Park St., Madison WI 53706. (608)263-2566. E-mail: madisonreview@yahoo.com. Web site: http://mendota .english.wisc.edu/ ~ MadRev. Established 1978. **Contact:** Poetry Editor.

Magazine Needs *The Madison Review*, published semiannually in May and December, seeks poems that are "smart and tight, that fulfill their own propositions." Does not want "religious or patriotic dogma and light verse." Has published poetry by Simon Perchik, Amy Quan Barry, Mitch Raney, Erica Meitner, and Henry B. Stobbs. Selects 15-20 poems from a pool of 750. Subscription: $15/ year, $25 for 2 years. Sample: $8.

How to Submit Submit up to 6 poems at a time. No simultaneous submissions. No e-mail submissions. Cover letter is preferred. Include SASE. Submissions must be typed. Guidelines available in magazine, for SASE, by e-mail, or on Web site. Usually responds in 9 months. Pays 2 contributor's copies.

Advice "Contributors: Know your market! Read before, during, and after writing. Treat your poems better than job applications!"

$◨ ◉ THE MAGAZINE OF FANTASY & SCIENCE FICTION

P.O. Box 3447, Hoboken NJ 07030. E-mail: FandSF@aol.com. Web site: www.fsfmag.com. Established 1949. **Contact:** Gordon Van Gelder, editor.

- *The Magazine of Fantasy & Science Fiction* is a past winner of the Hugo Award and World Fantasy Award.

Magazine Needs *The Magazine of Fantasy & Science Fiction*, published monthly 11 times/year, is "one of the longest-running magazines devoted to the literature of the fantastic." Wants only poetry that deals with the fantastic or the science-fictional. Has published poetry by Rebecca Kavaler, Elizabeth Bear, and Robert Frazier. *The Magazine of Fantasy & Science Fiction* is 160 pages, digest-sized, offset-printed, perfect-bound, with glossy cover, includes ads. Receives about 20-40 poems/ year, accepts about 1%. Press run is 35,000 (20,000 subscribers). Single copy: $4.50; subscription: $32.97. Sample: $5. Make checks payable to *The Magazine of Fantasy & Science Fiction*.

How to Submit Submit 1-3 poems at a time. No previously published poems or simultaneous submissions. No e-mail or disk submissions. Time between acceptance and publication is up to 2 years, but usually about 9 months. "I buy poems very infrequently—just when 1 hits me right." Seldom comments on rejected poems. Guidelines available for SASE or on Web site. Responds in up to 1 month. Always sends prepublication galleys. Pays $50/poem and 2 contributor's copies. Acquires first North American serial rights.

$◨ ◉ THE MAGAZINE OF SPECULATIVE POETRY (Specialized: horror; fantasy; science fiction; science)

P.O. Box 564, Beloit WI 53512. Established 1984. **Contact:** Roger Dutcher, editor.

Magazine Needs *The Magazine of Speculative Poetry*, published biannually, features "the best new speculative poetry. We are especially interested in narrative form, but open to any form, any length (within reason); interested in a variety of styles. We're looking for the best of the new poetry utilizing the ideas, imagery, and approaches developed by speculative fiction, and will welcome experimental techniques as well as the fresh employment of traditional forms." Has published poetry by Joanne Merriam, Jeannine Hall Gailey, Ann K. Schwader, and Kendall Evans. *The Magazine of Speculative Poetry* is 24-28 pages, digest-sized, offset-printed, saddle-stapled, with matte card cover. Receives about 500 poems/year, accepts less than 5%. Press run is 150-200. Subscription: $19 for 4 issues. Sample: $5.

How to Submit Submit 3-5 poems at a time. Lines/poem: "Some poems run 2 or 3 pages, but rarely anything longer. We're a small magazine, we can't print epics." No previously published poems or simultaneous submissions. "We like cover letters, but they aren't necessary. We like to see where you heard of us; the names of the poems submitted; a statement if the poetry manuscript is disposable; a big enough SASE; and if you've been published, some recent places." Poems should be double-spaced. Comments on rejected poems "on occasion." Guidelines available for SASE. Responds in up to 2 months. Pays 3¢/word ($7 minimum, $25 maximum) and 1 contributor's copy.

Acquires first North American serial rights. "All rights revert to author upon publication, except for permission to reprint in any 'Best of' or compilation volume. Payment will be made for such publication." Reviews books of speculative poetry. Query regarding unsolicited reviews, interviews, and articles. Send materials for review consideration.

⬛ 🔅 ⬭ MAGNAPOETS

13300 Tecumseh Rd. E., Suite 226, Tecumseh ON Canada N8N 4R8. E-mail: Magnapoets@gmail.com. Web site: www.magnapoets.com. Established 2008 **Contact:** Aurora Antonovic, editor-in-chief.
Magazine Needs *Magnapoets*, published semiannually in January and July, prints "all forms of poetry, as well as short stories and articles." Wants all forms of poetry, including free verse, formal poetry, tanka, haiku, senryu. Does not want "anything hateful, racist, bigoted, or overtly partisan." Considers poetry by teens. Has published poetry by Robert Pinsky, Kirsty Karkow, Elisha Porat, Peggy Lyles Wills, Curtis Dunlap, an'ya. *Magnapoets* is 36-40 pages, magazine-sized, digital press print format, saddle-stitched, with a glossy cover with full-sized color photograph or art. Single copy: $5 CAN; subscription: $10 CAN. Make checks payable to Aurora Antonovic.
How to Submit Submit 3 poems of free verse and formal poetry; for haiku and tanka, send up to 10 poems at a time, maximum 48 lines for longer poems. Accepts e-mail submissions (pasted into body of message); no fax or disk submissions. Cover letter is preferred. Include a 25-word (or less) bio. Reads submissions from March-May, and again from September-November. Time between acceptance and publication is 2 months. "Each editor edits his/her own section separately. Send submissions to each individual editor as specified. Currently, we have 6 editors: Ursula T. Gibson (free verse and form), Marie Lecrivain (short stories), David Herrle (special features), Matt Morden (haiku and senryu), Aurora Antonovic (tanka), Nick Zegarac (columnist). Never comments on rejected poems. Never publishes theme issues. Guidelines available in magazine and on Web site. Responds in 2 months. Pays 1 contributor's copy. Acquires first serial rights (magazine is distributed internationally). Rights revert to poets upon publication. Reviews books of poetry. Send materials for review consideration to Aurora Antonovic.
Additional Information "We publish themed anthologies twice a year. For information, see the Web site.
Advice "Send your best work. Follow the guidelines as detailed on the site."

⬭ 🔳 THE MAGNOLIA QUARTERLY (Specialized: membership required to submit)

P.O. Box 10294, Gulfport MS 39506. E-mail: writerpllevin@gmail.com. Web site: www.gcwriters.org. Established 1999. **Contact:** Phil L. Levin, poetry editor.
Magazine Needs *The Magnolia Quarterly* publishes poetry, fiction, nonfiction, reviews, and photography. **Membership required to submit to magazine.** Wants all styles of poetry. Does not want "pornography, racial or religious bigotry, far-left or far-right political poems." Has published poetry by Leonard Cirino, Catharine Savage Brosman, Angela Ball, Jack Bedell, and Larry Johnson. *The Magnolia Quarterly* is 30 pages, magazine-sized, stapled, with paper cover, includes ads. Single copy: $4; subscription: $15 (or included in $25 GCWA annual dues). Make checks payable to Gulf Coast Writers Assocation.
How to Submit Submit 1-5 poems at a time. Lines/poem: open. Considers previously published poems and simultaneous submissions. Accepts e-mail (as attachment) only. Cover letter is preferred. Reads submissions year round. Time between acceptance and publication varies. Guidelines available in magazine, for SASE, by e-mail, or on Web site. Responds in 2 weeks. No payment. Returns rights to poet upon publication.
Also Offers The Gulf Coast Writers Association, "a nationally recognized organization which strives to encourage and inspire writers throughout the Mississippi Gulf Coast regional area." Additional information available on Web site.

🔅 🌐 ⬭ MAGPIE'S NEST

176 Stoney Lane, Sparkhill, Birmingham B12 8AN England. E-mail: magpies-nest@tiscali.co.uk. Established 1979. **Contact:** Mr. Bal Saini, editor.
Magazine Needs *Magpie's Nest*, published quarterly, seeks "cutting-edge, modern poetry and fic-

tion that deals with the human condition.'' Does not want ''love poetry or self-obsessed work.'' *Magpie's Nest* receives about 200 poems/year, accepts about 25%. Press run is 200 (150 subscribers, 50 shelf sales). Single copy: $5; subscription: $20. Sample: $4.

How to Submit Submit 4 poems at a time. Lines/poem: 10 minimum, 40 maximum. Considers previously published poems and simultaneous submissions. Accepts e-mail submissions. Cover letter is preferred. ''Keep copies of submitted poems as those not used are binned.'' Reads submissions September 1-June 30 only. Time between acceptance and publication is 3 months. Seldom comments on rejected poems. Occasionally publishes theme issues. Responds in 3 months. Pays 1 contributor's copy. Reviews books of poetry and other magazines in 200 words, single-book format. Send materials for review consideration.

Advice ''Read past issues of the magazine to assess the editor's taste/preference.''

☑ MAIN STREET RAG

P.O. Box 690100, Charlotte NC 28227-7001. (704)573-2516. E-mail: editor@mainstreetrag.com. Web site: www.MainStreetRag.com. Established 1996. **Contact:** M. Scott Douglass, editor/publisher.

Magazine Needs *Main Street Rag*, published quarterly, prints ''poetry, short fiction, essays, interviews, reviews, photos, art, and cartoons (political, satirical). We like publishing good material from people who are interested in more than notching another publishing credit, people who support small independent publishers like ourselves.'' Will consider ''almost anything,'' but prefers ''writing with an edge—either gritty or bitingly humorous. Contributors are advised to visit our Web site prior to submission to confirm current needs.'' Has published poetry by Silvia Curbelo, Sean Thomas Dougherty, Denise Duhamel, Cathy Essinger, Ishle Yi Park, and Dennis Must. *Main Street Rag* is about 96 pages, digest-sized, perfect-bound, with 100 lb. 12-pt laminated color cover. Receives about 2,500 submissions/year; publishes 30-40 poems/issue. Press run is about 1,000 (300 subscribers, 15 libraries). Single copy: $8; subscription: $24/year, $45 for 2 years.

How to Submit Submit 6 pages of poetry at a time. No previously published poems or simultaneous submissions. **Accepts e-mail submissions from subscribers only**. Cover letter is preferred. ''No bios or credits—let the work speak for itself.'' Time between acceptance and publication is up to 1 year. Guidelines available for SASE, by e-mail, or on Web site. Responds within 6 weeks. Pays 1 contributor's copy. Acquires first North American print rights.

Contest/Award Offerings Main Street Rag's Annual Poetry Book Award and Main Street Rag's Annual Chapbook Contest (see separate listings in Contests & Awards).

Advice ''Small press independents exist by and for writers. Without their support (and the support of readers), we have no reason to exist. Sampling first is always appreciated.''

☷ $☑ THE MALAHAT REVIEW

University of Victoria, P.O. Box 1700, STN CSC, Victoria BC V8W 2Y2 Canada. (250)721-8524. Fax: (250)472-5051. E-mail: malahat@uvic.ca (inquiries only). Web site: www.malahatreview.ca. Established 1967. **Contact:** John Barton, editor.

Magazine Needs *The Malahat Review*, published quarterly, is ''a high-quality, visually appealing literary journal that has earned the praise of notable literary figures throughout North America. Its purpose is to publish and promote poetry and fiction of a very high standard, both Canadian and international.'' Wants ''various styles, lengths, and themes. The criterion is excellence.'' Has published poetry by Steven Heighton and Jan Zwicky. Receives about 2,000 poems/year, accepts about 100. Subscription: $40 CAD for individuals, $50 CAD for institutions (or U.S. equivalent). Sample: $16.45 USD.

How to Submit Submit 5-10 poems at a time. No previously published poems or simultaneous submissions. No e-mail submmissions; postal submissions only. Include SASE with Canadian stamps or IRC with each submission. Guidelines available for SASE (or SAE and IRC). Responds usually within 3 months. Pays $35 CAD per printed page, 2 contributor's copies, and 1 year's subscription. Acquires first world serial rights. Reviews Canadian books of poetry.

Contest/Award Offerings Presents the P.K. Page Founders' Award for Poetry, a $1,000 prize to the author of the best poem or sequence of poems to be published in *The Malahat Review*'s quarterly issues during the previous calendar year. Also offers the biennial Long Poem Prize and Far Horizons Award for Poetry (see separate listings in Contests & Awards).

▣ ◪ MANNEQUIN ENVY

E-mail: poetry@mannequinenvy.com. Web site: www.mannequinenvy.com. Established 2004. **Contact:** Patrick Carrington, poetry editor.

Magazine Needs *Mannequin Envy*, published quarterly online, is a journal of visual and literary arts. Wants "distilled writing that gets to the point without just painting a pretty picture. Improvisational, imperfect, innovative, quirky, non-linear, raw, brave. There is no shortage of really nice poems out there. We do not want 'nice.' We want to feel a physical reaction to your work. Nausea. Embarrassment. Arousal. Something. Make the mannequin turn and notice." Has published poetry by John Sweet, Lynn Strongin, Kelley White, Tim Mayo, and Charles Fishman. Receives about 2,000 poems/year, accepts about 10%.

How to Submit Submit 3-5 poems at a time. Considers simultaneous submissions; no previously published poems. Accepts e-mail submissions (pasted into body of message); no disk submissions. Cover letter is preferred. "Please check guidelines online." Reads submissions as follows: March 1-30 (Spring), May 1-30 (Summer), July 1-30 (Fall), and October 1-30 (Winter). "**Summer issue not open to regular submissions**. Featuring collections of the combined visual art and poetry of individual artists. Submit to Jennifer VanBuren, Editor, at editor@mannequinevy.com. See Web site for more details." Time between acceptance and publication is 1 month. Rarely comments on rejected poems. Guidelines available on Web site. Responds in 10 weeks. Always sends prepublication galleys. No payment. Acquires first rights; "we request the right to publish work in 1 anthology, in print or otherwise." Rights revert to poet upon publication. "We will nominate poets for the Pushcart Prize."

$◪ MANOA: A Pacific Journal of International Writing

1733 Donaghho Rd., Honolulu HI 96822. Fax: (808)956-3083. E-mail: mjournal-l@hawaii.edu. Web site: http://manoajournal.hawaii.edu. Established 1989. **Contact:** Frank Stewart, poetry editor.

● Poetry published in *Manoa* has also appeared in volumes of *The Best American Poetry*.

Magazine Needs *Manoa*, published twice/year, is a general interest literary magazine that considers work "in many forms and styles, regardless of the author's publishing history. However, we are not for the beginning writer. It is best to look at a sample copy of the journal before submitting." Has published poetry by Arthur Sze, Ai, Linda Gregg, Jane Hirshfield, and Ha Jin. *Manoa* is 240 pages, 7×10, offset-printed, flat-spined. Receives about 1,000 poems/year, accepts 1%. Press run is more than 2,500 (several hundred subscribers, 130 libraries, 400 shelf sales). "In addition, *Manoa* is available through Project Muse to about 900 institutional subscribers throughout the world." Subscription: $22/year. Sample: $10.

How to Submit Submit 3-5 poems at a time. No e-mail submissions. Seldom comments on rejected poems. Guidelines available on Web site. Responds in 6 weeks. Always sends prepublication galleys. Pays "competitive" amount plus 2 contributor's copies.

Advice "We are not a regional journal, but each issue features a particular part of Asia or the Pacific; these features, which include poetry, are assembled by guest editors. The rest of each issue features work by poets from the U.S. and elsewhere. We welcome the opportunity to read poetry from throughout the country, but we are not interested in genre or formalist writing for its own sake, or in casual impressions of the Asia-Pacific region."

◪ MANY MOUNTAINS MOVING: a literary journal of diverse contemporary voices

549 Rider Ridge Dr., Longmont CO 80501. (303)485-0800, ext. 2. E-mail: info@mmminc.org. Web site: www.mmminc.org. Established 1994. **Contact:** Poetry Editor.

● Poetry published in *Many Mountains Moving* has also been included in volumes of *The Best American Poetry* and *The Pushcart Prize*.

Magazine Needs *Many Mountains Moving: a literary journal of diverse contemporary voices*, published annually in the fall, welcomes "previously unpublished poetry, fiction, nonfiction, reviews, and art from writers and artists of all walks of life." Wants "all forms of poetry, welcoming writing with intelligence, wit, craft, and guile. We look for any form of excellent writing, and also appreciate work that reflects the diversity of our culture. Translations and book reviews are welcome." Has published Robert Bly, Lorna Dee Cervantes, Amiri Baraka, Allen Ginsberg, Yusef Komunyakaa, and Adrienne Rich. *Many Mountains Moving* is over 200 pages, digest-sized, with 4-color glossy cover. Receives 5,000 poems/year, accepts 1%. Press run is 600. Single copy: $12; subscription: $12/year.

How to Submit Submit 3-8 poems at a time. Considers simultaneous submissions; no previously published poems. Cover letter is encouraged. "See guidelines on the Web site for reading periods for paper submissions. Year-round online submissions **with a $2 reading fee** at www.mmm-submis sions.org." Seldom comments on rejected poems. Guidelines available on Web site. Responds within 3 months; "if we are seriously considering a submission, we may take longer." Sends prepublication galleys (PDFs by e-mail). Pays 1 contributors copy; additional copies available at discount. Acquires first North American serial rights and "rights to publish in a future edition of the *Best of Many Mountains Moving Anthology.*"

Contest/Award Offerings Many Mountains Moving Poetry Book Contest (see separate listing in Contests & Awards) and The Many Mountains Moving Poetry and Flash Fiction Contests. Guidelines available on Web site.

Advice "Although we feature many established poets, we also publish many new writers in every issue. We recommend that poets read through at least 1 issue to familiarize themselves with the type of work we generally publish."

MARGIE/THE AMERICAN JOURNAL OF POETRY

P.O. Box 250, Chesterfield MO 63006-0250. Fax: (636)532-0539. E-mail: margiereview@aol.com. Web site: www.margiereview.com. Established 2001. **Contact:** Robert Nazarene, founding editor.

● Multiple selections from *MARGIE* have appeared in *The Best American Poetry.*

Magazine Needs *MARGIE/The American Journal of Poetry*, published annually in the fall, features "superlative poetry. No limits as to school, form, or subject matter. Imaginative, risk-taking poetry which disturbs and/or consoles is of paramount interest. A distinctive voice is prized." Has published poetry by Billy Collins, Carol Muske-Dukes, Emmylou Harris, Charles Simic, Maxine Kumin, and Ted Kooser. *MARGIE* is about 400+ pages, digest-sized, professionally printed, perfect-bound, with glossy cover with art/graphics, includes ads. Receives about 40,000-50,000 poems/year, accepts less than 1%. **Available by subscription only.** Single copy: $15.95 (1 year subscription) for individuals, $19.95 for institutions and foreign (prices include shipping & handling). Make checks payable to *MARGIE, Inc.*

How to Submit Submit 3-5 poems at a time. Considers simultaneous submissions (notify with cover letter). Reads submissions according to the following schedule: open reading period is June 1-July 15 (one submission/poet during this time); **subscribers only** may submit up to 4 times annually, year round ("please mark 'Subscribe' on the outside of submission envelope"). Time between acceptance and publication is up to 1 year. Editor makes final decision. Sometimes comments on rejected poems. Guidelines available in magazine, for SASE, or on Web site. Responds in 1-3 weeks. Pays 1 contributor's copy. Acquires first rights. All rights revert to poet upon publication.

Contest/Award Offerings The Marjorie J. Wilson Award for Excellence in Poetry (see separate listing in Contests & Awards).

Advice "Read, read, read. Then: write. Be audacious, innovative, unafraid, distinctive."

$ ◎ THE MARTIAN WAVE (Specialized: science fiction related to exploration/ settlement of the Solar System)

P.O. Box 782, Cedar Rapids IA 52406-0782. E-mail: martianwave@samsdotpublishing.com. Web site: www.samsdotpublishing.com. Established 1997. **Contact:** J. Alan Erwine, editor. Member: The Speculative Literature Foundation (http://SpeculativeLiterature.org).

Magazine Needs *The Martian Wave*, published quarterly online, features "science fiction poetry and stories that are related in some way to the exploration and/or settlement of the Solar System." Does not want "anything other than science fiction." Considers poetry by children and teens. Has published poetry by Marge B. Simon, Kristine Ong Muslim, Christina Sng, Aurelio Rico Lopez III, s.c. virtes, and Tyree Campbell. Receives about 150 poems/year, accepts about 16 (12%).

How to Submit Submit up to 5 poems at a time. Lines/poem: prefers less than 100. No previously published poems or simultaneous submissions. Accepts e-mail submissions (pasted into body of message); no disk submissions. "Submission should include snail mail address and a short (1-2 lines) bio." Reads submissions year round. Submit seasonal poems 6 months in advance. Time between acceptance and publication is 1-2 months. Sometimes comments on rejected poems. Guidelines available on Web site. Responds in 4-6 weeks. Pays $5/poem. Acquires first North American serial rights.

Advice "It's up to the writer to take the first step and submit work. Some of our best poems have come from poets who weren't sure if they were good enough. Most important is our theme. The poem must be related to the exploration and/or settlement of the Solar System."

$🖉 THE MASSACHUSETTS REVIEW

South College, University of Massachusetts, Amherst MA 01003. (413)545-2689. E-mail: massrev@external.umass.edu. Web site: www.massreview.org. Established 1959. **Contact:** Deborah Gorlin and Ellen Watson, poetry editors.

• Work published in *The Massacusetts Review* has been included frequently in *The Best American Poetry*.

Magazine Needs *The Massachusetts Review*, published quarterly, prints "fiction, essays, artwork, and excellent poetry of all forms and styles." Has published poetry by Catherine Barnett, Billy Collins, and Dara Wier. *The Massachusetts Review* is digest-sized, offset-printed on bond paper, perfect-bound, with color card cover. Receives about 2,500 poems/year, accepts about 25. Press run is 1,600 (1,100-1,200 subscribers, 1,000 libraries, the rest for shelf sales). Subscription: $27/year U.S., $35 outside U.S., $37 for libraries. Sample: $9 U.S., $12 outside U.S.

How to Submit No previously published poems or simultaneous submissions. Reads submissions October 1-June 30 only. "Guidelines are available online at our Web site, as is our new online submission manager." Responds in 2 months. Pays 35¢/line (minimum of $10) plus 2 contributor's copies.

$◩ ◎ MATURE YEARS (Specialized: aging; Christian)

P.O. Box 801, 201 Eighth Ave. S., Nashville TN 37202. (615)749-6292. Fax: (615)749-6512. E-mail: matureyears@umpublishing.org. Established 1954. **Contact:** Marvin W. Cropsey, editor.

Magazine Needs *Mature Years*, published quarterly, aims to "help persons understand and use the resources of Christian faith in dealing with specific opportunities and problems related to aging. Poems may or may not be overtly religious. Poems should not poke fun at older adults, but may take a humorous look at them." Does not want "sentimentality and saccharine. If using rhymes and meter, make sure they are accurate." *Mature Years* is 112 pages, magazine-sized, perfect-bound, with full-color glossy paper cover. Press run is 55,000. Sample: $5.75.

How to Submit Lines/poem: 16 lines of up to 50 characters maximum. Accepts fax and e-mail submissions (e-mail preferred). Submit seasonal and nature poems for spring from December through February; for summer, March through May; for fall, June through August; and for winter, September through November. Time between acceptance and publication is up to 1 year. Guidelines available for SASE or by e-mail. Responds in 2 months. Pays $1/line upon acceptance.

◩ ◎ MEASURE: A REVIEW OF FORMAL POETRY (SPECIALIZED: METRICAL POETRY ONLY)

Dept. of English, The University of Evansville, 1800 Lincoln Ave., Evansville IN 47722. (812)488-2963. E-mail: pb28@evansville.edu. Web site: http://measure.evansville.edu. Established 2005. **Contact:** The Editors.

Magazine Needs *Measure: A Review of Formal Poetry* is "dedicated to publishing the best metrical, English-language verse from both the United States and abroad. In each issue we strive to bring you the best new poetry from both established and emerging writers, and we also reprint a small sampling of poems from the best books of metrical poetry published the previous year. Likewise, each issue includes interviews with some of our most important contemporary poets and offers short critical essays on the poetry that has helped to shape the craft." Wants "English-language metrical poetry with no particular stanza preference. See our Web site or a back issue for examples. *Measure* also reprints poems from books; send copy for consideration." Does not want "fixed forms written in free verse; syllabics; quantitative." Has published poetry by Timothy Steele, R.S. Gwynn, Philip Dacey, X.J. Kennedy, Rachel Hadas, and Charles Rafferty. *Measure* is 220 pages, digest-sized, perfect-bound, with glossy cover with color artwork. Receives about 1,500 poems/year, accepts about 10%. Press run is 1,000. Single copy: $10; subscription: $18 for one year, $34 for 2 years, $50 for 3 years. Make checks payable to *Measure*.

How to Submit Submit 3-5 poems at a time. Lines/poem: no minimum or maximum. No previously published poems or simultaneous submissions. No e-mail or disk submissions. Cover letter is preferred. "All submissions should be typed. Each poem should include the poet's name and phone number. A self-addressed stamped envelope must accompany the submission." Reads submissions year round. Time between acceptance and publication "depends." Never comments on rejected poems. Guidelines available in magazine, for SASE, or on Web site. Responds in 2-3 months. Pays 2 contributor's copies. Acquires one-time rights. Rights revert to poet upon publication.

Additional Information Prints the winners of the annual Howard Nemerov Sonnet Award (see separate listing in Contests & Awards).

☑ MÊLÉE

P.O. Box 1619, Alexander City AL 35010. E-mail: info@poetrymelee.com. Web site: www.poetryme lee.com. Established 2006. **Contact:** Lisa Ann Holmes or Chris Pappas, Jr., editors. Member: CLMP.

Magazine Needs *Mêlée*, published sporadically, seeks "poetry and essays that explore the symbiotic relationships between aesthetics and political/social activism. However, our intent is to publish the best work submitted to us regardless of topic. Poetry of any style or length and short essays on any topic will be considered. Content may or may not be of overtly political intent." Does not want "tired language." Has published poetry by Amiri Baraka, Lyn Lifshin, Ed Sanders, Maurice Manning, Beth Gylys, R.T. Castleberry, Robert Haslam, Jennifer Abbott, Linda Frost, and Steve Davenport. *Mêlée* is 24-40 pages, newsprint tabloid, saddle-stapled, with cover with b&w photos and art, includes ads. Receives about 1,000 poems/year, accepts about 10%. Press run is 4,000 (100 subscribers, 500 shelf sales); 2,400 distributed free. Single copy: $3.95; subscription: $14 (one year), $27 (2 years). Make checks payable to *Mêlée*.

How to Submit Submit up to 5 poems at a time. Lines/poem: any length considered. Considers simultaneous submissions; no previously published poems (even poems from internet publication). Prefers e-mail (as attachment in Word) submissions. For e-mail submissions with Word attachments, include name, address, phone number, and e-mail address in body of message. Cover letter is unnecessary, "but welcome." Reads submissions year round. Submit seasonal poems 4 months in advance. Time between acceptance and publication varies, "as does our publication schedule." Poems are circulated to an editorial board. "Both editors and guest readers read the poems submitted for publication." Sometimes comments on rejected poems. Sometimes publishes theme issues. Guidelines available on Web site. Response time varies, up to 9 months because of sporadic publication schedule. E-mails acceptance/rejection notification. Always sends prepublication galleys. Pays 5 contributor's copies. Acquires first rights; acquires electronic rights "upon negotiation with individual writers." Rights revert to poets upon publication.

Additional Information Reads for *Meridian*'s anthology, *Best New Poets* (www.bestnewpoets.org). Find *Mêlée*'s Blog at http://poetrymelee.blogspot.com/ or as link from the Web site www.poetrymel ee.com.

$☺ THE MENNONITE (Specialized: Christian)

P.O. Box 347, Newton KS 67114-0347. (316)283-5155, ext. 231. Fax: (316)283-0454. E-mail: gordon h@themennonite.org. Web site: www.themennonite.org. Established 1885. **Contact:** Gordon Houser, associate editor.

Magazine Needs *The Mennonite*, published twice/month, seeks "Christian poetry—usually free verse, not too long, with multiple layers of meaning." Does not want "sing-song rhymes or poems that merely describe or try to teach a lesson." Has published poetry by Jean Janzen and Julia

Kasdorf. *The Mennonite* is 32 pages, magazine-sized, with full-color cover, includes ads. Receives about 200 poems/year, accepts about 5%. Press run is 12,500 (11,000 subscribers). Single copy: $3; subscription: $43.95. Sample: $3.

How to Submit Submit up to 4 poems at a time. Considers previously published poems and simultaneous submissions. Accepts e-mail submissions (preferred). Cover letter is preferred. Time between acceptance and publication is up to 1 year. Seldom comments on rejected poems. Occasionally publishes theme issues. Guidelines available for SASE. Responds in 2 weeks. Pays $50-75 plus 1 contributor's copy. Acquires first or one-time rights.

◪ MERIDIAN

University of Virginia, P.O. Box 400145, Charlottesville VA 22904-4145. (434)982-5798. E-mail: MeridianUVA@yahoo.com. Web site: www.readmeridian.org. Established 1998. **Contact:** Poetry Editor.

• Work published in *Meridian* has appeared in *The Best American Poetry* and *The Pushcart Prize*.

Magazine Needs *Meridian*, published semiannually, prints poetry, fiction, nonfiction, interviews, and reviews. Has published poetry by David Kirby, Charles Wright, and Joelle Biele. *Meridian* is 190 pages, digest-sized, offset-printed, perfect-bound, with color cover. Receives about 2,500 poems/year, accepts about 30 (less than 1%). Press run is 1,000 (750 subscribers, 15 libraries, 200 shelf sales); 150 distributed free to writing programs. Single copy: $7; subscription: $12/year. Make checks payable to *Meridian*.

How to Submit Submit up to 4 poems at a time. Considers simultaneous submissions (with notification of acceptance elsewhere); no previously published poems. No e-mail or disk submissions; accepts postal and online submissions (**$2 upload fee for up to 4 poems**; no fee for postal submissions). Cover letter is preferred. Reads submissions September-May primarily (do not send submissions April 15-August 15; accepts online submissions year round). Time between acceptance and publication is 1-2 months. Seldom comments on rejected poems. Guidelines available on Web site. Responds in 1-4 months. Always sends prepublication galleys and author contracts. Pays 2 contributor's copies (additional copies available at discount). Reviews books of poetry.

Contest/Award Offerings *Meridian* Editors' Prize Contest offers annual $1,000 award. Submit online only; see Web site for formatting details. **Entry fee:** $16, includes one-year subscription to *Meridian*. **Deadline:** December; see Web site for current deadline.

☐ MERIDIAN ANTHOLOGY OF CONTEMPORARY POETRY

P.O. Box 970309, Boca Raton FL 33497. E-mail: LetarP@aol.com. Web site: www.MeridianAnthology.com. Established 2002. **Contact:** Phyliss L. Geller, editor/publisher; Marilyn Krepf, literary editor.

Magazine Needs *Meridian Anthology of Contemporary Poetry*, published annually in summer, seeks "poetry that is contemporary, insightful, and illuminating; that touches the nerves. It should have color, content, and be deciphering of existence." Does not want vulgarity, clichés. Has published poetry by Elizabeth Swados, Ann McGovern, Gladys Justin Carr, Alan Britt, and Doug Ramspeck. Has reprinted poetry (with poet's permission) by Philip Levine and Jane Hirshfield, Dorianne Laux, Marie Howe. *Meridian Anthology of Contemporary Poetry* is 110-168 pages, digest-sized, offset-printed, perfect-bound, with soft cover. Press run is 500-1,000. Single copy: Volume 6 for $16 in Summer 2008; Volume 5 is $16, Volume 4 is $14, Volume 3 is $13, $9 for Volume 2, $7 for Volume 1. $3 S/H for each additional anthology. Make checks payable to *Meridian Anthology of Contemporary Poetry*.

How to Submit Submit 1-5 poems at a time. Lines/poem: 78 maximum. Considers previously published poems and simultaneous submissions. No e-mail or disk submissions. Cover letter is preferred. Must include SASE. Reads submissions March-December. Time between acceptance and publication is up to one year. Seldom comments on rejected poems. Guidelines available for SASE or on Web site. Responds in 2-6 months, "depending on backlog." Acquires one-time rights. Please include consent to publish, form is available on Web site.

Additional Information "Volume 5, anniversary issue featured reprinted poems by Jane Hirshfield

and Marie Howe. Volume 4 featured Jane Hirshfield, Volume 3 featured Philip Levine). Editing services available: please go to our Web site for information.''
Advice ''A poem must have a reason for existence, some universal tendril.''

ℕ ◻ ◎ META-POIESIS (Specialized: high-school based publication)

P.O. Box 1619, Alexander City AL 35111.E-mail: editor@meta-poiesis.com. Web site: www.meta-poiesis.com. Established 2008. **Contact:** Lisa Holmes, managing editor.

Magazine Needs *Meta-Poiesis*, published annually in May online, is a ''high-school based, creative arts and multi-media class. They have an adult advisory board made up of published poets and writers that guides the selection and editing processes. Their mission is to learn how to select quality poetry and publish it in order to further promote aesthetic appreciation.'' Considers poetry by teens (''poets 15 years old to 115 years old''). Receives about 200 poems/year, accepts about 10%. Make donations payable to Melee, P.O. Box 1619, Alexander City, AL 35011.

How to Submit Submit up to 5 poems at a time. Considers simultaneous submissions with notification. (Considers poetry posted on a public Web site/blog/forum as published). Accepts e-mail submissions (as attachment); no fax or disk submissions. Cover letter is preferred. Reads submissions sporadically throughout the year. Time between acceptance and publication is 9-12 months. Poems are circulated to an editorial board. ''All poems are read by each student. They compile a list of favorite poems. Adult editors then sit in on discussions of the selected poems and each student is asked to narrow their selection to 3 poems. These are collected, sorted, and the final 30-50 poems are chosen by ballot process. The adult coordinator has final editorial rights.'' Sometimes comments on rejected poems. Never publishes theme issues. Guidelines available by e-mail and on Web site. Responds in 6-9 months. Always sends proofs. Acquires first rights and electronic rights for one-time publication in designated issue. Rights revert to poets upon publication.

$ ◙ MICHIGAN QUARTERLY REVIEW

University of Michigan, 3574 Rackham Bldg., 915 E. Washington St., Ann Arbor MI 48109. (734)764-9265. E-mail: mqr@umich.edu. Web site: www.umich.edu/ ~ mqr. Established 1962. **Contact:** Laurence Goldstein, editor-in-chief.

● Poetry published in *Michigan Quarterly Review* is included frequently in volumes of *The Best American Poetry* and *The Pushcart Prize* anthologies.

Magazine Needs *Michigan Quarterly Review* is ''an interdisciplinary, general interest academic journal that publishes mainly essays and reviews on subjects of cultural and literary interest.'' Wants all kinds of poetry except light verse. No specifications as to form, length, style, subject matter, or purpose. Has published poetry by Susan Hahn, Campbell McGrath, Carl Phillips, and Cathy Song. *Michigan Quarterly Review* is 160 pages, digest-sized, professionally printed, flat-spined, with glossy card cover. Receives about 1,400 submissions/year, accepts about 30. Press run is 2,000 (1,200 subscribers, half are libraries). Single copy: $7; subscription: $25. Sample: $4.

How to Submit No previously published poems or simultaneous submissions. No e-mail submissions. Cover letter is preferred. ''It puts a human face on the manuscript. A few sentences of biography is all I want, nothing lengthy or defensive.'' Prefers typed mss. Publishes theme issues. Upcoming themes available in magazine and on Web site. Guidelines available for SASE or on Web site. Responds in 6 weeks. Always sends prepublication galleys. Pays $8-12/page. Acquires first rights only. Reviews books of poetry. ''All reviews are commissioned.''

Contest/Award Offerings The Laurence Goldstein Poetry Award, an annual cash prize of $1,000, is given to the author of the best poem to appear in *Michigan Quarterly* during the calendar year. ''Established in 2002, the prize is sponsored by the Office of the President of the University of Michigan.''

Advice ''There is no substitute for omnivorous reading and careful study of poets past and present, as well as reading in new and old areas of knowledge. Attention to technique, especially to rhythm and patterns of imagery, is vital.''

$□ ◎ THE MID-AMERICA POETRY REVIEW (Specialized: poets living in MO, IL, AR, OK, KS, NE, IA)

The Mid-America Press, Inc., P.O. Box 575, Warrensburg MO 64093-0575. Established 1976 (press). **Contact:** Robert C. Jones, editor.

Magazine Needs *The Mid-America Poetry Review*, published 3 times/year, prints "well-crafted poetry, primarily from—but not limited to—poets living in Missouri, Illinois, Arkansas, Oklahoma, Kansas, Nebraska, and Iowa. We are open to all styles and forms; what we look for is poetry by writers who know both what they are doing and why." Has published poetry by Charles Guenther, Rhina P. Espaillat, Louis D. Brodsky, David Baker, Kate Northrop, and Gloria Vando. *The Mid-America Poetry Review* is 60-75 pages, digest-sized, offset-printed, perfect-bound, with matte paper cover. Receives about 1,000-1,500 poems/year, accepts about 15%. Press run is 750. Single copy: $6; subscription: $15/year. Make checks payable to The Mid-America Press, Inc.

How to Submit Submit 1-3 poems at a time. Lines/poem: 36 maximum. No previously published poems or simultaneous submissions. Cover letter is useful. "One-page cover letter (if included) should list items to be considered and contain brief paragraphs of information about author and previous publications. Type submissions, single- or double-spaced, on $8^{1}/_{2} \times 11$ white paper; include name, address, and telephone number in top left or right corner. Enclose SASE for notification/ guidelines. Do not send the only copy of your manuscript—unused submissions are recycled." Time between acceptance and publication may be up to 1 year. Sometimes comments on submissions. Guidelines available for SASE. Responds within 2 months. Sends prepublication galleys. Pays $5/ poem on acceptance, 2 contributor's copies on publication, and one-year subscription. Acquires first North American serial rights. Staff occasionally reviews books of poetry. Send materials for review consideration.

Additional Information The Mid-America Press, Inc. publishes 1-5 book-length poetry collections/ year. **"At present, the Press is not reading unsolicited book-length poetry manuscripts."** Award- winning publications from Mid-America Press, Inc. include *Uncurling* (2000) by Jeanie Wilson, *Light and Chance* (2001) by Ardyth Bradley, *Dreaming the Bronze Girl* (2002) by Serina Allison Hearn, and *The Graveyard Picnic* (2002) by William Ford. Order sample books by sending $13.95/book.

Advice "Read several copies of the magazine to see the range of subject matter and forms."

◙ THE MIDWEST QUARTERLY

Pittsburg State University, Pittsburg KS 66762. (620)235-4689. Fax: (620)235-4686. E-mail: smeats @pittstate.edu. Web site: www.pittstate.edu/engl/mwq/MQindex.html. Established 1959. **Contact:** Stephen Meats, poetry editor.

Magazine Needs *The Midwest Quarterly* publishes "articles on any subject of contemporary inter- est, particularly literary criticism, political science, philosophy, education, biography, and sociol- ogy. Each issue contains a section of poetry usually 12 poems in length." Wants "well-crafted poems, traditional or untraditional, that use intense, vivid, concrete, and/or surrealistic images to explore the mysterious and surprising interactions of the natural and inner human worlds." Does not want " 'nature poems,' per se, but if a poem doesn't engage nature in a significant way, as an integral part of the experience it is offering, I am unlikely to be interested in publishing it." Has published poetry by Peter Cooley, Jim Daniels, Naomi Shihab Nye, Jonathan Holden, William Kloefkorn, and Jeanne Murray Walker. *The Midwest Quarterly* is 130 pages, digest-sized, profession- ally printed, flat-spined, with matte cover. Press run is 650 (600 subscribers, 500 libraries). Receives about 4,000 poems/year, accepts about 50. Subscription: $15. Sample: $5.

How to Submit Submit no more than 5 poems at a time. Lines/poem: 60 maximum ("occasionally longer if exceptional"). Considers simultaneous submissions; no previously published poems. No fax or e-mail submissions. "Manuscripts should be typed with poet's name on each page. Submis- sions without SASE cannot be acknowledged." Comments on rejected poems "if the poet or poem seems particularly promising." Occasionally publishes theme issues or issues devoted to the work of a single poet. Guidelines available on Web site. Responds in 2 months. Pays 2 contributor's copies. Acquires first serial rights. Reviews books of poetry by *Midwest Quarterly*-published poets only.

Advice "Keep writing; read as much contemporary poetry as you can lay your hands on; don't let rejection discourage you from sending your work out to editors."

Diane Glancy

Words as sacred forces

I first came to know Diane Glancy's work through the competitions sponsored by the National Federation of State Poetry Societies (NFSPS). Year after year, their prize anthology included Glancy's winning poems; and in 2001, NFSPS honored Glancy as the winner of their Stevens Manuscript Competition, publishing her collection, *The Stones for a Pillow* (NFSPS Press).

Consequently, I was a little intimidated when I found myself sitting at Glancy's table at my first NFSPS national convention in 2004. By then I knew a lot more about the writer and her work: Glancy is of Cherokee and English/German descent and addresses issues of Native American culture in her writing. Her literary output is formidable, including fiction, essays, plays and screenplays as well as poetry. Her list of awards across these genres is staggering. And as I learned at that first NFSPS banquet, Glancy is down-to-earth, warm, and generous to writers at all levels.

Diane Glancy's profile at NativeWiki (www.nativewiki.org/Diane_Glancy) lists her many awards, which include the Minnesota Book Award in poetry (she's also been finalist in poetry for the Oklahoma Book Award); the Emily Dickinson Poetry Prize (1993, Poetry Society of America); a National Endowment for the Arts Fellowship in Poetry (2003); the Juniper Poetry Prize (2003, University of Massachusetts Press); and the Pablo Neruda Prize for Poetry (2001, Nimrod). There's also a thorough bibliography of Glancy's titles and links to online writing. Currently Glancy is on a four-year sabbatical from Macalester College (St. Paul, Minnesota) where she taught creative writing and Native American literature. Her most recent book of poetry is *Asylum in the Grasslands* (University of Arizona Press).

You've been very active in the National Federation of State Poetry Societies (NFSPS) through its annual competitions and national conventions. What is the value of belonging to an organization like NFSPS? Do you recommend it to fellow poets?

Yes, I recommend belonging to NFSPS. I think I have missed one year [of national conventions] since 1981, which speaks volumes for the organization.

I think, first of all, it is the members I like. There's a sense of camaraderie. NFSPS is a wonderful group of people I look forward to seeing each year. Secondly, I learn a lot about poetry at the conventions. You cannot hear poetry read from morning to night for three days solid without it becoming a learning experience. Thirdly, the conventions are fun.

At last year's NFSPS convention, you presented a wonderful workshop that involved everyone choosing a rock and letting it "speak" to us as a means of inspiring a poem. Could you talk a little more about the inspiration for that workshop? What other aspects of the natural world speak to you this way?

I have collected rocks for many years. When I moved from St. Paul to Kansas City in 2005, I had several boxes of rocks. I taped them closed, hoping the movers would think they belonged with the many boxes of books I also moved. I didn't want to explain about the voices of the rocks, and how I had collected them for years as souvenirs of sorts from all my travels. I want to say again, I actually hear nothing with my ears, but the rocks fill my imagination with their stories.

Each book or project seems to have its token, which is a rock. I don't think I could write without traveling. Many of my novels, such as *Pushing the Bear* [Harcourt Brace], *Stone Heart: A Novel of Sacajawea* [Overlook Press], *The Dance Partner, Stories of the Late 19th Century Ghost Dance* [Michigan State University Press], and a new manuscript, *The Reason for Crows*, are about historical characters or events. I always have to travel to the place where the events took place. I think the land carries voices, memories, visages of what happened upon it. It's where I get ideas, anyway. I usually pick up a rock and set it on the manuscript as I write. The rock for *Stone Heart* appears on the cover of the book. I think the rock for *The Reason for Crows* will be there also.

They are actually small pebbles. "Rock" sounds larger than I intend.

In an interview you once said, "Poetry can go down and swim with the underwater fish." This is an intriguing statement. Could you discuss this more?

I don't swim very well. I think it is frightening underwater. I think I meant that poetry requires taking a risk, letting one's personal voice speak in a poem, attaining a vulnerability.

You've attributed your writing in different genres to having a "broken past." Is writing in a variety of genres a way of dealing with each fragment individually, or does this help you make a whole out of those broken pieces?

I have been working on a collection of essays for several years. The present title is *The Dream of a Broken Field*. I guess the final message is that in brokenness, a greater meaning can enter. I kept thinking, what does a broken field dream? In the act of brokenness, something else takes place. As a Christian, I think of the breaking of bread during communion. Writing is in no way on the level of Christ's body breaking, of course, but there is a transference of the idea nonetheless—a brokenness that reaches a place that could not be reached without brokenness.

You once described words as "energy fields." Could you elaborate?

Words are energy. They are spirit forces. Maybe "sacred forces" is a better term. In Genesis, it says that God spoke the world into being. Words have power. They should not be underestimated. Writing poetry is one of those forces. It gets at what cannot be described with words when words are all we have to describe it. But in a particular arrangement, there is the formation of meaning that can't quite be gotten at.

I write narrative poems, but once in awhile I feel a "beyond" just beyond the poem. There's an interesting article, "A Way of Being: Some Observations on the Ends and Means of Poetry," by B. H. Fairchild in the Vol. 74, No. 1 issue of *New Letters* magazine. "Poetry reveals, opens up, significant experience by being the thing rather than being about the thing." Fairchild then quotes some of Sylvia Plath's poem "Blackberrying," in which a tossing field of blackberries becomes more of a sea than the sea just beyond it.

That is the energy field of language—when language transfers to something beyond it or acts as conduit for the "something beyond" to enter the field of consciousness, and all the world comes alive.

There seem to be various rituals involved in your writing process, such as when you washed a little of the Missouri River over the edge of your Sacajawea manuscript. Does this happen a lot? Is this a reflection of your Native American heritage working in mind and spirit?

I have a friend who lights a candle before she works. I usually just sit down and start writing. I'm from a practical background. I don't have many rituals. But, at the beginning of a project, such as looking for the voice of Sacajawea, I did wash some of the river over the edge of the manuscript, or over the notes I had been taking for the manuscript. In this particular manuscript, the river came together with the land. I usually work with land, so this was a new element I wanted to honor. I wanted to represent it correctly in the novel, so I asked its permission to use it. Or I asked it to speak. Or I asked that I would be able to hear its voice. It was an act of joining that voice to the paper. It seemed to work. Shortly after that, I heard a sentence for the book, "You know you are nothing they want." Maybe it was the little stone speaking about itself, but to me, it was Sacajawea.

Do you think there are enough voices speaking in current American poetry?

No. I think it takes many voices to tell the story of a nation. Every voice should be in a struggle to find its message, if it is to be a living voice.

—*Nancy Breen*

Nancy Breen is the former editor of *Poet's Market*. Her chapbooks include *Rites and Observances* (Finishing Line Press) and *How Time Got Away* (Pudding House Publications). She blogs at www.salmagundiexpress.wordpress.com.

◎ MIDWIFERY TODAY (Specialized: childbirth)

P.O. Box 2672, Eugene OR 97402-0223. (541)344-7438. Fax: (541)344-1422. E-mail: editorial@mid wiferytoday.com. Web site: www.midwiferytoday.com. Established 1986. **Contact:** Cheryl K. Smith, editor.

Magazine Needs *Midwifery Today*, published quarterly, provides "a voice for midwives and child-birth educators. We are a midwifery magazine. Subject must be birth or birth profession related." Does not want poetry that is "off subject or puts down the subject." *Midwifery Today* is 75 pages, magazine-sized, offset-printed, saddle-stapled, with glossy card cover with b&w photos and b&w artwork, includes ads. Press run is 5,000 (3,000 subscribers, 1,000 shelf sales). Subscription: $50. Sample: $10.

How to Submit No previously published poems. Accepts e-mail submissions (pasted into body of message or as attachment). Cover letter is required. Time between acceptance and publication is 1-2 years. Seldom comments on rejected poems. Publishes theme issues. Upcoming themes and deadlines available on Web site. Guidelines available for SASE or on Web site. Responds in 6 months. Pays 2 contributor's copies. Acquires first rights.

Advice "With our publication, please stay on the subject."

✖ $◻ MILLER'S POND

H&H Press (570)376-2821. Fax: (570)376-2674. E-mail: publisher@millerspondpoetry.com. Web site: http://millerspondpoetry.com. Established 1987. **Contact:** C.J. Houghtaling, publisher.

Magazine Needs *miller's pond*, published online with an annual print version each January, features contemporary poetry, interviews, reviews, and markets. Wants "contemporary poetry that is fresh, accessible, energetic, vivid, and flows with language and rhythm." Does not want "religious, horror, pornographic, vulgar, rhymed, preachy, lofty, trite, or overly sentimental work." Has published poetry by Vivian Shipley, Barbara Crooker, Philip Memmer, and Shoshauna Shy.

How to Submit As of 2009 *miller's pond* will be exclusively an e-zine and will not publish in hard copy format. "All submissions must be sent electronically from our Web site. Mail sent through the post office will be returned. No payment for accepted poems or reviews. Current guidelines, updates, and changes are always available on our Web site. Check there first before submitting anything."

Additional Information Books are available for sale via Web site, phone, or fax.

Advice "Believe in yourself. Perseverance is a writer's best 'tool.' Study the contemporary masters: Vivian Shipley, Billy Collins, Maxine Kumin, Colette Inez, Hayden Carruth. Please check our Web site before submitting."

⊚ MINAS TIRITH EVENING-STAR: JOURNAL OF THE AMERICAN TOLKIEN SOCIETY (Specialized: fantasy; Middle-Earth, Tolkien)

American Tolkien Society, P.O. Box 97, Highland MI 48357-0097. E-mail: editor@americantolkienso ciety.org. Web site: www.americantolkiensociety.org. Established 1967. **Contact:** Amalie A. Helms, editor.

Magazine Needs *Minas Tirith Evening-Star: Journal of the American Tolkien Society*, published quarterly, uses poetry of fantasy about Middle-Earth and Tolkien. Considers poetry by children and teens. Has published poetry by Thomas M. Egan, Anne Etkin, Nancy Pope, and Martha Benedict. *Minas Tirith Evening-Star* is digest-sized, offset-printed from typescript, with cartoon-like b&w graphics. Press run is 400. Single copy: $3.50; subscription: $12.50. Sample: $3. Make checks payable to American Tolkien Society.

How to Submit Considers previously published poems ("maybe"); no simultaneous submissions. Accepts e-mail and disk submissions. Cover letter is preferred. Sometimes comments on rejected poems. Occasionally publishes theme issues. Guidelines available for SASE or by e-mail. Responds in 2 weeks. Sometimes sends prepublication galleys. Pays 1 contributor's copy. Reviews related books of poetry; length depends on the volume ("a sentence to several pages"). Send materials for review consideration.

Additional Information Under the imprint of W.W. Publications, publishes collections of poetry of fantasy about Middle-Earth and Tolkien. Books/chapbooks are 50-100 pages. Publishes 2 chapbooks/year. For book or chapbook consideration, submit sample poems.

Also Offers Membership in the American Tolkien Society is open to all, regardless of country of residence, and entitles one to receive the quarterly journal. Dues are $12.50/year to addresses in U.S., $12.50 in Canada, and $15 elsewhere. Sometimes sponsors contests.

Advice "Adhere to the guidelines and show talent."

⊠ ⊘ ⊚ THE MINNESOTA REVIEW (SPECIALIZED: POLITICAL & SOCIAL ISSUES)

English Dept., Carnegie Mellon University, Baker Hall, Pittsburgh PA 15213. Fax: (412)268-7989. E-mail: editors@theminnesotareview.org. (inquiries only). Web site: www.theminnesotareview.org. Established 1960. **Contact:** Poetry Editor.

Magazine Needs *the minnesota review*, published biannually, seeks "poetry that explores some aspect of social or political issues and/or the nature of relationships." Does not want "nature poems, and no lyric poetry without the above focus." Has published poetry by Hollander and Fuentes Lemus. *the minnesota review* is about 200 pages, digest-sized, flat-spined, with b&w glossy card cover. Press run is 1,500 (800 subscribers). Subscription: $30/2 years for individuals, $45/year for institutions. Sample: $15.

How to Submit No fax or e-mail submissions. Cover letter is preferred. Include "brief intro with address." Address submissions to "Poetry Editor" (i.e., not to a specific editor by name). SASE with sufficient postage required for return of ms. Publishes theme issues. Upcoming themes available for SASE. Responds in up to 4 months. Pays 2 contributor's copies. "Rights revert to author at printing, though *the minnesota review* asks to be referenced whenever and wherever the poem is reprinted. Further, we reserve the right to post content on our Web site.''

N ◎ MOBIUS: THE JOURNAL OF SOCIAL CHANGE (Specialized: Socially and politically relevant poetry and fiction)

505 Christianson St, Madison WI 53714. (608)242-1009. E-mail: fmschep@charter.net. Web site: mobiusmagazine.com. Established 1989 **Contact:** F.J. Bergmann, poetry editor or Fred Schepartz, general editor

Magazine Needs *Mobius: The Journal of Social Change*, published quarterly, prints socially and politically relevant poetry and fiction and ''is distributed free in Madison, WI, and to libraries and subscribers.'' Wants any form of poetry on themes of social change. Does not want ''heavy-handed, transparent didacticism.'' Considers poetry by teens; however, the publication is not directed at children. Has published poetry by Greg Markee, Tom Neale, Richard Roe, Dennis Trudell, John Tuschen. *Mobius* is 14-24 pages, magazine-sized, offset print, saddle-stapled with cardstock cover and black-and-white art, includes ads. Receives about 500 poems/year, accepts about 20. Press run is 1000; distributed free to local coffee shops and bookstores. Single copy: $2.50; subscription: $10. Make checks payable to *Mobius*.

How to Submit Submit 5 poems at a time. Considers previously published poems and simultaneous submissions. Accepts e-mail submissions (pasted into body of message); no fax or disk submissions. Cover letter is unnecessary. Include short bio and mailing address; postal submissions must include e-mail address or SASE. Reads submissions year round. Time between acceptance and publication is up to 6 months. Sometimes comments on rejected poems. Never publishes theme issues. Guidelines available by e-mail and on Web site. Responds in 3 months. Pays 2 contributor's copies. Acquires one-time and electronic rights (''reserves right to publish on Web site also''). Rights revert to poets upon publication.

Advice ''Prose with line breaks is not poetry. Predictable rants will disappoint us.''

★ ◿ ◎ THE MOCCASIN (Specialized: members only)

The League of Minnesota Poets, 427 N. Gorman St., Blue Earth MN 56013. (507)526-5321. Web site: www.mnpoets.org. Established 1937. **Contact:** Meredith R. Cook, editor.

Magazine Needs *The Moccasin*, published annually in October, is the literary magazine of The League of Minnesota Poets. **Membership is required to submit work.** Wants ''all forms of poetry. Prefer strong short poems.'' Does not want ''profanity or obscenity.'' Considers poetry by children and teens who are student members of The League of Minnesota Poets (write grade level on poems submitted). Has published poetry by Diane Glancy, Laurel Winter, Susan Stevens Chambers, Doris Stengel, Jeanette Hinds, and Charmaine Donovan. *The Moccasin* is 40 pages, digest-sized, offset-printed, stapled, with 80 lb. linen-finish text cover with drawing and poem. Receives about 190 poems/year, accepts about 170. Press run is 200. Single copy: $5.25; subscription: free with LOMP membership. Sample: $2.25 for issues older than 1998. Make checks payable to LOMP and send to Angela Foster, LOMP Treasurer, 30036 St. Croix Rd, Pine City MN 55063.

How to Submit Submit 6 or more poems at a time. Lines/poem: 24 maximum (unless poem has won a prize from the National Federation of State Poetry Societies in its annual competition). Considers previously published poems; no simultaneous submissions. No disk submissions. Cover letter is preferred. ''No poems will be returned and no questions answered without a SASE.'' Reads submissions year round (deadline for each year's issue is mid-July). Sometimes comments on rejected poems. **Must be a member of The League of Minnesota Poets to submit.** Guidelines available in magazine. No payment; poet receives contributor's copy as part of LOMP membership subscription. Acquires one-time rights.

Also Offers To become a member of The League of Minnesota Poets, send $20 ($10 if high school student or younger) to Angela Foster, LOMP Treasurer, 30036 St. Croix Rd, Pine City MN 55063. Make checks payable to LOMP. You do not have to live in Minnesota to become a member of LOMP. ''Membership in LOMP automatically makes you a member of the National Federation of State Poetry Societies, which makes you eligible to enter its contests at a cheaper (members') rate.''

$ ☑ ◎ MODERN HAIKU (Specialized: haiku/senryu/haibun only; translations)

P.O. Box 7046, Evanston IL 60204-7046. Email: trumbullc@comcast.net. Web site: www.modernha iku.org. Established 1969. **Contact:** Charles Trumbull, editor.

Magazine Needs *Modern Haiku*, published 3 times/year in February, June, and October, is "the foremost international journal of English-language haiku and criticism. We are devoted to publishing only the very best haiku being written; also publish articles on haiku and have the most complete review section of haiku books." Wants "contemporary haiku in English (including translations into English) that incorporate the traditional aesthetics of the haiku genre, but which may be innovative as to subject matter, mode of approach or angle of perception, and form of expression. Haiku, senryu, and haibun only. No tanka or other forms. Same considerations, pro and con, given to work by children and teens." Has published haiku by Billy Collins, Lawrence Ferlinghetti, Sharon Olds, Paul Muldoon, and Gary Snyder. *Modern Haiku* is 120 pages (average), digest-sized, printed on heavy quality stock, with full-color cover illustrations. Receives about 12,000-14,000 submissions/year, accepts about 750. Press run is 650. Subscription: $26 ppd. Sample: $11 ppd in the U.S. **How to Submit** Submit "any number of haiku per letter-sized sheet." No e-mail submissions from North America. No previously published haiku or simultaneous submissions. Put name and address on each sheet. Include SASE. Guidelines available for SASE or on Web site. Responds in 6 weeks. Pays $1/haiku (but no contributor's copy). Acquires first North American serial rights. Staff and freelance reviews books of haiku in 350-1,000 words, usually single-book format. Send materials for review consideration with complete ordering information.

Contest/Award Offerings Sponsors the annual Robert Spiess Memorial Haiku Competition. Guidelines available for SASE or on Web site.

Advice "Study what haiku really are. We do not want sentimentality, pretty-pretty, or pseudo-Japanese themes. Juxtaposition of seemingly disparate entities that nonetheless create harmony is very desirable."

☑ MOTHER EARTH INTERNATIONAL JOURNAL

% National Poetry Association, 934 Brannan St., 2nd Floor, San Francisco CA 94103. (415)552-9261. Web site: www.nationalpoetry.org/npa/mother.html. Established 1976 (National Poetry Association), 1991 (*Mother Earth International Journal*). **Contact:** Herman Berlandt, editor/publisher.

Magazine Needs *Mother Earth International Journal* is "the only ongoing anthology of contemporary poetry in English translation from all regions of the world. It provides a forum for poets to comment in poetic form on political, economic, and ecological issues." Wants "bold and compassionate poetry that has universal relevance with an emphasis on the world's current political and ecological crisis." Does not want "self-indulgent or prosaic stuff that lacks imagination." Considers poetry by children and teens (ages 8-17). Has published poetry by Lawrence Ferlinghetti, Adrienne Rich, Corolyn Kizer, Mary Oliver, Alessio Zanelli, and Abba Korner. *Mother Earth International Journal* is 53 pages, $5^{1}/_{2} \times 8^{1}/_{2}$, offset-printed. Receives about 4,000 poems/year, accepts 15%. Press run is 2,000. Subscription: $12/year. Sample: $3.75. Make checks payable to Uniting the World Through Poetry. "We encourage the purchase of a copy or a year's subscription."

How to Submit Submit 4 poems at a time. Considers previously published poems and simultaneous submissions. Cover letter is preferred. Time between acceptance and publication is 4 months. Occasionally publishes theme issues (humanistic: love, peace, environmental). Guidelines available for SASE. Responds in 3 months. Sometimes sends prepublication galleys. Pays 2 contributor's copies. All rights revert to the author.

Contest/Award Offerings Sponsors a $50 prize for the best of "Your Two Best Lines," a benefit collage poem that will list all entries as a collective poem. **Entry fee:** "a $5 check should be enclosed with submission." (Send SASE or see http://internationalpoetrymuseum.org/ for information about the Poetry Film Festival and Songwriters Awards.)

Also Offers The National Poetry Association, currently working to establish an International Poetry Museum in San Francisco. For more information, visit http://internationalpoetrymuseum.org/.

Advice "*Mother Earth International Journal* is an ongoing anthology of world contemporary poetry. For subscribers, we reduced the subscription from $18 to $15 per year. While all future issues will include an American section, we hope that all who send in entries will subscribe to *Mother Earth International Journal* to get a truly world perspective of universal concerns."

◪ MOUNT OLIVE REVIEW

634 Henderson St., Mount Olive NC 28365. (919)658-2502. Established 1987. **Contact:** Dr. Pepper Worthington, editor.

Magazine Needs *Mount Olive Review* features "literary criticism, poetry, short stories, essays, and book reviews." Wants "modern poetry." Receives about 2,000 poems/year, accepts 8%. Press run is 500. Single copy: $10. Make checks payable to Mount Olive College Press.

How to Submit Submit 6 poems at a time. No previously published poems or simultaneous submissions. Cover letter is preferred. Time between acceptance and publication varies. Poems are circulated to an editorial board. Seldom comments on rejected poems. Responds in 6 months. Sometimes sends prepublication galleys. Acquires first rights. Reviews books/chapbooks of poetry and other magazines/journals. Send materials for review consideration.

▣ ◪ MUDLARK: AN ELECTRONIC JOURNAL OF POETRY & POETICS

Dept. of English, University of North Florida, Jacksonville FL 32224-2645. (904)620-2273. Fax: (904)620-3940. E-mail: mudlark@unf.edu. Web site: www.unf.edu/mudlark. Established 1995. **Contact:** William Slaughter, editor.

Magazine Needs *Mudlark: An Electronic Journal of Poetry & Poetics*, published online "irregularly, but frequently," offers 3 formats: issues of *Mudlark* "are the electronic equivalent of print chapbooks; posters are the electronic equivalent of print broadsides; and flash poems are poems that have news in them, poems that feel like current events. The poem is the thing at *Mudlark*, and the essay about it. As our full name suggests, we will consider accomplished work that locates itself anywhere on the spectrum of contemporary practice. We want poems, of course, but we want essays, too, that make us read poems (and write them?) differently somehow. Although we are not innocent, we do imagine ourselves capable of surprise. The work of hobbyists is not for *Mudlark*." Has published poetry by John Allman, Denise Duhamel, Taylor Graham, Susan Kelly-Dewitt, Frederick Pollack, and Michael Ruby. *Mudlark* is archived and permanently on view at www.unf.edu.

How to Submit Submit any number of poems at a time. Considers previously published poems ("inasmuch as issues of *Mudlark* are the electronic equivalent of print chapbooks, some of the individual poems in them might, or might not, have been previously published; if they have been, that previous publication must be acknowledged"); no simultaneous submissions ("because of our short turn-around time"). "Only poems that have not been previously published will be considered for *Mudlark* posters, the electronic equivalent of print broadsides, or for *Mudlark* flash poems." Accepts e-mail submissions; no fax submissions. Cover letter is optional. Time between acceptance and publication is up to 3 months. Seldom comments on rejected poems. Guidelines available for SASE, by e-mail, or on Web site. Responds in "1 day to 1 month, depending..." Always sends prepublication galleys "in the form of inviting the author to proof the work on a private Web site that *Mudlark* maintains for that purpose." No payment; however, "one of the things we can do at *Mudlark* to 'pay' our authors for their work is point to it here and there. We can tell our readers how to find it, how to subscribe to it, and how to buy it—if it is for sale. Toward that end, we maintain A-Notes (on the authors) we publish. We call attention to their work." Acquires one-time rights.

Advice "*Mudlark* has been reviewed well and often. At this early point in its history, *Mudlark* has established itself, arguably, as one of the few serious rivals in the first generation of the electronic medium, to print versions of its kind. Look at *Mudlark*, visit the Web site, spend some time there. Then make your decision: to submit or not to submit."

$ ◪ ◎ MYTHIC DELIRIUM (Specialized: science fiction; fantasy; horror; surreal; cross-genre)

3514 Signal Hill Ave. NW, Roanoke VA 24017-5148. E-mail: mythicdelirium@gmail.com. Web site: www.mythicdelirium.com. Established 1998. **Contact:** Mike Allen, editor. Member: Science Fiction Poetry Association, Science Fiction & Fantasy Writers of America.

Magazine Needs *Mythic Delirium*, published biannually, is "a journal of speculative poetry for the new millennium. All forms considered. Must fit within the genres we consider, though we have published some mainstream verse." Does not want "forced rhyme, corny humor, jarringly gross sexual material, gratuitous obscenity, handwritten manuscripts.'' Has published poetry by Sonya Taaffe, Theodora Goss, Joe Haldeman, Ursula K. Le Guin, Ian Watson, and Jane Yolen. *Mythic Delirium* is 32 pages, digest-sized, saddle-stapled, with color cover art, includes house ads. Receives about 750 poems/year, accepts about 5%. Press run is 150. Subscription: $9/year, $16/2 years. Sample: $5. Make checks payable to Mike Allen.

How to Submit Submit up to 6 poems at a time. No previously published poems or simultaneous submissions. Accepts e-mail submissions; no disk submissions. Cover letter is preferred. Time between acceptance and publication is 9 months. Often comments on rejected poems. Guidelines available for SASE, by e-mail, or on Web site. Responds in 5 weeks. Pays $5/poem, plus 1 contributor's copy. Acquires first North American serial rights.

Advice *"Mythic Delirium* isn't easy to get into, but we publish newcomers in every issue. Show us how ambitious you can be, and don't give up.''

NASSAU REVIEW

English Dept., Nassau Community College, Garden City NY 11530-6793. (516)572-7792. Established 1964. **Contact:** Editorial Board.

Magazine Needs *Nassau Review*, published annually in September, is a "creative and research vehicle for Nassau College faculty and the faculty of other colleges.'' Wants "serious, intellectual poetry of any form or style. Submissions from adults only. No college students; graduate students acceptable. Want only poems of high quality.'' Does not want "light or satiric verse.'' Has published poetry by Patti Tana, Dick Allen, David Heyen, Joan Sevick, and Mario Susko. *Nassau Review* is about 190 pages, digest-sized, flat-spined. Receives up to 1,900 poems/year, accepts about 20-25. Press run is 1,100. Sample: free.

How to Submit Submit 3 poems at a time (only once per yearly issue). No previously published poems or simultaneous submissions. Submit 3 copies of each poem. SASE required for reply. "Manuscripts will not be returned unless SASE includes sufficient postage.'' Reads submissions November 1-March 1 only. Guidelines available for SASE. Responds in up to 4 months. Pays 2 contributor's copies.

Contest/Award Offerings Sponsors an annual poetry contest with $200 award. **Deadline:** March 31.

Advice "We want professional-level, high-quality work!''

$ THE NATION

33 Irving Place, New York NY 10003. Web site: www.thenation.com/about/poetry_guidelines.mht ml. Established 1865. **Contact:** Peter Gizzi, poetry editor.

• Poetry published by *The Nation* has been included in *The Best American Poetry*.

Magazine Needs *The Nation*, published weekly, is a journal of left/liberal opinion, with arts coverage that includes poetry. The only requirement for poetry is "excellence.'' Has published poetry by W.S. Merwin, Maxine Kumin, James Merrill, May Swenson, Edward Hirsch, and Charles Simic.

How to Submit Submit up to 3 poems at a time, no more than 8 poems within the calendar year. No simultaneous submissions. No fax, e-mail, or disk submissions; send by First-Class Mail only. No reply without SASE.

THE NATIONAL POETRY REVIEW

P.O. Box 2080, Aptos CA 95001-2080. Web site: www.nationalpoetryreview.com. Established 2003. **Contact:** C.J. Sage, editor.

• Poetry appearing in *The National Poetry Review* has also appeared in *The Pushcart Prize*.

Magazine Needs *The National Poetry Review* seeks "the most stunning, memorable poems available. The editors celebrate Frost's declaration that the best poems begin in delight and end in wisdom. *TNPR* considers both experimental and 'mainstream' work.'' Does not want "overly self-centered or confessional poetry, simple autobiography, prose poems, or vulgarity.'' Has published poetry by Bob Hicok, Jennifer Michael Hecht, Larissa Szplorluk, Margot Schilpp, Sarah Hannah, and Ted Kooser. *The National Poetry Review* is 64 pages, perfect-bound, with full-color cover. Accepts less than 1% of submissions received. Single copy: $10; subscription: $15/year. Make checks payable to C.J. Sage only.

How to Submit Submit 3-5 poems at a time. Considers simultaneous submissions "with notification only." Submissions are accepted through e-mail only between June 1 and August 31 unless you are a subscriber or benefactor. Put your name in the subject line of your e-mail and send to tnprsubmissions@yahoo.com." Cover letter with bio is preferred. Subscribers and benefactors may submit any time during the year (please write 'subscriber' or 'benefactor' in the subject line). Reading period for non-subscribers is June through August only. See Web site before submitting." Time between acceptance and publication is no more than 1 year. "The editor makes all publishing decisions." Seldom comments on rejected poems. Guidelines available in magazine or on Web site. Usually responds in about 8 weeks. Pays 1 contributor's copy "and small honorarium if funds are available." Acquires first rights.

Contest/Award Offerings The Annie Finch Prize for Poetry, The Laureate Prize for Poetry, and *The National Poetry Review* Book Prize (see separate listings in Contests & Awards).

Advice "Read an issue or 2 before submitting. Send only your very best work."

⚡ ◪ NATURAL BRIDGE

Dept. of English, University of Missouri-St. Louis, One University Blvd., St. Louis MO 63121. E-mail: natural@umsl.edu. Web site: www.umsl.edu/~natural. Established 1999. **Contact:** O. Ayes, managing editor. Member: CLMP.

Magazine Needs *Natural Bridge*, published biannually, seeks "fresh, innovative poetry, both free and formal, on any subject. We want poems that work on first and subsequent readings—poems that entertain and resonate and challenge our readers. *Natural Bridge* also publishes fiction, essays, and translations." Has published poetry by Ross Gay, Beckian Fritz Goldberg, Joy Harjo, Bob Hicok, Sandra Kohler, and Timothy Liu. *Natural Bridge* is 150-200 pages, digest-sized, printed on 60 lb. opaque recycled, acid-free paper, true binding, with 12 pt. coated glossy or matte cover. Receives about 1,200 poems/year, accepts about 1%. Press run is 1,000 (200 subscribers, 50 libraries). Single copy: $8; subscription: $15/year, $25/2 years. Make checks payable to *Natural Bridge*.

How to Submit Submit 4-6 poems at a time. Lines/poem: no limit. Considers simultaneous submissions; no previously published poems. No e-mail or disk submissions. "Submissions should be typewritten, with name and address on each page. Do not staple manuscripts. Send SASE." Reads submissions July 1-August 31 and November 1-December 31. Time between acceptance and publication is 9 months. "Work is read and selected by the guest-editor and editor, along with editorial assistants made up of graduate students in our MFA program. We publish work by both established and new writers." Sometimes comments on rejected poems. Sometimes publishes theme issues. Upcoming themes available on Web site. Guidelines available in magazine or on Web site. Responds in 5 months after the close of the submission period. Sometimes sends prepublication galleys. Pays 2 contributor's copies plus one-year subscription. Rights revert to author upon publication.

Ⓝ ▣ $◻ ◎ NECROLOGY (Specialized: horror, science fiction, fantasy)

P.O. Box 510232, Saint Louis MO 63151. E-mail: editor@necrologymag.com. Web site: www.necrologymag.com. Established 2005. **Contact:** John Ferguson, editor.

Magazine Needs *Necrology Magazine*, published quarterly both in print and online, publishes "horror, science fiction, and fantasy. We publish short stories, poetry, artwork, and photos." Wants all styles and forms of poetry "as long as it stays in theme with the magazine. Our magazine is based on Lovecraftian style horror. While we do consider and accept other submissions, we look for those with a dark and deathly theme." Considers poetry by teens. *Necrology Magazine* runs approximately 70 pages, magazine-sized, includes ads. Receives about 40-50 poems/year, accepts about 5-10%. Press run is 1,500. Number of unique visitors: 1,000 monthly. Single copy: $4 print/$1 e-zine; subscription: $15 print/$4 e-zine. Make checks payable to *Necrology Magazine*.

How to Submit Submit 1-5 poems at a time. Considers previously published poems. Accepts e-mail submissions (as attachment) and disk submissions; no fax. Cover letter is unnecessary. Include SASE with disk and printed submissions. Reads submissions year round. Submit seasonal poems 9 months in advance. Time between acceptance and publication is 6-12 months. Often comments on rejected poems. Sometimes publishes theme issues. Upcoming themes available on Web site. Guidelines available by SASE, e-mail, and on Web site. Responds in 8 weeks. Pays $1-20 and 1 contributor's copy. Acquires one-time and electronic rights. Reviews books/chapbooks of poetry and other magazines/journals single-book format. Send materials for review consideration to John Ferguson.

⬛ NERVE COWBOY

P.O. Box 4973, Austin TX 78765. Web site: www.jwhagins.com/nervecowboy.html. Established 1995. **Contact:** Joseph Shields and Jerry Hagins, co-editors.

Magazine Needs *Nerve Cowboy*, published semiannually, features contemporary poetry, short fiction, and b&w drawings. Editors will also consider color artwork for the front cover of an issue. "Open to all forms, styles, and subject matter, preferring writing that speaks directly and minimizes literary devices." Wants "poetry of experience and passion which can find that raw nerve and ride it. We are always looking for that rare writer who inherently knows what word comes next." Has published poetry by Kathy Burkett, Gerald Locklin, Ann Menebroker, Joan Jobe Smith, Paul Agostino, and David J. Thompson. *Nerve Cowboy* is 64 pages, 7×8½, attractively printed, saddle-stapled, with matte card cover with b&w art. Accepts about 5% of submissions received. Press run is 400. Subscription: $16 for 4 issues. Sample: $6.

How to Submit Submit 3-7 poems at a time. Considers previously published poems with notification; no simultaneous submissions. Cover letter is preferred. Inclue bio and credits. Put name and mailing address on each page of ms. Seldom comments on rejected poems. Guidelines available for SASE or on Web site. Responds in 3 months. Pays 1 contributor's copy. Acquires first or one-time rights.

Contest/Award Offerings The *Nerve Cowboy* Chapbook Contest (see separate listing Contests & Awards).

⬛ $⬛ THE NEW CRITERION

The Foundation for Cultural Review, Inc., 900 Broadway, Suite 602, New York NY 10003. Web site: www.newcriterion.com. **Contact:** David Yezzi, poetry editor.

Magazine Needs *The New Criterion*, published monthly (except July and August), is a review of ideas and the arts, printing poetry of high literary quality. Has published poetry by Donald Justice, Andrew Hudgins, Elizabeth Spires, and Herbert Morris. *The New Criterion* is 90 pages, 7×10, flat-spined. Sample: $7.

How to Submit Accepts submissions by postal mail only. Cover letter is required. Responds in 3 months. Pays $2.50/line ($75 minimum).

Advice "To have an idea of who we are or what we stand for, poets should consult back issues."

$⬛ NEW ENGLAND REVIEW

Middlebury College, Middlebury VT 05753. (802)443-5075. E-mail: nereview@middlebury.edu. (inquiries only). Web site: http://go.middlebury.edu/nereview. Established 1978. **Contact:** Poetry Editor.

• Work published in *New England Review* is frequently included in *The Best American Poetry*.

Magazine Needs *New England Review*, published quarterly, is a prestigious, nationally distributed literary journal. Has published poetry by Carl Phillips, Lucia Perillo, Linda Gregerson, and Natasha Trethewey. *New England Review* is 200+ pages, 7×10, printed on heavy stock, flat-spined, with glossy cover with art. Receives 3,000-4,000 poetry submissions/year, accepts about 70-80 poems/year. Subscription: $25. Sample: $8. Overseas shipping fees plus $25 for subscription; plus $5 for single issues.

How to Submit Submit up to 6 poems at a time. No previously published poems or simultaneous submissions. Accepts submissions by postal mail only; accepts questions by e-mail. "Brief cover letters are useful." Address submissions to "Poetry Editor." Reads submissions postmarked September 1-May 31 only. Time between acceptance and publication is 3-6 months. Responds in up to 3 months. Always sends prepublication galleys. Pays $10/page ($20 minimum) plus 2 contributor's copies. Send materials for review consideration.

Advice "**Read** a few copies of the magazine before submitting work. Our response time is reasonable, so please do not send simultaneous submissions."

◙ NEW LETTERS

University of Missouri-Kansas City, 5101 Rockhill Rd., Kansas City MO 64110. (816)235-1168. Fax: (816)235-2611. E-mail: newletters@umkc.edu. Web site: www.newletters.org. Established 1934 (as *University Review*), 1971 (as *New Letters*). **Contact:** Robert Stewart, editor.

Magazine Needs *New Letters*, published quarterly, "is dedicated to publishing the best short fiction, contemporary poetry, literary articles, photography, and artwork by both established writers and new talents." Wants "fresh, new writing of all types. Short works are more likely to be accepted than very long ones." Has published poetry by Naomi Shihab Nye, Albert Goldbarth, Quincy Troupe, Ellen Bass, Joseph Millar, and Mia Leonin. *New Letters* is about 180 pages, digest-sized, professionally printed, flat-spined, with glossy 4-color cover with art. Press run is 3,600. Subscription: $22. Sample: $10.

How to Submit Submit no more than 6 poems at a time. No previously published poems. No e-mail submissions. Short cover letter is preferred. Guidelines available on Web site.

Contest/Award Offerings The annual *New Letters* Prize for Poetry (see separate listing in Contests & Awards).

Advice "Write with originality and freshness in language, content, and style. Avoid clichés in imagery and subject."

$◙ NEW ORLEANS REVIEW

Box 195, Loyola University, New Orleans LA 70118. (504)865-2295. Fax: (504)865-2294. Web site: www.loyno.edu/~noreview. Established 1968. **Contact:** Katie Ford, poetry editor.

Magazine Needs *New Orleans Review*, published twice/year, is an international journal of poetry, fiction, essays, book reviews, and interviews. Wants "dynamic writing that demonstrates attention to the language and a sense of the medium; writing that engages, surprises, moves us. We subscribe to the belief that in order to truly write well, one must first master the rudiments: grammar and syntax, punctuation, the sentence, the paragraph, the line, the stanza." Has published poetry by Chrisopher Howell, Martha Zweig, Lee Upton, Jeffrey Levine, Carlie Rosemurgy, and D.C. Berry. *New Orleans Review* is 120-200 pages, elegantly printed, perfect-bound, with glossy card cover. Receives about 3,000 mss/year. Press run is 1,500. Single copy: $8. Sample: $5.

How to Submit Submit 3-6 poems at a time. Considers simultaneous submissions "if we're notified immediately upon acceptance elsewhere"; no previously published poems. No fax submissions. Brief cover letter is preferred. Guidelines available on Web site. Responds in 2-4 months. Pays 2 contributor's copies and honorarium. Acquires first North American serial rights.

◙ ◙ NEW ORPHIC REVIEW

New Orphic Publishers, 706 Mill St., Nelson BC V1L 4S5 Canada. (250)354-0494. Web site: www3.te lus.net/neworphicpublishers-hekkanen. Established 1995 (New Orphic Publishers), 1998 (*New Orphic Review*). **Contact:** Margrith Schraner, associate editor. Editor-in-Chief: Ernest Hekkanen.

Magazine Needs *New Orphic Review*, published in May and October, is run "by an opinionated visionary who is beholden to no one, least of all government agencies like the Canada Council or institutions of higher learning. He feels Canadian literature is stagnant, lacks daring, and is terribly incestuous." Publishes poetry, novel excerpts, mainstream and experimental short stories, and articles on a wide range of subjects. Each issue includes a Featured Poet section. "*New Orphic Review* publishes authors from around the world as long as the pieces are written in English and are accompanied by a SASE with proper Canadian postage and/or U.S. dollars to offset the cost of postage." Wants "tight, well-wrought poetry over leggy, prosaic poetry. No 'fuck you' poetry; no rambling pseudo Beat poetry." Has published poetry by Robert Cooperman, Step Elder, Louis E. Bourgeios, and Art Joyce. *New Orphic Review* is 120-140 pages, magazine-sized, laser-printed, perfect-bound, with color cover, includes ads. Receives about 400 poems/year, accepts about 10%. Press run is 500. Subscription: $30 CAD for individuals, $35 CAD for institutions. Sample: $20 CAD.

How to Submit Submit 6 poems at a time. Lines/poem: 5 minimum, 30 maximum. Considers simultaneous submissions; no previously published poems. Cover letter is preferred. "Make sure a SASE (or SAE and IRC) is included." Time between acceptance and publication is up to 8 months. "The managing editor and associate editor refer work to the editor-in-chief." Seldom comments on rejected poems. Occasionally publishes theme issues. Guidelines available for SASE (or SAE and IRC). Responds in 2 months. Pays 1 contributor's copy. Acquires first North American serial rights.

Additional Information New Orphic Publishers publishes 4 paperbacks/year. However, **all material is solicited**.

Advice "Read the magazine before submitting."

$⬚ THE NEW RENAISSANCE

26 Heath Rd. #11, Arlington MA 02474-3645. E-mail: marccreate@aol.com. (inquiries only). Web site: www.tnrlitmag.net. Established 1968. **Contact:** Frank Finale, poetry editor. Editor-in-Chief: Louise T. Reynolds.

Magazine Needs *the new renaissance*, published spring and fall ("resources permitting'), is "intended for the 'renaissance' person—the generalist, not the specialist. We publish the best new writing and translations and offer a forum for articles on political, sociological topics; feature established as well as emerging visual artists and writers; highlight reviews of small press; and offer essays on a variety of topics from visual arts and literature to science. Open to a variety of styles, including traditional." Has published poetry by Anita Susan Brenner, Anne Struthers, Marc Widershien, Miguel Torga (trans. Alexis Levetin), Stephen Todd Booker, and Rabindranath Togore (trans. Wendy Barker and S. Togore). *the new renaissance* is 144-182 pages, digest-sized, professionally printed on heavy stock, flat-spined, with glossy color cover. Receives about 650 poetry submissions/year, accepts about 40. Press run is 1,500 (760 subscribers, 132 libraries). Single copy: $12.50 (current), $11.50 (recent), $7.50 (back issue); subscription: $30 for 3 issues in U.S., $35 in Canada, $38 all others. "All checks in U.S. dollars. A 3-issue subscription covers 18-22 months."

How to Submit Submit 3-6 poems at a time, "unless a long poem—then 1." Considers simultaneous submissions, if notified; no previously published poems "unless magazine's circulation was under 250." Always include SASE or IRC. Accepts submissions by postal mail only; "when accepted, we ask if a disk is available, and we prefer accepted translations to be available in the original language on disk. **All poetry submissions are tied to our Awards Program for poetry published in a 3-issue volume; judged by independent judges.**" **Entry fee:** $16.50 for nonsubscribers, $11.50 for subscribers, "for which they receive 2 back issues or a recent issue or an extension of their subscription. Submissions without entry fee are returned unread." Reads submissions January 2-June 30. Guidelines available for SASE. Responds in 5 months. Pays $21-40 (more for the occasional longer poem), plus 1 contributor's copy/poem. Acquires all rights but returns rights provided *the new renaissance* retains rights for any *the new renaissance* collection. Reviews books of poetry.

Contest/Award Offerings The Awards Program offers 3 prizes of $250, $125, and $50, with 3-4 Honorable Mentions of $25 each; all submissions are tied to the Awards Program (see above for entry fee).

Advice "Read, read, read! And support the literary magazines that support serious writers and poets. In 2002, more than 350 separate submissions came in, all without the required fee. Since our Poetry Awards Program has been in effect since 1995, and since we've notified all markets about our guidelines and entry fee, this just shows an indifferent, careless reading of our magazine's requirements."

⬚ NEW SOUTH

(formerly *GSU Review*), Campus Box 1894, Georgia State University, MSC 8R0322 Unit 8, Atlanta GA 30303-3083. (404)651-4804. Fax: (404)651-1710. E-mail: gsu_review@langate.gsu.edu. Web site: www.review.gsu.edu. Established 1980. **Contact:** Jenny Sadre-Orafai, poetry editor.

Magazine Needs *New South*, published semiannually, prints fiction, poetry, nonfiction, and visual art. Wants "original voices searching to rise above the ordinary. No subject or form biases." Does not want pornography or Hallmark verse. *New South* is 160 + pages. Press run is 2,000; 500 distributed free to students. Single copy: $5; subscription: $8/year; $14 for 2 issues. Sample: $3 (back issue).

How to Submit Submit up to 3 poems at a time. Considers simultaneous submissions (with notification in cover letter); no previously published poems. No e-mail submissions. Name, address, and phone/e-mail must appear on each page of ms. Cover letter is required. Include "a 3- to 4-line bio, a list of the work(s) submitted in the order they appear, and your name, mailing address, phone number, and e-mail address." Include SASE for notification. Time between acceptance and publication is 3-5 months. Seldom comments on rejected poems. Guidelines available for SASE, by e-mail, or on Web site. Pays 2 copies. Rights revert to poets upon publication.

Contest/Award Offerings The *New South* Annual Writing Contest offers $1,000 for the best poem; copy of issue to all who submit. Submissions must be unpublished. Submit up to 3 poems on any subject or in any form. "Specify 'poetry' on outside envelope." Guidelines available for SASE, by e-mail, or on Web site. **Deadline:** March 4. Competition receives 200 entries. Past judges include Sharon Olds, Jane Hirschfield, Anthony Hecht, Phillip Levine and Jake Adam York. Winner will be announced in the Spring issue.

Advice "Avoid clichéd and sentimental writing but as all advice is filled with paradox—write from the heart. We look for a smooth union of form and content."

▣ ⊕ ⊘ ◎ THE NEW VERSE NEWS (Specialized: current news, issues, & events)

E-mail: editor@newversenews.com. Web site: www.newversenews.com. Established 2005. **Contact:** James Penha, editor.

Magazine Needs *The New Verse News*, published online and updated "every day or 2," has "a clear liberal bias, but will consider various visions and views." Wants "poems, both serious and satirical, on current events and topical issues; will also consider prose poems and short-short stories and plays." Does not want "work unrelated to the news." Has published poetry by Rochelle Ratner, Bill Costley, Rochelle Owens, A.D. Winans, Mary Saracino, and Dave Lordan. Receives about 700 poems/year, accepts about 300.

How to Submit Submit 1-5 poems at a time. Lines/poem: no length restrictions. No previously published poems or simultaneous submissions. Accepts e-mail submissions (pasted into body of message); no disk submissions. Reads submissions year round. Submit seasonal poems 1 month in advance. "Normally, poems are published immediately upon acceptance." Poems are circulated to an editorial board. Sometimes comments on rejected poems. Guidelines available on Web site. Responds in 1-3 weeks. No payment. Acquires first rights. Rights revert to poet upon publication.

⊕ $⊘ THE NEW WRITER

P.O. Box 60, Cranbrook, Kent TN17 2ZR England. (44)(1580)212626. Fax: (44)(1580)212041. E-mail: admin@thenewwriter.com. Web site: www.thenewwriter.com. Established 1996. **Contact:** Catherine Smith, poetry editor.

Magazine Needs *The New Writer*, published 6 times/year, is "aimed at writers with a serious intent, who want to develop their writing to meet the high expectations of today's editors. The team at *The New Writer* is committed to working with its readers to increase the chances of publication through masses of useful information and plenty of feedback. More than that, we let you know about the current state of the market with the best in contemporary fiction and cutting-edge poetry, backed up by searching articles and in-depth features." Wants "short and long unpublished poems, provided they are original and undeniably brilliant. No problems with length/form, but anything over 2 pages (150 lines) needs to be brilliant. Cutting edge shouldn't mean inaccessible. No recent disasters—they date." Does not want " 'my baby/doggie' poems, God poems that sound like hymns, dum-dum rhymes, or comic rhymes (best left at the pub)." *The New Writer* is 56 pages, A4, professionally printed, saddle-stapled, with paper cover. Press run is 1,500 (1,350 subscribers); 50 distributed free to publishers, agents. Single copy: £6.25 in U.S. (5 IRCs required); subscription: £37.50 in U.S. "We have a secure server for subscriptions and entry into the annual Prose and Poetry Prizes on the Web site. Monthly e-mail newsletter included free of charge in the subscription package."

How to Submit Submit up to 6 poems at a time. Lines/poem: 150 maximum. Considers previously published poems. Accepts e-mail submissions (pasted into body of message). Time between acceptance and publication is up to 6 months. Often comments on rejected poems. **Offers criticism service: £12/6 poems.** Guidelines available for SASE (or SAE with IRC) or on Web site. Pays £3 voucher plus 1 contributor's copy. Acquires first British serial rights. Reviews books/chapbooks of poetry and other magazines. Send materials for review consideration.

Contest/Award Offerings Sponsors *The New Writer* Prose & Poetry Prizes annually. ''All poets writing in the English language are invited to submit an original, previously unpublished poem or a collection of 6-10 poems. Up to 25 prizes will be presented, as well as publication for the prize-winning poets in an anthology, plus the chance for a further 10 shortlisted poets to see their work published in *The New Writer* during the year.'' Guidelines available by e-mail or on Web site.

☑ NEW YORK QUARTERLY

P.O. Box 693, Old Chelsea Station, New York NY 10113. Web site: www.nyquarterly.org. Established 1969. **Contact:** Raymond Hammond, editor.

Magazine Needs *New York Quarterly*, published 3 times/year, seeks to print ''a cross-section of the best of contemporary American poetry.'' Has published poetry by Charles Bukowski, James Dickey, Lola Haskins, Lyn Lifshin, Elisavietta Ritchie, and W.D. Snodgrass. *New York Quarterly* is digest-sized, elegantly printed, flat-spined, with glossy color cover. Subscription: $28.

How to Submit Submit 3-5 poems at a time.Considers simultaneous submissions with notification. Include your name and address on each page. ''Include SASE; no international postage coupons.'' Guidelines available on Web site. Responds within 6 weeks. Pays in contributor's copies.

$☑ THE NEW YORKER

4 Times Square, New York NY 10036. E-mail: poetry@newyorker.com. Web site: www.newyorker.com. Established 1925. **Contact:** Paul Muldoon, poetry editor.

• Poems published in *The New Yorker* often have been included *The Best American Poetry*.

Magazine Needs *The New Yorker*, published weekly, prints poetry of the highest quality (including translations). Subscription: $47/year (47 issues), $77 for 2 years (94 issues).

How to Submit Submit no more than 6 poems at a time. No previously published poems or simultaneous submissions. Accepts e-mail submissions (pasted into body of message or as attachment). Include poet's name in the subject line and as the title of attached document. ''We prefer to receive no more than two submissions per writer per year.'' Pays top rates.

☑ NEW ZOO POETRY REVIEW

P.O. Box 36760, Richmond VA 23235. Web site: http://members.aol.com/newzoopoet. Established 1997. **Contact:** Angela Vogel, editor.

Magazine Needs *New Zoo Poetry Review*, published annually in January, prints ''free verse in well-crafted lyric and narrative forms. Our goal is to publish established poets alongside lesser-known poets of great promise.'' Wants ''serious, intellectual poetry of any form, length, or style. Rhyming poetry only if exceptional.'' Does not want ''light verse, song lyrics, or greeting card copy. If you're not reading the best of contemporary poetry, then *New Zoo Poetry Review* is not for you.'' Has published poetry by Heather McHugh, Leonard Gontarek, Frannie Lindsay, Marlys West, Natasha Sajé, and Martha Collins. *New Zoo Poetry Review* is 30-40 pages, digest-sized, photocopied, saddle-stapled, with card cover with with illustration or photo. Receives about 1,000 poems/year, accepts about 4%. Press run is 200. Single copy: $5.

How to Submit Submit 3-5 poems at a time. Considers simultaneous submissions; no previously published poems. Cover letter is required. Include SASE and brief bio. Seldom comments on rejected poems. Responds in 2 months. Pays 1 contributor's copy. Acquires first North American serial rights. ''Poets are discouraged from submitting more than once in a 12-month period. Please do not write to us for these submission guidelines. We understand and encourage simultaneous submissions and think threatening to 'blacklist' poets who do so responsibly is unfortunate. *NZPR* responds to submissions in an appropriate timeframe and seeks thereby to gather the best work out there.''

ℕ ◯ NIBBLE

6507 Melville Dr., Oakland CA.E-mail: nibblepoems@gmail.com. Established 1995 **Contact:** Jeff Fleming, editor.

Magazine Needs *nibble*, published bimonthly, is a journal of poetry ''focusing on short, concise, imagery-laden poems.'' Wants short poems. Does not want ''inaccessible, self-important poems.''

Considers poetry by children and teens. *nibble* is 16 pages, digest-sized, laser-printed, side-stapled, with a cardstock, imaged cover. Receives about 500 poems/year, accepts about 250. Press run is 250; 50 distributed free to schools. Single copy: $4. Make checks payable to Jeff Fleming.

How to Submit Submit up to 5 poems at a time. Cover letter is required. Reads submissions year round. Time between acceptance and publication is 2 months. Often comments on rejected poems. Sometimes publishes theme issues. Upcoming themes available by e-mail. Guidelines available for SASE and by e-mail. Responds in 2 weeks. Pays 1 contributor's copy. Acquires one-time rights. Reviews books and chapbooks of poetry.

Additional Information Occasionally will publish chapbooks.

◩ NIMROD: INTERNATIONAL JOURNAL OF POETRY AND PROSE

University of Tulsa, 600 S. College Ave., Tulsa OK 74104-3189. (918)631-3080. Fax: (918)631-3033. E-mail: nimrod@utulsa.edu. Web site: www.utulsa.edu/nimrod. Established 1956. **Contact:** Manly Johnson, poetry editor.

- Poetry published in *Nimrod* has been included in *The Best American Poetry*.

Magazine Needs *Nimrod: International Journal of Poetry and Prose*, published 2 times/year, is "an active 'little magazine,' part of the movement in American letters which has been essential to the development of modern literature." Publishes an awards issue in the fall, featuring the prizewinners of its national competition, and a thematic issue each spring. "Poems in non-award issues range from formal to freestyle with several translations." Wants "vigorous writing that is neither wholly of the academy nor the streets; typed manuscripts." Has published poetry by Diane Glancy, Judith Strasser, Steve Lautermilch, Virgil Suárez, and Jen-Mark Sens. *Nimrod* is about 200 pages, digest-sized, professionally printed on coated stock, perfect-bound, with full-color glossy cover. Receives about 2,000 submissions/year, accepts 1%. Press run is 2,500. Subscription: $17.50/year U.S., $19 foreign. Sample: $10. "Specific back issues available. Please send check or money order."

How to Submit Submit 5-10 poems at a time. No fax or e-mail submissions. Publishes theme issues. Guidelines available for SASE, by e-mail, or on Web site. Responds in up to 3 months. "During the months that the *Nimrod*/Hardman Awards competition is being conducted, reporting time on non-contest manuscripts will be longer." Pays 2 contributor's copies, plus reduced cost on additional copies.

Contest/Award Offerings The annual *Nimrod*/Hardman Writing Awards, including The Pablo Neruda Prize for Poetry (see separate listing in Contests & Awards).

Also Offers Sponsors the *Nimrod*/Hardman Awards Workshop, a one-day workshop held annually in October. Cost is about $50. Send SASE for brochure and registration form.

$◩ NINTH LETTER

Dept. of English, University of Illinois, 608 S. Wright St., Urbana IL 61801. E-mail: ninthletter@uiuc. edu. Web site: www.ninthletter.com. Established 2004. **Contact:** Jodee Stanley, editor. Member: CLMP; CELJ.

- *Ninth Letter* won Best New Literary Journal 2005 from the Council of Editors of Learned Journals (CELJ) and has had poetry selected for *The Pushcart Prize*, *Best New Poets*, and *The Year's Best Fantasy and Horror*.

Magazine Needs *Ninth Letter*, published semiannually, is "dedicated to the examination of literature as it intersects with various aspects of contemporary culture and intellectual life." Open to all forms of poetry. Wants "exceptional literary quality." Has published poetry by Cate Marvin, L.S. Asekoff, William Wenthe, Sharmila Voorakkara, Geri Doran, and T.R. Hummer. *Ninth Letter* is 176 pages, 9×12, offset-printed, perfect-bound, with 4-color cover with graphics. Receives about 9,000 poems/year, accepts about 40. Press run is 3,500 (500 subscribers, 1,000 shelf sales); 1,500 distributed free, 500 to contributors, media, and fundraising efforts. Single copy: $14.95; subscription: $21.95/year. Sample: $8.95 (back issue). Make checks payable to *Ninth Letter*.

How to Submit Submit no more than 6 poems or 10 pages at a time. No previously published poems or simultaneous submissions. No e-mail or disk submissions. Cover letter is preferred. "SASE must be included for reply." Reads submissions September 1-April 30 (inclusive postmark dates). Time between acceptance and publication is 5-6 months. Poems are circulated to an editorial board.

Sometimes comments on rejected poems. Guidelines available for SASE, by e-mail, or on Web site. Responds in 2 months. Always sends prepublications galleys. Pays $25/page and 2 contributor's copies. Acquires first North American serial rights. Rights revert to poet upon publication.

☑ NOMAD'S CHOIR

% Meander, 30-15 Hobart St., F4H, Woodside NY 11377. Established 1989. **Contact:** Joshua Meander, editor.

Magazine Needs *Nomad's Choir*, published quarterly, seeks "love poems, protest poems, mystical poems, nature poems, poems of humanity, poems with solutions to world problems and inner conflict, poems with hope; simple words, careful phrasing." Wants "free verse, rhymed poems, sonnets." Does not want "curse words in poems; little or no name-dropping; no naming of consumer products; no 2-page poems; no humor, no bias writing, no poems untitled." Has published poetry by Steven Baker, Angela Castillo, Murry Kaufman, and Joan Kitcher-White. *Nomad's Choir* is 12 pages, magazine-sized, typeset, saddle-stapled. Receives about 150 poems/year, accepts 50. Press run is 400; all distributed free. Subscription: $5. Sample: $1.50. Make checks payable to Joshua Meander.

How to Submit Submit 4 poems at a time, each on a different topic. Lines/poem: 9 minimum, 30 maximum. Responds in 2 months. Pays 1 contributor's copy.

Advice "Social commentary with beauty and hope gets first consideration."

$☑ NORTH AMERICAN REVIEW

University of Northern Iowa, 1222 West 27th St., Cedar Falls IA 50614-0516. (319)273-6455. Fax: (319)273-4326. E-mail: nar@uni.edu. Web site: http://webdelsol.com/NorthAmReview/NAR. Established 1815. **Contact:** Vince Gotera, poetry editor.

Magazine Needs *North American Review*, published 5 times/year, is "the oldest literary magazine in America." Wants "poetry of the highest quality; poems that are passionate about subject, language, and image. Especially interested in work that addresses contemporary North American concerns and issues, particularly with the environment, race, ethnicity, gender, sexual orientation, and class." Has published poetry by Debra Marquart, Nick Carbó, Yusef Komunyakaa, Virgil Suárez, Nance Van Winckel, and Dara Wier. *North American Review* is about 48 pages, magazine-sized, professionally printed, saddle-stapled, with glossy full-color paper cover. Receives about 10,000 poems/year, accepts 100. Press run is 2,500 (1,500 subscribers, 1,000 libraries). Subscription: $22 in U.S., $29 in Canada, $32 foreign. Sample: $5.

How to Submit Submit 3-6 poems at a time. No previously published poems or simultaneous submissions. No fax, e-mail, or disk submissions. Cover letter is preferred. Include brief bio and list poem titles. Include SASE. Time between acceptance and publication is up to 1 year. Guidelines available in magazine, for SASE, by e-mail, or on Web site. Responds in 4 months. Always sends prepublication galleys. Pays $1/line ($20 minimum, $100 maximum) and 2 contributor's copies. Acquires first North American serial rights only. Rights revert to poets upon publication.

Contest/Award Offerings The annual James Hearst Poetry Prize (see separate listing in Contest & Awards).

$◎ NORTH CAROLINA LITERARY REVIEW (Specialized: NC topics, work by NC authors)

Dept. of English, East Carolina University, Greenville NC 27858-4353. (252)328-1537. E-mail: bauerm@mail.ecu.edu. Web site: www.ecu.edu/nclr. Established 1992. **Contact:** Margaret Bauer, editor.

Magazine Needs *North Carolina Literary Review*, published annually in the summer, contains "articles and other works about North Carolina topics or by North Carolina authors." Wants "poetry by writers currently living in North Carolina, those who have lived in North Carolina, or those using North Carolina for subject matter." Has published poetry by Betty Adcock, James Applewhite, and A.R. Ammons. *North Carolina Literary Review* is 200 pages, magazine-sized. Receives about 100 submissions/year, accepts about 10%. Press run is 1,000 (350 subscribers, 100 libraries, 100 shelf sales); 100 distributed free to contributors. Subscription: $20 for 2 years, $36 for 4 years. Sample: $15.

How to Submit Submit 3-5 poems at a time. No e-mail submissions. Cover letter is required. "Submit two copies and include SASE or e-mail address for response." Reads submissions August 1-April 30 only. Time between acceptance and publication is up to 1 year. Often comments on rejected poems. Guidelines available for SASE, by e-mail, or on Web site. Responds in 3 months within reading period. Sometimes sends prepublication galleys. Pays 2-year subscription plus 1-2 contributor's copies. Acquires first or one-time rights. Reviews books of poetry by North Carolina poets in up to 2,000 words, multi-book format. Poets from North Carolina may send books for review consideration. Rarely reviews chapbooks.

☐ ◎ NORTH CENTRAL REVIEW (Specialized: undergraduate writers)

North Central College, CM #235, 30 N. Brainard St., Naperville IL 60540. (630)637-5291. Fax: (630)637-5221. E-mail: nccreview@noctrl.edu. Web site: http://blogs.noctrl.edu/review. Established 1936. **Contact:** The Editors ("editors change year to year, but postal and e-mail addresses don't").

Magazine Needs *North Central Review*, published semiannually, considers "work in all literary genres, including occasional interviews, from undergraduate writers globally. The journal's goal is for college-level, emerging creative writers to share their work publicly and create a conversation with each other. ALL styles and forms are welcome as submissions. The readers tend to value attention to form (but not necessarily fixed form), voice, and detail. Very long poems or sequences (running more than 4 or 5 pages) may require particular excellence because of the journal's space and budget constraints." Does not want "overly sentimental language and hackneyed imagery. These are all-too-common weaknesses that readers see in submissions; we recommend revision and polishing before sending work." Considers poetry by teens (undergraduate writers only). *North Central Review* is 120 pages, digest-sized, perfect-bound, with cardstock cover with 4-color design. Press run is about 750, distributed free to contributors and publication reception attendees. Single copy: $5; subscription: $10. Make checks payable to North Central College.

How to Submit Submit up to 5 poems at a time. Lines/poem: "no limit, but poems running more than 4-5 pages may undergo particular scrutiny." No previously published poems or simultaneous submissions. Accepts e-mail submissions (as Word attachments only); no fax submissions. Cover letter is preferred. Include name, postal address, phone number, and e-mail address (.edu address as proof of student status). If necessary (i.e., .edu address not available), include a photocopy of student ID with number marked out as proof of undergraduate status. Reads submissions September-March, with deadlines of February 15 and October 15. Time between acceptance and publication is 1-4 months. Poems are circulated to an editorial board. "All submissions are read by at least 3 staff members, including an editor." Rarely comments on rejected poems. Guidelines available on Web site, in magazine, for SASE, or by e-mail. Responds in 1-4 months. Pays 2 contributor's copies. Acquires one-time rights. Rights revert to poet upon publication.

Also Offers "For every issue, the staff holds a Publication Celebration and Reading featuring the work in the journal. Contributors are welcome to attend, but the staff recognizes that distance prohibits most contributors from joining in. So, NCC student contributors read their work, and staff also read selections from undergraduates elsewhere. Refreshments are served, and copies of the issue are free to those in attendance."

Advice "Don't send anything you just finished moments ago—rethink, revise, and polish. Avoid sentimentalitity and abstraction. That said, the *North Central Review* publishes beginners, so don't hesitate to submit and, if rejected, submit again."

◙ NORTH DAKOTA QUARTERLY

Merrifield Hall Room 110, 276 Centennial Dr. Stop 7209, Grand Forks ND 58202-7209. E-mail: ndq@und.nodak.edu. Web site: www.und.nodak.edu/org/ndq. Established 1910. **Contact:** Robert Lewis, editor.

Magazine Needs *North Dakota Quarterly* is published by the University of North Dakota. Seeks material related to the arts and humanities—essays, fiction, interviews, poems, reviews, and visual art. Wants poetry "that reflects an understanding not only of the difficulties of the craft, but of the vitality and tact that each poem calls into play." Has published poetry by Maxine Kumin, Paul

Muldoon, Robert Bagg, James Scully, Patricia Schneider, and Marianne Boruch. *North Dakota Quarterly* is about 200 pages, digest-sized, professionally designed and printed, perfect-bound, with full-color artwork on white card cover. Has 550 subscribers. Subscription: $25/year. Sample: $8.

How to Submit Submit 5 poems at a time. No previously published poems or simultaneous submissions. No e-mail submissions; accepts only typed hard-copy submissions by postal mail. Time between acceptance and publication varies. Responds in up to 6 weeks. Always sends prepublication galleys. Pays 2 contributor's copies. Acquires first serial rights.

Advice "We look to publish the best fiction, poetry, and essays that, in our estimation, we can. Our tastes and interests are best reflected in what we have been recently publishing, and we suggest that you look at some current numbers."

NORTHEAST ARTS MAGAZINE

P.O. Box 4363, Portland ME 04101. Established 1990. **Contact:** Mr. Leigh Donaldson, editor/publisher.

Magazine Needs *Northeast Arts Magazine*, published semiannually, seeks poetry, short fiction, essays, reviews, art, and photography that is "honest, clear, with a love of expression through simple language. We maintain a special interest in work that reflects cultural diversity in New England and throughout the world." Has published poetry by Steve Lutrell, Eliot Richman, Elizabeth R. Curry, Bob Begieburg, and Alisa Aran. *Northeast Arts Magazine* is 32 or more pages, digest-sized, professionally printed, with one-color coated card cover. Accepts 10-20% of submissions. Press run is 500-1,000; 50 distributed to arts organizations. Subscription: $10. Sample: $4.50.

How to Submit Lines/poem: 30 maximum. "A short bio is helpful." Reads submissions November 1-February 1 only. Guidelines available for SASE. Responds in 3 months. Pays 2 contributor's copies. Acquires first North American serial rights.

NORTHERN STARS MAGAZINE

North Star Publishing, N17285 Co. Rd. 400, Powers MI 49874. Established 1997. **Contact:** Beverly Kleikamp, editor.

Magazine Needs *Northern Stars Magazine*, published bimonthly, welcomes submissions of fiction, nonfiction, and poetry on any subject or style. "The main requirement is good clean family reading material—nothing you can't read to your child or your mother." Does not want "smut or filth." Considers poetry by children and teens. Has published poetry by Terri Warden, Gary Edwards, Sheila B. Roark, and C.L. Rymer. *Northern Stars Magazine* is 48 pages, digest-sized, photocopied, saddle-stapled, with soft cover. Single copy: $5; subscription: $21. Make checks payable to Beverly Kleikamp or *Northern Stars Magazine*.

How to Submit Submit up to 3 poems at a time. Lines/poem: 25 maximum. "Shorter poems stand a better chance of timely publication." Considers previously published poems; no simultaneous submissions. Cover letter is preferred. "Manuscripts must be typed; please do not submit handwritten material." Often comments on rejected poems. Guidelines available for SASE. "No payment, but nonsubscribers are notified of publication." All rights return to authors on publication.

Additional Information "I also publish chapbooks **for an 'affordable' price to the author**." Has published more than 100 chapbooks to date, including *Beholden* by Paul Truttman and *Butterfly Descending Sunlight* by Nancy M. Ryan. Chapbook prices and information available for SASE.

Contest/Award Offerings Sponsors contests for poetry and fiction/nonfiction in alternating issues (i.e., poetry contest in March-April issue, fiction/nonfiction in May-June). Guidelines available for SASE. **Entry fee:** $2.50/poem for nonsubscribers, $1/poem for subscribers. **Deadline:** 20th of month preceding publication. Publishes an annual chapbook of contest winners and honorable mentions in January.

Advice "Keep it clean, short, and interesting."

NORTHWEST REVIEW

369 PLC, University of Oregon, Eugene OR 97403. (541)346-3957. Fax: (541)346-1509. E-mail: jwitte@uoregon.edu. (inquiries only). Web site: http://nwr.uoregon.edu. Established 1957. **Contact:** John Witte, poetry editor.

• Poetry published by *Northwest Review* has been included in *The Best American Poetry*.

Magazine Needs *Northwest Review*, published 3 times/year in May, September, and January, states, "The only criterion for acceptance of material for publication is that of excellence. There are no restrictions on length, style, or subject matter, but we smile on originality." Has published poetry by Alan Dugan, Charles Bukowski, Ted Hughes, Olga Broumas, Gary Snyder, and William Stafford. *Northwest Review* is digest-sized, flat-spined. Receives about 3,500 submissions/year, accepts about 4%. Press run is 1,300. Single copy: $8; subscription: $22/year (3 issues). Sample: $4.

How to Submit Submit 6-8 poems at a time. No simultaneous submissions. No e-mail submissions; postal submissions only. Send only clear, clean copies. Guidelines available on Web site. Responds within 3 months. Pays 3 contributor's copies.

Advice "Persist."

$⬚ NORTHWOODS JOURNAL

Northwoods Press, P.O. Box 298, Thomaston ME 04861-0298. (207)226-7528. E-mail: cal@america nletters.org. Web site: www.americanletters.org. Established 1972 (Northwoods Press), 1993 (*Northwoods Journal*). **Contact:** Robert Olmsted, editor.

Magazine Needs *Northwoods Journal*, published quarterly, is a literary magazine for writers that publishes fiction, essays, reviews, nonfiction, and poetry. Interested in "all writers who feel they have something to say and who work to say it well. We have no interest in closet writers, vanity authors, or credit-seekers. All writers seeking an audience, working to improve their craft, and determined to 'get it right' are welcome here." *Northwoods Journal* is about 40 pages, digest-sized. Subscription: available only through membership in the Conservatory of American Letters (CAL) ($25/year). Sample: $6.50 and 6×9 SASE with $1.31 postage affixed.

How to Submit No previously published poems or simultaneous submissions. No e-mail submissions; submit by postal mail only. **Reading fee: $1 for 2 poems for CAL members, $1/poem for nonmembers.** "CAL offers 1 free read (up to 5 poems) per year if poetry is submitted simultaneously with membership or renewal." Make checks payable to CAL. Guidelines available for SASE or on Web site. "See guidelines before submitting anything." Pays 10¢ per line on average; "we do not provide free issues."

Additional Information Northwoods Press considers "books by working poets only. No subsidy permitted. No closet poets, vanity poets, or credit-seekers. All accepted books offer opportunity to include CD of author (or others) reading the book, or selections from the book. Original CD to be produced by author as we have no recording studio. No reading fee for book-length works. We would like to publish up to 12 books per year, but never receive enough quality manuscripts." Requires a personal marketing plan of prospective buyers and **membership in the Conservatory of American Letters (CAL)**.

Also Offers Publishes *The Annual Northwoods Anthology*. Considers poetry and fiction. **Deadline:** October 31. Guidelines available for #10 SASE or on Web site. Pays cash on acceptance.

Advice "Reading fees hold submissions down to a level that someone with 'yes' authority can actually read. They limit competition in a big way. We never get enough of anything. Reading this blurb does not equal 'knowing your market.' Read a few issues. Anyone who submits to a magazine or anthology they've never seen deserves whatever happens."

⬚ ⬚ ⬚ NTHPOSITION

E-mail: toddswift@clara.co.uk. Web site: www.nthposition.com. Established 2002. **Contact:** Todd Swift, poetry editor.

Magazine Needs *nthposition*, published monthly online, is an eclectic, London-based journal dedicated to poetry, fiction, and nonfiction "with a weird or innovative edge." Wants "all kinds of poetry—from spoken word to new formalist to linguistically innovative. We also publish political poetry." Does not want poetry from never-before-published authors. Has published poetry by Charles Bernstein, George Szirtes, Stephanie Bolster, and Mimi Khalvati. Receives about 2,000 poems/year, accepts about 10%.

How to Submit Submit 2-6 poems at a time. No previously published poems or simultaneous submissions. Accepts e-mail submissions only (pasted into body of message, no attachments).

Cover letter is required. "A brief author's bio is appreciated." Reads submissions throughout the year. Time between acceptance and publication is 4 months. "Poems are read and selected by the poetry editor, who uses his own sense of what makes a poem work online to select." Never comments on rejected poems. Occasionally publishes theme issues. Guidelines available by e-mail or on Web site. Responds in 6 weeks. No payment. Does not request rights but expects proper acknowledgement if poems reprinted later.

Also Offers Publishes special theme e-books from time to time, such as *100 Poets Against the War*.
Advice "Never give up; keep writing. Poetry is a life's work."

☐ ◎ NUTHOUSE (Specialized: humor)

Twin Rivers Press, P.O. Box 119, Ellenton FL 34222. Web site: http://hometown.aol.com/Nuthous 499/index2.html. Established 1989 (Twin Rivers Press) and 1993 (*Nuthouse*). **Contact:** Ludwig VonQuirk, editor.

Magazine Needs *Nuthouse*, published every 3 months, uses humor of all kinds, including homespun and political. Wants "humorous verse; virtually all genres considered." Has published poetry by Holly Day, Daveed Garstenstein-Ross, and Don Webb. *Nuthouse* is 12 pages, digest-sized, photocopied from desktop-published originals. Receives about 500 poems/year, accepts about 100. Press run is 100. Subscription: $5 for 4 issues. Sample: $1.50. Make checks payable to Twin Rivers Press.
How to Submit Considers previously published poems and simultaneous submissions. Time between acceptance and publication is 6 months to 1 year. Often comments on rejected poems. Responds within 1 month. Pays 1 contributor's copy/poem. Acquires one-time rights.

☐ THE OAK

1530 Seventh St., Rock Island IL 61201. (309)788-3980. Established 1991. **Contact:** Betty Mowery, poetry editor.

Magazine Needs *The Oak*, published quarterly, is a "publication for writers, featuring poetry and fiction." No restrictions as to form and style. Does not want "pornography or love poetry." Receives about 100 poems/year, accepts more than 50%. Press run is 250. Subscription: $10. Sample: $3. Make all checks payable to *The Oak*.
How to Submit Submit up to 5 poems at a time. Lines/poem: 35 maximum. Considers previously published poems and simultaneous submissions. "Include a SASE or manuscripts will not be returned." Responds in 1 week. "*The Oak* does not pay in dollars or copies, but you need not purchase to be published." Acquires first or second rights.
Contest/Award Offerings Sponsors numerous poetry contests. Guidelines available for SASE.
Also Offers Established in 1991, *The Gray Squirrel* is included in *The Oak* and accepts poetry and fiction from writers 60 years of age and older.
Advice "Write tight poems with a message; don't write about lost loves or crushes. Study the markets for word limit and subject. Always include SASE, or rejected manuscripts will not be returned."

⊞ ☐ OBSESSED WITH PIPEWORK

8 Abbot's Way, Pilton, Somerset BA4 4BN England. (44)(1749)890019. E-mail: cannula.dementia@ virgin.net. Established 1995. **Contact:** Charles Johnson, editor.

Magazine Needs *Obsessed with Pipework*, published quarterly, is "very keen to publish strong new voices—'new poems to surprise and delight' with somewhat of a high-wire aspect." Wants "original, exploratory poems—positive, authentic, oblique maybe—delighting in image and in the dance of words on the page." Does not want "the predictable, the unfresh, the rhyme-led, the clever, the didactic, the sure-of-itself. No formless outpourings, please." Has published poetry by David Hart, Jennifer Compton, Susan Wicks, Carol Burns, Lucille Gang Shulklapper, and Maria Jastrzebska. *Obsessed with Pipework* is 49 pages, A5, stapled, with card cover. Receives about 1,500 poems/ year, accepts about 10%. Press run is 70-100. Single copy: £3.50; subscription: £12. Sample: £2 if available. Make checks payable in pounds to Flarestack Publishing. Back issues are also available online at www.poetrymagazines.org.uk.
How to Submit Submit maximum of 6 poems at a time. No previously published poems or simulta-

neous submissions. Accepts e-mail submissions ("paste a maximum of 3 poems in the body of the message, as attached files may become lost or corrupted"). Cover letter is preferred. Often comments on rejected poems. Guidelines available for SASE or by e-mail. Responds in 2 months. Pays 1 contributor's copy. Acquires first rights.

Advice "Most beginning poets show little evidence of reading poetry before writing it! Join a poetry workshop. For chapbook publishing, we are looking for coherent first collections that take risks, make leaps, and show evidence of being written by a human being living in the 21st century."

⊕ ◐ OFFERTA SPECIALE

Bertola Carla Press, Corso De Nicola 20, Torino 10128 Italy. Established 1988. **Contact:** Carla Bertola, editor/director.

Magazine Needs *Offerta Speciale*, published semiannually in May and November, is an international journal. Has published poetry by Federica Manfredini (Italy), Bernard Heidsieck (France), and Richard Kostelanetz and E. Mycue (U.S.). *Offerta Speciale* is 56 pages, digest-sized, neatly printed, saddle-stapled, with glossy card cover. Receives about 300 poems/year, accepts about 40%. Press run is 500. Single copy: $25; subscription: $110. Make checks payable to Carla Bertola.

How to Submit Submit 3 poems at a time. No previously published poems or simultaneous submissions. Time between acceptance and publication is 1 year. Often comments on rejected poems. Guidelines available for SASE (or SAE and IRC). Pays 1 contributor's copy.

⊠ ◻ THE OLD RED KIMONO

Georgia Highlands College, 3175 Cedartown Highway SE, Rome GA 30161. E-mail: napplega@highlands.edu. Web site: www.highlands.edu/ork. Established 1972. **Contact:** Dr. Nancy Applegate, Kimberly Yarborough, and Randie Mayo, poetry editors.

Magazine Needs *The Old Red Kimono*, published annually, prints original, high-quality poetry and fiction. Has published poetry by Walter McDonald, Peter Huggins, Mildred Greear, John Cantey Knight, Kirsten Fox, and Al Braselton. *The Old Red Kimono* is 72 pages, magazine-sized, professionally printed on heavy stock, with colored matte cover with art. Receives about 1,000 submissions/year, accepts about 60-70. Sample: $3.

How to Submit Submit 3-5 poems at a time. Accepts e-mail submissions (pasted into body of message). Reads submissions September 1-March 1 only. Guidelines available for SASE or on Web site. Responds in 3 months. Pays 2 contributor's copies. Acquires first publication rights.

⊠ ◎ OPEN MINDS QUARTERLY (Specialized: writing by those who have experienced mental illness)

The Writer's Circle, 680 Kirkwood Dr., Building 1, Sudbury ON P3E 1X3 Canada. (705)675-9193, ext. 8286. E-mail: openminds@nisa.on.ca. Web site: www.nisa.on.ca. Established 1997. **Contact:** Dinah Laprairie, editor.

Magazine Needs *Open Minds Quarterly* provides a "venue for individuals who have experienced mental illness to express themselves via poetry, short fiction, essays, first-person accounts of living with mental illness, book/movie reviews." Wants "unique, well-written, provocative poetry." Does not want overly graphic or sexual violence. Considers poetry by children and teens. Has published poetry by Pamela MacBean, Sophie Soil, Alice Parris, and Kurt Sass. *Open Minds Quarterly* is 24 pages, magazine-sized, saddle-stapled, with 100 lb. stock cover with original artwork, includes ads. Receives about 300 poems/year, accepts about 30%. Press run is 750; 400 distributed free to potential subscribers, published writers, advertisers, and conferences and events. Single copy: $5.40 CAD, $5 USD; subscription: $35 CAD, $28.25 USD (special rates also available). Make checks payable to NISA/Northern Initiative for Social Action.

How to Submit Submit 1-5 poems at a time. Considers previously published poems and simultaneous submissions. Accepts e-mail and disk submissions. Cover letter is required. "Info in cover letter: indication as to 'consumer/survivor' of the mental health system status." Reads submissions year round. Submit seasonal poems at least 8 months in advance. Time between acceptance and publication is 6-18 months. "Poems are first reviewed by poetry editor, then accepted/rejected by the editor. Sometimes, submissions are passed on to a third party for input or a third opinion."

Seldom comments on rejected poems. Guidelines available for SASE, by fax, e-mail, or on Web site. Responds in up to 4 months. "Rarely" sends prepublication galleys. "All authors own their work—if another publisher seeks to reprint from our publication, we request they cite us as the source."

Also Offers "All material not accepted for our journal will be considered for The Writer's Circle Online, our Internet publication forum. Same guidelines apply. Same contact person."

Contest/Award Offerings "The Brainstorm Poetry Contest runs in first 2 months of each year. Contact the editor for information."

Advice "We are unique in that our outlets help to reduce the stigma surrounding mental illness by illustrating the creative talents of individuals suffering from mental illness."

▦ ◯ ORBIS: AN INTERNATIONAL QUARTERLY OF POETRY AND PROSE

17 Greenhow Ave., West Kirby, Wirral CH48 5EL England. E-mail: carolebaldock@hotmail.com. Established 1968. **Contact:** Carole Baldock, editor.

Magazine Needs *Orbis: An International Quarterly of Poetry and Prose* features "news, reviews, views, letters, prose, and quite a lot of poetry." Wants "more work from young people (this includes 20-somethings) and women writers." *Orbis* is 84 pages, digest-sized, professionally printed, flat-spined, with full-color glossy card cover. Receives "thousands" of submissions/year. Single copy: £4 UK, £5 overseas (€10, $11 USD); subscription: £15 UK, £20 overseas (€30, $40 USD).

How to Submit Submit up to 4 poems at a time. Accepts e-mail submissions "from outside UK only; send no more than 2 poems, pasted into body of message (no attachments)." For postal submissions, "1 poem/page; enclose SASE (or SAE and 2 IRCs) with all correspondence." Responds in up to 1 month. Reviews books and other magazines. Send books for review consideration to Nessa O'Mahony, 5 Walnut View, Brookwood, Scholarstown Road, Rathfarnham, Dublin 16, Ireland. Send magazines for review consideration to Nathan Jones, Belvedere Rd., Princes Park, Liverpool L8 3TF England.

Contest/Award Offerings Prizes in each issue: £50 for featured writer (3-4 poems); £50 Readers' Award for piece receiving the most votes; £50 split among 4 (or more) runners-up.

⭐ ◪ OSIRIS, AN INTERNATIONAL POETRY JOURNAL/UNE REVUE INTERNATIONALE (Specialized: bilingual; translations)

P.O. Box 297, Deerfield MA 01342-0297. E-mail: amoorhead@deerfield.edu. Established 1972. **Contact:** Andrea Moorhead, poetry editor.

Magazine Needs *Osiris*, published semiannually, prints contemporary poetry in English, French, and Italian without translation, and in other languages with translation, including Polish, Danish, and German. Wants poetry that is "lyrical, non-narrative, multi-temporal, post-modern, well-crafted. Also looking for translations from non-IndoEuropean languages." Has published poetry by Françoise Hàn (France), George Moore (USA), Flavio Ermini (Italy), Louise Warren (Quebec), Carlos de Oliveira (Portugal), and Ingrid Swanberg (USA). *Osiris* is 48-56 pages, digest-sized, perfect-bound. Press run is 500 (50 subscription copies sent to college and university libraries, including foreign libraries). Receives 200-300 submissions/year, accepts about 12. Single copy: $8; subscription: $16. Sample: $4.

How to Submit Submit 4-6 poems at a time. "Poems should be sent by postal mail. Include short bio and SASE with submission. Translators should include a letter of permission from the poet or publisher as well as copies of the original text." Responds in 1 month. Sometimes sends prepublication galleys. Pays 5 contributor's copies.

Advice "It is always best to look at a sample copy of a journal before submitting work, and when you do submit work, do it often and do not get discouraged. Try to read poetry and support other writers."

◪ OVER THE TRANSOM

825 Bush St. #203, San Francisco CA 94108. (415)928-3965. E-mail: jsh619@earthlink.net. Established 1997. **Contact:** Jonathan Hayes, editor.

Magazine Needs *Over The Transom*, published 2 times/year, is a free publication of art and literature. Open to all styles of poetry. "We look for the highest quality poetry and art that best fits the issue." Considers poetry by children and teens. Has published poetry by A.D. Winans, Dave Church, Glen Chesnut, Daniel J. Langton. *Over The Transom* is 32 pages, magazine-sized, saddle-stapled, with cardstock cover. Receives about 1,000 poems/year, accepts about 5%. Press run is 300 (100 subscribers); 150 distributed free to cafes, bookstores, universities, and bars. Single copy: free. Sample: $3. Make checks payable to Jonathan Hayes.

How to Submit Submit 5 poems at a time. Considers previously published poems and simultaneous submissions. Accepts e-mail submissions; no disk submissions. Must include a SASE with postal submissions. Reads submissions year round. Time between acceptance and publication is 2-6 months. Never comments on rejected poems. Occasionally publishes theme issues. Guidelines available for SASE or by e-mail. Responds in 2 months. Sometimes sends prepublication galleys. Pays 1 contributor's copy. Acquires first rights.

Advice "Editors have differing tastes, so don't be upset by rejection. Always send a SASE for response."

PACIFIC COAST JOURNAL

P.O. Box 56, Carlsbad CA 92018. E-mail: pcj@frenchbreadpublications.com. (inquiries only). Web site: www.frenchbreadpublications.com/pcj. Established 1992. **Contact:** Stillson Graham, editor.

Magazine Needs *Pacific Coast Journal*, published quasi-quarterly, is an "unprofessional literary magazine. Whatever you think that means, go with it." Has published poetry by Tom Holmes, Anne Babson, and A.D. Winans. *Pacific Coast Journal* is 40 pages, digest-sized, photocopied, saddle-stapled, with cardstock cover. Receives 750 poems/year, accepts about 3%. Press run is 200. Single copy: $4; subscription: $14. Sample: $3.

How to Submit Submit up to 6 poems or 12 pages at a time. Considers simultaneous submissions; no previously published poems. No e-mail submissions. Cover letter is preferred. Encourages the inclusion of e-mail address in lieu of SASE for response. Time between acceptance and publication is 3-18 months. Seldom comments on rejected poems. Guidelines available for SASE, by e-mail, or on Web site. Responds in 6-9 months (usually). Pays 1 contributor's copy. Acquires one-time rights.

Advice "We like experiments."

PACKINGTOWN REVIEW

English Dept., UH 2027, University of Illinois at Chicago, 601 S. Morgan St., Chicago IL 60607. E-mail: editors@packingtownreview.com. Web site: www.packingtownreview.com. Established 2007. **Contact:** Tasha Fouts or Snezana Zabic, editors-in-chief.

Magazine Needs *Packingtown Review*, published annually in November, prints poetry and imaginative and critical prose by emerging and established writers. "We welcome submissions of poetry, scholarly articles, drama, creative nonfiction, fiction, and literary translation, as well as genre-bending pieces." Wants "well crafted poetry. We are open to most styles and forms. We are also looking for poetry that takes risks and does so successfully. We will consider articles about poetry." Does not want "uninspired and unrevised work." *Packingtown Review* is 250 pages, magazine-sized. Press run is 500. Single copy: $14; subscription: $14. Make checks payable to *Packingtown Review*.

How to Submit Submit 3-5 poems at a time. Considers simultaneous submissions (with notification); no previously published poems (considers poems posted on a public Web site/blog/forum previously published, but not those posted on a private, password-protected forum). No e-mail or disk submissions. Cover letter is required. "Please include a SASE. If you have simultaneously submitted these poems, please indicate in the cover letter and let us know ASAP if a poem is accepted elsewhere." Reads submissions year round. Poems are circulated to an editorial board. Sometimes comments on rejected poems. Sometimes publishes theme issues. Guidelines available on Web site. Responds in 3 months. Always sends prepublication galleys. Pays 2 contributor's copies. Acquires first North American serial rights. Rights revert to poets upon publication. Review books/chapbooks of poetry and other magazines/journals. Send materials for review consideration to Madeleine Monson-Rosen.

Magazines/Journals

◎ PARADOXISM (Specialized: avant-garde, experimental)

University of New Mexico, Gallup NM 87301. E-mail: smarand@unm.edu. Web site: www.gallup.u nm.edu/~smarandache/a/Paradoxism.htm. Established 1990. **Contact:** Florentin Smarandache, editor.

Magazine Needs *Paradoxism*, published annually, prints "avant-garde poetry, experiments, poems without verses, literature beyond the words, anti-language, non-literature and its literature, as well as the sense of the non-sense; revolutionary forms of poetry. Paradoxism, a 1980s movement of anti-totalitarian protest, is based on excessive use of antitheses, antinomies, contradictions, paradoxes in creation." Wants "avant-garde poetry, 1-2 pages, any subject, any style (lyrical experiments)." Does not want "classical, fixed forms." Has published poetry by Paul Georgelin, Mircea Monu, Ion Rotaru, Michéle de LaPlante, and Claude LeRoy. *Paradoxism* is 52 pages, digest-sized, offset-printed, with soft cover. Press run is 500; distributed "to its collaborators, U.S. and Canadian university libraries, and the Library of Congress as well as European, Chinese, Indian, and Japanese libraries."

How to Submit No previously published poems or simultaneous submissions. Do not submit during the summer. "We do not return published or unpublished poems or notify the author of date of publication." Responds in up to 3 weeks. Pays 1 contributor's copy.

Additional Information Paradoxism Association also publishes 2 poetry paperbacks and 1-2 chapbooks/year, including translations. "The poems must be unpublished and must meet the requirements of the Paradoxism Association." Responds to queries in 2 months; to mss in up to 3 weeks. Pays 50 author's copies. Sample e-books available on Web site at www.gallup.unm.edu/~smarand ache/eBooksLiterature.htm.

Advice "We mostly receive traditional or modern verse, but not avant-garde (very different from any previously published verse). We want anti-literature and its literature, style of the non-style, poems without poems, non-words and non-sentence poems, very upset free verse, intelligible unintelligible language, impersonal texts personalized, transformation of the abnormal to the normal. Make literature from everything; make literature from nothing!"

◎ PASSAGES NORTH

English Dept., Northern Michigan University, 1401 Presque Isle Ave., Marquette MI 49855. (906)227-1203. E-mail: passages@nmu.edu. Web site: http://myweb.nmu.edu/~passages. Established 1979. **Contact:** Austin Hummell, poetry editor.

Magazine Needs *Passages North*, published annually in spring, prints poetry, short fiction, creative nonfiction, essays, and interviews. Publishes work by established and emerging writers. Has published poetry by Moira Egan, Frannie Lindsay, Ben Lerner, Bob Hicok, and Gabe Gudding. *Passages North* is 250 pages. Circulation is 1,500. Single copy: $13; subscription: $13/year, $23 for 2 years. Sample: $3 (back issue).

How to Submit Submit up to 6 poems at a time. Considers simultaneous submissions. Time between acceptance and publication is 6 months. Reads submissions September-May only. Responds in 2 months. Pays 2 contributor's copies.

Contest/Award Offerings Sponsors the Elinor Benedict Poetry Prize every other year. 1st Prize: $1,000, plus 2 Honorable Mentions. **Entry fee:** $10 for 1-3 poems (each entrant receives the contest issue of *Passages North*). Make checks payable to Northern Michigan University. **Deadline:** reads entries October 15-January 22. Guidelines available for SASE, by e-mail, or on Web site.

◎ PATERSON LITERARY REVIEW

Poetry Center, Passaic County Community College, Cultural Affairs Dept., One College Blvd., Paterson NJ 07505-1179. (973)684-6555. Fax: (973)523-6085. E-mail: mgillan@pccc.edu. Web site: www .pccc.edu/poetry. Established 1979. **Contact:** Maria Mazziotti Gillan, editor/executive director.

● The Poetry Center Library at Passaic County Community College has an extensive collection of contemporary poetry and seeks small press contributions to help keep it abreast.

Magazine Needs *Paterson Literary Review*, published annually, is produced by the The Poetry Center at Passaic County Community College. Wants poetry of "high quality; clear, direct, powerful work." Has published poetry by Diane di Prima, Ruth Stone, Marge Piercy, and Laura Boss. *Paterson*

Literary Review is 300-400 pages, magazine-sized, professionally printed, saddle-stapled, with glossy 4-color card cover. Press run is 1,000. Sample: $13.

How to Submit Submit up to 5 poems at a time. Lines/poem: 100 maximum. Considers simultaneous submissions. Reads submissions December 1-March 31 only. Responds within 1 year. Pays 1 contributor's copy. Acquires first rights.

Contest/Award Offerings The Allen Ginsberg Poetry Awards and The Paterson Poetry Prize (see separate listings in Contests & Awards).

Also Offers Publishes *The New Jersey Poetry Resource Book* ($5 plus $1.50 p&h) and *The New Jersey Poetry Calendar*. The Distinguished Poets Series offers readings by poets of international, national, and regional reputation. Poetryworks/USA is a series of programs produced for UA Columbia-Cablevision. See Web site for details about these additional resources.

▦ ◐ PATTAYA POETRY REVIEW

Classic Village, 95/31 Moo 10 Nong Phrue, Banglamung, Chonburi 20150 Thailand. 6681 7177 941. E-mail: jsutta@yahoo.com. Established 2003. **Contact:** Jiraporn Sutta, editor.

Magazine Needs *Pattaya Poetry Review*, published quarterly, prints poetry. Wants "all types and styles, especially traditional forms." *Pattaya Poetry Review* is 16 pages, digest-sized, with cardstock cover. Receives about 200 poems/year, accepts about 20%. Press run is 70. Single copy: $9; subscription: $16.

How to Submit Submit no more than 3 poems at a time. Considers previously published poems and simultaneous submissions. Accepts e-mail submissions; no disk submissions. Reads submissions year round. Time between acceptance and publication is 3 months. Sometimes comments on rejected poems. Guidelines available. Responds in 3 months. Sometimes sends prepublication galleys. Pays 1 contributor's copy. Returns rights upon written request. Send materials for review consideration to Jiraporn Sutta.

◧ PAVEMENT SAW

Pavement Saw Press, P.O. Box 6291, Columbus OH 43206-0291. E-mail: info@pavementsaw.org. Web site: www.pavementsaw.org. Established 1992. **Contact:** David Baratier, editor.

Magazine Needs *Pavement Saw*, published annually in August, wants "letters and short fiction, and poetry on any subject, especially work." Does not want "poems that tell; no work by a deceased writer, and no translations." Dedicates 15-20 pages of each issue to a featured writer. Has published poetry by Simon Perchik, Sofia Starnes, Alan Catlin, Adrianne Kalfopoulou, Jim Daniels, and Mary Weems. *Pavement Saw* is 88 pages, digest-sized, perfect-bound. Receives about 9,000 poems/year, accepts less than 1%. Press run is 550. Single copy: $8; subscription: $14. Sample: $7. Make checks payable to Pavement Saw Press.

How to Submit Submit 5 poems at a time. Lines/poem: 1-2 pages. Considers simultaneous submissions, "as long as poet has not published a book with a press run of 1,000 or more"; no previously published poems. No e-mail submissions; postal submissions only. Cover letter is required. "No fancy typefaces." Seldom comments on rejected poems. Guidelines available in magazine or for SASE. Responds in 4 months. Sometimes sends prepublication galleys. Pays at least 2 contributor's copies. Acquires first rights.

Additional Information Pavement Saw Press also publishes books of poetry. "Most are by authors who have been published in the journal." Published "7 titles in 2005 and 7 titles in 2006; 5 were full-length books ranging from 80 to 240 pages."

Contest/Award Offerings Transcontinental Poetry Award and Pavement Saw Press Chapbook Award (see separate listings in Contests & Awards).

◧ PEARL

3030 E. Second St., Long Beach CA 90803-5163. (562)434-4523 or (714)968-7530. E-mail: pearlmag@aol.com. (inquiries only). Web site: www.pearlmag.com. Established 1974. **Contact:** Joan Jobe Smith, Marilyn Johnson, and Barbara Hauk, poetry editors.

Magazine Needs *Pearl*, published semiannually in May and November, is interested "in accessible, humanistic poetry that communicates and is related to real life. Humor and wit are welcome, along with the ironic and serious. No taboos, stylistically or subject-wise." Does not want "sentimental, obscure, predictable, abstract, or cliché-ridden poetry. Our purpose is to provide a forum for lively, readable poetry that reflects a wide variety of contemporary voices, viewpoints, and experiences—that speaks to real people about real life in direct, living language, profane or sublime. Our Spring/Summer issue is devoted exclusively to poetry, with a 12- to 15-page section featuring the work of a single poet." Has published poetry by Fred Voss, David Hernandez, Lisa Glatt, Jim Daniels, Nin Andrews, and Frank X. Gaspar. *Pearl* is 112-136 pages, digest-sized, offset-printed, perfect-bound, with glossy cover. Press run is 700. Subscription: $21/year (includes a copy of the Pearl Poetry Prize-winning book). Sample: $8.

How to Submit Submit 3-5 poems at a time. Lines/poem: no longer than 40 lines preferred, each line no more than 10-12 words, to accommodate page size and format. Considers simultaneous submissions ("must be acknowledged as such"); no previously published poems. No e-mail submissions; postal submissions only. Cover letter is appreciated. "Handwritten submissions and unreadable printouts are not acceptable." Reads submissions January-June only. Time between acceptance and publication is up to 1 year. Guidelines available for SASE or on Web site. Responds in 2 months. Sometimes sends prepublication galleys. Pays 1 contributor's copy. Acquires first serial rights.

Additional Information Pearl Editions publishes the winner of the Pearl Poetry Prize only (see separate listing in Contests & Awards). All other books and chapbooks are by invitation only.

Advice "Advice for beginning poets? Just write from your own experience, using images that are as concrete and sensory as possible. Keep these images fresh and objective. Always listen to the music."

◼ $◪ THE PEDESTAL MAGAZINE

E-mail: pedmagazine@carolina.rr.com (inquiries only; make submissions through online submission form). Web site: www.thepedestalmagazine.com. Established 2000. **Contact:** John Amen, editor-in-chief. Member: CLMP.

Magazine Needs *The Pedestal Magazine*, published bimonthly online, prints "12-15 poems per issue, as well as fiction, interviews, and book reviews. We are open to a wide variety of poetry, ranging from the highly experimental to the traditionally formal." Has published poetry by W.S. Merwin, Philip Levine, Nikki Giovanni, and Sharon Olds. Receives about 5,000 poems/year, accepts about 1%. "We have a readership of approximately 13,000 per month."

How to Submit Submit up to 6 poems at a time. Lines/poem: open. Considers simultaneous submissions; no previously published poems. No e-mail or disk submissions. "Submissions are accepted via a submission form provided in the 'Submit' section of the Web site. Our submissions schedule is posted in the guidelines section." Time between acceptance and publication is 2-4 weeks. Poems are circulated to an editorial board. Sometimes comments on rejected poems. Sometimes publishes theme issues. Guidelines available on Web site. Responds in 4-6 weeks. Always sends prepublication galleys (by e-mail). Pays $30/poem. Acquires first rights. Reviews books/chapbooks of poetry in 850-1,000 words. "Please query via e-mail prior to sending books or related materials."

◪ PEGASUS

P.O. Box 61324, Boulder City NV 89006. Established 1986. **Contact:** M.E. Hildebrand, editor.

Magazine Needs *Pegasus*, published quarterly, is "for serious poets who have something to say and know how to say it using sensory imagery." Does not want "religious, political, and pornographic themes." Has published poetry by John Grey, Elizabeth Perry, Diana K. Rubin, Lyn Lifshin, Robert K. Johnson, and Nikolas Macioci. *Pegasus* is 32 pages, digest-sized, desktop-published, saddle-stapled, with colored paper cover. Publishes 10-15% of the poetry received. Circulation is 200. Subscription: $20. Sample: $6.

How to Submit Submit 3-5 poems at a time. Lines/poem: 3 minimum, 40 maximum. Considers previously published poems, provided poet retains rights; no simultaneous submissions. Guidelines available for SASE. Responds in 2 weeks. Publication is payment. Acquires first or one-time rights.

★ ◻ ◎ THE PEGASUS REVIEW (Specialized: theme-driven issues)

P.O. Box 88, Henderson MD 21640-0088. (410)482-6736. E-mail: bounds1@comcast.net. (inquiries only). Established 1980. **Contact:** Art Bounds, editor.

Magazine Needs *The Pegasus Review*, now a quarterly, focuses on a specific theme for each issue and issued in calligraphic format. "Since themes might change it is advisable to contact editor about current themes. With us, brevity is the key. Themes may be submitted in the way of poetry, short-short fiction and essays." Has published work by Dorothy Bussemer, Katherine Sherin-Zauner, and Michael Keshigian. Press run is 120 (100 subscribers, 2 libraries). Subscription: $12. Sample: $2.50, including shipping and handling.

How to Submit Submit 3-5 poems at a time. Lines/poem: 24 maximum. Considers previously published poems, "if there is no conflict or violation of rights agreement," and simultaneous submissions, "but author must notify proper parties once specific material is accepted." No e-mail submissions. "Brief cover letter with specifics as they relate to one's writing background are welcome." Include name and address on each page. "The usual SASE would be appreciated, unless told to recycle material." Responds within 1 month, often with a personal response. Pays 2 contributor's copies and an occasional book award. Themes for 2009: January - Parenthood; April - Nature; July - Books and Reading; and October - Ideas.

Advice "Perseverance is the key word. Continue to write as well as circulating your work. Consider any editorial comments that might be made on a submission, although the final decision is up to the author. Constantly hone your craft. Keep abreast of current marketing information with the latest writing publications."

◢ "THE PEN": THE POETRY EXPLOSION NEWSLETTER

P.O. Box 4725, Pittsburgh PA 15206. (866)234-0297. E-mail: arthurford@hotmail.com. Established 1984. **Contact:** Arthur C. Ford, Sr., editor.

Magazine Needs *"The Pen": The Poetry Explosion Newsletter*, published quarterly, is "dedicated to the preservation of poetry." Wants "poetry and prose from all walks of life." Does not want "vulgarity." Considers poetry by children and teens; "if under 18 years old, parent or guardian should submit!" Has published poetry by Iva Fedorka. *The Pen* is 12-16 pages, saddle-stapled, mimeographed on both sides. Receives about 300 poems/year, accepts 80. The Poetry Explosion Newsletter is 12-14 pages, magazine-sized, mimeographed, stapled, and includes ads. Press run is 850. Subscription: $20/year, $38 for 2 years. Send $4 for sample copy and more information. Make checks payable to Arthur C. Ford.

How to Submit Submit up to 5 poems at a time. Lines/poem: 40 maximum. Considers previously published poems and simultaneous submissions. No e-mail submissions. Include large SASE if you want work returned. **Reading fee: $1.** Sometimes publishes theme issues. Guidelines available for SASE. Responds in up to 3 weeks. Comments on rejected poems "sometimes, but not obligated." **Poetry critiques available for 15¢/word.** Pays 1 contributor's copy. Send materials for review consideration.

Advice "Be fresh, honest, and legible!"

★ ▦ ◢ PENNINE INK

Mid Pennine Arts, The Gallery, Yorke St., Burnley BB11 1HD England. +44(0)1282 432 992. E-mail: sheridansdandl@yahoo.co.uk. Established 1983. **Contact:** Laura Sheridan, editor.

Magazine Needs *Pennine Ink*, published annually in January, prints poems and short prose pieces. *Pennine Ink* is 48 pages, A5, with b&w illustrated cover. Receives about 400 poems/year, accepts about 40. Press run is 200. "Contributors wishing to purchase a copy of *Pennine Ink* should enclose £3 ($6 USD) per copy."

How to Submit Submit up to 6 poems at a time. Lines/poem: 40 maximum; prose: no longer than 1,000 words. Considers previously published poems and simultaneous submissions. Accepts e-mail submissions. Seldom comments on rejected poems. Responds in 3 months. Pays 1 contributor's copy.

Advice "Submissions should be accompanied by a suitable SASE (or SAE with IRCs) for return of work."

⊞ ⊕ ⊘ PENNINE PLATFORM

Frizingley Hall, Frizinghall Rd., Bradford, West Yorkshire BD9 4LD England. Web site: www.pennin eplatform.co.uk. Established 1973. **Contact:** Nicholas Bielby, poetry editor.

Magazine Needs *Pennine Platform*, published 2 times/year in May and November, seeks any kind of poetry but concrete. "All styles—things good of their kind." Has published poetry by Gerard Benson, Miklos Radnoti (trans. Thomas Land), Mike Shields, Sam Smith, William Connely, and Milner Place. *Pennine Platform* is 60 pages, A5, digitally printed, stapled, with matte card cover with graphics. Receives about 1,000 submissions/year, accepts about 100. Circulation is 300 including libraries and universities. Subscription: £8.50 UK, £10 rest of Europe, £12 ROW (all payable in sterling only). Sample: £4.50 UK, £6 ROW.

How to Submit Submit up to 6 poems at a time. Lines/poem: open, "but poems of fewer than 40 lines have a better chance." Submissions must be typed. Comments on all poems (if SAE or e-mail address is provided). Responds in up to 6 months. Pays 1 contributor's copy. Acquires first serial rights. Reviews books of poetry, multi-book format. Send materials for review consideration.

Advice "Pay attention to technique. Intelligent thoughtfulness and intelligent humor both appreciated. Religious poetry (but not religiosity) accepted."

⊘ PENNSYLVANIA ENGLISH

Penn State DuBois, DuBois PA 15801-3199. (814)375-4814. E-mail: ajv2@psu.edu. (inquiries only). Established 1988. **Contact:** Antonio Vallone, editor.

Magazine Needs *Pennsylvania English*, published annually, is "sponsored by the Pennsylvania College English Association." Wants poetry of "any length, any style." Has published poetry by Liz Rosenberg, Walt MacDonald, Amy Pence, Jennifer Richter, and Jeff Schiff. *Pennsylvania English* is up to 200 pages, digest-sized, perfect-bound, with full-color cover. Press run is 500. Subscription: $10/year.

How to Submit Submit 3 or more poems at a time. Considers simultaneous submissions; no previously published poems. No e-mail submissions. Submissions must be typed. Include SASE. Guidelines available for SASE. Responds in 6 months. Pays 2 contributor's copies.

Advice "Poetry does not express emotions; it evokes emotions. Therefore, it should rely less on statements and more on images."

⊘ ◎ THE PENWOOD REVIEW (Specialized: spirituality, the sacred)

P.O. Box 862, Los Alamitos CA 90720-0862. E-mail: submissions@penwoodreview.com. Web site: www.penwoodreview.com. Established 1997. **Contact:** Lori M. Cameron, editor.

Magazine Needs *The Penwood Review*, published semiannually, seeks "to explore the spiritual and sacred aspects of our existence and our relationship to God." Wants "disciplined, high-quality, well-crafted poetry on any subject. Rhyming poetry must be written in traditional forms (sonnets, tercets, villanelles, sestinas, etc.)." Does not want "light verse, doggerel, or greeting card-style poetry. Also, nothing racist, sexist, pornographic, or blasphemous." Has published poetry by Kathleen Spivack, Anne Babson, Hugh Fox, Anselm Brocki, Nina Tassi, and Gary Guinn. *The Penwood Review* is about 40 pages, magazine-sized, saddle-stapled, with heavy card cover. Press run is 50-100. Single copy: $6; subscription: $12.

How to Submit Submit 3-5 poems at a time. Lines/poem: less than 2 pages preferred. No previously published poems or simultaneous submissions. Accepts e-mail submissions (pasted into body of message). Cover letter is preferred. 1 poem to a page with the author's full name, address, and phone number in the upper right corner. Time between acceptance and publication is up to 1 year. "Submissions are circulated among an editorial staff for evaluations." Never comments on rejected poems. Responds in up to 4 months. Pays with subscription discount of $10 and, with subscription, 1 additional contributor's copy. Acquires one-time rights.

⊘ PEREGRINE

Amherst Writers & Artists, 190 University Dr., Suite 1, Amherst MA 01002. (413)253-3307. E-mail: peregrine@amherstwriters.com. Web site: www.amherstwriters.com. Established 1983. **Contact:** Nancy Rose, editor.

Magazine Needs *Peregrine*, published annually, features poetry and fiction. Open to all styles, forms, and subjects except greeting card verse. "*Peregrine* has provided a forum for national and international writers since 1983, and is committed to finding excellent work by new writers as well as established authors. We publish what we love, knowing that all editorial decisions are subjective." Has published poetry by Willie James King, Virgil Suárez, Susan Terris, Janet Aalfs, Dianalee Velie, and Ralph Hughes. *Peregrine* is 104 pages, digest-sized, professionally printed, perfect-bound, with glossy cover. Press run is 1,000. Single copy: $15. Sample: $12. Make checks payable to AWA Press.

How to Submit Submit 3-5 poems at a time. Lines/poem: 60 maximum (including spaces). Considers simultaneous submissions; no previously published poems. No e-mail submissions. Include cover letter with bio, 30 words maximum; indicate line count for each poem. Enclose sufficiently stamped SASE for return of mss; if disposable copy, enclose #10 SASE for response. Reads submissions January 2 - March 31 (postmark) only. Each ms read by several readers; final decisions made by the editor. Guidelines available for #10 SASE or on Web site. Pays 2 contributor's copies. Acquires first rights.

Advice "Check guidelines before submitting your work. Familiarize yourself with *Peregrine*."

✪ ⬗ PERMAFROST: A LITERARY JOURNAL

% English Dept., University of Alaska Fairbanks, P.O. Box 755720, Fairbanks AK 99775. E-mail: fbpfrost@uaf.edu. Web site: www.uaf.edu/english/permafrost. Established 1977. **Contact:** Poetry Editor.

Magazine Needs *Permafrost: A Literary Journal*, published in May, contains poems, short stories, creative nonfiction, b&w drawings, photographs, and prints. "We survive on both new and established writers, hoping and expecting to see the best work out there. We publish any style of poetry provided it is conceived, written, and revised with care. While we encourage submissions about Alaska and by Alaskans, we also welcome poems about anywhere, from anywhere. We have published work by E. Ethelbert Miller, W. Loran Smith, Peter Orlovsky, Jim Wayne Miller, Allen Ginsberg, and Andy Warhol." *Permafrost* is about 200 pages, digest-sized, professionally printed, flat-spined. Subscription: $8/year, $16/2 years, $22/3 years. Sample: $4.

How to Submit Submit 3-5 poems at a time. Considers simultaneous submissions. "Poems should be typed, single- or double-spaced, and formatted as they should appear in print." Reads submissions by March 15 deadline (does not accept submissions March 15-September 1). Sometimes comments on poems. Guidelines available for SASE or on Web site. Responds in about 2 months. Pays 1 contributor's copies; reduced contributor rate on additional copies.

Contest/Award Offerings The Midnight Sun Poetry Chapbook Contest (formerly the Susan Blalock Contest; see separate listing).

⬗ ◎ PERSPECTIVES (Specialized: Christian)

Dept. of English, Hope College, Holland MI 49422-9000. **Contact:** Rhoda Janzen, poetry editor.

Magazine Needs *Perspectives*, published 10 times/year, aims "to express the Reformed faith theologically; to engage in issues that Reformed Christians meet in personal, ecclesiastical, and societal life; and thus to contribute to the mission of the church of Jesus Christ." Wants "poems excellent in craft and significant in subject, both traditional and free in form. We publish 1-2 poems every other issue." Has published poetry by Ann Hostetler, Paul Willis, and Priscilla Atkins. *Perspectives* is 24 pages, magazine-sized, Web offset-printed, saddle-stapled, with paper cover containing b&w illustration. Receives about 300 poems/year, accepts 6-20. Press run is 3,300. Subscription: $30. Sample: $3.50.

How to Submit No previously published poems or simultaneous submissions. Cover letter is preferred. Include SASE. "Submissions without SASE will not be returned." Time between acceptance and publication is 3-12 months. Responds in 3-6 months. Pays 5 contributor's copies. Acquires first rights.

◻ ◎ PHILADELPHIA STORIES (Specialized: submissions from PA, NJ, DE resident poets)

2021 S. 11th St., Philadelphia PA 19148. E-mail: info@philadelphiastories.org. Web site: www.philadelphiastories.org. Established 2003. **Contact:** Conrad Weiser. Member: CLMP.

Magazine Needs *Philadelphia Stories*, published quarterly, publishes "literary fiction, poetry, and art from Pennsylvania, New Jersey, and Delaware—and provide it to the general public free of charge." Wants "polished, well crafted poems." Does not want "first drafts." Considers poetry by teens. Has published poetry by Daniel Abdal-Hayy Moore, Scott Edward Anderson, Sandy Crimmins, Liz Dolan, Alison Hicks, and Margaret A. Robinson. *Philadelphia Stories* is 24 pages, magazine-sized, saddle-stapled, with 4-color cover with original art, includes ads. Receives about 600 poems/year, accepts about 15%. Press run is 12,000 per quarter, distributed free. Subscription: "we offer $20 memberships that include home delivery." Make checks payable to *Philadelphia Stories*.

How to Submit Submit 3 poems at a time. Lines/poem: 36. Considers simultaneous submissions; no previously published poems. Accepts submissions through online submission form at www.philadelphiastories.org/submissions; no disk submissions. Cover letter is preferred. Reads submissions year round. Time between acceptance and publication is 3 months. Poems are circulated to an editorial board. "Each poem is reviewed by a preliminary board that decides on a final list; the entire board discusses this list and chooses the mutual favorites for print and Web." Guidelines available on Web site. Responds in 3 months. "We send a layout proof to check for print poems." Acquires one-time rights. Rights revert to poets upon publication. Reviews books of poetry.

☑ PHOEBE: A JOURNAL OF LITERATURE AND ART

MSN 2D6, George Mason University, 4400 University Dr., Fairfax VA 22030-4444. (703)993-2915. E-mail: phoebe@gmu.edu. (inquiries only). Web site: www.gmu.edu/pubs/phoebe. Established 1970. **Contact:** Poetry Editor.

Magazine Needs *Phoebe: A Journal of Literature and Art*, published semiannually in September and February, looks "for imagery that will make your thumbs sweat when you touch it." Has published poetry by C.D. Wright, Russell Edson, Yusef Komunyakaa, Rosemarie Waldrop, and Leslie Scalapino. Press run is 3,000, with 35-40 pages of poetry in each issue. Receives 4,000 submissions/year. Single copy: $6; subscription: $12/year.

How to Submit Submit up to 5 poems at a time. No simultaneous submissions. No e-mail submissions; postal submissions only. Include SASE and a short bio. Reads submissions September 1-April 15 (postmark); mss postmarked April 16-August 31 will not be read. Guidelines available for SASE or on Web site. Responds in up to 3 months. Pays 2 contributor's copies or one-year subscription.

Additional Information Check http://phoebejournal.blogspot.com. for additional information and commentary about *Phoebe*.

Contest/Award Offerings The Greg Grummer Poetry Award (see separate listing in Contests & Awards).

☑ THE PINCH

Dept. of English, University of Memphis, Memphis TN 38152-6176. (901)678-4591. Fax: (901)678-2226. E-mail: thepinch@memphis.edu. Web site: www.thepinchjournal.com. or www.mfainmemphis.com. Established 1980. **Contact:** Kristen Iversen, editor-in-chief.

Magazine Needs *The Pinch* (previously *River City*), published semiannually (fall and spring), prints fiction, poetry, interviews, creative nonfiction, and visual art. Has published poetry by Albert Goldbarth, Maxine Kumin, Jane Hirshfield, Terrance Hayes, S. Beth Bishop, and Naomi Shahib Nye. *The Pinch* is 160 pages, 7×10, professionally printed, perfect-bound, with colorful glossy cover and color art and photography. Press run is 1,500. Sample: $10.

How to Submit Submit no more than 5 poems at a time. No e-mail submissions. Include SASE. "We do not read in the summer months." Reads submissions according to these deadlines only: August 15-November 1 (Spring issue) and January 15-March 15 (Fall issue). Guidelines available for SASE, by e-mail, or on Web site. Responds in up to 3 months. Pays 2 contributor's copies.

Contest/Award Offerings Offers an annual award in poetry. 1st Prize: $1,000 and publication; 2nd- and 3rd-Prize poems may also be published. Any previously unpublished poem of up to 2 pages is eligible. No simultaneous submissions. Poems should be typed and accompanied by a cover letter. Author's name should not appear anywhere on ms. Manuscripts will not be returned. Guidelines available for SASE, by e-mail, or on Web site. **Entry fee:** $15 for up to 3 poems (includes one-year subscription). **Deadline:** January 15-March 15 (inclusive postmark dates). Winners will be notified in July; published in subsequent issue.

▣ ◯ THE PINK CHAMELEON—ONLINE
E-mail: dpfreda@juno.com. Web site: www.geocities.com/thepinkchameleon/index.html. Established 1985 (former print version), 1999 (online version). **Contact:** Mrs. Dorothy P. Freda, editor.
Magazine Needs *The Pink Chameleon—Online* published annually, prints "family-oriented, upbeat poetry, any genre in good taste that gives hope for the future." Wants "poems about nature, loved ones, rare moments in time." Does not want "pornography, cursing, swearing; nothing evoking despair." Considers poetry by children and teens. Receives about 50 poems/year, accepts about 50%.
How to Submit Submit 1-4 poems at a time. Lines/poem: 6 minimum, 24 maximum. Considers previously published poems; no simultaneous submissions. Accepts e-mail submissions only (pasted into body of message; "please, no attachments"). Use plain text and include a brief bio. Reads submissions January-April and September-October. Time between acceptance and publication is up to 1 year depending on date of acceptance. "As editor, I reserve the right to edit for grammar, spelling, sentence structure, flow; omit redundancy and any words or material I consider in bad taste." Often comments on rejected poems. Guidelines available by e-mail or on Web site. Responds in 1 month. No payment. Acquires one-time, one-year publication rights. All rights revert to poet in 6 months to a year, depending on date of acceptance.
Advice "Always keep a typed hard copy or a back-up disk of your work for your files. Mail can go astray. And I'm human, I can accidentally delete or lose the submission."

◪ PINYON
Dept. of Languages, Literature & Communications, Mesa State College, 1100 North Ave., Grand Junction CO 81051. E-mail: pinyonpoetry@hotmail.com. Established 1995. **Contact:** Randy Phillis, editor.
Magazine Needs *Pinyon*, published annually in June, prints "the best available contemporary American poetry and fiction. No restrictions other than excellence. We appreciate a strong voice." Does not want "inspirational, light verse, or sing-song poetry." Has published poetry by Mark Cox, Barry Spacks, Wendy Bishop, and Anne Ohman Youngs. *Pinyon* is about 120 pages, magazine-sized, perfect-bound. Receives about 4,000 poems/year, accepts 2%. Press run is 300; 100 distributed free to contributors, friends, etc. Subscription: $8/year. Sample: $4.50. Make checks payable to Pinyon, MSC.
How to Submit Submit 3-5 poems at a time. No previously published poems or simultaneous submissions. Cover letter is preferred. "Name, address, e-mail, and phone number on each page. SASE required." Reads submissions August 1-December 1. "Three groups of assistant editors, led by an associate editor, make recommendations to the editor." Seldom comments on rejected poems. Guidelines available for SASE. Responds in February. Pays 2 contributor's copies. Acquires one-time rights.
Advice "Send us your best work!"

Ⓝ ◪ PIRENE'S FOUNTAIN
3616 Glenlake Dr, Glenview IL 60026. E-mail: pirenepublisher@gmail.com. Web site: pirenesfountain.com. Established 2008. **Contact:** Ami Kaye, publisher.
Magazine Needs *Pirene's Fountain* is published online 3 times per year in January, May, and October. Does not want "blatantly religious/political themes, anything obscene, pornographic, or discriminatory in nature." Receives about 600 poems/year, accepts about 20%.
How to Submit Submit 3-8 poems at a time. Considers previously published poems and simultaneous submissions. Considers poetry posted on a public Web site/blog/forum and poetry posted on a private, password-protected forum as published. Accepts e-mail submissions pasted into body of message; no fax or disk submissions. Cover letter is unnecessary but 50-100 word bio is required. Reads submissions during the months of November, April, and September. Submit seasonal poems

anytime. Time between acceptance and publication is 4 to 6 weeks. Poems are circulated to an editorial board. Never comments on rejected poems. Sometimes publishes theme issues. Guidelines available on Web site. Responds in 4 to 5 weeks. Poets retain copyright to their own work, rights revert to poets upon publication.

Also Offers "We offer a poetry discussion group on Facebook, entitled 'PF Poetry.' Membership on Facebook is free and approval from a PF officer is required. E-mail publisher for details if interested."

Advice "Please read submission guidelines carefully and send in *at least* 3 poems."

N ◗ PLAIN SPOKE

6199 Steubenville Road SE, Amsterdam OH 43903. (740)543-4333. E-mail: plainspoke@gmail.com. Web site: www.plainspoke.net. Established 2007. **Contact:** Cindy Kelly, editor.

Magazine Needs *Plain Spoke*, published quarterly, publishes "poetry heavy in sense images and with a clear, plain-spoken voice." Wants "Americana, nostalgia, narrative." Does not want "esoteric, universal, cliché." Has published poetry by Claudia Burbank, Hannah Craig, Amy Sargent. *Plain Spoke* is 36-52 digest-sized, laser-printed, saddle-stitched, with a color art on cardstock cover. Receives about 2,500 poems/year, accepts about 5%. Press run is 300. Single copy: $6; subscription: $20. Make checks payable to Amsterdam Press.

How to Submit Submit up to 6 poems at a time, preferably under 40 lines. Considers simultaneous submissions, no previously published poems (considers poetry posted on a public Web site/blog/forum). Accepts e-mail submissions (pasted into body of message) and disk submissions; no fax submissions. Cover letter is required. Paper submissions require an SASE. Reads submissions year round. Submit seasonal poems 3 months in advance. Time between acceptance and publication is 1-4 months. Poems are circulated to an editorial board. Sometimes comments on rejected poems. Never publishes theme issues. Guidelines available for SASE, by e-mail, and on Web site. Responds in 1 week. Pays 1 contributor's copy. Acquires first North American serial rights. Rights revert to poets upon publication. Reviews books and chapbooks of poetry in single-book format. Send materials for review consideration to Reviews Editor, *Plain Spoke*.

◗ ◎ PLAINSONGS (Specialized: Great Plains poems encouraged)

Dept. of English, Hastings College, Hastings NE 68902-0269. (402)461-7352. Fax: (402)461-7756. E-mail: plainsongs@hastings.edu. (inquiries only). Established 1980. **Contact:** Laura Marvel Wunderlich, editor.

Magazine Needs *Plainsongs*, published 3 times/year, considers poems "on any subject, in any style, but free verse predominates. Plains region poems encouraged." *Plainsongs*' title suggests not only its location on the Great Plains, but its preference for the living language, whether in free or formal verse. "*Plainsongs* is committed to poems only, to make space without visual graphics, bios, reviews, or critical positions." Has published poetry by Judith Tate O'Brien, Andrew H. Oerke, Lyn Lifshin, Larsen Bowker, and Louis Daniel Brodsky. *Plainsongs* is 40 pages, digest-sized, laser-set, printed on thin paper, saddle-stapled, with one-color matte card cover with generic black logo. "Published by the English department of Hastings College, the magazine is partially financed by subscriptions. Although editors respond to as many submissions with personal attention as they have time for, the editor offers specific observations to all contributors who also subscribe." Subscription: $15 for 3 issues. Sample: $5.

How to Submit Submit up to 6 poems at a time, with name and address on each page. No fax, e-mail, or disk submissions; postal submissions only. Reads submissions according to the following deadlines: July 15 for Winter issue; November 15 for Spring issue; March 15 for Fall issue. Responds 7-8 weeks after deadline. Guidelines available for SASE. Pays 2 contributor's copies and one-year subscription. Acquires first rights.

Contest/Award Offerings 3 poems in each issue receive a $25 prize. "A short essay in appreciation accompanies each award poem."

Advice "We like poems that seem to be aware of modernist and post-modernist influences during the last hundred years, not necessarily by imitation or allusion, but by using the tools provided by that rich heritage. Poets need to read and absorb the work of other poets."

$☑ PLEIADES

Pleiades Press, Dept.of English, University of Central Missouri, Warrensburg MO 64093. (660)543-8106. E-mail: pleiades@ucmo.edu. Web site: http://www.ucmo.edu/englphil/pleiades/. Established 1990. **Contact:** Kevin Prufer, editor.

• Poems published in *Pleiades* have appeared in *The Best American Poetry* and *The Pushcart Prize*.

Magazine Needs *Pleiades*, published semiannually in April and October, prints poetry, fiction, literary criticism, belles lettres (occasionally), and reviews. Open to all writers. Wants "avant-garde, free verse, and traditional poetry, and some quality light verse." Does not want anything "pretentious, didactic, or overly sentimental." Has published poetry by James Tate, Joyce Carol Oates, Brenda Hillman, Wislawa Szymborska, Carl Phillips, and Jean Valentine. *Pleiades* is 160 pages, digest-sized, perfect-bound, with heavy coated cover with color art. Receives about 9,000 poems/year, accepts fewer than 1%. Press run is 2,500-3,000; about 200 distributed free to educational institutions and libraries across the country. Single copy: $6; subscription: $12. Sample: $5. Make checks payable to Pleiades Press.

How to Submit Submit 3-5 poems at a time. Considers simultaneous submissions with notification; no previously published poems. Cover letter is preferred. Include brief bio. Time between acceptance and publication "can be up to 1 year. Each poem published must be accepted by 2 readers and approved by the poetry editor." Seldom comments on rejected poems. Guidelines available for SASE or on Web site. Responds in up to 3 months. Payment varies. Acquires first and second serial rights.

$☑ PLOUGHSHARES

Emerson College, 120 Boylston St., Dept. P, Boston MA 02116. (617)824-8753. Web site: www.pshares.org. Established 1971. **Contact:** Poetry Editor.

• Work published in *Ploughshares* has been selected frequently for *The Best American Poetry*.

Magazine Needs *Ploughshares*, published 3 times/year, is "a journal of new writing guest-edited by prominent poets and writers to reflect different and contrasting points of view. Translations are welcome if permission has been granted." Editors have included Carolyn Forché, Gerald Stern, Rita Dove, Chase Twichell, and Marilyn Hacker. Has published poetry by Donald Hall, Li-Young Lee, Robert Pinsky, Brenda Hillman, and Thylias Moss. *Ploughshares* is 200 pages, digest-sized. Receives about 2,500 poetry submissions/year. Press run is 7,000. Subscription: $24 domestic, $36 foreign. Sample: $10.95 current issue, $8.50 back issue.

How to Submit Submit 1-3 poems at a time. Considers simultaneous submissions if indicated as such; no previously published poems. Postal submissions only, include SASE. Cover letter is preferred. Reads submissions August 1-March 31 (postmark); mss submitted April 1-July 31 will be returned unread. "We suggest you read a few issues (online or in print) before submitting. Check our Web site for any special guidelines." Responds in up to 5 months. Always sends prepublication galleys. Pays $25/printed page ($50 minimum, $250 maximum), plus 2 contributor's copies and a subscription.

$◯ ◎ POCKETS (Specialized: Christian; poetry by/for children; thematic issues)

1908 Grand Ave., P.O. Box 340004, Nashville TN 37203-0004. E-mail: pockets@upperroom.org. Web site: www.pockets.org. **Contact:** Lynn W. Gilliam, editor.

Magazine Needs *Pockets*, published monthly (except February), is an interdenominational magazine for children ages 6-11. "Each issue is built around a specific theme, with material (including poetry) that can be used by children in a variety of ways. Submissions do not need to be overly religious; they should help children experience a Christian lifestyle that is not always a neatly wrapped moral package but is open to the continuing revelation of God's will." Considers poetry by children.

How to Submit Lines/poem: 24 maximum. Considers previously published poems (first reprint only). No fax or e-mail submissions. Submissions should be typed, double-spaced, on 8½×11 paper, accompanied by SASE for return. "Those who wish to save postage and are concerned about paper conservation may send a SASP for notification of accepted manuscripts. Please list the titles of the submissions on the postcards. We will recycle the paper the submission is printed on.'' Reads submissions year round. Publishes theme issues; themes are available each year the end of December. Guidelines available on Web site (under Adults/Writer's Corner). Pays $2/line ($25 minimum). Pays on acceptance; may place mss on long-term hold for specific issues. Acquires newspaper, periodical, and electronic rights.

POEM

Huntsville Literary Association, P.O. Box 2006, Huntsville AL 35804. Web site: www.hla-hsv.org. Established 1967. **Contact:** Rebecca Harbor, editor.

Magazine Needs *Poem*, published twice/year in May and November, consists entirely of poetry. ''We publish both traditional forms and free verse.'' Wants poems ''characterized by compression, rich vocabulary, significant content, and evidence of 'a tuned ear and practiced pen.' We want coherent work that moves through the particulars of the poem to make a point. We equally welcome submissions from established poets as well as from less-known and beginning poets.'' Does not want translations. Has published poetry by Kathryn Kirkpatrick, Peter Serchuk, and Kim Bridgford. *Poem* is 90 pages, digest-sized, flat-spined, printed on good stock paper, with a clean design and a matte cover. Prints more than 60 poems/issue, generally featured 1 to a page. Press run is 500. Single copy: $10; subscription: $20. Sample: $7 (back issue).

How to Submit Send 3-5 poems at a time. No previously published poems or simultaneous submissions. Include SASE. Reads submissions year round. Guidelines available for SASE or on Web site. Responds in 1-2 months. Pays 2 contributor's copies. Acquires first serial rights.

POEMELEON: A JOURNAL OF POETRY

3509 Bryce Way, Riverside CA 92506. (951)218-4464. E-mail: editor@poemeleon.org. Web site: www.poemeleon.org. Established 2005. **Contact:** Cati Porter, editor Member: CLMP, Online Literary Association.

- Poems from recent issues have been selected for inclusion in Verse Daily's Web Monthly Feature, NewPages' WordsMatter: A Selection of Poetry & Prose on the Web, and Best New Poets 2007.

Magazine Needs *Poemeleon: A Journal of Poetry*, published semiannually online, wants all forms and styles of poetry. Does not want ''overly religious or sentimental, greeting card verse. If you have to ask yourself whether it's right for *Poemeleon*, it's probably not.'' Has published poetry by Tony Barnstone, Catherine Daly, Ann Fisher-Wirth, Richard Garcia, Eloise Klein Healy, Bob Hicok. Poemeleon receives about 1,000 poems/year, accepts about 150-200. Number of unique visitors: 25,000/year.

How to Submit Submit 3-5 poems at a time. Considers previously published poems (as long as they have not appeared online) and simultaneous submissions (''as long as we are notified promptly if a poem is taken elsewhere''). Considers poetry posted on a public Web site/blog/forum as published. Accepts e-mail submissions (pasted into body of message, as attachment, or by the upload form located on the guidelines page of the Web site.); no fax or disk submissions. Cover letter is preferred. ''Each issue is devoted to a particular type of poetry (past issues include poems of place, ekphrastic poems, poems in form, and the prose poem). Please check the guidelines page for specifics before submitting.'' Reads submissions year round. Time between acceptance and publication is about 2 months. Poems are circulated to an editorial board. Sometimes comments on rejected poems. Regularly publishes them issues. Upcoming themes and guidelines available on Web site. Responds in 2-4 months. Always sends prepublication galleys. Acquires one-time rights. Rights revert to poets upon publication. Reviews books and chapbooks of poetry.

Contest/Award Offerings Mystery Box Contest offers a prize of the Mystery Box and publication on the Web site. Submit 1 poem. Guidelines available on Web site. **Entry fee:** none. **Deadline:** none.

Advice ''Please read our guidelines before submitting.''

POEMS & PLAYS

English Dept., Middle Tennessee State University, Murfreesboro TN 37132. (615)898-2712. Established 1993. **Contact:** Gaylord Brewer, editor.

Magazine Needs *Poems & Plays*, published annually in the spring, is an "eclectic publication for poems and short plays." No restrictions on style or content of poetry. Has published poetry by Naomi Wallace, Kate Gale, James Doyle, and Charles Harper Webb. *Poems & Plays* is 88 pages, digest-sized, professionally printed, perfect-bound, with coated color card cover. Receives 1,500 poems per issue, publishes 30-35 "typically." Press run is 800. Subscription: $10 for 2 issues. Sample: $6.

How to Submit No previously published poems or simultaneous submissions. Reads submissions October-November only. "Work is circulated among advisory editors for comments and preferences. All accepted material is published in the following issue." Sometimes comments on rejected poems. Responds in 2 months. Pays 1 contributor's copy. Acquires first publication rights only.

Contest/Award Offerings Considers chapbook mss (poems or short plays) of 20-24 pages for The Tennessee Chapbook Prize. "Any combination of poems or plays, or a single play, is eligible. The winning chapbook is printed within *Poems & Plays*." Winning author receives 50 copies of the issue. SASE required. **Entry fee:** $10 (includes 1 copy of the issue). **Deadline:** same as for the magazine (October-November). Past winners include Julie Lechevsky and Nancy Naomi Carlson. "The chapbook competition annually receives over 150 manuscripts from the U.S. and around the world."

⬛ $⬜ POESIA (Specialized: venue for Northwest AK poets)

Indian Bay Press, One West Mountain St., Fayetteville AR 72701. (479)444-9323. Fax: (479)444-9326. E-mail: editor@indianbaypress.com. Web site: www.indianbaypress.com. Established 2003. **Contact:** Jay Ross, editor.

Magazine Needs *Poesia*, published biannually, prints poetry and poetry reviews of all genres. "Although we accept manuscripts worldwide, our purpose is to offer a venue that currently does not exist for unpublished writers in Northwest Arkansas. We accept and encourage submissions of poetry and poetry review from foreign poets." *Poesia* is digest-sized, offset-printed, perfect-bound, includes ads. Receives about 1,000 poems/year, accepts about 30-40%. Press run is 2,000; 15% distributed free for promotions. Single copy: $9.95; subscription: $18/year, $32 for 2 years. Make checks payable to Indian Bay Press.

How to Submit Submit 3 poems at a time. No previously published poems or simultaneous submissions. Accepts e-mail (as attachment) submissions in word document format only or CD submissions. Cover letter is required. "Include name, address, SASE, and biographical information, as well as previous publishing credits." Reads submissions year round. Time between acceptance and publication is 3 months. Never comments on rejected poems. Guidelines available on Web site. Responds in 1 week. Pays $10/poem and 2 contributor's copies. Acquires one-time rights. Rights revert to author upon publication. Reviews books and chapbooks of poetry in 250-500 words, single-book format. Send materials for review consideration to Attn: Editor, Indian Bay Press.

Contest/Award Offerings Sponsors the annual Oliver W. Browning Poetry Competition. Offers 1st Prize: $500; 2nd Prize: $150; 3rd Prize: Honorable Mention. Submit 3 poems. **Entry fee:** $18 (includes subscription to *Poesia*). **Deadline:** October 15. Guidelines available in magazine or on Web site.

⬜ ◎ POESY MAGAZINE (Specialized: Boston, MA & Santa Cruz, CA)

P.O. Box 7823, Santa Cruz CA 95061. (831)239-4419. E-mail: info@poesy.org. Web site: www.poesy.org. Established 1991. **Contact:** Brian Morrisey, editor/publisher.

Magazine Needs *POESY Magazine*, published quarterly, is "an anthology of American poetry. *POESY*'s main concentrations are Boston, Massachusetts and Santa Cruz, California, 2 thriving homesteads for poets, beats, and artists of nature. Our goal is to unite the 2 scenes, updating poets on what's happening across the country." Wants to see "original poems that express observational impacts with clear and concise imagery. Acceptence is based on creativity, composition, and relation to the format of *POESY*." Does not want "poetry with excessive profanity. We would like to endorse creativity beyond the likes of everyday babble." Has published poetry by Lawrence Ferlinghetti, Jack Hirschman, Edward Sanders, Todd Moore, Diane Di Prima, and Julia Vinograd. *POESY* is 16 pages, magazine-sized, newsprint, glued/folded, includes ads. Receives about 1,000 poems/year, accepts about 10%. Press run is 1,000; most distributed free to local venues. Single copy: $1; subscription: $12/year. Sample: $2. Make checks payable to Brian Morrisey.

How to Submit Submit 3-5 poems at a time. Lines/poem: 32 maximum. No previously published poems or simultaneous submissions. Accepts e-mail (submissions@poesy.org) and disk submissions. "Snail mail submissions are preferred with a SASE." Cover letter is preferred. Reads submissions year round. Time between acceptance and publication is 1 month. "Poems are accepted by the Santa Cruz editor/publisher based on how well the poem stimulates our format." Guidelines available in magazine, for SASE, by e-mail, or on Web site. Responds in 1 month. Sometimes sends prepublication galleys. Pays 3 contributor's copies. Acquires one-time rights. Reviews books/chapbooks of poetry and other magazines/journals in 1,000 words, single-book format. Send materials for review consideration to *POESY*, % Brian Morrisey.

Advice "Stay away from typical notions of love and romance. Become one with your surroundings and discover a true sense of natural perspective."

☑ POET LORE

The Writer's Center, 4508 Walsh St., Bethesda MD 20815. (301)654-8664. Fax: (801)730-6233. E-mail: postmaster@writer.org. Web site: www.writer.org. Established 1889. **Contact:** Jason DeYoung, managing editor.

Magazine Needs *Poet Lore*, published semiannually, is "dedicated to the best in American and world poetry as well as timely reviews and commentary." Wants "fresh uses of traditional forms and devices, but any kind of excellence is welcome." Has published poetry by Ai, Denise Duhamel, Jefferey Harrison, Eve Jones, Carl Phillips, and Ronald Wallace. *Poet Lore* is 144 pages, digest-sized, professionally printed, perfect-bound, with glossy card cover. Receives about 4,200 poems/year, accepts 125. Press run is at least 800. Single copy: $9; subscription: $18. "Add $1/single copy for shipping; add $5 postage for subscriptions outside U.S."

How to Submit Considers simultaneous submissions "with notification in cover letter." No e-mail or disk submissions. "Submit typed poems, with author's name and address on each page; SASE is required." Guidelines available for SASE or on Web site. Responds in 3 months. Pays 2 contributor's copies. Reviews books of poetry. Send materials for review consideration.

☑ POETALK

P.O. Box 11435, Berkeley CA 94712-2435. E-mail: poetalk@aol.com. Web site: www.bayareapoetscoalition.org. Established 1974. **Contact:** Maggie Morley, editor.

Magazine Needs *POETALK*, currently published 1-2 issues/year, is the poetry journal of the Bay Area Poets Coalition (BAPC) and publishes about 65 poets in each issue. "*POETALK* is open to all. No particular genre. Rhyme must be well done." *POETALK* is 36 pages, digest-sized, photocopied, saddle-stapled, with heavy card cover. Press run is 400. Subscription: $8/year. Sample: $2.

How to Submit Submit 3-5 poems at a time, no more than twice/year. Lines/poem: under 35 preferred; longer poems of outstanding quality considered. Considers previously published poems and simultaneous submissions, but must be noted. Cover letter is preferred. Include SASE. "Manuscripts should be clearly typed, single-spaced, and include author's name and mailing address on every page. Include e-mail address if you have one." Usually responds in up to 6 months. Pays 1 contributor's copy. All rights revert to author upon publication.

Contest/Award Offerings Sponsors yearly contest. **Deadline:** submit October 1-November 15 (postmark). Guidelines available in early September for SASE, by e-mail, or see posting on Web site.

Also Offers Bay Area Poets Coalition holds monthly readings (in Berkeley, CA). BAPC has 150 members. BAPC Membership: $15/year (includes subscription to *POETALK* and other privileges); extra outside U.S.

Advice "If you don't want suggested revisions, you need to say so clearly in your cover letter or indicate on each poem submitted."

⊞ ◻ ◎ POETIC HOURS (Specialized: subscriptions encouraged; raises money for charity)

43 Willow Rd., Carlton, Nolts NG4 3BH England. E-mail: erranpublishing@hotmail.com. Web site:

www.poetichours.homestead.com. Established 1993. **Contact:** Nicholas Clark, editor.

Magazine Needs *Poetic Hours*, published semiannually, aims "to encourage and publish new poets, i.e., as a forum where good but little known poets can appear in print; and **to raise money for third world and other charities**. *Poetic Hours* features articles and poetry by subscribers and others." Wants "any subject; rhyme preferred but not essential; suitable for wide-ranging readership." Does not want "gothic, horror, extremist, political, self-interested." *Poetic Hours* is 40 pages, A4, saddle-stapled. Receives about 500 poems/year, accepts about 40%. Press run is about 400. Subscription: £7 sterling; overseas payments in sterling (Europe and EC) or U.S. dollars ($20 from U.S. or Canada). Subscribe online from Web site or send bankers checks (UK only) or cash. Sample: £3.75. Make checks payable to Erran Publishing.

How to Submit Submit 3-4 poems at a time. Lines/poem: 30 maximum. Considers previously published poems; no simultaneous submissions. Accepts e-mail (preferred; pasted into body of message) and disk (non-returnable) submissions. Cover letter is required. "Poets are encouraged to subscribe or buy a single copy, though not required." Time between acceptance and publication is 3 months. "Poems are read by editors and, if found suitable, are used." Always comments on rejected poems. Responds "within a week, whenever possible." Acquires one-time rights.

Additional Information *Poetic Hours* is non-profit-making; all proceeds go to various charities, particularly well-building and children's charities. A page of each issue is set aside for reporting how money is spent.

Also Offers Poetic Hours Online (www.poetichours.homestead.com/PoeticHoursOnline.html) features original content **by invitation of editor only.**

Advice "We welcome newcomers and invite those just starting out to have the courage to submit work. The art of poetry has moved from the hands of book publishers down the ladder to the new magazines. This is where all the best poetry is found."

POETIC LOGIC (Specialized: FL resident poets; renga; radio feature)

E-mail: poeticlogic@earthlink.net. Web site: www.wmfe.org Established 2002. **Contact:** Sara Schlossman, producer/editor; Charlene L. Edge, associate reader.

Magazine Needs *Poetic Logic* is a "radio feature that runs on National Public Radio (NPR) Affiliate WMFE 90.7FM. We feature poets from the central Florida listening area and poets who are visiting our state for a reading, teaching position, book tour, vacation, etc. We have had U.S. Poets Laureate and many internationally known poets on our program in addition to Florida's resident poets." Considers poetry by children and teens, "but if child is under 11th-grade level, work must be submitted by teacher on behalf of student." Has featured poetry by Teri Witek, Ilyse Kesnetz, Terry Godbey, Mark Jarman, Philip F. Deaver, Billy Collins. Also maintains extensive audio archives going back to inception of program.

How to Submit Submit 5 poems at a time. Lines/poem: prefers no more than 40. Considers previously published poems and simultaneous submissions. E-mail submissions ONLY; pasted into body of message. Cover letter is preferred. Include short bio. Reads submissions year round "but slower in summer and in winter holiday season." Submit seasonal poems 2 months in advance. Time between acceptance and publication is 1-3 months. Sometimes comments on rejected poems. Guidelines available on Web site. Responds in 2-4 months. Acquires electronic rights. "We like to post a printed version of chosen poem(s) on our Web site for 1 week; all rights revert to author."

Also Offers "The *Poetic Logic* Renga Chain began in April of 2005 and is still going strong. Contributors sign up, are assigned a sequence number, and when their number is up, compose a tanka to link with the previous contributor's work. The Renga is open to all Florida residents. Guidelines for joining this work-in-progress are on the Web site. For submissions from outside the listening area: we now accept submissions from across the U.S. for *Poetic Logic* to be posted on our Web site. Same submission guidelines as above."

Advice "Read the work of the poets we have listed as it shows our broad spectrum of preferences."

POETIC MATRIX, A PERIODIC LETTER

P.O. Box 1223, Madera CA 93639. (559)673-9402. E-mail: poeticmatrix@yahoo.com. Web site: www.poeticmatrix.com. Established 1997 in Yosemite. **Contact:** John Peterson, editor/publisher.

Magazine Needs *Poetic Matrix, a periodic letteR*, published 2 times/year online, seeks poetry that "creates a 'place in which we can live' rather than telling us about the place; poetry that draws from the imaginal mind and is rich in the poetic experience—hence the poetic matrix." Does not want poetry that talks about the experience. Has published poetry by Lyn Lifshin, Tony White, Gail Entrekin, James Downs, Joan Michelson, and Brandon Cesmat.

How to Submit Accepts e-mail submissions (pasted into body of message, no attachments). Guidelines available by e-mail or on Web site. Acquires one-time rights.

Additional Information "*Poetic Matrix* has a call for manuscripts for the Slim Volume Series every 2 years. See Web site for when reading dates are set and for additional guidelines and awards. The Slim Volume Series is for manuscripts of 65-75 pages." **Charges reading fee of $17.**

Advice "We seek writing of quality, with passion and intelligence."

◎ POETICA MAGAZINE, REFLECTIONS OF JEWISH THOUGHT

P.O. Box 11014, Norfolk VA 23517. Fax: (757)399-3936. E-mail: poeticamag@aol.com. Web site: www.poeticamagazine.com. Established 2002. **Contact:** Michal Mahgerefteh, publisher/editor.

Magazine Needs *Poetica Magazine, Reflections of Jewish Thought*, published 3 times/year, offers "an outlet for the many writers who draw from their Jewish backgrounds and experiences to create poetry/prose/short stories, giving both emerging and recognized writers the opportunity to share their work with the larger community." Does not want long pieces, haiku, rhyming poetry. Considers poetry by children and teens, grades 6-12. *Poetica* is 64 pages, digest-sized, desktop-published, saddle-stapled, with glossy cardstock cover with b&w art, includes some ads. Receives about 500 poems/year, accepts about 60%. Press run is 350. Single copy: $5; subscription: $14.

How to Submit Submit 3 poems at a time. Lines/poem: 2 pages maximum. Considers simultaneous submissions. No e-mail or disk submissions. Cover letter is optional. Reads submissions year round. Time between acceptance and publication is 1 year. Seldom comments on rejected poems. Occasionally publishes theme issues. Guidelines available for SASE or on Web site. Responds in 1 month. Pays 1 contributor's copy. Poet retains all rights.

Contest/Award Offerings Offers annual poetry contest with up to $50 awarded for First Prize; up to 5 Honorable Mentions. Selected poems will be published in future issues of *Poetica*. Accepts simultaneous submissions. No limit on number of entries (3 poems constitute an entry). Submit 2 copies of each poem, single-spaced, no more than 1 poem/page. Include poet's name on all pages. No e-mail submissions. Include SASE for results only; mss will not be returned. Guidelines available on Web site. **Entry fee:** $12 for up to 3 poems. **Deadline:** March 31 annually. Judge: Jane Ellen Glasser. Notifies winners by June.

Advice "'A fierce light beats upon the Jew'—reflect it in your writings. Tikun Olam is encouraged."

$⊡ POETRY

444 N. Michigan Ave., Suite 1850, Chicago IL 60611. E-mail: poetry@poetrymagazine.org (send Letters to the Editor to editors@poetrymagazine.org). Web site: www.poetrymagazine.org. Established 1912. **Contact:** The Editors.

● Work published in *Poetry* is frequently included in *The Best American Poetry* and *The Pushcart Prize: Best of the Small Presses.*

Magazine Needs *Poetry*, published monthly by The Poetry Foundation (see separate listing in Organizations), "has no special manuscript needs and no special requirements as to form or genre: We examine in turn all work received and accept that which seems best." Has published poetry by the major voices of our time as well as new talent. *Poetry* is 5½×9, elegantly printed, flat-spined. Receives 90,000 submissions/year, accepts about 300-350. Press run is 16,000. Single copy: $3.75; subscription: $35 ($38 for institutions). Sample: $5.50.

How to Submit Submit no more than 4 poems at a time. No previously published poems or simultaneous submissions. Electronic submission preferred. When submitting by post put return address on outside of envelope; include SASE. Submissions must be typed, single-spaced, with poet's name and address on every page. Guidelines available for SASE. Responds in 1-2 months. Pays $10/line (with a minimum payment of $150). Reviews books of poetry in multi-book formats of varying lengths. Does not accept unsolicited reviews.

Contest/Award Offerings 7 prizes (Bess Hokin Prize, Levinson Prize, Frederick Bock Prize, J. Howard and Barbara M.J. Wood Prize, John Frederick Nims Memorial Prize, Friends of Literature Prize, Union League Civic and Arts Poetry Prize) ranging from $300 to $5,000 are awarded annually to poets whose work has appeared in the magazine that year. Only verse already published in *Poetry* is eligible for consideration; no formal application is necessary.

Also Offers *Poetry*'s Web site offers featured poems, letters, reviews, interviews, essays, and Web-exclusive features.

THE POETRY CHURCH MAGAZINE (Specialized: subscribers only; Christian)

Feather Books, P.O. Box 438, Shrewsbury SY3 0WN England. Phone/fax: 44 (0)1743 872177. E-mail: john@waddysweb.freeuk.com. (inquiries only). Web site: www.waddysweb.freeuk.com. Established 1982 (Feather Books); 1996 (*The Poetry Church Magazine*). **Contact:** Rev. John Waddington-Feather, editor.

Magazine Needs *The Poetry Church Magazine*, published quarterly, contains Christian poetry, prayers, and hymns. Wants "Christian or good religious poetry." Does not want "unreadable blasphemy." **Publishes subscribers' work only.** Considers poetry by children over age 10. Has published poetry by Laurie Bates, Joan Sheridan Smith, Idris Caffrey, Isabella Strachan, Walter Nash, and Susan Glyn. *The Poetry Church Magazine* is 40 pages, digest-sized, photocopied, saddle-stapled, with illustrated cover. Receives about 1,000 poems/year, accepts about 500. Press run is 1,000. Single copy: free; subscription: £12 for 4 issues ($20 USD). Make checks payable in sterling to Feather Books. Payment can also be made through Web site.

How to Submit Submit 2 poems at a time. Lines/poem: usually around 20, "but will accept longer." Considers previously published poems and simultaneous submissions. Cover letter is preferred (with information about the poet). No e-mail submissions; postal submissions only. Include SASE, or SAE and IRC. Submissions must be typed. **Publishes "only subscribers' poems as they keep us solvent."** Time between acceptance and publication is 4 months. "The editor does a preliminary reading, then seeks the advice of colleagues about uncertain poems." Responds within 1 week. Poets retain copyright.

Additional Information Feather Books publishes the Feather Books Poetry Series, collections of around 20 Christian poems and prayers. Has recently published the Glyn family, Walter Nash, David Grieve, and Rosie Morgan Barry. "We have now published 300 poetry collections by individual Christian poets." Books are usually photocopied, saddle-stapled, with illustrated covers. "We do not insist, but **most poets pay for their work. Enquire for current costs.** If they can't afford it, but are good poets, we stand the cost. We expect poets to read *The Poetry Church Magazine* to get some idea of our standards."

Also Offers Each winter and summer, selected poems appear in *The Poetry Church Collection*, the leading Christian poetry anthology used in churches and schools.

Advice "We find it better for poets to master rhyme and rhythm before trying free verse. Many poets seem to think that if they write 'down' a page they're writing poetry, when all they're doing is writing prose in a different format. But good free verse is accpted."

POETRY INTERNATIONAL

Dept. of English & Comparative Literature, San Diego State University, 5500 Campanile Dr., San Diego CA 92182-8140. (619)594-1522. Fax: (619)594-4998. E-mail: poetryinternational@rohan.sdsu .edu. Web site: http://poetryinternational.sdsu.edu. Established 1996. **Contact:** Fred Moramarco, editor.

Magazine Needs *Poetry International*, published annually in November, is "an eclectic poetry magazine intended to reflect a wide range of poetry being written today." Wants "a wide range of styles and subject matter. We're particularly interested in translations." Does not want "cliché-ridden, derivative, or obscure poetry." Has published poetry by Adrienne Rich, Robert Bly, Hayden Carruth, Kim Addonizio, Maxine Kumin, and Gary Soto. *Poetry International* is 200 pages, perfect-bound, with coated cardstock cover. Press run is 1,500. Single copy: $12; subscription: $24/2 years (plus s&h).

How to Submit Submit up to 5 poems at a time. Considers simultaneous submissions, "but prefer not to''; no previously published poems. No fax or e-mail submissions. Reads submissions September 1-30 only. Time between acceptance and publication is 8 months. Poems are circulated to an editorial board. Seldom comments on rejected poems. Responds in up to 4 months. Pays 2 contributor's copies. Acquires all rights. Returns rights ''50/50,'' meaning they split with the author any payment for reprinting the poem elsewhere. ''We review anthologies regularly.''

Advice ''We're interested in new work by poets who are devoted to their art. We want poems that matter—that make a difference in people's lives. We're especially seeking good translations and prose by poets about poetry.''

⊕ ☑ POETRY KANTO

Kanto Gakuin University, Kamariya-cho 3-22-1, Kanazawa-ku, Yokohama 236-8502 Japan. E-mail: alan@kanto-gakuin.ac.jp. Web site: http://home.kanto-gakuin.ac.jp/∼kg061001/. Established 1984 by William I. Elliott. **Contact:** Alan Botsford, editor.

Magazine Needs *Poetry Kanto*, published annually in October by the Kanto Gakuin University, is Japan's leading annual bilingual, bicultural poetry magazine. Features ''outstanding poetry that navigates the divide of ocean and language. We seek exciting, well-crafted contemporary poetry in English, and also encourage and publish high-quality English translations of modern and emerging Japanese poets. All translations must be accompanied by the original poems.'' See Web site for sample poems. Has published poetry by Harryette Mullen, Ilya Kaminsky, Beth Ann Fennelly, Vijay Seshadri, Michael S. Collins, Mari L'Esperance, Michael Sowder, and Sarah Arvio. *Poetry Kanto* is 120 pages, 6×9, professionally printed on coated stock, perfect-bound, with glossy cover. Press run is 1,000; many are distributed free to schools, poets, and presses. The magazine is unpriced. Sample: send SAE with IRCs.

How to Submit Submit 5 poems at a time maximum. No previously published poems or simultaneous submissions. Prefers e-mail submissions (as attachment in Word). Cover letter is required. Include brief bio. All postal submissions require SAE and IRCs. Reads submissions December-April. Guidelines available on Web site. Pays 3-5 contributor's copies.

Advice ''From forebears, learn; from the future, write; in the present, live.''

☑ POETRY NORTHWEST

4232 SE Hawthorne Blvd., Portland OR 97215. (503)236-0615. E-mail: editors@poetrynw.org. Web site: www.poetrynw.org. Established 1959. **Contact:** David Biespiel, editor.

Magazine Needs *Poetry Northwest* is published semiannually in March and October. ''The mission of *Poetry Northwest* is to publish the best poetry written in English. In the words of founding editor Carolyn Kizer, we aim to 'encourage the young and the inexperienced, the neglected mature, and the rough major talents and the fragile minor ones.' All styles and aesthetics will find consideration.'' Has published poetry by Theodore Roethke, Czeslaw Milosz, Anne Sexton, Harold Pinter, Thom Gunn, and Philip Larkin. *Poetry Northwest* is 40+ pages, magazine-sized, Web press-printed, saddle-stapled, with 4-color cover, includes ads. Receives about 10,000 poems/year, accepts about 1%. Press run is 2,000. Single copy: $8. Sample: $9. Make checks payable to *Poetry Northwest*.

How to Submit Submit 4 poems at a time maximum. No previously published poems or simultaneous submissions. No e-mail or disk submissions. Cover letter is required. Time between acceptance and publication is 2 months. Sometimes comments on rejected poems. Sometimes publishes theme issues. Upcoming themes available in magazine or by e-mail. Guidelines available on Web site. Responds in 4-6 weeks (''except during July and August; submissions sent during these months will be considered in September''). Always sends prepublication galleys. Pays 2 contributor's copies. Acquires all rights. Returns rights to poets upon request. Reviews books of poetry in single- and multi-book format.

⊕ ☑ POETRY NOTTINGHAM

11 Orkney Close, Stenson Fields, Derbyshire DE24 3LW England. Established 1946. Web site: http://nottinghampoetrysociety.co.uk. **Contact:** Adrian Buckner, editor.

Magazine Needs *Poetry Nottingham*, published 3 times/year, features articles and reviews in addition to poetry. Open to submissions from UK and overseas. Has published poetry from Europe,

Australasia, the U.S., and Japan. *Poetry Nottingham* is 6×8, perfect-bound, professionally printed. Receives about 2,000 submissions/year, accepts about 120. Press run is 250. Single copy: £4; subscription: £12 UK, £20 overseas. Checks payable to Poetry Nottingham Publications. Subscribers who wish to pay in U.S. dollars please send check for $25, payable to Karen Crosbie, to 1036 Menlo Avenue, Apt 103, Los Angeles, CA, 90006. Single copy $7.

How to Submit Submit up to 6 poems at a time. No previously published poems. Cover letter is required. "Send SAE and 3 IRCs for stamps. No need to query." Responds in 2 months. Pays 1 contributor's copy. Staff reviews books of poetry, usually confined to UK publications.

Contest/Award Offerings The Nottingham Open Poetry Competition offers cash prizes, annual subscriptions, and publication in *Poetry Nottingham*. Open to all. Guidelines available on Web site.

Advice "We seek to provide an uncluttered environment for poems of wit, poems of concise lyrical intensity, and poems that are bold enough to expand on a theme."

POETRY NOW

1719 25th St., Sacramento CA 95816.916-451-5569. E-mail: grahampoet@aol.com. Web site: http://sacramentopoetrycenter.org. Contact: Frank Dixon Graham, editor.

Magazine Needs *Poetry Now* is published about 10 times per year, "in newsletter style, with some graphic art design work. The publication serves the members of the Sacramento Poetry Center and other interested readers. Poetry now is frequently available on the poetry center's Web site in a downloadable format. The newsletter includes a calendar of local events, reviews, interviews, and poetry." Wants all styles and forms of poetry. "Accepts work primarily from the Northern California poets, but will take a look at poets elsewhere." Has published poetry by Francisco Alarcon, Alice Anderson, Quinton Duvall, Bob Stanley, Joyce Odam, and Allegra Silberstein. Receives about 300 poems/year, accepts about 40%. Press run suits the demand of membership with some extra copies for bookstore distribution. Membership to the Poetry Center, with a subscription of *Poetry Now* and its sister publication, *Tule Review*, is $30.

How to Submit Submit a few poems at a time, generally no more than 1-page poems. Looking for unpublished work, but will consider previously published work by writers with a published collection or book of poems. Prefer to receive e-mail submissions with a brief bio, no cover letter necessary. Reads submissions year round. Time of acceptance is up to 60 days.

Contest/Award Offerings SPC has an annual poetry contest: deadline is usually in January/February. Check with the newsletter to find details.

Advice "Study the works of poets you love. Attend a group meeting of experienced and published poets, like Sacramento Poetry Center's workshop. Find your genre, submit often, and keep the faith."

POETRY SALZBURG REVIEW

University of Salzburg, Dept. of English, Akademiestrasse 24, Salzburg A-5020 Austria. (43)(662)8044-4422. Fax: (43)(662)8044-167. E-mail: editor@poetrysalzburg.com. Web site: www.poetrysalzburg.com. Established 2001. **Contact:** Dr. Wolfgang Goertschacher, editor.

Magazine Needs *Poetry Salzburg Review*, published twice/year, contains "articles on poetry, mainly contemporary, and 60 percent poetry. Also includes essays on poetics, review-essays, interviews, artwork, and translations. We tend to publish selections by authors who have not been taken up by the big poetry publishers. Nothing of poor quality." Has published poetry by Paul Muldoon, Alice Notley, Samuel Menashe. *Poetry Salzburg Review* is about 200 pages, A5, professionally printed, perfect-bound, with illustrated card cover. Receives about 5,000 poems/year, accepts 5%. Press run is 500. Single copy: $12; subscription: $22 (cash preferred; subscribers can also pay with PayPal). Make checks payable to Wolfgang Goertschacher. "No requirements, but it's a good idea to subscribe to *Poetry Salzburg Review*."

How to Submit No previously published poems or simultaneous submissions. Accepts e-mail submissions (as attachment). Time between acceptance and publication is 6 months. Seldom comments on rejected poems. Occasionally publishes theme issues. Responds in 2 months. No payment. Acquires first rights. Reviews books/chapbooks of poetry as well as books on poetics. Send materials for review consideration.

▣ ◉ POETRYBAY

P.O. Box 114, Northport NY 11768. (631)427-1950. Fax: (631)367-0038. E-mail: poetrybay@aol.c om. Web site: www.poetrybay.com. Established 2000. **Contact:** George Wallace, editor.

Magazine Needs *Poetrybay*, published semiannually online, seeks ''to add to the body of great contemporary American poetry by presenting the work of established and emerging writers. Also, we consider essays and reviews.'' Has published poetry by Robert Bly, Yevgeny Yevtushenko, Marvin Bell, Diane Wakoski, Cornelius Eady, and William Heyen.

How to Submit Submit 5 poems at a time. Considers simultaneous submissions; no previously published poems. Accepts e-mail submissions (pasted into body of message); no disk submissions. Time between acceptance and publication is 2 months. Seldom comments on rejected poems. Occasionally publishes theme issues. Guidelines available on Web site. Sometimes sends prepublication galleys. Acquires first-time electronic rights. Reviews books/chapbooks of poetry and other magazines/journals. Send materials for review consideration.

⚔ ◪ THE POET'S ART (Specialized: family-friendly writing)

171 Silverleaf Lane, Islandia NY 11749. (631)439-0427. E-mail: davidirafox@yahoo.com. (inquiries only). Established 2000. **Contact:** David Fox, editor.

Magazine Needs *The Poet's Art*, published quarterly, is ''a family-style journal, accepting work from the unpublished to the well known and all levels in between.'' Wants ''family-friendly, positive poetry; any form considered. Topics include humor, nature, religion, inspirational, children's poetry, or anything else that fits the family-friendly genre.'' Does not want ''violent, vulgar, or overly depressing work. Work is read and accepted by the mentally-ill population, but they should keep in mind this is a family-friendly journal.'' Considers poetry by children and teens, ''any age, as long as it's good quality; if under 18, get parents' permission.'' Has published poetry by Anselm Brocki, Susan Carole, Peter Layton, Mary L. Ports, Melanie Monterey Eyth, and Amber Rothrock. *The Poet's Art* is 40 or more pages, magazine-sized, photocopied, paper-clipped or stapled, with computer cover, includes ads. Receives about 100 poems a year, accepts about 50%. Press run is 30 + . ''Due to limited supplies, only those who submit or whose review is accepted receive a copy; foreign contributors must pay for a copy. (There are no samples or subscriptions offered by this magazine.)''

How to Submit Submit ''as many poems that will fit on 1 page'' at a time (''you can submit more, if compelled to do so; extra accepted pieces will be spread over a few issues''). Lines/poem: rarely accepts anything over 1 page. Considers simultaneous submissions (''list any other small press journals (if any) poems titles''). No e-mail or disk submissions; postal submissions only. Cover letter is preferred. ''It's only polite. And include a SASE—a must! (I have been lax in this rule about SASEs, but I will now throw any submissions without a SASE away!)'' Reads submissions year round, ''but poets should be aware we are currently backlogged into December of 2009, as of this listing. I review all poems submitted and then decide what I wish to publish.'' Never comments on rejected poems. Reviews chapbooks of poetry and other magazines/journals, ''but editors and authors must write reviews themselves. After all, who knows your magazine/journal or chapbook better than you? (Little-known/newer journals sent in by editors or contributors get first consideration for reviews).'' Send to David Fox.

Advice ''We enjoy and value loyalty, but remember to send your work out to as many magazines/ journals as you can. Poetry is meant to be shared. Family-friendly poetry for this journal, please!''

⚏ ▣ ◉ POET'S ESPRESSO

P.O. Box 121, Farmington CA 95230. E-mail: poetsespresso@yahoo.com. Web site: www.poetsespr esso.com. Established 2005. **Contact:** Donald R. Anderson and Nikki Quismondo, co-editors/co-publishers.

• Received 7.0 out of 10 rating from www.neufutur.com. for June/July 2007 issue.

Magazine Needs *Poet's Espresso*, published bimonthly online and in print, is ''a small black and white publication of poetry, art, photography, recipes, and local events.'' Sponsored by the Writers' Guild, a club of San Joaquin Delta College. ''We value variety, appropriateness for most age groups, and poetry that goes well with the season of the issue.'' Does not want ''profanity, racially prejudiced, or otherwise offensive material. Or submissions that are excessively long." Considers poetry by children and teens. "Please include contact info of parent if from a minor." Has published poetry by Marie J. Ross, Nikki Quismondo, and others. *Poet's Espresso* (print edition) is 24-28 pages, digest-sized, printed "on College's industrial printers," stapled, with colored paper cover with b&w photograph/artwork, includes ads ("which are free and only if associated with us"). Accepts about 90 poems/year. Press run is 500+; 450+ distributed free in the Central Valley, Sacramento, and Bay Areas (to coffee shops, colleges, bookstores, and restaurants). Number of unique visitors (online): "small count with rapid growth." Single copy: $1.50; subscription: $7/year (6 issues). Sample: free in return for online or published review. Make checks payable to Donald Anderson.

How to Submit Submit "as many poems as you wish" at a time. Lines/poem: "from quote-size up to 80." Considers previously published poems and simultaneous submissions. (Considers poems posted on public Web site/blog/forum and/or on private, password-protected forum as previously published.) Accepts e-mail (as attachment in MS Word [.doc], MS Works [.wps], rich text [.rtf], or notepad [.txt] formats) and disk submissions; no fax submissions. "If postal submissions, submit copies, not originals. Include SASE." Cover letter is unnecessary. "A 2 to 4 line biography about the poet is required, written in third person. Biography photo is optional. You may include info for readers to contact you, if you wish. You may include biography text or photo(s) in postal submission or in e-mail." Reads submissions year round. "Deadline for submissions are on the 22nd-25th of the month prior to the issue." Submit seasonal poems 1 week in advance. Time between acceptance and publication is up to 2 months. "The co-editors decide on submissions based upon space and meeting the guidelines." Sometimes comments on rejected poems. Regularly publishes theme issues. Guidelines available for SASE, by e-mail, or on Web site. Responds in up to 2 months. Sometimes sends prepublication galleys (upon request). Pays 1 contributor's copy (maybe more, if by request). Acquires one-time rights for print edition; acquires electronic rights "to keep an archived issue available online indefinitely in the future." Rights revert to poets upon publication ("rights remain with author to publish in any way; rights are given to *Poet's Espresso* for indefinite archive on Web site and 1 issue of the newsletter"). Reviews books/chapbooks of poetry and other magazines/journals in single- or multi-book format. Send materials for review consideration by e-mail or to Donald R. Anderson and Nikki Quismondo by postal mail.

Additional Information "If you have a collection of poetic works that you wish to submit, we will consider them for publishing in paperback black and white (or more costly color) book form. However, we cannot afford to pay our contributors at this time, and global distribution and copies of the book are an expense that needs discussion prior to acceptance. For info on other works we have published, please visit the Web site for the book Sun Shadow Mountain at www.sunshadowmountain.com."

Advice "Help the reader visualize the scene or story in your poem. If a word or line can be left out and still achieve the effect you want, then it probably needs to be."

▣ ◯ THE POET'S HAVEN

Web site: www.PoetsHaven.com. Established 1997. **Contact:** Vertigo Xi'an Xavier, publisher.

Magazine Needs *The Poet's Haven* is a Web site "featuring poetry, artwork, stories, reviews, essays, and much more." Wants work that's "emotional, personal, and intimate with the author or subject. Topics can cover just about anything." Does not want "material that is obscene, excessively vulgar, pornographic, racist, or religious." Has published poetry by Danielle Briganti, Jacob Erin-Cilberto, Rebecca Guile Hudson, Elisha Porat, and Katherine Zaleski. Work published on *The Poet's Haven* is left on the site permanently. Receives about 1,000 poems/year, accepts about 80%.

How to Submit Considers previously published poems and simultaneous submissions. Accepts submissions through online form only. Time between acceptance and publication is about 2 weeks. Never comments on rejected poems. Guidelines available on Web site. No payment for online publication; pays 1 contributor's copy for print edition. Acquires rights to publish on the Web site permanently and in any future print publications. Poet retains rights to have poems published elsewhere, "provided the other publishers do not require first-time or exclusive rights."

Additional Information Has published print editions as *The Poet's Haven Digest*. On indefinite hiatus as of April 2007. Check Web site for updated information or to order sample copies.

Also Offers Message forums, chat room, publisher's blog, open-mic events, a podcast, and Web site hosting for authors and artists.

▣ ◯ POET'S INK

E-mail: poet_Kelly@yahoo.com. Web site: www.PoetsInk.com. Established 2005. **Contact:** Kelly Morris.

Magazine Needs *Poet's Ink*, published monthly online, seeks "poetry of all kinds. Work by new poets is published alongside that of more experienced poets." Does not want "bad rhyme, clichés, poetry riddled with abstractions." Considers poetry by teens. "Will be judged by the same standards as poetry by adults." Has published poetry by Alexandria Webb, Julie Allen, Colin Baker, Jessica Healy, and Shelby Norris. Receives about 150 poems/year, accepts about 20%.

How to Submit Submit 3-5 poems at a time. Lines/poem: 2 minimum, 100 maximum ("longer poems better not be long-winded!"). Considers previously published poems and simultaneous submissions. Accepts e-mail submissions (as attachment); no disk submissions. Cover letter is preferred. "No funky formatting of poems!" Reads submissions year round. Time between acceptance and publication is 1 month. Often comments on rejected poems. Sometimes publishes theme issues. Guidelines available by e-mail or on Web site. Responds in 1-2 weeks. Acquires one-time rights. Rights revert to poets upon publication.

Advice "Read guidelines carefully before submitting. Take advantage of all the advice you get, but also follow your heart."

▣ ⊕ ✒ POETS ON THE LINE

P.O. Box 20292, Brooklyn NY 11202-0292. E-mail: llerner@mindspring.com. Web site: www.echon yc.com/~poets. Established 1995 (founded by Andrew Gettler and Linda Lerner). **Contact:** Linda Lerner, editor.

• **Currently not accepting unsolicited work.**

✒ ◎ THE POET'S PEN (Specialized: members/subscribers preferred)

The Society of American Poets (SOAP), 6500 Clito Road, Statesboro GA 30461. (912)587-4400. E-mail: DrRev@msn.com. Established 1984. **Contact:** Dr. Charles E. Cravey, editor.

Magazine Needs *The Poet's Pen*, published quarterly by The Society of American Poets, is "open to all styles of poetry and prose—both religious and secular." Does not want "gross or 'X-rated' poetry without taste or character." Has published poetry by Najwa Salam Brax, Henry Goldman, Henry W. Gurley, William Heffner, Linda Metcalf, and Charles Russ. *The Poet's Pen* uses poetry **primarily by members and subscribers**, but outside submissions are also welcome. Subscription: included in membership, $30/year ($25 for students). Sample: $10.

How to Submit Submit 3 poems at a time/quarter. Considers simultaneous submissions and previously published poems, if permission from previous publisher is included. Include name and address on each page. "Submissions or inquiries will not be responded to without a #10 business-sized SASE. We do stress originality and have each new poet and/or subscriber sign a waiver form verifying originality." Publishes seasonal/theme issues. Guidelines available in magazine, for SASE, or by e-mail. Sometimes sends prepublication galleys. Always comments on rejected poems.

Contest/Award Offerings Sponsors several contests each quarter, with prizes totaling $100-250. Also offers Editor's Choice Awards each quarter. The President's Award for Excellence is a prize of $50. **Deadline:** November 1. Also publishes a quarterly anthology from poetry competitions in several categories with prizes of $25-100. Guidelines available for SASE or by e-mail.

Advice "Be honest with yourself above all else. Read the greats over and again and study styles, grammar, and what makes each unique. Meter, rhythm, and rhyme are still the guidelines that are most acceptable today."

✪ ⧓ ◯ POETS' PODIUM (Specialized: subscribers given priority)

2-3265 Front Rd., E. Hawksbury ON K6A 2R2 Canada. E-mail: kennyel@hotmail.com. Web site: http://geocities.com/poetspodium/. Established 1993. **Contact:** Ken Elliott, Catherine Heaney Barrowcliffe, Robert Piquette, or Ron Barrowcliffe, associate editors.

The Prose Poem

Fish or fowl?

The prose poem seems to be a contradiction in terms and remains an oddity to many, even though its history is long and vigorous. The discussion in *The New Princeton Encyclopedia of Poetry and Poetics* (Princeton University Press) stresses its French antecedents and hybrid nature. Some critics suggest a much older origin, citing Greek poetics and fragments from Sappho. Whatever their source, prose poems flourish in contemporary literary journals, where you can find a diverse group of excellent models.

In elementary school, many of us were taught to recognize a poem by its vertical orientation on the page and its linear birth, composed line by line rather than sentence by sentence. (Alas, many teachers added rhyme as a requisite, thus sending forth generations of children who grew up thinking poems weren't poems unless they appeared in rhyming stanzas.)

Because certain identifiers were so ingrained, many readers still balk at the idea of paragraphs as poetry. Charles Simic, the current U.S. Poet Laureate, wrote, "The prose poem has the unusual distinction of being regarded with suspicion not only by the usual haters of poetry, but also by many poets themselves."

Rather than ambiguous paradox, prose poems in fact contain all the density, resonance and impact of any other poem—that is, the good ones do. True, they refuse to live on tidy shelves in the poetry closet with neat labels. They challenge our idea of what poetry is supposed to be. Creatures of habit, we are out of kilter in their clutches

Do you always choose a seat in the same theater section? Do you always park on the west side of the mall, or sit in the same pew? Do you feel slightly off-center if that space is taken? It's because your orientation is now changed. Things you "knew before" are no longer part of your support base; comfort levels clank to the bottom of the well.

Prose poems contain all the elements and conventions of poetry except one: the line. Because poets are accustomed to working with the line, relying on its flexibility, considering the weight of end words, the effects of various line break options, and opportunities for multiple meanings, doing away with line work altogether is a little like stepping into space.

Think of a tall building with many windows. You are a literary Peeping Tom, notebook in hand, traveling in your private, silent hovercraft. Up you go—but there's a problem. By the time you catch a glimpse inside one window, you are already passing by another, then veering around the corner to yet another. And thus prose poems are built, a window for each; but the view is limited to a partially revealed world. Every prose poem establishes its own habitat, its own theater and voice. Poets and readers alike hopefully enjoy being surprised by its many possibilities, enough to return for another visit. It's almost a funhouse, where readers are lured through mirrors by the trickster coyote-in-residence.

Professor and ethicist Michael Bugeja, author of many books including the classic *The Art and Craft of Poetry* (Writer's Digest Books), reminds us that prose structure emerges from sentences and paragraphs in a self-contained unit. He defines the prose poem as "a short, textured piece of writing without the added meaning derived from lines and stanzas." Like other poems it can be lyric, dramatic or narrative in nature. It can be written as a single paragraph, a longer piece with dialogue and multiple voices, or even in sequences, such as in Bob Collén's series of postcard poems.

Poets using the form include Robert Hass, Charles Simic, James Tate, Robert Bly, Russell Edson, Pablo Neruda, Campbell McGrath, John Ashbery, Naomi Shihab Nye; and the earlier poets Beaudelaire, Rimbaud, Turgenev and Poe. Even as they resume prominence on the literary stage, prose poems become changelings under the gifted pens of emerging writers. Recent collections include *Great American Prose Poems: From Poe to the Present*, edited by David Lehman (Scribner); *Boxing Inside the Box: Women's Prose Poetry*, edited by Holly Iglesias (Quale Press); and *No Boundaries: Prose Poems by 24 American Poets*, edited by Ray Gonzalez (Tupelo Press). A study of Arabic prose poets, *The Prose Poem and the Journal Shi'r*, is newly published in the U.K. by Orared Haidar. And I must mention Peter Johnson, who led the way into the forest of small press journals, where he championed the form and devoted a journal to it, one I wish would be resurrected.

What makes a prose poem distinctly a poem? Prose poems refuse to line up as a matched set, but they often do share certain characteristics. Sonic and visual effects are important. You will encounter tensions, something at stake. Imagery may be impressionistic but must be strong, as are rhythms. Length is variable, but generally short. I am reminded of watercolors, dreamscapes and jazz riffs. Prose poems seem closer to improvisation than to more formal structures such as the concerto, villanelle or even DNA—but do not be misled. They are not for the lazy writer.

Some poets craft surreal work, while others choose sharper edges and stark, theatrical realism; that is, not true realism but a composed one, much as fictional dialogue resembles, but is not real conversation. I often feel as though a door opens into someone else's dream, only to have it shut again (with that final punctuation) before I learn the ending. A prose poem often begins *in media res* and closes without explanation, certainly without resolution or "summing up." (Good training for poets, especially for those inclined to over-explain or write the poem and then comment, thus ruining a perfectly good poem by going on too long!)

The line between them may be thin, but in my view a prose poem is not flash fiction because of its charged language and emotional impact. A story line may be present, but as Lyn Lifshin suggests, plot is not necessary. Lyn, whose new books are *Another Woman Who Looks Like Me* (Black Sparrow-David Godine) and *The Licorice Daughter: My Year with Ruffian* (Texas Review Press) says:

In the same way that experimenting with line length—long narrow
poems, a form many think I use often, but also 'heavier' longer
lined, more varied lengths that can give the poem a more rooted,
almost grounded feeling, not as airy, a prose poem can change the
impact, the emphasis, the rhythm—even the focus can shift. Putting
the poem in that form improves some works, takes away from others.
I think it's good to experiment—try the different forms.

Former U.S. Poet Laureate Ted Kooser, in *The Poetry Home Repair Manual* (University of Nebraska Press), speaks of the continuum of writing with technical nonfiction articles on one end, moving along to journalism, where we often follow the writers we admire because of their style or what they tell us about themselves; then to personal narrative and essay, where expert practitioners employ figurative language, analogies and linguistic processes, where speech sounds and rhythms play against one another. Kooser encourages us to recognize the blurring of terms all along this imaginary line. He points out that in all these writings, even the most evocative, a few words changed here or there will not affect the final product to any large extent. But this is not the case with poems in any form, including prose poetry, where diction (word choice), the single syllable, or even spacing are critical decisions for the poet. Kooser says that while formal poems are intimidating to some readers, "we are all so accustomed to the appearance of prose that we enter a prose poem without much fear."

In the writing process, though, Kooser agrees with Lifshin that final form and format may change:

> Sometimes the poem begun in lined-out verse winds
> up as a prose poem, and vice versa. The quality of the
> poetry always counts for more than does the satisfaction
> of a literary shape.

Thinking of Kooser's continuum, I asked personal essay expert Susan Bono (Tiny Lights Publications) what makes the personal essay peculiarly itself rather than a prose poem. She responded, "An essay is about the writer's attempt to come to terms with some question or problem; it requires a shift in perspective as the narrative unfolds. The more a piece of writing focuses on the experience itself . . . the more like poetry it feels."

John Amen, editor of the popular electronic journal, *The Pedestal Magazine* (www.thepedestal magazine.com), had this to say:

> Humans love to create categories, and the prose poem, like most
> hybridizations, reflects an attempt to transcend categorization and
> move beyond rigid parameters. Any writer who has used the form
> has come to it for his or her own stylistic and musical reasons.
> Ultimately, it remains a rebel form and, in this culture at least, rebel
> forms are regarded suspiciously. We at *Pedestal* love to see well hewn
> prose poems; many editors, however, remain strangely (and oftentimes
> secretly) prejudiced against the form, regardless of its illustrious history.

One secret of the creative brain, for scientific or artistic invention of any kind, including the best poetry, is this: At a critical moment, the poet accomplishes art by *seeing* another way and giving us this vision as a gift. Prose poems perform as actors, or jokes, or early-morning dreams; they occupy no box, but they speak in our voices and demand that we listen.

—*Sandra Soli*

Sandra Soli is a freelance writer and editor in Oklahoma City. Her poems have appeared in *The New York Quarterly, Southern Poetry Review, Negative Capability, Ellipsis* and elsewhere. Her work has won or been a finalist for major national competitions and nominated for AWP's Intro Award and the Pushcart Prize. Her chapbooks are *Silvering the Flute* and the newly released *What The Trees Know*.

Magazine Needs *Poets' Podium*, published quarterly, is a newsletter that aims "to promote the reading and writing of the poetic form, especially among those being published for the first time." Poetry specifications are open. "**Priority is given to valued subscribers.** Nevertheless, when there is room in an issue, we will publish nonsubscribers." Does not want poetry that is "gothic, erotic/sexual, gory, bloody, or that depicts violence." Subscription: $10 USD. Sample: $3 USD.

How to Submit Submit 3 poems at a time. Lines/poem: 4 minimum, 25 maximum. Considers previously published poems and simultaneous submissions. Cover letter is required. Include SASE (or SAE and IRC), name, address, and telephone number; e-mail address if applicable. Time between acceptance and publication varies. Guidelines available for SASE (or SAE and IRC), or by fax or by e-mail. Pays 3 contributor's copies. All rights remain with the author.

Advice "Poetry is a wonderful literary form. Try your hand at it. Send us the fruit of your labours."

☆ ☑ THE PORTLAND REVIEW

Portland State University, P.O. Box 347, Portland OR 97207-0347. (503)725-4533. Fax: (503)725-4534. Web site: www.portlandreview.org. Established 1956. **Contact:** Patrick Haas, editor.

Magazine Needs *The Portland Review*, published 3 times/year by Portland State University, seeks "submissions exhibiting a unique and compelling voice, and content of substance. Experimental poetry welcomed." Has published poetry by Gaylord Brewer, Richard Bentley, Charles Jensen, Mary Biddinger, and Jerzy Gizella. *The Portland Review* is about 130 pages. Receives about 1,000 poems/year, accepts about 30. Press run is 1,000 for subscribers, libraries, and bookstores nationwide. Single copy: $9; subscription: $28/year, $54/2 years. Sample: $8.

How to Submit Submit up to 5 poems at a time. Considers simultaneous submissions; no previously published poems. Accepts postal submissions only. Include phone number, e-mail address, and other contact information on ms. Indicate whether you wish ms returned; if so, include SASE (otherwise mss will be recycled automatically). Reads submissions year round except during the months of June, July, and August. Guidelines available for SASE or on Web site. "Our Web site is a general introduction to our magazine, with samples of our poetry, fiction, and art." Responds in up to 4 months. Pays 1 contributor's copy. Acquires first North American rights.

Advice "Include a SASE and specify if submissions need to be returned. Otherwise, they will be recycled."

☑ ◎ POST POEMS (Specialized: poems under 7 lines; poetry postcard series)

Raw Dog Press, 151 S. West St., Doylestown PA 18901-4134. Web site: http://rawdogpress.braveho st.com. Established 1977. **Contact:** R. Gerry Fabian, poetry editor.

Magazine Needs Post Poems, published annually by Raw Dog Press, is a postcard series. Wants "short poetry (3-7 lines) on any subject. The positive poem or the poem of understated humor always has an inside track. No taboos, however. All styles considered. Anything with rhyme had better be immortal." Has published poetry by Don Ryan, John Grey, and the editor, R. Gerry Fabian. Send SASE for catalog to buy samples.

How to Submit Submit 3-5 poems at a time. Lines/poem: 3-7. Cover letter is optional. SASE is required. Always comments on rejected poems. Guidelines available on Web site. Pays in contributor's copies. Acquires all rights. Returns rights on mention of first publication. Sometimes reviews books of poetry.

Additional Information Raw Dog Press welcomes new poets and detests second-rate poems from "name" poets. "We exist because we are dumb like a fox, but even a fox takes care of its own." Send SASE for catalog to buy samples.

Also Offers Offers criticism for a fee; "if someone is desperate to publish and is willing to pay, we will use our vast knowledge to help steer the manuscript in the right direction. We will advise against it, but as P.T. Barnum said..."

Advice "I get poems that do not fit my needs. At least 1 quarter of all poets waste their postage because they do not read the requirements. Also, there are too many submissions without a SASE and they go directly into the trash!"

◙ POTOMAC REVIEW: A JOURNAL OF ARTS & HUMANITIES

Montgomery College, 51 Mannakee St., Rockville MD 20850. (240)567-4100. E-mail: potomacrevie weditor@montgomerycollege.edu. Web site: www.montgomerycollege.edu/potomacreview. Established 1994. **Contact:** Julie Wakeman-Linn, editor.

Magazine Needs *Potomac Review: A Journal of Arts & Humanities,* published semiannually in November and May, wants "stories with unique setting and plots, as well as fiction that has a compelling voice. We welcome poetry, both free verse and in-form (translations accepted). Essays and creative nonfiction are also welcome." Considers poetry by children and teens. Has published work by David Wagoner, William Jollif, Mary Collins, Patricia Schultheis, Joan Siegal, and Paul Freidinger. *Potomac Review* is 150 pages, digest-sized, 50 lb paper; 65 lb cover stock. Receives about 2,500 poems/year, accepts 3%. Subscription: $18/year (includes 2 issues). Sample: $10.

How to Submit Submit up to 3 poems (5 pages maximum) at a time. Considers simultaneous submissions; no previously published poems. Cover letter is preferred. Include brief bio; enclose SASE. Time between acceptance and publication is up to 1 year. Poems are read "in house," then sent to poetry editor for comments and dialogue. Often comments on rejected poems. Does not publish theme issues. Guidelines available on Web site. Responds within 3 months. Pays 2 contributor's copies and offers 40% discount on additional copies.

Contest/Award Offerings Sponsors an annual poetry contest and annual fiction contest. Guidelines available in magazine (fall/winter issue), for SASE, or on Web site.

Advice "Read a current issue to see what kind of work delights us. We like a wide variety of subjects, and we especially love memorable characters and evocative imagery. Keep checking Web site for updates and changes."

▣ ◙ THE POTOMAC

2020 Pennsylvania Ave. NW, Suite 443, Washington DC 20006. E-mail: nathan_21045@yahoo.com. Web site: www.webdelsol.com/The_Potomac. Established 2004. **Contact:** Charles Rammelkamp, editor. Member: Web del Sol.

Magazine Needs *The Potomac,* published quarterly online, features political commentary, cutting-edge poetry, flash fiction, and reviews. Open to all forms of poetry by new and established writers. Has published poetry and fiction by Robert Cooperman, Michael Salcman, Joanne Lowery, Pamela Painter, and L.D. Brodsky. Receives a "variable" number of poems/year, accepts about 50-60. Sample: free online.

How to Submit Submit any number of poems at a time. Considers simultaneous submissions; no previously published poems. Accepts e-mail submissions (as attachment) only; no postal or disk submissions. Cover letter is preferred. Reads submissions year round. Time between acceptance and publication is 3 months. Often comments on rejected poems. Guidelines available on Web site. Responds in 2 months. Sometimes sends prepublication galleys. No payment. Acquires one-time rights. Reviews books/chapbooks of poetry and other magazines/journals in up to 2,000 words, single- and multi-book format. Send materials for review consideration.

Advice "We welcome the opportunity to read work from new writers."

⬙ $◙ ◎ THE PRAIRIE JOURNAL

Prairie Journal Press, P.O. Box 61203, Brentwood Post Office, 217-3630 Brentwood Rd. NW, Calgary AB T2L 2K6 Canada. E-mail: prairiejournal@yahoo.com. Web site: www.geocities.com/prairiejour nal. Established 1983. **Contact:** A. Burke, editor.

Magazine Needs *The Prairie Journal,* published twice/year, seeks poetry "of any length; free verse, contemporary themes (feminist, nature, urban, non-political), aesthetic value, a poet's poetry." Does not want to see "most rhymed verse, sentimentality, egotistical ravings. No cowboys or sage brush." Has published poetry by Liliane Welch, Cornelia Hoogland, Sheila Hyland, Zoe Lendale, and Chad Norman. *The Prairie Journal* is 40-60 pages, digest-sized, offset-printed, saddle-stapled, with card cover, includes ads. Receives about 1,000 poems/year, accepts 10%. Press run is 600; the rest are sold on newsstands. Subscription: $10 for individuals, $18 for libraries. Sample: $8 ("use postal money order"). No U.S. stamps.

How to Submit No previously published poems or simultaneous submissions. No e-mail submissions. "We will not be reading submissions until such time as an issue is in preparation (twice yearly), so be patient and we will acknowledge, accept for publication, or return work at that time." Guidelines available for postage ("no U.S. stamps, please"; get IRCs from USPS) or on Web site. Sometimes sends prepublication galleys. Pays $10-50 and 1 contributor's copy. Acquires first North American serial rights. Reviews books of poetry, "but must be assigned by editor. Query first."

Additional Information For chapbook publication by Prairie Journal Press, **Canadian poets only** (preferably from the plains region). Has published *Voices From Earth*, selected poems by Ronald Kurt and Mark McCawley, and *In the Presence of Grace* by McCandless Callaghan. "We also publish anthologies on themes when material is available." Query first, with 5 sample poems and cover letter with brief bio and publication credits. Responds to queries in 2 months; to mss in 6 months. Payment in modest honoraria.

Also Offers Publishes "Poems of the Month" online. Submit up to 4 poems **with $1 reading fee** by postal mail.

Advice "Read recent poets! Experiment with line length, images, metaphors. Innovate."

◙ PRAIRIE SCHOONER

201 Andrews Hall, P.O. Box 880334, University of Nebraska, Lincoln NE 68588-0334. (402)472-0911. Fax: (402)472-9771. E-mail: jengelhardt2@unl.edu. Web site: http://prairieschooner.unl.edu. Established 1926. **Contact:** James Engelhardt, managing editor.

• Poetry published in *Prairie Schooner* has been selected for inclusion in *The Best American Poetry* and *The Pushcart Prize*.

Magazine Needs *Prairie Schooner*, published quarterly, prints poetry, fiction, personal essays, interviews, and reviews. Wants "poems that fulfill the expectations they set up." No specifications as to form, length, style, subject matter, or purpose. Has published poetry by Alicia Ostriker, Marilyn Hacker, D.A. Powell, Stephen Dunn, and David Ignatow. *Prairie Schooner* is about 200 pages, digest-sized, flat-spined. Receives about 5,500 submissions/year, uses about 300 pages of poetry. Press run is 2,500. Single copy: $9; subscription: $28. Sample: $6.

How to Submit Submit 5-7 poems at a time. No simultaneous submissions. No fax or e-mail submissions; postal submissions only. Reads submissions September 1-May 1 (mss must be received during that period). Guidelines available for SASE or on Web site. Responds in 4 months, "sooner if possible." Always sends prepublication galleys. Pays 3 contributor's copies. Acquires all rights. Returns rights upon request without fee. Reviews books of poetry. Send materials for review consideration.

Contest/Award Offerings "All manuscripts published in *Prairie Schooner* automatically will be considered for our annual prizes." These include The Strousse Award for Poetry ($500), the Bernice Slote Prize for Beginning Writers ($500), the Hugh J. Luke Award ($250), the Edward Stanley Award for Poetry ($1,000), the Virginia Faulkner Award for Excellence in Writing ($1,000), the Glenna Luschei Prize for Excellence ($1,500), and the Jane Geske Award ($250). Also, each year 10 Glenna Luschei Awards ($250 each) are given for poetry, fiction, and nonfiction. All contests are open only to those writers whose work was published in the magazine the previous year. Editors serve as judges. Also sponsors The *Prairie Schooner* Book Prize (see separate listing Contests & Awards).

Also Offers Editor-in-Chief Hilda Raz also promotes poets whose work has appeared in her pages by listing their continued accomplishments in a special section (even when their work does not concurrently appear in the magazine).

☐ ◎ PRAYERWORKS (Specialized: praying; the elderly)

P.O. Box 301363, Portland OR 97294-9363. (503)761-2072. E-mail: jay4prayer@aol.com. Established 1988. **Contact:** V. Ann Mandeville, editor.

Magazine Needs *PrayerWorks*, published weekly, is a newsletter "encouraging elderly people to recognize their value to God as prayer warriors." Established as a ministry to people living in retirement centers, *PrayerWorks* features "prayers, ways to pray, stories of answered prayers, teaching on a Scripture portion, articles that build faith, and poems." *PrayerWorks* is 4 pages, digest-sized, desktop-published, photocopied, folded. Receives about 50 poems/year, accepts about 25%. Press run is 1,000. Subscription: free.

How to Submit Submit 5 poems at a time. Considers previously published poems and simultaneous submissions. Accepts e-mail submissions (WordPerfect or Microsoft Word attachments). Cover letter is preferred. 1 poem/page. Time between acceptance and publication is usually within 1 month. Seldom comments on rejected poems. Publishes theme issues relating to the holidays (submit holiday poetry 2 months in advance). Guidelines available for SASE. Responds in 3 weeks. Pays 5 or more contributor's copies.

N ☉ PRESA

P.O. Box 792, Rockford MI 49341.E-mail: presapress@aol.com. Web site: www.presapress.com. Established 2003. **Contact:** Roseanne Ritzema, assistant editor.

Magazine Needs *Presa*, published twice/year, prints poems, reviews, essays, photos, criticism, and prose. Wants "imagistic, surreal, experimental, and personal poetry. Dedicates 6-8 pages of each issue to a featured poet." Does not want "political or didactic poetry." Has published poetry by Antler, Eric Greinke, Richard Kostelanetz, Donald Lev, Simon Perchik, and Jared Smith. *Presa* is 48-64 pages, digest-sized laser printed on 20-24 lb. paper, saddle-stitch bound with a color cover artwork on card stock; includes ads. Receives about 2,500 poems/year, accepts about 5%. Press run is 500. Single copy: $8.50; subscription: $15. Make checks payable to Presa Press.

How to Submit Submit 3-5 poems at a time. Considers previously published poems. (Considers poetry posted on a public Web site/blog/forum and poetry posted on a private, password-protected forum as published.) Accepts postal submissions only. Cover letter is preferred. Reads submissions year round. Time between acceptance and publication is 8-12 weeks. Poems are circulated to an editorial board. Never comments on rejected poems. Never publishes theme issues. Guidelines available in magazine, for SASE, and by e-mail. Responds in 4-8 weeks. Pays 2 contributor's copies. Acquires first North American serial rights and the right to reprint in anthologies. Rights revert to poets upon publication. Reviews books and chapbooks of poetry. Send materials for review consideration to Larry Hill.

Advice "Read an issue or check our Web site."

⬆ $☉ PRISM INTERNATIONAL

Creative Writing Program, University of British Columbia, Buchanan E462, 1866 Main Mall, Vancouver BC V6T 1Z1 Canada. E-mail: prism@interchange.ubc.ca. Web site: http://prism.arts.ubc.ca. Established 1959. **Contact:** Editor (rotating title).

• *PRISM international* is one of the top literary journals in Canada.

Magazine Needs *PRISM international*, published quarterly, prints poetry, drama, short fiction, creative nonfiction, and translation into English in all genres. "We have no thematic or stylistic allegiances: Excellence is our main criterion for acceptance of manuscripts." Wants "fresh, distinctive poetry that shows an awareness of traditions old and new. We read everything." Considers poetry by children and teens. "Excellence is the only criterion." Has published poetry by Margaret Avison, Elizabeth Bachinsky, John Pass, Warren Heiti, Don McKay, Bill Bissett, and Stephanie Bolster. *PRISM international* is 80 pages, digest-sized, elegantly printed, flat-spined, with original color artwork on a glossy card cover. Receives 1,000 submissions/year, accepts about 80. Circulation is for 1,200 subscribers. Subscription: $28/year, $46 for 2 years. Sample: $11. "Subscribers outside of Canada, please pay in U.S. dollars."

How to Submit Submit up to 6 poems at a time. No previously published poems or simultaneous submissions. No e-mail submissions. Cover letter is required. Include brief introduction and list of previous publications. Poems must be typed or computer-generated (font and point size open). Include SASE (or SAE with IRCs). "Note: American stamps are not valid postage in Canada. No SASEs with U.S. postage will be returned. Translations must be accompanied by a copy of the original." Guidelines available for SASE (or SAE with IRCs), by e-mail, or on Web site. Responds in up to 6 months. Pays $40/printed page (for poetry) and one-year subscription; plus an additional $10/printed page to selected authors for publication online. Editors sometimes comment on rejected poems. Acquires first North American serial rights.

Contest/Award Offerings The editorial board awards an annual $500 prize to an outstanding poetry contributor in each volume.

Advice "While we don't automatically discount any kind of poetry, we prefer to publish work that challenges the writer as much as it does the reader. We are particularly looking for poetry in translation."

$⬚ ◎ PROVINCETOWN ARTS (Specialized: Cape Cod & area art colony culture)

P.O. Box 35, 650 Commercial St., Provincetown MA 02657. (508)487-3167. E-mail: cbusa@comcast. net. Web site: www.provincetownarts.org. Established 1985. **Contact:** Christopher Busa, editor.

Magazine Needs *Provincetown Arts*, published annually in July, prints quality poetry, focusing "broadly on the artists and writers who inhabit or visit the tip of Cape Cod." Seeks to "stimulate creative activity and enhance public awareness of the cultural life of the nation's oldest continuous art colony. Drawing upon a century-long tradition rich in visual art, literature, and theater, *Provincetown Arts* publishes material with a view towards demonstrating that the artists' colony, functioning outside the urban centers, is a utopian dream with an ongoing vitality." Has published poetry by Bruce Smith, Franz Wright, Sandra McPherson, and Cyrus Cassells. *Provincetown Arts* is about 170 pages, magazine-sized, perfect-bound, with full-color glossy cover. Press run is 10,000. Sample: $10.

How to Submit Submit up to 3 poems at a time. No e-mail submissions; "all queries and submissions should be sent via postal mail." Submissions must be typed. Reads submissions October-February. Guidelines available for SASE. Responds in 3 months. Usually sends prepublication galleys. Pays $25-100/poem plus 2 contributor's copies. Acquires first rights. Reviews books of poetry in 500-3,000 words, single- or multi-book format. Send materials for review consideration.

Additional Information The Provincetown Arts Press has published 8 volumes of poetry. The Provincetown Poets Series includes *At the Gate* by Martha Rhodes, *Euphorbia* by Anne-Marie Levine (a finalist in the 1995 Paterson Poetry Prize), and *1990* by Michael Klein (co-winner of the 1993 Lambda Literary Award).

◲ ◎ PUDDING MAGAZINE: THE INTERNATIONAL JOURNAL OF APPLIED POETRY (Specialized: popular culture; virtual journalism)

81 Shadymere Lane, Columbus OH 43213. (614)986-1881. Web site: www.puddinghouse.com. Established 1979. **Contact:** Jennifer Bosveld, editor.

Magazine Needs *Pudding Magazine: The International Journal of Applied Poetry*, published "every several months," seeks "what hasn't been said before. Speak the unspeakable. Long poems okay as long as they aren't windy." *Pudding* also serves as "a forum for poems and articles by people who take poetry arts into the schools and the human services." Wants "poetry on popular culture, rich brief narratives, i.e. 'virtual journalism' (see Web site)." Does not want "preachments or sentimentality; obvious traditional forms without fresh approach." Has published poetry by Knute Skinner, David Chorlton, Mary Winters, and Robert Collins. *Pudding* is 70 pages, digest-sized, offset-composed on Microsoft Word PC. Press run is 1,500. Subscription: $29.95 for 4 issues. Sample: $8.95.

How to Submit Submit 3-10 poems at a time. Previously published submissions "respected, but include credits"; no simultaneous submissions. Cover letter is preferred ("cultivates great relationships with writers"). "Submissions without SASEs will be discarded. No postcards." Sometimes publishes theme issues. Guidelines available on Web site only. Responds on same day (unless traveling). Pays 1 contributor's copy; $10 and 4 contributor's copies to featured poets. Returns rights "with *Pudding* permitted to reprint." Send anthologies and books for review consideration or listing as recommended.

Also Offers "Our Web site is one of the greatest poetry Web sites in the country—calls, workshops, publication list/history, online essays, games, guest pages, calendars, poem of the month, poet of the week, much more." The Web site also links to the site for The Unitarian Universalist Poets Cooperative and American Poets Opposed to Executions, both national organizations.

Advice "Editors have pet peeves. I won't respond to postcards. I require SASEs. I don't like cover letters that state the obvious, poems with trite concepts, or meaning dictated by rhyme. Thoroughly review our Web site; it will give you a good idea about our publication history and editorial tastes."

⊞ ✒ PULSAR POETRY MAGAZINE

Ligden Publishers, 34 Lineacre, Grange Park, Swindon, Wiltshire SN5 6DA England. (44)(01793)875941. E-mail: pulsar.ed@btopenworld.com. Web site: www.pulsarpoetry.com. Established 1992. **Contact:** David Pike, editor.

Magazine Needs *Pulsar Poetry Magazine*, published every March and September, "encourages the writing of poetry from all walks of life. Contains poems, reviews, and editorial comments." Wants "hard-hitting, thought-provoking work; interesting and stimulating poetry." Does not want "racist material. Not keen on religious poetry." Has published poetry by A.C. Evans, Chris Hardy, Kate Edwards, Elizabeth Birchall, and Michael Newman. *Pulsar* is 40-44 pages, A5, professionally printed, saddle-stapled, with glossy full-color cover, includes ads. Press run is 300; several distributed free to newspapers, etc. Subscription: $18 (£8 UK). Sample: $9. Make checks payable to Ligden Publishers.

How to Submit Submit 3 poems at a time. No previously published poems or simultaneous submissions. Accepts e-mail submissions (pasted into body of message). "Send no more than 2 poems via e-mail; file attachments will not be read." Cover letter is preferred. Include SAE with adequate IRCs for a reply only (mss not returned if non-UK). Manuscripts should be typed. Time between acceptance and publication is about 1 month. "Poems can be published in next edition if it is what we are looking for. The editor and assistant read all poems." Seldom comments on rejected poems. Guidelines available for SASE (or SAE and IRC) or on Web site. Responds within 1 month. Pays 1 contributor's copy. Acquires first rights. "Originators retain copyright of their poems." Staff reviews poetry books and CDs (mainstream); word count varies. Send materials for review consideration.

Advice "Give explanatory notes if poems are open to interpretation. Be patient and enjoy what you are doing. Check grammar, spelling, etc. (should be obvious). Note: we are a nonprofit-making society."

◻ PULSE ONLINE LITERARY JOURNAL

7781 SVL Box, Victorville CA 92395-5117 (contest only address, all other submissions by email). (760)243-8034. E-mail: mainepoet@mac.com. Web site: www.heartsoundspress.com. Established 1997. **Contact:** Carol Bachofner, poetry editor.

Magazine Needs *Pulse Online Literary Journal* is open to formal poetry as well as free verse. Wants "your best. Send only work revised and revised again! Translations welcome." Does not want "predictable, sentimental, greeting card verse. No gratuitous sexuality or violence. No religious verse or predictable rhyme." Has published poetry by Walt McDonald and Lyn Lifshin. Receives about 400 poems/year, accepts about 10-15%.

How to Submit Submit 3-5 poems at a time. Lines/poem: up to 120. Considers previously published poems. Only accepts email submissions (pasted into body of email); no disk submissions. Cover letter is required. "Send bio of 50-100 words with submission." Reads submissions year round. Submit seasonal poems 2 months in advance. Time between acceptance and publication is 3-4 weeks. Sometimes comments on rejected poems. Sometimes publishes theme issues. Upcoming themes for 2009 are January-March: weather; April-September: Urban Landscape; September-December: Movements. Guidelines available on Web site. Responds in 3-4 weeks. Acquires first rights. Reviews books/chapbooks of poetry.

Contest/Award Offerings Sponsors the annual Pulse Poetry Prize. Offers 1st Prize: $90; 2nd Prize: $45; 3rd Prize: $20; plus 3 Honorable Mentions and publication to prizewinners. Submit 3 poems up to 120 lines each. **Entry fee:** $10/entry (multiple entries okay with additional fee for each). **Deadline:** August 2008. Guidelines available by e-mail or on Web site.

Also Offers "Ask about our Poetry Abroad in London program. E-mail for info. Spend up to 3 weeks visiting and learning your craft in Literary London with possible college credit. Proposed trip Fall 2010. Also ask about Scribblers Writing Academy (online only until 2011, then also face-to-face classes will be available."

Advice "Be relentless in the revision process. Read widely. Write every day."

$◎ PURPOSE (Specialized: Mennonite; poetry for young adults & adults)

Mennonite Publishing Network, 616 Walnut Ave., Scottdale PA 15683-1999. (724)887-8500. E-mail: horsch@mph.org. **Contact:** James E. Horsch, editor.

Magazine Needs *Purpose*, published by Mennonite Publishing Network (the official publisher for the Mennonite Church in the U.S. and Canada), is a "religious young adult/adult monthly." Focuses on "action-oriented, discipleship living." *Purpose* is digest-sized with 4-color printing throughout. Press run is 8,000. Receives about 2,000 poems/year, accepts 150. Sample: (with guidelines) $2 and 9×12 SAE.

How to Submit Lines/poem: up to 12. Considers simultaneous submissions. Prefers e-mail submissions. Postal submissions should be double-spaced, typed on one side of sheet only. Responds in 6 months. Guidelines available electronically or for SASE. Pays $7.50 to $20 per poem plus 2 contributor's copies.

⊕ $☐ QUANTUM LEAP (Specialized: subscribers favored)

Q.Q. Press, York House, 15 Argyle Terrace, Rothesay, Isle of Bute PA20 0BD Scotland. Established 1997. **Contact:** Alan Carter, editor.

Magazine Needs *Quantum Leap*, published quarterly, uses "all kinds of poetry—free verse, rhyming, whatever—as long as it's well written and preferably well punctuated, too. We rarely use haiku." Has published poetry by Pamela Constantine, Ray Stebbing, Leigh Eduardo, Sky Higgins, Norman Bissett, and Gordon Scapens. *Quantum Leap* is 40 pages, digest-sized, desktop-published, saddle-stapled, with card cover. Receives about 2,000 poems/year, accepts about 15%. Press run is 200. Single copy: $13; subscription: $40. Sample: $10. Make checks payable to Alan Carter. "All things being equal in terms of a poem's quality, **I will sometimes favor that of a subscriber (or someone who has at least bought an issue) over a nonsubscriber**, as it is they who keep us solvent."

How to Submit Submit 6 poems at a time. Lines/poem: 36 ("normally"). Considers previously published poems (indicate magazine and date of first publication) and simultaneous submissions. Cover letter is required. "Within the UK, send a SASE; outside it, send IRCs to the return postage value of what has been submitted." Time between acceptance and publication is usually 3 months "but can be longer now, due to magazine's increasing popularity." Sometimes comments on rejected poems. Guidelines available for SASE (or SAE and 2 IRCs). Responds in 3 weeks. Pays £2 sterling. Acquires first or second British serial rights.

Additional Information Under the imprint "Collections," Q.Q. Press offers **subsidy arrangements** "to provide a cheap alternative to the 'vanity presses'—poetry only." Charges **£150 sterling ($300 USD) plus postage** for 50 32-page (A4) books. Write for details. Order sample books by sending $12 (postage included). Make checks payable to Alan Carter.

Contest/Award Offerings Sponsors open poetry competitions as well as competitions for subscribers only. Send SAE and IRC for details.

Advice "Submit well thought-out, well presented poetry, preferably well punctuated, too. If rhyming poetry, make it flow and don't strain to rhyme. I don't bite, and I appreciate a short cover letter, but not a long, long list of where you've been published before! Please do not add U.S. stamps to IRCs. They have no validity here. If you want to increase the value, just send extra IRCs."

☑ QUARTERLY WEST

Dept. of English/LNCO 3500, University of Utah, 255 S. Central Campus Dr., Salt Lake City UT 84112-9109. (801)581-3938. E-mail: quarterlywest@yahoo.com. (inquiries only). Web site: www.u tah.edu/quarterlywest. Established 1976. **Contact:** Kathryn Cowles and Stacy Kidd, poetry editors; Paul Ketzle and Brenda Sieczkowski, editors.

• Poetry published in *Quarterly West* has appeared in *The Best American Poetry* and in numerous Pushcart Prize anthologies.

Magazine Needs *Quarterly West*, published semiannually, seeks "original and accomplished literary verse—free or formal." Also considers translations (include originals with submissions). No greeting card or sentimental poetry. Has published poetry by Quan Barry, Medbh McGuckian, Alice Notley, Brenda Shaughnessy, Bob Hicok, David Kirby, and Linh Dinh. *Quarterly West* is 160 pages, digest-sized, offset-printed, with 4-color cover art. Receives 2,500 submissions/year, accepts less than 1%. Press run is 1,500 (500 subscribers, 300-400 libraries). Subscription: $14/year, $25 for 2 years. Sample: $8.50.

How to Submit Submit 3-5 poems at a time. Considers simultaneous submissions, with notification; no previously published poems. No e-mail submissions; postal submissions only. Reads submissions September 1-May 1. Seldom comments on rejected poems. Guidelines available on Web site. Responds in up to 6 months. Pays 2 contributor's copies and money when possible. Acquires first North American serial rights. Returns rights with acknowledgment and right to reprint. Reviews books of poetry in 1,000-3,000 words.

$□ ◎ ELLERY QUEEN'S MYSTERY MAGAZINE (Specialized: mystery/suspense)

475 Park Ave. S., 11th Floor, New York NY 10016. E-mail: elleryqueen@dellmagazines.com (inquries only). Web site: www.themysteryplace.com. Established 1941. **Contact:** Janet Hutchings.
Magazine Needs *Ellery Queen's Mystery Magazine*, published 10 times/year, uses primarily short stories of mystery, crime, or suspense—little poetry. *Ellery Queen's Mystery Magazine* is 144 pages (double-issue, published twice/year, is 240 pages), digest-sized, professionally printed on newsprint, flat-spined, with glossy paper cover. Single copy: $5 by check to publisher, available for $4.99 on newsstands; subscription: $55.90.
How to Submit Considers simultaneous submissions; no previously published poems. No e-mail submissions; postal submissions only. Include SASE with submissions. Guidelines available for SASE or on Web site. Responds in 3 months. Pays $15-65 and 3 contributor's copies.

◢ QUERCUS REVIEW

Quercus Review Press, Modesto Junior College, Division of Literature & Language Arts, 435 College Ave., Modesto CA 95350. (209)575-6183. E-mail: pierstorffs@mjc.edu. Web site: www.quercusreview.com. Established 1999. **Contact:** Sam Pierstorff, editor.
Magazine Needs *Quercus Review*, published annually in May/June, prints high-quality poetry, fiction, and b&w art. "We publish numerous nationally recognized and award-winning writers from across the nation." Wants "writing with a pulse. Writing that reflects a unique voice." Does not want "rhyme, religious, or cliché writing." Considers poetry by children and teens. Has published poetry by X.J. Kennedy, Gerald Locklin, Naomi Shihab Nye, Amiri Baraka, Charles Harper Webb, and Dorianne Laux. *Quercus Review* is 112 pages, digest-sized, professionally printed, perfect-bound, with full-color cover. Receives about 3,500 poems/year, accepts less than 10%. Press run is 500; 100 distributed free to contributors and local bookstores. Single copy: $8; subscription: $20 for 2 years (includes 2 issues of *Quercus Review*, plus annual book award winner). Make checks payable to "MJC (QR)."
How to Submit Submit 3-5 poems at a time. Lines/poem: prefers 40 maximum, but will consider longer. No previously published poems or simultaneous submissions. No e-mail or disk submissions. Cover letter is required. Include brief bio and SASE. Reads submissions year round. Time between acceptance and publication is usually 3 weeks to 3 months. "Poems are selected by 5-person staff of editors, which rotates annually." Guidelines available on Web site. Sometimes sends prepublication galleys. Pays 1 contributor's copy, 30% discount on additional copies. Acquires first rights.
Contest/Award Offerings Quercus Review Press Poetry Series Book Award (see separate listing in Contests & Awards).
Advice "Avoid overusing the world 'soul,' but feel free to drown us in fresh imagery and bold language. We like poems with a pulse. Make us laugh or cry, but don't bore or try too hard to impress us."

◢ QUEST

Freiburger Hall, Lynn University, 3601 N. Military Trail, Boca Raton FL 33431. E-mail: jdaily@lynn.edu. Established 1997. **Contact:** John Daily, editor.
Magazine Needs *Quest*, published annually in April, is a literary and arts journal. Wants "poems with a clear voice that use careful diction to create poetry in which sound and sense work together, creating fresh perception." Does not want "poems that rely on profanity or shock value." Has published poetry by Jeff Morgan, John Daily, Eugene Martel, Andrea Best, Fred Cichocki, Johanne Perron. *Quest* is digest-sized, laser-printed, saddle-stapled, with 32 lb. bright white coverstock cover

printed with 4-color process. Receives about 100 poems/year, accepts about 25. Press run is 200 (one library subscriber); 150 distributed free to Lynn University faculty, staff, and students. Single copy: $5. Make checks payable to Lynn University.

How to Submit Submit up to 3 poems at a time. No previously published poems or simultaneous submissions. No e-mail or disk submissions. Cover letter is preferred. "Include adequate SASE if you want work returned." Reads submissions mid-September to mid-January. Time between acceptance and publication is up to 7 months. "English Department faculty review submissions." Seldom comments on rejected poems. Guidelines available for SASE. Responds in up to 4 months. Pays 1 contributor's copy. Acquires one-time rights.

Advice "Even the freest of verse has its roots in the formal elements."

☑ ◎ RADIX MAGAZINE (Specialized: poetry that expresses a Christian world-view)

E-mail: RadixMag@aol.com. Web site: www.radixmagazine.com. Established 1969. **Contact:** Luci Shaw, poetry editor. Editor: Sharon Gallagher.

Magazine Needs *Radix Magazine*, published quarterly, is named for the Latin word for "root" and "has its roots both in the 'real world' and in the truth of Christ's teachings." Wants poems "that reflect a Christian world-view, but aren't preachy." Has published poetry by John Leax, Walter McDonald, Evangeline Paterson, and Luci Shaw. *Radix* is 32 pages, magazine-sized, offset-printed, saddle-stapled, with 60-lb. self cover. Receives about 50 poems/year, accepts about 20%. Press run varies. Sample: $5. Make checks payable to *Radix Magazine*.

How to Submit Submit 1-4 poems at a time. No previously published poems or simultaneous submissions. Accepts e-mail submissions only. Submit seasonal poems 6 months in advance. Time between acceptance and publication is 3 months to 3 years. "We have a serious backlog. The poetry editor accepts or rejects poems and sends the accepted poems to the editor. The editor then publishes poems in appropriate issues. If more than one poem is accepted from any poet, there will probably be a long wait before another is published, because of our backlog of accepted poems." Seldom comments on rejected poems. Occasionally publishes theme issues. Responds in 2 months. Pays 2 contributor's copies. Acquires first rights. Returns rights upon request. Reviews books of poetry.

Advice "*Radix* has a distinctive voice and often receives submissions that are completely inappropriate. Familiarity with the magazine is recommended before sending any submissions."

☑ ◎ THE RAINTOWN REVIEW (Specialized: formal/traditional poetry)

E-mail: Oelfkej@aol.com. Web site: www.centralavepress.com/html. Established 1996. **Contact:** John Oelfke, editor.

Magazine Needs *The Raintown Review*, published 2 times/year in February and August, contains poetry "and the occasional literary criticism or review." Wants well-crafted poems. "We are primarily a venue for formal/traditional poetry." Has published poetry by William Baer, Joseph S. Salemi, Richard Moore, Annie Finch, and many others. *The Raintown Review* is 120 pages, perfect-bound. Receives about 900 poems/year, accepts 10-15%. Press run is 150 (most go to subscribers and contributors). Subscription: $24/year, $45 for 2 years, $65 for 3 years. Sample: $12. Make checks/money orders payable to Central Ave Press, 2132A Central SE #144, Albuquerque NM 87106.

How to Submit Submit 3-5 poems at a time. Lines/poem: no restrictions. Considers previously published poems (with acknowledgment of previous publication) and simultaneous submissions. Accepts e-mail submissions only (pasted into body of message); no postal submissions. Comments on rejected poems if requested at the time of submission. Guidelines available on Web site. Usually responds in 2 weeks, if possible. Pays 1 contributor's copy. Acquires one-time rights.

☑ ◎ RATTAPALLAX (Specialized: the diversity of world cultures)

532 La Guardia Place, Suite 353, New York NY 10012. E-mail: info@rattapallax.com. Web site: www.rattapallax.com. Established 1998. **Contact:** Poetry Editor.

Magazine Needs *Rattapallax*, published semiannually, is named for "Wallace Steven's word for the sound of thunder. The magazine includes a DVD featuring poetry films and audio files. *Rattapallax* is looking for the extraordinary in modern poetry and prose that reflect the diversity of world cultures. Our goals are to create international dialogue using literature and focus on what is relevant to our society.'' Has published poetry by Anthony Hecht, Sharon Olds, Lou Reed, Marilyn Hacker, Billy Collins, and Glyn Maxwell. *Rattapallax* is 112 pages, magazine-sized, offset-printed, perfect-bound, with 12-pt. CS1 cover. Receives about 5,000 poems/year, accepts 2%. Press run is 2,000 (100 subscribers, 50 libraries, 1,200 shelf sales); 200 distributed free to contributors, reviews, and promos. Single copy: $7.95; no subscriptions. Make checks payable to *Rattapallax*.

How to Submit Submit 3-5 poems at a time. Considers simultaneous submissions; no previously published poems. Accepts e-mail submissions (sent as simple text) from outside the U.S. and Canada; all other submissions must be sent via postal mail (SASE required). Cover letter is preferred. Reads submissions year round; issue deadlines are June 1 and December 1. Time between acceptance and publication is 6 months. ''The editor-in-chief, senior editor, and associate editor review all the submissions and then decide on which to accept every week. Near publication time, all accepted work is narrowed, and unused work is kept for the next issue.'' Often comments on rejected poems. Guidelines available by e-mail or on Web site. Responds in 2 months. Always sends prepublication galleys. Pays 2 contributor's copies. Acquires first rights.

☑ RATTLE

12411 Ventura Blvd., Studio City CA 91604. (818)505-6777. E-mail: timgreen@rattle.com. Web site: www.rattle.com. Established 1994. **Contact:** Timothy Green, editor.

Magazine Needs *RATTLE*, published semiannually in June and December, includes poems, essays, reviews, interviews with poets, and a tribute section dedicated to a specific ethnic or vocational group. Wants ''high-quality poetry of any form. Nothing unintelligible.'' Considers some poetry by children and teens (ages 10-18). Has published poetry by Lucille Clifton, Charles Simic, Mark Doty, Sharon Olds, Billy Collins, and Stephen Dunn. *RATTLE* is 196 pages, digest-sized, neatly printed, perfect-bound, with 4-color coated card cover. Receives about 8,000 submissions/year, accepts 200. Press run is 4,000. Subscription: $16/year, $28/2 years, $34/3 years. Sample: $10. Make checks payable to *RATTLE*.

How to Submit Submit up to 5 poems at a time. Considers simultaneous submissions ''if notified immediately by e-mail or phone should they be taken elsewhere.'' Accepts e-mail submissions (pasted into body of message). Cover letter is required (with e-mail address, if possible). Include bio. For postal submissions, put name, address, and phone number on each page in upper right corner; include SASE. Reads submissions year round. Seldom comments on rejected poems (unless requested by the author). Guidelines available in magazine, by e-mail, or on Web site. Responds in up to 2 months. Pays 2 contributor's copies. Rights revert to poet upon publication. Reviews books of poetry in 375 words or less. Send materials for review consideration.

Additional Information Welcomes essays up to 2,000 words on poetry or the writing process. Publishes a biannual electronic issue in March and September, e-mailed as a PDF to 4,000 subscribers, featuring excerpts from poetry collections, chapbooks, reviews, and print issue previews.

Contest/Award Offerings The *RATTLE* Poetry Prize (see separate listing in Contests & Awards).

Ⓝ ▣ $☑ ◎ RAVING DOVE (Specialized: Anti-war, anti-violence, peace-related, human rights)

P.O. Box 28, West Linn OR 97068.E-mail: editor@ravingdove.org. Web site: www.ravingdove.org. Established 2004. **Contact**: Jo-Ann Moss, editor.

● Nonprofit status granted by U.S. government.

Magazine Needs *Raving Dove*, published 3 times a year, ''is an online literary journal which publishes original poetry, nonfiction, fiction, photography, and art with universal anti-war, anti-violence, peace-related, and human rights themes. Our material is about the pain of war and the vision of peace-in all their manifestations and in all their appearances throughout time. *Raving Dove* is a 501(c)(3) nonprofit organization.'' Wants free verse only, any length. Does not want anything other than free verse. Has published poetry by Howard Camner, Marguerite Bouvard, John Kay, Harry Youtt. Receives about 750 poems/year, accepts about 30. Number of visitors is ''2,000/month and growing.''

How to Submit Considers simultaneous submissions. Accepts e-mail submissions as attachment;

no fax or disk submissions. Cover letter is unnecessary. "Poetry Submission" must appear as the subject of the e-mail; all submissions must include full name, general geographic location, and a brief, third-person bio. Weblinks are permitted. Reads submissions year round. Time between acceptance and publication is no more than 4 months. Sometimes comments on rejected poems. Guidelines available on Web site. Always sends prepublication galleys ("the link to the poet's Web page at *Raving Dove* is sent prior to publication"). Responds in 4 months. Pays $10 per poem. Acquires first North American seria, one-time, elcectronic, and other rights (see submission guidelines on Web site for further information). Rights revert to poets at the end of the issue in which the poetry appears.

Advice "*Raving Dove* is not a political journal. Material for or against one specific person or entity will not be considered, fictitious or otherwise. Our material is about the pain of war and the vision of peace-in all their manifestations and in all their appearances throughout time. Please follow submission guidelines very carefully. Guidelines can be found at http://www.ravingdove.org/sub missions."

☑ RB'S POETS' VIEWPOINT

330 S. Third St., Lot 67, Coleman MI 48618-9587. Established 1989. **Contact:** Robert Bennett, editor.

Magazine Needs *RB's Poets' Viewpoint*, published bimonthly, features poetry and cartoons. Wants "general and religious poetry, sonnets, and sijo." Does not want "vulgar language." Has published poetry by Robert D. Spector, Ruth Ditmer Ream, Ruth Halbrooks, and Delphine Ledoux. *RB's Poets' Viewpoint* is 34 pages, digest-sized, photocopied, saddle-stapled. Receives about 400 poems/year, accepts about 90%. Press run is 60. Subscription: $8. Sample: $2. Make checks payable to Robert Bennett.

How to Submit Submit 3 poems at a time. Lines/poem: 21 maximum. Considers previously published poems and simultaneous submissions. Submissions should be typed single-spaced. **Reading fee: $1.50/poem.** Reads submissions February, April, June, August, October, and December only. Time between acceptance and publication is 1 month. "Poems are selected by 1 editor." Often comments on rejected poems. Guidelines available for SASE. Responds in 1 month. Pays 1 contributor's copy. Acquires one-time rights.

Contest/Award Offerings Sponsors contests for general poetry, religious poetry, sonnets, and sijo with 1st Prizes of $20, $6, and $5, respectively, plus publication in *RB's Poets' Viewpoint*. **Entry fee:** 50¢/poem (sijo), $1.50/poem (all others). Guidelines available for SASE.

$☺ RED LIGHTS (Specialized: English-language tanka)

33 Riverside Dr., Suite 4-G, New York NY 10023-8025. (212)875-9342. E-mail: deucedk@aol.com. Established 2004. **Contact:** Pamela Miller Ness, editor.

Magazine Needs *red lights*, published semiannually in January and June, is devoted to English-language tanka and tanka sequences. Wants "print-only tanka, mainly 'free-form' but also strictly syllabic 5-7-5-7-7; will consider tanka sequences and tan-renga." Considers poetry by children and teens. Has published poetry by Sanford Goldstein, Michael McClintock, Laura Maffei, Linda Jeannette Ward, Jane Reichhold, and Michael Dylan Welch. *red lights* is 28-36 pages, $8\frac{1}{2} \times 3\frac{3}{4}$, offset-printed, saddle-stapled, with Japanese textured paper cover; copies are numbered. Receives about 1,200 poems/year, accepts about 20%. Press run is 150. Single copy: $6; subscription: $12 U.S., $13 USD Canada, $15 USD foreign. Ma⅝ke checks payable to Pamela Miller Ness.

How to Submit Submit 10 tanka or 2 sequences at a time (maximum). No previously published poems or simultaneous submissions. No e-mail or disk submissions. Include SASE. Reads submissions year round. Time between acceptance and publication "depends on submission time." Often comments on rejected poems. Guidelines available for SASE. Responds in 2 weeks. Pays $1/tanka. Acquires first rights.

Contest/Award Offerings "Each issue features a '*red lights* featured tanka' on the theme of 'red lights.' Poet whose poem is selected receives 1 contributor's copy in addition to $1."

Additional Information "The center 4 pages are devoted to the 'Featured Tanka Poet,' selected by invitation. Twelve previously published poems are featured."

$⬜ ◎ THE RED MOON ANTHOLOGY OF ENGLISH LANGUAGE HAIKU

P.O. Box 2461, Winchester VA 22604-1661. (540)722-2156. E-mail: jim.kacian@redmoonpress.com. Web site: www.redmoonpress.com. Established 1996. **Contact:** Jim Kacian, editor/publisher.

Magazine Needs *The Red Moon Anthology of English Language Haiku*, published annually in February, is "a collection of the best haiku published in English around the world." Considers poetry by children and teens. Has published haiku and related forms by Roberta Beary, Thomas Heffernan, Peggy Willis Lyles, and Marcus Larsson. *The Red Moon Anthology of English Language Haiku* is 184 pages, digest-sized, offset-printed on quality paper, with 4-color heavy-stock cover. Receives several thousand submissions/year, accepts less than 2%. Print run is 1,000 for subscribers and commercial distribution. Subscription: $16.95 plus $4 p&h. Sample available for SASE or by e-mail.

How to Submit Submit up to 5 haiku or related works at a time, published within the calendar year. **Considers previously published poems only.** Accepts e-mail and disk submissions. Include SASE for postal submissions. Time between acceptance and publication varies according to time of submission. Poems are circulated to an editorial board. "Only haiku published within the calendar year will be considered." Guidelines available for SASE or by e-mail. Pays $1/page. Acquires North American serial rights.

Also Offers *contemporary haibun*, "an annual volume of the finest English-language haibun and haiga published anywhere in the world." (See separate listing in this section.)

Advice "Haiku is a burgeoning and truly international form. It is nothing like what your fourth-grade teacher taught you years ago, and so it is best if you familiarize yourself with what is happening in the genre (and its close relatives) today before submitting. We strive to give all the work we publish plenty of space in which to resonate, and to provide a forum where the best of today's practitioners can be published with dignity and prestige."

⬜ RED ROCK REVIEW

English Dept. J2A, Community College of Southern Nevada, 3200 E. Cheyenne Ave., North Las Vegas NV 89030. (702)651-4094. Fax: (702)651-4639. E-mail: richard.logsdon@csn.edu. Web site: http://sites.csn.edu/english/redrockreview/. Established 1994. **Contact:** Dr. Richard Logsdon, editor. Poetry Editor: Jeanie French. Associate Editor: Todd Moffett.

Magazine Needs *Red Rock Review*, published semiannually in May and December, prints "the best poetry available," as well as fiction, creative nonfiction, and book reviews. Has published poetry by Dorianne Laux, Kim Addonizio, Ellen Bass, Cynthia Hogue, and Dianne di Prima. *Red Rock Review* is about 130 pages, magazine-sized, professionally printed, perfect-bound, with 10-pt. CS1 cover. Accepts about 15% of poems received/year. Press run is 750. Sample: $5.50.

How to Submit Submit 2-3 poems at a time. Lines/poem: 80 maximum. Considers simultaneous submissions; no previously published poems. Accepts disk submissions. Cover letter and SASE are required. Submissions should be "mailed flat, not folded, into a letter-sized envelope." Reads submissions September-May. Time between acceptance and publication is 3-5 months. "Poems go to poetry editor, who then distributes them to 3 readers." Seldom comments on rejected poems. Guidelines available for SASE or on Web site. Responds in 3-5 months. Pays 2 contributor's copies. Acquires first North American serial rights. Reviews books/chapbooks of poetry in 500-1,000 words, multi-book format. Send materials for review consideration.

⬜ RED WHEELBARROW

De Anza College, 21250 Stevens Creek Blvd., Cupertino CA 95014. (408)864-8600. E-mail: SplitterRandolph@deanza.edu. Web site: www.deanza.edu/redwheelbarrow. Established 1976 (as *Bottomfish Magazine*). **Contact:** Randolph Splitter, editor, or Poetry Editor.

• " **Please note:** We are not affiliated with Red Wheelbarrow Press or any similarly named publication."

Magazine Needs *Red Wheelbarrow*, published annually in spring or summer, is a college-produced, national magazine. Wants "diverse voices." Has published poetry by Mark Brazaitis, James Doyle, Sharon Doyle, Arthur Gottlieb, Lyn Lifshin, Guadalupe Garcia McCall, Mario Susko, and Jianqing Zheng. *Red Wheelbarrow* is about 250 pages, book-sized, printed on heavy stock with b&w graphics, perfect-bound. Press run is on demand. Single copy: $10. Sample: $2.50 (for back issue).

How to Submit Submit up to 5 poems at a time. Accepts e-mail submissions. Include SASE or e-mail address for reply. Reads submissions September-January (January 31 deadline). Responds in 2-6 months, depending on backlog. Pays 1 contributor's copy.
Advice "We seek diverse voices from around the country and the world."

REDIVIDER

Dept. of Writing, Literature, and Publishing, Emerson College, 120 Boylston St., Boston MA 02118. E-mail: redividerpoetry@gmail.com. Web site: www.redividerjournal.org. Established 1990 (as *Beacon Street Review*). **Contact:** Poetry Editor (changes annually, see Web site). Member: CLMP.
Magazine Needs *Redivider*, published semiannually, prints high-quality poetry, art, fiction, and creative nonfiction. Wants "all styles of poetry. Most of all, we look for language that seems fresh and alive on the page, that tries to do something new. Read a sample copy for a good idea." Does not want "greeting card verse or inspirational verse." Has published poetry by Bob Hicok, Billy Collins, Paul Muldoon, Tao Lin, Claudia Emerson, and Bobby Byrd. *Redivider* is 100 + pages, digest-sized, offset-printed, perfect-bound, with 4-color artwork on cover. Receives about 1,000 poems/year, accepts about 30%. Press run is 1,000. Single copy: $6; subscription: $10. Make checks payable to *Redivider* at Emerson College.
How to Submit Submit 3-6 poems at a time. Considers simultaneous submissions, but requires notification if your work is taken elsewhere; no previously published poems. For online submissions, e-mail poems as a single file. Cover letter is required. Reads submissions year round. Seldom comments on rejected poems. Guidelines available in magazine, for SASE, by e-mail, or on Web site. Responds in 5 months. Pays 2 contributor's copies. Acquires first North American serial rights. Reviews books of poetry in 500 words, single-book format. Send materials for review consideration, Attn: Review Copies. "Book reviews and interviews are internally generated."
Advice "We want your finished product—don't send your experimental first draft!"

THE REDNECK REVIEW, an online poetry journal

P.O. Box 8718, Atlanta GA 31106. E-mail: editor@redneckreview.com. Web site: www.redneckreview.com. Established 2000. **Contact:** Penya Sandor, editor.
Magazine Needs *The Redneck Review*, published semiannually online, is "born out of the rich literary tradition of the South." Wants "writing that is interesting, has energy, and doesn't feel like homework." Considers poetry by children and teens. Has published poetry by Denise Duhamel, Marie Howe, Walt McDonald, Hal Sirowitz, Ben Satterfield, and Jean Trounstine. Publishes about 15-20 poems/issue.
How to Submit Submit no more than 5 poems at a time. Considers previously published poems and simultaneous submissions. Accepts e-mail and disk submissions. Cover letter is preferred. "If sending submissions by postal mail, include SASE unless you have an e-mail address. Poems won't be returned." Time between acceptance and publication "depends." Often comments on rejected poems. Guidelines available on Web site. Response time varies. Sometimes sends prepublication galleys. No payment. "Authors retain rights, but we ask that they mention our journal if they publish the poem again." Send materials for review consideration to *The Redneck Review*.
Advice "There are many respectable literary journals that publish well-written but dull writing. We would prefer to read literature that is electric, not just technically well crafted."

REFLECTIONS LITERARY JOURNAL (Specialized: work from NC resident/native poets)

P.O. Box 1197, Roxboro NC 27573. (336)599-1181, ext. 231. E-mail: reflect@piedmontcc.edu. Established 1999. **Contact:** Dawn Langley, editor.
Magazine Needs *Reflections Literary Journal*, published annually in spring, prints poetry, short fiction, and creative nonfiction. Wants any styles and forms of poetry, including translations. Does not want material using obscenities, or culturally insensitive material. **Accepts submissions from NC authors only (residents or natives).** "If time and space permit, we'll consider submissions from southeastern U.S. authors and from authors we've previously published." Has published poetry by Robert Cooperman, Fredrick Zydek, Bruce Bennett, Fred Chappell, Shari O'Brien, and

Daniel Green. *Reflections Literary Journal* is 100-150 pages, digest-sized. Receives about 400 poems/year, accepts about 5%. Press run is 250 (20 subscribers, 4 libraries, 150 shelf sales); 75 distributed free to contributors, editors, advisors, local schools, and cultural sites. Single copy: $7; subscription: $7. Sample: $5 (back issue). Make checks payable to *Reflections Literary Journal*.

How to Submit Submit 5 poems maximum at a time. Lines/poem: no longer than 1 page (single-spaced). Considers previously published poems and simultaneous submissions (if notified). Accepts e-mail submissions (pasted into body of message or as attachment in MS Word). "Include a 25-word bio with submission. Include 2 copies of each poem—1 with name and address, 1 without. Affix adequate postage to SAE for return of manuscript if desired, or use First-Class stamps on SAE for notification. Poems are read by an 8- to 12-member editorial board who rank submissions through 'blind' readings. Board members refrain from ranking their own submissions." Sometimes comments on rejected poems. Guidelines available in magazine, for SASE, or by e-mail. Responds in up to 9 months (in March or April). Pays 1 contributor's copy. Acquires first North American serial rights (if poem is unpublished) or one-time rights (if poem is previously published).

☆ ⊕ ◎ RENDITIONS: A CHINESE-ENGLISH TRANSLATION MAGAZINE

Research Centre for Translation, Chinese University of Hong Kong, Shatin, N.T., Hong Kong. (852)2609-7407. Fax: (852)2603-5110. E-mail: renditions@cuhk.edu.hk. Web site: www.renditions .org. **Contact:** Dr. Anders Hansson, editor.

Magazine Needs *Renditions: A Chinese-English Translation Magazine*, published twice/year in May and November, uses "exclusively translations from Chinese, ancient and modern." All poems are printed with Chinese and English texts side by side. Has published translations of the poetry of Yang Lian, Gu Cheng, Shu Ting, Mang Ke, and Bei Dao. *Renditions* is about 150 pages, magazine-sized, elegantly printed, perfect-bound, with glossy card cover. Single copy: $19.90; subscription: $29.90/year, $49.90/2 years, $69.90/3 years.

How to Submit Submissions should be accompanied by Chinese originals. Accepts e-mail and fax submissions. "Chinese originals should be sent by postal mail because of formatting problems. Include 2 copies each of the English translation and the Chinese text to facilitate refereeing. Use British spelling." Sometimes comments on rejected translations. Publishes theme issues. Guidelines available on Web site. Responds in 2 months. Manuscripts usually not returned.

Additional Information Also publishes a hardback series (Renditions Books) and a paperback series (Renditions Paperbacks) of Chinese literature in English translation. "Will consider" book mss; query with sample translations.

◪ RHINO

P.O. Box 591, Evanston IL 60204. Web site: www.rhinopoetry.org. Established 1976. **Contact:** Deborah Nodler Rosen, Helen Degen Cohen, or Jackie White, co-editors.

- *RHINO* poems have been reprinted in *The Best American Poetry*, nominated for Pushcart Prizes, and won repeated Illinois Arts Council awards.

Magazine Needs *RHINO*, published annually in spring, prints poetry, short-shorts, and translations. Wants "work that reflects passion, originality, engagement with contemporary culture, and a love affair with language. We welcome free verse, formal poetry, innovation, and risk-taking." Has published poetry by Geoffrey Forsyth, Victoria Anderson, F. Daniel Rzicznek, and Ricardo Pau-Llosa. *RHINO* is 150 pages, 7×10, printed on high-quality paper, with card cover with art. Receives 8,000-10,000 submissions/year, accepts 90-100, or 1%. Press run is 1,000. Single copy: $12. Sample: $5 (back issue).

How to Submit Submit 3-5 poems or 1-3 short-shorts once during reading period. Considers simultaneous submissions with notification; no previously published poems. Include SASE. Expects electronic copy upon acceptance; sends proofs. Reads submissions April 1-October 1. Guidelines available for SASE or on Web site. Responds in up to 3-6 months. Pays 2 contributor's copies. Acquires first rights only.

⊕ $◪ THE RIALTO

P.O. Box 309, Alysham, Norwich, Norfolk NR11 6LN England. Web site: www.therialto.co.uk. Established 1984. **Contact:** Michael Mackmin, editor.

Magazine Needs *The Rialto*, published 3 times/year, seeks "to publish the best new poems by established and beginning poets. We seek excellence and originality." Has published poetry by Alice Fulton, Jenny Joseph, Les Murray, George Szirtes, Philip Gross, and Ruth Padel. *The Rialto* is 64 pages, A4, with full-color cover. Receives about 12,000 poems/year, accepts about 1%. Press run is 1,500. Single copy: £7.50; subscription: £23 (prices listed are for U.S. and Canada). Make checks payable to *The Rialto*. "Checks in sterling only, please. Online payment also available on Web site."

How to Submit Submit up to 6 poems at a time. Considers simultaneous submissions; no previously published poems. Cover letter is preferred. "SASE or SAE with IRCs essential. U.S. readers please note that U.S. postage stamps are invalid in UK." Time between acceptance and publication is up to 4 months. Seldom comments on rejected poems. Responds in up to 4 months. "A large number of poems arrive every week, so please note that you will have to wait at least 10 weeks for yours to be read." Pays £20/poem. Poet retains rights.

Additional Information "*The Rialto* has recently commenced publishing first collections by poets. Please do not send book-length manuscripts. Query first."

Contest/Award Offerings Sponsors an annual young poets competition. Details available in magazine and on Web site.

Advice Before submitting, "you will probably have read many poems by many poets, both living and dead. You will probably have put aside each poem you write for at least 3 weeks before considering it afresh. You will have asked yourself, 'Does it work technically?'; checked the rhythm, the rhymes (if used), and checked that each word is fresh and meaningful in its context, not jaded and tired. You will hopefully have read *The Rialto*."

🖉 ◎ RIBBONS: TANKA SOCEITY OF AMERICA JOURNAL

5921 Cayutaville Rd, Alpine NY 14805. E-mail: davidb@htva.net. Web site: www.tankasocietyofamerica.com. Established 2000. **Contact:** Dave Bacharach, editor.

Magazine Needs *Ribbons: Tanka Society of America Journal*, published quarterly, seeks and regularly prints "the best tanka poetry being written in English, together with reviews, critical and historical essays, commentaries, and translations." Wants "poetry that exemplifies the very best in English-language tanka, which we regard as 'the queen of short form poetry,' having a significant contribution to make to the short poem in English. All schools and approaches are welcome." Tanka should "reflect contemporary life, issues, values, and experience, in descriptive, narrative, and lyrical modes." Does not want "work that merely imitates the Japanese masters." Considers poetry by children and teens. "We have no age restrictions." Has published poetry by Cherie Hunter Day, Marianne Bluger, Sanford Goldstein, Larry Kimmel, John Stevenson, and George Swede. *Ribbons* is 60-72 pages, 6×9 perfect-bound, with color cover and art. Receives about 2,000 poems/year, accepts about 20%. Press run is 275; 15 distributed free. Single copy: $10; subscription: $25. Make checks payable to Tanka Society of America and contact Carole MacRury, Secretary/Treasurer (e-mail: macrury@whidbey.com; 1636 Edwards Dr., Point Roberts, WA 98281).

How to Submit Submit 1-8 poems at a time. Lines/poem: 5 minimum; sequences of up to 50 total lines considered. No previously published poems or simultaneous submissions. Prefers e-mail submissions (pasted into body of message); no disk submissions. "Postal submissions must include SASE." Reads submissions year round. "See the publication or contact the editor for specific deadlines for each issue." Time between acceptance and publication is 2 months. Sometimes comments on rejected poems. Regularly publishes theme issues. Guidelines available in magazine or on Web site. Responds in 4-8 weeks. No payment. Acquires one-time rights. Rights revert to poet upon publication. Reviews books/chapbooks of poetry and other magazines/journals in 250-1,200 words, single- or multi-book format. Send materials for review consideration to the editor or to Michael McClintock, President, Tanka Society of America, 9230 N. Stoneridge Lane, Fresno CA 93720.

Additional Information "Features in each issue include 'Poet and Tanka' (various writers); 'Tanka Cafe' by Michael McClintock; 'Tanka Favorites,' essays by various writers, book reviews, and topical and historical essays and commentaries. About 200 new tanka appear in each issue. McClintock's 'Tanka Cafe' uses up to 45 poems per issue on a given theme, with critical commentary relating to contemporary tanka in English trends, styles, techniques, and subject matter."

Contest/Award Offerings The annual Tanka Society of America International English-Language Tanka Competition (see separate listing in Contests & Awards). "Additionally, a Members' Choice Award of $25 is given each quarter for a poem appearing in the 'Tanka Cafe' feature; non-cash Editor's Choice Awards are also featured in each issue."

Advice "Work by beginning as well as established English-language tanka poets is welcome; first-time contributors are encouraged to study the tanka form and contemporary examples before submitting. No particular school or style of tanka is preferred over another; our publications seek to showcase the full range of English-language tanka expression and subject matter through the work of new and established poets in the genre from around the world."

✪ ◪ RIVER OAK REVIEW

Elmhurst College, 190 Prospect Ave., Elmhurst IL 60126. (630)617-6483. Web site: www.riveroakreview.org. Established 1993. **Contact:** Ann Frank Wake, poetry editor.

Magazine Needs *River Oak Review*, published biannually, prints high-quality poetry, short fiction, and creative nonfiction. "We are a national journal striving to publish midwestern poets in each issue." Has published poetry by Wendy Bishop, Jim Elledge, James Doyle, Ken Meisel, and Robin Becker. *River Oak Review* is at least 128 pages, digest-sized, neatly printed, perfect-bound, with glossy color cover with art. Publishes about 5% of poetry received. Press run is 500. Single copy: $10; subscription: $10/year, $20/2 years. Sample: $5. Make checks payable to *River Oak Review*.

How to Submit Submit 4-6 poems at a time. No previously published poems or simultaneous submissions. SASE required. Reads submissions year round. Sometimes comments on rejected poems. Guidelines available for SASE or on Web site. Tries to respond in 3 months. Pays 2 contributor's copies. Acquires first North American serial rights.

Advice "Mary Oliver suggests that poets should read modern poetry for at least 2 hours for every hour they spend writing. Our experience as editors bears this out. We agree in principle with Stanley Kunitz, who told his poetry students to 'End on an image and don't explain it!' While we don't mean this literally, we do think that a 'less is more' philosophy usually results in better poems."

✪ $◪ RIVER STYX MAGAZINE

3547 Olive St., Suite 107, St. Louis MO 63103-1014. Web site: www.riverstyx.org. Established 1975. **Contact:** Richard Newman, editor.

- Poetry published in *River Styx* has been selected for inclusion in past volumes of *The Best American Poetry*, *Beacon's Best*, *Best New Poets* and *The Pushcart Prize*.

Magazine Needs *River Styx Magazine*, published 3 times/year in April, August, and December, is "an international, multicultural journal publishing both award-winning and previously undiscovered writers. We feature poetry, short fiction, essays, interviews, fine art, and photography." Wants "excellent poetry—original, energetic, musical, and accessible." Does not want "chopped prose or opaque poetry that isn't about anything." Has published poetry by Jennifer Perrine, Louis Simpson, Molly Peacock, Marilyn Hacker, Yusef Komunyakaa, Andrew Hudgins, and Catie Rosemurgy. *River Styx Magazine* is 100-120 pages, digest-sized, professionally printed on coated stock, perfect-bound, with color cover, includes ads. Receives about 8,000 poems/year, accepts 60-75. Press run is 2,500 (1,000 subscribers, 80 libraries). Subscription: $20/year, $35/2 years. Sample: $7.

How to Submit Submit 3-5 poems at a time. Manuscripts should be "legible copies with name and address on each page." Reads submissions May 1-November 30 only. No electronic submissions. Time between acceptance and publication is up to 1 year. Sometimes comments on rejected poems. Publishes 1 theme issue/year. Upcoming themes available in magazine or on Web site. Guidelines available for SASE or on Web site. Responds in up to 5 months. Pays 2 contributor's copies and one-year subscription, plus $15/page. Acquires one-time rights.

Contest/Award Offerings Sponsors an annual poetry contest. Past judges include Alan Shapiro, Dorianne Laux, Ellen Bryant Voigt, Philip Levine, Mark Doty, and Naomi Shihab Nye. **Deadline:** May 31. Guidelines available for SASE or on Web site.

N E O ◎ ROAD NOT TAKEN: THE JOURNAL OF FORMAL POETRY, THE (Specialized: formal poetry)

E-mail: jimatshs@yahoo.com. Web site: www.journalofformalpoetry.com. Established 2007. **Contact:** Dr. Jim Prothero, co-editor.

Magazine Needs *The Road Not Taken: the Journal of Formal Poetry*, published quarterly online, prints formal poetry "in the tradition of Frost, Wordsworth, Tennyson, Hopkins, etc." Wants "formal poetry only. Nature and spiritual poetry always of interest but not required. Also essays/blogs on the topic of formal poetry would be of interest." Does not want free verse. Accepts poetry by children and teens; no age limitations, "it just has to be excellent."

How to Submit Submit 5 poems at a time. Considers previously published poems; no simultaneous submissions. (Considers poetry posted on a public Web site/blog/forum as published.) Accepts e-mail submissions (pasted into body of message); no fax or disk submissions. Cover letter is unnecessary. Reads submissions year round. Submit seasonal poems 3 months in advance. Time between acceptance and publication is 2 months. Poems are circulated to an editorial board. "There are 2 editors, Dr. Jim Prothero and Dr. Don Williams. Poems must meet both of our approval." Sometimes comments on rejected poems. Never publishes theme issues. Guidelines available by e-mail and on Web site. Responds in 1 month. Acquires one-time rights. Rights revert to poets upon publication.

Advice "Frost is really our patron here. We like skilled formal poetry and nature or spiritual topics are of interest."

E ◑ ◎ ROADRUNNER HAIKU JOURNAL (Specialized: haiku, senryu, short haiku-like poetry)

E-mail: roadrunner_haiku@cox.net or ztemttocs@gmail.com. Web site: www.roadrunnerjournal.n et. Established 2004. **Contact:** Jason Sanford Brown, Scott Metz, editors; Richard Gilbert, translation editor.

Magazine Needs *Roadrunner Haiku Journal*, published quarterly online, is "an international Web journal that publishes the most innovative modern haiku written today." Wants haiku, senryu, and short haiku-like poetry. Does not want tanka, haiga, or haibun. Considers poetry by children and teens. Has published poetry by Fay Aoyagi, Dhugal Lindsay, Dietmar Tauchner, and Diane Wakoski. Receives about 5,000 poems/year, accepts about 5%. Distributed free online. Number of unique visitors: 25,000/year.

How to Submit Submit 5-15 poems at a time. Lines/poem: "less than 5 or so." No previously published poems or simultaneous submissions. Accepts e-mail submissions (pasted into body of message, with "Roadrunner Submission" and poet's name in subject line); no disk submissions. Cover letter is unnecessary. "Please include a short bio." Reads submissions year round. Time between acceptance and publication is less than 3 months. Poems are circulated to an editorial board. Sometimes comments on rejected poems. Guidelines available on Web site. Responds in 2 weeks. Sometimes sends prepublication galleys. Acquires first rights. Rights revert to poets upon publication.

◑ THE ROCKFORD REVIEW

P.O. Box 858, Rockford IL 61105. E-mail: daveconnieross@aol.com. Web site: http://writersguild1. tripod.com. Established 1971. **Contact:** David Ross, editor.

Magazine Needs *The Rockford Review*, published twice/year by the Rockford Writers' Guild, features poetry and prose by members and other contributors from across the country and abroad. Wants "experimental or traditional poetry that provides fresh insight into the human condition in a literal or satirical voice." Open to veterans and novices alike. "We delight in discovering new talent." Considers poetry by children and teens. *The Rockford Review* is about 100 pages, digest-sized, professionally printed, perfect-bound. Press run is 350. Single copy: $9; subscription: $20 (includes the Guild's monthly newsletter, *Write Away*).

How to Submit Submit up to 3 poems at a time. Lines/poem: 50 maximum. Considers simultaneous submissions; no previously published poems (including those published on the Internet). No e-mail submissions; accepts postal submissions only. Cover letter is required. "Include your name, address, phone number, e-mail address (if available), a 3-line bio, and an affirmation that the poems are unpublished electronically or in print." SASE required for return. Guidelines available for SASE or on Web site. Responds in 2 months. Pays 1 contributor's copy and an invitation to be a guest of honor at annual summer Gala Reading & Reception in July. Acquires first North American serial rights.

Contest/Award Offerings Editor's Choice Prizes of $25 are awarded each issue. Also sponsors an Ides of March Poetry and Prose Contest for adults and youth, with cash prizes and publication in the summer *Rockford Review*. Details available on Web site.

Also Offers Rockford Writers' Guild is a nonprofit corporation established 60 years ago "to promote good writing of all forms and to nurture literary artists of all stages." Monthly meetings and newsletters offer practical tips on writing/marketing from professional guest poets, and open mics for contests/works in progress. Levels of membership/dues: $35/year. Further information available for SASE, by e-mail, or on Web site.

Advice "If the heart/soul of your poetry raises/answers questions about coping with the human condition, try us first—we're on the same page."

$☑ ◎ ROCKY MOUNTAIN RIDER MAGAZINE (Specialized: horses; cowboy poetry; Northern Rockies region)

P.O. Box 1011, Hamilton MT 59840. (406)363-4085 or (800)509-1537. Fax: (406)363-1056. E-mail: info@rockymountainrider.com. Web site: www.rockymountainrider.com. Established 1993. **Contact:** Natalie Riehl, editor.

Magazine Needs *Rocky Mountain Rider Magazine*, published monthly, is a regional all-breed horse magazine. Wants "cowboy poetry; western or horse-themed poetry." *Rocky Mountain Rider Magazine* is 68 + pages, magazine-sized, Web offset-printed on newsprint, stapled. Publishes 0-2 poems/issue. Press run is 16,000; distributed free through 530 locations in 11 states.

How to Submit Submit 1-10 poems at a time. Lines/poem: keep length to no more than 5 stanzas. Considers previously published poems and simultaneous submissions. No e-mail submissions; postal submissions only. Cover letter is preferred. Include SASE. Seldom comments on rejected poems. Occasionally publishes theme issues. Guidelines available for SASE. Pays $10/poem. Acquires one-time rights. Reviews books of poetry. Send materials for review consideration.

☐ ◎ RUAH: A JOURNAL OF SPIRITUAL POETRY (Specialized: poetry of a spiritual nature)

Power of Poetry, 5890 Birch Ct., Oakland CA 94618-1627. Fax: (510)596-1860. E-mail: cjrenzop@yahoo.com. Web site: http://popruah.opwest.org. Established 1990. **Contact:** Armando P Ibáñez, O.P., general editor.

Magazine Needs *Ruah: A Journal of Spiritual Poetry*, published annually in June, provides "a 'noncombative forum' for poets who have had few or no opportunities to publish their work." Theme: spiritual poetry. Has 3 sections: general poems, featured poet, and chapbook contest winners. Wants "poetry that is of a 'spiritual nature,' i.e., describes an experience of the Transcendent. No religious affiliation preferences; no style/format limitations." Does not want "Satanic verse." Has published poetry by Jean Valentine, Alberto Rios, Luci Shaw, and Wendell Berry. *Ruah* is 60-80 pages, digest-sized, photocopied, perfect-bound, with glossy cardstock cover with color photo. Receives about 350 poems/year, accepts 10-20%. Press run is 250 (about 100 subscribers, 7 libraries, 10 shelf sales); 50 distributed free to authors, reviewers, and inquiries. Subscription: donated cost of $10 plus $1.75 s&h. Sample: $5 plus $1.75 s&h. Make checks payable to Power of Poetry/DSPT.

How to Submit Submit 3-5 poems at a time. Lines/poem: no more than 4 typed pages. Considers simultaneous submissions; no previously published poems. Accepts fax, e-mail (as MS Word 97 file attachments or pasted into body of message), and disk submissions. Submit poems January 1-March 31 only; reads submissions April-June only. Time between acceptance and publication is up to 6 months. "Poems are reviewed by writers and/or scholars in field of creative writing/literature." Guidelines available for SASE or by e-mail. Responds in 2 weeks. Pays 1 contributor's copy/poem. Acquires first rights, including right to publish poems on Web site.

Contest/Award Offerings The New Eden Chapbook Competition (see separate listing in Contests & Awards).

Advice *"Ruah* is a gathering place in which new poets can come to let their voices be heard alongside and in the context of 'more established' poets. The journal hopes to provide some breakthrough experiences of the Divine at work in our world."

🌐 ☑ S.W.A.G., THE MAGAZINE OF SWANSEA'S WRITERS AND ARTISTS

Dan-y-Bryn, 74 CWM Level Rd., Brynhyfryd, Swansea SA5 9DY Wales. Established 1992. **Contact:** Peter Thabit Jones, chairman/editor.

Magazine Needs *S.W.A.G., The Magazine of Sansea's Writers and Artists*, published semiannually, contains poetry, prose, articles, and illustrations. "Our purpose is to publish good literature." Wants "first-class poetry—any style." Has published poetry by Adrian Mitchell, Alan Llwyd, Mike Jenkins, and Dafydd Rowlands. *S.W.A.G.* is 48 pages, A4, professionally printed on coated paper, saddle-stapled, with glossy paper cover. Press run is 500. Subscription: £5. Sample: £2.50 plus postage (includes guidelines).

How to Submit Submit 6 poems at a time. Lines/poem: 40 maximum. No previously published poems or simultaneous submissions. Cover letter is required. Submissions must be typed. Time between acceptance and publication is 4-6 months. Poems are circulated to an editorial board. "Editor chooses/discusses choices with board." Guidelines available for SASE (or SAE with IRCs). Responds ASAP. Pays 2 contributor's copies plus a copy of S.W.A.G.'s newsletter. Staff reviews books of poetry (half page to full page). Send materials for review consideration.

Also Offers The Swansea Writers and Artists Group (S.W.A.G.) also publishes a newsletter containing information on the group's events. Send SASE for details on the organization. "We also publish Welsh-language poetry."

Advice "Interested poets should obtain sample beforehand (to see what we offer)."

☑ ◎ SAHARA (Specialized: poetry of Central New England; subscribers preferred)

P.O. Box 20705, Worcester MA 01602. (508)798-5672. E-mail: SaharaJournal@aol.com. Established 2000. **Contact:** Lydia Mancevice, managing editor.

Magazine Needs *Sahara*, published annually at the end of the year, is "dedicated to the poetry of our region, Central New England." Wants "unaffected, clear writing in any style. Poems may exist, but they should mean something, too." Does not want "pointless obscenities." Considers poetry by children and teens. Has published poetry by Robert Cording, Martin Espada, Laura Jehn Menides, Judith Ferrara, Wally Swist, and John Hodgen. *Sahara* is 90 pages, digest-sized, offset-printed, perfect-bound, with b&w printed card cover with graphics. Receives about 600 poems/year, accepts about 10%. Press run is 300 (70 subscribers, 10 libraries, 100-150 shelf sales). Single copy: $12; subscription: $20 for 2 years. Make checks payable to Elizabethan Press.

How to Submit Submit 5 poems at a time. No previously published poems or simultaneous submissions. No fax, e-mail, or disk submissions. Cover letter is required. "Please state the titles of the poems and include a bio." Reads submissions continually. Submit seasonal poems 6 months in advance. Time between acceptance and publication is at least 6 months. "Material is circulated among several editors and must find at least 1 strong advocate to be considered." Seldom comments on rejected poems. **"Subscribers are preferred."** Responds in up to 9 months. Sometimes sends prepublication galleys. Pays 1 contributor's copy. Acquires one-time rights. Reviews books/chapbooks of poetry in 300-600 words. Send materials for review consideration.

Advice "Keep revising and submitting your work."

✖ ☑ SALT HILL

English Dept., Syracuse University, Syracuse NY 13244. (315)443-1984. E-mail: salthilljournal@gmail.com. Web site: http://salthill.syr.edu/. Established 1994. **Contact:** Poetry Editor.

Magazine Needs *Salt Hill*, published semiannually, is "published by a group of writers affiliated with the Creative Writing Program at Syracuse University." Has published poetry by Campbell McGrath, Dean Young, Kim Addonizio, and James Tate. *Salt Hill* is 120-150 pages, digest-sized, perfect-bound, includes ads. Receives about 3,000 poems/year, accepts about 2%. Press run is 1,000. Subscription: $15/year. Sample: $8 domestic, $11 foreign.

How to Submit Submit 5 poems at a time. Considers simultaneous submissions; no previously published poems. Cover letter is preferred. Include a brief bio. Time between acceptance and publication is up to 8 months. Seldom comments on rejected poems. Guidelines available for SASE. Responds in up to 9 months. Pays 2 contributor's copies. Acquires one-time rights.

▣ $◻ ◎ SAM'S DOT CURRENT EVENTS (Specialized: fantasy; science fiction; horror)

(formerly *Between Kisses*), P.O. Box 782, Cedar Rapids IA 52406-0782. E-mail: sdpshowcase@yahoo .com. Web site: www.samsdotpublishing.com. Established 2002. **Contact:** Tyree Campbell, editor. Member: The Speculative Literature Foundation.

Magazine Needs *Sam's Dot Current Events*, published bimonthly online, presents fantasy, science fiction, sword and sorcery, alternate history, horror short stories, poems, illustrations, and movie and book reviews. Wants fantasy, science fiction, spooky horror, and speculative poetry. Does not want "horror with excessive blood and gore." Considers poetry by children and teens. Has published poetry by Bruce Boston, Karen A. Romanko, Erin Donahoe, Cythera, Kristine Ong Muslim, and Aurelio Rico Lopez III. Receives about 150 poems/year, accepts about 35 (23%).

How to Submit Submit up to 5 poems at a time. Lines/poem: prefers less than 100. Considers previously published poems; no simultaneous submissions. Accepts e-mail submissions (pasted into body of message); no disk submissions. "Submission should include snail mail address and a short (1-2 lines) bio." Reads submissions year round. Submit seasonal poems 6 months in advance. Time between acceptance and publication is 1-2 months. Often comments on rejected poems. Guidelines available on Web site. Responds in 4-6 weeks. Pays $2/poem, $1/reprint. Acquires first North American serial rights. Reviews books/chapbooks of poetry. Send materials for review consideration to Tyree Campbell.

Advice "*Sam's Dot Current Events* is a good place for beginning writers to submit their work."

◪ THE SAME

P.O. Box 494, Mount Union PA 17066. E-mail: riverfrontreadings@yahoo.com. Web site: http:// tsmag.itgo.com. Established 2000. **Contact:** Philip Miller, editor.

Magazine Needs *The Same*, published semiannually, prints nonfiction (essays, reviews, literary criticism), poetry, and short fiction. Wants "eclectic poetry (formal to free verse,'mainstream' to experimental, all subject matter.)" Considers poetry by children and teens. Has published poetry by Phyllis Becker, Graham Duncan, Patricia Lawson, Holly Posner, Stephen Stepanchev, and Robert Weaver. *The Same* is 50-100 pages, desktop-published, perfect-bound, with cardstock cover. Receives about 2,000 poems/year, accepts about 5%. Press run is 250 (125 subscribers/shelf sales). Single copy: $5; subscription: $10 for 2 issues, $18 for 4 issues. Make checks payable to Philip Miller.

How to Submit Submit 1-7 poems at a time. Lines/poem: 120 maximum. No previously published poems or simultaneous submissions "without query." Prefers e-mail submissions (pasted into body of message). Cover letter is optional. "Include SASE if you want a snail mail response. If you don't want your manuscript returned, you may omit the SASE if we can respond by e-mail." Please query before submitting fiction and non-fiction. Reads submissions year round. Time between acceptance and publication can be up to 11 months. Sometimes comments on rejected poems. Guidelines available for SASE, by e-mail, or on Web site. Responds within 2 months. Pays one contributor's copy. Acquires first North American serial rights and online rights for up to 9 months; returns rights to poet.

Additional Information Publishes 1-3 chapbooks/year. **Solicited mss only.** Chapbooks are 24-32 pages, desktop-published, saddle-stapled, with cardstock covers. Pays 25 author's copies (out of a press run of 100).

Advice "Our motto is 'Everyone else is different, but we're the same!' We are eclectic and non-doctrinaire."

✪ ◻ ◎ SAMSARA: THE MAGAZINE OF SUFFERING (Specialized: suffering/healing)

P.O. Box 467, Ashburn VA 20147. E-mail: rdfgoalie@gmail.com. Web site: www.samsaramagazine. net. Established 1993. **Contact:** R. David Fulcher, editor.

Magazine Needs *Samsara, The Magazine of Suffering*, published biannually, prints poetry and fiction dealing with suffering and healing. "Both metered verse and free verse poetry are welcome if dealing with the theme of suffering/healing." Has published poetry by Michael Foster, Nicole Provencher, and Jeff Parsley. *Samsara* is 80 pages, magazine-sized, desktop-published, with color cardstock cover. Receives about 200 poems/year, accepts about 15%. Press run is 300 (200 subscribers). Single copy: $5.50; subscription: $10. Sample: $4.50. Make checks payable to R. David Fulcher.

How to Submit Submit up to 5 poems at a time. Lines/poem: 3 minimum, 100 maximum. Considers simultaneous submissions "if noted as such"; no previously published poems. Cover letter is preferred. No e-mail submissionis; accepts submissions by postal mail only. Time between acceptance and publication is 3 months. Seldom comments on rejected poems. Guidelines available for SASE or on Web site. Responds in 2 months. Pays 1 contributor's copy. Acquires first North American serial rights. Reviews books/chapbooks of poetry in 500 words, single-book format. Send material for review consideration.

☑ THE SARANAC REVIEW

CVH, Plattsburgh State University, 101 Broad St., Plattsburgh NY 12901. (518)564-2241. E-mail: saranacreview@plattsburgh.edu. Web site: http://research.plattsburgh.edu/saranacreview. Established 2004. **Contact:** Poetry Editor.

Magazine Needs *The Saranac Review*, published annually in the fall, wants poetry from both U.S. and Canadian writers. Does not want "amateurish or 'greeting card' poetry." Has published poetry by Neil Shepard, Don Revell, Jim Daniels, and Naomi Ayala. *The Saranac Review* is magazine-sized, with color photo or painting on cover, includes ads. Press run is 1500. Single copy: $9/$11CA; subscription: $8/year, $15 for 2 years, $22 for 3 years, $35 for 5 years ($15/year for institutions—multi-year subscriptions receive 15% institutional discount); all Canadian subscriptions add $3/year. Make checks payable to Subscriptions/*The Saranac Review*.

How to Submit Submit no more than 3 poems at a time. Considers simultaneous submissions if notified; no previously published poems. No e-mail or disk submissions. Cover letter is appreciated. Include phone and e-mail contact information (if possible) in cover letter. Manuscripts will not be returned without SASE. Reads submissions September 1-February 15 (firm). Poems are circulated to an editorial board. Sometimes comments on rejected poems. Guidelines available on Web site. Responds in 3-6 months. Pays 2 contributor's copies. Acquires first rights.

✕ ▣ $◯ ◎ SCIFAIKUEST (Specialized: scifaiku, horror-ku, tanka, senryu, haibun, and other minimalist poetry forms)

P.O. Box 782, Cedar Rapids IA 52406-0782. E-mail: gatrix65@yahoo.com. Web site: www.samsdotpublishing.com. Established 2003. **Contact:** Tyree Campbell, managing editor. Member: The Speculative Literature Foundation.

• *Scifaikuest* was voted #1 poetry magazine in the 2004 Preditors & Editors poll.

Magazine Needs *Scifaikuest*, published quarterly both online and in print, features "science fiction/fantasy/horror minimalist poetry, especially scifaiku, and related forms. We also publish articles about various poetic forms and reviews of poetry collections. The online and print versions of *Scifaikuest* are different." Wants "artwork, scifaiku and speculative minimalist forms such as tanka, haibun, ghazals, senryu. No 'traditional' poetry." Has published poetry by Tom Brinck, Oino Sakai, Deborah P. Kolodji, Aurelio Rico Lopez III, Joanne Morcom, and John Dunphy. *Scifaikuest* (print edition) is 32 pages, digest-sized, offset-printed, perfect-bound, with color cardstock cover, includes ads. Receives about 500 poems/year, accepts about 160 (32%). Press run is 100/issue; 5 distributed free to reviewers. Single copy: $7; subscription: $20/year, $37 for 2 years. Make checks payable to Tyree Campbell/Sam's Dot Publishing.

How to Submit Submit 5 poems at a time. Lines/poem: varies, depending on poem type. No previously published poems or simultaneous submissions. Accepts e-mail submissions (pasted into body of message). No disk submissions; artwork as e-mail attachment or inserted body of e-mail. "Submission should include snail mail address and a short (1-2 lines) bio." Reads submissions year round. Submit seasonal poems 6 months in advance. Time between acceptance and publication is 1-2 months. "Editor Teri Santitoro makes all decisions regarding acceptances." Often comments on rejected poems. Guidelines available on Web site. Responds in 6-8 weeks. Pays $1/poem, $4/review or article, and 1 contributor's copy. Acquires first North American serial rights.

Advice "It's up to the writer to take the first step and submit work. Some of our best poems have come from poets who weren't sure if they were good enough. A basic knowledge of writing traditional haiku is helpful."

🌐 ◢ SEAM

P.O. Box 1051, Sawston, Cambridge CB22 3WT England. E-mail: seam.magazine@googlemail.com. (inquiries only). Web site: www.seampoetry.co.uk. Established 1994. **Contact:** Anne Berkeley, editor.

Magazine Needs *Seam*, published twice/year in spring and autumn, seeks "good contemporary poetry." Wants "high-quality poems that engage the reader." Has published poetry by Mike Barlow, Jane Holland, Sheenagh Pugh, Julian Stannard, George Szirtes, and Tamar Yoseloff. *Seam* is 72 pages, A5, perfect-bound, with b&w cover. Receives about 2,000 poems/year, accepts about 5%. Press run is 300. Subscription: £8/year (£12 or $18 overseas). Sample: £4.50 (£5.50 or $9 overseas). Payments accepted through PayPal.

How to Submit Submit 5-6 poems at a time. No simultaneous submissions or previously published poems (if published in UK). No e-mail submissions. Type each poem on 1 sheet of paper (A4 size). Sometimes comments on rejected poems. Pays 1 contributor's copy.

◢ SEEMS

P.O. Box 359, Lakeland College, Sheboygan WI 53082-0359. (920)565-1276 or (920)565-3871. Fax: (920)565-1206. E-mail: kelder@excel.net. Web site: www.seems.lakeland.edu. Established 1971. **Contact:** Karl Elder, editor.

Magazine Needs *SEEMS*, published irregularly, prints poetry, fiction, and essays. Two of the issues are considered chapbooks, and the editor suggests sampling *SEEMS* #14, "What Is The Future Of Poetry?" ($5), consisting of essays by 22 contemporary poets; "if you don't like it, return it, and we'll return your $5." "Explain That You Live: Mark Strand with Karl Elder" (*SEEMS* #29) is available for $3. Has published poetry by Philip Dacey, William Hathaway, William Heyen, Sapphire, and Frank Stanford. *SEEMS* is handsomely printed, nearly square ($7 \times 8\frac{1}{4}$), saddle-stapled. Publishes less than .5% of submissions received. Press run is 500 (more than 250 subscribers, 20 libraries). Single copy: $4; subscription: $16 for 4 issues.

How to Submit Lines/poem: open. No simultaneous submissions. No fax or e-mail submissions. Cover letter is optional. Include biographical information, SASE. Reads submissions year round. There is a 1- to 2-year backlog. "People may call or fax with virtually any question, understanding that the editor may have no answer." Guidelines available on Web site. Responds in up to 3 months (slower in summer). Pays 1 contributor's copy. Acquires first North American serial rights and permission to publish online. Returns rights upon publication.

Additional Information *Word of Mouth* (alias Seems)—with focus on work that integrates economy of language, "the musical phrase," forms of resemblance, and the sentient—will consider unpublished poetry, fiction, and creative nonfiction. Subsequent issues may include themes and will alternate with chapbooks from Word of Mouth Books (query for the no-fee, any-genre, chapbook contest: elderk@lakeland.edu). See the editor's Web site at www.karlelder.com. " Links to my work and an interview may provide insight for the potential contributor."

Advice "Visit the *SEEMS* Web site."

⬛ ◢ SENECA REVIEW

Hobart and William Smith Colleges, Geneva NY 14456. (315)781-3392. Fax: (315)781-3348. E-mail: senecareview@hws.edu. Web site: www.hws.edu/senecareview/. Established 1970. **Contact:** David Weiss, editor.

• Poetry published in *Seneca Review* has been included in *The Best American Poetry* and The Pushcart Prize anthologies.

Magazine Needs *Seneca Review*, published semiannually, seeks "serious poetry of any form, including translations. Also essays on contemporary poetry and lyrical nonfiction. You'll find plenty of free verse here—some accessible and some leaning toward experimental—with emphasis on voice, image, and diction. All in all, poems and translations complement each other and create a distinct editorial mood in each issue." Does not want "light verse." Has published poetry by Seamus Heaney, Rita Dove, Denise Levertov, Stephen Dunn, and Hayden Carruth. *Seneca Review* is 100 pages, digest-sized, professionally printed on quality stock, perfect-bound, with matte card cover. Receives 3,000-4,000 poems/year, accepts about 100. Press run is 1,000. Subscription: $11/year, $20 for 2 years, $28 for 3 years. Sample: $7.

How to Submit Submit 3-5 poems at a time. No previously published poems or simultaneous submissions. No e-mail submissions; postal submissions only. SASE required. Reads submissions September 1-May 1 only. "Submit only once during the annual reading period." Guidelines available on Web site. Responds in up to 3 months. Pays 2 contributor's copies and a 2-year subscription.

✦ ☑ ◎ SENSATIONS MAGAZINE (Specialized: 16th Century America to 21st Century America, themes)

P.O. Box 132, Lafayette, NJ 07848. E-mail: editor@sensationsmag.com. Web site: www.sensations mag.com. Established 1987. **Contact:** David Messineo, publisher/poetry editor.

• Three-time winner, American Literary Magazine Awards 1994-1996.

Magazine Needs *Sensations Magazine*, published semiannually, prints poetry, fiction, and research on American history. Wants "free verse and form on theme." Does not want "basic monosyllabic rhyme." Has published poetry by Moira Bailis, Mary Florio, Vera Gelyn, Dean Kostos, Michael Brown, Brett Rutherford. *Sensations Magazine* is 100 pages, magazine-sized, printed on acid-free paper, center-stapled, with a full-color glossy cover. Receives about 1000 poems/year, accepts about 50. Press run is 150 (100 subscribers, 30 libraries, 5 distributed free to indexing organizations and anthology contests. Single copy: $12; subscription: 20/2 issues. Make checks payable to "The Six Centuries Club."

How to Submit Submit 6 poems at a time. Considers previously published poems and simultaneous submissions. Does not accept fax, or disk submissions, will only accept email version if accepted for publication. Cover letter is preferred. See Web site for number of lines, "click 'submit' button, then 'poetry' button," and other guidelines. Reads submissions within 2 months after January deadline. Time between acceptance and publication is up to 2 months. Sometimes comments on rejected poems. Regularly publishes theme issues. Must purchase minimum $20/2 issue subscription. Pays $120 for best batch of 6 poems. Acquires one-time rights and electronic rights. Rights revert to poets upon publication. Reviews books of poetry in single-book format. Only reviews books published by active subscribers.

Also Offers "*Sensations Magazine* frequently sponsors events and holds a writer's retreat every 2 years. See 'attend' button on Web site for details."

Advice "Our thanks to all the working poets who have enabled this little independent journal to put out over 42 issues across 20 consecutive years without 1 dollar in federal, state, local, or university grant funding. Still here to serve, still eager to read your very best work."

$☑ THE SEWANEE REVIEW

University of the South, 735 University Ave., Sewanee TN 37383-1000. (931)598-1246. E-mail: lcouch@sewanee.edu. Web site: www.sewanee.edu/sewanee_review. Established 1892 ("thus being our nation's oldest continuously published literary quarterly"). **Contact:** George Core, editor.

Magazine Needs *Sewanee Review*, published quarterly, is open "to all styles and forms: formal sequences, metered verse, structured free verse, sonnets, and lyric and narrative forms—all accessible and intelligent. Fiction, criticism, and poetry are invariably of the highest establishment standards. Many of our major poets appear here from time to time." Has published poetry by Wendell Berry, George Bilgere, Catherine Savage Brosman, David Mason, Leslie Norris, and Christian Wiman. *The Sewanee Review* is nearly 200 pages, conservatively bound in matte paper, always of the same typography. Press run is 2,600. Subscription: $25/year for individuals, $33/year for institutions. Sample: $8.50 U.S., $9.50 foreign.

How to Submit Submit up to 6 poems at a time. Lines/poem: 40 maximum. No simultaneous submissions. No e-mail submissions; postal submissions only. "Unsolicited works should not be submitted between June 1 and August 31. A response to any submission received during that period will be greatly delayed." Guidelines available in magazine or on Web site. Responds in 2 months. Pays per line, plus 2 contributor's copies (and reduced price for additional copies). Solicits brief, standard, and essay-reviews.

Contest/Award Offerings Winners of the Allen Tate Prize and the Aiken Taylor Award for Modern American Poetry are determined by the editorial board and a prize committee; poets cannot apply for these awards.

Advice "Please keep in mind that for each poem published in *The Sewanee Review*, approximately 250 poems are considered."

☐ ◎ SHEMOM (Specialized: parenting)

2486 Montgomery Ave., Cardiff CA 92007. E-mail: pdfrench@cox.net. Established 1997. **Contact:** Peggy French, editor.

Magazine Needs *Shemom*, published 3 times/year, is a zine that "celebrates parenting and the joys and struggles that present themselves on that journey." Includes poetry, essays, book and CD reviews, recipes, art, and children's poetry. Open to any style, but prefers free verse. "We showcase writers of all ages that reflect on life's varied experiences. We often feature hiaku." *Shemom* is 10-20 pages. Receives about 100 poems/year, accepts 50%. Press run is 60 (30 subscribers). Single copy: $3.50; subscription: $12/4 issues. Make checks payable to Peggy French.

How to Submit Submit 3 poems at a time. Considers previously published poems and simultaneous submissions. Accepts e-mail submissions (as attachment or pasted into body of message). "Prefer e-mail submission, but not required; if material is to be returned, please include a SASE." Time between acceptance and publication is 3 months. Guidelines available for SASE or by e-mail. Responds in 2 months. Pays 1 contributor's copy. Acquires one-time rights.

$☑ SHENANDOAH

Mattingly House, 2 Lee Ave., Washington and Lee University, Lexington VA 24450-0303. (540)458-8765. Fax: (540)458-8461. E-mail: lleech@wlu.edu. Web site: http://shenandoah.wlu.edu. Established 1950. **Contact:** Lynn Leech, managing editor.

• Poetry published in *Shenandoah* has been included in *The Best American Poetry*.

Magazine Needs *Shenandoah*, published triannually at Washington and Lee University, is open to all styles and forms. Has published poetry by Mary Oliver, Andrew Hudgins, W.S. Merwin, and Rita Dove. *Shenandoah* is 224+ pages, digest-sized, professionally printed, perfect-bound, with full-color cover. Press run is 2,000+. Subscription: $22/year, $40 for 2 years, $54 for 3 years. Sample: $8.

How to Submit Considers simultaneous submissions "only if we are immediately informed of acceptance elsewhere." No e-mail submissions. All submissions should be typed on 1 side of the paper only, with name and address clearly written on the upper right corner of the ms. Include SASE. Reads submissions September 1-May 30 only. Responds in 3 months. Pays $2.50/line, one-year subscription, and 1 contributor's copy. Acquires first publication rights. Staff reviews books of poetry in 7-10 pages, multi-book format. Send materials for review consideration. (Most reviews are solicited.)

Contest/Award Offerings Sponsors the annual James Boatwright III Prize for Poetry, a $1,000 prize awarded to the author of the best poem published in *Shenandoah* during a volume year. The Glasgow/Shenandoah Prize for emerging writers $2,500 awarded for poetry on alternate years. 2009 prize is for poetry. Includes publication of new work in Shenandoah. Eligibility: All writers of poetry with only 1 published book in that genre. To apply, send first book, up to 5 poems and biographical information along with an SASE and a check for the entry fee. **Entry fee:** $25 (includes 1 year subscription to Shenandoah). **Deadline**: March 15-March 31, 2009. Attn: R.T. Smith, The Glasgow Prize.

☑ ◎ THE SHEPHERD (Specialized: religious; inspirational)

1530 Seventh St., Rock Island IL 61201. (309)788-3980. Established 1996. **Contact:** Betty Mowery, poetry editor.

Magazine Needs *The Shepherd*, published quarterly, features inspirational poetry from all ages. Wants "something with a message but not preachy." Subscription: $10. Sample: $3. Make all checks payable to *The Oak*.

How to Submit Submit up to 5 poems at a time. Lines/poem: 35 maximum. Considers previously published poems. Include SASE with all submissions. Responds in one week. "*The Shepherd* does not pay in dollars or copies, but you need not purchase to be published." Acquires first or second rights. All rights revert to poet upon publication.

Contest/Award Offerings Sponsors poetry contest. Guidelines available for SASE.

◎ SHIRIM, A JEWISH POETRY JOURNAL (Specialized: reflections of Jewish living)

259 St. Joseph Ave., Long Beach CA 90803. (310)476-2861. Established 1982. **Contact:** Marc Dworkin, editor.

Magazine Needs *Shirim, A Jewish Poetry Journal*, published semiannually, prints "poetry that reflects Jewish living without limiting to specific symbols, images, or contents." Has published poetry by Robert Mezcy, Karl Shapiro, and Grace Schulmon. *Shirim* is 40 pages, 4×5, desktop-published, saddle-stapled, with cardstock cover. Press run is 200. Subscription: $7. Sample: $4.

How to Submit Submit 4 poems at a time. No previously published poems or simultaneous submissions. Cover letter is preferred. Seldom comments on rejected poems. Regularly publishes theme issues. Responds in 3 months. Acquires first rights.

◙ SIERRA NEVADA COLLEGE REVIEW

999 Tahoe Blvd., Incline Village NV 89451. E-mail: sncreview@sierranevada.edu. Web site: www.si erranevada.edu/zSNCReview/. Established 1990. **Contact:** June Sylvester Saraceno, advisory editor.

Magazine Needs *Sierra Nevada College Review*, published annually in May, features poetry and short fiction by new writers. Wants "image-oriented poems with a distinct, genuine voice. Although we don't tend to publish 'light verse,' we do appreciate, and often publish, poems that make us laugh. No limit on length, style, etc." Does not want "sentimental, clichéd, or obscure poetry." Has published poetry by Virgil Suárez, Simon Perchik, Carol Frith, and Marisella Veiga. *Sierra Nevada College Review* is about 75 pages, with art on cover. Receives about 500 poems/year, accepts about 50. Press run is 500. Subscription: $10/year. Sample: $5.

How to Submit Submit up to 5 poems at a time. Considers simultaneous submissions; no previously published poems. Accepts e-mail submissions (pasted into body of message, no attachments). Reads submissions September 1-March 1 only. Sometimes comments on rejected poems. Guidelines available for SASE, by e-mail, or on Web site. Responds in about 3 months. Pays 2 contributor's copies.

Advice "We're looking for poetry that shows subtlety and skill."

◙ THE SILT READER

Temporary Vandalism, P.O. Box 6184, Orange CA 92863-6184. E-mail: tvrec@yahoo.com. Web site: http://home.surewest.net/aphasiapress. Established 1991 (Temporary Vandalism Recordings), 1999 (*The Silt Reader*). **Contact:** Robert Roden and Barton M. Saunders, editors.

Magazine Needs *The Silt Reader*, published semiannually in January and August, is a small print magazine. "Form, length, style, and subject matter can vary. It's difficult to say what will appeal to our eclectic tastes." Does not want "strictly rants, overly didactic poetry." Has published poetry by M. Jaime-Becerra, Gerald Locklin, Simon Perchik, Margaret Garcia, and Don Winter. *The Silt Reader* is 32 pages, 4¼×5½, photocopied, saddle-stapled, with colored card cover, includes ads. Accepts less than 5% of poems received. Press run is 500. Sample: $2. Make checks payable to Robert Roden.

How to Submit Submit 5 poems at a time. Considers previously published poems and simultaneous submissions. No e-mail submissions. Cover letter is preferred. Submissions should be neatly typed. Time between acceptance and publication is 12-16 months. "Two editors' votes required for inclusion." Seldom comments on rejected poems. Responds in up to 6 months. Guidelines available for SASE or on Web site. Pays 2 contributor's copies. Acquires one-time rights.

Additional Information Temporary Vandalism publishes 2 chapbooks/year. **"We are not currently accepting any unsolicited full-length manuscripts for publishing."** Chapbooks are usually 40 pages, photocopied, saddle-stapled, with an initial press run of 100 (reprint option if needed). For sample chapbooks, send $5 to the above address.

☐ ◎ SKIPPING STONES: A MULTICULTURAL MAGAZINE (Specialized: poetry by young writers under 18; bilingual; multicultural and social issues; nature/ecology)

P.O. Box 3939, Eugene OR 97403. (541)342-4956. E-mail: editor@skippingstones.org. Web site: www.skippingstones.org. Established 1988. **Contact:** Arun Toké, editor.
   • *Skipping Stones* has been the recipient of EdPress, NAME, and Parent's Guide Awards, among others.

Magazine Needs *Skipping Stones: A Multicultural Magazine*, published bimonthly during the school year (5 issues), "encourages cooperation, creativity, and celebration of cultural and ecological richness." Wants "poetry by young writers under age 18, on multicultural and social issues, family, freedom—uplifting. No adult poetry, please." *Skipping Stones* is magazine-sized, saddle-stapled, printed on recycled paper. Receives about 500-1,000 poems/year, accepts 10%. Press run is 2,500. Subscription: $25. Sample: $5.

How to Submit Submit up to 5 poems at a time. Lines/poem: 30 maximum. Considers simultaneous submissions; no previously published poems. Accepts e-mail submissions. Cover letter is preferred. "Include your cultural background, experiences, and the inspiration behind your creation." Time between acceptance and publication is 6-9 months. "A piece is chosen for publication when all the editorial staff feel good about it." Seldom comments on rejected poems. Publishes multi-theme issues. Guidelines available for SASE. Responds in up to 4 months. Pays 1 contributor's copy, offers 25% discount for more. Acquires first serial rights and non-exclusive reprint rights.

Contest/Award Offerings Sponsors Annual Youth Honor Awards for 7- to 17-year-olds. Theme is "Multicultural, Social, International, and Nature Awareness." Guidelines available for SASE or on Web site. **Entry fee:** $3 (entitles entrant to a free issue featuring the 10 winners). **Deadline:** June 25.

☑ SLANT: A JOURNAL OF POETRY

Box 5063, University of Central Arkansas, 201 Donaghey Ave., Conway AR 72035-5000. (501)450-5107. Web site: www.uca.edu/english/Slant/. Established 1987. **Contact:** James Fowler, editor.

Magazine Needs *Slant: A Journal of Poetry*, published annually in May, aims "to publish a journal of fine poetry from all regions of the United States and beyond." Wants "traditional and 'modern' poetry, even experimental; moderate length, any subject on approval of Board of Readers." Doesn't want "haiku, translations." Has published poetry by Susan H. Case, Philip Dacey, Maureen Tolman Flannery, Nancy Scott, Peter Swanson, and Paul Willis. *Slant* is 120 pages, professionally printed on quality stock, flat-spined, with matte card cover. Receives about 1,300 poems/year, accepts 70-75. Press run is 175 (70-100 subscribers). Sample: $10.

How to Submit Submit up to 5 poems at a time. Lines/poem: poems should be of moderate length. No previously published poems or simultaneous submissions. Submissions should be typed; include SASE. "Put name, address (including e-mail if available), and phone number at the top of each page." Accepts submissions September 1-November 15. Comments on rejected poems "on occasion." Guidelines available in magazine, for SASE, or on Web site. Responds in 3-4 months from November 15 deadline. Pays 1 contributor's copy. Poet retains rights.

Advice "We tend to publish those poems whose execution, line by line, does full justice to their conception. Often the decision to accept comes down to the matter of craft, language."

☐ ◎ SLATE & STYLE (Specialized: by & for blind writers)

2704 Beach Dr., Merrick NY 11566. (516)868-8718. E-mail: LoriStay@aol.com. Web site: http://home.earthlink.net/~uinen/writers_division/. Established 1982. **Contact:** Loraine Stayer, editor.

Magazine Needs *Slate & Style*, published quarterly, is the magazine of the Writers' Division of the National Federation of the Blind. Published for blind writers, *Slate & Style* is available on cassette, in large print, in Braille, and by e-mail, and includes resources and articles of interest to blind writers. "We prefer contributors be blind writers, or at least writers by profession or inclination. New writers welcome. No obscenities. Will consider all forms of poetry including haiku. Interested in new talent." Considers poetry by children and teens, "but please specify age." Has published poetry by Mary Brunoli, Kerry Elizabeth Thompson, Katherine Barr, and Nancy Scott. *Slate & Style* (print format) is 28-32 pages, magazine-sized, stapled. Press run is 200 (160 subscribers, 4-5 libraries). Subscription/membership: $10/year (regardless of format). Sample: $3.

How to Submit Submit 3 poems at a time once or twice/year. Lines/poem: 5-36. No previously published poems or simultaneous submissions. Accepts submissions by e-mail (pasted into body of message). "On occasion we receive poems in Braille. I prefer print, since Braille slows me down. Typed is best." Cover letter is preferred. Reads submissions according to the following deadlines: February 16, May 15, August 15, November 15; "do not submit manuscripts in July." Comments on rejected poems "if requested." Guidelines available in magazine, for SASE, by e-mail, or on Web site. Responds in 2 weeks "if I like it." Pays 1 contributor's copy. Reviews books of poetry. Send materials for review consideration.

Contest/Award Offerings Sponsors an annual poetry contest, awarding 1st Prize: $100; 2nd Prize: $50; 3rd Prize: $25. Honorable mentions may also be awarded, and winning poems will be published in magazine. **Entry fee:** $5 for up to 3 poems. Make check or money order payable to NFB Writers' Division. "Include cover letter with title and your identifying information." **Deadline:** June 1. Guidelines available for SASE, by e-mail, or on Web site.

Advice "Before you send us a poem, read it aloud. Does it sound good to you? We put our poetry into tape format, so we want it to sound and look good."

☑ SLIPSTREAM

Dept. W-1, P.O. Box 2071, Niagara Falls NY 14301-0071. (716)282-2616 (after 5 PM, EST). E-mail: editors@slipstreampress.org. Web site: www.slipstreampress.org. Established 1980. **Contact:** Dan Sicoli, Robert Borgatti, and Livio Farallo, poetry editors.

Magazine Needs *Slipstream*, published annually in spring, is "about 95% poetry, with some artwork. We like new work with contemporary urban flavor. Writing must have a cutting edge to get our attention. We like to keep an open forum, any length, subject, style. Best to see a sample to get a feel. Like city stuff as opposed to country." Wants "poetry that springs from the gut, screams from dark alleys, inspired by experience." Does not want "pastoral, religious, traditional, rhyming" poetry. Has published poetry by Terry Godbey, Gerald Locklin, David Chorlton, Martin Vest, Beth Royer, and Mofolasayo Ogundiran. *Slipstream* is 80-100 pages, $7 \times 8^{1/2}$, professionally printed, perfect-bound. Receives more than 2,500 poetry submissions/year, accepts less than 10%. Press run is 500 (400 subscribers, 10 libraries). Subscription: $20 for 2 issues and 2 chapbooks. Sample: $10.

How to Submit No e-mail submissions. Sometimes comments on rejected poems. Publishes theme issues. Guidelines available for SASE or on Web site. Responds in up to 2 months "if SASE included." Pays 1-2 contributor's copies.

Contest/Award Offerings *Slipstream* Poetry Chapbook Contest (see separate listing in Contests & Awards).

Advice "Do not waste time submitting your work 'blindly.' Sample issues from the small press first to determine which ones would be most receptive to your work."

☑ SMARTISH PACE

P.O. Box 22161, Baltimore MD 21203. E-mail: sreichert@smartishpace.com. Web site: www.smarti shpace.com. and www.myspace.com/smartishpace. Established 1999. **Contact:** Stephen Reichert, editor.

Magazine Needs *Smartish Pace*, published in April, contains poetry and translations. "*Smartish Pace* is an independent poetry journal and is not affiliated with any institution." No restrictions on style or content of poetry. Has published poetry in the past year by Carl Dennis, B.H. Fairchild, David Lehman, Alda Merini, Campbell McGrath, Gregory Orr, and Diane Wakowski. *Smartish Pace* is about 140 pages, digest-sized, professionally printed, perfect-bound, with full-color cover featuring contemporary artwork. Receives about 5,000 poems/year, accepts 1%. Press run is 1,100. Subscription: $20. Sample: $10.

How to Submit Submit no more than 6 poems at a time. Considers simultaneous submissions; no previously published poems. Cover letter with bio and SASE required. Submit seasonal poems 8 months in advance. Time between acceptance and publication is up to 1 year. Guidelines available for SASE or on Web site. Responds in 1-5 months. Pays 1 contributor's copy. Acquires first rights. Encourages unsolicited reviews, essays, and interviews. Send materials for review consideration. All books received will also be listed in the Books Received section of each issue and on the Web site along with ordering information and a link to the publisher's Web site.

Contest/Award Offerings *Smartish Pace* hosts the annual Erskine J. Poetry Prize and the Beullah Rose Poetry Prize (for women) (see separate listings in Contests & Awards).

Also Offers Also available on Web site: Poets Q&A, where readers can ask questions of poets and read their responses. Recent participants have included Robert Pinsky, Jorie Graham, Stephen Dunn, Carl Dennis, Eavan Boland, Campbell McGrath, and Robert Hass.

Advice "Visit our Web site. Read a few issues."

$⬛ ◎ SNOWY EGRET (Specialized: nature-oriented poetry)

P.O. Box 29, Terre Haute IN 47808. Web site: www.snowyegret.net. Established 1922 by Humphrey A. Olsen. **Contact:** Philip Repp, editor.

Magazine Needs *Snowy Egret*, published in spring and autumn, specializes in work that is "nature-oriented: poetry that celebrates the abundance and beauty of nature or explores the interconnections between nature and the human psyche." Has published poetry by Conrad Hilberry, Lyn Lifshin, Gayle Eleanor, James Armstrong, and Patricia Hooper. *Snowy Egret* is 60 pages, magazine-sized, offset-printed, saddle-stapled. Receives about 500 poems/year, accepts about 30. Press run is 400. Sample: $8; subscription: $15/year, $25 for 2 years.

How to Submit Guidelines available for #10 SASE. Responds in 1 month. Always sends prepublication galleys. Pays $4/poem or $4/page plus 2 contributor's copies. Acquires first North American and one-time reprint rights.

Advice "First-hand, detailed observation gives poetry authenticity and immediacy."

⬛ ◎ SO TO SPEAK: A Feminist Journal of Language and Art (Specialized: women/feminism)

George Mason University, 4400 University Dr., MSN 2C5, Fairfax VA 22030-4444. (703)993-3625. E-mail: sts@gmu.edu. (inquiries only). Web site: www.gmu.edu/org/sts. Established 1991. **Contact:** Poetry Editor.

Magazine Needs *So to Speak*, published semiannually, prints "high-quality work relating to feminism, including poetry, fiction, nonfiction (including book reviews and interviews), photography, artwork, collaborations, lyrical essays, and other genre-questioning texts." Wants "work that addresses issues of significance to women's lives and movements for women's equality and are especially interested in pieces that explore issues of race, class, and sexuality in relation to gender." *So to Speak* is 100-128 pages, digest-sized, photo-offset-printed, perfect-bound, with glossy cover, includes ads. Receives about 800 poems/year, accepts 10%. Press run is 1,000 (75 subscribers, 100 shelf sales); 500 distributed free to students/contributors. Subscription: $12. Sample: $7.

How to Submit Submit 3-5 poems at a time. Considers simultaneous submissions; no previously published poems. No e-mail submissions. "Please submit poems as you wish to see them in print. Be sure to include a cover letter with full contact info, publication credits, and awards received." Reads submissions August 15-October 15 and December 31-March 15. Time between acceptance and publication is 6-8 months. Seldom comments on rejected poems. Responds in 3 months if submissions are received during reading period. Pays 2 contributor's copies. Acquires one-time rights.

Contest/Award Offerings *So to Speak* holds an annual poetry contest that awards $500. Guidelines available for SASE, by e-mail, or on Web site.

✪ ☐ ◎ SO YOUNG! (Specialized: aging; holistic health)

Anti-Aging Press, Inc., P.O. Box 142174, Coral Gables FL 33114. (305)662-3928. Fax: (305)661-4123. E-mail: julia2@gate.net. Established 1992 (press), 1996 (newsletter). **Contact:** Julia Busch, editor.

Magazine Needs *So Young!*, published quarterly, is a newsletter covering "anti-aging/holistic health/humorous/philosophical topics; dedicated to a youthful body, face, mind, and spirit." Wants "short, upbeat, fresh, positive poetry for the mid-30s and older adult. Work can be humorous, philosophical fillers." Does not want "off-color, suggestive poems, or anything relative to first night, maudlin memories, politics, religion, or unrequited love affairs." *So Young!* is 16 pages, magazine-sized (8×11 sheets, 3-hole-punched, stapled), unbound. Receives several hundred poems/year, accepts 4-6. Press run is 700. Subscription: $35. Sample: $9.

How to Submit Submit up to 5 poems at a time. Considers previously published poems and simultaneous submissions. Accepts e-mail submissions (preferred, pasted into body of message). Cover letter unnecessary. Time between acceptance and publication "depends on poem subject matter— usually 6-8 months." Guidelines available for SASE. Responds in 2 months. Pays 10 contributor's copies. Acquires one-time rights.

⬛ ◎ SONG OF THE SAN JOAQUIN (Specialized: subjects pertinent to the San Joaquin Valley)

P.O. Box 1161, Modesto CA 95353-1161. E-mail: SSJQ03psj@yahoo.com. Web site: www.Chaparral Poets.org/SSJ.html. Established 2003. **Contact:** The Editor.

Magazine Needs *Song of the San Joaquin*, published quarterly, features "subjects about or pertinent to the San Joaquin Valley of Central California. This is defined geographically as the region from Fresno to Stockton, and from the foothills on the west to those on the east." Wants all forms and styles of poetry. "Keep subject in mind." Does not want "pornographic, demeaning, vague, or trite approaches." Considers poetry by children and teens. Has published poetry by Joyce Odam, Wilma Elizabeth McDaniel, Margarita Engle, Marnelle White, Frederick Zydek, and Nancy Haskett. *Song of the San Joaquin* is 60 pages, digest-sized, direct-copied, saddle-stapled, with cardstock cover with glossy color photo. Press run is 200 (25 copies to libraries); 40 distributed free to contributors.

How to Submit Submit up to 3 poems at a time. Lines/poem: open ("however, poems under 40 lines have the best chance"). Considers previously published poems; no simultaneous submissions. Accepts e-mail submissions; no disk submissions. Cover letter is preferred. "SASE required. All submissions must be typed on 1 side of the page only. Proofread submissions carefully. Name, address, phone number, and e-mail address should appear on all pages. Cover letter should include any awards, honors, and previous publications for each poem, and a biographical sketch of 75 words or less." Reads submissions "periodically throughout the year." Submit seasonal poems at least 3 months in advance. Time between acceptance and publication is 3-6 months. "Poems are circulated to an editorial board of 7 who then decide on the final selections." Seldom comments on rejected poems. Occasionally publishes theme issues. Upcoming themes available for SASE, by e-mail, or on Web site. Guidelines available in magazine, for SASE, by e-mail, or on Web site. Responds in up to 3 months. Pays 1 contributor's copy. Acquires one-time rights.

Additional Information "Poets of the San Joaquin, which sponsors this publication, is a chapter of California Federation of Chaparral Poets, Inc., and publishes an annual anthology of members' works. Information available for SASE or by e-mail."

Contest/Award Offerings Poets of the San Joaquin holds an annual local young poets' contest as well as regular poetry contests. Guidelines available for SASE or by e-mail.

Advice "Know the area about which you write. Poems do not need to be agricultural or nature-oriented but should reflect the lifestyles of the California Central Valley."

⬛ SOUL FOUNTAIN

90-21 Springfield Blvd., Queens Village NY 11428. (718)479-2594. E-mail: davault@aol.com. Web site: www.TheVault.org. Established 1997. **Contact:** Tone Bellizzi, editor.

Magazine Needs *Soul Fountain*, published 4 times/year, is produced by The Vault, a not-for-profit arts project of the Hope for the Children Foundation, "committed to empowering young and emerging artists of all disciplines at all levels to develop and share their talents through performance, collaboration, and networking." Prints poetry, art, photography, short fiction, and essays. Open to all. "We publish quality submitted work, and specialize in emerging voices. We favor visionary, challenging, and consciousness-expanding material." Does not want "poems about pets, nature, romantic love, or the occult. Sex and violence themes not welcome." Welcomes poetry by teens. *Soul Fountain* is 28 pages, magazine-sized, offset-printed, saddle-stapled. Subscription: $24. Sample: $6. Make checks payable to Hope for the Children Foundation.

How to Submit Submit 2-3 poems at a time. Lines/poem: 1 page maximum. Considers previously published poems and simultaneous submissions. Accepts e-mail submissions (pasted into body of message). Poems should be camera-ready. "When e-mailing a submission, it is necessary to include your mailing address. Cover letter not needed. SASE with postal mail submissions is not necessary, but $2 in postage is appreciated." Time between acceptance and publication is up to 1 year. Guidelines available for SASE or on Web site. Pays 1 contributor's copy.

☑ THE SOUTH CAROLINA REVIEW

Center for Electronic & Digital Publishing, Strode Tower Room 611, Box 340522, Clemson SC 29634-0522. (864)656-3151 or 656-5399. Fax: (864)656-1345. Web site: www.clemson.edu/caah/cedp/scrintro.htm. Established 1968. **Contact:** Wayne Chapman, editor.

Magazine Needs *The South Carolina Review*, published semiannually, is a literary magazine "recognized by the *New York Quarterly* as one of the top 20 of this type." Wants "any kind of poetry as long as it's good. Interested in seeing more traditional forms." Does not want "stale metaphors, uncertain rhythms, or lack of line integrity." Has published poetry by Stephen Cushman, Alberto Ríos, and Virgil Suárez. *The South Carolina Review* is 200 pages, digest-sized, professionally printed, flat-spined. Receives about 1,000 submissions of poetry/year, accepts about 100. Press run is 500 (350 subscribers, 250 libraries). Sample: $16.

How to Submit Submit 3-10 poems at a time. No previously published poems or simultaneous submissions. Cover letter is preferred. "Editor prefers a chatty, personal cover letter plus a list of publishing credits. Manuscript format should be according to new MLA Stylesheet." Submissions should be sent "in an 8×10 manila envelope so poems aren't creased." Do not submit during June, July, August, or December. Occasionally publishes theme issues. Responds in 2 months. Pays in contributor's copies. Staff reviews books of poetry.

☑ ◎ SOUTH DAKOTA REVIEW (Specialized: American West subjects & work by Western authors)

Dept. of English, University of South Dakota, 414 E. Clark St., Vermillion SD 57069. (605)677-5184 or 677-5966. Fax: (605)677-6409. E-mail: bbedard@usd.edu. Web site: www.usd.edu/sdreview/. Established 1963. **Contact:** Brian Bedard, editor.

Magazine Needs *South Dakota Review*, published quarterly, prints "poetry, fiction, criticism, and scholarly and personal essays. When material warrants, emphasis is on the American West; writers from the West; Western places or subjects. There are frequent issues with no geographical emphasis; periodic special issues on one theme, one place, or one writer." Wants "originality, sophistication, significance, craft—i.e., professional work." Has published poetry by Allan Safarik, Joanna Gardner, Nathaniel Hansen, and Jeanine Stevens. Press run is 500-600 (450 subscribers, half libraries). Single copy: $10; subscription: $30/year, $45/2 years. Sample: $8.

How to Submit Submit 3-5 poems at a time. No e-mail submissions. Cover letter is required. Must include SASE. Reads submissions year round. Time between acceptance and publication is up to 6 months. Sometimes comments on rejected poems. Publishes theme issues. Guidelines available for SASE or on Web site. Responds in 2-3 months ("sometimes longer if still considering manuscript for possible use in a forthcoming issue"). Pays 1 contributor's copy and a one-year subscription. Acquires first North American serial rights and reprint rights.

Advice "We tend to favor the narrative poem, the concrete crafted lyric, the persona poem, and the meditative place poem. Yet we try to leave some room for poems outside those parameters to keep some fresh air in our selection process."

☆ ☐ THE SOUTHEAST REVIEW

Dept. of English, Florida State University, Tallahassee FL 32306. (850)644-2773. E-mail: serpoetry@gmail.com. Web site: www.southeastreview.org. Established 1979. **Contact:** Rebecca Hazelton, poetry editor.

Magazine Needs *The Southeast Review*, published biannually, looks for "the very best poetry by new and established poets." *The Southeast Review* is 160 pages, digest-sized. Receives about 5,000 poems/year, accepts less than 4%. Press run is 1,000 (500 subscribers, 100 libraries, 200 shelf sales); 100 distributed free. Single copy: $8; subscription: $15/year. Sample: $6. Make checks payable to *The Southeast Review*.

How to Submit Submit 3-5 poems at a time. Considers simultaneous submissions; no previously published poems. Accepts submissions by postal mail only; SASE required. Cover letter is preferred ("very brief"). Reads submissions year round. Time between acceptance and publication is up to 1 year. Seldom comments on rejected poems. Guidelines available for SASE, by e-mail, or on Web site. Responds in up to 3 months. Pays 2 contributor's copies. Acquires first North American serial rights. Reviews books and chapbooks of poetry. "Please query the Book Review Editor (serbookreview@gmail.com) concerning reviews."

Contest/Award Offerings Sponsors an annual poetry contest. Winner receives $500 and publication; 9 finalists will also be published. **Entry fee:** $15 for 3 poems. **Deadline:** March 1. Guidelines available on Web site.

⦿ SOUTHERN HUMANITIES REVIEW

9088 Haley Center, Auburn University, Auburn AL 36849-5202. E-mail: shrengl@auburn.edu. Web site: www.auburn.edu/shr. Established 1967. **Contact:** Dan Latimer and Virginia M. Kouidis, co-editors.

Magazine Needs *Southern Humanities Review*, published quarterly, is "interested in poems of any length, subject, genre. Space is limited, and brief poems are more likely to be accepted. Translations welcome, but also send written permission from the copyright holder." Has published poetry by Donald Hall, Andrew Hudgins, Margaret Gibson, Stephen Dunn, Walt McDonald, and R.T. Smith. *Southern Humanities Review* is 100 pages, digest-sized. Press run is 800. Subscription: $15/year. Sample: $5.

How to Submit Submit 3-5 poems at a time. No previously published poems or simultaneous submissions. No e-mail submissions. "Send poems in a business-sized envelope. Include SASE. Avoid sending faint computer printout." Responds in 2 months, "possibly longer in summer." Always sends prepublication galleys. Pays 2 contributor's copies. Copyright reverts to author upon publication. Reviews books of poetry in approximately 750-1,000 words. Send materials for review consideration.

Contest/Award Offerings Sponsors the Theodore Christian Hoepfner Award, a $50 prize for the best poem published in a given volume of *Southern Humanities Review*.

Advice "For beginners, we recommend study and wide reading in English and classical literature, and, of course, American literature—the old works, not just the new. We also recommend study of or exposure to a foreign language and a foreign culture. Poets need the reactions of others to their work: criticism, suggestions, discussion. A good creative writing teacher would be desirable here, and perhaps some course work, too; and then submission of work, attendance at workshops. And again, the reading: history, biography, verse, essays—all of it. We want to see poems that have gone beyond the language of slippage and easy attitudes."

⭐ ⦿ SOUTHERN POETRY REVIEW

Dept. of Languages, Literature and Philosophy, Armstrong Atlantic State University, 11935 Abercorn St., Savannah GA 31419-1997. (912)921-5633. E-mail: rrparham@aug.edu. Web site: www.spr.armstrong.edu. Established 1958. **Contact:** Robert Parham, editor. Member: CLMP.

● Work appearing in *Southern Poetry Review* received a 2005 Pushcart Prize.

Magazine Needs *Southern Poetry Review*, published semiannually, is the second oldest poetry journal in the region. Wants "poetry eclectically representative of the genre; no restrictions on form, style, or content." Does not want fiction, essays, or reviews. Has published poetry by Cathy Smith Bowers, Albert Goldbarth, Robert Morgan, Linda Pastan, Margaret Gibson, and R. T. Smith. *Southern Poetry Review* is 70-80 pages, digest-sized, perfect-bound, with 80 lb. matte cardstock cover with b&w photography, includes ads. Receives about 5,000 poems/year, accepts about 2%. Press run is 1,200. Single copy: $6; subscription: $12 individuals, $15 institutions. Make checks payable to *Southern Poetry Review*.

How to Submit Submit 5-7 poems at a time (10 pages maximum). Lines/poem: subject to limitations of space. Considers simultaneous submissions (with notification in cover letter); no previously published poems ("previously published" includes poems published or posted online). No e-mail or disk submissions. Cover letter is preferred. "Include SASE for reply; manuscript returned only if sufficient postage is included." Reads submissions year round. Time between acceptance and publication is 6 months. Poems are circulated to an editorial board ("multiple readers, lively discussion and decision-making"). Sometimes comments on rejected poems. Guidelines available in magazine, for SASE, by e-mail, or on Web site. Responds in 3 months. Always sends prepublication galleys. Pays 2 contributor's copies. Acquires one-time rights.

Advice "We suggest that before submitting, writers read a current issue to get a feel for our journal."

$⊘ THE SOUTHERN REVIEW

Louisiana State University, Old President's House, Baton Rouge LA 70803. (225)578-5108. Fax: (225)578-5098. E-mail: southernreview@lsu.edu. Web site: www.lsu.edu/thesouthernreview. Established 1935 (original series), 1965 (new series). **Contact:** The Editors.

• Work published in *The Southern Review* has been included frequently in *The Best American Poetry* and *The Pushcart Prize* as well as *The Beacon's Best of 1999*.

Magazine Needs *The Southern Review*, published quarterly, prints "fiction, poetry, critical essays, and book reviews, with emphasis on contemporary literature in the U.S. and abroad. Selections are made with careful attention to craftsmanship and technique and to the seriousness of the subject matter." Wants "any variety of poetry that is well crafted, though we cannot normally accommodate excessively long poems (i.e., 10 pages and over)." Has published poetry by Mary Oliver, Sydney Lea, Madeline DeFrees, Brendan Galvin, Claudia Emerson, and Jay Rogoff. *The Southern Review* is 240 pages, digest-sized, flat-spined, with matte card cover. Receives about 6,000 poetry submissions/year. Press run is 2,900 (2,100 subscribers, 70% libraries). Subscription: $25. Sample: $8.

How to Submit Submit up to 1-4 pages of poetry at a time. No previously published poems. No fax or e-mail submissions. "We do not require a cover letter, but we prefer one giving information about the author and previous publications." Reads submissions September-May. Guidelines available for SASE or on Web site. Responds in 1-2 months. Pays $30/printed page plus 2 contributor's copies. Acquires first North American serial rights. Staff reviews books of poetry in 3,000 words, multibook format. Send materials for review consideration.

$⊘ SOUTHWEST REVIEW

Southern Methodist University, P.O. Box 750374, Dallas TX 75275-0374. (214)768-1037. Fax: (214)768-1408. E-mail: swr@mail.smu.edu. Web site: www.smu.edu/southwestreview. Established 1915. **Contact:** Willard Spiegelman, editor.

• Poetry published in *Southwest Review* has been included in *The Best American Poetry* and *The Pushcart Prize*.

Magazine Needs *Southwest Review*, published quarterly, prints fiction, essays, poetry, and occasional interviews. "We always suggest that potential contributors read several issues of the magazine to see for themselves what we like. We demand very high quality in our poems; we accept both traditional and experimental writing, but avoid unnecessary obscurity and private symbolism. We place no arbitrary limits on length but find shorter poems easier to fit into our format than longer ones. We have no specific limitations as to theme. Poems tend to be lyric and narrative free verse combining a strong voice with powerful topics or situations. Diction is accessible and content often conveys a strong sense of place." Has published poetry by Albert Goldbarth, John Hollander, Mary Jo Salter, James Hoggard, Dorothea Tanning, and Michael Rosen. *Southwest Review* is 144 pages, digest-sized, professionally printed, perfect-bound, with matte text stock cover. Receives about 1,000 poetry submissions/year, accepts about 32. Press run is 1,500. Subscription: $24. Sample: $6.

How to Submit No previously published poems or simultaneous submissions. Submit by mail or on Web site. Mailed manuscripts must be typed and should include SASE for a response. Guidelines available for SASE or on Web site. Responds within 1 month. Always sends prepublication galleys. Pays cash plus contributor's copies.

Contest/Award Offerings The Elizabeth Matchett Stover Memorial Award presents $250 to the author of the best poem or groups of poems (chosen by editors) published in the preceding year. Also offers The Morton Marr Poetry Prize (see separate listing in Contests & Awards).

THE SOW'S EAR POETRY REVIEW

217 Brookneill Dr., Winchester VA 22602. E-mail: errol@kitenet.net. (inquiries only). Web site: www.sows-ear.kitenet.net. Established 1988. **Contact:** Kristin Zimet, submissions editor.

Magazine Needs *The Sow's Ear Poetry Review*, published quarterly, wants fine poetry of all styles and lengths. "Excellent art in black and white complements the poems. We often take more than 1 poem by an author we like. The 'Community of Poets' feature presents group submissions; define 'community' as broadly as you like. The 'Crossover' feature showcases works that marry the written word with another art form (for example, lyrics with music, word collages, or special calligraphy)." Has published poetry by Robert Morgan, Elizabeth Spires, Virgil Suárez, Susan Terris, and Franz Wright. *The Sow's Ear Poetry Review* is 32 pages, magazine-sized, professionally printed, saddle-stapled, with matte card cover. Receives about 3,000 poems/year, accepts about 75. Press run is 700 (600 subscribers, 15 libraries). Subscription: $20. Sample: $5. For subscriptions, contact Errol Hess, Managing Editor, 355 Mt. Lebanon Rd., Donalds SC 29638.

How to Submit Submit up to 5 poems at a time. Considers simultaneous submissions "if you tell us promptly when work is accepted elsewhere"; no previously published poems, although will consider poems from chapbooks if they were never published in a magazine. No e-mail submissions; postal submissions only. Include brief bio and SASE. Guidelines available for SASE, by e-mail, or on Web site. Responds in 3 months. Pays 2 contributor's copies. Acquires first publication rights. Inquire about reviews, interviews, and essays.

Contest/Award Offerings *The Sow's Ear* Poetry Competition and *The Sow's Ear* Chapbook Contest (see separate listings in Contests & Awards).

Advice "Four criteria help us judge the quality of submissions: 1) Does the poem make the strange familiar or the familiar strange, or both? 2) Is the form of the poem vital to its meaning? 3) Do the sounds of the poem make sense in relation to the theme? 4) Does the little story of the poem open a window on the Big Story of the human situation?"

SP QUILL QUARTERLY MAGAZINE

Shadow Poetry, 1209 Milwaukee St., Excelsior Springs MO 64024. Phone/fax: (208)977-9114. E-mail: spquill@shadowpoetry.com. Web site: www.shadowpoetry.com/magazine/spquill.html. Established 2000 (Shadow Poetry Web site), 2003 (*SP Quill*). **Contact:** Marie Summers, chief editor. Poetry Editor: Andrea Dietrich.

Magazine Needs *SP Quill Quarterly Magazine* is "an interactive chapbook-style magazine for poets and writers, filled with poetry, flash fiction, book reviews, articles, contests, profiles/bios, quotes, and more." Wants high-quality poetry, flash fiction, and quotes. Does not want "anything in poor taste, or poorly crafted poetry." Considers poetry by children (parental permission required) and teens. *SP Quill Quarterly Magazine* is 52-60 pages, digest-sized, saddle-stapled, with cardstock cover with b&w artwork (cover design remains the same from issue to issue). Receives about 500 poems/ quarter, accepts less than 10%. Single copy: $8 U.S., $10 international; subscription: $25/year U.S., $30/year international. Make checks/money orders payable to Shadow Poetry.

How to Submit Submit up to 3 poems at a time. Lines/poem: 3 minimum, 30 maximum. No previously published poems or simultaneous submissions. Accepts fax, e-mail, disk, and postal submissions as well as submissions through online form. Cover letter is preferred. "Name of author, street address, and e-mail address must accompany all submissions, no exceptions. A small author bio may accompany submission. If work is accepted, participants will be contacted by mail or e-mail before magazine release date." Reads submissions by the following deadlines: November 20 (Winter issue), February 28 (Spring issue), May 31 (Summer issue), and August 31 (Fall issue). Welcomes seasonal poems for the appropriate issue. Time between acceptance and publication is 3 weeks or more. "Poems are decided upon and edited by the poetry editor and chief editor. Final drafts will be e-mailed or mailed to the accepted poet." Never comments on rejected poems. Publishes special issues; "submit up to eight cinquain for a special Spring issue and/or 3 etheree for a special Fall issue. For definitions of these poetry types, please visit the Shadow Poetry Web site.'' Guidelines available in magazine or on Web site. Acquires first rights. Reviews books/chapbooks of poetry.

Additional Information Shadow Poetry sponsors Shadows Ink Poetry Contest, Shadow Poetry's Annual Chapbook Competition, and *White Lotus* Haiku Competition (see separate listings in Contests & Awards).

▣ $◻ ◎ SPACEPORTS & SPIDERSILK (Specialized: fantasy, science fiction, mild horror for older children and teens)

(formerly *KidVisions*), P.O. Box 782, Cedar Rapids IA 52406-0782. E-mail: kidvisions@samsdotpubl ishing.com. Web site: www.samsdotpublishing.com. Established 2002. **Contact:** Lisa M. Bradley, editor. Member: The Speculative Literature Foundation.

Magazine Needs *Spaceports & Spidersilk*, published quarterly online, prints ''fantasy, science fiction, sword and sorcery, alternate history, myths/folktales, spooky short stories, poems, illustrations, puzzles, nonfiction articles, and movie and book reviews, all for a reading audience of 9-18 years old.'' Wants ''fantasy, science fiction, spooky horror, and speculative poetry'' appropriate to age group. Does not want ''horror with excessive blood and gore.'' Considers poetry by children and teens. Has published poetry by Bruce Boston, Karen A. Romanko, Guy Belleranti, Aurelio Rico Lopez III, and Kristine Ong Muslim. Receives about 180 poems/year, accepts about 30 (16%).

How to Submit Submit up to 5 poems at a time. Lines/poem: 25 maximum. Considers previously published poems; no simultaneous submissions. Accepts e-mail submissions only (pasted into body of message). ''Submission should include snail mail address and a short (1-2 lines) bio.'' Reads submissions year round. Submit seasonal poems 6 months in advance. Time between acceptance and publication is 1-3 months. Often comments on rejected poems. Guidelines available on Web site. Responds in 4-6 weeks. Pays $2/original poem, $1/reprint. Acquires first, exclusive worldwide electronic rights for 90 days. Reviews books/chapbooks of poetry. Send materials for review consideration to Tyree Campbell.

Advice ''We prefer to see material from younger writers whenever possible.''

⊕ ◻ SPEEDPOETS ZINE

86 Hawkwood St., Brisbane QLD 4122 Australia. (61)(7)3420-6092. E-mail: speedpoets@speedpoet s.org. Web site: www.speedpoets.org. Established 2002. **Contact:** Graham Nunn, editor.

Magazine Needs *SpeedPoets Zine*, published monthly, showcases ''the community of poets that perform at the monthly SpeedPoets readings in Brisbane, as well as showcasing poets from all around the world.'' Wants ''shorter, experimental pieces.'' Does not want long submissions. Has published poetry by Robert Smith, Steve Kilbey, Brentley Frazer, Jayne Fenton Keane, Graham Nunn, and Marie Kazalia. *SpeedPoets Zine* is 28 pages, digest-sized, photocopied, folded and stapled, with color cover. Press run is 50. Single copy: $5. Make checks payable to Graham Nunn (in AUD only, or send well-concealed cash).

How to Submit Submit 2 poems at a time. Lines/poem: 25 maximum. Considers previously published poems. Accepts e-mail submissions (pasted into body of message); no disk submissions. Cover letter is preferred. Reads submissions year round. Time between acceptance and publication is 2 weeks. Sometimes comments on rejected poems. Guidelines available by e-mail. Responds in 2 weeks. Rights revert to poet upon publication.

$◻ ◎ SPIDER (Specialized: children ages 6-9)

Carus Publishing, 70 E. Lake St., Suite 300, Chicago IL 60601. Web site: www.cricketmag.com. Established 1994. **Contact:** Submissions Editor.

Magazine Needs *SPIDER*, published monthly, is a reading and activity magazine for children ages 6-9. ''It's specially written and edited for children who have reached that amazing age when they first get excited about reading on their own.'' Wants ''serious and humorous poetry, nonsense rhymes.'' *SPIDER* is 38 pages, 8×10, staple-bound. Receives more than 1,200 submissions/month, accepts 25-30. Circulation is 70,000. Subscription: $35.97/year (12 issues). Sample: $5; sample pages available on Web site.

How to Submit Submit no more than 5 poems at a time. Lines/poem: no more than 20. Considers previously published poems. Responds in 6 months. Guidelines available for SASE or on Web site. Pays up to $3/line on publications. Acquires North American publication rights for previously published poems; rights vary for unpublished poems.

Advice "Our standards are very high, and we will accept only top-quality material. Before attempting to write for *SPIDER*, be sure to familiarize yourself with this age child and with the magazine itself."

☑ SPILLWAY

P.O. Box 7887, Huntington Beach CA 92615-7887. (714)968-0905. E-mail: spillway@tebotbach.org. Web site: www.tebotbach.org. Established 1991. **Contact:** Mifanwy Kaiser, senior editor/managing editor or J.D. Lloyd, editor.

Magazine Needs *Spillway*, published annually in August, celebrates "writing's diversity and power to affect our lives." Open to all voices, schools, and tendencies. "We publish poetry, translations, reviews, essays, black-and-white photography, and color artwork and photography for the cover." Has published poetry by David Lehman, Richard Jones, Virgil Suárez, Gerry Locklin, Charles Harper Webb, and Eleanor Wilner. *Spillway* is about 176 pages, digest-sized, attractively printed, perfect-bound, with 2-color or 4-color card cover. Press run is 2,000. Single copy: $12; subscription: $21 for 2 issues, $33 for 4 issues. All prices include s&h. Make checks payable to *Spillway*. "We recommend ordering a sample copy before you submit, though acceptance does not depend upon purchasing a samply copy."

How to Submit Submit 3-6 poems at a time (6 pages maximum total). Considers previously published poems ("only in rare instances") and simultaneous submissions ("say where also submitted"). Email submissions only (Microsoft Word document attachment); no disk or fax submissions. Cover letter is required. Include brief bio. Responds in up to 6 months. Pays 1 contributor's copy. Acquires one-time rights. Reviews books of poetry in 500-2,500 words. Send materials for review consideration.

☑ SPINNING JENNY

% Black Dress Press, P.O. Box 1373, New York NY 10276. Web site: www.spinning-jenny.com. Established 1994. **Contact:** C.E. Harrison, editor.

Magazine Needs *Spinning Jenny*, published once/year in the fall (usually September), has published poetry by Tina Cane, Michael Morse, Ryan Murphy, and Sheilah Coleman. *Spinning Jenny* is 96 pages, digest-sized, perfect-bound, with heavy card cover. "We accept less than 5% of unsolicited submissions." Press run is 1,000. Single copy: $8; subscription: $15 for 2 issues.

How to Submit Submit up to 6 poems at a time. No previously published poems or simultaneous submissions. Accepts e-mail submissions (pasted into body of message, no attachments; see Web site for address). Reads submissions September 15-May 15 only. Seldom comments on rejected poems. Guidelines available for SASE, by e-mail, or on Web site. Responds within 4 months. Pays 3 contributor's copies. Authors retain rights.

☑ ◎ SPITBALL: THE LITERARY BASEBALL MAGAZINE (Specialized: writing about baseball)

5560 Fox Rd., Cincinnati OH 45239. Web site: www.angelfire.com/oh5/spitball. Established 1981. **Contact:** Mike Shannon, editor-in-chief.

Magazine Needs *Spitball: The Literary Baseball Magazine*, published semiannually, is "a unique magazine devoted to poetry, fiction, and book reviews exclusively about baseball. Newcomers are very welcome, but remember that you have to know the subject; we do, and our readers do. Perhaps a good place to start for beginners is one's personal reactions to the game, a game, a player, etc., and take it from there." **Writers submitting to *Spitball* for the first time must buy a sample copy (waived for subscribers).** "This is a one-time-only fee, which we regret, but economic reality dictates that we insist those who wish to be published in *Spitball* help support it, at least at this minimum level." *Spitball* is 96 pages, digest-sized, computer-typeset, perfect-bound. Receives about 1,000 submissions/year, accepts about 40. Press run is 1,000. Subscription: $12. Sample: $6.

How to Submit Submit a "batch" of poems at a time ("we prefer to use several of same poet in an issue rather than a single poem"). Lines/poem: open. No previously published poems or simultaneous submissions. Cover letter is required. Include brif bio and SASE. "Many times we are able to publish accepted work almost immediately." Pays 2 contributor's copies.

Additional Information "All material published in *Spitball* will be automatically considered for inclusion in the next *Best of Spitball* anthology."

Contest/Award Offerings 1) Poems submitted to *Spitball* will be considered automatically for Poem of the Month, to appear on the Web site. 2) "We sponsor the Casey Award (for best baseball book of the year) and hold the Casey Awards Banquet in late February or early March. Any chapbook of baseball poetry should be sent to us for consideration for the 'Casey' plaque that we award to the winner each year."

Advice "Take the subject seriously. We do. In other words, get a clue (if you don't already have one) about the subject and about the poetry that has already been done and published about baseball. Learn from it—think about what you can add to the canon that is original and fresh— and don't assume that just anybody with the feeblest of efforts can write a baseball poem worthy of publication. And most importantly, stick with it. Genius seldom happens on the first try."

🌐 ▢ SPLIZZ

4 St. Marys Rise, Burry Port, Carms SA16 0SH Wales. E-mail: splizzmag@yahoo.co.uk. Established 1993. **Contact:** Amanda Morgan, editor.

Magazine Needs *Splizz*, published quarterly, features poetry, prose, reviews of contemporary music, and background to poets. Wants "any kind of poetry. We have no restrictions regarding style, length, subjects." Does not want "anything racist or homophobic." Has published Colin Cross (UK), Anders Carson (Canada), Paul Truttman (U.S.), Jan Hansen (Portugal), and Gregory Arena (Italy). *Splizz* is 60-64 pages, A5, saddle-stapled, includes ads. Receives about 200-300 poems/year, accepts about 90%. Press run is 150 (35 subscribers). Single copy: £2 UK; subscription: £8 UK. Email for current rates. Payments accepted in cash or paypal to splizz@tiscali.co.uk. No checks please.

How to Submit Submit 5 poems at a time. No previously published poems or simultaneous submissions. Accepts e-mail submissions (as attachment). Cover letter is required. Include short bio. Typed submissions preferred. Name and address must be included on each page of submitted work. Include SAE with IRCs. Time between acceptance and publication is 4 months. Often comments on rejected poems. **Charges criticism fee.** "Just enclose SAE/IRC for response, and allow 1-2 months for delivery. For those sending IRCs, please ensure that they have been correctly stamped by your post office." Guidelines available in magazine, for SASE (or SAE and IRC), or by e-mail. Responds in 2 months. Sometimes sends prepublication galleys. Reviews books/chapbooks of poetry or other magazines in 50-300 words. Send materials for review consideration. E-mail for further enquiries.

Advice "Beginners seeking to have their work published, send your work to *Splizz*, as we specialize in giving new poets a chance to see their work published alongside more established writers."

◑ THE SPOON RIVER POETRY REVIEW

4241/English Dept., Illinois State University, Normal IL 61790-4241. Web site: www.litline.org/spoon. Established 1976. **Contact:** Bruce Guernsey, editor and Tara Reeser, associate editor.

Magazine Needs *The Spoon River Poetry Review*, published semiannually, features "newer and well-known poets from around the country and world." Also features one Illinois poet per issue at length for the magazine's Illinois Poet Series. Wants "compelling original poetry and translations that have a strong sense of the line." Also considers submissions for the journal's new feature, "Poets on Teaching," a 1,000 word practical essay written for, and by, teachers of poetry writing. *The Spoon River Poetry Review* is 128 pages, digest-sized, laser-set, with card cover, includes ads. Receives about 3,000 poems/month, accepts 1%. Press run is 1,500. Subscription: $16. Sample: $10 (includes guidelines).

How to Submit Submit 3-5 poems at a time. No simultaneous submissions "unless we are notified immediately if a submission is accepted elsewhere. Include name and address, including e-mail address, on every poem." Do not submit mss April 15-September 15. Comments on rejected poems "many times, if a poet is promising." Guidelines available in magazine or on Web site. Responds in 3 months. Pays a year's subscription. Acquires first North American serial rights. Reviews books of poetry. Send materials for review consideration.

Contest/Award Offerings Sponsors *The Spoon River Poetry Review* Editor's Prize Contest (see separate listing in Contests & Awards).

Advice "Read and workshop with poets who are better than you. Subscribe to at least 5 literary magazines per year, especially those you'd like to be published in."

◘ SPOUT MAGAZINE

P.O. Box 581067, Minneapolis MN 55458-1067. E-mail: editors@spoutpress.org. Web site: www.sp outpress.org. Established 1989. **Contact:** Michelle Filkins, poetry editor.

Magazine Needs *Spout*, published approximately 3 times/year, aims to provide "a paper community of unique expression." Wants "poetry of the imagination; poetry that surprises. We enjoy the surreal, the forceful, the political, the expression of confusion." No light verse, archaic forms or language. Has published poetry by Gillian McCain, Larissa Szporluk, Matt Hart, Joanna Fuhrman, Josie Rawson, and Richard Siken. *Spout* is 40-60 pages, saddle-stapled, with cardstock or glossy cover (different color each issue). Receives about 400-450 poems/year, accepts about 10%. Press run is 200-250 (35-40 subscribers, 100-150 shelf sales). Single copy: $5; subscription: $15.

How to Submit Submit up to 5 poems at a time. Considers previously published poems and simultaneous submissions. Cover letter is preferred. Time between acceptance and publication is 2-3 months. "Poems are reviewed by 2 of 3 editors; those selected for final review are read again by all three." Seldom comments on rejected poems. Guidelines available for SASE or on Web site. Responds in 4 months. Pays 1 contributor's copy.

Advice "Read a copy of the magazine to understand our editorial biases."

◘ ◎ SPRING: THE JOURNAL OF THE E.E. CUMMINGS SOCIETY (Specialized: poems in the spirit of E.E. Cummings; submissions from subscribers only)

129 Lake Huron Hall, Grand Valley State University, Allendale MI 49401-9403. (616)331-3071. Fax: (616)331-3430. E-mail: websterm@gvsu.edu. Web site: www.gvsu.edu/english/cummings/ Index.html. **Contact:** Michael Webster, editor.

Magazine Needs *Spring: The Journal of the E.E. Cummings Society*, published annually (usually in the fall), is designed "to maintain and broaden the audience for E.E. Cummings, and to explore various facets of his life and art." **Contributors are required to subscribe.** Wants poems in the spirit of Cummings, primarily poems of one page or less. Does not want "amateurish" work. Has published poetry by John Tagliabue, Jacqueline Vaught Brogan, and Gerald Locklin. *Spring* is about 180 pages, digest-sized, offset-printed, perfect-bound, with light cardstock cover. Press run is 500 (200 subscribers, 25 libraries, 300 shelf sales). Subscription or sample: $17.50.

How to Submit No previously published poems or simultaneous submissions. Accepts fax and e-mail (as attachment) submissions. Cover letter is required. Reads submissions May-August only. Seldom comments on rejected poems. Guidelines available for SASE. Responds in 6 months. Pays 1 contributor's copy.

$◻ ◎ ST. ANTHONY MESSENGER (Specialized: Catholic; spirituality/inspirational)

28 W. Liberty St., Cincinnati OH 45202-6498. Fax: (513)241-0399. Web site: www.americancatholic .org. **Contact:** Christopher Heffron, poetry editor.

- *St. Anthony Messenger* poetry occasionally receives awards from the Catholic Press Association Annual Competition.

Magazine Needs *St. Anthony Messenger*, published monthly, is a mgazine for Catholic families, mostly with children in grade school, high school, or college. Some issues feature a poetry page that uses poems appropriate for their readership. Poetry submissions are always welcome despite limited need. "We seek to publish accessible poetry of high quality. Spiritual/inspirational in nature a plus, but not required." Considers poetry by young writers, ages 14 and older. *St. Anthony Messenger* is 56-pages. Press run 310,000. Sample: free for 9×12 SASE.

How to Submit Submit "a few" poems at a time. Lines/poem: under 25. No previously published poems. Accepts fax and e-mail submissions. "Do not send us your entire collection of poetry. Poems must be original . Please include your social security number with your submission." Submit seasonal poems several months in advance. Guidelines available for SASE, by fax, or on Web site. Pays $2/line on acceptance plus 2 contributor's copies. Acquires first worldwide serial rights.

⬥ ▦ 🌐 $⃝ ✎ STAND MAGAZINE

School of English, University of Leeds, Leeds LS2 9JT England. 00 (44)(0)113 3434794. E-mail: stand@leeds.ac.uk. Web site: www.standmagazine.org. Established 1952 (by Jon Silkin). **Contact:** Jon Glover and John Whale, editors. (U.S. Editor: David Latané, Dept. of English, Virginia Commonwealth University, Richmond VA 23284-2005; dlatane@vcu.edu.)

Magazine Needs *Stand Magazine*, published quarterly, "seeks more subscriptions from U.S. readers and also hopes that the magazine will be seriously treated as an alternative platform to American literary journals." *Library Journal* calls *Stand* "one of England's best, liveliest, and truly imaginative little magazines." Has published poetry by John Ashbery, Mary Jo Bang, Brian Henry, and Michael Mott. *Stand* is about 64 pages, A5 (landscape), professionally printed on smooth stock, flat-spined, with matte color cover, includes ads. Press run is 2,000 (1,000+ subscribers, 600 libraries). Subscription: $49.50. Sample: $13.

How to Submit No fax or e-mail submissions. Cover letter is required, "assuring us that work is not also being offered elsewhere." Publishes theme issues. Always sends prepublication galleys. Pays £20 for first poem and £5 for each subsequent poem over 6 lines, and one contributor's copy. Acquires first world serial rights for 3 months after publication. If work appears elsewhere, *Stand* must be credited. Reviews books of poetry in 3,000-4,000 words, multi-book format. Send materials for review consideration.

🌐 $⃝ ✎ STAPLE MAGAZINE

114-116 St. Stephen's Rd., Sneinton, Nottingham NG2 4FJ England. Established 1982 (redesigned 2001). **Contact:** Wayne Burrows, editor.

Magazine Needs *Staple*, published 3 times/year, accepts "poetry, short fiction, and articles about the writing process and general culture in relation to writing." *Staple* is about 100 pages, perfectbound. Press run is 500 (350 subscribers). Single copy: £5.99; subscription: £15/year, £20/year overseas. Sample: £3.50 (back issue).

How to Submit Submit 6 poems or 1-2 stories/essays at a time. No previously published poems or simultaneous submissions. Cover letter is preferred. Include SAE and 2 IRCs. Reads submissions by the following deadlines: end of March, July, and November. Sometimes comments on rejected poems. Responds in up to 3 months. Pays £5/poem, £10/story/essay.

$⃝ 🎦 STAR*LINE (Specialized: science fiction, fantasy, horror)

Science Fiction Poetry Association, 1412 NE 35th St., Ocala FL 34479. E-mail: SFPASL@aol.com. Web site: www.sfpoetry.com. Established 1978. **Contact:** Marge Simon, editor.

Magazine Needs *Star*Line*, published bimonthly by the Science Fiction Poetry Association (see separate listing in Organizations), is a newsletter and poetry magazine. "Open to all forms—free verse, traditional forms, light verse—as long as your poetry shows skilled use of the language and makes a good use of science fiction, science, fantasy, horror, or speculative motifs." Considers poetry by children and teens. Has published poetry by Lawrence Schimel, Kendall Evans, Charlie Jacob, Terry A. Garey, and Timons Esaias. *Star*Line* is digest-sized, photocopied, saddle-stapled. Receives about 300-400 submissions/year, accepts about 80. Has 250 subscribers. Subscription: $13 for 6 issues. Sample: $2. Send requests for copies/membership information to Samantha Henderson, SFPA Treasurer, P.O. Box 4846, Covina, CA 91723. Send submissions to *Star*Line* only.

How to Submit Submit 3-5 poems at a time. Lines/poem: preferably under 50. No simultaneous submissions. Accepts e-mail submissions (preferred; pasted into body of message, no attachments). Cover letter is preferred (brief). Submissions must be typed. Responds in 1 month. Pays $3 for 10 lines or less; $5 for 11-50 lines; 10¢ per line rounded to the next dollar for 51+ lines. Buys first North American serial rights. Reviews books of poetry "within the science fiction/fantasy field" in 50-500 words. Open to unsolicited reviews. Send materials for review consideration.

Also Offers The Association also publishes *The Rhysling Anthology*, a yearly collection of nominations from the membership "for the best science fiction/fantasy long and short poetry of the preceding year."

✖ ☑ ◎ THE WALLACE STEVENS JOURNAL (Specialized: poems about/in the spirit of Wallace Stevens)

Arts and Sciences, Clarkson University, Box 5750, Potsdam NY 13699-5750. (315)268-3987. Fax: (315)268-3983. E-mail: serio@clarkson.edu. Web site: www.wallacestevens.com. Established 1977. **Contact:** Prof. Joseph Duemer, poetry editor (jduemer@clarkson.edu).

Magazine Needs *The Wallace Stevens Journal*, published semiannually by the Wallace Stevens Society, uses "poems about or in the spirit of Wallace Stevens or having some relation to his work. No bad parodies of Stevens's anthology pieces." Has published poetry by David Athey, Jacqueline Marcus, Charles Wright, X.J. Kennedy, A.M. Juster, and Robert Creeley. *The Wallace Stevens Journal* is 96-120 pages, digest-sized, typeset, flat-spined, with glossy cover with art. Receives 200-300 poems/year, accepts 15-20. Press run is 700. Subscription: $30 (includes membership in the Wallace Stevens Society). Sample: $10.

How to Submit Submit 1-4 poems at a time. No previously published poems, "though we have made a few exceptions to this rule." No fax or e-mail submissions, "though requests for information are fine." Cover letter is encouraged, but keep brief. Send clean, readable copy. Responds in up to 10 weeks. Always sends prepublication galleys. Pays 2 contributor's copies. Acquires all rights. Returns rights with permission and acknowledgment. Staff reviews books of poetry. Send materials for review consideration "only if there is some clear connection to Stevens."

Advice "Please don't submit to *The Wallace Stevens Journal* if you have not read Stevens. We like parodies, but they must add a new angle of perception. Most of the poems we publish are not parodies but meditations on themes related to Wallace Stevens and those poets he has influenced. Those wishing to contribute might want to examine a previous issue."

▣ $◻ STICKMAN REVIEW: An Online Literary Journal

721 Oakwater Lane, Port Orange FL 32128. E-mail: poetry@stickmanreview.com. Web site: www.stickmanreview.com. Established 2001.

Magazine Needs *Stickman Review*, published semiannually online, is dedicated to printing great poetry, fiction, nonfiction, and artwork. Wants poetry "that is literary in intent; no restrictions on form, subject matter, or style." Does not typically want "rhyming poetry."

How to Submit Submit 5 poems at a time. Considers simultaneous submissions; no previously published poems. Accepts e-mail submissions only (as attachment in Word, .rtf or .txt, or pasted into body of message); no postal submissions. Cover letter is preferred. Reads submissions year round. Time between acceptance and publication is 4-6 months. "Currently, the editors-in-chief review all submissions." Sometimes comments on rejected poems. Guidelines available on Web site. Responds in up to 4 months. Pays $10/poem, up to $20/author. Acquires first rights.

Advice "Keep writing and submitting. A rejection is not necessarily a reflection upon the quality of your work. Be persistent, trust your instincts, and sooner or later, good things will come."

$◻ ◎ STONE SOUP, THE MAGAZINE BY YOUNG WRITERS AND ARTISTS (Specialized: poetry by/for children 13 or younger)

Submissions Dept., P.O. Box 83, Santa Cruz CA 95063. (831)426-5557. Fax: (831)426-1161. E-mail: editor@stonesoup.com. Web site: www.stonesoup.com. Established 1973. **Contact:** Ms. Gerry Mandel, editor.

● *Stone Soup* has received Parents' Choice and Edpress Golden Lamp Honor Awards.

Magazine Needs *Stone Soup*, published 6 times/year, showcases writing and art by children ages 13 and under. Wants free verse poetry. Does not want rhyming poetry, haiku, or cinquain. *Stone Soup* is 48 pages, 7×10, professionally printed in color on heavy stock, saddle-stapled, with coated cover with full-color illustration. Receives 5,000 poetry submissions/year, accepts about 12. Press run is 20,000 (14,000 subscribers, 5,000 shelf sales, 1,000 other). Subscription: membership in the Children's Art Foundation includes a subscription, $37/year. Sample: $5.

Daniel Thomas Moran

Talking poems, Whitman, and root canals

How often does a dental patient find the administering hands of a poet treating his cavity or performing her root canal? According to Daniel Thomas Moran, there probably aren't many. Moran, a widely published poet and former Poet Laureate of Suffolk County, New York, believes he may be the only contemporary dentist who also has a career as a poet.

Moran is the author of six volumes of poetry, the most recent of which is *Looking for the Uncertain Past* (Poetry Salzburg, The University of Salzburg). His work has appeared in a wide range of prestigious journals, including *Confrontation, Nassau Review, Oxford, Commonweal, Parnassus, Rattapallax, LUNGFULL!, Poetry Salzburg Review,* and *The Journal of the American Medical Association.* From 1997-2005 he served as Vice-President of The Walt Whitman Birthplace Association in West Hills, New York, where he instituted The Long Island School of Poetry Reading Series. Moran has been Literary Correspondent to Long Island Public Radio where he hosted "The Long Island Radio Magazine." He's a participating writer to The Passwords Project, an international collaboration between visual artists and writers based in Austria. He served as Poet Laureate from 2005 to 2007 by appointment of The Legislature of Suffolk County, New York. A native of New York City, Moran lives on Shelter Island with his wife Karen; there he is also a practicing doctor of dentistry.

As a student of biology and dental surgery, how did you get interested in writing poetry?

I was actually writing poetry long before I went to college. I loved to write, but I wanted to do it for the love of it and not to feed myself. There are too many hungry poets in the world already. I have come to conclude after many years that the same kinds of passions and sensibilities which drive scientists also drive poets, i.e. the desire for understanding, a fascination with the mysteries of life and the physical world, a passion for the intricate and the complex, and even a certain cynicism. In my capacity as a doctor, I have learned a great deal about how human beings function; and I have met many fascinating people in the course of my daily work, many of whom have inspired and informed my poetry.

When did you first start publishing your poetry?

I did not get serious about my writing until after I earned my Doctoral Degree in 1983, because that kind of intensive study did not allow time for the distracted thinking that leads to poetry. In 1987, at the age of 30, I did my first poetry reading; and after I finished, a woman approached me and asked if she could print one of the poems I read in a small literary magazine she published. I still know that woman, and I even recently thanked her again for doing me that honor 20 years ago. After that, the man who owned the bookshop where I read suggested I look at *Poet's Market*. I continue to do that to this day and recommend the same to poets I teach.

Does your work as a dentist influence your poetry? Does it suggest any special themes?

My work as a dentist does influence my poetry, mostly because of the psychology of treating people. Doctors get to see the best and the worst in people; then they have to deal with it in creative ways. Many of the things I know about life were learned because of the intimacy involved in caring for people who are, at times, anxious and in some kind of distress. It takes a lot out of me, but I have never stopped understanding that it is a great privilege.

Writing poems and having people wanting to read them is also a privilege. To have both of those things in my life make me a very fortunate man. I have also been asked many times if I write poems about teeth. Never. Who wants to read a poem about teeth? Anyway, I cannot improve on the poetry of a smile.

Have you come across any other poet/dentists?

Some years ago, the librarian at The University of Michigan Dental Library, Patricia Anderson, who was a poetry lover, did a search of the world's literature to find dentists who are also recognized poets. She did find there had been a couple in history, but at the moment I seem to be the only one. That makes me, among other things, a certifiable oddity. That does not mean that other dentists have not written poetry, but that I may be the only living dentist who also has a career as a poet. There are a good many physician poets, the most notable being William Carlos Williams, who won two Pulitzer Prizes. I am often compared to him, which is all right with me, but I would be most pleased if The Pulitzer Committee saw fit to do so. I might guess that I'm more likely to find myself doing a root canal on one of them.

Do your patients know you're a poet? Are they familiar with your work?

My patients all know that I'm a poet, and many of them have my books. I don't have magazines in my waiting room, only collections of my poems, something a magician would refer to as a "forced choice." The walls of my office are filled with the artwork of friends, and so my office looks more like a gallery than a dental office, which makes both me and my patients feel more content to be there.

I have often read poems to people before I start work if I have something appropriate. I have also given poems and books to people when the spirit moves me. When I was a child, my family dentist used to reward me after an appointment by letting me pick a toy ring from a box of them he kept in his desk. I don't have a box of rings, but occasionally I give out a sonnet. I once heard that a woman I saw one time decided that she did not want a dentist "who had his head in the clouds" and went to someone else. I have treated more than 3,000 patients in my career, and that is the only time that has happened.

For years people would refer to "The Art of Medicine." There is something to that, as far as I can see. I think an artist makes a better doctor. I know now that there is a woman somewhere who disagrees with me.

We Mortals

*We long for
the perfection
in these things
of the world,
Life certain in
its bilateral symmetry,
Generations strung
like pearls on
an imagined wire.
We squint at the sun.
We marvel at the
plaintive syllables
of songbirds.
We admire
tallness and clarity.
Feeling the
vibrations of it all
beneath our feet,
We rhapsodize
distances suggested
upon moonless nights
daring to name the ineffable.
We write poems and
chant to the mysteries.
We dance round fires
in clearings we have
made in the forest.
We weep for the
spirits of fallen trees.
Facing death
we avert our eyes.
When great things succumb,
We tell ourselves
they were never there.
Thirsty, we lie on
our backs, allowing
our mouths to fill
with rainwater, and
hope to rise, like blossoms
from the dust.*

(© Daniel Thomas Moran; reprinted with permission)

Do you identify yourself as a dentist when you're giving readings or in your bio notes in magazines? How do readers respond? What's the most interesting comment you've received?

The fact that I'm a dentist comes up all the time, and I feel fine about that entirely. When I first started doing poetry readings, I didn't tell my patients that I was a poet because I was concerned that they would think I wasn't serious about being a dentist. At my readings,

I also did not tell people that I was a dentist because I was concerned that they wouldn't think I was a serious poet.

Now I am 50 years old, I have been a dentist for 25 years, and I have had several hundred poems published, including six collections. I have also seen three kids through their teen years. I don't worry about much of anything anymore.

As far as interesting comments, I can't think of any off hand; but I did have a very interesting thing happen which bridged my two lives as poet and dentist. At a reading a few years back, an elderly woman actually died. My wife and I did CPR on her and revived her. I found out she was 96 years old, and she lived for nearly another year after that. Nothing like that has ever happened in my office and I hope it stays that way. There is a part of me that still cannot believe that really happened.

Marvin Bell once asked me what the strangest thing was that ever happened to me at a reading. He's a great poet, but he could not beat that story in a month of Sundays.

You're the former vice-president of the Walt Whitman Birthplace Association. Please describe the organization and some of its activities, including the Long Island School of Poetry Reading Series.

The Walt Whitman Birthplace Association was formed in the early 1950s to purchase, preserve and maintain the actual house where Walt Whitman was born on Long Island. There is now a wonderful visitor's center, used to host many school and tour groups and even run some cultural events.

I might argue that that house might be the most significant artistic historic site in America. Think how much would not have happened had Whitman not been born there in 1819. It cannot be conceived of, really.

I initiated The Long Island School of Poetry Reading Series as a way to honor and to feature the poets of Long Island on a continuing basis. As Poet Laureate of Suffolk County, New York, where that homestead is, I also edited an historic anthology of the best poets presently living in Suffolk County called *The Light of City and Sea*. Suffolk has had a staggering array of great poets over the years since Whitman; in fact, far too many to mention. But today we have people like Allen Planz and Grace Schulman, Harvey Shapiro and Siv Cedering, Stanley Moss and Phil Schultz, Philip Appleman and Louis Simpson, to name just a few. These are not only fine poets, but they are important poets. I am still amazed that I can say I know them.

What were your responsibilities as Poet Laureate of Suffolk County? What do you think the value of the Poet Laureate position is to the community at large and to poetry in society? What's your perspective on the ever-growing movement to appoint poets laureate for more narrowly defined locales?

As Poet Laureate of Suffolk County, I had no defined responsibilities. What I did was to become a cheerleader on behalf of the poets of Suffolk and to let its four million inhabitants know that they have some very remarkable people among them doing things they should know about.

I also tried to be a teacher and to involve children and adults in writing and reading poetry, hoping that they could find some wonder and some solace in what poetry had to offer. Poetry is the voice of the human spirit; who could turn away from that wisdom and insight and not be missing something crucial?

I think it's good that many people are seeing the need for poets laureate and many states and counties are creating such positions. But that comes with a great caveat. Poets are, by nature, not politicians; and heaven knows there is virtually no evidence of poetry in politicians. When the two mix, the results can be unfortunate and even disheartening. Human beings are capable of both great miracles and great mischief.

How would you characterize your poetry? How have you developed as a poet over time?

The poetry I write doesn't seem to fit a particular category, but I've been called a lyric poet by some reviewers. I just write what strikes me at the moment; and because I have the great advantage of never having studied poetry, I can do it with complete abandon. A dear friend who is a poet professor once told me that she especially liked a poem I had written in "heroic couplets." I thanked her; but I have not the vaguest idea what a "heroic couplet" might be, and I have no intention of trying to find out.

Last year I was sent a copy of a term paper which was written by a poetry student in Salzburg, Austria. It addressed a poem of mine which had its first draft completed on a napkin in a restaurant in Greenwich Village. I needed a dictionary to read her take on the poem, but she got an "A" and that made me happy.

I'm one of the few poets I know who never taught at the college level. After many years, I've decided that what I had originally thought a weakness might be my true strength. I cannot tell whether what I write is wrong or right. I only know that I did the best I could do and that it pleases me. If my wife Karen also likes it, then I'm a success. Time will judge how I fit into the great fabric of poetry. I'll be content and proud if, when I'm gone, someone says that I was a poet.

As far as developing as a poet over time, I not only hope that to be the case; it is crucial, if not for that to be the case, at least that one think it is the case. How else could one go on writing? To this day, there are times I can read my own work and think it is really quite good, and other times when I think that for the sake of mankind I should set fire to the whole pile. If I stop thinking those things, it will be time to stop altogether.

Describe The Passwords Project? How did you become involved?

I've made a lot of friends among the artistic community in Austria as a result of some readings I did there in 2003. I was asked to be part of this project, which seeks to use the work of writers to inspire visual artists via a Web site; then the works get posted on the site. It involves some 40 people from some 12 countries and five continents who communicate with each other through art. We've done exhibitions as well in Austria, Mexico, Colombia, Beijing, and Washington, D.C. It's been quite a thrill to think that words I've written have inspired someone I've never met in China or Italy or England.

Anyone can see what has been done by going to www.password.or.at. Art can change the world even in small ways. All of this is just further confirmation of all the wonderful places I've been as a result of writing poems. How fortunate can one be?

—*Nancy Breen*

Nancy Breen is the former editor of *Poet's Market*. Her chapbooks include *Rites & Observances* (Finishing Line Press) and *How Time Got Away* (Pudding House Publications). She blogs at www.salmagundiexpress.wordpress.com.

How to Submit No simultaneous submissions. No e-mail submissions. "Submissions can be any number of pages, any format. Include name, age, home address, and phone number. Don't include SASE; we respond only to those submissions under consideration and cannot return manuscripts." Guidelines available on Web site. Responds in up to 6 weeks. Pays $40, a certificate, and 2 contributor's copies plus discounts. Acquires all rights. Returns rights upon request. Open to reviews by children.

◻ THE STORYTELLER

2441 Washington Rd., Maynard AR 72444. (870)647-2137. E-mail: storyteller1@hightowercom.com. Web site: www.thestorytellermagazine.com. Established 1996. **Contact:** Regina Williams, editor.

Magazine Needs *The Storyteller*, published quarterly, "is geared to, but not limited to, new writers and poets." Wants "any form, any subject, any style, but must have a meaning. Do not throw words together and call it a poem." Does not want "explicit sex, violence, horror, or explicit language. I would like it to be understood that I have young readers, ages 9-18." Considers poetry by children and teens. Has published poetry by Patrick Lobrutto, Bryan Byrd, and Gerald Zipper. *The Storyteller* is 72 pages, magazine-sized, desktop-published, with slick cover with original pen & ink drawings, includes ads. Receives about 300 poems/year, accepts about 40%. Press run is 700 (more than 600 subscribers). Single copy: $6 U.S., $8 Canada and foreign; subscription: $20 U.S., $24 Canada & foreign.

How to Submit Submit 3 poems at a time. Lines/poem: up to 40. Considers previously published poems and simultaneous submissions, "but must state where and when poetry first appeared." No e-mail submissions; postal submissions only. "However, if accepted, you will be asked to send material by e-mail, if possible." Cover letter is preferred. Manuscripts must be typed and double-spaced. "Make sure name and address are on each page submitted. We are getting many submissions without names." Time between acceptance and publication is 9 months. "Poems are read and discussed by staff." Sometimes comments on rejected poems. Guidelines available for SASE or on Web site. Responds in 1 week. Pays $1 per poem; does not provide contributor's copies. Acquires first or one-time rights. Reviews books/chapbooks of poetry by subscribers only. Send materials for review consideration to Jamie Johnson, assistant editor.

Contest/Award Offerings Sponsors a quarterly contest. "Readers vote on their favorite poems. Winners receive a copy of the magazine and a certificate. We also nominate for the Pushcart Prize." See Web site for yearly contest announcements and winners.

Advice "Be professional. Do not send 4 or 5 poems on 1 page. Send us poetry written from the heart."

ℕ ▣ ◿ THE STRAY BRANCH

8490 White Cedar Dr Apt 543, Miamisburg OH 45342. (937)305-9262. E-mail: thestraybranchlitmag @yahoo.com. Web site: www.thestraybranch.org. Established 2008. Contact: D. Spencer-Berk, editor/publisher.

Magazine Needs *The Stray Branch*, published twice per year, is an online journal "open to form and style but prefers free verse. Open to subject matter but prefers edgy, raw material written from the gut that reflects the heart and human experience. Wants poetry by real people that can be understood by all readers. *The Stray Branch* prefers works of a darker nature." Does not want "over-schooled, arrogant, self-righteous, religious, political, overly sentimental, overly erotic, or happy and light, pretty poetry." Has published poetry by Andy Robertson, Keith Estes, and Justin Blackburn.

How to Submit Submit 6 poems at a time. "Maximum length for poems is no longer than 1 page, shorter poems are preferred and stand a better chance." Considers previously published poems; no simultaneous submissions. (Considers poetry posted on a public Web site/blog/forum and poetry posted on a private, password-protected forum as published.) Accepts e-mail submissions (pasted into body of message); no fax or disk submissions. Cover letter is unnecessary. Reads submissions October-April. Sometimes comments on rejected poems. Guidelines available on Web site. Responds in 3 weeks. Acquires one-time rights. Rights revert to poets upon publication.

☐ STRAYLIGHT

University of Wisconsin-Parkside, English Dept., 900 Wood Rd., P.O. Box 2000, Kenosha WI 53141. (262)595-2139. Fax: (262)595-2271. E-mail: straylight@litspot.net. Web site: www.litspot.net/stray light. Established 2005. **Contact:** Poetry Editor.

Magazine Needs *Straylight*, published biannually, seeks "poetry of almost any style as long as it's inventive." *Straylight* is digest-sized. Single copy: $6; subscription: $10. Make checks payable to *Straylight*.

How to Submit Submit 3-6 poems at a time. No previously published poems or simultaneous submissions. Accepts e-mail submissions (preferred, as .rtf or .doc attachment); no fax or disk submissions. Cover letter is required. "Include contact information on all pages of submission." Reads submissions August 15-April 15. Submit seasonal poems 3 months in advance. Time between acceptance and publication is 6 months. Never comments on rejected poems. Sometimes publishes theme issues. Upcoming themes available on Web site. Guidelines available for SASE or on Web site. Responds in 2 months. Pays 2 contributor's copies. Acquires first North American serial rights. Rights revert to poet upon publication.

Advice "We suggest you buy a sample copy to get a feel for what we publish."

▣ ▦ ☑ STRIDE MAGAZINE

Stride Publications, 4b Tremayne Close, Devoran, Cornwall TR3 6QE England. E-mail: submissions @stridemagazine.co.uk (submissions) or editor@stridemagazine.co.uk (inquiries). Web site: www .stridemagazine.co.uk. Established 1982. **Contact:** Rupert Loydell, editor.

Magazine Needs *Stride Magazine*, published online, is "a gathering of new poetry, short prose, articles, news, reviews, and whatever takes our fancy. *Stride* is regularly updated with new contributions."

How to Submit Submit 4-5 poems at a time. Accepts e-mail submissions (pasted into body of message; no attachments). "Attachments or snail mail without SAEs will not be considered or replied to."

Additional Information "At the moment, **Stride Publications is unable to consider any manuscript submissions.**" Check www.stridebooks.co.uk for updates.

☐ ◎ STRUGGLE: A MAGAZINE OF PROLETARIAN REVOLUTIONARY LITERATURE (Specialized: working class, social issues)

P.O. Box 13261, Detroit MI 48213-0261. (313)273-9039. E-mail: timhall11@yahoo.com. Web site: www.strugglemagazine.net. Established 1985. **Contact:** Tim Hall, editor.

Magazine Needs *Struggle: A Magazine of Proletarian Revolutionary Literature*, published quarterly, focuses "on the struggle of the working people and all oppressed against the rich, dealing with such issues as racism, poverty, women's rights, aggressive wars, workers' struggle for jobs and job security, the overall struggle for a non-exploitative society, a genuine socialism." The poetry and songs printed are "generally short, any style; subject matter must criticize or fight—explicitly or implicitly—against the rule of the billionaires. We welcome experimentation devoted to further-ing such content. We are open to both subtlety and direct statement." Has published poetry by John R. Guthrie, Linda Ann Strang, Ariono'-jovan Labu, Jamie Lee Clark, Sara Littlecrow-Russell, and Allan Douglass Coleman. *Struggle* is 36 pages, digest-sized, photocopied. Subscription: $10/ year (4 issues). Sample: $3. Make checks payable to "Tim Hall—Special Account."

How to Submit Submit up to 8 poems at a time. Accepts e-mail submissions (pasted into body of message, no attachments), but prefers postal mail. "Writers must include SASE. Name and address must appear on the opening page of each poem." Accepted work usually appears in the next or following issue. Comments on rejected poems "with every submission." Responds in 4 months, if possible, but often becomes backlogged. Pays one contributor's copy. "If you are unwilling to have your poetry published on our Web site, please inform us."

Advice "Show passion and fire. Humor also welcome. Prefer powerful, colloquial language over academic timidity. Look to Neruda, Lorca, Bly, Whitman, Braithwaite, Tupac Shakur, Muriel Ru-keyser. Experimental, traditional forms both welcome. Especially favor: works reflecting rebellion by the working people against the rich; works against racism, sexism, militarism, imperialism;

works critical of our exploitative culture; works showing a desire for—or fantasy of—a non-exploitative society; works attacking the Republican 'anti-terrorism' war frenzy and the Democrats' surrender to it.''

⊕ ◑ ◎ STUDIO, A JOURNAL OF CHRISTIANS WRITING (Specialized: christian; spirituality)

727 Peel St., Albury NSW 2640 Australia. Phone/fax: (61)(2)6021-1135. E-mail: studio00@bigpond. net.au. Established 1980. **Contact:** Paul Grover, publisher.

Magazine Needs *Studio, A Journal of Christians Writing*, published quarterly, prints "poetry and prose of literary merit, offering a venue for previously published, new, and aspiring writers, and seeking to create a sense of community among Christians writing." Also publishes occasional articles as well as news and reviews of writing, writers, and events of interest to members. Wants "shorter pieces [of poetry] but with no specification as to form or length (necessarily less than 200 lines), subject matter, style, or purpose. People who send material should be comfortable being published under this banner: *Studio, A Journal of Christians Writing*." Has published poetry by John Foulcher, Les Murray, and other Australian poets. *Studio* is 36 pages, digest-sized, professionally printed on high-quality recycled paper, saddle-stapled, with matte card cover. Press run is 300 (all subscriptions). Subscription: $60 AUD for overseas members. Sample: $10 AUD (airmail to U.S.).

How to Submit Lines/poem: less than 200. Considers simultaneous submissions. Cover letter is required. Include brief details of previous publishing history, if any. SAE with IRC required. "Submissions must be typed and double-spaced on one side of A4 white paper. Name and address must appear on the reverse side of each page submitted." Response time is 2 months. Time between acceptance and publication is 9 months. Pays 1 contributor's copy. Acquires first Australian rights. Reviews books of poetry in 250 words, single-book format. Send materials for review consideration.

Contest/Award Offerings Conducts a biannual poetry and short story contest.

Advice "The trend in Australia is for imagist poetry and poetry exploring the land and the self. Reading the magazine gives the best indication of style and standard, so send for a sample copy before sending your poetry. Keep writing, and we look forward to hearing from you."

◑ STUDIO ONE

Mary Commons, College of St. Benedict, St. Joseph MN 56374. E-mail: studio1@csbsju.edu. Web site: http://clubs.csbsju.edu/studio1. Established 1976. **Contact:** Editor (changes yearly).

Magazine Needs *Studio One*, published annually in May, is a "literary and visual arts magazine designed as a forum for local, regional, and national poets/writers. No specifications regarding form, subject matter, or style of poetry submitted." Considers poetry by children and teens. Has published poetry by Bill Meissner, Eva Hooker, and Larry Schug. *Studio One* is 50-80 pages, typeset, with soft cover. Receives 600-800 submissions/year. No subscriptions, but a sample copy can be obtained by sending a self-addressed, stamped manila envelope and $6 for p&h. Make checks payable to *Studio One*.

How to Submit Submit no more than 5 poems at a time. Lines/poem: "poetry no more than 2 pages stands a better chance of publication." Considers simultaneous submissions; no previously published poems. Accepts e-mail submissions (pasted into body of message); "clearly show page breaks and indentations." Reads submissions by March 1 deadline for spring publication. Seldom comments on rejected poems.

✪ ◑ SUN POETIC TIMES

12301 Blanco Road #316, San Antonio, TX 78216. (210)325-8122. E-mail: sunpoets@hotmail.com. Established 1994. **Contact:** Rod C. Stryker, editor.

Magazine Needs *Sun Poetic Times*, published 2-4 times/year, is a literary and visual arts magazine featuring "all types of literary and visual art from all walks of life. We take all types." Has published poetry by Naomi Shihab Nye, Chris Crabtree, Trinidad Sanchez, Jr., and Garland Lee Thompson, Jr. *Sun Poetic Times* is 24-28 pages, magazine-sized, attractively printed, saddle-stapled, with cardstock cover. Receives about 300 poems/year, accepts about 20%. Press run is 250 (100 shelf sales).

Subscription: $10/2 issues, $20/4 issues. Sample: $5 and SASE. Make checks payable to *Sun Poetic Times*.

How to Submit Submit 3-5 poems at a time. Lines/poem: "one page in length if typed, 2 pages if handwritten (legibly)." Considers simultaneous submissions; no previously published poems. Accepts e-mail submissions (pasted into body of message; no attachments). Cover letter is preferred. "In cover letters, we like to hear about your publishing credits, reasons you've taken up the pen, and general B.S. like that (biographical info)." Time between acceptance and publication is up to one year. Seldom comments on rejected poems. Occasionally publishes theme issues. Guidelines available for SASE or by e-mail. Responds in up to 9 months. Pays 1 contributor's copy. Rights revert back to author upon publication.

$☑ THE SUN

107 N. Roberson St., Chapel Hill NC 27516. Web site: www.thesunmagazine.org. Established 1974. **Contact:** Sy Safransky, editor.

Magazine Needs *The Sun*, published monthly, is "noted for honest, personal work that's not too obscure or academic. "We favor poetry that is accessible and emotionally evocative." We avoid traditional, rhyming poetry, as well as limericks and haiku. We're open to almost anything else: free verse, prose poems, short and long poems." Has published poetry by Ellen Bass, Christopher Bursk, Steve Kowit, Alison Luterman, Ellery Akers, and Tess Gallagher. *The Sun* is 48 pages, magazine-sized, offset-printed on 50 lb. paper, saddle-stapled. Press run is 80,000 (70,000 subscribers, 500 libraries). Receives 3,000 submissions of poetry/year, accepts about 30. Subscription: $36. Sample: $5.

How to Submit Submit up to 6 poems at a time. Considers previously published poems buy strongly prefers unpublished work; no simultaneous submissions. "Poems should be typed and accompanied by a cover letter and SASE." Guidelines available for SASE or on Web site. Responds within 3-6 months. Pays $100-500 on publication plus contributor's copies and subscription. Acquires first serial or one-time rights.

☑ SUNSTONE

343 N. Third W., Salt Lake City UT 84103-1215. (801)355-5926. Established 1974. **Contact:** Dixie Partridge, poetry editor.

Magazine Needs *Sunstone*, published 5 times/year, prints "scholarly articles of interest to an open, Mormon audience; personal essays; fiction and poetry." Wants "both lyric and narrative poetry that engages the reader with fresh, strong images, skillful use of language, and a strong sense of voice and/or place." Does not want "didactic poetry, sing-song rhymes, or in-process work." Has published poetry by Susan Howe, Anita Tanner, Robert Parham, Ryan G. Van Cleave, Robert Rees, and Virgil Suárez. *Sunstone* is 80 pages, magazine-sized, professionally printed, saddle-stapled, with semi-glossy paper cover. Receives more than 500 poems/year, accepts 40-50. Press run is 5,000. Subscription: $36 for 6 issues. Sample: $8 postpaid.

How to Submit Submit up to 5 poems at a time. Lines/poem: 40 maximum. No previously published poems or simultaneous submissions. Include name and address on each poem. Time between acceptance and publication is 2 years or less. Seldom comments on rejected poems. Guidelines available for SASE. Responds in 3 months. Pays 5 contributor's copies. Acquires first North American serial rights.

Advice "Poems should not sound like a rewording of something heard before. Be original; pay attention to language, sharp imagery. Contents should deepen as the poem progresses. We've published poems rooted strongly in place, narratives seeing life from another time or culture, poems on religious belief or doubt—a wide range of subject matter."

☑ ⊚ SUPERIOR CHRISTIAN NEWS (Specialized: Christian; translations into English; Rocky Mountain West)

Superior Poetry Press, P.O. Box 424, Superior MT 59872. Established 1995. **Contact:** Ed and Guna Chaberek, editors.

Magazine Needs *Superior Christian News*, published quarterly, prints "the best and most interesting of new Christian poets, as well as mainstream poets, we can find. Also, we encourage lively translation into English from any language." Wants "Christian, Western, or humorous poetry; translations." Considers poetry by children and teens; the only restriction is quality, not age. Has published poetry by Bob Kimm, Simon Perchik, John Grey, makyo, and Charles L. Wright. *Superior Christian News* is 12-24 pages, digest-sized, photocopied. Receives about 1,500 poems/year, accepts 5%. Press run is 100; 5 distributed free to libraries. Single copy: $3; $10 for 4 issues.

How to Submit Submit 3-5 poems at a time. Lines/poem: 40 maximum. No previously published poems or simultaneous submissions (unless stated). Cover letter is preferred. Include short bio. Time between acceptance and publication is 3 months. Seldom comments on rejected poems. Guidelines available for SASE. Responds in 1 week. Pays 1 contributor's copy. Acquires first rights.

Additional Information *Superior Christian News* is now repositoried at the University of Wisconsin (Madison) Memorial Library. Christian-oriented articles (300-500 words) also considered.

Advice "Original—be original."

▣ ◎ SWELL (Specialized: gay/lesbian/bisexual/transgendered)

E-mail: swelleditor@gmail.com. Web site: www.swellzine.com. Established 1980. **Contact:** Jill Craig, editor.

Magazine Needs *Swell*, published quarterly online by NewTown Writers (see separate listing in Organizations), aims "to reach beyond the traditional boundaries of the printed word, exploring the limits of form, structure, and content, while giving a voice to emerging writers." Wants "work that reflects a spectrum of perspectives as diverse as the community from which it was born. Ideal publication candidates approach GLBT issues in a fresh way or present universal topics from a unique point of view."

How to Submit Lines/poem: no works over 3,000 words total. Welcomes multiple submissions as long as the total submitted is under the maximum word count. Accepts e-mail submissions only (as attachment in Word). Responds in 1-2 months. Rights revert to poet upon publication.

✪ ◪ SYCAMORE REVIEW

Dept. of English, Purdue University, 500 Oval Dr., West Lafayette IN 47907-2038. (765)494-3783. Fax: (765)494-3780. E-mail: sycamore@purdue.edu. Web site: www.sycamorereview.com. Established 1988 (first issue May 1989). **Contact:** Poetry Editor (see Web site for current editor).

• Poetry published by *Sycamore Review* has appeared in *The Best American Poetry* and *The Pushcart Prize.*

Magazine Needs *Sycamore Review*, published semiannually in January and June, uses "personal essays, short fiction, short shorts, drama, translations, and quality poetry in any form. We aim to publish many diverse styles of poetry from formalist to prose poems, narrative, and lyric." Has published poetry by Denise Duhamel, Jonah Winter, Amy Gerstler, Mark Halliday, Dean Young, and Ed Hirsch. *Sycamore Review* is about 120 pages, 8x8, professionally printed, flat-spined, with matte color cover. Press run is 1,000 (200 subscribers, 50 libraries). Subscription: $12 ($14 outside U.S.). Sample: $7. Indiana residents add 5% sales tax. Make checks payable to Purdue University.

How to Submit Submit 3-6 poems at a time. with name and address on each page. Include SASE. Considers simultaneous submissions, if notified immediately of acceptance elsewhere; no previously published poems except translations. No fax or e-mail submissions. Cover letter is required. "Include phone number, short bio, and previous publications, if any, in cover letter." Put name and address on each page of ms, include SASE. Reads submissions August 1-March 1 only. Guidelines available for SASE or on Web site. Responds in 4-5 months. Pays 2 contributor's copies. Acquires first North American rights. After publication, all rights revert to author. Staff reviews books of poetry. Send materials for review consideration to editor-in-chief.

Advice "Poets who do not include a SASE do not receive a response."

Ⓝ ◪ TAIGA

E-mail: taigapoetry.gmail.com. Web site: www.taigapoetry.blogspot.com. Established 2007. **Contact:** Brooklyn Copeland and Cortney Settle, co-editors.

Magazine Needs *Taiga*, published semiannually, is "a journal of poetry, original and translated.

We publish a Summer Issue and a Winter Issue each year. We're open to receiving work poets with few or no publication credits, as well as poets who have published several books already. For English language poems, we like to publish edgy, refined verse. For translations, our primary focus is on the Scandinavian, Baltic, and Slavic languages.'' *Taiga* is 60-80 pages digest-sized, saddle-stitched, with a cardstock cover and clean, minimal graphic design. Accepts about 6% of poems received for publication. Press run is 200. Single copy: $6.

How to Submit Submit 1-3 poems at a time, no more than 40 lines. Considers simultaneous submissions. Accepts e-mail submissions (pasted into body of message); no fax or disk submissions. Cover letter is required. ''A cover letter lets us know who you are. Please let us know how you found out about *Taiga*, your name, age, whereabouts, previous publications, and any other involvement you might have with poetry writing or publishing. If we don't see a cover letter at all, we delete your submission without reading the poetry or bothering to reply. Also, bearing in mind our quick turnaround, do not send additional work in the same reading period unless specifically advised to do so by one of the editors. Seeing your name in our inbox a second time without invitation is also grounds for deletion without response.'' Reads submissions November-February for Summer issue, June-August for Winter issue. Time between acceptance and publication is 3-4 months. Rarely comments on rejected poems. ''Translations must have permission from the translated poet for the work to be published in *Taiga*. We also like to publish the original language alongside the English version, so please take care to make all necessary arrangements before submitting to us.'' Never publishes theme issues. Guidelines available on Web site. Responds in 1-6 weeks. Sometimes sends prepublication galleys. Pays 1 free copy with 50% discount on all other issues of *Taiga* purchased at any time.'' Acquires one-time rights. Rights revert to poets upon publication. Reviews chapbooks of poetry and other magazines/journals in 200 words. ''Contact us via email to make arrangements.''

Additional Information ''We also publish 2-4 titles each year in the Tundra Chapbook Series. Most titles are solicited, but watch the blog for updates about the reading period.''

Advice ''Please stay current on your reading of journals and magazines. We all have access to so many great publications that are available for free online, so there's no excuse for sending outdated work. We tend to post a list of *Taiga*'s contributor's on our blog, so when in doubt, search for their names online and try to tune in to their caliber. Also, don't forget to order sample copies from small presses. It's the best way to support a publication, and you'll often get a beautiful, limited-edition piece of art for what you would have dropped in a coffee shop.''

🌐 $⊘ TAKAHE

P.O. Box 13 335, Christchurch 8001 New Zealand. (64)(3)359-8133. Web site: http://www.takahe.o rg.nz. Established 1990. **Contact:** James Norcliffe, poetry editor.

Magazine Needs *Takahe*, published 3 times/year, features stories and poetry by both established and emerging writers. ''While insisting on correct British spelling (or recognized spellings in foreign languages), smart quotes, and at least internally consistent punctuation, we, nonetheless, try to allow some latitude in presentation. Any use of foreign languages must be accompanied by an English translation.'' No style, subject, or form restrictions. Has published poetry by Virgil Suárez, Keith Flynn, Steve de Franco, Elizabeth Smithers, and Michael Harlow. *Takahe* is 60 pages, A4 size. Receives about 500 poems/year, accepts about 10%. Press run is 400. Single copy: $8.50 NZD; subscription: $25 NZD within New Zealand, $35 NZD elsewhere.

How to Submit No simultaneous submissions. No e-mail submissions. ''**Please note:** U.S. stamps should not be used on SAEs. They do not work in New Zealand. Please enclose IRCs or supply e-mail address.'' Cover letter is required. ''Advise if you have e-mail.'' Time between acceptance and publication is 4 months. Often comments on rejected poems. Guidelines available for SASE. Responds in 4 months. ''Payment varies, but currently $30 NZD total for any and all inclusions in an issue, plus 2 contributor's copies. Overseas contributors receive a year's subscription in lieu of cash.'' Acquires first or one-time rights.

Additional Information *Takahe* is published by Takahe Collective Trust, a nonprofit organization formed to help new writers and get them into print alongside established poets.

Contest/Award Offerings The Takahe Poetry Competition awards 1st Prize: $250 NZD; 2nd Prize:

$100 NZD; plus one-year subscriptions to *Takahe* to 2 runners-up. Submit as many poems as you wish, but each much be named separately on the entry form. Submissions must be unpublished and may not be entered in other contests. Poems must be in English and typed on A4 paper, with no identifying information on the ms. Include SASE with entry for results and/or return of entries (or SAE with IRCs for overseas entrants; may also add $2 NZD to entry fee for handling and postage). All entries considered for publication in *Takahe*. Guidelines and entry form available on Web site. **Entry fee:** $5 NZD/poem. **Deadline:** September 30 for 2008. 2008 judge: Michael Harlow. Winners announced in December.

$◻ ◎ TALES OF THE TALISMAN (Specialized: science fiction; fantasy; horror)

P.O. Box 2194, Mesilla Park NM 88047-2194. E-mail: hadrosaur@zianet.com. Web site: www.talesofthetalisman.com. Established 1995. **Contact:** David Lee Summers, editor.

Magazine Needs *Tales of the Talisman*, published quarterly, prints "well-written, thought-provoking science fiction and fantasy." Wants "strong visual imagery. Strong emotion from a sense of fun to more melancholy is good." Does not want "graphic/gory violence or poetry that strays too far from the science fiction/fantasy genre." Has published poetry by Terrie Leigh Relf, Alessio Zanelli, L.B. Sedlacek, and Lyn Lifshin. *Tales of the Talisman* is 86 pages, $8^{1}/_{4} \times 10^{1}/_{2}$, printed on 60 lb. white paper, perfect-bound, with full-color cardstock cover. Receives about 500 poems/year, accepts up to 5%. Press run is 200 (100 subscribers). Single copy: $8; subscription: $20/year. Make checks payable to Hadrosaur Productions.

How to Submit Submit 1-5 poems at a time. Considers previously published poems; no simultaneous submissions. Accepts e-mail submissions (pasted into body of message); no disk submissions. "For e-mail submissions, place the word 'Hadrosaur' in the subject line. Submissions that do not include this will be destroyed unread. Postal submissions will not be returned unless sufficient postage is provided." Cover letter is preferred. Time between acceptance and publication is one year. Often comments on rejected poems. Guidelines available for SASE or on Web site. Responds in 1 month. Sends prepublication galleys on request. Pays $4/poem plus 1 contributor's copy. Acquires one-time rights.

Advice "Read absolutely everything you can get your hands on, especially poetry outside your genre of choice, and ask 'What if?' This is a great source for original speculative poems."

Ⓝ ◩ $◙ TALISMAN: A SEED-BED FOR THE ADVANCEMENT OF AN AESTHETIC

E-mail: ariel.kalinowski2@gmail.com. Web site: www.caravantalisman.blogspot.com.

Magazine Needs *Talisman: A Seed-Bed for the Advancement of an Aesthetic*, published weekly, "is a collection of poetry, poetics, and links that advance a synthesis of the formal methodologies of post-modernism with the archetypical human concerns of religion, nature, politics, and culture." Wants "work that operates within the nexus of: (a) journalistic and anthropological realism, (b) contemporary symbolism, surrealism, and/or imagism, (c) radical, experimental and/or hybrid form. Your work must draw from at least 2 of these areas. If you draw from 3, we'll be extremely impressed. Additionally, extra points for work that has (a) a strong intuitive emotional component, is (b) short and is (c) about the world, rather than the writer's psyche."

How to Submit Submit 5 poems at a time. Considers previously published poems and simultaneous submissions. Accepts e-mail submissions (as attachment); no fax or disk submissions. Cover letter is preferred. Reads submissions year round. Poems are circulated to an editorial board. Never comments on rejected poems. Never publishes theme issues. Guidelines available in magazine. Pays $10. Acquires one-time rights. Rights revert to poets upon publication.

Also Offers "If your work is accepted, you may have the opportunity to participate in our ART/POETRY FUSION projects at Talisman @ The Arts for Peace Gallery in NYC. Check Web site."

◻ ◎ TAPESTRIES (Specialized: for senior citizen audience)

MWCC Life Program, 444 Green St., Gardner MA 01440. (978)630-9176. Fax: (978)632-6155. E-mail: alanahb@earthlink.net or p_cosentino@mwcc.mass.edu. Web site: www.mwcc.mass.edu/LLL/tapestriesGuidelines.html. Established 2001. **Contact:** Patricia B. Cosentino, editor.

Magazine Needs *Tapestries*, published annually in November, is an anthology of poetry, short stories, essays, and nonfiction. Themes on family, heritage, tradition, folklore local history, imaginative pieces; also for 2008-9 celebration poems of 30 lines on the rebuilding of the Freedom Tower, NYC. Wants any style poetry; no restrictions on form. Does not want "political, propaganda, pornographic, or sexually explicit material as this is a 'family' magazine of high literary quality. We do not exclude religious poems, but they must have non-sectarian universality." Has published poetry by Maxine Kumin, Victor Howes, Diana Der-Hovanessian, Marge Piercy, Salma Jayyusi, F.D. Reeve, Ghazi-al-Gosaibi, and Lucinda Franks. *Tapestries* is 100 pages, magazine-sized, offset-printed, tape-bound, with card stock cover. Receives about 1,000 poems/year, accepts about 10%. Press run is 500. Copy: $10 includes S&H. Make checks payable to MWCC Life Program. We provide tear sheets to all contributors if they prefer not to buy a copy of the magazine. "We are subsidized in part by the Massachussets Cultural Council and other grants."

How to Submit Submit 3-5 poems at a time. Lines/poem: 30. Considers previously published poems and simultaneous submissions. No disk, fax, or e-mail submissions. Cover letter is preferred (only if work is previously published). Submit two copies, with name and address on only one copy. Include SASE." Reads submissions by March 31 deadline. Time between acceptance and publication is 4 months. Poems are circulated to an editorial board. Rarely comments on rejected submissions. Occasionally publishes a theme issue. Upcoming themes available on Web site. Guidelines available on Web site. No payment. Acquires first North American serial rights. Rights revert to author 90 days after publication.

Advice "Try to avoid use of first person point of view in poems. It dilutes the essence of the work. We want humor and wisdom in the submissions. Absolutely imperative to include SASE; all submissions must include proper postage. If writer wants return of hard copy, the SASE must provide the full postage on the return envelope."

◢ TAPROOT LITERARY REVIEW

P.O. Box 204, Ambridge PA 15003. (724)266-8476. E-mail: taproot10@aol.com. Established 1986. **Contact:** Tikvah Feinstein, editor.

Magazine Needs *Taproot Literary Review*, published annually, is "a very respected anthology with increasing distribution. We publish some of the best poets in the U.S. We enjoy all types and styles of poetry from emerging writers to established writers to those who have become valuable and old friends who share their new works with us." Has published poetry by Kate Wells, Ayaz Daryl Nielsen, Robert Cooperman, Karen R. Porter, Ellaraine Lockie, Shirley Barasch, Rebecca Foust, and Ed Galling. *Taproot Literary Review* is about 95 pages, offset-printed on white stock, with one-color glossy cover. Circulation is 500. Single copy: $8.95; subscription: $7.50. Sample: $5.

How to Submit Submit up to 5 poems at a time. Lines/poem: 35 maximum. No previously published poems or simultaneous submissions. Accepts submissions by e-mail (pasted into body of message), but "we would rather have a hard copy. Also, we cannot answer without a SASE." Cover letter is required (with general information). Reads submissions September 1-December 31 only. Guidelines available for SASE. Sometimes sends prepublication galleys. Pays 1 contributor's copy; additional copies are $6.50 each. Open to receiving books for review consideration. Send query first.

Contest/Award Offerings Sponsors the annual Taproot Writer's Workshop Annual Writing Contest. 1st Prize: $25 and publication in *Taproot Literary Review*; 2nd and 3rd Prizes: publication. Submit 5 poems of literary quality, in any form, on any subject except porn, religion, and politics. **Entry fee:** $12/5 poems (no longer than 35 lines each); fee includes copy of *Taproot*. **Deadline:** December 31. Winners announced the following March.

Advice "We publish the best poetry we can in a variety of styles and subjects, so long as it's literary quality and speaks to us. We love poetry that stuns, surprises, amuses, and disarms."

◢ TAR RIVER POETRY

Erwin Building Mailroom, East Carolina University, Greenville NC 27858-4353. (252)328-6783. E-mail: TarRiverPoetry@gmail.com. Web site: http://core.ecu.edu/engl/trp. Established 1978. **Contact:** Luke Whisnant, editor; Carolyn Elkins, associate editor.

Magazine Needs *Tar River Poetry*, published twice/year, is an " 'all-poetry' magazine that publishes 40-50 poems per issue, providing the talented beginner and experienced writer with a forum that features all styles and forms of verse." Wants "skillful use of figurative language; poems that appeal to the senses." Does not want "sentimental, flat-statement poetry." Has published poetry by William Stafford, Sharon Olds, Carolyn Kizer, A.R. Ammons, and Claudia Emerson. Has also published "many other well-known poets, as well as numerous new and emerging poets." *Tar River Poetry* is 64 pages, digest-sized, professionally printed on salmon stock, with matte card cover with photo. Receives 6,000-8,000 submissions/year, accepts 80-100. Press run is 900 (500 subscribers, 125 libraries). Subscription: $12. Sample: $6.50.

How to Submit Submit no more than 5 poems at a time. No previously published poems or simultaneous submissions. Accepts e-mail submissions only; no print submissions. "Detailed submission instructions appear on the Web site, along with writer's guidelines." Check Web site for reading periods: "we do not read manuscripts from May through August—submissions will be returned unread." Rarely comments on rejections "due to volume of submissions." Guidelines available for SASE or on Web site. Responds in 6 weeks. Pays 2 contributor's copies. Acquires first rights. Reviews books of poetry in 4,000 words maximum, single- or multi-book format. Query for reviews.

Advice "Writers of poetry should first be readers of poetry. Read and study traditional and contemporary poetry."

⛧ ⬚ TAR WOLF REVIEW

P.O. Box 2038, Clarkrange TN 38553. E-mail: tarwolfpoets@hotmail.com. Web site: www.tarwolfreview.org. Established 2003. **Contact:** DeAnna Stephens Vaughn, poetry editor.

Magazine Needs *Tar Wolf Review*, published annually, prefers "free verse that uses innovative language and imagery to discuss unique subjects or to re-see traditional ones, but we'll consider formal verse that meets these standards." Wants "work that expresses a unique perspective and insight. Past issues have featured lyric free verse, lyric-narrative, and prose poetry. We enjoy work that experiments with form, diction, syntax, and juxtaposition of imagery." Does not want "poetry with obvious rhymes and meanings; cliché-ridden, pornographic, or maudlin poetry. Not interested in poems about poems or the process of writing." Has published poetry by Trent Busch, William Doreski, Gayle Elen Harvey, Ruth Holzer, Jacqueline Kolosov, and Gary Metras. *Tar Wolf Review* is 64 pages, digest-sized, saddle-stapled, with 110 lb. cover with color or b&w art. Receives about 1,900 poems/year, accepts about 4%. Press run is 80-100. Single copy: $6 plus $1.42 shipping; subscription: $12 plus $2.84 shipping. Make checks or money orders payable to *Tar Wolf Review*.

How to Submit Submit 3-5 poems at a time. Lines/poem: 90 maximum, including spaces. Considers simultaneous submissions (with notification); no previously published poems. No e-mail or disk submissions. Cover letter is preferred. "Present the poems as you would like them to appear in their published forms. Include name and contact information on each page, and a cover letter with a bio of 40 or fewer words. Submissions without SASEs will be discarded unread. Multiple submissions will be returned unread or discarded." Reads submissions year round. Time between acceptance and publication is 1 month to 1 year. Sometimes comments on rejected poems. Guidelines available for SASE or on Web site. Responds within 6 months. Pays at least 1 contributor's copy. Acquires first North American serial rights.

Advice "Consider how each line stands on its own and whether it contributes to the poem's effect. Read a diverse selection of poets, especially ones whose work is very different from your own."

▣ ⬚ TARPAULIN SKY

E-mail: editors@tarpaulinsky.com (inquiries) or submissions@tarpaulinsky.com (submissions). Web site: www.tarpaulinsky.com. Established 2002. **Contact:** Poetry Editors. Editor: Christian Peet.

Magazine Needs *Tarpaulin Sky*, published biannually in print and online, features "highest-quality poetry, prose, cross-genre work, art, photography, interviews, and reviews. We are open to all styles and forms, providing the forms appear inevitable and/or inextricable from the poems. We are especially fond of inventive/experimental and cross-/trans-genre work. The best indication of our aesthetic is found in the journal we produce: Please read it before submitting your work. Also, hardcopy submissions may be received by different editors at different times; check guidelines before submitting." Has published poetry by Jenny Boully, Matthea Harvey, Bin Ramke, Eleni Sikelianos, Juliana Spahr, and Joshua Marie Wilkinson. Receives about 3,000 poems/year.

Magazines/Journals

How to Submit Submit 4-6 poems at a time. Considers simultaneous submissions; no previously published poems. Accepts e-mail submissions (''best received as attachments in .rtf or .pdf formats''); no disk submissions. Cover letter is preferred. Reads submissions year round. Time between acceptance and publication is 2-6 months. ''Poems are read by all editors. We aim for consensus.'' Rarely comments on rejected poems. Guidelines available for SASE, by e-mail, or on Web site. Responds in 1-4 months. Pays in contributor's copies and ''by waiving readings fees for Tarpaulin Sky Press Open Reading Periods.'' Always sends prepublication galleys (electronic). Acquires first rights. Reviews books/chapbooks of poetry.

▣ ☑ TATTOO HIGHWAY

E-mail: submissions@tattoohighway.org. Web site: www.tattoohighway.org. Established 1998. **Contact:** Sara McAulay, editor.

Magazine Needs *Tattoo Highway*, published biannually online, is a journal of poetry, literary prose, new media, and art. ''We're open to most styles; only criterion is quality.'' Wants ''language that is fresh, vivid, and original; writing that is smart and a little edgy, that engages with the world beyond the writer's own psyche. We like formal poetry if well handled.'' Does not want ''self-pity, navel-contemplation, clichés, workshop hackery.'' Has published poetry by Judith Skillman, Barry Spacks, Kelley White, Taylor Graham, Erin Murphy, Patrick Carrington, and Laura McCullough. Receives about 800 poems/year, accepts about 50.

How to Submit Submit up to 5 poems at a time. Considers previously published poems (if they've appeared in small-circulation print journals; unpublished work preferred) and simultaneous submissions (''but please let us know promptly if you place your piece elsewhere''). Accepts e-mail submissions (pasted into body of message) only. ''For hypertext or New Media (Flash, etc.) submissions, please provide a URL where we may view the work.'' Reading periods vary; ''typically last about three months. Blind readings by editorial board. Several rounds of 'triage' during the reading period, usually handled by e-mail. Face-to-face editorial meeting shortly after submission deadline, where final selections are made. Editor and poetry editor have final say.'' Sometimes comments on rejected poems. ''If a poem has its moments, though it doesn't quite work, we try to acknowledge that. We encourage near-misses to try us again.'' Regularly publishes theme issues. Guidelines available on Web site. Responds in up to 3 months (''usually within 1 week of deadline''). Always sends prepublication galleys. No payment. Acquires first electronic rights; rights revert to author 90 days after online publication date.

Contest/Award Offerings ''Picture Worth 500 Words'' contest for poetry/prose. No entry fee; small prizes. See guidelines on Web site.

Advice ''Read some past issues before submitting.''

▣ ◎ THE TEACHER'S VOICE (Specialized: the American teacher experience, from pre-K to university professor)

P.O. Box 150384, Kew Gardens NY 11415. E-mail: editor@the-teachers-voice.org. Web site: www. the-teachers-voice.org. Established 2005. **Contact:** Andrés Castro, founder/managing editor.

Magazine Needs *The Teacher's Voice*, was founded as an experimental hardcopy literary magazine and is now free and online. ''We publish poetry, short stories, creative nonfiction, and essays that reflect the many different American teacher experiences.'' Wants ''all styles and forms. We ask to see critical creative writing that takes risks without being overly self-indulgent or inaccessible. We welcome work that ranges from 'art for art's sake' to radically social/political. Writing that illuminates the most pressing/urgent issues in American education and the lives of teachers gets special attention.'' Has published poetry by Edward Francisco Sapphire, Hal Sirowitz, and Antler. Receives about 1,000 poems/year, accepts about 10%.

How to Submit Submit 3-5 poems at a time. Lines/poem: no limits. Considers previously published poems (if rights are held by the author) and simultaneous submissions (contact if submission has been accepted elsewhere). No e-mail or disk submissions. Send up to 5 pages of poetry or prose pieces under 2,000 words. Cover letter is preferred: ''are you a teacher, administrator, parent, student, librarian, custodian, coach, security officer, etc? We do not accept responsibility for submissions or queries not accompanied by a SASE with adequate postage.'' Reads submissions year round. Time between acceptance and publication is 1-6 months. Poems are circulated to an editorial board. Sometimes comments on rejected poems. "We respond if the author asks for feedback that addresses a specific aspect or issue." Guidelines available in magazine, for SASE, or on Web site. Sometimes sends prepublication galleys "if requested." Acquires first rights and electronic reprint rights. Rights revert to poet "after work is first electronically published and archived on this site; no material on this site may be reproduced in any form without permission from their individual authors." No longer accepts online submissions.

Additional Information "This year, we are going to release our second annual Teacher's Voice Chapbook Contest selection as well as last year's runner-up, a 'Best of 2008' chapbook, and other limited press collections if funds allow. Since we publish open as well as theme issues (that require enough thematic pieces to be compiled) and do rely on readership financial support, our publishing schedule and format may vary from year to year. Our production goal is to showcase strong cohesive collections that support our mission and satisfy the needs of particular issues. For the moment, our new focus on electronic publishing is a matter of survival that offers many new possibilities and opportunities in keeping with the changing times."

Contest/Award Offerings Sponsors *The Teacher's Voice* Annual Chapbook Contest and *The Teacher's Voice* Annual Poetry Contest for Unpublished Poets. Guidelines for both contests available for SASE, by e-mail, or on Web site.

Also Offers "*The Teacher's Voice*'s sibling Don Quixote Poetry Project was established to bring free workshops to schools, libraries, and community centers in underserved communities in New York City. Information is available on our Web site."

Advice "Please, be daring. Take some personal risks. If you find it comfortable to write about your students only from a distance or if they and you are not part of surrounding social and political institutions, we may not be for you. Sadly and realistically, many teachers are afraid, given the personally revealing or critical nature of their writing, to jeopardize their positions in their schools and communities—especially if new and untenured. If you must, feel free to include a pseudonym in your cover letter. If you are a teacher, become a poet. If you are a poet, become a teacher."

✪ 🌐 ☑ TEARS IN THE FENCE

38 Hod View, Stourpaine, Nr. Blandford Forum, Dorset DT11 8TN England. (44)(1258)456803. Fax: (44)(1258)454026. E-mail: david@davidcaddy.wanadoo.co.uk. Web site: www.myspace.com/tearsinthefence. Established 1984. **Contact:** David Caddy, general editor.

Magazine Needs *Tears in the Fence*, published 3 times/year, is a "small press magazine of poetry, fiction, interviews, essays, and reviews. We are open to a wide variety of poetic styles. Work that is unusual, perceptive, and risk-taking as well as imagistic, lived, and visionary will be close to our purpose. However, we like to publish a variety of work." Considers poetry by children and teens. Has published poetry by Nathaniel Tarn, Jennifer K Dick, John James, Don Winter, Chris McCabe, Donna Hilbert, and Mary Maher. *Tears in the Fence* is 144 pages, A5, docutech-printed on 110-gms. paper, perfect-bound, with matte card cover. Press run is 800 (522 subscribers). Subscription: $20/4 issues. Sample: $7.

How to Submit Submit 6 poems at a time. Accepts e-mail (pasted into body of message) and disk submissions. Cover letter with brief bio is required. Poems must be typed; include SASE. Time between acceptance and publication is 8 months "but can be less." Responds in 3 months. Pays one contributor's copy. Reviews books of poetry in 2,000-4,000 words, single- or multi-book format. Send materials for review consideration.

Also Offers The magazine runs a regular series of readings in London, and an annual international literary festival.

Advice "I think it helps to subscribe to several magazines in order to study the market and develop an understanding of what type of poetry is published. Use the review sections and send off to magazines that are new to you."

☑ ◎ TEXAS POETRY CALENDAR (Specialized: poems with a TX connection)

Dos Gatos Press, 1310 Crestwood Rd., Austin TX 78722. (512)467-0678. Fax: (408)580-8523. E-mail: editors@dosgatospress.org. Web site: www.dosgatospress.org. Established 2004 (under current editorship). **Contact:** Scott Wiggerman or David Meischen, co-editors.

Magazine Needs *Texas Poetry Calendar*, published annually in August, features a "week-by-week calendar side-by-side with poems with a Texas connection." Wants "a wide variety of styles, voices, and forms, including rhyme—though a Texas connection is preferred. Humor is welcome! Poetry *only!*" Does not want "children's poetry, erotic poetry, profanity, obscure poems, previously published work, or poems over 35 lines." *Texas Poetry Calendar* is about 144 pages, digest-sized, offset-printed, spiral-bound, with 2-color cardstock cover. Receives about 600 poems/year, accepts about 70-75. Press run is 1,500; 70 distributed free to contributors. Single copy: $12.95 plus $3 shipping. Make checks payable to Dos Gatos Press.

How to Submit Submit 3 poems at a time. Lines/poem: 35 maximum, "including spaces and title." Considers simultaneous submissions; no previously published poems. No fax, e-mail, or disk submissions. Cover letter is required. "Include a short bio (100 words or less) and poem titles in cover letter. Also include e-mail address and phone number. Do not include poet's name on the poems themselves!" Reads submissions year round. Time between acceptance and publication is 3-4 months. Poems are circulated to an editorial board. Never comments on rejected poems. **"Entry fee for the *Texas Poetry Calendar* Awards ($5 for 3 poems) is required for all submissions—all poems submitted are eligible for cash awards."** (See Contest/Award Offerings below.) Guidelines available in magazine, by e-mail, or on Web site. Responds "only once a year, in spring." Sometimes sends prepublication galleys. Pays 1 contributor's copy. Acquires first, electronic, and reprint rights.

Contest/Award Offerings Sponsors the annual Texas Poetry Calendar Awards, offering 1st Prize: $150; 2nd Prize: $75; 3rd Prize: $40. "Award-winning poems receive special recognition in the calendar in which they are printed." Submit 3 poems. Guidelines available in magazine, by e-mail, or on Web site. **Entry fee:** $5 for 3 poems. **Deadline:** March 20 (postmark). "Judged by a nationally known poet—Robert McDowell, Naomi Shihab Nye, Kathleen Pierce, and Benjamin Alire Saenz."

$🖉 ◎ THEMA (Specialized: specific theme per issue)

Thema Literary Society, P.O. Box 8747, Metairie LA 70011-8747. E-mail: thema@cox.net. Web site: http://members.cox.net/thema. Established 1988. **Contact:** Gail Howard, poetry editor.

Magazine Needs *THEMA*, published triannually, uses poetry related to specific themes. "Each issue is based on an unusual premise. Please, please send SASE for guidelines before submitting poetry to find out the upcoming themes." Does not want "scatologic language, alternate lifestyle, explicit love poetry." Has published poetry by Phil Gruis, John Grey, Amy Dengler, and Fredrick Zydek. *THEMA* is 120 pages, digest-sized professionally printed, with glossy card cover. Receives about 400 poems/year, accepts about 8%. Press run is 400 (230 subscribers, 30 libraries.) Subscription: $20 U.S./$30 foreign. Sample $10 U.S./$15 foreign.

How to Submit Submit up to 3 poems at a time. Include SASE. "All submissions should be typewritten on standard 8½×11 paper. Submissions are accepted all year, but evaluated after specified deadlines." Specify target theme. Editor comments on submissions. Upcoming themes and guidelines available in magazine, for SASE, by e-mail, or on Web site. Pays $10/poem and 1 contributor's copy. Acquires one-time rights.

Advice "Do not submit to *THEMA* unless you have one of *THEMA*'s upcoming themes in mind. And be sure to specify which one!"

🖵 ◻ THICK WITH CONVICTION

E-mail: twczine@yahoo.com. Web site: www.angelfire.com/poetry/thickwithconviction. Established 2005. **Contact:** Sara Blanton, Kristina Blanton, or Mandy Callen, editors.

Magazine Needs *Thick With Conviction*, published quarterly online, is "run by three quirky twenty-something women who are desperately searching for new and interesting ideas in poetry. We'd like to be moved to anger or tears." Wants all genres of poetry, "poems that make us exhale a deep sigh after reading them. Basically, if we can't feel the words in front of us, we're not going to be happy. We'd like to expose the world to poets who may not get the kind of exposure that more experienced poets do." Does not want "teen angst poems, religious poems, or greeting card tripe." Considers poetry by teens. Has published poetry by Taylor Graham, Corey Mesler, Kendall A. Bell, Tanya Ranta, Rachel Bunting, and Simon Perchik. Receives about 300 poems/year, accepts about 15%.

How to Submit Submit 3-5 poems at a time. Lines/poem: no limit. Considers previously published poems; no simultaneous submissions. Accepts e-mail submissions (pasted into body of message; "any attachments will be deleted"); no disk submissions. Cover letter is required. Reads submissions year round. Submit seasonal poems 3 months in advance. Time between acceptance and publication is 3 months. Never comments on rejected poems. Guidelines available on Web site. Responds in "roughly 1 to 2 weeks." Acquires one-time rights. Rights revert to poet upon publication.

Advice "Take the time to read the poems on our Web site. If your style is similar, we'll most likely enjoy your work. The most important thing a writer can do is read, read, read. The more you read, the more your writing will grow and blossom. Be sure to have thick skin, and don't let rejections get you down."

☑ THIRD COAST
Dept. of English, Western Michigan University, Kalamazoo MI 49008-5331. (269)387-2675. Web site: www.wmich.edu/thirdcoast. Established 1995. **Contact:** Poetry Editors.

Magazine Needs *Third Coast*, published semiannually in March and September, is a national literary magazine of poetry, prose, creative nonfiction, translations, and drama. Wants "excellence of craft and originality of thought. Nothing trite." Has published poetry by Myronn Hardy, Sean Thomas Dougherty, Terrance Hayes, Margo Schlipp, Mark Halliday, and Philip Levine. *Third Coast* is 176 pages, digest-sized, professionally printed, perfect-bound, with 4-color cover with art. Receives about 2,000 poems/year, accepts about 1%. Press run is 3,500 (850 subscribers, 50 libraries, 2,400 shelf sales). Single copy: $8; subscription: $14/year, $26 for 2 years, $38 for 3 years. Sample: $6 (back issue).

How to Submit Submit up to 5 poems at a time. Considers simultaneous submissions with notification; no previously published poems. No electronic submissions. Cover letter is preferred. "Poems should be typed single-spaced, with the author's name on each page. Stanza breaks should be double-spaced." Poems are circulated to assistant poetry editors and poetry editors; poetry editors make final decisions. Seldom comments on rejected poems. Guidelines available on Web site. Responds in 4 months. Pays 2 contributor's copies plus one-year subscription. Acquires first rights.

Contest/Award Offerings Sponsors an annual poetry contest. 1st Prize: $1,000 and publication; 4 finalists receive notification in prize-winners issue, possible publication, and a 3-year subscription. Guidelines available on Web site. **Entry fee:** $15, includes one-year subscription to *Third Coast*.

⊞ ☐ THE THIRD HALF
K.T. Publications, 16 Fane Close, Stamford, Lincolnshire PE9 1HG United Kingdom. (44)(1780)754193. Established 1989. **Contact:** Kevin Troop, editor.

Magazine Needs *The Third Half*, published regularly, is a literary magazine containing "free-flowing and free-thinking material on most subjects. Open to all ideas and suggestions." Showcases 4 poets/issue. "Each poet has 24 pages." Does not want "badly written or obscene scribbling." Has published poetry by Gillian Bence-Jones, R. Tomas, Raymond Humphreys, and Mario Petrucci. *The Third Half* is perfect-bound, with glossy cover. Press run is 100-500. Single copy: £5.50 in UK. Sample: £10 overseas. Make checks payable to K.T. Publications.

How to Submit Submit 6 poems at a time. No previously published poems. Accepts disk submissions. Cover letter is preferred. Include SAE. Time between acceptance and publication "depends on the work and circumstances." **There is a £5 reading fee to cover costs.** Seldom comments on rejected poems. Sometimes publishes theme issues ("as themes present themselves"). Responds in 2 days. Always sends prepublication galleys. Pays 1-6 contributor's copies. "Copyright belongs to the poets/authors throughout."

Also Offers A "reading and friendly help service to writers. Costs are reasonable." Write for details.

Advice "Keep writing; be patient."

☑ ◎ THOUGHTS FOR ALL SEASONS: THE MAGAZINE OF EPIGRAMS (Specialized: epigrams; rhyming poetry; humor; themes)
86 Leland Rd., Becket MA 01223. Established 1976. **Contact:** Prof. Em. Michel Paul Richard, editor.

Magazine Needs *Thoughts for All Seasons*, published irregularly, is "designed to preserve the epigram as a literary form; satirical. All issues are commemorative. Volume 6 celebrates the centennial of the publication of *The Devil's Dictionary* by Ambrose Bierce." Has published poetry by Kendal Bush, William D. Barney, and Jill Williams. *Thoughts for All Seasons* is 80 pages, offset-printed from typescript, saddle-stapled, with card cover. Accepts about 15% of material submitted. Press run is 500-1,000. "There are several library subscriptions, but most distribution is through direct mail or local bookstores and newsstand sales." Single copy: $6.50 (includes p&h).

How to Submit Submit at least one or 2 pages (10-12 epigrams or 2-4 poems) at a time. Considers simultaneous submissions; no previously published epigrams "unless a thought is appended which alters it." Include SASE and one-paragraph bio. Comments on rejected poems. Publishes theme issues. Guidelines available in magazine or for SASE. Responds in 1 week. Pays 1 contributor's copy, additional discounted copies.

Advice "Preference given to rhyming poetry, including original limericks. Nonsense verse with good imagery also acceptable. No haiku!"

$◨ THE THREEPENNY REVIEW

P.O. Box 9131, Berkeley CA 94709. (510)849-4545. Web site: www.threepennyreview.com. Established 1980. **Contact:** Wendy Lesser, editor.

- Work published in *The Threepenny Review* has been included in *The Best American Poetry* and *The Pushcart Prize*.

Magazine Needs *The Threepenny Review*, published quarterly, is "a national review of literature, performing and visual arts, and social articles aimed at the intelligent, well-read (but not necessarily academic) reader." Wants "formal, narrative, short poems (and others). No bias against formal poetry; in fact, a slight bias in favor of it." Has published poetry by Anne Carson, Frank Bidart, Seamus Heaney, Robert Pinsky, and Louise Glück. *The Threepenny Review* is a 36-page tabloid. Receives about 4,500 submissions of poetry/year, accepts about 40 poems. Press run is 10,000 (8,000 subscribers, 150 libraries). Subscription: $25. Sample: $12.

How to Submit Submit up to 5 poems at a time. Lines/poem: 100 maximum ("exceptions are possible"). No previously published poems or simultaneous submissions. **Do not submit mss September-December.** Guidelines available for SASE or on Web site. Responds in up to 2 months. Pays $200/poem plus one-year subscription. Acquires first serial rights. Guidelines available for SASE.

◪ $◨ TICKLED BY THUNDER

14076-86A Ave., Surrey BC V3W 0V9 Canada. E-mail: info@tickledbythunder.com. Web site: www. tickledbythunder.com. Established 1990. **Contact:** Larry Lindner, editor/publisher.

Magazine Needs *Tickled by Thunder*, published up to 4 times/year, uses poems "about fantasy particularly; writing or whatever. Require original images and thoughts. Welcome humor and creative inspirational verse." Does not want "anything pornographic, childish, unimaginative." Has published poetry by Laleh Dadpour Jackson and Helen Michiko Singh. *Tickled by Thunder* is 24 pages, digest-sized, published on Macintosh. Has 1,000 readers/subscribers. Subscription: $12 CAD/4 issues. Sample: $2.50 CAD.

How to Submit Submit 3-5 poems at a time. Lines/poem: up to 40 ("keep them short—not interested in long, long poems"). No e-mail submissions. Cover letter is required. Include "a few facts about yourself and brief list of publishing credits." Comments on rejected poems "80% of the time." Guidelines available for SASE or on Web site. Responds in up to 6 months. Pays 2¢/line, $2 CAD maximum. Acquires first rights. Reviews books of poetry in up to 300 words. Open to unsolicited reviews. Send materials for review consideration.

Contest/Award Offerings Offers a poetry contest 4 times/year. Prize: cash, publication, and subscription. **Entry fee:** $5 CAD for one poem; free for subscribers. **Deadlines:** the 15th of February, May, August, and October.

Additional Information Publishes **author-subsidized chapbooks**. "We are interested in student poetry and publish it in our center spread: *Expressions*." Send SASE (or SAE and IRC) for details.

◪ TIGER'S EYE: A JOURNAL OF POETRY

Tiger's Eye Press, P.O. Box 2935, Eugene OR 97402. E-mail: tigerseyepoet@yahoo.com. Web site: www.tigerseyejournal.com. Established 2001. **Contact:** Colette Jonopulos and JoAn Osborne, editors.

Magazine Needs *Tiger's Eye: A Journal of Poetry*, published semiannually, features both established and undiscovered poets. "Besides publishing the work of several exceptional poets in each issue, we feature two poets in interviews, giving the reader insight into their lives and writing habits." Wants "both free verse and traditional forms; no restrictions on subject or length. We welcome sonnets, haibun, haiku, ghazals, villenelles, etc. We pay special attention to unusual forms and longer poems that may have difficulty being placed elsewhere. Poems with distinct imagery and viewpoint are read and re-read by the editors and considered for publication." Has published poetry by Shawn Fawson, Anne Blonstein, Cheryl Loetscher, Patrick Carrington, and Hari Bhajan Khalsa. *Tiger's Eye* is 64 pages, saddle-stitched. Receives 1,000 poems/year, accepts 100. Press run is 300. Single copy: $5; subscription: $10 for 2 issues. Make checks payable to Tiger's Eye Press.

How to Submit Submit 3-5 poems at a time. Considers simultaneous submissions with notification if a poem is accepted elsewhere; no previously published poems. No e-mail submissions. Cover letter is required. Include brief bio. SASE for notification only; no submissions are returned. Reads submissions year-round; deadlines are February 28 and August 31. Time between acceptance and publication is 3 months. "All poems are read by the editors, then filed as poems we definitely want to publish, those we are still considering, and those we aren't publishing. Our two featured poets are chosen, then letters and e-mails are sent out." Seldom comments on rejected poems. Guidelines available in magazine or on Web site. Responds in 6 months. Always sends prepublication galleys. Pays one contributor's copy to each poet, 2 to featured poets. Acquires one-time rights.

Additional Information *Tiger's Eye* nominates for The Pushcart Prize.

Contest/Award Offerings Tiger's Eye Annual Poetry Contest (see separate listing in Contests & Awards).

Advice "We accept poems submitted by new poets with as much enthusiasm as those submitted by established poets. Poems with clean images, unique subjects, and strong voices have a good chance of being published in *Tiger's Eye*."

✪ ◪ TIMBER CREEK REVIEW

P.O. Box 16542, Greensboro NC 27416. E-mail: timber_creek_review@hoopsmail.com. Established 1994. **Contact:** John M. Freiermuth, editor.

Magazine Needs *Timber Creek Review*, published quarterly, prints short stories, literary nonfiction, and poetry. Wants all types of poetry. Does not want religious or pornographic poetry. Has published poetry by Kelly Whiddon, Maureen A. Sherbondy, L. Lee Harper, Gregory Muller, Jacqueline de Weeverm, and Steve Rhodes. *Timber Creek Review* is 80-84 pages, digest-sized, laser-printed, stapled, with colored paper cover. Receives about 1,000 poems/year, accepts about 8%. Press run is 150 (120 subscribers, 2 libraries, 30 shelf sales). Single copy: $4.75; subscription: $17. Make checks payable to J.M. Freiermuth.

How to Submit Submit 3-6 poems at a time. Lines/poem: 3 minimum, "rarely over 30." Considers simultaneous submissions; no previously published poems. No e-mail or disk submissions. Cover letter is required. Reads submissions year round. Submit seasonal poems 10 months in advance. Time between acceptance and publication is 3-6 months. Never comments on rejected poems. Occasionally publishes theme issues. Guidelines available for SASE or by e-mail. Responds in up to 6 months. Pays one contributor's copy. Acquires first North American serial rights.

Advice "Turn off your TV and read that poety magazine that published your last poem, and maybe someone else will read your poem, too!"

◪ ◎ TIME OF SINGING, A MAGAZINE OF CHRISTIAN POETRY (Specialized: literary Christian poetry)

P.O. Box 149, Conneaut Lake PA 16316. E-mail: timesing@zoominternet.net. Web site: www.timeo fsinging.bizland.com. Established 1958-1965, revived 1980. **Contact:** Lora H. Zill, editor.

Magazine Needs *Time of Singing, A Magazine of Christian Poetry*, published 4 times/year, seeks "poems that 'show' rather than 'tell.' The viewpoint is unblushingly Christian—but in its widest and most inclusive meaning." Wants free verse and well-crafted rhyme; would like to see more forms. Does not want "collections of uneven lines, sermons that rhyme, unstructured 'prayers,' and trite sing-song rhymes." Has published poetry by John Grey, Luci Shaw, Bob Hostetler, Frances P. Reid, Tony Cosier, Barbara Crooker, and Charles Waugaman. *Time of Singing* is 44 pages, digest-sized, offset from typescript. Receives more than 800 submissions/year, accepts about 175. Press run is 300 (150 subscribers). Subscription: $17 USD, $21 USD Canada, $30 USD overseas. Sample: $4, or 2 for $6 (postage paid).

How to Submit Submit up to 5 poems at a time. Lines/poem: prefers less than 40, "but will publish up to 60 lines if exceptional." Considers previously published poems (indicate when/where appeared) and simultaneous submissions. Accepts e-mail submissions (pasted into body of message or as attachment). Poems should be single-spaced. Time between acceptance and publication is up to one year. Comments "with suggestions for improvement if close to publication." Guidelines available for SASE, by e-mail, or on Web site. Responds in 2 months. Pays 1 contributor's copy.

Contest/Award Offerings Sponsors theme contests for specific issues. Guidelines available for SASE, by e-mail, or on Web site.

Advice "Study the craft. Be open to critique. A poet is often too close to his/her work and needs a critical, honest eye. *Time of Singing* publishes more literary-style verse, not greeting card style."

◩ ◎ TO TOPOS: POETRY INTERNATIONAL (Specialized: humanism; pacifism; altermondialism)

OSU Dept. of Foreign Languages & Literatures, 210 Kidder Hall, Corvallis OR 97331. (541)737-2146. Fax: (541)737-3563. E-mail: jkrause@oregonstate.edu. Web site: http://oregonstate.edu/dept/forei gn_lang/totopos/index.html. Established 1997. **Contact:** Joseph Krause, editor.

• *To Topos* is funded through Poetry Enterprises, a nonprofit association.

Magazine Needs *To Topos: Poetry International*, published semiannually in June and December, is "committed to fostering human rights on an environmentally fragile planet. Its focus is altermon-dialist, recognizing that the causes of poverty and injustice are often related to race, gender, nationality, and the effacement of earth-given resources. Most issues are thematically focused. Previous themes have included Incarceration, Peace and the Sea, Forests, North African Voices (guest-edited by Nabil Boudraa), Contemporary Hungarian Poets (guest-edited by Eniko Bollobaso), and Indigenous American Voices (guest-edited by Allison Hedge Coke). *To Topos* is open to both aspiring and recognized poets, and primarily interested in living poets who believe words carry the gift of positive social change. We particularly invite submissions from refugees and the borderless. The harmony of craft and message should be the primary consideration prior to submitting texts. Black and white photography and imagery are particularly welcome to complement specific themes." Wants "poetry from all over the world and in any language, so long as it is accompanied by an English translation. The journal espouses a vision of pacifism and human rights but is not anchored in a political current." Does not want "self-serving poetry." Has published poetry by Leonard Cirino, Khadija Al Mourabit, Gérard Bocholier, Sándor Csoóri, Joy Harjo, and Mairead Byrne. *To Topos* is 50-120 pages, digest-sized, docutech-printed, perfect-bound, with cardstock cover with graphics, includes ads (from Amnesty International only). Receives 100-300 poems/issue "depending on the theme," accepts 30-50%. Press run is 250-300; distributed to the international poetry community and to contributors. Single copy: $9; subscription: $18.

How to Submit Submit no more than 6 poems at a time. Considers previously published poems (with the permission of the original copyright holder) and simultaneous submissions. Accepts e-mail (as attachment) and disk submissions; no fax submissions. Cover letter is preferred. "Include brief bio (2-4 lines) and SASE." Reads submissions year round. Time between acceptance and publication is 1-6 months. Poems are circulated to an editorial board. "Guest Editor makes initial selection; co-editors finalize, often seeking advice from consulting editors." Rarely comments on rejected poems. Regularly publishes theme issues. Guidelines available in magazine or on Web site. Pays 1 contributor's copy. Acquires one-time rights. Rights revert to poet upon publication. Reviews books of poetry in 250 words, single-book format. "We review books relevant to theme. Books reviewed are selected by the editors. Contact editors to suggest titles."

Advice "The mission of this journal is to reveal the human face of poetry as a statement of urgency in today's world. *To Topos* is open to all aesthetic and stylistic orientations, but submissions should be a seed for social change along humanist principles without indulging in political or nationalist rhetoric."

◼ ◪ ◎ TORCH: POETRY, PROSE, AND SHORT STORIES BY AFRICAN AMERICAN WOMEN

E-mail: info@torchpoetry.org (inquiries); poetry@torchpoetry.org (submissions). Web site: www.t orchpoetry.org. Established 2006. **Contact:** Amanda Johnston, editor.

Magazine Needs *Torch: Poetry, Prose, and Short Stories by African American Women*, published semiannually online, provides "a place to celebrate contemporary poetry, prose, and short stories by experienced and emerging writers alike. We prefer our contributors to take risks, and offer a diverse body of work that examines and challenges preconceived notions regarding race, ethnicity, gender roles, and identity." Has published poetry by Sharon Bridgforth, Patricia Smith, Shia Shabazz, Ana-Maurine Lara, and Remica L. Bingham. Receives about 250+ submissions/year, accepts about 20. Number of unique visitors: 300+/month.

How to Submit Submit 3-7 poems at a time. Lines/poem: 40 maximum. No previously published poems or simultaneous submissions. Accepts e-mail submissions only (as one attachment). Send to poetry@torchpoetry.org with "Poetry Submission" in subject line. "Poems should be individually typed on separate pages." Cover letter is preferred (in the body of the e-mail). Reads submissions April 1-August 31 only. Time between acceptance and publication is 2-7 months. Sometimes comments on rejected poems. Sometimes publishes theme issues. Guidelines available on Web site. Always sends prepublication galleys. No payment. Acquires rights to publish accepted work in online issue and in archives. Rights revert to poets upon publication.

Also Offers "Within *Torch*, we offer a special section called Flame that features an interview, biography, and work sample by an established writer as well as an introduction to their Spark—an emerging writer who inspires them and adds to the boundless voice of creative writing by Black women." A free online newsletter is available; see Web site.

Advice "Black women, write freely. Know that your words are wanted, needed, and safe here. Read the previous issues online for examples of the type of writing *Torch* publishes."

◪ TRESTLE CREEK REVIEW

English Dept., North Idaho College, 1000 W. Garden Ave., Coeur d'Alene ID 83814-2199. (208)769-3394. E-mail: tcr@nic.edu. Established 1982-83. **Contact:** Lori Wallin, editor.

Magazine Needs *Trestle Creek Review*, published annually by North Idaho College, accepts submissions of poetry, fiction, creative nonfiction, and b&w art from NIC students and residents of Idaho's five northern counties only. "We're fairly eclectic and favor poetry strong on image and sound." Does not want "the romantic, the formulaic, and the clichéd." Has published poetry by Sean Brendan-Brown, E.G. Burrows, Ron McFarland, and Mary Winters. *Trestle Creek Review* is 57 pages, digest-sized, professionally printed on heavy buff stock, saddle-stapled, with matte cover with art. Receives 300 submissions/year, accepts about 30. Press run is 500. Single copy: $8.40. Sample: $5.25 (back issue).

How to Submit Submit 3-5 poems at a time, or fiction/creative nonfiction mss of no more than 5,000 words. Multiple submissions by the same author will be returned without consideration. No previously published poems or simultaneous submissions. Accepts e-mail submissions; no fax submissions. Cover letter with "address, phone number, e-mail address, brief bio, and SASE is required with all submissions whether electronic or hard copy." Accepts submissions to January 31 deadline (for May publication). Responds by May 30. Pays 5 contributor's copies.

Advice "Be neat; be precise; don't romanticize or cry in your beer; strike the surprising, universal note. Know the names of things."

◼ ◪ ◎ TRIPLOPIA (Specialized: thematic issues)

E-mail: editor@triplopia.org. Web site: www.triplopia.org. Established 2001. **Contact:** Tara A. Elliott, poetry editor.

Magazine Needs *TRIPLOPIA* is "an internationally oriented, Web-based quarterly with a solid emphasis on excellence and accessibility. We favor work that is both accessible and of significant use to the working writer." Wants "attention to craft as well as a range of voice." Does not want "poetry that has to force its way through an overt agenda." Considers poetry by teens. Has published poetry by Joy Harjo, Steve Kowit, Bob Holman, Angie Estes, Barbara Crooker, and Frannie Lindsay. Receives about 1,600 poems/year, accepts about 100. Number of unique visitors: 31,350/issue. "Each issue is widely publicized on Internet poetry sites/forums and individually to our large mailing list."

How to Submit Submit 5-6 poems at a time. Lines/poem: "no preference." Considers previously published poems; no simultaneous submissions. Accepts e-mail submissions; no disk submissions. "For work in special formats, please paste into body of e-mail and include an explanatory note in your submission. We will invite you to send an attachment once your material is under consideration." Cover letter is unnecessary. Reads submissions January 15-February 20; April 15-May 20; July 15-August 20; and October 15-November 20. Time between acceptance and publication is one month. Poems are circulated to an editorial board. Sometimes comments on rejected poems. Regularly publishes theme issues. Upcoming themes and guidelines available on Web site. Responds in 2 months. Always sends prepublication galleys. No payment, but provides links to contributor's other publications and maintains work in archives. Acquires one-time rights. Rights revert to poets upon publication.

Contest/Award Offerings Sponsors the Best of the Best Competition (see separate listing in Contests & Awards).

Advice "We at *TRIPLOPIA* do everything in our power and imagination to promote and honor our contributors. We publish multiple pieces; contribute to major competitions including Pushcart and Best of the Net; offer our own competition (see Best of the Best in the Contests & Awards section); respond to submissions quickly; invite contributors back as reviewers; link to their work and Web sites in extensive bio notes; keep their work accessible in our archive; and are meticulous about galley proofs. We believe that we are there to support artists, not the other way around."

✖ ◪ TULANE REVIEW

122 Norman Mayer, New Orleans LA 70118. (504)865-5160. Fax: (504)862-8958. E-mail: litsoc@tulane.edu. Web site: www.tulane.edu/~litsoc. Established 1988. **Contact:** Whitney Johnson, editor.

• *Tulane Review* is the recipient of an AWP Literary Magazine Design Award.

Magazine Needs *Tulane Review*, published biannually, is a national literary journal seeking quality submissions of prose, poetry, and art. "We consider all types of poetry." Wants "imaginative poems with bold, inventive images." Has published poetry by Virgil Suárez, Tom Chandler, Gaylord Brewer, and Ryan Van Cleave. *Tulane Review* is 80 pages, 7×9, perfect-bound, with 100# cover with full-color artwork. Receives about 1,200 poems/year, accepts about 30. Single copy: $5; subscription: $10. Make checks payable to *Tulane Review*.

How to Submit Submit up to 6 poems at a time. Lines/poem: 1-2 pages. Considers simultaneous submissions; no previously published poems. Accepts e-mail submissions; no fax or disk submissions. Cover letter is required. "Include brief biography." Reads submissions year round. Time between acceptance and publication is 3 months. "Poems are reviewed anonymously by a review board under a poetry editor's supervision. Recommendations are given to the editor, who makes final publication decisions." Often comments on rejected poems. Guidelines available in magazine, for SASE, by e-mail, or on Web site. Responds in 2 months. Pays 3 contributor's copies. Acquires first North American serial rights.

◪ ◎ THE TULE REVIEW (Specialized: poets living in the greater Sacramento area)

Sacramento Poetry Center, 1719 25th St., Sacramento CA 95816. (916)451-5569. E-mail: tulereview @sacramentopoetrycenter.org. Web site: www.sacramentopoetrycenter.org. **Contact:** Brad Buchanan, managing editor.

Magazine Needs *The Tule Review*, published semiannually, uses "poetry, book reviews, and essays concerning contemporary poetry; occasionally includes an audio CD." Wants "all styles and forms of poetry." Primarily publishes poets living in the greater Sacramento area, but accepts work from anywhere. Has published poetry by Gary Snyder, Diane DiPrima, Jack Hirschman, Julia Connor, and Douglas Blazek. *The Tule Review* is 24-32 pages, digest-sized, saddle-stapled, with b&w cover artwork. Receives about 500 poems/year, accepts about 10-20%. Press run is 500; 80 distributed free to contributors and for review. Single copy: $6 ppd; subscription: $25/year (includes *Poetry Now*, a monthly publication). Make checks payable to Sacramento Poetry Center.

How to Submit Submit 3-6 poems at a time. Lines/poem: 96 maximum. Considers previously published poems; no simultaneous submissions. Accepts e-mail (pasted into body of message or as attachment) and disk submissions. "If you attach poems, put all poems into one attachment." Cover letter is required. Reads submissions year round. Submit seasonal poems 6 months in advance. Time between acceptance and publication is 1-6 months. Poems are circulated to an editorial board. Sometimes comments on rejected poems. Sometimes publishes theme issues. Upcoming themes available in magazine, by e-mail, or on Web site. Guidelines available in magazine, for SASE, by e-mail, or on Web site. Responds in 3-4 months. Pays 2 contributor's copies. Acquires first North American serial rights. Rights revert to poet upon publication. Reviews books/chapbooks of poetry and other magazines/journals.

Advice "Send us your best work!"

☾ ◎ TUNDRA: THE JOURNAL OF THE SHORT POEM (Specialized: poems of 13 or fewer lines, including haiku and tanka)

22230 NE 28th Place, Sammamish WA 98074-6408. E-mail: WelchM@aol.com. Web site: http://hometown.aol.com/welchm/Tundra.html. Established 1999. **Contact:** Michael Dylan Welch, editor/publisher.

Magazine Needs *Tundra: The Journal of the Short Poem* showcases all short poetry, including haiku, tanka, and other genres. Wants "short poems of 13 or fewer lines rooted in immediate and objective imagery, including haiku and tanka." Does not want religious, topical, or confessional poetry. Has published poetry by Dana Gioia, X.J. Kennedy, Jane Hirshfield, Peter Pereira, Robert Bly, and Madeleine DeFrees. *Tundra* is 128 pages, digest-sized, offset-printed, perfect-bound, with glossy cover. Receives about 14,000 poems/year, accepts less than 1%. Press run is 1,200 (700 subscribers, 10 libraries, 50 shelf sales); 10 distributed free to such places as poetry centers. Single copy: $9; subscription: $21 for 3 issues. Make checks payable to Michael Dylan Welch.

How to Submit Submit 3-5 poems at a time ("up to 10 is okay if as short as haiku"). No previously published poems or simultaneous submissions. Accepts e-mail submissions (pasted into body of message; no attachments); no disk submissions. "Always include your full postal address with each e-mail submission." Cover letter is optional; "okay the first time you submit, but unnecessary thereafter unless you write something you are sure the editor needs to know. *Tundra* does not publish bios, so there's no need to include them except for the editor's information. Please include a #10 SASE with sufficient postage for return of the manuscript or for a response." Reads submissions year round. Time between acceptance and publication "varies, but is sometimes up to a year. The editor makes the sole decision, and may occasionally offer suggestions on poems whether accepted or returned. The editor will clearly indicate if he wants to see a revision." Recommends reading an issue before submitting, "but no purchase or subscription is required." Guidelines available for SASE, by e-mail, or on Web site. Responds in 3-4 months. Sometimes sends prepublication galleys. Pays 1 contributor's copy. Acquires first rights. "Rights revert to author after publication, but we may want to include selected poems on a Web site in the future." Reviews books/chapbooks of poetry in 500-2,000 words, single- and multi-book format. Send materials for review consideration to Michael Dylan Welch.

Advice "If your work centers on immediate and objective imagery, *Tundra* is interested. All poems must be 13 or fewer lines, with only very rare exceptions (where each line is very short). If you think that a haiku is merely 5-7-5 syllables, then I do not want to see your work (see 'Becoming a Haiku Poet' online at www.haikuworld.org/begin/mdwelch.apr2003.html. for reasons why). Due to the excessive volume of inappropriate submissions for *Tundra* in the past, I now encourage only well-established poets to submit."

Magazines/Journals

$ ◎ TURTLE MAGAZINE FOR PRESCHOOL KIDS (Specialized: ages 2-5)

Children's Better Health Institute, 1100 Waterway Blvd., Indianapolis IN 46202. Web site: www.cbh i.org. or www.turtlemag.org.

Magazine Needs *Turtle Magazine for Preschool Kids*, published by Children's Better Health Institute, is a magazine for children ages 2-5. "Colorful and entertaining...perfect for reading aloud." Wants light-hearted poetry appropriate for the age group. Reviews submissions for possible use in all Children's Better Health Institute publications.

How to Submit Manuscripts must be typewritten with poet's contact information in upper right-hand corner of each poem's page. SASE required. Submit seasonal material at least 8 months in advance. Guidelines available for SASE or on Web site. Responds in about 3 months. Pays $25 minimum for poetry. Acquires all rights.

Advice "We receive too many poetry submissions that are about kids, not for kids. Or, the subject matter is 1 that adults think children would or should like. Reading our guidelines is not enough. Careful study of current issues will acquaint writers with each title's 'personality.'"

☑ 24.7

30 Forest St., Providence RI 02906. (401)521-4728. Established 1994. **Contact:** David Church, poetry editor.

• **Considers solicited submissions only.** Has published poetry by George Held, A.D. Winans, Ann Menebroker, Charles Plymell, and Gerry Nicosia.

◩ U.S. 1 WORKSHEETS

P.O. Box 127, Kingston NJ 08528-0127. Established 1973. **Contact:** Nancy Scott, managing editor.

Magazine Needs *U.S. 1 Worksheets*, published annually, uses high-quality poetry and, on occasion, short fiction. "We prefer complex, well-written work." Has published poetry by Alicia Ostriker, BJ Ward, James Richardson, Lois Marie Harrod, and Baron Wormser. *U.S. 1 Worksheets* is 96 pages, perfect-bound, with b&w cover art. Press run is 500. Subscription: 2 years for $15; sample copy $8. Back issues $5.

How to Submit Submit up to 5 poems at a time. Considers simultaneous submissions if indicated; no previously published poems. "We use a rotating board of editors. We read May through June, and can no longer return manuscripts. Enclose SASE for reply." Pays 1 contributor's copy.

Also Offers The U.S. 1 Poets' Cooperative co-sponsors (with the Princeton Public Library) a series of monthly poetry readings (U.S. 1 Poets Invite) at the Princeton Public Library. "There is no formal membership, only the willingness of participants to share their work."

Advice "Send us your best. Please note submission dates. We receive many good poems we cannot consider because they arrive far outside our reading period."

▣ ◯ ◎ UGLY ACCENT: A LITERARY ADVERSARIA BROUGHT TO YOU BY THE MIDWEST

2310 40th Pl. NW, #302, Washington DC 20007. E-mail: poetry@uglyaccent.com. Web site: www.u glyaccent.com. Established 2006. **Contact:** Matt Friauf, poetry editors.

Magazine Needs *UGLY ACCENT: A Literary Adversaria Brought to You by the Midwest*, published quarterly online, seeks "to publish new talent, specifically those with some degree of separation to the Midwest. We wish to glorify the cesspool of talent that this part of the nation breeds." Has published poetry by Ron Czerwien, Eddie Kilowatt, Gene Tanta, Paul Gaszak, Karla Huston, and Bronwen Tate. Receives about 350 poems/year, accepts about 80 (22%).

How to Submit Submit 5 poems at a time. Lines/poem: open. Considers previously published poems and simultaneous submissions. Accepts e-mail submissions (as attachment); no disk submissions. Cover letter is preferred. Include 50-word bio with submission. Reads submissions year round. Time between acceptance and publication is 6 months. Poems are circulated to an editorial board. Often comments on rejected poems. Sometimes publishes theme issues. Guidelines available on Web site. Responds in 3-4 months. Pays 1 contributor's copy. Acquires one-time rights and right to publish work in online archives. Rights revert to poets upon publication. Reviews books/chapbooks of poetry. Send materials for review consideration to the attention of Matt Friauf.

Advice "We are looking for writers with subtlety and a predilection for experimentation with language and form. We believe that poetry should test the elasticity of language and utilize the form for all its worth. Self-absorbed poems will not be tolerated; sure, all poems are autobiographical to some extent, but at least pretend to care about something else.''

⊞ ☑ UNDERSTANDING MAGAZINE

127 Milton Rd. W., 7 Duddingston House Courtyard, Edinburgh EH15 1JG Scotland. Phone/fax: (44)(131)661-1156. Established 1989. **Contact:** Denise Smith.

Magazine Needs *Understanding Magazine*, published annually, features "poetry, short stories, parts of plays, reviews, and articles." Wants "original poetry." Has published poetry by Susanna Roxman, D. Zervanou, Thom Nairn, Alexis Stamatis, Byron Leodaris, and Keith Bennett. *Understanding* is A5, perfect-bound. Receives 2,000 poems/year. Press run is 1,000. Single copy: £5.50; subscription: £11. Sample: £3. Make checks payable to Dionysia Press Ltd.

How to Submit Submit up to 5 poems at a time. No previously published poems or simultaneous submissions. No fax submissions. Time between acceptance and publication is 6 months to a year. Poems are circulated to an editorial board. Often comments on rejected poems. Guidelines available for SASE or by fax. Responds in 6 months or more. Always sends prepublication galleys. Pays 1 contributor's copy. Acquires all rights. Returns rights after publication. Staff reviews books/chapbooks of poetry or other magazines. Send materials for review consideration.

Contest/Award Offerings Sponsors poetry competitions with cash prizes. Guidelines and themes available for SASE.

Advice "Be original."

◙ UNMUZZLED OX

105 Hudson St., New York NY 10013. Established 1971. **Contact:** Michael Andre, poetry editor.

Magazine Needs Unmuzzled Ox, published semi-annually, is a literary tabloid. Each edition is built around a theme or specific project. **"The chances of an unsolicited poem being accepted are slight since I always have specific ideas in mind."** Has published poetry by Allen Ginsberg, Robert Creeley, and Denise Levertov. Subscription: $20.

How to Submit Only unpublished work will be considered, but poems may be in French as well as English.

Advice "I suggest contributors read carefully an issue before sending in an unsolicited manuscript."

⚃ ◻ UP AND UNDER: THE QND REVIEW

P.O. Box 115, Hainesport NJ 08036. E-mail: qndpoets@yahoo.com. Web site: www.quickanddirtyp oets.com. Established 2004. **Contact:** Rachel Bunting, editor.

Magazine Needs *Up and Under: The QND Review*, published annually in March, is "a journal with an eclectic mix of poetry: sex, death, politics, IKEA, Mars, food, and jug handles alongside a smorgasbord of other topics covered in such diverse forms as the sonnet, villanelle, haiku, and free verse. We are interested in excellent poetry with no bias between free verse or traditional forms." Does not want "greeting card verse, graphic pornography." Has published poetry by Dan Maguire, Gina Larkin, Leonard Gontarek, Autumn Konopka, John Grey and Taylor Graham. *Up and Under* is 50-60 pages, digest-sized, laser-printed, saddle-stapled, with card cover with photograph, includes ads. Receives about 300 poems/year, accepts about 30 (or 10%). Press run is 100. Single copy: $7. Chapbooks are available online or through U.S. Mail. Make checks payable to Rachel Bunting.

How to Submit Submit up to 5 poems at a time. Lines/poem: no limit. Considers simultaneous submissions (with notification); no previously published poems. Accepts e-mail submissions (pasted into body of message). Reads submissions September 1-December 30. Time between acceptance and publication is 3-6 months. Poems are circulated to an editorial board. Sometimes comments on rejected poems. Guidelines available in magazine, for SASE, or on Web site. Responds in 2-3 months. Pays 1 contributor's copy. Acquires one-time rights.

Advice "Take a moment to read the poems featured on our Web site before submitting. We prefer poetry that uses concrete imagery to engage all 5 senses."

★ ⊕ ⊘ ◎ URTHONA MAGAZINE (Specialized: Buddhism)

Abbey House, Abbey Road, Cambridge CB5 8HQ England. +44(0)1223-362513. E-mail: urthonama g@onetel.com. Web site: www.urthona.com. Established 1992. **Contact:** Poetry Editor.

Magazine Needs *Urthona*, published biannually, explores the arts and Western culture from a Buddhist perspective. Wants "poetry rousing the imagination." Does not want "undigested autobiography, political, or New Age-y poems." Has published poetry by Peter Abbs, Robert Bly, and Peter Redgrove. *Urthona* is 60 pages, A4, offset-printed, saddle-stapled, with 4-color glossy cover, includes ads. Receives about 300 poems/year, accepts about 40. Press run is 1,200 (200 subscribers, plus shelf sales in Australia and America). "See Web site for current subscription rates." Sample (including guidelines): $7.99 USD, $8.99 CAD.

How to Submit Submit 6 poems at a time. No previously published poems or simultaneous submissions. Accepts e-mail submissions (as attachment). Cover letter is preferred. Time between acceptance and publication is up to 8 months. Poems are circulated to an editorial board and are read and selected by poetry editor. Other editors have right of veto. Responds within 6 months. Pays 1 contributor's copy. Acquires one-time rights. Reviews books/chapbooks of poetry and other magazines in 600 words. Send materials for review consideration.

▣ ⊘ VALPARAISO POETRY REVIEW: Contemporary Poetry and Poetics

Dept. of English, Valparaiso University, Valparaiso IN 46383-6493. (219)464-5278. Fax: (219)464-5511. E-mail: vpr@valpo.edu. Web site: www.valpo.edu/english/vpr/. Established 1999. **Contact:** Edward Byrne, editor.

Magazine Needs *Valparaiso Poetry Review: Contemporary Poetry and Poetics*, published semiannually online, accepts "submissions of unpublished or previously published poetry, book reviews, author interviews, and essays on poetry or poetics that have not yet appeared online and for which the rights belong to the author. Query for anything else." Wants poetry of any length or style, free verse or traditional forms. Has published poetry by Charles Wright, Billy Collins, John Balaban, Stanley Plumly, and Annie Finch. Receives about 2,000 poems/year, accepts about 1%.

How to Submit Submit 3-5 poems at a time (no more than 5). Considers previously published poems ("original publication must be identified to ensure proper credit") and simultaneous submissions. Accepts e-mail submissions (pasted into body of message, no attachments); no fax or disk submissions. **Postal submissions preferred.** Cover letter is preferred. Include SASE. Reads submissions year round. Time between acceptance and publication is 6-12 months. Seldom comments on rejected poems. Guidelines available on Web site. Responds in up to 6 weeks. Acquires one-time rights. "All rights remain with author." Reviews books of poetry in single- and multi-book format. Send materials for review consideration.

⊕ ⊘ VAN GOGH'S EAR: BEST WORLD POETRY & PROSE

French Connection Press, 12 rue Lamartine, Paris 75009 France. (33)(1)4016-0535. Fax: (33)(1)4016-0701. E-mail: frenchcx@tiscali.fr. Web site: www.frenchcx.com. Established 2002. **Contact:** Ian Ayres, founder/editor.

• Poetry published in *Van Gogh's Ear* has appeared in *The Best American Poetry*.

Magazine Needs *Van Gogh's Ear*, published annually in April, is an anthology series "devoted to publishing powerful poetry and prose in English and English translations by major voices and innovative new talents from around the globe." Has published poetry by Marilyn Monroe, Tony Curtis, Yoko Ono, James Dean, Xaviera Hollander, and Charles Manson. *Van Gogh's Ear* is 280 pages, digest-sized, offset-printed, perfect-bound, with 4-color matte cover with commissioned artwork. Receives about 1,000 poems/year, accepts about 30%. Press run is 2,000 (105 subscribers, 25 libraries, 1,750 shelf/online sales); 120 distributed free to contributors and reviewers. Single copy: $19; subscription: $36 for 2 years. "As a 501(c)(3) nonprofit enterprise, *Van Gogh's Ear* needs the support of individual poets, writers, and readers to survive. Any donation, large or small, will help *Van Gogh's Ear* continue to publish the best cross-section of contemporary poetry and prose. Because of being an anglophone publication based in France, *Van Gogh's Ear* is unable to get any grants or funding. Your contribution will be tax-deductible. Make donation checks payable to Committee on Poetry-*VGE*, and mail them (donations **only**) to the Allen Ginsberg Trust, P.O. Box

582, Stuyvesant Station, New York NY 10009. All U.S. checks/money orders for reading fees, subscriptions, and purchases must be made out to French Connection Press and sent to Michael Hathaway, 522 E. South Ave., St. John KS 67576-2212.''

How to Submit Submit 6 poems or 2 prose pieces at a time. Lines/poem: 165 maximum (1,500 words maximum for prose). No previously published poems or simultaneous submissions. No fax, e-mail, or disk submissions. Cover letter is preferred. "**Send to the French Connection Press address only!** Please include SASE (or SAE with IRCs) or e-mail address along with a brief bio of up to 120 words.'' Reads submissions May 1-October 31. **Charges $10 (USD) reading fee for non-subscribers.** Time between acceptance and publication is one year. "Every submission is closely read by all members of the editorial board and voted upon." Seldom comments on rejections. "Our continued existence, and continued ability to read your work, depends mainly on subscriptions/donations. Therefore, we must ask that you at least purchase a sample copy before submitting work." Guidelines available in anthology or on Web site. Responds in 9 months. Always sends prepublication galleys. Pays 1 contributor's copy. Acquires one-time rights.

Advice "The goal of *Van Gogh's Ear* is for each volume to transport all who experience it into multifaceted realities that transcend color and culture through the uncensored pens of legendary and new talents from all walks of life. 'Intensity' is the key. And we are more than open to poets/writers who haven't been published before. Being published isn't as important as the work itself. Please note: Volume 7 will be the final volume of *Van Gogh's Ear*. We are currently accepting submissions for that volume.''

▣ ◪ VERSAL

Amsterdam, The Netherlands. E-mail: versal@wordsinhere.com. Web site: www.wordsinhere.com. Established 2002. **Contact:** Megan M. Garr, editor.

Magazine Needs *Versal*, published annually by wordsinhere, is the only English-language literary magazine in the Netherlands and publishes new poetry, prose, and art from around the world. "We publish writers with an instinct for language and line break, content and form that is urgent, involved, and unexpected." Has published poetry by Naomi Shihab Nye, Marilyn Hacker, Julie Marie Wade, Myronn Hardy, and Jennifer Gandel Ridgeway. *Versal* is 100 pages, 20cm×20cm, offset-printed, perfect-bound, with acid-free full-color cover. Receives about 1,000+ poems/year, accepts about 4%. Single copy: $15 USD or €10. Ordering information available on Web site.

How to Submit Submit 3-5 poems at a time. Considers simultaneous submissions; no previously published poems. Accepts e-mail submissions only (online submission system can be found on Web site. Cover letter is required. Cover letter is required (in body of e-mail). Reads submissions September 15-January 15. Time between acceptance and publication is 4-6 months. Poems are circulated to an editorial board. Sometimes comments on rejected poems. Guidelines available on Web site. Responds in 3 months. Sends prepublication PDF galleys. Pays 1 contributor's copy. Acquires one-time rights. Rights revert to poet upon publication.

Advice "Write as much as you can. Follow the guidelines. Resist the urge to send us poems about tulips, windmills, or sex and drug adventures. Support independent literary publishing: Buy copies of *Versal* and any other lit mag you find.''

◪ ◪ VERSE

Dept. of English, University of Richmond, Richmond VA 23173. Web site: http://versemag.blogspot.com. Established 1984. **Contact:** Brian Henry and Andrew Zawacki, editors.

● **NOTE:** *Verse* **is closed to unsolicited submissions.**

Poetry published in *Verse* has also appeared in *The Best American Poetry* and *The Pushcart Prize*.

Magazine Needs *Verse*, published 3 times/year, is "an international poetry journal which also publishes interviews with poets, essays on poetry, and book reviews." Wants "no specific kind; we look for high-quality, innovative poetry. Our focus is not only on American poetry, but on all poetry written in English, as well as translations." Has published poetry by James Tate, John Ashbery, Barbara Guest, Gustaf Sobin, and Rae Armantrout. *Verse* is 128-416 pages, digest-sized, professionally printed, perfect-bound, with card cover. Receives about 5,000 poems/year, accepts

1%. Press run is 1,000. Single copy: $10; subscription: $18 for individuals, $39 for institutions. Sample: $6.

How to Submit *Verse* is closed to unsolicited submissions until further notice; check Web site for any updates. Unsolicited submissions will be recycled.

Advice "Read widely and deeply. Avoid inundating a magazine with submissions; constant exposure will not increase your chances of getting accepted."

$ 🖸 THE VIRGINIA QUARTERLY REVIEW

P.O. Box 400223, Charlottesville VA 22904-4223. (434)924-3124. Fax: (434)924-1397. Web site: www.vqronline.org. Established 1925.

Magazine Needs *The Virginia Quarterly Review* uses about 45-50 pages of poetry in each issue. No length or subject restrictions. Issues have largely included lyric and narrative free verse, most of which features a strong message or powerful voice. *The Virginia Quarterly Review* is 288-336 pages, digest-sized, flat-spined. Press run is 7,000.

How to Submit Submit up to 5 poems at a time. No simultaneous submissions. Accepts online submissions only at http://vqronline.org/submission/. Responds in 3 months or longer, "due to the large number of poems we receive." Guidelines available on Web site; do not request by fax. Pays $5/line.

Contest/Award Offerings Sponsors the Emily Clark Balch Prize for Poetry, an annual award of $1,000 given to the best poem or group of poems published in the *Review* during the year. 2006 winner was Susan B. A. Somers-Willett.

🖸 VOICINGS FROM THE HIGH COUNTRY

4920 S. Oak St., Casper WY 82601. Established 2000. **Contact:** Ella J. Cvancara, editor.

Magazine Needs *Voicings from the High Country*, published annually in the spring, seeks "poetry with substance, not just pretty words; understandable, rather than obscure; poetry that goes beyond the self. Biased toward free verse that is worldly rather than introspective, tells a story, and uses many/most/all of the five senses." Also considers haiku, senryu, and tanka (for a haiku page). Does not want "rhyming, pornography, violent language, 'Hallmark' verse, political poems, or overtly religious poetry. No poetry that's unsure of why it was written, is demeaning to the human spirit, or untitled." Has published poetry by guest poets David Lee, the first poet laureate of Utah, and Robert Roripaugh, former poet laureate of Wyoming. *Voicings from the High Country* is 35-40 pages, digest-sized, computer-generated, stapled, with 110 lb. cardstock cover. Receives about 200 poems/year, accepts about 15%. Press run is 75; 30 distributed free to contributors. Single copy: $6. Make checks payable to Ella J. Cvancara.

How to Submit Submit 3 poems at a time. Lines/poem: 35 maximum. Considers previously published poems; no simultaneous submissions. Accepts submissions by postal mail only; no disk submissions. Cover letter is required. Include a 3- to 5-line bio. "Submit each poem on a separate page with name and address in upper right corner; typed or computer-generated. Include SASE for response." Reads submissions July 1-February 1 only. Time between acceptance and publication is 3 months. "Poems are circulated to a three-member editorial board with the names of the poets removed. Poems are ranked according to a system." Seldom comments on rejected poems. Guidelines available for SASE. Responds in 6 months. Pays one contributor's copy. Acquires one-time rights.

Advice "Beginners often write about themselves. Reach beyond yourself, avoid clichés, search for fresh language. Use metaphor and simile. Strike a spark with words."

🗀 🎯 WATERWAYS: POETRY IN THE MAINSTREAM (Specialized: thematic issues)

Ten Penny Players, Inc., 393 Saint Pauls Ave., Staten Island NY 10304-2127. (718)442-7429. E-mail: tenpennyplayers@si.rr.com. Web site: www.tenpennyplayers.org. Established 1977. **Contact:** Barbara Fisher and Richard Spiegel, poetry editors.

Magazine Needs *Waterways: Poetry in the Mainstream*, published 11 times/year, prints work by adult poets. "We publish theme issues and are trying to increase an audience for poetry and the printed and performed word. While we do 'themes,' sometimes an idea for a future magazine is inspired by a submission, so we try to remain open to poets' inspirations. Poets should be guided, however, by the fact that we are children's and animal rights advocates and are a NYC press. We are open to reading material from people we have never published, writing in traditional and experimental poetry forms." Does not want "haiku or rhyming poetry; never use material of an explicit sexual nature." Has published poetry by Ida Fasel, Will Inman, and Richard Kostelanetz. *Waterways* is 40 pages, $4\frac{1}{4} \times 7$, photocopied from various type styles, saddle-stapled, with matte card cover. Accepts 60% of poems submitted. Press run is 150. Subscription: $33. Sample: $3.50.

How to Submit Submit less than 10 poems at a time (for first submission). Considers simultaneous submissions. Accepts e-mail submissions (pasted into body of message). "Since we've taken the time to be very specific in our response, writers should take seriously our comments and not waste their emotional energy and our time sending material that isn't within our area of interest. Sending for our theme sheet and a sample issue and then objectively thinking about the writer's own work is practical and wise. Manuscripts that arrive without a return envelope are not sent back." Sometimes comments on rejected poems. Guidelines available for SASE or on Web site. Responds in less than 1 month. Pays 1 contributor's copy. Acquires one-time publication rights.

Additional Information Ten Penny Players publishes chapbooks "by children and young adults only—not by submission—they come through our workshops in the library and schools. Adult poets are published through our Bard Press imprint, **by invitation only**. Books evolve from the relationship we develop with writers we publish in *Waterways* and to whom we would like to give more exposure."

Advice "We suggest that poets attend book fairs and check our Web site. It's a fast way to find out what we're publishing. Without meaning to sound 'precious' or unfriendly, the writer should understand that small press publishers doing limited editions and all production work in-house are working from their personal artistic vision and know exactly what notes will harmonize, effectively counterpoint, and meld. Many excellent poems submitted to *Waterways* are sent back to the writers because they don't relate to what we are trying to create in a given month."

☑ WAVELENGTH: POEMS IN PROSE AND VERSE

1753 Fisher Ridge Rd., Horse Cave KY 42749-9706. Established 1999. **Contact:** David P. Rogers, editor/publisher.

Magazine Needs *Wavelength: Poems in Prose and Verse*, published twice /year, seeks "poems that use lively images, intriguing metaphor, and original language. Long poems OK; would like to see more prose poems. Rhyme is almost always a liability. All subjects and styles considered as long as the poem is thought-provoking or uses language in an innovative way." Does not want "rhymed, very religious—anything that sacrifices creativity for convention." Has published poetry by Robert Cooperman, Lyn Lifshin, Francis Blessington, Ann Taylor, Albert Haley, and Virgil Suárez. *Wavelength* is 35 (or more) pages, digest-sized, laser-printed, perfect-bound, with heavy cardstock cover with illustration. Receives about 450 poems/year, accepts 5-10%. Press run is 100 (25 subscribers, 20-25 shelf sales); 50 distributed free to the public. Single copy: $6; subscription: $15 for 3 issues. Make checks payable to Dr. David P. Rogers.

How to Submit Submit 1-5 poems at a time. Considers previously published poems and simultaneous submissions, "but please do not withdraw the poem after we've accepted it." No disk submissions. Cover letter is required. "Brief bio preferred. Poet's name and address must appear on every page. SASE or no response. Poets who want poems returned should include sufficient postage." Submit seasonal poems 3 months in advance. Time between acceptance and publication is up to one year. Seldom comments on rejected poems. "Please do not write for guidelines. Just send a courteous submission following the guidelines in this listing." Responds in 4 months. Pays one contributor's copy. Acquires one-time rights. Reviews books/chapbooks of poetry in 100-150 words, single-book format. Send materials for review consideration.

Advice "Read and write every day. If a poem still seems good a year after you wrote it, send it out. Be original. Say something clever, and ask what will the reader get out of it? Editor has a weakness for synesthesia. The cover letter will not get your poems published if they're not what we need, but it gives you a chance to create interest in them—why not take it?"

$⊠ WEBER: THE CONTEMPORARY WEST

Weber State University, 1214 University Circle, Ogden UT 84408-1214. (801)626-6473. E-mail: weberjournal@weber.edu. Web site: http://weberjournal.weber.edu. Established 1983. **Contact:** Michael Wutz, editor.

• Poetry published in *Weber* has appeared in *The Best American Poetry*.

Magazine Needs *Weber: The Contemporary West*, published 3 times/year, is "an interdisciplinary journal interested in relevant works covering a wide range of topics." Wants "three or four poems; we publish multiple poems from a poet." Does not want "poems that are flippant, prurient, singsong, or preachy." Has published poetry by Stephen Dunn, Carolyn Forché, William Kloefkorn, Gailmarie Pahmeier, Mark Strand, Janet Sylvester, David Lee, and Robert Dana. *Weber* is 144 pages, 7½×10, offset-printed on acid-free paper, perfect-bound, with color cover. Receives about 250-300 poems/year, accepts 30-40. Press run is 1,200 (1,000 subscribers, 90 libraries). Subscription: $20 ($30 for institutions). Sample: $10 (back issue).

How to Submit Submit 3-4 poems at a time, 2 copies of each (one without name). Considers simultaneous submissions; no previously published poems. Cover letter is preferred. Time between acceptance and publication is 12 months. Poems are selected by an anonymous (blind) evaluation. Seldom comments on rejected poems. Publishes theme issues. Guidelines available in magazine, for SASE, by e-mail, or on Web site. Responds in up to 3 months. Always sends prepublication galleys. Pays $30-50/poem (depending on fluctuating grant monies) and 2 contributor's copies. Acquires all rights. Copyright reverts to author after first printing.

Contest/Award Offerings The Dr. Sherwin W. Howard Poetry Award, a $500 cash prize, is awarded annually to the author of the best set of poems published in *Weber* during the previous year. The competition is announced each year in the Spring/Summer issue.

Advice "This journal is refereed by established poets—beginners not encouraged."

⊞ $⊘ WESTERLY (Specialized: Australia, Asia, Indian Ocean region)

English, Communication, and Cultural Studies, University of Western Australia, Crawley 6009 Western Australia. (61)(8)6488-2101. Fax: (61)(8)6488-1030. E-mail: westerly@cyllene.uwa.edu.au. Web site: http://westerly.uwa.edu.au. Established 1956. **Contact:** Andrew Taylor, poetry editor.

Magazine Needs *Westerly*, published annually in November, prints quality short fiction, poetry, literary critical, socio-historical articles, and book reviews with special attention given to Australia, Asia, and the Indian Ocean region. "We don't dictate to writers on rhyme, style, experimentation, or anything else. We are willing to publish short or long poems. We do assume a reasonably well-read, intelligent audience. Past issues of *Westerly* provide the best guides. Not consciously an academic magazine." *Westerly* is about 200 pages, digest-sized, "electronically printed." Press run is 1,200. Subscription: $16 (USD), $23.95 (AUD).

How to Submit Submit up to three poems or one short story (two if quite short-suggested maximum length 5,000 words) at a time. No simultaneous submissions. Accepts fax and e-mail (as attachment in Word 6 format). "If submission is short, include in body of e-mail." Cover letter is preferred. "Cover letters should be brief and non-confessional." All manuscripts must show the name and address of the sender and should be typed (double-spaced) on 1 side of the paper only. Reads submissions by June 30 deadline. Time between acceptance and publication "can be up to 1 year depending on when work is submitted. Please wait for a response before forwarding any additional submissions for consideration." Responds in 4 months. Pays minimum of $50 AUD plus 1 contributor's copy. Acquires first publication rights; requests acknowledgment on reprints. Reviews books of poetry in multi-book format in an annual review essay. Send materials for review consideration.

Contest/Award Offerings The Patricia Hackett Prize (value approximately $750 AUD) is awarded annually for the best contribution published in the previous year's issue of *Westerly*.

Advice "Be sensible. Write what matters to you, but think about the reader. Don't spell out the meanings of the poems and the attitudes to be taken to the subject matter—i.e., trust the reader. Don't be swayed by literary fashion. Read the magazine, if possible, before sending submissions."

✪ $⊘ WESTERN HUMANITIES REVIEW

University of Utah, 255 S. Central Campus Dr., Room 3500, Salt Lake City UT 84112-0494. (801)581-6070. Fax: (801)585-5167. E-mail: whr@mail.hum.utah.edu. Web site: www.hum.utah.edu/whr. Established 1947. **Contact:** P.J. Carlisle, managing editor.

• Poetry published in *Western Humanities Review* has been selected for *The Best American Poetry* as well as the Pushcart Prize anthologies.

Magazine Needs *Western Humanities Review*, published semiannually in April and October, prints poetry, fiction, and a small selection of nonfiction. Wants "quality poetry of any form, including translations." Has published poetry by Christopher Cunningham, Ravi Shankar, Aaron Fogel, Justin Dodd, J. Ely Shipley. Innovative prose poems may be submitted as fiction, non-fiction to the appropriate editor. Has published prose by Michael Martone, Craig Dworkin, Lance Olsen, Steve Almond. *Western Humanities Review* is 112-144 pages, digest-sized, professionally printed on quality stock, perfect-bound, with coated card cover. Receives about 1500 submissions/year, accepts less than 10%. Press run is 1,000. Subscription: $16 to individuals in the U.S. Sample: $10.

How to Submit Considers simultaneous submissions but no more than five poems per reading period. No fax or e-mail submissions. Reads submissions October 1-May 31 only. Time between acceptance and publication is 1-4 issues. Managing editor makes an initial cut, then the poetry editor makes the final selections. Seldom comments on rejected poems. "We do not publish writer's guidelines because we think the magazine itself conveys an accurate picture of our requirements." Responds in up to 6 months. Pays $5/published page and 2 contributor's copies. Acquires first serial rights then rights revert to author.

Contest/Award Offerings Sponsors an annual contest for Utah writers.

▨ ◉ WESTVIEW: A JOURNAL OF WESTERN OKLAHOMA (Specialized: particularly interested in southwest writers)

Southwestern Oklahoma State University, 100 Campus Dr., Weatherford OK 73096. Established 1981. **Contact:** James Silver, editor.

Magazine Needs *Westview: A Journal of Western Oklahoma*, published semiannually, is "particularly interested in writers from the Southwest; however, we are open to quality work by poets from elsewhere. We publish free verse, prose poems, and formal poetry." Has published poetry by Carolynne Wright, Miller Williams, Walter McDonald, Robert Cooperman, Alicia Ostriker, and James Whitehead. *Westview* is 64 pages, magazine-sized, perfect-bound, with full-color glossy card cover. Receives about 500 poems/year, accepts 7%. Press run is 700 (300 subscribers, about 25 libraries). Subscription: $15/2 years. Sample: $5.

How to Submit Submit 5 poems at a time. Cover letter is required. Including biographical data for contributor's note. Comments on submissions "when close." Manuscripts are circulated to an editorial board. Responds within 4-6 months. Pays 1 contributor's copy.

◖ WESTWARD QUARTERLY: THE MAGAZINE OF FAMILY READING

Laudemont Press, P.O. Box 250, Kirkland IL 60146. (800)440-4043. E-mail: wwquarterly@aol.com. Web site: http://members.aol.com/wwquarterly. Established 1999. **Contact:** Shirley Anne Leonard, editor.

Magazine Needs *WestWard Quarterly: The Magazine of Family Reading* prints poetry. Wants "all forms, including rhyme—we welcome inspirational, positive, reflective, humorous material promoting nobility, compassion, and courage." Does not want "experimental or avant-garde forms, offensive language, depressing or negative poetry." Considers poetry by children and teens. Has published poetry by Margaret Been, Brian Felder, Grace Hartley, Leland Jamieson, Michael Keshigian, and J. Alvin Speers. *WestWard Quarterly* is 32 pages, digest-sized, laser-printed, saddle-stapled, with inkjet color cover with scenic photos, includes ads. Receives about 2,000 poems/year, accepts about 8%. Press run is 120 (60 subscribers). Single copy: $4; subscription: $15/year ($18 foreign). Make checks payable to Laudemont Press.

How to Submit Submit up to 5 poems at a time. Lines/poem: 40 maximum. Considers previously published poems and simultaneous submissions. Prefers e-mail submissions (pasted into body of message); no disk submissions. Reads submissions year round. Submit seasonal poems 3 months in advance. Time between acceptance and publication is "months." Often comments on rejected poems. Guidelines available for SASE, by e-mail, or on Web site. Responds in "weeks." Pays 1 contributor's copy. Acquires one-time rights.

Contest/Award Offerings Offers a quarterly prize of one-half of entry fees per contest. Submit poems up to 40 lines. **Entry fee:** $1 for subscribers, $2 for nonsubscribers. **Deadline:** March 31, June 30, September 30, December 31. Guidelines available in magazine, for SASE, by e-mail, or on Web site.

Also Offers "Every issue has an article on improving writing skills and/or writing different forms of poetry."

◙ WHISKEY ISLAND MAGAZINE

English Dept., Cleveland State University, Cleveland OH 44115. (216)687-2056. Fax: (216)687-6943. E-mail: whiskeyisland@csuohio.edu. Web site: www.csuohio.edu/whiskey_island. Established 1968. **Contact:** Poetry Editor. (Student editors change yearly.)

Magazine Needs *Whiskey Island Magazine,* published semiannually, prints poetry, prose, and art. Wants "writing that engages the reader immediately. It's always good to be interesting early." Has published poetry by Nin Andrews, George Bilgere, and Mary Biddinger. *Whiskey Island Magazine* is about 100 pages, digest-sized, professionally printed, perfect-bound, with glossy stock cover. Receives 1,000-1,500 poetry mss/year, accepts 6%. Press run is 750. Subscription: $12 domestic, $20 overseas. Sample: $6. Make checks payable to *Whiskey Island Magazine.*

How to Submit Submit 3-5 poems at a time. No previously published poems. Cover letter is required. Include brief bio and SASE for reply only, with name, address, e-mail, and phone number on each page of ms. Reads submissions year round. Poems are circulated to an editorial committee. Guidelines available in magazine, for SASE, by e-mail, or on Web site. Responds within 4 months. Pays 2 contributor's copies and one-year subscription.

Contest/Award Offerings Sponsors an annual poetry contest. $500 prize and publication to winning entry. **Entry fee:** $10. **Deadline:** entries accepted October 1-March 31. Guidelines available by e-mail or on Web site.

◙ ◎ WHITE LOTUS: A JOURNAL OF SHORT ASIAN VERSE AND HAIGA

Shadow Poetry, 1209 Milwaukee St., Excelsior Springs MO 64024. Phone/fax: (208)977-9114. E-mail: whitelotus@shadowpoetry.com. Web site: www.shadowpoetry.com/magazine/whitelotus.html. Established 2005 (Shadow Poetry Web site established 2000). **Contact:** Marie Summers, chief editor. Associate Editor: Kathy Lippard Cobb.

Magazine Needs *White Lotus,* published semiannually, is a "specialized journal of haiku, senryu, tanka, and haiga. Editors'/readers' choice awards are also featured. Articles, book reviews, and sumi-e are welcome." Wants "only haiku, senryu, tanka, haiga, and sumi-e of the highest quality from poets ages 13 and up. The top ten placing entries in Shadow Poetry's annual *White Lotus* Haiku Competition are published in the Spring/Summer issue." *White Lotus* is 32-60 pages, digest-sized, saddle-stapled, with glossy b&w cover; back cover reserved for a color-printed haiga. Receives about 500 haiku/senryu per issue, prints less than 10%. Single copy: $10 US/Int'l; subscription: $15/year US, $20/yr Int'l. Make checks/money orders payable to Shadow Poetry.

How to Submit Submit up to 10 haiku/senryu/tanka at a time, with correct seasonal theme (if applicable) in accordance with the next issue to be released. No previously published poems or simultaneous submissions. Accepts fax, e-mail, and disk submissions, as well as submissions through online form and by postal mail. Cover letter is preferred. "Name of author, street address, and e-mail address must accompany all submissions, no exceptions. If work is accepted, participants will be contacted by mail or e-mail within one month of submissions." Reads submissions according to the following deadlines: June 30 (Fall/Winter issue) and December 31 (Spring/Summer issue). Never comments on rejected poems. Guidelines available in magazine or on Web site. Sends prepublication galleys. "Final drafts will be e-mailed or mailed to the accepted poet." Acquires first rights.

Additional Informatin Shadow Poetry sponsors Shadows Ink Poetry Contest, Shadow Poetry's Annual Chapbook Competition, and *White Lotus* Haiku Competition (see separate listings in Contests & Awards.

◙ WHITE PELICAN REVIEW

P.O. Box 7833, Lakeland FL 33813. Established 1999. **Contact:** Nancy Wiegel, editor.

Magazine Needs *White Pelican Review,* published semiannually in April and October, is dedicated to printing poetry of the highest quality. Wants "writing that goes beyond competency to truly masterful acts of imagination and language." Has published poetry by Paul Hostovsky, Michael Hettich, Corrine De Winter, James Doyle, and Lou Suarez. *White Pelican Review* is about 48 pages, digest-sized, photocopied from typescript, saddle-stapled, with matte cardstock cover. Receives about 5,000 poems/year, accepts 3%. Circulation is 500. Single copy: $4; subscription: $8/year for individuals, $10/year for institutions. Make checks payable to *White Pelican Review*.

How to Submit Submit 3-5 poems at a time. Lines/poem: "optimal length is 32 lines plus title, although longer poems are given full consideration." No previously published poems or simultaneous submissions. Cover letter is required. SASE is a must. "Please include name, address, telephone number, and (if available) e-mail address on each page. No handwritten poems." Reads submissions year round. Time between acceptance and publication is 1-6 months. Poems are circulated to an editorial board. Seldom comments on rejected poems. Guidelines available for SASE. Responds in 6 months. Pays 1 contributor's copy. Acquires one-time rights.

Contest/Award Offerings The Hollingsworth Prize of $100 is offered to the most distinguished poem published in each issue. No contest or fee is involved.

▣ ◻ WILD GOOSE POETRY REVIEW

Central Piedmont Community College, Levine Campus, P.O. Box 35009, Charlotte NC 28235-5009. (704)330-4397. E-mail: Patricia.Bostian@cpcc.edu. Web site: www.wildgoosepoetryreview.com. Established 2005. **Contact:** Patricia Kennedy Bostian, editor.

Magazine Needs *Wild Goose Poetry Review*, published quarterly online, is a poetry journal with essays, reviews, and interviews. Wants "poetry that exudes a sense of place, that is well-crafted, with an eye to imagery and an ear to music." Does not want "erotica, abstract stream-of-consciousness, or gratuitous obscenities." Has published poetry by Anthony Abbott. Receives about 1,000 poems/year, accepts about 12%.

How to Submit Submit 3-5 poems at a time. Lines/poem: "no poems longer than two pages accepted." Considers simultaneous submissions; no previously published poems. Accepts e-mail submissions only (pasted into body of message); no disk submissions. Cover letter is preferred. Reads submissions year round. Time between acceptance and publication is up to 6 months. Poems are circulated to an editorial board. Comments on rejected poems. Guidelines available on Web site. Responds in 4-6 weeks. Rights revert to poet upon publication. Reviews books/chapbooks of poetry in 500 words. Send materials for review consideration to Patricia Bostian.

Advice "Read, read, read. Inspiration does not a poem make. Revise, revise, revise."

▣ ◪ WILD VIOLET

P.O. Box 39706, Philadelphia PA 19106-9706. E-mail: wildvioletmagazine@yahoo.com. Web site: www.wildviolet.net. Established 2001. **Contact:** Alyce Wilson, editor.

Magazine Needs *Wild Violet*, published quarterly online, aims "to make the arts more accessible, to make a place for the arts in modern life." Wants "poetry that is well crafted, that engages thought, that challenges or uplifts the reader. We have published free verse, haiku, blank verse, and other forms. If the form suits the poem, we will consider any form." Does not want "abstract, self-involved poetry; poorly managed form; excessive rhyming; self-referential poems that do not show why the speaker is sad, happy, or in love." Has published poetry by Lyn Lifshin, Erik Kestler, Anselm Brocki, Berwyn Moore, and Doug Bolling. Accepts about 15% of work submitted.

How to Submit Submit 3-5 poems at a time. Considers simultaneous submissions; no previously published poems. Accepts e-mail submissions (pasted into body of message, or as text or Word attachment); no disk submissions. Cover letter is preferred. Reads submissions year round. Submit seasonal poems 3 months in advance. Time between acceptance and publication is 3 months. "Decisions on acceptance or rejection are made by the editor." Seldom comments on rejected poems, unless requested. Occasionally publishes theme issues. Guidelines available by e-mail or on Web site. Responds in up to 6 weeks. Pays by providing a bio and link on contributor's page. Requests electronic rights to publish and archive accepted works. Reviews books/chapbooks of poetry in 250 words, single-book format. Query for review consideration.

Contest/Award Offerings Sponsors an annual poetry contest, offering 1st Prize: $100 and publication in *Wild Violet*; 2 Honorable Mentions will also be published. Guidelines available by e-mail or on Web site. **Entry fee:** $5/poem. Judged by independent judges.

Advice "Read voraciously; experience life and share what you've learned. Write what is hardest to say; don't take any easy outs."

WILLARD & MAPLE

163 S. Willard St., Box 34, Burlington VT 05401. E-mail: willardandmaple@champlain.edu. Established 1996. **Contact:** Poetry Editor.

Magazine Needs *Willard & Maple*, published annually in spring, is "a student-run literary magazine from Champlain College's Professional Writing Program that publishes a wide array of poems, short stories, creative essays, short plays, pen & ink drawings, photos, and computer graphics." Wants "creative work of the highest quality." Does not want any submissions over 5 typed pages in length; all submissions must be in English. Considers poetry by children and teens. Has published poetry by Geof hewitt, Rachel Orsini, Jason Briody, Suki Fredericks, and N.B. Smith. *Willard & Maple* is 200 pages, digest-sized, digitally printed, perfect-bound. Receives about 500 poems/year, accepts about 20%. Press run is 600 (80 subscribers, 4 libraries); 200 are distributed free to the Champlain College writing community. Single copy: $15. Make checks payable to Champlain College.

How to Submit Submit up to 5 poems at a time. Lines/poem: 100 maximum. Considers simultaneous submissions; no previously published poems. Accepts e-mail and disk submissions. Cover letter is required. "Please provide current contact information including an e-mail address. Single-space submissions, one poem/page." Reads submissions September 1 -March 31. Time between acceptance and publication is less than 1 year. "All editors receive a blind copy to review. They meet weekly throughout the academic year. These meetings consist of the submissions being read aloud, discussed, and voted upon." Seldom comments on rejected poems. Occasionally publishes theme issues. Upcoming themes available by e-mail. Responds in less than 6 months. Pays 2 contributor's copies. Acquires one-time rights. Reviews books/chapbooks of poetry and other magazines/journals in 1,200 words. Send materials for review consideration to the poetry editor.

Advice "The power of imagination makes us infinite."

THE WILLIAM AND MARY REVIEW

Campus Center, The College of William and Mary, P.O. Box 8795, Williamsburg VA 23187-8795. (757)221-3290. E-mail: review@wm.edu. Web site: www.wm.edu/so/wmreview/. Established 1962. **Contact:** Poetry Editors.

Magazine Needs *The William and Mary Review*, published annually in May, is "dedicated to publishing new work by established poets as well as work by new and vital voices." Has published poetry by Cornelius Eady, Minnie Bruce Pratt, Edward Field, Dan Bellm, Forrest Gander, and Walter Holland. *The William and Mary Review* is about 100 pages, digest-sized, professionally printed on coated paper, perfect-bound, with 4-color card cover. Receives about 2,000 poems/year, accepts 10-12. Press run is 1,600 (50 library subscriptions, about 150 shelf sales). Sample: $5.50.

How to Submit Submit up to 5 poems at a time. Accepts submissions by postal mail only. Cover letter is required. Include address, phone number, e-mail address (if available), and brief bio note. SASE required. Type one poem/page. Reads submissions September 1-February 1 only. Responds in up to 6 months. Pays 5 contributor's copies.

Advice "Submit considered, well-crafted poetry. Seeking originality of topic and clarity of language. New writers are encouraged to submit."

WILLOW REVIEW

College of Lake County, 19351 W. Washington St., Grayslake IL 60030-1198. (847)543-2956. Fax: (847)543-3956. E-mail: com426@clcillinois.edu. Web site: www.clcillinois.edu/community/willowreview.asp. Established 1969. **Contact:** Michael F. Latza, editor.

● *Willow Review* is partially supported by a grant from the Illinois Arts Council, a state agency.

Magazine Needs *Willow Review*, published annually, is interested in poetry, creative nonfiction, and fiction of high quality. "We have no preferences as to form, style, or subject, as long as each poem stands on its own as art and communicates ideas." Has published poetry by Lisel Mueller, Lucien Stryk, David Ray, Louis Rodriguez, John Dickson, and Patricia Smith. *Willow Review* is 88-96 pages, digest-sized, professionally printed, flat-spined, with a 4-color cover featuring work by an Illinois artist. Press run is 1,000. Subscription: $18 for 3 issues, $30 for 5 issues. Sample: $5 (back issue).

How to Submit Submit up to 5 poems at a time. Considers simultaneous submissions "if indicated in the cover letter"; no previously published poems. No e-mail submissions; postal submissions only. Include SASE; **"manuscripts will not be returned unless requested." Reads submissions September-May.** Guidelines available on Web site. Pays 2 contributor's copies. All rights remain with the author.

Contest/Award Offerings Prizes totaling $400 are awarded to the best poetry and short fiction/creative nonfiction in each issue.

Also Offers The College of Lake County Reading Series (4-7 readings/academic year) has included Thomas Lux, Isabel Allende, Donald Justice, Galway Kinnell, Lisel Mueller, Amiri Baraka, and others. One reading is for contributors to *Willow Review*. Readings, usually held on Thursday evenings and widely publicized in Chicago and suburban newspapers, are presented to audiences of about 150 students and faculty of the College of Lake County and other area colleges, as well as residents of local communities.

▣ ◻ THE WILLOW

The Smithtown Poetry Society, P.O. Box 793, Nesconset NY 11767. (631)656-6690. Fax: (631)656-6690. E-mail: editor@thesmithtownpoetrysociety.com. Web site: www.thesmithtownpoetrysociety .com. Established 1991. **Contact:** Sheryl Minter.

Magazine Needs *The Willow*, published quarterly online, features "new and upcoming poets alongside known poets. We also feature art, short stories, and poetry, regardless of length, that inspire intelligent thought and originality." Wants all forms of poetry. Does not want "poetry written without thought or in sing-song rhyme." Considers poetry by children and teens. Has published poetry by Marian Ford and Najwa Brax. Receives about 1,000 poems/year, accepts about 15%. Press run is 600; 300 distributed free to coffee shops. Single copy: $7; subscription: $20. Make checks payable to S. Minter.

How to Submit Submit up to 3 poems at a time. Lines/poem: 30 maximum (longer poems are considered but may take longer to publish, depending on magazine space; query before submitting). Considers previously published poems; no simultaneous submissions. Accepts disk submissions; no fax or e-mail submissions. Cover letter is preferred. "All submissions must be typed, double-spaced, with submitter's name and address clearly printed. Please include a SASE for all submissions if you would like your original work returned." Reads submissions year round. Submit seasonal poems 6 months in advance. **Charges $1 reading fee.** Time between acceptance and publication is up to one year. Poems are circulated to an editorial board. Sometimes comments on rejected poems. Guidelines available in magazine, for SASE, by e-mail, or on Web site. Responds in 1 month.

Contest/Award Offerings The Smithtown Poetry Society Yearly Contest is open to all poets and offers 50% of the contest proceeds as first prize; "the other half goes to the distribution of *The Willow*." Submit up to 3 poems, 20 lines maximum each. **Entry fee:** $5. **Deadline:** June 1. Guidelines available in magazine, for SASE, or on Web site. "All submissions may be edited for grammar and punctuation."

◪ ◉ WINDFALL: A JOURNAL OF POETRY OF PLACE (Specialized: poetry of place, specifically in the Pacific Northwest)

Windfall Press, P.O. Box 19007, Portland OR 97280-0007. E-mail: bsiverly@comcast.net. Web site: www.hevanet.com/windfall. Established 2002. **Contact:** Bill Siverly and Michael McDowell, co-editors.

Magazine Needs *Windfall: A Journal of Poetry of Place*, published semiannually in March and September, is "looking for poems of place, specifically places in the Pacific Northwest (the broad bioregion extending from the North Slope of Alaska to the San Francisco Bay Area, and from the Rocky Mountains to the Pacific Coast). 'Place' can be named or unnamed; but if unnamed, then location should be clearly implied or suggested by observed detail. The poet does not have to be living in the Pacific Northwest, but the poem does. We favor poetry based on imagery derived from sensory observation. *Windfall* also favors poetry that occurs in lines and stanzas.'' Does not want ''language poetry, metapoetry, surrealism, 'Internet poetry' (constructed from search engine information rather than experience), abstract, or self-centered poetry of any kind.'' Has published poetry by Judith Barrington, Gloria Bird, Barbara Drake, Clem Starck, Tom Wayman, and Robert Wrigley. *Windfall* is 52 pages, digest-sized, stapled, with art on covers (''all are drawings or prints by Portland artist Sharon Bronzan''). Receives about 160 poems/year, accepts about 60. Press run is 250. Single copy: $5; subscription: $10/year. Make checks payable to Windfall Press.

How to Submit Submit 5 poems at a time. Lines/poem: up to 50. Considers simultaneous submissions; no previously published poems. Accepts e-mail submissions (as attachment). Cover letter is preferred. ''SASE required for submissions by U.S. mail.'' Reads submissions ''after the deadlines for each issue: February 1 for Spring, and August 1 for Fall.'' Time between acceptance and publication is 2 months. Never comments on rejected poems. Guidelines available in magazine or on Web site. Responds in 2 weeks to 6 months (''depends on when poems are submitted in the biannual cycle''). Pays 2 contributor's copies. Acquires first North American serial rights. ''Poem may appear in sample pages on *Windfall* Web site.'' Rights revert to poet upon publication.

Advice ''In every issue of *Windfall*, editors Siverly and McDowell present an afterword that explores some aspect or tradition of poetry of place in the spirit of informing and inspiring new poems. Poets submitting to *Windfall* should check our Web site where all afterwords are posted and can be downloaded. Sample pages from most issues are also available. We are serious about our emphasis on poetry of place in the Pacific Northwest, and we are looking for poems that are based in direct experience and close observation in built or natural settings. At the end of the age of oil, we want to encourage poetry that goes back to its roots.''

$⬚ ◎ WISTERIA: A JOURNAL OF HAIKU, SENRYU, & TANKA

P.O. Box 150932, Lufkin TX 75915-0932. E-mail: wisteriajournal@gmail.com (inquiries and submissions). Web site: www.wistaria.blogspot.com. Established 2006. **Contact:** T.A. Thompson, publisher and editor, editor staff: Gary Hotham.

Magazine Needs *Wisteria: A Journal of Haiku, Senryu, & Tanka*, published quarterly, is a small journal printing only haiku, senryu, and tanka forms. Published work by Sanford Goldstein, Stanford M. Forrester, Wanda D. Cook, Michael Dylan Welch, and Kirsty Karkow. *Wisteria* is 24 pages, $4\frac{1}{4} \times 5\frac{1}{2}$, self-published, laser-printed, saddle-stapled, with cardstock cover with photo. Press run is 200; 25 distributed free to poetry publishers and small presses that publish haiku, senryu, and tanka. Accepts about 7% of poems submitted. Single copy: $3; subscription: $10/year. Make checks payable to T.A. Thompson (cash and money orders also accepted).

How to Submit Submit 5-7 poems at a time. No previously published poems or simultaneous submissions. No e-mail or disk submissions. E-mail and postal submissions only. ''Please include name, address, e-mail in upper right corner of manuscript. SASE required for reply.'' Reads submissions year round. Time between acceptance and publication is 6 months. Sometimes comments on rejected poems. Guidelines available in magazine or on Web site. Responds in 1 month. Pays $1 maximum honorarium for postal submissions only. Acquires first rights. Rights revert to poet upon publication.

Contest/Award Offerings The Pinewood Haiku Contest (see separate listing in Contests & Awards).

Advice ''Study the history of haiku and how contemporary English language has influenced this form today.''

⬚ THE WORCESTER REVIEW

Worcester County Poetry Association, Inc., 1 Ekman St., Worcester MA 01607. (508)797-4770. E-mail: wcpaboard@yahoo.com. Web site: www.geocities.com/wreview. Established 1973. **Contact:** Rodger Martin, managing editor.

Magazine Needs *The Worcester Review*, published annually by the Worcester County Poetry Association, encourages ''critical work with a New England connection; no geographic limitation on poetry and fiction.'' Wants ''work that is crafted, intuitively honest and empathetic.'' Has published poetry by Kurt Brown, Cleopatra Mathis, and Theodore Deppe. *The Worcester Review* is 160 pages, digest-sized, professionally printed in dark type on quality stock, perfect-bound, with matte card cover. Press run is 750. Subscription: $25 (includes membership in WCPA). Sample: $6.

How to Submit Submit up to 5 poems at a time ("I recommend 3 or less for most favorable readings"). Considers previously published poems "only on special occasions" and simultaneous submissions "if indicated." Cover letter is required. Include brief bio. Poems should be typed on $8^1/_2 \times 11$ paper, with poet's name in upper left corner of each page. Include SASE for return of ms. Comments on rejected poems "if manuscript warrants a response." Guidelines available for SASE or on Web site. Responds in up to 9 months. Pays 2 contributor's copies plus subscription. Acquires first rights.

Advice "Read some. Listen a lot."

◢ WRITE ON!! POETRY MAGAZETTE

P.O. Box 901, Richfield UT 84701-0901. E-mail: jimnipoetry@yahoo.com. Established 1998. **Contact:** Jim Garman, editor.

Magazine Needs *Write On!! Poetry Magazette*, published monthly, features "poetry from poets around the world." Wants poetry of "any style; all submissions must be suitable for all ages to read." Does not want "adult or vulgar material." Considers poetry by children and teens. Has published poetry by Cathy Porter, B.Z. Niditch, Gerald Zipper, and Betty Shelley. *Write On!!* is 24 pages, digest-sized, photostat-copied, saddle-stapled. Receives about 500 poems/year, accepts about 50%. Press run is 50. Single copy: $4. Sample: $3. Make checks payable to Jim Garman.

How to Submit Submit 1-6 poems at a time. Lines/poem: 6 minimum, 28 maximum. Considers previously published poems and simultaneous submissions. Accepts e-mail submissions (pasted into body of message, no attachments). Reads submissions year round. Submit seasonal poems 2 months in advance. Time between acceptance and publication is one month. Never comments on rejected poems. Occasionally publishes theme issues. Guidelines available by e-mail. Responds in "approximately" 3 weeks. No payment or free copies provided. "*WRITE ON!!* contains no ads, no sponsors, all costs are out of pocket or from those desiring a copy." Acquires one-time rights, "which return to author upon publication."

Advice "Send only your best material after it has been refined."

◢ WRITER'S BLOC

Dept. of Language & Literature, Texas A&M University-Kingsville, MSC 162, Kingsville TX 78363-8202. E-mail: c-downs@tamuk.edu. (inquiries only). Web site: www.tamuk.edu/langlit/writer's.htm. Established 1980. **Contact:** C. Downs, faculty sponsor.

Magazine Needs *Writer's Bloc*, published annually in October, prints poetry, fiction, creative nonfiction, and graphic art. "About half of our pages are devoted to the works of Texas A&M University-Kingsville Space students and half to the works of writers and artists from all over the world." Wants quality poetry; no restrictions on content or form. *Writer's Bloc* is 80-96 pages, digest-sized. Press run is 300-500. Subscription: $7. Sample: $7.

How to Submit Submit no more than 3 pages of poetry at a time ("prose poems okay"). Lines/poem: 50 maximum. No previously published poems or simultaneous submissions. No e-mail submissions; postal submissions only. "Submissions should be typed, double-spaced; SASE required for reply." Reads submissions September-January only. "Manuscripts are published upon recommendation by a staff of students and faculty." Seldom comments on rejected poems. Guidelines available in magazine or for SASE. "Acceptance letters are sent out in October." Pays 1 contributor's copy.

$ ◢ ◎ WRITERS' JOURNAL

P.O. Box 394, Perham MN 56573. (218)346-7921. Fax: (218)346-7924. E-mail: writersjournal@writersjournal.com. Web site: www.writersjournal.com. Established 1980. **Contact:** Esther M. Leiper, poetry editor.

Magazine Needs *WRITERS'' Journal*, published bimonthly, offers "advice and guidance, motivation, and inspiration to the more serious and published writers and poets." Features 2 columns for poets: "Esther Comments" offers critiques of poems sent in by readers, and "Every Day with Poetry" discusses a wide range of poetry topics, often—but not always—including readers' work. Wants "a variety of poetry: free verse, strict forms, concrete, Oriental. Since we appeal to those of different skill levels, some poems are more sophisticated than others, but those accepted must move, intrigue, or otherwise positively capture me. 'Esther Comments' is never used as a negative force to put a poem or a poet down. Indeed, I focus on the best part of a given work and seek to suggest means of improvement on weaker aspects." Does not want anything "vulgar, preachy, or sloppily written." Considers poetry by children (school-age). Has published poetry by Lawrence Schug, Diana Sutliff, and Eugene E. Grollmes. *WRITERS' Journal* is 64 pages, magazine-sized, professionally printed, with paper cover. Receives about 900 submissions/year, accepts about 25 (including those used in columns). Press run is 26,000. Single copy: $5.99; subscription: $19.97/year U.S., add $15 for Canada/Mexico, $30 for Europe, all others add $35. Sample: $6.

How to Submit Submit 3-4 poems at a time. Lines/poem: 25 maximum. No e-mail submissions; postal submissions only. Responds in up to 5 months. Pays $5/poem plus 1 contributor's copy.

Contest/Award Offerings Sponsors poetry contests for previously unpublished poetry. Submit serious verse only, on any subject or in any form, 25 lines maximum. "Submit in duplicate: one with name and address, one without." Received 300 entries/contest. Winners announced in *The WRITERS' Journal* and on Web site. **Entry fee:** $3/poem for each contest. **Deadline:** April 30, August 30, and December 30. Guidelines available for SASE or on Web site.

◪ ◎ XAVIER REVIEW (Specialized: focus on African American, Caribbean, Southern literature)

Xavier University, 1 Drexel Dr., New Orleans LA 70125-1098. (504)520-7303. Fax: (504)520-7917. Web site: www.xula.edu/review. Established 1980 (review), 1988 (press). **Contact:** Dr. Nicole P. Greene, editor (review) or Dr. Thomas Bonner, executive editor (press).

Magazine Needs *Xavier Review*, published semiannually, is a journal of poetry, fiction, translations, essays, and reviews (contemporary literature) for professional writers, libraries, colleges, and universities. "Our content includes a focus on African American, Caribbean, and Southern literature, as well as works that touch on issues of religion and spirituality. We do, however, consider quality works on all themes." Has published poetry by Chris Waters, Lisa Sisk, Mark Taksa, Glenn Sheldon, Christine DeSimone, and Holly Pettit. Press run is 300. Subscription: $10/year for individuals, $15/year for institutions. Sample: $5.

How to Submit Submit 3-5 poems at a time. Include SASE. "Overseas authors only may submit by e-mail attachment." Pays 2 contributor's copies; offers 40% discount on additional copies.

Additional Information Xavier Review Press publishes book-length works of poetry and prose. Recent publications include *Turning Up the Volume* by Patrice Melnick and *Vespers at Mount Angel* by Stella Nesanovich. Books are available through Web site or by e-mailing rskinner@xula.edu. Query via e-mail: tbonner@xula.edu. **"Manuscripts should not be sent without permission of the editor."**

◪ YALOBUSHA REVIEW

d University of Mississippi, Dept. of English, Bondurant Hall, P.O. Box 1848, University MS 38677-1848. E-mail: yreditor@yahoo.com. Web site: www.olemiss.edu/yalobusha. Established 1995. **Contact:** Poetry Editor.

Magazine Needs *Yalobusha Review*, published annually in spring, promotes "new writing and art, creative nonfiction, fiction, and poetry." Does not want anything over 3 pages. Has published poetry by Charles Wright, Blas Falconer, Aimee Nezhukumatathil. *Yalobusha Review* is 126 pages, digest-sized, with glossy cover. Receives 300-400 poems/year, accepts about 15%. Press run is 1,000; 50 are distributed free to chosen writers/artists. Single copy: $10. Sample: $8. Make checks payable to *Yalobusha Review*.

How to Submit Submit 3-5 poems at a time maximum. Lines/poem: one page minimum, 3 pages maximum. No previously published poems, simultaneous submissions okay. No e-mail or electronic submissions; postal submissions only. Cover letter is required. Include SASE. Reads submissions July 15-November 1. Time between acceptance and publication is 4 months. Poems are circulated to an editorial board. Never comments on rejected poems. Guidelines available for SASE or on Web site. Responds in up to 4 months. Pays 2 contributor's copies. Acquires all rights. Returns full rights upon request.

Contest/Award Offerings The Yellowwood Poetry Award (see separate listing in Contests & Awards).

Advice "We don't accept poetry with flat language. We are usually most attracted to narrative poetry, but will consider all styles."

⬛ ▦ ◪ YASOU EZINE

2025 Taraval St. Rear, San Francisco CA 94116. (415)665-0294. E-mail: joanneolivieri@sbcglobal.net. Web site: http://yasouezine.tripod.com. Established 2000. **Contact:** Joanne Olivieri, editor.

Magazine Needs *Yasou Ezine*, published online 3 times/year in March, July, and November, is "an eclectic mix of poetry, short stories, art, photography and commentaries. We publish work which is geared towards celebrating life to it's fullest and accept work by beginning as well as seasoned writers. We also accept artwork and photography. All artists considered." Does not want "anything of a violent or sexually explicit nature." Considers poetry by children and teens. Has published poetry by Taylor Graham, B.Z. Niditch, Colleen Breuning, C. David Hay, Paula Timpson, and Genny Harten-Borleis. Receives about 500 poems/year, accepts about 25%. Number of unique visitors: "hundreds per month." Sample: free online.

How to Submit Submit 3 poems at a time. Lines/poem: no limit. Considers previously published poems and simultaneous submissions. (Considers poetry posted on a public Web site/blog/forum and poetry posted on a private, password-protected forum as published.) Considers e-mail submissions (pasted into body of e-mail message); no disk submissions. Cover letter is unnecessary. "Read our guidelines page." Reads submissions year round. Time between acceptance and publication is 3 months. Never comments on rejected poems. Guidelines available on Web site. Responds in 1 week. Never sends prepublication galleys. Pays "for featured poet in each issue. We pay in cash, plus either a music CD or poetry chapbook." Rights revert to poets upon publication. Reviews chapbooks of poetry. "**For a modest fee of $5**, we will review chapbooks of poetry and publish the review in the following issue along with a link to the poet's Web site. Make checks payable to Joanne Olivieri."

Contest/Award Offerings Sponsors annual poetry contest. "The ezine sponsors a poetry contest annually at which time the rules and awards will be listed on our Web site. Please check Web site regularly for detailed information."

Advice "We encourage beginners to submit their work. We pride ourselves on recognizing the uniqueness of each poet and affording them the opportunity to be published. All styles and forms welcome."

◪ YEMASSEE

Dept. of English, University of South Carolina, Columbia SC 29208. (803)777-2085. E-mail: editor@yemasseejournal.org. Web site: www.yemasseejournal.org. Established 1993. **Contact:** Darien Cavanaugh and Jonathan Maricle, co-editors.

Magazine Needs *Yemassee*, published semiannually, features "primarily fiction and poetry, but we are also interested in one-act plays, brief excerpts of novels, essays, reviews, and interviews with literary figures. Our essential consideration for acceptance is the quality of the work; we are open to a variety of subjects and writing styles." Does not want "poems of such a highly personal nature that their primary relevance is to the author; bad Ginsberg." Has published poetry by Nick Finney, Kwame Dawes, Pamela McClure, Rafael Campo, David Kirby, and Susan Ludvigson. *Yemassee* is 80-100 pages, perfect-bound. Receives about 400 poems/year, accepts about 90% unsolicited. Press run is 500. Subscription: $15 for 2 issues ($10 for students). Sample: $5. Make checks payable to Education Foundation/English Literary Magazine Fund.

How to Submit Submit up to 5 poems at a time. Lines/poem: less than 50, "but poems of exceptional quality are considered regardless of length." No previously published poems (in any form, print or electronic). Considers simultaneous submissions if identified as such and notified of acceptance elsewhere. No fax or e-mail submissions. Include SASE. Cover letter is required. "Each issue's contents are determined on the basis of blind selections. Therefore, we ask that all works be submitted without the author's name or address anywhere on the manuscript. Include this information along with the title(s) of the work(s) in a cover letter. For longer submissions, please include an approximate word count." Reads submissions August 15-May 15. Time between acceptance and publication is up to 4 months. "Staff reads and votes on 'blind' submissions." Often comments on rejected poems. Guidelines available on Web site. Responds in up to 2 months after submission deadline. Pays 2 contributor's copies with the option to purchase additional copies at a reduced rate. Acquires first rights.

Contest/Award Offerings The Pocataligo Poetry Contest (see separate listing in Contests & Awards).

🖥 📝 ◎ ZEEK: A JEWISH JOURNAL OF THOUGHT AND CULTURE (Specialized: Jewish writers/themes preferred)

330 Seventh Ave., 21st Floor, New York NY 10001. E-mail: zeek@zeek.net. Web site: www.zeek.net. Established 2002. **Contact:** Richard Chess, poetry editor. Associate Editor: Dan Friedman.

Magazine Needs *Zeek: A Jewish Journal of Thought and Culture*, published monthly online and in print, seeks poetry that is "poetically daring, with shades of the numinous as it manifests in moments non-poets would ignore." Does not want "clichéd, 'inspirational,' or ethnocentric writing; something that could serve as a greeting card, political poster, etc.; cynicism." Has published poetry by Hal Sirowitz, Rodger Kamenetz, Linda Zisquit, Yerra Sugarman, Shirley Kaufman, others. *Zeek* (print version) is 96 pages, digest-sized, perfect-bound, includes photography. Receives about 500 poems/year, accepts about 20. Press run (print) is 2,000 (200 subscribers); online version gets 60,000 hits/month. Single copy: $7; subscription: $14/year. Make checks payable to Zeek Media Inc.

How to Submit Submit 3 poems at a time. Considers simultaneous submissions; no previously published poems. Accepts e-mail submissions only (pasted into body of message). Short cover letter is acceptable. Reads submissions year round. Time between acceptance and publication varies. "Poetry editor has final approval, but editorial board of four can propose or reject." Seldom comments on rejected poems. Occasionally publishes theme issues. Guidelines available on Web site. Responds anywhere from 1 month to 1 year. Pays 5 contributor's copies (to poets published in print edition). Acquires one-time rights. Reviews books of poetry.

Advice "If someone else can say it, let them. If no one else can say it, say *that*."

Book/Chapbook Publishers

Every poet dreams of publishing a collection of his or her work. However, it's surprising how many poets still envision putting out a thick, hardbound volume containing hundreds of poems. In reality, poetry books are usually slim, often paperback, with varying levels of production quality, depending on the publisher.

More common than full-length poetry books (i.e., 50-150 pages by modern standards) are poetry *chapbooks*, small editions of approximately 24-32 pages. They may be printed on quality paper with beautiful cover art on heavy stock; or they may be photocopied sheets of plain printer paper, folded and stapled or hand-sewn along the spine.

In this section you'll find a variety of presses and publishers of poetry books and chapbooks. However, it's a reflection of how poetry publishing works in the early 21st century that many book/chapbook publishing opportunities appear in the Contest & Awards section instead. To thoroughly search for a publisher/press, consult the Chapbook Publishers index (starting on page 482) and the Book Publishers index (starting on page 486) for a complete roundup of publishers that are listed in this edition of *Poet's Market*.

HOW LISTINGS ARE FORMATTED

Content of each listing was provided or verified by a representative of the press or publisher (poetry editor, managing editor, owner, etc.). Here is how that content is arranged in each listing:

Symbols. Icons at the beginning of each listing offer visual signposts to specific information about the book/chapbook publisher: (**N**) this market is recently established and new to *Poet's Market*; (★) this market did not appear in the 2008 edition; (■) this market publishes primarily online (some books and chapbooks are indeed published online, sometimes as a PDF that can be printed out); (❖) this market is located in Canada or (🌐) outside the U.S. and Canada; (**$**) this market pays a monetary amount (as opposed to a given number of author's copies); (◻) this market welcomes submissions from beginning poets; (◑) this market prefers submissions from skilled, experienced poets, will consider work from beginning poets; (◐) this market prefers submissions from poets with a high degree of skill and experience; (◎) this market has a specialized focus (listed in parentheses after publisher/press name); (⊘) this market does not consider unsolicited submissions; and (⊘) this market is closed to *all* submissions. (Keys to these symbols are listed on the inside covers of this book and on page 3.)

Contact information. Next you'll find the information you need to contact the press or publisher, according to what was provided for each listing: name (in bold) of the publisher/ press (with areas of specialization noted in parentheses where appropriate); regular mail address; telephone number; fax number; e-mail address; Web site address; year the publisher/press was established; the name of the person to contact (or an editorial title); and membership in small press/publishing organization(s). (**Note:** If a publisher or press wants electronic submissions exclusively, no street address may be given.)

Book/Chapbook Needs. This section provides an overview of the publisher/press, including such helpful information as editorial preferences; how manuscripts are considered; the number and kinds of books and/or chapbooks produced; a list of recently published titles; and production information about the titles (number of pages, printing/binding details, type of cover, press run).

How to Submit. This section states whether a poet should query with samples or send the complete manuscript; possible reading periods; reading fees, if applicable; response time; payment amount/terms; and how to order sample copies.

Additional Information. Editors/publishers may use this section to explain other types of publishing activities (such as broadsides, postcards or anthologies), elaborate on some aspect of production—anything beyond the basic details of the submission process that readers may find of interest.

Contest/Award Offerings. This section discusses prizes and competitions associated with the publisher, with either brief guidelines or a cross-reference to a separate listing in the Contests & Awards section.

Also Offers. Describes other offerings associated with this publisher (i.e., sponsored readings, Web site activities such as blogs and forums, related poetry groups, etc.).

Advice. Provides direct quotes from the editor/publisher about everything from pet peeves to tips on writing to views on the state of poetry today.

GETTING STARTED, FINDING A PUBLISHER

If you don't have a publisher in mind, read randomly through the listings, making notes as you go. (Don't hesitate to write in the margins, underline, use highlighters; it also helps to flag markets that interest you with Post-It Notes). Browsing the listings is an effective way to familiarize yourself with the kind of information presented and the publishing opportunities that are available at various skill levels.

If you're thinking of a specific publisher by name, however, begin with the General Index. Here all *Poet's Market* listings are alphabetized along with publishers from the 2007 edition that don't appear in this book (the latter are accompanied by a two-letter code explaining the publisher's absence; a key to these codes appears at the beginning of the General Index.) In addition, publishers/presses that have changed names since the 2007 edition are listed in the General Index, cross-referenced to the new names.

REFINE YOUR SEARCH

To supplement the General Index, we provide several more specific indexes to help you refine your marketing plan for your manuscript. Not every listing appears in one of these indexes, so use them only to reinforce your other research efforts. As mentioned earlier, the Chapbook Publishers Index and Book Publishers Index are good places to start when you have a poetry collection to submit. In addition, the following indexes may be helpful:

Openness to Submissions Index breaks out markets according to the symbols (○ ◐ ◑ ◎) that appear at the beginning of each listing—signposts that indicate the level of writing an editor/publisher prefers to see. (For an explanation of these symbols, see page 3, the inside covers of this book, or the handy tear-out bookmark just inside the front cover.)

Geographical Index sorts publishers/presses by state and by countries outside the U.S. Some publishers are more open to poets from their region, so use this index when you're pinpointing local opportunities.

Subject Index groups all markets into categories according to areas of special focus. These include all specialized markets (appearing with the ◎ symbol) as well as broader categories such as online markets, poetry for children, markets that consider translations, and others. Save time when looking for a specific type of publisher/press by checking this index first.

THE NEXT STEP

Once you know how to interpret the listings in this section and identify markets for your work, the next step is to start submitting your poetry collection. See "Getting Started (and Using This Book)" on page 2 and "Frequently Asked Questions" on page 7 for advice, guidelines for preparing your manuscript and proper submissions procedures.

❖ $⬜ ◎ ⓘ ADASTRA PRESS (Specialized: letterpress-printed, hand-sewn chapbooks)
16 Reservation Rd., Easthampton MA 01027-1227. Established 1980. **Contact:** Gary Metras, publisher.

• Chosen Publisher of the Year 2006 by *Contemporary Poetry Review*.

Book/Chapbook Needs "Adastra is primarily a chapbook publisher using antique equipment and methods, i.e., hand-set type, letterpress printing, hand-sewn bindings. Any titles longer than chapbook length are by special arrangement and are from poets who have previously published a successful chapbook or two with Adastra. Editions are generally released with a flat-spine paper wrapper, and some titles have been bound in cloth. Editions are limited, ranging from 200- to 400-copy print runs. Some of the longer titles have gone into reprint, and these are photo-offset and perfect-bound. Letterpress chapbooks by themselves are not reprinted as single titles. Once they go out of print, they are gone. I am biased against poems that rhyme and/or are religious in theme. Sequences and longish poems are always nice to present in a chapbook format. Competition is keen. Less than 0.5% of submissions are accepted." Published chapbooks include *Poetic License* by Susan Terris, *Digger's Blues* by Jim Daniels, *Behind Our Memories* by Michael Hettich, and *Three* by Stephen Philbrick. Publishes 2-4 chapbooks/year. Sample hand-crafted chapbook: $8 postpaid.

How to Submit Chapbook mss should be 12-18 pages, double-spaced. No full-length mss will be considered. Submit in February of each year. Responds by April. Time between acceptance and publication can be as long as 2 years. Pays 10% of press run.

Advice "Adastra Press is a one-man printer/publisher but releases more poetry titles per year than Random House, one of the largest trade book publishers in the world. I approach book-making as an art, and design each chapbook to fit the poetry. As *The Virginia Quarterly Review* wrote, Adastra is 'one of our most interesting smaller presses'; and Contemporary Poetry Review in 2007 selected Adastra as Publisher of the Year, beating literary and corporate giant Farrah, Straus & Giroux. Small, independent publishers, such as Adastra Press, are worthwhile and recognizable. Adastra is open to a wide range of poets. The criteria is moving and memorable poetry that speaks to the reader."

⬜ AHSAHTA PRESS
MFA Program in Creative Writing, Boise State University, 1910 University Dr., Boise ID 83725-1525. (208)426-3134. Fax: (208)426-4373. E-mail: ahsahta@boisestate.edu. Web site: http://ahsahtapress.boisestate.edu. Established 1976. **Contact:** Janet Holmes, editor.

Book/Chapbook Needs Ahsahta Press, which originally published contemporary poets of the American West, has since expanded its scope "to publish poets nationwide, seeking out and publishing the best new poetry from a wide range of aesthetics—poetry that is technically accomplished, distinctive in style, and thematically fresh." Has published *Bone Pagoda* by Susan Tichy, *Case Sensitive* by Kate Greenstreet, *Quarantine* by Brian Henry, *Fence Above the Sea* by Brigitte Byrd, *Spell* by Dan Beachy-Quick, and *Saving the Appearances* by Liz Waldner.

How to Submit Considers multiple and simultaneous submissions. Reading period is temporarily suspended due to backlog, but the press publishes runners-up as well as winners of the Sawtooth Poetry Prize. Forthcoming, new, and backlist titles available on Web site. Most backlist titles: $9.95; most current titles: $16.

Contest/Award Offerings The Sawtooth Poetry Prize (see separate listing in Contests & Awards).

Advice "Ahsahta seeks distinctive, non-imitative, unpredictable, and innovatively crafted work. Please check our Web site for examples of what we publish."

Ⓝ $⬜ AMSTERDAM PRESS
6199 State Hwy 43, Amsterdam OH 43903.Estab. 2007. 740-543-4333. E-mail: plainspoke@gmail.com. Web site: www.amsterdampress.net. **Contact:** Cindy Kelly, editor.

Book/Chapbook Needs Amsterdam Press, publishes chapbooks and broadsides, wants "poetry of place, poetry grounded in sense images, poetry that leaps, and has a clear voice." Does not want "esoteric poetry that focuses on the universal." Manuscripts are selected through open submission. Chapbooks are 36 pages, laser-printed, saddle-stitched, with card cover and black and white art/graphics.

How to Submit Query first, with a few sample poems and a cover letter with brief bio and publication credits. Chapbook mss may include previously published poems. "Previously published poetry must be recognized on a separate page of mss." Responds to queries in 1-3 months; to mss in 1-3 months. Pays honorarium of $25-100 and 10 author's copies out of a press run of 100-300. Order sample books/chapbooks by sending $8 to Amsterdam Press, 6199 Steubenville Road SE, Amsterdam, OH 43903.

⊕ ◎ ⊘ ARC PUBLICATIONS (Specialized: UK writers; world and overseas poets; translations)

Nanholme Mill, Shaw Wood Rd., Todmorden, Lancashire OL14 6DA England. E-mail: arc.publicatio ns@btconnect.com. Web site: www.arcpublications.co.uk. Established 1969. **Contact:** Tony Ward, managing editor or Angela Jarman (music editor).

Book/Chapbook Needs Publishes "contemporary poetry from new and established writers from the UK and abroad, specializing in the work of world poets writing in English, and the work of overseas poets in translation."

How to Submit *"At present we are not accepting submissions but keep updated by visiting the Web site."*

⊠ ARCTOS PRESS

P.O. Box 401, Sausalito CA 94966-0401. (415)331-2503. E-mail: runes@aol.com. Web site: http:// members.aol.com/RUNES. Established 1997. **Contact:** CB Follett, editor.

Book/Chapbook Needs Arctos Press, under the imprint HoBear Publications, publishes 1-2 paperbacks/year. "We publish quality, perfect-bound books and anthologies of poetry, usually theme-oriented, in runs of 1,500." Has published *GRRRRR, A Collection of Poems About BEARS* (anthology); *Prism*, poems by David St. John; *Fire Is Favorable to the Dreamer*, poems by Susan Terris; and others.

How to Submit "We do not accept unsolicited manuscripts unless a current call has been posted in *Poets & Writers* and/or elsewhere, at which time up to 5 poems related to the theme should be sent." Considers previously published poems (if author holds the rights) and simultaneous submissions ("if we are kept informed"). Accepts submissions by postal mail only. Upcoming themes and guidelines available for SASE or on Web site. Pays 1 author's copy; discounts available on additional copies.

$⊘ AUSABLE PRESS

1026 Hurricane Rd., Keene NY 12942-9719. E-mail: editor@ausablepress.org. Web site: www.ausab lepress.org. Established 1999. **Contact:** Chase Twichell, editor. Member: CLMP.

Book/Chapbook Needs Ausable Press wants poetry "that investigates and expresses human consciousness in language that goes where prose cannot." Interested in work by new poets. Does not want "children's poetry or poetry for children, chapbooks, light verse, inspirational poetry, illustrated poetry, or peviously self-published work." Has published poetry by C.K. Williams, Steve Orlen, Linton Kwesi Johnson, Bruce Weigl, Laura Kasischke, and Laure-Anne Bosselaar. Publishes 4-6 books/year, paperback, offset-printed; number of pages varies.

How to Submit "Due to a backlog of accepted manuscripts, Ausable Press will not be holding open submissions in 2008. We hope to resume in 2009. Please check our Web site for updates and new guidelines."

⊘ THE BACKWATERS PRESS

3502 N. 52nd St., Omaha NE 68104-3506. (402)451-4052. E-mail: gkosmicki@cox.net. Web site: www.thebackwaterspress.homestead.com. **Contact:** Greg Kosmicki, editor.

Book/Chapbook Needs "The Backwaters Press continues to accept manuscripts for consideration for publication through the Open Submissions category. We're looking for manuscripts between 65 and 80 pages in length. **There is a $25 reading fee.**"

How to Submit "Please see the Web site for complete details, or send a self-addressed, stamped envelope to 'Guidelines' at the above address, or e-mail with a subject line of 'Open Submission Guidelines.' " Books available through The Backwaters Press or Amazon.com.

Advice "The Backwaters Press is dedicated to publishing the best new literature we can find. Send your best work."

☑ ☑ BARNWOOD PRESS

4604 47th Ave., S, Seattle WA 98118-1824. (206)225-6887. E-mail: barnwoodpress@earthlink.net. Web site: www.barnwoodpress.org. Established 1975. **Contact:** Tom Koontz, editor.

Book/Chapbook Needs Barnwood Press publishes 1 paperback and 1 chapbook of poetry/year. Has recently published *New and Selected Poems* by Robert Ronnow, *Hitler's Mustache* by Peter Davis, *Sheer* by Martha Collins, and *Whatever You Can Carry: Poems of the Holocaust* by Stephen Herz. Chapbooks are usually 12-32 pages, offset-printed, saddle-stapled, with paper covers with art; size varies.

How to Submit Query first with a few sample poems and cover letter with brief bio and publication credits. Responds to queries and mss in 1 month. Order sample books/chapbooks through Web site.

☑ ◎ ☑ BELHUE PRESS (Specialized: gay male poetry)

2501 Palisade Ave., Suite A1, Riverdale, Bronx NY 10463. E-mail: belhuepress@earthlink.net. Web site: www.perrybrass.com. Established 1990. **Contact:** Tom Laine, editor.

Book/Chapbook Needs Belhue Press is a small press specializing in gay male poetry. "We are especially interested in books that get out of the stock poetry market." Wants "hard-edged, well-crafted, fun, and often sexy poetry. No mushy, self-pitying, confessional, boring, indulgent, teary, or unrequited love poems—yuck! Poet must be willing to promote book through readings, mailers, etc." Publishes 3 paperbacks/year; no chapbooks. **"We have a $10 sample and guideline fee.** Please send this before submitting any poetry. We have had to initiate this due to a deluge of bad, amateur, irrelevant submissions. After fee, we will give constructive criticism when necessary."

How to Submit Query first, with 6 pages of poetry and cover letter with brief bio and publication credits. Considers previously published poems and simultaneous submissions. Time between acceptance and publication is 1 year. Often comments on rejected poems. Will request criticism fees "if necessary." Responds "fast" to queries and submitted mss. No payment information provided.

Advice "The only things we find offensive are stupid, dashed off, 'fortune cookie' poems that show no depth or awareness of poetry. We like poetry that, like good journalism, tells a story."

$☑ BIRCH BROOK PRESS

P.O. Box 81, Delhi NY 13753. Fax: (607)746-7453. E-mail: birchbrook@copper.net (inquiries only). Web site: www.birchbrookpress.info. Established 1982. **Contact:** Tim Tolnay, poetry editor. Member: American Academy of Poets, Small Press Center, Publishers Marketing Association, American Typefounders Fellowship.

Book/Chapbook Needs Birch Brook Press began publishing in 1982 and "is a letterpress book printer/typesetter/designer that uses monies from these activities to publish several titles of its own each year with cultural and literary interest." Specializes in literary work, flyfishing, baseball, outdoors, theme anthologies, translations of classics, and books about books. Has published *Daimonion Sonata* by Steven Owen Shields, *Human/Nature* by Lance Lee, *Confessions of a Rational Lunatic* by Marcus Rome, *Jack's Beans* by Tom Smith, and *The Alchemy of Words* by Edward Francisco. Publishes 4 paperbacks and/or hardbacks/year. Specializes "mostly in anthologies with specific themes." Books are "handset letterpress editions printed in our own shop." **Offers occasional co-op contract.**

How to Submit Query first with sample poems, or send entire ms. No e-mail submissions; submissions by postal mail only. "Must include SASE with submissions." Occasionally comments on rejected poems. Guidelines available for SASE. Pays from $5-25 for publication in anthology. Royalty on co-op contracts. Order sample books by visiting our online catalog at: www.birchbookpress.info.

Advice "Send your best work, and see other Birch Brook Press books."

$⬛ BLACK LAWRENCE PRESS

521 56th Street 2F, Brooklyn NY 11220. E-mail: editors@blacklawrencepress.com. Web site: www. blacklawrencepress.com. Established 2003. **Contact:** Colleen Ryor, editor.

Book/Chapbook Needs Black Lawrence Press seeks "to publish intriguing books of literature: novels, short story collections, poetry. Will also publish the occasional translation (from the German and French)." Has published poetry by D.C. Berry, James Reidel, and Stefi Weisburd. Publishes 10-12 books/year, mostly poetry and fiction. Manuscripts are selected through open submission and competition (see below). Books are 48-400 pages, offset-printed or high-quality POD, perfect-bound, with matte 4-color cover.

How to Submit "Regular submissions are considered on a year-round basis. Please check the general submissions page on our Web site for the most up-to-date guidelines information before submitting." Responds in up to 4 months for mss, "sometimes longer depending on backlog." Pays royalties. Sample books available through Web site.

Contest/Award Offerings The St. Lawrence Book Award, The Hudson Prize, and The Black River Chapbook Competition (see separate listings in Contests & Awards).

⬛ BLUE LIGHT PRESS

3600 Lyon St., San Francisco CA 94123. (415)440-8668 or (641)472-7882. E-mail: bluelightpress@aol.com. Established 1988. **Contact:** Diane Frank, chief editor.

Book/Chapbook Needs Blue Light Press publishes 3 paperbacks, 2 chapbooks/year. "We like poems that are imagistic, emotionally honest, and push the edge—where the writer pushes through the imagery to a deeper level of insight and understanding. No rhymed poetry." Has published poetry by Alice Rogoff, Ken McCullough, Becky Sakellariou, Tom Centolella, Stewart Florsheim, and Christopher Buckley. Chapbooks are 30 pages, digest-sized, professionally printed, with original art on an elegant matte cover. Chapbooks available for $8 plus $2 p&h; books for $15.95 plus $2 p&h.

How to Submit Submission guidelines for non-contest submissions available for SASE or by e-mail. Does not accept e-mail submissions. **Deadline:** December 15, 2007.

Contest/Award Offerings The Blue Light Poetry Prize and Chapbook Contest (see separate listing in Contests & Awards).

Also Offers "We have an online poetry workshop with a wonderful group of American and international poets—open to new members 3 times per year. Send an e-mail for info. We work in person with local poets, and will edit/critique poems by mail; $40 for four poems."

Advice "Read some of the books we publish, especially 1 of the anthologies. We like to publish poets with a unique vision and gorgeous or unusual language; poems that push the edge. Stay in the poem longer and see what emerges in your vision and language."

$⬛ BOA EDITIONS, LTD.

250 N. Goodman Street, Suite 306, Rochester, NY 14607. (585)546-3410. Web site: www.boaeditions.org. Established 1976. **Contact:** Thom Ward, poetry editor and Peter Conners, fiction editor.

Book/Chapbook Needs BOA Editions, a Pulitzer Prize-winning, not-for-profit publishing house acclaimed for its work, reads poetry mss for the American Poets Continuum Series (new poetry by distinguished poets in mid- and late career), the Lannan Translations Selection Series (publication of 2 new collections of contemporary international poetry annually, supported by The Lannan Foundation of Santa Fe, NM), and The A. Poulin, Jr. Poetry Prize (to honor a poet's first book; mss considered through competition—see separate listing in Contests & Awards). Has published poetry by W.D. Snodgrass, John Logan, Isabella Gardner, Richard Wilbur, and Lucille Clifton. Also publishes introductions by major poets of those less well-known (Gerald Stern wrote the foreword for Li-Young Lee's *Rose*, for example). BOA now also publishes fiction manuscripts for its American Reader Series. Check BOA's Web site for when the house is accepting fiction manuscripts.

How to Submit Check Web site for reading periods for the American Poets Continuum Series and The Lannan Translation Selection Series. "Please adhere to the general submission guidelines for each series." Guidelines available for SASE or on Web site. Pays advance plus 10 author's copies.

Contest/Award Offerings The A. Poulin, Jr. Poetry Prize (see separate listing in Contests & Awards).

Also Offers Available for download from Web site are reading and teaching guides for selected titles; and Season Sampler chapbooks, which provide introductions to BOA poets and their work.

◢ ◎ ☑ BOTTOM DOG PRESS, INC. (Specialized: writing from the Midwest; working lives; Zen Buddhism)

P.O. Box 425, Huron OH 44839. (419)433-5560, ext. 20784. E-mail: LsmithDog@aol.com. Web site: http://members.aol.com/lsmithdog/bottomdog. **Contact:** Larry Smith, director. Associate Editors: David Shevin and Laura Smith.

   • Imprint: Bird Dog Publishing

Book/Chapbook Needs Bottom Dog Press, Inc., "is a nonprofit literary and educational organization dedicated to publishing the best writing and art from the Midwest." Has published poetry by Jeff Gundy, Jim Daniels, Maj Ragain, Diane di Prima, and Sue Doro. Publishes the Midwest Series, Working Lives Series, and Harmony Series (105 books to date).

How to Submit Guidelines available on Web site.

Advice "Please read some of our books and send us a query before submitting anything."

◢ BRICKHOUSE BOOKS, INC.

306 Suffolk Rd., Baltimore MD 21218. (410)235-7690. E-mail: charriss@towson.edu. Web site: www.towson.edu/~harriss/!bhbwebs.ite/bhb.htm. Established 1970. **Contact:** Clarinda Harriss, editor/director.

   • Imprints: New Poets Series, Chestnut Hills Press, and Stonewall.

Book/Chapbook Needs BrickHouse Books "is open to submissions of all kinds (poetry, novellas, plays, etc.), so long as they do not exceed 128 pages." New Poets Series brings out first books by promising new poets. Poets who have previously had book-length mss published are not eligible. Prior publication in journals and anthologies is strongly encouraged. Wants "excellent, fresh, non-trendy, literate, intelligent poems. Any form (including traditional), any style." BrickHouse Books and New Poets Series pay 20 author's copies (out of a press run of 500), the sales proceeds going back into the corporation to finance the next volume. "BrickHouse has been successful in its effort to provide writers with national distribution; in fact, The New Poets Series was named an Outstanding Small Press by the prestigious Pushcart Awards Committee, which judges some 5,000 small press publications annually." Chestnut Hills Press publishes **author-subsidized books**; "high-quality work only, however. Chestnut Hills Press has achieved a reputation for prestigious books, printing only the top 10% of manuscripts Chestnut Hills Press and New Poets Series receive." Chestnut Hills Press authors receive proceeds from sale of their books. The Stonewall series publishes work with a gay, lesbian, or bisexual perspective. BrickHouse Books and its subdivisions have published books by Rane Aroyo, Gale Acuff, Harris George, Jan-Mitchell Sherrill, Donald Richardson, and Richard Fein. Books are 42-200 pages. Chapbooks available for $10; full-length books for $15-25.

How to Submit Send a 50- to 55-page manuscript, **$10 reading fee**, and cover letter including bio and publication credits. "Do not query by phone or fax; e-mail or postal mail queries only. Do not send anything by certified mail; BHB is unable to sign for such deliveries." Considers simultaneous submissions. No e-mail submissions. "Cover letters should be very brief, businesslike, and include an accurate list of published work. Indicate if manuscript is to be considered for BrickHouse, New Poets Series, Chestnut Hills Press, or Stonewall." Manuscripts accepted for publication must be available on a CD provided by the author. Sometimes comments briefly on rejected poems. Responds in up to 1 year. Manuscripts "are circulated to an editorial board of professional, publishing poets. BrickHouse is backlogged, but the best 10% of the manuscripts it receives are automatically eligible for Chestnut Hills Press consideration," **a subsidy arrangement**. Send $5 and a 7×10 SASE for a sample volume.

◢ ◎ CAROLINA WREN PRESS (Specialized: women; minorities; gay/lesbian)

120 Morris St., Durham NC 27701. (919)560-2738. Fax: (919)560-2759. E-mail: carolinawrenpress@ earthlink.net. Web site: www.carolinawrenpress.org. Established 1976. **Contact:** Andrea Selch, president.

Book/Chapbook Needs Publishes 1 poetry book/year, "usually through our poetry series. Primarily women and minorities, though men and majorities also welcome." Has published *Downriver* by Jeanne Leiby, as well as poetry by William Pitt Root, George Elliott Clarke, Jaki Shelton Green, Evie Shockley, and Erica Hunt.

How to Submit Query first, with 10 pages of sample poems and cover letter with brief bio and publication credits. Include SASE for reply only. Accepts e-mail queries, but send only letter and description of work; no large files. Reads unsolicited poetry submissions February 1-June 1. "Your best bet is to submit as part of our biennual poetry contest held in autumn of even-numbered years (e.g., 2008, 2010)." Guidelines available for SASE, by e-mail, or on Web site. Responds to queries in 3 months; to mss in 6 months. Payment varies.

Contest/Award Offerings Carolina Wren Press Poetry Contest for a First Book (see separate listing in Contests & Awards).

◑ ☑ COFFEE HOUSE PRESS

27 N. Fourth St., Suite 400, Minneapolis MN 55401. (612)338-0125. Web site: www.coffeehousepress.org. Established 1984. **Contact:** Christopher Fischbach, senior editor.

- Books published by Coffee House Press have won numerous honors and awards. Example: *The Book of Medicines* by Linda Hogan won the Colorado Book Award for Poetry and the Lannan Foundation Literary Fellowship.

Book/Chapbook Needs Publishes 4-5 poetry books/year. Wants poetry that is "challenging and lively; influenced by the Beats, the NY School, LANGUAGE and post-LANGUAGE, or Black Mountain." Has published poetry collections by Victor Hernandez Cruz, Anne Waldman, Eleni Sikelianos, and Paul Metcalf.

How to Submit Query first, with 8-12 sample poems and cover letter with brief bio and publication credits. "Please include a SASE for our reply and/or the return of your manuscript. Absolutely no phone, fax, or e-mail queries." Seldom comments on rejected poems. Responds to queries in 1 month; to mss in up to 8 months. Always sends prepublication galleys. Catalog available for SASE.

Also Offers Online sign-up for free e-newsletter.

▨ $☑ ◎ COTEAU BOOKS (Specialized: Canadian writers only)

Thunder Creek Publishing Co-op, 2517 Victoria Ave., Regina SK S4P 0T2 Canada. (306)777-0170. Fax: (306)522-5152. E-mail: coteau@coteaubooks.com. Web site: www.coteaubooks.com. Established 1975. **Contact:** Acquisitions Editor.

Book/Chapbook Needs Coteau Books is a "small literary press that publishes poetry, fiction, drama, anthologies, criticism, young adult novels—**by Canadian writers only**." Has published *The Crooked Good* by Louise Bernice Halfe, *Wolf Tree* by Randy Lundy, and *Predicting the Next Big Advertising Breakthrough Using a Potentially Dangerous Method* by Daniel Scott Tysdal.

How to Submit Submit mss (80-100 poems only) typed with at least 12-point font. No simultaneous or non-Canadian submissions. No e-mail or fax submissions. Cover letter is required. Include publishing credits and bio, and SASE for return of ms. Responds to queries and mss in 4 months. Always sends prepublication galleys. Author receives 10% royalties and 10 author's copies. Order samples by sending 9×12 SASE for catalog.

Additional Information Web site includes title and ordering information, author interviews, awards, news and events, submission guidelines, and links.

Advice "Generally, poets should have a number of publishing credits (single poems or series) in literary magazines and anthologies before submitting a manuscript."

☑ ◎ CROSS-CULTURAL COMMUNICATIONS (Specialized: bilingual, translations, multicultural)

239 Wynsum Ave., Merrick NY 11566-4725. (516)868-5635. Fax: (516)379-1901. E-mail: cccpoetry@aol.com. Web site: www.cross-culturalcommunications.com. Established 1971. **Contact:** Stanley H. or Bebe Barkan, or Mia Barkan Clarke.

- See www.thedrunkenboat.com (Summer 2002 issue) for a profile and www.Poetryvlog.com for a video.

Book/Chapbook Needs "*Cross-Cultural Review* began as a series of chapbooks (6-12 per year) of collections of poetry translated from various languages, and continues as the Holocaust, Women Writers, Latin American Writers, African Heritage, Italian Heritage, International Artists, Art & Poetry, Jewish, Israeli, Yiddish, Hebrew, Arabic, Armenian, American, Bengali, Brazilian (Portuguese), Bulgarian, Cajun, Catalan, Chicano, Chinese, Dutch & Flemish, Estonian, Finnish, Gypsy (Roma), Korean, Macedonian, Native American, Polish, Romanian, Russian, Serbian, Sicilian, Swedish, Scandinavian, Turkish, Ukrainian, Welsh, and Long Island and Brooklyn Writers Chapbook Series (with a number of other permutations in the offing)—issued simultaneously in palm-sized and regular paperback and cloth-binding editions, and boxed and canned editions, as well as audiocassette, CD, DVD, and videocassette. The Cross-Cultural International Writers Series, focusing on leading poets from various countries, includes titles by Leo Vroman (Holland) and Pablo Neruda (Chile). The Holocaust Series is for survivors. In addition to publications in these series, Cross-Cultural Communications has published anthologies and postcard and broadside portfolio collections by dozens of poets from many countries, a number in special bilingual limited editions, including such poets and translators as Joan Alcover, Francisco Arriví, Fuad Attal, Laura Boss, Darrell Bourque, Bohdan Boychuk, Gwendolyn Brooks, Siv Cedering, Vince Clemente, David Curzon, Aleksey Dayen, Arthur Dobrin, John Dotson, Eva Feiler, Ruth Feldman, Nancy Festinger, Charles Fishman, Cola Franzen, Carlos Ernesto García, David Gershator, Maria Mazziotti Gillan, Estelle Gilson, Daniela Gioseffi, Isaac Goldemberg, Theofil Halama, Talât Sait Halman, Joan Carol Hand, Langston Hughes, Menke Katz, Ko Won, Stanley Kunitz, Carilda Oliver Labra, Vladimir Levchev, Manuel van Loggem, Eeva-Liisa Manner, Beverly Matherne, D.H. Melhem, Elizabeth Gamble Millar, Ifeanyi A. Menkiti, Vinícius de Moraes, Fernand Moutet, Biljana D. Obradovic, Raymond R. Patterson, Ritva Poom, Gabriel Preil, Stanislao G. Pugliese, Clementine Rabassa, Gregory Rabassa, Orna Rav-Hon, Kay Richards, Rainer Maria Rilke, Stephen A. Sadow, Marco Scalabrino, Edith Södergran, Sherill St. Germain, Rainer Schulte, Louis Simpson, William Stafford, Adam Szyper, Tino Villanueva, Daniel Weissbort, Claire Nicolas White, and A.D. Winans, with complementary artwork by various international artists, such as Yaacov Agam (France/Israel), Eduardo Arranz-Bravo (Catalonia), Elise Asher (USA), Nicolò D'Alessandro (Sicily), Pablo Picasso (Spain), Mark Polyakov (Russia/USA), Edward Tabachnik (Canada), Tchouki (Bulgaria), Alfred Van Loen (Holland/USA), and George Zimmerman (Romania/USA).'' Sample chapbook: $10 postpaid.

How to Submit Guidelines available for SASE. Pays 10% of print run.

Additional Information New: *Cross-Cultural Review Chapbook* (CCRCB), an occasional series of 16-48 page limited edition chapbooks (print runs of 100-150 copies) focusing on poetry (bilingual preferred). Sample: $15 postpaid. Pays 5-10 copies.

Also Offers ''Cross-Cultural Communications continues, on an occasional basis, to organize events for international poets and writers. In April-May 2008, CCC will host a national tour for two Welsh poets: Peter Thabit Jones, editor of *The Seventh Quarry*, and Aeronwy Thomas (daughter of Dylan Thomas).''

$ 💬 ⊘ JOHN DANIEL & COMPANY

Daniel & Daniel Publishers, Inc., P.O. Box 2790, McKinleyville CA 95519. (707)839-3495. Fax: (707)839-3242. E-mail: dandd@danielpublishing.com. Web site: www.danielpublishing.com. Established 1980; reestablished 1985. **Contact:** John Daniel, editor.

Book/Chapbook Needs John Daniel & Company, an imprint of Daniel & Daniel Publishers, Inc., is a general small press publisher, specializing in literature, both prose and poetry. ''Book-length manuscripts of any form or subject matter will be considered, but we do not want to see pornographic, libelous, illegal, or sloppily written poetry.'' Has published *Calls from a Lighted House* by Jeanne Lohman, *How Far Light Must Travel* by Judi K. Beach, and *Aching for Tomorrow* by Frank Meyskens. Publishes about 6 flat-spined poetry paperbacks/year. Books average 80 pages. Press runs average between 500-1,000. No longer issues a print catalog, but all books are shown and described on Web site.

How to Submit Query first, with 12 sample poems and cover letter with brief bio and publication credits. Considers simultaneous submissions. No fax or e-mail submissions. Responds to queries in 2 weeks; to mss in 2 months. Always sends prepublication galleys. Pays 10% royalties of net receipts. Acquires English-language book rights. Returns rights upon termination of contract.

Advice "We receive over 1,000 unsolicited manuscripts and query letters per year. We publish only a few books per year, of which fewer than half are received unsolicited. Obviously the odds are not with you. For this reason, we encourage you to send out multiple submissions, and we do not expect you to tie up your chances while waiting for our response. Also, poetry does not make money, alas. It is a labor of love for both publisher and writer. But if the love is there, the rewards are great."

DIAL BOOKS FOR YOUNG READERS (Specialized: poetry for children/teens)

345 Hudson St., New York NY 10014. Web site: www.penguin.com. **Contact:** Submissions.

Book/Chapbook Needs Dial publishes some illustrated books of poetry for children. Has published poetry by J. Patrick Lewis and Nikki Grimes.

How to Submit "Submit entire picture book manuscripts, or the first 3 chapters of longer works. Please include a cover letter with brief bio and publication credits." Considers simultaneous submissions; no previously published poems. "Please note that, **unless interested in publishing them, Dial will not respond to unsolicited submissions.** Please do not include a self-addressed, stamped envelope with your submission. If Dial is interested, you can expect a reply from us within 4 months." Payment varies.

DIONYSIA PRESS LTD.

127 Milton Rd. W., 7 Duddingston House Courtyard, Edinburgh EH15 1JG Scotland. Phone/fax: (44)(131)661-1156. Established 1989. **Contact:** Denise Smith.

Book/Chapbook Needs Dionysia Press Ltd. publishes 2-10 paperbacks and chapbooks of poetry/year. "Sometimes we select from submissions or competitions." Has published *Chagall Takes a Fall* by Thom Nairn; *Imagining Seals* by Susanne Roxman; *Skies of Sand* by D. Smith; *Psychostasia* by Byron Leodaris; *Like Words and the Body Without a Passkey* by Zefi Daraki (author), Tom Nairn and D. Zervanou (translators); and *Rattlesnake Road* by Tom Bryan. Books are usually A5, perfect-bound, with hard covers with art.

How to Submit Query first, with a few sample poems and a cover letter with brief bio and publication credits. Responds to queries in 2-6 months. Pays in author's copies. "We usually get arts council grants, or poets get grants for themselves." For sample books or chapbooks, write to the above address.

DOLPHIN-MOON PRESS

P.O. Box 22262, Baltimore MD 21203. Established 1973. **Contact:** James Taylor, president.

Book/Chapbook Needs Dolphin-Moon is "a limited-edition (500-1,000 copies) press that emphasizes quality work (regardless of style), often published in unusual/'radical' format." The writer is usually allowed a strong voice in the look/feel of the final piece. "We've published magazines, anthologies, chapbooks, pamphlets, perfect-bound paperbacks, records, audio cassettes, and comic books. All styles are read and considered, but the work should show a strong spirit and voice. Although we like the feel of 'well-crafted' work, craft for its own sake won't meet our standards either." Has published work by Teller, Michael Weaver, John Strausbaugh, Josephine Jacobsen, and William Burroughs.

How to Submit Query first, with 6-10 sample poems and a cover letter with brief bio and publication credits. "Please, no submission of complete manuscripts unless requested." No fax or e-mail submissions. Responds to queries and full-length submissions (if invited) in up to 1 month. Always sends prepublication galleys. Pays in author's copies (negotiable, usually 10% of the press run). Acquires first edition rights. Send SASE for catalog to purchase samples, or send $15 for a "sampler" (guaranteed to be up to $25 worth of publications).

Advice "Our future plans are to continue as we have since 1973, publishing the best work we can by local, up-and-coming, and nationally recognized writers—in a quality package."

ÉCRITS DES FORGES (Specialized: French)

1497 Laviolette, Trois-Rivières QC G9A 5G4 Canada. (819)379-9813. Fax: (819)376-0774. E-mail: ecrits.desforges@tr.cgocable.ca. Web site: www.ecritsdesforges.com. Established 1971. **Contact:** Gaston Bellemare, président. Directrice Générale: Maryse Baribeau.

Book/Chapbook Needs Écrits des Forges publishes poetry only that is "authentic and original as a signature. We have published poetry from more than 1,000 poets coming from most of the franco-phone countries: André Romus (Belgium), Amadou Lamine Sall (Sénégal), Nicole Brossard, Claude Beausoleil, Jean-Marc Desgent, and Jean-Paul Daoust (Québec)." Publishes 45-50 paperback books of poetry/year. Books are usually 80-88 pages, digest-sized, perfect-bound, with 2-color covers with art.

How to Submit Query first with a few sample poems and a cover letter with brief bio and publication credits. Responds to queries in up to 6 months. Pays royalties of 10-20%, advance of 50% maximum, and 25 author's copies. Order sample books by writing or faxing.

Also Offers Sponsors the Festival international de la poésie/International Poetry Festival (see separate listing in Conferences, Workshops & Festivals).

⚏ ◙ FINISHING LINE PRESS

P.O. Box 1626, Georgetown KY 40324. (859)514-8966. E-mail: FinishingBooks@aol.com. Web site: www.finishinglinepress.com. Established 1998. **Contact:** Leah Maines, poetry editor.

• Member of CLMP

Book/Chapbook Needs Finishing Line Press seeks to "discover new talent" and hopes to publish chapbooks by both men and women poets who have not previously published a book or chapbook of poetry. Has published *Parables and Revelations* by T. Crunk, *Family Business* by Paula Sergi, *Putting in a Window* by John Brantingham, and *Dusting the Piano* by Abigail Gramig. Publishes 50-60 poetry chapbooks/year. Chapbooks are usually 25-30 pages, digest-sized, laser-printed, saddle-stapled, with card covers with textured matte wrappers.

How to Submit Submit up to 26 pages of poetry with cover letter, bio, acknowledgments, and **$12 reading fee**. Responds to queries and mss in up to 1 month. Pay varies; pays in author's copies. "Sales profits, if any, go to publish the next new poet." Sample chapbooks available by sending $6 to Finishing Line Press or through Web site.

Contest/Award Offerings The Finishing Line Press Open Chapbook Competition and the New Women's Voices Chapbook Competition (see separate listings in Contests & Awards).

Advice "We are very open to new talent. If the poetry is great, we will consider it for a chapbook."

◙ ◎ FLOATING BRIDGE PRESS (Specialized: WA poets)

PO Box 18814, Seattle, WA 98118. E-mail: floatingbridgepress@yahoo.com. Web site: www.floatingbridgepress.org Established 1994. **Contact:** The Editor.

Book/Chapbook Needs Floating Bridge Press publishes chapbooks and anthologies by Washington State poets, selected through an annual competition (see below). Has published *In the Convent We Become Clouds* by Annette Spaulding-Convy, *Toccata & Fugue* by Timothy Kelly, and *The Former St. Christopher* by Michael Bonacci, among others. The press also publishes *Floating Bridge Review*, an annual anthology featuring the work of Washington State poets. *Floating Bridge Review* is 86-144 pages, digest-sized, offset-printed, perfect-bound, with glossy cardstock cover. For a sample chapbook or anthology, send $13 postpaid.

Contest/Award Offerings For consideration, **Washington State poets only** should submit a chapbook ms of 20-24 pages of poetry. In addition to publication, the winner receives $500, 15 author's copies, and a reading in the Seattle area. All entrants receive a copy of the winning chapbook and will be considered for inclusion in *Floating Bridge Review*. Poet's name must not appear on the ms. Include a separate page with ms title, poet's name, address, phone number, and acknowledgments of any previous publications. Include SASE for results only; mss will not be returned. **Entry fee:** $12. **Deadline:** usual reading period is November 1-February 15 (postmark). Considers previously published individual poems and simultaneous submissions. Manuscripts are judged anonymously.

⚏ ⊞ ◙ ◎ GALAXY PRESS (Specialized: experimental, romantic, neuromantic)

71 Recreation St., Tweed Heads NSW 2485 Australia. (61)(7)5536-1997. Established 1978. **Contact:** Lance Banbury, editor.

Book/Chapbook Needs Galaxy Press publishes "original avant-garde poetry and critical accounts as well as contemporary lyrics and prose poems." Latest guest imprint (November 2005) is a selection of the poetry of Wolf Larsen of Chicago. Latest in-house imprint (August, 2007) is an essay on selected novels of Robert Louis Stevenson. Books are usually 16-20 pages, 15×21cm, offset/lithograph-printed, with glossy color card covers. Press run is 100. Obtain sample books or chapbooks by "written request."

How to Submit Considers simultaneous submissions. Cover letter is preferred. Often comments on rejected poems. Responds to queries in 2 weeks. Pays 5 author's copies.

Advice "Interests tend toward the Romantic and Neuromantic styles; a radical approach to imagery and emotions always welcome."

GERTRUDE PRESS (Specialized: gay, lesbian, bisexual, transgendered, queer-identified & allied)

P.O. Box 83948, Portland OR 97283. E-mail: editor@gertrudepress.org. Web site: www.gertrudepress.org. Established 1998. **Contact:** Eric Delehoy, founding editor.

Book/Chapbook Needs Gertrude Press, a nonprofit 501(c)(3) organization, showcases and develops "the creative talents of lesbian, gay, bisexual, trans, queer-identified, and allied individuals." Has published *Bone Knowing* by Kate Grant. Gertrude Press publishes 2 chapbooks/year (1 fiction, 1 poetry) as well as *Gertrude,* a semiannual literary journal (see separate listing in Magazines/Journals). Manuscripts are chosen through competition only (see below). Chapbooks are 20-24 pages, offset-printed, saddle-stapled, with cardstock cover with art.

How to Submit Refer to guidelines for Gertrude Press Poetry Chapbook Contest (see separate listing in Contests & Awards). Order sample chapbooks for $10.

Contest/Award Offerings The Gertrude Press Poetry Chapbook Contest (see separate listing in Contests & Awards).

GHOST PONY PRESS (Specialized: contemporary lyric; experimental)

P.O. Box 260113, Madison WI 53726-0113. (608)238-0175. E-mail: ghostponypress@hotmail.com. Web site: www.geocities.com/abraxaspress/. Established 1980. **Contact:** Ingrid Swanberg, editor/publisher.

Book/Chapbook Needs Ghost Pony Press has published 3 books of poetry by próspero saíz, including *the bird of nothing & other poems* (168 pages, 7×10, with sewn and wrapped binding; paperback available for $20, signed and numbered edition for $35). Also published *zen concrete & etc.* by d.a. levy (268 pages, magazine-sized, perfect-bound, illustrated; paperback available for $27.50).

How to Submit Query first, with a few sample poems (5-10) and cover letter with brief bio and publication credits. Include SASE. Considers previously published material for book publication. Accepts submissions by postal mail only; no e-mail submissions. Editor sometimes comments briefly on rejected poems. No promised response time. "We currently have a considerable backlog." Payment varies per project. Send SASE for catalog to buy samples.

GINNINDERRA PRESS (Specialized: Australian poets only)

P.O. Box 6753, Charnwood ACT 2615 Australia. E-mail: smgp@optusnet.com.au. Web site: www.ginninderrapress.com.au. Established 1996. **Contact:** Stephen Matthews, publisher.

● Please note: No longer accepting mss from writers residing outside of Australia.

Book/Chapbook Needs Ginninderra Press works "to give publishing opportunities to new writers." Has published poetry by Alan Gould and Geoff Page. Books are usually up to 72 pages, A5, laser-printed, saddle-stapled or thermal-bound, with board covers.

How to Submit Query first, with a few sample poems and a cover letter with brief bio and publication credits. Considers previously published poems; no simultaneous submissions. No fax or e-mail submissions. Time between acceptance and publication is 2 months. Seldom comments on rejected poems. Responds to queries in 1 week; to mss in 2 months.

GOOSE LANE EDITIONS (Specialized: Canadian poets only)

500 Beaverbrook Court, Ste 300, Fredericton NB E3B 5X4 Canada. (506)450-4251. Fax: (506)459-4991. Web site: www.gooselane.com. Established 1954. **Contact:** Ross Leckie, poetry editor.

Book/Chapbook Needs Goose Lane is a small literary press publishing Canadian fiction, poetry, and nonfiction. **Considers mss by Canadian poets only.** Receives about 400 mss/year, publishes 15-20 books/year, 4 of which are poetry collections. Has published *Beatitudes* by Herménégilde Chiasson and *Falsework* by Gary Geddes.

How to Submit "Call to inquire whether we are reading submissions." Accepts submissions by postal mail only. Guidelines available on Web site. Always sends prepublication galleys. Authors may receive royalties of up to 10% of retail price on all copies sold. Copies available to author at 40% discount.

Advice "Many of the poems in a manuscript accepted for publication will have been previously published in literary journals such as *The Fiddlehead*, *The Dalhousie Review*, or *The Malahat Review*."

ⓝ ◎ GOTHIC PRESS (Specialized: gothic, horror, dark fantasy)

2272 Quail Oak, Baton Rouge LA 70808.Estab. 1979. 225-766-2906. E-mail: gothicpt12@aol.com. Web site: www.gothicpress.com. Contact: Gary William Crawford, editor. Member, Science Fiction Poetry Association, Horror Writers Association.

Book/Chapbook Needs Gothic Press publishes gothic, horror, and dark fantasy poetry in their Gothic Chapbook series. Wants poetry in "any form or style as long as gothic or horror elements are present." Does not want science fiction. Has published Bruce Boston, Joey Froehlich, Scott C. Hocstad. Manuscripts are selected through open submission. Chapbooks are 10-80 pages, offset, saddle-stapled, with cardstock cover or interior illustration by commission. Send samples of art.

How to submit Query first, with a few sample poems and a cover letter with brief bio and publication credits. Book/chapbook mss may include previously published poems. Responds to queries in 1 week; to mss in 4 weeks. Pays 10% advance against royalty. Order sample books/chapbooks by sending $6.

Advice: "Know Gothic literature well.

◖ ⦸ GRAYWOLF PRESS

2402 University Ave., Suite 203, Saint Paul MN 55114. Web site: www.graywolfpress.org. Established 1974. **Contact:** Jeff Shotts, poetry editor.

● Poetry published in Graywolf Press collections has been included in *The Pushcart Prize*, and many books have won major awards.

Book/Chapbook Needs Graywolf Press is considered one of the nation's leading nonprofit literary publishers. "Graywolf introduces and promotes some of the most exciting and creative writers of our times." Considers only mss by poets widely published in magazines and journals of merit; **does not generally consider unsolicited mss by considers queries.** Has published poetry by Vijay Seshadri, Tess Gallagher, Tony Hoagland, Natasha Trethewey, Matthea Harvey, D.A. Powell, and many more. Publishes around 9 collections of poetry, 1-2 collections of poetry in translation, and 1-2 collections of essays on poetry/year.

How to Submit *No unsolicited mss.* Query first, with 10 pages of poetry (as a sample from the ms) and cover letter with brief bio and publication credits. SASE required for reply. No e-mail queries. Reads queries postmarked January 15-December 1 only. Responds to queries in 3-6 months. Order sample books through Web site, or request catalog through online submission form.

★ ❖ ◎ ⦸ GUERNICA EDITIONS INC. (Specialized: pluriculturalism; international translation)

P.O. Box 117, Station P, Toronto ON M5S 2S6 Canada. (416)658-9888. Fax: (416)657-8885. E-mail: guernicaeditions@cs.com. Web site: www.guernicaeditions.com. Established 1978. **Contact:** Antonio D'Alfonso, poetry editor.

Book/Chapbook Needs "We wish to bring together the different and often divergent voices that exist in Canada and the U.S. We are interested in translations. We are mostly interested in poetry and essays on pluriculturalism." Has published poetry by Pier Paolo Pasolini, Marianne Micros, Laurence Hutchman, and Bruno Ramirez.

How to Submit Query with 1-2 pages of sample poems. Send SASE (Canadian stamps only) or SAE and IRCs for catalog.

Advice "We are interested in promoting a pluricultural view of literature by bridging languages and cultures. We specialize in international translation."

⊘ HELIKON PRESS

120 W. 71st St., New York NY 10023. Established 1972. **Contact:** Robin Prising and William Leo Coakley, poetry editors.

Book/Chapbook Needs "We try to publish the best contemporary poetry in the tradition of English verse. We read (and listen to) poetry and ask poets to build a collection around particular poems. We print fine editions illustrated by good artists."

How to Submit *"Unfortunately, we cannot encourage submissions."*

◎ HIGH LYRICAL EXPERIMENTS (Specialized: experimental; paradoxism; outer-art)

P.O. Box 141, Rehoboth NM 87322. E-mail: M_L_Perez@yahoo.com. Web site: www.gallup.unm.e du ~ smarandache/ebooksliterature.htm. Established 1990. **Contact:** M. Lou, publisher.

Book/Chapbook Needs High Lyrical Experiments publishes 2-3 poetry paperbacks/year. Wants experimental poetry dealing with paradoxism. No classical poetry. See Web site for poetry samples. Has published poetry by Anatol Ciocanu, Nina Josu, and Al Bantos.

How to Submit Submit 3-4 poems at a time. No previously published poems or simultaneous submissions. Cover letter is preferred. Submit seasonal poems 1 month in advance. Time between acceptance and publication is 1 year. Seldom comments on rejected poems. Responds to queries in 1 month. Pays 100 author's copies. Order sample books by sending SASE.

Also Offers Free e-books available on Web site.

$⊘ ◎ ⊘HIGH PLAINS PRESS (Specialized: WY and the American West)

P.O. Box 123, Glendo WY 82213. (307)735-4370. Fax: (307)735-4590. E-mail: editor@highplainspre ss.com. Web site: www.highplainspress.com. Established 1985. **Contact:** Nancy Curtis, poetry editor.

Book/Chapbook Needs High Plains Press considers books of poetry "about Wyoming and the American West, particularly poetry based on historical people/events or nature. We mainly publish historical nonfiction, but do publish 1 book of poetry every year." Has published *Bitter Creek Junction* by Linda Hasselstrom, *Beasts in Snow* by Jane Wohl, and *The White Dove: A Celebration of Father Kino* by Jane Candia Coleman.

How to Submit Query first with 3 sample poems (from a 50-poem ms). Accepts submissions by e-mail (as attachment); no fax or disk submissions. Time between acceptance and publication is up to 2 years. Guidelines available for SASE or by fax or e-mail. Responds in 2 months. Always sends prepublication galleys. Pays 10% of sales. Acquires first rights. Catalog available on request; sample books: $5.

Advice "Look at our previous titles."

▦ ◎ ⊘HILLTOP PRESS (Specialized: science fiction, dark fantasy)

4 Nowell Place, Almondbury, Huddersfield, West Yorkshire HD5 8PB England. Web site: www.bbr-online.com/catalogue (online catalog). Established 1966. **Contact:** Steve Sneyd, editor.

Book/Chapbook Needs Hilltop Press publishes mainly science fiction poetry, plus some dark fantasy poetry. Publications in print include: a series of books on poetry in U.S. and UK SFanzines; collections, new and reprint, by individual science fiction poets including Andrew Darlington, Gavin Salisbury, Mary Ladd, Mark Sonnenfeld, John F. Haines, and Jimmie Dickie; dark fantasy, including Medusa poems anthology and work including family myth verse play by Frances Elizabeth Campbell, and ballad and Arthurian reprints. Orders from the U.S. can be placed through the Web site of BBR Solutions Ltd. (see above).

How to Submit *Does not accept unsolicited mss.*Query (with SAE/IRC) with proposals for relevant projects.

Advice "My advice for beginning poets is: a) Persist—don't let any 1 editor discourage you. 'In poetry's house are many mansions.' What 1 publication hates another may love; b) Be prepared for long delays between acceptance and appearance of work—the small press is mostly self-financed and part-time, so don't expect it to be more efficient than commercial publishers; c) Always keep a copy of everything you send out, put your name and address on everything you send, and always include adequately stamped SAE.''

⊕ $⊘ ◎ ⊠ HIPPOPOTAMUS PRESS (Specialized: modernism)

22 Whitewell Rd., Frome, Somerset BA11 4EL England. Phone/fax: (44)(1373)466653. E-mail: rjhip popress@aol.com. Established 1974. **Contact:** Roland John, poetry editor.

Book/Chapbook Needs Hippopotamus Press publishes 6 books/year. ''The Hippopotamus Press is specialized, with an affinity with Modernism. No Typewriter Poetry, Concrete Poetry, or Surrealism.''

How to Submit Query first, with a few sample poems and cover letter with brief bio and publication credits. Considers simultaneous submissions and previously published poems. Responds in 6 weeks. Pays 7½-10% royalties plus author's copies. Request book catalog to purchase sample books.

⊌ ◎ ⊠ HOLIDAY HOUSE, INC. (Specialized: poetry for children/teens)

Editorial Dept., 425 Madison Ave., New York NY 10017. Web site: www.holidayhouse.com. Established 1936.

Book/Chapbook Needs A trade children's book house. Has published hardcover books for children by John Updike and Walter Dean Myers. Publishes one poetry book/year, averaging 32 pages.

How to Submit *'' The acceptance of complete book manuscripts of high-quality children's poetry is limited.''* Send a query with SASE before submitting.

✪ ⊠ $⊌ ◎ ⊠ HOUSE OF ANANSI PRESS (Specialized: work by Canadian authors)

110 Spadina Ave., Suite 801, Toronto ON M5V 2K4 Canada. (416)363-4343. Fax: (416)363-1017. Web site: www.anansi.ca. Established 1967.

Book/Chapbook Needs House of Anansi publishes literary fiction and poetry by Canadian and international writers. ''We seek to balance the list between well-known and emerging writers, with an interest in writing by Canadians of all backgrounds. We publish Canadian poetry only, and poets must have a substantial publication record—if not in books, then definitely in journals and magazines of repute.'' Does not want ''children's poetry or poetry by previously unpublished poets.'' Has published *Power Politics* by Margaret Atwood and *Ruin & Beauty* by Patricia Young. Books are generally 96-144 pages, trade paperbacks with French sleeves, with matte covers.

How to Submit Canadian poets should query first with 10 sample poems (typed double-spaced) and a cover letter with brief bio and publication credits. Considers simultaneous submissions. Poems are circulated to an editorial board. Often comments on rejected poems. Responds to queries within 1 year, to mss (if invited) within 4 months. Pays 8-10% royalties, a $750 advance, and 10 author's copies (out of a press run of 1,000).

Advice ''To learn more about our titles, check our Web site or write to us directly for a catalog. We strongly advise poets to build up a publishing résumé by submitting poems to reputable magazines and journals. This indicates 3 important things to us: 1, that he or she is becoming a part of the Canadian poetry community; 2, that he or she is building up a readership through magazine subscribers; and 3, it establishes credibility in his or her work. There is a great deal of competition for only 3 or 4 spots on our list each year—which always includes works by poets we have previously published.''

⊘ ALICE JAMES BOOKS

University of Maine at Farmington, 238 Main St., Farmington ME 04938. Phone/fax: (207)778-7071. E-mail: ajb@umf.maine.edu. Web site: www.alicejamesbooks.org. Established 1973. **Contact:** Contest Coordinator.

Book/Chapbook Needs ''The mission of Alice James Books, a cooperative poetry press, is to seek out and publish the best contemporary poetry by both established and beginning poets, with particular emphasis on involving poets in the publishing process.'' Has published poetry by Jane Kenyon, Jean Valentine, B.H. Fairchild, and Matthea Harvey. Publishes flat-spined paperbacks of high quality, both in production and contents. Does not want children's poetry or light verse. Publishes 6 paperback books/year, 80 pages each, in editions of 1,500.

How to Submit Manuscripts are selected through competitions (see below).

Contest/Award Offerings The Kinereth Gensler Awards and The Beatrice Hawley Award (see separate listings in Contests & Awards).

✪ ⊘ KATYDID BOOKS

1 Balsa Rd., Santa Fe NM 87508. Web site: http://katydidbooks.com. Established 1973. **Contact:** Karen Hargreaves-Fitzsimmons and Thomas Fitzsimmons, editors/publishers.

Book/Chapbook Needs Katydid Books publishes 1 paperback/year and 1 hardback/year. "We publish a series of poetry: Asian Poetry in Translation (distributed by University of Hawaii Press)."

How to Submit *Currently not accepting submissions.*

⊕ ◯ ◎ ⊘ KITE BOOKS (Specialized: poetry for children)

K.T. Publications, 16 Fane Close, Stamford, Lincolnshire PE9 1HG England. (44)(1780)754193. Established 1989. **Contact:** Kevin Troop, editor.

Book/Chapbook Needs K.T. Publications and Kite Books publish "as much as possible each year" of poetry, short stories, and books for children—"at as high a standard as humanly possible." Has published *Freezing the Frame* by Michael Bangerter and *Insect Nights* by Hannah Welfare. Books are usually 50-60 pages, A5, perfect-bound, with glossy covers.

How to Submit Query first, with up to 6 sample poems and a cover letter with brief bio and publication credits. "Also include suitable SAE with IRCs—so that I do not end up paying return postage every time."

Also Offers A "reading and friendly help service to writers. Costs are reasonable." Write for details.

Advice "Keep writing; be patient."

⊕ ⊘ ◎ ⊘ LAPWING PUBLICATIONS (Specialized: work by Irish poets)

1 Ballysillan Dr., Belfast BT14 8HQ Northern Ireland. Phone/fax: (44)(2890)295800. E-mail: lapwin g.poetry@ntlworld.com. Web site: http://www.freewebs.com:80/lapwingpoetry/. Established 1989. **Contact:** Dennis Greig, editor.

• Lapwing will produce work only if and when resources to do so are available.

Book/Chapbook Needs Lapwing publishes "emerging Irish poets and poets domiciled in Ireland, plus the new work of a suitable size by established Irish writers." Publishes 6-10 chapbooks/year. Wants poetry of all kinds, but, "no crass political, racist, sexist propaganda, even of a positive or 'pc' tenor." Has published Zlatko Tomicic (*Croatia My Love*), Said (Iranian-German)—Goethe Medallion 2006—(*The Place I Die I Shall Not Belong*), Ilmar Lehtpere and Kristina Ehin (Estonian)—Popescue European Translation Award 2007—(*My Brother is Going Off to War*). Pamphlets up to 32 pages, chapbooks up to 44 pages, books 48-112 pages. Belfast binding (saddle-stitched signatures in a perfect binding 'look'), Belfast Japanese side stitch square spined, simple saddle-stitched otherwise.)

How to Submit "Submit 6 poems in the first instance; depending on these, an invitation to submit more may follow." Considers simultaneous submissions. Accepts e-mail submissions (pasted into body of message). Cover letter is required. Poems are circulated to an editorial board. "All submissions receive a first reading. If these poems have minor errors or faults, the writer is advised. If poor quality, the poems are returned. Those 'passing' first reading are retained, and a letter of conditional offer is sent." Often comments on rejected poems. Responds to queries in 1 month; to mss in 2 months. Pays 20 author's copies; no royalties. "After initial publication, irrespective of the quantity, the work will be permanently available using 'print-on-demand' production; such publications will not always be printed exactly as the original, although the content will remain the same."

Advice "Clean; check spelling, grammar, punctuation, layout (i.e., will it fit a book page?); clear text. Due to limited resources, material will be processed well in advance of any estimated publishing date. All accepted material is strictly conditional on resources available, no favoritism. The

Irish domestic market is small, the culture is hierarchical, poet/personality culture predominates, literary democracy is limited.''

◖ ◎ ☑ LOONFEATHER PRESS (Specialized: for MN-area writers)

P.O. Box 1212, Bemidji MN 56619. E-mail: books@loonfeatherpress.com. Web site: http://loonfeat herpress.com. Established 1979. **Contact:** Poetry Editors.

Book/Chapbook Needs Loonfeather Press publishes a limited number of quality poetry books. Has published *Imaginarium* by Lynn Levin (a 2005 ForeWord Finalist); *The Rhubarb King* by Sharon Chmielarz; and *Traces in Blood, Bone, & Stone: Contemporary Ojibwe Poetry*, edited by Kimberly Blaeser.

How to Submit *Does not accept unsolicited mss.*Does accept query letters/e-mails. Check Web site for updates.

◖ LOUISIANA STATE UNIVERSITY PRESS

3990 West Lakeshore Dr., Baton Rouge LA 70808. (225)578-6434. Fax: (225)578-6461. E-mail: jeaster@lsu.edu. Web site: www.lsu.edu/lsupress. Established 1935. **Contact:** John Easterly, executive editor.

Book/Chapbook Needs A highly respected publisher of collections by poets such as Claudia Emerson, David Kirby, Brendan Galvin, Fred Chappell, Marilyn Nelson, and Henry Taylor. Publisher of the Southern Messenger Poets series edited by Dave Smith.

How to Submit *"Currently accepting poetry submissions, but the lists are full through 2010."*

◖ ◎ ☑ LUNA BISONTE PRODS (Specialized: experimental, avant-garde)

137 Leland Ave., Columbus OH 43214-7505. Web site: www.johnmbennett.net. Established 1967. **Contact:** John M. Bennett, editor/publisher.

Book/Chapbook Needs Luna Bisonte Prods considers book submissions. "Interested in avant-garde and highly experimental work only." Has published poetry by Jim Leftwich, Sheila E. Murphy, Al Ackerman, Richard Kostelanetz, Carla Bertola, Olchar Lindsann, and many others.

How to Submit Query first, with a few sample poems and cover letter with brief bio and publication credits. "Keep it brief. Chapbook publishing usually depends on grants or other subsidies, and is usually by solicitation. **Will also consider subsidy arrangements on negotiable terms.**" A sampling of various Luna Bisonte Prods products is available for $20.

Advice "Be blank."

☑ MAD RIVER PRESS

State Road, Richmond MA 01254. (413)698-3184. Established 1986. **Contact:** Barry Sternlieb, editor.

Book/Chapbook Needs Mad River publishes 2 broadsides/year and occasional chapbooks, "all types of poetry, no bias."

How to Submit *Does not read unsolicited submissions.*

✪ ☑ MAMMOTH BOOKS

MAMMOTH press, inc., 7 Juniata St., DuBois PA 15801. Established 1996. **Contact:** Antonio Vallone, publisher.

Book/Chapbook Needs MAMMOTH books, an imprint of MAMMOTH press inc., publishes 4 or more paperbacks/year of creative nonfiction, fiction, and poetry. "We are open to all types of literary poetry." Has published *The House of Sages* by Philip Terman, *The Never Wife* by Cynthia Hogue, *These Happy Eyes* by Liz Rosenberg, and *Subjects for Other Conversations* by John Stigall. Books are usually 5×7 or 6×9, digitally printed, perfect-bound; covers vary (1- to 4-color).

How to Submit *Not currently reading unsolicited mss.* Order sample books by writing to the above address.

Advice "Read big. Write big. Publish small. Join the herd."

◖ ◎ MARYMARK PRESS (Specialized: experimental, avant-garde)

45-08 Old Millstone Dr., East Windsor NJ 08520. (609)443-0646. Established 1994. **Contact:** Mark Sonnenfeld, editor/publisher.

Book/Chapbook Needs Marymark Press's goal is "to feature and promote experimental writers. I will most likely be publishing broadsides, give-out sheets, and chapbooks this year. I want to see experimental writing of the outer fringe. Make up words, sounds, whatever, but say something you thought never could be explained. Disregard rules, if need be." No traditional, rhyming, or spiritual verse; no predictable styles. Has published poetry by Stephanie Hiteshew, Eric Greinke, James Michael Ward, Judith L. Lundin, and Dyani Johns.

How to Submit Submit 3 poems at a time. Considers previously published poems and simultaneous submissions. Cover letter is preferred. "Copies should be clean, crisp, and camera-ready. I do not have the means to accept electronic submissions. A SASE should accompany all submissions, and include a telephone number if at all possible." Time between acceptance and publication is 1 month. Seldom comments on rejected poems. Guidelines available for SASE. Responds to queries and mss in up to 2 weeks. Pays at least 10 author's copies (out of a press run of 200-300). **May offer subsidy arrangements.** "It all depends upon my financial situation at the time. Yes, I might ask the author to subsidize the cost. It could be worth their while. I have good connections in the international small press." Order sample publications by sending a 6×9 SAE. "There is no charge for samples."

Advice "Experiment with thought, language, the printed word."

☐ ☑ MAVERICK DUCK PRESS

E-mail: maverickduckpress@yahoo.com. Web site: www.maverickduckpress.com. Established 2005. **Contact:** Kendall A. Bell, editor.

Book/Chapbook Needs Maverick Duck Press is a "publisher of chapbooks from undiscovered talent. We are looking for fresh and powerful work that shows a sense of innovation or a new take on passion or emotion. Previous publication in print or online journals will increase your chances of us accepting your manuscript." Does not want "unedited work." Recently published *Worshipfully* by Lauren Reynolds, *Chariots of Flame* by J. Michael Wahlgren, *14 Ways to Die* by Kendall A. Bell, *Sad Town* by Jon Ballard, and *Warm Summer Memories* by Michael Keshigian. Publishes 6-8 chapbooks/year. Manuscripts are selected through open submission. Chapbooks are 20-30 pages, photocopied, saddle-stapled, with cardstock covers (poet must provide desired cover art).

How to Submit Query first, with a few sample poems and a cover letter with brief bio and publication credits. Chapbook mss may include previously published poems. "Previous publication is always a plus, as we may be more familiar with your work. Chapbook manuscripts should have at least 20 poems." Pays 20 author's copies (out of a press run of 50).

Advice "Write and revise often. Read a lot of other poets. Your manuscript should be the strongest of your work."

$ ☑ ◎ MEADOWBROOK PRESS (Specialized: anthologies; children's humor)

5451 Smetana Dr., Minnetonka MN 55343. Web site: www.meadowbrookpress.com. Established 1975. **Contact:** Poetry Editor.

Book/Chapbook Needs Meadowbrook Press is "currently seeking poems to be considered for future funny poetry book anthologies for children." Wants humorous poems aimed at children ages 6-12. "Poems should be fun, punchy, and refreshing. We're looking for new, hilarious, contemporary voices in children's poetry that kids can relate to." Has published poetry by Shel Silverstein, Jack Prelutsky, Jeff Moss, Kenn Nesbitt, and Bruce Lansky. Published anthologies include *Kids Pick the Funniest Poems*, *A Bad Case of the Giggles*, and *Miles of Smiles*.

How to Submit "Please take time to read our guidelines, and send your best work." Submit up to 10 poems at a time; 1 poem to a page with name and address on each; include SASE. Lines/poem: 25 maximum. Considers simultaneous submissions. Time between acceptance and publication is 1-2 years. Poems are tested in front of grade school students before being published. Guidelines available for SASE or on Web site. Responds only if interested. Pays $50-100/poem plus 1 contributor's copy.

◎ ☑ MIDWEST VILLAGES & VOICES (Specialized: Midwestern poetry)

P.O. Box 40214, St. Paul MN 55104. (612)822-6878. Established 1979.

Book/Chapbook Needs Midwest Villages & Voices is a cultural organization and small press publisher of Midwestern poetry and prose.

How to Submit "We encourage and support Midwestern writers and artists. However, **at this time submissions are accepted by invitation only.** Unsolicited submissions are not accepted."

☑ MILKWEED EDITIONS
1011 Washington Ave. S., Suite 300, Minneapolis MN 55415-1246. (612)332-3192. Fax: (612)215-2550. E-mail: editor@milkweed.org. Web site: www.milkweed.org. Established 1984. **Contact:** Poetry Reader.

Book/Chapbook Needs Milkweed Editions is "looking for poetry manuscripts of high quality that embody humane values and contribute to cultural understanding." Not limited in subject matter. Open to writers with previously published books of poetry or a minimum of 6 poems published in nationally distributed commercial or literary journals. Considers translations and bilingual mss. Has published *Hallelujah Blackout* by Alex Lemon, *Music for Landing Planes By* by Eireann Lorsung, *Atlas* by Katrina Vandenberg, and *Willow Room, Green Door* by Deborah Keenan.

How to Submit Submit 60 pages or more, typed on high-quality white paper. No fax or e-mail submissions. Do not send originals. Include SASE for reply. Reads unsolicited mss in January and June **only**, but accepts mss all year. "In the event that manuscripts are not accepted for publication, we prefer to recycle them. If you need your work returned, **please enclose a check for $5 rather than a stamped mailer**." Guidelines available for SASE or on Web site. Responds in up to 6 months. Order sample books through Web site.

☑ ☑ MOUNT OLIVE COLLEGE PRESS
634 Henderson St., Mount Olive NC 28365. (919)658-2502. Established 1990. **Contact:** Dr. Pepper Worthington, editor.

Book/Chapbook Needs Mount Olive Press publishes 2 books/year. Books are usually digest-sized.

How to Submit Submit 12 sample poems. Guidelines available for SASE. Responds to queries and mss in 3 months. Obtain sample books by writing to the above address.

◎ ☑ MOVING PARTS PRESS (Specialized: translations; Latino/Chicano)
10699 Empire Grade, Santa Cruz CA 95060-9474. (831)427-2271. E-mail: frice@movingpartspress.com. Web site: www.movingpartspress.com. Established 1977. **Contact:** Felicia Rice, poetry editor.

Book/Chapbook Needs Moving Part Press publishes handsome, innovative books, broadsides, and prints that "explore the relationship of word and image, typography and the visual arts, the fine arts and popular culture." Published *Codex Espangliensis: from Columbus to the Border Patrol* (1998) with performance texts by Guillermo Gómez-Peña and collage imagery by Enrique Chagoya; *Cosmogonie Intime/An Intimate Cosmogony* (2005), a limited edition artists' book with poems by Yves Peyré, translated by Elizabeth R. Jackson, and drawings by Ray Rice.

How to Submit *Does not accept unsolicited mss.*

◙ ☑ ☑ MULTICULTURAL BOOKS
Suite 307, 6311 Gilbert Rd., Richmond BC V7C 3V7 Canada. (604)277-3864. E-mail: jrmbooks@hotmail.com. Web site: www.thehypertexts.com. Established 1985. **Contact:** Joe M. Ruggier, publisher.

Book/Chapbook Needs Multicultural Books publishes poetry and related literature as well as fiction and various forms of nonfiction. Publishes 1-6 books/year "depending on availability and quality." Manuscripts are selected through open submission. Books are 120+ pages, digitally photocopied, perfect-bound, with heavy color cardstock cover.

How to Submit Query first, with a few sample poems and a cover letter with brief bio and publication credits. Book mss may include previously published poems. "The only criteria is quality of work and excellence." Responds to queries in 2 months; to mss in 2 months. **Offers author-subsidy as well as publisher-subsidy options**; the selection process for the latter is extremely competitive and quality-conscious. "Authors who feel their work may be up to standard are welcome to query us with a sample or else submit an entire manuscript. All interested parties may consult our guidelines as well as our sample publication contract on Web site." Order sample books/chapbooks by contacting Joe M. Ruggier.

◎ ☑ NEW NATIVE PRESS (Specialized: translations; marginalized & endangered languages)

P.O. Box 661, Cullowhee NC 28723. (828)293-9237. E-mail: newnativepress@hotmail.com. Web site: www.newnativepress.com. Established 1979. **Contact:** Thomas Rain Crowe, publisher.

Book/Chapbook Needs New Native Press has "selectively narrowed its range of contemporary 20th- and 21st-century literature to become an exclusive publisher of writers in marginalized and endangered languages. All books published are bilingual translations from original languages into English." Publishes about 2 paperbacks/year. Has published *Kenneth Patchen: Rebel Poet in America* by Larry Smith; Gaelic, Welsh, Breton, Cornish, and Manx poets in an all-Celtic-language anthology of contemporary poets from Scotland, Ireland, Wales, Brittany, Cornwall, and Isle of Man, entitled *Writing The Wind: A Celtic Resurgence* (The New Celtic Poetry); and *Selected Poems* by Kusumagraj (poet from Bombay, India) in the Marathi language. Books are sold by distributors in 4 foreign countries, and in the U.S. by Baker & Taylor, Amazon.com, library vendors, and Small Press Distribution. Books are typically 80 pages, offset-printed on glossy 120 lb. stock, perfect-bound, with professionally designed color cover.

How to Submit Query first, with 10 sample poems and cover letter with brief bio and publication credits. Considers previously published poems and simultaneous submissions. Time between acceptance and publication is up to 1 year. Always comments on rejected poems. Responds in 2 weeks. Pays in author's copies ("amount varies with author and title").

Advice "We are looking for work indicative of rare and unique talent—and original voices—using language experimentally and symbolically, if not subversively."

◙ NEW ORLEANS POETRY JOURNAL PRESS

2131 General Pershing St., New Orleans LA 70115. (504)891-3458. Established 1956. **Contact:** Maxine Cassin, publisher/editor. Co-Editor: Charles de Gravelles.

- "For the present, due to Hurricane Katrina, all correspondence should be sent to Maxine Cassin at 140 Wylie Dr., #4, Baton Rouge LA 70808."

Book/Chapbook Needs "We prefer to publish relatively new and/or little-known poets of unusual promise or those inexplicably neglected." Does not want to see "cliché or doggerel, anything incomprehensible or too derivative, or workshop exercises. First-rate lyric poetry preferred (not necessarily in traditional forms)." Has published books by Everette Maddox, Charles Black, Malaika Favorite, Martha McFerren, Paul Petrie, Charles de Gravelles, and Ralph Adamo.

How to Submit *This market is currently closed to all submissions.*

Advice "Read as much as possible! Write only when you must, and don't rush into print! No poetry should be sent without querying first! Publishers are concerned about expenses unnecessarily incurred in mailing manuscripts. Telephoning is not encouraged."

▨ ◻ NEW RIVERS PRESS

MSU Moorhead, 1104 Seventh Ave. S., Moorhead MN 56563. E-mail: nrp@mnstate.edu. Web site: www.newriverspress.com. Established 1968. **Contact:** Donna Carlson, managing editor.

Book/Chapbook Needs New Rivers Press publishes collections of poetry, novels or novellas, translations of contemporary literature, and collections of short fiction and nonfiction. "We will continue to publish books regularly by new and emerging writers, especially those with a connection to Minnesota or to New York City, but we also welcome the opportunity to read work of every character and to publish the best literature available by new and emerging authors nationwide. Each October and November, through the MVP competition (see below), we choose 3 books, 1 of them national (genre will vary by year) and 2 regional." Has published *The Pact* by Walter Roers, *Nice Girls* by Cezarija Abartis, *Mozart's Carriage* by Dan Bachhuber, *The Volunteer* by Candace Black, *The Hunger Bone* by Deb Marquart, and *Real Karaoke People* by Ed Bok-Lee, and *Terrain Tracks* by Purvi Shah.

How to Submit Book-length mss of poetry, short fiction, novellas, or creative nonfiction are all considered. No fax or e-mail submissions. Guidelines and catalog available on Web site.

Contest/Award Offerings The Minnesota Voices Project (MVP) awards $1,000, a standard book contract, and publication of a book-length ms by New Rivers Press. Every third year, the poetry competition is national, open to anyone residing in the U.S.; 2 additional annual prizes (1 prose, 1 in any genre) are open only to residents of Minnesota or New York City. Entrants may submit only 1 ms to the MVP competition annually. All previously published poems must be acknowledged. Considers simultaneous submissions "if noted as such. If your manuscript is accepted elsewhere during the judging, you must notify New Rivers Press immediately. If you do not give such notification and your manuscript is selected, your signature on the entry form gives New Rivers Press permission to go ahead with publication." Submit 50-80 pages of poetry. Entry form (required) and guidelines available on Web site. **Entry fee:** none. **Deadline:** submit September 15-November 1 (postmark). 2007 poetry winner was Kelsea Habecker (*Hollow Out*). 2007 judge: Charles Simic.

$⊘ ◎ ⊘ OOLIGAN PRESS (Specialized: gives preference to translated poetry, prose poetry, traditional verse, and works from local poets)

Portland State University, P.O. Box 751, Portland OR 97207-0751. Web site: www.publishing.pdx.edu. Established 2001. **Contact:** Acquisitions Committee.

Book/Chapbook Needs As a general trade press, Ooligan Press is "open to publishing limited collections of poetry (this genre represents only a small percentage of the overall list)." Open to "all forms of style and verse; however, we give special preference to translated poetry, prose poetry, and traditional verse. We place special value on collections of works from local poets. Although spoken word, slam, and rap poetry are of interest to the press, we will not consider such work if it does not translate well to the written page." Has published *American Scream & Palindrome Apocalypse* by Durbravaka Oraic-Tolid, translated by Julienne Eden Busic, and *Deer Drinks the Moon*, edited by Liz Nakazawa. Manuscripts are selected through open submission. Books are offset-printed, perfect-bound, with soft covers.

How to Submit Query by postal mail, with a few sample poems, a brief bio including poet's publication credits, and a SASE. Book mss may include previously published poems. Accepts simultaneous submissions. See Web site for explanation of acquisition process and complete submission guidelines. Responds to queries in 3 months. Payment varies, but generally 6-12% of retail price and 25 author's copies. Order sample books through Web site.

⊠ ⊘ ORCHISES PRESS

P.O. Box 20602, Alexandria VA 22320-1602. E-mail: lathbury@gmu.edu. Web site: http://mason.gmu.edu/lathbury. Established 1983. **Contact:** Roger Lathbury, poetry editor.

• Orchises Press prefers not to receive unsolicited mss.

◐ OUTRIDER PRESS, INC.

2036 North Winds Drive, Dyer IN 46311. (219)322-7270. Fax: (219)322-7085. E-mail: outriderpress @sbcglobal.net. Web site: www.outriderpress.com. **Contact:** Whitney Scott, editor. Estab. 1988. Small literary press and hand bindery; publishes many first-time authors. Publishes paperback originals. Books: 70 lb. paper; offset printing; perfect bound. Average print order: 2,000. **Published 25-30 debut authors within the last year.** Distributes titles through Baker & Taylor.

• Was a *Small Press Review* "Pick" for 2000.

Needs Ethnic, experimental, family saga, fantasy (space fantasy, sword and sorcery), feminist, gay/lesbian, historical, horror (psychological, supernatural), humor, lesbian, literary, mainstream/contemporary, mystery (amateur slueth, cozy, police procedural, private eye/hard-boiled), new age/mystic, psychic/supernatural, romance (contemporary, futuristic/time travel, gothic, historical, regency period, romantic suspense), science fiction (soft/sociological), short story collections, thriller/espionage, western (frontier saga, traditional). Published *Telling Time*, by Cherie Caswell Dost; *If Ever I Cease to Love*, by Robert Klein Engler.

How to Contact Accepts unsolicited mss. Query with SASE. Accepts queries by mail. Include estimated word count, brief bio, list of publishing credits. Agented fiction 10%. Responds in 3 weeks to queries; 4 months to mss. Accepts simultaneous submissions, electronic submissions, submissions on disk. Sometimes comments on rejected mss. In affiliation with Tallgrass Writers Guild, publishes an annual anthonlogy with cash prizes. 2009 themes is: "Fearsome Fascinations: Vampires, Zombies. Artificial Intelligence (with hostile intent) and other frights. As always, broadly interpreted." Deadline is February 27, 2009. For details and complete guidelines, e-mail outriderpres s@sbcglobal.net.

Terms Pays honorarium. Publishes ms 6 months after acceptance. Ms guidelines for SASE.

Advice "It's always best to familiarize yourself with our publications. We're especially fond of humor/irony."

✪ ◗ ◎ ⊘ PATH PRESS, INC. (Specialized: African American, Third World)

P.O. Box 2925, Chicago IL 60690. (847)424-1620. Fax: (847)424-1623. E-mail: pathpressinc@aol.c om. Established 1969. **Contact:** Bennett J. Johnson, president.

Book/Chapbook Needs Path Press is a small publisher of books and poetry primarily "by, for, and about African American and Third World people." Open to all types of poetic forms; emphasis is on high quality. Books are "hardback and quality paperbacks."

How to Submit Query first, with a few sample poems and cover letter with brief bio and publication credits. Submissions should be typewritten in ms format. Accepts submissions by e-mail (as attachment).

$ ◖ ◎ ⊘ PELICAN PUBLISHING COMPANY (Specialized: regional/various; poetry books for children)

1000 Burmaster St., Gretna LA 70053. E-mail: editorial@pelicanpub.com. Web site: www.pelicanpu b.com. Established 1926. **Contact:** Nina Kooij, editor-in-chief.

Book/Chapbook Needs Pelican Publishing Company is a medium-sized publisher of popular histories, cookbooks, regional books, children's books, and inspirational/motivational books. Considers poetry for "hardcover children's books only, preferably with a regional focus. However, our needs for this are very limited; we publish 15 juvenile titles per year, and most of these are prose, not poetry." Has published *Librarian's Night Before Christmas* by David Davis and *Santa's Revenge* by James Rice. Two of Pelican's popular series are prose books about Gaston the Green-Nosed Alligator by James Rice, and Clovis Crawfish by Mary Alice Fontenot. Has a variety of books based on "The Night Before Christmas," adapted to regional settings such as Cajun, prairie, and Texas. Books are 32 pages, magazine-sized, include illustrations.

How to Submit *Currently not accepting unsolicited mss.*Query first with a cover letter including "work and writing backgrounds and promotional connections." No previously published poems or simultaneous submissions. Guidelines available for SASE or on Web site. Responds to queries in 1 month; to mss (if invited) in 3 months. Always sends prepublication galleys. Pays royalties. Acquires all rights. Returns rights upon termination of contract. Typically, Pelican books sell for $15.95. Write for catalog or visit Web site to buy samples.

Advice "We try to avoid rhyme altogether, especially predictable rhyme. Monotonous rhythm can also be a problem."

⊘ PERUGIA PRESS (Specialized: first or second poetry book by a woman)

P.O. Box 60364, Florence MA 01062. E-mail: info@perugiapress.com. Web site: www.perugiapress. com. Established 1997. **Contact:** Susan Kan, director.

Book/Chapbook Needs Perugia Press publishes 1 collection of poetry each year, by a woman at the beginning of her publishing career (first or second books only). "Our books appeal to people who have been reading poetry for decades, as well as those who might be picking up a book of poetry for the first time. Slight preference for narrative poetry." Has published *Beg No Pardon* by Lynn Thompson, *Kettle Bottom* by Diane Gilliam Fisher, *Lamb* by Frannie Lindsay, *The Disappearing Letters* by Carol Edelstein, *Seamless* by Linda Tomol Pennisi, and *Red* by Melanie Braverman. Books are an average of 88 pages, offset-printed, perfect-bound. Print run is 500-1,200. Order sample books through Web site.

How to Submit "We are not accepting general submissions at this time." *Manuscripts are selected through competition only.*

Contest/Award Offerings The Perugia Press Prize (see separate listing in Contests & Awards).

☑ ◎ ☑ PLAN B PRESS (Specialized: experimental, concrete, visual poetry)

3412 Terrace Dr., #1731, Alexandria VA 22302. (215)732-2663. E-mail: planbpress@att.net. Web site: www.planbpress.com. Established 1999. **Contact:** stevenallenmay, president.

Book/Chapbook Needs Plan B Press is a "small publishing company with an international feel. Our intention is to have Plan B Press be part of the conversation about the direction and depth of literary movements and genres. Plan B Press's new direction is to seek out authors rarely-to-never published, sharing new voices that might not otherwise be heard. Plan B Press is determined to merge text with image, writing with art." Publishes poetry and short fiction. Wants "experimental poetry, concrete/visual work." Does not want "sonnets, political or religious poems, work in the style of Ogden Nash." Has published poetry by Lamont B Steptoe, Michele Belluomini, Jim Mancinelli, Lyn Lifshin, Robert Miltner, and stevenallenmay. Publishes 1 poetry book/year and 5-10 chapbooks/year. Manuscripts are selected through open submission and through competition (see below). Books/chapbooks are 24-48 pages, with covers with art/graphics.

How to Submit Query first, with a few sample poems and a cover letter with brief bio and publication credits. Book/chapbook mss may include previously published poems. Guidelines available on Web site. Responds to queries in 1 month; to mss in 3 months. Author keeps royalties. Pays varying number of author's copies; press run varies per book. Order sample books/chapbooks by writing to Plan B Press or through Web site.

Contest/Award Offerings The annual Plan B Press Poetry Chapbook Contest (see separate listing in Contests & Awards).

Advice "Writing reveals the mirror to your soul. Don't think about words until you are in the editing phase, and then only look for errors. Whatever sense your work makes is for the reader to ascertain, not you. You are a beacon, a transmitter."

☐ PLATONIC 3WAY PRESS

P.O. Box 844, Warsaw IN 46581. (317)457-3505. E-mail: mail@platonic3waypress.com. Web site: www.Platonic3WayPress.com. Established 2005. **Contact:** Steve Henn, Oren Wagner, and Don Winter, co-editors.

Book/Chapbook Needs Platonic 3Way Press wants "poetry that celebrates honesty and humor, poetry with some bite to it." Does not want "cute bunny poems, overtly political poems, knee-jerk, poorly executed anti-(fill in the blank) poems." Publishes 1 chapbook/year. Manuscript selected through the Evil Genius Chapbook Contest only (see separate listing in Contests & Awards). "Winners selected by votes of the 3 editors." Chapbooks are 16-30 pages, high resolution photocopied, usually saddle-stapled, with cardstock cover and graphics that "vary according to the project."

How to Submit Submissions accepted through the Evil Genius Chapbook Contest only (see separate listing in Contests & Awards).

Also Offers *Fight These Bastards*, a journal of literature and art (see separate listing in Magazines/Journals) as well as the Painfully Platonic chapbook series (submissions by invitation only).

Advice "Looking for the poetry of revolt—against the Academy, against the poetic mainstream. Looking for poetry accessible beyond the ivory towers of academia and outside the bonds of religious or politically correct restrictions."

✪ $☑ POETIC MATRIX PRESS

P.O. Box 1223, Madera CA 93639. (559)673-9402. E-mail: poeticmatrix@yahoo.com. Web site: www.poeticmatrix.com. Established 1997. **Contact:** John Peterson, editor/publisher.

Book/Chapbook Needs Poetic Matrix Press publishes books (70-120 pages). "Poetic Matrix Press hosts a Slim Volume Series call for submissions of manuscripts every 2 years of between 70-80 pages. The manuscript selected will be published with full-color cover, perfect binding, and ISBN. The selected poet will receive 100 copies of the completed book and a $200 honorarium."

How to Submit Guidelines and submission dates available for SASE or by e-mail. **Charges reading fee for Slim Volume Series submissions only.** For chapbook and book information, contact the publisher. "Inquire about Author Assisted Financial Development publications for additional publishing options."

Advice "We seek writing of quality, with passion and intelligence."

🌐 ☑ ☑ POETRY SALZBURG

University of Salzburg, Dept. of English, Akademiestrasse 24, Salzburg A-5020 Austria. (43)(662)8044-4422. Fax: (43)(662)8044-167. E-mail: editor@poetrysalzburg.com. Web site: www. poetrysalzburg.com. Established 1971 (as University of Salzburg Press). **Contact:** Dr. Wolfgang Goertschacher, editor.

Book/Chapbook Needs Poetry Salzburg publishes "collections of at least 100 pages by mainly poets not taken up by big publishers." Publishes 6-8 paperbacks/year. Books are usually 100-350 pages, A5, professionally printed, perfect-bound, with card covers.

How to Submit Query first, with a few sample poems and a cover letter with brief bio and publication credits. Suggests authors publish in *Poetry Salzburg Review* (see separate listing in Magazines/Journals) first. Responds to queries in 4 weeks; to mss in about 3 months. Payment varies.

Ⓝ ☺ PRESA :S: PRESS

PO Box 792, Rockford MI 49341. Estab. 2003. E-mail: presapress@aol.com. Web site: www.presapress.com. **Contact:** Roseanne Ritzema, assistant editor.

Book/Chapbook Needs Presa :S: Press publishes "perfect-bound paperbacks and saddle-stitched chapbooks of poetry." Wants "imagistic poetry where form is an extension of content, surreal, experimental, and personal poetry." Does not want "overtly political or didactic material." Has published poetry books by Kirby Congdon, Hugh Fox, Eric Greinke, Lyn Lifshin, Stanley Nelson, and A.D. Winans. Publishes 3 poetry books/year, 3 chapbooks/year, and an anthology. Manuscripts are selected through open submission. Books are 84-144 pages, laser-printed on 24 lb. paper, perfect-bound paperback with a laminated, color art cover. Chapbooks are 40-60 pages, laser-printed on 20-24 lb. paper, saddle-stitched with a color art cover. Anthologies are 250-325 pages, laser-printed, perfect-bound paperback with a laminated color art cover.

How to Submit Query first, with a few sample poems and a cover letter with brief bio and publication credits. Book/chapbook mss may include previously published poems. Responds to queries in 2-4 weeks; to mss in 8-12 weeks. Pays 25 author's copies out of a press run of 500.

☺ ◎ ☑ PRESS HERE (Specialized: haiku, tanka)

22230 NE 28th Place, Sammamish WA 98074-6408. E-mail: WelchM@aol.com. Established 1989. **Contact:** Michael Dylan Welch, editor/publisher.

• Press Here publications have won the 1st-place Merit Book Award and other awards from the Haiku Society of America.

Book/Chapbook Needs Press Here publishes award-winning books of haiku, tanka, and related poetry by the leading poets of these genres, as well as essays, criticism, and interviews about these genres. "We publish work only by those poets who are already frequently published in the leading haiku and tanka journals." Does not want any poetry other than haiku, tanka, and related genres. Has published poetry by Lee Gurga, paul m., Paul O. Williams, Pat Shelley, Cor van den Heuvel, and William J. Higginson. Publishes 2-3 poetry books/year, plus occasional books of essays or interviews. Manuscripts are selected through open submission. Books are 32-112 pages, offset-printed, perfect-bound, with glossy paperback covers.

How to Submit Query first, with a few sample poems and a cover letter with brief bio and publication credits. Book mss may include previously published poems ("previous publication strongly preferred"). "All proposals must be by well-established haiku or tanka poets, and must be for haiku or tanka poetry, or criticism/discussion of these genres. If the editor does not already know your work well from leading haiku and tanka publications, then he is not likely to be interested in your manuscript." Responds to queries in up to 1 month; to mss in up to 2 months. Pays a negotiated percentage of author's copies (out of a press run of 200-1,000). Catalog available for #10 SASE.

Advice "Press Here publishes only 2-3 titles per year by leading haiku and tanka poets. For Press Here to publish your book, you will likely already know other Press Here books and the work of their authors, and the editor would most likely already know you and your work. If not, then establish yourself in these genres first by publishing extensively in the leading haiku or tanka journals."

◎ PRINCETON UNIVERSITY PRESS (Specialized: poetry in translation only)

41 William St., Princeton NJ 08540. (609)258-4900. Fax: (609)258-6305. Web site: www.press.princ eton.edu. **Contact:** Hanne Winarsky, editor.

Book/Chapbook Needs "The Lockert Library of Poetry in Translation embraces a wide geographic and temporal range, from Scandinavia to Latin America to the subcontinent of India, from the Tang Dynasty to Europe of the modern day. It especially emphasizes poets who are established in their native lands and who are being introduced to an English-speaking audience. The series, nearly all of whose titles are bilingual editions, calls attention to some of the most widely-praised poetry available today. In the Lockert Library series, each book is given individual design treatment rather than stamped into a series mold. We have published a wide range of poets from other cultures, including well-known writers such as Hölderlin and Cavafy, and those who have not yet had their due in English translation, such as Göran Sonnevi. Manuscripts are judged with several criteria in mind: the ability of the translation to stand on its own as poetry in English; fidelity to the tone and spirit of the original, rather than literal accuracy; and the importance of the translated poet to the literature of his or her time and country."

How to Submit Submit hard copy of proposal with sample poems or full ms. Cover letter is required. Reads submissions year round. Manuscripts will not be returned. Comments on finalists only. Responds in 3-4 months.

☑ THE PUDDIN'HEAD PRESS

P.O. Box 477889, Chicago IL 60647. (708)656-4900. E-mail: phbooks@compuserve.com. Web site: www.puddinheadpress.com. Established 1985. **Contact:** David Gecic, editor-in-chief.

Book/Chapbook Needs The Puddin'head Press is interested in "well-rounded poets who can support their work with readings and appearances." Wants "quality poetry by active poets who read and lead interesting lives. We occasionally publish chapbook-style anthologies and let poets on our mailing lists know what type of work we're interested in for a particular project." Does not want experimental, overly political poetry, or poetry with overt sexual content; no shock or novelty poems. Has published poetry by Jared Smith, Carol Anderson, Larry Janowski, Sandy Goldsmith, and Norman Porter. Puddin'head Press publishes 2-3 books and 2-3 chapbooks per year. Books/ chapbooks are 30-100 pages, perfect-bound or side-stapled ("we use various formats").

How to Submit "Please e-mail us for submission guidelines." Poets must include SASE with submission. Responds to queries in 2 months; to mss in 6 months. Pays various royalty rates "depending on the publication. We usually have a press run of 500 books." **About 10% of books are author subsidy-published.** Terms vary. Order sample books/chapbooks by sending $10 (price plus postage) to The Puddin'head Press (also available through Amazon). "Please visit our Web site and see what we publish."

Additional Information "In the last several years we have been increasingly active across the country. There are numerous readings and events that we sponsor. We do our own distribution, primarily in the Midwest, and also do distribution for other small presses. Please send a SASE for a list of our current publications and publication/distribution guidelines. We sell poetry books, not just print them. Submitted poetry is evaluated for its marketability and quality."

Also Offers "Extensive Web site with rare and used books, extensive links to who's who in poetry and online marketing."

Advice "It is difficult to find a quality publisher. Poets must have patience and find a press that will work with them. A good relationship between poet and publisher is important. Many good books will never be seen because the poet/publisher relationship is not healthy. If a poet is involved in the literary world, he will find a publisher, or a publisher will find him."

$☑ ☑ QED PRESS/CYPRESS HOUSE

155 Cypress St., Fort Bragg CA 95437. (800)773-7782. Fax: (707)964-7531. E-mail: joeshaw@cypres shouse.com. Web site: www.cypresshouse.com. Established 1985. **Contact:** Joe Shaw, editor.

Book/Chapbook Needs QED Press publishes "clear, clean, intelligent, and moving work." Wants "concrete, personal, and spare writing. No florid rhymed verse." Has published poetry by Victoria Greenleaf, Luke Breit, Paula Tennant (Adams), and Cynthia Frank. Publishes 1-2 paperback poetry books/year. Books are usually about 100 pages (75-80 poems), digest-sized, offset-printed, perfect-bound, with full-color covers.

How to Submit ''We prefer to see ten representative poems.'' Considers simultaneous submissions. Cover letter and SASE for return of materials are required. Time between acceptance and publication is up to 1 year. Poems are circulated to an editorial board. Responds to queries and mss in 1 month. Pays royalties of 7-12% and 25 author's copies (out of a press run of 500-1,000). Order sample books through Web site.

Also Offers Book packaging, and promotion and marketing services to start-up publishers. ''We are not a vanity press.''

$☑ ◎ ☑RATTAPALLAX PRESS (Specialized: the diversity of world cultures)

532 La Guardia Place, Suite 353, New York NY 10012. E-mail: info@rattapallax.com. Web site: www.rattapallax.com. Established 1998. **Contact:** Poetry Editor.

Book/Chapbook Needs Rattapallax Press publishes ''contemporary poets and writers with unique, powerful voices.'' Publishes 5 paperbacks and 3 chapbooks/year. Books are usually 64 pages, digest-sized, offset-printed, perfect-bound, with 12-pt. CS1 covers.

How to Submit Query first, with a few sample poems and cover letter with brief bio and publication credits. Include SASE. Requires authors to first be published in *Rattapallax* (see separate listing in Magazines/Journals). Responds to queries in 1 month; to mss in 2 months. Pays royalties of 10-25%. Order sample books from Web site.

◙ ◎ ☑RED MOON PRESS (Specialized: English-language haiku & related forms)

P.O. Box 2461, Winchester VA 22604-1661. (540)722-2156. E-mail: jim.kacian@redmoonpress.com. Web site: www.redmoonpress.com. Established 1993. **Contact:** Jim Kacian, editor/publisher.

Book/Chapbook Needs Red Moon Press ''is the largest and most prestigious publisher of English-language haiku and related work in the world.'' Publishes 6-8 volumes/year, usually 3-5 anthologies and individual collections of English-language haiku, as well as 1-3 books of essays, translations, or criticism of haiku. Under other imprints, the press also publishes chapbooks of various sizes and formats.

How to Submit Query with book theme and information, and 30-40 poems or draft of first chapter. Responds to queries in 2 weeks, to mss (if invited) in 3 months. ''Each contract separately negotiated.''

Advice ''Haiku is a burgeoning and truly international form. It is nothing like what your fourth-grade teacher taught you years ago, and so it is best if you familiarize yourself with what is happening in the genre (and its close relatives) today before submitting. We strive to give all the work we publish plenty of space in which to resonate, and to provide a forum where the best of today's practitioners can be published with dignity and prestige. All our books have either won awards or are awaiting notification. We intend to work hard to keep it that way.''

⬕ $◙ ◎ ☑RONSDALE PRESS (Specialized: Canadian poets only)

3350 W. 21st Ave., Vancouver BC V6S 1G7 Canada. (604)738-4688. Fax: (604)731-4548. E-mail: ronsdale@shaw.ca. Web site: www.ronsdalepress.com. Established 1988. **Contact:** Ronald B. Hatch, director.

Book/Chapbook Needs Publishes 3 flat-spined paperbacks of poetry per year—**by Canadian poets only**—classical to experimental. ''Ronsdale looks for poetry manuscripts that show the writer reads and is familiar with the work of some of the major contemporary poets. It's also essential that you have published some poems in literary magazines. We have never published a book of poetry when the author has not already published a goodly number in magazines.'' Has published *Return to Open Water* by Harold Rhenisch, *Mother Time* by Joanne Arnott, *Cobalt 3* by Kevin Roberts, *Poems for a New World* by Connie Fife, *Steveston* by Daphne Marlatt, and *After Ted & Sylvia* by Crystal Hurdle.

How to Submit Query first, with a few sample poems and cover letter with brief bio and publication credits. Considers previously published poems and simultaneous submissions. Often comments on rejected poems. Responds to queries in 2 weeks, to mss in 2 months. Pays 10% royalties and 10 author's copies. Write for catalog to purchase sample books.

Advice "Ronsdale looks for Canadian poetry with echoes from previous poets. To our mind, the contemporary poet must be well-read."

ROSE ALLEY PRESS
4203 Brooklyn Ave. NE, #103A, Seattle WA 98105-5911. (206)633-2725. E-mail: rosealleypress@jun o.com. Web site: www.rosealleypress.com. Established 1995. **Contact:** David D. Horowitz, editor/ publisher.
- Rose Alley Press does not presently read unsolicited manuscripts.

$☐ ◎ ☑ SAM'S DOT PUBLISHING (Specialized: scifaiku, horror-ku, other minimalist poetry forms)
P.O. Box 782, Cedar Rapids IA 52406-0782. E-mail: gatrix65@yahoo.com. Web site: www.samsdotp ublishing.com. Established 2003. **Contact:** Tyree Campbell, managing editor. Member: The Speculative Literature Foundation.
Book/Chapbook Needs Sam's Dot Publishing prints collections of scifaiku, horror-ku, and minimalist poetry. Publishes 2-3 chapbooks/year and one anthology/year. Manuscripts are selected through open submission. Chapbooks are 32 pages, offset-printed, saddle-stapled, with cardstock covers.
How to Submit Query first, with a few sample poems and a cover letter with brief bio and publication credits. Chapbook mss may include previously published poems. Responds to queries in 2 weeks; to mss in 4-6 weeks. Pays royalties of 12.5% minimum and 1-2 author's copies (out of a press run of 50-100). Order sample chapbooks by sending $8 to Tyree Campbell/Sam's Dot Publishing.
Advice "It's up to the writer to take the first step and submit work. Some of our best poems have come from poets who weren't sure if they were good enough. A basic knowledge of writing traditional haiku is helpful."

★ ◨ ☑ SARABANDE BOOKS, INC.
2234 Dundee Rd., Suite 200, Louisville KY 40205. (502)458-4028. Fax: (502)458-4065. E-mail: info@ sarabandebooks.org. Web site: www.SarabandeBooks.org. Established 1994. **Contact:** Sarah Gorham, editor-in-chief. Member: CLMP.
Book/Chapbook Needs Sarabande Books publishes books of poetry of 48 pages minimum. Wants "poetry that offers originality of voice and subject matter, uniqueness of vision, and a language that startles because of the careful attention paid to it—language that goes beyond the merely competent or functional." Has published poetry by Mark Jarman, Louise Glück, Charles Wright, Sydney Lea, Cleopatra Mathis, and Eleanor Lerman. Manuscripts are selected through open submission and competition. "At least half of our list is drawn from contest submissions to the Kathryn A. Morton Prize in Poetry."
How to Submit Query first, with 10 sample poems and cover letter with brief bio and publication credits. Include SASE. **Open reading period for non-contest submissions:** September only. Guidelines available for SASE, by e-mail, or on Web site.
Contest/Award Listings The Kathryn A. Morton Prize in Poetry (see separate listing).
Advice "We recommend that you request our catalog and familiarize yourself with our books. Our complete list shows a variety of style and subject matter."

☐ ☑ SEAWEED SIDESHOW CIRCUS
P.O. Box 234, Jackson WI 53037. (414)791-1109. Fax: (262)644-0249. E-mail: sscircus@aol.com. Web site: http://hometown.aol.com/SSCircus/sscweb.html. Established 1994. **Contact:** Andrew Wright Milam, editor.
Book/Chapbook Needs Seaweed Sideshow Circus is "a place for young or new poets to publish a chapbook." Has published *Main Street* by Steven Paul Lansky and *The Moon Incident* by Amy McDonald. Publishes one chapbook/year. Chapbooks are usually 30 pages, digest-sized, photocopied, saddle-stapled, with cardstock covers.
How to Submit Query first, with 5-10 sample poems and cover letter with brief bio and publications credits. Responds to queries in 3 weeks; to mss in 3 months. Pays 10 author's copies (out of a press run of 100). Order sample chapbooks by sending $6.

⊕ ✉ SECOND AEON PUBLICATIONS

19 Southminster Rd., Roath, Cardiff CF23 5AT Wales. Phone/fax: (44)(29)2049-3093. E-mail: peter @peterfinch.co.uk. Web site: www.peterfinch.co.uk. Established 1966. **Contact:** Peter Finch, poetry editor.

- Does not accept unsolicited mss.

✉ STEEL TOE BOOKS

Western Kentucky University, 1906 College Heights Blvd. #11086, Bowling Green KY 42101-1086. (270)745-5769. E-mail: tom.hunley@wku.edu. Web site: www.steeltoebooks.com. Established 2003. **Contact:** Dr. Tom C. Hunley, director.

Book/Chapbook Needs Steel Toe Books publishes ''full-length, single-author poetry collections. Our books are professionally designed and printed. We look for workmanship (economical use of language, high-energy verbs, precise literal descriptions, original figurative language, poems carefully arranged as a book); a unique style and/or a distinctive voice; clarity; emotional impact; humor (word plays, hyperbole, comic timing); performability (a Steel Toe poet is at home on the stage as well as on the page).'' Does not want ''dry verse, purposely obscure language, poetry by people who are so wary of being called 'sentimental' they steer away from any recognizable human emotions, poetry that takes itself so seriously that it's unintentionally funny.'' Has published poetry by James Doyle, Jennifer Gresham, Ken Waldman, Martha Silano, Mary Biddinger, John Guzlowski, and Jeannine Hall Gailey. Publishes 1-3 poetry books/year. Manuscripts are selected through open submission. Books are 48-64 pages, perfect-bound, with full-color covers with art/graphics.

How to Submit ''Check the Web site for news about our next open reading period.'' Book mss may include previously published poems. Responds to mss in 3 months. Pays 20% royalties and 10 author's copies. Order sample books by sending $12 to Steel Toe Books.

✉ SWAN SCYTHE PRESS

2052 Calaveras Ave., Davis CA 95616-3021. E-mail: sandyjmc@mindspring.com. Web site: www.s wanscythe.com. Established 1999. **Contact:** Sandra McPherson, editor/publisher.

- Swan Scythe Press has been awarded a California Arts Council Multicultural Entry Grant and a Fideicomiso para la Cultura Mexico-EUA/US-Mexico Fund for Culture Grant.

Book/Chapbook Needs ''After publishing 25 chapbooks, a few full-sized poetry collections, and 1 anthology, Swan Scythe Press is resting. **We cannot at this time consider manuscripts**, but our books are still for sale. A multi-ethnic press primarily publishing emerging writers, we have also published established poets such as Ted Joans and Jordan Smith.'' Has published poetry by Emmy Pérez, Maria Melendez, John Olivares Espinoza, Karen An-hwei Lee, Pos Moua, and Walter Pavlich. Order sample books/chapbooks by sending $11 to Swan Scythe Press or order through Web site.

How to Submit *Not considering mss at this time.*

✪ $◻ ✉ SYNERGEBOOKS (Specialized: poetry with religious overtones)

1235 Flat Shoals Rd., King NC 27021. (336)994-2405. Fax: (336)994-8403. E-mail: inquiries@synerg ebooks.com. Web site: www.synergebooks.com. Established 1999. **Contact:** Deb Staples, acquisitions editor. Member: EPIC; PMA.

Book/Chapbook Needs SynergEbooks specializes in ''quality works by talented new writers in every available digital format, including CD-ROMs and paperback. Poetry must have a very unique twist or theme and must be edited. We are looking specifically for poetry with religious overtones.'' Does not accept unedited work. Has published poetry by Theresa Jodray, Brenda Roberts, Vanyell Delacroix, Joel L. Young, and Chuck Kelly. SynergEbooks publishes up to 40 titles/year, less than 1% of them poetry. Books are usually 45-150 pages, print-on-demand, with paperback binding. ''There is no guarantee that a book will be put into print.''

How to Submit Query by e-mail preferred, with a few sample poems and a cover letter with brief bio and publication credits. ''We prefer no simultaneous submissions, but inform us if this is the case.'' Accepts e-mail submissions (as attachment) only. ''Please do not send poetry via postal mail. Valid, working e-mail address is required.'' Guidelines available on Web site. Responds to queries in 1 month; to mss in up to 5 months. Pays royalties of 15-40% for electronic formats; up to 30% for paperbacks.

Book/Chapbook Publishers

Advice "We are inundated with more poetry than prose every month; but we will accept the occasional anthology with a unique twist that is original and high quality. New poets welcome."

✅ ⊚ TARPAULIN SKY PRESS (Specialized: cross- & trans-genre work)

P.O. Box 190, Saxtons River, VT 05154. E-mail: editors@tarpaulinsky.com (inquiries). Web site: www.tarpaulinsky.com. Established 2006. **Contact:** Elena Georgiou and Christian Peet, editors.

Book/Chapbook Needs Tarpaulin Sky Press publishes cross- and trans-genre works as well as innovative poetry and prose. Produces full-length books and chapbooks, hand-bound books and trade paperbacks, and offers both hand-bound and perfect-bound paperback editions of full-length books. "We're a small, author-centered press endeavoring to create books that, as objects, please our authors as much their texts please us." Has published books and chapbooks by Jenny Boully, Danielle Dutton, Joyelle McSweeney, Chad Sweeney, Andrew Michael Roberts, and Max Winter, as well as a collaborative book by Noah Eli Gordon as Joshua Marie Wilkinson.

How to Submit Writers whose work has appeared in or been accepted for publication in *Tarpaulin Sky* (see separate listing in Magazines/Journals) may submit chapbook or full-length manuscripts at any time, with no reading fee. Tarpaulin Sky Press also considers chapbook and full-length manuscripts from writers whose work has not appeared in the journal, but **asks for a $20 reading fee**. Make checks/money orders to Tarpaulin Sky Press. Cover letter is preferred. Reads periods may be found on the Web site.

✅ ☑ TEBOT BACH

P.O. Box 7887, Huntington Beach CA 92615-7887. (714)968-0905. E-mail: info@tebotbach.org. Web site: www.tebotbach.org. **Contact:** Mifanwy Kaiser, editor/publisher.

Book/Chapbook Needs Tebot Bach (Welsh for "little teapot") publishes books of poetry. Has published *The House in the Heart* by Willie James King, *Swagger and Remorse* by Richard Fox, *Dragon Ship* by Daniel F. Polikoff, and *A Café in Boca* by Sam Pereira.

How to Submit Query first, with a few sample poems and cover letter with brief bio and publication credits. Include SASE. Responds to queries and mss, if invited, in 3 months. Time between acceptance and publication is up to 2 years. Write to order sample books.

Contest/Award Offerings The Patricia Bibby First Book Award (see separate listing in Contests & Awards).

Also Offers An anthology of California poets, published annually in April. Must be current or former resident of California in order to submit, but no focus or theme required for poetry. Submit up to 6 poems with "California Anthology" written on lower left corner of envelope. Accepts submissions by e-mail (pasted into body of message or as attachment in Word). Deadline for submission is in August. Also publishes *Spillway: A Literary Journal* (see separate listing in Magazines/Journals).

$ ✅ ☑ TOKYO ROSE RECORDS/CHAPULTEPEC PRESS

4222 Chambers, Cincinnati OH 45223. E-mail: chapultepecpress@hotmail.com. Web site: www.TokyoRoseRecords.com. Established 2001. **Contact:** David Garza.

Book/Chapbook Needs Chapultepec Press publishes books of poetry/literature, essays, social/political issues, art, music, film, history, popular science; library/archive issues, and bilingual works. Wants "poetry that works as a unit, that is caustic, fun, open-ended, worldly, mature, relevant, stirring, evocative. Bilingual. Looking for authors who have a publishing history. No poetry collections without a purpose, that are mere collections. Also looking for broadsides/posters/illuminations." Publishes 1-2 books/year. Books are usually 1-100 pages.

How to Submit Query first with a few sample poems, or a complete ms, and a cover letter with brief bio and publication credits. Pays advance or author's copies. Order sample books by sending $4 payable to David Garza.

☑ THE UNIVERSITY OF CHICAGO PRESS

1427 E. 60th St., Chicago IL 60637. (773)702-7700. Fax: (773)702-2705. Web site: www.press.uchicago.edu. Established 1891. **Contact:** Randolph Petilos, poetry editor.

● Submissions by invitation only!

Book/Chapbook Needs The University of Chicago Press publishes scholarly books and journals. "We may only publish 4 books of new poems in the Phoenix Poets series per year, and perhaps 4 books of poetry in translation per year. We occasionally publish a book of poems outside Phoenix Poets, or as a reprint from other houses." Has published poetry by Connie Voisine, Matthew Schwartz, Elise Partridge, Gabriela Mistral, Luis de Góngora, and Andrea Zanzotto.

How to Submit *By invitation only.* No unsolicited mss.

▣ ◔ ◎ ☑ VEHICULE PRESS (Specialized: work by Canadian poets only)

P.O. Box 125 Station Place du Parc, Montreal QC H2X 4A3 Canada. (514)844-6073. Fax: (514)844-7543. E-mail: vp@vehiculepress.com. Web site: www.vehiculepress.com. **Contact:** Carmine Starnino, poetry editor.

Book/Chapbook Needs Vehicule Press is a "literary press with a poetry series, Signal Editions, publishing the work of Canadian poets only." Publishes flat-spined paperbacks. Has published *How We All Swiftly* by Don Coles, *Red Ledger* by Mary Dalton, and *Reaching for Clear* by David Solway. Publishes Canadian poetry that is "first-rate, original, content-conscious."

How to Submit Query before submitting.

$☑ ◎ WASHINGTON WRITERS' PUBLISHING HOUSE (Specialized: Washington, D.C.- and Baltimore-area poets only)

P.O. Box 15271, Washington D.C., 20003. Web site: www.washingtonwriters.org. Established 1973. **Contact:** Moira Egan, president. Member: CLMP.

● Individual books by WWPH authors have been nominated for and/or won many awards, e.g. the Towson University Prize.

Book/Chapbook Needs Washington Writers' Publishing House publishes books by Washington, D.C.- and Baltimore-area poets through its annual book competition. "No specific criteria, except literary excellence." Has published books by Carly Sachs, Piotr Gwiazda, Moira Egan, Jane Satterfield, Jean Nordhaus, and Gray Jacobik. Publishes 1-2 poetry books/year.

How to Submit Washington Writers' Publishing House considers book-length mss for publication by poets living within 60 driving miles of the U.S. Capitol (Baltimore area included) through competition only (see below).

Contest/Award Offerings Offers $500 and 100 copies of published book. Manuscripts may include previously published poems. Submit 3 copies of a poetry ms of 50-60 pages, single-spaced (poet's name should not appear on ms pages). Include separate page of publication acknowledgments plus 2 cover sheets: one with ms title, poet's name, address, telephone number, and e-mail address, the other with ms title only. Include SASE for results only; mss will not be returned (will be recycled). Guidelines available for SASE or on Web site. **Entry fee:** $20. **Deadline:** July 1-November 1 (postmark). Order sample books by sending $12 plus $2 s&h to Washington Writers' Publishing House, P.O. Box 15271, Washington DC 20003.

Advice "Washington Writers' Publishing House is a nonprofit cooperative poetry press reflecting the cultural and racial diversity of the Greater Washington-Baltimore area. The winning poet becomes a member of the organization and should be prepared to participate actively in the work of the press, including such areas as publicity, distribution, production, and fundraising. Our tradition of poets actively working on behalf of other poets is essential to the continued vitality and success of WWPH. Contest entrants should be willing to make this commitment should their work be selected for publication. Membership in WWPH is an opportunity to work together with many of the best writers in the region."

$◎ ☑ WEST END PRESS (Specialized: social/political concerns; multicultural)

P.O. Box 27334, Albuquerque NM 87125. (505)345-5729. Established 1976. **Contact:** John Crawford, publisher.

Book/Chapbook Needs West End Press publishes poetry, fiction, and drama with a social/cultural interest. Open as to form. Does not want "purely aesthetic, precious, self-involved poetry." Has published poetry by Laura Tohe, Joseph Bruchac, Charles Potts, and Michael Henson. Publishes 2

poetry books/year; occasional chapbooks and anthologies. Books/chapbooks are 48-96 pages, off-set-printed, perfect-bound, with glossy 4-color covers.
How to Submit Query first, with a few sample poems and a cover letter with brief bio and publication credits. Book/chapbook mss may include previously published poems. Responds to queries in 6 weeks; to mss in 3 months. Pays royalties of 6%; 10% author's copies (out of a press run of 600-1,500). Order sample books/chapbooks postage-free by sending $8.95 to West End Press.
Advice "We prefer crude vigor to polished banality."

☑ ☑ WHITE EAGLE COFFEE STORE PRESS

P.O. Box 383, Fox River Grove IL 60021-0383. E-mail: WECSPress@aol.com. Web site: http://members.aol.com/wecspress. Established 1992.
Book/Chapbook Needs White Eagle is a small press publishing 2-3 chapbooks/year. "Alternate chapbooks are published by invitation and by competition. Author published by invitation becomes judge for next competition." Wants "any kind of poetry. No censorship at this press. Literary values are the only standard." Does not want "sentimental or didactic writing." Has published poetry by Timothy Russell, Connie Donovan, Scott Lumbard, Linda Lee Harper, Scott Beal, Katie Kingston, and Brian Brodeur. Sample: $6.95.
How to Submit *Regular submissions by invitation only.*
Contest/Award Offerings Winner receives $500 and 25 author's copies. All entrants will receive a copy of the winning chapbook. Considers previously published poems and simultaneous submissions, with notice. Submit complete chapbook ms (20-24 pages), paginated, with table of contents. Poet's name should not appear on ms pages. Include 2 cover sheets: 1 with ms title, poet's name, address, phone number, and brief biography; second with ms title and 125-word statement about poet's work to be included in chapbook (poet's name should not appear on second cover sheet). Include list of credits for previously published poems. No e-mail submissions. Include SASE for results only; mss will not be returned. Guidelines available for SASE or on Web site. **Entry fee:** $15. **Deadline:** October 31 (postmark) for 2008. "Each competition is judged by either the author of the most recent chapbook published by invitation or by previous competition winners." Responds 3 months after deadline.
Advice "Poetry is about a passion for language. That's what we're about. We'd like to provide an opportunity for poets of any age who are fairly early in their careers to publish something substantial. We're excited by the enthusiasm shown for this press and by the extraordinary quality of the writing we've received."

☑ ◎ ☑ WOODLEY MEMORIAL PRESS (Specialized: work by KS poets)

English Dept., Washburn University, 1700 SW College Ave., Topeka KS 66621. E-mail: karen.barron @washburn.edu. Web site: www.washburn.edu/reference/woodley-press. Established 1980. **Contact:** Paul Fecteau, managing editor.
Book/Chapbook Needs Woodley Memorial Press publishes 1-2 flat-spined paperbacks/year, "most being collections of poets from Kansas or with Kansas connections. Terms are individually arranged with author on acceptance of manuscript." Has published *Rebecca Orders Lasagna* by John Jenkinson, *Thailand Journal* by Denise Low, and *Kansas Poems of William Stafford*. Sample books may be ordered from Woodley Memorial Press.
How to Submit Guidelines available on Web site. Responds to queries in 2 weeks; to mss in 6 months. Time between acceptance and publication is 1 year.
Advice "We look for experienced writers who are part of their writing and reading communities."

Contests & Awards

This section contains a wide array of poetry competitions and literary awards. These range from state poetry society contests (with a number of modest monetary prizes) to prestigious honors bestowed by private foundations, elite publishers and renowned university programs. Because these listings reflect such a variety of skill levels and degrees of competitiveness, it's important to read each carefully and note its unique requirements. *Never* enter a contest without consulting the guidelines and following directions to the letter (including manuscript formatting, number of lines or pages of poetry accepted, amount of entry fee, entry forms needed and other details).

Important note: As we gathered information for this edition of *Poet's Market*, we found that some competitions hadn't yet established their 2009 fees and deadlines. In such cases, we list the most recent information available as a general guide. Always consult current guidelines for updates before entering any competition.

WHERE TO ENTER?

While it's perfectly okay to "think big," being realistic may improve your chances of winning a prize for your poetry. Many of the listings in the Contests & Awards section begin with symbols that reflect their level of difficulty:

Contests ideal for beginners and unpublished poets are coded with the (◻) symbol. That's not to say these contests won't be highly competitive—there may be a large number of entries. However, you may find these entries are more on a level with your own, increasing your chances of being "in the running" for a prize. Don't assume these contests reward low quality, though. If you submit less than your best work, you're wasting your time and money (in postage and entry fees).

Contests for poets with more experience are coded with the (◐) symbol. Beginner/unpublished poets are usually still welcome to enter, but the competition is keener here. Your work may be judged against that of widely published, prize-winning poets, so consider carefully whether you're ready for this level of competition. (Of course, nothing ventured, nothing gained—but those entry fees *do* add up.)

Contests for accomplished poets are coded with the (◕) symbol. These may have stricter entry requirements, higher entry fees and other conditions that signal these programs are not intended to be "wide open" to all poets.

Specialized contests are coded with the (◉) symbol. These may include regional contests; awards for poetry written in a certain form or in the style of a certain poet; contests for women, gay/lesbian, ethnic, or age-specific poets (for instance, children or older adults); contests for translated poetry only; and many others.

There are also symbols that give additional information about contests. The (ⓝ) symbol indicates the contest is newly established and new to *Poet's Market*; the (⭐) symbol indicates this contest did not appear in the 2008 edition; the (⬥) symbol identifies a Canadian contest or award and the (🌐) symbol an international listing. Sometimes Canadian and international contests require that entrants live in certain countries, so pay attention when you see these symbols.

ADDITIONAL CONTESTS & AWARDS

Contest information also appears in listings in other sections of the book (Magazines/Journals, Book/Chapbook Publishers, Conferences, Workshops & Festivals and Organizations). To make sure you don't overlook these opportunities, we've cross-referenced them under Additional Contests & Awards at the back of this section. For details about a contest associated with a market in this list, go to that market's page number.

WHAT ABOUT ENTRY FEES?

Most contests charge entry fees, and these are usually quite legitimate. The funds are used to cover expenses such as paying the judges, putting up prize monies, printing prize editions of magazines and journals, and promoting the contest through mailings and ads. If you're concerned about a poetry contest or other publishing opportunity, see "Is It a 'Con'?" on page 36 for advice on some of the more questionable practices in the poetry world.

OTHER RESOURCES

Widen your search for contests beyond those listed in *Poet's Market*. Many Internet writer's sites have late-breaking announcements about competitions old and new (see Additional Resources on page 466). Often these sites offer free electronic newsletter subscriptions, sending valuable information right to your e-mail inbox.

The writer's magazines at your local bookstore regularly include listings for upcoming contests, as well as deadlines for artist's grants at the state and national level. (See Additional Resources on page 466 for a few suggestions; also, Grants on page 424.) The Association of Writers & Writing Programs (AWP) is a valuable resource, including its publication, *Writer's Chronicle*. (See Organizations, page 445.) State poetry societies are listed throughout this book; they offer many contests, as well as helpful information for poets (and mutual support). To find a specific group, search the General Index for listings under your state's name or look under "poetry society" or "society."

Don't overlook your local connections. City and community newspapers, radio and TV announcements, bookstore newsletters and bulletin boards, and your public library can be terrific resources for competition news, especially regarding regional contests.

ADDITIONAL FEATURES

The Contests & Awards section includes an Insider Report in which **Amy Ratto Parks** tackles how to handle the personal artist statement in writing residency applications (page 388).

$✍ AKRON POETRY PRIZE

The University of Akron Press, Akron OH 44325-1703. (330)972-5342. Fax: (330)972-8364. E-mail: uapress@uakron.edu. Web site: www.uakron.edu/uapress. **Contact:** Elton Glaser, award director. Offers annual award of $1,000 plus publication of a book-length ms. Submissions must be unpublished. Considers simultaneous submissions (with notification of acceptance elsewhere). Submit 60-100 pages maximum, typed, single-spaced or double-spaced, with SASE for results. Manuscripts will not be returned. Do not send mss bound or enclosed in covers. Guidelines available for SASE or by fax, e-mail, or on Web site. **Entry fee:** $25. **Deadline:** entries accepted May 15-June 30 only. Competition receives 450-550 entries. 2007 winner ws Brian Brodeur (*Other Latitudes*). 2008 judge: Rita Dove. Winner will be announced in September by letter (if SASE enclosed with entry) or on Web site. Copies of winning books are available from UAP or through your local bookstore. The University of Akron Press "is committed to publishing poetry that, as Robert Frost said, 'begins in delight and ends in wisdom.' Books accepted must exhibit 3 essential qualities: mastery of language, maturity of feeling, and complexity of thought."

$✍ AGHA SHAHID ALI PRIZE IN POETRY

The University of Utah Press, 1795 E. South Campus Dr., #101, Salt Lake City UT 84112. (801)581-6771. Fax: (801)581-3365. E-mail: sarah.hoffman@utah.edu. Web site: www.uofupress.com/Agha-Shahid-Ali. Established 2003. The University of Utah Press and the University of Utah Department of English offer an annual award of $1,000, publication of a book-length poetry ms, and a reading in the Guest Writers Series. Poems must be unpublished as a collection, but individual poems may have been previously published elsewhere. Considers simultaneous submissions; "however, entrants must notify the Press immediately if the collection submitted is accepted for publication elsewhere during the competition." Submit 48-64 typed pages of poetry, with no names or other identifying information appearing on title page or within ms. Include cover sheet with complete contact information (name, address, telephone, e-mail address). Submissions must be in English. Mss will not be returned; include SASE for notification only. Guidelines available on Web site. **Entry fee:** $25/book submission. **Deadline:** must be postmarked during February 1-March 31, 2008. Competition receives over 300 mss/year. 2007 winner was Susan McCabe. 2008 judge: Medbh McGuckian. Winner announced on press Web site after September 1; series editor contacts winning poet. Copies of winning books are available for $12.95 from University of Utah Press ((800)621-2736 for order fulfillment) or through Web site.

$ ALLIGATOR JUNIPER'S NATIONAL WRITING CONTEST

Prescott College, Prescott AZ 86301. E-mail: aj@prescott.edu. Web site: www.prescott.edu/highlights/alligator_juniper/index.html. Established 1995. *Alligator Juniper*, published annually in May, awards $500 each to first prize winners in poetry, fiction, and creative nonfiction. Additional winners selected for publication are paid 4 contributor's copies. Submissions must be unpublished. Considers simultaneous submissions ("inform us in your cover letter and contact us immediately if your work is accepted elsewhere"). Submit up to 5 poems at a time with reading fee (separate fee for each additional entry). Submissions must be typed with numbered pages; single-spaced okay for poetry entries. Cover letter is required with the following statement: "I have read and understand the guidelines for *Alligator Juniper*'s national writing contest." Include SASE for results only; mss are not returned. "All entrants receive a personal letter from one of our staff regarding the status of their submissions." No e-mail submissions. Guidelines available for SASE, by e-mail, or on Web site. **Entry fee:** $10/entry (5 poems or 5 pages of poetry). Each entrant receives a copy of *Alligator Juniper*, a $10 value. **Deadline:** submit May 1-October 1 (postmark). 2007 winner was Elton Glaser. Winner announced in late January. *Alligator Juniper* is available for $10.

$✍ THE AMERICAN POET PRIZE FOR POETRY

The American Poetry Journal, P.O. Box 2080, Aptos CA 95001-2080. E-mail: editor@americanpoetryjournal.com. Web site: www.americanpoetryjournal.com. Established 2004. **Contact:** J.P. Dancing Bear, editor. The American Poet Prize for Poetry offers $500 and publication in *The American Poetry*

Journal (see separate listing in Magazines/Journals). All entries will be considered for publication, and all entrants receive a year's subscription. Submissions must be unpublished. Considers simultaneous submissions with notification. Accepts multiple submissions with separate fee for each entry (3 poems). Submit up to 3 original poems (10 pages maximum total). Include cover with poem titles, poet's name, contact information (including e-mail address), and bio. Include SASP for confirmation of delivery of ms and SASE for results only. Guidelines available on Web site. **Entry fee:** $15; all entrants receive a year's subscription to *The American Poetry Journal.* Make checks payable to Dancing Bear. **Deadline:** June 30. Judge: all selections and winners made by the editor. Personal friends, relatives, and/or students of the editor are NOT eligible for the contest (their entry fees will be refunded).

$☑ THE AMERICAN POETRY JOURNAL BOOK PRIZE

P.O. Box 2080, Aptos CA 95001-2080. E-mail: editor@americanpoetryjournal.com. Web site: www.americanpoetryjournal.com. Established 2004. **Contact:** J.P. Dancing Bear, editor. *The American Poetry Journal* Book Prize awards $500 and book publication. Submit 48-60 paginated pages of poetry, table of contents, acknowledgments, bio, and e-mail address (for results). No SASE required; mss will be recycled. Guidelines available on Web site. **Entry fee:** $20. Make checks payable to J.P. Dancing Bear. **Deadline:** February 28 (check Web site for updates). 2006 winner was Theodore Worozbyt (*The Dauber Wings*).

$☑ THE AMERICAN POETRY REVIEW/HONICKMAN FIRST BOOK PRIZE

117 S. 17th St., Suite 910, Philadelphia PA 19103. (215)496-0439. Fax: (215)569-0808. Web site: www.aprweb.org. Established 1972. Annual award to encourage excellence in poetry, and to provide a wide readership for a deserving first book of poems. Offers $3,000, publication of a book-length ms, and distribution by Copper Canyon Press through Consortium. Open to U.S. citizens writing in English and who have not yet published a book-length collection of poems which was assigned an ISBN. Guidelines available on Web site. **Entry fee:** $25/book ms. **Deadline:** October 31. 2008 winner was Matthew Dickman (*All American Poem*). 2008 judge: Claudia Keelan.

$☑ ANABIOSIS PRESS CHAPBOOK CONTEST

2 South New St., Bradford MA 01835. (978)469-7085. E-mail: rsmyth@anabiosispress.org. Web site: www.anabiosispress.org. **Contact:** Richard Smyth, editor. The Anabiosis Press Chapbook Contest offers $100 plus publication of the winning chapbook and 75 copies of the first run. Submit 16-20 pages of poetry on any subject. Include separate pages with a biography, table of contents, and acknowledgments for any previous publications. Include SASE with correct postage for return of ms. **Entry fee:** $11 (all entrants receive a copy of the winning chapbook). Make checks payable to The Anabiosis Press. **Deadline:** June 30 (postmark). Winners announced by September 30. 2006 winner was Jackie White (*Bestiary Charming*).

$☑ THE ANHINGA PRIZE FOR POETRY

Anhinga Press, Tallahassee FL 32302. (850)442-1408. Fax: (850)442-6323. E-mail: info@anhinga.org. Web site: www.anhinga.org. Established 1973. **Contact:** Rick Campbell, poetry editor. The annual Anhinga Prize awards $2,000 and publication to a book-length poetry ms. Guidelines available for SASE or on Web site. **Entry fee:** $25. **Deadline:** submit February 15-May 1. Past judges include Donald Hall, Joy Harjo, Robert Dana, Reginald Shepherd, and Sidney Wade. Past winners include Frank X. Gaspar, Julia Levine, Keith Ratzlaff, and Lynn Aarti Chandhok.

$ARIZONA LITERARY CONTEST & BOOK AWARDS

Arizona Authors Association, 6145 W. Echo Lane, Glendale, AZ 85302. (623)847-9343. E-mail: info@azauthors.com. Web site: www.azauthors.com. **Contact:** Toby Heathcote, president. Arizona Authors Association sponsors annual literary contest in poetry, short story, essay, unpublished novels, and published books (fiction, nonfiction, and children's literature). Awards publication in *Arizona Literary Magazine*, publication of novel by AuthorHouse, and $100 1st Prize, $50 2nd Prize, and $25 3rd Prize in each category. Poetry submissions must be unpublished. Considers simultaneous submissions. Submit any number of poems on any subject up to 42 lines. Entry form and guidelines available for SASE. **Entry fee:** $10/poem. **Deadline:** reads submissions January 1-July 1. Competition receives 1,000 entries/year. Recent poetry winners include Cappy Love Hanson and Margaret C Weber. Judges: Arizona authors, editors, and reviewers. Winners announced at an award banquet by November 8.

⚇ $□ ART AFFAIR POETRY CONTEST

P.O. Box 54302, Oklahoma City OK 73154. Web site: www.shadetreecreations.com. **Contact:** Barbara Shepherd. The annual Art Affair Poetry Contest offers 1st Prize: $40 and certificate; 2nd Prize: $25 and certificate; and 3rd Prize: $15 and certificate. Open to any poet. Poems must be unpublished. No simultaneous submissions. Multiple entries accepted with separate entry fee for each. Submit one original poem on any subject, in any style, no more than 60 lines (put line count in the upper right-hand corner of first page). Include cover page with poet's name, address, phone number, and ms title. Do not include SASE; mss will not be returned. Guidelines available on Web site. **Deadline:** October 1, 2008 (postmark). **Entry Fee:** $3/poem. Make check payable to Art Affair. 2007 winners were Pat King (1st and 2nd Prize) and Maria Rachel Hooley (3rd Prize). Winners' list will be published on the Art Affair Web site in December.

$□ ◎ THE ART OF MUSIC ANNUAL WRITING CONTEST (Specialized: music-related writing)

Piano Press, Del Mar CA 92014-0085. (619)884-1401. Fax: (858)755-1104. E-mail: pianopress@pianopress.com. Web site: www.pianopress.com. Established 1998. **Contact:** Elizabeth C. Axford, M.A., owner, Piano Press. The Art of Music Annual Writing Contest offers cash prizes and publication in *The Art of Music: A Collection of Writings*. 1st Prize: $150; 2nd Prize: $100; 3rd Prize: $50; also presents winners with a copy of each anthology, and a certificate. In addition, the top entries are published in the anthology. Open to all writers ages 4 and up; signature of a parent or guardian is required for entrants under 18 years old. Entry may consist of an original music-related poem, short story, essay, song lyric, or cover illustration. Manuscripts must be titled and typed, with no identifying information on any page. No entries will be returned. Each entry must be accompanied by an official form. Guidelines and entry form available on Web site. **Entry fee:** $20. Make checks/money orders payable to Piano Press. All entrants receive a copy of *The Art of Music: A Collection of Writings*, Volume 1 or Volume 2 (designate preference on entry form). **Deadline:** June 30 (postmark). Judges: published poets, authors, and songwriters. Winners announced by mail by October 31. Copies of anthologies available through Web site.

$□ ◎ ARTIST TRUST (Specialized: WA resident artists)

1835 12th Ave., Seattle WA 98122. (206)467-8734. Fax: (206)467-9633. E-mail: info@artisttrust.org. Web site: www.artisttrust.org. **Contact:** Heather Helbach-Olds, Director of Programs. Artist Trust is a nonprofit arts organization that provides grants to artists (including poets) who are residents of the state. Applications for Grants for Artist Projects (GAP) are accepted each year in February; awards grants of up to $1,500. Applications for Fellowship Program are accepted in June of odd-numbered years; awards $6,500 merit-based awards. **Deadline:** GAP, last Friday of February annually; Fellowship, second Friday of June in odd-numbered years. Each competition receives 200-300 literary entries/year. Most recent winners include Stacey Levine, Ann Pancake, and Brenda Miller. Also publishes a newsletter (4 times/year) full of information on arts-related topics and cultural issues; *Possibilities* (published 6 times/year), full of listings of opportunities for artists of all disciplines; and *Artists' Assets* (published annually) full of resources for artists of all disciplines.

⊕ $□ AUSTRALIAN-IRISH HERITAGE WRITER'S PRIZE

Australian-Irish Heritage Association, P.O. Box 1583, Subiaco WA 6904 Australia. (61)(8)9384-1368. E-mail: aiha@irishheritage.net. Web site: www.irishheritage.net. Established 1997. **Contact:** Pavla Walsh, coordinator. Offers annual awards. See Web site for current year's entry details.

$⊘ AUTUMN HOUSE POETRY PRIZE

Autumn House Press, P.O. Box 60100, Pittsburgh PA 15211. (412)381-4261. E-mail: msimms@autumnhouse.org. Web site: http://autumnhouse.org. Established 1999. **Contact:** Michael Simms, editor. Offers annual prize of $2,500 and publication of book-length ms with national promotion. Submission must be unpublished as a collection, but individual poems may have been previously published elsewhere. Considers simultaneous submissions. Submit 50-80 pages of poetry ("blind judging—2 cover sheets requested"). Guidelines available for SASE, by e-mail, or on Web site. **Entry fee:** $25/ms. **Deadline:** June 30 annually. Competition receives 700 entries/year. 2007 winner was Miriam Levine. 2008 judge: Naomi Shihab Nye. Winners announced through mailings and through ads in *Poets & Writers*, *American Poetry Review*, and *Writer's Chronicle* (extensive publicity for winner). Copies of winning books available from Amazon.com, Barnes & Noble, Borders, and other retailers. "Autumn House is a nonprofit corporation with the mission of publishing and promoting poetry. We have published books by Gerald Stern, Ruth L. Schwartz, Ed Ochester, Andrea Hollander Budy, Jo McDougall, and others." Advice: "Include only your best poems."

$⊘ THE MURIEL CRAFT BAILEY MEMORIAL AWARD

4956 St. John Dr., Syracuse NY 13215. (315)488-8077. E-mail: poetry@comstockreview.org. Web site: www.comstockreview.org. The annual Muriel Craft Bailey Memorial Award offers 1st Prize: $1,000; 2nd Prize: $250; 3rd Prize: $100; Honorable Mentions; plus publication of winners and selected finalists in *The Comstock Review* (see separate listing in Magazines/Journals). May offer discounted copies or subscriptions to entrants. Submissions must be unpublished. No simultaneous submissions. Submit poems of 40 lines each, single-spaced. Put poet's name, address, phone number, and e-mail address on reverse side (back) of each page. "We read each poem 'blind,' so we do not want to see your name on the front of the poem." Poems with identification visible to judges on the front side of page will not be read. Include SASE for results only; no poems will be returned. Guidelines availableon Web site after April 1st yearly. **Entry fee:** $4/poem. Make checks payable to *The Comstock Review* (combine fees on a single check for multiple entries). **Deadline:** reads April 1-July 1 (postmark). 2006 winners were Allan Peterson (1st), Greg Larson (2nd), and Lynn Levin (3rd). 2007 judge: Carolyn Forché; initial screening by editorial team from *The Comstock Review*. Winners notified in September.

▢ ◎ THE BAILEY PRIZE (Specialized: open to upper-level undergraduate & graduate-level writing students)

The Chrysalis Reader, 1745 Gravel Hill Rd., Dillwyn VA 23936. (434)983-3021. Fax: (434)983-1074. E-mail: chrysalis@hovac.com. Web site: www.swedenborg.com/chrysalis. **Contact:** The Editor. Celebrating more than 20 years of publishing established and emerging writers, *The Chrysalis Reader* offers The Bailey Prize, an annual publishing prize for undergraduate and graduate-level students. *The Chrysalis Reader*, published yearly in the fall, is an anthology of poetry, fiction, and non-fiction. Winners will be published in CR (see separate listing in Magazines/Journals), receive 3 copies of the issue, and have their work available online after print publication. The Bailey Prize is open to nominations by instructors of undergraduate and graduate-level courses. Instructors may submit a maximum of 3 nominations from their students' output within one academic year. Nominations may be any combination of previously unpublished poetry (100 lines maximum) or fiction or nonfiction (3,100 words maximum). "We welcome both traditional and experimental writing with an emphasis on insightful writing related to the Chrysalis Reader's annual theme. The 2009 them is Lenses." Submit one copy of each entry with writer's contact information. Include a cover letter and SASE. No email or disk submissions. No nominated entries will be returned. Guidelines available on Web site. **Entry fee:** none. **Deadline:** All entries must be dated on or before May 31 to be considered for that year's publishing cycle.

$⊘ BAKELESS LITERARY PUBLICATION PRIZES

Break Loaf Writers' Conference, Middlebury College, Middlebury VT 05753. (802)443-2018. E-mail: jabates@middlebury.edu. Web site: www.bakelessprize.org. **Contact:** Ms. Jennifer Bates, contest coordinator. The Bread Loaf Writers' Conference (see separate listing in Conferences, Workshops

& Festivals) sponsors the Bakeless Literary Publication Prizes for new authors of literary works in poetry, fiction, and creative nonfiction. Awards publication by Houghton Mifflin of a book-length ms, and a fellowship to attend the Bread Loaf Writers' Conference. Submissions must be unpublished as a collection, but individual poems may have been previously published elsewhere. Considers simultaneous submissions, "but contestants are asked to notify the contest coordinator immediately if a manuscript has been accepted for publication elsewhere." Submit at least 50 pages of poetry, typed double- or single-spaced on letter-size paper. Good-quality photocopies or letter-quality printed mss acceptable. Include 2 cover pages: one with poet's name, address, phone number, ms title, and genre (poetry) indicated; one with only ms title and genre. Poet's name must not appear on any ms page. Do not include author's note, bio, or acknowledgments page. Include SASP for confirmation of ms receipt and SASE for results only; mss will not be returned. Guidelines available on Web site. **Entry Fee:** $10/submission. Make checks payable to Middlebury College. **Deadline:** Submissions accepted between September 15 and November 1. Winners announced in May.

$ ☑ ◎ THE WILLIS BARNSTONE TRANSLATION PRIZE (Specialized: translations from any language)

1800 Lincoln Ave., Evansville IN 47722. Phone/fax: (812)488-1042. E-mail: evansvillereview@evansville.edu. Web site: http://english.evansville.edu/EvansvilleReview.htm. Established 1989. **Contact:** Kirby Snell, poetry editor. The annual Willis Barnstone Translation Prize offers an annual award of $1,000 and publication in *The Evansville Review* for translated poems from any language and any time period, ancient to contemporary. Submissions must be unpublished. Each translated poem must not exceed 200 lines. "Please staple the translation to a copy of the original (which identifies the original poet) and put the name, address, and phone number of the translator(s) on the back of the translation page." Accepts multiple entries (up to 10/translator). Include SASE for results; mss will not be returned. Guidelines available for SASE or on Web site. **Entry fee:** $5 for the first poem, $3 for each subsequent poem. Make checks payable to The University of Evansville. **Deadline:** December 1. Competition receives 400 entries/year. Winner will be announced in April in *The Evansville Review* and to entrants who provided SASEs.

$ ☑ BARROW STREET PRESS BOOK CONTEST

P.O. Box 1831, New York NY 10156. E-mail: info@barrowstreet.org. Web site: www.barrowstreet.org. Established 2002. **Contact:** Contest Coordinator. Barrow Street Press publishes one poetry book/year through the annual Barrow Street Press Book Contest. Winner receives $1,000 and publication. Submit a 50- to 70-page ms of original, previously unpublished poetry in English. Manuscript should be typed, single-spaced on white $8^{1}/_{2} \times 11$ paper. Clear photocopies acceptable. Include 2 title pages and an acknowledgments page listing any poems previously published in journals or anthologies. Author's name, address, and daytime phone number should appear on first title page only, and nowhere else in ms. Include SASE for results only; no mss will be returned. Guidelines available on Web site. **Entry fee:** $25; include mailer with $2.13 postage for copy of winning book. Make checks payable to Barrow Street. **Deadline:** June 30, 2008. 2007 winner was Ely Shipley (*Boy with Flowers*). 2007 judge: Phillis Levin.

⟳ $ ☑ THE SHAUNT BASMAJIAN CHAPBOOK AWARD

P.O. Box 340, Station B, London ON N6A 4W1 Canada. Phone/fax: (519)660-0548. E-mail: cpa@sympatico.ca. Web site: www3.sympatico.ca/cpa. Established 1996. **Contact:** Wayne Ray, contest director. The Shaunt Basmajian Chapbook Award, named in honor of one of the founding members of the Canadian Poetry Association (see separate listing in Organizations), offers $100 CAD and publication, plus 50 copies. Submissions must be unpublished as a collection, but individual poems may have been previously published elsewhere. Considers simultaneous submissions. Submit up to 20 pages of poetry, typed single-spaced and paginated, with collection title on each page. Include separate sheet with ms title, poet's name, address, and phone number (poet's name must not appear on ms pages). Manuscripts will not be returned. Guidelines available for SASE and on Web site. **Entry fee:** $15 CAD. Make checks/money orders payable to the Canadian Poetry Association.

Deadline: April 30 (postmark) annually. Judge: members of the London Chapter committee. Winning chapbooks available for $6 CAD.

$□ ◎ BELLEVUE LITERARY REVIEW MAGLIOCCO PRIZE FOR POETRY (Specialized: humanity, health, and healing)

Bellevue Literary Review, New York University School of Medicine, OBV-A612, 550 First Ave., New York NY 10016. (212)263-3973. E-mail: info@BLReview.org. Web site: www.BLReview.org. Established 2005. **Contact:** Stacy Bodziak. The annual Magliocco Prize for Poetry recognizes outstanding writing related to themes of health, healing, illness, the mind, and the body. Offers $1,000 for best poem and publication in *Bellevue Literary Review* (see separate listing in Magazines/Journals). All entries will be considered for publication. No previously published poems (including Internet publication) or simultaneous submissions. Submit up to 3 poems (5 pages maximum). Electronic (online) submissions only (as Word document with *.doc extension); combine all poems into one document and use first poem as document title. See guidelines for additional submission details. Guidelines available for SASE or on Web site. **Entry fee:** $15/submission, limit of 2 submissions per person (one-year subscription available for additional $5). **Deadline:** August 1. Winner announced in December. 2009 judge: Naomi Shihab Nye. Previous judges include Edward Hirsch (2006), Rafael Campo (2007), and Marie Howe (2008).

$◑ GEORGE BENNETT FELLOWSHIP

Phillips Exeter Academy, 20 Main St., Exeter NH 03833-2460. Web site: http://www.exeter.edu/about_us/about_us_537.aspx. Established 1968. **Contact:** Charles Pratt, selection committee coordinator. Provides an annual $10,000 fellowship plus residency (room and board) to a writer with a ms in progress. The Fellow's only official duties are to be in residence while the academy is in session and to be available to students interested in writing. The committee favors writers who have not yet published a book-length work with a major publisher. Application materials and guidelines available for SASE or on Web site. **Entry fee:** $5. **Deadline:** December 1. Competition receives 190 entries. Recent award winners were Maggie Dietz (2002-2003), Nia Stephens (2003-2004), and Erin Soros (2004-2005). Winners will be announced by mail in March. "Please, no telephone calls or e-mail inquiries."

$◑ ◎ BEST OF OHIO WRITERS WRITING CONTEST (Specialized: OH resident writers)

2570 Superior Ave. E, Ste 203, Cleveland, OH 44114-4252. (216) 694-0000. E-mail: peggy@the-lit.org. Web site: www.the-lit.org. Offers annual contest for poetry, fiction, creative nonfiction, and "Writers on Writing" (any genre). 1st Prize: $150; 2nd Prize: $50; plus publication for 1st-prize winner of each category in a special edition of *Muse*. Submit up to 3 typed poems, no more than 2 pages each, unpublished mss only. Open only to Ohio residents. "Entries will be judged anonymously, so please do not put name or other identification on manuscript. Attach entry form (or facsimile) to submission. Manuscripts will not be returned." Include SASE for results. Entry form and guidelines available for SASE, by e-mail, or on Web site. **Entry fee:** $15/first entry in each category (includes one-year subscription or renewal to *Ohio Writer*); $2 for each additional entry in same category (limit 3/category). **Deadline:** July 31. Judges have included Will Greenway, Susan Grimm, Ron Antonucci, and Paula Maclain. Winners announced in the October-December issue of *Muse*.

■ $◎ BEST OF THE BEST COMPETITION (Specialized: poems that have won first place in other competitions)

E-mail: bestofthebest@triplopia.org. Web site: www.triplopia.org. Established 2006. **Contact:** Tracy Koretsky, contest coordinator. *TRIPLOPIA* (see separate listing in Magazines/Journals) sponsors an annual award of $100, Pushcart Prize nomination, author interview, and publication for a poem that has previously won first place in other competitions. Submission may be previously published. Submit one poem of 2 pages maximum, any subject, form, or style. **Must specify what competition the poem won previously.** Guidelines available by request via e-mail. **Entry fee:** none. **Deadline:** Entries accepted ONLY April 1-June 1. Will consider only the first 100 eligible entries. See 2006 winner Jan Steckel ("Tiresias") www.triplopia.org/inside.cfm?ct = 674 and 2007 winner Christina Lovin, "Coal Country" www.triplopia.org/inside.cfm?ct = 806. Annual judge: Tracy Koretsky with *TRIPLOPIA* editors Gene Justice and Tara A. Elliott. Winner will be contacted by e-mail by July 1." *TRIPLOPIA* is an internationally oriented, Web-based quarterly with a solid emphasis on excellence and accessibility."

$☑ THE PATRICIA BIBBY FIRST BOOK AWARD

Tebot Bach, P.O. Box 7887, Huntington Beach CA 92615-7887. E-mail: info@tebotbach.org. Web site: www.tebotbach.org. Established 2005. **Contact:** Mifanwy Kaiser. The Patricia Bibby First Book Award offers $1,000 and publication of a book-length poetry manuscript by Tebot Bach (see separate listing in Book/Chapbook Publishers). Open to "all poets writing in English who have not committed to publishing collections of poetry of 36 poems or more in editions of over 400 copies." Submissions must be unpublished as a collection, but individual poems may have been previously published elsewhere. Considers simultaneous submissions, but Tebot Bach must be notified immediately by e-mail if the collection is accepted for publication. Partial guidelines: Submit 50-84 pages of poetry, letter-quality, single-spaced; clear photocopies acceptable. Use binder clip; no staples, folders, or printer-bound copies. Include 2 title pages: 1 (not fastened to ms) with ms title, poet's name, address, phone number, and e-mail address; the second (fastened to ms) with ms title only. Also include table of contents. Include SASP for notification of receipt of entry and SASE for results only; mss will not be returned. Complete guidelines available by e-mail or on Web site. **Reading fee:** $25. Make checks/money orders payable to Tebot Bach with reading fee and title of ms. on the notation line. **Deadline:** October 31 (postmark) annually. Winner announced each year in April. Judges are selected annually.

$☑ ◎ BINGHAMTON UNIVERSITY MILT KESSLER POETRY BOOK AWARD
(Specialized: poets over 40)

Binghamton University Creative Writing Program, P.O. Box 6000, Binghamton NY 13902. (607)777-2713. Fax: (607)777-2408. E-mail: cwpro@binghamton.edu. Web site: http://english.binghamton.edu/cwpro. Established 2001. **Contact:** Maria Mazziotti Gillan, award director. Offers annual award of $1,000 for a book of poetry judged best of those published that year by a poet over the age of 40. "Submit books published that year; do not submit manuscripts." Entry form and guidelines available for SASE, by e-mail, or on Web site. **Entry fee:** none; "just submit 3 copies of book." **Deadline:** March 1. Competition receives 500 books/year. 2006 winner was Christopher Bursk. Winner will be announced in June in *Poets & Writers* and on Web site, or by SASE if provided. *(***NOTE:** Not to be confused with the Milton Kessler Memorial Prize for Poetry sponsored by Harpur Palate*)*.

$☑ THE BLACK RIVER CHAPBOOK COMPETITION

Black Lawrence Press, P.O. Box 9, Watertown NY 13601. E-mail: info@blacklawrencepress.com. Web site: www.blacklawrencepress.com. Established 2003. **Contact:** Colleen Ryor, editor. The semiannual Black River Chapbook Competition awards $300, publication by Black Lawrence Press (see separate listing in Book/Chapbook Publishers), and 25 copies to the winner. Considers simultaneous submissions, but notify immediately if ms is accepted elsewhere. Submit 16-40 pages of poetry, paginated, with cover letter with brief bio and contact information (include valid e-mail address), acknowledgments page (if applicable), and table of contents. No e-mail submissions. Include SASE or e-mail address for results only; mss will not be returned. Guidelines available on Web site. **Entry fee:** $15/entry; multiple submissions accepted with entry fee for each. Make checks/money orders payable to Black Lawrence Press. **Deadline:** October 31 (fall) and May 31 (spring) (postmark).

$☑ BLUE LIGHT POETRY PRIZE AND CHAPBOOK CONTEST

3600 Lyon St., San Francisco CA 94123. (415)440-8668 or (641)472-7882. E-mail: bluelightpress@aol.com. Established 1988. **Contact:** Diane Frank, chief editor. The Blue Light Poetry Prize and Chapbook Contest offers a cash prize and publication by Blue Light Press (see separate listing in Book/

Chapbook Publishers). "The winner will receive a $100 honorarium and 50 copies of his or her book, which can be sold for $8 each, for a total of $500." Submit ms of 10-24 pages, typed or printed with a laser or inkjet printer. No e-mail submissions. Include SASE for notification of receipt of ms, SASE for contest results only; no mss will be returned. Guidelines available with SASE or by e-mail. **Entry fee:** $10. Make checks payable to Blue Light Press. **Deadline:** June 1 for chapbook contest. Winner announced October 1. January 31 for full-length ms contest. Send e-mail for guidelines. Winner announced May 1.

✖ $◙ BLUE LYNX PRIZE FOR POETRY

Eastern Washington University Press, 534 E Spokane Falls Blvd, Ste 203., Spokane WA 99202. 1-800-508-9095. Fax: (509)368-6596. E-mail: ewupress2@mail.ewu.edu. Web site: http://ewupress.ewu.edu. **Contact:** editorial assistant for prizes. Offers annual award of $1,500 and publication by EWU Press for a book-length ms. For U.S. authors only. Must be unpublished as a collection, but individual poems may have been previously published elsewhere. Submit 48 pages of poetry minimum, paginated, on any subject, in any form. Include table of contents. Include SASE for notification; no mss will be returned. Guidelines available for SASE, by e-mail, or on Web site. **Entry fee:** $25. Make checks payable to EWU Press. **Deadline:** May 15 annually. Competition receives 400 entries/year. 2007 winner was B.T. Shaw (*This Dirty Little Heart*). 2007 judge: Alberto Ríos. Winner announced in fall of contest year. Copies of winning books available from EWU Press.

✖ $◙ THE BOSTON REVIEW ANNUAL POETRY CONTEST

Boston Review, 35 Medford St., Suite 302, Somerville MA 02143. (617)591-0505. Fax: (617)591-0440. E-mail: review@bostonreview.net (inquiries only). Web site: www.bostonreview.net. Established 1975. **Contact:** Contest Coordinator. Offers $1,500 and publication in *Boston Review* (see separate listing in Magazines/Journals). "Any poet writing in English is eligible, unless he or she is a current student, former student, or close personal friend of the judge." Submissions must be unpublished. Considers simultaneous submissions with notice of acceptance elsewhere. Submit up to 5 poems, no more than 10 pages total, in duplicate. Include cover sheet with poet's name, address, and phone number; no identifying information on the poems themselves. No mss will be returned. Guidelines available for SASE or on Web site. **Entry fee:** $20 ($30 for international submissions); all entrants receive a one-year subscription to *Boston Review*. Make checks payable to *Boston Review*. **Deadline:** June 1 (postmark). Winner announced in early November on Web site. 2007 winner was Elizabeth Willis. 2008 Judge: John Koethe.

✖ ✖ $◙ BPNICHOL CHAPBOOK AWARD (Specialized: works published in Canada)

316 Dupont St., Toronto ON M5R 1V9 Canada. (416)964-7919. Fax: (416)964-6941. Web site: www.pcwf.ca. **Contact:** Philip McKenna. Established 1985. Sponsored by the Phoenix Community Works Foundation. The bpNichol Chapbook Award offers $1,000 CAD for the best poetry chapbook (10-48 pages) in English published in Canada. Poet or publisher may submit 3 copies (not returnable) and a brief curriculum vitae of the author with address, telephone number, and e-mail. Guidelines available on Web site. **Deadline:** March 30. Competition receives between 40-60 entries on average. 2007 winner was Jake Kennedy (*Hazard*).

$◙ THE BRIAR CLIFF REVIEW FICTION, POETRY AND CREATIVE NONFICTION CONTEST

3303 Rebecca St., Sioux City IA 51104-2100. Web site: www.briarcliff.edu/bcreview. **Contact:** Jeanne Emmons, poetry editor. *The Briar Cliff Review* (see separate listing in Magazines/Journals) sponsors an annual contest offering $1,000 and publication to each First Prize winner in fiction, poetry, and creative nonfiction. Previous year's winner and former students of editors ineligible. Winning pieces accepted for publication on the basis of First-Time Rights. Considers simultaneous submissions, "but notify us immediately upon acceptance elsewhere." Submit 3 poems, single-spaced on 8½×11 paper, no more than 1 poem/page. Include separate cover sheet with author's name, address, e-mail, and poem title(s); no name on ms. Include SASE for results only; mss will not be returned. Guidelines available on Web site. **Entry fee:** $20 for 3 poems. "All entrants receive a copy of the magazine (a $15 value) containing the winning entries." **Deadline:** November 1. Judge: the editors of *The Briar Cliff Review*.

$☑ BRIGHT HILL PRESS POETRY BOOK AWARD

P.O. Box 193, 94 Church St., Treadwell NY 13846-0193. (607)829-5055. Fax: (607)829-5054. E-mail: wordthur@stny.rr.com. Web site: www.brighthillpress.org. Established 1992. **Contact:** Bertha Rogers, editor-in-chief/founding director. Member: Council of Literary Magazines and Presses, NYC. The annual Bright Hill Press Poetry Book Award offers $1,000, publication of a book-length ms, and 25 author's copies. Submissions must be unpublished as a collection, but individual poems may have been previously published elsewhere. Considers simultaneous submissions if Bright Hill Press is notified of acceptance elsewhere. Submit 48-65 pages of poetry, paginated and secured with bulldog or spring clip. Include bio, table of contents, and acknowledgments page. Include 2 title pages: 1 with ms title, poet's name, address, and phone number; 1 with ms title only. Include SASE for results only; mss will not be returned. Guidelines available for SASE, by e-mail, or on Web site. **Entry fee:** $20 for Word Thursdays/Bright Hill Press members; $22 for nonmembers. **Deadline:** was November 30 (postmark) for 2006. Competition receives over 300 entries/year. Winners will be announced in summer of the year following the contest. Copies of winning books available from Bright Hill Press (see Web site); include **with entry only** a sturdy 6×8 or 9×12 envelope with $1.65 postage affixed to receive a free copy of an award-winning Bright Hill Press poetry book (affix $2 postage for padded envelope). "Publish your poems in literary magazines before trying to get a whole manuscript published. Publishing individual poems is the best way to hone your complete manuscript."

$☑ BRIGHT HILL PRESS POETRY CHAPBOOK AWARD

P.O. Box 193, 94 Church St., Treadwell NY 13846-0193. (607)829-5055. Fax: (607)829-5054. E-mail: wordthur@stny.rr.com. Web site: www.brighthillpress.org. Established 1992. **Contact:** Bertha Rogers, editor-in-chief/founding director. Member: Council of Literary Magazines and Presses, NYC. The annual Bright Hill Press Chapbook Award offers $300, publication of a chapbook-length ms, and 25 author's copies. Submissions must be unpublished as a collection, but individual poems may have been previously published elsewhere. Considers simultaneous submissions if Bright Hill Press is notified of acceptance elsewhere. Submit 16-24 pages of poetry, paginated and secured with bulldog or spring clip. Include bio, table of contents, and acknowledgments page. Include 2 title pages: 1 with ms title, poet's name, address, and phone number; 1 with ms title only. Include SASE for results only; mss will not be returned. Guidelines available for SASE, by e-mail, or on Web site. **Entry fee:** $10 for Word Thursdays/Bright Hill Press members; $12 for nonmembers. Multiple entries accepted with separate fee for each. **Deadline:** July 31 (postmark). Competition receives over 300 entries/year. Copies of winning chapbooks available from Bright Hill Press (see Web site); include **with entry only** a 5×7 SASE with $1.31 postage affixed and receive a free copy of a recent winning Bright Hill Press poetry chapbook. "Publish your poems in literary magazines before trying to get a whole manuscript published. Publishing individual poems is the best way to hone your complete manuscript."

$☑ BRITTINGHAM PRIZE IN POETRY

University of Wisconsin Press, Dept. of English, 600 N. Park St., University of Wisconsin, Madison WI 53706. E-mail: rwallace@wisc.edu. Web site: www.wisc.edu/wisconsinpress/index.html. Established 1985. **Contact:** Ronald Wallace, poetry series editor. The annual Brittingham Prize in Poetry is one of 2 prizes awarded by The University of Wisconsin Press (see separate listing for the Felix Pollak Prize in Poetry in this section). Offers $1,000 plus publication, with an additional $1,500 honorarium to cover expenses of a reading in Madison. Submissions must be unpublished as a collection, but individual poems may have been published elsewhere (publication must be acknowledged). Considers simultaneous submissions if notified of selection elsewhere. Submit 50-80 unbound ms pages, typed single-spaced (with double spaces between stanzas) or double-spaced. Clean photocopies are acceptable. Include title page with poet's name, address, and telephone number. No translations. Include SASE for results only; mss will not be returned. Guidelines available for SASE or on Web site. **Entry fee:** $25. **NOTE:** $25 fee applies to consideration of same entry for the Felix Pollak Prize in Poetry—1 fee for 2 contest entries. Make checks/money orders payable to University of Wisconsin Press. **Deadline:** submit September 1-30 (postmark). 2008 Brittingham Prize winner was Philip Pardi (*Meditations on Rising and Falling*). Qualified readers will screen all mss. Judge: "a distinguished poet who will remain anonymous until the winners are announced in mid-February."

✪ $◩ BRODINE/BRODINSKY POETRY COMPETITION

Connecticut Poetry Society, P.O. Box 270554, West Hartford CT 06127-0554. E-mail: connpoetry@comcast.net. Web site: www.ct-poetry-society.org. **Contact:** Contest Director. The Brodine/Brodinsky Poetry Competition, sponsored by the Connecticut Poetry Society, is open to all poets. Offers prizes of $150, $100, and $50; winning poems will be published in *Connecticut River Review*. Submit up to 3 unpublished poems, any form, 40 line limit. Include 2 copies of each poem: 1 with complete contact information and one with NO contact information. Include SASE for results only (no poems will be returned). Winning poems must be submitted by disc or e-mail following notification. **Entry fee:** $10 for up to 3 poems. Make checks payable to Connecticut Poetry Society. **Deadline:** submit May 1-July 31 (postmark). 2007 judge: Steve Straight.

✪ $◩ ◎ DOROTHY BRUNSMAN POETRY PRIZE (Specialized: poets living west of the central time zone)

Bear Star Press, 185 Hollow Oak Dr., Cohasset CA 95973. (530)891-0360. E-mail: online form. Web site: www.bearstarpress.com. Established 1996. **Contact:** Beth Spencer, editor/publisher. The annual Dorothy Brunsman Poetry Prize awards $1,000 and publication by Bear Star Press to the best book-length ms by a poet who resides in the Western states (within Mountain or Pacific time zones, plus Alaska and Hawaii). "The contest also serves as our best pool for finding new voices." Submission must be unpublished as a collection, but individual poems may have been previously published elsewhere (as long as poet retains copyright). Considers simultaneous submissions (contact immediately if ms status changes). Submit ms of 50-65 pages of original poetry, in any form, on any subject. Use a plain 10-12 point font. Include separate cover sheet with poet's name, address, and phone number; no identifying information on mss pages. Include SASP for notification of receipt (do not send by Registered Mail) and SASE for results; mss will not be returned. Guidelines available for SASE or on Web site. **Entry fee:** $20. **Deadline:** November 30 (postmark); reads mss in September, October, and November. 2008 winner was Kathryn Cowles (*Eleanor, Eleanor, Not Your Real Name*). Judge: mss judged in house. Winner notified on or before February 1; winner information posted on Web site. Copies of winning books available through Web site. "Send your best work; consider its arrangement. A 'wow' poem early on keeps me reading."

$◎ BURNING BUSH POETRY PRIZE (Specialized: community-centered values, democratic processes)

Burning Bush Publications, P.O. Box 4658, Santa Rosa CA 95402. Web site: www.bbbooks.com. Offers annual award of $200 plus publication in online e-zine, *In Our Own Words* (see separate listing in Magazines/Journals), to a poet whose writing "inspires others to value human life and the natural world instead of short-term economic advantage; speaks for community-centered values and democratic processes, especially those whose voices are seldom heard; demonstrates poetic excellence; and educates readers of the relevance of the past to the present and future." Prefers unpublished work, "but published poems may be submitted. If published before, please include where, when, and any acknowledgment information we may need." Submit 3 poems maximum, any style or form. Include index card with name, address, e-mail, phone, and title of each poem submitted. Also include SASE with sufficient postage for return of work. "Submissions without SASE will not be returned. If your poem is selected for the Poetry Prize, we will need a brief (50 words) biographical statement from you." Guidelines available on Web site. **Entry fee:** $10. **Deadline:** June 1. Competition receives 100 entries/year. 2007 winner was C.S. Cooley. Winner announced in late July.

$⊡ BURNSIDE REVIEW CHAPBOOK COMPETITION

P.O. Box 1782, Portland OR 97207. E-mail: sid@burnsidereview.org. Web site: www.burnsidereview.org. Established 2004. **Contact:** Sid Miller, editor. The annual *Burnside Review* Chapbook Competition awards $200, publication, and 25 author's copies to winning poet. Guidelines available for SASE or on Web site. **Entry fee:** $15. **Deadline:** March 15-June 30. 2007 winner was Nicholas Reading(*The Party in Question*). (See separate listing for *Burnside Review* in Magazines/Journals.)

$THE WITTER BYNNER FOUNDATION FOR POETRY, INC.

P.O. Box 10169, Santa Fe NM 87504. (505)988-3251. Fax: (505)986-8222. E-mail: bynnerfoundation @aol.com. Web site: www.bynnerfoundation.org. **Contact:** Steven Schwartz, executive director. Awards grants, ranging from $1,000 to $10,000, exclusively to nonprofit organizations for the support of poetry-related projects in the area of: 1) support of individual poets through existing nonprofit institutions; 2) developing the poetry audience; 3) poetry translation and the process of poetry translation; and 4) uses of poetry. ''May consider the support of other creative and innovative projects in poetry.'' Letters of intent accepted annually August 1-December 31; requests for application forms should be submitted to Steven Schwartz, executive director. Additional information available by fax, e-mail, or on Web site. **Deadline:** Applications, if approved, must be returned to the Foundation postmarked by February 1.

⚘ $◎ CAA POETRY AWARD (Specialized: Canadian poets)

Canadian Authors Association, Box 419, Campbellford ON K0L 1L0 Canada. (705)653-0323. Fax: (705)653-0593. E-mail: admin@CanAuthors.org. Web site: www.CanAuthors.org. **Contact:** Alec McEachern, national director. The CAA Poetry Award offers $1,000 CAD and a silver medal to Canadian writers for a poetry collection (by a single poet) published during the year. Guidelines available on Web site. **Entry fee:** $35 CAD/title. **Deadline:** December 15; except for works published after December 1, in which case the postmark deadline is January 15. Competition receives 100 entries/year. 2006 winner was Barry Dempster (*The Burning Alphabet*); 2007 winner was Sarah Klassen (*A Curious Beatitute*). All awards are given at the CAA Awards Banquet at the annual conference.

✪ $⊡ GERALD CABLE BOOK AWARD

Silverfish Review Press, P.O. Box 3541, Eugene OR 97403. (541)344-5060. E-mail: sfrpress@earthlink.net. Web site: www.silverfishreviewpress.com. Established 1979. **Contact:** Rodger Moody, editor. Offers annual award of $1,000, publication by Silverfish Review Press, and 100 author copies to the best book-length ms of original poetry by an author who has not yet published a full-length collection. No restrictions on the kind of poetry or subject matter; no translations. Individual poems may have been previously published elsewhere, but must be acknowledged. Considers simultaneous submissions (notify immediately of acceptance elsewhere). Submit at least 48 pages of poetry, no names or identification on ms pages. Include separate title sheet with poet's name, address, and phone number. Include SASP for notification of receipt and SASE for results; no mss will be returned. Accepts e-mail submissions in Word, plain text, or rich text; send entry fee and SASE by regular mail. Guidelines available for SASE, by e-mail, or on Web site. **Entry fee:** $20. Make checks payable to Silverfish Review Press. **Deadline:** October 15 (postmark). 2006 winner was Daneen Wardrop (*The Odds of Being*). Winner announced in March. Copies of winning books available through Web site. ''All entrants who enclose a 7 × 10 envelope and $1.65 in postage will receive a free copy of a recent winner of the book award.''

$⊡ CAROLINA WREN PRESS POETRY CONTEST FOR A FIRST BOOK

120 Morris St., Durham NC 27701. (919)560-2738. Fax: (919)560-2759. E-mail: carolinawrenpress@ earthlink.net. Web site: www.carolinawrenpress.org. Established 1976. **Contact:** Contest Director. The biennial Carolina Wren Press Poetry Contest for a First Book offers $1,000 and publication by Carolina Wren Press (see separate listing in Book/Chapbook Publishers). Open only to poets who have published no more than 1 full-length collection (48 pages or more). Submissions must be unpublished as a collection, but individual poems may have been previously published elsewhere.

Manuscripts that have been previously self-published or that are available online in their entirety are not eligible. Considers simultaneous submissions (notify immediately of acceptance elsewhere). Submit 2 copies of a poetry ms of 48-60 pages. Page count should include title page, table of contents, and optional dedication page. See guidelines for complete formatting and submission details. Include SASE for results only; mss will not be returned. Guidelines available for SASE, by e-mail, or on Web site (in July). **Entry fee:** $20. **Deadline:** December 1, 2008 (postmark). 2008 judge: Minnie Bruce Pratt. Copies of winning books available through Web site, Amazon, or local bookstore.

$ ☑ ◎ CAVE CANEM POETRY PRIZE (Specialized: African American)

Cave Canem Foundation, Inc., 584 Broadway, Suite 508, New York NY 10012. E-mail: dantemichea ux@ccpoets.org. Web site: www.cavecanempoets.org. Established 1999 (prize) and 1996 (foundation). **Contact:** Alison Meyers, Cave Canem director. Offers "annual first book award dedicated to presenting the work of African American poets who have not been published by a professional press. The winner will receive $500 cash, publication, and 50 copies of the book." **U.S. poets only.** Considers simultaneous submissions, but they should be noted. "If the manuscript is accepted for publication elsewhere during the judging, immediate notification is requested." Send 2 copies of manuscript of 50-75 pages. The author's name should not appear on the manuscript. 2 title pages should be attached to each copy. The first must include the poet's name, address, telephone number, and the title of the manuscript; the second should list the title only. Number the pages." Include SASE for notification of receipt of ms; mss will not be returned. Guidelines available for SASE or on Web site. **Entry fee:** $15. **Deadline:** May 17 annually. 2007 winner was Ronaldo V. Wilson (*The Narrative of the Brown Boy and the White Man*, The University of Pittsburgh Press). 2008 judge: Clarence Major. Winners will be announced by press release in October of year of contest. Copies of winning books are available from "any bookseller, because the publishers are Graywolf Press, University of Georgia Press, and University of Pittsburgh Press. Cave Canem sponsors a weeklong retreat each summer and a regional workshop in New York. It sponsors readings in various parts of the country. The winner of the prize and the judge are featured in an annual reading." Recommends "being at a stage in your development where some of your poems have already been published in literary journals. Manuscripts not adhering to guidelines will not be forwarded to judge nor returned to applicant."

⊠ $ ☑ THE CENTER FOR BOOK ARTS' ANNUAL POETRY CHAPBOOK COMPETITION

28 W. 27th St., 3rd Floor, New York NY 10001. (212)481-0295. E-mail: info@centerforbookarts.org. Web site: www.centerforbookarts.org. Established 1995. **Contact:** Alexander Campos, executive director. Offers $500 cash prize, a $500 reading honorarium, and publication of winning manuscript in a limited edition letterpress-printed and handbound chapbook (10 copies reserved for poet). Must be unpublished as a collection, but individual poems may have been published elsewhere. Submit no more than 500 lines or 24 pages on any subject, in any form; may be collection or sequence of poems or a single long poem. Bind with a simple spring clip. Include table of contests and acknowledgments page. Include 2 cover pages: 1 with ms title, poet's name, address, phone number, and e-mail; 1 without poet's identification. (Page count does not include table contents, acknowledgments page, titles pages, or cover sheet.) Include #10 SASE for results; mss will not be returned. Guidelines and entry form available for SASE, by e-mail, or on Web site. **Entry fee:** $25. Make checks payable to The Center for the Book Arts. **Deadline:** December 1 (postmark). Competition receives 500-1,000 entries/year. 2007 winner was Eric Pankey (*Objects and Mementos*). 2009 judges: Kim Addonizio and Sharon Dolin. Winner announced in April. Copies of winning chapbooks available through Web site. "Center for Book Arts is a nonprofit organization dedicated to the traditional crafts of bookmaking and contemporary interpretations of the book as an art object. Through the Center's Education, Exhibition, and Workspace Programs, we ensure that the ancient craft of the book remains a viable and vital part of our civilization."

$ ☑ CIDER PRESS REVIEW BOOK AWARD

777 Braddock Lane, Halifax PA 17032. E-mail: editor@ciderpressreview.com (inquiries only). Web site: http://ciderpressreview.com/bookaward. Established 1999. **Contact:** Contest Director. The

annual *Cider Press Review* Book Award offers $1,000, publication, and 25 author's copies. CPR acquires first publication rights. Initial print run is not less than 1,000 copies. Submissions must be unpublished as a collection, but individual poems may have been previously published elsewhere. Submit book-length ms of 48-80 pages. "Submissions can be made online using the submission form on the Web site or by mail. If sending by mail, include 2 cover sheets—1 with title, author's name, and complete contact information; and 1 with title only, all bound with a spring clip. Include SASE for results; manuscripts cannot be returned. Online submissions must be in Word for PC or PDF format, and should not include title page with author's name. The editors strongly urge contestants to use online delivery if possible." **Entry fee:** $25. All entrants will receive a copy of the winning book. **Deadline:** submit September 1-November 30 (postmark). 2006 winner was Anne Caston (*Judah's Lion*). 2008 judge: Lucille Clifton.

$□ CNW/FFWA FLORIDA STATE WRITING COMPETITION

Florida Freelance Writers Association, P.O. Box A, North Stratford NH 03590-0167. (603)922-8338. E-mail: contest@writers-editors.com. Web site: www.writers-editors.com. Established 1978. **Contact:** Dana K. Cassell, award director. Offers annual awards for nonfiction, fiction, children's literature, and poetry. Awards for each category are 1st Prize: $100 plus certificate; 2nd Prize: $75 plus certificate; 3rd Prize: $50 plus certificate; plus Honorable Mention certificates. Poetry submissions must be unpublished. Submit any number of poems on any subject in traditional forms, free verse, or children's. Entry form and guidelines available for SASE or on Web site. **Entry fee:** $3/poem (members), $5/poem (nonmembers). **Deadline:** March 15. Competition receives 350-400 entries/year. Competition is judged by writers, librarians, and teachers. Winners will be announced on May 31 by mail and on Web site.

$□ COLORADO PRIZE FOR POETRY

Center for Literary Publishing, Dept. of English, Colorado State University, Fort Collins CO 80523. (970)491-5449. E-mail: creview@colostate.edu. Web site: http://coloradoprise.colostate.edu. Estab. 1995. **Contact:** Stephanie G'Schwind, editor. The annual Colorado Prize for Poetry awards an honorarium of $1,500 and publication of a book-length ms. Submission must be unpublished as a collection, but individual poems may have been published elsewhere. Submit approximately 40-100 pages of poetry (no set minimum or maximum) on any subject, in any form, double- or single-spaced. Include 2 titles pages: one with ms title only, the other with ms title and poet's name, address, and phone number. Enclosed SASP for notification of receipt and SASE for results; mss will not be returned. Guidelines available for SASE or by e-mail. **Entry fee:** $25; includes one-year subscription to *Colorado Review* (see separate listing in Magazines/Journals). **Deadline:** submission period was October 1-January 11 for 2008. Winner announced in May. 2007 winner was Craig Morgan Teicher (*Brenda Is in the Room & Other Poems*). 2008 judge: Martha Ronk.

$□ CRAB ORCHARD SERIES IN POETRY FIRST BOOK AWARD

Dept. of English, Mail Code 4503, Faner Hall 2380, Southern Illinois University Carbondale, 1000 Faner Dr., Carbondale IL 62901. Web site: www.siu.edu/~crborchd. Established 1995. **Contact:** John Tribble, series editor. The Crab Orchard Series in Poetry First Book Award offers $2,500 ($1,000 prize plus $1,500 honorarium for a reading at Southern Illinois University Carbondale) and publication. "Manuscripts should be 50-75 pages of original poetry, in English, by a U.S. citizen or permanent resident who has neither published, nor committed to publish, a volume of poetry 40 pages or more in length (individual poems may have been previously published). Current students and employees of Southern Illinois University and authors published by Southern Illinois University Press are not eligible." See guidelines for complete formatting instructions. Guidelines available for SASE or on Web site. **Entry fee:** $25/submission; includes a copy of the summer/fall *Crab Orchard Review* (see separate listing in Magazines/Journals). Make checks payable to Crab Orchard Series in Poetry. **Deadline:** see guidelines or check Web site. 2007 winner was Sean Nevin (*Oblivio Gate*).

$□ CRAB ORCHARD SERIES IN POETRY OPEN COMPETITION AWARDS

Dept. of English, Mail Code 4503, Faner Hall 2380, Southern Illinois University Carbondale, 1000 Faner Dr., Carbondale IL 62901. Web site: www.siu.edu/~crborchd. Established 1995. **Contact:**

Jon Tribble, series editor. The Crab Orchard Series in Poetry Open Competition Awards offer 1st Prize: $3,500 and publication of a book-length ms; and 2nd Prize: $1,500 and publication of a book-length ms. "Cash prize totals reflect a $1,500 honorarium for each winner for a reading at Southern Illinois University Carbondale. Publication contract is with Southern Illinois University Press. Entrants must be U.S. citizens or permanent residents." Submissions must be unpublished as a collection, but individual poems may have been previously published elsewhere. Considers simultaneous submissions, but series editor must be informed immediately upon acceptance. Manuscripts should be typewritten or computer-generated (letter quality only, no dot matrix), single-spaced; clean photocopy is recommended as mss are not returned. See guidelines for complete formatting instructions. Guidelines available for SASE or on Web site. **Entry fee:** $25/submission; includes a copy of the winning *Crab Orchard Review* (see separate listing in Magazines/Journals). Make checks payable to Crab Orchard Series in Poetry. **Deadline:** see guidelines or check Web site. 2007 winners were Ciaran Berry (1st prize, *Sphere of Birds*) and Jake Adam York (2nd prize, *A Murmuration of Starlings*).

$☑ LOIS CRANSTON MEMORIAL POETRY PRIZE

Calyx, Inc., P.O. Box B, Corvallis OR 97339. E-mail: calyx@proaxis.com. Web site: www.calyxpress .org. Established 2002. *CALYX* (see separate listing in Magazines/Journals) offers the annual Lois Cranston Memorial Poetry Prize of $300, publication in *CALYX*, and a one-volume subscription. Finalists will be published on the *CALYX* Web site and receive a one-volume subscription. No previously published poems or simultaneous submissions. Submit up to 3 poems/entry (6 pages total maximum). Include separate cover letter with poet's name, address, phone number, e-mail address, and title(s) of poem(s). No names on poems. No mss will be returned. Guidelines available for SASE, by e-mail, or on Web site. **Entry fee:** $15 for up to 3 poems. Make checks payable to *CALYX*. **Deadline:** submit March 1-May 31 (inclusive postmark dates). Winners notified by October 30 and announced on *Calyx*'s Web site. 2006 winner is Lorraine Healy ("A Poem Before We Face the Business of Death"). 2007 judge: Paulann Peterson.

☐ CREATIVITY UNLIMITED PRESS® ANNUAL POETRY COMPETITION

30819 Casilina Dr., Rancho Palos Verdes CA 90275. E-mail: ihf@cox.net. Established 1978. **Contact:** Shelley Stockwell-Nicholas, PhD, editor. Annual invitation to submit offers possible widespread publication, with full credit to the author—Creativity Unlimited Press® uses poetry submitted in published texts and newsletters. "We often use poems as chapter introductions in self-help books. Short, clever, quippy, humorous, and delightful language encouraged. No inaccessible, verbose, esoteric, obscure poetry." Enter no more than 2 pages/poem, double-spaced, 1 side of page. Submissions may be previously published "provided writer has maintained copyright and notifies us." Accepts e-mail submissions. **Deadline:** December 31.

$☑ DANA AWARD IN POETRY

200 Fosseway Dr., Greensboro NC 27455. (336)644-8028 (for emergency questions only). E-mail: danaawards@pipeline.com. Web site: www.danaawards.com. Established 1996. **Contact:** Mary Elizabeth Parker, award chair. Offers annual award of $1,000 for the best group of 5 poems. Submissions must be unpublished and not under promise of publication when submitted. Considers simultaneous submissions. Submit 5 poems on any subject, in any form; no light verse. Include separate cover sheet with name, address, phone, e-mail address, and titles of poems. Entries by regular mail only. Include SASE for winners list only; no mss will be returned. Guidelines available for SASE, by e-mail, or on Web site. **Entry fee:** $15 for 5 poems. **Deadline:** October 31 (postmark). Competition receives 400-500 poetry entries. Recent judges: Enid Shomer and Michael White. Winner will be announced in early spring by phone, letter, and e-mail.

$☐ DANCING POETRY CONTEST

Artists Embassy International, 704 Brigham Ave., Santa Rosa CA 95404-5245. (707)528-0912. E-mail: jhcheung@aol.com. Web site: www.DANCINGPOETRY.com. Established 1993. **Contact:** Judy Cheung, contest chair. Annual contest offers 3 Grand Prizes of $100, five 1st Prizes of $50, ten 2nd Prizes of $25, and twenty 3rd Prizes of $10. The 3 Grand Prize-winning poems will be choreographed, costumed, premiered, and videotaped at the annual Dancing Poetry Festival at Palace of the Legion of Honor, San Francisco; Natica Angilly's Poetic Dance Theater Company will perform the 3 Grand Prize-winning poems. In addition, "all prizes include an invitation to read your prize poem at the festival, and a certificate suitable for framing." Submissions must be unpublished or poet must own rights. Submit 2 copies of any number of poems, 40 lines maximum (each), with name, address, phone number on 1 copy only. Foreign language poems must include English translations. Include SASE for winners list. No inquiries or entries by fax or e-mail. Entry form available for SASE. **Entry fee:** $5/poem or $10 for 3 poems. **Deadline:** May 15 annually. Competition receives about 500-800 entries. 2006 Grand Prize winners were Joyce P. Hardy, Gerard F. Keogh, Jr., and Sandra W. Soli. Judges for upcoming contest: members of Artists Embassy International. Winners will be announced by mail; Grand Prize winners will be contacted by phone. Ticket to festival will be given to all winners. Artist Embassy International has been a nonprofit educational arts organization since 1951, "Furthering intercultural understanding and peace through the universal language of the arts."

$□ LYNN DECARO POETRY COMPETITION FOR HIGH SCHOOL STUDENTS (Specialized: student poets in grades 9-12)

Connecticut Poetry Society, P.O. Box 270554, West Hartford CT 06127-0554. E-mail: connpoetry@comcast.net. Web site: www.ct-poetry-society.org. **Contact:** Contest Director. The Lynn DeCaro Poetry Competition honors the memory of Lynn DeCaro, a promising young member of Connecticut Poetry Society who died of leukemia in 1986. Offers prizes of $75, $50, and $25; prize poems will be published in *Long River Run II*. Open to high school students (grades 9-12). Send up to 3 unpublished poems, any form, 40 line limit. Include 2 copies of each poem: one with complete contact information and one with NO contact information. Both copies must be marked: Lynn DeCaro Competition. Include SASE for results only (no poems will be returned). Winning poems must be submitted by disk or e-mail following notification. **Entry fee:** none. **Deadline:** submit December 1-March 15. 2008 judge: Stephen Campiglio.
d.

$◩ DEHN POETRY COMPETITION FOR COLLEGE UNDERGRADUATES

Connecticut Poetry Society, P.O. Box 270554, West Hartford CT 06127-0554. E-mail: connpoetry@comcast.net. Web site: www.ct-poetry-society.org. **Contact:** Contest Coordinator. The Dehn Poetry Competition honors Adolf and Virginia Dehn, visual artists who supported creativity and excellence in all art forms. Offers prizes of $150, $100, and $50; prize poems will be published in *Long River Run II*. Submit up to 3 unpublished poems, any form, 40 line limit. Include 2 copies of each poem: 1 with complete contact information including college or university affiliation and 1 with NO contact information. Both copies must be marked: Dehn Poetry Competition. Include SASE for results only (no poems will be returned). Winning poems must be submitted by disk or e-mail following notification. **Entry fee:** $10 for up to 3 poems. Make checks payable to Connecticut Poetry Society. **Deadline:** submit December 1-March 15.

$◙ DEL SOL PRESS ANNUAL POETRY PRIZE

89 Elm Ridge Rd., Stow MA 01775. E-mail: editor@webdelsol.com. Web site: http://webdelsol.com/DelSolPress. Established 2003. **Contact:** Michael Neff, publisher. Offers annual award of a $1,200 honorarium, book publication, and 20 author copies. Submissions may include previously published poems and may be entered in other contests. "Poet should have some prior publication of individual poems." Submit 50-100 typed ms pages; start each poem on new page. Type or word-process on standard white paper, 1 side of page only. Paginate consecutively with a table of contents. Bind with a binder clip (no paperclips). Include 2 cover pages: 1 with poet's contact information (phone, e-mail, address), 1 with the ms title only. Poet's name should not appear on the manuscript itself. Attach publications acknowledgments, if any. Include SASP for notification of receipt of ms; no mss will be returned. Guidelines available on Web site. **Entry fee:** $24 (includes copy of winning book if 8×10 SASE with sufficient postage is sent with entry). Make checks payable

to Web del Sol. **Deadline:** mid-January; see Web site for current deadline. Most recent winner was David Ray Vance (*Vitreous*). 2006 judge: Thomas Lux. Winners will be announced on Web site. Copies of winning books available from Del Sol Press. "Web del Sol is the nation's largest online publisher of contemporary periodicals and hosts many poetry-related journals, including *Perihelion* (www.webdelsol.com/Perihelion), as well as columns and articles on poetry. It also hosts online publication-oriented poetry workshops (www.webdelsol.com/Algonkian/Poetry)." Advice: "Send only your best. Our standards are high. Check the poetry we publish onwww.webdelsol.com."

$◨ DIAGRAM/NEW MICHIGAN PRESS CHAPBOOK CONTEST

648 Crescent NE, Grand Rapids MI 49503. E-mail: nmp@thediagram.com. Web site: www.newmich iganpress.com/nmp. Established 2000. **Contact:** Ander Monson, editor. The annual *DIAGRAM/ New Michigan Press Chapbook Contest* offers $1,000 plus publication and author's copies, with discount on additional copies. Also publishes 2-4 finalist chapbooks each year. Submit 18-44 pages of poetry, fiction, mixed-genre, or genre-bending work (images okay if b/w). Include SASE. Guidelines available on Web site. **Entry fee:** $15. **Deadline:** April 1.

⬓ $◻ JAMES DICKEY PRIZE FOR POETRY

Georgia State University, P.O. Box 3999, Atlanta GA 30302-3999. (404)413-5833. Fax: (404)413-5877. Web site: www.webdelsol.com/Five_Points. Established 1996. **Contact:** Megan Sexton, editor. The annual James Dickey Prize for Poetry awards $1,000 and publication in *Five Points*. Submissions must be unpublished. Submit up to 3 typed poems, no more than 50 lines each. Include name and address on each poem. Enclose 2 SASEs: 1 to acknowledge receipt of ms, 1 for results. Guidelines available for SASE or on Web site. **Entry fee:** $20 domestic, $30 foreign (includes one-year subscription). Make checks payable to Georgia State University. **Deadline:** November 30. Winner announced in spring.

$◧ "DISCOVERY" POETRY CONTEST: THE JOAN LEIMAN JACOBSON POETRY PRIZES

Unterberg Poetry Center, 92nd Street Y, 1395 Lexington Ave., New York NY 10128. (212)415-5759 (voicemail). Web site: www.92y.org/poetry. **Contact:** Contest Coordinator. The "Discovery" Poetry Contest is designed to attract large audiences to poets who have not yet published a book. Awards a cash prize to 4 winners, plus a reading at The Unterberg Poetry Center and publication in a literary journal of national distribution, to be announced. New guidelines available on Web site. Endowed by Joan L. and Dr. Julius H. Jacobson, II.

$◧ DREAM HORSE PRESS NATIONAL POETRY CHAPBOOK PRIZE

P.O. Box 2080, Aptos CA 95001-2080. E-mail: dreamhorsepress@yahoo.com. Web site: www.drea mhorsepress.com. Established 1999. **Contact:** J.P. Dancing Bear, editor/publisher. The Dream Horse Press National Poetry Chapbook Prize offers an annual cash prize and multiple copies of a handsomely printed chapbook (prize amounts change yearly, check Web site for current information; 2008 prize was $500 and 25 copies). All entries will be considered for publication. Submissions may be previously published in magazines/journals but not in books or chapbooks. Considers simultaneous submissions with notification. "Submit 16-24 double-spaced pages of poetry in a readable font with acknowledgments, bio, e-mail address for results, and entry fee. Poet's name should not appear anywhere on the manuscript." Accepts multiple submissions (with separate fee for each entry). Manuscripts will be recycled after judging. Guidelines available on Web site. **Entry fee:** changes annually; check Web site (2008 fee was $15). Make checks/money orders made payable to Dancing Bear. **Deadline:** check Web site (2008 deadline was May 31). 2007 winner was Charles Sweetman (*Incorporated*). 2007 judge: C.J. Sage.

$◧ T.S. ELIOT PRIZE FOR POETRY

Truman State University Press, 100 E. Normal, Kirksville MO 63501-4221. (660)785-7336. Fax: (660)785-4480. E-mail: tsup@truman.edu. Web site: http://tsup.truman.edu. Press established 1986. **Contact:** Nancy Rediger. Offers annual award of $2,000 and publication. "The manuscript may include individual poems previously published in journals or anthologies, but may not include a significant number of poems from a published chapbook or self-published book.'' Submit 60-100 pages. Include 2 title pages: 1 with poet's name, address, phone number, and ms title; the other with ms title only. Include SASE for acknowledgment of ms receipt only; mss will not be returned. Guidelines available for SASE or on Web site. **Entry fee:** $25. **Deadline:** October 31. Competition receives more than 500 entries/year. 2008 winner was Victoria Brockmeier (*My Maiden Cowboy Names*). 2008 judge: Grace Schulman.

$ T.S. ELIOT PRIZE (Specialized: collections published in the UK & Ireland)

The Poetry Book Society, 4th Floor, 2 Tavistock Place, London WC1H 9RA England. (44)(207)833-9247. Fax: (44)(207)833-2990. E-mail: info@poetrybooks.co.uk. Web site: www.poetrybooks.co.uk. Established 1993. **Contact:** Chris Holifield, award director. Offers annual award for the best poetry collection published in the UK/Republic of Ireland each year. Prize: $29,500 to winner and $1,960 to shortlisted poets (donated by Mrs. Valerie Eliot). Submissions must be previously published and may be entered in other contests. Book/manuscript must be submitted by publisher and have been published (or scheduled to be published) the year of the contest. Entry form and guidelines available for SASE or by fax or e-mail. **Deadline:** early August. Competition receives 100 entries/year. 2007 winner was Sean O'Brien (*The Drowned Book*). Recent judges: Peter Porter (chair), W N Herbert and Sujata Bhatt. Also runs a Shadowing Scheme for schools. The 2008 winner will be announced in January 2009.

$ EMERGING VOICES

PEN USA, % Antioch University, 400 Corporate Pointe, Culver City CA 90230. (310)862-1555, ext. 358. Fax: (310)862-1556. E-mail: ev@penusa.org. Web site: www.penusa.org. **Contact:** Christine Lanoie-Newman, director. Annual program offering $1,000 stipend and 8-month fellowship to writers in the early stages of their literary careers. Program includes one-on-one sessions with mentors, seminars on topics such as editing or working with agents, courses in the Writers' Program at UCLA Extension, and literary readings. Participants selected according to potential and lack of access to traditional publishing and/or educational opportunities. No age restrictions; selection is not based solely on economic need. Participants need not be published, but ''the program is directed toward poets and writers of fiction and creative nonfiction with clear ideas of what they hope to accomplish through their writing. Mentors are chosen from PEN's comprehensive membership of professional writers and beyond. Participants are paired with established writers sharing similar writing interests and often with those of the same ethnic and cultural backgrounds.'' Program gets underway in January. See Web site for brochure and complete guidelines. **Deadline:** September 5, 2008 (for 2009 cycle). ''Materials must arrive in the PEN offices by the submission deadline—no exceptions.''

$ ERSKINE J. POETRY PRIZE

P.O. Box 22161, Baltimore MD 21203. E-mail: sreichert@smartishpace.com. Web site: www.smartishpace.com. Established 1999. **Contact:** Stephen Reichert, editor. The annual Erskine J. Poetry Prize offers 1st Prize: $200 and publication of the winning poem in *Smartish Pace* (see separate listing in Magazines/Journals); 2nd and 3rd Prizes: winning poems will be published in *Smartish Pace*. Winners also receive additional Internet and advertising exposure. Honorable mention (usually 5 to 12) also published in Smartish Pace. All entries will be considered for publication in *Smartish Pace*. Submit 3 poems, with poet's name, address, e-mail, telephone number (preferred), and ''Erskine J.'' at the top of each page of poetry submitted. Include bio. Entries may be submitted online or by e-mail (as attachment) or regular mail. Include SASE with postal entries. Guidelines available on Web site. **Entry fee:** $5/3 poems; additional poems may be submitted for $1/poem (limit of 12 poems). Make checks/money orders payable to *Smartish Pace*. **Deadline:** August 15, 2008. 2007 winners were Dawn McGuire (1st prize), Joan Lowery (2nd prize), and Danielle Sellers (3rd prize). Judge: Stephen Reichert (editor).

$ THE EVIL GENIUS CHAPBOOK CONTEST

Platonic 3Way Press, P.O. Box 844, Warsaw IN 46581. (317)457-3505. E-mail: evilgenius@platonic3waypress.com. Web site: www.Platonic3WayPress.com. Established 2005. **Contact:** Oren Wagner,

Steve Henn, and Don Winter, co-editors. The annual Evil Genius Chapbook Contest offers $50, publication, 50 author's copies, and "some publicity. We will submit the winning chap for review by various nationally recognized magazines and reviewers." Considers simultaneous submissions "as long as you keep us informed of the status." Submit 16-23 poems. Include SASE for reply or return of ms. Guidelines available in *Fight These Bastards* (see separate listing in Magazines/Journals), published by Platonic 3Way Press (see separate listing in Book/Chapbook Publishers), or on Web site. **Entry fee:** $12; includes a copy of the winning chapbook. "All other proceeds go to the continuing publication of *Fight These Bastards*." Make checks, bank drafts, or money orders made payable to Platonic 3Way Press. **Deadline:** was July 1 for 2007; see Web site or Spring issue of *Fight These Bastards* for 2008. "Winners will be announced in fall issues of *Fight These Bastards*."

⬀ $⊘ FAR HORIZONS AWARD FOR POETRY

The Malahat Review, University of Victoria, P.O. Box 1700, Stn CSC, Victoria BC V8W 2Y2 Canada. (250)721-8524. Fax: (250)472-5051. E-mail: malahat@uvic.ca. Web site: www.malahatreview.ca. **Contact:** Awards Coordinator. The biennial Far Horizons Award for Poetry offers $500 CAD, publication in *The Malahat Review* (see separate listing in Magazines/Journals), and payment at the rate of $40 CAD per printed page upon publication. Open to "emerging poets from Canada, the United States, and elsewhere" who have not yet published a full-length book (48 pages or more). Submissions must be unpublished. No simultaneous submissions. Submit up to 3 poems per entry, each poem not to exceed 60 lines; no restrictions on subject matter or aesthetic approach. Include separate page with poet's name, address, e-mail, and poem title(s); no identifying information on mss pages. No e-mail submissions. Do not include SASE for results; mss will not be returned. Guidelines available on Web site. **Entry fee:** $25 CAD, $30 USD ($35 USD for entries from Mexico and outside North America); includes a one-year subscription to *The Malahat Review*. **Deadline:** May 1 (postmark) of alternate years (2010, 2012, etc.). 2006 winner: Rhonda Douglas. Winner and finalists contacted by e-mail. Winner announced in fall in *The Malahat Review*, on Web site, and in quarterly e-newsletter, *Malahat lite*.

$⊘ THE WILLIAM FAULKNER-WILLIAM WISDOM CREATIVE WRITING COMPETITION

The Pirate's Alley Faulkner Society, Inc., 624 Pirate's Alley, New Orleans LA 70116. (504)586-1609. Fax: (504)522-9725. E-mail: faulkhouse@aol.com. Web site: www.wordsandmusic.org. Established 1992. **Contact:** Rosemary James, award director. Offers annual publication in *The Double Dealer*, cash prize of $750, gold medal, and all-expense-paid trip to New Orleans from any continental U.S. city. "Foreign nationals are eligible, but the society pays transportation to awards ceremony from U.S. cities only. Winners must be present at annual meeting to receive award." Submissions must be previously unpublished. Submit 1 poem of no more than 750 words on any subject in any English-language form. Multiple entries permitted. Entry form (required for each entry) and guidelines available for SASE or on Web site. **Entry fee:** $25/entry. **Deadline:** submit January 15-April 15 (postmark). "No entries before January 15, please." Competition receives 1,600 (for 7 categories) entries/year. 2007 winner was Emily Lupita Plum. 2007 judge: Nicole Cooley. Winners are announced on the society's Web site between January 1 and January 15. "Competition is keen. Send your best work."

$⊘ THE FIDDLEHEAD POETRY PRIZE

8405 Bay Parkway, C8, Brooklyn NY 11214. E-mail: fiddleheadprize@blacklawrencepress.com. Web site: www.adirondackreview.homestead.com. Established 2000. **Contact:** Diane Goettel, editor. With Black Lawrence Press, *The Adirondack Review* (see separate listing in Magazines/Journals) offers The Fiddlehead Poetry Prize, to be awarded once each year for a previously unpublished poem. Winner receives $300 and publication in *The Adirondack Review*. Honorable Mention poems will also be published and receive an honorarium of $30. Considers simultaneous submissions if notified immediately of acceptance elsewhere. Submit up to 3 original poems, unpublished in either print or on-line publications. Submissions should be sent to fiddleheadprize@blacklawrencepress.com with poet's name, address, phone number, and e-mail address included. E-mail should be titled FIDDLEHEAD PRIZE SUBMISSION in subject line; poems must be pasted into body of message. Guidelines available by e-mail (from diane@blacklawrencepress.com) or on Web site. **Entry fee:** $5 for 1 poem, $8 for 2 poems, $10 for 3 poems. Make payment through Web site via PayPal. **Deadline:** May 1. Winners announced during the summer. Judges: *The Adirondack Review* editors.

$☑ THE FIELD POETRY PRIZE

Oberlin College Press, Oberlin College, 50 N. Professor St., Oberlin OH 44074. (440)775-8408. E-mail: oc.press@oberlin.edu (inquiries only). Web site: www.oberlin.edu/ocpress. Established 1969. **Contact:** David Young. The annual *FIELD* Poetry Prize for a book-length collection of poems offers $1,000 and publication in the *FIELD* Poetry Series. Submit non-returnable ms of 50-80 pages. Guidelines available for SASE or on Web site. **Entry fee:** $22; includes one-year subscription to *FIELD* (see separate listing in Magazines/Journals). Make checks payable to Oberlin College Press. **Deadline:** submit during May only (postmark). 2007 winner was J. W. Marshall (*Meaning a Cloud*).

$☑ THE ANNIE FINCH PRIZE FOR POETRY

The National Poetry Review, P.O. Box 2080, Aptos CA 95001-2080. E-mail: editor@nationalpoetryreview.com. Web site: www.nationalpoetryreview.com. **Contact:** C.J. Sage, editor. The Annie Finch Prize for Poetry offers $300 plus publication in *The National Poetry Review* (see separate listing in Magazines/Journals). All entries will be considered by the editor for publication. Submissions must be unpublished and uncommitted. Considers simultaneous submissions, "but if the work is selected by *The National Poetry Review* for the prize or for publication, it must be withdrawn from elsewhere unless you have withdrawn it from us two weeks before our acceptance." Submit up to 3 poems/ entry (10 pages maximum per group of 3). Include cover letter with bio and contact information, including e-mail address for results. Guidelines available on Web site. **Entry fee:** $15/entry; accepts multiple submissions with separate entry fee for each 3-poem group. "If you include a small book-sized SASE with $1.30 postage with your entry, we will provide you a copy of the winner's issue." Make checks payable to *The National Poetry Review* . **Deadline:** April 30 (postmark). 2006 final judge: Bob Hicok.

$☑ THE FINISHING LINE PRESS OPEN CHAPBOOK COMPETITION

Finishing Line Press, P.O. Box 1626, Georgetown KY 40324. (859)514-8966. E-mail: FinishingBooks @aol.com. Web site: www.finishinglinepress.com. Established 1998. **Contact:** Leah Maines, poetry editor. The Finishing Line Press Open Chapbook Competition offers a $1,000 cash award and publication. All entries will be considered for publication. Open to all poets regardless of past publications. Submit up to 26 pages of poetry. Include bio, acknowledgments, and cover letter. Guidelines available by e-mail or on Web site. **Entry fee:** $15. **Deadline:** July 15 (postmark) for 2008.

Ⓝ $◯ THE FLIP KELLY POETRY PRIZE

6199 Steubenville Road SE, Amsterdam OH 43903.740-543-4333. E-mail: plainspoke@gmail.com. Web site: www.plainspoke.net. Established 2007. **Contact:** Cindy Kelly, editor. The Flip Kelly Poetry Prize offers a 1st prize of $100 honorarium & Feature spread in Winter 2009 issue of *Plain Spoke*. Runners-Up receive a small feature in the same issue. All entries are considered for future publication in *Plain Spoke* (see separate listing under Magazines /Journals and Amsterdam Press under Book/Chapbook publishers). Submissions must be unpublished (considers poetry posted on a public Web site/blog/forum published). Poems may be entered in other contests and/or under consideration elsewhere. Submit 3 poems and entry form with poet's name, address, phone number, and poem titles. Guidelines and entry forms available for SASE, by e-mail, and on Web site. Entry fee: $15/3 poems. Deadline: November 1, 2008. 2008 judge: TBA. Winners will be announced January 15, 2009 (or sooner). Copies of *Plain Spoke* with winning entries will be available from www.plainspoke.net for $6. "Amsterdam Press was founded in 2007." Advice: "We favor the plain-spoken over the esoteric. We like specific, not universal."

$☑ FLUME PRESS CHAPBOOK COMPETITION

California State University at Chico, 400 W. First St., Chico CA 95929-0830. (530)898-5983. E-mail: flumepress@csuchico.edu. Web site: www.csuchico.edu/engl/flumepress. Established 1984.

Contact: Casey Huff, poetry editor. Flume Press selects chapbooks for publication through its biennial competition (alternates between poetry and fiction). Winner receives $500 and 25 author's copies. Submission must be unpublished as a collection, but individual poems may have been previously published. Considers simultaneous submissions if poet agrees to withdraw ms from other competitions if chosen as a winner by Flume. Submit 24-30 pages, including title, table of contents, and acknowledgments page. Include cover sheet with poet's name and address; poet's name should not appear on ms pages. Include SASE for return of ms and comments. Guidelines available on Web site. **Entry fee:** $20 (each entrant receives a copy of the winning chapbook). **Deadline:** December 1 (postmark); check Web site for appropriate year for poetry. Chapbooks available for $10 from Flume Press.

$🖉 THE 49TH PARALLEL POETRY AWARD

Bellingham Review, Western Washington University, Mail Stop 9053, Bellingham WA 98225. (360)650-4863. E-mail: bhreview@cc.wwu.edu. Web site: www.wwu.edu/~bhreview. **Contact:** Contest Director. The annual 49th Parallel Poetry Award offers 1st Prize of $1,000, plus publication in and a year's subscription to *Bellingham Review* (see separate listing in Magazines/Journals). Runners-up and finalists may be considered for publication. Submissions must be unpublished and not accepted for publication elsewhere. Considers simultaneous submissions, but work must be withdrawn from the competition if accepted for publication elsewhere. Submit up to 3 poems. "Poems within a series will each be treated as a separate entry." For each entry, include a 3×5 index card stating the title of the work, the category (poetry), the poet's name, phone number, address, and e-mail. "Make sure writing is legible on this card. Author's name must not appear anywhere on the manuscript." Include SASE for results only; mss will not be returned. Guidelines available for SASE or on Web site. **Entry fee:** $18 for first entry (up to 3 poems); $10 each additional poem. Make checks payable to *Bellingham Review*. "Everyone entering the competition will receive a complimentary two-issue subscription to *Bellingham Review*." **Deadline:** entries must be postmarked December 1-March 15, 2008. 2007 winner was Luisa A. Igloria ("The Clear Bones"). 2007 judge: Carolyne Wright. Winners will be announced by July 2008.

$🖉 THE ROBERT FROST FOUNDATION ANNUAL POETRY AWARD (Specialized: poems written in the spirit of Robert Frost)

The Robert Frost Foundation, Lawrence Library, 51 Lawrence St., Lawrence MA 01841. (978)725-8828. E-mail: frostfoundation@comcast.net. Web site: www.frostfoundation.org. Established 1997. Offers annual award of $1,000. Submissions may be entered in other contests. Submit up to 3 poems of not more than 3 pages each (2 copies of each poem, 1 with name, address, and phone number), written in the spirit of Robert Frost. Guidelines available for SASE and on Web site. **Entry fee:** $10/poem. **Deadline:** September 15. Competition receives over 600 entries/year. 2007 Winner was Barbara Adams. Winners will be announced at the annual Frost Festival and by SASE following the Festival (late October). Winning poem can be viewed on Web site.

$🖉 ◎ KINERETH GENSLER AWARD (Specialized: New England, NY, NJ residents)

Alice James Books, 238 Main St., Farmington ME 04938. Phone/fax: (207)778-7071. E-mail: ajb@umf.maine.ed. Web site: www.alicejamesbooks.org. Established 1973. **Contact:** Contest Coordinator. The Kinereth Gensler Award offers $2,000 and publication by Alice James Books (see separate listing in Book/Chapbook Publishers); winners become members of the Alice James Books cooperative, with a 3-year commitment to the editorial board. **Entrants must reside in New England, New York, or New Jersey.** Submissions must be unpublished as a collection, but individual poems may have been previously published elsewhere (in publications of less than 48 pages). Submit 2 copies of ms of 50-70 pages, typed single-spaced and paginated, with table of contents and acknowledgments page; bio is optional. Use binder clips; no staples, folders, or printer-bound copies. Title page of each ms copy must include poet's name, address, and phone number. Enclose SASP for acknowledgment of receipt of ms, #10 SASE for results; mss will not be returned. Guidelines available for SASE or on Web site. **Entry fee:** $25/ms. Make checks/money orders payable to Alice James Books. For a free book (does not apply to books not yet published), include an additional

6×9envelope with $2 in postage attached; write title of selection on back of envelope. **Deadline:** October 2008. 2006 winners were Bill Rasmovicz (*The World in Place of Itself*), Ann Killough (*Dog in the Road*), and Peter Waldor (*The Warmth of The Ones I Love*). Judges: members of the Alice James Books Editorial Board. Winners announced in December. Copies of winning books available through Web site.

$⊘ ◎ GERTRUDE PRESS POETRY CHAPBOOK CONTEST (Specialized: gay, lesbian, bisexual, transgendered, queer-identified & allied)

P.O. Box 83948, Portland OR 97283. E-mail: editor@gertrudepress.org (inquiries only). Web site: www.gertrudepress.org. Established 1998. **Contact:** Eric Delehoy, founding editor. Gertrude Press (see separate listing in Books/Chapbooks) sponsors an annual chapbook competition. Offers $50, publication, and 50 author copies (out of a press run of 200) to the winning poet. Individual poems may have been previously published; unpublished poems are welcome. Submit 16-20 pages of poetry (postal submissions only). "Poetry may be of any subject matter, and writers from all backgrounds are encouraged to submit." Include list of acknowledgments and cover letter indicating how poet learned of the contest. Guidelines available in *Gertrude* (see separate listing in Magazines/Journals), for SASE, by e-mail, or on Web site. **Entry fee:** $15; includes copy of the winning chapbook. **Deadline:** submit September 1-January 15 (postmark) annually. 2007 winner was Michael Montlack.

$⊘ ALLEN GINSBERG POETRY AWARDS

Poetry Center, Passaic County Community College, One College Blvd., Paterson NJ 07505-1179. (973)684-6555. E-mail: mgillan@pccc.edu. Web site: www.pccc.edu/poetry. Established 1979. **Contact:** Maria Mazziotti Gillan, editor/executive director. The Allen Ginsberg Poetry Awards offer annual prizes of 1st Prize: $1,000, 2nd Prize: $200, and 3rd Prize: $100. All winning poems, honorable mentions, and editor's choice poems will be published in *Paterson Literary Review* (see separate listing in Magazines/Journals). Winners will be asked to participate in a reading that will be held in the Paterson Historic District. Submissions must be unpublished. Submit up to 5 poems (no poem more than 2 pages long). Send 4 copies of each poem entered. Include cover sheet with poet's name, address, phone number, and poem titles. Poet's name should not appear on poems. Include SASE for results only; poems will not be returned. Guidelines available for SASE or on Web site. **Entry fee:** $15 (includes subscription to *Paterson Literary Review*). Write "poetry contest" in memo section of check and make payable to PCCC. **Deadline:** April 1 (postmark). Winners will be announced the following summer by mail and in newspaper announcements. 2007 winners were Kenneth Hart and Glenn Morazzini (1st), R.G. Evans and Linda Radice (2nd), and Patti Conroy (3rd).

⚃ $◎ GOVERNOR GENERAL'S LITERARY AWARDS (Specialized: Canadian citizens/ permanent residents; English- and French-language works)

The Canada Council for the Arts, P.O. Box 1047, 350 Albert St., Ottawa ON K1P 5V8 Canada. (613)566-4414, ext. 5573. Fax: (613)566-4410. E-mail: christian.mondor@canadacouncil.ca. Web site: www.canadacouncil.ca/prizes/GGLA. Established 1957. **Contact:** Robyn Pollex, program assistant. Established by Parliament, the Canada Council for the Arts "provides a wide range of grants and services to professional Canadian artists and art organizations in dance, media arts, music, theater, writing, publishing, and the visual arts." The Governor General's Literary Awards, valued at $25,000 CAD each, are given annually for the best English-language and best French-language work in each of 7 categories, including poetry. Non-winning finalists each receive $1,000 CAD. Books must be first edition trade books written, translated, or illustrated by Canadian citizens or permanent residents of Canada and published in Canada or abroad during the previous year (September 1 through the following September 30). Collections of poetry must be at least 48 pages long, and at least half the book must contain work not published previously in book form. In the case of translation, the original work must also be a Canadian-authored title. Books must be submitted by publishers with a Publisher's Submission Form, which is available on request from the Writing and Publishing Section of the Canada Council for the Arts. Guidelines and current deadlines on the Web site and available by mail, telephone, fax, or e-mail.

$⊘ GRANDMOTHER EARTH NATIONAL AWARD

Grandmother Earth Creations, P.O. Box 2018, Cordova TN 38088. (901)309-3692 or (901)216-4496 (cell). E-mail: Gmoearth@aol.com. Web site: www.grandmotherearth.org. Established 1994. **Contact:** Frances Cowden, award director. Offers annual award of $1,250 with varying distributions each year; $1,250 minimum in awards for poetry and prose; $200 first, etc., plus publication in anthology; non-winning finalists considered for anthology if permission is given. Submissions may be published or unpublished. Considers simultaneous submissions. Submit at least 3 poems, any subject, in any form. Include SASE for winners list. Guidelines available for SASE or on Web site. **Entry fee:** $10 for 3 works, $2 each additional work. Entry fee includes a copy of the anthology. **Deadline:** July 15. 2006 winners were Carol Carpenter, Marcia Camp, Timothy Russell, and Lene' Gary. 2007 judge: Nancy Breen. Winners will be announced in October at the Mid-South Poetry Festival in Memphis. Copies of winning poems or books available from Grandmother Earth Creations.

$◯ THE GREAT BLUE BEACON POETRY CONTEST

1425 Patriot Dr., Melbourne FL 32940. (321)253-5869. E-mail: ajircc@juno.com. Established 1997. **Contact:** A.J. Byers, award director. Offers prizes approximately 3 times/year, as announced, of 1st Prize: $25; 2nd Prize: $15; 3rd Prize: $10. "Winning poem to be published in *The Great Blue Beacon*. Prize amounts will be increased if sufficient entries are received." Submissions must be unpublished. Considers simultaneous submissions. Submit up to 3 poems maximum on any subject, in any form. Submit 3 typed copies of each entry, no more than 24 lines/poem. On 1 copy, put poet's name, address, and telephone number in the upper left-hand corner of the first page; no name or address on the second or third copies. "Contestants must send SASE or e-mail address with entry to receive notification of results. Follow guidelines, particularly line limits. Submit your best work." Guidelines available for SASE or by e-mail. **Entry fee:** $3/poem ($2 for subscribers to *The Great Blue Beacon*). Make checks payable to Andy Byers. **Deadline:** see guidelines. Competition receives 200-300 entries/year. Most recent winners were Anna Evans (NJ), 1st and 2nd places; and Barbara Anton (FL). Winners are announced approximately 2 months after deadline date. *The Great Blue Beacon* is a quarterly newsletter for all writers. Sample copy: $1 and 60¢ postage (or IRC). Subscription: $10/year; students $8; $14 outside the U.S.

$⊘ GREAT LAKES COLLEGES ASSOCIATION NEW WRITERS AWARD

GLCA, 535 W. William, Ste. 301, Ann Arbor MI 48103. (734)661-2350. Fax: (734)661-2340. E-mail: shackelford@glca.org. Web site: www.glca.org. **Contact:** Deanna Shackelford, program coordinator. Director of Program Development: Gregory Wegner. Offers annual award to the best first book of poetry, fiction, and creative non-fiction among those submitted by publishers. The winning authors tour several of the 12 GLCA-member colleges (as invited) reading, lecturing, visiting classes, doing workshops, and publicizing their books. Each writer receives an honorarium of at least $500 from each college visited, as well as travel expenses, hotel accommodations, and hospitality. Usually, 1 winner (fiction) tours in the fall, and the other winner (poetry) tours in the spring, following the competition. Submissions must be previously published. Publishers should submit 4 copies of galleys or the printed book plus a statement of the author's agreement to commit to the college tour. Guidelines available for SASE, by e-mail, or on Web site. **Deadline:** Late spring 2008. Additional details will be available on the GLCA Web site. 2007 poetry winner was Jay Hopler (*Green Squall*); fiction winner was Tony D'Souza (*Whiteman*). Winners will be announced in May.

$⊘ THE GREEN ROSE PRIZE IN POETRY

New Issues Poetry & Prose, Western Michigan University, 1903 W. Michigan Ave., Kalamazoo MI 49008-5463. (269)387-8185. Fax: (269)387-2562. Web site: www.wmich.edu/newissues. Established 1996. The Green Rose Prize in Poetry offers $2,000 and publication of a book of poems by an established poet who has published one or more full-length collections of poetry. *New Issues* may publish as many as 3 additional mss from this competition. Considers simultaneous submissions, but *New Issues* must be notified of acceptance elsewhere. Submit a ms of at least 48 pages, typed, single-spaced preferred. Clean photocopies acceptable. Do not bind; use manila folder or metal clasp. Include cover page with poet's name, address, phone number, and title of the ms. Also include brief bio, table of contents, and acknowledgments page. No e-mail or fax submissions. Include SASP for notification of receipt of ms and SASE for results only; mss will be recycled. Guidelines available for SASE, by fax, e-mail, or on Web site. **Entry fee:** $20. Make checks payable to *New Issues Poetry & Prose*. **Deadline:** submit May 1-September 30 (postmark). Winner is announced in January or February on Web site. 2008 winner was Patty Seyburn (*Hilarity*). Judge: *New Issues* editors. The winning manuscript will be published Spring 2010.

$✅ GREG GRUMMER POETRY AWARD

MSN 2D6, George Mason University, 4400 University Dr., Fairfax VA 22030-4444. (703)993-2915. E-mail: phoebe@gmu.edu (inquiries only). Web site: www.gmu.edu/pubs/phoebe. Established 1970. **Contact:** Contest Coordinator. The Greg Grummer Poetry Award offers $1,000 and publication in *Phoebe: A Journal of Literature and Art* (see separate listing in Magazines/Journals) for winner, possible publication for finalists, and a copy of awards issue to all entrants. Submissions must be unpublished. Submit up to 4 poems (not to exceed 20 pages total), any subject, any form, with name on cover page only. Include SASE for results only; mss will not be returned. Guidelines available for SASE or on Web site. **Entry fee:** $15/entry. Make checks/money orders payable to *Phoebe*/GMU. **Deadline:** December 1 (postmark). Contest receives 300-400 submissions. Back copy of awards issue available for $6.

⊠ $✅ GUGGENHEIM FELLOWSHIPS

John Simon Guggenheim Memorial Foundation, Writing Fellowships, 90 Park Ave., New York NY 10016. (212)687-4470. E-mail: fellowships@gf.org. Web site: www.gf.org. Established 1925. Guggenheim Fellowships are awarded each year to poets, as well as fiction and creative nonfictions writers, "on the basis of unusually distinguished achievement in the past and exceptional promise for future accomplishment." 2007 Fellowships were awarded to 25 writers; amounts averaged $40,211 each. Submit career summary, statement of intent, and no more than 3 published books. Guidelines, application form (required), and additional information available for SASE, by e-mail, or on Web site. **Deadline:** was September 15 for 2008 awards. **Entry fee:** none. 2007 Fellowship recipients in poetry were Christopher Buckley, Greg Delanty, Erica Funkhouser, A. Van Jordan, Dana Levin, Malena Mörling, D. Nurkse, Kathleen Peirce, and Lawrence Raab.

$✅ THE DONALD HALL PRIZE IN POETRY

AWP Award Series in Poetry, The Association of Writers & Writing Programs, Carty House, Mail Stop 1E3, George Mason University, Fairfax VA 22030-4444. E-mail: chronicle@awpwriter.org (inquiries only). Web site: www.awpwriter.org. Established 2003. The Association of Writers & Writing Programs (AWP) sponsors an annual competition for the publication of excellent new book-length works, the AWP Award Series, which includes The Donald Hall Prize in Poetry. Offers annual award of $4,000 and publication for the best book-length ms of poetry (book-length defined for poetry as 48 pages minimum of text). Open to published and unpublished poets alike. "Poems previously published in periodicals are eligible for inclusion in submissions, but manuscripts previously published in their entirety, including self-published, are not eligible. As the series is judged anonymously, no list of acknowledgments should accompany your manuscript. You may submit your manuscript to other publishers while it is under consideration by the Award Series, but you must notify AWP immediately in writing if your manuscript is accepted elsewhere. Your manuscript must be submitted in accordance with the eligibility requirements, format guidelines, and entry requirements or it will be disqualified." Complete guidelines, including important formatting information, eligibility requirements, and required entry form available on Web site. **Entry fee:** $10 (AWP members) or $25 (nonmembers). Make checks/money orders payable in U.S. dollars only to AWP. **Deadline:** mss must be postmarked between January 1-February 28. 2007 winner was Sharon Dolin (*Burn and Dodge*). 2008 judge: Lynn Emanuel.

$ BEATRICE HAWLEY AWARD

Alice James Books, 238 Main St., Farmington ME 04938. Phone/fax: (207)778-7071. E-mail: ajb@u mf.maine.ed. Web site: www.alicejamesbooks.org. Established 1973. **Contact:** Contest Coordinator. The Beatrice Hawley Award offers $2,000 and publication by Alice James Books (see separate listing in Book/Chapbook Publishers). Winners have no cooperative membership commitment. "In addition to the winning manuscript, one or more additional manuscripts may be chosen for publication." Entrants must reside in the U.S. Submissions must be unpublished as a collection, but individual poems may have been previously published elsewhere (in publications of less than 48 pages). Submit 2 copies of ms of 50-70 pages, typed single-spaced and paginated, with table of contents and acknowledgments page; bio is optional. Use binder clips; no staples, folders, or printer-bound copies. Title page of each ms copy must include poet's name, address, and phone number. Include SASP for acknowledgment of receipt of ms, #10 SASE for results only; mss will not be returned. Guidelines available for SASE or on Web site. **Entry fee:** $25/ms. Make checks/money orders payable to Alice James Books (write "Beatrice Hawley Award" on memo line). **Deadline:** December 1 (postmark) for 2008. 2006 winner was Henrietta Goodman (*Take What You Want*). Judges: members of the Alice James Books Editorial Board. Winners announced in April. Copies of winning books available through Web site.

$⬛ JAMES HEARST POETRY PRIZE

North American Review, University of Northern Iowa, 1222 West 27th St., Cedar Falls IA 50614-0516. (319)273-6455. Fax: (319)273-4326. E-mail: nar@uni.edu. Web site: http://webdelsol.com/NorthAmReview/NAR. **Contact:** Vince Gotera, poetry editor. The James Hearst Poetry Prize offers 1st Prize: $1,000; 2nd Prize: $100; and 3rd Prize: $50. All winners and finalists will be published in *North American Review* (see separate listing in Magazines/Journals). Submissions must be unpublished. No simultaneous submissions. Submit up to 5 poems, 2 copies each; **NO NAMES** on ms pages. Cover sheet is required (MS Word or PDF). Include SASP for acknowledgment of receipt of ms and #10 SASE for results (or provide e-mail address on cover sheet); mss will not be returned. Guidelines available for SASE, by fax, e-mail, or on Web site. **Entry fee:** $18 (includes one-year subscription). Make checks/money orders payable to *North American Review*. **Deadline:** October 31 (postmark).

🌐 $◎ FELICIA HEMANS PRIZE FOR LYRICAL POETRY (Specialized: University of Liverpool members & students)

The University of Liverpool, Foundation Building, Brownlow Hill, Liverpool L69 72X England. (44)(151)794-2458. E-mail: wilderc@liv.ac.uk. Established 1899. **Contact:** Chief Operating Officer, University of Liverpool. Offers annual award of £30. Open to past or present members and students of the University of Liverpool. Considers simultaneous submissions. Submit 1 poem. Guidelines available for SASE only. **Deadline:** May 1. Competition receives 12-15 entries. Judges are the Professors of English Literature in the University. The winner and all other competitors will be notified by mail in June.

$⬛ THE ALFRED HODDER FELLOWSHIP

Program in Creative Writing, 185 Nassau St., Princeton NJ 08542. (609)258-4096. Fax: (609)258-2230. E-mail: jbraude@princeton.edu. Web site: www.princeton.edu/arts/hodder_fellowship. **Contact:** Janine Braude. "Stipends of $58,000 will be given to 3 writers of exceptional promise to pursue independent projects and teach 1 course in the humanities at Princeton University during the 2007-2008 academic year. Typically the fellows are poets, playwrights, novelists, creative nonfiction writers, and translators who have published 1 highly acclaimed work and are undertaking a significant new project that might not be possible without the 'studious leisure' afforded by the fellowship." Preference is given to applicants outside academia. Candidates for the Ph.D. are not eligible. Submit a résumé, sample of previous work (10 pages maximum, not returnable), a project proposal of 2-3 pages, and SASE. Guidelines available on Web site. **Deadline:** January 1 (postmark). Announcement of the Hodder Fellow is posted on the Web site in March.

$⬛ TOM HOWARD/JOHN H. REID POETRY CONTEST

Tom Howard Books, % Winning Writers, 351 Pleasant St., PMB 222, Northampton MA 01060-3961. (866)946-9748. Fax: (413)280-0539. E-mail: johnreid@mail.qango.com. Web site: www.winn

ingwriters.com. Established 2003. **Contact:** John H. Reid, award director. Offers annual award of 1st Prize: $1,000; 2nd Prize: $400; 3rd Prize: $200; 7 High Distinction Awards of $100 each; 10 Highly Commended Awards of $70 each; and 10 Commended Awards of $50 each. The top 10 entries will be published on the Winning Writers Web site. Submissions may be published or unpublished and may have won prizes elsewhere. Considers simultaneous submissions. Submit poems in any form, style, or genre. "There is no limit on the number of lines or poems you may submit." No name on ms pages; type or computer-print on letter-size white paper, single-sided. Submit online or by regular mail. Guidelines available for SASE or on Web site. **Entry fee:** $6 USD for every 25 lines (exclude poem titles and any blank lines from line count). **Deadline:** December 15-September 30. Competition receives about 1,000 entries/year. 2006 winner was Debbie Camelin ("Intimidation"). 2006 judges: John H. Reid and Dee C. Konrad. Winners announced in February at WinningWriters.com. Entrants who provide valid e-mail addresses will also receive notification.

$☑ HENRY HOYNS & POE/FAULKNER FELLOWSHIPS (Specialized: MFA candidates in creative writing)

Creative Writing Program, 219 Bryan Hall, P.O. Box 400121, University of Virginia, Charlottesville VA 22904-4121. (434)924-6675. Fax: (434)924-1478. E-mail: SHB7F@virginia.ed. Web site: http://www.engl.virginia.edu/creativewriting/admissions.shtml. **Contact:** Sydney Blair, program director. Annual fellowships in poetry and fiction of varying amounts for candidates for the MFA in creative writing. Sample poems/prose required with application. **Deadline:** January 2, 2008. Competition receives 400-500 entries.

$☑ THE HUDSON PRIZE

(Formerly the Ontario Prize), Black Lawrence Press, 521 56th Street 2F, Brooklyn NY 11220. E-mail: editors@blacklawrencepress.com. Web site: www.blacklawrencepress.com. Established 2003. **Contact:** Colleen Ryor, editor. The Hudson Prize is awarded annually for an unpublished collection of poetry or short stories. Winner receives $1,000, publication by Black Lawrence Press (see separate listing in Book/Chapbook Publishers), 10 author copies, and an interview in *The Adirondack Review* (see separate listing in Magazines/Journals). Finalists will receive a copy of the winning book. All finalists will be considered for standard publication. Accepts simultaneous submissions, but notify immediately if ms is accepted elsewhere. Submit book-length ms, paginated, with cover letter with brief bio and contact information (including valid e-mail), table of contents, and an acknowledgments page (if applicable). "Finalists will be notified and asked to submit another copy of the manuscript for final judging." Include 2 cover pages: 1 with ms title, brief bio, and poet's contact information (including e-mail); the second with ms title only. Clip together the cover letter, cover pages, acknowledgments, and entry fee. No e-mail submissions. Include SASE or e-mail address for results only; mss will not be returned. Guidelines available on Web site. **Entry fee:** $25. Make checks/money orders payable to Black Lawrence Press. **Deadline:** March 31.

$☑ THE LYNDA HULL MEMORIAL POETRY PRIZE

Crazyhorse, Dept. of English, College of Charleston, 66 George St., Charleston SC 29424. (843)953-7740. E-mail: crazyhorse@cofc.edu. Web site: http://crazyhorse.cofc.edu. Established 1960. **Contact:** Prize Director. The annual Lynda Hull Memorial Poetry Prize offers $2,000 and publication in *Crazyhorse* (see separate listing in Contests & Awards). All entries will be considered for publication. Submissions must be unpublished. Submit online or by mail up to 3 original poems (no more than 10 pages). Include cover page (placed on top of ms) with poet's name, address, e-mail, and telephone number; no identifying information on mss (blind judging). Accepts multiple submissions with separate fee for each. Include SASP for notification of receipt of ms and SASE for results only; mss will not be returned. Guidelines available for SASE or on Web site. **Entry fee:** $16/ms for new entrants; $14/ms for poets who have entered the *Crazyhorse* prizes before (indicate on ms cover page). Fee includes a one-year/2 issue subscription to *Crazyhorse*; for each poetry ms entered and fee paid, subscription is extended by 1 year. Make checks payable to *Crazyhorse*; credit card payments also accepted (see Web site for details). **Deadline:** September 1-December 15 (postmark). Winners announced by April. 2007 winner: Jude Nutter ("Frank O'Hara in Paradise"). 2007 judge: Marvin Bell.

⬛ $⬜ INKWELL ANNUAL POETRY CONTEST

Inkwell, Manhattanville College, 2900 Purchase St., Purchase NY 10577. (914)323-7239. Fax: (914)323-3122. E-mail: inkwell@mville.edu. Web site: www.inkwelljournal.org. Established 1995. **Contact:** Contest Coordinator. The *Inkwell* Annual Poetry Competition awards $1,000 grand prize and publication in *Inkwell* (see separate listing in Magazines/Journals) for best poem. Submissions must be unpublished. Submit up to 5 poems at a time, no more than 40 lines/poem, typed in 12 pt. font. Include cover sheet with poet's name, address, phone number, e-mail, and poems titles and line counts. No name or address should appear on mss. Also include Submission Checklist (download from Web site). Indicate "Poetry Competition" on envelope. Include SASE for results only; mss will not be returned. Guidelines available on Web site. **Entry fee:** $10 for first poem, $5 for each additional poem (USD only). Make checks payable to Manhattanville—*Inkwell*. **Deadline:** August 1-October 30 (postmark). 2008 judge: Major Jackson.

$☑ THE IOWA POETRY PRIZES

The University of Iowa Press, 100 Kuhl House, 119 West Park Rd., Iowa City IA 52242-1000. (319)335-2000. E-mail: uipress@uiowa.edu. Web site: www.uiowapress.org. The University of Iowa Press offers the annual Iowa Poetry Prizes for book-length mss (50-150 pages) "written originally in English" by new or established poets. Winners will be published by the Press under a standard royalty contract. Poems from previously published books may be included only in mss of selected or collected poems, submissions of which are encouraged. Considers simultaneous submissions if Press is immediately notified if the book is accepted by another publisher. Guidelines available on Web site. **Entry fee:** $20. **Deadline:** postmarked during April only. 2006 winners were *American Spikenard* by Sarah Vap and *Sunday Houses the Sunday House* by Elizabeth Hughey.

$☑ THE IOWA REVIEW AWARD IN POETRY

308 EPB, University of Iowa, Iowa City IA 52242. (319)335-0462. E-mail: iowa-review@uiowa.edu. Web site: www.iowareview.org. Established 1970. **Contact:** Contest Coordinator. *The Iowa Review* Award in Poetry, Fiction, and Nonfiction presents $1,000 to each winner in each genre, $500 to runners-up. Winners published in *The Iowa Review* (see separate listing in Magazines/Journals). Submissions must be unpublished. Considers simultaneous submissions (with notification of acceptance elsewhere). Submit up to 10 pages of poetry, double- or single-spaced; one poem or several. Include cover page with poet's name, address, e-mail and/or phone number, and title of each work submitted. Personal identification must not appear on ms pages. Label mailing envelope "Contest: Poetry." Include SASP for confirmation of receipt of entry, SASE for results. Guidelines available on Web site. **Entry Fee:** $15 for entry only; $25 for entry and yearlong subscription. Make checks payable to *The Iowa Review*. **Deadline:** submit January 1-31 (postmark). 2007 winners were John Colasacco (1st Prize) and Mary Flanagan and Nancy Kathleen Pearson (runners-up). 2008 judge: Heather McHugh.

$◎ JOSEPH HENRY JACKSON AWARD (Specialized: northern CA or NV residents ages 20-35)

% Intersection for the Arts, 446 Valencia St., San Francisco CA 94103. (415)626-2787. Fax: (415)626-1636. Web site: www.theintersection.org. Established 1955. **Contact:** Awards Coordinator. The Joseph Henry Jackson Award offers $2,000 to the author of an unpublished work-in-progress of fiction (novel or short stories), nonfictional prose, or poetry. Applicants must be residents of northern California or Nevada for 3 consecutive years immediately prior to the March 31 deadline and must be between the ages of 20 and 35 as of the deadline. Guidelines and entry form (required) available on Web site. **Entry fee:** none. **Deadline:** March 31. Competition receives 150-180 entries. 2007 winner was Peter Nathaniel Malae (fiction, "What We Are").

$☑ ◎ JAPANESE LITERARY TRANSLATION PRIZE (Specialized: Japanese into English)

Donald Keene Center of Japanese Culture, Columbia University, 507 Kent Hall, New York NY 10027. (212)854-5036. Fax: (212)854-4019. E-mail: donald-keene-center@columbia.edu. Web site:

www.donaldkeenecenter.org. **Contact:** Miho Walsh, associate director. Established 1981. The Donald Keene Center of Japanese Culture at Columbia University annually awards $6,000 for the Japan-U.S. Friendship Commission Prize for the Translation of Japanese Literature. A prize is given for the best translation of a modern work of literature or for the best classical literary translation, or the prize is divided between a classical and a modern work. Submissions may be previously published. Considers simultaneous submissions. Translated works submitted for consideration may include: a) unpublished mss; b) works in press; c) translations published after January 1, 2007. Submit 7 hard copies of book-length ms or published book. Entry form and guidelines available for SASE, by fax, e-mail, or on Web site. **Deadline:** March 1, 2009. Competition receives 20-25 entries/year. 2007 award winners were Anthony H. Chambers for his translation of *Tales of Moonlight and Rain* by Akinari Ueda, and Kozue Uzawa and Amelia Fielden for their translation of tanka poems in *Ferris Wheel: 101 Modern and Contemporary Tanka.*Winners are announced through press releases and on Web site.

✪ $▢ JOHN WOOD COMMUNITY COLLEGE CREATIVE WRITING CONTEST

Business Office/Writing Contest, John Wood Community College, 1301 S. 48th St., Quincy IL 62305. (217)641-4940. Fax: (217)641-4900. E-mail: klangston@jwcc.edu. Web site: www.jwcc.edu. Established 1990. **Contact:** Kelli Langston, contest coordinator, or Janet McGovern ((217)641-4905; jmcgovern@jwcc.edu). Offers annual award for original, unpublished poetry, fiction, and nonfiction. Categories include non-rhyming poetry, traditional rhyming poetry, plus a category for all other poetry forms (i.e., haiku, limerick, etc.). 1st, 2nd, and 3rd Prizes awarded in each category, plus Honorable Mention certificates. Cash prizes based on dollar total of entry fees. Guidelines available for SASE, by fax, e-mail, or on Web site. **Entry fee:** $5/poem; $7/nonfiction or fiction piece. **Deadline:** entries accepted January 15-April 3. Competition receives 50-100 entries. ''We are offering a new critiquing service of works submitted to the contest. **If you wish a written critique, you must include an additional $5 per poem and/or $15 per story (include up to 3 pages).** Critiques will be sent as soon as possible after judging.''

$◙ JUNIPER PRIZE FOR POETRY

University of Massachusetts Press, Amherst MA 01003. (413)545-2217. Fax: (413)545-1226. E-mail: info@umpress.umass.edu. Web site: www.umass.edu/umpress. Established 1964. **Contact:** Carla Potts. The University of Massachusetts Press offers the annual Juniper Prize for Poetry, awarded in alternate years for first and subsequent books. Prize includes publication and $1,500 in addition to royalties. In even-numbered years (2008, 2010, etc.), only ''subsequent'' books will be considered: mss whose authors have had at least 1 full-length book or chapbook (of at least 30 pages) of poetry published or accepted for publication. Self-published work is not considered to lie within this ''books and chapbooks'' category. In odd-numbered years (2009, 2011, etc.), only ''first books'' will be considered: mss by writers whose poems may have appeared in literary journals and/or anthologies but have not been published, nor accepted for publication, in book form. Considers simultaneous submissions, ''but if accepted for publication elsewhere, please notify us immediately. Manuscripts by more than 1 author, entries of more than 1 manuscript simultaneously or within the same year, and translations are not eligible.'' Submit paginated ms of 50-70 pages of poetry, with paginated contents page, credits page, and information about previously published books. Include 2 cover sheets: 1 with contact information, one without. Manuscripts will not be returned. Guidelines available for SASE or on Web site. **Entry fee:** $20. **Deadline:** submit August 1-September 29 (postmark). 2007 winner was Theodore Worozbyt (*Letters of Transit*). Winners announced in April on Web site. Copies of winning books available through Web site.

✪ $▢ ◎ BARBARA MANDIGO KELLY PEACE POETRY AWARDS

Nuclear Age Peace Foundation, PMB 121, 1187 Coast Village Rd., Suite 1, Santa Barbara CA 93108-2794. (805)965-3443. Fax: (805)568-0466. Web site: www.wagingpeace.org. Established 1996. Offers an annual series of awards ''to encourage poets to explore and illuminate positive visions of peace and the human spirit.'' Awards $1,000 to adult contestants, $200 to youth in each 2 categories (13-18 and 12 and under), plus Honorable Mentions in each category. Submissions must be unpublished. Submit up to 3 poems in any form, unpublished and in English; maximum 30 lines/poem. Send 2 copies; put name, address, e-mail, phone number, and age (for youth) in upper right-hand corner of 1 copy of each poem. Title each poem; do not staple individual poems together. "Any entry that does not adhere to ALL of the contest rules will not be considered for a prize. Poets should keep copies of all entries as we will be unable to return them." Guidelines available for SASE or on Web site. **Entry fee:** $15 for up to 3 poems; no fee for youth entries. **Deadline:** July 1 (postmark). Judges: a committee of poets selected by the Nuclear Age Peace Foundation. Winners will be announced by October 1 by mail and on Web site. Winning poems from current and past contests are posted on the Foundation's Web site. "The Nuclear Age Peace Foundation reserves the right to publish and distribute the award-winning poems, including Honorable Mentions."

$ ☑ ◎ HAROLD MORTON LANDON TRANSLATION AWARD (Specialized: any language into English)

The Academy of American Poets, 584 Broadway, Suite 604, New York NY 10012-3210. (212)274-0343. Fax: (212)274-9427. E-mail: cevans@poets.org. Web site: www.poets.org. Award established 1976. **Contact:** CJ Evans, awards coordinator. Offers one $1,000 award each year to recognize a published translation of poetry from any language into English. Guidelines available for SASE or on Web site. **Deadline:** December 31 (postmark) of year in which book was published. 2007 winners were Robert Fagles and Susanna Nied. 2007 judge: Jerome Rothenberg.

$ ☑ THE JAMES LAUGHLIN AWARD

The Academy of American Poets, 584 Broadway, Suite 604, New York NY 10012. (212)274-0343. Fax: (212)274-9427. E-mail: cevans@poets.org. Web site: www.poets.org. Offered since 1954. **Contact:** CJ Evans, awards coordinator. Offers $5,000 prize to recognize and support a poet's second book (ms must be under contract to a publisher). Submissions must be made by a publisher in ms form. The Academy of American Poets purchases copies of the Laughlin Award-winning book for distribution to its members. Poets must be U.S. citizens. Entry form, signed by the publisher, required. Entry form and guidelines available for SASE (in January) or on Web site. **Deadline:** submissions accepted between January 1 and May 15. Winners announced in August. 2007 winner was Brenda Shaughnessy for *Human Dark with Sugar*. 2008 judges: Rae Armantrout, Claudia Rankine, and Bruce Smith.

$ ☑ THE LAUREATE PRIZE FOR POETRY

The National Poetry Review, P.O. Box 2080, Aptos CA 95001-2080. E-mail: editor@natonalpoetryreview.com. Web site: www.nationalpoetryreview.com. **Contact:** C.J. Sage, editor. The Laureate Prize for Poetry, an annual award of $300 and publication in *The National Poetry Review* (see separate listing in Magazines Journals), "will honor 1 new poem that *TNPR* believes has the greatest chance of standing the test of time and becoming part of the literary canon." Submissions must be unpublished and uncommitted (not promised for first publication elsewhere). Considers simultaneous submissions, "but if the work is selected by *TNPR* for the prize or for publication, it must be withdrawn from elsewhere unless you have withdrawn it from us 2 weeks before our acceptance." Submit up to 3 poems (10 page maximum per group of 3). Include a brief bio, contact information, and poet's e-mail address for results. Guidelines available on Web site. **Entry fee:** $15/entry; accepts multiple submissions with separate entry fee for each 3-poem group. "If you include a small booksized SASE with $1.30 postage with your entry, we will provide you a copy of the winner's issue." Make checks payable to *The National Poetry Review*. **Deadline:** August 31 (postmark).

☼ $ ◎ THE STEPHEN LEACOCK MEMORIAL MEDAL FOR HUMOUR (Specialized: humor by Canadian citizens)

Stephen Leacock Associates, P.O. Box 854, Orillia ON L3V 3P4 Canada. (705)835-7061. Fax: (705)835-7062. E-mail: spruce@encode.com. Web site: www.leacock.ca. **Contact:** Marilyn Rumball, corresponding secretary. Award Chairman: Judith Rapson. Annual award of the Silver Leacock Medal for Humour and T.D. Canada Trust cash award of $10,000. Presented for a book of humor in prose, verse, drama, or any book form—by a Canadian citizen. "Book must have been published in the current year and no part of it may have been previously published in book form.'' Submit 10 copies of book, 8×10 b&w photo, bio, and entry fee. **Entry fee:** $100 CAD. **Deadline:** December 31. Competition receives 40-50 entries. 2007 winner of the Leacock Memorial Medal was Stuart McLean for ''Secrets from the Vinyl Cafe.'' The committee also publishes *The Newspacket* 3 times/ year.

$☐ THE LEAGUE OF MINNESOTA POETS CONTEST

Web site: www.mnpoets.org (see Web site for current contact information). **Contact:** Christina Flaugher, contest chair. Annual contest offers 18 different categories, with 3 prizes in each category ranging from $10-125. See guidelines for poem lengths, forms, and subjects. Guidelines available for #10 SASE, by e-mail, or on Web site. **Entry fee:** (nonmembers) $1/poem per category; $2/poem (limit 6) for Grand Prize category; (members) $5 for 17 categories; $1/poem (limit 6) for Grand Prize category. Make checks payable to LOMP Contest. **Deadline:** July 31. Nationally known, non-Minnesota judges. Winners will be announced at the October LOMP Conference and by mail. Additional information regarding LOMP membership available on Web site.

$☑ THE LEDGE POETRY AWARDS COMPETITION

P.O. Box 310153, Jamaica NY 11431. Web site: www.theledgemagazine.com. **Contact:** Contest Director. Offers annual awards of 1st Prize: $1,000; 2nd Prize: $250; 3rd Prize: $100; and all 3 winners will be published in *The Ledge* (see separate listing in Magazines/Journals). All entries will be considered for publication. Submissions must be unpublished. Considers simultaneous submissions. ''No restrictions on form or content. Excellence is the only criterion.'' Submit 3 poems. Include SASE for results or return of ms. Guidelines available on Web site. **Entry fee:** $10 for the first 3 poems, $3 for each additional poem; $20 subscription to *The Ledge* gains free entry for the first 3 poems. **Deadline:** April 30 (postmark). Winners announced in September.

$☑ THE LEDGE POETRY CHAPBOOK CONTEST

The Ledge Press, P.O. Box 310153, Jamaica NY 11431. Web site: www.theledgemagazine.com. **Contact:** Contest Director. The Ledge Poetry Chapbook Contest offers an annual prize of $1,000, publication by The Ledge Press, and 25 chapbook copies. Considers simultaneous submissions. Accepts multiple submissions with separate entry fee for each. ''No restrictions on form or content. Excellence is the only criterion.'' Submit 16-28 pages of poetry with bio and acknowledgements, if any. Include title page with poet's name, address, and e-mail address (if applicable). Include SASE for results or return of ms. Guidelines available on Web site. **Entry fee:** $18; all entrants will receive a copy of the winning chapbook upon publication. **Deadline:** October 31. Sample chapbooks available for $8 postpaid. Winner announced in March.

▣ $☑ ◎ LITERAL LATTÉ FOOD VERSE AWARDS (Specialized: poems with food as ingredient)

200 East 10th St., Suite 240, New York NY 10003. Web site: www.literal-latte.com. **Contact:** Contest Director. The annual *Literary Latté* Food for Verse Awards offers 1st Prize: $500 for best poem with food as an ingredient. All entries considered for publication in *Literal Latté* (see separate listing in Magazines/Journals). Submissions must be unpublished. Include cover page with poet's name, address, phone number, and poem titles/first lines; no identifying information on mss pages. Include SASE or e-mail for results. Guidelines available for SASE, by e-mail, or on Web site. **Entry fee:** $10 for up to 6 poems, $15 for 12 poems. Make checks/money orders payable to *Literal Latté*. **Deadline:** January 15 (postmark).

▣ $☑ LITERAL LATTÉ POETRY AWARDS

200 East 10th St., Suite 240, New York NY 10003. Web site: www.literal-latte.com. **Contact:** Contest Director. The annual *Literal Latté* Poetry Awards offer 1st Prize: $1,000; 2nd Prize: $300; 3rd Prize: $200. All entries considered for publication in *Literal Latté* (see separate listing in Magazines/Journals). Submissions must be unpublished. All styles welcome, 2,000 words maximum. Include cover page with poet's name, address, and telephone number; no identifying information on ms

pages. Include SASE or e-mail for results. Guidelines available for SASE, by e-mail, or on Web site. **Entry fee:** $10 for up to 6 poems, $15 for 12 poems. Make checks/money orders payable to *Literal Latté*. **Deadline:** July 15 (postmark).

$⊘ FRANCES LOCKE MEMORIAL POETRY AWARD

The Bitter Oleander Press, 4983 Tall Oaks Dr., Fayetteville NY 13066-9776. (315)637-3047. Fax: (315)637-5056. E-mail: info@bitteroleander.com. Web site: www.bitteroleander.com. Established 1974. **Contact:** Paul B Roth. The Frances Locke Memorial Poetry Award offers $1,000, publication in *The Bitter Oleander* (see separate listing in Magazines/Journals), and 5 contributor's copies. Submit up to 5 poems, each no more than 2 pages in length, legibly typed or computer generated. Include poet's name, address, and phone number or e-mail on each poem. Include a short biography with submission. No e-mail submissions. Include SASE for results only; mss will not be returned. Guidelines available on Web site. **Entry fee:** $10 for up to 5 poems, $2 each additional poem. **Deadline:** June 15 (postmark). 2007 winner: Maureen Alsop ('' *Sky Hour Lumiére, Circa 1936*'').

⚡ $⊘ ◎ LONG POEM PRIZE (Specialized: long poem or poem cycle)

The Malahat Review, University of Victoria, P.O. Box 1700, Stn CSC, Victoria BC V8W 2Y2 Canada. (250)721-8524. Fax: (250)472-5051. E-mail: malahat@uvic.ca. Web site: www.malahatreview.ca. **Contact:** Awards Coordinator. The biennial Long Poem Prize offers 2 awards of $500 CAD each for a long poem or cycle (10-20 printed pages). Includes publication in *The Malahat Review* (see separate listing in Magazines/Journals) and payment at $40 CAD per printed page upon publication. Open to ''entries from Canadian, American, and overseas authors.'' Submissions must be unpublished. No simultaneous submissions. Submit a single poem or cycle of poems, 10-20 published pages (a published page equals 32 lines or less, including breaks between stanzas); no restrictions on subject matter or aesthetic approach. Include separate page with poet's name, address, e-mail, and title; no identifying information on mss pages. No e-mail submissions. Do not include SASE for results; mss will not be returned. Guidelines available on Web site. **Entry fee:** $35 CAD, $40 USD ($45 USD for entries from Mexico and outside North America); includes one-year subscription to *The Malahat Review*. **Deadline:** February 1 (postmark) of alternate years (2009, 2011, etc.). 2007 winners: Aurian Haller, Harold Rhenisch. 2007 Judges: Margo Button, Brian Bartlett, and John Pass. Winners and finalists notified by e-mail. Winners announced in summer in *The Malahat Review*, on Web site, and in quarterly e-newsletter, *Malahat lite*.

$⊘ THE LOUISIANA LITERATURE PRIZE FOR POETRY

SLU Box 10792, Southeastern Louisiana University, Hammond LA 70402. (504)549-5022. Web site: http://louisianaliterature.org. **Contact:** Contest Director. The *Louisiana Literature* Prize for Poetry offers $400 and publication in *Louisiana Literature* (see separate listing in Magazines/Journals). All entries considered for publication. Open to U.S. residents only. Submissions must be unpublished. Submit 1-5 poems, totaling 250 lines, on any topic. Include poet's name and address on each poem. Include SASP for notification of receipt of ms, SASE for results only; mss will not be returned. Guidelines available for SASE or on Web site. **Entry fee:** $12 for 1-5 poems; includes one-year subscription to *Louisiana Literature*. **Deadline:** April 15.

$◡ ◎ NAOMI LONG MADGETT POETRY AWARD (Specialized: African American)

Lotus Press, P.O. Box 21607, Detroit MI 48221. (313)861-1280. Fax: (313)861-4740. E-mail: lotupress@aol.com. Web site: www.lotuspress.org. Established 1972. **Contact:** Constance Withers. Offers annual award of $500 and publication by Lotus Press, Inc. for a book-length ms by an African American poet. ''Individual poems may be previously published, but poems published in a collection of your own work, self-published or not, will not be considered. Please do not submit a manuscript which you have submitted, or which you plan to submit during the period of consideration, to another publisher. However, you may enter another competition as long as you notify us that you have done or plan to do so. If you are notified that your manuscript has won another award or prize, you must inform us of this immediately. If you have already had a book published by Lotus Press, you are ineligible. However, inclusion in a Lotus Press anthology does not disqualify you." Submit 2 complete copies of 60-90 page ms, exclusive of table of contents or other optional introductory material. **See guidelines for special formatting instructions.** Enclose stamped, self-addressed postcard to confirm receipt of material; no SASE as mss will not be returned. Mail by First Class Priority; no Certified, Federal Express, or other mail requiring a signature. **Deadline:** entries must be received between January 2 and March 31. Guidelines available for SASE, by e-mail, or on Web site. Winner and judges announced no later than June 1. Copies of winning books available from Lotus Press at the address above. Advice: "Read some of the books we have published, especially award winners. Read a lot of good contemporary poetry. Those who have worked over a period of years at developing their craft will have the best chance for consideration. The work of novices is not likely to be selected."

$✅ MAIN STREET RAG'S ANNUAL CHAPBOOK CONTEST

P.O. Box 690100, Charlotte NC 28227-7001. (704)573-2516. E-mail: editor@mainstreetrag.com. Web site: www.MainStreetRag.com. Established 1996. **Contact:** M. Scott Douglass, editor/publisher. Annual chapbook contest by *Main Street Rag* (see separate listing in Magazines/Journals) offers 1st Prize: $500 and 50 copies of chapbook. "As many as 19 runners-up have been published in previous contests, and every manuscript entered is considered for publication." All entrants receive a copy of the winning chapbook. Submit 24-32 pages of poetry, no more than 1 poem/page. Guidelines available for SASE, by e-mail, or on Web site. **Entry fee:** $15. **Deadline:** May 31. 2006 winner was Stacey Waite (*Love Poem to Androgyny*).

$✅ MAIN STREET RAG'S ANNUAL POETRY BOOK AWARD

P.O. Box 690100, Charlotte NC 28227-7001. (704)573-2516. E-mail: editor@mainstreetrag.com. Web site: www.MainStreetRag.com. Established 1996. **Contact:** M. Scott Douglass, editor/publisher. *Main Street Rag*'s Annual Poetry Book Award offers 1st Prize: $1,000 and 50 copies of book; runners-up may also be offered publication. Submit 48-80 pages of poetry, no more than 1 poem/page (individual poems may be longer than 1 page). Guidelines available for SASE, by e-mail, or on Web site. **Entry fee:** $20 (or $25 to include a copy of the winning book). **Deadline:** January 31. 2007 winner was Heather Davis (*The Lost Tribe of Us*).

$✅ MANY MOUNTAINS MOVING POETRY BOOK CONTEST

Many Mountains Moving Press, 549 Rider Ridge Dr., Longmont CO 80501. E-mail: jeffreyethan@att.net. Web site: www.mmminc.org. The Many Mountains Moving Poetry Book Contest offers $1000 and publication of a book-length poetry ms by Many Mountains Moving Press. Open to all poets writing in English. More than half of ms may not have been published as a collection, but individual poems and chapbook-length sections may have been previously published if publisher gives permission to reprint. Accepts email submissions (as an attachment, without any identification in the mss. itself). Considers simultaneous submissions "if the poet agrees to notify MMM Press of acceptance elsewhere." Submit 50-100 typed pages of poetry, single- or double-spaced. Include cover letter with ms title, brief bio, poet's name, address, phone number, and e-mail address(es). Poet's name must not appear anywhere on ms. Acknowledgments may be sent but are not required. Include SASE for results only; no mss will be returned. Guidelines available on Web site. **Entry fee:** $20; entitles entrant to free back issue of *Many Mountains Moving*, discount on subscription, and discount on any 1 of selected Many Mountains Moving Press books (use order form, available on Web site). Make checks/money orders payable to Many Mountains Moving Press. **Deadline:** June 1(postmark). 2008 judge TBA.

$✅ ◎ THE MORTON MARR POETRY PRIZE (Specialized: traditional poetry forms)

Southern Methodist University, P.O. Box 750374, Dallas TX 75275-0374. (214)768-1037. Fax: (214)768-1408. E-mail: swr@mail.smu.edu. Web site: www.smu.edu/southwestreview. Established 1915. **Contact:** Prize Coordinator. The annual Morton Marr Poetry Prize awards 1st Prize: $1,000 and 2nd Prize: $500 to a poet who has not yet published a first book of poetry. Winners will be published in *Southwest Review* (see separate listing in Magazines/Journals). Submit 6 poems in a "traditional" form (e.g., sonnet, sestina, villanelle, rhymed stanzas, blank verse, et al). Include cover letter with poet's name, address, and other relevant information; no identifying information on entry pages. Manuscripts will not be returned. Guidelines available on Web site. **Entry fee:** $5/poem. **Deadline:** September 30 (postmark). 2007 winners: Gretchen Steele Pratt (1st Place), Bradford Gray Telford (2nd Place), Elizabeth Rosen (HM), and Chloë Joan López (HM).

$☑ MARSH HAWK PRESS POETRY PRIZE

P.O. Box 206, East Rockaway NY 11518-0206. E-mail: marshhawkpress1@aol.com. Web site: www.MarshHawkPress.org. Established 2001. **Contact:** Prize Director. The Marsh Hawk Press Poetry Prize offers $1,000 plus publication of a book-length ms. Submissions must be unpublished as a collection, but individual poems may have been previously published elsewhere. Submit 48-70 pages of original poetry in any style in English, typed single-spaced, paginated, and bound with a spring clip. Include 2 title pages: 1 with ms title, poet's name, and contact information only; 1 with ms title only (poet's name must not appear anywhere in the ms). Also include table of contents and acknowledgments page. Include SASE for results only; will not be returned. Electronic upload available on Web site. Guidelines available on Web site. **Entry fee:** $20. Make check/money order payable to Marsh Hawk Press. **Deadline:** see Web site. 2007 winner was Karin Randolph (*Either She Was*). 2008 judge: Thylias Moss.

$☑ THE LENORE MARSHALL POETRY PRIZE

The Academy of American Poets, 584 Broadway, Suite 604, New York NY 10012. (212)274-0343. Fax: (212)274-9427. E-mail: jkronovet@poets.org. Web site: www.poets.org. Established 1975. **Contact:** Jennifer Kronovet, awards coordinator. Offers $25,000 for the most outstanding book of poems published in the U.S. in the previous year. Contest is open to books by living American poets published in a standard edition (40 pages or more in length with 500 or more copies printed). Self-published books are not eligible. Publishers may enter as many books as they wish (books must be submitted in the year after their publication). Four copies of each book must be submitted and none will be returned. Guidelines, required entry form available for SASE or on Web site. **Entry fee:** $25/title. **Deadline:** entries must be submitted between April 1 and June 15. Finalists announced in October; winner announced in November. 2006 winner was Eleanor Lerman for *Our Post-Soviet History Unfolds*. 2006 judges: Carl Dennis, Tony Hoagland, and Carol Muske-Dukes.

$☑ MIDNIGHT SUN POETRY CHAPBOOK CONTEST

(formerly Susan Blalock Poetry Chapbook Contest), *Permafrost*, Chapbook Division, % English Dept., University of Alaska Fairbanks, P.O. Box 755720, Fairbanks AK 99775. E-mail: fbpfrost@uaf.edu. Web site: www.uaf.edu/english/permafrost. Established 1977. **Contact:** Poetry Editor. The Midnight Sun Poetry Chapbook Contest offers $100, publication, and 30 author's copies. Submit a ms of no more than 34 pages. Include SASE. Guidelines available on Web site. **Entry fee:** $10, includes a one-issue subscription to *Permafrost* (see separate listing in Magazines/Journals). **Deadline:** March 15.

$☐ MILFORD FINE ARTS COUNCIL NATIONAL POETRY CONTEST

Milford Fine Arts Council, 40 Railroad Ave., South, Milford CT 06460. Web site: www.milfordarts.org. Established 1976. **Contact:** Tom Bouton, Writer's Group chairperson. Offers annual award of 1st Prize: $100; 2nd Prize: $50; 3rd Prize: $25; plus winners will be published in Milford Fine Arts Council's annual publication, *High Tide*. Submissions must be unpublished. No simultaneous submissions. Poems entered may not have won any other prizes or honorable mentions. Poets must be 18 years and older. "Poems must be typed single-spaced on white standard paper, 10-30 lines (including title), no more than 48 characters/line, on any subject, in any style, rhymed or unrhymed. Use standard font, clear and legible, 1 poem/page, no script or fax. NO foul language. No bio or date, only the words 'Unpublished Original' typed above the poem." Include poet's name, address, ZIP code, and phone number or e-mail address in the middle back of the submitted poem, no identifying information on the front of the page. Poems will be judged on form, clarity, originality, and universal appeal. "Entries may be considered for publication in *High Tide*. If you do not want your poems considered for publication, then you *must* print on the back of the poem (below your name, address, and ZIP code) 'For National Poetry Contest Only.' "

Include SASE for results only, with NOTIFICATION printed on bottom left corner of envelope; no poems will be returned. Guidelines available for SASE or on Web site. **Entry fee:** $3 for one poem, $6 for 3 poems, $2 for each additional poem after 3. Contestants may enter an unlimited number of poems (will be judged individually, not as a group). Check or money order accepted, no cash. **Deadline:** March 31, 2009.

$✍ EDNA ST. VINCENT MILLAY "BALLAD OF THE HARP WEAVER" AWARD (Specialized: narrative poems)

Verdure Publications, P.O. Box 640387, Beverly Hills FL 34464-0387. E-mail: verdure@tampabay.rr. com. Established 1989. **Contact:** Madelyn Eastlund, editor. The annual Edna St. Vincent Millay "Ballad of the Harp Weaver" Award offers $50 and publication in *Harp-Strings Poetry Journal* (see separate listing in Magazines/Journals) for a narrative poem, 40-100 lines. Guidelines available for SASE. **Entry fee:** $5 for 1-3 poems. Make checks payable to Madelyn Eastlund. **Deadline:** July 15.

$✍ MISSISSIPPI REVIEW PRIZE

118 College Dr. #5144, Hattiesburg MS 39406-0001. (601)266-4321. Fax: (601)266-5757. E-mail: rief@mississippireview.com. Web site: www.mississippireview.com. The *Mississippi Review* Prize offers an annual award of $1,000 each in poetry and fiction. Winners and finalists comprise 1 issue of *Mississippi Review*. Submissions must be unpublished. Submit up to 3 poems/entry (totaling 10 pages or less). No limit on number of entries. Put "*MR* Prize" plus poet's name, address, phone number, e-mail address, and title(s) on page 1 of entry. Manuscripts will not be returned. **Entry fee:** $15/entry. Make checks payable to *Mississippi Review*. Each entrant receives a copy of the prize issue. **Deadline:** submit April 1-October 1 (postmark). Winners announced in January.

$☐ MISSISSIPPI VALLEY POETRY CONTEST

Midwest Writing Center, P.O. Box 3188, Rock Island IL 61204. (563)359-1057. **Contact:** Max J. Molleston, chairman. Offers annual prizes of approximately $1,000 for unpublished poems in categories for students (elementary, junior, and senior high), adults, Mississippi Valley, senior citizens, jazz, religious, humorous, rhyming, haiku, ethnic, and history. Submissions must be unpublished. **Entry fee:** (adults) $10 for up to 5 poems, no limit to number of entries; (children) $5 for up to 5 poems. Send check or U.S. dollars. **Deadline:** April 1. Professional readers present winning poems to a reception at an award evening in May. Competition receives 700 entries.

✪ $✍ ◎ MONEY FOR WOMEN (Specialized: women's concerns, feminism)

Barbara Deming Memorial Fund, Inc., P.O. Box 309, Wilton NH 03085-0309. **Contact:** Susan Pliner, executive director. Offers biannual small grants of up to $1,500 to feminists in the arts "whose work addresses women's concerns and/or speaks for peace and justice from a feminist perspective." Submissions may be previously published and entered in other contests. Application form available for SASE. Entrants must use application form with correct deadline date. Applicants must be citizens of U.S. or Canada. **Application fee:** $20. **Deadline:** June 30. Receives 400 applications/year. 2007 grantees in poetry were Ana-Maurine Lara, Faith Shearin, Francine Marie Tolf, and Laura Van Prooyen. Winners announced in November. Also offers the *Gertrude Stein Award* for outstanding work by a lesbian, and the *Fannie Lou Hamer Award* for work which combats racism and celebrates women of color.

$✍ JENNY MCKEAN MOORE WRITER IN WASHINGTON

Dept. of English, George Washington University, Washington DC 20052. (202)994-6515. Fax: (202)994-7915. E-mail: dmca@gwu.edu. Web site: www.gwu.edu/~english. Offers fellowship for a visiting lecturer in creative writing, currently about $55,000 for 2 semesters. Stipend varies slightly from year to year, depending on endowment payout. Teaching duties involve 2 workshops per semester—one for undergraduate students, the other free to the community. Apply with résumé and writing sample of 25 pages or less. Books may be submitted but will not be returned without SASE. Awarded to writers in different genres each year, typically alternating between poets and fiction writers. Check Web site for specific genre each year. **Deadline:** November 15.

The Personal Artist Statement

Expressing what you want to accomplish

In the past 10 years, the number of people pursuing the writing life has skyrocketed. Chalk it up to a change in the economy or a change in values, but no matter how you view it, the evidence is there: People are leaving the nine-to-five cubicle behind.

We know this because advanced degrees in Creative Writing have slowly moved toward the top of the most popular graduate programs, and applications for writing residencies are breaking new records every year. However, as more and more people gather their applications materials and pray for more time to write, the competition only increases in intensity. If you want to create a successful application, you have to be able to distinguish your writing from the rest of the crowd.

Finding time to write

These days, many poets choose a graduate program before applying for a writing residency. However, you don't need an advanced degree to earn a residency. Many graduate programs offer their students two to three years of writing and study, while residencies allow writers and artists unimpeded time and space in which to work—and residencies are very popular. Each year thousands of people apply for writing residencies, with only a very small percentage accepted. Caroline Crumpacker, Director of the Millay Colony of the Arts, says they received "well over 400 applications this year for 48 spots. It was very tight. We had to turn down some extremely talented artists."

Although graduate programs and writing residencies are two fundamentally very different creative settings, their application processes are similar. While every group has its own specific requirements, most programs ask applicants to submit a writing sample, a CV or résumé, and a statement of artistic intentions, also known as the personal statement or the artist statement.

It is the personal artist statement that seems to cause the most confusion for writers. Most poets are familiar with writing a CV or résumé, and most have a whole slew of poems for the writing sample. But what in the world goes into the personal statement? For many poets, writing *about* their own poetry can be the only thing harder than actually writing the poem.

The past, present and future of your poems

To get to the heart of the personal statement, let's first consider its context.

When you're applying for graduate school or a writing residency, the selection committee is usually looking for a number of things. They want to be convinced of your seriousness and dedication as a writer; they want to see that you have specific goals and intentions for your work; they want to see self-awareness about your writing; and they have to be interested in your writing itself. Every group has limited space and a limited budget, so they want to make sure the writers they select will make good use of their time by producing innovative, professional-level work.

Each piece of your application provides the selection committee with a slightly different kind of evidence about who you are and what you want to do with your writing. The CV gives them background about your experience, education and awards or publications. The writing sample gives them, quite simply, a sample of your work. *The personal artist's statement, then, is a proposal for what you hope to accomplish; and it is a platform for you to explain your work to the jury or selection committee.*

"The best statements can really augment an application by clearly contextualizing a work sample within the artist's own oeuvre and the larger field in which the artist is working," says Crumpacker. "A strong statement will then discuss, clearly and simply, what the artist proposes to work on during a residency."

A few points to keep in mind

Here are some specific things to think about when you're sitting down to compose your artist statement:

Use clear, specific language. Many people believe that flowery, abstract discussions make them seem more artistic. "Unfortunately, many artists do not write compelling or, often, comprehensible statements," says Crumpacker. "Sometimes I can read an entire artist's statement and still not know what an artist is doing and in what medium. There is a lot of airy abstract writing that ends up being kind of meaningless."

Remember that these committees are reading hundreds of these essays and would rather spend their time and patience on reviewing the work sample.

Define clear goals for yourself. You are more likely to be a successful applicant if you have a specific idea about how you want to direct your thinking and writing. Comments like "I want to grow as a writer" or "I want to push my form in new directions" are vague because both of these things ought to be happening all the time. Comments such as "I plan to write a series of long poems about childbirth traditions" or "I plan to complete a manuscript of poems that explores contemporary folklore" give a committee a very specific idea about what you plan to be working on.

Be honest. Ruth Gundle, Director of the Soapstone Retreat for Women, suggests that poets write honestly about their work and goals. She says, "These are little windows into the applicant and are usually surprisingly revealing. The point isn't to be original, but to use your writerly skills to answer the questions concisely and candidly."

Prageeta Sharma, the Director of the Creative Writing Program at the University of Montana, echoes Gundle's comment about honesty. "Reflecting on what isn't working even works to your benefit because it shows you understand yourself as a writer," she says

Make your statement complement your work sample. Crumpacker explains, "This can take a number of different styles. Some people will want to talk only about the work at hand, and others will bring in critical theory or other ideas to elaborate on their work and its relevance. Either way, we should be able to understand what the artist is doing and wants to do."

Sharma suggests examining your own history as a student of writing and discuss "your influences, what you think your range is, and what you're ready to do"

Make sure your details are correct. When you send out a number of applications, it's very easy to make small editing mistakes that make you look unprofessional from the get-go. Sharma says, "This is really basic, but check to make sure you get the details right. Make sure the school's name and faculty's names are accurate and spelled correctly."

Survey the field. Whether you're interested in graduate school or a residency, there are hundreds of options out there. You (and your wallet) will be happier if you do some research before applying. "I would look at a number of residencies before applying," Crumpacker says. "There are a lot of them in the Northeast alone, and each one has its own style and benefits. I think it is important to choose the right one. Some are more social and networky, others more remote and work-oriented. Still others mix the two."

Devote ample time to the writing sample. Even though we've been talking mainly about the artist's statement, most programs pay the most attention to the writing sample. Make sure you do as well. Choose a mix of older, more polished poems and new, more innovative work that will show where you want to go. Crumpacker says that at the Millay Colony, "We give [readers] detailed instructions on how to evaluate an applicant's work—assessing technical expertise, creative ingenuity and ambition in relation both to the pool of applicants and the larger field in which the artist is working."

Don't use the personal statement as an opportunity to brag. Sharma says that there's no need to brag on yourself in the personal statement. She notes that while it's okay to "be proud of (your) accomplishments and what (you've) learned from them," you should use the statement as a chance to talk about your growth as a writer, rather than simply reiterate the information in the CV. Most programs put the most weight on the writing sample; remember to use the personal statement space to give your writing sample context.

Don't squander statement space praising the regional beauty. Many residency programs take place in beautiful parts of the country, but most selection committees are less interested in whether you're excited by the scenery—they're more interested in finding out if you're a good fit. Sharma says, "Make sure it's more than a regional choice. Pick the program and the faculty, and let us know *why* you're a good fit."

Don't give up if you're not accepted right away. "We urge unsuccessful applicants to reapply," says Gundle. "Even the same reader would choose different writers from one year to the next. It's a very subjective process. I would urge writers not to feel daunted if they are not awarded a residency the first or even second time they try."

Graduate writing programs and writing residencies are both popular but competitive means to finding time to write. In a field where everyone's goal is to be innovative and unique, distinguishing your work from the competition can seem daunting. Remember not to rely on your perceptions about what everyone else is doing; instead, look hard at what *you're* doing. Spend the time understanding your own work, and make sure you're being clear about where you want to go.

—*Amy Ratto Parks*

Amy Ratto Parks teaches English at the University of Montana. Her chapbook, *Bread and Water Body*, was the winner of the Merriam Frontier Chapbook Prize.

$⊘ SAMUEL FRENCH MORSE POETRY PRIZE

Dept. of English, 406 Holmes, Northeastern University, Boston MA 02115. (617)373-4546. Fax: (617)373-2509. E-mail: g.rotella@neu.edu. Web site: www.english.neu.edu. **Contact:** Prof. Guy Rotella, editor. Offers annual prize of book publication (ms 50-70 pages) by NU/UPNE and $1,000. Open to U.S. poets who have published no more than 1 book of poetry. Entry must be unpublished in book form but may include poems previously published elsewhere. Manuscripts will not be returned. Guidelines available on Web site (under "Publications"). **Entry fee:** $20. **Deadline:** August 1 for inquiries; September 15 for single copy of ms. Competition receives approximately 400 entries/year. Recent winners include Jennifer Atkinson, Ted Genoways, and Dana Roeser. Previous judges: Marilyn Hacker, Rosanna Warren, Robert Cording, and Ellen Bryant Voigt.

$⊘ THE KATHRYN A. MORTON PRIZE IN POETRY

Sarabande Books, Inc., P.O. Box 4456, Louisville KY 40205. E-mail: info@sarabandebooks.org. Web site: www.SarabandeBooks.org. Established 1994. **Contact:** Sarah Gorham, editor-in-chief. Member: CLMP. The Kathryn A. Morton Prize in Poetry is awarded annually to a book-length ms (at least 48 pages). Winner receives $2,000, publication, and a standard royalty contract. All finalists are considered for publication. Entry form and SASE are required. Guidelines available for SASE, by e-mail, or on Web site. **Entry fee:** $25. **Deadline:** submit January 1-February 15 (postmark) only. Competition receives approximately 1,400 entries. 2007 winner was Monica Ferrell's *Beasts for the Chase*, selected by Jane Hirshfield. 2008 judge is Lynn Emanuel. "To avoid conflict of interest, students in a degree-granting program or close friends of a judge are ineligible to enter the contest in the genre for which their friend or teacher is serving as judge. Sarabande, as a member of CLMP, complies with its Contest Code of Ethics."

$⊘ NATIONAL BOOK AWARD

The National Book Foundation, 95 Madison Ave., Suite 709, New York NY 10016. (212)685-0261. E-mail: nationalbook@nationalbook.org. Web site: www.nationalbook.org. Presents $10,000 in each of 4 categories (fiction, nonfiction, poetry, and young people's literature), plus 16 short-list prizes of $1,000 each to Finalists. Submissions must be previously published and **must be entered by the publisher**. General guidelines available on Web site; interested publishers should phone or e-mail the Foundation. **Entry fee:** $125/title. **Deadline:** see Web site for current year's deadline. 2006 poetry winner was Nathaniel Mackey for *Splay Anthem*.

$⊘ THE NATIONAL POET HUNT CONTEST

Schoolcraft College, 18600 Haggerty Rd., Livonia MI 48152-2696. (734)462-4400, ext. 5327. Fax: (734)462-4679. E-mail: macguffin@schoolcraft.edu. Web site: www.schoolcraft.edu/macguffin. Established 1996. **Contact:** Carol Was, poetry editor. The National Poet Hunt Contest offers 1st Prize: $500 and publication in a future issue of *The MacGuffin*; may also award 2 Honorable Mentions and publication. Open to all writers. Submissions must be unpublished and may be entered in other contests. Submit 5 typed poems on any subject, in any form. Put name and address on separate 3×5 index card only. Include SASE for winners' list only; entries will not be returned. Guidelines available for SASE, by fax, e-mail, or on Web site. **Entry fee:** $15/entry (5 poems). Make checks payable to Schoolcraft College. **Deadline:** check Web site for current deadline. 2008 judge: Vivian Shipley.

⊕ $⊘ NATIONAL POETRY COMPETITION

Poetry Society, 22 Betterton Street, London WC2H 9BX United Kingdom. E-mail: info@poetrysociety.org.uk. Web site: www.poetrysociety.org.uk. Established 1978. **Contact:** Competition Organiser. The National Poetry Competition offers 1st Prize: £5,000; 2nd Prize: £1,000; 3rd Prize: £500; plus 10 commendations of £50 each. Winners will be published in *Poetry Review* (see separate listing in Magazines/Journals), and on the Poetry Society Web site and will receive a year's free membership in the Poetry Society (see separate listing in Organizations). Open to anyone aged 17 or over. Entries "received from all around the world. All entries are judged anonymously and past winners include both published and previously unknown poets." Submissions must be unpublished (poems posted on Web sites are considered published). Submit original poems in English, on any subject, no more than 40 lines/poem, typed on 1 side only of A4 paper, double- or single-spaced. Each poem must be titled. No identifying information on poems. Do not staple ms pages. Accepts online submissions; full details available on the National Poetry Competition pages on the Poetry Society Web site. Entry form (required) available for A5 SAE (1 entry form covers multiple entries, may be photocopied). Include SAE or SAP for notification of receipt of postal entries (confirmation of online entries will be e-mailed at time of submission); mss will not be returned. Guidelines available on Web site. **Entry fee:** £5 for first poem, £3 for each subsequent entry (Poetry Society members can enter a second poem free of charge). "Only sterling (checks, postal orders, money orders, or credit cards) will be accepted. All other payments will be returned. Checks must be drawn from UK banks." Make checks payable to the Poetry Society. **Deadline:** October 31. 2008 judges: Jack Mapanje, Frieda Hughes, and Brian Patten. Winners and commended poets notified in February 28, 2009.

$ ⊠ THE NATIONAL POETRY REVIEW BOOK PRIZE

E-mail: nationalpoetryreview@yahoo.com. Web site: www.nationalpoetryreview.com. *The National Poetry Review* Book Prize offers $1000, publication of a book-length ms, and 15 author copies. All entries will be considered for publication. Submit 45-80 pages of poetry. Include cover letter with bio and acknowledgments page. **See Web site for entry address and details.** Include e-mail address for results (no SASEs; mss will not be returned). Guidelines available on Web site. **Fee:** $25. Make checks payable to *The National Poetry Review* . **Deadline:** November 30 (postmark).

$ ◎ HOWARD NEMEROV SONNET AWARD

The Formalist, 320 Hunter Dr., Evansville IN 47711. Web site: www2.evansville.edu/theformalist/. Established 1994. Although *The Formalist* has ceased publication, it continues to sponsor the annual Howard Nemerov Sonnet Award. Offers $1,000 prize; winner and 11 finalists will be published in *Measure: An Annual Review of Formal Poetry* (see separate listing in Magazines/Journals). Submit original, unpublished sonnets, no translations; sonnet sequences acceptable, but each sonnet will be considered individually. Poets may enter as many sonnets as they wish. Poet's name, address, phone number, and e-mail address should be listed on the **back** of each entry. Enclose SASE for contest results; mss will not be returned. Guidelines available for SASE or on Web site. **Entry fee**: $3/sonnet. Make all checks payable to *The Formalist*. **Deadline:** November 15 (postmark). Past winners include Rhina P. Espaillat, Marion Shore, Deborah Warren, and A.M. Juster. 2008 judge: Timothy Steele.

$ ⊠ THE PABLO NERUDA PRIZE FOR POETRY

d*Nimrod*, Literary Contest—Poetry, The University of Tulsa, 600 S. College, Tulsa OK 74104. Web site: www.utulsa.edu/nimrod. **Contact:** Contest Coordinator. The annual *Nimrod* Literary Awards include The Pablo Neruda Prize for Poetry, which offers 1st Prize: $2,000 and publication in *Nimrod: International Journal of Poetry and Prose* (see separate listing in Magazines/Journals); and 2nd Prize: $1,000 and publication. *Nimrod* retains the right to publish any submission. Submissions must be unpublished. Work must be in English or translated by original author. Submit 3-10 pages of poetry (1 long poem or several short poems). Poet's name must not appear on ms. Include cover sheet with poem title(s), poet's name, address, phone and fax numbers, and e-mail address (poet must have a U.S. address by October of contest year to enter). Mark "Contest Entry" on submission envelope and cover sheet. Include SASE for results only; mss will not be returned. Guidelines available for #10 SASE or on Web site. **Entry fee:** $20; includes one-year subscription (2 issues) to *Nimrod*. Make checks payable to *Nimrod*. **Deadline:** entries accepted January 1-April 30 (postmark). 200 winners were Natalie Diaz (1st Prize, "When My Brother Was an Aztec" and Others) and Keet Je Kuipers (2nd Prize, "Barn Elegy" and Others). Winners will be announced on *Nimrod's* Web site.

$ ⊠ NERVE COWBOY CHAPBOOK CONTEST

P.O. Box 4973, Austin TX 78765. Web site: www.jwhagins.com/ChapContest.html. Established 1995. **Contact:** Joseph Shields and Jerry Hagins, co-editors. The *Nerve Cowboy* Chapbook Contest offers 1st Prize: $200, publication, and 50 author's copies; 2nd Prize: $100, publication, and 30 author's copies. Submit 24-40 pages of poetry and/or short fiction. Include SASE for return of ms. Guidelines available on Web site. **Entry fee:** $10 (all entrants receive a copy of the winning chapbook and a discount on the 2nd Prize chapbook). Make checks payable to *Nerve Cowboy*. **Deadline:** January 31st of each year. Winners included David J. Thompson, 1st Prize, *Even the Fallen* and 2nd Prize, *The Book of the Toothpicker*.

$□ ◎ NEW EDEN CHAPBOOK COMPETITION (Specialized: spiritual poetry)

Power of Poetry, 5890 Birch Ct., Oakland CA 94618-1627. Fax: (510)596-1860. E-mail: pluma@earth link.net. Web site: http://popruah.opwest.org. Established 1990. **Contact:** Armando Ibanez, O.P., general editor. The New Eden Chapbook Competition offers $100, publication of the chapbook within a volume of the literary annual *Ruah* (see separate listing in Magazines/Journals), and 25 copies of that issue. "The New Eden Chapbook Competition is named in honor of Leo Thomas, O.P., founder of 'Healing Ministry,' a parish-based program which provides spiritual support for those in need of healing. The essence of Fr. Thomas' life and ministry recollects how Divine healing leads to a renewed experience of the Original Blessedness found in the garden of Eden. The Chapbook Contest recognizes that poetry, particularly spiritual poetry, leads us to this place of healing particularly when it helps us touch the Divine." Entries must be unpublished as a collection, but individual poems may have been previously published. Submit up to 24 pages of verse, any style. Include 2 title pages: 1 with name, address, and phone number, the other with title only. Provide table of contents and acknowledgments page. Include SASE for results. Guidelines available on Web site. **Entry fee:** $10 (includes the previous issue of *Ruah*). **Deadline:** December 31 postmark (submit September-December).

$▧ THE NEW ISSUES POETRY PRIZE

New Issues Poetry & Prose, Dept. of English, Western Michigan University, 1903 W. Michigan Ave., Kalamazoo MI 49008-5463. (269)387-8185. Fax: (269)387-2562. Web site: www.wmich.edu/newissues. Established 1996. The New Issues Poetry Prize offers $2,000 plus publication of a book-length ms. Open to "poets writing in English who have not previously published a full-length collection of poems." Additional mss will be considered from those submitted to the competition for publication in the New Issues Press Poetry Series. Considers simultaneous submissions, but New Issues must be notified of acceptance elsewhere. Submit ms of at least 48 pages, typed, single-spaced preferred. Clean photocopies acceptable. Do not bind; use manila folder or metal clasp. Include cover page with poet's name, address, phone number, and title of the ms. Also include brief bio and acknowledgments page. No e-mail or fax submissions. Include SASP for notification of receipt of ms and SASE for results only; no mss will be returned. Guidelines available for SASE, by fax, by e-mail, or on Web site. **Entry fee:** $15. Make checks payable to New Issues Poetry & Prose. **Deadline:** November 30 (postmark). Winning manuscript will be named in April 2009 and published in Spring 2010. 2007 winner was Sandra Beasley (*Theories of Falling*). "A national judge selects the prize winner and recommends other manuscripts. The editors decide on the other books considering the judge's recommendation, but are not bound by it." 2008 judge: Carl Phillips.

$▧ NEW LETTERS PRIZE FOR POETRY

University of Missouri-Kansas City, University House, 5101 Rockhill Rd., Kansas City MO 64110-2499. E-mail: newletters@umkc.edu. Web site: www.newletters.org. Established 1986. **Contact:** Contest Coordinator. The annual *New Letters* Poetry Prize awards $1,500 and publication in *New Letters* (see separate listing in Magazines/Journals) to the best group of 3-6 poems. All entries will be considered for publication in *New Letters*. Submissions must be unpublished. Considers simultaneous submissions with notification upon acceptance elsewhere. Accepts multiple entries with separate fee for each. Submit up to 6 poems (need not be related). Include 2 cover sheets: 1 with poet's name, address, e-mail, phone number, prize category (poetry), and ms title(s); the second with category and ms title only. No identifying information on ms pages. Accepts electronic submissions. Include SASP for notification of receipt of ms and entry number, and SASE for results only (send only 1 envelope if submitting multiple entries); mss will not be returned. Guidelines available for SASE or on Web site. **Entry fee:** $15 for first entry, $10 for each subsequent entry; includes cost of a one-year subscription, renewal, or gift subscription to *New Letters* (shipped to any address within the U.S.). Make checks payable to *New Letters*. **Deadline:** May 18 (postmark). 2007 winner was Jennifer Maier. 2007 judge: Mary Jo Salter. "Current students and employees of the University of Missouri-Kansas City, and current volunteer members of the *New Letters* and BkMk Press staffs, are not eligible."

⬛ $⬜ NEW MILLENNIUM AWARD FOR POETRY

New Millennium Writings, Room EM, P.O. Box 2463, Knoxville TN 37901. Web site: www.newmille nniumwritings.com. **Contact:** Don Williams, editor. Offers 2 annual awards of $1,000 each. Submissions must be unpublished and may be entered in other contests. Submit up to 3 poems, 5 pages maximum. No restrictions on style, form, or content. Include name, address, phone number, and a #10 SASE for notification. All contestants receive the next issue at no additional charge. Entry form available on Web site. Include SASE or e-mail address for results; mss will not be returned. Guidelines available for SASE or on Web site. **Entry fee:** $17. Make checks payable to *New Millennium Writings*. **Deadline:** June 17 and November 17 (each deadline may be extended once; check Web site for updates). Competition receives 2,000 entries/year. "2 winners and all finalists will be published." Most recent award winner was Ellen Sullins.

$⬜ NEW RIVER POETS TRIANNUAL POETRY AWARDS

New River Poets, 36929 Grace Ave., Zephyrhills FL 33542. Established 2000. **Contact:** Verna Thornton, awards coordinator. Offers 1st Prize: $75; 2nd Prize: $50; 3rd Prize: $40; plus 5 Honorable Mentions at $5 each. Submissions may be previously published and may have previously won prizes. Considers simultaneous submissions. Submit up to 4 poems of no more than 42 lines each. Subject and form are poet's choice; "please identify structured form." Send 2 copies of each poem on 8½×11 white paper; list deadline in upper right-hand corner of both copies. On second copy only, in upper right-hand corner under deadline, list poet's name and full address. Include #10 SASE with entry. **Entry fee:** up to 4 poems for $5; $1 each additional poem; no limit. Make checks payable to New River Poets and mail to Verna Thornton at the above address. **Deadline:** February 15, June 15, and October 15 (all postmark). "Winning entries will be selected by a highly qualified poet or a panel of established poets. New River Poets is a chartered chapter of the Flordia State Poets Association, Inc., and a member of the National Federation of State Poetry Societies (NFSPS). Its purpose is to acknowledge and reward outstanding poetic efforts."

$⬜ ◎ NEW WOMEN'S VOICES CHAPBOOK COMPETITION

Finishing Line Press, P.O. Box 1626, Georgetown KY 40324. (859)514-8966. E-mail: FinishingBooks @aol.com. Web site: www.finishinglinepress.com. Established 1998. **Contact:** Leah Maines, poetry editor. The New Women's Voices Chapbook Competition offers $1,000 and publication by Finishing Line Press for a chapbook-length ms by a woman poet who has not yet published a full-length collection (previous chapbook publication is okay). All entries will be considered for publication; up to 10 entries will be selected for the New Women's Voices series. Submit up to 26 pages of poetry. Include bio, acknowledgments, and SASE. Guidelines available on Web site. **Entry fee:** $15. **Deadline:** February 15 (postmark). Judge: Varies.

$⬜ ◎ NFSPS COLLEGE/UNIVERSITY LEVEL POETRY AWARDS (Specialized: student writing)

P.O. Box 520698, Salt Lake City UT 84152-0698. (801)484-3113. Fax: (801)606-3444. E-mail: SBSeni or@juno.com. Web site: www.nfsps.org. **Contact:** N. Colwell Snell, chairman. Offers 2 annual awards of $500 each; 1 as the Edna Meudt Memorial Award, the second as the Florence Kahn Memorial Award. Each prize includes publication of winning ms, with 75 copies awarded to the respective poet. Recipients will be invited to read at the annual NFSPS (National Federation of State Poetry Societies) convention; NFSPS will provide an additional travel stipend to be presented at the convention to recipients in attendance (winners are responsible for the balance of convention costs). Open to all freshmen, sophomores, juniors, and seniors of an accredited university or college.

Submit a ms of 10 original poems, 1 poem to each page, single-spaced, each poem titled. Each poem must be no more than 46 lines (including spaces between stanzas) and have no more than 50 characters/line (including spaces between words and punctuation). Manuscript must be titled and must include cover page with name, address, phone number in upper left-hand corner; ms title centered on page. May include dedication page. No other identification on any page other than cover page. **NOTE:** A current, official NFSPS application, completed and duly notarized, must accompany ms at time of submission. No e-mail submissions or special deliveries; First Class Mail only. Entry form and guidelines available for SASE or on Web site. Send 4 copies of the manuscript. **Entry fee:** none. **Deadline:** notarized applications and mss received on or before February 1 (no entry mailed before January 1). Winners will be selected on or before March 31 and announced after April 15. Each recipient's state poetry society is also notified. Copies of winning books available on NFSPS Web site.

$☐ NFSPS COMPETITIONS

30 West Lester Ave., D-27, Salt Lake City UT 84107. (801)281-5529. E-mail: theda_bassett2002@yahoo.com. Web site: www.nfsps.org. **Contact:** Theda Bassett, contest chair. NFSPS sponsors a national contest with 50 different categories each year, including the NFSPS Founders Award of 1st Prize: $1,500; 2nd Prize: $500; 3rd Prize: $250. Rules for all contests are given in a brochure available from Madelyn Eastlund, editor of *Strophes* newsletter, at 310 South Adams St., Beverly Hills FL 34465 (e-mail: verdure@tampabay.rr.com); or from Theda Bassett at the address above; or on the NFSPS Web site. **Entry fee:** (for members) $1/poem or $8 total for 8 or more categories, plus $5/poem for NFSPS Founders Award (limit 4 entries in this category alone). All poems winning over $15 are published in the *ENCORE Prize Poem Anthology*. NFSPS also sponsors the annual Stevens Poetry Manuscript Competition and the NFSPS College/University Level Poetry Awards (see separate listings this section).

✴ $☑ THE NIGHTBOAT POETRY PRIZE

Nightboat Books, P.O. Box 656, Beacon NY 12508. E-mail: editor@nightboat.org. Web site: www.nightboat.org. Established 2003. **Contact:** Stephen Motika. The Nightboat Poetry Prize offers an annual award of $1,000 plus book publication; finalists are announced. Submissions must be unpublished as a collection, but individual poems may have been previously published in journals; and collection may be entered simultaneously in other ms contests. Submit 48-100 pages of poetry (suggested length only), single-spaced, paginated, 1 poem/page, 1 side only. Manuscript must be typed, bound only by a clip. Include 2 title pages (1 with book title, name, address, telephone, and e-mail address; 1 with book title only), table of contents, and acknowledgments page. Poet's name should not appear anywhere in the ms, except on the first title page. Bio optional. Entry form and guidelines available for SASE, by e-mail, or on Web site. **Entry fee:** $20. **Deadline:** November 15 (postmark). 2006 winner was Jonathan Weinert (*In the Mode of Disappearance*). 2006 judge: Brenda Hillman. Winner announced by March on Web site, in *Poets & Writers Magazine*, and in a written letter to all entrants. "Nightboat Books has published books by Michael Burkard, Fanny Howe, Joshua Kryah, Douglas A. Martin, Juliet Patterson, and Natalie Stephens."

$☑ JESSE BRYCE NILES MEMORIAL CHAPBOOK AWARD

4956 St. John Dr., Syracuse NY 13215. (315)488-8077. E-mail: poetry@comstockreview.org. Web site: www.comstockreview.org. The Jesse Bryce Niles Memorial Chapbook Award runs every other year, next in 2009, and offers $1,000 plus publication and 50 author's copies; each entrant also receives a copy. Submissions must be unpublished as a collection, but individual poems may have been previously published in journals. Considers simultaneous submissions "as long as the poet notifies us immediately upon acceptance elsewhere." Submit 25-34 pages of poetry, single-spaced (1 page = 38 lines maximum, including spacing between lines; poems may run longer than 1 page). **Manuscripts either too short or too long will be disqualified.** "Do not count title page, acknowledgments, dedication, or bio in the page length. Do not send illustrations, photos, or any other graphics attached to the poems. You may submit a table of contents, which may list the manuscript name only, not the poet's name (not counted in page total for manuscript)." Manuscripts should be paginated and secured with a binder clip; no staples or plastic covers. Include 2 cover pages: 1 with ms title, poet's name, address, phone number, and e-mail address; second with ms title only. List acknowledgments on a separate, removable page with same identifying information. Poet's name should not appear on poems. Include SASE for results only; mss will not be returned. Guidelines available for SASE or on Web site. **Entry fee:** $15/chapbook. **Deadline:** submit August 1-September 30 (postmark). **Offered every other year.** 2005 winner was J.F. Connolly (*Among the Living*). 2007 judge: Kathleen Bryce Niles; all entries are screened by the editors of *The Comstock Review* (see separate listing in Magazines/Journals). Winner is notified in December. Copies of winning chapbooks are available for $10 saddle-stitched, $11.50 perfect-bound. E-mail for ordering details.

▦ $◎ NSW PREMIER'S LITERARY AWARD "THE KENNETH SLESSOR PRIZE" (Specialized: Australian citizens only)

Arts NSW, P.O. Box A226, Sydney South NSW 1235 Australia. E-mail: mail@arts.nsw.gov.au. Web site: www.arts.nsw.gov.au. Established 1980. Offers annual award of $15,000 AUD for a book of poetry (collection or long poem) published in the previous year. **Open to Australian citizens only.** Books may be nominated by poets or by their agents or publishers. Write for entry form and guidelines or check Web site. **Deadline:** November (check guidelines). Winners will be announced in May. "Obtain copy of guidelines before entering."

$□ OHIO POETRY DAY CONTESTS

Ohio Poetry Day Association, Dept. of English, Heidelberg College, 310 East Market, Tiffin OH 44883. Web site: www.ohiopoetryassn.com. Established 1937. **Contact:** Bill Reyer, contest chair. Offers annual slate of 30-40 contest categories. Prizes range from $75 down; all money-winning award poems are published in an annual anthology (runs over 100 pages). Submissions must be unpublished. Submit 1 poem/category on topic and in form specified. Some contests open to everyone, but others open only to Ohio poets. "Each contest has its own specifications. Entry must be for a specified category, so entrants need rules." Entry form and guidelines available for SASE. **Entry fee:** $10 inclusive, unlimited number of categories. **Deadline:** usually end of May; see guidelines for each year's deadline. Competition receives over 4,000 entries/year. Winners and judges for most recent contest listed in winners' anthology. Judges are never announced in advance. Winners list available in August for SASE (enclose with poem entries); prizes given in October. Copies of annual prize anthologies available from Amy Jo Zook, contest treasurer (3520 State Route 56, Mechanicsburg OH 43044) for $9 plus postage (prices can differ from year to year). "Ohio Poetry Day is the umbrella. Individual contests are sponsored by poetry organizations and/or individuals across the state. OPD sponsors several and selects the Poet of the Year; have four memorial funds." Join mailing list at any time by sending contact information by postcard or letter. Advice: "Revise, follow rules, look at individual categories for a good match."

✪ $◩ OHIO STATE UNIVERSITY PRESS/THE JOURNAL AWARD IN POETRY

180 Pressey Hall, 1070 Carmack Rd., Columbus OH 43210-1002. (614)292-6930. Fax: (614)292-2065. E-mail: ohiostatepress@osu.edu. Web site: www.ohiostatepress.org. **Contact:** Patt McLaughlin. Each year *The Journal* selects one full-length book ms for publication by Ohio State University Press. Winner also receives the Charles B. Wheeler Prize of $3,000. Each entrant receives a one-year subscription (2 issues) to *The Journal*. Manuscript must be unpublished as a collection, but poems may have been published elsewhere and must be identified as such. Submit at least 48 pages of original poetry, typed; clear photocopies acceptable. Include cover page and contact information; poet's name or other identification must not appear on ms pages. Include SASP for notification of receipt of ms and SASE for results; no mss will be returned. Guidelines available for SASE, by e-mail, or on Web site. **Entry fee:** $25. Make checks/money orders payable to The Ohio State University. **Deadline:** entry must be postmarked within the month of September. 2007 winner was Mark Svenvold (*Empire Burlesque*).

$◎ OHIOANA POETRY AWARD (Helen and Laura Krout Memorial) (Specialized: native & resident OH authors)

Ohioana Library Association, 274 E. First Ave., Suite 300, Columbus OH 43201. (614)466-3831.

Fax: (614)728-6974. E-mail: ohioana@ohioana.org. Web site: www.ohioana.org. **Contact:** Linda Hengst, executive director. Offers annual Ohioana Book Awards. Up to 6 awards may be given for books (including books of poetry) by authors born in Ohio or who have lived in Ohio for at least 5 years. The Ohioana Poetry Award of $1,000 (with the same residence requirements), made possible by a bequest of Helen Krout, is given yearly "to an individual whose body of published work has made, and continues to make, a significant contribution to poetry, and through whose work as a writer, teacher, administrator, or in community service, interest in poetry has been developed." **Deadline:** nominations to be received by December 31. Competition receives several hundred entries. 2007 award winners were Kathy Fagan (poetry award) and Martha Collins and Bruce Weigl (book award/poetry tie so 2 books received awards). *Ohioana Quarterly* regularly reviews books by Ohio authors and is available through membership in Ohioana Library Association ($25/year).

$☑ THE ORPHIC PRIZE FOR POETRY

Dream Horse Press, P.O. Box 2080, Aptos CA 95001-2080. E-mail: dreamhorsepress@yahoo.com. Web site: www.dreamhorsepress.com. Established 1999. **Contact:** J.P. Dancing Bear, editor/publisher. The Orphic Prize for Poetry offers an annual award of $1,000 and publication of a book-length ms by Dream Horse Press. All entries will be considered for publication. Both free and formal verse styles are welcome. Submissions may be entered in other contests, "but if your manuscript is accepted for publication elsewhere, you must notify Dream Horse Press immediately." Submit 48-80 pages of poetry, paginated, with table of contents, acknowledgments, and bio. Include separate cover letter with poet's name, biographical information, and e-mail address (when available). Poet's name should not appear anywhere on the ms. Manuscripts will be recycled after judging. Guidelines available on Web site. **Entry fee:** $25/ms entered. Entry fees are non-refundable. Make checks/money orders payable to Dancing Bear. **Deadline:** December 1 for 2008; check Web site for deadlines and details for subsequent years. 2006 winner was Gaylord Brewer (*The Martini Diet*). Judge: judging will be anonymous.

◼ $☐ PACIFIC NORTHWEST WRITERS ASSOCIATION (PNWA) LITERARY CONTEST

PMB 2717-1420 NW Gilman Blvd, Ste 2, Issaquah, WA 98027. (425)673-2665. Fax: (206) 824-4559. E-mail: pnwa@pnwa.org. Web site: www.pnwa.org. Established 1956. **Contact:** Kelli Liddane. "Calling all writers. Submit your writing to 12 categories for our annual literary contest." **Entry fee:** $35 for PNWA members, $50 for non-PNWA members per category. **Deadline:** February. Check Web site for specific date. Over $12,000 in prize monies. Winners will be announced at awards banquet at annual PWNA Summer Writers Conference in Seattle, WA. "The Pacific Northwest Writers Association, a nonprofit organization, is dedicated to Northwest writers and the development of writing talent from pen to publication through education, accessibility to the publishing industry, and participation in an interactive vital writer community. In addition to the annual literary contest, PNWA hosts an annual conference each summer in the Seattle area. See Web site for further membership and conference details."

$☑ THE PATERSON POETRY PRIZE

Poetry Center, Passaic County Community College, One College Blvd., Paterson NJ 07505-1179. (973)684-6555. E-mail: mgillan@pccc.edu. Web site: www.pccc.edu/poetry. Established 1979. **Contact:** Maria Mazziotti Gillan, editor/executive director. The Paterson Poetry Prize offers an annual award of $1,000 for the strongest book of poems (48 or more pages) published in the previous year. The winner will be asked to participate in an awards ceremony and to give a reading at The Poetry Center. Minimum press run: 500 copies. Publishers may submit more than 1 title for prize consideration; 3 copies of each book must be submitted. Include SASE for results; books will not be returned (all entries will be donated to the Poetry Center Library). Guidelines and application form (required) available for SASE or on Web site. **Entry fee:** none. **Deadline:** February 1 (postmark). Winners will be announced in *Poets & Writers Magazine* and on Web site. 2007 winners were Christopher Bursk (*The First Inhabitants of Arcadia*) and Patricia Smith (*Teahouse of the Almighty*). The award splits between 2 winners.

⊠ $☑ PAUMANOK POETRY AWARD

English Dept., Knapp Hall, Farmingdale State University of New York, 2350 Broadhollow Rd., Farmingdale NY 11735. E-mail: brownml@farmingdale.edu. Web site: www.farmingdale.edu. Established 1990. **Contact:** Dr. Margery Brown, director. Offers 1st Prize of $1,000 plus an all-expense-paid feature reading in their 2008-2009 visiting writers series. (*Please note:* travel expenses within the continental U.S. only.) Also awards two 2nd Prizes of $500 plus expenses for a reading in the series. Submit cover letter, 1 paragraph literary bio, and 3-5 poems (no more than 10 pages total), published or unpublished. Include cover page with name, address, and phone number. Guidelines available for SASE or on Web site. **Entry fee:** $25. Make checks payable to Farmingdale State University of New York, VWP. **Deadline:** by September 15 (postmark). Include SASE for results (to be mailed by late December); results also posted on Web site. Competition receives over 600 entries. 2006 winners were Jennifer Rose (1st Prize) and Jesse Arthur Stone and Vivian Shipley (runners-up).

$☑ PAVEMENT SAW PRESS CHAPBOOK AWARD

321 Empire Street, Montpelier, OH 43206-0291. E-mail: info@pavementsaw.org. Web site: www.pavementsaw.org. Established 1992. **Contact:** David Baratier, editor. Pavement Saw Press Chapbook Award offers $500, publication, and 50 author copies. Open to all poets regardless of previous publication history. Submit up to 32 pages of poetry. Include signed cover letter with poet's name, address, phone number, e-mail, publication credits, a brief biography, and ms title. Also include 2 cover sheets: 1 with poet's contact information and ms title, 1 with the ms title only. Do not put poet's name on mss pages except for first title page. No mss will be returned. Guidelines available for SASE or on Web site. **Entry fee:** $15. "Every entrant will receive the equivalent cost of the entry fee in Pavement Saw Press titles." Make checks payable to Pavement Saw Press. **Deadline:** December 30 (entries must be postmarked by this date to be eligible). 2007 winner was Susan Terris (*Marriage License*).

$☑ PEARL POETRY PRIZE

Pearl Editions, 3030 E. Second St., Long Beach CA 90803-5163. (562)434-4523 or (714)968-7530. E-mail: pearlmag@aol.com. Web site: www.pearlmag.com. Established 1974. **Contact:** Joan Jobe Smith, Marilyn Johnson, and Barbara Hauk, poetry editors. The annual Pearl Poetry Prize awards $1,000, publication, and 25 author's copies for a book-length ms. Guidelines available for SASE or on Web site. **Entry fee:** $20 (includes a copy of the winning book). **Deadline:** submit May 1-July 15 only. 2006 winner was Kevin Griffith (*Denmark, Kangaroo, Orange*). 2007 judge: David Hernandez.

$◻ ◎ JUDITH SIEGEL PEARSON AWARD (Specialized: subject concerning women)

Wayne State University/Family of Judith Siegel Pearson, 5057 Woodward Ave., Suite 9408, Detroit MI 48202. (313)577-2450. Fax: (313)577-8618. E-mail: rhonda@wayne.edu. **Contact:** Rhonda Agnew, competition coordinator. Offers an annual award of up to $200 for the best creative or scholarly work on a subject concerning women. The type of work accepted rotates each year: drama and nonfictional prose in 2008; poetry in 2009; essays in 2010, fiction in 2011. Open to all interested writers and scholars. Submissions must be unpublished. Submit 4-10 poems (20 pages maximum). Guidelines available for SASE or by fax or e-mail. **Deadline:** March 3.

$◎ PEN CENTER USA LITERARY AWARD IN POETRY (Specialized: writers living west of the Mississippi)

PEN Center USA, % Antioch University Los Angeles, 400 Corporate Pointe, Culver City CA 90230. (310)862-1555, ext. 361. Fax: (310)862-1556. E-mail: awards@penusa.org. Web site: www.penusa.org. **Contact:** Awards Coordinator. Offers annual $1,000 cash award to a book of poetry professionally published during the previous calendar year. Open to writers living west of the Mississippi. Submit 4 copies of the entry. Entry form and guidelines available for SASE, by fax, e-mail, or on Web site. **Entry fee:** $35. **Deadline:** December 14. 2006 winner was Brian Turner for *Here, Bullet* (Alice James Books). 2006 judges: Terry Wolverton, Elena Karina Byrne, and Sholeh Wolpe. Winner will be announced in the summer and honored at a ceremony in Los Angeles in November.

$☑ PENNSYLVANIA POETRY SOCIETY ANNUAL CONTEST

6 Kitchen Ave., Harvey's Lake PA 18618. E-mail: sarah62@comcast.net. Web site: www.NFSPS.o rg. **Contact:** Sarah Kelly Marston, Contest Chair, 126 Strayer Dr., Carlisle PA 17013. Annual contest offers Grand Prize awards of $100, $50, and $25; other categories offer $25, $15, and $10. May enter 5 poems for Grand Prize at $2 each for members and nonmembers alike. Also offers prizes in other categories of $25, $15, and $10 (1 entry/category); only 1 poem accepted in each of remaining categories. A total of 18 categories open to all, 4 categories for members only. Guidelines available for SASE or on Web site. **Entry fee:** for members entering categories 1-22, $5 inclusive; for nonmembers entering categories 2-18, $2 each. **Deadline:** January 15. Also offers: *The Pegasus Contest* for PA students only, grades 5-12. Guidelines available for SASE (to Marilyn Downing, Pegasus Contest Chair, 137 Apple Lane, Hershey PA 17033) or on Web site. **Deadline:** February 1. *Carlisle Poets Contest* opens to all poets. Guidelines available for SASE (to Joy Campbell, Contest Chair 10 Polecat Rd., Landisburg PA 17040) or e-mail archjoy@embarqmail.com. **Deadline:** October 31. The Society publishes a quarterly newsletter, *Penns to Paper*, with member poetry and challenges, plus an annual soft-cover book of prize poems from the annual contest. Winning Pegasus Contest poems are published in a booklet sent to schools. PPS membership dues: $17/fiscal year. Make checks payable to PPS, Inc. and mail to Steven Concert, Membership Liaison, 6 Kitchen Ave., Harvey's Lake PA 18618.

$☑ ◎ PERUGIA PRESS PRIZE (Specialized: first or second poetry book by a woman)

P.O. Box 60364, Florence MA 01062. E-mail: info@perugiapress.com. Web site: www.perugiapress. com. Established 1997. **Contact:** Susan Kan, director. The Perugia Press Prize for a first or second poetry book by a woman offers $1,000 and publication. Poet must be a living U.S. resident with no more than 1 previously published book of poems (chapbooks don't count). Submissions must be unpublished as a collection, but individual poems may have been previously published in journals, chapbooks, and anthologies. Considers simultaneous submissions if notified of acceptance elsewhere. Submit 48-72 pages (white paper) "with legible typeface, pagination, and fastened with a removable clip. No more than 1 poem per page." 2 cover pages required: 1 with ms title, poet's name, address, telephone number, and e-mail address; and 1 with ms title only. Include table of contents and acknowledgments page. No e-mail submissions. No translations or self-published books. Multiple submissions accepted if accompanied by separate entry fee for each. Include SASE for winner notification only; mss will be recycled. Guidelines available on Web site. **Entry fee:** $22. Make checks payable to Perugia Press. **Deadline:** submit August 1-November 15 (postmark). "Use USPS only, not FedEx or UPS." Winner announced by April 1 by e-mail or SASE (if included with entry). Judges: panel of Perugia authors, booksellers, scholars, etc.

$☑ THE RICHARD PETERSON POETRY PRIZE

Dept. of English, Mail Code 4503, Faner Hall 2380, Southern Illinois University Carbondale, 1000 Faner Dr., Carbondale IL 62901. Web site: www.siu.edu/~crborchd. Established 1995. **Contact:** Jon Tribble, managing editor. The Richard Peterson Poetry Prize offers $1,500 plus publication in the Winter/Spring issue of *Crab Orchard Review* (see separate listing in Magazines/Journals). "Submissions must be unpublished original work not under consideration elsewhere, written in English by a U.S. citizen or permanent resident. Name, address, telephone number, and/or e-mail address should appear only on the title page of manuscript; author's name should not appear on any subsequent pages. Mark 'poetry' on outside of envelope. Include #10 SASE for notification of winners." See guidelines for complete formatting instructions. Guidelines available for SASE or on Web site. **Entry fee:** $10/entry (3 poems, 100 line limit per poem, no more than 1 poem per page; poet may submit up to 3 separate entries if not entering the fiction or nonfiction categories of the contest). Each fee entitles entrant to a copy of the winter/spring *Crab Orchard Review* featuring the prize winner; include complete address. Make checks payable to *Crab Orchard Review*. **Deadline:** see guidelines or check Web site.

$◎ PEW FELLOWSHIPS IN THE ARTS (Specialized: PA resident of Bucks, Chester, Delaware, Montgomery, or Philadelphia County; 25 or older)

230 S. Broad St., Suite 1003, Philadelphia PA 19102. (215)875-2285. Fax: (215)875-2276. Web

site: www.pewarts.org. Established 1991. **Contact:** Melissa Franklin, award director. "The Pew Fellowships in the Arts provide financial support directly to artists so they may have the opportunity to dedicate themselves wholly to the development of their artwork for up to 2 years. Up to 12 fellowships of $50,000 each (in 3 different categories) awarded each year." Must be a Pennsylvania resident of Bucks, Chester, Delaware, Montgomery, or Philadelphia County for at least 2 years; must be 25 or older. Matriculated students, full or part-time, are not eligible. Application and guidelines available mid-August. **Deadline:** December of the preceding year. Judges: panel of artists and art professionals. Winner will be announced by letter.

$✉ ◎ JAMES D. PHELAN AWARD (Specialized: CA-born writers ages 20-35)

% Intersection for the Arts, 446 Valencia St., San Francisco CA 94103. (415)626-2787. Fax: (415)626-1636. Web site: www.theintersection.org. Established 1935. **Contact:** Awards Coordinator. The James D. Phelan Award offers $3,000 to the author of an unpublished work-in-progress of fiction (novel or short stories), nonfictional prose, poetry, or drama. Applicants must be California-born (although they may now reside outside of the state), and must be between the ages of 20 and 35 as of the March 31 deadline. Guidelines and entry form (required) available on Web site. **Entry fee:** none. **Deadline:** March 31. Competition receives 150-180 entries. 2007 winner was Tung-Hui Hu (poetry, "Greenhouses, Lighthouses").

$✉ ◎ PINEWOOD HAIKU CONTEST

Wisteria, P.O. Box 150932, Lufkin TX 75915-0932. E-mail: wisteriajournal@gmail.com (inquiries only). Web site: www.wistaria.blogspot.com. Established 2006. **Contact:** T.A. Thompson, founder. The annual Pinewood Haiku Contest offers 1st Prize: $100; 2nd Prize: $50; 3rd Prize: $25. Winners will be published in the April issue of *Wisteria: A Journal of Haiku, Senryu, and Tanka*. For contemporary English-language haiku; no rules as to syllable or line count. Submissions must be unpublished. Submit 2 copies of each haiku, typed, on a 3×5 index card. 1 card only should include the poet's name, address, and e-mail for contact purposes. Only 1 haiku/card. No e-mail submissions. Guidelines available for SASE or on Web site. **Entry fee:** $2/poem or 3 poems for $5; 3 poems maximum, cash or money order only, no checks. Make money orders payable to T.A. Thompson. **Deadline:** accepts entries November 1-February 14. Winners will be notified by e-mail and postal mail; no SASE required.

$✉ PLAN B PRESS POETRY CHAPBOOK CONTEST

3412 Terrace Dr., #1731, Alexandria VA 22302. (215)732-2663. E-mail: teammay@att.net. Web site: www.planbpress.com. Established 1999. **Contact:** Contest Coordinator. The annual Plan B Press Poetry Chapbook Contest offers $175, publication by Plan B Press (see separate listing in Book/Chapbook Publishers), and 50 author's copies. Poems may be previously published individually. Accepts multiple submissions with separate fee for each. Submit up to 24 poems (48 pages total maximum) in English. Include table of contents and list of acknowledgments. Include e-mail address or SASE for notification of winner; mss will not be returned. Author retains copyright of poems, but Plan B reserves rights to layout and/or cover art and design. Guidelines available on Web site. **Entry fee:** $15. **Deadline:** was March 1 for 2008. 2007 winner was Ellen Sullins (*Elsewhere*). 2008 final judge: Kimmika Williams.

$✉ THE POCATALIGO POETRY CONTEST

Yemassee, Dept. of English, University of South Carolina, Columbia SC 29208. (803)777-2085. E-mail: editor@yemasseejournal.org. Web site: www.yemasseejournal.org. Established 1993. Contact: Contest Coordinator. The annual Pocataligo Poetry Contest offers a $500 prize and publication in *Yemassee* (see separate listing in Magazines/Journals). Submissions must be unpublished. Considers simultaneous submissions with notice of acceptance elsewhere. Accepts multiple entries with separate $10 fee and SASE for each. Submit 3-5 poems (15 pages total), typed. Include cover letter with poet's name, contact information, and poem title(s); no identifying information on ms pages except poem title (which should appear on every page). Include SASE for results only; mss will not be returned. Guidelines available on Web site. **Entry fee:** $10. Make checks payable to Educational Foundation/English Literary Magazine Fund. **Deadline:** February 15 (postmark) annually.

$☑ POETIC LICENSE CONTEST

Mkashef Enterprises, P.O. Box 688, Yucca Valley CA 92286-0688. E-mail: alayne@inetworld.net. Web site: www.asidozines.com. Established 1998. **Contact:** Alayne Gelfand, poetry editor. Offers biannual poetry contest with awards of 1st Prize: $500; 2nd Prize: $100; 3rd Prize: $40; plus publication in anthology and 1 copy. 5 honorable mentions receive 1 copy; other poems of exceptional interest will also be included in the anthology. Themes and deadlines available for SASE. Submissions may be previously published. Submit any number of poems, any style, of up to 50 lines/poem. Include name, address, and phone number on each poem. Enclose a SASE for notification of winners. Accepts e-mail (as attachment or pasted into body of message), disk, or postal submissions. "Judges prefer original, accessible, and unforced works." Guidelines available for SASE or by e-mail. **Entry fee:** $1/poem. **Deadline:** available for SASE or by e-mail. "We're looking for fresh word usage and surprising imagery. Please keep in mind that our judges prefer non-rhyming poetry. Each contest seeks to explode established definitions of the theme being spotlighted. Be sure to send SASE or e-mail for current theme and deadline."

$☑ POETRY 2009 INTERNATIONAL POETRY COMPETITION

Atlanta Review, P.O. Box 8248, Atlanta GA 31106. E-mail: dan@atlantareview.com (inquiries only). Web site: www.atlantareview.com. Established 1994. **Contact:** Dan Veach, editor/publisher. *Atlanta Review* (see separate listing in Magazines/Journals) sponsors an annual international poetry competition, offering $2,009 Grand Prize, 20 International Publication Awards (winners will be published in *Atlanta Review*), and 30 International Merit Awards (includes certificate, Honorable Mention in *Atlanta Review*, and free issue). Poems must not have been published in a nationally distributed print publication. Put your name and address on each page (e-mail and phone optional). Include SASE for results only (outside of U.S., SAE only, no IRC required); no entries will be returned. Guidelines available on Web site. **Entry fee:** $5 for the first poem, $3 for each additional poem. Make checks payable to *Atlanta Review*. "Checks in your national currency are acceptable at the current exchange rate. We also accept uncancelled stamps from your country." **Deadline:** May 8, 2009. Winners will be announced in August; Contest Issue published in October. Contest Issue available for $4, or free with $10 subscription to *Atlanta Review*.

$☑ THE POETRY CENTER BOOK AWARD

1600 Holloway Ave., San Francisco CA 94132. (415)338-2227. Fax: (415)338-0966. E-mail: poetry@sfsu.edu. Web site: www.sfsu.edu/~poetry. Established 1980. **Contact:** Elise Ficarra, business manager. Offers award to an outstanding book of poems published by an individual author in the current year. Awards one prize of $500 and an invitation to read at The Poetry Center. Books by a single author; no collaborative works, anthologies, or translations. Must be published and copyrighted during year of contest. Publisher, author, or reader may submit entries. **Entry fee:** $10. **Deadline:** July 1-January 31 annually (e.g., entries published during 2008 will be accepted up until January 31, 2009). Competition receives 200-250 entries annually. 2005 winner was Dara Wier (*Reverse Rapture*, Verse Press). Winner will be announced on Web site and through press release. "The Poetry Center and American Poetry Archives at San Francisco State University were established in 1954. Its archives include the largest circulating tape collection of writers reading their own work in the United States."

$☑ ◎ THE POETRY COUNCIL OF NORTH CAROLINA ANNUAL POETRY CONTEST
(Specialized: NC residents or anyone with NC connection)

Web site: http://share.triangle.com/node/11095. Check recent blog posts for contest dates and guidelines. **Contact:** check Web site for current contact information. The Poetry Council of North Carolina is "an organization whose sole purpose is to sponsor annual adult and student poetry contests and to publish the winning poems in our book, *Bay Leaves*. There is no membership fee. All winners are invited to read their poems at Poetry Day in the fall of each year, either late September or early October." Open to residents and anyone with a "North Carolina connection" (persons born in NC, transients from other states who either attend school or work in NC, and NC residents temporarily out of state). Offers 4 adult and 2 student contests with prizes ranging from

$10 to $25; all winning poems plus Honorable Mentions will be published in *Bay Leaves* (50+ pages, perfect-bound). Guidelines available for SASE or on Web site. **Entry fee:** $3/poem, 1 poem/ contest. **Deadline:** see Web site. Competition receives 200+ entries/year. Winners list available for SASE, also appears in *Bay Leaves* and on Web site. Copies of *Bay Leaves* available from Poetry Council of North Carolina. "Please read the guidelines carefully. Send only your best work. You can enter only 1 poem in each contest."

$⬛ POETRY SOCIETY OF AMERICA AWARDS

Poetry Society of America, 15 Gramercy Park, New York NY 10003. (212)254-9628. E-mail: psa@po etrysociety.org. Web site: www.poetrysociety.org. Offers the following awards **open to PSA members only**: *The Writer Magazine/Emily Dickinson Award* ($250, for a poem inspired by Dickinson though not necessarily in her style); *Cecil Hemley Memorial Award* ($500, for a lyric poem that addresses a philosophical or epistemological concern); *Lyric Poetry Award* ($500, for a lyric poem on any subject); *Lucille Medwick Memorial Award* ($500, for an original poem in any form on a humanitarian theme); *Alice Fay Di Castagnola Award* ($1,000 for a manuscript-in-progress of poetry or verse-drama). The following awards are **open to both PSA members and nonmembers**: *Louise Louis/Emily F. Bourne Student Poetry Award* ($250, for the best unpublished poem by a student in grades 9-12 from the U.S.); *George Bogin Memorial Award* ($500, for a selection of 4-5 poems that use language in an original way to reflect the encounter of the ordinary and the extraordinary and to take a stand against oppression in any of its forms); *Robert H. Winner Memorial Award* ($2,500, to acknowledge original work being done in mid-career by a poet who has not had substantial recognition, open to poets over 40 who have published no more than one book). Entries for the *Norma Farber First Book Award* ($500) and the *William Carlos Williams Award* (purchase prize between $500 and $1,000, for a book of poetry published by a small press, non-profit, or university press) **must be submitted directly by publishers**. Complete submission guidelines for all awards are available on Web site. **Entry fee:** all of the above contests are free to PSA members; nonmembers pay $15 to enter any or all of contests 6-8; $5 for high school students to enter single entries in the student poetry competition; high school teachers/administrators may submit unlimited number of students' poems (one entry/student) to student poetry award for $20. **Deadline:** submissions accepted October 1-December 21 (postmark). Additional information available on Web site.

$⬜ POETS' DINNER CONTEST

2214 Derby St., Berkeley CA 94705-1018. (510)841-1217. **Contact:** Dorothy V. Benson. Contestant must be present to win. Submit 3 anonymous typed copies of original, unpublished poems in not more than 3 of the 8 categories (Humor, Love, Nature, Beginnings & Endings, Spaces & Places, People, Theme [Earth], and Poet's Choice). Winning poems (Grand Prize, 1st, 2nd, 3rd) are read at an awards banquet and Honorable Mentions are presented. Cash prizes awarded; Honorable Mention receives books. The event is nonprofit. "Since 1927 there has been an annual awards banquet sponsored by the ad hoc Poets' Dinner Committee, currently at Francesco's in Oakland." Guidelines available for SASE. **Entry fee:** none. **Deadline:** January 15. Competition receives about 300 entries. Recent contest winners include Stephen Sadler (Grand Prize), Linda Prather, Amy Miller, Joyce Odam, Gregory DeHart, Tom Odegard, Laverne Frith, Joan Gelfand (1st Prizes). 2007 Judges: Kathleen Norris, Jonah Bornstein, Andrea Hollander Budy, Patricia Clark, Suzanne C. Smith, Vincent Nixon. *Remembering*, an anthology of winning poems from the Poets' Dinner over the last 25 years, is available by mail for $6 plus tax from Dorothy V. Benson at the contest address.

$⬛ FELIX POLLAK PRIZE IN POETRY

University of Wisconsin Press, Dept. of English, 600 N. Park St., University of Wisconsin, Madison WI 53706. E-mail: rwallace@wisc.edu. Web site: www.wisc.edu/wisconsinpress/index.html. Established 1994. **Contact:** Ronald Wallace, poetry series editor. The annual Felix Pollack Prize in Poetry is one of 2 prizes awarded by the University of Wisconsin Press (see separate listing for the Brittingham Prize in Poetry). Offers $1,000 plus publication, with an additional $1,500 honorarium to cover expenses of a reading in Madison. Submissions must be unpublished as a collection, but individual poems may have been published elsewhere (publication must be acknowledged). Considers simultaneous submissions if notified of selection elsewhere. Submit 50-80 unbound ms pages, typed single-spaced (with double spaces between stanzas) or double-spaced. Clean photocopies are acceptable. Include title page with poet's name, address, and telephone number. No translations. Include SASE for results only; mss will not be returned. Guidelines available for SASE or on Web site. **Entry fee:** $25. **NOTE:** $25 fee applies to consideration of same entry for the Brittingham Prize in Poetry—1 fee for 2 contest awards. Make checks/money orders payable to University of Wisconsin Press. **Deadline:** submit September 1-30 (postmark). 2007 Pollak Prize winner was Barbara Goldberg (*The Royal Baker's Daughter*). Qualified readers will screen all mss. Judge: "a distinguished poet who will remain anonymous until the winners are announced in mid-February."

$⬛ PORTLANDIA CHAPBOOK CONTEST

The Portlandia Group, PMB 225, 6663 SW Beaverton-Hillsdale Hwy., Portland OR 97225. E-mail: braucher@portlandia.com. Established 1999. **Contact:** Karen Braucher, award director. Offers biennial prize of $200, publication of chapbook, and 30 copies. Submissions must be unpublished as a collection, but individual poems may have been previously published in journals. Considers simultaneous submissions. Submit 24 pages of poetry with table of contents, acknowledgments, and bio. Include 2 title pages: 1 with ms title and personal info, the other with ms title only. Include SASE for results only; no mss will be returned. "See guidelines for the year you are submitting." Guidelines available for SASE or by e-mail. **Entry fee:** $12/entry, includes copy of winning chapbook. **Deadline:** March 1 for 2008 (check biennial guidelines). Competition receives about 200 entries/year. Past winners include Judith Taylor, Kurt S. Olsson, Elisa A. Garza, John Surowiecki, Ron Drummond, and John Pursley III. Copies of winning chapbooks ($8, includes shipping) are available from The Portlandia Group.

⬛ $⬛ ◎ THE JACKLYN POTTER YOUNG POETS COMPETITION (Specialized: Washington, DC-area high school students)

The Word Works, 1200 North Quaker Lane, Alexandria VA 22302. (703)931-5177. Web site: www. worksdc.com. **Contact:** W. Perry Epes, director. The annual Jacklyn Potter Young Poets Competition is open to Washington, DC-are high school students. 2 winners receive an honorarium and read their original work at the Joaquin Miller Cabin in Rock Creek Park in an appearance with an established poet. The winners and other notable entrants will be recommended for a reading at the Nora School Poetry Series held in Silver Spring, MD. Submit 5-6 poems with poet's name, address, and phone number in the upper right corner of every ms page. Include a separate cover page with poet's name, address, phone number, e-mail address, name of school, grade, expected graduation date, and listed titles of poems submitted. Include SASE for results. **Deadline:** submit January 1-March 31.

$⬛ A. POULIN, JR. POETRY PRIZE

BOA Editions, Ltd., 260 East Ave., Rochester NY 14604. (585)546-3410. Web site: www.boaeditions .org. Established 1976. **Contact:** Thom Ward, poetry editor. BOA Editions, Ltd. (see separate listing in Book/Chapbook Publishers) sponsors the annual A. Poulin, Jr. Poetry Prize for a poet's first book. Awards $1,500 and publication. Individual poems may have been previously published. Considers simultaneous submissions. Submit 48-100 pages of poetry, paginated consecutively, typed or computer-generated in 11 pt. font. Bind with spring clip (no paperclips). Include cover/ title page with poet's name, address, and telephone number. Also include table of contents; list of acknowledgments; and entry form (available for download on Web site). Multiple entries accepted with separate entry fee for each. No e-mail submissions. Include SASP for notification of receipt and SASE for results. Mss will not be returned. Guidelines available on Web site in May. **Entry fee:** $25. **Deadline:** submit August 1-November 30 annually. 2008 judge: Jean Valentine. Winner announced in March.

$⬛ THE PRAIRIE SCHOONER BOOK PRIZE SERIES

University of Nebraska Press, 201 Andrews Hall, P.O. Box 880334, University of Nebraska, Lincoln NE.68588-0334. (402)472-0911. Fax: (402)472-9771. E-mail: psbookprize@gmail.com. Web site:

http://prairieschooner.unl.edu. Established 1926. **Contact:** Contest Director. The annual *Prairie Schooner* Book Prize Series offers $3,000 and publication of a book-length collection of poetry by the University of Nebraska Press; one runner-up receives $1,000. Individual poems may have been previously published elsewhere. Considers simultaneous submissions if notified immediately of acceptance elsewhere. Submit at least 50 pages of poetry with acknowledgments page (if applicable). Poet's name should not appear on ms pages. Xeroxed copies are acceptable. Bind with rubber band or binder clip only. Include 2 cover pages: one with poet's name, address, phone number, and e-mail address; the other with ms title only. Include SASP for acknowledgment of receipt of ms and #10 SASE for results only; mss will not be returned. Guidelines available for SASE, by e-mail, or on Web site. **Entry fee:** $25. Make checks payable to *Prairie Schooner*. **Deadline:** January 15-March 15 annually. 2006 winner was Paul Guest (*Notes for My Body Double*). Winners announced on Web site in early July, with results mailed shortly thereafter. (See separate listing for *Prairie Schooner* in Magazines/Journals.)

$☑ THE PSA NATIONAL CHAPBOOK FELLOWSHIPS

Poetry Society of America, 15 Gramercy Park, New York NY 10003. (212)254-9628. E-mail: psa@poetrysociety.org. Web site: www.poetrysociety.org. Established 2002. The PSA National Chapbook Fellowships offer 2 prizes of $1,000 and publication of winning chapbook mss, with distribution by the Poetry Society of America. Open to any U.S. resident who has not published a full-length poetry collection. **(Poets who apply to this contest may not apply to The PSA New York Chapbook Fellowships.)**Does not accept entries by fax or e-mail. Guidelines available for SASE or on Web site. **Entry fee:** $12 for both PSA members and nonmembers. Make checks/money orders payable to Poetry Society of America. **Deadline:** submit October 1-December 21 (postmarked). 2006 winners were Dan Chelotti (*The Eights*) and Maureen Thorson (*Mayport*). Most recent judges: Harryette Mullen and Mark Strand. Additional information available on Web site.

$☑ ◎ THE PSA NEW YORK CHAPBOOK FELLOWSHIPS (Specialized: open to NYC residents only)

Poetry Society of America, 15 Gramercy Park, New York NY 10003. (212)254-9628. E-mail: psa@poetrysociety.org. Web site: www.poetrysociety.org. Established 2002. The PSA New York Chapbook Fellowships offer 2 prizes of $1,000 and publication of each of winning chapbook mss, with distribution by the Poetry Society of America. Open to any New York City resident (in the 5 boroughs) who is 30 or under and has not published a full-length poetry collection. **(Poets who apply to this contest may not apply to The PSA National Chapbook Fellowships.)** Does not accept entries by fax or e-mail. Guidelines available for SASE or on Web site. **Entry fee:** $12 for both PSA members and nonmembers. Make checks/money orders payble to Poetry Society of America. **Deadline:** submit October 1-December 21 (postmarked). 2006 winners were Jessica Fjeld (*On animate life: its profligacy, organ meats, &c*) and Maya Pindyck (*Locket, Master*). Most recent judges: Rae Armantrout and Kevin Young. Additional information available on Web site.

Ⓝ ☐ PSALMS POETRY PRAYER CONTEST

1465 NW 70 Lane, Margate FL 33063.954-977-5211. Fax: 954-917-8414. E-mail: editor@aprayeraday.org. Web site: www.aprayeraday.org. Established 2007. **Contact:** R. Lee Williams, PhD., editor. Psalms Poetry Prayer quarterly contest offers $100 for first place, $50 for second place, $25 for third place, and "as many honorable mentions as merit publication in magazine and annual book." Open to beginners. Poems may be previously published "if author holds copyright." Simultaneous submissions acceptable but "must be notified if author loses copyright." Submit any number of poems up to 24 lines/poem in any form. Guidelines available on Web site. **Entry fee:** $5 per poem. **Deadline:** 30 days before publication—will be held for next issue. Competition receives 100 entries per contest. Most recent winner for 2007 was Jean Bellovio. 2008/09 judges: Kelly Salazar, R. Lee Williams, Paul Howard. Winner announced by mail when selected. Copies of winning books available. Advice: "See Web site— read and reread 23 Psalms."

$☑ THE PULITZER PRIZE IN LETTERS

The Pulitzer Prize Office, 709 Journalism, Columbia University, New York NY 10027. (212)854-3841. Fax: (212)854-3342. E-mail: pulitzer@www.pulitzer.org. Web site: www.pulitzer.org. **Con-**

tact: the Pulitzer Prize Board. The Pulitzer Prize for Letters annually awards 2 prizes of $10,000 each and a certificate for the most distinguished books of poetry and fiction published during the preceding year (U.S. authors only). Anyone, including the author, may submit a book that's eligible. Submit 4 copies of published books (or galley proofs if book is being published after October 15), completed entry form, 1 photograph, and 1 biography. Entry form and guidelines available for SASE, by fax, or on Web site. **Entry fee:** $50. **Deadline:** October 15. Competition receives about 150 entries/year. 2007 poetry winner was Natasha Trethewey for *Native Guard* (Houghton Mifflin). 2007 judges: Cynthia Huntington, Rafael Campo, and Claudia Emerson.

$⚃ QUERCUS REVIEW PRESS POETRY SERIES BOOK AWARD

Quercus Review Press, Modesto Junior College, Div. of Literature & Language Arts, 435 College Ave., Modesto CA 95350. (209)575-6183. E-mail: pierstorffs@mjc.edu. Web site: www.quercusreview.com. Established 1999. **Contact:** Contest Coordinator. Quercus Review Press publishes 1 poetry book/year selected through the Poetry Series Book Award. Offers $1000, publication, and 50 author's copies. Book mss may include previously published poems. Submit 46-96 pages in ms format. Include cover letter and SASE. Guidelines available on Web site. **Entry fee:** $20 ($25 to receive a copy of winning book). **Deadline:** June-October 17 (postmark). 2006 winner was Neil Carpathios (*At the Axis of Imponderables*).

⚃ $⚃ QWF A.M. KLEIN PRIZE FOR POETRY (Specialized: books by Quebec authors)

Quebec Writers' Federation, 1200 Atwater Ave., Montreal QC H3Z 1X4 Canada. Phone/fax: (514)933-0878. E-mail: admin@qwf.org. Web site: www.qwf.org. **Contact:** Lori Schubert, executive director. Offers annual awards of $2,000 CAD each for poetry, fiction, nonfiction, first book, and translation. Submissions must be previously published. Open to authors "who have lived in Quebec for at least 3of the past 5 years." Submit 4 copies of a book of at least 48 pages. Entry forms and instructions available at qwf.org in April. **Entry fee:** $20 CAD/submission. **Deadline:** May 31 for books published between October 1 and May 15; August 1 for books published between May 15 and September 30 (bound proofs are acceptable; the finished book must be received by September 30). Poetry competition receives approximately 10 entries. 2007 winner was Susan Elmslie (*I, Nadja and Other Poems*). Winners announced in November. "QWF was formed in 1988 to honor and promote literature written in English by Quebec authors." QWF also publishes *QW-RITE*, "a newsletter offering information and articles of interest to membership and the broader community and has an online literary journal, *carte blanche*, at http://www.carte-blanche.org/."

$⚃ ◎ THE RAIZISS/DE PALCHI TRANSLATION AWARDS (Specialized: Italian poetry translated into English)

The Academy of American Poets, 584 Broadway, Suite 604, New York NY 10012. (212)274-0343. Fax: (212)274-9427. E-mail: cevans@poets.org. Web site: www.poets.org. Established 1934. **Contact:** CJ Evans, awards coordinator. Awarded for outstanding translations of modern Italian poetry into English. A $5,000 book prize and a $20,000 fellowship are awarded in alternate years. Guidelines and entry form available for SASE or on Web site. **Deadline:** see Web site for current deadlines for book and fellowship awards. 2006 fellowship winner was Adria Bernardi. Winner announced in January.

$⚃ RATTLE POETRY PRIZE

RATTLE, 12411 Ventura Blvd., Studio City CA 91604. (818) 505-6777. E-mail: timgreen@rattle.com. Web site: www.rattle.com. Established 2006. The *RATTLE* Poetry Prize awards 1st Prize of $5,000, plus ten $100 Honorable Mentions. Additional entries may be offered publication as well. Open to writers worldwide (see Web site for special international guidelines). Poems must be written in English (no translations). No previously published poems or works accepted for publication elsewhere. No simultaneous submissions. Submit no more than 4 poems/entry. Multiple entries by a single poet accepted; however, each 4-poem group must be treated as a separate entry with its own cover sheet and entry fee. Include cover sheet with poet's name, address, e-mail address, phone number, and poem titles. No contact information should appear on poems. Include SASE for results only; no poems will be returned. **Note:** Poems also may be entered through online submission on Web site. Guidelines available by e-mail or on Web site. **Entry fee:** $16; includes one-year subscription to *RATTLE* (see separate listing in Magazines/Journals). Make checks/money orders payable to *RATTLE* (for credit card entries, see Web site). **Deadline:** August 1 (postmark). 2007 winner was Albert Haley ("Barcelona"). Judge: editors of *RATTLE* in blind review. Winners announced in September.

$ ◎ MARGARET REID POETRY CONTEST FOR TRADITIONAL VERSE

Tom Howard Books, % Winning Writers, 351 Pleasant St., PMB 222, Northampton MA 01060-3961. (866)946-9748. Fax: (413)280-0539. E-mail: johnreid@mail.qango.com. Web site: www.winningwriters.com. Established 2004. **Contact:** John Reid, award director. Offers annual award of 1st Prize: $1,000; 2nd Prize: $400; 3rd Prize: $200; 7 High Distinction Awards of $100 each; 10 Highly Commended Awards of $70 each; and 30 Commended Awards of $50 each. The top 10 entries will be published on the Winning Writers Web site. Submissions may be published or unpublished, may have won prizes elsewhere, and may be entered in other contests. Submit poems in traditional verse forms, such as sonnets, ballads, odes, blank verse, and haiku. No limit on number of lines or number of poems submitted. No name on ms pages; type or computer-print on letter-size white paper, single-sided. Guidelines available for SASE or on Web site. Submit online or by mail. **Entry fee:** $6 USD for every 25 lines (exclude poem title and any blank lines from count). **Deadline:** November 15-June 30. 2006 winner was Susan Keith ("Remembrance"). 2006 judges: John H. Reid and Dee C. Konrad. Winners announced in September at WinningWriters.com; entrants who provide valid e-mail addresses also receive notification.

✪ $ ◻ MARY ROBERTS RINEHART AWARDS

Mail Stop Number 3E4, English Dept., George Mason University, Fairfax VA 22030-4444. (703)993-1180. E-mail: ddeulen@gmu.edu. Web site: www.gmu.edu/departments/writing. **Contact:** Danielle Deulen, English graduate coordinator. 3 annual grants of $1,000-2,000 each are awarded in spring for the best nominated ms in fiction, nonfiction, and poetry. "Grants are made only for unpublished works by writers who have not yet published a book or whose writing is not regularly appearing in nationally circulated commercial or literary magazines. Writers may see a grant in only 1 category in any given year; an author not granted an award 1 year may apply in succeeding years, but once a writer receives an award, he or she may not apply for another, even in a different genre. Grant recipients must be U.S. citizens." **A writer's work must be nominated in writing by an established author, editor, or agent.** Nominations must be accompanied by a sample of the nominee's work (10 pages of individual or collected poems/30 pages of fiction or nonfiction). Guidelines available for SASE, by e-mail, or on Web site. **Deadline:** November 30 (postmark). "Grants will be announced early in the following March on the awards Web page. Candidates who wish to receive a printed announcement should submit a #10 SASE." Competition receives over 300 entries.

$ ◻ ◎ RIVERSTONE POETRY CHAPBOOK AWARD

Riverstone, A Press for Poetry, P.O. Box 1421, Carefree AZ 85377. Established 1992. Web site: www.riverstonepress.org.
• **Will not be reading mss in 2008-2009.**
The Riverstone Poetry Chapbook Award offers $100, publication, and 50 copies to the winner. Submissions may include previously published poems. Considers simultaneous submissions. Submit chapbook ms of 16-24 pages of poetry; include "poems in their proposed arrangement, title page, table of contents, and acknowledgments. All styles welcome." Accepts multiple entries with separate entry fees. Include SASE for contest results; no mss will be returned. Guidelines available for SASE or on Web site. **Entry fee:** $10. "All entrants will receive a copy of the most recent winning chapbook." **Deadline:** check Web site for when Riverstone starts reading mss again. Order sample chapbooks by sending $5 plus $1 shipping.

◎ ROANOKE-CHOWAN POETRY AWARD (Specialized: NC resident authors)

The North Carolina Literary & Historical Association, 4610 Mail Service Center, Raleigh NC 27699-4610. (919)807-7290. Fax: (919)733-8807. E-mail: michael.hill@ncmail.net. Web site: www.ah.dcr.

state.nc.us/affiliates/lit-hist/awards/awards.htm. **Contact:** Michael Hill, awards coordinator. Offers annual award for "an original volume of poetry published during the 12 months ending June 30 of the year for which the award is given." Open to "authors who have maintained legal or physical residence, or a combination of both, in North Carolina for the 3 years preceding the close of the contest period." Submit 3 copies of each entry. Guidelines available for SASE or by fax or e-mail. **Deadline:** July 15. Competition receives about 15 entries. 2006 winner was James Applewhite (*Selected Poems*). Winner announced by mail October 15.

$⬙ ◎ BEULLAH ROSE POETRY PRIZE (Specialized: poetry by women)

P.O. Box 22161, Baltimore MD 21203. E-mail: cbanks@smartishpace.com. Web site: www.smartish pace.com. Established 1999. **Contact:** Clare Banks, associate editor. The annual Beullah Rose Poetry Prize for exceptional poetry by women offers 1st Prize: $200 and publication of the winning poem in *Smartish Pace* (see separate listing in Magazines/Journals); 2nd and 3rd Prizes: winning poems will be published in *Smartish Pace*. Winners also receive additional Internet and advertising exposure. Submit 3 poems, with poet's name, address, e-mail, telephone number (preferred), and "Beulah Rose Poetry Prize" at the top of each page of poetry submitted. Include bio. Entries may be submitted online or by e-mail (as attachment) or regular mail. Include SASE with postal entries. Guidelines available on Web site. **Entry fee:** $5 for 3 poems; additional poems may be submitted for $1/poem (12 poem maximum). Make checks/money orders payable to *Smartish Pace*. **Deadline:** November 1. Judges: Clare Banks and Traci O'Dea, associate editors.

⬙ $⬙ ◎ ANNA DAVIDSON ROSENBERG AWARDS FOR POEMS ON THE JEWISH EXPERIENCE

Jewish Community Center of San Francisco, 3200 California St., San Francisco CA 94118. (415)292-1200. Fax: (415)276-1550. E-mail: taubecenter@jccsf.org. Web site: www.jccsf.org. Established 1987 by Judah L. Magnus Museum and the children of Anna Davidson Rosenberg. Offers prizes of $1,000, $500, and Honorable Mentions for original, unpublished poems (in English) on the Jewish Experience. Open to all interested writers. Submit up to 3 poems (no more than 10 pages total). "Manuscripts should be submitted in quadruplicate, with a cover note listing the author's name, address, phone number, and e-mail address." No names on poems; entries judged anonymously. "Submissions will not be returned; please do not send your only copies." No fax or e-mail submissions. Guidelines available on Web site. **Entry fee:** none. **Deadline:** was December 1 (postmark) for 2007. 2007 judges: Marcia Falk, Joshua Rivkin, and Susan Terris. Winners announced no later than March 1 at www.jccsf.org and at www.dorothyprizes.org. Reception, award ceremony, and poetry reading in April.

$⬙ ERNEST SANDEEN PRIZE IN POETRY

Dept. of English, University of Notre Dame, Notre Dame IN 46556-5639. (574)631-7526. Fax: (574)631-4795. E-mail: creativewriting@nd.edu. Web site: http://www.nd.edu/~alcwp/sandeen. html. Established 1994. **Contact:** Director of Creative Writing. The Sandeen Prize in Poetry offers $1,000 (a $500 award and a $500 advance against royalties from the Notre Dame Press) and publication of a book-length ms. Open to poets who have published at least 1 volume of poetry. "Please include a photocopy of the copyright and the title page of your previous volume. Vanity press publications do not fulfill this requirement. We will pay special attention to second volumes. Please include a vita and/or a biographical statement that includes your publishing history. We will be glad to see a selection of reviews of the earlier collection." Submit 2 copies of ms (inform if ms is available on computer disk). Include SASE for acknowledgment of receipt of ms and SASE for return of ms. **Entry fee:** $15; includes one-year subscription to *Notre Dame Review* (see separate listing in Magazines/Journals). Make checks payable to University of Notre Dame. **Deadline:** submit May 1- September 1. 2007 winner was Jude Nutter (*The Curator of Silence*). Winners announced by the end of January.

$⬙ SAWTOOTH POETRY PRIZE

Ahsahta Press, MS1525, 1910 University Dr., Boise State University, Boise ID 83725-1525. (208)426-2195. Fax: (208)426-4373. E-mail: ahsahta@boisestate.ed. Web site: http://ahsahtapress.boisestate

.edu. The Sawtooth Poetry Prize, sponsored by Ahsahta Press (see separate listing in Books/Chapbooks), honors a book of original poetry in English by a single author. Offers a $1,500 honorarium upon publication and 25 author's copies. Translations are not eligible for this award. "Students and former students of Boise State University and of this year's judge may not enter; close friends of the judge are also not considered eligible." Considers simultaneous submissions, "but entrants are asked to notify Ahsahta Press immediately if a manuscript becomes committed elsewhere." Submit 48-100 pages of poetry, single-spaced, printed on 1 side of $8\frac{1}{2} \times 11$ or A4 page only. Number pages consecutively. Include acknowledgments page and biographical note, which will be removed before judging. Include 2 title pages: 1 with poet's name, address, phone number, and e-mail address (if available); and 1 without. Poet's name should not appear anywhere else on ms; only the anonymous title page will be sent to the readers and judge. Contain pages in a plain manila folder or bind manuscript with a secure clip; do not bind ms in a notebook. Include SASP for notification of receipt of ms and SASE (#10 business) for results; mss will not be returned. Guidelines available on Web site. **Entry fee:** $25/ms. Make checks payable to Ahsahta Press. (See Web site for payment options outside the U.S.) "Entrants will receive a copy of the winning book when it is printed if they include a 7×10 self-addressed mailer with $3.95 postage. Our books measure 6×8 and will not fit in smaller-sized mailers." **Deadline:** submit January 1-March 1 (postmark). "In addition to announcements in national publications, the winning book and author will be featured on the Ahsahta Web site, as will lists of finalists and semi-finalists." 2007 winner was Rusty Morrison with *the true keeps calm biding its story*. 2008 judge: C.D. Wright. "Ahsahta Press, a member of the Council of Literary Magazines and Presses, conforms to the CLMP Code of Ethics and participated in its drafting." Winner will be announced in May 2008.

$ ☺ ◎ HELEN SCHAIBLE SHAKESPEAREAN/PETRARCHAN SONNET CONTEST

Poets' Club of Chicago, 1212 S. Michigan Ave., Apt. 2702, Chicago IL 60605. **Contact:** Tom Roby, president and contest chair. The annual Helen Schaible Shakespearean/Petrarchan Sonnet Contest is open to anyone. **For sonnets only!** Offers 1st Prize: $50; 2nd Prize: $35; 3rd Prize: $15; plus 3 Honorable Mentions and 3 Special Recognitions (non-cash). Submit only 1 entry (2 copies) of either a Shakespearean or a Petrarchan sonnet, which must be original and unpublished. Entry must be typed on $8\frac{1}{2} \times 11$ paper, double-spaced. Name and address in the upper right-hand corner on only 1 copy. All necessary guidelines appear in this listing. Include SASE with entry to receive winners' list. **Entry fee:** none. **Deadline:** September 1 (postmark). Competition receives 150 entries/year. 2007 contest winners were Susan McClean, Allene Rasmussen Nichols, and Beth Staas. Winners will be notified by mail by November 1, 2008. The Poets' Club of Chicago meets monthly at Chicago's Chopin Theater to critique their original poetry, which the members read at various venues in the Chicago area and publish in diverse magazines and books. Members also conduct workshops at area schools and libraries by invitation. "Read the guidelines—1 sonnet only!"

$ ☐ ◎ MONA SCHREIBER PRIZE FOR HUMOROUS FICTION & NONFICTION

15442 Vista Haven Place, Sherman Oaks CA 91403. E-mail: brashcyber@pcmagic.net. Web site: www.brashcyber.com. Established 2000. **Contact:** Brad Schreiber. Offers annual awards of 1st Prize: $500; 2nd Prize: $250; 3rd Prize: $100. All winners are posted on Web site and receive a copy of *What Are You Laughing At?: How to Write Funny Screenplays, Stories & More* by Brad Schreiber. Submissions must be unpublished and may be entered in other contests. Submit any number of poems, 750 words maximum/poem. Include contact information on each poem submitted. Guidelines available on Web site. **Entry fee:** $5/poem. **Deadline:** December 1 annually. Competition receives 340-350 entries/year. Judge: Brad Schreiber. Winners announced December 24 by phone (if U.S. and Canada) or by e-mail. "Take risks in form, content, theme, and language."

$ ☐ ◎ CLAUDIA ANN SEAMAN POETRY AWARD (Specialized: students grades 9-12)

The Community Foundation of Dutchess County, 80 Washington St., Suite 201, Poughkeepsie NY 12601. (845)452-3077. Fax: (845)452-3083. Web site: www.CFDCNY.org. **Contact:** Nevill Smythe, Vice President/Programs. Established 1983. Annual national contest offering award of $500 (1st Prize). Open to U.S. students grades 9-12. Submissions must be unpublished. Considers simultaneous submissions. Submit 1-2 unpublished poems on any subject, in any form. "Entry must contain student and school names, addresses, and phone numbers and the name of the English or writing teacher." Entry guidelines available on Web site. **Entry fee:** none. **Deadline:** June 1. Winner contacted by phone or in writing. Copies of last year's winning poem may be obtained by contacting the Community Foundation by phone, in writing, or on Web site. "The Community Foundation is a nonprofit organization serving Dutchess and Ulster County, New York, and the surrounding area; it administers numerous grant programs, scholarship funds, and endowment funds for the benefit of the community. This is an excellent opportunity for young, previously unpublished poets to earn recognition for their work. Since there's no fee, there is little to lose; realize, however, that a national contest will have more entries than a regional competition."

$☐ SHADOW POETRY'S ANNUAL CHAPBOOK COMPETITION

Shadows Ink Publications, 1209 Milwaukee St., Excelsior Springs MO 64024. Fax: (208)977-9114. E-mail: shadowpoetry@shadowpoetry.com. Web site: www.shadowpoetry.com. Established 2000. **Contact:** James Summers, award director. Offers biannual award of $250, 50 copies of published chapbook, and 25% royalties paid on each copy sold through Shadow Poetry (retail only). Submissions must be unpublished as a whole (collection). No simultaneous submissions. (Winning poet retains copyrights and may publish individual poems elsewhere later.) Submit ms of 16-40 pages, acknowledgments, table of contents, poet bio, etc., in addition to the poetry. Poetry to be submitted on any subject, in any form, in good taste. "Cover letter required with name, address, phone, age, and e-mail address. Enclose cover letter, manuscript, and cover ideas/art, if applicable, in #90 (9×12) envelope. Include #10 SASE for winner notification and SASP for entry receipt (optional)." Guidelines available for SASE or on Web site. **Entry fee:** $18/ms. Make checks/money orders payable to Shadow Poetry. **Deadline:** December 31. "Notification of winner on April 10 by e-mail and SASE." Copies of winning or sample chapbooks available from Shadow Poetry for $8.45 (see Web site for titles).

$☐ SHADOWS INK POETRY CONTEST

Shadows Ink Publications, 1209 Milwaukee St., Excelsior Springs MO 64024. Fax: (208)977-9114. E-mail: shadowpoetry@shadowpoetry.com. Web site: www.shadowpoetry.com. Established 2000. **Contact:** James Summers, award director. Offers annual award of 1st Prize: $100 and publication in chapbook (plus 20 copies of published work); 2nd Prize: $75; 3rd Prize: $35; top 3 winners also receive a certificate, printed copy of winning poem, and a ribbon. The top 40 placing poems will be published in a *Shadows Ink Poetry Chapbook*, and all poets appearing in this publication will receive 1 free copy (additional copies available for $5 each plus shipping). Submissions must be unpublished. No simultaneous submissions. (Winning poets retain copyrights and may publish poems elsewhere later.) Submit maximum of 10 poems, 24 line limit each, on any subject, in any form. "Entry form must be present with mail-in entries. Submit entries in duplicate with name, address, phone number, and e-mail address (when available) on upper left-hand corner of one sheet. Enclose #10 SASE for winners list. Include an additional SASE for entry receipt (optional). If no SASE is included for receipt, Shadow Poetry will e-mail an entry confirmation to the contestant, if applicable." Entry form and guidelines available for SASE or on Web site. **Entry fee:** $5/poem. Make checks/money orders payable to Shadow Poetry. **Deadline:** December 31. Competition receives 150 entries/year. "Winners will be announced February 1 by e-mail and to those who requested a winners list. Results will also be posted on the Shadow Poetry Web site."

$☑ SLAPERING HOL PRESS CHAPBOOK COMPETITION

300 Riverside Dr., Sleepy Hollow NY 10591-1414. (914)332-5953. Fax: (914)332-4825. E-mail: info @writerscenter.org. Web site: www.slaperingholpress.org. Established 1990. **Contact:** Margo Stever. The Slapering Hol Press Chapbook Competition offers an annual award of $1,000, publication, 10 author's copies, and a reading at The Hudson Valley Writers' Center (see separate listing in Organizations). Open only to poets who have not previously published a book or chapbook. Submit 16-20 pages of poetry (collection or one long poem), any form or style. Manuscript should be anonymous with separate cover sheet containing name, address, phone number, e-mail address,

a bio, and acknowledgments. Include SASE for results only; manuscripts will not be returned. Guidelines available for SASE, by fax, e-mail, or on Web site. **Entry fee:** $15. Make checks payable to The Hudson Valley Writers' Center. **Deadline:** May 15. Winner will be announced in September. Competition receives more than 300 entries. 2006 winner was Mary Kaiser (*Falling Into Velázquez*). Winning chapbooks available through Web site and www.amazon.com.

$☑ SLIPSTREAM POETRY CHAPBOOK CONTEST

Dept. W-1, P.O. Box 2071, Niagara Falls NY 14301-0071. (716)282-2616 (after 5 PM, EST). E-mail: editors@slipstreampress.org. Web site: www.slipstreampress.org. Established 1980. **Contact:** Contest Director. The annual Slipstream Poetry Chapbook Contest awards $1,000, publication of a chapbook ms, and 50 author's copies. All entrants receive copy of winning chapbook and an issue of *Slipstream* (see separate listing in Magazines/Journals). Considers simultaneous submissions if informed of status. Accepts previously published work with acknowledgments. Submit up to 40 pages of poetry, any style, format, or theme. Manuscripts will not be returned. Guidelines available for SASE or on Web site. **Entry fee:** $20. **Deadline:** December 1. 2008 winner was Douglas Goetsch (*Your Whole Life*). Winner announced late spring/early summer.

$◉ HELEN C. SMITH MEMORIAL AWARD FOR BEST BOOK OF POETRY (Specialized: TX-born/-resident poets)

Web site: www.smu.edu/english/creativewriting/the_texas_institute_of_letters.htm. Established 1936. The Texas Institute of Letters gives annual awards for books by Texas authors, including the Helen C. Smith Memorial Award for Best Book of Poetry, a $1,200 award. Books must have been first published in the year in question, and entries may be made by authors or by their publishers. Complete guidelines and award information available on Web site. **Deadline:** see Web site. Receives about 30 entries/year. 2006 winner was John Brieuth (*As Long As It's Big*).

$◯ KAY SNOW WRITING AWARDS

Willamette Writers, 9045 SW Barbur Blvd., Suite 5A, Portland OR 97219-4027. (503)452-1592. Fax: (503)452-0372. E-mail: wilwrite@willamettewriters.com. Web site: www.willamettewriters.com. Established 1986. **Contact:** Pat Macaodha, award director. Offers annual awards of 1st Prize: $300; 2nd Prize: $150; 3rd Prize: $50 in several genres, including poetry. Submissions must be unpublished. Submit up to 2 poems (1 entry fee), maximum 5 pages total, on any subject, in any style or form, single-spaced, 1 side of paper only. Entry form and guidelines available for SASE or on Web site. **Entry fee:** $10 for members of Willamette Writers; $15 for nonmembers. **Deadline:** January 15-April 23 (postmarked) for 2008. Competition receives 150 entries. 2007 poetry winners were Matt Schumacher, Corey Thompson, and Frank Ratti. Winners will be announced July 27th. "Write and send in your very best poem. Read it aloud. If it still sounds like the best poem you've ever heard, send it in."

$☑ THE RICHARD SNYDER MEMORIAL PUBLICATION PRIZE

Ashland Poetry Press, 401 College Ave., Ashland University, Ashland OH 44805. (419)289-5957 or (419)289-5110. Web site: www.ashland.edu/aupoetry. Established 1969. **Contact:** Sarah Wells, managing editor. Offers annual award of $1,000 plus book publication in a paper-only edition of 1,000 copies. Submissions must be unpublished in book form. Considers simultaneous submissions. Submit 50-80 pages of poetry. **Entry fee:** $25. **Deadline:** April 30 annually. Competition receives 350 entries/year. 2007 Winner was Helen Wallace (*Shimming the Glass House*). Annual judge: Robert Phillips. Winners will be announced in *Writer's Chronicle* and *Poets & Writers*. Copies of winning books available from Small Press Distribution, Baker & Taylor, and directly from the Ashland University Bookstore online. The Ashland Poetry Press publishes 2-4 books of poetry/year.

Ⓝ $◯ SOCIETY OF SOUTHWESTERN AUTHORS WRITING CONTEST

P.O. Box 35484, Tucson AZ 85740. (520)293-6373. Fax: (520)293-6363. E-mail: douglashutchison@comcast.net. Web site: www.ssa-az.org. Established 1972. **Contact:** Mary Ann Hutchison, contest chair. Society of Southwestern Authors Writing Contest offers annual awards for: short story, personal essay/memoirs, poetry, short stories for children, ages 6-12. Cash prizes: 1st-$300; 2nd-$150; 3rd-$75; honorable mention-$25; award certificates; first through honorable mention printed in the Society's annual anthology magazine, *The Story Teller*. All winners receive copies of *The Story Teller*. Open to beginners. Submissions must be unpublished. No simultaneous submissions. Submit 40 lines maximum on any subject. All forms welcome. Entry forms and guidelines available on Web site or may be requested by email or send SASE to post office address. **Entry fee:** $10 per poem. **Deadline:** May 31, 2008. Competition receives 95 poems on average each year. 2007 winners: Suzanne Morrone, Marlene Baird, Dixon Hearne, Robert Nordmeyer. 2007 judges: Jim Cox, Ned Mackey, Don Nickerson. Winner notified by mail within a month of being selected. Awards presented at awards luncheon held on the 3rd Sunday of October or sent by mail if winner cannot be present. Copies of winning anthologies available for $10 per copy from SSA. "SSA is a non-profit association of writers and other publishing professionals, founded in 1972. Its objective is to conduct a program of activities designed to promote mutually-supportive friendship among writers, provide recognition of members' achievements, and encourage and assist persons seeking to become published writers. In addition to the writing contest, it sponsors an annual conference in September." **Advice** "All contest entrants are asked to read all the requirements thoroughly, and then reread them, to avoid disqualification. However, SSA is writer friendly and encouraging new writers is high on our list."

$☑ SOUL-MAKING LITERARY COMPETITION

National League of American Pen Women, Nob Hill, San Francisco Bay Area Branch, 1544 Sweetwood Dr., Colma CA 94015-2029. Phone/fax: (650)756-5279. E-mail: PenNobHill@aol.com. Web site: www.soulmakingcontest.us. Established 1993. **Contact:** Eileen Malone, award director. Annual open contest offers cash prizes in each of 9 literary categories, including poetry and prose poem. 1st Prize: $100; 2nd Prize: $50; 3rd Prize: $25. Submissions in some categories may be previously published. Submit 3 one-page poems on soul-making theme; any form for open poetry category. No names or other identifying information on mss; include 3×5 card with poet's name, address, phone, fax, e-mail, title(s) of work, and category entered. Include SASE for results only; mss will not be returned. Guidelines available on Web site. **Entry fee:** $5/entry. **Deadline:** November 30. Competition receives 300 entries/year. Names of winners and judges are posted on Web site. Winners announced in January by SASE and on Web site. Winners are invited to read at the Koret Auditorium, San Francisco. Event is televised.

$☑ THE SOW'S EAR CHAPBOOK COMPETITION

355 Mount Lebanon Rd., Donalds SC 29638-9115. E-mail: errol@kitenet.net. Web site: www.sows-ear.kitenet.net. Established 1988. **Contact:** Errol Hess, managing editor. *The Sow's Ear Poetry Review* (see separate listing in Magazines/Journals) sponsors an annual chapbook competition. Offers $1,000, publication as the Spring issue of the magazine, and 25 author's copies. Open to adults. Submissions may be previously published individually if poet holds publication rights. Considers simultaneous submissions, "but if your chapbook is accepted elsewhere, you must withdraw promptly from our competition." Submit 22-26 pages of poetry; no length limit on poems, but no more than 1 poem on a page. Include title page and table of contents. Poet's name should not appear on poems, title page, or table of contents. Include separate sheet with chapbook title, poet's name, address, phone number, e-mail address (if available), and publication credits for submitted poems, if any. Include SASE or e-mail address for results only; entries will not be returned. Guidelines available for SASE, by e-mail, or on Web site. **Entry fee:** $20; includes subscription. Make checks payable to *The Sow's Ear Poetry Review*. Submit in March and April. **Deadline:** May 1 (postmark).

$☑ THE SOW'S EAR POETRY COMPETITION

355 Mount Lebanon Rd., Donalds SC 29638-9115. E-mail: errol@kitenet.net. Web site: www.sows-ear.kitenet.net. Established 1988. **Contact:** Errol Hess, managing editor. *The Sow's Ear Poetry Review* (see separate listing in Magazines/Journals) sponsors an annual contest for unpublished poems.

Offers $1,000 and publication in *The Sow's Ear Poetry Review*; also offers the option of publication for top finalists. Submit up to 5 unpublished poems. Include separate sheet with poem titles, poet's name, address, phone number, and e-mail address (if available). "We will check with finalists before sending to final judge." Poet's name should not appear on poems. Include SASE for results only; entries will not be returned. Guidelines available for SASE, by e-mail, or on Web site. **Entry fee:** $20 for up to 5 poems. Contestants receive a year's subscription. Make checks payable to *The Sow's Ear Poetry Review*. **Deadline:** November 1 (postmark). Past judges include Gregory Orr and Marge Piercy. "4 criteria help us judge the quality of submissions: 1) Does the poem make the strange familiar or the familiar strange, or both? 2) Is the form of the poem vital to its meaning? 3) Do the sounds of the poem make sense in relation to the theme? 4) Does the little story of the poem open a window on the Big Story of the human situation?"

$⬚ SPIRE PRESS POETRY CONTEST

532 LaGuardia Place, Suite 298, New York NY 10012. E-mail: editor@spirepress.org. Web site: www.spirepress.org. Established 2002. **Contact:** Shelly Reed, award director. Offers annual award of publication with royalty contract and promotion; cash prizes (see guidelines for each year). Submissions must be unpublished. Considers simultaneous submissions as long as Spire Press is informed. Submit a chapbook ms of 18-40 pages of poetry in any form (shorter poems preferred). Include SASE. **Entry fee:** $18/ms. **Deadline:** May 1. Competition receives 400 entries/year. 2006 winner was Matthew Hittinger (*Pear Slip*). Winners will be announced on Web site after contest deadline. Copies of winning chapbooks available through Web site, Amazon, selected bookstores, and Spire Press.

$◑ THE SPOON RIVER POETRY REVIEW EDITORS' PRIZE

4241 Dept. of English, Publications Unit, Illinois State University, Normal IL 61790-4241. Web site: www.litline.org/spoon. Established 1976. **Contact:** Prize Director. The *Spoon River Poetry Review* Editors' Prize awards $1,000 to 1 winning poem; 2 runners-up will receive $100 each. Winning poem, runners-up, and honorable mentions will be published in the fall issue of *The Spoon River Poetry Review* (see separate listing in Magazines/Journals). Submissions must be unpublished. Submit 2 copies of 3 poems, maximum 10 pages total. On each page of 1 copy only include poet's name, address, and phone number. No fax or e-mail submissions. Include SASE for results only; mss will not be returned. Guidelines available for SASE or on Web site. **Entry fee:** $16; includes one-year subscription or gift subscription. (Indicate preference and include recipient's name and address.) **Deadline:** April 15 (postmark). 2007 winner was M.B. McLatchey.

✦ $⬚ SPS STUDIOS BIANNUAL POETRY CARD CONTEST

Blue Mountain Arts, Inc., P.O. Box 1007, Dept. E, Boulder CO 80306. Web site: www.sps.com. SPS Studios offers a biannual poetry contest with prizes of $300, $150, and $50 for each competition (winning poems are also published on the SPS Web site). "Poems can be rhyming or non-rhyming, although we find that non-rhyming poetry reads better. We suggest you write about real emotions and feelings and that you have some special person or occasion in mind as you write. Poems are judged on the basis of originality and uniqueness. English-language entries only, please. Enter as often as you like." All entries must be the original creation of the submitting poet, who must own all rights to the entries. Poet gives permission to SPS Studios, Inc. to publish and display the entry on the Web (in electronic form only) if the entry is selected as a winner or finalist. Contest is open to everyone except employees of SPS Studios and their families. Submit entries through online form or by postal mail. "If submitting by regular mail, please do not send us the only copy of your work. If you'd like your entry material returned, enclose a SASE. Label each submission with your name, snail mail address, phone number, and e-mail address (if you have 1)." Guidelines available on Web site. **Entry fee:** none. **Deadline:** June 30 and December 31. Winners will be contacted within 45 days of the deadline date.

$◑ THE ST. LAWRENCE BOOK AWARD

Black Lawrence Press, 521 56th Street 2F Brooklyn NY 11220. E-mail: editors@blacklawrencepress.com. Web site: www.blacklawrencepress.com. Established 2003. **Contact:** Colleen Ryor, editor.

The St. Lawrence Book Award is awarded annually for a first collection of poetry or short stories. Prize includes $1,000, publication, 10 author copies, and an interview with the winner in *The Adirondack Review* (see separate listing in Magazines/Journals). Prizes awarded on publication. Finalists will receive a copy of the winning book. All finalists will be considered for standard publication. "Entrants must not have had a full-length book published. Chapbooks do not count as full-length books." Considers simultaneous submissions, but notify immediately if ms is accepted elsewhere. Submit book-length ms, paginated, with cover letter with brief bio and contact information (including valid e-mail), table of contents, and an acknowledgments page (if applicable). "Finalists will be notified and asked to submit another copy of the manuscript for final judging." Include 2 cover pages: 1 with ms title, brief bio, and poet's contact information (including e-mail); the second with ms title only. Clip together the cover letter, cover pages, acknowledgments, and entry fee. No e-mail submissions. Include SASE or e-mail address for results only; mss will not be returned. Guidelines available on Web site. **Entry fee:** $25. Make checks/money orders payable to Black Lawrence Press. **Deadline:** August 31 annually. 2005 winner was Stefi Weisburd (*The Wind-Up Gods*).

✪ 🌐 ☯ THE ANN STANFORD POETRY PRIZE

% Master of Professional Writing Program, 3501 Trousdale Parkway, Mark Taper Hall, THH 355J, University of Southern California, Los Angeles CA 90089-0355. (213)740-3253. E-mail: scr@college.usc.edu. Web site: www.usc.edu/scr. Established 1982. **Contact:** Contest Coordinator. The Ann Stanford Poetry Prize offers 1st Prize: $1,000; 2nd Prize: $200; 3rd Prize: $100. Winners will be published in the Fall edition of *Southern California Review* (see separate listing in Magazines/Journals). Submissions must be unpublished. Submit up to 5 poems. Include cover sheet with poem titles, poet's name, address, phone number, and e-mail. No identification on submission pages. Incomplete submissions will not be accepted. Include SASE for results. Guidelines available on Web site. **Entry fee:** $10 for up to 5 poems. All entrants receive a free issue of Southern California Review. **Deadline:** April 30.

✪ $☯ WALLACE E. STEGNER FELLOWSHIPS

Creative Writing Program, Stanford University, Stanford CA 94305-2087. (650)725-1208. Fax: (650)723-3679. E-mail: mpopek@stanford.edu. Web site: www.stanford.edu/dept/english/cw. **Contact:** Mary Popek, program administrator. Offers 5 fellowships in poetry of $26,000 plus tuition of over $6,000/year for promising writers who can benefit from 2 years of instruction and criticism at the Writing Center. "We do not require a degree for admission. No school of writing is favored over any other. Chronological age is not a consideration." **Deadline:** December 1 (postmark). Competition receives about 600 entries/year for poetry. 2007/2008 fellows in poetry were James Arthur, Elizabeth Bradfield, Sean Hill, Laura McKee and Joshua Rivkin.

✪ $☯ THE WALLACE STEVENS AWARD

The Academy of American Poets, 584 Broadway, Suite 604, New York NY 10012-3210. (212)274-0343. Fax: (212)274-9427. Web site: www.poets.org. Award established 1994. Awards $100,000 annually to recognize outstanding and proven mastery in the art of poetry. **No applications are accepted.** 2006 winner was Michael Palmer. 2006 judges: Robert Hass, Fanny Howe, Susan Stewart, Arthur Sze, and Dean Young.

$▢ STEVENS POETRY MANUSCRIPT CONTEST

22614 N. Santiam Hwy., Lyons OR 97358. E-mail: eberry@wvi.com. Web site: www.nfsps.com. **Contact:** Eleanor Berry, contest chair. National Federation of State Poetry Societies (NFSPS) offers annual award of $1,000, publication of ms, and 50 author's copies. Individual poems may have been previously published in magazines, anthologies, or chapbooks, but not the entire ms as a collection. Simultaneous submissions allowed. Submit 48-70 pages of poetry by a single author, typewritten, or computer printed, 1 poem or column of poetry to a page. Pages numbered, with table of contents, but no author identification anywhere in ms. Include 2 title pages; 1 with no author identification, the other with name of poet, address, phone number, email address and state poetry society member affiliation, if applicable. No staples or binders; plain manila folder and/or manuscript clip permitted. No illustrations. No disk submissions; no certified or registered mail. Optional: Include SASE for results only; mss will not be returned. Guidelines available for SASE or on Web site. **Entry fee:** $20 for NFSPS members; $25 for nonmembers. Make checks/money orders payable to NFSPS. **Deadline:** October 15 (postmark). Winners announced in January following deadline; entrants who include an email address or SASE will be notified of winner. Book will be published by June and sold at annual NFSPS convention and winning poet (if present) will read from it. Copies of books available through NFSPS Web site.

$🖉 THE RUTH STONE PRIZE IN POETRY

Vermont College, 36 College St., Montpelier VT 05602. (802)828-8633. Fax: (802)828-8649. E-mail: hungermtn@tui.edu. Web site: http://www.tui.edu/hungermtn/index.asp. Established 2002. **Contact:** Caroline Mercurio, managing editor. The annual Ruth Stone Prize in Poetry offers $1,000 and publication in *Hunger Mountain: The Vermont College Journal of Arts & Letters* (see separate listing in Magazines/Journals); 2 Honorable Mentions also published. Submit up to 3 poems, not to exceed 6 pages. **Entry fee:** $15 (includes copy of prize issue). **Deadline:** December 10. Guidelines available in magazine, for SASE, by fax, e-mail, or on Web site. "Include SASE and index card with poem titles and address; do not put name on poems."

$🖉 MAY SWENSON POETRY AWARD

Utah State University Press, 7800 Old Main Hill, Logan UT 84322-7800. (435)797-1362. Fax: (435)797-0313. E-mail: michael.spooner@usu.edu. Web site: www.usu.edu/usupress. Established 1996. **Contact:** Michael Spooner, director. The annual May Swenson Poetry Award offers $1,000 and publication by Utah State University Press for a full-length poetry collection. No restrictions on form or subject. Submit 50-100 pages of original poetry. Include cover sheet with poet's name and address. Include SASE for results; mss will not be returned. Guidelines available on Web site. **Entry fee:** $25; includes copy of winning book. **Deadline:** September 30 (postmark). 2008 winner was Idris Anderson (*Mrs. Ramsay's Knee*). 2009 Judge: Billy Collins.

$🖉 ◎ TANKA SOCIETY OF AMERICA INTERNATIONAL ENGLISH-LANGUAGE TANKA COMPETITION

Web site: www.tankasocietyofamerica.com. Offers cash awards and publication of winning poems in *Ribbons* (see separate listing in Magazines/Journals), the journal of the Tanka Society of America (see separate listing in Organizations). All rights revert to poets after publication. Open to all except TSA officers and judges. Submissions must be unpublished. No simultaneous submissions. Submit any number of original tanka, in English. Guidelines and details available in March issue of *Ribbons* or on Web site.

$🖉 TIGER'S EYE POETRY CONTEST

P.O. Box 2935, Eugene OR 97402. E-mail: tigerseyepoet@yahoo.com. Web site: www.tigerseyejournal.com. The *Tiger's Eye* Poetry Contest offers $500, $100, and $50 to the top 3 poems submitted; in addition, 1 contest entrant will be awarded an editors' choice chapbook contract, with winner receiving 50 copies and publication in the Mid-Spring issue of *Tiger's Eye* (see separate listing in Magazines/Journals). No previously published poems. Considers simultaneous submissions. Submit 3 poems that represent your best work. No restrictions on form, subject, or length. "We welcome sonnets, haibun, haiku, ghazals, villenelles, etc., as well as free verse and experimental poetry." Include cover page with poet's name and contact information; no identifying information on mss pages. Guidelines available on Web site. **Entry fee:** $10 for 3 poems. **Deadline:** February 28 (postmark). 2008 judge: Carol Alena Aronoff.

$🖉 ◎ TOWSON UNIVERSITY PRIZE FOR LITERATURE (Specialized: book MD writer)

Towson University, College of Liberal Arts, Towson MD 21252. (410)704-2128. Fax: (410)704-6392. E-mail: eduncan@towson.edu. Web site: www.towson.edu. **Contact:** Chair of the English Dept. Offers annual prize of $1,000 "for a single book or book-length manuscript of fiction, poetry, drama, or imaginative nonfiction by a Maryland writer. The prize is granted on the basis of literary and aesthetic excellence as determined by a panel of distinguished judges appointed by the university. The first award, made in the fall of 1980, went to novelist Anne Tyler.'' Work must have been published within the 3 years prior to the year of nomination or must be scheduled for publication within the year in which nominated. Submit 5 copies of work in bound form or in typewritten, double-spaced ms form. Entry form and guidelines available for SASE or on Web site (search "Towson Prize for Literature"). **Deadline:** June 15. Competition receives 8-10 entries. 2007 winner was Ron Tanner (*A Bed of Nails*, Bkmk Press).

$☑ TRANSCONTINENTAL POETRY AWARD

Pavement Saw Press,321 Empire Street, Montpelier, OH 43543. E-mail: info@pavementsaw.org. Web site: www.pavementsaw.org. Established 1992. **Contact:** David Baratier, editor. The Transcontinental Poetry Award offers $1,000, publication, and a percentage of the print run for a first book. "Each year, Pavement Saw Press will seek to publish at least 1 book of poetry and/or prose poems from manuscripts received during this competition, which is open to anyone who has not previously published a volume of poetry or prose. Writers who have had volumes of poetry and/or prose under 40 pages printed, or printed in limited editions of no more than 500 copies, are eligible." Submit 48-70 pages of poetry (1 poem/page), paginated and bound with a single clip. Include 2 cover sheets: 1 with ms title, poet's name, address, phone number, and e-mail, if available, the second with ms title only (this sheet should be clipped to ms). Also include one-page cover letter (a brief biography, ms title, poet's name, address, and telephone number, e-mail, and poet's signature) and acknowledgments page (journal, anthology, chapbook, etc., and poem published). Include SASP for acknowledgment of receipt; SASE unnecessary as result will be sent with free book and no mss will be returned. Guidelines available for SASE or on Web site. **Entry fee:** $20. "All U.S entrants will receive books, chapbooks, and journals equal to, or more than, the entry fee. Add $3 (USD) for other countries to cover the extra postal charge." Make checks payable to Pavement Saw Press. **Deadline:** reads submissions in June, July, and until August 15 (must have August 15 or earlier postmark).

$☑ ◎ TUFTS POETRY AWARDS (Specialized: for emerging poet & for first book)

The Center for the Arts and Humanities at Claremont Graduate University, 160 E. 10th St., Harper East B7, Claremont CA 91711-6165. (909)621-8974. Web site: www.cgu.edu/tufts. Established 1992. **Contact:** Susan Hampson, special events coordinator. The annual Kingsley Tufts Poetry Award offers $100,000 for a work by an emerging poet, "1 who is past the very beginning but has not yet reached the acknowledged pinnacle of his/her career." The Kate Tufts Discovery Award ($10,000) is for a first book. Books considered for the 2009 awards must have been published between September 15, 2007 and September 15, 2008. Entry form and guidelines available for SASE or on Web site. **Deadline:** September 15, 2008. 2008 winners are Tom Sleigh (*Space Walk*) and Jannice Harrington (*Even the Hollow My Body Made is Gone*). Winners announced in February. Check Web site for updated deadlines and award information.

$☑ ◎ WAR POETRY CONTEST (Specialized: war-themed poetry)

Winning Writers, 351 Pleasant St., PMB 222, Northampton MA 01060-3961. (866)946-9748. Fax: (413)280-0539. E-mail: adam@winningwriters.com. Web site: www.winningwriters.com. Established 2002. **Contact:** Adam Cohen, award director. Offers annual award of 1st Prize: $2,000; 2nd Prize: $1,200; 3rd Prize: $600; 12 Honorable Mentions of $100 each. All prizewinners receive online publication at WinningWriters.com; selected finalists may also receive online publication. Submissions must be unpublished. Considers simultaneous submissions. Submit 1-3 poems of up to 500 lines total on the theme of war, any form, style, or genre. No name on ms pages, typed or computer-printed on letter-size white paper, single-sided. Submit online or by regular mail. Guidelines available for SASE or on Web site. **Entry fee:** $15 for group of 1-3 poems. **Deadline:** November 15-May 31. Competition receives about 800 entries/year. 2006 winner was Ed Frankel for "Instrumentum Vocale" and "Gladium Vocale." 2006 judge: Jendi Reiter. Winners announced on November 15 at WinningWriters.com and in free e-mail newsletter. Entrants who provided valid e-mail addresses will also receive notification. (See separate listing for the Wergle Flomp Humor Poetry Contest in this section and for Winning Writers in the Additional Resources section.)

$⧉ ⊚ ROBERT PENN WARREN AWARDS (Specialized: free verse only)

P.O. Box 5, Windsor VT 05089. (802)674-2315. Fax: (802)674-5767. E-mail: newvtpoet@aol.com. Web site: www.newenglandwriters.org. Established 1986. **Contact:** Susan Anthony, contest coordinator. The Robert Penn Warren Awards are given annually for free verse poems. Offers 1st Prize: $300; 2nd Prize: $200; 3rd Prize: $100; 10 Honorable Mentions; 10 Commendables; 10 Editor's Choice; winning poems published in *The Anthology of New England Writers*. Submissions must be unpublished. No simultaneous submissions. Submit 3 poems of 10-30 lines each, each poem titled, no name/address on ms. Include 3×5 card with name, address, and titles of poems. Mss will not be returned. Guidelines available for SASE, by e-mail, or on Web site. **Entry fee:** $5 for 3 poems (unlimited entries). Make checks payable to New England Writers (see separate listing in Organizations). **Deadline:** submit January through June 15 (postmark) only. Winners announced at the New England Writers Conference in July; winners are notified and posted on Web site.

$⧉ WASHINGTON POETS ASSOCIATION ANNUAL POETRY CONTEST

Washington Poets Association, 2442 NW Market St., Seattle WA 98107. E-mail: treasurer@washingtonpoets.org. Web site: www.washingtonpoets.org. Established 1971. **Contact:** Jed Myers, contest chair (2007). Sponsored annually by the Washington Poets Association (see separate listing in Organizations), offers over $1,000 total in cash awards plus Honorable Mentions. Entries accepted in 4 categories: *William Stafford Award* (any form), *Carlin Aden Award* (traditional rhyme/meter), *Charlie Proctor Award* (humorous, any form), and *Francine Porad Award* (haiku). Submissions must be unpublished and must not have won awards in other contests. Submit as many poems as you like up to 50 lines each, 1 poem to a page. Entry form required. See guidelines for complete instructions. Include SASE for notification; poems will not be returned. Entry form and guidelines available on Web site. **Entry fee:** $5 general fee, plus $1/poem entered. **Deadline:** was March 1 for 2008; March 15 for Francine Porad Award. Winners are notified by SASE after judges' decisions. "Washington Poets Association reserves the right to publish winning poems in its newsletter and Web site and is granted permission to print Award and Honorable Mention poems in future anthologies."

ℕ ⊙ THE CATHY WASHINGTON PRIZE

The Sacramento Poetry Center. P.O. Box 160406, Sacramento CA 95816. (916)451-5569. E-mail: buchanan@csus.edu. Web site: www.sacramentopoetrycenter.org. Established: 2008. **Contact:** Brad Buchanan. The Cathy Washington Prize offers an annual prize of book publication, $1000, and 50 free copies of the winning book. Submissions must be unpublished as a collection, but individual poems may have been previously published elsewhere. Considers simultaneous submissions, with notification. Submit 48-70 pages of poetry. Include 2 title pages: name and contact information (including email address, if possible) should appear on first title page only. Staff, volunteers, or board members of the Sacramento Poetry Center, or their relations, may not submit manuscripts for consideration in this contest. Guidelines available for SASE, on Web site, or by e-mail. **Entry fee:** $20. Check should be made out to The Sacramento Poetry Center. **Deadline:** April 1, 2009. Winner announced in June by email. Copies of winning books available for $12 from The Sacramento Poetry Center. "The Sacramento Poetry Center is a non-profit organization dedicated to furthering the cause of poetry in the Sacramento area and nationwide. We welcome work from anyone, anywhere."

Advice "Never lose heart. SPC supports the CLMP Code of Ethics and will adhere to its precepts regarding contests, so we're as fair as it gets."

$⧉ THE WASHINGTON PRIZE

The Word Works, P.O. Box 42164, Washington DC 20015. E-mail: editor@wordworksdc.com (inquiries only). Web site: www.wordworksdc.com. Established 1981. **Contact:** Miles Moore, prize administrator. The Washington Prize offers $1,500 and publication of a book-length ms of original poetry in English by a living American poet (U.S. or Canadian citizen or resident). Submit a ms of 48-64 pages. Include title page with poet's name, address, phone number, e-mail address, and signature. Poet's name and contact information should appear on the title page only. Also include table of contents (with ms title) and a cover letter containing acknowledgments and a brief bio. Ackowledgments and biographical material must not appear elsewhere in the ms. Use a binder clip to secure the ms. Indicate the information source where you learned about the Washington Prize (for example, AWP newsletter, *Poets & Writers Magazine*, the Word Works Web site). Send entries to this address only by First Class Mail: Steven B. Rogers, Washington Prize Director, Word Works Washington Prize, 3201 Taylor St., Mt. Rainier MD 20712. Enclose SASE for results only; no mss will be returned. **Entry fee:** $25 (includes copy of winning book). Make checks payable to The Word Works. **Deadline:** submit January 15-March 1 (postmark). Winners will be announced in July. 2007 winner was Prartho Sereno (*Call from Paris*).

$⬛ ROBERT WATSON LITERARY PRIZES

The Greensboro Review, MFA Writing Program, 3302 HHRA Building, University of North Carolina at Greensboro, Greensboro NC 27402-6170. Web site: www.greensystematically.org. Established 1966. **Contact:** Contest Coordinator. The annual Robert Watson Literary Prizes include a $500 award for poetry. All entries meeting guidelines will be considered for publication in *The Greensboro Review* (see separate listing in Magazines/Journals). Submissions must be unpublished. No simultaneous submissions. Submit poems of any length, typed. No e-mail submissions. Include SASE for results or (with additional postage) for return of ms (mss will not be returned unless specifically requested by author). Guidelines available in magazine, for SASE, or on Web site. **Entry fee:** none. **Deadline:** September 15 (postmark) annually.

$⬛ ◎ WERGLE FLOMP HUMOR POETRY CONTEST (Specialized: parody of vanity contest entries)

Winning Writers, 351 Pleasant St., PMB 222, Northampton MA 01060-3961. (866)946-9748. Fax: (413)280-0539. E-mail: adam@winningwriters.com. Web site: www.winningwriters.com. Established 2002. **Contact:** Adam Cohen, award director. Offers annual award of 1st Prize: $1,359; 2nd Prize: $764; 3rd Prize: $338; plus 12 Honorable Mentions of $72.95 each. All prizewinners receive online publication at WinningWriters.com. Submissions may be previously published. Considers simultaneous submissions. Submit 1 poem of any length, in any form, but must be "a humor poem that has been submitted to a 'vanity poetry contest' as a joke. See Web site for examples." Entries accepted only through Web site; no entries by regular mail. Guidelines available on Web site. **Entry fee:** none. **Deadline:** August 15-April 1. Competition receives about 1,000 entries/year. 2006 winner was Nicholas Moore for "How to Write a Poem." 2006 judge: Jendi Reiter. Winners announced on August 15 at WinningWriters.com and in free e-mail newsletter. "Please read the past winning entries and the judge's comments published at WinningWriters.com. Guidelines are a little unusual—please follow them closely."

🌐 $◎ WESTERN AUSTRALIAN PREMIER'S BOOK AWARDS (Specialized: native & resident poets of Western Australia)

State Library of Western Australia, Alexander Library Bldg., Perth Cultural Centre, Perth WA 6000 Australia. (61)(8)9427-3330. Fax: (61)(8)9427-3336. E-mail: doug.george@slwa.wa.gov.au. Web site: www.slwa.wa.gov.au/pba.html. Established 1982. **Contact:** Doug George, awards manager. Offers annual poetry prize of $7,500 AUD for a published book of poetry. Winner also eligible for Premier's Prize of $20,000 AUD. Submissions must be previously published. Open to poets born in Western Australia, current residents of Western Australia, or poets who have resided in Western Australia for at least 10 years at some stage. Entry form and guidelines available for SASE or on Web site. **Entry fee:** none. **Deadline:** January 4 for 2008. Competition receives about 10-15 entries in poetry category per year (130 overall). 2006 poetry winner was Dennis Haskell for *All the Time in the World*. Judges: Mr. Andrew Taylor, Ms. Chloe Mauger, Prof. Ed Jaggard, and Ms. Lucille Fisher. Winners announced in June each year (i.e., June 2008 for 2007 awards) at a presentation dinner given by the Premier of Western Australia. "The contest is organized by the State Library of Western Australia, with money provided by the Western Australian State Government to support literature."

$◎ WHITE LOTUS HAIKU COMPETITION

Shadow Poetry, 1209 Milwaukee St., Excelsior Springs MO 64024. Fax: (208)977-9114. E-mail: shadowpoetry@shadowpoetry.com. Web site: www.shadowpoetry.com. Established 2000. **Contact:** James Summers, award director. Offers annual award of 1st Prize: $100; 2nd Prize: $50; 3rd Prize: $25, plus the top 3 winners also receive a certificate, a printed copy of winning haiku, and a ribbon. The top 10 placing haiku will be published in the Spring/Summer issue of *White Lotus Magazine* (see separate listing in Magazines/Journals). Submissions must be previously unpublished. No simultaneous submissions. Submit free form haiku or 5/7/5, written in the traditional 3-line format. "Haiku entries are accepted on $8\frac{1}{2} \times 11$ paper or on 3×5 index cards, submitted in duplicate, neatly handwritten or typed. The poet's name, address, phone number, and e-mail address (if applicable) should appear in the upper left-hand corner of 1 sheet or on the back of 1 index card. Repeat this method for multiple submissions." Include #10 SASE for notification of receipt of ms (optional) and/or a for results. "If no SASE is included for receipt, Shadow Poetry will e-mail an entry confirmation to the contestant, if applicable." Entry form and guidelines available for SASE or on Web site. **Entry fee:** $5 for 3 haiku or $2 per each individual haiku (entries are unlimited). Make checks/money orders payable to Shadow Poetry. **Deadline:** December 31. Winners announced February 1 each year "by e-mail and to those who requested a winners list with SASE. Results will also be posted on the Shadow Poetry Web site and printed in *White Lotus*."

$◪ THE WHITE PINE PRESS POETRY PRIZE

White Pine Press, P.O. Box 236, Buffalo NY 14201. E-mail: wpine@whitepine.org. Web site: www. whitepine.org. Established 1973. **Contact:** Dennis Maloney, editor. The White Pine Press Poetry Prize offers $1,000 plus publication for a book-length collection of poems by a U.S. author. Submissions must be unpublished as a collection, but individual poems may have been previously published elsewhere. Submit 60-80 pages of poetry, typed, with table of contents. Include cover sheet with poet's name, address, e-mail address, and phone number. No e-mail submissions. Include SASP for notification of receipt of ms and SASE for results only; mss will not be returned. Guidelines available for SASE or on Web site. **Entry fee:** $20. Make checks payable to White Pine Press. **Deadline:** submit July 1-November 30 (postmark). 2008 winner was Al Maginnes (*Ghost Alphabet*). Judge: poet of national reputation. Winning books available from local booksellers and White Pine Press.

$◖ THE WALT WHITMAN AWARD

The Academy of American Poets, 584 Broadway, Suite 604, New York NY 10012. (212)274-0343. Fax: (212)274-9427. E-mail: jkronovet@poets.org. Web site: www.poets.org. Award established 1975. **Contact:** Jennifer Kronovet, awards coordinator. Offers $5,000, publication of a poet's first book by Louisiana State University Press, and a 1 month residency at the Vermont Studio Center. The Academy of American Poets purchases copies of the Whitman Award-winning book for distribution to its members. Submit mss of 50-100 pages. Poets must be American citizens. Entry form required; entry form and guidelines available for SASE (in August) or on Web site. **Entry fee:** $25. **Deadline:** November 30. 2006 winner was Anne Pierson Wiese (*Floating City*). 2007 judge: August Kleinzahler. Winner announced in May.

$◪ STAN AND TOM WICK POETRY PRIZE

Wick Poetry Center, 301 Satterfield Hall, Kent State University, P.O. Box 5190, Kent OH 44242-0001. (330)672-2067. Fax: (330)672-3333. E-mail: wickpoet@kent.edu. Web site: http://dept.kent.edu/wick. Established 1994. **Contact:** Maggie Anderson, director. Offers annual award of $2,000 and publication by Kent State University Press. Open to poets writing in English who have not yet published a full-length collection. Submissions must be unpublished as a collection, but individual poems may have been previously published elsewhere. Considers simultaneous submissions as long as the Wick Poetry Center receives notice upon acceptance elsewhere. Submit 50-70 pages of poetry. Include cover sheet with poet's name, address, telephone number, e-mail address, and title of ms. Guidelines available for SASE or on Web site. **Entry fee:** $20. **Deadline:** submit February 1-May 1. Competition receives 700-800 entries.

$ THE RICHARD WILBUR AWARD (Specialized: American poets only)

Dept. of English, University of Evansville, 1800 Lincoln Ave., Evansville IN 47722. (812)488-2963. Web site: http://english.evansville.edu/english/WilburAwardGuidelines.htm. **Contact:** William Baer, series director. Offers a biennial award (even-numbered years) of $1,000 and book publication to "recognize a quality book-length manuscript of poetry." Submissions must be unpublished original poetry collections ("although individual poems may have had previous journal publications") and "public domain or permission-secured translations may comprise up to 1/3 of the manuscript." Considers simultaneous submissions. Open to all American poets. Submit ms of 50-100 typed pages, unbound, bound, or clipped. Manuscripts should be accompanied by 2 title pages: 1 with ms title, author's name, address, and phone number; 1 with ms title only. Include SASE for results only; mss are not returned. Guidelines available for SASE or on Web site. **Entry fee:** $25/ms. **Deadline:** December 1. Competition receives 300-500 entries. Winning ms is published and copyrighted by the University of Evansville Press.

$ MARJORIE J. WILSON AWARD FOR BEST POEM CONTEST

MARGIE/The American Journal of Poetry, P.O. Box 250, Chesterfield MO 63006-0250. E-mail: margie review@aol.com. Web site: www.margiereview.com. The Marjorie J. Wilson Award for Best Poem Contest offers $2,500 and publication in *MARGIE* (see separate listing in Magazines/Journals). All entries will be considered for publication. Submissions must be unpublished. Considers simultaneous submissions. Submit 3 poems, 60-line limit/poem. Include single cover sheet with poet's name, address, phone number, e-mail (if available), and poem titles. No names should appear on the poems themselves; do not send originals. Include SASE for results only; submissions will not be returned. Guidelines available for SASE or on Web site. **Entry fee:** $15 for 3 poems; $5 for each additional poem. Make checks payable to MARGIE, Inc. **Deadline:** March 31 (postmark). 2006 winner was Jill Drumm ("Just Like You Had Flown Away"). 2007 judge: David Wagoner.

$ WORKING PEOPLE'S POETRY COMPETITION

Blue Collar Review, P.O. Box 11417, Norfolk VA 23517. E-mail: red-ink@earthlink.net (inquiries only). Web site: www.partisanpress.org. The Working People's Poetry Competition offers $100 and a one-year subscription to *Blue Collar Review* (see separate listing in Magazines/Journals). "Poetry should be typed as you would like to see it published, with your name and address on each page. Include cover letter with entry." Guidelines available on Web site. **Entry fee:** $15. Make checks payable to Partisan Press. **Deadline:** May 1. 2007 winner was Erika Meyers.

$ THE YALE SERIES OF YOUNGER POETS (Specialized: U.S. poets under age 40)

Yale University Press, P.O. Box 209040, New Haven CT 06520-9040. Web site: http://yalepress.yale.edu/yupbooks/youngerpoets.asp. **Contact:** Contest Coordinator. Established 1919. The Yale Series of Younger Poets offers publication and royalties to 1 winning book-length ms. Open to U.S. citizens under age 40 at the time of entry who have not published a volume of poetry; poets may have published a limited edition chapbook of 300 copies or less. Poems may have been previously published in newspapers and periodicals and used in the book ms if so identified. No translations. Submit 48-64 pages of poetry, paginated, printed single-sided, with each new poem starting on a new page. Do not bind or staple ms; loose sheets may be placed in an envelope of appropriate size. Include 2 cover sheets: 1 showing ms title, poet's name, address, telephone number, e-mail address, and page count; the second with manuscript title only. Also include table of contents and acknowledgments page, as well as a brief bio at the end of ms (optional). Include SASP for notification of receipt of ms and SASE for results; mss will not be returned. No e-mail submissions. Guidelines (with additional submission details) available on Web site. **Entry fee:** $15. Make checks/money orders payable to Yale University Press. **Deadline:** submit October 1-November 15 (postmark). 2006 winner was Jessica Fisher (*Frail-Craft*).

$⬙ THE W.B. YEATS SOCIETY ANNUAL POETRY COMPETITION

W.B. Yeats Society of New York, National Arts Club, 15 Gramercy Park S, New York NY 10003. (212)780-0605. Web site: www.YeatsSociety.org. Established 1990. **Contact:** Andrew McGowan, president. Offers annual $250 cash prize for 1st Place, $100 cash prize for 2nd Place, and optional Honorable Mentions. Open to beginner as well as established poets. Winners are invited to read their poems at an awards event held each spring in New York; also inducted as Honorary Members of the W.B. Yeats Society, a 501(c)(3) charitable organization (see separate listing in Organizations). Submissions must be unpublished. Considers simultaneous submissions. Submit any number of unpublished poems in any style or form, up to 60 lines each, typed on letter-size paper without poet's name. Guidelines available for SASE or on Web site; no entry form required. **Entry fee:** $8 for first poem, $7 for each additional poem. Attach a 3×5 card to each entry containing the poem's title along with the poet's name, address, and phone/fax/e-mail. **Deadline:** February 1 annually. Receives 200-300 entries/year. 2007 winners were Charlotte Muse, J. Michael Parish, M. Lee Alexander, and Maureen Waters. 2007 judge: Marie Ponsot. Winners selected by March 31 and announced in April. Winning entries and judge's report are posted on the Society's Web site. Printed report available for SASE.

$⬙ THE YELLOWWOOD POETRY AWARD

d*Yalobusha Review*, Dept. of English, University of Mississippi, P.O. Box 1848, University MS 38677-1848. Established 2007. Web site: www.olemiss.edu/Yalobusha/contest.html. The annual Yellowwood Poetry Award offers $500, publication in *Yalobusha Review* (see separate listing in Magazines/Journals), exclusive publication on Web site, and 2 contributor's copies to winner. First North Amerian Rights retained by *Yalobusha Review*. Submit 3-5 poems. Include cover letter with poet's contact information and poem titles. Poet's name should not appear on poems. Include SASE for results only. Guidelines available on Web site. **Entry fee:** $10. Make checks/money orders payable to *Yalobusha Review*. **Deadline:** October 1, 2008. Judge: all submissions will be ranked by *Yalobusha Review* editors; final judge is Ann Fisher-Wirth. Winner notified by December 15, 2008.

ADDITIONAL CONTESTS & AWARDS

The following listings also contain information about contests and awards. Turn to the page numbers indicated for details about their offerings.

Grants

State & Provincial

rts councils in the United States and Canada provide assistance to artists (including poets) in the form of fellowships or grants. These grants can be substantial and confer prestige upon recipients; however, **only state or province residents are eligible**. Because deadlines and available support vary annually, query first (with a SASE) or check Web sites for guidelines.

UNITED STATES ARTS AGENCIES

Alabama State Council on the Arts, 201 Monroe St., Montgomery AL 36130-1800. (334)242-4076. E-mail: staff@arts.alabama.gov. Web site: www.arts.state.al.us.

Alaska State Council on the Arts, 411 W. Fourth Ave., Suite 1-E, Anchorage AK 99501-2343. (907)269-6610 or (888)278-7424. E-mail: aksca_info@eed.state.ak.us. Web site: www.eed. state.ak.us/aksca.

Arizona Commission on the Arts, 417 W. Roosevelt St., Phoenix AZ 85003-1326. (602)771-6501. E-mail: info@azarts.gov. Web site: www.azarts.gov.

Arkansas Arts Council, 1500 Tower Bldg., 323 Center St., Little Rock AR 72201. (501)324-9766. E-mail: info@arkansasarts.com. Web site: www.arkansasarts.com.

California Arts Council, 1300 I St., Suite 930, Sacramento CA 95814. (916)322-6555. E-mail: info@caartscouncil.com. Web site: www.cac.ca.gov.

Colorado Council on the Arts, 1625 Broadway, Suite 2700, Denver CO 80202. (303)892-3802. E-mail: online form. Web site: www.coloarts.state.co.us.

Connecticut Commission on Culture & Tourism, Arts Division, One Financial Plaza, 755 Main St., Hartford CT 06103. (860)256-2800. Web site: www.cultureandtourism.org.

Delaware Division of the Arts, Carvel State Office Bldg., 4th Floor, 820 N. French St., Wilmington DE 19801. (302)577-8278 (New Castle Co.) or (302)739-5304 (Kent or Sussex Counties). E-mail: delarts@state.de.us. Web site: www.artsdel.org.

District of Columbia Commission on the Arts & Humanities, 410 Eighth St. NW, 5th Floor, Washington DC 20004. (202)724-5613. E-mail: cah@dc.gov. Web site: http://dcarts .dc.gov.

Florida Arts Council, Division of Cultural Affairs, R.A. Gray Building, Third Floor, 500 S. Bronough St., Tallahassee FL 32399-0250. (850)245-6470. E-mail: info@florida-arts.org. Web site: http://dcarts.dc.gov.

Georgia Council for the Arts, 260 14th St., Suite 401, Atlanta GA 30318. (404)685-2787. E-mail: gaarts@gaarts.org. Web site: www.gaarts.org.

Guam Council on the Arts & Humanities Agency, P.O. Box 2950, Hagatna GU 96932. (671)646-2781. Web site: www.guam.net.

Hawaii State Foundation on Culture & the Arts, 2500 S. Hotel St., 2nd Floor, Honolulu HI 96813. (808)586-0300. E-mail: ken.hamilton@hawaii.gov. Web site: http.state.hi.us/sfca.

Idaho Commission on the Arts, 2410 N. Old Penitentiary Rd., Boise ID 83712. (208)334-2119 or (800)278-3863. E-mail: info@arts.idaho.gov. Web site: www.arts.idaho.gov.

Illinois Arts Council, James R. Thompson Center, 100 W. Randolph, Suite 10-500, Chicago IL 60601. (312)814-6750. E-mail: iac.info@illinois.gov. Web site: www.state.il.us/agency/iac.

Indiana Arts Commission, 150 W. Market St., Suite 618, Indianapolis IN 46204. (317)232-1268. E-mail: IndianaArtsCommission@iac.in.gov. Web site: www.in.gov/arts.

Iowa Arts Council, 600 E. Locust, Des Moines IA 50319-0290. (515)281-6412. Web site: www.iowaartscouncil.org.

Kansas Arts Commission, 700 SW Jackson, Suite 1004, Topeka KS 66603-3761. (785)296-3335. E-mail: KAC@arts.state.ks.us. Web site: http://arts.state.ks.us.

Kentucky Arts Council, 21st Floor, Capital Plaza Tower, 500 Mero St., Frankfort KY 40601-1987. (502)564-3757 or (888)833-2787. E-mail: kyarts@ky.gov. Web site: http://artscouncil.ky.gov.

Louisiana Division of the Arts, Capitol Annex Bldg., 1051 N. 3rd St., 4th Floor, Room #420, Baton Rouge LA 70804. (225)342-8180. Web site: www.crt.state.la.us/arts.

Maine Arts Commission, 193 State St., 25 State House Station, Augusta ME 04333-0025. (207)287-2724. E-mail: MaineArts.info@maine.gov. Web site: www.mainearts.com.

Maryland State Arts Council, 175 W. Ostend St., Suite E, Baltimore MD 21230. (410)767-6555. E-mail: msac@msac.org. Web site: www.msac.org.

Massachusetts Cultural Council, 10 St. James Ave., 3rd Floor, Boston MA 02116-3803. (617)727-3668. E-mail: mcc@art.state.ma.us. Web site: www.massculturalcouncil.org.

Michigan Council of History, Arts, and Libraries, 702 W. Kalamazoo St., P.O. Box 30705, Lansing MI 48909-8205. (517)241-4011. E-mail: artsinfo@michigan.gov. Web site: www.michigan.gov/hal/0,1607,7-160-17445_19272---,00.html.

Minnesota State Arts Board, Park Square Court, 400 Sibley St., Suite 200, St. Paul MN 55101-1928. (651)215-1600 or (800)866-2787. E-mail: msab@arts.state.mn.us. Web site: www.arts.state.mn.us.

Mississippi Arts Commission, 501 N. West St., Suite 701B, Woolfolk Bldg., Jackson MS 39201. (601)359-6030. Web site: www.arts.state.ms.us.

Missouri Arts Council, 815 Olive St., Suite 16, St. Louis MO 63101-1503. (314)340-6845 or (866)407-4752. E-mail: moarts@ded.mo.gov. Web site: www.missouriartscouncil.org.

Montana Arts Council, 316 N. Park Ave., Suite 252, Helena MT 59620-2201. (406)444-6430. E-mail: mac@mt.gov. Web site: www.art.state.mt.us.

National Assembly of State Arts Agencies, 1029 Vermont Ave. NW, 2nd Floor, Washington DC 20005. (202)347-6352. E-mail: nasaa@nasaa-arts.org. Web site: www.nasaa-arts.org.

Nebraska Arts Council, 1004 Farnam St., Plaza Level, Omaha NE 68102. (402)595-2122 or (800)341-4067. Web site: www.nebraskaartscouncil.org.

Nevada Arts Council, 716 N. Carson St., Suite A, Carson City NV 89701. (775)687-6680. E-mail: online form. Web site: http://dmla.clan.lib.nv.us/docs/arts.

New Hampshire State Council on the Arts, 2½ Beacon St., 2nd Floor, Concord NH 03301-4974. (603)271-2789. Web site: www.nh.gov/nharts.

New Jersey State Council on the Arts, 225 W. State St., P.O. Box 306, Trenton NJ 08625. (609)292-6130. Web site: www.njartscouncil.org.

New Mexico Arts, Dept. of Cultural Affairs, P.O. Box 1450, Santa Fe NM 87504-1450. (505)827-6490 or (800)879-4278. Web site: www.nmarts.org.

New York State Council on the Arts, 175 Varick St., New York NY 10014. (212)627-4455. Web site: www.nysca.org.

North Carolina Arts Council, 109 East Jones St., Cultural Resources Building, Raleigh NC 27601. (919)807-6500. E-mail: ncarts@ncmail.net. Web site: www.ncarts.org.

North Dakota Council on the Arts, 1600 E. Century Ave., Suite 6, Bismarck ND 58503. (701)328-7590. E-mail: comserv@state.nd.us. Web site: www.state.nd.us/arts.

Commonwealth Council for Arts and Culture (Northern Mariana Islands), P.O. Box 5553, CHRB, Saipan MP 96950. (670)322-9982 or (670)322-9983. E-mail: galaidi@vzpacifica.net. Web site: www.geocities.com/ccacarts/ccacwebsite.html.

Ohio Arts Council, 727 E. Main St., Columbus OH 43205-1796. (614)466-2613. Web site: www.oac.state.oh.us.

Oklahoma Arts Council, Jim Thorpe Building, 2101 N. Lincoln Blvd., Suite 640, Oklahoma City OK 73105. (405)521-2931. E-mail: okarts@arts.ok.gov. Web site: www.arts.state.ok.us.

Oregon Arts Commission, 775 Summer St. NE, Suite 200, Salem OR 97301-1280. (503)986-0082. E-mail: oregon.artscomm@state.or.us. Web site: www.oregonartscommission.org.

Pennsylvania Council on the Arts, 216 Finance Bldg., Harrisburg PA 17120. (717)787-6883. Web site: www.pacouncilonthearts.org.

Institute of Puerto Rican Culture, P.O. Box 9024184, San Juan PR 00902-4184. (787)724-0700. E-mail: www@icp.gobierno.pr. Web site: www.icp.gobierno.pr.

Rhode Island State Council on the Arts, One Capitol Hill, Third Floor, Providence RI 02908. (401)222-3880. E-mail: info@arts.ri.gov. Web site: www.arts.ri.gov.

South Carolina Arts Commission, 1800 Gervais St., Columbia SC 29201. (803)734-8696. E-mail: info@arts.state.sc.us. Web site: www.southcarolinaarts.com.

South Dakota Arts Council, 711 E. Wells Ave., Pierre SD 57501-3369. (605)773-3301. E-mail: sdac@state.sd.us. Web site: www.artscouncil.sd.gov.

Tennessee Arts Commission, 401 Charlotte Ave., Nashville TN 37243-0780. (615)741-1701. Web site: www.arts.state.tn.us.

Texas Commission on the Arts, E.O. Thompson Office Building, 920 Colorado, Suite 501, Austin TX 78701. (512)463-5535. E-mail: front.desk@arts.state.tx.us. Web site: www.arts.state.tx.us.

Utah Arts Council, 617 E. South Temple, Salt Lake City UT 84102-1177. (801)236-7555. Web site: http://arts.utah.gov.

Vermont Arts Council, 136 State St., Drawer 33, Montpelier VT 05633-6001. (802)828-3291. E-mail: online form. Web site: www.vermontartscouncil.org.

Virgin Islands Council on the Arts, 5070 Norre Gade, St. Thomas VI 00802-6872. (340)774-5984. Web site: http://vicouncilonarts.org.

Virginia Commission for the Arts, Lewis House, 223 Governor St., 2nd Floor, Richmond VA 23219. (804)225-3132. E-mail: arts@arts.virginia.gov. Web site: www.arts.state.va.us.

Washington State Arts Commission, 711 Capitol Way S., Suite 600, P.O. Box 42675, Olympia WA 98504-2675. (360)753-3860. E-mail: info@arts.wa.gov. Web site: www.arts.wa.gov.

West Virginia Commission on the Arts, The Cultural Center, Capitol Complex, 1900 Kanawha Blvd. E., Charleston WV 25305-0300. (304)558-0220. Web site: www.wvculture.org/arts.

Wisconsin Arts Board, 101 E. Wilson St., 1st Floor, Madison WI 53702. (608)266-0190. E-mail: artsboard@arts.state.wi.us. Web site: www.arts.state.wi.us.

Wyoming Arts Council, 2320 Capitol Ave., Cheyenne WY 82002. (307)777-7742. E-mail: ebratt@state.wy.us. Web site: http://wyoarts.state.wy.us.

CANADIAN PROVINCES ARTS AGENCIES

Alberta Foundation for the Arts, 10708-105 Ave., Edmonton AB T5H 0A1. (780)427-9968. Web site: www.affta.ab.ca/index.shtml.

British Columbia Arts Council, P.O. Box 9819, Stn. Prov. Govt., Victoria BC V8W 9W3. (250)356-1718. E-mail: BCArtsCouncil@gov.bc.ca. Web site: www.bcartscouncil.ca.

The Canada Council for the Arts, 350 Albert St., P.O. Box 1047, Ottawa ON K1P 5V8. (613)566-4414 or (800)263-5588 (within Canada). Web site: www.canadacouncil.ca.

Manitoba Arts Council, 525-93 Lombard Ave., Winnipeg MB R3B 3B1. (204)945-2237 or (866)994-2787 (in Manitoba). E-mail: info@artscouncil.mb.ca. Web site: www.artscouncil.mb.ca.

New Brunswick Arts Board (NBAB), 634 Queen St., Suite 300, Fredericton NB E3B 1C2. (506)444-4444 or (866)460-2787. Web site: www.artsnb.ca.

Newfoundland & Labrador Arts Council, P.O. Box 98, St. John's NL A1C 5H5. (709)726-2212 or (866)726-2212. E-mail: nlacmail@nfld.net. Web site: www.nlac.nf.ca.

Nova Scotia Department of Tourism, Culture, and Heritage, Culture Division, 1800 Argyle St., Suite 601, P.O. Box 456, Halifax NS B3J 2R5. (902)424-4510. E-mail: cultaffs@gov.ns.ca. Web site: www.gov.ns.ca/dtc/culture.

Ontario Arts Council, 151 Bloor St. W., 5th Floor, Toronto ON M5S 1T6. (416)961-1660 or (800)387-0058 (in Ontario). E-mail: info@arts.on.ca. Web site: www.arts.on.ca.

Prince Edward Island Council of the Arts, 115 Richmond St., Charlottetown PE C1A 1H7. (902)368-4410 or (888)734-2784. E-mail: info@peiartscouncil.com. Web site: www.peiartscouncil.com.

Québec Council for Arts & Literature, 79 boul. René-Lévesque Est, 3e étage, Québec QC G1R 5N5. (418)643-1707 or (800)897-1707. E-mail: info@calq.gouv.qc.ca. Web site: www.calq.gouv.qc.ca.

The Saskatchewan Arts Board, 2135 Broad St., Regina SK S4P 1Y6. (306)787-4056 or (800)667-7526 (Saskatchewan only). E-mail: sab@artsboard.sk.ca. Web site: www.artsboard.sk.ca.

Yukon Arts Funding Program, Cultural Services Branch, Dept. of Tourism & Culture, Government of Yukon, Box 2703 (L-3), Whitehorse YT Y1A 2C6. (867)667-8589 or (800)661-0408 (in Yukon). E-mail: arts@gov.yk.ca. Web site: www.tc.gov.yk.ca/216.html.

Conferences, Workshops & Festivals

There are times when we want to immerse ourselves in learning. Or perhaps we crave a change of scenery, the creative stimulation of being around other artists, or the uninterrupted productivity of time alone to work.

That's what this section of *Poet's Market* is all about, providing a selection of writing conferences and workshops, artist colonies and retreats, poetry festivals, and even a few opportunities to go travelling with your muse. These listings give the basics: contact information, a brief description of the event, lists of past presenters, and offerings of special interest to poets. Contact an event that interests you for additional information, including up-to-date costs and housing details. **(Please note that most directors had not finalized their 2009 plans when we contacted them for this edition of *Poet's Market*. However, where possible, they provided us with their 2008 dates, costs, faculty names or themes to give you a better idea of what each event has to offer.)**

Before you seriously consider a conference, workshop or other event, determine what you hope to get out of the experience. Would a general conference with one or two poetry workshops among many other types of sessions be acceptable? Or are you looking for something exclusively focused on poetry? Do you want to hear poets speak about poetry writing, or are you looking for a more participatory experience, such as a one-on-one critiquing session or a group workshop? Do you mind being one of hundreds of attendees, or do you prefer a more intimate setting? Are you willing to invest in the expense of travelling to a conference, or would something local better suit your budget? Keep these questions and others in mind as you read these listings, view Web sites and study conference brochures.

Some listings are coded with symbols to provide certain "information at a glance." The (N) symbol indicates a recently established conference/workshop; the ( ) symbol indicates this conference/workshop did not appear in the 2008 edition; the ( ) symbol denotes a Canadian event and the ( ) symbol one located outside the U.S. and Canada.

The Additional Conferences & Workshops list at the end of this section cross-references conference, workshop and festival information in other sections of this book. To find out more, go to the page number indicated for each listing.

⬛ ◎ AMERICAN CHRISTIAN WRITERS CONFERENCES

P.O. Box 110390, Nashville TN 37222. (800)21-WRITE. E-mail: ACWriters@aol.com. Web site: www.ACWriters.com. Established 1981. **Contact:** Reg Forder, director. Annual 2-day events. Holds 30 conferences/year in cities including Houston, Boston, Minneapolis, Chicago, St. Louis, Detroit, Atlanta, Miami, Phoenix, and Los Angeles. Location: usually a major hotel chain like Holiday Inn. Average attendance: 40-80.

Purpose/Features Open to anyone. Conferences cover fiction, poetry, writing for children. Offers poets ms critiques.

Costs/Accommodations Cost: $99-169. Participants responsible for all meals. Accommodations available on site.

Additional Information Also sponsors an annual Caribbean Christian Writers Conference Cruise each November. Additional information available for SASE, by e-mail, or on Web site.

◉ ANAM CARA WRITER'S AND ARTIST'S RETREAT

Eyeries, Beara, Co. Cork, Ireland. (353)(027)74441. Fax: (353)(027)74448. E-mail: anamcararetreat @eircom.net. Web site: www.anamcararetreat.com. **Contact:** Sue Booth-Forbes, director. Offers up to one-month individual retreats as well as workshops for writers and artists. Length of workshops varies with subject and leader/facilitator. Location: "Beara is a rural and hauntingly beautiful part of Ireland that is kept temperate by the Gulf Stream. The retreat sits on a hill overlooking Coulagh Bay, the mountains of the Ring of Kerry, and the Slieve Mishkish Mountains of Beara. The village of Eyeries is a short walk away." Average attendance: 5 residents at the retreat when working individually; 12-18 workshop participants.

Purpose/Features "Anam Cara is open to novice as well as professional writers and artists. Applicants are asked to provide a written description on the focus of their work while on retreat. Residencies are on a first-come, first-deposit-in basis." 2007 workshops included sessions on poetry, painting, haiku, creative nonfiction, and fiction.

Costs/Accommodations 2007 cost: residency fee ranges from €600-700/week for individual retreats, depending on room, and includes full room and board; editorial consulting; laundry; sauna; hot tub overlooking Coulagh Bay; 5 acres of gardens, meadows, riverbank and cascades, river island, swimming hole, and several unique working spots, such as the ruin of a stone mill and a sod-roofed beehive hut. Overflow from workshops stay in nearby B&Bs, a 10-minute walk or 2-minute drive away. Transportation provided if needed. Details regarding transporation to Anam Cara available on Web site.

Additional Information Requests for specific information about rates and availability can be made through the Web site; also available by fax or e-mail. Brochure available on request.

◉ ART WORKSHOPS IN GUATEMALA

4758 Lyndale Ave. S., Minneapolis MN 55419-5403. (612)825-0747. E-mail: info@artguat.org. Web site: www.artguat.org. Established 1995. **Contact:** Liza Fourre, director. Annual 10-day creative writing courses, held in February, March, July, and October. Location: workshops held in Antigua, the old colonial capital of Guatemala. Average attendance: limit 10 students.

Purpose/Features Art Workshops in Guatemala provides "the perfect getaway for creative writers of all skill levels looking for a memorable and inspiring writing/travel experience." For 2007, offered poets "Journey of the Soul" (with Sharon Doubiago, July 21-30) and "Snapshots in Words" (with Roseann Lloyd).

Costs/Accommodations 2008 cost: $1,695. Includes "tuition, lodging in a beautiful old colonial home, a hearty breakfast, ground transportation, and some pretty interesting cultural field trips."

Additional Information Individual poetry critiques included. Call, write, e-mail, or check Web site.

BREAD LOAF WRITERS' CONFERENCE

Middlebury College, Middlebury VT 05753. (802)443-5286. Fax: (802)443-2087. E-mail: blwc@mid dlebury.edu. Web site: www.middlebury.edu/~blwc. **Contact:** Noreen Cargill, administrative manager. Director: Michael Collier. Established 1926. Annual 11-day event. 2008 dates: August 13-

24. Location: mountain campus of Middlebury College. Average attendance: 200+.

Purpose/Features Conference is designed to promote dialogue among writers and provide professional critiques for students. Offers poets workshops, lectures, faculty readings, and ms critiques. 2007 poetry presenters included Eavan Boland, Michael Collier, Brigit Pegeen Kelly, James Longenbach, Steve Orlen, Arthur Sze, and Natasha Trethewey.

Costs/Accommodations 2008 cost: $2,345 (general applicant) or $2,245 (auditor), including tuition, room, and board. Conference fellowships and scholarships available. See Web site for eligibility guidelines, application deadlines, and other important information.

Additional Information Sponsors the Bakeless Literary Publication Prizes, an annual book series competition for new authors of literary works in poetry, fiction, and creative nonfiction (see separate listing in Contests & Awards).

CATSKILL POETRY WORKSHOP

Hartwick College, Oneonta NY 13820. (607)431-4448. Fax: (607)431-4457. E-mail: frostc@hartwick .edu. Web site: http://info.hartwick.edu/library/catskill/poetry.htm. **Contact:** Carol Frost, director. Annual weeklong event. 2007 dates: July 9-15. Location: Pine Lake campus of Hartwick College, a small, private college in the Catskill Mountain area (includes private chef and rustic cottages). Average attendance: 20-25.

Purpose/Features Open to "talented adult writers" of poetry. Offerings cover "traditional meters, free verse lineation, and uses of metaphor; individual instruction." 2007 poetry instructors included Stephen Dunn, Carol Frost, Lynn Emanuel, Jay Hopler, Tom Sleigh, Chase Twichell, and Michael Waters.

Costs/Accommodations 2007 cost: $1,250, including tuition, room and board; $900 for commuters, tuition and lunch included. Accommodations available on site.

Additional Information Direct contact with 4 faculty poets, including one individual conference scheduled for each participant. Registration forms available for SASE and on Web site.

◎ CAVE CANEM (Specialized: African American poets)

584 Broadway, Suite 508, New York NY 10012. (212)941-5720. E-mail: dantemicheaux@ccpoets.o rg. Web site: www.cavecanempoets.org. Established 1996. **Contact:** Alison Myers, executive director. Three-year fellowship, completed in five years. Successful candidates participate in an annual residency. Usually held last week in June. Location: University of Pittsburgh at Greensburg, PA. Average attendance: 54.

Purpose/Features Open to African American poets. Participants selected based on a sample of 6-8 poems. Offerings include workshops by fellows and faculty, evening readings. 2008 faculty included co-founders Toi Derricotte, Cornelius Eady, Colleen J. McElroy, Carl Phillips, Claudia Rankine, and Reginald Shepherd. Guest poet: Ntozake Shange.

Costs/Accommodations 2008 cost: $500, including room and board. Tuition is free. For complete information, contact Cave Canem.

Additional Information Poets should submit 6-8 poems with cover letter. 2009 deadline: March 17, 2009, receipt with accepted poets notified by April 30. Cave Canem Foundation also sponsors the Cave Canem Poetry Prize (see separate listing in Contests & Awards section).

CHAUTAUQUA WRITERS' CENTER

Box 1377, Chautauqua NY 14722. (216)295-1824. E-mail: pataverbach@hotmail.com. Web site: http://writers.ciweb.org. Established 1988. **Contact:** Clara Silverstein, program director. Annual season of 9 separate weeklong workshops held late June to late August. Participants may attend one week or more. Location: Victorian lakeside village in western New York; most Writers' Center programs offered in the CLSC Alumni Hall. Average attendance: no more than 12 workshop particpants and 5 non-participaing auditors may enroll in each workshop to assure individual attention.

Purpose/Features Provides "a lively community of writers at all levels of development who cultivate the courage, craft, and vision necessary to grow as artists" under the tutelage of nationally recognized poets-in-residence. Poetry workshops meet 2 hours daily, 8:30-10:30 a.m. 2008 poetry faculty includes Susan Grimm, Margaret Gibson, Philip Terman, Geraldine Connolly, Todd Davis,

Philip Brady, Jim Daniels, Terrance Hayes, and Laura Kasischke. Other features include prose workshops, free Sunday afternoon readings by writers-in-residence, Brown Bag lunches and lectures every Tuesday and Friday at 12:15 p.m,, and open mic events every Sunday.

Costs/Accommodations 2008 cost: $100/weeklong workshop. Participants responsible for gate fees ($325/week), housing, and meals. See Web site for accommodations options, which range from the Atheneum Hotel to local rooming houses and condos.

Additional Information Most workshop leaders offer private half hour conferences. Fee: $25, payable directly to leader. Additional information available by phone, e-mail, or on Web site. Also sponsors The Chautauqua Writers' Festival (see separate listing in this section). Publishes *Chautauqua Literary Journal* (see separate listing in Magazines/Journals).

COLGATE WRITERS' CONFERENCE

Office of Summer Programs, Colgate University, 13 Oak Dr., Hamilton NY 13346. (315)228-7770. Fax: (315)228-6543. E-mail: info@cvwc.net. Web site: www.cvwc.net. **Contact:** Matthew Leone, conference director. Established 1996. Annual weeklong event. 2007 dates: June 22-28. Location: Colgate University, "an expansive campus, with classrooms, dormitories, libraries, and recreational facilities all in close proximity to each other." Average attendance: 75.

Purpose/Features Open to "all serious writers or aspirants." Offers poets workshops, lectures, readings, and ms critiques. 2008 poetry staff included Bruce Smith, Peter Balakian, and David Thoreen.

Costs/Accommodations 2008 cost: for poetry workshop, $995 (tuition, room, and board); $750 for day students. Meal plan available for day students. Accommodations available on site.

Additional Information Each applicant must submit a ms with his/her application. Brochure and registration form available for SASE or on Web site.

THE COLRAIN POETRY MANUSCRIPT CONFERENCE

Concord Poetry Center, 40 Stow. St., Concord MA 01742. (978)897-0054. E-mail: cpc@concordpoetry.org. Web site: www.colrainpoetry.com. Established 2004. **Contact:** Joan Houlihan, director. Usually held 4-5 times/year in 3-day, weekend sessions. Location: Colrain, MA, Greenfield, MA, and others. Average attendance: 20 poets.

Purpose/Features "The first poetry conference realistically designed to set poets who have a completed manuscript or a manuscript-in-progress on a path toward book publication. Three-day intensive conference includes a manuscript preparation workshop and in-depth meetings with poetry press editors." Also offers evening poetry readings, an editorial panel Q&A, and an after-conference strategy session. 2007 faculty include Joan Houlihan, Frederick Marchant, Jeffrey Levine (Tupelo Press), Martha Rhodes (Four Way Books), Jeffrey Shotts (Graywolf Press).

Costs/Accommodations 2008 cost: $995-1395, includes lodging, meals, and tuition.

Additional Information Details, application, and registration form available on Web site.

◎ THE CONFERENCE ON POETRY AND TEACHING (Specialized: for high school & middle school teachers)

The Frost Place, P.O. Box 74, Franconia NH 03580. (603)823-5510. E-mail: rfrost@ncia.net. Web site: www.frostplace.org. **Contact:** Jim Schley and Baron Wormser, co-directors. Annual event. 2008 dates: June 30-July 4.

Purpose/Features Designed for high school and middle school classroom teachers. Brings together poets and teachers to address how poetry can be taught most effectively. Offers first-hand experience about how poems are created and how poets view their art. 2008 guest poetry faculty includes Alice B. Fogel, Mekeel McBride, Shara McCallum, and J.D. Scrimgeour.

Costs/Accommodations 2008 cost: $600 plus $86 for daily lunch and 2 dinners. Additional cost of $405 for 3 graduate credits through Plymouth State University. Overnight accommodations available locally.

Additional Information To apply, send letter describing current teaching situation and literary interests. Additional information available on Web site.

GERALDINE R. DODGE POETRY FESTIVAL

Geraldine R. Dodge Poetry Program, P.O. Box 1239, Morristown NJ 07962-1239. (973)540-8442 ext. 5. Web site: www.dodgepoetry.org. Established 1986. Biennial 4-day event usually held in early fall. 2008 dates: September 25-28; check Web site for 2010 dates. Location: Waterloo Village in Stanhope, NJ. Average attendance: nearly 17,000 in 2006.

Purpose/Features Biennial celebration of poetry for poets, students, teachers, and the general public. Presents panels, talks, and workshops covering a range of topics and issues related to poetry; offers an ambitious schedule of poetry readings featuring the cream of contemporary poets. 2008 featured poets included Billy Collins, Taha Muhammad Ali, Lucille Clifton, Martin Espada, Edward Hirsch, Ted Kooser, and many more. Costs/Accommodations Fee charged; check Web site for latest information. Passes can be purchased for multiple days. Participants responsible for own lodging and meals. Information on overnight accommodations in area hotels available on Web site.

Additional Information Sign up online for mailing list for future brochures and announcements.

✂ ◎ FESTIVAL INTERNATIONAL DE LA POÉSIE (Specialized: poetry readings in French)

Maison de la Poésie, 1497 Laviolette, C.P. 335, Trois-Rivières QC G9A 5G4 Canada. (819)379-9813. Fax: (819)376-0774. E-mail: info@fiptr.com. Web site: www.fiptr.com. Established 1985. President/Founder: Gaston Bellemare. Annual 10-day poetry festival. 2008 dates: 3-12 October 08. Location: Trois Rivières, Quebec, Canada. Average attendance: 35,000-40,000.

Purpose/Features The International Poetry Festival/Festival international de la poésie has become "a veritable literary Happening." Showcases 125 poets from 30 countries spanning 5 continents. Poets participate in over 350 events in more than 90 different venues, including cafes, bars, restaurants, art galleries, theatres, and museums. Readings are all in French. Program and list of participating poets available on Web site.

Costs/Accommodations Dinner and lunch reservations recommended at restaurants where poetry readings take place. Accommodations available at local inns, pensions, motels, and hotels. Information on travel and overnight accommodations available from the Tourism Bureau (Office de Tourisme et des Congrès de Trois-Rivières) at www.tourismetroisrivieres.com.

Additional Information Offers several festival prizes for published and unpublished poets. Guidelines available on Web site.

FINE ARTS WORK CENTER

24 Pearl St., Provincetown MA 02657. (508)487-9960, ext. 103. Fax: (508)487-8873. E-mail: workshops@fawc.org. Web site: www.fawc.org. Established 1968. **Contact:** Dorothy Antczak, summer program director. Offers more than 80 weeklong workshops in poetry, fiction, and creative nonfiction. Location: The Fine Arts Work Center in Provincetown.

Purpose/Features The Fine Arts Work Center in Provincetown is "a nonprofit organization dedicated to providing emerging writers and visual artists with time and space in which to pursue independent work in a community of peers." Seven-month fellowships are awarded to poets and fiction writers in the emerging stages of their careers; professional juries make admissions decisions. The 2008 Summer Workshop program runs from June 15 through August 22, 2008.

Costs/Accommodations 2008 cost: Summer Workshop Program fees range $600-725. Accommodations available at the Work Center for $625 for 6 nights. Additional accommodations available locally.

Additional Information See Web site for details and an application form.

FROST PLACE ANNUAL FESTIVAL OF POETRY

The Frost Place, P.O. Box 74, Franconia NH 03580. (603)823-5510. E-mail: rfrost@ncia.net. Web site: www.frostplace.org. Established 1978. Executive Director: Jim Schley. Annual weeklong conference. 2008 dates: July 27-August 2. Location: Robert Frost's historic house and barn, now a center for poetry and the arts. Average attendance: 55-65.

Purpose/Features Open to poets only. Offers daily craft talk, reading, and organized critique of participant work. 2008 guest faculty: Cornelius Eady, Susan Howe, Chase Twichell, Jean Valentine, and David Wojahn; workshop leaders Patrick Donnelly, Linda Susan Jackson, Ilya Kaminsky, and Ellen Dore Watson; James Hoch, resident poet.

Costs/Accommodations 2007 cost: $900, participant; reduced fee for auditors. Room and board available locally; information sent upon acceptance to program.

Additional Information For participants, application should be accompanied by 3 pages of your own poetry and $25 reading fee. Auditors apply by brief letter describing literary interests, accompanied by $15 reading fee. Additional information available on Web site.

THE FROST PLACE SEMINAR

The Frost Place, P.O. Box 74, Franconia NH 03580. (603)823-5510. E-mail: rfrost@ncia.net. Web site: www.frostplace.org. **Contact:** Jeanne Marie Beaumont, seminar director. Held annually in early August following the Frost Place Annual Festival of Poetry. 2008 dates: August 3-8. Average attendance: limited to 16 participants.

Purpose/Features Priority given to those who have participated in the Festival of Poetry at least once before. Offers daily lecture on poetry of the past, workshop focusing on participant poems, and evening reading. 2008 poetry staff: Jeanne Marie Beaumont, Andrea Hollander Budy, David Trinidad, and Rachel Hadas.

Costs/Accommodations 2008 cost: $800 tuition; $140 (separate check) for meals.

Additional Information Admission competitive. To apply, send cover letter outlining goals for your participation and 3 pages of your own poetry as well as $25 reading fee. Additional information available on Web site.

⬛ ◉ FURIOUS FLOWER POETRY CENTER COLLEGIATE CONFERENCE (Specialized: African American poetry)

James Madison University, 800 S. Main St., Harrisonburg VA 24401. (540)568-8883. Fax: (540)568-8888. E-mail: hawortex@jmu.edu. Web site: www.jmu.edu/furiousflower. **Contact:** Elizabeth Haworth, assistant director. "This is a new conference to be held in 2009. It will be the collegiate version of the Furious Flower Poetry Conferences of 1994 and 2004." Three-day event. 2009 dates: TBA. Location: James Madison University, Harrisonburg, VA. Average attendance: 300.

Purpose/Features Open to college-level poets. Offers "meetings with and feedback from established African American poets" plus workshops, lectures, faculty readings, participant readings, and ms critiques.

Costs/Accommodations 2009 costs: TBA. Participants responsible for some meals. Accommodations available on site. Information available on Web site as details are finalized closer to the conference date.

Additional Information Offers poetry contest as part of conference. Guidelines available on Web site closer to the date of conference. Brochure and registration form will be available on Web site as 2009 conference approaches. "After 2009, the next Furious Flower Poetry Conference will be 2014."

GREEN LAKE WRITERS CONFERENCE

Green Lake Conference Center, W2511 State Highway 23, Green Lake WI 54941-9599. 920-294-7327 or 920-294-3323. E-mail: janwhite@glcc.org. Web site: www.glcc.org. Established 1948. **Contact:** Jan White. Annual weeklong event. 2008 dates: August 17-22, 2008 (60th annual conference). 2009: August 23-28. Location: Green Lake, WI.

Purpose/Features "Attendees may be well-published or beginners, may write for secular and/or Christian markets. Leaders are experienced writing teachers. Spend 11½ contact hours in the workshop of your choice: fiction, nonfiction, poetry, inspirational/devotional. Also take in as many seminars as you wish to enhance specific skills: marketing, humor, songwriting, writing for children, self-publishing, writing for churches, interviewing, memoir writing, the magazine market. Evening: panels of experts will answer your questions. Social and leisure activities.

Costs/Accommodations Brochure and scholarship info from Web site or contact Jan White.

Additional Information GLCC is in South Central Wisconsin, has 1000 acres, 2½ miles of shoreline on Wisconsin's deepest lake, and offers a beautiful resort setting. Hotels, lodges, and all meeting rooms are a/c. Affordable rates, excellent meals. Party and writers' showcase.

INDIANA UNIVERSITY WRITERS' CONFERENCE

464 Ballantine Hall, Indiana University, Bloomington IN 47405. (812)855-1877. Fax: (812)855-9535. E-mail: writecon@indiana.edu. Web site: www.indiana.edu/~writecon. Established 1940. **Contact:** Bob Bledsoe, director. Annual week-long event. 2008 dates: June 8-13. Location: Bloomington campus of Indiana University. Average attendance: 100.

Purpose/Features Open to all. Offers poets workshops, classes, readings, and ms critiques. 2008 poetry presenters included Jean Valentine, Reginald Shepherd, and Ross Gay.

Costs/Accommodations 2008 cost: $500 for workshop (including all classes); $250 for classes only. $50 application fee. Accommodations available on site. Information on overnight accommodations available on Web site.

Additional Information Poetry workshop applicants must submit up to 10 pages of poetry with application. Brochure and registration form available for SASE, by e-mail, or on Web site.

IOWA SUMMER WRITING FESTIVAL

C215 Seashore Hall, University of Iowa, Iowa City IA 52242. (319)335-4160. Fax: (319)335-4039. E-mail: iswfestival@uiowa.edu. Web site: www.uiowa.edu/~iswfest. Established 1987. **Contact:** Amy Margolis, director. Annual 6-week event. 2007 dates: June 10-July 27. Includes one-week and weekend workshops at the University of Iowa campus. Average attendance: 150/week.

Purpose/Features "Open to all adults 21 and over who have a desire to write." Offers poets workshops, lectures, discussions, and participant readings in either weeklong or weekend formats. Participants in weeklong workshops have private conference/critique with workshop leader. 2007 poetry staff included Jane Mead, Christine Hemp, Bruce Bond, Jim Heynen, Michael Morse, Michael Dennis Browne, Katie Ford, and Vince Gotera.

Costs/Accommodations 2007 cost: $250 for a weekend course and $500-525 for a one-week course. Participants responsible for most meals. Accommodations available at area hotels. Information on overnight accommodations available by phone or on Web site.

Additional Information Brochure and registration form available upon request or on Web site.

◎ THE IWWG SUMMER CONFERENCE

The International Women's Writing Guild, P.O. Box 810, Gracie Station, New York NY 10028. (212)737-7536. Fax: (212)737-9469. E-mail: iwwg@iwwg.org. Web site: www.iwwg.org. Established 1978. **Contact:** Hannelore Hahn, executive director. 2008 dates: June 13-20. Location: Skidmore College in Saratoga Springs, NY. Average attendance: 500 maximum.

Purpose/Features Open to all women. Around 65 workshops offered each day. 2008 poetry staff included Barbara Garro, Marj Hahne, D.H. Melhem, Myra Shapiro, and Susan Baugh.

Costs/Accommodations 2008 cost: $1,085 (single), $945 (double) for IWWG members; $1,130 (single), $990 (double) for nonmembers. Includes program and room and board for 7 nights, 21 meals at Skidmore College. Shorter conference stays available, such as 5 days or weekend. Commuters welcome.

Additional Information Post-conference retreat weekend also available. Additional information available for SASE, by e-mail, or on Web site.

JENTEL ARTIST RESIDENCY PROGRAM

Jentel Foundation, 130 Lower Piney Creek Rd., Banner WY 82832. (307)737-2311. Fax: (307)737-2305. E-mail: jentel@jentelarts.org. Web site: www.jentelarts.org. Established 2000. One-month residencies throughout the year, scheduled the 15th of 1 month through the 13th of the following month. Application deadlines are September 15 and January 15 annually. Location: Banner, WY. Average attendance: 2 writers in any genre (also 4 visual artists in any media).

Purpose/Features Residency program for writers and visual artists who are U.S. citizens or from the international community currently residing in the U.S., are 25 years and older, and are not matriculated students. "Set in a rural ranch setting in the foothills of the Big Horn Mountains of North Central Wyoming, Jentel offers unfettered time and space to focus on the creative process, experience of Wyoming landscape, and interact as desired with a small community of writers and artists." Special features include Jentel Presents, a monthly evening of slide presentations and readings by residents in 1 of the surrounding communities.

Costs/Accommodations Residents are responsible for travel expenses and personal items. "Jentel provides a private accommodation in a shared living space, a comfortable private studio, and a stipend to help defray the cost of food and personal expenses. Staff takes residents grocery shopping weekly after the stipend is distributed. Staff will pick up and drop off residents at the airport and bus station in Sheridan, 20 miles from the ranch setting of Jentel." Accommodation provided in a large house with common living and dining areas; fully equipped kitchen; library with computer, printer, and Wireless Internet access; media room with television, DVD/video player, and CD player; spacious private bedroom; and separate private studio.

Additional Information Brochure and application form available for self-addressed mailing label and 58 cents postage, or on Web site.

THE KENYON REVIEW WRITERS WORKSHOP

Kenyon College, Gambier OH 43022. (740)427-5207. E-mail: reacha@kenyon.edu. Web site: www. kenyonreview.org/workshops. **Contact:** Anna Duke Reach, director of summer programs and special events. Annual 8-day event. 2008 dates: June 14-21. Location: the Kenyon College campus. Average attendance: 10/class.

Purpose/Features Offers the time, setting, and community for writers to practice and develop their art. Focuses on the generation and revision of new work, although participants may bring works-in-progress. Offers poets one-on-one meetings with instructors, exercises and discussions, and public readings by distinguished visiting writers and workshop participants. 2008 poetry instructors were David Baker and Meghan O'Rourke.

Costs/Accommodations 2008 cost: $1,995 (includes tuition, room, and meals). A $200 discount is offered to returning participants. Participants are housed in modern campus apartments with computer access.

Additional Information College and non-degree graduate credit available. Online application form and writing sample submission available on Web site. Early application is encouraged as space is limited.

⋈ ◎ KUNDIMAN POETRY RETREAT (Specialized: Asian American)

245 Eighth Ave #151, New York NY 10011.E-mail: info@kundiman.org. Web site: www.kundiman. org. Established 2002. **Contact:** Sarah Gambito, executive director.

Annual 5 day retreat in the last week of June. 2008 dates were June 25-29. Location: The University of Virginia, Charlottesville, VA. Average attendance: 18.

Purpose/Features Open to Asian American poets. Offers poets workshops, lectures, faculty readings, participant readings, and mentorship sessions. 2008 poetry presenters include Bei Dao, Tan Lin, and Aimee Nezhukumatathil. Costs/Accommodations $325—includes all housing and meal costs. Tuition is free to accepted fellows. Accommodations available on site.

Additional Information Guidelines available on Web site. Brochure and registration form available on Web site. "Open to Asian American poets. Renowned faculty will conduct workshops and provide one-on-one mentorship sessions with fellows. Readings and informal social gatherings will also be scheduled. Fellows selected based on sample of 6-8 poems and short essay answer. Applications should be received between February 1-March 1."

◎ LIFE PRESS CHRISTIAN WRITERS' CONFERENCE

P.O. Box 2018, Cordova TN 38088. (901)309-3692. E-mail: gmoearth@aol.com. Web site: www.gra ndmotherearth.org. Established 1998. **Contact:** Frances Cowden. Annual one-day event. 2008 date: August 2. Location: Cordova, TN. Average attendance: 45.

Purpose/Features Open to all writers. Offers poets workshops, lectures, readings, and ms critiques. 2007 staff included Robert Hall, Florence Bruce, Cindy Beebe, and Sarah Hull Gurley.

Costs/Accommodations 2008 cost: $35 registration fee (includes one contest entry, critique of all entries, continental breakfast and lunch); $30 (includes registration with entries plus food, but no critique); or $25 (includes food, no entries); $20 fee for spouses. Information on overnight accommodations available in brochure.

Additional Information Individual poetry critiques available. Poets should submit a limit of 6 works/

category and $10 fee. "One payment for all entries—send with entries." Sponsors contest for "poetry and prose in general, open to all writers. Other contests require attendance." National Awards for poetry (open to everyone, 50-line limit) are $50, $25, $15, and $10. Conference Awards for poetry (open to those who register for the conference, 30-line limit) are $50, $15, and $10. **Entry fee:** "$5 entitles you to one entry; $2 for each additional entry." **Deadline:** July 6 for 2008. Critique from the judges is available for $10 for all entries. Guidelines available for SASE.

◎ MONTEREY COWBOY POETRY & MUSIC FESTIVAL

1120 Forest Ave., #319, Pacific Grove CA 93950. (800)722-9652. E-mail: info@montereycowboy.com. Web site: www.montereycowboy.com. Established 1998. **Contact:** J.P. "Mick" Vernon, president. Annual 2-day, 3-night event. 2008 dates: December 6, 7, and 8th. Location: Monterey Conference Center. Average attendance: 2,000.

Purpose/Features Open to the general public. Celebrates cowboy poetry and music. Offerings include 9 separate shows of varying theme, most featuring 2 poets and 2 musicians; a few feature strictly poets. Other special features include an open mic at noon on Saturday and Sunday, and a Western art and gear show.

Costs/Accommodations 2007 cost: admission either $15 or $35; an All-Event Pass, $190. Covers admission costs only; participants responsible for own housing and meals. Information on overnight accommodations available. Accommodations include special rates at area hotels.

Additional Information Brochure available on Web site.

MONTEVALLO LITERARY FESTIVAL

Sta. 6420, University of Montevallo, Montevallo AL 35115. (205)665-6420. Fax: (205)665-6422. E-mail: murphyj@montevallo.edu. Web site: www.montevallo.edu/English. Established 2003. **Contact:** Dr. Jim Murphy, director. Annual 2-day event. 2007 dates: April 13-14. Location: several sites on the bucolic University of Montevallo campus. Average attendance: 60-100.

Purpose/Features Presents "a unique opportunity for participants to interact with some of the top writers in the country. Participants attend workshops in poetry, prose, or drama, working closely on their own writing with some of the country's most distinguished poets, fiction writers, playwrights, and writers of nonfiction." Offers poets readings, panels, workshops, and ms critiques. 2008 poetry workshop leader: Claudia Emerson. Prior poetry workshop leaders have included Angela Ball, Don Bogen, Andrew Hudgins, Rodney Jones, Jeff Thomson, Natasha Trethewey, Catherine Bowman, and Frank X Walker.

Costs/Accommodations 2007 cost: $45 for festival, including meals; $95 for festival, including meals and workshop. Offers overnight accommodations at Ramsay Conference Center on campus; rooms $40/night. Call (205)665-6280 for reservations. Free on-campus parking. Additional information available at www.montevallo.edu/cont_ed/ramsay.shtm.

Additional Information Poetry workshop participants submit up to 5 pages of poetry; e-mail as Word doc to Jim Murphy (murphyj@montevallo.edu) at least 2 weeks prior to festival. Brochure available on Web site. Information on upcoming festival available in February.

NAPA VALLEY WRITERS' CONFERENCE

Napa Valley College, 1088 College Ave., St. Helena CA 94574. (707)967-2900. E-mail: writecon@napavalley.edu. Web site: www.napawritersconf.org. **Contact:** Anne Evans, managing director; or Nan Cohen, poetry director. Established 1981. Annual weeklong event. 2008 dates: July 27-August 1. Location: Upper Valley Campus in the historic town of St. Helena, 25 miles north of Napa in the heart of the valley's wine growing community. Excellent cuisine provided by Napa Valley Cooking School. Average attendance: 48 in poetry and 48 in fiction.

Purpose/Features "Serious writers of all backgrounds and experience are welcome to apply." Offers poets workshops, lectures, faculty readings, ms critiques, and meetings with editors. "Poetry session provides the opportunity to work both on generating new poems and on revising previously written ones." 2008 poetry faculty includes Mark Doty, Nick Flynn, Brenda Hillman, and Claudia Rankine in poetry with Ron Carlson, Lan Samantha Chang, Ehud Havazelet, and Ann Parker in fiction.

Costs/Accommodations 2008 cost: $750, including breakfast, lunch, 2 dinners, and attendance at all conference events. Scholarships are available. Information on overnight accommodations available. Limited accommodations in local homes available on a first-come, first-served basis; $30 one-time placement fee.

Additional Information All applicants are asked to submit a qualifying ms with their registration (no more than 5 poems) as well as a brief description of their writing background. Include $10 reading fee and $75 tuition deposit with application. 2008 application deadline: May 22. Brochure and registration form available for SASE or on Web site.

⬚ ◻ NELSON CENTER FOR THE ARTS RESIDENCY, KIMMEL HARDING

801 3rd Corso, Nebraska City NE 68410.402-874-9600. Fax: 402-874-9600. E-mail: pfriedli@khncent erforthearts.org. Web site: www.khncenterforthearts.org. Established 2001. **Contact:** Pat Friedli, assistant director. Annual event consisting of 2, 4, 6, or 8 week stays.

Location Kimmel Harding Nelson Center for the Arts, Nebraska City, NE. Average attendance: 50 residencies are awarded each year.

Purpose/Features Open to all skill levels. See Web site for details.

Costs/Accommodations $25 application fee, participant responsible for all meals. Accommodations available on site. Information on overnight accommodations available on Web site.

⬚ PIMA WRITERS' WORKSHOP

Pima College, 2202 W. Anklam Rd., Tucson AZ 85709-0170. (520)206-6084. E-mail: mfiles@pima.e du. Established 1987. **Contact:** Meg Files, director. Annual 3-day event. 2008 dates: May 30-June 1. Location: Pima College's Center for the Arts, "includes a proscenium theater, a black box theater, a recital hall, and conference rooms, as well as a courtyard with amphitheater." Average attendance: 300.

Purpose/Features Open to all writers, beginning and experienced. Offers poets workshops, ms critiques, writing exercises, and workshop's atmosphere—"friendly and supportive, practical and inspirational." Past poetry staff has included Peter Meinke, Steve Kowit, David Citino, and others.

Costs/Accommodations 2008 cost: $80, can include individual consultation. Participants responsible for own meals. Information on overnight accommodations available.

Additional Information Brochure and registration form available for SASE or by fax or e-mail.

S.O.M.O.S., SOCIETY OF THE MUSE OF THE SOUTHWEST

P.O. Box 3225, 233B Paseo del Pueblo Sur, Taos NM 87571. (505)758-0081. Fax: (505)758-4802. E-mail: somos@laplaza.com. Web site: www.somostaos.org. Established 1983. **Contact:** Dori Vinella, executive director. "We offer readings, special events, and workshops at different times during the year." Length of workshops varies. Location: various sites in Taos. Average attendance: 10-50.

Purpose/Features Open to anyone. "We offer workshops in various genres—fiction, poetry, nature writing, etc." Past workshop presenters have included Denise Chavez, Marjorie Agosin, Judyth Hill, Robin Becker, Sawnie Morris, and Lise Goett. Other special features include the 2-day Annual Taos Storytelling Festival in October, a Winter Writers Series (January-February), and Summer Writer's Series (July-August).

Costs/Accommodations See Web site for current information.

Additional Information Additional information available by fax, e-mail, or on Web site. "Taos has a wonderful community of dedicated and talented writers who make S.O.M.O.S. workshops rigorous, supportive, and exciting." Also publishes *Chokecherries*, an annual anthology.

⬚ SAGE HILL SUMMER WRITING EXPERIENCE

P.O. Box 1731, Saskatoon SK S7K 3S1 Canada. Phone: (306)652-7395. Fax: (306)244-0255. E-mail: sage.hill@sasktel.net. Web site: www.sagehillwriting.ca. Established 1990. **Contact:** Steven Ross Smith, executive director. Annual 10-day adult summer program. 2008 dates: July 21-30. Location: St. Michael's Retreat, Lumsden, Saskatchewan. Average attendance: varies according to specific workshop (usually 5-11 participants).

New! Spring Poetry Colloquium, a 14-day program for 8 writers working with 2 instructors, Erin Mouré and John Pass. 2008: May 14-27; similar dates for 2009.

Purpose/Features Open to writers, 19 years of age and older, who are working in English. No geographic restrictions. Offers poets workshops, labs, colloquia, and readings. 2007 poetry staff included Jeanette Lynes, John Steffler, and Nicole Brossard.

Costs/Accommodations 2008 summer program cost: $1,095 CAD, including instruction, accommodations, meals, and all facilities. Accommodations available on site. Spring program cost: $1395.

Additional Information Writing sample and $50 CAD deposit required with application. Additional information available for SASE, by phone, e-mail, or on Web site.

THE SANDHILLS WRITERS CONFERENCE

Augusta State University, Augusta GA 30904. (706)729-2417. Fax: (706)729-2247. E-mail: akellman @aug.edu. Web site: www.sandhills.aug.edu. Established 1975. **Contact:** Anthony Kellman, conference director. Annual 3-day event usually held the third weekend in March. 2009 dates: March 19-21. Location: campus of Augusta State University. Facilities are handicapped accessible. Average attendance: 100.

Purpose/Features Designed to ''hone the creative writing skills of participants and provide networking opportunities.'' Open to all aspiring writers. Offers poets craft lectures, ms evaluations, and readings. 2008 poetry presenters included Peter Makuck.

Costs/Accommodations 2007 cost: $156 full conference registration; $110 conference-only registration (no ms critique); $76 full conference student registration. All registrations include 2 lunches. Accommodations available at area hotels. Information on overnight accommodations available on Web site.

Additional Information Offers poetry contest as part of conference; also offers scholarships to college students. Guidelines available by e-mail or on Web site. Brochure and registration form available for SASE or on Web site.

SANTA BARBARA WRITERS CONFERENCE

P.O. Box 6627, Santa Barbara CA 93160. (805)964-0367. E-mail: info@sbwritersconference.com. Web site: www.sbwritersconference.com. Established 1973. **Contact:** Marcia Meier, executive director. Annual event. 2008 dates: June 21-26. Location: Fess Parker's Doubletree Resort in Santa Barbara. Average attendance: 450.

Purpose/Features Open to everyone. Covers all genres of writing. Offers poets workshops, lectures, faculty readings, participant readings, ms critiques, master classes, young writers program, and meetings with agents and editors. 2008 poetry presenters included Christopher Buckley and Perie J. Longo.

Costs/Accommodations 2008 cost: $625 before March 1, $825 after (including all workshops and lectures, closing dinner, and final awards breakfast). Accommodations available on site or nearby. Information on overnight accommodations available by e-mail or on Web site.

Additional Information Offers poetry contest as part of conference. Guidelines available on Web site. Brochure and registration form available on Web site.

⬛ SASKATCHEWAN FESTIVAL OF WORDS

Moose Jaw Cultural Centre, 217 Main St. N., Moose Jaw SK S6H 0W1. (306)691-0557. Fax: (306)693-2994. E-mail: word.festival@sasktel.net. Web site: www.festivalofwords.com. Established 1997. **Contact:** Donna Lee Howes, artistic director. Annual 4-day event. 2008 dates: July 17-20. Location: Moose Jaw Library/Art Museum complex in Crescent Park. Average attendance: about 4,000 admissions.

Purpose/Features ''The Saskatchewan Festival of Words celebrates the imaginative uses of language, and features fiction and nonfiction writers, screenwriters, poets, children's authors, songwriters, dramatists, and film makers. Our festival is an ideal place for people who love words to mingle, promote their books, get acquainted, share ideas, conduct impromptu readings, and meet their fans.'' Offers poets workshops, readings, and open mics. 2006 poetry program presenters included Daniel Scott Tysdal, Karen Solie, David Seymour, and Jeanette Lynes.

Costs/Accommodations 2007 cost: $8 CAD for adults; some adult events with front-line entertainment and meals cost $15-20 CAD. "Patrons can save up to 50% by purchasing a festival pass, especially before the end of June." Accommodations available at local inns, campgrounds, and bed & breakfast establishments. Information on overnight accommodations available for SASE or by phone or e-mail.

Additional Information Complete information about festival presenters, events, costs, and schedule available on Web site. Festival presented by Living Skies Festival of Words, Inc.

SBWC MARCH POETRY CONFERENCE

PO Box 6627, Santa Barbara CA 93160.805-964-0367. E-mail: info@sbwritersconference.com. Web site: www.sbwritersconference.com. Established 2009. **Contact:** Marcia. Meier, executive director. Annual event. 2008 dates: March 28-30. Average attendance: 100.

Purpose/Features Open to everyone. Offers poets workshops, faculty readings, ms critiques, seminars, and a master class with a featured poet. 2008: Philip Levine.

Costs/Accommodations $325 for commuter students. This includes all workshops and lunches and dinners from Friday dinner through Sunday lunch. Cost including lodging at retreat center is $495 for a double-occupancy room and all meals. Accommodations available on site.

Additional Information Brochure and registration form available on Web site.

SEWANEE WRITERS' CONFERENCE

735 University Ave., Sewanee TN 37383-1000. (931)598-1141. E-mail: cpeters@sewanee.edu. Web site: www.sewaneewriters.org. Established 1990. **Contact:** Cheri B. Peters, creative writing programs manager. Annual 12-day event held the last 2 weeks in July. Location: the University of the South ("dormitories for housing, Women's Center for public events, classrooms for workshops, Sewanee Inn for dining, etc."). Attendance: about 120.

Purpose/Features Open to poets, fiction writers, and playwrights who submit their work for review in a competitive admissions process. "Participants belong to a workshop devoted to constructive critique of members' manuscripts; in addition, each participant has an individual, private manuscript conference with a faculty member. Readings, craft lectures, panels, and Q&A sessions round out the formal offerings; numerous social functions offer opportunities for informal exchange and networking. Workshops are genre-based rather than theme-based." 2008 poetry faculty featured Daniel Anderson, Claudia Emerson, Andrew Hudgins, Mark Jarman, Brad Leithauser, Mary Jo Salter, Mark Strand, and Greg Williamson. Guest poets Leigh Anne Couch, Charles Martin, and Nigel Thompson will give readings, as will conference director Wayatt Prunty; Martin and Thompson will lead a short workshop on poetry translation.

Costs/Accommodations 2008 cost: $1,700, inclusive of single rooms with shared bathroom facilities. Each year scholarships and fellowships based on merit are available on a competitive basis.

Additional Information A ms should be sent in advance after admission to the conference. Write for brochure and application forms; no SASE necessary. Additional information available on Web site.

SPLIT ROCK ARTS PROGRAM

University of Minnesota, 360 Coffey Hall, 1420 Eckles Ave., St. Paul MN 55108-6084. (612)625-8100. Fax: (612)624-6210. E-mail: splitrockarts@umn.edu. Web site: www.cce.umn.edu/splitrockarts. Established 1983. **Contact:** Anastasia Faunce, program director. Summer series of weeklong and 3-day workshops in creative writing, visual art, and design. 2008 dates: June 15-August 1. Locations: University's Twin Cities campus and Cloquet Forestry Center in Northern MN. Average attendance: 500.

Purpose/Features Open to anyone over 18 years old interested in literary and visual arts and design. Offers writers a variety of intensive workshops with renowned faculty. 2009 faculty to be determined. 2008 writing faculty included Michael Dennis Browne, Patricia Weaver Francisco, Philip Gerard, Rigoberto González, Tayari Jones, Lance Larsen, Valerie Miner, Kyoko Mori, Scott Russell Sanders, Ruth Schwartz, Catherine Watson, and more.

Costs/Accommodations 2008 cost: $550 tuition (noncredit); undergraduate/graduate credit available for additional fee. Scholarships available. Participants responsible for most meals. Accommodations available on site or at area hotels.

Additional Information Print catalogs available in February. Registration opens in late February. Additional information available on Web site.

SQUAW VALLEY COMMUNITY OF WRITERS POETRY WORKSHOP

P.O. Box 1416, Nevada City CA 95959. (530)470-8440. E-mail: info@squawvalleywriters.org. Web site: www.squawvalleywriters.org. Established 1969. **Contact:** Brett Hall Jones, executive director. Annual 7-day event. 2008 dates: July 19-26. Location: The Squaw Valley USA's Lodge in the Sierras near Lake Tahoe. Average attendance: 60 for poetry.

Purpose/Features The Poetry Program is founded "on the belief that when poets gather in a community to write new poems, each poet may well break through old habits and write something stronger and truer than before. To help this happen we work together to create an atmosphere in which everyone might feel free to try anything. In the mornings we meet in workshops to read to each other the work of the previous 24 hours; each participant also has an opportunity to work with each staff poet. In the late afternoons we gather for a conversation about some aspect of craft. On several late afternoons staff poets hold brief individual conferences." 2008 poetry presenters include Lucille Clifton, Robert Hass, Sharon Olds, C.D. Wright, and Dean Young.

Costs/Accommodations 2008 cost: $750 for poetry tuition (includes 6 evening meals), $25 reading/application fee. Accommodations extra. "We arrange housing for participants in local houses and condominiums at a variety of rates." Information on overnight accommodations available on Web site.

Additional Information A limited amount of financial aid is available. Brochure available by e-mail (include mailing address for response) or on Web site. Also publishes the annual *Squaw Valley Community of Writers Omnium Gatherum and Newsletter* containing "news and profiles on our past participants and staff, craft articles, and book advertising."

STEAMBOAT SPRINGS WRITERS CONFERENCE

P.O. Box 774284, Steamboat Springs CO 80477. (970)879-8079. E-mail: sswriters@cs.com. Web site: www.steamboatwriters.com. Established 1982. **Contact:** Harriet Freiberger, director. Annual one-day event usually held in mid-July. Location: a "renovated train station, the Depot is home of the Steamboat Springs Arts Council—friendly, relaxed atmosphere." Average attendance: 35-40 (registration limited).

Purpose/Features Open to anyone. Conference is "designed for writers who have limited time. Instructors vary from year to year, offering maximum instruction during a weekend at a nominal cost." Previous poetry instructors include David Mason, Renate Wood, Jim Tipton, and Donald Revell.

Costs/Accommodations 2008 cost: $35 members, $45 nonmembers before May 19; then $45 and $55 respectively. Includes seminar and catered luncheon. "A variety of lodgings available."

Additional Information Brochure and registration form available for SASE, by e-mail, or on Web site. Optional: Friday evening dinner (cost not included in registration fee); readings by participants (no cost).

TAOS SUMMER WRITERS' CONFERENCE

University of New Mexico, Dept. of English Language and Literature, MSC03 2170, 1 University of New Mexico, Albuquerque NM 87131-0001. (505)277-5572. Fax: (505)277-2950. E-mail: taosconf@ unm.edu. Web site: www.unm.edu/~taosconf. Established 1999. **Contact:** Sharon Oard Warner, director. Annual 5-day (weeklong) and 2-day (weekend) workshops usually held mid-July. Location: Sagebrush Inn in Taos. Average attendance: 180 total; 100 places available in each weekend, 180 places available in weeklong workshops. Class size limited to 12/class, usually smaller.

Purpose/Features Open to everyone, beginners to experienced. Minimum age is 18. Friendly, relaxed atmosphere with supportive staff and instructors. Offers both weekend and weeklong workshops in such areas as fiction, poetry, memoir, publishing, screenwriting, and craft, with master classes in novel, poetry, and memoir. One-on-one consultations with agents and editors available.

Workshop presenters have included Pam Houston, Antonya Nelson, Hilda Raz, Demetria Martinez, and John Dufresne. Special features include evening readings and panels, open mic sessions, and tours of the D.H. Lawrence Ranch.

Costs/Accommodations 2008 cost: $300 for weekend, $600 for weeklong sessions, discounted tuition rate of $250 per weekend workshop with weeklong workshop or master class, including workshop registration and special events. Nearest airport is Albuquerque International Sunport. Taos is about 170 miles north of Albuquerque. Information on overnight accommodations available. Sagebrush Inn, Comfort Suites, and Quality Inn offer special rates.

Additional Information Brochure and registration form available by e-mail or on Web site. "Taos is a unique experience of a lifetime. The setting and scenery are spectacular; historical and natural beauty abound. Our previous attendees say they have been inspired by the place and by the friendly, personal attention of our instructors."

⚡ UNIVERSITY OF WISCONSIN-MADISON'S SCHOOL OF THE ARTS AT RHINELANDER

715 Lowell Center, 610 Langdon St., Madison WI 53703. (608)263-3494. Fax: (608)262-1694. E-mail: mmcclenaghan@dcs.wisc.edu. Web site: www.dcs.wisc.edu/lsa/writing/index.html. Established 1964. **Contact:** Miranda McClenaghan, director. Annual 5-day event. 2008 dates: July 20-25. Location: James Williams Junior High School in Rhinelander. Average attendance: 300.

Purpose/Features Open to all levels and ages. Offers poets workshops and related workshops in creativity. 2007 poetry staff included Ellen Kort, Mary Sue Koeppel and Laurel Yourke.

Costs/Accommodations 2008 cost: registration costs ranged from $199-349; university credit fees are additional. Information on overnight accommodations available.

Additional Information Catalog available in mid-March. Additional information available by phone, e-mail, or on Web site.

WESLEYAN WRITERS CONFERENCE

Wesleyan University, Middletown CT 06457. (860)685-3604. Fax: (860)685-2441. E-mail: agreene@ wesleyan.edu. Web site: www.wesleyan.edu/writers. Established 1956. **Contact:** Anne Greene, director. Annual 5-day event. 2008 dates: June 15-20. Location: the campus of Wesleyan University "in the hills overlooking the Connecticut River, a brief drive from the Connecticut shore. Wesleyan's outstanding library, poetry reading room, and other university facilities are open to participants." Average attendance: 100.

Purpose/Features "The conference welcomes everyone interested in the writer's craft. Participants are a diverse, international group. Both new and experienced writers are welcome. You may attend all of the seminars, including poetry, the novel, short story, fiction techniques, literary journalism, memoir, and multi-media work." Offers poets workshops, seminars, lectures, readings, ms critiques, meetings with editors and agents, and special panel presentations. Recent poetry presenters include Honor Moore, Peter Gizzi, Elizabeth Willis, Sherwin Bitsui, Laura Cronk.

Costs/Accommodations See Web site for current rates. 2007 cost: $830 day student rate (includes tuition only); $1,050 day student rate, full program (includes tuition and meals); $1,250 boarding student rate (includes tuition, meals, room for 5 nights). Accommodations available on site or at area hotels. Information on overnight accommodations available on Web site.

Additional Information Registration for critiques must be made before the conference. Additional information available by phone, fax, or on Web site.

WHIDBEY ISLAND WRITERS' CONFERENCES

The Whidbey Island Writers' Association, P.O. Box 1289, Langley WA 98260. (360)331-6714. E-mail: writers@writeonwhidbey.org. Web site: www.writeonwhidbey.org. Established 1997. Annual event. 2009 dates: February 27-March 1. Location: South Whidbey High School and various sites in the Whidbey Island area. Average attendance: 250.

Purpose/Features Open to writers of every genre and skill level. Offers poets workshops, lectures, readings, author critiques, and "Author Fireside Chats." 2008 poetry presenters included Lorraine Healy, Gloria Burgess, Nancy Pagh, and Molly Larson Cook.

Costs/Accommodations 2008 cost: $375 WIWA members, $395 nonmembers. Participants responsible for most meals. Accommodations available at area hotels. Information on overnight accommodations available on Web site.

Additional Information Offers Benefactor's Award Writing Contest as part of conference. Open to conference attendeees only. Guidelines available on Web site. Program and registration form available on Web site. Brochure available by calling (360)331-6714.

WINTER POETRY & PROSE GETAWAY IN CAPE MAY

18 North Richards Ave., Ventnor NJ 08406. (609)823-5076. E-mail: info@wintergetaway.com. Web site: www.wintergetaway.com. Established 1994. **Contact:** Peter E. Murphy, founder/director. Annual 4-day event. 2009 dates: January 16-19. Location: The Grand Hotel on the Oceanfront in Historic Cape May, NJ. Average attendance: 200 (10 or fewer participants in each poetry workshop).

Purpose/Features Open to all writers, beginners and experienced, over the age of 18. ''The poetry workshop meets for an hour or so each morning before sending you off with an assignment that will encourage and inspire you to produce exciting new work. After lunch, we gather together to read new drafts in feedback sessions led by experienced poet-teachers who help identify the poem's virtues and offer suggestions to strengthen its weaknesses. The groups are small, and you receive positive attention to help your poem mature. In late afternoon, you can continue writing, attend a panel or demonstration lesson, or schedule your personal tutorial session with one of the poets on staff.'' 2008 poetry presenters included Pulitzer Prize recipient Stephen Dunn, Renee Ashley, Kurt Brown, Catherine Doty, Douglas Goetsch, James Richardson, and many more.

Costs/Accommodations 2008 cost: $375 registration, including 2 lunchs, 3 receptions, 3 days of workshops, and a 20-minute tutorial with one of the poets on staff. Accommodations, including breakfast, started at $215 for a double room or $375 for a single. A $25 Early Bard Discount is available if paid in full by November 15.

Additional Information Brochure and registration form available by mail or on Web site. ''The Winter Getaway is known for its challenging and supportive atmosphere that encourages imaginative risk-taking and promotes freedom and transformation in the participants' writing.''

◎ THE YOUNG POETS CONFERENCE

The Frost Place, P.O. Box 74, Franconia NH 03580. (603)823-5510. E-mail: rfrost@ncia.net. Web site: www.frostplace.org. **Contact:** Jim Schley, executive director. Annual event. 2008 dates: April 25-27.

Purpose/Features Designed for high school students along with high school and middle school classroom teachers. ''An intensive poetry experience in a historic New England inn, with time for writing, revision, workshops, readings, and games; and with a field trip to the nearby Frost Place, Robert Frost's former home.'' 2008 faculty poets included Eloise Bruce and Rick Agran.

Costs/Accommodations 2008 costs: $300. Includes local housing and meals.

Additional Information To apply, send a brief letter describing interests in poetry and noting current year in school, mailing address, phone number, and e-mail address. Also enclose 3 original poems and a letter of recommendation from a teacher. Additional information available on Web site.

ADDITIONAL CONFERENCES, WORKSHOPS & FESTIVALS

The following cross-references listings in other sections of this book that include information about conferences, workshops, conventions and festivals. Among these are state and local poetry groups that may offer a variety of workshop opportunities for their members.

Resources

Resources

Organizations

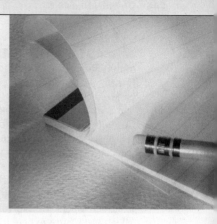

There are many organizations of value to poets. These groups may sponsor workshops and contests, stage readings, publish anthologies and chapbooks or spread the word about publishing opportunities. A few provide economic assistance or legal advice. The best thing organizations offer, though, is a support system to which poets can turn for a pep talk, a hard-nosed (but sympathetic) critique of a manuscript or simply the comfort of talking and sharing with others who understand the challenges, and joys, of writing poetry.

Whether national, regional or as local as your library or community center, each organization has something special to offer. The listings in this section reflect the membership opportunities available to poets with a variety of organizations. Some groups provide certain services to both members and nonmembers.

These symbols may appear at the beginning of some listings: The (N) symbol indicates a recently established organization new to *Poet's Market*; the ( ) symbol indicates this organization did not appear in the 2008 edition; the ( ) symbol denotes a Canadian organization and the ( ) symbol one headquartered outside the U.S. and Canada.

Since some organizations are included in listings in the other sections of this book, we've cross-referenced these listings under Additional Organizations at the end of this section. For further details about an organization associated with a market in this list, go to that market's page number.

To find out more about groups in your area (including those that may not be listed in *Poet's Market*), contact your YMCA, community center, local colleges and universities, public library and bookstores (and don't forget newspapers and the Internet). If you can't find a group that suits your needs, consider starting one yourself. You might be surprised to discover there are others in your locality who would welcome the encouragement, feedback and moral support of a writer's group.

🌐 ACADEMI—YR ACADEMI GYMREIG/THE WELSH ACADEMY

Mount Stuart House, 3rd Floor, Cardiff CF10 5FQ Wales. (44)(29)2047-2266. Fax: (44)(29)2049-2930. E-mail: post@academi.org. Web site: www.academi.org. Established 1959. **Contact:** Peter Finch, chief executive. Academi is the Welsh National Literature Promotion Agency and Society of Writers and is open to "the population of Wales and those outside Wales with an interest in Welsh writing." Currently has 2,000 members. Levels of membership/dues: associate, full, and fellow; £15/year (waged) or £7.50/year (unwaged). Offerings include promotion of readings, events, conferences, exchanges, tours; employment of literature-development workers; publication of a quarterly events magazine; publication of a literary magazine in Welsh (*Taliesin*) and another (*NWR*) in English. Sponsors conferences/workshops and contests/awards. Publishes *A470: What's On In Literary Wales*, a magazine appearing quarterly containing information on literary events in Wales. Available to nonmembers for £15 (annual subscription). Academi is also a resident company of the Wales Millenium Centre, where it runs the Glyn Jones Center, a resource centre for writers and the public. Additional information available for SASE (or SAE and IRC), by fax, e-mail, or on Web site.

THE ACADEMY OF AMERICAN POETS

584 Broadway, Suite 604, New York NY 10012-5243. (212)274-0343. Fax: (212)274-9427. E-mail: academy@poets.org. Web site: www.poets.org. Executive Director: Tree Swenson. Established 1934. The Academy of American Poets was founded to support the nation's poets at all stages of their careers and to foster the appreciation of contemporary poetry. Levels of membership/dues: begin at $35/year (contributing member). Administers The Walt Whitman Award; The James Laughlin Award; The Harold Morton Landon Translation Award; The Lenore Marshall Poetry Prize; The Raiziss/de Palchi Translation Award; and The Wallace Stevens Award. (For further details, see individual listings in the Contests & Awards section.) Also awards The Fellowship of the Academy of American Poets ($25,000 to honor distinguished poetic achievement, no applications accepted) and The University & College Poetry Prizes. Publishes *American Poet*, an informative semiannual journal sent to all Academy members. The Academy's other programs include National Poetry Month (April), the largest literary celebration in the world; the Poetry Audio Archive, a 700-volume audio library capturing the voices of contemporary American poets for generations to come; an annual series of poetry readings and special events; and Poets.org, which includes thousands of poems, hundreds of essays and interviews, lesson plans for teachers, a National Poetry Almanac, a national Calendar of Events, and the National Poetry Map.

ARIZONA AUTHORS ASSOCIATION

6145 W Echo Lane, Glendale, AZ 85302. (623)847-9343. E-mail: info@azauthors.com. Web site: www.azauthors.com. Established 1978. **Contact:** Toby Heathcotte, president. Provides education and referral for writers and others in publishing. Statewide organization. Currently has 200 members. Levels of membership/dues: Published, Unpublished (seeking publication), Professional (printers, agents, and publishers), and Student; $45/year for authors, $30/year students, $60/year professionals. Sponsors conferences, workshops, contests, awards. Sponsors annual literary contest in poetry, short story, essay, unpublished novels, and published books (fiction, children's, and nonfiction). Publishes *Arizona Literary Magazine* and *Arizona Authors Newsletter*. Members meet monthly. Additional information available on Web site.

THE ASSOCIATION OF WRITERS AND WRITING PROGRAMS (AWP)

Mail Stop 1E3, George Mason University, Fairfax VA 22030-4444. (703)993-4301. E-mail: services@awpwriter.org (membership contact). Web site: www.awpwriter.org. Established 1967. Offers a variety of services for writers, teachers, and writing programs, including networking and resources, job placement assistance (helps writers find jobs in teaching, editing, and other related fields), writing contests, literary arts advocacy, and forums. Levels of membership/dues: annual individual membership is $65/year; $110 for 2 years; students who provide photocopy of valid student ID pay $40/year (all prices apply to U.S. residents only). Membership includes 6 issues of *The Writer's Chronicle* (containing information about grants and awards, publishing opportunities, fellowships, and writing programs); access to the online *AWP Job List* (employment opportunity listings for writers); access to AWP eLink, a members-only Web site; a 50% discount on AWP Award Series entry fees; discount on registration for annual conference; and more. *The Writer's Chronicle* is available by subscription only for $20/year (6 issues). The AWP Award Series for novel, poetry, fiction, and creative nonfiction includes the Donald Hall Prize for Poetry (see separate listing in Contests & Awards). Additional information available on Web site.

THE BEATLICKS

940 W. Van Patten, Las Cruces NM 88005. E-mail: beatlickjoe@yahoo.com. Web site: www.beatlick .com. Established 1988. **Contact:** Joe Speer, editor. International organization open to "anyone interested in literature." Currently has 200 members. "There is no official distinction between members, but there is a core group that does the work, writes reviews, organizes readings, etc." Offerings include publication of work (have published poets from Australia, Egypt, India, and Holland) and reviews of books and venues. Publishes *Beatlick News* 4 times/year, a networking tool designed to inform poets of local events and to bring awareness of the national scene. "We include poems, short fiction, art, photos, and articles about poets and venues." Submit short pieces, no vulgar language. "We try to elevate the creative spirit. We publish new voices plus well-established talents." Subscription: $15/year. Additional information available for SASE or by e-mail. "We promote all the arts."

BRIGHT HILL LITERARY CENTER

P.O. Box 193, 94 Church St., Treadwell NY 13846-0193. (607)829-5055. Fax: (607)829-5054. E-mail: wordthur@stny.rr.com. Web site: www.brighthillpress.org. Established 1992. **Contact:** Bertha Rogers, founding director. Bright Hill Literary Center serves residents in the Catskill Mountain region, greater New York, and throughout the U.S. Includes the Bright Hill Library & Internet Center, with "thousands of volumes of literary journals, literary prose and poetry, literary criticism and biography, theater, reference, art, and children's books available for reading and research (noncirculating, for the time being). Wireless Internet access is available." Sponsors workshops for children and adults. Sponsors contests/awards (Bright Hill Press book and chapbook competitions; see separate listings in Contests & Awards). Publishes 5-7 books of poetry each year.

☑ BURNABY WRITERS' SOCIETY

6584 Deer Lake Ave., Burnaby BC V5G 3T7 Canada. E-mail: info@bws.bc.ca. Web site: www.bws.b c.ca. Established 1967. **Contact:** Eileen Kernaghan. Corresponding membership in the society, including a newsletter subscription, is open to anyone, anywhere. Currently has 100 members. Levels of membership/dues: regular ($30 CAD); students/seniors ($20 CAD/year). Sample newsletter in return for SASE with Canadian stamp. Holds monthly meetings at The Burnaby Arts Centre (located at 6450 Deer Lake Ave.), with a business meeting at 7:30 followed by a writing workshop or speaker. Members of the society stage regular public readings of their own work. Sponsors open mic readings for the public. Sponsors a poetry contest open to British Columbia residents. Competition receives about 100-200 entries/year. Past contest winners include Mildred Tremblay, Irene Livingston, and Kate Braid. Additional information available on Web site.

CALIFORNIA STATE POETRY SOCIETY

CSPS/CQ, P.O. Box 7126, Orange CA 92683. Web site: www.californiaquarterly.blogspot.com. **Contact:** Membership Chair. The California State Poetry Society "is dedicated to the adventure of poetry and its dissemination. Although located in California, its members are from all over the U.S. and abroad." Levels of membership/dues: $30/year. Benefits include membership in the National Federation of State Poetry Societies (NFSPS); 4 issues of *California Quarterly* (see separate listing in Magazines/Journals), *Newsbriefs*, and *The Poetry Letter*. Sponsors monthly and annual contests. Additional information available for SASE or on Web site.

☑ CANADIAN POETRY ASSOCIATION

331 Elmwood Dr., Suite 4-212, Moncton NB E1A 1X6 Canada. Phone/fax: (506)204-1732. E-mail: info@canadianpoetryassoc.com. Web site: www.canadianpoetryassoc.com. Established 1985.

"We promote all aspects of the reading, writing, publishing, purchasing, and preservation of poetry in Canada. The CPA promotes the creation of local chapters to organize readings, workshops, publishing projects, and other poetry-related events in their area." Membership is open to anyone with an interest in poetry, including publishers, schools, libraries, booksellers, and other literary organizations. Levels of membership/dues: $30 CAD/year; seniors, students, and fixed income, $20 CAD; International, $40 USD. Publishes a magazine, *Poemata*, featuring news articles, chapter reports, poetry by new members, book reviews, markets information, announcements, and more. Membership form available for SASE or on Web site. Also sponsors The CPA Annual Poetry Contest, with 3 cash prizes plus up to 5 Honorable Mentions. **Open to the public.** Winning poems published in *Poemata* and on CPA Web site. **Deadline:** January 30, 2008. Guidelines available for SASE or on Web site.

COLUMBINE POETS OF COLORADO

P.O. Box 6245, Westminster CO 80021. (303)431-6774. E-mail: anitajg5@aol.com. Web site: www. Nazcaresources.com/columbine. Established 1978. **Contact:** Anita Jepson-Gilbert, secretary/treasurer. Statewide organization open to anyone interested in poetry. Currently has 100 members. An affiliate of the National Federation of State Poetry Societies (NFSPS). Levels of membership/dues: Members at Large, who do not participate in the local chapters but who belong to the National Federation of State Poetry Societies and to the Colorado Society; and local members, who belong to the national, state, and local chapters in Denver or Salida, Colorado ($15 state and national; $35 local, state, and national). Offerings for the Denver Chapter include weekly workshops and monthly critiques. Sponsors contests, awards for students and adults. Sponsors the Annual Poets Fest, where members and nationally known writers give readings and workshops that are open to the public. Members meet weekly. Additional information available for SASE, by phone, e-mail, or on Web site.

✖ CONNECTICUT POETRY SOCIETY

P.O. Box 702, Manchester CT 06040. E-mail: connpoetry@comcast.net. Web site: www.ct-poetry-society.org/. Established 1978. **Contact:** Christine Beck, president. The Connecticut Poetry Society is a nonprofit organization dedicated to the promotion and enjoyment of poetry through chapter meetings, contests, and poetry-related events. Statewide organization open to non-Connecticut residents. Currently has about 150 members. Levels of membership/dues: full, $25/year; student, $10/year. Membership benefits include automatic membership in The National Federation of State Poetry Societies (NFSPS); a free copy of *The Connecticut River Review*, a national poetry journal published by CPS (see separate listing in Magazines/Journals); opportunity to publish in *Long River Run II*, a members-only poetry journal; quarterly CPS and NFSPS newsletters; annual April poetry celebration; and membership in any of 10 state chapters. Sponsors conferences and workshops. Sponsors *The Connecticut River Review* Annual Poetry Contest, The Brodinsky-Brodine Contest, The Winchell Contest, The Lynn Decaro High School Competition, and The Dehn Poetry Competition (see separate listings in Contests & Awards). Members and nationally known writers give readings that are open to the public. Members meet monthly. Additional information available by SASE or on Web site.

COUNCIL OF LITERARY MAGAZINES AND PRESSES (CLMP)

154 Christopher St., Suite 3C, New York NY 10014. (212)741-9110. E-mail: info@clmp.org. Web site: www.clmp.org. Established 1967. "Dedicated to supporting and actively promoting the field of independent literary publishing." Open to publishers who are primarily literary in nature, have published at least one issue/title prior to applying for membership, publish at least one issue/title annually on an ongoing basis, have a minimum print run of 500 per issue or title, do not charge authors a fee, are not primarily self-publishing, and do not primarily publish children's/students' work. Currently has over 500 members. Levels of membership/dues: based on publishing organization's annual budget. See Web site for complete member application process. Benefits include free and discounted monographs, subscription to e-mail listserves and online databases, annual copy of *The Literary Press and Magazine Directory*, plus many valuable services. Additional information available by e-mail or on Web site.

◎ FURIOUS FLOWER POETRY CENTER (Specialized: African American poetry)

MSC 3802, James Madison University, Harrisonburg VA 22807. (540)568-8883. Fax: (540)568-8888. E-mail: bradshnr@jmu.edu. Web site: www.jmu.edu/furiousflower. Established 1999. **Contact:** Natalia Bradshaw-Parson. Executive Director: Dr. Joanne Gabbin. A non-membership-based organization. "The mission of the Furious Flower Poetry Center is to advance the genre of African American poetry by providing opportunities for education, research, and publication." Sponsors workshops and conferences related to African American poetry, including an annual poetry camp for children of the community. Sponsored national conferences in 1994 and 2004. Nationally known writers give readings that are open to the public. Sponsors open mic readings for the public; also sponsors the Central Shenandoah Valley Slam Team. Additional information available by e-mail or on Web site.

GREATER CINCINNATI WRITERS' LEAGUE

Web site: www.cincinnatiwritersleague.org. Established 1930. **Contact:** GCWL President (see Web site for current contact information). Purpose is to "support those who write poetry in the Cincinnati area and to promote excellence in poetry writing. We believe in creative freedom, with open, constructive critique as a learning tool." Currently has 30 members and participants ("many are published poets"). Membership/Dues: $25/year. Offerings include monthly meetings with critique or a workshop on a subject of interest to poets. Poems submitted by members are critiqued by guest critics (published poets who are also teachers or professors of poetry and/or creative writing). Group discussion of critiqued poems follows. Sponsors fall poetry contest with cash prizes; also sponsors a category of the annual Ohio Poetry Day contest with cash prizes. Occasionally publishes an anthology. Members occasionally give readings that are open to the public (see Web site for meeting time and place). Additional information available on Web site.

◎ HAIKU SOCIETY OF AMERICA

578 3rd Ave., San Francisco CA 94118-3903. E-mail: lstparker@cs.com. Web site: www.hsa-haiku.org. Established 1968. **Contact:** Lane Parker, secretary. The Haiku Society of America is composed of haiku poets, editors, critics, publishers, and enthusiasts dedicated to "promoting the creation and appreciation of haiku and related forms (haibun, haiga, renku, senryu, sequences, and tanka) among its members and the public." Currently has over 800 members. Levels of membership/dues: $33 U.S.; $30 seniors or full-time students (in North America); $35 USD in Canada and Mexico; $45 USD for all other areas. Membership benefits include a year's subscription (3 issues in 2007) to the Society's journal, *Frogpond* (see separate listing in Magazines/Journals), and to the quarterly *HSA Newsletter*; the annual information sheet; an annual address/e-mail list of HSA members; and eligibility to submit work to the members' anthology. Administers the following annual awards: The Harold G. Henderson Awards for haiku, The Gerald Brady Awards for senryu, The Bernard Lionel Einbond Awards for renku, The Merit Book Awards, and The Nicholas Virgilio Haiku Awards for youth. Guidelines available in the newsletter or on Web site. Meets quarterly at various locations throughout the U.S. Additional information available for SASE or on Web site.

THE HUDSON VALLEY WRITERS' CENTER

300 Riverside Dr., Sleepy Hollow NY 10591. (914)332-5953. Fax: (914)332-4825. E-mail: info@writerscenter.org. Web site: www.writerscenter.org. Established 1988. **Contact:** Jerri Lynn Fields, executive director. "The Hudson Valley Writers' Center is a nonprofit organization devoted to furthering the literary arts in our region. Its mission is to promote the appreciation of literary excellence, to stimulate and nurture the creation of literary works in all sectors of the population, and to bring the diverse works of gifted poets and prose artists to the attention of the public." Open to all. Currently has 350 members. Levels of membership/dues: individual ($35/year), family ($50/year), senior/student ($25/year), and friend ($100/year and up). Offerings include public readings by established and emerging poets/writers, workshops and classes, monthly open mic nights, paid and volunteer outreach opportunities, and an annual chapbook competition with Slapering Hol Press (see separate listing in Contests & Awards). Additional information available for SASE, by fax, e-mail, or on Web site.

⊚ INTERNATIONAL WOMEN'S WRITING GUILD

P.O. Box 810, Gracie Station, New York NY 10028. (212)737-7536. Fax: (212)737-9469. E-mail: iwwg@iwwg.org. Web site: www.iwwg.org. Established 1976. **Contact:** Hannelore Hahn, founder/ executive editor. A network for the personal and professional empowerment of women through writing. Levels of membership/dues: $45/year (domestic and overseas). The Guild publishes a bimonthly 32-page journal, *Network*, which includes members' achievements, contests, calendar, and extensive publishing opportunities. Other benefits include regional/local writing groups and kitchen tables, agent list, and dental and vision insurance. "We offer a minimum of 8 writing workshops throughout the U.S., including the weeklong summer conference held at Skidmore College in Saratoga Springs, New York. Poetry workshops are interspersed in the conference programs." Additional information available by fax, e-mail, or on Web site.

⊚ IOWA POETRY ASSOCIATION (Specialized: IA residents only)

2325 61st St., Des Moines IA 50322. (515)279-1106. Web site: www.iowapoetry.com. Established 1945. **Contact:** Lucille Morgan Wilson, editor. Statewide organization open to "anyone interested in poetry, with a residence or valid address in the state of Iowa." Currently has about 425 members. Levels of membership/dues: Regular ($8/year) and Patron ($15 or more/year; "same services, but patron members contribute to cost of running the association"). Offerings include "semiannual workshops to which a poem may be sent in advance for critique; annual contest—also open to nonmembers—with no entry fee; *IPA Newsletter*, published 5 or 6 times/year, including a quarterly national publication listing of contest opportunities; and an annual poetry anthology, *Lyrical Iowa*, containing prize-winning and high-ranking poems from contest entries, available for $10 postpaid. No requirement for purchase to ensure publication." Semiannual workshops "are the only 'meetings' of the association." Additional information available for SASE or on Web site.

THE KENTUCKY STATE POETRY SOCIETY

E-mail: www.cscott@kcu.edu. Web site: www.kystatepoetrysociety.org. Established 1966. **Contact:** A. Carol Scott, president. Regional organization open to all. Member of The National Federation of State Poetry Societies (NFSPS). Currently has about 230 members. Levels of membership/ dues: students ($5); adults ($20); senior adults ($15); other categories: Life; Patron; Benefactor. Offerings include association with other poets; information on contests and poetry happenings across the state and nation; annual state and national contests; national and state annual conventions with workshops, selected speakers, and open poetry readings. Sponsors workshops, contests, awards. Membership includes the quarterly *KSPS Newsletter*. Also includes a quarterly newsletter, *Strophes*, of the NFSPS; and the KSPS journal, *Pegasus*, published 3 times/year: a Spring/ Summer and Fall/Winter issue which solicits good poetry for publication (need not be a member to submit), and a Prize Poems issue of 1st Place contest winners in over 30 categories. Members or nationally known writers give readings that are open to the public. Members meet annually. Membership information available by e-mail or on Web site.

⧆ THE LEAGUE OF CANADIAN POETS

92 Yonge St., Suite 608, Toronto ON M4W 3C7 Canada. (416)504-1657. E-mail: readings@poets.ca. Web site: www.poets.ca. Established 1966. **Contact:** Ingrel Madrus, Readings/Membership Coordinator. A nonprofit national association of professional publishing and performing poets in Canada. Its purpose is "to enhance the status of poets and nurture a professional poetic community to facilitate the teaching of Canadian poetry at all levels of education and to develop the audience for poetry by encouraging publication, performance, and recognition of Canadian poetry nationally and internationally. As well as providing members and the public with many benefits and services, the League speaks for poets on many issues such as freedom of expression, Public Lending Right, CanCopy, contract advice, and grievance." Open to all Canadian citizens and landed immigrants; applications are assessed by a membership committee. Currently has 600 members. Levels of membership/dues: Full ($175 CAD); Associate ($60 CAD); Student ($20 CAD); and Supporting ($100 CAD). Membership benefits include a one-year subscription to monthly e-newsletter, discount on Gift Shop purchases, listing in online members' catalog, and more (benefits increase with member-

ship level). Sponsors The Pat Lowther Memorial Award (for a book of poetry by a Canadian woman published in the preceding year; $1,000 CAD prize) and The Gerald Lampert Memorial Award (recognizes the best first book of poetry published by a Canadian in the preceding year; $1,000 CAD). Additional information available on Web site.

THE LIT
2570 Superior Ave., Suite 203, Cleveland, OH 44114. E-mail: judith@the-lit.org. Web site: www.the-lit.org. Established 1974. **Contact:** Judith Mansour-Thomas, executive director. Founded "to foster a supportive community for poets and writers throughout Northern Ohio and to expand the audience for creative writing among the general public." Currently has 300 members. Levels of membership/dues: $25/year. Membership benefits include subscription to *Muse Magazine* and discounts on services and facilities at the Literary Center. The Literary Center offers classes and an event space for writers and readers. The Lit conducts a monthly workshop where poets can bring their work for discussion. Publishes a monthly calendar of literary events in NE Ohio; a quarterly magazine, *Muse*, which includes articles on the writing life, news, markets, and an annual writing contest in all genres; and 2 chapbooks/year featuring an anthology of work by area poets. "The Lit also sponsors a dramatic reading series, 'Poetry: Mirror of the Arts,' which unites poetry and other art forms performed in cultural settings; and 'Writers & Their Friends,' a biennial literary showcase of new writing (all genres), performed dramatically by area actors, media personalities, and performance poets." Additional information available for SASE, by e-mail, or on Web site.

THE LOFT LITERARY CENTER
Suite 200, Open Book, 1011 Washington Ave. S, Minneapolis MN 55414. (612)215-2575. E-mail: loft@loft.org. Web site: www.loft.org. Established 1974. The largest and most comprehensive literary center in the country, serving both writers and readers with a variety of educational programs, contests and grants, and literary facilities. Levels of membership/dues: Individual ($60/year); Household ($75/year); Low Income/Full-Time Student ($25/year); Donor ($125/year). Membership benefits include discounted tuition, admission charges, and contest fees; check-out privileges at The Loft's Rachel Anne Gaschott Resource Library; rental access to the Book Club Meeting Room and writers' studios; a year's subscription to *A View from the Loft*; and more. Sponsors classes/workshops, contests, and grants (information available on Web site). Sponsors readings by local and national writers. Additional information about The Loft and associated services and programs available on Web site.

MAINE POETS SOCIETY
E-mail: ahammond5@verizon.net. Established 1936. **Contact:** Anne Hammond. Maine Poets Society is an organization "committed to fostering poetry in Maine and beyond. Membership open to all poets who reside at least part-time in Maine." Levels of membership/dues: $15. Make checks payable to Anne Hammond, Treasurer. E-mail Anne for mailing address. Membership benefits include access to writing groups and round robins as well as a subscription to *Stanza*, a newsletter published 3 times/year containing contest-winning poems. Sponsors 3 contests/year with cash prizes for 1st, 2nd, and 3rd Prize; open to members only. Meets third Saturday of February, May, and September. "Our locations change to allow Mainers from across the state to easily join us." Additional information available by e-mail.

MASSACHUSETTS STATE POETRY SOCIETY, INC.
64 Harrison Ave., Lynn MA 01905. E-mail: msps.jcmaes@comcast.net. Web site: http://mastatepoetrysociety.tripod.com/. Established 1959. **Contact:** Jeanette C. Maes, president. Dedicated to the writing and appreciation of poetry and promoting the art form. Statewide organization open to anyone with an interest in poetry. Currently has 200 members. Levels of membership/dues: $15/year. Member benefits include subscription to *Bay State Echo*, published 5 times/year with members' news and announcements; members-only contests; round-robin critique groups; members-only annual anthology; workshops at society meetings; and automatic membership in National Federation of State Poetry Societies (NFSPS). Sponsors contests open to all poets. Guidelines avail-

able for SASE or on Web site. Members or nationally known writers give readings that are open to the public. Sponsors open mic readings for members and the public for National Poetry Day. Members meet 5 times/year. Additional information available for SASE or on Web site.

MOUNTAIN WRITERS SERIES

Mountain Writers Center, 2804 S.E. 27th Ave., #2, Portland OR 97202. (503)232-4517. E-mail: pdxmws@mountainwriters.org. Web site: www.mountainwriters.org. **Contact:** Bob Kreider, program associate. Established 1973. "Mountain Writers Series is an independent nonprofit organization dedicated to supporting writers, audiences, and other sponsors by promoting literature and literacy through artistic and educational literary arts events in the Pacific Northwest." Currently has about 150 members. Levels of membership/dues: Basic ($50); Student/Retired ($25); Family ($75); Contributing ($100); Supporting ($500); and Patron ($1,000). Mountain Writers Series offers intensive one-day and 2-day workshops, weekend master classes, 5-week, 8-week, and 10-week courses about writing." Authors who have participated recently include David James Duncan, Linda Gregg, C.K. Williams, Li-Young Lee, Kim Addonizio, and David St. John. Sponsors readings that are open to the public. Nationally and internationally known writers are sponsored by the Mountain Writers Series Northwest Regional Residencies Program (reading tours) and the campus readings program (Pulitzer Prize winners, Nobel Prize winners, MacArthur Fellows, etc.). Additional information available for SASE, by fax, e-mail, or on Web site.

NATIONAL FEDERATION OF STATE POETRY SOCIETIES, INC. (NFSPS)

Web site: www.nfsps.org. Established 1959. "NFSPS is a nonprofit organization exclusively educational and literary. Its purpose is to recognize the importance of poetry with respect to national cultural heritage. It is dedicated solely to the furtherance of poetry on the national level and serves to unite poets in the bonds of fellowship and understanding." Currently has 7,000 members. Any poetry group located in a state not already affiliated, but interested in affiliating, with NFSPS may contact the membership chairman (see Web site). In a state where no valid group exists, help may also be obtained by individuals interested in organizing a poetry group for affiliation. Most reputable state poetry societies are members of the National Federation and advertise their various poetry contests through the NFSPS quarterly newsletter *Strophes* (sample copy available for SASE and $1), edited by Madelyn Eastlund, 310 South Adams St., Beverly Hills FL 34465 (e-mail: verdure@tampab ay.rr.com). **Beware of organizations calling themselves state poetry societies (however named) that are not members of NFSPS, as such labels are sometimes used by vanity schemes trying to sound respectable.** NFSPS holds an annual 3-day convention in a different state each year with workshops, an awards banquet, and addresses by nationally known poets. Sponsors an annual 50-category national contest (see separate listing for NFSPS Competitions in Contests & Awards). Additional information available by e-mail or on Web site.

NATIONAL WRITERS ASSOCIATION

10940 S. Parker Rd., #508, Parker CO 80134. (303)841-0246. Fax: (303)841-2607. E-mail: natlwriters assn@hotmail.com. Web site: www.nationalwriters.com. Established 1937. **Contact:** Sandy Whelchel, executive director. National organization with regional affiliations open to writers. Currently has 3,000 members. Levels of membership/dues: Professional ($85); Regular ($65) and Student ($30). Hosts an annual Summer Conference where workshops, panels, etc., are available to all attendees, including poets. Also offers a yearly poetry writing contest with cash awards of $100, $50, and $25. **Entry fee:** $10/poem. **Deadline:** October 1. Send SASE for judging sheet copies. Publishes *Authorship*, an annual magazine. Sample copy available for 9×12 envelope with $1.21 postage. Available to nonmembers for $20. Additional information available for SASE, by fax, e-mail, or on Web site.

NEVADA POETRY SOCIETY

P.O. Box 7014, Reno NV 89510. (775)322-3619. Established 1976. **Contact:** Sam Wood, president. Statewide organization. Currently has 30 members. Levels of membership/dues: Active and Emeritus ($10). Offerings include membership in the National Federation of State Poetry Societies (NF-

SPS), which includes a subscription to their publication, *Strophes*; monthly challenges followed by critiquing of all new poems; lessons on types of poetry. Members of the society are occasionally called upon to read to organizations or in public meetings. Members meet monthly. Additional information available for SASE. "We advise poets to enter their poems in contests before thinking about publication."

NEW ENGLAND WRITERS

P.O. Box 5, Windsor VT 05089. (802)674-2315. Fax: (802)674-5767. E-mail: newvtpoet@aol.com. Web site: www.newenglandwriters.org. Established 1986. **Contact:** Susan Anthony, director. New England Writers was founded "to encourage precision and ingenuity in the practice of writing and speaking, whatever the form and style." Currently has 500 members. Levels of membership/dues: $10/year (regular); $7/year (senior citizens and students). Publishes the semiannual newsletter, *NewScript*. Sponsors the New England Writers Conference. Additional information available for SASE, by e-mail, or on Web site.

NEW HAMPSHIRE WRITERS' PROJECT

2500 North River Rd., Manchester NH 03106. (603)314-7980. Fax: (603)314-7981. E-mail: info@nh writersproject.org. Web site: www.nhwritersproject.org. Established 1988. **Contact:** Barbara Yoder, executive director. Statewide organization open to writers at all levels in all genres. Currently has 700+ members. Levels of membership/dues: $45/year; $25/year for seniors and students. Offerings include workshops, seminars, an annual conference, and a literary calendar. Sponsors daylong workshops and 4- to 6-week intensive courses. Also sponsors the biennial New Hampshire Literary Awards for outstanding literary achievement (including The Jane Kenyon Award for Outstanding Book of Poetry). Publishes *NH Writer*, a bimonthly newsletter for and about New Hampshire writers. Members and nationally known writers give readings that are open to the public. Additional information available for SASE, by fax, e-mail, or on Web site.

NEW YORK CENTER FOR INDEPENDENT PUBLISHING

The General Society of Mechanics & Tradesmen, 20 W. 44th, New York NY 10036. (212)764-7021. Fax: (212)840-2046. E-mail: info@smallpress.org. Web site: www.smallpress.org. Established 1984. "The Small Press Center is a nonprofit educational program and resource center for independent publishing, as well as a membership organization of independent and small press publishers and their enthusiasts." National organization open to "any person, company, or organization that supports the small press." Levels of membership/dues: Friends Membership ($50 Individual, $75 Dual/Family, $100 Contributing Friends, $250 Literary Benefactors, $300 Corporate Sponsors, $500 Patrons); Publisher Membership ($75 for one year; $100 for 2 years). Membership benefits include the quarterly *Small Press Center Newsletter*; discounts on workshops, lectures, and audiotapes; invitations to readings and special events; and discount on *Books on Writing & Publishing: A Bibliography in Progress*, with 1,700 listings (additional or unique benefits available according to membership type and level). Sponsors the Small Press Book Fair in March and the New York Round Table Writers' Conference (www.writersconferencenyc.org) in April. Offers "a place in which the public may examine and order the books of independent publishers, free from commercial pressures. The Center is open five days a week." Additional information available for SASE, by fax, e-mail, or on Web site.

◎ THE NORTH CAROLINA POETRY SOCIETY (Specialized: NC poets)

Officers change annually; please contact through Web site at www.ncpoetrysociety.org. Established 1932. Purpose is "to foster the writing of poetry; to bring together in meetings of mutual interest and fellowship the poets of North Carolina; to encourage the study, writing, and publication of poetry; and to develop a public taste for the reading and appreciation of poetry." Statewide and out-of-state organization open to "all interested persons." Currently has about 320 members. Levels of membership/dues: Adult ($25/year) and Student ($10/year). NCPS conducts 6 general meetings and numerous statewide workshops each year; sponsors annual poetry contests with categories for adults and students (open to anyone, with small fee for nonmembers; December/January deadline; cash prizes); publishes the contest-winning poems in the annual anthology *Pinesong*; publishes a newsletter; and supports other poetry activities. Also sponsors the annual Brockman/Campbell Book Award for a book of poetry (over 20 pages) by a North Carolina poet (native-born or current resident for 3 years). Prize: $200. **Entry fee:** $10 for nonmembers. **Deadline:** May 1. Competitions receive 300 entries/year. Nationally known writers give readings that are open to the public. Sponsors open mic readings that are open to the public. Additional information available on Web site.

⋈ NORTH CAROLINA WRITERS' NETWORK

P.O. Box 954, Carrboro NC 27510. (919)967-9540. Fax: (919)929-0535. E-mail: mail@ncwriters.org. Web site: www.ncwriters.org. Established 1985. Supports the work of writers, writers' organizations, independent bookstores, little magazines and small presses, and literary programming statewide. Currently has 1,400 members. Levels of membership/dues: $75/year; seniors/students, $55/year. Membership benefits include *The Writers' Network News*, a 24-page bimonthly newsletter containing organizational news, national market information, and other literary material of interest to writers; and access to the NCWN Library & Resource Center, other writers, workshops, writer's residencies, conferences, readings and competitions, and NCWN's critiquing and editing service. Annual fall conference features nationally known writers, publishers, and editors, held in a different North Carolina location each November. Sponsors competitions in short fiction, nonfiction, and poetry for North Carolina residents and NCWN members. Guidelines available for SASE or on Web site.

OHIO POETRY ASSOCIATION

129 Columbus Rd., Fredericktown OH 43019. (740)694-5013. E-mail: bob@poeticaljourneys.com. Web site: www.ohiopoetryassn.com. Established in 1929 as Verse Writers' Guild of Ohio. **Contact:** Bob Casey, president. Promotes the art of poetry, and furthers the support of poets and others who support poetry. Statewide membership with additional members in several other states, Japan, and England. Affiliated with the National Federation of State Poetry Societies (NFSPS). Open to poets and writers of all ages and ability, as well as to non-writing lovers of poetry. Currently has about 215 members. Levels of membership/dues: Regular ($18); Student (including college undergrads, $8); Associate ($8); Senior ($15); Life; and Honorary. Member benefits include regular contests; meeting/workshop participation; assistance with writing projects; networking; twice-yearly magazine, *Common Threads* (see separate listing in Magazines/Journals), publishing only poems by members; quarterly *Ohio Poetry Association Newsletter*; quarterly NFSPS newsletters (*Strophes*); automatic NFSPS membership; and contest information and lower entry fees for NFSPS contests. Members are automatically on the mailing list for Ohio Poetry Day contest guidelines (OPA financially supports Ohio Poetry Day; see separate listing in Contests & Awards). Individual chapters regularly host workshops and seminars. Members and nationally known writers give readings that are open to the public (at quarterly meetings; public is invited). Sponsors open mic readings for members and the public. Past readers have included Lisa Martinovic, David Shevin, Michael Bugeja, David Citino, and Danika Dinsmore. Members meet quarterly (September, December, March, May). Additional information available by e-mail or on Web site. "In short, OPA provides poets with opportunities to share info, critique, publish, sponsor contests, and just socialize."

PEN AMERICAN CENTER

588 Broadway, Suite 303, New York NY 10012. (212)334-1660. E-mail: pen@pen.org. Web site: www.pen.org. Established 1922. PEN American Center "is the largest of the 141 centers of International PEN, the world's oldest human rights organization and the oldest international literary association. PEN American Center works to advance literature, to defend free expression, and to foster international literary fellowship." The 2,900 members of the PEN American Center include poets, playwrights, essayists, editors, novelists (for the original letters in the acronym PEN), as well as translators and those editors and agents who have made a substantial contribution to the literary community. Levels of membership/dues: $75 Member (must meet standard qualifications to become a Member; see Web site); $40 Associate Member and $20 Student (both open to everyone). Membership benefits include subscription to *PEN America Journal*, discounts on admission to pub-

lic programs, discounted access to *Grants and Awards Available to American Writers* (an online database), access to online bulletin board, and more (additional benefits at Member level, including reciprocal privileges in PEN American Center branches and in foreign centers for those traveling abroad). Sponsors public literary programs, forums on current issues, visits by prominent authors to inner-city schools, the promotion of international literature to U.S. readers, and grants and loans to writers with emergency financial need. Publishes *PEN America Journal* (available through Web site and selected bookstores, or by subscription at $18/year); and *Grants and Awards Available to American Writers* online (access available through membership or nonmember subscription of $12/year). Administers the PEN/Joyce Osterwell Award for Poetry for a new and emerging American poet of literary character ($5,000), and the PEN Award for Poetry in Translation ($3,000) for book-length translations of poetry into English from any language. Also sponsors the annual PEN World Voices: The New York Festival of International Literature. Additional information on membership and all programs and activities available on Web site.

PITTSBURGH POETRY EXCHANGE

P.O. Box 4279, Pittsburgh PA 15203. (412)481-POEM. Web site: http://pghpoetryexchange.pghfree. net. **Contact:** Michael Wurster, coordinator. Established 1974. A community-based volunteer organization for local poets, it functions as a service organization and information exchange, conducting ongoing workshops, readings, forums, and other special events to promote poets and poetry. No dues or fees. "Any monetary contributions are voluntary, often from outside sources. We've managed not to let our reach exceed our grasp." Currently has about 30 members (with a mailing list of 300). Reading programs are primarily committed to local and area poets, with honorariums of $25-85. Sponsors a minimum of 3 major events each year in addition to a monthly workshop (first Monday, 8 p.m, City Books); these include reading programs in conjunction with community arts festivals, such as South Side Poetry in October—a series of readings throughout the evening at various shops, galleries, and bookstores. Poets from out of town may contact the Exchange for assistance in setting up readings at bookstores to help sell their books. "We have been partnering with Autumn House Press in co-sponsoring events and bringing some of its authors to town." Members meet on an ongoing basis, at least twice monthly. Additional information available for SASE or on Web site. "Pittsburgh is a very exciting literary town."

▥ POETRY BOOK SOCIETY

4th Floor, 2 Tavistock Place, London WC1H 9RA England. (44)(207)833-9247. E-mail: info@poetry books.co.uk. Web site: www.poetrybooks.co.uk; www.childrenspoetrybookshelf.co.uk; www.poet rybookshoponoline.com. Established 1953. A book club that promotes "the best newly published contemporary poetry to as wide an audience as possible." Levels of membership/dues: £40/year Full Member; £12/year Associate Member; £50/year Full International Member. All members receive a subscription to the quarterly *PBS Bulletin*, 25% discount on almost all poetry books published in the UK, and advance notice of poetry events; Full Members also receive 4 PBS Choice selections free. New members receive a welcome gift. The PBS selectors also recommend other books of special merit each quarter. Sponsors The Children's Poetry Bookshelf (a poetry book club for children ages 7-11) and Poetry Bookshop Online, selling all poetry in print in the UK and Ireland. The Poetry Book Society is subsidized by the Arts Council of England. Additional information available by e-mail or on Web site.

THE POETRY FOUNDATION

444 N. Michigan Ave., Suite 1850, Chicago IL 60611-4034. (312)787-7070. Fax: (312)787-6650. E-mail: mail@poetryfoundation.org. Web site: http://poetryfoundation.org. Established 2003. President: John Barr. The Poetry Foundation is "an independent literary organization committed to a vigorous presence for poetry in our culture. It exists to discover and celebrate the best poetry and to place it before the largest possible audience." Initiatives include publishing *Poetry* magazine (see separate listing in Magazines/Journals); funding and promoting Ted Kooser's American Life in Poetry newspaper project (in partnership with the Library of Congress); funding and promotion of Poetry Out Loud: National Recitation Contest (in partnership with the National Endowment for the

Arts and state arts associations); and commissioning "Poetry in America: A Research Study," the first scientific study of American attitudes toward poetry (available for download from Web site). The Poetry Foundation also added to its existing awards (the Ruth Lilly Poetry Prize, an annual award of $100,000, and the Ruth Lilly Poetry Fellowship, 2 annual awards of $15,000 to young poets to support their further studies in poetry) by establishing a family of prizes called the Pegasus Awards to honor under-recognized poets and types of poetry (The Neglected Masters Award, The Emily Dickinson First Book Award, The Mark Twain Poetry Award, The Randall Jarrell Award in Criticism, The Children's Poet Laureate, and The Verse Drama Award). In addition, The Poetry Foundation established and maintains a major Web site for English-language poetry, which includes access to a major archive of poems, poetry-related articles and essays, a news blog, and other features. Additional information available on Web site.

⊞ ⊕ POETRY LIBRARY

The Saison Poetry Library, Royal Festival Hall, London SE1 8XX UK. (44)(207)921-0943/0664. Fax: (44)(207)921-0939. E-mail: info@poetrylibrary.org.uk. Web site: www.poetrylibrary.org.uk; www.poetrymagazines.org.uk. Established 1953. **Contact:** Chris McCabe and Miriam Valencia, assistant librarians. A "free public library of modern poetry. It contains a comprehensive collection of all British poetry published since 1912 and an international collection of poetry from all over the world, either written in or translated into English. As the United Kingdom's national library for poetry, it offers loan and information services and a large collection of poetry magazines, cassettes, compact discs, videos, records, poem posters, and cards; also press cuttings and photographs of poets."

POETRY SOCIETY OF AMERICA

15 Gramercy Park, New York NY 10003. (212)254-9628. Web site: www.poetrysociety.org. Established 1910. Executive Director: Alice Quinn. The Poetry Society of America is a national nonprofit organization for poets and lovers of poetry. Levels of membership/dues: Student ($25); Member ($45); Supporter ($65); Sustainer ($100); Patron ($250); Benefactor ($500); and Angel ($1,000). All paid members receive *Crossroads: The Journal of the Poetry Society of America*; additional benefits available as membership levels increase. Sponsors readings and lectures as well as the Poetry in Motion program. Provides free-to-join PSA electronic mailing list for news of upcoming events. PSA also sponsors a number of competitions for members and nonmembers.

POETRY SOCIETY OF NEW HAMPSHIRE

31 Reservoir, Farmington NH 03835. (603)332-0732. E-mail: frisella@worldpath.net. Established 1964. **Contact:** Patricia L. Frisella, president. A statewide organization for anyone interested in poetry. Currently has 200 members. Levels of membership/dues: Junior ($10); Regular ($20). Offerings include annual subscription to quarterly magazine, *The Poet's Touchstone*; critiques, contests, and workshops; public readings; and quarterly meetings with featured poets. *The Poet's Touchstone* is available to nonmembers for $4.50 (single issue). Members and nationally known writers give readings that are open to the public. Sponsors open mic readings for members and the public. Additional information available for SASE or by e-mail. "We do sponsor a national contest four times a year with $100, $50, and $25 prizes paid out in each one. People from all over the country enter and win."

THE POETRY SOCIETY OF SOUTH CAROLINA (PSSC)

P.O. Box 1090, Charleston SC 29402. E-mail: poetrysocietysc@aol.com. Web site: www.poetrysocietysc.org. Established 1920. **Contact:** Susan Meyers, president. The Poetry Society of South Carolina supports "the reading, writing, study, and enjoyment of poetry." Statewide organization open to anyone interested in poetry. Offers programs in Charleston that are free and open to the public September-May (except for members-only holiday party in December). Currently has 150 members. Levels of membership/dues: $15 student, $25 individual, $35 family, $50 patron, and $100 business or sponsor. Membership year runs July 1-June 30. Membership benefits include discounts to PSSC-sponsored seminars and workshops held in various SC locations; a copy of the annual *Yearbook* of contest-winning poems; eligibility to read at the open mic and to enter contests without a fee; and an invitation to the annual holiday party. Sponsors a monthly Writers' Group, a January open mic reading featuring PSSC members, a Charleston Poetry Walk during Piccolo Spoleto in June, and a May Forum leading to an audience-selected poetry prize. Sponsors two yearly contests, totaling 20-25 contest categories, some with themes; some are open to all poets, others open only to SC residents or PSSC members. Guidelines available on Web site. **Deadline:** November 15 (Fall round) and February 15 (Spring round). Also offers the Skylark Prize, a competition for SC high school students. Sometimes offers a chapbook competition. Members and nationally known writers give readings that are open to the public. Poets have included Billy Collins, Henry Taylor, Cathy Smith Bowers, and Richard Garcia, as well as emerging poets from the region. Additional information available by e-mail or on Web site.

POETRY SOCIETY OF TENNESSEE

4383 Garner Pl., Bartlett TN 38135. E-mail: mrdcolonel@aol.com. Web site: www.tpstn.org. Established in 1953. **Contact:** Michael Dennington, president. Purpose is "to promote the creative poetry of its members, poetry in the community, improving poetry writing skills, and creative poetry among young people." Statewide, "but we have some associate members out of state." Affiliated with the National Federation of State Poetry Societies (NFSPS). Organization open to anyone interested in poetry. Currently has 115 members. Levels of membership/dues: $20/year for adults; $5 for students. Offerings include monthly speakers, contests, and poetry readings; an annual poetry festival; and 2 student poetry contests each year. Sponsors conferences/workshops. "We publish a yearly anthology of poems, *Tennessee Voices*, that has won in various festival, monthly, and special contests." Also publishes a newsletter called *Tennessee Voices* 4-6 times/year as needed; contains information on meetings and speakers, contests and winners, various activities, etc. Not available to nonmembers. "We have readings four times a year at various bookstores and restaurants in Memphis. Nonmembers are invited to participate also." Additional information available for SASE, by e-mail, or on Web site. "Our meetings are held at 2 p.m. on the first Saturday of each month from September through May at the Evergreen Presbyterian Church across from the campus of Rhodes College in Memphis." Contest brochure available after June 1 for SASE or on Web site.

THE POETRY SOCIETY OF TEXAS

7231 Alto Caro Dr., Dallas TX 75248. (972)490-4605. E-mail: dallasstacy@sbcglobal.net. Web site: www.poetrysocietyoftexas.org. **Contact:** Marilyn Stacy. Established 1921. "The purpose of the society shall be to secure fuller public recognition of the art of poetry, to encourage the writing of poetry by Texans, and to kindle a finer and more intelligent appreciation of poetry, especially the work of living poets who interpret the spirit and heritage of Texas." Poetry Society of Texas is a member of the National Federation of State Poetry Societies (NFSPS). Has 25 chapters in cities throughout the state. Currently has 300 members. Levels of membership/dues: Active ($25) for native Texans, Citizens of Texas, or former Citizens of Texas who were active members; Associate ($25) for all who desire to affiliate; also Student ($12.50); Sustaining; Benefactors; and Patrons of the Poets. Offerings include annual contests with prizes in excess of $5,000 as well as monthly contests (general and humorous); 8 monthly meetings; annual awards banquet; annual summer conference in a different location each year; round-robin critiquing opportunities sponsored at the state level; and Poetry in Schools with contests at state and local chapter levels. "Our monthly state meetings are held at the Preston Royal Branch of the Dallas Public Library. Our annual awards banquet is held at the Crown Plaza Suites in Dallas. Our summer conference is held at a site chosen by the hosting chapter. Chapters determine their meeting sites." PST publishes *A Book of the Year*, which presents annual and monthly award-winning poems, coming contest descriptions, minutes of meetings, by-laws of the society, history, and information. Also publishes the *Poetry Society of Texas Bulletin*, a monthly newsletter that features statewide news documenting contest winners, state meeting information, chapter and individual information, news from the NFSPS, and announcements of coming activities and offerings for poets. "*A Book of the Year* is available to nonmembers for $8." Members and nationally known writers give readings. "All of our meetings are open to the public." Additional information available for SASE, by e-mail, or on Web site.

⊕ THE POETRY SOCIETY

22 Betterton St., London WC2H 9BX United Kingdom. (44)(207)420-9880. Fax: (44)(207)240-4818. E-mail: info@poetrysociety.org.uk. Web site: www.poetrysociety.org.uk. Established 1909. One of Britain's most dynamic arts organizations, with membership open to all. "The Poetry Society exists to help poets and poetry thrive in Britain today. Our members come from all over the world, and their support enables us to promote poetry on a global scale." Publishes *Poetry Review* (see separate listing in Magazines/Journals), Britain's most prominent poetry magazine, and *Poetry News*, the Society's newsletter, as well as books and posters to support poetry in the classroom. Runs the National Poetry Competition (see separate listing in Contests & Awards) and The Foyle Young Poets of the Year Award (for poets aged 11-17), as well as many other competitions, services, and education projects for readers and writers of poetry. "Visit the Web site for a full idea of the range of activities The Poetry Society is engaged with."

POETS & WRITERS, INC.

90 Broad St., Suite 2100, New York NY 10004. (212)226-3586. Web site: www.pw.org. Established 1970. Poets & Writers' mission is "to foster the professional development of poets and writers, to promote communication throughout the U.S. literary community, and to help create an environment in which literature can be appreciated by the widest possible public." The largest nonprofit literary organization in the nation, P&W offers information, support, resources, and exposure to poets, fiction writers, and nonfiction writers at all stages in their careers. Sponsors the Readings/ Workshops Program, through which P&W sponsors more than 1,700 literary events in New York, California, and other cities in the U.S. Publishes the online *Directory of American Poets and Writers* with a searchable database of over 7,000 writers; *Poets & Writers Magazine* (print); and *Poets & Writers Online*, whichoffers topical information, the Speakeasy Message Forum (a central meeting place for writers), and links to over 1,500 Web sites of interest to writers. Sponsors the Writers Exchange Contest (emerging poets and fiction writers are introduced to literary communities outside their home states); the Jacobson Poetry Prize ($50,000 award for an early to mid-career poet; no nominations accepted); the Barnes & Noble Writers for Writers Award; and the Amy Award (see separate listing in Contests & Awards).

POETS HOUSE

594 Broadway, Ste 510, New York NY 10012. (212)431-7920. Fax: (212)431-8131. E-mail: info@poet shouse.org. Web site: www.poetshouse.org. **Note: Poets House will to Battery Park City in Fall 2008; see Web site for details.** Established 1985. Poets House, a national poetry library and literary center, is a "home for all who read and write poetry." Levels of membership/dues: begin at $40/ year; along with other graduated benefits, each new or renewing member receives free admission to all regularly scheduled programs. Resources include the 50,000-volume poetry collection, conference room, exhibition space, and a Children's Room. Over 200 annual public programs include panel discussions and lectures, readings, seminars and workshops, and The People's Poetry Gathering. In addition, Poets House continues its collaboration with public library systems, Poetry in The Branches, a multi-faceted program model to help libraries nationwide create a complete environment for poetry locally (see Web site for information). Finally, each April Poets House hosts the Poets House Showcase, a comprehensive exhibit of the year's new poetry releases from commercial, university, and independent presses across the country. (**Note: Poets House is not a publisher.**) Copies of new titles become part of the library collection, and comprehensive listings for each of the books are added to *Directory of American Poetry Books*, a free, searchable online database featuring over 20,000 poetry titles published 1996-2007. "Poets House depends, in part, on tax-deductible contributions of its nationwide members." Additional information available by fax, e-mail, or on Web site.

QUINCY WRITERS GUILD

1282 W Lakeshore Dr, Fowler, IL 62338. (217)885-3327. E-mail: chillebr@adams.net. Established 1989. **Contact:** Carol Hillebrenner, treasurer. Purpose is "to encourage writers to write and, if they wish, get published." Regional organization open to all those who love to write and want mutual support in their passion. Currently has 18 members. Levels of membership/dues: $15/year. Offers "support, encouragement, whatever information we can gather for each other, and an occasional newsletter and special speakers on the writing craft." Meets at Bickford Cottage the first Monday of most months. Sponsors conferences/workshops. Publishes a newsletter about upcoming meetings and "anything the editor thinks might interest others." E-mail newsletter is free for one year. Additional information available by e-mail.

◎ SCIENCE FICTION POETRY ASSOCIATION (Specialized: science fiction, fantasy, horror)

PO Box 4846, Covina, CA 91723. E-mail: SFPATreasurer@gmail.com. Web site: www.sfpoetry.com. Established 1978. **Contact:** Samantha Henderson, treasurer. The Science Fiction Poetry Association was founded "to bring together poets and readers interested in science fiction poetry (poetry with some element of speculation, usually science fiction, fantasy, or horror)." Levels of membership/dues: $21 USD (U.S., Canada, Mexico) for one-year memberships/renewals; $25 USD for overseas. Membership benefits include 6 issues/year of *Star*Line* (see separate listing in Magazines/Journals), a journal filled with poetry, reviews, articles, and more; one issue of the annual *Rhysling Anthology* of the best science fiction poetry of the previous year; opportunity to nominate one short poem and one long poem to be printed in the anthology, and to vote for which poems should receive that year's Rhysling award; half-priced advertising on the SFPA Web site, with greater subject matter leeway than non-members; eligibility to vote for SFPA officers (or run for officer); mailings with the latest news. Additional information available on Web site.

⊕ SCOTTISH POETRY LIBRARY

5 Crichton's Close, Edinburgh EH8 8DT Scotland. (44)(131)557-2876. Fax: (44)(131)557-8393. E-mail: inquiries@apl.org.uk. Web site: www.spl.org.uk. **Contact:** Julie Johnstone, librarian. Director: Robyn Marsack. A reference information source and free lending library; also lends by post and from its 13 outreach collections. Arranges poetry-writing workshops throughout Scotland, mainly for young people. The library has a web-based catalog available at www.spl.org.uk, which allows searches of all the library's resources, including books, magazines, and audio material—over 10,000 items of Scottish and international poetry. Need not be a member to borrow material; memberships available strictly to support the library's work. Levels of membership/dues: £20 individual; £10 concessionary; £30 organizational. Benefits include semiannual newsletter, annual report, new publications listings, book offers, special events, and use of members' room at the library. The School of Poets is open to anyone; "at meetings, members divide into small groups in which each participant reads a poem, which is then analyzed and discussed." Meetings normally take place at 7:30 p.m. on the second Tuesday of each month at the library. Also offers a Critical Service in which groups of up to 6 poems, not exceeding 200 lines in all, are given critical comment by members of the School: 15 for each critique (with SAE). Publishes the *Scottish Poetry Index*, a multi-volume indexing series, photocopied, spiral-bound, that indexes poetry and poetry-related material in selected Scottish literary magazines from 1952 to present; an audio CD of contemporary Scottish poems, *The Jewel Box* (January 2000); and various anthologies available from www.spl.org.uk. A wide range of poetry events takes place throughout the year. Additional information available by e-mail or on Web site.

SMALL PUBLISHERS ASSOCIATION OF NORTH AMERICA (SPAN)

P.O. Box 1306, Buena Vista CO 81211. (719)475-1726. Fax: (719)471-2182. E-mail: info@spannet.org. Web site: www.spannet.org. **Contact:** Scott Flora, executive director. Established 1996. Founded to "advance the image and profits of independent publishers and authors through education and marketing opportunities." Open to "authors, small- to medium-sized publishers, and the vendors who serve them." Currently has 1,300 members. Levels of membership /dues: Regular ($95/year); Associate Vendor ($120/year). Offers marketing ideas, sponsors annual conference. Publishes *SPAN Connection*, "a 24-page monthly newsletter jam-packed with informative, money-making articles." Available to nonmembers for $8/issue. Additional information available for SASE, by fax, or on Web site.

◎ TANKA SOCIETY OF AMERICA

1636 Edward's Dr., Point Roberts WA 98281. E-mail: macrury@whidbey.com. Web site: www.tank asocietyofamerica.com. Established 2000. **Contact:** Carole MacRury, secretary. The Tanka Society of America, a nonprofit volunteer organization, aims to further the writing, reading, study, and appreciation of tanka poetry in English. Open to anyone interested in tanka. Membership dues for USA, Canada, and International are available on Web site. Membership offerings include the quarterly *Ribbons: Tanka Society of America Journal* (see separate listing in Magazines/Journals) and eligibility to submit poems to annual members' anthology. The Tanka Society of American also conducts an annual international tanka competition with cash awards and publication of winning poems. Additional information available by e-mail or on Web site.

UNIVERSITY OF ARIZONA POETRY CENTER

1508 E. Helen St., P.O. Box 210150, Tucson AZ 85721. (520)626-3765. Fax: (520)621-5566. E-mail: poetry@u.arizona.edu. Web site: www.poetrycenter.arizona.edu. **Contact:** Gail Browne, executive director. Established 1960. Open to the public, the University of Arizona Poetry Center is a contemporary poetry archive and a nationally acclaimed poetry collection that includes over 60,000 items. Programs and services include a library with a noncirculating poetry collection and space for small classes; poetry-related meetings and activities; facilities, research support, and referral information about poetry and poets for local and national communities; Reading Series; community creative writing classes and workshops; bilingual Poets-in-Preschools program; high school poet-in-residence; a one-month summer residency offered each year to an emerging writer selected by jury; and poetry awards, readings, and special events for high school, undergraduate, and graduate students. Additional information available for SASE, by fax, e-mail, or on Web site. "One can become a 'Friend of the Poetry Center' by making an annual contribution."

THE UNTERBERG POETRY CENTER OF THE 92ND STREET Y

1395 Lexington Ave., New York NY 10128. (212)415-5759. E-mail: unterberg@92y.org. Web site: www.92y.org/poetry. Established 1939. The Unterberg Poetry Center offers "students of all ages the opportunity to hone their skills as writers and deepen their appreciation as readers." Offers annual series of readings by major literary figures (weekly readings late September through May), writing workshops, master classes in fiction and poetry, and lectures and literary seminars. Also co-sponsors the "Discovery" Poetry Contest (see separate listing in Contests & Awards).

WASHINGTON POETS ASSOCIATION

Web site: www.washingtonpoets.org. Established 1971. **Contact:** president. The Washington Poets Association seeks to "serve and inspire individuals and communities across the state by supporting the creation, presentation, and appreciation of poetry through events, publications, recognition, and education." Regional organization open to poets and fans of poetry. Currently has 345 members. Levels of membership/dues: $15/year. Membership benefits include e-newsletter; discounted admission to Burning Word Festival and other events; ability to submit to WPA anthology, Cascade Journal (plus one free copy and discounts on the purchase of additional copies); and advance notification of contests, events, readings, and publishing opportunities. Sponsors conferences/workshops, including the annual Burning Word Festival (see separate listing in Conferences, Workshops & Festivals). Also sponsors On the Road poetry workshops for underserved areas in Washington state. Sponsors the Washington Poets Association Annual Poetry Contest (see separate listing in Contests & Awards). Publishes quarterly newsletter, *Word!*; available to nonmembers free on Web site. Members and nationally known writers give readings that are open to the public. Sponsors open mic readings for the public "scheduled weekly, monthly, and quarterly at venues across the state." Additional information available on Web site.

⚡ WEST VIRGINIA POETRY SOCIETY (WVPS)

% Holly Cross, president, PO Box 295, Nitro WV 25143. E-mail: wvpoetry@yahoo.com. Web site: http://www.wvpoetrysociety.org/. Established 1950. **Contact:** Holly Cross, president. "Our purpose: To encourage creative writing and an appreciation of poetry; to foster the establishment of active community chapters of WVPS." Has statewide, regional, and national membership; "not limited to West Virginia residents." Affiliated with the National Federation of State Poetry Societies (NFSPS). Open to "all poets and lovers of poetry." Currently has about 250 members. Levels of membership/dues: $20, local/community chapters of WVPS. Membership benefits include *WV Crossroads*, a quarterly newsletter; annual poetry contests; state and national conventions "with outstanding presenters"; and state membership automatically includes membership in NFSPS. Sponsors conferences/workshops and contests/awards. Members also receive *Laurels*, a quarterly anthology, and the NFSPS newsletter, *Strophes*. Members and nationally known writers give readings that are open to the public. Sponsors "annual contests with hundreds of dollars in prize money across thirty categories. Members enter for free, non-members pay a small fee. Information is on the Web site and is sent out to members in brochure form. We will also send the brochure to anyone if they send an SASE." Also sponsors open mic readings for members and the public. "Meetings and annual conventions may be attended by nonmembers. Many readings are in conjunction with special occasions such as National Poetry Month/Day." Local chapters of WVPS meet monthly and at the annual convention (state and national). "WVPS exists to raise awareness of the incredibly talented poets in our state, to network with poets all over the world, to encourage the instruction of poetry in public schools, to support one another and improve our craft. Many people find that if they pay the $20 to join WVPS their money will go much further. If you enter 20 or more categories in the annual contests (state and national), you might as well go ahead and join WVPS, submit the poems for free, and gain all of the other added benefits of membership. Don't hesitate to contact me with any questions, concerns, ideas, or suggestions you may have. I try to be as accessible to the members as possible. We have a strong group of very supportive people who know their stuff. If you would like to be part of such a group, join us!"

WISCONSIN FELLOWSHIP OF POETS
E-mail: kppi2105@sbcglobal.net. Web site: www.wfop.org. Established 1950. **Contact:** Peter Piaskoski, Membership Chair, 2105 E. Lake Bluff Blvd., Shorewood WI 53211. President: Peter Sherrill. Statewide organization open to residents and former residents of Wisconsin who are interested in the aims and endeavors of the organization. Currently has 450 members. Levels of membership/dues: Active ($25); Student ($12.50). Sponsors biannual conferences, workshops, contests and awards. Publishes *Wisconsin Poets' Calendar*, poems of Wisconsin (resident) poets. Also publishes *Museletter*, a quarterly newsletter. Members or nationally known writers give readings that are open to the public. Sponsors open mic readings. Additional information available for SASE to WFOP membership chair at the above address, by e-mail, or on Web site.

THE WORD WORKS
P.O. Box 42164, Washington DC 20015. E-mail: editor@wordworksdc.com. Web site: www.wordworksdc.com. Established 1974. **Contact:** Karren L. Alenier, president. Word Works is "a nonprofit literary organization publishing contemporary poetry in single-author editions, usually in collaboration with a visual artist." Levels of membership/dues: $35 (basic), $50 (sustaining). Membership benefits at the basic level include choice of 2 books from The Word Works book list, newsletter, and 20% discount on additional book orders; in addition to these benefits, sustaining members are eligible for on-line critique of several poems (member needs access to an e-mail account). Sponsors an ongoing poetry reading series, educational programs, and the Hilary Tham Capital Collection (publishing mostly poets from metropolitan Washington, DC). Sponsors The Washington Prize and The Jacklyn Potter Young Poets Competition (see separate listings in Contests & Awards). Additional information available on Web site.

THE WRITER'S CENTER
4508 Walsh St., Bethesda MD 20815. (301)654-8664. Fax: (801)730-6233. E-mail: postmaster@writer.org. Web site: www.writer.org. Established 1976. **Contact:** Gregory Robison, executive director. Voluntary, membership organization open to all skill levels. "The Writer's Center is a nonprofit community of writers supporting each other in the creation and marketing of literary texts." Levels of membership/dues: $40/year individual; $25/year full-time student; $50/year family. Annually

conducts hundreds of workshops; hosts literary events, readings, and conferences; publishes *Writer's Carousel*, a quarterly magazine of articles and writing news for members. Also publishes *Poet Lore*, America's oldest poetry journal (see separate listing in Magazines/Journals). Additional information available by e-mail or on Web site.

✪ ✪ ◎ WRITERS GUILD OF ALBERTA

11759 Groat Rd., Edmonton AB T5M 3K6 Canada. (780)422-8174. Fax: (780)422-2663. E-mail: mail@writersguild.ab.ca. Web site: www.writersguild.ab.ca. Established 1980. Founded to "provide a community of writers which exists to support, encourage, and promote writers and writing; to safeguard the freedom to write and read; and to advocate for the well-being of writers." Provincial organization open to emerging and professional writers. Currently has over 1,000 members. Offerings include retreats/conferences; monthly events; bimonthly magazine that includes articles on writing and a market section; weekly electronic bulletin with markets and event listings; and the Stephan G. Stephansson Award for Poetry (Alberta residents only). Additional information available by phone, e-mail, or on Web site.

THE WRITERS ROOM

740 Broadway, 12th Floor, New York NY 10003. (212)254-6995. Fax: (212)533-6059. E-mail: writers room@writersroom.org. Web site: www.writersroom.org. Established 1978. Provides a "home away from home" for any writer who needs space to work. Open 24 hours a day, 7 days a week, **for members only**. Currently has about 350 members. Emerging and established writers may apply. Levels of membership/dues: vary from $400 to $600/half year, plus one-time initiation fee of $75. Large loft provides desk space, Internet access, storage, and more. Call for application or download from Web site.

✪ WRITERS' FEDERATION OF NOVA SCOTIA

1113 Marginal Rd., Halifax NS B3H 4P7 Canada. (902)423-8116. Fax: (902)422-0881. E-mail: talk@writers.ns.ca. Web site: www.writers.ns.ca. Established 1975. **Contact:** Jane Buss, executive director. Pupose is "to foster creative writing and the profession of writing in Nova Scotia; to provide advice and assistance to writers at all stages of their careers; and to encourage greater public recognition of Nova Scotian writers and their achievements." Regional organization open to anybody who writes. Currently has 800 members. Levels of membership/dues: $40 CAD annually ($20 CAD students). Offerings include resource library with over 2,500 titles, promotional services, workshop series, annual festivals, manuscript reading service, and contract advice. Sponsors the Atlantic Writing Competition for unpublished works by beginning writers, and the annual Atlantic Poetry Prize for the best book of poetry by an Atlantic Canadian. Publishes *Eastword*, a bimonthly newsletter containing "a plethora of information on who's doing what; markets and contests; and current writing events and issues." Members and nationally known writers give readings that are open to the public. Additional information available on Web site.

✪ ✪ THE WRITERS' UNION OF CANADA (Specialized: Canadian citizens or landed immigrants only)

90 Richmond St. East, Suite 200, Toronto ON M5C 1P1 Canada. (416)703-8982. Fax: (416)504-9090. E-mail: info@writersunion.ca. Web site: www.writersunion.ca. Established 1973. Dedicated to advancing the status of Canadian writers by protecting the rights of published authors, defending the freedom to write and publish, and serving its members. National organization open to poets who have had a trade book published by a commercial or university press; must be a Canadian citizen or landed immigrant. Currently has over 1,600 members. Levels of membership/dues: $185 CAD/year. Offerings include contact with peers, contract advice/negotiation, grievance support, and electronic communication. Sponsors conferences/workshops. Sponsors Annual General Meeting, usually held in May, where members debate and determine Union policy, elect representatives, attend workshops, socialize, and renew friendships with their colleagues from across the country. Publishes *The Writers' Union of Canada Newsletter* 4 times/year. Regional reps meet with members when possible. For writers not eligible for membership, the Union offers, for a fee, publications on

publishing, contracts, and more; a Manuscript Evaluation Service for any level writer; Contract Services, including a Self-Help Package; and 3 annual writing competitions for developing writers. Additional information available for SASE (or SAE and IRC), by fax, e-mail, or on Web site.

W.B. YEATS SOCIETY OF NEW YORK

National Arts Club, 15 Gramercy Park S, New York NY 10003. Web site: www.YeatsSociety.org. Established 1990. **Contact:** Andrew McGowan, president. Founded ''to promote the legacy of Irish poet and Nobel Laureate William Butler Yeats through an annual program of lectures, readings, poetry competition, and special events.'' National organization open to anyone. Currently has 450 members. Levels of membership/dues: $25/year; $15/year students. Sponsors The W.B. Yeats Society Annual Poetry Competition (see separate listing in Contests & Awards). Also sponsors conferences/ workshops. Each April, presents an all-day Saturday program, ''A Taste of Yeats Summer School in Ireland.'' Nationally known writers give readings that are open to the public. Members meet approximately monthly, September to June. Additional information available on Web site.

ADDITIONAL ORGANIZATIONS

The following listings also contain information about organizations. Turn to the page numbers indicated for details about their offerings.

Resources

Resources

Additional Resources

This section lists publications and Web sites that focus on information about writing and publishing poetry. While few provide markets for your work, some of these resources do identify promising leads for your submission efforts. You'll also find advice on craft, poet interviews, reviews of books and chapbooks, events calendars and other valuable material. For print publications, we provide contact information; however, you may also find these publications in your library or bookstore or be able to order them through your favorite online booksellers.

These symbols may appear at the beginning of some listings: The (N) symbol indicates a recently established resource new to *Poet's Market*; the (✗) symbol indicates this resource did not appear in the 2008 edition; the (✦) symbol denotes a Canadian resource and the (⊕) symbol one headquartered outside the U.S. and Canada.

Internet resources for poetry continue to grow, and there are far too many to list here. However, among the following listings you'll find those key sites every poet should bookmark. Although we confirmed every address at press time, URLs can become outdated quickly; if a site comes up "not found," enter the name of the site in a search engine to check for a new address.

Some listings in the other sections of this book include references to informative print publications (such as handbooks and newsletters) and online resources. We've cross-referenced these markets in the Additional Resources of Interest list at the end of this section. To find out more about a resource associated with one of these markets, go to that market's page number.

THE ACADEMY OF AMERICAN POETS

Web site: www.poets.org. One of the most comprehensive poetry Web sites on the Internet.

ALIENFLOWER

Web site: www.alienflower.org. Where poets to share ideas about poetry and its place in society; includes advice, articles, exercises, and The Modern Poet's I Ching.

☑ AMERICAN LIFE IN POETRY

Web site: www.americanlifeinpoetry.org. A project initiated by Ted Kooser, former U.S. Poet Laureate, to provide newspapers and online publications with a free weekly column featuring a brief poem by a contemporary American poet, with introductory commentary by Kooser. Funded and supported by The Poetry Foundation (publisher of *Poetry* magazine) in partnership with the Library of Congress. Current and archived columns are available on the website or by weekly e-mail (free registration available online). **Does not consider unsolicited poetry submissions.**

ASK.COM

Web site: www.ask.com. Internet search engine.

ASSOCIATION OF WRITERS AND WRITING PROGRAMS (AWP)

Web site: www.awpwriter.org. Home site for AWP; offers membership information, AWP contest guidelines, articles and advice, and career links for writing and publishing. Also links to the Writers' Conferences & Centers (WC&C) online resource. AWP publishes *The Writer's Chronicle*. (See separate listing for Association of Writers and Writing Programs in the Organizations section.)

⚏ CANADA POST

Web site: www.canadapost.ca. Provides all necessary information about postal mail to, from, and within Canada. Includes *Canada Postal Guide* online (several chapters printable as PDF).

⚏ CANADIAN POETRY: STUDIES, DOCUMENTS, REVIEW

Dept. of English, University of Western Ontario, London ON N6A 3K7 Canada. E-mail: canadianpoet ry@uwo.ca. Web site: www.canadianpoetry.ca. **Contact:** Prof. D.M.R. Bentley, general editor; R.J. Shroyer, associate editor. Established 1977. A refereed journal devoted to the study of poetry from all periods in Canada, published semiannually (Spring/Summer and Fall/Winter). Subscription: $15 CAD. **Publishes no poetry except as quotations in articles.** Also offers Canadian Poetry Press Scholarly Editions. Details available for SASE or on Web site.

CAVE CANEM

Web site: www.cavecanempoets.org. Site for the Cave Canem group offers "A Home for Black Poetry" on the Internet. Includes information about Cave Canem programs, publications, and calendar; an online newsletter and forum; and extensive links. (See separate listings in the Contests & Awards and Conferences & Workshops sections.)

COUNCIL OF LITERARY MAGAZINES & PRESSES (CLMP)

154 Christopher St., Suite 3C, New York NY 10014. (212)741-9110. E-mail: info@clmp.org. Web site: www.clmp.org. Established 1967. Dedicated "to supporting and actively promoting the field of independent literary publishing." Online resources for nonmembers include a thorough Frequently Asked Questions (FAQ) section covering CLMP, writing, and publishing; a Literary Landscape section offering information about independent publishing and an index to member journals and publishers; a comprehensive links page; and information about joining CLMP. (See separate listing in Organizations section.)

DOGPILE

Web site: www.dogpile.com. Uses metasearch technology to "search the search engines" and return results from Google, Yahoo! Search, MSN, Ask.com, About, MIVA, LookSmart, and more.

DUSTBOOKS

P.O. Box 100, Paradise CA 95967. (800)477-6110. Fax: (530)877-0222. E-mail: publisher@dustbooks.com. Web site: www.dustbooks.com. Dustbooks publishes a number of books useful to writers. Send SASE for catalog or check website. Regular publications include *The International Directory of Little Magazines & Small Presses*, published annually with 900 pages of magazine and book publisher listings, plus subject and regional indexes. *Directory of Poetry Publishers* has similar information for over 2,000 poetry markets. *Small Press Review* is a bimonthly magazine carrying updates of listings in *The International Directory*, small press needs, news, announcements, and reviews.

ELECTRONIC POETRY CENTER

Web site: http://epc.buffalo.edu. Online resource offering links to magazines, presses, blogs, and other sites of interest on the Internet; includes an international digital poetry festival.

GOOGLE

Web site: www.google.com. Internet search engine; includes hundreds of user groups for/about poets and poetry.

HAIKU SOCIETY OF AMERICA

Web site: www.hsa-haiku.org. Includes membership and organization information, submission guidelines for *Frogpond* (HSA's quarterly magazine), contest guidelines, announcements, haiku and senryu archives, links, and more.

INDEPENDENT PUBLISHER ONLINE

Jenkins Group Inc., 1129 Woodmere, Traverse City MI 49686. (800)706-4636 or (231)933-0445 (main). E-mail: online form. Web site: www.independentpublisher.com. **Contact:** Jim Barnes, managing editor. For 25 years, the mission at *Independent Publisher* has been to recognize and encourage the work of publishers who exhibit the courage and creativity necessary to take chances, break new ground, and bring about change in the world of publishing. The Independent Publisher Book Awards, conducted annually to honor the year's best independently published titles (including poetry), accept entries from independent publishers worldwide who publish for the North American market, ranging from self-publishers to major university presses. The "IPPY" Awards were launched in 1996 to bring increased recognition to unsung titles published by independent authors and publishers.

INTERNAL REVENUE SERVICE

Web site: www.irs.ustreas.gov. Includes U.S. federal tax information, resources, publications, and forms for individuals and businesses.

⊕ KUDOS, FOR PEOPLE WHO PRIZE WRITING

(formerly Competitions Bulletin) 17 Greenhow Ave., West Kirby, Wirral CH48 5EL England. E-mail: carolebaldock@hotmail.com. Established 2000. **Contact:** Carole Baldock, editor. Publishes information about contests, anthology collections, etc., as well as details of magazines (particularly new ones), requests for submissions, and publication opportunities. "Details of well over £100,000 in prize money each issue, 50-plus competitions for poetry, around 40 for short stories. Plus collections, anthologies, playwriting, nonfiction, books, etc." *Competitions Bulletin* is 28 pages, digest-sized, professionally printed. For convenience, can be e-mailed overseas as a PDF file. Single copy: £2.50 UK; Overseas, €5, $7; subscription: 6 issues pa, £15 UK; Overseas, £20, €30, $40 USD.

▣ THE LEAGUE OF CANADIAN POETS

Web site: www.poets.ca. Web site includes membership information, details of League programs and projects, an online members' catalog, guidelines to League-sponsored contests, bookstore and gift shop, links, and much more. (See separate listing in Organizations.)

THE LIBRARY OF CONGRESS

Web site: www.loc.gov/poetry. The poetry pages on the Web site of The Poetry & Literature Center of the Library of Congress feature links to information about U.S. Poet Laureates past and present; a list of readings, news, and events related to poetry; an online search for recorded poetry archives at the Library of Congress; Webcasts of 2 series, *Poet Vision* and *The Poet and the Poem*; links to the Poetry 180 Project (promoting poetry to high school students) and The Learning Page (with extensive resources, Internet links, and lesson plans to help educators explore literature and poetry with their students); and much more.

🌐 LIGHT'S LIST OF LITERARY MAGAZINES

Web site: www.bluechrome.co.uk (for orders). Established 1986. *Light's List* is an annual publication that lists 1,500 small press magazines publishing creative writing in English and artwork. Listings consist of names, addresses, prices, page counts, frequency, and brief notes of interest for magazines published in the United Kingdom, Europe, United States, Canada, Australia, Africa, and Asia. The 22nd edition (2007) is the first to be published by bluechrome. Single copy: £7.99. Editor John Light can be reached at Photon Press, 37 The Meadows, Berwick-Upon-Tweed, Northumberland TD15 1NY England; (44)(1289)306523; photon.press@virgin.net; www.photonpress.co.uk **(information only, no orders)**.

NATIONAL FEDERATION OF STATE POETRY SOCIETIES (NFSPS)

Web site: www.nfsps.org. Site for this national umbrella organization includes NFSPS contest information, contact information and links to affiliated state poetry societies, and an online version of the quarterly newsletter *Strophes*.

NEW YORK CENTER FOR INDEPENDENT PUBLISHING

20 West 44th St., New York NY 10036. (212)764-7021. E-mail: nycip@nycip.org. Web site: www.nycip.org. Provides information to and about independent and small publishers. "The Small Press Center provides access to education and expertise in the field of independent publishing, encouraging excellence and free expression in publishing through workshops, lectures, book fairs, exhibits, and a reference collection. The Center is committed to preserving the craft and art of publishing through a library dedicated to its history." Web site includes resources, publisher news, and member directory. (See separate listing in Organizations.)

PARNASSUS: POETRY IN REVIEW

205 W. 89th St., #8F, New York NY 10024-1835. (212)362-3492. Fax: (212)875-0148. Web site: www.parnassuspoetry.com. Established 1972. **Contact:** Herbert Leibowitz, publisher/editor. *Parnassus: Poetry in Review* provides "comprehensive and in-depth coverage of new books of poetry, including translations from foreign poetry." Subscription: $24/year for individuals, $46/year for libraries. Back issues available; see website. Make checks payable to Poetry in Review Foundation. **Not open to unsolicited poetry.**

THE POET'S CORNER

Web site: www.theotherpages.org/poems. Text site that includes 6,725 works by 780 poets, plus poet bios and photos, indexes, and The Daily Poetry Break.

POETRY DAILY

Web site: www.poems.com. Established in 1997, Poetry Daily presents a new poem every day from a recently published book or journal, a weekly prose feature, plus news, reviews, and special features. Register online for a free weekly e-mail newsletter. Poetry Daily is published by the Poetry Daily Association, a not-for-profit organization supported by tax deductible contributions, sponsorships, and grants.

THE POETRY FOUNDATION

444 North Michigan Ave., Suite 1850, Chicago IL 60611-4034. (312)787-7070. Fax: (312)787-6650. E-mail: mail@poetryfoundation.org. Web site: http://www.poetryfoundation.org. Established

2003. John Barr, president. The Poetry Foundation is an independent literary organization "committed to a vigorous presence for poetry in our culture. It exists to discover and celebrate the best poetry and to place it before the largest possible audience. Initiatives include publishing *Poetry* magazine (see separate listing in Magazines/Journals); funding and promoting Ted Kooser's American Life in Poetry newspaper project (in partnership with the University of Nebraska at Lincoln); funding and promotion of Poetry Out Loud: National Recitation Contest (in partnership with the National Endowment for the Arts and state arts associations); funding the News Hour with Jim Lehrer Poetry series, an exploration of the role of poetry in society including profiles of contemporary poets and current debates and issues in poetry; and commissioning "Poetry in America: A Research Study," the first scientific study of American attitudes toward poetry (available for download from website). The Poetry Foundation also added to its existing awards (the Ruth Lilly Poetry Prize, an annual award of $100,000, and the Ruth Lilly Poetry Fellowship, 5 annual awards of $15,000 to young poets to support their further studies in poetry (The Neglected Masters Award, The Emily Dickinson First Book Award, The Mark Twain Poetry Award, The Randall Jarrell Award in Criticism, The Children's Poet Laureate, and The Verse Drama Award). In addition, The Poetry Foundation established and maintains www.poetryfoundation.org, a comprehensive online resource featuring a free archive of more than 6,500 poems, poetry-related articles and essays, a poetry best-seller list, poetry news, a blog, poetry videos, and several podcasts. Additional information available on website.

POETRY SOCIETY OF AMERICA
Web site: www.poetrysociety.org. Includes membership and award information, poet resources, and more. (See separate listing in Organizations.)

THE POETRY SOCIETY
22 Betterton St., London WC2H 9BX United Kingdom. (44)(207)420-9880. Fax: (44)(207)240-4818. E-mail: info@poetrysociety.org.uk. Web site: www.poetrysociety.org.uk. Established 1909. One of Britain's most dynamic arts organizations. Web site offers membership information, events calendar, links, news, Society contest guidelines, the "Poetry Landmarks of Britain" interactive map, and much more. (See separate listing in Organizations.)

POETS & WRITERS ONLINE
Web site: www.pw.org. Includes searchable *Directory of American Poets and Writers*, excerpts from *Poets & Writers Magazine*, informational resources, and more. (See separate listing for Poets & Writers, Inc. in Organizations.)

PUSHCART PRESS
P.O. Box 380, Wainscott NY 11975. (631)324-9300. **Contact:** Bill Henderson, editor. The Pushcart Press, an affiliate publisher of W.W. Norton & Co., publishes the acclaimed *The Pushcart Prize* annual anthology, the winner of the Pushcart Editor's Book Award, and other quality literature, both fiction and nonfiction. "*The Pushcart Prize* was named among the most influential projects in the history of American publishing by *Publishers Weekly*." The most recent edition of *The Pushcart Prize* is available for $35 (hardcover) or $16.95 (paperback).

RAIN TAXI REVIEW OF BOOKS
P.O. Box 3840, Minneapolis MN 55403. E-mail: info@raintaxi.com. Web site: www.raintaxi.com. Established 1996. *Rain Taxi Review of Books* is a quarterly publication produced in both print and online versions (the latter with completely different material). The print version is available by subscription and for free in select bookstores nationwide. "We publish reviews of books that are overlooked by mainstream media, and each issue includes several pages of poetry reviews, as well as author interviews and original essays." Poets and publishers may send books for review consideration. Subscription: $15 domestic, $30 international. Sample: $4. "We DO NOT publish original poetry. **Please don't send poems.**"

TANKA SOCIETY OF AMERICA

Web site: www.tankasocietyofamerica.com. Offers membership information, contest guidelines and winning poems, and definitions and discussion of tanka.

U.S. COPYRIGHT OFFICE

Web site: www.copyright.gov. Offers copyright basics and FAQ, step-by-step directions for registering work for copyright, full schedule of related fees, records search, and other information.

U.S. POSTAL SERVICE

Web site: www.usps.com. Extensive site includes postage rates, mail preparation and mailing directions, online postage and label printing, domestic and foreign shipping options, and much more.

WEB DEL SOL

Web site: http://webdelsol.com. Must-see site for anyone interested in contemporary literary arts. Web del Sol "is a collaboration on the part of scores of dedicated, volunteer editors, writers, poets, artists, and staff whose job it is to acquire and frame the finest contemporary literary art and culture available in America, and abroad, and to array it in such a manner that it speaks for itself...at WDS we employ the traditional and electronic means necessary to bring a whole new readership to the contemporary literary arts."

WINNINGWRITERS.COM

Web site: www.winningwriters.com. Quality resources for poets and writers, including *Poetry Contest Insider* (quarterly, published online, subscription required), a variety of links, manuscript tips, "bad contest" warning signs, Winning Writers contests, and more. Register online for free e-mail newsletter. (See separate listing for Wergle Flomp Humor Poetry Contest and War Poetry Contest in Contests & Awards.)

WRITER BEWARE

Web site: www.sfwa.org/beware. Science Fiction and Fantasy Writers of America, Inc. offers this resource on their Web site devoted to scam alerts, common publishing practices that take advantage of writers, case studies, "thumbs down" lists of publishers and agents, and the Writer Beware blog.

WRITER'S DIGEST BOOKS

4700 East Galbraith Rd., Cincinnati OH 45236. (800)448-0915. Web sites: www.writersdigest.com; www.fwbookstore.com. Writer's Digest Books publishes an array of books useful to all types of writers. In addition to *Poet's Market*, books for poets include *The Rhythm Method, Razzmatazz and Memory: How to Make Your Poetry Swing* by Keith Flynn; *Writing Metrical Poetry* by William Baer; *Creating Poetry* and *The Poetry Dictionary* by John Drury, and *The Art and Craft of Poetry* by Michael J. Bugeja. Also of interest to poets are *The Portable MFA* and *The Writer's Digest Writing Clinic* (both of which include sections on poetry), and *The Pocket Muse* by Monica Wood (stimulating inspiration for all writers, including poets). Call or write for a complete catalog or log on to www.fw bookstore.com. **PLEASE NOTE:** *Writer's Digest Books does not publish poetry.*

YAHOO!

Web site: www.yahoo.com. Internet search engine; site includes thousands of Yahoo! Groups for poets and poetry, many genre- or culture-specific.

YOUNG POETS

E-mail: ypeditor@gmail.com. Web site: www.youngpoets.ca. Established 2001. **Contact:** Shannon Cowan, editorial coordinator. A project of The League of Canadian Poets, the Young Poets site provides separate sections and content for Youth and Teachers. The Youth section includes resources, an online forum, games and activities, collaborative poetry, and *Re:verse*, a zine for young poets. The "Teacher's Staff Lounge" includes workshop ideas, poetry teaching links, information on Poets in the Schools, a digital history of Canadian poetry, a "poem in progress" feature with commentary from the poet, and an online forum for teachers.

ADDITIONAL RESOURCES OF INTEREST

The following listings also contain information about instructive publications and online resources for poets. Turn to the page numbers indicated for details about their offerings.

Resources

Resources

Poets in Education

Whether known as PITS (Poets in the Schools), WITS (Writers in the Schools), or similar names, programs exist nationwide that coordinate residencies, classroom visits and other opportunities for experienced poets to share their craft with students. Many state arts agencies include such "arts in education" programs in their activities (see Grants on page 424 for contact information). Another good source is the National Assembly of State Arts Agencies (see below), which offers an online directory of contact names and addresses for arts education programs state-by-state. The following list is a mere sampling of programs and organizations that link poets with schools. Contact them for information about their requirements (some may insist poets have a strong publication history, others may prefer classroom experience) or check their Web sites where available.

The Academy of American Poets, 584 Broadway, Suite 604, New York NY 10012-5243. (212)274-0343. E-mail: academy@poets.org. Web site: www.poets.org (includes links to state arts in education programs).

Arkansas Writers in the Schools, WITS Director, 333 Kimpel Hall, University of Arkansas, Fayetteville AR 72701. (479)575-5991. E-mail: wits@cavern.uark.edu. Web site: www.uar k.edu/ ~ wits.

California Poets in the Schools, 1333 Balboa St. #3, San Francisco CA 94118. (415)221-4201. E-mail: info@cpits.org. Web site: www.cpits.org.

e-poets.network, a collective online cultural center that promotes education through video-conferencing (i.e., "distance learning"); also includes the *Voces y Lugares* project. Web site: http://learning.e-poets.net (includes online contact form).

Idaho Writers in the Schools, Log Cabin Literary Center, 801 S. Capitol Blvd., Boise ID 83702. (208)331-8000. E-mail: info@thecabinidaho.org. Web site: www.thecabinidaho.org.

Indiana Writers in the Schools, University of Evansville, Dept. of English, 1800 Lincoln Ave., Evansville IN 47722. (812)488-2962. E-mail: rg37@evansville.edu. Web site: http:// english.evansville.edu/WritersintheSchools.htm.

Michigan Creative Writers in the Schools, ArtServe Michigan, 17515 W. Nine Mile Rd., Suite 1025, Southfield MI 48075. (248)557-8288 **OR** 1310 Turner St., Suite B, Lansing MI 48906. (517)371-1720 (toll free at (800)203-9633). E-mail: online form. Web site: www.art servemichigan.org.

National Assembly of State Arts Agencies, 1029 Vermont Ave. NW, 2nd Floor, Washington DC 20005. (202)347-6352. E-mail: nasaa@nasaa-arts.org. Web site: www.nasaa-arts.org.

National Association of Writers in Education (NAWE), P.O. Box 1, Sheriff Hutton, York YO60 7YU England. (44)(1653)618429. Web site: www.nawe.co.uk.

Oregon Writers in the Schools, Literary Arts, 224 NW 13th Ave., Suite 306, Portland OR 97209. (503)227-2583. E-mail: john@literary-arts.org. Web site: www.literary-arts.org/wits.

PEN in the Classroom (PITC), Pen Center USA, % Antioch University, 400 Corporate Pointe, Culver City CA 90230. (310)862-1555. E-mail: pitc@penusa.org. Web site: www.penusa.org/go/classroom.

"Pick-a-Poet," The Humanities Project, Arlington Public Schools, 1439 N. Quincy St., Arlington VA 22207. (703)228-6299. E-mail: online form. Web site: www.humanitiesproject.org.

Potato Hill Poetry, 6 Pleasant St., Suite 2, South Natick MA 01760. (888)5-POETRY. E-mail: info@potatohill.com. Web site: www.potatohill.com (includes online contact form).

Seattle Writers in the Schools (WITS), Seattle Arts & Lectures, 105 S. Main St., Suite 201, Seattle WA 98104. (206)621-2230. Web site: www.lectures.org/wits.html.

Teachers & Writers Collaborative, 520 Eighth Ave., Suite 2020, New York NY 10018. (212)691-6590 or (888)BOOKS-TW (book orders). E-mail: info@twc.org. Web site: www.twc.org. A catalog of T&W books is available online, or call toll-free to request a print copy.

Texas Writers in the Schools, 1523 W. Main, Houston TX 77006. (713)523-3877. E-mail: mail@witshouston.org. Web site: www.writersintheschools.org.

Writers & Artists in the Schools (WAITS), COMPAS, Landmark Center, Suite 304, 75 Fifth St. West, St. Paul MN 55102-1496. (651)292-3254. E-mail: daniel@compas.org. Web site: www.compas.org.

Youth Voices in Ink, Badgerdog Literary Publishing, Inc., P.O. Box 301209, Austin TX 78703-0021. (512)538-1305. E-mail: info@badgerdog.org. Web site: www.badgerdog.org.

Resources

RESOURCES

Glossary of Listing Terms

A3, A4, A5. Metric equivalents of $11^3/4 \times 16^1/2$, $8^1/4 \times 11^3/4$, and $5^7/8 \times 8^1/4$ respectively.

Acknowledgments page. A page in a poetry book or chapbook that lists the publications where the poems in the collection were originally published; may be presented as part of the copyright page or as a separate page on its own.

Anthology. A collection of selected writings by various authors.

Attachment. A computer file electronically "attached" to an e-mail message.

AUD. Abbreviation for Australian Dollar.

b&w. Black & white (photo or illustration).

Bio. A short biographical statement often requested with a submission.

CAD. Abbreviation for Canadian Dollar.

Camera-ready. Poems ready for copy camera platemaking; camera-ready poems usually appear in print exactly as submitted.

Chapbook. A small book of about 24-50 pages.

Circulation. The number of subscribers to a magazine/journal.

CLMP. Council of Literary Magazines and Presses; service organization for independent publishers of fiction, poetry, and prose.

Contributor's copy. Copy of book or magazine containing a poet's work, sometimes given as payment.

Cover letter. Brief introductory letter accompanying a poetry submission.

Coverstock. Heavier paper used as the cover for a publication.

Digest-sized. About $5^1/2 \times 8^1/2$, the size of a folded sheet of conventional printer paper.

Download. To "copy" a file, such as a registration form, from a Web site.

Electronic magazine. See *online magazine*.

E-mail. Mail sent electronically using computer and modem or similar means.

Euro. Currency unit for the 27 member countries of the European Union; designated by EUR or the € symbol.

FAQ. Frequently Asked Questions.

Font. The style/design of type used in a publication; typeface.

Galleys. First typeset version of a poem, magazine, or book/chapbook.

GLBT. Gay/lesbian/bisexual/transgender (as in "GLBT themes").

Honorarium. A token payment for published work.

Internet. A worldwide network of computers offering access to a variety of electronic resources.

IRC. International Reply Coupon; a publisher can exchange IRCs for postage to return a manuscript to another country.

JPEG. Short for *Joint Photographic Experts Group*; an image compression format that allows digital images to be stored in relatively small files for electronic mailing and viewing on the Internet.

Magazine-sized. About $8^1/2 \times 11$, the size of an unfolded sheet of conventional printer paper.

ms. Manuscript.

mss. Manuscripts.

Multi-book review. Several books by the same author or by several authors reviewed in one piece.

Offset-printed. Printing method in which ink is transferred from an image-bearing plate to a "blanket" and then from blanket to paper.

Online magazine. Publication circulated through the Internet or e-mail.

p&h. Postage & handling.

p&p. Postage & packing.

"Pays in copies." See *contributor's copy*.

PDF. Short for *Portable Document Format*, developed by Adobe Systems, that captures all elements of a printed document as an electronic image, allowing it to be sent by e-mail, viewed online, and printed in its original format.

Perfect-bound. Publication with glued, flat spine; also called "flat-spined."

POD. See *print-on-demand*.

Press run. The total number of copies of a publication printed at one time.

Previously published. Work that has appeared before in print, in any form, for public consumption.

Print-on-demand. Publishing method that allows copies of books to be published as they're requested, rather than all at once in a single press run.

Publishing credits. A poet's magazine publications and book/chapbook titles.

Query letter. Letter written to an editor to raise interest in a proposed project.

Reading fee. A monetary amount charged by an editor or publisher to consider a poetry submission without any obligation to accept the work.

Rich Text Format. Carries the .rtf filename extension. A file format that allows an exchange of text files between different word processor operating systems with most of the formatting preserved.

Rights. A poet's legal property interest in his/her literary work; an editor or publisher may acquire certain rights from the poet to reproduce that work.

ROW. "Rest of world."

Royalties. A percentage of the retail price paid to the author for each copy of a book sold.

Saddle-stapled. A publication folded, then stapled along that fold; also called "saddle-stitched."

SAE. Self-addressed envelope.

SASE. Self-addressed, stamped envelope.

SASP. Self-addressed, stamped postcard.

Simultaneous submission. Submission of the same manuscript to more than one publisher at the same time.

Subsidy press. Publisher who requires the poet to pay all costs, including typesetting, production, and printing; sometimes called a "vanity publisher."

Tabloid-sized. 11×15 or larger, the size of an ordinary newspaper folded and turned sideways.

Text file. A file containing only textual characters (i.e., no graphics or special formats).

Unsolicited manuscript. A manuscript an editor did not ask specifically to receive.

URL. Stands for "Uniform Resource Locator," the address of an Internet resource (i.e., file).

USD. Abbreviation for United States Dollar.

Web site. A specific address on the Internet that provides access to a set of documents (or "pages").

Resources

Glossary of Poetry Terms

This glossary is provided as a quick-reference only, briefly covering poetic styles and terms that may turn up in articles and listings in *Poet's Market*. For a full understanding of the terms, forms, and styles listed here, as well as common literary terms not included, consult a solid textbook or handbook, such as John Drury's *The Poetry Dictionary* (Writer's Digest Books). (Ask your librarian or bookseller for recommendations.)

Abstract poem: conveys emotion through sound, textures, and rhythm and rhyme rather than through the meanings of words.

Acrostic: initial letters of each line, read downward, form a word, phrase, or sentence.

Alliteration: close repetition of consonant sounds, especially initial consonant sounds. (Also known as *consonance*.)

Alphabet poem: arranges lines alphabetically according to initial letter.

American cinquain: derived from Japanese haiku and tanka by Adelaide Crapsey; counted syllabic poem of 5 lines of 2-4-6-8-2 syllables, frequently in iambic feet.

Anapest: foot consisting of 2 unstressed syllables followed by a stress (- - ′).

Assonance: close repetition of vowel sounds.

Avant-garde: work at the forefront—cutting edge, unconventional, risk-taking.

Ballad: narrative poem often in ballad stanza (4-line stanza with 4 stresses in lines 1 and 3, 3 stresses in lines 2 and 4, which also rhyme).

Ballade: 3 stanzas rhymed *ababbcbC* (*C* indicates a refrain) with envoi rhymed *bcbC*.

Beat poetry: anti-academic school of poetry born in '50s San Francisco; fast-paced free verse resembling jazz.

Blank verse: unrhymed iambic pentameter.

Caesura: a deliberate rhetorical, grammatical, or rhythmic pause, break, cut, turn, division, or pivot in poetry.

Chant: poem in which one or more lines are repeated over and over.

Cinquain: any 5-line poem or stanza; also called "quintain" or "quintet." (See also *American cinquain*.)

Concrete poetry: see *emblematic poem*.

Confessional poetry: work that uses personal and private details from the poet's own life.

Consonance: see *alliteration*.

Couplet: stanza of 2 lines; pair of rhymed lines.

Dactyl: foot consisting of a stress followed by 2 unstressed syllables (′ - -).

Didactic poetry: poetry written with the intention to instruct.

Eclectic: open to a variety of poetic styles (as in "eclectic taste").

Ekphrastic poem: verbally presents something originally represented in visual art, though more than mere description.

Elegy: lament in verse for someone who has died, or a reflection on the tragic nature of life.

Emblematic poem: words or letters arranged to imitate a shape, often the subject of the poem.

Enjambment: continuation of sense and rhythmic movement from one line to the next; also called a "run-on" line.

Envoi: a brief ending (usually to a ballade or sestina) no more than 4 lines long; summary.

Epic poetry: long narrative poem telling a story central to a society, culture, or nation.

Epigram: short, witty, satirical poem or saying written to be remembered easily, like a punchline.

Epigraph: a short verse, note, or quotation that appears at the beginning of a poem or section; usually presents an idea or theme on which the poem elaborates, or contributes background information not reflected in the poem itself.

Epitaph: brief verse commemorating a person/group of people who died.

Experimental poetry: work that challenges conventional ideas of poetry by exploring new techniques, form, language, and visual presentation.

Fibs: short form based on the mathematical progression known as tje Fibonacci sequence; syllable counts for each line are 1/1/2/3/5/8/13 (count for each line is derived by adding the counts for the previous two lines).

Flarf: a malleable term that may refer to 1) poetic and creative text pieces by the Flarflist Collective; any poetry created from search engine (such as Google) results; any intentionally bad, zany, or trivial poetry.

Foot: unit of measure in a metrical line of poetry.

Found poem: text lifted from a non-poetic source such as an ad and presented as a poem.

Free verse: unmetrical verse (lines not counted for accents, syllables, etc.).

Ghazal: Persian poetic form of 5-15 unconnected, independent couplets; associative jumps may be made from couplet to couplet.

Greeting card poetry: resembles verses in greeting cards; sing-song meter and rhyme.

Haibun: originally, a Japanese form in which elliptical, often autobiographical prose is interspersed with haiku.

Haikai no renga: see *renku*.

Hay(na)ky: a 3-line form, with 1 word in line 1, 2 words in line 2, and 3 words in line 3.

Haiku: originally, a Japanese form of a single vertical line with 17 sound symbols in a 5-7-5 pattern. In English, typically a 3-line poem with fewer than 17 syllables in no set pattern, but exhibiting a 2-part juxtapositional structure, seasonal reference, imagistic immediacy, and a moment of keen perception of nature or human nature. The term is both singular and plural.

Hokku: the starting verse of a renga or renku, in 5, 7, and then 5 sound symbols in Japanese; or in three lines, usually totaling fewer than 17 syllables, in English; the precursor for what is now called haiku. (See also *haiku*).

Iamb: foot consisting of an unstressed syllable followed by a stress (- ').

Iambic pentameter: consists of 5 iambic feet per line.

Imagist poetry: short, free verse lines that present images without comment or explanation; strongly influenced by haiku and other Oriental forms.

Kyrielle: French form; 4-line stanza with 8-syllable lines, the final line a refrain.

Language poetry: attempts to detach words from traditional meanings to produce something new and unprecedented.

Limerick: 5-line stanza rhyming *aabba*; pattern of stresses/line is traditionally 3-3-2-2-3; often bawdy or scatalogical.

Line: basic compositional unit of a poem; measured in feet if metrical.

Linked poetry: written through the collaboration of 2 or more poets creating a single poetic work.

Long poem: exceeds length and scope of short lyric or narrative poem; defined arbitrarily, often as more than 2 pages or 100 lines.

Lyric poetry: expresses personal emotion; music predominates over narrative or drama.

Metaphor: 2 different things are likened by identifying one as the other (A = B).

Meter: the rhythmic measure of a line.

Minute: a 12-line poem consisting of 60 syllables, with a syllabic line count of 8,4,4,4,8,4,4,4, 8,4,4,4; often consists of rhyming couplets.

Modernist poetry: work of the early 20th century literary movement that sought to break with the past, rejecting outmoded literary traditions, diction, and form while encouraging innovation and reinvention.

Narrative poetry: poem that tells a story.

New Formalism: contemporary literary movement to revive formal verse.

Nonsense verse: playful, with language and/or logic that defies ordinary understanding.

Octave: stanza of 8 lines.

Ode: a songlike, or lyric, poem; can be passionate, rhapsodic, and mystical, or a formal address to a person on a public or state occasion.

Pantoum: Malayan poetic form of any length; consists of 4-line stanzas, with lines 2 and 4 of one quatrain repeated as lines 1 and 3 of the next; final stanza reverses lines 1 and 3 of the previous quatrain and uses them as lines 2 and 4; traditionally each stanza rhymes *abab*.

Petrarchan sonnet: octave rhymes *abbaabba*; sestet may rhyme *cdcdcd, cdedce, ccdccd, cddcdd, edecde,* or *cddcee*.

Prose poem: brief prose work with intensity, condensed language, poetic devices, and other poetic elements.

Quatrain: stanza of 4 lines.

Refrain: a repeated line within a poem, similar to the chorus of a song.

Regional poetry: work set in a particular locale, imbued with the look, feel, and culture of that place.

Renga: originally, a Japanese collaborative form in which 2 or more poets alternate writing 3 lines, then 2 lines for a set number of verses (such as 12, 18, 36, 100, and 1,000). There are specific rules for seasonal progression, placement of moon and flower verses, and other requirements. (See also *linked poetry*.)

Rengay: an American collaborative 6-verse, thematic linked poetry form, with 3-line and 2-line verses in the following set pattern for 2 or 3 writers (letters represent poets, numbers indicate the lines in each verse): A3-B2-A3-B3-A2-B3 or A3-B2-C3-A2-B3-C2. All verses, unlike renga or renku, must develop at least one common theme.

Renku: the modern term for renga, and a more popular version of the traditionally more aristocratic renga. (See also *linked poetry*.)

Rhyme: words that sound alike, especially words that end in the same sound.

Rhythm: the beat and movement of language (rise and fall, repetition and variation, change of pitch, mix of syllables, melody of words).

Rondeau: French form of usually 15 lines in 3 parts, rhyming *aabba aabR aabbaR* (*R* indicates a refrain repeating the first word or phrase of the opening line).

Senryu: originally, a Japanese form, like haiku in form, but chiefly humorous, satirical, or ironic, and typically aimed at human foibles. (See also *haiku* and *zappai*.)

Sequence: a group or progression of poems, often numbered as a series.

Sestet: stanza of 6 lines.

Sestina: fixed form of 39 lines (6 unrhymed stanzas of 6 lines each, then an ending 3-line stanza), each stanza repeating the same 6 non-rhyming end-words in a different order; all 6 end-words appear in the final 3-line stanza.

Shakespearean sonnet: rhymes *abab cdcd efef gg*.

Sijo: originally a Korean narrative or thematic lyric form. The first line introduces a situation or problem that is countered or developed in line 2, and concluded with a twist in line 3. Lines average 14-16 syllables in length.

Simile: comparison that uses a linking word (*like, as, such as, how*) to clarify the similarities.

Sonnet: 14-line poem (traditionally an octave and sestet) rhymed in iambic pentameter; often presents an argument but may also present a description, story, or meditation.

Spondee: foot consisting of 2 stressed syllables (' ').

Stanza: group of lines making up a single unit; like a paragraph in prose.

Strophe: often used to mean "stanza"; also a stanza of irregular line lengths.

Surrealistic poetry: of the artistic movement stressing the importance of dreams and the subconscious, nonrational thought, free associations, and startling imagery/juxtapositions.

Tanka: originally, a Japanese form in one or 2 vertical lines with 31 sound symbols in a 5-7-5-7-7 pattern. In English, typically a 5-line lyrical poem with fewer than 31 syllables in no set syllable pattern, but exhibiting a caesura, turn, or pivot, and often more emotional and conversational than haiku.

Tercet: stanza or poem of 3 lines.

Terza rima: series of 3-line stanzas with interwoven rhyme scheme (*aba, bcb, cdc* . . .).

Trochee: foot consisting of a stress followed by an unstressed syllable (′ -).

Villanelle: French form of 19 lines (5 tercets and a quatrain); line 1 serves as one refrain (repeated in lines 6, 12, 18), line 3 as a second refrain (repeated in lines 9, 15, 19); traditionally, refrains rhyme with each other and with the opening line of each stanza.

Visual poem: see *emblematic poem*.

Waka: literally, "Japanese poem," the precursor for what is now called tanka. (See also *tanka*.)

War poetry: poems written about warfare and military life; often written by past and current soldiers; may glorify war, recount exploits, or demonstrate the horrors of war.

Zappai: originally Japanese; an unliterary, often superficial witticism masquerading as haiku or senryu; formal term for joke haiku or other pseudo-haiko.

Zeugma: a figure of speech in which a single word (or, occasionally, a phrase) is related in one way to words that precede it, and in another way to words that follow it.

Resources

Chapbook Publishers Index

A poetry chapbook is a slim volume of 24-50 pages (although chapbook lengths can vary; some are even published as inserts in magazines). Many publishers and journals solicit chapbook manuscripts through competitions. Read listings carefully, check Web sites where available, and request guidelines before submitting. See Frequently Asked Questions on page 7 for further information about chapbooks and submission formats.

Book Publishers Index

The following are magazines and publishers that consider full-length book manuscripts (over 50 pages, often much longer). See Frequently Asked Questions on page 7 for further information about book manuscript submission.

Special Indexes

Openness to Submissions Index

In this section, all magazines, publishers, and contests/awards with primary listings in *Poet's Market* are categorized according to their openness to submissions (as indicated by the symbols that appear at the beginning of each listing). Note that some markets are listed in more than one category.

◻ WELCOMES SUBMISSIONS FROM BEGINNING POETS

PREFERS SUBMISSIONS FROM EXPERIENCED POETS, WILL CONSIDER WORK FROM BEGINNING POETS

Special Indexes

Special Indexes

❤ PREFERS SUBMISSIONS FROM SKILLED, EXPERIENCED POETS, FEW BEGINNERS

Special Indexes

◎ MARKET WITH A SPECIALIZED FOCUS

Special Indexes

Special Indexes

Geographical Index

This section offers a breakdown of U.S. publishers and conferences/workshops arranged alphabetically by state or territory, followed by listings for Canada, Australia, France, Ireland, Japan, the United Kingdom, and other countries—a real help when trying to locate publishers in your region as well as conferences and workshops convenient to your area.

Book/Chapbook Publishers

Special Indexes

Book/Chapbook Publishers

Special Indexes

Conferences, Workshops & Festivals

NORTH CAROLINA
Magazines/Journals

Book/Chapbook Publishers

NORTH DAKOTA
Magazines/Journals

OHIO
Magazines/Journals

Special Indexes

Book/Chapbook Publishers

**Conferences, Workshops &
Festivals**

OKLAHOMA
Magazines/Journals

Book/Chapbook Publishers

OREGON
Magazines/Journals

Special Indexes

Subject Index

This index focuses on markets indicating a specialized area of interest, whether regional, poetic style, or specific topic (these markets show a ◎ symbol at the beginning of their listings). It also includes markets we felt offered special opportunities in certain subject areas. Subject categories are listed alphabetically, with additional subcategories indicated under the "Specialized" heading (in parentheses behind the market's name). **Please note:** 1) This index only partially reflects the total markets in this book; many do not identify themselves as having specialized interests and so are not included here. 2) Many specialized markets have more than one area of interest and will be found under multiple categories. 3) When a market appears under a heading in this index, it does not necessarily mean it considers *only* poetry associated with that subject, poetry *only* from that region, etc. It's still best to read all listings carefully as part of a thorough marketing plan.

Bilingual/Foreign Language

Form/Style (Asian)

Gay/Lesbian/Bisexual/Transgendered

Poetry by Children (considers submissions)

Poetry by Teens (considers submissions)

Psychic/Occult

Regional

Religions (various)

Religious Poetry

Science Fiction

Spirituality/Inspirational

Translations

Special Indexes

General Index

Market listings that appeared in the 2008 edition of *Poet's Market* but do not appear in this edition are identified with a two-letter code explaining why the listing was omitted: **(NR)**—no response to our request for updated information; **(RR)**—removed by request; **(UC)**—unable to contact; **(OB)**—out of business; **(UF)**—uncertain future; **(HA)**—on hiatus; **(ED)**—editorial decision.

B

Special Indexes

Special Indexes